October

To Eric,
With best wishes — Joe

My best wishes or better! Chuck

An Introduction to Proto-Indo-European and the Early Indo-European Languages

An Introduction to Proto-Indo-European and the Early Indo-European Languages

Joseph Voyles &
Charles Barrack

Bloomington, Indiana, 2009

ISBN: 978-0-89357-342-3

Cover design by Stephanie Welch

Library of Congress Cataloging-in-Publication Data

Voyles, Joseph B., 1938-
An introduction to proto-Indo-European and the early Indo-European languages / Joseph Voyles & Charles Barrack.
p. cm.
Includes bibliographical references and index.
ISBN 978-0-89357-342-3
1. Proto-Indo-European language. 2. Indo-European languages. I. Barrack, Charles Michael, 1938- II. Title.
P572.V68 2009
410--dc22

2009018476

Slavica Publishers
Indiana University
2611 E. 10th St.
Bloomington, IN 47408-2603
USA

[Tel.] 1-812-856-4186
[Toll-free] 1-877-SLAVICA
[Fax] 1-812-856-4187
[Email] slavica@indiana.edu
[www] http://www.slavica.com/

Dedicated to the memory of our friends

Francis X. Allard (July 12, 1942–December 24, 2000)

Julia Barrack (July 4, 1914–January 17, 2002)

Christa E. Haenel (December 12, 1901–June 15, 1999)

Contents

3 Latin

4 Ancient Greek

5 Old Irish

Abbreviations

abl	ablative
abs	absolute
acc	accusative
act	active
adj	adjective
adv	adverb
C	a single consonant or the feature "consonantal" when occurring in a matrix
com	common
comp	comparative
cond	conditional
conj	conjunction or conjunct
dat	dative
dem	demonstrative
dep	deponent
der	derivation or derivational
du	dual
encl	enclitic
Eng	English
env	environment
ev	eventually
f	and following page
fem	feminine
fut	future
gen	genitive
ger	gerund
Gk	Greek
Gmc	Germanic
Go	Gothic
Hit	Hittite
IE	Indo-European
imp	imperative
imperf	imperfect
ind	indicative
indef	indefinite
indep	independent
inf	infinitive
infl	inflection or inflectional
inj	injunctive
instr	instrumental
inter	interrogative
Lat	Latin
loc	locative
masc	masculine
med	medial
mid	middle
Mod Germ	Modern German
morph cond	morphologically conditioned
morph str	morpheme structure
n	endnote
NB	nota bene = note
neut	neuter
nom	nominative
nondep	nondeponent
NWGmc	Northwest Germanic
obl	oblique
OCSlav	Old Church Slavic
OEng	Old English
OIce	Old Icelandic
OHGerm	Old High German
OIr	Old Irish
OLat	Old Latin
opt	optative
OSax	Old Saxon
part	participle
pass	passive
perf	perfect
phon cond	phonologically conditioned
PIE	Proto-Indo-European
pl	plural
pluperf	pluperfect
pos	positive
poss	possessive
prep	preposition
pres	present
pret	preterite
pron	pronoun
refl	reflexive

rel	relative
s	a syllable
sg	singular
Skt	Sanskrit
subj	subjunctive
suf	suffix
sup	superlative or supine
syl	syllable
V	a single vowel
voc	vocative
VV	a long vowel or a diphthong
V(V)	V or VV (see immediately above)
V̄	a long vowel
V́	a vowel with primary stress
V̀	a vowel with secondary stress
V(:)	a long vowel (V:) or a short vowel (V)
x^l	a form triggering OIr rule 2b LEN (lenition)
x_n^m	a sequence consisting of at least n and at most m number of segments or other constituents such as syllables
x^n	a form triggering OIr rule 3a ECLIP (eclipsis)
→	a synchronic derivation
<	"developed from" in a diachronic derivation
>	"developing to" in a diachronic derivation
><	contemporaneity of two changes
#	a boundary between a prefix and a root
##	a word boundary
/…/	a phonemic or broad transcription
[…]	a phonetic or narrow transcription
<…>	a graphemic transcription
+	a word-internal morpheme boundary
*x	a reconstructed form
**x	a false or nonoccurring form
Ø	zero or a deletion in a rule

Preface

The impetus for this book arose from our forty-plus-year experience in teaching classes in the early Germanic languages, the history of the German language and courses on Proto-Indo-European at the University of Washington. During these years we found that gifted and inspired students often lacked the necessary background to form enlightened opinions on various aspects of Indo-European linguistics.

We recur in this connection to our citation of Oswald Szemerényi in the first paragraph of our first chapter. Szemerényi says there that anyone interested in a depth-probe of Indo-European needs to possess the "basic equipment" of Latin, Greek, Sanskrit et al. The present book is intended to provide preliminary access to this "basic equipment". There exists to our knowledge no such synoptic introduction to the phonological and morphological history of the early Indo-European languages.

In acquiring the basic equipment posited by Szemerényi, the reader may either work through any of our chapters in detail or skim the chapters and use the book as a reference work. After a perusal of the present work and perhaps other books on Indo-European, the reader may well come to conclusions which differ from ours. We strongly encourage this endeavor. We should add that we have attempted to keep our exposition more or less theory-neutral: e.g. the laryngeal theory, for which Voyles holds no brief, while Barrack is in some instances sympathetic to it; or the glottalic theory, which neither of us supports. In both these instances we have attempted to include the argumentation on both sides and let the reader form his or her own opinion. Indeed, we encourage our readers to craft their own hypotheses about Indo-European based on the present work as well as others which they may consult.

Regarding the consultation of other works, we suggest that the reader might consider "adopting" an Indo-European language of choice and analyzing it in the way done here. We also suggest that the reader should not be reluctant to consult a grammar written in French, Spanish, German or Russian—even if the reader is unfamiliar with that language: linguistic terminology is fairly universal and the reader would be surprised at how much one can understand. We also suggest that in a first reading of the grammar of the language the reader has adopted, that he or she not work out all the exercises in detail, but read the grammar rather as a novel—and not as a mathematical text. In this way the reader will gain an understanding of the basic structure of the language.

We believe that any of the works listed in our bibliography are worthy of consideration. Those which we have found particularly useful are starred below; and two of them are double-starred. These sources are Atkinson (1953, for Greek), Auty (1960, for Old Church Slavic), *Baldi (1983, for general Indo-European), Beekes (1995, for general Indo-European), Brandenstein (1959, for Greek), *Brugmann et al. (1897–1918, for general Indo-European), *Buck (1962, for Greek and Latin), *Diels (1932 and 1934, for Old Church Slavic), *Fortson (2004, for general Indo-European), *Friedrich (1960, for Hittite), **Held et al. (1988, for Hittite), Hirt (1912, for Greek), *Kent (1940 and 1946, for Latin), *Kronasser (1956, for Hittite), Leskien (1922, for Old Church Slavic), Meier-Brügger (2000, for general Indo-European), Ó Siadhail (1988, for Modern Irish), Sihler (1995, for Greek and Latin), Sturtevant (1933, for Hittite), **Szemerényi (1990, for general Indo-European) and Wright (1954, for Gothic).

Finally, our gratitude for the principal stimulus for this book must be extended to our students, many of whom pressed us for explicit formulations of the rules (including such well-known changes as Verner's Law, which to our knowledge had not been explicitly formulated previous to our research: we give an explicit account of it in Chapter 2) and who encouraged us to write this book. Second, we wish to thank the students and faculty of the Department of Germánics and of the Department of Linguistics at the University of Washington who have supported our work in numerous ways. In particular, Voyles wishes to thank Sol Saporta, who in his capacity as chair of the Department of Linguistics first asked him in the mid-1960's to teach courses in Indo-European and historical linguistics for the department. Without these stimuli this book would most likely not have been written.

Third—and most emphatically—we both wish to thank George Fowler, the editor of the Slavica Series, who perceptively and tactfully shepherded our manuscript through our infelicities of form and presentation into its present version. George did his best: any remaining formal errors are purely our own.

Joseph Voyles
joevoy@u.washington.edu

Charles Barrack
cbarrack@u.washington.edu

Department of Germanics
University of Washington
Box 353130
Seattle, WA 98195-3130 USA

Chapter 1

Terminology and Method
A Reconstructed Portion of Proto-Indo-European

I Introduction

Oswald Szemerényi (1990:12) has made the following observation: "Anyone who wishes to become familiar with the problems of the Indo-European languages and to work in this field will need to start with the basic equipment of Latin, Greek, Old Indic [Sanskrit] and Gothic, and in the course of time to add further important languages such as Hittite, Old Church Slavic, etc."

The present work is intended to provide this basic equipment. The following chapters contain descriptions of the phonological and morphological history of the earliest attested languages in the major Indo-European subfamilies. These are Chapter 2 where we consider the Gothic language of the Germanic group, Chapter 3 with Latin of the Italic and later Romance-language family, Chapter 4 with Ancient Greek (which we call here simply Greek), Chapter 5 with Old Irish of the Celtic family, Chapter 6 with Old Church Slavic of the Balto-Slavic family, Chapter 7 with Sanskrit from the Indo-Iranian group and finally Chapter 8 with Hittite from the Anatolian group of languages. (Note that "Indo-European" often refers to the later Indo-European languages such as those just cited, while "Proto-Indo-European" (PIE) designates the reconstructed proto-language.)

Each of the Chapters 2 through 8 is structured as follows:

I Introduction

A description of the sources and the location of the language.

II Phonological changes from PIE into the language

A. Overview of the changes in their relative chronology.

B. The changes explicitly formulated.

C. The evidence for the relative chronology of the changes.

III Resulting phonology of the language

IV Historical morphology of the language

The paradigms are given with their PIE antecedents.

A. Overview of the paradigms.

B. The morphology of the language.

V Exercises

VI Sample text in the language with a phonological and morphological analysis of it

VII Key

Any of these chapters may either be worked through in detail or skimmed and used as a reference work. We further recommend as an exercise that the reader might consider adopting an Indo-European language and putting it under an analysis like those modeled here. Some possibilities are Tocharian, Armenian, Albanian, Lithuanian or any of the more familiar Indo-European languages such as French, Italian, Dutch or English.

II Terminology and Method

2.1 Synchronic Description

We begin with an outline of the structure of a grammar as we envision it and as we employ the concept and the relevant terms. We consider the basic structure of a grammar to be as follows:

(1) Deep level: (a) basic structure
(b) presupposition.

(2) Transformational level: transformational rules.

(3) Morphological level: morphemes and morphological rules.

(4) Phonological level: phonological rules.

(5) Output: a sentence of the language which is produced by the application of some of these rules.

In the following we shall cite some examples of the function of these concepts and rules in the so-called derivational histories of several sentences. The "derivational history" of a sentence means those synchronic rules which have applied in order for the sentence to be produced.

2.1.1 Deep Level

As our first example we consider the basic structure and derivational history of this sentence:

(a) John is American and intelligent.

As its deep structure we posit the following.
A deep structure may be described in two ways:

(a')

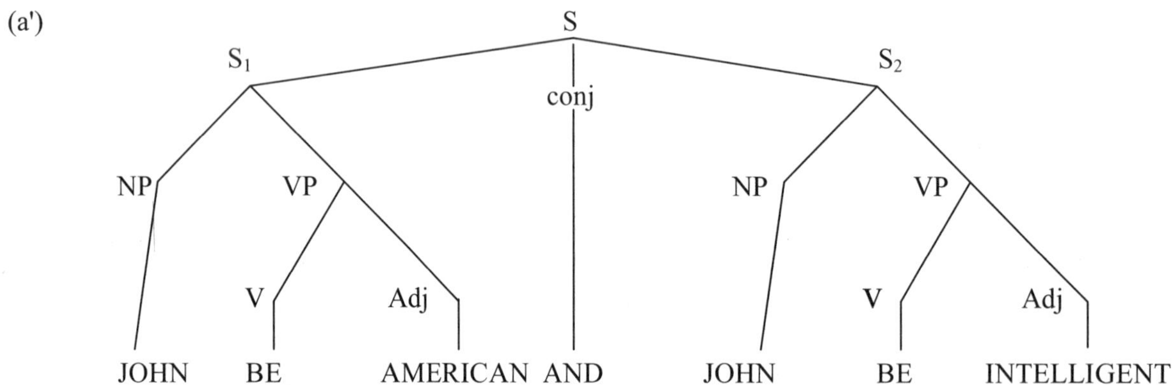

or,

(a'') $[_{S}\ [_{S_1}\ [_{NP}\ \text{JOHN}\ ]_{NP}\ [_{VP}\ [_{V}\ \text{BE}\ ]_{V}\ [_{Adj}\ \text{AMERICAN}\ ]_{Adj}\ ]_{VP}\ ]_{S_1}$

$[_{conj}\ \text{AND}\ ]_{conj}\ [_{S_2}\ [_{NP}\ \text{JOHN}\ ]_{NP}\ [_{VP}\ [_{V}\ [\text{BE}]\ ]_{V}\ [_{AdJ}\ \text{INTELLIGENT}\ ]_{Adj}\ ]_{VP}\ ]_{S_2}\ ]_{S}$

The formalizations (a') and (a'') indicate that the sentence (a), i.e. S, consists at its basic level of two sentences, S_1 and S_2, conjoined by the conj AND. Each of the component sentences S_1 and S_2 consists of a subject noun phrase (NP) and a verb phrase (VP), which itself consists of the verb BE plus an adj. (As we shall see directly, this deep structure must pass through a transformational rule which deletes JOHN and BE in S_2.)

The basic structure just cited entails the view that the fundamental word-order in English sentences is SVO — namely subject plus verb plus the rest of the sentence. On the other hand, it is usually (and probably correctly) assumed that the basic word-order of PIE was SOV. In this connection, it is very likely that all the Indo-European languages we consider here were also SOV, with the exception of Old Irish in Chapter 5 which was VSO.

We now turn to our notion of presupposition. A "presupposition" is an assumption or belief on the part of the speaker which affects the grammatical structure of a sentence. We can illustrate this concept by formulating an alternative version of sentence (a) above, which is as follows:

(b) John is American, but intelligent.

That is, both sentences (a) and (b) share the same deep-level structure. This means that they both are logically the same and have the same truth value (on which more below). However, the transformational insertion of "but" for deep-level AND as opposed to "and" is the result of a presupposition. The presupposition on the part of the speaker is that the concatenation of S_1 and S_2 in the deep structure of sentence (b) above might be considered to involve a contradiction. (All the Indo-European languages considered here have distinct words for "and" vs. "but" based on this presupposition. It is possible that all human languages distinguish between words for "and" vs. "but". This is not the case for logical formalisms or computer languages.)

Other instances of presuppositions occur in connection with some of the verb moods, as in our descriptions of the PIE subjunctive and optative in section 3.2 below. An example of such a subjunctive sentence is the following:

(c) If he were here, I'd leave.

The basic structure of this sentence is this:

(c') $[_S\ [_{S_1}$ HE BE HERE$]_{S_1}$ $[_{conj}$ IMPLY $]_{conj}$ $[_{S_2}$ I LEAVE $]_{S_2}\ ]_S$

That is, the sentence S consists of two sentences, S_1 and S_2, conjoined by a conjunction of implication. However, the presupposition obtains that both S_1 and S_2 (but not the entire sentence S) are false. Hence they are marked as +subj.

A sentence derived from the same deep structure, but without the presupposition that S_1 and S_2 are false, is this:

(c'') Whenever he's here, I leave.

2.1.2 Transformational Level

A transformational rule in our usage of the term changes one sentence structure into another while retaining the truth value of both sentences. One example is the relation between the deep structure (a') JOHN BE AMERICAN AND JOHN BE INTELLIGENT and the sentence (a) "John is American and intelligent" described in 2.1.1 above. The transformational rule involved in the derivational history of the sentence deletes the subject and the verb in S_2. This transformation is sometimes called "conjunction reduction".

Two additional transformations are in the derivational history of the following sentence:

(a) Never have I seen such a thing.

The deep structure of the sentence is something like this:

(a') I HAVE NEVER SEEN SUCH A THING.

The two transformations are called "topicalization" and "subject-verb permutation". The first of these preposes NEVER. The second permutes the order subject-verb to verb-subject. It is because of such transformations that basically SVO or SOV languages can under various circumstances show different surface sequences.

2.1.3 Morphological Level

Morphemes have been defined as "the minimally significant grammatical units" of a language. Speakers of a language can usually identify intuitively the morphemes of that language.
For example, in the following sentence,

(a) The man runs.

a speaker of English will consider the first two words monomorphemic and the third as consisting of two morphemes, namely run- and -s.

Morphemes like <man> and <run> consist of three kinds of features: (i) semantic or meaning features, (ii) grammatical or syntactic features and (iii) phonological features.The morphemes <man> and <run> cited above may be illustrated with the following matrices in which (i) represents the semantics, (ii) the grammatical features and (iii) the phonology:

(i) MAN	(i) RUN
(ii) Noun, 3sg, i-class...	(ii) Verb, strong...
(iii) /mæn/	(iii) /rən/

These matrices indicate that the two morphemes have meaning, which we have delineated under (i) by writing in capitals. They also have grammatical features, some of which we give under (ii). Those for <man> indicate that it is a noun in the third person singular; the feature "i-class" indicates that the noun belongs to a class which forms its plural in a particular way (namely as in /mɛn/ <men> and not as **/mænz/ **<mans>). Similarly <run> is a verb of the strong class, which means that it forms its past and perfect participle by PIE "ablaut" or vowel alternation (namely as <run, ran, run> and not as, say, **<run, runned, runned>). The phonological features under (iii) are given in phonemic transcription, of which more below.

Most of the features such as Noun and Verb in the two morphemes just cited are "inherent" or "lexical". This means that they are idiosyncratic and as such simply a part of what a speaker must know in order to use the morphemes in the language.

There are other features of morphemes which are "variable". These features change according to the function of the morpheme in a particular context. For example, in the derivational history of sentence (a) and after the application of the transformational rules, the structure of the sentence is this:

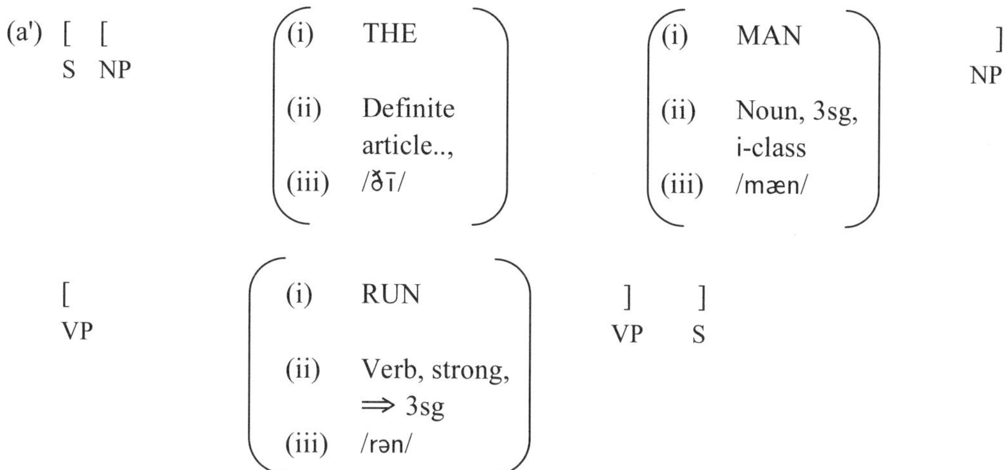

Here the variable feature 3sg has been copied into the RUN matrix by a transformation (⇒) called "agreement".

The morphological rule which applies to structure (a') is a rule of English which adds <-s> to non-modal verbs (i.e., to all verbs except those like <can> or <shall>) in the 3sg pres ind. The paradigms in part 3.2.2 Morphology in this chapter as well as in part IV Historical Morphology in each of the following chapters provide instances of the application of morphological rules.

These paradigms contain endings of "inflection". "Derivation" and derivative suffixes differ from inflection in that while inflection is the result of productive morphological rules like the one just described which inserts the 3sg pres indic ending <-s>, derivative suffixes are generally less productive and put morphemes into different form-classes. For example, Eng <drive> is a verb which can occur with an inflectional suffix <drive+s>. It can also occur as a noun with a derivative suffix, <driv+er> which can in turn take an inflectional suffix <driv+er+s>.

We include here two more pieces of terminology. First, a "root" is a constituent of a word which consists of only one morpheme plus a possible inflectional ending. E.g., Eng (drive)+s or PIE *(mog^h)+ō 'I can'. Second, a "stem" consists of a root plus a derivative suffix plus a possible inflectional ending. E.g., Eng (driv+er)+s or PIE nom sg fem *(mog^h+t)+is 'ability'.

2.1.4 Phonological Level

These rules determine the final phonetic form of a sentence. We often write the input to the phonological level in slashes /.../ and its final output in brackets [...]. The former is a "phonemic" or "broad" transcription and contains less detail. The latter is a "phonetic" or "narrow" transcription and contains more detail. (In this connection we note that <...> designates the traditional orthography of a form. Usually we cite attested forms with no special markings; hence we do not italicize them.)

Given the phonological rules of a language, the more detailed phonetic transcription [...] is predictable from the less detailed phonemic one /.../. For example, the PIE word */song^{hw}ā́/ 'oracle, song' is phonetically *[soŋg^{hw}ā́] with the velar nasal [ŋ]. The PIE phonological rule which predicts that /n/ in this particular environment is phonetically [ŋ] is 3.1.2d NASAL ASSIM given below. The segments within the slashes /.../ are called "phonemes". Those within brackets are "allophones". In the present example, /n/ has two allophones, [n] and [ŋ] as predicted by the PIE NASAL ASSIM rule noted above.

The environments of phonological rules are either phonologically conditioned (phon cond) or morphologically conditioned (morph cond) — or a mixture of both. An example of the former is the rule 3.1.2d NASAL ASSIM given below whereby the occurrence of the nasals [m, n, ŋ] is predictable on the basis of the following obstruent consonants. An environment is morph cond if, unlike the preceding one, it cannot be stated in purely phonological terms. An example of this is the word-stress rule of PIE (namely 3.1.2h WORD STRESS below) or that of early Sanskrit (change 11 SANSKRIT STRESS in Chapter 7). In both these rules the placement of the stress can be determined only by such factors as the case of a noun or the tense of a verb — all of which are non-phonological.

Some phonological rules are optional. An example is the following rule which occurs in some dialects of English:

bv → vv

E.g., the word "obvious" may be pronounced by speakers of this dialect either as /ábviəs/ or as /ávviəs/. It is likely that the changes we cite in part II The Phonological Changes of each of the following chapters were at their inception optional rules.

Some rules we call "persistent". This means that the rule continues to apply even after chronologically later changes have occurred.

An example of a persistent rule occurring in all the Indo-European languages we consider here is the PIE rule 3.1.2d NASAL ASSIM, whereby the nasal consonants [m, n, ŋ] occur contingent upon the following obstruent, namely [p, b^{h}, b; t, d^{h}, d; k$^{(w)}$, g$^{h(w)}$, g$^{(w)}$] respectively. During the history of Greek as described in Chapter 4, the change occurred whereby the PIE labiovelars /k^{w}, g^{hw}, g^{w}/ became /t, t^{h}, d; p, p^{h}, b; and k, k^{h}, g/ respectively, under specific conditions.

After the Greek change 5a LABIOVEL happens, the persistent rule 3.1.2d NASAL ASSIM, which has remained in the grammar, automatically reapplies. Hence the following derivation from PIE into Greek: PIE nom sg fem */song^{hw}ā́/ 'song, oracle, voice' (3.1.2d NASAL ASSIM, applying as a synchronic rule) → *[soŋg^{hw}ā́] (the Greek changes 2a ASPIR DEVOI and 3e s-h-Ø in Chapter 4) > *hoŋk^{hw}ā́ (Greek 5a LABIOVEL) > *hoŋp^{h}ā́ (persistent rule 3.1.2d NASAL ASSIM applying as a synchronic rule) → *homp^{h}ā́ (Greek 6a ā-TO-ē and 7b GRASSMANN) > Gk omp^{h}έ́. (Note that in this derivation we have used the symbols → and >. The first designates a synchronic derivation from a phonemic /.../ to a phonetic [...] form. The > designates a diachronic or historical derivation from an earlier to a later stage of the language. Note also that this Greek word is cognate with the English word "song".)

2.2 Comparative Method

The term "comparative method" is the rather misleading appellation used to describe the process by which one reconstructs an earlier language from at least two genetically related later languages.The method may be represented schematically as follows:

Data: Grammars of two or more attested and genetically related "daughter" languages — G_1, G_2...G_n.

Theory: Hypotheses on the nature of language and language change such as the following: "All languages have subordinate clauses." "If a language is SOV, it usually has postpositions." "If a language is SOV, then adjectives usually follow nouns." "All languages have at least one vowel." Or "If a language has only one nasal consonant, it is /n/."

Conclusions: Given the data and the hypotheses (which may be either true or false), one can derive at least four types of conclusions: (which consequently may also be either true or false). The conclusions are these. (i) A reconstructed grammar of a proto-language, *G. (In actual practice, lexical items are what are usually reconstructed instead of an entire grammar.) (ii) Rules of historical change. (iii) Relative chronologies for some of the changes. (Examples of these are in the following chapters.) (iv) A genetic tree indicating the relationships among the daughter languages and the reconstructed proto-language. (Such trees are constructed under the assumption that daughter languages which share a number of changes probably belong to the same subfamily. E.g., Gothic and English belong to the Germanic family.)

Handbooks of historical linguistics usually provide exercises in comparative method by citing cognates from daughter languages from which one then posits an appropriate proto-form. We can illustrate this with the following two-member cognate set.

Skt aɟāmi 'I drive' (where /ɟ/ is as in "Joe") — Lat agō 'idem'

The task here is to reconstruct a PIE root (disregarding the endings -āmi and -ō) and to posit a proto-form and plausible rules of historical change. There are at least two possible theories:

(i) PIE *aɟ- with a change ɟ > g in Latin.
(ii) PIE *ag- with a change g > ɟ in Sanskrit.

Earlier scholarship tended to opt for theory i under the assumption that an earlier attested language like Sanskrit would be more likely to reflect the proto-language than would a later attested one like Latin. Later scholarship, however, has leaned toward theory ii under the assumption that a change of ɟ > g as posited under theory i does not seem to occur. But a change like g > ɟ as posited under theory ii has been seen to occur in various languages. Such changes are often referred to as "palatalizations".

The preceding example, albeit brief, adequately illustrates the nature of comparative method. For now, theory ii offers the preferable account; this is of course not to say that it will not some day be superseded. Note that in such competitions between two (or among several) theories, there is usually no dispute about the data. The disagreements almost invariably concern opposing basic beliefs, namely the hypotheses. As the philosopher M.S. Gram once observed in this connection (personal communication), the best way to argue for a particular theory is to attack the other theories' hypotheses — or as Gram put it, to "kick them in the axiom".

III A Portion of Proto-Indo-European

Below we give in outline a possible reconstruction of PIE phonology and morphology. After considering this and the data in the following chapters as well as elsewhere, the reader may come to different conclusions about PIE. We encourage this endeavor.

3.1 PIE Phonology

In this section we give first an inventory of the phonological segments which we posit for PIE; second, we give eight of the major phonological rules of PIE; and finally we summarize four of the disputed issues on PIE phonology.

3.1.1 Inventory of Segments

As in the following chapters, we cite the segments first in articulatory terms and second in terms of phonological features. The formulation in articulatory terms is this:

Obstruent Consonants

labial	dental	alveolar	velar	labiovelar
p	t		k	k^w
b^h	d^h		g^h	g^{hw}
b	d		g	g^w
		{ s / z }[1]		

Sonorant Consonants

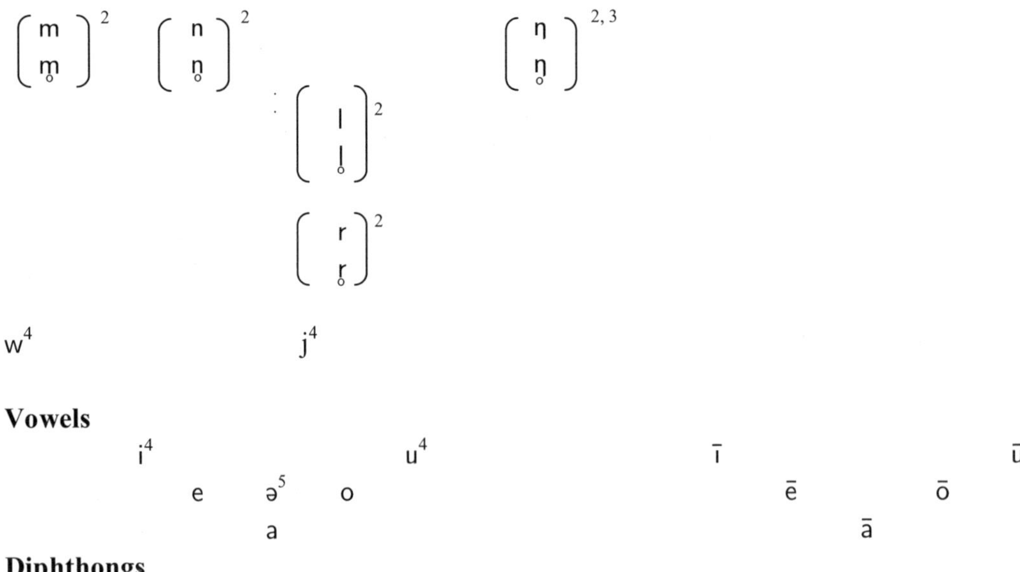

Vowels

i[4] u[4] ī ū

e ə[5] o ē ō

a ā

Diphthongs

ai, au, ei, eu, oi, ou, əi, əu
āi, āu, ēi, ēu, ōi, ōu

PIE Segments in Terms of Phonological Features: Consonants

	p	t	k	kʷ	bʰ	dʰ	gʰ	gʰʷ	b	d	g	gʷ	s	z[6]	m	m̥	n	n̥	ŋ	ŋ̥	l	l̥	r	r̥	w	j
consonantal	+	+	+	+	+	+	+	+	+	+	+	+	+	+	+	+	+	+	+	+	+	+	+	+	–	–
sonorant	–	–	–	–	–	–	–	–	–	–	–	–	–	–	+	+	+	+	+	+	+	+	+	+	+	+
vocalic	–	–	–	–	–	–	–	–	–	–	–	–	–	–	–	+	–	+	–	+	–	+	–	+	–	–
high	–	–	+	+	–	–	+	+	–	–	+	+	–	–	–	–	–	–	+	+	–	–	–	–	+	+
back	–	–	+	+	–	–	+	+	–	–	+	+	–	–	–	–	–	–	+	+	–	–	–	–	+	–
low	–	–	–	–	–	–	–	–	–	–	–	–	–	–	–	–	–	–	–	–	–	–	–	–	–	–
anterior	+	+	–	–	+	+	–	–	+	+	–	–	+	+	+	+	+	+	–	–	+	+	+	+	–	–
coronal	–	+	–	–	–	+	–	–	–	+	–	–	+	+	–	–	+	+	–	–	+	+	+	+	–	–
voiced	–	–	–	–	+	+	+	+	+	+	+	+	–	+	+	+	+	+	+	+	+	+	+	+	+	+
continuant	–	–	–	–	–	–	–	–	–	–	–	–	+	+	–	+	–	+	–	+	+	+	+	+	+	+
nasal	–	–	–	–	–	–	–	–	–	–	–	–	–	–	+	+	+	+	+	+	–	–	–	–	–	–
strident	–	–	–	–	–	–	–	–	–	–	–	–	+	+	–	–	–	–	–	–	–	–	–	–	–	–
delayed release	–	–	–	–	–	–	–	–	–	–	–	–	–	–	–	–	–	–	–	–	–	–	–	–	–	–
round	–	–	–	+	–	–	–	+	–	–	–	+	–	–	–	–	–	–	–	–	–	–	–	–	+	–
lateral	–	–	–	–	–	–	–	–	–	–	–	–	–	–	–	–	–	–	–	–	+	+	–	–	–	–
palatal	–	–	–	–	–	–	–	–	–	–	–	–	–	–	–	–	–	–	–	–	–	–	–	–	–	+
aspirated	–	–	–	–	+	+	+	+	–	–	–	–	–	–	–	–	–	–	–	–	–	–	–	–	–	–
stressed	–	–	–	–	–	–	–	–	–	–	–	–	–	–	–	±	–	±	–	±	–	±	–	±	–	–
long	–	–	–	–	–	–	–	–	–	–	–	–	–	–	–	–	–	–	–	–	–	–	–	–	–	–

PIE Segments in Terms of Phonological Features: Vowels

	a	e	i	o	u	ā	ē	ī	ō	ū	ə
consonantal	–	–	–	–	–	–	–	–	–	–	–
sonorant	+	+	+	+	+	+	+	+	+	+	+
vocalic	+	+	+	+	+	+	+	+	+	+	+
high	–	–	+	–	+	–	–	+	–	+	–
back	+	–	–	+	+	+	–	–	+	+	+
low	+	–	–	–	–	+	–	–	–	–	–
voiced	+	+	+	+	+	+	+	+	+	+	+
continuant	+	+	+	+	+	+	+	+	+	+	+
nasal	–	–	–	–	–	–	–	–	–	–	–
round	–	–	–	+	+	–	–	–	+	+	–
tense	–	–	–	–	–	+	+	+	+	+	–
stressed	±	±	±	±	±	±	±	±	±	±	±[7]
long	–	–	–	–	–	+	+	+	+	+	–

3.1.2 Eight PIE Phonological Rules

Below are eight phonological rules which have been reconstructed for PIE. We note for each rule whether it is morph cond or phon cond.

3.1.2a The Ablaut Rule (ABLAUT)

This rule is morph cond. Its basic structure is this:

V → e(:), o(:) or Ø / in a morph cond environment

That is, virtually any morpheme — whether a prefix, root or suffix — can occur with its vowel nucleus as any one of these five possibilities: /e, ē, o, ō/ or zero. The occurrence of each of these possibilities is determined by a morph cond environment.

Reflexes of these alternations occur in all Indo-European languages. Perhaps the clearest illustration of Ablaut is the strong verb paradigm in Germanic as described in Chapter 2 on Gothic, morphology section 6.1.1. An example is in the Gothic 1st class strong verb paradigm. We cite the 1st person forms: PIE pres *g^{h}réibō 'seize', past sg *g^{h}róiba, past pl *g^{h}ribmé (ev) > Go grīpa <greipa>, grēp <graip>, gripum <gripum>. This is an instance of /e-o-Ø/ ablaut.

Two additional examples are these. The first is from Latin in Chapter 3, morphological section 6.4, in the present perfect. E.g., the PIE 1sg pres *mów+ējō 'I move' vs. the 1sg perf *mṓw+ai (ev) > Lat moveō and mōvī. This is /o-ō/ ablaut. The second example is from Chapter 7, rule 7a MON in Sanskrit. The alternation is /Ø-e-ē/ ablaut. E.g., PIE 1pl perf *pe+pØt+ime 'fall', 3sg pres *pét+eti 'idem' and 3sg pres causative *pēt+éjeti 'cause to fall' (ev) > Skt paptima, pátati and pātáyati.

It is generally assumed that the earlier version of ABLAUT was a phon cond rule. If so, the original conditioning may have been a function of the PIE rule 3.1.2h WORD STRESS.

3.1.2b The Diphthong Rule (DIPH)

This rule is phon cond. It specifies that the only diphthongs possible in the language are those given in the inventory of segments in 3.1.1 above. The rule is this:

V V → [V, -high] [V, +high, -long]
1 2 1 2

(with the proviso that no morpheme boundary occurs between the two vowels). That is, the first segment of a diphthong must be a non-high vowel, either long or short (but not /i(:)/ or /u(:)/); and the second segment must be either /i/ or /u/. The DIPH rule continues to apply during the development of various Indo-European languages. E.g., the derivation into Greek of the PIE thematic 1sg pres act opt $*$léik^w+o+ī+mi 'leave' (in which -o- is the thematic vowel and -ī- the optative marker; then reinterpretation of -o+ī- as monomorphemic -oī-) > $*$léik^{w}oīmi (DIPH applying as a persistent rule to the illegitimate diphthong /oī/ to produce the admissable /oi/) →$*$léik^{w}oimi (ev) > Gk leípoimi. Additional examples of the persistent application of the DIPH rule are in Chapter 7 in our account of Skt rule 7a MON.

3.1.2c Alternation of /i – j/ and /u – w/ (i – j/u – w ALT)

This rule is phon cond and remains in the grammars of all the PIE languages considered here. It is this:

[–stress, i/j or u/w] → (a) j or w / —— V
(b) i or u / —— C or ##

That is, (a) unstressed /i/ or /u/ becomes /j/ or /w/ before a vowel; and (b) /j/ or /w/ becomes /i/ or /u/ before a consonant or word-finally — i.e., when not followed by a vowel.

E.g., (a) PIE 3sg pres athematic verb $*$éi+ti 'goes' vs. its thematic counterpart $*$éi+e+ti 'idem' (i-j/u-w ALT) → $*$éiti and $*$éjeti (ev) > Skt ēti and áyati. PIE nom sg $*$b^{h}ā́g^{h}u+s 'elbow' vs. the ablauting nom pl $*$b^{h}ā́g^{h}eu+es (i-j/u-w ALT) → $*$b^{h}ā́g^{h}us and $*$b^{h}ā́g^{h}ewes (the Greek changes 2a Aspirate Devoicing, 6a ā-TO-ē, 6d u(:)-TO-y(:), 7b Grassmann) > $*$pḗk^{h}ys and $*$pḗk^{h}ewes (Greek 7c w-Deletion) > $*$pḗk^{h}ys and $*$pḗk^{h}ees (ev) > Gk pêk^{h}ys and pḗk^{h}eis. (b) PIE $*$b^{h}ónd^{h}jā 'bond, tie' (ev) > Pre-Go Gmc $*$bándj (i-j/u-w ALT applying as a persistent rule) → Go bandi. PIE perf act part masc $*$te+tud+wōt+s 'having pushed' vs. ablauting neut $*$te+tud+wØt (i-j/u–w ALT) → $*$tetudwōts and $*$tetudut (3.1.2h WORD STRESS) → $*$tetudwṓts and $*$tetudút.

3.1.2d Assimilation of Nasal Segments (NASAL ASSIM)

This rule is phon cond and remains in the grammar to apply as a persistent rule.

[C, +nasal] → [α place features] / —— (C, +obstruent / α place features)

(where no morpheme boundary intervenes between the nasal and the obstruent)

That is, within a morpheme the only nasal to occur immediately before /p, b^h, b/ is /m/ (or vocalic [m̥]), before /t, d^h, d, s/ is /n/ (or vocalic [n̥]) and before /k, g^h, g/ is [ŋ] (or vocalic [ŋ̊]). The latter nasals [ŋ, ŋ̊], unlike /m/ or /n/, occur only in this environment. We have considered them allophones of /n/.

E.g., PIE $*$amb^{h}í 'around' as opposed to a non-form like $**$anb^{h}í, $*$b^{h}end^h- 'bind' as opposed to $**$b^{h}emd^h- and $*$aŋg^h- 'narrow' (usually written phonemically as $*$ang^h-) as opposed to $**$amg^h-. An example of the persistent application of NASAL ASSIM is the derivation of PIE $*$song^{hw}ā́ 'song, oracle' into Gk omp^{h}ḗ as described in 2.1.4 above.

3.1.2e The Rule for Obstruent Clusters (OBST CL)

This rule consisted of two ordered parts. It is phon cond; and part 2 remains to apply as a persistent rule in the development of the Indo-European languages considered here. Part 1 is sometimes referred to as "Bartolomae's Law". The rule is this:

$$(1)\quad \begin{bmatrix} b^h \\ g^h \end{bmatrix}_1 + t_2 \rightarrow \begin{bmatrix} b \\ g \end{bmatrix}_1 + d^h_2$$

(in which "+" is a word-internal morpheme boundary)

$$(2)\quad \begin{bmatrix} \text{C, –sonorant} \\ \alpha\text{voiced} \end{bmatrix} \rightarrow [\beta\text{voiced}] \;/\; \_\_\_\_ \;(+)\; [\text{C, –sonorant, } \beta\text{voiced}]$$

That is, (1) the sequences /b^h + t/ or /g^h + t/ become /bd^h/ or /gd^h/. (2) Obstruent clusters, whether or not occurring over a morpheme boundary, are uniformly voiced or voiceless depending upon the final obstruent consonant in the sequence.

E.g., (1) PIE perf pass part nom sg masc *lab^h+t+ós 'seized' (OBSTR CL) → *labd^{h}ós (ev) > Skt labdhás; PIE nom sg i-class noun *kúg^h+t+is 'thought' (OBSTR CL) → *kúgd^{h}is (ev) > Go (ga)hugds. (2) perf pass part nom sg masc *jug+t+ós 'yoked' and *sed+t+ós 'set' (OBSTR CL) → *juktos and *settós (ev) > Skt yuktás and sattás. PIE nom sg of the masc o-class noun (consisting of *ni- 'in' plus *sd-, the Ø-grade ablaut of 'sit' plus the nom sg masc o-class ending *-os) *nisdós (OBSTR CL) → *nizdós (ev) > Skt nīḍás 'nest'. Similarly, the PIE nom sg masc o-class noun consisting of *upo- 'upon' plus the Ø-grade ablaut of *pVd- 'foot' plus the nom sg masc o-class ending, namely *upo+pd+ós 'noise, foot-stamping' (OBSTR CL) → *upobdós (ev) > Skt upabdás.

3.1.2f Sievers' Law (SIEVERS)

This rule was originally phon cond. By the time of most of the attested Indo-European languages (with the possible exception of Sanskrit) the rule had either dropped from the grammar; or its reflex had, as in Gothic by change 9h LOSS OF SIEVERS, become morph cond.

The rule was first formulated by Eduard Sievers (1878: 129) and later elaborated upon by Franklin Edgerton (1934: 235). A possible early version is this:

$$j \rightarrow ij \;\Big/\; \begin{bmatrix} \text{(a) } VC \\ \text{(b) } V_2^3 \\ \text{(c) } s_2 \end{bmatrix} C_1^n \_\_\_\_$$

That is, /j/ becomes /ij/ if following a "long sequence" which ends in one or more consonants (C_1^n). A long sequence is either (a) a vowel followed by at least two consonants (VCC_1^n), (b) a long vowel or diphthong followed by at least one consonant ($V_2^3\, C_1^n$) or (c) at least two syllables followed by at least one consonant ($s_2C_1^n$). Some sources consider the rule to have applied also to /w/ to produce /uw/. (See Barrack 1998 for a detailed discussion of the environment of Sievers' Law and its fate in Indo-European, specifically in Germanic.)

E.g., PIE 3sg pres *nosjéti ‘saves’ and *kousjéti ‘hears’ (SIEVERS) → *nosjéti and *kousijéti (ev) > Go nasjiþ vs. háuseiþ /hɔ̄́sīþ/.

3.1.2g The Syllabic Sonorant Rule (SYL SON)

This rule is both phon cond and morph cond, the latter in that it must take into account word-internal and word-external morpheme boundaries.

$$[\text{C}, +\text{sonorant}] \quad \rightarrow \quad [+\text{vocalic}] \;\Big/\; \begin{Bmatrix} \text{(a) [-vocalic]} \\ \text{(b) \#\#} \\ \text{(c) +} \end{Bmatrix} \;\_\_\; \begin{Bmatrix} \text{(a) [-vocalic]} \\ \text{(b) \#\#} \\ \text{(c) +} \end{Bmatrix}$$

That is, the segments /l, m, n, ŋ, r/ are syllabic [l̥, m̥, n̥, ŋ̥, r̥] when occurring in the nine possible non-vocalic environments shown above. These are (aa) between two non-vocalic segments, (ab) between a non-vocalic segment and a word-final boundary and (ac) between a non-vocalic segment and a word-internal morpheme boundary. Similarly, (ba) word-initially and followed by non-vocalic segment, (bb) between two word-boundaries (which probably does not occur), (bc) word-initially and followed by a word-internal morpheme boundary, and so on.

E.g., (aa) PIE */kntóm/ ‘100’ (SYL SON) → *[kn̥tóm] (ev) > Skt śatám; (ab) PIE acc sg */pód+m/ ‘foot’ (SYL SON) → *[pód+m̥] (ev) > Gk póda; (ac) PIE perf pass part */bʰr+ón/ ‘carried’ (SYL SON) → *[bʰr̥+ ó n] (ev) > Go baúran /bóran/; (ba) PIE */mbʰí/ ‘around’ (SYL SON) → *[m̥bʰí] (ev) > Gk ampʰí; (bb) Ø (i.e., no such example); (bc) the PIE negative prefix */n+/ (SYL SON) → [n̥+] (ev) > Go un-, Lat in-, Gk an-.

3.1.2h The Rule of Word Stress (WORD STRESS)

This rule is morph cond. We assume that the PIE word-stress rule is most nearly reflected in the early Greek stress rule 2f1 GREEK STRESS and in the early Skt rule 11(1) SANSKRIT STRESS.

The PIE rule stresses words in six configurations. They are these.

(a) ##[C_0—], i.e. on the first syllable.
s

(b) [C_0, inflectional suffix —], i.e. on an inflectional suffix.
s

(c) [C_0, derivative suffix —], i.e. on a derivative suffix.
s

(d) ##s[C_0—], i.e. on the second syllable.
s

(e) Alternation in a paradigm between the first syllable and and the inflectional ending (= a and b above).

(f) Alternation in a paradigm between the derivative suffix and the inflectional ending (= c and b above).

Exactly which of these six stress patterns accrues to a word is determined by one of the following three morph cond parameters:

(A) A particular derivative suffix.

(B) A particular marked lexical item.

(C) A particular combination of syntactic and morphological features such as case, number, tense, mood or person in a particular form class.

E.g., the following PIE words. (aA) Nom sg masc sup *kak+ist+os 'worst' (WORD STRESS) → *kákistos; (aB) nom sg masc *rēg+ōn 'king' (WORD STRESS) → *rḗgōn; (aC) voc sg *deiw+e 'god' (WORD STRESS) → *déiwe. (bA) Nom sg masc adj *paid+ik+os 'childish' (WORD STRESS) → *paidikós; (bB) nom sg *jug+os 'yoke' (WORD STRESS) → *jugós; (bC) Ø, i.e. no such example. (cA) Nom sg neut *paid+i+om 'child' (WORD STRESS) → *paidíom, (cB) Ø, (cC) Ø. (dA) Ø; (dB) nom sg *pətēr and gen sg *pətr+os (WORD STRESS) → *pətḗr and *pətrós; (dC) Ø. (eA) Ø, (eB) Ø, (eC) Ø-class masc acc sg *gūp+m̥ 'vulture' and gen sg *gūp+os (WORD STRESS) → *gū́pm̥ and *gūpós (ev) > Gk gŷpa and gȳpós. (fA) Ø; (fB) Ø; (fC) 1sg pres *sun+eu+mi 'I press' and ablauting 1 pl pres *sun+u+mos (WORD STRESS) → *sunéumi and *sunumós (ev) > Skt sunṓmi and sunumás. (Further examples of the application of the PIE WORD STRESS rule are to be found in Chapters 4 and 7 under the Greek change 2f GREEK STRESS and Sanskrit 11 SANSKRIT STRESS, respectively.)

In the following table we summarize the morph cond conditions which can trigger PIE WORD STRESS. (Here + = "yes" and – = "no".)

		A	B	C
		Derivat. Suffix	**Lexical Item**	**Syntax**
a	**First Syllable**	+	+	+
b	**Inflection**	+	+	–
c	**Derivat. Suffix**	+	–	–
d	**Second Syllable**	–	+	–
e/f	**Alternating**	–	–	+

3.1.3 Four Disputed Questions

3.1.3.1 Aspirated Voiceless Stops

Some sources posit for the PIE phoneme inventory a series of voiceless aspirated obstruent stops, /p^h, t^h, k^h/. This is plausible because it assumes a typologically more likely PIE obstruent system. If these consonants in fact existed in PIE, then in all the Indo-European languages considered here — except for Sanskrit — the reflexes of the aspirated voiceless obstruents would be the same as the reflexes of the unaspirated series as provided by their respective rules. And for Sanskrit one may under this theory assume that the PIE voiceless aspirate stops were retained. (An alternative explanation for the occurrence of the Sanskrit voiceless aspirate stops is to assume that they arose from the corresponding voiceless unaspirated stops when immediately followed by a laryngeal. See on this our formulation of the Sanskrit change la LARYNGEALS iii in Chapter 7.)

3.1.3.2 The Glottalic Theory

This view of the PIE obstruent system has been proposed in several sources, among them Gamkrelidze and Ivanov (1973, 1984 and 1994) as well as Hopper (1973 and 1977). According to this theory, PIE had the following series of obstruents (as opposed to those which we have posited in 3.1.1 above). We designate each series by its first member, e.g. p = /p, t, k, k^w/, b^h = /b^h, d^h, g^h, g^{hw}/, etc.

Traditional inventory	=	Glottalic inventory
p		p^h [8]
b^h		b^h [8]
b		p' [9]

Which of these reconstructions, the traditional or the glottalic, more closely reflects PIE is a matter of debate. If one adopts the glottalic view, one must then assume one or more rules to change the glottalized consonants into their non-glottalic reflexes in all the later Indo-European daughter languages including those considered here. (For a negative appraisal of the Glottalic Theory, see Barrack (2002 and 2003).)

3.1.3.3 Laryngeals

The laryngeal theory has been described in various terms and in various sources, among them Beekes (1969), Lehmann (1955), Lindemann (1987) and Sturtevant (1942). Opposition to the theory is voiced in Szemerényi (1990: 136).

According to a common version of this theory, there were three laryngeal segments in PIE. These are usually denoted by the symbols "h_1", "h_2" and "h_3" while "h" may be used to designate any of the three laryngeals. The phonetic content of the laryngeals is usually left unspecified. They are sometimes assumed to have been back consonants such as [h, ʔ, x].

One version of laryngeal theory holds that there was originally only one vowel in early PIE, namely /e/. The later PIE vowels then arose through these changes:

(a)	h_1e → Øe	**(b)**	eh_1 → ēØ	**(c)**	ih → īØ
	h_2e → Øa		eh_2 → āØ		uh → ūØ
	h_3e → Øo		eh_3 → ōØ		
	1 2 1 2		1 2 1 2		1 2 1 2

That is, (a) /e/ preceded by the respective laryngeal becomes /e, a, o/ and the laryngeal is lost; (b) /e/ followed by the respective laryngeal becomes /ē, ā, ō/ and the laryngeal is lost; and (c) [i] and [u] (which are sometimes considered allophones of /j/ and /w/ in non-vocalic environments) followed by any laryngeal become /ī/ and /ū/ and the laryngeal is lost.

E.g., (a) early PIE *$h_1$es- 'be', *$h_2$eg- 'drive' and *h_3ek^w- 'eye' (ev) > later PIE *es-, *ag- and *ok^w-; (b) early PIE *d^heh_1- 'put', *steh_2- 'stand' and *gneh_3- 'know' (ev) > later PIE *d^hē-, *stā- and *gnō-; and (c) early PIE nom sg *kih+s 'worm' and *suh+s 'pig' (ev) > later PIE *kīs and *sūs.

One argument adduced in support of the laryngeal theory is the fact that it renders the morpheme structure of early PIE symmetric. That is, all roots are of the form $C_1V_1C_1$, i.e. they must begin with one or more consonants (C_1), contain one or more vowels (V_1) and end in one or more consonants (C_1). E.g., *steig^h- 'climb', *pod- 'foot' and *b^hend^h- 'tie' — and at the laryngeal stage of early PIE, *d^heh₁*, *steh₂- etc. At the later stage this symmetry was destroyed by the occurrence of the forms *d^hē-, *stā-, etc.

A counter-argument here is to quarrel with the basic axiom and ask why one should assume that an asymmetric morpheme structure should necessarily have been preceded by a symmetric one.

In Chapters 4, 7 and 8 we give the laryngeal-changing rules purportedly occurring in those languages which have been cited as illustrative of laryngeal influence. These are the Greek change la LARYNGEALS, the Sanskrit change la LARYNGEALS and the Hittite change lb LARYNGEALS.

3.1.3.4 Palatal vs. Velar Stops

In the preceding section 3.1 we have posited the velar and labiovelar series / k, k^w; g^h, g^hw; g, g^w/. Some sources posit the following back stops for PIE:

palatal	velar	labiovelar
k'	k	k^w
g^h'	g^h	g^hw
g'	g	g^w

Here there is an additional segment /k', g^h', g'/. Our reasons for not positing the palatal segments are given in our discussion of the Sanskrit change 4b 2ND PAL in Chapter 7. Additional treatment of the same issue is under the Sanskrit change 2a 1ST PAL in Chapter 7 as well as in Chapter 6 under the Old Church Slavic changes 1c EARLIEST PAL and 5b 1ST PAL.

3.2 PIE Morphology

In each of the following chapters we give a complete description of the morphology of that Indo-European sub-dialect from which the respective Indo-European daughter language developed. These later sub-dialects can differ. This can be clearly seen from the numerals. For example, the Indo-European antecedent of Lat septem '7' is *septḿ̥ while that of Go sibun '7' is *sepń̥t. Similarly, the OCSlav gen sg vlĭka 'wolf' devolves from an Indo-European abl sg *wl̥̍k^wōd. That is, in the later Indo-European sub-dialect from which Slavic developed the earlier ablative singular had already taken over the function of the genitive singular.

Below we reconstruct the PIE morphology as having been closest to that of Ancient Greek and Sanskrit. This view is not universally accepted: Baldi (1999:29) considers Hittite to reflect early PIE morphology. We do not subscribe to this view for the reasons set forth in Chapter 8.

3.2.1 Overview

We assume the following structure for PIE morphology. Our numeration below follows that which we use in the following chapters. We give our PIE morphology in outline. For more detail, see Chapters 2 through 8, in particular Chapter 4 on Greek and Chapter 7 on Sanskrit.

Outline of Proto-Indo-European Morphology

3.2.2 Morphology

We assume the basic morphology of PIE to have been as follows. More details on the sub-dialects are to be found in Chapters 2 through 8.

1 Nouns

Regarding nouns, adjectives, numerals and pronouns we make the following four assumptions. First, there was in PIE no definite article. Second, there were three morph cond genders — masculine, feminine. and neuter. Third, there were three numbers — singular, dual and plural. Fourth and finally, there were eight cases. We illustrate their basic functions with English examples. (Additional examples may be found in Chapters 2 through 8, particularly in the texts in section IV of each chapter.)

a. **Nominative**. Subject of a sentence or after a linking verb like 'be'. E.g.,
   (a) The man came home.
   (b) She was that woman.

b. **Vocative**. Direct address. E.g.,
   (a) Father, come here.

c. **Accusative**. Direct object of most verbs or direction into. E.g.,
   (a) I see the dog.
   (b) The children ran home.

d. **Genitive**. This case has more varied uses than any of the others. Its main function is to indicate an open relationship between two nouns or NPs. The nature of this relationship is left to the imagination of the speaker and hearer. This type of situation constitutes a presupposition as we have described the concept in 2.1.1 above. Another use of the genitive is to mark the objects of certain verbs. The meanings of these verbs are often perceptional such as 'perceive, hear, remember' or the like. E.g.,

   (a) This is John's tree. (The relation between the nouns John and tree is open: it can mean the tree John owns, the tree John is always talking about, the tree John planted as a child, etc.)
   (b) I remember mama.

e. **Locative**. Location at some place. E.g.,
   (a) The child stays home.

f. **Dative**
   Indirect object of many verbs taking two objects, motion up to, object of verbs usually meaning 'help, serve, thank' and the so-called "ethical dative". This latter dative indicates that

some sort of presuppositional relationship exists between the sentence and the noun in the dative. E.g.,

(a) I gave that man the book.
(b) He walked to the tree.
(c) The woman helped that man.
(d) The farmer's sheep all died on him. (This is the ethical dative; it is not a locative. It shows that the fact of the sheep's death affected the farmer.)

g. **Ablative**
Motion away from and often after comparative adjectives. E.g.,
(a) They walked away from the town.
(b) Mary was smarter than John.

h. **Instrumental**
Means by which something occurs and attendant circumstance. The latter is called the "instrumental absolute". E.g.,

(a) Mary killed John with a knife.
(b) With John gone, Mary could start having fun.

Basic Noun and Adjective Inflectional Endings

	Sg	**Du**	**Pl**
nom	-m[10]	-V̄(i/u)[11,12]	-(e)s
	-s	-e[12]	-a[13]
	-Ø		
acc	-m	"	-ns
	-Ø[10]		-a[13]
gen	-(e/o)s(jo)	-ous	-o(:)m[14]
loc	-i	"	-su
dat	-Vi[11]	-b^hi(ō)n	-b^h(j)os[15]
		-mō	-is[15]
			-mis[15]
abl	-V̄d[11]	"	"
instr	-b^hi	"	-$b^h$is
	-mi		-mis
	-V̄[11]		-ōis

In the following paradigms the nominative and accusative neuter forms are identical. In all these paradigms the neuter endings are like those of the masculine except for the nominative and accusative — singular, dual and plural. Nouns and adjectives were declined the same in PIE. They were lexically marked as belonging to any one of the classes described below. (We list these classes with the same numeration as we use in Chapters 2 through 8 on the individual Indo-European daughter languages.)

1.1 o- and jo-Class (Masculine, Neuter)

Nouns of this class have ablauting -o(:)/e(:)/Ø- between the stem and the ending. E.g., the following masc noun, *deiwós, 'god'.

sg nom	*deiw+ó+s	**du nom**	*deiw+ṓ+u	**pl nom**	*deiw+ṓ+s
voc	*déiw+e				
acc	*deiw+óm			**acc**	*deiw+ó+ns
abl	*deiw+ṓd				

E.g., the following neut noun, *jugóm 'yoke'

sg nom	*jug+ó+m[16]	**du nom**	*jug+ṓ+i[16]	**pl nom**	*jug+á[16]

Some of these nouns have a thematic -jo-. E.g., the following nominative singular forms.

masc *kór+j+os 'army'
neut *gŋ̥́+j+om 'tribe, family'

1.2 ā- and jā-Class (Feminine)

Nouns of this class have an intermediate -ā- or –jā- between the stem and the ending. E.g., *b^{h}ugā́ 'flight' and *wóikjā 'house'[17].

sg nom	*b^{h}ug+ā́+Ø	**du nom**	*b^{h}ug+ā́+i	**pl nom**	*b^{h}ug+ā́+s
	*wóik+jā+Ø		*wóik+jā+i		*wóik+jā+s

1.3 i-Class (Masculine, Feminine, Neuter)

Nouns of this class have an intermediate -Vi- (where V = ablauting e(:)/o(:)/Ø) between the stem and the ending. The masculine and feminine nouns have the same endings. The declension of the neuter nouns differs from that of the masc/fem only in the nom/acc sg and pl. E.g., the masculine noun *egnís 'fire' and the neuter noun *wṓri 'water'.

sg nom	*egn+í+s	**du nom**	* egn+ī́	**pl nom**	*egn+éi+es[18]
voc	*égn+ei+Ø				

sg nom	*wṓr+i+Ø	**du nom**	*wṓr+ī	**pl nom**	*wṓr+i+a[19]

1.4 u-Class (Masculine, Feminine, Neuter)

Nouns of this class have an intermediate -Vu- (where V = ablauting e(:)/o(:)/Ø) between the stem and the ending. As with the i-class immediately above, the masculine and feminine nouns have the same endings. And the declension of the neuter nouns differs from that of the masc/fem only in the nom/acc sg and pl. E.g. masculine noun *kótrus 'enemy' and the neuter noun *méd^{h}u 'honey'.

sg nom	*kótr+u+s	**du nom**	*kótr+ū	**pl nom**	*kótr+eu+es[20]
voc	*kótr+u+Ø				

sg nom	*médʰ+u+Ø	**du nom**	*médʰ+ū	**pl nom**	*médʰ+u+a[20]

1.5 Athematic classes (Masculine, Feminine, Neuter)

These nouns have no intermediate thematic vowel between the stem and the inflectional ending. The Ø-class athematic nouns consist of the root plus the endings; the other athematic nouns have a stem consisting of a root plus a suffix (which was probably in origin a derivative suffix) plus the inflectional endings.

In all athematic classes the masculine and feminine nouns take the same endings. The neuter nouns also have these same endings except for the nom/acc sg, dual and pl. In the following we list the seven athematic classes in the alphabetical sequence of the particular suffix occurring within the stem. The classes are the Ø-class with no suffix, the r/n-class, the root-class, the tVr-class, the Vn-class, the Vnt-class and the Vs-class (where in all instances V = ablauting e(:)/o(:)/Ø).

1.5.1 Ø-Class

Two examples follow: The first is masc *pḗds 'foot'[21, 22].

sg nom	*pḗd+s	**du nom**	*pḗd+e[22]	**pl nom**	*pḗd+es[22]
acc	*péd+m[22, 23]				
gen	*ped+és[22]				*ped+ṓm[22]

An example of a neuter noun is the nom/acc of *gʷégʷn̥t 'world'.

sg	*gʷégʷn̥t+Ø	**du**	*gʷégʷn̥t+ī	**pl**	*gʷégʷn̥t+a

1.5.2 r/n-Class

It would seem that most of these nouns were neuter. The stem suffix is -Vr in the nom and acc sg/dual/pl and -Vn in the other cases (where V = ablauting e(:)/o(:)/Ø).
E.g., the neuter noun *wódor, 'water'

sg nom	*wód+or+Ø	**sg gen**	*wód+en+es

1.5.3 Root class

Most, if not all of these nouns are masculine or feminine. These nouns consist of roots ending in a vowel plus the endings of the Ø-class above. These nouns tend to have ablaut in their roots. E.g., the masculine noun *diēús 'god'.

sg nom	*diēú+s[24]	**sg voc**	*díēu+Ø[24]	**sg acc**	*díØu+m[25]

1.5.4 tVr-Class

These nouns designate family members or constitute agent nouns such as *dō+tḗr 'giver'. E.g., masc *pətḗr 'father'.

sg nom *pətḗr+Ø **sg voc** *pə́ter+Ø[26] **sg acc** *pətér+m[26, 27]

cf. fem sg nom *mātḗr+Ø 'mother'[26, 28]

1.5.5 Vn-Class

E.g., the masculine noun *rḗgōn 'king'

sg nom *rḗg+ōn+Ø **sg voc** *rḗg+on+Ø **pl dat** *rḗg+Øn+b^{h}jos[29]

Neuter nouns of this class have the same endings as the masc/fem except for the nom/acc pl. E.g., the neuter noun *nṓmn 'name'.

sg nom *nōm+Øn +Ø[30] **du nom** *nōm+Øn+ī[30] **pl nom** *nōm+Øn+a

1.5.6 Vnt-Class

These nouns and adjectives are in origin present active participles. E.g., the following masculine noun *odónts 'tooth'.[31]

sg nom *od+ónt+s **sg voc** *ód+ont+Ø **sg acc** *od+ónt+m̥

1.5.7 Vs-Class

E.g., the neuter noun *ménos 'mind'

sg nom *mén+os+Ø **du nom** *mén+os+ī **pl nom** *mén+os+a

2 Adjectives

The adjectives in PIE were declined like the corresponding nouns. Adjs were lexically marked as belonging to one of the four following adjective classes. Aside from adjs of the o-/jo- and ā/jā-classes under 2.1 below, the masculine and feminine adjs in the other three classes take the same endings.

2.1 o-/jo- and ā-/jā-Class

The masculine and neuter adjectives are o-/jo-class . The feminine adjectives are ā-/jā-class. E.g., *b^{h}lénd^{h}- 'blind'.

nom sg masc *b^{h}lénd^{h}+o+s **nom sg fem** *b^{h}lénd^{h}+ā+Ø **nom sg neut** *b^{h}lénd^{h}+o+m

An example of a jo-/jā-class adjective, *med^h- ‘mid, central’, follows.

nom sg masc	*méd^h+jo+s	**nom sg fem**	*méd^h+jā+Ø	**nom sg neut**	*méd^h+jo+m

2.2 i-Class

E.g., *kúk^w- ‘pure’:

nom sg masc/fem	*kúk^w+i+s	**nom sg neut**	*kúk^w+i+Ø

2.3 u-Class

E.g., *ten-́ ‘thin’:

nom sg masc/fem	*ten+ú+s	**nom sg neut**	*ten+ú+Ø

2.4 Athematic classes

Adjectives occur in each of the athematic classes listed under 1.5 above. The adjective *k^{w}etus+pod- ‘4-footed’ is athematic Ø-class.

nom sg masc/fem	*k^{w}etus+pod+s	**nom sg neut**	*k^{w}etus+pod+Ø

2.5 Comparison

There seem to have been several suffixes for constructing comparative and superlative adjectives. These adjectives. were generally in the o-/ā-class. They were stressed on the first syllable by rule 3.1.2h(aA) WORD STRESS. E.g., the following nominative singular masculine form

positive	*kak+ó+s ‘bad’	**comparative**	*kák+is+os ‘worse’	**superlative**	*kák+ist+os ‘worst’

3 Adverbs

There seem to have been no specific suffixes for forming deadjectival or denominal advs. Rather, various neuter case endings were usually used. E.g., neut acc sg *sn̥t+jó+m ‘in truth, truly’.

4 Numerals

The Indo-European languages considered here and presumably PIE had cardinal (“one, two, three”) and ordinal (“first, second, third”) numerals. It is a well-known phenomenon that numerals in a sequence can affect one another. For instance, the word-initial /d/ in OCSlav dévętɪ ‘9’ comes from désętɪ ‘10’. If this had not occurred, one would have OCSlav **névętɪ. Since these changes have tended to occur frequently, the later PIE antecedents of the numerals can vary somewhat from language to language. (See on this Chapters 2 through 8.)

5 Pronouns

These are of three basic types: the first person "I, we two, we"; the second person "you, you two, you all"; and the third person "he, she, it; those two; they". There are also the reflexive "oneself" and relative "who, whom, that" and interrogative "who?, what?" pronouns. The pronouns took singular, dual and plural forms. Below we give these pronouns in outline form. For more detail, see Chapters 2 through 8.

5.1 First person

sg	*eg-	**sg**	*m-	**du**	*w-	**pl**	*w-	**pl**	*n̥s
nom	'I'	**obl**	'me'	**all cases**	'we two'	**nom**	'we'	**obl**	'us'

5.2 Second person

sg	*t-	**du**	*j/w-	**pl**	*j/w-
	'you'		'you two'		'you all'

5.3 Third person

These pronouns are deictic and as such mean 'he, she, it, they, this, that, these, those'. The endings of these pronouns are generally those of the nouns and adjectives except for those indicated in the following paradigm:

nom sg masc	*i+s, *s+o+s, *t+i+s[32]	**nom sg fem**	*i+ā, *s+ā *t+ā	**nom sg neut**	*i+d, *s+o+d, *t+i+d[33]
dat sg masc/neut	*i+smō, *s+o+smō, *t+i+smō[33]				
nom pl masc/fem	*i+i, *s+i, *t+i				

5.4 Reflexive

These pronouns mean 'myself, yourself, oneself, themselves'. The basic formative is *s- and it occurs only in the obl cases. E.g.,

acc sg	*s+o+m	**acc sg**	*s+ā+m	**acc sg**	*s+o+d
masc		**fem**		**neut**	

5.5 Relative

The exact form of the PIE relative pronoun is not clear since the various Indo-European languages show various different relative pronouns. (See on this Chapters 2 through 8.)

5.6 Interrogative

In some Indo-European languages these pronouns can also function as indefinites meaning 'whoever, whatever'. They invariably begin with $*k^w$-. E.g.,

nom sg masc	$*k^w$+o+s 'who?'	**nom sg fem**	$*k^w$+ā 'who?'	**nom sg neut**	$*k^w$+o+d 'what?'

6 Verbs

The Indo-European languages evince numerous similarities in their noun, adjective, and pronoun declensions. But the verb paradigms in the various Indo-European languages differ substantially. In some of these languages such as Latin or Gothic there is a conjugational system. So for example in Latin a verb with an infinitive in -āre almost invariably has its perfect in -āvi (amāre 'love', portāre 'carry': amāvi, portāvi). And in Gothic a Class 1 strong verb with its present in -ī- forms its past singular in -ē- (/grīpan/ 'seize', /skrīban/ 'write': /grēp/ /skrēf/).

In other languages such as Greek and Sanskrit, predictions like these are for the most part not possible. So for example two Greek or Sanskrit verbs which form their present in the same way can form their aorists differently. Here we assume that the presence of predictable verb conjugations is an innovation of languages like Gothic and Latin and that the PIE verb was characterized by the lack of predictability of Greek and Sanskrit.

Accordingly, we assume for the PIE verb a structure like that given in tables i and ii below. Table i shows the variable features — namely those which can change contingent upon the context. Table ii shows the lexical or inherent features — namely those that are idiosyncratic. They indicate the basic form-class of the verb. (The features in these tables in columns are mutually exclusive. Not all the logical possibilities are realized. The x's and active/middle/passive notations in the (e)-columns of table i indicate which are. The middle voice has the reflexive meaning 'to "verb" for oneself or on one's own behalf'. Many such verbs denote bodily functions such as breathing. The optative is used under two main conditions. First, it is used when the truth value of a clause S is in doubt or unknown. Second, it is used when the speaker presupposes (in this case, hopes) that the clause S should turn out to be true. An example from English is the verb in the formulaic sentence "Long live the queen!" Another is the embedded S in a sentence like "The judge ordered that the man be fined." (as opposed to **"... is fined.").)

(i) Variable Features

The first part of this table lists the purely verbal features. The second gives the features of deverbative adjectives and nouns.

Verbal Inflection

(a) Person	(b) Number	(c) Voice	(d) Mood
1. 1st	1. singular	1. active[34]	1. indicative[35]
2. 2nd	2. dual	2. middle[34]	2. subjunctive[35]
3. 3rd	3. plural	3. ?passive[34]	3. imperative[36]
			4. optative[37]

(i) Variable Features (cont.):

Verbal Inflection (cont.)

(e)	Tense Occurring in	Indicative	Subjunctive	Imperative	Optative
1.	present	x	x	x	x [38]
2.	imperfect	x	?	?	?
3.	aorist	x	?	?	?
4.	perfect	x	?	?	?
5.	?future [39]	x	?	?	?

The imperfect designates a past event which lasted for some time as in the English sentences "I was writing." and "I used to write." The perfect designates a past event which has been completed. E.g., the English sentence "I have written (and finished) this letter." The aorist designates a past event without regard to the length of time it may have taken to complete. E.g., the English sentence "I wrote (once or continually)." (See on the aorist Chapter 4, Greek.)

Adjectival and Nominal Inflection:

(a) Person	(b) Number	(c) Voice	(d) Mood
	1. singular	1. active[34]	1. ? infinitive[40]
Ø	2. dual	2. middle[34]	2. participle
	3. plural	3. passive[34]	

(e)	Tense Occurring in	Infinitive[40]	Participle
1.	present	active[40]	active/middle
2.	imperfect	?	?
3.	aorist	?	?
4.	perfect	?	active/middle/passive
5.	future	?	?

(ii) Inherent Features:

(a) Inflectional Type	(b) Class Type
1. deponent[34]	1. thematic[41]
2. nondeponent[34]	2. athematic[41]

(c) Class for present and imperfect formations[42]

1.	j-class	**thematic**	e.g. *níg^{w}+j+ō	'I wash'
2.	n-class	"	e.g. *tém+n+ō	'I cut'
3.	sk-class	"	e.g. *gnṓ+sk+ō	'I know
4.	Ø-class	"	e.g. *léik^{w}+Ø+ō	'I leave'
5.	nV-class	**athematic**	e.g. *per+nā́+mi	'I bring in'
6.	reduplicating class	"	e.g. *di+dṓ+mi	'I give'
7.	Ø-class	"	e.g. *éi+Ø+mi	'I go'

The following paradigms instantiate four basic types of endings. These are the following: (i) the primary endings which occur in the present ind paradigm (6.1.1 below); (ii) the secondary endings which occur in the imperfect and aorist tenses as well as in the optative mood (as in 6.2, 6.3, 6.1.4 and 6.1.8 below); (iii) the perfect endings (in 6.4 below) and (iv) the imperative endings (in 6.1.3 and 6.1.7).

6.1 Present

In the following present paradigms we cite examples of thematic and athematic verbs.

6.1.1 Present Active Indicative

The following paradigm is thematic.

sg	**1**	*léik^{w}+ō 'leave'	**du**	**1**	*léik^{w}+o+mes	**pl**	**1**	*léik^{w}+o+me
	2	*léik^{w}+e+si		**2**	*léik^{w}+e+thes[43]		**2**	*léik^{w}+e+te
	3	*léik^{w}+e+ti		**3**	*léik^{w}+e+tes		**3**	*léik^{w}+o+nti

6.1.2 Present Active Subjunctive The subjunctive is formed in thematic verbs by lengthening the thematic vowel of the indicative forms and in athematic verbs by inserting the corresponding short vowel between the root and the ending. E.g.,

	1	*léik^{w}+ō 'leave'		**1**	*dwéis+o+mi 'hate'
thematic sg	**2**	*léik^{w}+ē+si	**athematic sg**	**2**	*dwéis+e+si
	3	*léik^{w}+ē+ti		**3**	*dwéis+e+ti

6.1.3 Present Active Imperative We list here only the 2nd person forms. PIE may also have had 1st and 3rd person imperative forms as described in Chapter 4 (Greek) and Chapter 7 (Sanskrit). The thematic and athematic endings are the same. E.g.,

sg 2	*b^{h}ér+e 'carry'	**du 2**	*b^{h}ér+e+thes	**pl 2**	*b^{h}ér+e+te

6.1.4 Present Active Optative

The optative endings for thematic and athernatic verbs are the same. However, the intermediate optative formant for thematic verbs is *-oi- and that for athematic verbs is *-jē- in the singular and *-ī- in the dual and plural. These formants were probably ablauting variants of a single ending, namely *-ī-. The ablauting variants would have been *-o+ī-, *-ī+ē- and *-ī+Ø-. The *-o+ī- was then reformed to the acceptable diphthong *-oi- by the PIE rule 3.1.2b DIPH; and the *-ī+ē- sequence was reformed to the more usual *-jē- by rule 3.1.2c i-j/u-w ALT.

The thematic conjugation is as follows.

sg	**1**	*léik^w+oi+m 'leave'	**du**	**1**	*léik^w+oi+we	**pl**	**1**	*léik^w+oi+me
	2	*léik^w+oi+s		**2**	*léik^w+oi+tom		**2**	*léik^w+oi+te
	3	*léik^w+oi+t		**3**	*léik^w+oi+tām		**3**	*léik^w+oi+nt

The athematic conjugation takes the same endings. E.g.,

sg	**1**	*dwís+jē+m 'hate'	**du**	**1**	* dwís+ī+we	**pl**	**1**	* dwís+ī+me

6.1.5 Present Middle Indicative

The thematic conjugation is this:

sg	**1**	*b^{h}ér+ai (or) *b^{h}ér+ō+r 'I carry for myself, am carried'[44]	**du**	**1**	*b^{h}ér+o+w+ai	**pl**	**1**	*b^{h}ér+o+med^h+ai
	2	*b^{h}ér+e+s+ai		**2**	*b^{h}ér+e+th+ai		**2**	*b^{h}ér+e+t+ai
	3	*b^{h}ér+e+t+ai		**3**	*b^{h}ér+e+t+ai		**3**	*b^{h}ér+o+nt+ai

The endings of the athematic conjugation are like those of the thematic conjugation except for the 1sg E.g.,

sg	**1**	*d^{h}í+d^{h}e+m+ai 'I set for myself, am set'
	2	*d^{h}í+d^{h}e+s+ai

6.1.6 Present Middle Subjunctive

This paradigm is like that of the present active subjunctive in that thematic verbs lengthen the thematic vowel and athematic verbs insert the corresponding short thematic vowel between the root and the ending. E.g.,

thematic sg	1	*b^{h}ér+ō+ai 'carry for myself'[45]
"	2	*b^{h}ér+ē+s+ai
athematic sg	1	*d^{h}í+d^{h}e+o+m+ai 'set for myself'
"	2	*d^{h}í+d^{h}e+e+s+ai[46]

6.1.7 Present Middle Imperative

We cite only the 2nd person forms. The endings are the same for both thematic and athematic paradigms. E.g., the following thematic verb:

sg	2	*b^{h}ér+ai 'carry for yourself, be carried'	**du**	2	*b^{h}ér+ai+thes	**pl**	2	*b^{h}ér+ai+te

6.1.8 Present Middle Optative

The thematic and athematic endings are the same. The intermediate formatives may vary: the thematic verbs take *-oi- and the athematic ones *-ī-. The endings are the secondary middle ones. E.g., the following thematic verb:

sg	1	*b^{h}ér+oi+mām 'carry for myself, be carried'	**du**	1	*b^{h}ér+oi+mo	**pl**	1	*b^{h}ér+oi+med^{h}e
	2	*b^{h}ér+oi+so		2	*b^{h}ér+oi+thām		2	*b^{h}ér+oi+tām
	3	*b^{h}ér+oi+to		3	*b^{h}ér+oi+tām		3	*b^{h}ér+oi+nto

The athematic verbs take the same endings but with the intermediate vowel *-ī-. E.g.,

sg	1	*dwís+ī+mām 'hate for myself, be hated'	**du**	1	*dwís+ī+mo	**pl**	1	*dwís+ī+med^{h}e

6.2 Imperfect

The imperfect had only two paradigms, the indicative active and middle.

6.2.1 Imperfect Active Indicative

The endings are the secondary ones. Following is a thematic verb.

sg	1	*é+b^{h}er+o+m 'carried'	**du**	1	*é+b^{h}er+o+we	**pl**	1	*é+b^{h}er+o+me
	2	*é+b^{h}er+e+s		2	*é+b^{h}er+e+tom		2	*é+b^{h}er+e+te
	3	*é+b^{h}er+e+t		3	*é+b^{h}er+e+tām		3	*é+b^{h}er+o+nt

The athematic conjugation has the same endings as the thematic, but lacks the intermediate thematic vowel. E.g.,

sg	1	*é+d^{h}i+d^{h}ē+m 'set'[47]
	2	*é+d^{h}i+d^{h}ē+s

6.2.2 Imperfect Middle Indicative

This paradigm consists of the imperfect active indicative root as in 6.2.1 plus the secondary endings of the present middle optative in 6.1.8. E.g.,

sg	**1**	*é+b^her+o+mām 'I carried for myself, was carried'	**1**	*é+dweis+mām 'I hated for myself, was hated'
	2	*é+b^her+e+so	**2**	*é+dweis+so

6.3 Aorist

There seem to have been several ways to form the aorist. (See on this Chapter 7 on Sanskrit.) Two of the aorist formatives were the following: first, there is an s-aorist by which an *-s- plus the endings are added to the root; and second, a Ø-aorist which adds the aorist endings directly to the root. The endings are those of the imperfect under 6.2 above.

6.3.1 Aorist Active Indicative

E.g., the following 1sg forms:

s-aorist	*é+b^her+s+om 'I carried'[48]	*é+leik^w+s+om 'I left'[48]
Ø-aorist	*é+b^hr̥+om[48, 49]	*é+lik^w+om[48, 49]

6.3.2 Aorist Middle Indicative

E.g., the following 1sg forms:

s-aorist	*é+b^her+s+omām 'carried for myself'	*é+d^hē+s+omām 'set for myself'
Ø-aorist	*é+b^hr̥+omām	*é+d^hē+omām[50]

6.4 Perfect

This tense is usually formed by reduplicating the word-initial consonant(s), adding /e/ and prefixing this syllable to the root. The stress is on the root in the active singular and on the ending otherwise. The root in the singular usually has e/o-ablaut; the dual and plural roots have the Ø-grade. (See on this the Sanskrit rule in Chapter 7, morphology section 6.3.)

6.4.1 Perfect Active Indicative E.g.,

sg	1	*te+téud+a 'I have pushed'	**du**	1	*te+tud+wé	**pl**	1	*te+tud+mé
	2	*te+téud+tha[51]		2	*te+tud+éthur		2	*te+tud+té[51]
	3	*te+téud+e		3	*te+tud+étur		3	*te+tud+úr

Some few verbs form their perfect conjugation without reduplication, but with the usual ablaut and stress patterns. E.g., the following 1st person forms.

sg	*wóid+a 'I have seen, know'	**du**	*wid+wé	**pl**	*wid+mé

6.4.2 Perfect Middle Indicative

This paradigm was an amalgam consisting basically of the perfect active endings plus the present middle indicative marker *-ai. The stress was likely on this ending.

sg	1	*te+tud+ái[52] 'I have been pushed'	**du**	1	*te+tud+wái	**pl**	1	*te+tud+mái
	2	*te+tud+thái		2	*te+tud+ethurái		2	*te+tud+tái
	3	*te+tud+ái[52]		3	*te+tud+eturái		3	*te+tud+urái

6.5 Participles

Below we cite the nominative singular masculine, feminine and neuter forms.

6.5.1 Present Active Participle

This is a Vnt-class athematic adjective as described in 1.5.6 above.

masc	*b^{h}ér+ont+s 'carrying'	**fem**	*b^{h}ér+ont+s	**neut**	*b^{h}ér+ont+Ø

6.5.2 Present Middle Participle

This is an o-and ā-class adjective as described in 2.1 above.

masc	*b^{h}ér+omen+os 'carrying for oneself'	**fem**	*b^{h}ér+omen+ā	**neut**	*b^{h}ér+omen+om

6.5.3 Perfect Active Participle

This is a Vs-class adjective as described in 1.5.7 above.

masc	*te+tud+wṓt+s[53] 'having pushed'	**fem**	*te+tud+wṓt+s[53]	**neut**	*te+tud+úØt+Ø[54]

6.5.4 Perfect Passive Participle

The two formatives are *-Vn- and *-Vt- (where V is ablauting /e/ or /o/). The perfect passive participle is an o- and a-class adjecive as described in 2.1 above.

masc	*b^{h}r̥+ón+os (or) *b^{h}r̥+ót+os 'carried'	**fem**	*b^{h}r̥+ón+ā (or) *b^{h}r̥+ót+ā	**neut**	*b^{h}r̥+ón+om (or) *b^{h}r̥+ót+om

IV A Proto-Indo-European Text

The linguist August Schleicher composed a PIE fable in 1868. In 1939 Hermann Hirt rewrote the fable in his version of PIE. Hirt (1939: 113–114) cites both versions. We give both these versions below as well as our own version of the fable. (In the Key to the present chapter we give a translation of the fable which we have set as an exercise.)

The view has often been expressed that the reconstruction of a PIE text is somehow illicit and that the only legitimate reconstruction is of phonology, morphological paradigms as given in 3.2.2 above or of lexical items such as given in etymological dictionaries like Pokorny (1959 and 1969).

This view is erroneous. Rather, the reconstruction of a text is indeed a legitimate endeavor. But, the ontological status of such a text is different from that of a reconstructed proto-form such as *[pətḗr] 'father'. One assumes for a form like the preceding that it occurred on occasion and was so pronounced.

However, in the case of the text cited below we do not assume that it was in its entirety ever spoken. But we do assume that if it had been spoken to a speaker of PIE, it would have been understood much as we have translated it in part 5 of the Key to this chapter.

Schleicher's version is as follows. From it one can see that Schleicher assumed that PIE was much like Sanskrit.

> Avis akvāsas ka. Avis, jasmin varnā na ā ast, dadarka akvams, tam, vāgʰam garum vagʰantam, tam, bʰāram magʰam, tam, manum āku bʰarantam. Avis akvabʰjams ā vavakat: kard agʰnutai mai vidanti manum akvams agantam. Akvāsas ā vavakant: krudʰi avai, kard agʰnutai vividvant-svas: manus patis varnām avisāms karnauti svabʰjam gʰarmam vastram avibʰjams ka varnā na asti. Tat kukruvants avis agram ā bʰugat.

Hirt's 1939 version is this:

> Owis eḱwōses-kʷe. Owis, jesmain wьlənā ne ēst, dedorḱe eḱwons, tom, wogʰom gʷьrum wegʰontm̥, tom, bʰorom megam, tom ǵʰьmonm̥ ōku bʰerontm̥. Owis eḱwomos ewьwekʷet: ḱērd agʰnutai moi widontei gʰьmonm̥ eḱwons aǵontm̥. eḱwoses ewьwekʷont: ḱludʰi, owei! Ḱērd aghnutai widontmos: ǵʰьmo, potis, wьlənām owjōm kʷr̥neuti sebʰoi gʰʷermom westrom; owimos-kʷe wьlənā ne esti. Tod ḱeḱruwos owis aǵrom ebʰuget.

Our version of the fable is as follows. We give (a) a phonetic transcription of the forms as they appear after the application of the phonological rules in 3.1.2 above. We mark the stress on polysyllabic words. We include the usual punctuation such as cola, commas and periods. In (b) we give a gloss; and in (c) a grammatical description of the word.

1	**a**	ówis	ékwōs	kʷe.	ówis,	?[55]
	b	*sheep*	*horse*	*and*	*sheep*	*on which*
	c	nom sg	nom pl	enclitic	nom sg	rel pron
		i-class fem	o-class masc	conj	i-class fem	loc sg fem

2	**a**	wĺ̥nā	ne	é+es+t,	dedórke	ékwons,
	b	*wool*	*not*	*be*	*see*	*horse*
	c	nom sg	adv	3sg	3sg	acc pl
		ā-class fem		imperf	perf act	o-class masc
3	**a**	tom	wógʰom	gʷr̥úm	wégʰontm̥,	tom,
	b	*the one*	*wagon*	*heavy*	*move*	*the other*
	c	pron acc	acc sg	acc sg masc	pres act part	pron acc
		sg masc	o-class masc	u-class adj	Vnt-class adj	sg masc
4	**a**	bʰórom	mégm̥,	tom	gʰḿ̥onm̥	ōkú
	b	*burden*	*large*	*yet another*	*man*	*quick*
	c	acc sg	acc sg masc	pron acc	acc sg	adv
		o-class masc	Ø-class adj	sg masc	Vn-class masc	
5	**a**	bʰérontm̥.	ówis	ékwobʰjos	éweket:	kerd
	b	*carry*	*sheep*	*horse*	*speak*	*heart*
	c	pres act part	nom sg	dat pl	3sg imperf	nom sg
		Vnt-class adj	i-class fem	o-class masc	act	Ø-class neut
		acc sg masc				
6	**a**	áŋgʰetai	moi	wídontei	gʰḿ̥onm̥	ékwons
	b	*be oppressed*	*I*	*see*	*man*	*horse*
	c	3sg pres	1st pers	pres act part	acc sg	acc pl
		mid indic	pron dat sg	Vnt-class adj	Vn-class masc	o-class masc
				dat sg		
7	**a**	ágontm̥,	ékwōs	wewekúr:	klúdʰe,	ówei!
	b	*drive*	*horse*	*speak*	*listen*	*sheep*
	c	pres act part	nom pl	3 pl perf act	2 sg pres act	voc sg
		Vnt-class acc sg.	o-class masc		imp	i-class fem
8	**a**	kerd	áŋgʰetai	wídontbʰjos:[56]	gʰḿ̥on,	pótis,
	b	*heart*	*be oppressed*	*see*	*man*	*master*
	c	nom sg	3sg pres	pres act part	nom sg	nom sg
		Ø-class neut	mid ind	Vnt-class adj	Vn-class masc	i-class masc
				dat pl		
9	**a**	wĺ̥nām	ówijōm	kʷr̥néti	soi	gʰʷermóm
	b	*wool*	*sheep*	*make*	*oneself*	*warm*
	c	acc sg	gen pl	3sg pres	refl pron	o/ā-class adj
		ā-class fem	i-class fem	indic	dat sg	neut acc sg

10						
a	wéstrom;	ówib^{h}jos	k^{w}e	ẃ̥nā	ne	ésti.
b	*clothing*	*sheep*	*and*	*wool*	*not*	*be*
c	acc sg o-class neut	dat pl i-class fem	encl conj	nom sg ā-class fem	adv	3sg pres indic

11					
a	tod	keklṓts	ówis	agróm	éb^{h}uget.
b	*this*	*hear*	*sheep*	*field*	*flee*
c	pron acc sg neut	perf act part Vs-class adj nom sg fem	nom sg i-class fem	acc sg o-class masc	3sg aorist

V Exercises

(1) Consider the following traditionally reconstructed PIE forms. Reformulate them in terms of the glottalic theory as described in 3.1.3.2 above.

a. *ag- 'drive'.
b. *ang^h- 'narrow'.
c. Nom sg *b^{h}ā́g^h+u+s 'elbow'.
d. *b^{h}end^h- 'bind'.
e. Nom sg *b^{h}ugā́ 'flight'.
f. 3sg perf *dedórke 'has seen'.
g. 1sg pres *dwéismi 'I hate'.
h. 3sg pres *éiti 'goes'.
i. *es- 'be'.
j. 1sg pres *g^{h}réibō 'seize'.
k. *gnō- 'know'.
l. *kn̥tóm '100'.
m. *m̥b^{h}í 'around'.
n. *meg- 'large'.
o. 1sg pres *mów+ējō 'I move' vs. 1 sg perf *mṓw+a.
p. Nom sg *od+ónt+s 'tooth'.
q. *ok^w- 'eye'.
r. Nom sg fem ówis 'sheep'.
s. *ōkú 'quickly'.
t. *pətḗr 'father'.
u. *sed- 'sit'.
v. *song^{hw}ā́ 'song, oracle'.
w. *stā- 'stand'.

(2) Consider the traditionally reconstructed PIE forms cited immediately above. Reformulate them in terms of the laryngeal theory as described in 3.1.3.3 above.

(3) Consider the following formalizations of both possible and impossible phonological changes. State each rule in normal English and construct a possible example of its application. Using your intuition, state which changes seem to you plausible and which ones bogus.

a.	ai, au	→	ɛ̄, ɔ̄ / ___ [–vocalic]
b.	d	→	l
c.	dw	→	b / ##___
d.	f, θ, x	→	ƀ, ð, ǥ / [V, –stress] ___ { [+sonorant] / ## }
e.	h	→	x / ___ [+vocalic]
f.	j	→	Ø
g.	kʷ	→	p
h.	l	→	r (tongue-trilled)
i.	m	→	n / [V, –stress] ___##
j.	n	→	(b, d, g) / [V, -stress] (b, d, g) ___ [+vocalic]
k.	o(:)	→	ö(:)
l.	p	→	kʷ
m.	pʰ, tʰ, kʰ	→	f, θ, x
n.	s	→	h
o.	s	→	x / k, r, i(:), u(:) ___ V
p.	sr	→	str
q.	t	→	s / ___ [V, +high]
r.	u(:)	→	y(:)
s.	Vmj	→	Vnj
t.	w	→	Ø
u.	x	→	h / ___ [+vocalic]
v.	z	→	r (tongue-trilled)
w.	Ø	→	e / ## ___ sC

(4) Consider the following sets of cognates. Posit a possible PIE antecedent using the phoneme inventory in 3.1.1 above. Posit changes which seem to you plausible; state these changes.

a.	Gk	ágō 'I drive'
	Lat	ágō 'idem'
	Skt	áǰā- 'idem'
b.	Gk	hādýs 'sweet'
	Skt	svādús 'idem'
	Eng	sweet

c. Go baíra /béra/ 'I carry'
Gk pʰérō 'idem'
Lat férō 'idem'
Skt bʰárā- 'idem'

d. Go wit- 'know'
Gk id- 'idem'
Lat vid- 'see'

e. Considering the vowels in the cognate sets a through d above, reconstruct a possible Indo-European antecedent for the following set. What is the problem in this reconstruction?

Go fáðar 'father'
Gk patér 'idem'
Lat páter 'idem'
Skt pitár 'idem'

(5) Consider the PIE fable in section 4 above. Give a smooth translation of this text.

VII Key

(1) The glottalic reconstructions are these:

(a) *ak'-, (b) *angʰ-, (c) *bʰā́gʰus, (d) *bʰendʰ-, (e) *bʰuk'ā́, (f) *t'et'órkʰe, (g) *t'weismi, (h) éitʰi, (i) *es-, (j) *gʰréip'ō, (k) *k'nō-, (l) *kʰn̥tʰóm, (m) *m̥bʰí, (n) mek'-, (o) mówējō and *mṓwa, (p) *ot'óntʰs, (q) *okʰʷ-, (r) *ówis, (s) *ōkʰú, (t) *pʰətʰḗr, (u) *set'-, (v) *songʰʷā́, (w) *stʰā-.

(2) Possible laryngeal reconstructions are these:

(a) *$h_2$eg-, (b) *$h_2$engʰ-, (c) *bʰéh_2gʰus, (d) *bʰendʰ-, (e) *bʰugéh_2, (f) *ded$h_3$érke, (g) *dwéismi, (h) *$h_1$éiti, (i) *$h_1$es-, (j) *gʰréibeh_3, (k) *gneh_3, (l) *kn̥t$h_3$ém, (m) *m̥bʰí, (n) *meg-, (o) *m$h_3$éwe$h_2$jeh_3 and *méh_3wh_2e, (p) *$h_3$ed$h_3$énts, (q) *$h_3$ekʷ-, (r) *$h_3$éwis, (s) *e$h_3$kú, (t) *phtéh_1r, (u) *sed-, (v) *s$h_3$engʰʷéh_2, (w) *steh_2-.

(3) The changes and their status are as follows:

a. The diphthongs /ai/ and /au/ become the long lax vowels /ɛ̄/ and /ɔ̄/ when followed by a nonvocalic segment. E.g., *pait, *paut → *pɛ̄t, *pɔ̄t. This change can occur as in the Go change 7a ai/au-MONOPH.
b. /d/ becomes /l/ everywhere. This change does not occur.

c. /dw/ becomes /b/ word-initially. E.g., *dwo → *bo. This change can occur as in the Latin change 8b dw-CHANGES.

d. /f, θ, x/ become voiced /ƀ, ð, ǥ/ if preceded by an unstressed vowel and if followed by any sonorant segment or if word-final. E.g., *afá → aƀá. This change can occur as in the Gothic change 3 VERNER.

e. /h/ becomes /x/ before a vocalic segment. E.g., *aha → *axa. This change does not occur.

f. /j/ disappears. E.g., *ja → *a. This change can occur as in the OIr change 9b j-DELE.

g. /k^w/ becomes /p/. E.g., *k^wa → *pa. This change has occurred in the history of some Celtic languages. See on this the OIr change 7a k^w-to -k.

h. /l/ becomes tongue-trilled /r/. E.g., *ala → *ara. This change can occur as in the Sanskrit change 9b l/r ALT.

i. /m/ becomes /n/ word-finally if preceded by an unstressed vowel. E.g., *álam → *álan. This change can occur as in the Go change 7c NASAL LOSS.

j. /n/ is assimilated to a preceding /b, d, g/ if the preceding vowel is unstressed; and the /n/ must precede a vowel. E.g., *abná, *egnó → *abbá, *eggó. This change can occur as in the Gothic change 4b n-ASSIM.

k. Short or long /o(:)/, regardless of environment, becomes fronted to /ö(:)/. E.g., *dōn → *dȫn. This change does not occur.

l. /p/ becomes /k^w/. E.g., *pa → *k^wa. This change does not occur.

m. Aspirated /p^h, t^h, k^h/ become the continuants /f, θ, x/. E.g., *p^ha, *t^ha, *k^ha → *fa, *θa, *xa. This change can occur as in the Gothic change 2 1ST SS.

n. /s/ becomes /h/. E.g., *sō → *hō. This change can occur as in the Greek change 3e s-h-Ø.

o. /s/ becomes /x/ if preceded by /k, r, i(:), or u(:)/ and if followed by a vowel. E.g., *aksa, *arsa, *isu, *usu → *akxa, *arxa, *ixu, *uxu. This change can occur as in the OCSlav change 3 RUKI.

p. The sequence /sr/ becomes /str/. E.g., *sro →*stro. This change can occur as in the OCSlav change 2a C CL.

q. /t/ becomes/s/ if preceding a high vowel, namely /i(:) or u(:)/. E.g., *tu → *su. This change can occur as in the Greek change 4b t-TO-s.

r. Short and long /u(:)/ become the front and still rounded /y(:)/. E.g., *tu → *ty. This change can occur as in the Greek change 6d u(:)-TO-y(:).

s. /m/ becomes /n/ if preceded by a vowel and followed by /j/. E.g., *amjo → *anjo. This change can occur as in the Latin change 3a C+j CHANGES.

t. /w/ is everywhere deleted. E.g., *awi → *ai. This change can occur as in the Greek change 7c w-DELE.

u. /x/ becomes /h/ if followed by a vowel. E.g.,*xal → *hal. This change can occur as in the Go change 5e x-TO-h.

v. /z/ becomes tongue-trilled /r/. E.g., *aza →*ara. This change can occur as in the Latin change 3d s-TO-r.

w. /e/ is inserted word-initially if the word begins with /s/ plus another consonant. E.g., *sma → *esma. This change can occur as for example in the history of several later Romance languages such as Spanish.

(4) The PIE reconstructions and the changes are as follows:

a. The PIE form is *ágō. The changes are g > ɟ and ō > ā in Skt.
b. The PIE form is *swādús. The changes are sw > h and u > y in Greek; w > v in Sanskrit and (ev) ā > ī (spelled <ee>) and d > t in English.
c. The PIE form is *b^hérō. The changes are b^h > b and word-final unstressed ō > a in Gothic; b^h> p^h in Greek; b^h > p^h > f in Latin; and e > a and ō > ā in Sanskrit.
d. The PIE form is *wid-. The changes are d > t in Gothic, w > Ø in Greek and w > v in Latin.
e. The problem is that cognate set (a) has /a/ throughout and set (d) has /i/ throughout. So if one reconstructs PIE *pitér, one would expect Go **fiðar, Gk **pitér and Lat **píter. If one reconstructs PIE *patér, one would expect Skt **patár. One way out of this is to reconstruct an entirely different vowel. The common assumption has been that if the PIE short vowels were /i, e, a, o, u/ and an extra vowel was needed, that vowel would likely be /ə/. Hence the reconstructed PIE form is often assumed to have been *pətér. Then the changes are ə > i in Sanskrit and ə > a in the other daughter languages. Another suggestion has been to posit a laryngeal in *phtér and the changes h > i in Sanskrit and h > a otherwise.

(5) A translation of the fable in section 4 above is the following.

"The sheep and the horses. A sheep on which there was no wool saw horses, one pulling a heavy wagon, one a great burden and another swiftly carrying a man. The sheep said to the horses: 'My heart is oppressed when I see a man driving horses.' The horses spoke: 'Listen, sheep! Our heart is oppressed seeing that man, the master, makes the sheep's wool into warm clothing for himself; and for the sheep there is no wool.' Having heard this the sheep fled into the field."

VIII Notes

[1] The /s, z/ alternation is predictable by the PIE phonological rule 3.1.2e OBSTR CL below. Another way of stating this alternation is that the phoneme /s/ has two allophones [s, z] as determined by OBSTR CL.
[2] The syllabic with subscript vs. nonsyllabic alternations are predictable by PIE rule 3.1.2g SYL SON below.
[3] The [n, ŋ] alternation occurs according to the PIE rule 3.1.2d NASAL ASSIM.
[4] The phonemes /w/ and /j/ are often written as /u̯/ and /i̯/; /j/ can also be written /y/. The alternations /i/-/j/ and /u/-/w/ occur from rule 3.1.2c i-j/u-w ALT cited below.
[5] This segment, if it did in fact exist in the PIE inventory, occurred rarely. The rationale for its reconstruction is explained in (4e) in the Key to this chapter.
[6] We shall refer to +consonantal and –sonorant segments as "obstruents".
[7] The notation "±" indicates that any +vocalic segment may be either stressed or not according to rule 3.1.2h WORD STRESS as outlined below.
[8] Under the glottalic theory the segments and /p^h/ and /b^h/ had allophones such that /p^h/ = [p^h, p] and /b^h/ = [b^h, b] in certain environments which to our knowledge have not been made explicit in the literature.
[9] The series represented by /p'/ consists of tense, unaspirated and glottalized consonants of a type frequently found in many non-IE languages such as Korean.

[10] The -m is the o-class neuter ending. For the other classes the neuter ending is -Ø. The -Ø is also the nom sg fem ending of the ā- and jā-class (1.2 below) as well as the nom sg masc/fem of the athematic tVr- and Vn-classes (1.5.4 and 1.5.5 below).
[11] The V(:) in these endings is the stem vowel of the particular class.
[12] The ending –e accrues to the athematic classes. For the other classes the ending is –V̄(i/u).
[13] This is the neuter ending. It is also reconstructed as -ə or as -ā.
[14] The Gothic antecedent may have been an ablauting ending -ēm.
[15] The reflex of -b^h(j)os occurs in Latin, Old Irish and Sanskrit; that of -is occurs in Greek; and that of -mis occurs in Gothic and OCSlav . The Hittite endings devolve from the genitive singular.
[16] Recall that the neuter nominative and accusative endings are identical. Aside from these forms, the neuter endings are those of the masculine.
[17] Phonological rule 3.1.2f SIEVERS applies in the synchronic derivation of this form: */wóik+jā/ (SIEVERS) → *[wóikijā].
[18] The derivation of this form is */egn+éi+es/ (PIE rule 3.1.2c i-j/u–w ALT) → *[egnéjes].
[19] The derivation is */wṓr+i+a/ (3.1.2c i-j/u–w ALT) → *wṓrja (3.1.2f SIEVERS) → *[wṓrija].
[20] The derivation of these forms is */kótr+eu+es/ and */med^h+u+a/ (3.1.2c i-j/u–w ALT) → *[kótrewes] and *[méd^{h}wa].
[21] The synchronic derivation is */pḗd+s/ (PIE rule 3.1.2e OBSTR CL) → *[pḗts].
[22] The stress in these forms is determined by the PIE rule 3.1.2h(eC) WORD STRESS.
[23] The derivation is */péd+m/ (PIE rule 3.1.2g Syl Son) → *[pédm̥].
[24] The derivation of these forms is */diēú+s/ and */ díēu/ (PIE rule 3.1.2c i-j/u-w ALT) → *[djēús] and *[díēu].
[25] The root in this case has Ø-grade ablaut. Its derivation is */díu+m/ (rule 3.1.2g SYL SON) → *díu+m̥ (rule 3.1.2c i-j/u–w ALT) → *[díwm̥].
[26] The stress pattern in these words is set by provisos aC and bB of rule 3.1.2h WORD STRESS.
[27] The derivation is */pəter+m/ (rule 3.1.2g SYL SON) → *pəterm̥ (3.1.2h(dB) WORD STRESS) → *[pətérm̥].
[28] Masculine and feminine nouns take the same endings.
[29] The Vn-suffix shows ō/o/Ø-ablaut. Derivation: *rḗg+Øn+b^{h}jos (rule 3.1.2g SYL SON) → *[rḗgn̥b^{h}jos].
[30] The derivation of these forms is */nṓm+Øn+Ø/ and */nṓm+Øn+ī/ (rule 3.1.2g SYL SON applying only to the first form) → *[nṓmn̥] and *[nṓmnī].
[31] This is the o-grade ablaut of the verb *ed- 'eat'. Some languages have the Ø-grade ablaut form for this noun such as *Ød+ent+s (ev) > Lat dens 'tooth'.
[32] The pronominal roots are *i-, *s- and *t-. They occur in several Indo-European languages.
[33] These endings are exclusively pronominal, as opposed to the other endings, which are also adjectival and nominal.
[34] The notions of active and passive are familiar as in the active sentence "I see." vs. the passive. "I am seen." Some sources dispute the existence of a passive in PIE. We assume that the PIE passive took the same endings as the middle. Also in this connection we note that some verbs are deponent (dep). Such verbs take middle endings, but have active meanings. E.g., the verb' *sék^w+ō+r (possibly *sék^w+ai) 'I follow'.
[35] The indicative is an unmarked mood and is used to express a simple assertion. The subjunctive is used in a clause, main or subordinate, when the speaker presupposes that its truth value (i.e., whether it is true or false) is not known. An example of this is the VP "is coming" in the sentence "I don't know whether he is coming." In PIE the verb meaning "is coming" (*g^{w}em-) in this construction would be marked as +subj (*g^{w}ém+ē+ti vs. indic *g^{w}ém+e+ti). Another function of the subjunctive is to mark verbs in clauses whose truth values are presupposed to be false. For example, the two clauses in the sentence "If he were here, I'd leave." cited in 2.1.1 above. Recall that in this sentence the two constituent clauses S_1 and S_2 are presupposed to be false. Hence their verbs are marked as +subj.

[36] The imperative expresses a strong wish or command, as for instance in the sentence "Go home!" Although the imperative usually occurs in the 2nd person, it can also occur in the 1st and 3rd persons as well. (See Chapter 3 Latin and Chapter 8 Hittite.)

[37] Since the functions of the optative and the subjunctive can occasionally overlap (as for example in the presupposition that the truth value of a clause S is in doubt), the optative often takes on a subjunctive function in the later Indo-European languages. (See on this Chapter 2 Gothic, 4 Greek and 5 Old Irish.)

[38] On the basis of the early Indo-European languages cited in Chapters 2 through 8, we consider it likely that PIE verbs in the present occurred in the indicative, subjunctive, imperative and optative. However, the other tenses (imperfect, aorist, perfect and future) probably occurred only in the indicative.

[39] Some assume that PIE had no future-tense formative. If this is true, then the present paradigms below would surely have been used on occasion to express future meanings.

[40] It is not obvious that PIE had an infinitive since these constructions vary considerably in the attested Indo-European languages.

[41] The terms "thematic" and "athematic" refer to the presence vs. the absence of a vowel between a root and an inflectional ending. E.g., 3sg pres ind thematic *b^{h}ér+e+ti 'carries' vs. the 3sg pres indic athematic *dwéis+Ø+ti 'hates'.

[42] These class formatives occur after the verb root only in the present and imperfect tenses — and not elsewhere. Hence the 3sg pres *gnṓ+sk+eti 'knows' and the 3sg imperf *é+gnō+sk+et 'used to know' vs. the 3sg aorist *é+gnō+t 'knew'.

[43] There was possibly a laryngeal /h/ in this ending. The athematic verbs have the same endings as the thematic ones except for two features: first, the 1 singular ending is *-mi; and second, there is no thematic vowel between the root and the ending. E.g.,

sg	1	*dwéis+Ø+mi 'hate'	2	*dwéis+Ø+si	3	*dwéis+Ø+ti

[44] There may have been a PIE -r suffix for middle and passive verb forms. See on this Chapter 3 Latin, Chapter 5 Old Irish.

[45] The thematic 1st singular may have taken the athematic ending *-m to result in *b^{h}ér+ō+m+ai.

[46] The sequence /e+e / in this form would result in /ē/, *d^{h}íd^{h}ēsai.

[47] The root *d^{h}ē- is the ē-ablaut grade of *d^{h}e-.

[48] As noted earlier, a verb of any form class can form its aorist either as an s-aorist or a Ø-aorist.

[49] Verbs taking the Ø-aorist usually show Ø-grade ablaut in order to be distinguished from the imperfect forms, with which they would otherwise be identical.

[50] The imperfect of this verb would not be identical with the Ø-aorist form because the irnperfect would have the reduplicative syllable as in the 1sg imperf *é+d^{h}i+d^{h}ē+omām.

[51] The derivation of these forms is *te+téud+tha and *te+tud+té (rule 3.1.2e OBSTR CL) → *tetéuttha and *tetutté.

[52] The active endings *-a and *-e are totally replaced here.

[53] The suffixes in these forms have ō-grade ablaut.

[54] The suffix has Ø-grade ablaut. The derivation is *te+tud+wØt+Ø (3.1.2c i-j/u-w ALT) → *tetudut (3.1.2h WORD STRESS) → *tetudút.

[55] The form of the PIE relative pronoun is not clear. The loc sg fem may have been *j+āi.

[56] The derivation of this form is *wídont+b^{h}jos (rule 3.1.2e OBSTR CL) → *widondb^{h}jos.

Chapter 2

Gothic

I Introduction

The earliest extensively attested Germanic language is Gothic (Go). We posit as the first split in the Germanic linguistic community the bifurcation between East Germanic and Northwest (NW) Germanic. The only East Germanic language attested is Gothic. The NW Germanic community later split into North Germanic and West Germanic. The only North Germanic language we cite here is Old Icelandic. (Other North Germanic languages are Old, Middle and Modern Norwegian, Swedish and Danish. Middle and Modern Icelandic are conservative in their developments and as such stand close to Old Icelandic.) The West Germanic languages we cite are Old English, Modern English, Old High German, Modern German and Old Saxon. (Other West Germanic languages are Frisian and Dutch.)

The earliest Gothic consists of a translation of a sizeable portion of the New Testament by the Gothic bishop Wulfila, who is sometimes referred to as Ulfilas. The translation was done around 350 AD, although the main manuscript — the so-called Codex Argenteus "Silver Codex" — dates from the 500's AD.

At Wulfila's time the West Goths, to which community Wulfila belonged, were living in today's Bulgaria. It is surmised that the East Germanic peoples, from whom the Goths eventually emerged, had left the Germanic homeland in southern Scandinavia at around 0 AD.

To record Gothic Wulfila devised an alphabet which he based mainly on that of Greek with occasional recourse to the alphabets of Latin and the runic inscriptions. We cite our Gothic forms for the most part in the traditional romanization of the original Wulfilian orthography. One aspect of this romanization involves the graphemes <ai> and <au>, which Wulfila used to represent long /ɛ̄/ and short /e/ as well as long /ɔ̄/ and short /o/, respectively. Most editors have used accent marks to distinguish the long and short vowels: <ái> = /ɛ̄/, <aí> = /e/; <áu> = /ɔ̄/, <aú> = /o/. We have followed this practice, although we often give phonemic and phonetic transcriptions of the Gothic forms: baíran /beran/ 'carry' vs. áins /ɛ̄ns/ 'one' and baúrans /borans/ 'born' vs. áuk /ɔ̄k/ 'also'. We usually do not mark Gothic word stress, particularly when it is word-initial. We differ from the traditional romanization in that we indicate vowel length with the macron: traditional <berum> 'we carried' is our <bērum> and <forum> 'we traveled' is our <fōrum>. (Some additional minor transcriptional conventions are discussed in III Gothic phonology.)

II The Changes from PIE into Gothic

A. Overview of the Changes and their Chronology

The stages are ordered. The changes within each stage may have been in any order or roughly simultaneous.

STAGE 1 (ca. 3000 BC or later)

B. The Changes

1a Simplification of Geminate Consonants (GEM C SIMP)

This rule remains as a phon cond alternation in the Gothic grammar. Part (a) was inherited from PIE; part (b) is probably a Germanic innovation.

$$C_aC_a \rightarrow C_a \;/\; \text{(a)}\;\_\_\_ \begin{Bmatrix} C \\ ?\#\# \end{Bmatrix} \;\text{or}\; \begin{Bmatrix} C \\ \#\# \end{Bmatrix} \_\_\_ \qquad \text{(b)}\; VV\;\_\_\_$$

That is, two like consonants are simplified (a) if preceding another consonant or possibly if word-final or if following another consonant or if word-initial; or (b) if following a long vowel or diphthong — and with no intervening morpheme boundary.

E.g., (a) 2 sg pres /kann+t/ 'you can' → [kant], written <kant> or <kannt>; 3 sg pres /kann/ 'he can' → [kan], written <kann>. (b) There is no Gothic word with the morpheme structure VVC_aC_a with no morpheme boundary between the VV and the geminate C_aC_a. Hence Go nēmum 'we took', not **nēmmum.

1b Voicing and Devoicing of Obstruent Clusters (OBSTR VOI/DEVOI)

This rule is inherited from PIE and remains in the grammar as a phon cond rule.

$$\begin{bmatrix} +\text{obstruent} \\ \alpha\text{voiced} \end{bmatrix} \rightarrow [\beta\text{voiced}] \;/\; \_\_\_ \begin{bmatrix} +\text{obstruent} \\ \beta\text{voiced} \end{bmatrix}$$

That is, in a two-obstruent consonant cluster the first obstruent is voiced if the second one is and voiceless if the second one is voiceless. E.g., PIE inf *tong+jonom 'think' vs. 1 sg past *tong+tōm (OBSTR VOI/DEVOI) > *tongjonom and *tonktōm (2 1ST SS) > *þonkjonom and þonxtōm (ev) > Go þankjan vs. þāhta /θā^{n}hta/. (Note the necessary chronology OBSTR VOI/DEVOI > 2 1ST SS.) A possible addendum to OBSTR VOI/DEVOI may have been a proviso that if the first obstruent in the cluster was aspirated and voiced, then the second consonant became aspirated and voiced as well. E.g., PIE nom sg fem *kug^{h}+t+is 'mind' (OBSTR VOI/DEVOI) > *kug^{h}d^{h}is (2 1ST SS, 3 VERNER) > *huǥðiz (ev) > Go hugds 'thought'.

1c A Rule of /s/-/z/ Alternation (s-z RULE)

This rule may represent an expansion in the environment of 1b OBSTR VOI/DEVOI and as such be roughly contemporaneous with it. It remains in the grammar as a persistent phon cond rule until after the time of 2 1ST SS.

$$\begin{array}{lll} s \rightarrow z \;/ & [+\text{sonorant}]\;\_\_\_ & [C, +\text{voiced}] \\ z \rightarrow s \;/ & [+\text{sonorant}]\;\_\_\_ & [C, -\text{voiced}] \end{array}$$

That is, after a sonorant segment /z/ occurs if the following consonant (obstruent or sonorant /l, m, n, r/) is voiced and /s/ if the following consonant is voiceless. Only /s/ occurs word-initially.

E.g., PIE nom sg *ni+sd+os 'an in-sitting, nest' (1b OBSTR VOI/DEVOI applying synchronically) → *nizdos (2 1ST SS, 3 VERNER) > *niztoz (s-z RULE applying synchronically) → *nistoz (ev) > Go nists. PIE nom sg *persnā 'heel' (2 1ST SS) > *fersnā (s-z RULE, ev) > Go faírzna /ferzna/. The /s/ remains word-initially: PIE nom sg snoig^{hw}os 'snow' (ev) > Go snáiws /snɛ̄ws/, not **znáiws.

1d Insertion of /s/ (s-INSERTION)

This change seems to have been from the outset morph cond. It remains as such in the Gothic grammar.

$$\emptyset \rightarrow s \,/\, \begin{Bmatrix} \text{n} \\ \text{Verb root} \end{Bmatrix} \;\_\_\_\; \begin{Bmatrix} \text{t} \\ \text{Derivative suffix} \end{Bmatrix}$$

That is, an /s/ is inserted after a verb root ending in /n/ and before the nominalizing derivative suffix -t. E.g., PIE nom sg *on+t+is 'favor' (s-INSERTION) > *onstis (2 1ST SS, ev) > Go ansts. This derivation indicates a chronology s-INSERTION > 2 1ST SS. Otherwise the derivation would be *ontis (2 1ST SS) > *onþis (ev) > Go **anþs.

1e The Change of /tt/ and /ts/ to /ss/ (tt/ts-TO-ss)

This change remains in the Gothic grammar as a morph cond rule. Its early version is this.

t	+ t or s	→	s	+ s
1	2 3		1	2 3

where + = a word-internal morpheme boundary between a verb root and a suffix.

That is, the sequences t + t or t + s, whenever they arise through the concatenation of two morphemes, are realized as s + s. E.g., PIE 1 sg past *wid+t+ōm 'I saw, know' (1b OBSTR VOI/DEVOI) > *wittōm (tt/ts-TO-ss, ev) > Go wissa. The rule is morph cond in Gothic in that it does not apply to a /t+s/ sequence in the nom sg of nouns: e.g., Go ansts 'favor', not **anss. We assume that tt/ts-TO-ss occurred before 2 1ST SS. Otherwise one could have a derivation like wit+t+ōm 'I knew' (2 1ST SS, ev) > Go **wiþta instead of wissa.

2 The First Sound Shift AKA Grimm's Law (1ST SS)

This change — or rather series of changes — results for the most part in a restructured phonemic inventory. A remnant of it described below remains as a phon cond rule of Germanic and of Gothic. The 1ST SS change may be represented schematically as follows:

	PIE		Gmc
(a)	p t k k^{w}	>	f þ x x^{w}
(b)	b^{h} d^{h} g^{h} g^{hw}	>	ƀ ð ǥ ǥ^{w}
(c)	b d g g^{w}	>	p t k k^{w}

E.g., (a) PIE nom sg *pōd+s 'foot', *tū 'you', *kerd+ōn 'heart', *k^{w}od 'what' (1ST SS, ev) > Go fōtus, þū, haírta /herta/, ƕa /h^{w}a/. (b) PIE 1 sg *b^{h}erō 'I carry', nom sg *d^{h}r̥+om 'door', *g^{h}ort+ōn 'yard', 1 sg *seng^{hw}ō 'I sing' (1ST SS, ev) > Go baíra /bera/, daúr /dor/, garda [ǥarda], siggwa [siŋgwa]. (c) PIE nom sg masc *d^{h}eubos 'deep', 1 sg *sedō 'I sit', nom sg *jugom 'yoke', *g^{w}en+ōn 'woman' (1ST SS, ev) > Go diups, sita, juk, qinō /k^{w}inō/.

It is clear that the 1ST SS did not occur as a single change. A likely sequence of events is the successive addition to the grammar of the following three rules:

1) [C, +obstruent, –voiced] → [+aspirated] / { [+sonorant] / ## } ___

2) [C, +obstruent, +aspirated] → [+continuant]

3) [C, +obstruent, +voiced, –continuant] → [–voiced]

That is, (1) PIE p, t, k, k^w → p^h, t^h, k^h, k^{hw} if preceded by a vowel, /l, m, n, r/ or if word-initial. (2) PIE p^h, t^h, k^h, k^{hw}; b^h, d^h, g^h, g^{hw} → f, þ, x, x^w; ƀ, ð. ǥ, $ǥ^w$. (3) PIE b, d, g, g^w → p, t, k, k^w. We thus posit developments like these: PIE *pōd- 'foot', *b^her- 'carry', *nokt- 'night' (1ST SS part 1) > *p^hōd- 'foot', *b^her- 'carry', *nok^{h}t- 'night' (1ST SS part 2) > *fōd-, *ƀer-, *noxt- (1ST SS part 3) > *fōt-, *ƀer-, *noxt- (ev) > Go fōtus, baíra /bera/, nahts /nahts/.

These rules eventually became obligatory. This resulted in the restructuring of the Germanic phoneme inventory to include the new phonemes /f, þ, x, x^w; ƀ, ð, ǥ, $ǥ^w$; p, t, k, k^w/. Then the three 1ST SS rules were dropped from the grammar.

A possible remnant of the 1ST SS is the following phon cond rule, which seems to exist in most Germanic languages:

(C, +obstruent, –voiced, –continuant) → [+aspirated] / { [+sonorant] / ## } ___
[–aspirated] / elsewhere

That is, the voiceless obstruent stops /p, t, k/ are phonetically aspirated [p^h, t^h, k^h] if following a sonorant (a vowel or /l, m, n, r/) or if word-initial; otherwise (if following an obstruent consonant) these consonants are unaspirated [p, t, k]. E.g., the synchronic derivation of the Gothic inf /standan/ 'to stand' and /twalif/ '12' (1ST SS synchronically) → [st$^=$andan] but [t^{h}walif].

A possible indicator of the date of the 1ST SS is the occurrence in several Germanic languages of the word for 'hemp': OIce hampr, OEng hænep and OHGerm hanaf (the /f/ from an earlier /p/ through regular change). The Germanic antecedent was a masc o-class noun *xanapaz (later *hanapaz by 5e x-TO-h). The argument for dating the 1ST SS (in Streitberg 1943: 135-6) is that this word was borrowed from some non-PIE source into several Indo-European languages, among them Greek kannabis and Persian kanab. The original word was something like kanab. The word appears to have been borrowed into Greek sometime during the 400's BC. The Greek historian Herodotus (ca. 484-425 BC) records the use (and presumably the knowledge) of the plant as something recent. Now the form *kanab clearly underwent all three stages of 1ST SS in Gothic. If the borrowing of *kanab into pre-Germanic PIE occurred at about the same time as its borrowing into Greek, then the beginning of stage 1 of 1ST SS may have been around 400 BC, if not somewhat later.

3 Verner's Law (VERNER)

The reflex of VERNER in later Germanic and Gothic is first, a series of restructured lexical items and second, a morph cond rule. The early phon cond version of this change is this:

[C, +obstruent, –voiced] → [+voiced] / (V(V) –stress) [C, +sonorant]$_0$ ___ { [+sonorant] / ## }

That is, a voiceless obstruent consonant /f, θ, x, x^w, s/ becomes voiced /ƀ, ð, ǥ, $ǥ^w$, z/ if preceded by an unstressed long or short vowel or a diphthong (with the possibility of an intervening sonorant consonant /l, m, n, r/) and if followed by a sonorant segment (a vowel or /j, w, l, m, n, r/) or if word-final (##). The stress referred to here is still that of PIE. Hence the relative chronology VERNER > 4a GMC STRESS.

E.g., PIE nom sg *patér 'father' (2 1ST SS stages 1 and 2) > *faθér (VERNER) > faðér (4a GMC STRESS, 9c a -TO-e) > Go fadar [fáðar]. PIE 1 sg past (perf) > *se+slḗb+a 'I slept' (VERNER) > *sezlḗba (2 1ST SS stage 3) > *sezlḗpa (ev) > Go saízlēp /sezlḗp/. PIE pret-pres verb 1 sg *tórpa 'I need' vs. 1 pl *tr̥pmé 'we need' (2 1ST SS stages 1 and 2) > *θórfa and *θr̥fmé (VERNER) > *θórfa and *θr̥ƀmé (4a GMC STRESS, 6c SYL SON, ev) > Go þarf vs. þaúrbum /θorbum/.

We make two observations on the relative chronology of VERNER. First, we assume it occurs after stage 1 of 4a GMC STRESS. (Our reasons for that assumption are given in our discussion of 4a GMC STRESS.) Second, we assume that VERNER occurred during 2 1ST SS — before stage 3 and after either stage 1 or stage 2. Thus if VERNER occurred after stage 1 and before stage 2, it would change /pʰ, tʰ, etc./ to /bʰ, dʰ, etc./, which would then become /ƀ, ð, etc./ by 2 1ST SS stage 2. If VERNER occurred after 2 1ST SS stage 2, it would change /f, θ, etc./ to /ƀ, ð, etc./. In either locus, VERNER produces the same results.

But in its present formulation VERNER must apply before 2 1ST SS stage 3. If VERNER applied after stage 3, it would in some instances incorrectly revoice Gmc /p, t, k,/ < PIE /b, d, g/ by 2 1ST SS stage 3. E.g., PIE 1 pl past *gʰribmé 'we seized' (2 1ST SS all three stages) > *ǥripmé (VERNER) > **ǥribmé (ev) > Go **gribum instead of the correct form gripum.

As noted above, one reflex of VERNER is the existence of restructured forms such as Go fadar [fáðar] < PIE patér with [ð] throughout the paradigm. Another reflex is a morph cond rule which voices the root-final consonants /f, θ, h/ to /ƀ, ð, ǥ/ in the third and fourth principal parts of some some strong verbs. (On this see IV Historical Gothic morphology, section 6.1.1.) For the reasons discussed under 4a GMC STRESS, the alternation /f ~ ƀ/ etc. does not occur in the strong verbs of Gothic. However the alternation is found in some of the Gothic pret-pres verbs such as the 1 sg þarf 'need' vs. the 1 pl þaúrbum noted above.

4a The Gradual Development of Germanic Word Stress (GMC STRESS)

The eventual development of the Gmc stress rule progressed through the following three stages. The changes result in the Germanic and Gothic grammar as a mostly phon cond rule.

Stage 1. The earlier PIE rule 3.1.2h Word Stress given in Chapter 1 remains in the grammar as a morph cond rule, but it changes its morphological conditioning. Shortly before the time of 3 VERNER, the rule had become this.

V → [+stressed] / in these environments:

(a) For substantives (which are forms taking case endings, namely nouns, adjectives, inflected numerals, pronouns and participles) the environment is this:

(aa) $+[C_o \text{---}]_s s_o\#\#$

i.e., on the first syllable of an inflectional ending in (morph cond) any oblique case (= any case except the nominative, vocative, or accusative — hence in the present instance, the genitive or dative) in a substantive of the o-class and in any plural oblique case in substantives of the other classes.

(ab) $\#\#[C_o \text{---}]_s$ otherwise i.e., on the first syllable of the word.

(b) For verbs the environment is this:

(ba) $+[C_o \text{---}]_s s_o\#\#$

i.e., on the first syllable of an inflectional ending in (morph cond) the 3rd and 4th principal parts of strong verbs (i.e., in the past plural indicative, past subjunctive and past participle); in all forms of most weak verbs; and in the present plural, present subjunctive, past plural, and past subjunctive of preterite-present verbs.

(bb) $\#\#[C_o —]_s s_o\#\#$

i.e., on the first syllable of the word, but not if the first syllable is in one of the verbal prefixes listed under stage 3 below.

E.g., (a) PIE o-class nom sg *d^{h}og^{hw}os 'day', gen sg *d^{h}og^{hw}eso, dat pl *d^{h}og^{hw}omis vs. the same cases of the ā-class noun *g^{h}eb^{h}ā 'gift', *g^{h}eb^{h}ās and *g^{h}eb^{h}āmis (GMC STRESS stage 1) → *d^{h}óg^{hw}os, *d^{h}og^{hw}éso, *d^{h}og^{hw}ómis, *g^{h}éb^{h}ā, *g^{h}éb^{h}ās, and *g^{h}eb^{h}ā́mis. (b) PIE strong verb paradigm 1 sg pres *deukō 'lead', 1 sg past *douka, 1 pl past *dukme, perf part *dukon (GMC STRESS stage 1) → *déukō, *dóuka, *dukmé, *dukón. PIE weak verb paradigm 1 sg pres *nosjō 'save', 1 sg past *nositōm (GMC STRESS stage 1) → *nosjṓ, *nositṓm. Finally, PIE pret-pres verb 1 sg pres *torpa 'need' and 1 pl pres *tr̥pme (GMC STRESS stage 1) → *tórpa, *tr̥pmé. (Additional examples of the application of GMC STRESS stage 1 can be found in IV Historical Gothic Morphology where we give the late PIE antecedents of the Gothic and NW Germanic forms.)

We posit the stress pattern of stage 1 because it provides the necessary environment for the application of 3 VERNER. E.g., nom sg *d^{h}og^{hw}os 'day' vs. gen sg *d^{h}og^{hw}eso (GMC STRESS stage 1) → *d^{h}óg^{hw}os vs. *d^{h}og^{hw}éso (2 1st SS, 3 VERNER) > *ðóǥ^{w}oz vs. *ðoǥ^{w}éso (GMC STRESS stages 2 and 3, ev) > NWGmc *dáǥaz vs. *dáǥes (ev through regular change) > OIce dagr vs. dags. Similarly, the strong verb paradigm cited above *déukō 'lead', *dóuka, *dukmé, *dukón (2 1ST SS, 3 VERNER) > *téuxō, *tóuxa, *tuǥmé, *tuǥón (GMC STRESS stages 2 and 3, ev) > OSax teohan, tōh, tuǥun, (ǥi)toǥan.

Stage 2. The change at this stage occurs only in East Germanic and before the time of 3 VERNER. Hence its reflexes are noticeable in Gothic, but not in the NW Germanic languages. The change consists of a modification of parts (ab) and (bb) of the stage 1 rule, which remains in the grammar. The modifications are as follows.

V → [+stressed] / in the environments

(ab') $\#\# [C_0 —]_s$

i.e., on the first syllable of the word in all singular forms and in the nominative and accusative plural of all substantives. (Hence the only substantive forms left with ending stress are the genitive and dative plural.)

(bb') $\#\# [C_0 —]_s$

i.e., on the first syllable of the word (excepting the verbal prefixes noted below) in all strong verbs and in many weak ones as well. (Hence the only verbs left with ending stress are in the preterite-present paradigms and some weak verbs.) That is, word-initial stress begins to become general. An example of (ab') is the derivation of the genitive singular of the o-class noun *d^{h}og^{hw}éso into Gothic dagiz+uh (where -uh is an enclitic meaning 'and') vs. a NW Germanic language such as OSax daǥes: *d^{h}og^{hw}eso (2 1ST SS, GMC STRESS stage 1) > *ðoǥ^{w}éso (GMC STRESS stage 2 applying only in East Germanic) > East Gmc *ðóǥ^{w}eso vs. NWGmc *ðoǥ^{w}éso (3 VERNER) > *ðóǥ^{w}ezo vs. *ðoǥ^{w}éso (ev) > Go dagiz vs. OSax daǥes.

An example of (bb') is the derivation of the strong verb paradigm for 'lead' into Gothic and Old Saxon (abbreviated OSax below). The principal parts are the 1 sg pres, 1 sg past, 1 pl past and the past part.

	1 Sg Pres	1 Sg Past	1 Pl Past	Past Part
PIE	*deukō	*douka	*dukme	*dukon
		2 1ST SS, GMC STRESS Stage 1		
PGmc	*téuxō	*tóuxa	*tuxmé	*tuxón
		GMC STRESS Stage 2 applying only in East Germanic		
EGmc	*téuxō	*tóuxa	*túxme	*túxon
NWGmc	*téuxō	*tóuxa	*tuxmé	*tuxón
		3 VERNER		
EGmc	*téuxō	*tóuxa	*túxme	*túxon
NWGmc	*téuxō	*tóuxa	*tuǥmé	*tuǥón
		GMC STRESS Stage 3, eventually		
Go	tiuhan	táuh	taúhum	taúhans
OSax	teohan	tōh	tuǥun	ǥitoǥan

Another example of (bb') is the derivation of the infinitive of the weak verb 'save' into Gothic and Old Saxon from PIE *nosjonom:

2 1ST SS, Germanic Word Stress Stage 1

PGmc *nosjónom

Germanic Word Stress Stage 2 applying only in East Germanic

EGmc *nósjonom

NWGmc *nosjónom

3 VERNER

EGmc *nósjonom

NWGmc *nozjónom

Germanic Word Stress Stage 3, eventually

Go nasjan

OSax nerian

Stage 3. At this stage the word-initial stress beginning to occur in stage 2 was now totally generalized to virtually all paradigms throughout the entire Germanic area (which we assume at this time to have consisted of two mutually intelligible dialects, namely East Germanic and NW Germanic). This then is the final version of the Germanic word–stress rule, which remains as a mostly phon cond rule in the grammars of all early Germanic languages:

$$V \rightarrow [+\text{stressed}] \ / \ \text{in the environment} \ \#\#[C_0 \ \text{—} \ ]_{s}$$

in all words except for the following verbal prefixes: *ant-, *bi-, *ga-, *fur-, *uz- or the reduplicative prefix in the past of Class 7 strong verbs (see IV Historical Gothic Morphology 6.1.1).

That is, the stress is now on the first syllable of a word except for the verbal prefixes noted. Examples of these prefixes occur in VI A Gothic text below. They may also be found in the verbs of most modern Germanic languages such as ModEng forgét, aríse (the a- < Gmc *uz-), etc. An example of the reduplicating prefix is the derivation of the PIE 1 sg past *seslḗba 'I slept' (2 1ST SS, GMC STRESS stage 1) > *seslḗpa (3 VERNER, GMC STRESS stages 2 and 3 not applying, ev) > Go saízlēp /sezlēp/.

4b Assimilation of /n/ (n-ASSIM)

The existence of this change is disputed. If it did in fact occur, it restructured various lexical items and then was dropped as a rule from the grammar. The early version of the change is this:

$$\underset{1}{[C, +\text{voiced}]} \ \underset{2}{n} \quad \rightarrow \quad \underset{1}{[C, +\text{voiced}]} \ \underset{2}{[C, +\text{voiced}]} \ / \ [V, -\text{stress}] \ \_\_\_\_$$

That is, a sequence consisting of a voiced consonant plus /n/ and preceded by an unstressed vowel (the stress being that of 4a GMC STRESS stage 1) becomes the same two consonants.

E.g., PIE adv *pernṓ 'far' (2 1ST SS) > *fernṓ (n-ASSIM) > *ferrṓ (4a GMC STRESS stage 3) > *ferro (8a MORA LOSS) > Go faírra /férra/. Note also the etymologically related adjective, nom sg masc *pérnjos 'old' (where n-ASSIM cannot apply because of the stressed vowel, ev) > Go faírneis /férnīs/, not **faírreis.

Additional examples of n-ASSIM are to be found among the ā-class weak verbs, particularly as they occur in the West Germanic languages. (Such verbs were formed with the derivative suffix -n- and often have a repetitive or intensitive meaning.) E.g., PIE in *ligʰ+n+ā́nom 'lick' (2 1ST SS stages 1 and 2) >*lignā́nom (n-ASSIM) > *liggā́nom (? an early stage of 5d OBSTR-TO-STOP)> *liggā́nom (2 1ST SS stage 3) > *likkā́nom (ev) > NWGmc *líkkōn, Eng lick. (Note that given our formulation of n-ASSIM geminating only voiced consonants, it must precede stage 3 of 2 1ST SS.) Another such verb is PIE inf *duk+nā́nom 'pull repeatedly' (the intensive form of *duk- 'pull') (3 VERNER, ev) > *dugnā́nom (n-ASSIM) > *duggā́nom (2 1ST SS stage 3, ev) > West Gmc *túkkōn (ev) > Eng tuck. (Note here the necessary chronology 3 VERNER > n-ASSIM.)

There do not seem to be such verbs in Gothic as the West Gmc *likkōn 'lick' or *tukkōn 'tuck' noted above. The reason for their absence from Gothic is the fact that by the time of n-ASSIM the East Germanic and as such the pre-Gothic word stress was by 4a GMC STRESS stage 2 already for the most part on the word-initial syllable of most weak verbs. Hence n-ASSIM would not have applied to these verbs. However, there are a few Gothic forms where n-ASSIM may have applied. E.g., PIE oblique plural of the neut Vn-class noun *terkń- 'hole' (2 1ST SS, 3 VERNER) > *θergń- (n-ASSIM, ev) > *θérkk- (1a GEM C SIMP applying as a synchronic rule, ev) > Go nom sg þaírkō /θerkō/. The Gothic prep þaírh /θerh/ 'through' is from PIE *térk with root stress to which n-ASSIM cannot apply.

5a Shortening of the PIE Long Diphthongs (DIPH SHORTENING)

This change restructured the phonemic inventory and was then dropped from the grammar. The PIE long diphthongs were /āi, ēi, ōi, āu, ēu, ōu/. The change was as follows:

[V, +long] → [–long] / ___ i or u (except for stressed /ḗi, ṓu/).

E.g., PIE *plṓ+is 'more', *oktṓu '8', *kḗir 'here', nom sg *pṓun 'fire' (2 1ST SS, 3 VERNER) > *flṓiz, *óxtōu, *xḗir, *fṓun (4a GMC STRESS) > *flṓiz, *óxtōu, *xḗir, *fṓun (DIPH SHORTENING) > *flóiz, *óxtou, xḗir, *fṓun (6b o-TO-a) > *fláiz, *áxtau, *xḗir, fṓun (9d ēi/ōu-TO-ē/ō, ev) > OIce fleire, Go ahtáu /áhtɔ̄/, hēr, fōn. (Note that the stress condition for DIPH SHORTENING is that of Germanic. Hence the relative chronology is 4a GMC STRESS > DIPH SHORTENING > 6b o-TO-a as well as 9d ēi/ōu-TO-ē/ō.)

5b The Labiovelar Changes (LABIOVELARS)

These changes restructure various lexical items and then are dropped from the grammar. The eventual development of the PIE LABIOVELARS /k^w, g^{hw}, g^w/ by the changes 2 1ST SS, 3 VERNER and 5e x-TO-h results in Gmc /h^w, $ǥ^w$, k^w/. We posit two successive stages for LABIOVELARS.

Stage 1.

h^w, k^w → h, k / (a) ## ___ o(:) or u(:)
(b) ___ C or ##

(c) ## ___ o(:)
$ǥ^w$ → w / (d) l, r, n e(:) or i(:) ___ a(:), o(:) or u(:)
(e) a(:), o(:) or u(:) ___ l, r, n, e(:) or i(:)

That is, /h^w/ (which is possibly still /x^w/ at this time) and /k^w/ lose their rounding (a) word-initially before a round vowel or (b) if followed by a consonant or if word-final. Otherwise /h^w/ and /k^w/ remained. Further, /$ǥ^w$/ becomes /w/ (c) word-initially before /o(:)/, (d) after /l, r, n, e(:), i(:)/ and before /a(:), o(:), u(:)/ and (e) vice versa. Otherwise /$ǥ^w$/ remains.

Stage 2.

$ǥ^w$ → ǥ

That is, the remaining /$ǥ^w$/ becomes /ǥ/ everywhere. (We assume that by this time 5d OBSTR-TO-STOP had applied whereby the continuant /$ǥ^w$/ becomes a stop /g^w/ if following /n/ = [ŋ]. Hence LABIOVELARS stage 2 does not apply to the sequence /ng^w/.)

E.g., PIE nom sg *k^wólsos 'neck', *k^wálos 'whale', *g^wṓus 'cow', *g^wŋ̥ā 'woman' and ablauting *g^wḗnā 'woman', *g^{hw}órmos 'warm , *mág^{hw}ilā 'maiden', *mág^{hw}us 'boy', *snóig^{hw}os 'snow' and the inf *séng^{hw}onom 'to sing' (2 1ST SS, 3 VERNER, possibly 5e x-TO-h, ev) > *h^wólsoz, *h^wáloz, *k^wṓuz, *k^wŋ̥́ā, *k^wḗnā, *$ǥ^w$órmoz, *máǥ^{w}ilā, *máǥ^{w}uz, *snóiǥ^{w}oz, *séng^{w}onom (LABIOVELARS) > *hólsoz, *h^wáloz, *kṓuz, *k^wŋ̥́ā, *k^wḗnā, *wórmoz, *máwilā, *máǥuz, *snóiwoz, *séngwonom (6a ā-TO-ō, 6b o-TO-a, 6c SYL SON, ev) > *hálsaz, *h^wálaz, *kṓuz, *kúnō, *k^wḗnō, *wármaz, *máwilō, *máǥuz, *snáiwaz, *síngwanam (ev) > OHGerm hals, Eng whale, OEng cū /kū/, OIce kona, Eng queen, Go warms, Go mawila, Go magus [maǥus], Go snáiws /snɛ̄ws/, Go siggwan [siŋgwan].

We note the following chronologies. First, the environment of LABIOVELARS must segregate the voiced from the voiceless LABIOVELARS. This assumes the prior application of 2 1ST SS and 3 VERNER. Second, at the time of LABIOVELARS, PIE /o/ and /a/ as well as /ā/ and /ō/ must have still been distinguished. Hence LABIOVELARS preceded 6a ā-TO-ō and 6b o-TO-a.

The precise conditioning of LABIOVELARS is disputed. Here we follow Voyles (1992: 45). Differing formulations are found in Sievers (1878: 149), Kieckers (1928: 78), Lehmann (1955: 63) and in Seebold (1967).

5c Various Morpheme-Structure Changes (MS CHANGES)

These changes restructure various lexical items and then are dropped from the grammar. They are valid for all Germanic languages. We formulate them in their version as it would have been after lc s-z RULE, 2 1ST SS, 3 VERNER and 4a GMC STRESS.

(a) Changes of two-segment sequences

ðl	→	ll	
ln	→	ll	
mr	→	br	/ ## ____
nm	→	mm	/ [V, –stress] ____
nw	→	nn	
zm, zn	→	mm, nn	

(b) Changes of three-segment sequences.

rƀm	→	rm
sr	→	str

E.g., (a) PIE nom sg *stadʰlos 'stall' (2 1ST SS) > *staðlos (MS CHANGES, ev) > Eng stall; PIE nom sg masc *pl̥n +os 'full' (MS CHANGES, ev) > Go fulls; PIE nom sg *mrengōn 'brink, edge' (MS CHANGES, ev) > Eng brink; PIE dat pl *gʰm̥ónmis 'men' (2 1ST SS, 3 VERNER, 4a GMC STRESS) > *ǥḿ̥onmiz (MS CHANGES) > *ǥḿ̥ommiz (ev) > Go gumam; PIE nom sg *genwus 'cheek' (ev) > Go kinnus 'chin'; PIE dat sg masc *bʰlendʰósmō 'blind' (2 1ST SS, 4a GMC STRESS stage 1, 3 VERNER) > bléndozmō (MS CHANGES, ev) > Go blindamma; PIE nom sg masc *orbʰmos 'poor' (2 1ST SS, ev) > *orƀmos (MS CHANGES) > *ormoz (ev) > Go arms; PIE nom sg masc *sroumos 'stream' (MS CHANGES, ev) > Gmc straumaz (ev) > Eng stream.

5d The Change of Certain Voiced Obstruents to Stops (OBSTR-TO-STOP)

This change remains in the Gothic grammar as a phon cond rule. After 2 1ST SS and 3 VERNER, the Germanic voiced obstruents were all continuants, namely /ƀ, ð, ǥ, ǥʷ, z/. Under certain conditions the first four of these become stops by the time of the first attested Germanic languages. The environments vary somewhat. The basic rule is as follows.

ƀ, ð, ǥ⁽ʷ⁾	→	b, d, g⁽ʷ⁾	/ (a) [C, +nasal] ___ (b) if geminated (c) ## (ƀ, ð only)	in all Germanic languages
			(d) any C ___	only in Gothic

E.g., PIE inf *bʰéndʰonom 'bind', nom sg *lómbʰom 'lamb', nom sg *dʰē+t́- 'deed', inf *gʰóngʰonom 'go', nom sg *gʰortṓn 'garden, yard' and the inf *kapjónom 'have' (2 1ST SS, 3 VERNER) > *ƀénðonom, *lómƀom, *ðēð́-, *ǥónǥonom, *ǥorðṓn, *xaƀjónom (4a GMC STRESS, OBSTR-TO-STOP, ev) > Go bindan, OSax lamb, Go dēþs, gangan [ǥaŋganJ, garda [ǥarda] and haban [haƀan] — as opposed to

OSax hebbian [hebbian] where [ƀƀ] has become [bb] by the synchronic reflex of part (b). (Note here the necessary chronologies 2 1ST SS > OBSTR-TO-STOP and 3 VERNER > OBSTR-TO-STOP.) Finally, PIE nom sg *kus+d^h+om 'hoard' (1b OBSTR VOI/DEVOI) > *kuzd^{h}om (2 1ST SS) > *xuzđom (OBSTR-TO-STOP) > *xuzdom (5e x-TO-h, ev) > Go huzd.

Finally, some Germanic languages — unlike Gothic — do not have voiced obstruent stops in environment (d) of OBSTR-TO-STOP. E.g., PIE *selb^h 'self' (2 1ST SS) > *selƀ (OBSTR-TO-STOP, ev) > OEng seolf (from *selƀ where OBSTR-TO-STOP has not applied) vs. Go silb [silb] where it has.

5e The Change of /x$^{(w)}$/ to /h$^{(w)}$/ (x-TO-h)

In the early Germanic languages, except for Gothic, this change remains as a phon cond rule in the grammar. In Gothic the change restructures the phoneme inventory and then is dropped from the grammar.

x$^{(w)}$ → h$^{(w)}$ / (a) ____ [+sonorant] in all early Germanic languages except Gothic
(b) in all occurrences in Gothic

That is, /x/ or /x^w/ becomes /h, h^w/ (a) before /l, m, n, r, j, w/ or a vowel (otherwise /x, x^w/ remain); and (b) /x$^{(w)}$/ becomes /h$^{(w)}$/ everywhere in Gothic E.g., (a) PIE nom sg *kŕ̥̥nom 'horn', *nóktis 'night', 1 sg pres *déukō 'lead' vs. past *dóuka, 1 sg pres *sék^{w}ō 'see' vs. past *sók^{w}a and 1 sg pres *klóubō 'run' (2 1ST SS, 3 VERNER, 4a GMC STRESS, which we leave unmarked, ev) > early Germanic *xr̥nom, *noxtiz, *teuxō, *touxa, *sex^{w}ō, *sox^{w}a, *xloupō (ev) > OSax horn [horn], naht [naxt], tiuhu [tiuhu], tōh [tɔ̄x], sihu [sihu], sah [sax] and hlōpu [hlɔ̄pu]. (b) The same antecedents result in Gothic haúrn [horn], nahts [nahts], tiuha [tiuha], táuh [tɔ̄h], saíƕa /seh^{w}a/, saƕ /sah^w/ and hláupa /hlɔ̄pa/. (Note the necessary chronology 2 1ST SS > x-TO-h. The 1ST SS produces /x/ to which x-TO-h applies.)

6a The Change of /ā/ to /ō/ (ā-TO-ō)

This change restructures the phonemic inventory of the language and then is dropped from the grammar.

ā → ō

That is, /ā/ (stressed or unstressed) becomes /ō/. E.g., PIE nom sg *b^{h}ā́gā 'beech, (later) book', gen sg *g^{h}éb^{h}ās 'gift' (2 1ST SS, 3 VERNER, 4a GMC STRESS, ev) > early Gmc *bā́kā, *ǥéƀāz (ā-TO-ō) > *bṓkō, *ǥéƀōz (8a MORA LOSS, ev) > Go bōka, gibōs. This change must follow 5b LABIOVELARS. E.g., PIE nom sg fem *k^{w}ā 'who?' (2 1ST SS) > *x^{w}ā (to which 5b LABIOVELARS does not apply, then ā-TO-ō, ev) > Go ƕō /h^{w}ō/. If the order were ā-TO-ō > 5b LABIOVELARS, the Gothic form would be **hō. As for the absolute chronology of this change, we estimate its date at about 50 BC. Our reason for this assumption is the attestation in Caesar (100-44 BC) of the place name silva Bācenis "Beech Wood". The form Bācenis reflects an early Germanic *bāk- (later *bōk-) from PIE *b^{h}āg-. The occurrence of Bācenis indicates that by Caesar's time 2 1ST SS had occurred, but not yet ā-TO-ō.

6b The Change of /o/ to /a/ (o-TO-a)

This change restructures the phonemic inventory of the language and then drops from the grammar.

o → a

That is, /o/ becomes /a/ in all environments, stressed or unstressed. E.g., PIE nom sg *d^{h}óg^{hw}os 'day', inf *póronom 'travel', *oktṓu '8' (2 1ST SS, 3 VERNER, 4a GMC STRESS, 5a DIPH SHORTENING, ev) > early Gmc *dóǥoz, *fóronom, *óxtou (o-TO-a, ev) > Go dags, faran, ahtáu /áhtɔ̄/.

6c The Change in the PIE Syllabic Sonorant Consonants (SYL SON)

This change restructures various lexical items and inflectional endings and then is dropped from the grammar. The change is as follows:

l̥, r̥, m̥, n̥ → ul, ur, um, un

E.g., PIE inf *tŋ̥́g+jonom *[tŋ̥́gjonom] 'seem', *tĺ̥+onom 'tolerate', past pass. part. *wr̥t+ónos 'become' (2 1ST SS, 3 VERNER, 4a GMC STRESS, ev) > early East Gmc) *θŋ̥́kjonom, *θĺ̥onom, *wŕ̥θonoz (SYL SON) > later East Gmc *θúnkjonom, *θúlonom, *wúrθonoz (7b 1ST UMLAUT, ev) > Go þugkjan /θúnkjan/ [θúŋkjan], þulan /θúlan/, waúrþans /wórθans/. Note here the necessary chronology SYL SON > 7b 1ST UMLAUT.

7a Monophthongization of /ai/ and /au/ (ai/au-MONOPH)

This change probably began in the East Germanic area and spread from there into NW Germanic It occurred in three stages. The first two stages restructure the phonemic inventory of the language and then are dropped from the grammar. The rule at the third stage remains in the grammar of Gothic as a phon cond rule.

Stage 1. This change first occurred in East Germanic

ai, au → ɛ̄, ɔ̄ / [–stress] [C_0 –stress ____ C_0]##
s-2 s-1

That is, unstressed /ai/ and /au/ became long and lax /ɛ̄/ and /ɔ̄/ if in a word-final syllable (s-1) which is preceded by another unstressed syllable (s-2). (The stress is that of Germanic: hence the chronology 4a GMC STRESS > ai/au-MONOPH.)

E.g., PIE 3 sg pass ind *bʰérotai 'is carried' (2 1ST SS, 3 VERNER, 6b o-TO-a, ev) > *bératai (ai/au-MONOPH stage 1) > *béraðɛ̄ (8a MORA LOSS) > *béraðe (9c e-TO-a) > Go baírada [béraða]. Note the necessary chronologies 6b o-TO-a > ai/au-MONOPH, and ai/au-MONOPH stage 1 > 8a MORA LOSS.

Stage 2. This change occurred throughout the Germanic area and after 8a MORA LOSS.

ai, au → ɛ̄, ɔ̄ / [–stress, ____]

That is, now any remaining unstressed /ai, au/ become /ɛ̄, ɔ̄/ (later +tense /ē, ō/ in NW Germanic). E.g., PIE nom pl masc *bʰléndʰoi 'blind', gen sg *súnous 'son', 1 sg past *kapoitṓm 'I had' (ev up to 6b o-TO-a) > *bléndai, *súnauz, *háƀaiðōm (ai/au-MONOPH stage 2) > *bléndai, *súnauz, *háƀaiðōm (to which 8a MORA LOSS does not apply since it has already occurred, ev) > Go blindái [blíndɛ̄], sunáus [súnɔ̄s], habáida [háƀɛ̄ða].

Stage 3. The rule at this stage, which is an expansion of that of stage 2, is exclusively East Germanic and Gothic.

ai, au → ɛ̄, ɔ̄ / [+stress ____] { [–vocalic] / ## }

That is, stressed /ai, au/ become /ɛ̄, ɔ̄/ everywhere except before a vowel. E.g., PIE nom sg masc *óinos 'one', *kóukos 'high' (ev up to 6b o-TO-a) > early Germanic *áinaz, *háuhaz (ai/au-MONOPH stage 3, ev) > Go áins /ɛ̄ns/, háuhs /hɔ̄hs/. Instances of the application of ai/au-MONOPH stage 3 as a synchronic rule of Gothic are these: /bai/ 'both' as well as /bai+ōθ/, inf /tau+jan/ 'do' vs. 1 sg past

/tau+ida/ (au/au-MONOPH stage 3) → bε̄, baiō̄θ, tɔ̄jan, tauida (PIE 3.1.2c i-j/u-w Alt, still in the grammar as a synchronic rule, ev) → bai [bε̄], bajōþ [bajōθ], táujan [tɔ̄jan], tawida [tawiðа].

7b The Change of First Umlaut (1ST UMLAUT)

The term "umlaut" designates a process of vowel assimilation. By the time of 1ST UMLAUT the first dialect division in Germanic between East and NW Germanic was under way. Below we give the pre-Gothic East Germanic version of the change. It occurred in three chronological stages. All three stages remain as largely phon cond rules in the phonology of Gothic.

Stage 1.

e → i / [V, +stress] … [−stress, ___] [any segment except /r, h$^{(w)}$/]

where "..." does not contain a word boundary ##.

That is, unstressed /e/ when following the stressed vowel within a word is raised to /i/ except when followed by /r/, /h/ or /h^{w}/. E.g., PIE 3 sg pres *b^{h}éreti 'carries' (ev up to 1ST UMLAUT) > early Germanic *béreði (1ST UMLAUT stage 1) > *bériði (8a MORA LOSS, 9b CONT OBSTR DEVOICING) > Go baíriþ /bériθ/. Note that 1ST UMLAUT cannot apply to PIE 1 sg past *seslḗba 'I slept' or to PIE nom sg masc *ánteros 'other' (ev) > Go saíslēp /seslḗp/, not **sislēp, and anþar /ánθar/, not **anþir.

Stage 2.

e → i / [+stress, ___] [any segment except /r, h$^{(w)}$/]

A stressed /e/ is raised to /i/ except when followed by /r/, /h/ or /h^{w}/. E.g., PIE inf *g^{h}éb^{h}onom 'to give' and *g^{h}réibonom 'to seize' (ev through 1ST UMLAUT stage 2) > *ǥíƀanam and *ǥríipanam, i.e. *ǥrī́panam, (ev) > Go giban and greipan /grī́pan/.

Stage 3

i, u → e, o / [+stress, ___] /r, h$^{(w)}$/

That is, the stressed +high vowels /i, u/ become –high if followed by /r/, /h/, or /h^{w}/. This rule constitutes an expansion of the rule of stage 2. At that stage /e/ was raised to /i/ except before /r/, /h/ or /h^{w}/. Now the vowels /i/ and /u/ are lowered in the converse environment. E.g., PIE past pass part *b^{h}r̥ónos 'carried', nom sg masc *wíros 'man', nom sg fem *d^{h}úkter'daughter' (ev through 6c SYL SON) > *búranaz, *wíraz, *dúhter (1ST UMLAUT stage 3) > *bóranaz, *wéraz, *dóhter (ev) > Go baúrans /bórans/, waír /wér/, daúhtar /dóhtar/.

The stress placement for 1ST UMLAUT is that of Germanic. Hence we assume the chronology 4a GMC STRESS > 1ST UMLAUT. Further, as can be seen in the derivation of Go baúrans 'carried' above, 6c SYL SON must precede 1ST UMLAUT. Finally, since 6b o-TO-a does not affect the /o/ produced by 1ST UMLAUT, we assume the sequence 6b o-TO-a > 1ST UMLAUT. (Assuming the change 6a ā-TO-ō may have been roughly contemporaneous with 6b o-TO-a, we also posit the sequence 6a ā-TO-ō > 1ST UMLAUT.) We estimate the date of 1ST UMLAUT at ca. 50 AD. A possible reflex of 1ST UMLAUT occurs in Tacitus (ca. 55–120 AD) in the tribal name Ingvaeones, the first syllable of which derives from an earlier *eng-. But there also occurs in Tacitus the name Fenni 'Finns' (instead of **Finni) where 1ST UMLAUT has not yet applied. Later the same name occurs as Phinnoi in the Greek historian Ptolomy from about 100 AD. The NW Germanic version of 1ST UMLAUT resembles that of Gothic. Its basic form is this:

(a) e → i / (aa) ___ C_0 i(:), j, u(:), w
(ab) ___ [C, +nasal]C

(b) i, u → e, o / ___ C_0[V, –high]

where $C_0 \neq$ [C, +nasal]C

That is, (a) /e/ becomes /i/ (aa) if followed by a possible consonant or consonant cluster followed in turn by the +high sonorants /i(:), j, u(:), w/ or (ab) if followed by the sequence nasal consonant plus any other consonant. (b) Otherwise, the +high vowels /i, u/ become –high /e, o/ if followed by a consonant or consonant cluster plus a –high vowel, namely a(:), e(:), o(:); but the consonant cluster cannot be a nasal consonant plus another consonant.

Hence at this stage there were beginning to be the first dialectal variations within Germanic. E.g. PIE inf *gʰébʰonom 'give', 3 sg pres *gʰébʰeti 'gives' and *wérteti 'turns' (ev) > East Gmc Go giban, gibiþ, waírþiþ /wérθiθ/ vs. NWGmc OSax geban, gibid, wirthid.

7c The Loss of Word-Final Nasal Consonants in Unstressed Syllables (NASAL LOSS)

This change occurred in three chronological stages, all of which remained for a time as persistent rules in the grammar. By the time of Gothic, however, the NASAL LOSS rule had been deleted from the grammar. Its Gothic reflex was in the form of restructured inflectional endings.

Stage 1

m → n / [V, –stress] ___ ##

That is, /m/ becomes /n/ if word-final and preceded by an unstressed vowel.

Stage 2

At this stage the first-stage rule remains in the grammar under (a) below. In addition another rule (b) is added. Either (a) or (b), but not both, can apply.

(a) m → n / [V, –stress] ___ ## (as above)

(b) [V, –stress] n ## → [same V, but +nasal] Ø same
1 2 3 1 2 3

That is, (a) is as it was at stage 1. (b) Word-final /n/ if preceded by an unstressed vowel is deleted and the preceding vowel is nasalized.

Stage 3

At this stage rules (a) and (b) remain from the previous stages. In addition, rule (c) below is also added. Only one of these three rules can apply to a given form. So the rules at this stage are the following:

(a) m → n / [V, –stress] ___ ## (as above)

(b) [V, –stress] n ## → [same V, but +nasal] Ø same (as above)
1 2 3 1 2 3

(c) [V, –stress, +nasal] → [V, –stress, –nasal] / — ##

That is, a word-final unstressed nasal vowel is denasalized.

We give as examples two derivations. First, PIE acc sg masc *bʰléndʰom 'blind' and dʰógʰʷom 'day' (ev through 6b o-TO-a) > early Gmc *bléndam *dáǥam (NASAL LOSS stage 1) > *bléndan *dáǥan. At this time the particle *-ōn (itself from earlier *-ōm by Nasal Loss) was added to the adjective. The further derivation is then *bléndanōn *dáǥan (NASAL LOSS stage 2) > *bléndanō^n *dáǥa^n (NASAL LOSS stage 3) > *bléndanō dáǥa (8a MORA LOSS, ev) > Go blindana dag. (Note here the necessary chronology NASAL LOSS > 8a MORA LOSS.)

Second, PIE gen pl *gʰebʰṓm 'gift' and acc sg *gʰébʰām 'idem' (ev through 6a ā-TO-ō , but before stage 3 of 4a GMC STRESS) > early Gmc *ǥeƀṓm or *ǥéƀōm (NASAL LOSS stage 1) > *ǥeƀṓm vs. *ǥéƀōn (NASAL LOSS stage 2) > *ǥeƀṓm vs. *ǥéƀō^n (NASAL LOSS stage 3 applying as a persistent rule) > *ǥéƀōn vs. *ǥéƀō (NASAL LOSS stage 3 reapplying as a persistent rule) > *ǥéƀō^n vs. *ǥéƀō (7b 1ST UMLAUT, 8a MORA LOSS) > *ǥíƀō^n vs. *ǥíƀa (NASAL LOSS stage 3 reapplying as a persistent rule) > Go gibō vs. giba.[1]

8a The Loss of a Mora in Unstressed Word-Final Syllables (MORA LOSS).

The term "mora" designates a segment of time within a syllable and consists of a single short vowel or a single consonant. Hence the change MORA LOSS involves the loss of a single consonant, a single short vowel or a unit of vowel length ($\bar{V}$ = VV → V). After MORA LOSS had become obligatory, it was dropped from the grammar. Its reflex in Gothic is in the form of restructured word-final syllables. Under MORA LOSS we subsume three changes occurring in unstressed word-final syllables. Although these changes may seem at first glance disparate, we shall see directly that they must have occurred contemporaneously; hence we consider them as manifestations of one and the same process. Like 7b 1ST UMLAUT, MORA LOSS differs somewhat in its East Germanic and NW Germanic versions. Below we give the East Germanic version.

$$\text{(a)}\quad \begin{pmatrix} +\text{consonant} \\ +\text{obstruent} \\ +\text{coronal} \\ -\text{strident} \end{pmatrix} \rightarrow \varnothing \quad / \; [\text{V}, -\text{stress}]\; C_0 \;\_\_\; \#\#$$

$$\text{(b)}\quad [\text{V}, -\text{stress}, +\text{long}] \rightarrow [\text{-long}] \quad / \;\_\_\; \#\#$$

$$\text{(c)}\quad [\text{V}, -\text{long}, -\text{stress}] \rightarrow \varnothing \; / \; \text{(ca) } [+\text{stress, long syllable}]\; C_1 \begin{pmatrix} -\text{round} \\ \_\_ \end{pmatrix} (\text{z})\#\#$$

$$\text{(cb) } [-\text{stress}]\; C_1 \;\_\_\; (\text{z})\; \#\#$$

That is, (a) the segments /t, θ, ð, d/ if word-final and in an unstressed syllable are deleted. (b) Word-final unstressed long vowels are shortened (whereby $\bar{V}$ = VV → V). (ca) A short unstressed vowel is deleted if it follows a long stressed syllable, is not rounded (i.e., is /a, e, i/) and if it is word-final or precedes a word-final /z/. (A long syllable is one containing a long vowel or diphthong, or one ending in at least one consonant. For an explanation of the notion of syllable as we use the concept here, see Chapter 3 Latin, change 6c LATIN STRESS.) (cb) Finally, a short unstressed vowel is deleted if it follows an unstressed syllable and if it is word-final or precedes a word-final /z/.

E.g., (a) PIE adv *apterṓd 'from behind', 3 sg pres subj *bʰéroit 'carry', *dékn̥t '10' (ev through 7a ai/au-MONOPH) > early Germanic *áfterōt, *bérēð, *téhund (MORA LOSS) > *áfterō, *bérē, *téhun (9c e-TO-a) > Go aftarō, baírái /bérē/, taíhun /téhun/.

E.g., (b) PIE 1 sg pres ind. *bʰérō 'I carry' (2 1ST SS) > early Gmc *bérō (MORA LOSS) > *béro (ev) > Go baíra /béra/ vs. OHGerm biru. Note here that while the Gothic reflex of earlier word-final /o/ is /a/, the NW Germanic reflex is /u/. The reason for this variation is that by the time of MORA LOSS, there were no unstressed /o/'s in Germanic because 6b o-TO-a had already occurred and because 7b 1ST UMLAUT, which had also already occurred, produced only stressed /o/'s. When changes like MORA LOSS occur which create new segments in a language or place segments in environments where they do not otherwise occur (here an /o/ not under stress), the new segments are often mapped onto phonetically close ones already existing in the language. In the case at hand, East Germanic Gothic identified the unstressed /o/ with the phonetically close /a/ (Go baíra), while NW Germanic identified it with /u/ (OHGerm biru).

E.g., (ca) PIE nom sg *ózdos 'branch', 2 sg imp *ā́g^{h}es 'fear', 1 sg pret pres *wóida 'know', nom sg *kléptus 'thief' (ev through 7b 1ST UMLAUT) > *ástaz, *ṓǥiz, *wáita, *hlíftuz (MORA LOSS ca) > *ástz, *ṓǥz, *wáit /wḗt/, *hliftuz (9b CONT OBSTR DEVOICING, ev) > Go asts, ōgs [ōxs], wait /wḗt/, hliftus. (cb) PIE dat pl *d^{h}og^{hw}ómis 'days', 3 sg pres *b^{h}éreti 'carries' (ev through 7b 1ST UMLAUT) > *dáǥamiz,*bériδ (9b CONT OBSTR DEVOICING, 9i mz-TO-mm, ev) > Go dagam, baíriþ /bériθ/.

The following derivations indicate that MORA LOSS (a), (b) and (c) are contemporaneous and thus represent one and the same process.

(i) PIE adv *apterṓd 'from behind' (ev) > early Gmc *áfterōt (MORA LOSS a, deletion of consonants) > *áfterō (ev) > Go aftarō. If the sequence were MORA LOSS a (deletion of consonants) > MORA LOSS b (vowel shortening), then the incorrect **aftero and ev Go **aftara would occur. Hence the sequence must be MORA LOSS b > MORA LOSS a.

(ii) PIE 3 sg pres *b^{h}éreti 'carries' (ev) > early Gmc *bériδi (MORA LOSS c, deletion of short vowels) > *bériδ (ev) > Go baíriþ /bériθ/. If the sequence were MORA LOSS c (deletion of short vowels) > MORA LOSS a (deletion of consonants), then the incorrect **beri and ev Go **baíri would occur. Hence the sequence must be MORA LOSS a > MORA LOSS c.

(iii) PIE 1 sg pres *g^{h}réibō 'seize' (ev) > early Gmc *ǥrī́pō (MORA LOSS b, vowel shortening) > *ǥrī́pa (ev) > Go greipa /grī́pa/. If the sequence were MORA LOSS b (vowel shortening) > MORA LOSS c (deletion of short vowels), then the incorrect **ǥrī́p and ev Go **greip would occur. Hence the sequence must be MORA LOSS c > MORA LOSS b.

In the preceding we deduced the following chronologies:

(i) MORA LOSS b > MORA LOSS a,
(ii) MORA LOSS a > MORA LOSS c,
(iii) MORA LOSS c > MORA LOSS b.

If " > " here is interpreted as "must precede", the conclusions are contradictory. From (i) b > a and (ii) a > c, it follows that b > c, which contradicts (iii). From (iii) c > b and (i) b > a, it follows that c > a, which contradicts (ii). And from (ii) a > c and (iii) c > b, it follows that a > b, which contradicts (i). Hence the chronologies (i, ii iii) all lead to contradictions.

A way to make sense of this is to interpret ">" in the above statements as "cannot follow". If this is done, then by (i) b > a "MORA LOSS b cannot follow MORA LOSS a"; and by its contrary a > b "MORA LOSS a cannot follow MORA LOSS b", MORA LOSS a and b must be contemporaneous. And so on for the other sequences. We formalize this with "><". Hence the chronologies are now these:

(i') MORA LOSS a > < MORA LOSS b,
(ii') MORA LOSS a > < MORA LOSS c,
(iii') MORA LOSS c > < MORA LOSS b.

Hence the three changes MORA LOSS a, b and c are contemporaneous and represent one and the same process.Two further chronological considerations are these. First, MORA LOSS must be formulated in terms of Germanic stress. Hence it must follow 4a GMC STRESS. Second, there seems to have been no unstressed /o/ at the time of MORA LOSS. Hence we assume MORA LOSS followed 6b o-TO-a and probably 7b 1ST UMLAUT as well.

8b Deletion of Some Occurrences of [ŋ] (ŋ-DELETION)

This change occurs in the pre-history of all Germanic languages. It remains in their grammars, including that of Gothic, as a morph cond rule. The early version of the change is this.

V	ŋ	x or h	→	{ same V, but +long and +nasal }	Ø	same
1	2	3		1	2	3

That is, in the sequence vowel plus [ŋ] plus [h] or [x], the vowel is lengthened and nasalized, the [ŋ] is deleted and the [x] or [h] remain. (The [ŋ] is an allophone of /n/ by the PIE rule 3.1.2d NASAL ASSIM, which remains in the grammar as a persistent rule. The [x, h] variation assumes the prior application of 5e x-TO-h. By Gothic times only [h] occurs.) E.g., PIE inf *pónkonom 'seize', 3 sg past *tŋ̥́k+tēt 'seemed', inf *ténkonom 'thrive' (2 1ST SS, 6b o-TO-a, 6c SYL SON, 7b 1ST UMLAUT, ev) > early Gmc *fánhana, *þúnxtēð, *θínhana (ŋ-DELETION) > *fā́^{n}hana, *θū́^{n}xtēð, *θī́^{n}hana (8a MORA LOSS, ev) > Go fāhan /fā́^{n}han/, þūhta /θū́^{n}hta/, þeihan /θī́^{n}han/.

Note that in these derivations ŋ-DELETION must be preceded by 2 1ST SS, 6b o-TO-a, 6c SYL SON and 7b 1ST UMLAUT for the correct forms to be derived. Since ŋ-DELETION is evident in all Germanic languages but must follow 7b 1ST UMLAUT, which differs in its East Germanic and NW Germanic version, it seems that ŋ-DELETION spread over the East and NW Germanic dialect areas while they were still contiguous.

The long vowels resulting from ŋ-DELETION remained nasalized until fairly late Germanic times. E.g., later Gmc inf *fā^{n}han 'seize' vs. inf *lātan 'let' (ev) > OEng fōn vs. lǣtan. Note in the preceding the different development of nasalized /ā^{n}/ vs. oral /ā/. Another indication of the existence of long nasal vowels in later Germanic is the so-called *First Grammatical Treatise* written in Old Icelandic by an anonymous author at around 1150 AD. The author records the presence of long nasal vowels in the historically appropriate forms. E.g., early Gmc nom sg masc *hanhaz 'shark' (ŋ-DELETION) > *hā^{n}haz (ev) > OIce /hā^{n}r/. (See on this Voyles 1992: 61.) These nasal vowels may well have been present in Gothic, although there is no orthographic evidence for them.

Since ŋ-DELETION applies after 6b o-TO-a, 6c SYL SON and 7b 1ST UMLAUT, the only vowels it produces are /ī^{n}, ā^{n}, ū^{n}/. Hence one reflex of ŋ-DELETION in Gothic may be the presence of these vowels in the phonemic inventory. Another reflex is a morph cond rule of ŋ-DELETION remaining in Gothic. It accounts for such alternations as the inf þankian 'think' vs. the 1 sg past þāhta /θā^{n}hta/ 'thought'. The synchronic derivation of the latter is /θank+t+a/ (synchronic reflex of 1b Obstr Devoicing and 2 1ST SS) → þanxta (reflex of ŋ-DELETION) → [θā^{n}hta].

9a The change of Unstressed /am/ to /um/ (am-TO-um)

This change and all those of stage 9 apply to Gothic and to no other attested Germanic languages. The am-TO-um change restructures a few endings and then is dropped from the grammar.

a → u / [–stress ___] m [–stress]$_2$
s

That is, unstressed /a/ becomes/u/ if followed by /m/ and at least two other unstressed syllables within the word. E.g., PIE dat sg masc *ne##oinózmē+kʷum 'no##1 + and' (ev) > early Gmc *ni##áinazmēhun (5c MS CHANGES) > *ni##áinammēhun (am-TO-um) > Go ni áinummēhun 'no one'.[2]

9b Devoicing of Continuant Obstruent Consonants (CONT OBSTR DEVOICING)

This change remains in the grammar of Gothic as a phon cond rule.

$$\begin{pmatrix} \text{C, +obstruent} \\ \text{+continuant} \\ \text{+voiced} \end{pmatrix} \rightarrow [\text{–voiced}] \ / \ \_\_ \ \begin{Bmatrix} [\text{–voiced}] \\ \#\# \end{Bmatrix}$$

That is, the voiced continuant obstruents [ƀ, ð, ǥ, z] are devoiced to [f, θ, x, s] if followed by any voiceless segment (namely a voiceless obstruent consonant) or if word-final.

As examples we cite synchronic derivations of Gothic. E.g., nom sg hlēƀ+z 'loaf' vs. gen sg hlēƀ+iz (CONT OBSTR DEVOICING) → hlēƀs vs. hlēƀis (CONT OBSTR DEVOICING reapplying) → [hlēfs] hláifs vs. [hlēƀis] /hlēbis/ hláibis. Voc sg frōð 'wise' vs. gen sg masc frōð+iz (CONT OBSTR DEVOICING)→ frōþ vs. frōdis [frōðis]. And nom sg daǥ+z 'day' vs. gen sg daǥ+iz (CONT OBSTR DEVOICING) → dags [daxs] vs. dagis [daǥis]. Note that CONT OBSTR DEVOICING cannot apply in such instances as the 3 sg past band [band] 'tied', not **banþ **[banθ], because the voiced obstruent [d] is –continuant by 5d OBSTR-TO-STOP, which had applied before CONT OBSTR DEVOICING.

Although inflectional endings usually occur word-finally and as such undergo CONT OBSTR DEVOICING, their underlying forms may be seen when they occur with the Gothic enclitic -uh 'and'. E.g., gen sg hláibis [hlēƀis] 'loaf' to which CONT OBSTR DEVOICING has applied vs. hláibizuh [hlēƀiz+uh] to which it has not.

In the examples given above the graphemic alternations <b - f>, <d - þ> and <z - s> occur as a result of CONT OBSTR DEVOICING. There is no graphemic indication of the [ǥ] - [x] alternation, which is what we posit. A possible reason for this is that the alternations /b/ ([ƀ]) - /f/, /d/ ([ð]) - /θ/ and /z/ - /s/ constitute phonemic contrasts in Gothic. E.g., aba /aba/ 'man' vs. afar /afar/ 'but', háidus /hēdus/ 'state' vs. háiþiwisks /hēθiwisks/ 'heathenish' and hazjan 'praise' vs. nasjan 'save'. Since these segments constitute separate phonemes, they were differentiated in the Gothic orthography. However, [ǥ] and [x] do not contrast phonemically. Since 5e x-TO-h has already occurred, [x] arises from [ǥ] only through CONT OBSTR DEVOICING. Hence orthographic <g> is used for both [g] and [x]. Another possible reason for the sole occurrence of <g> in such forms may be that CONT OBSTR DEVOICING at first applied only to the –back continuant obstruents [ƀ, ð, z] and had by Gothic times not yet extended its domain to include [ǥ].

9c The Change of Posttonic Unstressed /e/ to /a/ (e-TO-a)

This change restructures various lexical items and then is dropped from the grammar.

e → a / [V, +stress] ... [–stress, ___]

where "..." does not contain a word-boundary ##.

That is, unstressed /e/ occurring after the main stress in a word becomes /a/. (This change must occur after 7b 1ST UMLAUT. Hence these /e/'s occur only before /r, h or hʷ/.)

E.g., PIE nom sg *bʰrā́ter 'brother' (ev) > Gmc *brṓθer (e-TO-a) > Go brōþar. The e-TO-a change cannot affect an /e/ in pretonic position. E.g., PIE 1 sg past *lelṓda 'I let' (ev) > Gmc *lelṓt (e-TO-a not applying) > Go laílṓt /lelṓt/.

9d The Change of /ḗi,ṓu/ to /ḗ, ṓ/ (ēi/ōu-TO-ē/ō)

This change restructures a few lexical items and is then dropped from the grammar. By 5a DIPH SHORTENING the PIE long diphthongs were shortened, except for/ḗi/ and /ṓu/, where the stress is that of Germanic. These remaining long diphthongs then change:

ḗi, ṓu → ḗ, ṓ

E.g., PIE *kḗir 'here', nom sg *pṓun 'fire' (ev) > Gmc *hḗir, *fṓun (ēi/ōu-TO-ē/ō) > Go hēr, fōn.

9e Deletion and Assimilation of /h/ (h-DELETION)

The obligatory part (a) of this change restructures certain lexical items and then is dropped from the grammar. The optional parts (b, c, d) remain as phon cond rules in the phonology of Gothic.

h → (a) Ø / ___C_3
(b) Ø / ___C_1^2
(c) Ø /[V, –stress] ___ ##
(d) [αfeatures] / ___ ## [C, αfeatures]
(b–d) optional

That is, (a) is /h/ deleted obligatorily before a sequence of three or more consonants. (b, c) /h/ is deleted optionally before one or two consonants or after an unstressed vowel in word-final position. (d) Word-final /h/ can optionally assimilate over a word boundary to a following word-initial consonant.

E.g., (a) PIE nom sg *wr̥g+stw+om 'work' (1b OBSTR VOI/DEVOI) > *wr̥kstwom (2 1ST SS, 5e x-TO-h, 6c SYL SON, 7b 1ST UMLAUT, 7c NASAL LOSS, 8a MORA LOSS) > *worhstw (h-DELETION)> Go waúrstw /worstw/. (b) Underlying Go hiuhma 'crowd' (h-DELETION) → /hiuma/ or /hiuhma/. (c) Underlying Go ƕileikuh /hʷílīk+uh/ 'what kind of' (h-DELETION) → ƕileiku /hʷílīku/ or ƕileikuh /hʷílīk+uh/. (d) Underlying Go jah##θan 'and then' (h-DELETION) → jaþ þan or jah þan.

Regarding the chronology of this change, it seems likely that it would have occurred after 5e x-TO-h. For a glide [h] would be more apt to undergo the deletion and assimilation changes of h-DELETION rather than a full-fledged consonant like [x].

9f Insertion of /j/ (j-INSERTION)

This change remains as an optional phon cond rule of Gothic.

Ø → j / [V, +stress] ___ + V

where "+" is a word-internal morpheme boundary and where at least one of the vowels (V) is usually /i(:)/.

That is, /j/ is optionally inserted between two vowels, the first one stressed, at a morpheme boundary. E.g., the Gothic synchronic derivations: underlying gen pl θrí+ē '3', 1 pl pres sí+um 'we are', 3 sg pres sɛ́+iθ 'sows' (j-INSERTION) → þrījē, sijum or sium, and sáijiþ or sáiiþ, i.e. /sɛ́jiθ/ or /sɛ́iθ/.

9g Later Monophthongization of /ai/ and /au/ (LATER ai/au-MONOPH)

This change is stage 3 of 7a ai/au-MONOPH. It remains in the grammar of Gothic as a phon cond rule.

9h The Loss of Sievers' Law from the Grammar (LOSS OF SIEVERS)

In later Germanic but still pre-Gothic times the PIE rule 3.1.2f SIEVERS was dropped from the grammar. Recall that in its PIE version, SIEVERS changed /j/ to /ij/ after a "long sequence" as defined below.

However, when SIEVERS was dropped, it did not disappear without a trace. It left the following morph cond rule as its Gothic reflex.

ji → ī / (a) VC ⎫ C_1^n — in certain noun, adjective and verb paradigms.
(b) VV ⎬
(c) s_2 ⎭

That is, /ji/ becomes /ī/ in certain paradigms if following a "long sequence", namely a stem consisting of (a) a syllable ending in at least two consonants, (b) a syllable containing a long vowel or diphthong, or (c) at least two syllables. In any case, the long sequence must end in at least one consonant. E.g., the Gothic synchronic derivations gen sg herdj+is 'shepherd' vs. harj+is 'army' (LOSS OF SIEVERS) → haírdeis /hérdīs/ vs. harjis; 3 sg pres hɔ̄sj+iθ 'hears', mikilj+iθ 'praises' vs. nasj+iþ 'saves' (LOSS OF SIEVERS) → háuseiþ /hɔ̄́sīθ/, mikileiþ /míkilīθ/ vs. nasjiþ.

The eventual development of the Gothic morph cond rule may be illustrated by the following seven-stage historical derivation:

(1) PIE 1 sg pres *nosj+ṓ 'save' vs. *kousj+ṓ 'hear' and 3 sg pres *nosj+éti vs. *kousj+éti (PIE 3.1.2f SIEVERS applying as a synchronic rule) →
(2) *nosjṓ, *kousijṓ; *nosjéti, *kousijéti (ev through 6b o-TO-a) >
(3) *násjō, *háusijō; *násjeði, *háusijeði (7b 1ST UMLAUT) >
(4) *násjō, *háusijō; *násjiði, *háusijiði (reinterpretation of /iji/ as /ī/) >
(5) *násjō, *háusijō; *násjiði, *háusīði (8a MORA LOSS, 9b CONT OBSTR DEVOICING, 9g LATER ai/au-MONOPH) >
(6) *násja, *hɔ̄́sija; *násjiθ, *hɔ̄́sīθ (LOSS OF SIEVERS as a synchronic rule from the grammar) >
(7) Go nasja, háusja /hɔ̄́sja/; nasjiþ, háuseiþ /hɔ̄́sīθ/.

(Note the necessary chronology 7b 1ST UMLAUT > LOSS OF SIEVERS in the preceding derivation.)

9i The Change of /mz/ to /mm/ (mz-TO-mm)

After the rule for this change became obligatory, it resulted in the restructuring of certain inflectional endings. It was then dropped from the grammar.

mz → mm

E.g., PIE dat pl *$d^h og^{hw}$ómis 'days' (ev through 6b o-TO-a) > *dágamiz (8a MORA LOSS) > *dágamz (mz–to-mm, note here the necessary chronology 8a MORA LOSS > mz-TO-mm) > *dágamm (la GEM C SIMP applying as a persistent synchronic rule) → Go dagam.

9j The Change of /r/ and /n/ to /l/ (r/n-TO-l)

This change restructures various lexical items and then is dropped from the grammar.

r or n → l / ##...r or n (respectively)... —
where "..." contains no instances of word boundaries "##".

That is, /r/ or /n/ occurring within a word and preceded by /r/ or /n/, respectively, becomes /l/.

E.g., PIE nom sg masc *neu+gn+ók+os 'newly or just born' (through 9b CONT OBSTR DEVOICING) > *níuknahs (r/n-TO-l) > Go niuklahs, not **niuknahs. Note also the restructuring of the Latin loan word orarium 'handkerchief' to Go aúrali /órali/ instead of **aúrari.

9k Thurneysen's Law (THURNEYSEN)

This change remains as a morph cond rule of Gothic phonology. It applies fairly generally in Gothic, although a few marked lexical forms elude it. As we shall illustrate below, the change was in fact a morpheme-structure condition which arose from the effects of changes 2 1ST SS, 3 VERNER and 4a GMC STRESS. It is as follows:

$$[\text{C}, +\text{obstruent}, +\text{continuant}, -\text{voiced}] \quad \rightarrow \quad [+\text{voiced}]$$

$$/ \begin{pmatrix} \text{V} \\ +\text{stress} \end{pmatrix} \begin{pmatrix} \text{C} \\ -\text{voiced} \end{pmatrix}_1 \begin{pmatrix} \text{C} \\ +\text{sonorant} \end{pmatrix}_0 \begin{pmatrix} \text{V} \\ -\text{stress} \end{pmatrix} \quad \_\_\_ \quad [+\text{sonorant}]$$

1 2 3 4 5 6

where no word boundary ## intervenes between any of the six segments.

That is, the voiceless obstruent continuant consonants /f, θ, h, s/ become voiced /b, d, g, z/ (i.e., [ƀ, ð, ǥ, z] in position (5) above if followed by (6) any sonorant segment /l, m, n, r/ or any vowel; and if immediately preceded by (4) an unstressed vowel, itself optionally preceded by one or more sonorant consonants (3), preceded in turn by at least one voiceless consonant (2) which immediately follows a stressed vowel. All these segments occur within a single word.

Thus THURNEYSEN in effect prohibits within a word this sequence:

$$\begin{pmatrix} \text{C}, +\text{obstruent} \\ +\text{continuant} \\ -\text{voiced} \end{pmatrix} \quad [\text{V}, -\text{stress}] \quad \begin{pmatrix} \text{C}, +\text{obstruent} \\ +\text{continuant} \\ -\text{voiced} \end{pmatrix}$$

As examples we cite the following synchronic derivations of Go nom sg neut fást+ufni 'act of fasting' (THURNEYSEN) → fastubni [fástuƀni]; likewise nom sg neut wáld+ufni 'power' (to which THURNEYSEN cannot apply) → waldufni. Similarly, underlying nom sg fem ɔ̄θ+iθ+a 'desert' vs. dɔ̄b+iθ+a 'deafness' (THURNEYSEN) → áuþida [ɔ̄́θiða] vs. dáubiþa [dɔ̄́ƀiθa]. As noted above, a few lexically marked forms do not undergo THURNEYSEN: e.g. underlying θwást+iθ+a 'security' (ev) → þwastiþa as opposed to **þwastida **[θwástiða]. (See on this Voyles 1992:92–3.)

The origin of THURNEYSEN is to be found in the sequence of changes 2 1ST SS, 3 VERNER and 4a GMC STRESS. The chronology of the changes is as follows. (We use the bilabials/p, b^h, b/ as illustrative of their respective series.)

Stage 1.	1ST SS	p	→	p^h
Stage 2a.	1ST SS	p^h, b^h	→	f, ƀ
b.	VERNER	p^h or f	→	b^h or ƀ
Stage 3a.	1ST SS	b	→	p
b.	GMC STRESS			

(In the preceding the a and b changes may occur in either sequence within that stage.)

Given this chronology, then there must have been a period between stages 2 and 3 when the morpheme-structure constraints of early Germanic excluded the following sequences:

(a) **V f [V, –stress] f V
(b) **V ƀ [V, –stress] f V

The constraints (a) and (b) existed because after stages 1 and 2 above, only the following three sequences could occur in early Germanic.

(c) V́ f V ƀ V < PIE V́ p V p V
(d) V ƀ V́ f V < PIE V p V́ p V
(e) V ƀ V ƀ V́ < PIE V p V p V́

Hence neither of the sequences (a) or (b) above can occur at this time.

Then after stage 3, sequence (b) becomes a possibility. Here is how: PIE V p V́ p V (2 1ST SS, 3 VERNER) > early Gmc V ƀ V́ f V (4a GMC STRESS) > V́ ƀ V f V. But sequence (a), namely **V f [V, –stress] f V, remained excluded. And it is precisely this sequence that THURNEYSEN excludes:

[V, +stress]	f	[V, –stress]	f	V	→	same	same	same	ƀ	same
1	2	3	4	5		1	2	3	4	5

9l Vowel Deletion with Enclitics (V-DELETION WITH ENCLITICS)

This change remains in Gothic as a morph cond rule. It affects only the enclitics -uh 'and' as well as -ei (a marker of a subordinate clause). The rule is this:

(a) -uh → -h / [V, +long or +stress, not necessarily both] ___
(b) [V, –long, –stress] → Ø / ___ –uh or –ei

That is, (a) the /u/ in -uh is deleted after a long or a stressed vowel; and (b) a short unstressed vowel is deleted before the enclitics -uh or -ei. E.g., the synchronic derivations (a) gen pl θízē+uh 'these' → þizēh /θízēh/, nom sg masc sá+uh 'this' → sah; (b) nom sg neut θáta+uh 'this' → þatuh, acc sg masc θána+ī 'whom' → þanei /θanī/.

9m Lowering and Laxing of Long Vowels (V-LOWERING)

This change remains in the phonology of Gothic as a morph cond rule.

(V, +long, –low, +stress) → [–high, –tense] / ___ + V

That is, long and stressed /ī́, ḗ/ and /ū́, ṓ/ become /ɛ̄́/ and /ɔ̄́/respectively, if followed by a word-internal morpheme boundary and a vowel.

E.g., Gmc inf *bū́an 'build' (V-LOWERING) > Go báuan /bɔ̄́an/. The rule applies synchronically in the following instances: underlying inf sḗ+an 'sow' vs. the noun sē+θ+s 'seed' (V-LOWERING) → sáian /sɛ̄́an/ vs. sēþs, to which V-LOWERING cannot apply; and 3 sg past stō+ida 'judged' vs. inf stō+jan (V-LOWERING) → stáuida /stɔ̄́ida/ vs. stōjan.

9n A Glide-TO-Consonant Change (*VERSCHÄRFUNG*)

This change is referred to as "Holtzmann's Law" or "*Verschärfung*". It left some restructured forms and was then dropped from the grammar. The precise nature of this change is disputed; it seems to have occurred in two chronological stages. (See on this Voyles 1992: 94–5.)

(1)

V́	j	+	e(:), i(:)	→	same	j j	same	same
V́	w	+	a(:), o(:), u(:)		"	w w	"	"
1	2	3	4		1	2	3	4

(2)
j j → d j (possibly ddj)
ww → g w (possibly ggw)

That is, (1) /j/ and /w/ following a stressed vowel are doubled — /j/ if followed by a word-internal morpheme boundary "+" and a front vowel and/w/ if followed by a word-internal morpheme boundary and a back vowel. (2) The resulting geminated glides /jj/ and /ww/ become the respective obstruent stops /dj/ and /gw/(or possibly /ddj/ and /ggw/ depending on how one interprets the orthographic evidence).

E.g., PIE gen pl *dwoi+ḗm '2' (PIE 3.1.2c i-j/u-w ALT applying synchronically) → *dwojḗm (ev through 7c NASAL LOSS) > East Gmc *twáj+ē (*VERSCHÄRFUNG*) > Go twaddjē. PIE nom sg masc u-class adj. *g^{h}lówus 'exact' (ev through 9b CONT OBSTR DEVOICING) > *gláwuz (*VERSCHÄRFUNG* and ev) > Go glaggwuba 'exactly'. *VERSCHÄRFUNG* cannot apply to a form like PIE nom sg masc adj. •g^{w}íwos 'alive' (ev) > Go qius /k^{w}íus/, not **qiggws.

Some instances of the /jj/ sequence which undergoes stage 2 do not arise from stage 1, but rather from morpheme concatenation. E.g., PIE inf *d^{h}áj+jonom 'suckle' (ev through 8a MORA LOSS) > *dájjan (*VERSCHÄRFUNG* stage 2) > Go daddjan.

9o Deletion of Word-Final /z/ (z-DELETION)

This change remains in the Gothic grammar as a morph cond rule in that it applies only to the nom sg masc forms of those nouns and and adjectives (but not adverbs) which fit its conditioning.

z → Ø / [V, –long] r or s — ##

That is, /z/ is deleted word-finally if preceded by a short vowel followed in turn by /r/ or /s/. E.g., nom sg masc nouns *wíros 'man', *d^{h}rúsos 'fall', adj. *ánteros 'other' (ev through 9c e-TO-a) > *wérz, *drúsz, *ánθarz (z-DELETION) > Go waír /wer/, drus, anþar. Our formulation of z-DELETION assumes the prior application of 8a MORA LOSS (and possibly 9b CONT OBSTR DEVOICING).

As a morph cond rule remaining in the Gothic grammar, this rule applies to the nominative singular masculine of nouns and adjectives of the type shown above. Hence underlying Go nom sg wer+z 'man' vs. dag+z 'day' vs. comp adv werz 'worse' (z-DELETION applying synchronically, ev) → waír /wer/, dags, but waírs /wers/.

9p A Change of /z/ to /r/ (z-TO-r)

This change remains as a morph cond rule in the grammar of Gothic.

z → r / (a) — #r
(b) optional — ## r

That is, /z/ becomes /r/ (a) obligatorily over a prefix boundary when the following morpheme begins with an /r/ and (b) optionally over a word boundary when the following word begins with an /r/. E.g., the synchronic derivations of (a) the inf *ūz#rī́san 'arise' (z-TO-r) → ūrreisan /ūrrīsan/ and (b) the sequence ##ūz##rik^{w}iza## 'out of darkness' (z-TO-r) → ūr riqiza. If z-TO-r does not apply, then 9b CONT OBSTR DEVOICING does producing Go ūs riqiza.

C. The Relative Chronology

The ">" means "must precede"; and "> <" means "at approximately the same time as".

1a GEM C SIMP > 2 1ST SS (see la).
1b OBSTR VOI/DEVOI > < lc s-z RULE (see 1c), > le tt/ts-TO-ss (see le), > 2 1ST SS (see 1b).
1c s-z RULE > 2 1ST SS (see 1c), > 5c MS CHANGES (see 5c).
1d s-INSERTION > 2 1ST SS (see 1d).
1e tt/ts-TO-ss > 2 1ST SS (see 1e).
2 1ST SS > 3 VERNER (at least stages 1 and 2 of 1ST SS precede VERNER, see 3), > 4b n-ASSIM (see 4b), > 5b LABIOVELARS (see 5b), > 5c MS CHANGES (see 5c), > 5d OBSTR-TO-STOP (see 5d), > 5e x-TO-h (see 5e), > 8b ŋ-DELETION (see 8b), > 9k THURNEYSEN (see 9k).

3 VERNER > 2 1ST SS stage 3 (see 3), > 4a GMC STRESS (see 4a), > 4b n-ASSIM (see 4b), > 5b LABIOVELARS (see 5b) , > 5c MS CHANGES (see 5c), > 5d OBSTR-TO-STOP (see 5d), > 9k THURNEYSEN (see 9k).

4a GMC STRESS > 3 VERNER (the first 2 stages of 4a precede 3, see 4a), > 5a DIPH SHORTENING (see 5a), > 5c MS CHANGES (see 5c), > 7a ai/au MONOPH (see 7a), > 7b 1ST UMLAUT (see 7b), >< 7c NASAL LOSS (see 7c), > 8a MORA LOSS (see 8a), > 9d ē i/ō u-TO-ē/ō (see 9d), > 9k THURNEYSEN (see 9k).

4b n-ASSIM > 2 1ST SS stage 3 only (see 4b), > 4a GMC STRESS stages 1 and 2 (see 4a), > 5d OBSTR-TO-STOP (see 4a).

5a DIPH SHORTENING > 6b o-TO-a (see 5a).

5b LABIOVELARS > 6a ā-TO-ō (see 6a), > 6b o-TO-a (see 5b).

5c MS CHANGES > 9a am-TO-um (see 9a).

5d OBSTR-TO-STOP > 5b LABIOVELARS stage 2 (see 5b), > 9b CONT OBSTR DEVOICING (see 9b).

5e x-TO-h > 9e h-DELETION (see 9e).

6a ā-TO-ō > 7b 1ST UMLAUT (see 7b).

6b o-TO-a > 7a ai/au-MONOPH (see 7a), > 7b 1ST UMLAUT (see 7b), > 8a MORA LOSS (see 8a), > 8b ŋ-DELETION (see 8b).

6c SYL SON > 7b 1ST UMLAUT (see 6c and 7b), > 8b ŋ-DELETION (see 8b).

7a ai/au-MONOPH > 8a MORA LOSS (see 7a), > 9c e-TO-a (see 7a).

7b 1ST UMLAUT > 8a MORA LOSS (see 8a), > 8b ŋ-DELETION (see 8b), > 9c e-TO-a (see 9c), > 9h LOSS OF SIEVERS (see 9h).

7c NASAL LOSS > 4a GMC STRESS stage 3 (see 7c), > 8a MORA LOSS (see 7c).

8a MORA LOSS > 7a ai/au-MONOPH stage 2 (see 7a), > 9i mz-TO-mm (see 9i), > 9o z-DELETION (see 9o).

The following rules do not necessarily precede any other rules:

(8b) ŋ-DELETION; (9a) am-TO-um; (9b) CONT OBSTR DEVOICING; (9c) e-TO-a; (9d) ēi/ōu-TO-ē/ō; (9e) h-DELETION; (9f) j-INSERTION; (9g) LATER ai/au-MONOPH; (9h) LOSS OF SIEVERS; (9i) mz-TO-mm; (9j) r/n-TO-l; (9k) THURNEYSEN; (9l) V-DELETION WITH ENCLITICS; (9m) V-LOWERING; (9n) *VERSCHÄRFUNG*; (9o) z-DELETION ; (9p) z-TO-r.

III Gothic Phonology

After the changes described in the previous section, the inventory of segments in the phonology of Gothic at about 350 AD was as follows.

Obstruent Consonants

labial	dental	alveolar	velar	labiovelar	glottal	labioglottal
f	θ	s			h	h^w[3]
		z				
[b ƀ][4]	[d ð][4]		[g ǥ][4] [x][5]			
p[6]	t[6]		k[6]	k^w[3, 6]		

Sonorant Consonants

m [n ŋ][7]

l

r

w j

Vowels

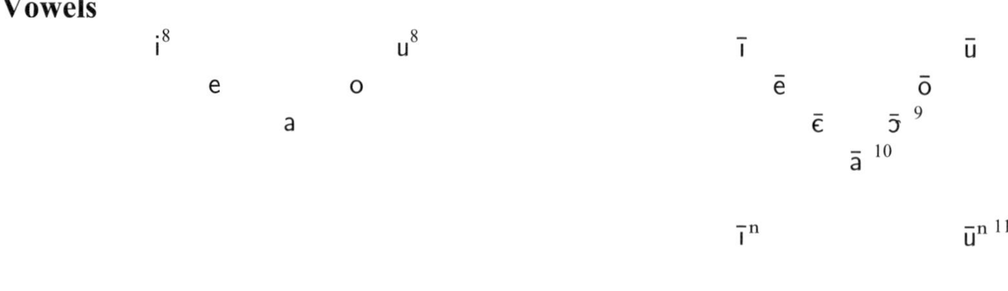

Diphthongs

aj, aw, iu[9]

The Gothic Segments in Terms of Phonological Features: Consonants

	f	θ	s	x	h	h^w	z	b	d	g	ƀ	ð	ǥ	p	t	k	k^w	m	n	ŋ	l	r	w	j
consonantal	+	+	+	+			+	+	+	+	+	+	+	+	+	+	+	+	+	+	+	+	−	−
sonorant	−	−	−	−			−	−	−	−	−	−	−	−	−	−	−	+	+	+	+	+	+	+
vocalic	−	−	−	−			−	−	−	−	−	−	−	−	−	−	−	−	−	−	−	−	−	−
high	−	−	−	+			−	−	−	+	−	−	+	−	−	+	+	−	−	+	−	−	+	+
back	−	−	−	+			−	−	−	+	−	−	+	−	−	+	+	−	−	+	−	−	+	−
low	−	−	−	−			−	−	−	−	−	−	−	−	−	−	−	−	−	−	−	−	−	−
anterior	+	+	+	−			+	+	+	−	+	+	−	+	+	−	−	+	+	−	+	+	−	−
coronal	−	+	+	−			+	−	+	−	−	+	−	−	+	−	−	−	+	−	+	+	−	−
voiced	−	−	−	−	−	−	+	+	+	+	+	+	+	−	−	−	−	+	+	+	+	+	+	+
continuant	+	+	+	+	+	+	+	−	−	−	+	+	+	−	−	−	−	−	−	−	+	+	+	+
nasal	−	−	−	−			−	−	−	−	−	−	−	−	−	−	−	+	+	+	−	−	−	−
strident	−	−	+	−			+	−	−	−	−	−	−	−	−	−	−	−	−	−	−	−	−	−
delayed release	−	−	−	−	−	−	−	−	−	−	−	−	−	−	−	−	−	−	−	−	−	−	−	−
round	−	−	−	−	−	+	−	−	−	−	−	−	−	−	−	−	+	−	−	−	−	−	+	−
lateral	−	−	−	−			−	−	−	−	−	−	−	−	−	−	−	−	−	−	+	−	−	−
palatal	−	−	−	−			−	−	−	−	−	−	−	−	−	−	−	−	−	−	−	−	−	+
tense	−	−	−	−			−	−	−	−	−	−	−	−	−	−	−	−	−	−	−	−	−	−
aspirated	−	−	−	−	+	+	−	−	−	−	−	−	−	−	−	−	−	−	−	−	−	−	−	−
stressed	−	−	−	−			−	−	−	−	−	−	−	−	−	−	−	−	−	−	−	−	−	−
long	−	−	−	−			−	−	−	−	−	−	−	−	−	−	−	−	−	−	−	−	−	−

Gothic Segments in Terms of Phonological Features: Vowels

	a	e	i	o	u	ā	ē	ɛ̄	ī	ō	ɔ̄	ū	ā^{n}	ī^{n}	ū^{n}
consonantal	−	−	−	−	−	−	−	−	−	−	−	−	−	−	−
sonorant	+	+	+	+	+	+	+	+	+	+	+	+	+	+	+
vocalic	+	+	+	+	+	+	+	+	+	+	+	+	+	+	+
high	−	−	+	−	+	−	−	−	+	−	−	+	−	+	+
back	+	−	−	+	+	+	−	−	−	+	+	+	+	−	+
low	+	−	−	−	−	+	−	−	−	−	−	−	+	−	−
voiced	+	+	+	+	+	+	+	+	+	+	+	+	+	+	+
continuant	+	+	+	+	+	+	+	+	+	+	+	+	+	+	+
nasal	−	−	−	−	−	−	−	−	−	−	−	−	+	+	+
round	−	−	−	+	+	−	−	−	−	+	+	+	−	−	+
tense	−	−	−	−	−	+	+	−	+	+	−	+	+	+	+
stressed	±	±	±	±	±	±	±	±	±	±	±	±	+	+	+
long	−	−	−	−	−	+	+	+	+	+	+	+	+	+	+

Certain of the changes have remained as rules in the grammar of Gothic. Those below labeled "morph cond" are morphologically conditioned and apply either to lexically marked items or to morphosyntactically defined classes. Those marked "phon cond " are phonologically conditioned and apply more or less generally. The symbol "Ø" after a change means that it has restructured lexical items and/or changed the inventory of underlying segments and has then been dropped from the grammar. For those changes remaining as rules in the grammar we cite an illustrative derivation. Additional examples can be found in the discussions of the particular rules.

1a GEM C SIMP (phon cond): gen sg /mann+z/ 'man' vs. gen pl /mann+ē/ (GEM C SIMP, ev) → mans or mannē.

1b OBSTR VOI/DEVOI (phon cond): the sequence /st/ can occur as in standan, not **/zt/ or **/sd/.

1c s-z RULE: Ø.

1d s-INSERTION (morph cond): nom sg /an+t+z/ 'favor' (s-INSERTION, ev) → ansts.

1e tt/ts-TO-ss (morph cond): 1 sg past /wit+t+a/ 'knew' (tt/ts-TO-ss) → wissa.

2 1ST SS (a phon cond remnant): /twalif/ '12' (1ST SS remnant) → [t^{h}walif], but inf /standan/ 'stand' (1ST SS remnant) → [st˭and˭an].

3 VERNER (morph cond): 1 sg /θarf/ 'need' vs. 1 pl /θorf+um/ (VERNER) → þarf vs. þaúrbum.

4a GMC STRESS (phon cond): nom sg /katiluz/ 'kettle', inf /bi#lɛ̄bjan/'leave', 1 sg past /se+slēp/ 'slept' (GMC STRESS, ev) → katilus /kátilus/, biláibjan /bilɛ̄́bjan/, saíslēp /seslḗp/. (Since Germanic stress is fairly straightforward, we usually do not mark it in our transcriptions of Gothic words.)

4b n-ASSIM: Ø.

5a DIPH SHORTENING: Ø.

5b LABIOVELARS: Ø.

5c MS CHANGES: Ø.

5d OBSTR-TO-STOP (phon cond): inf /haban/ 'have' and /bindan/ 'tie' (OBSTR-TO-STOP) → [haƀan] vs. [bindan].

5e x-TO-h: Ø.

6a ā-TO-ō: Ø

6b o-TO-a: Ø

6c SYL SON: Ø.

7a ai/au-MONOPH stages 1 and 2: Ø, stage 3 (phon cond): underlying /bai/ 'both' vs. /bai+ōθ/ (ai/au-MONOPH, ev) → bái /bɛ̄/ vs. bajōþ /bajōθ/.

7b 1ST UMLAUT (phon cond): infs. /bindan/ 'tie' vs. /wirθan/ 'become' — a verb of the same class — (1ST UMLAUT) → bindan vs. waírþan [werθan].

7c NASAL LOSS: Ø.

8a MORA LOSS: Ø.

8b ŋ-DELETION (morph cond): 1 sg past /θank+ta/ 'I thought' (1b OBSTR VOI/DEVOI applying as a synchronic rule) → θanhta (ŋ-DELETION) → þāhta /θā^{n}hta/.

9a am-TO-um: Ø.

9b CONT OBSTR DEVOICING (phon cond): nom sg /hlɛ̄b+z/ 'loaf' vs. gen sg /hlɛ̄b+iz/ (5d OBSTR-TO-STOP applying synchronically) → hlɛ̄bz and hlɛ̄biz/ (CONT OBSTR DEVOICING) → hláifs [hlɛ̄fs] and hláibis [hlɛ̄ƀis].

9c e-TO-a: Ø.

9d ēi/ōu-TO-ē/ō: Ø

9e h-DELETION (phon cond): /jah##θan/ 'and then' (h-DELETION applying optionally) → jaþ þan or jah þan.

9f j-INSERTION (phon cond): 3 sg /sē+ið/ 'sows' (9b CONT OBSTR DEVOICING applying synchronically) → sɛ̄+iθ (j-INSERTION applying optionally) → sáiiþ [sɛ̄iθ] as well as sáijiþ [sɛ̄jiθ].

9g Later ai/au-MONOPH (phon cond): see 7a ai/au-MONOPH above.

9h LOSS OF SIEVERS (morph cond): 3 sg /hɔ̄sj+ið/ 'hears' vs. /nasj+ið/ 'saves' (9b CONT OBSTR DEVOICING applying synchronically) → hɔ̄sjiθ vs. nasjiθ (LOSS OF SIEVERS) → háuseiþ /hɔ̄sīθ/ vs. nasjiþ /nasjiθ/.

9i mz -TO-mm: Ø.

9j r/n -TO-l: Ø.

9k THURNEYSEN (morph cond): nom sg /ɔ̄́θ+iθ+a/ 'desert' (THURNEYSEN) → áuþida [ɔ̄́θiða].

9l V-DELETION WITH ENCLITICS (morph cond): gen pl /θízē+uh/ 'and of these' (V-DELETION WITH ENCLITICS) → þizēh.

9m V-LOWERING (morph cond): inf /stō+jan/ 'judge' vs. the 1 sg past /stō-+ida/ (V-LOWERING, ev) → stōjan vs. stáuida [stɔ̄iða].

9n *VERSCHÄRFUNG*: Ø.

9o z-DELETION (morph cond): nom sg /wer+z/'man' vs. /dag+z/ (z-DELETION) → waír /wer/, not **waírs, vs. dags, not **dag.

9p z-TO-r (morph cond): inf /ūz#rīsan/ 'arise' (z-TO-r) → ūrreisan [ūrrīsan].

IV Historical Gothic Morphology

A. Overview

B. Gothic Morphology

In each paradigm below the Gothic forms of ca. 350 AD are cited in the left-hand column, the reconstructed NW Germanic forms of about the same time in the center column and the PIE forms with the pre-Germanic stress of 4a GMC STRESS stage 1 in the right-hand column. The Gothic and NW Germanic forms are usually cited without their stress being marked since this is easily derivable from 4a GMC STRESS.

1 Nouns

Nouns as well as the other substantives such as adjectives, pronouns and numerals occur in the singular and plural. The cases are nominative, vocative, accusative, genitive and dative with remnants of the locative and instrumental. In all paradigms the vocative plural is homophonous with the nominative plural and as such is not marked. Where the vocative singular is not cited, it is the same as the nominative singular.

1.1 o-Class (Masculine, Neuter)

E.g., the masculine noun, dags 'day':

		Go	NWGmc	PIE
sg	nom	dags	*daǥaz	*d^{h}óg^{hw}os
	voc	dag	*daǥ	*d^{h}óg^{hw}e
	acc	dag	*daǥa	*d^{h}óg^{hw}om
	gen	dagis[12]	*daǥes	*d^{h}og^{hw}éso
	dat		*daǥē	*d^{h}og^{hw}ṓi
		daga		*d^{h}og^{hw}ḗ/ṓ[13]
	loc	Ø	*daǥi	*d^{h}og^{hw}éi
pl	nom	dagōs[12]	*daǥōz	*d^{h}óg^{hw}ōs
	acc	dagans[12]	*daǥanz	*d^{h}óg^{hw}ons
	gen	dagē	*daǥō^{n}	*d^{h}og^{hw}ḗm$^{(\alpha)}$
	dat	dagam	*daǥamz	*d^{h}og^{hw}ómis

(α) The history of the Gothic gen pl dagē is not clear. The problem is that virtually all Indo-European languages have genitive plural reflexes of *-ōm, while no language, except possibly Gothic, has *-ēm, which could be an ablauting variant of *-ōm. On the various theories see Jones 1979: 64–73.

Neut o-class nouns have the same endings as the masculine nouns, except for the following.
E.g., the neuter noun, wáurd /word/, 'word':

		Go	NWGmc	PIE
sg	nom/acc	wáurd	*worda	*wŕ̥d^{h}om
pl	nom/acc	wáurda	*wordu	*wŕ̥d^{h}ā

The jo-class nouns have historically the same endings as those of the o-class. However, through regular phonological change the jo-class endings can differ by Gothic times. E.g., the masculine nouns harjis 'army' and haírdeis /herdīs/ 'shepherd', and the neuter nouns kuni 'tribe' and reiki /rīki/ 'realm':

		Go	NWGmc	PIE
masc sg	**nom**	harjis	*harjaz	*kórjos
		haírdeis	*herðijaz	*kérd^{h}ijos[14]
neut sg	**nom/acc**	kuni	*kunja	*gń̥jom
		reiki	*rīkija	*rī́gijom[15]

Occasionally sources posit a so-called wo-class. The endings are those of the o-class. E.g., snáiws /snēws/ 'snow':

		Go	NWGmc	PIE
masc sg	**nom**	snáiws	*snaiwaz	*snóig^{hw}os

1.2 ā-Class (Feminine)

E.g., the noun, giba 'gift':

		Go	NWGmc	PIE
sg	**nom**	giba	*ǥeƀu	*g^{h}éb^{h}ā[16]
	acc	giba	*ǥeƀō	*g^{h}éb^{h}ām[17]
	gen	gibōs	*ǥeƀōz	*g^{h}éb^{h}ās
	dat	gibái	*ǥeƀē	*g^{h}éb^{h}āi[18]
pl	**nom**	gibōs	*ǥeƀōz	*g^{h}éb^{h}ās
	acc	gibōs	*ǥeƀōnz	*g^{h}éb^{h}āns[α]
	gen	gibō	*ǥeƀō^n	*g^{h}eb^{h}ṓm
	dat	gibōm	*ǥeƀōmz	*g^{h}eb^{h}ā́mis[19]

(α) The Gothic accusative plural is from the original nominative plural.

There is also a jā-class. Historically the same as those of the ā-class, the jā-class endings of long-stem nouns have come to differ in the nominative singular. E.g., the nouns bandi 'bond' and banja 'wound':

	Go	NWGmc	PIE
nom sg	bandi	*bandiju	*b^{h}ónd^{h}jā[20]
	banja	*banju	*b^{h}ánjā[20]

1.3 i-Class (Masculine, Feminine)

E.g., the noun, gasts 'guest':

		Go	NWGmc	PIE
sg	**nom**	gasts	*ǥastiz	*gʰóstis
	voc	gast	*ǥast	*gʰósti
	acc	gast	*ǥasti	*gʰóstim
	gen	gastis	*ǥastes	*gʰost+éso[α]
	dat	gasta	*ǥastē	*gʰost+ṓi, *gʰost+ḗ [α]
pl	**nom**	gasteis /gastīs/	*ǥastīz	*gʰóstei+es[21]
	acc	gastins	*ǥastinz	*gʰóstins
	gen	gastē	*ǥastō^{n}	*gʰost+ḗm[α]
	dat	gastim	*ǥastimz	*gʰostímis

(α) These endings are from the o-class.

The feminine i-class nouns have the same plural endings as the masculine. E.g. the noun qēns 'lady':

		Go	NWGmc	PIE
sg	**nom**	qēns /kʷēns/	*kʷēniz	*gʷḗnis
	acc	qēn	*kʷēni	*gʷḗnim
	gen	qēnáis /kʷēnɛ̄s/	*kʷēnīz	*gʷḗnois, *gʷḗneis[22]
	dat	qēnái	*kʷēnī	*gʷḗnoi, *gʷḗnei[22]

1.4 u-Class (Masculine, Feminine, Neuter)

E.g., the masculine noun, sunus 'son':

		Go	NWGmc	PIE
sg	**nom**	sunus	*sunuz	*súnus
	voc	sunu,	*sunu,	*súnu,
		sunáu /sunɔ̄/	*sunō	*súnou[23]
	acc	sunu	*sunu	*súnum
	gen	sunáus	*sunōz	*súnous
	dat	sunáu	*sunō, *sunju	*súnou[24], *súneu
pl	**nom**	sunjus	*sunjuz	*súneu+es[25]
	acc	sununs	*sununz	*súnuns
	gen	suniwē	*suniwō^{n}	*suneu+ḗm[25]
	dat	sunum	*sunumz	*sunúmis

The endings of the neuter nouns of this class are the same as those above except for the following:

		Go		NWGmc	PIE
sg	nom/acc	faíhu /fehu/	'cattle'	*fehu	*péku
pl		*faíhiwa		*fehiwu	*pékeu+ā[26]

1.5 Athematic Classes

The masculine and feminine paradigms of these classes have the same endings.

1.5.1 Ø-Class (Masculine, Feminine, Neuter)

E.g., the feminine noun, baúrgs /borgs/ 'city':

		Go	NWGmc	PIE
sg	nom	baúrgs	*burǥz	*bʰŕ̥̥gʰ+s[27]
	voc	baúrg	*burǥ	*bʰŕ̥̥gʰ
	acc	baúrg	*burǥ	*bʰŕ̥̥gʰm̥
	gen	baúrgs	*burǥz	*bʰŕ̥̥gʰes[28]
	dat	baúrg	*burǥ	*bʰŕ̥̥gʰi
pl	nom	baúrgs	*burǥz	*bʰŕ̥̥gʰes[28]
	acc	baúrgs	*burǥz	*bʰŕ̥̥gʰes[(α)]
	gen	baúrgē	*burǥō^n	*bʰr̥̥gʰḗm
	dat	baúrgim	*burǥumz	*bʰr̥̥gʰḿ̥̥is[(β)]

(α) The Gothic accusative plural is derived from the PIE nominative plural. Otherwise the derivation would be PIE *bʰŕ̥̥gʰn̥s (ev) > Go **baúrguns as opposed to baúrgs.

(β) The Gothic ending –im is from the i-class. Otherwise one would expect the derivation PIE *bʰr̥gʰḿ̥̥is (ev) > Go **baúrgum. Other Ø-class nouns tend in various other instances to pass into the i-class. E.g., the Go Ø-class nom pl nahts 'nights' from PIE *noktes is in later West Gmc i-class *naxtīz (ev) > OHGerm nachti > ModGerm Nächte.

The masc Ø-class nouns such as Go reiks /rīks/ 'ruler' have basically the same endings as baúrgs. However, by Gothic times Ø-class nouns are tending to go into other classes. E.g., the gen sg of reiks is reikis with the ending from the o-class, PIE *rī́g+eso. (Gmc *rīk- is actually a pre-1ST SS borrowing from Celtic *rīg- from PIE *rēg- by the Old Irish change 1b ē-TO-ī.)

There are no neuter nouns of this class in Gothic since they have gone into the o-class. However, neut Ø-class nouns do occur in other Germanic languages such as OEng nom acc sg ealu 'ale', gen pl ealoþa. We assume that neuter nouns of this class had the same endings as those of the masculine and feminine except for the nominative/accusative:

		Go	NWGmc	PIE
nom/acc	sg	*alu	*alu	*alút[29]
	pl	*aluda [áluða]	*aluθu	*alútā[30]

1.5.2 r/n-Class (Neuter)

This class is sometimes referred to as "heteroclitic" (Krause 1953: 160). We call it the PIE r/n-class. The PIE stems alternated, ending in /r/ in the nominative/accusative, singular and plural, and in /n/ otherwise. Gothic analogized the paradigm with /n/; the other Germanic languages usually with /r/. The endings are those of the neut Ø-class. E.g., the singular forms, watō 'water' and fōn 'fire':

	Go	NWGmc	PIE
nom/acc	watō		*wód+ōn
		*watar	*wód+or
	fōn		*pṓu+n[31]
		*fuer	*pú+er[31]
gen	watins		*wód+en+s
		*watares[32]	*wód+or+eso[32]
	funins		*pú+n+en+s[31]
		*fueres[32]	*pú+er+eso[32]

1.5.3 (t)Vr-Class (Masculine, Feminine)

These nouns denote family members. The PIE suffix is *-(t)Vr, where V = an ablauting vowel. The endings of the masculine and feminine nouns such as Go fem daúhtar /dóhtar/ 'daughter' and masc brōþar 'brother' are the same. A masculine paradigm follows:

		Go	NWGmc	PIE
sg	**nom**	brōþar	*brōθer	*b^{h}rā́ter[33]
	acc	brōþar	*brōθer	*b^{h}rā́term̥
	gen	brōþrs	*brōθrz	*b^{h}rā́tres[(α)]
	dat	brōþr	*brōθr	*b^{h}rā́tri
pl	**nom**	brōþrjus[(β)]	*brōθrz	*b^{h}rā́tres[(β)]
	acc	brōþruns[(β)]	*brōθrunz	*b^{h}rā́trn̥s[(β)]
	gen	brōþrē	*brōθrō^{n}	*b^{h}rātrḗm
	dat	brōþrum	*brōθrumz	*b^{h}rātŕ̥mis

(α) The derivation is *b^{h}rā́tres (2 1ST SS, 3 VERNER) > *brā́θrez (6a ā-TO-ō, 8a MORA LOSS) > *brṓθrz (9b CONT OBSTR DEVOICING) > Go brōþrs.

(β) From a PIE nom pl *b^{h}rā́tres one would expect Go **brōþrs by a derivation like that of gen sg brōþrs above. But the accusative plural would develop as follows: PIE *b^{h}rā́trn̥s (2 1ST SS, 3 VERNER, 6a ā-TO-ō) > *brṓθrn̥z (6c SYL SON) > *brṓθrunz (9b CONT OBSTR DEVOICING) > Go brōþruns. Since the accusative plural ending is now homophonous with that of the u-class sununs 'sons', the u-class nominative plural was added to Ø-class nouns: brōþrjus after sunjus.

1.5.4 Vn-Class (Masculine, Feminine, Neuter)

The stem suffix of this class is -Vn, where V is an ablauting vowel. The noun guma 'man' demonstrates the masculine paradigm:

		Go	NWGmc	PIE
sg	**nom**	guma[34]	*ǥomō[34]	*g^{h}ḿ̥+ōn
	acc	guman	*ǥoman	*g^{h}ḿ̥+on+m̥
	gen	gumins	*ǥominz	*g^{h}ḿ̥+en+es
	dat	gumin	*ǥomin	*g^{h}ḿ̥+en+i
pl	**nom**	gumans	*ǥomanz	*g^{h}ḿ̥+on+es$^{(\alpha)}$
	acc	gumans	*ǥomanz	*g^{h}ḿ̥+on+es$^{(\alpha)}$
	gen	gumanē	*ǥomanō	*g^{h}m̥+on+ḗm
	dat	gumam	*ǥomamz	*g^{h}m̥+onḿ̥is[35]

(α) The accusative plural is from an original nominative plural. The derivation is *g^{h}ḿ̥ones (2 1ST SS, 3 VERNER) > *ǥḿ̥+on+ez (6b o-TO-a, 6c SYL SON, 7b 1ST UMLAUT) > *ǥúmaniz (8a MORA LOSS) > *ǥúmanz (9b CONT OBSTR DEVOICING) > Go gumans. A PIE acc pl *g^{h}ḿ̥onn̥s would result in Go **gumanuns.

The feminine nouns of this class have the same endings as the masculine; however, the -Vn suffix has ō-grade ablaut throughout. E.g., the noun tuggō /tuŋgō/ 'tongue':

		Go	NWGmc	PIE
sg	**nom**	tuggō	*tungō	*dń̥g^{h}ōn
	acc	tuggōn	*tungōn	*dń̥g^{h}ōn +m̥

Some Vn-class fem nouns have the suffix -īn. These are usually deadjectival nouns. E.g.,

		Go	NWGmc	PIE
sg	**nom**	háuhei /hɔ̄hī/ 'height'	*hauhī	*kóuk+īn

The neut Vn-class nouns decline as demonstrated by the noun haírtō /hertō/'heart':

		Go	NWGmc	PIE
sg	**nom/acc**	haírtō	*hertō	*kérd+ōn
	gen	haírtins	*hertinz	*kérd+en+es
	dat	haírtin	*hertin	*kérd+en+i
pl	**nom/acc**	haírtōna	*hertōnu	*kérd+ōn+ā
	gen	haírtōnē	*hertōnō^n	*kerd+ōn+ḗm
	dat	haírtam	*hertamz	*kerd+ómis[36]

A few masculine and neuter nouns show the Ø-grade in the –Vn suffix in the plural cases. E.g., the following dative plural forms of the masculine noun aba 'man' and the neuter noun watō 'water':

	Go	NWGmc	PIE
masc	abnam	*aƀnamz	*ab^{h}+n+ómis
neut	watnam	*watnamz	*wod+n+ómis

There are also jVn-class masculine and feminine nouns. Many of these are derived agent nouns. The endings are those of the other masculine and feminine nouns, e.g., the following nominative singular forms:

	Go	NWGmc	PIE
masc	arbja 'heir'	*arƀijō	*órb^{h}jōn[(α)]
fem	arbjō 'heiress'	*arƀijō	*órb^{h}jōn[(α)]

(α) The phonological development of PIE *órb^{h}jōn results in Go arbja. In the Go fem arbjō the /ō/ was reimported into the nominative singular from the oblique cases.

1.5.5 Vnt-Class (Masculine, Perhaps Feminine)

This paradigm consists of agent nouns constructed from present active participles of verbs. The endings of the genitive singular and dative plural are from the o-class. Otherwise the endings are those of the Ø-class baúrgs 'city' above. E.g., the masculine noun, nasjands 'savior':

		Go	NWGmc	PIE
sg	**nom**	nasjands	*nazjandz	*nósjont+s
	gen	nasjandis	*nazjandes	*nosjont+éso
pl	**dat**	nasjandam	*nazjandamz	*nosjont+ómis

1.5.6 Vs-Class (Neuter)

In Gothic, the nouns of this class have gone into the o-class. The early NW Germanic paradigm was as follows:

		NWGmc	PIE
sg	**nom/acc**	*kalƀaz 'calf'	*gólb^{h}+os
	gen	*kalƀizes	*golb^{h}+es+éso[(α)]
	dat	*kalƀizē	*golb^{h}+es+ṓi[(α)]
pl	**nom/acc**	*kalƀizu	*gólb^{h}+es+ā
	gen	*kalƀizō^{n}	*golb^{h}+es+ṓm[(α)]
	dat	*kalƀizamz	*golb^{h}+es+ómis[(α)]

(α) These endings are from the o-class.

In the earlier stages of the West Germanic languages, the reflex of the -iz suffix, namely -ir, is found in all cases except the nominative/accusative singular. The endings are those of the neut o-class. E.g., nom sg *kalƀ, gen sg *kalƀires. Later the -ir suffix was added only in the plural.

In Gothic the Vs-class nouns were through regular phonological change absorbed into the neut o-class. E.g., the PIE short-stem nom sg *ség^h+es 'victory' vs. the long-stem *wéik+es 'town' and nom pl *ség^h+es+ā *wéik+es+ā (through 7b 1ST UMLAUT) > *síǥiz, *wī́hiz; *siǥizo, *wī́hizō (8a MORA LOSS) > *síǥiz, *wī́hz; *síǥizā, *wī́hzā (9b CONT OBSTR DEVOICING) > Go sigis, weihs /wīhs/ 'place'; *siǥisa, weihsa.

2 Adjectives

As in all early Germanic languages, in Gothic there are two basic adjective declensions, the so-called strong and the weak. Any adjective can participate in either paradigm.

The distinction between the two declensions was semantic and pragmatic in nature. That means that the strong declension was used when an indefinite reference was intended (namely something like "some or another x"), while the weak declension was used to indicate a definite reference (something like "this or that specific x"). E.g., pre-Germanic PIE nominative singular masculine strong declension *b^{h}lénd^{h}os *wíros 'some blind man' vs. nominative singular masculine weak declension *b^{h}lénd^{h}ōn *wíros 'the or that specific blind man' (ev) > NWGmc *blíndaz *wéraz vs. *blíndō *wéraz and Go blinds waír /wer/ vs. blinda waír.

2.1 Strong Adjective Declension

The endings of these adjectives are those of the o-, ā-, jo-, jā-, i- or u-class nouns. Membership in these classes is lexically marked, i.e., idiosyncratic. Most adjectives belong to the o- and ā-class, whose declination is as follows.

2.1.1 o- and ā-Class

The endings of the masculine and neuter are of the o-class; those of the feminine are from the ā-class. E.g., the adjective blinds 'blind':

			Go	**NWGmc**	**PIE**
masc	**sg**	**nom**	blinds	*blindaz	*b^{h}lénd^{h}os[α]
		acc	blindana	*blindanō	*b^{h}lénd^{h}om+ōm[37]
		gen	blindis	*blindes	*b^{h}lend^{h}éso[α]
		dat	blindamma	*blindammu	*b^{h}lend^{h}ósmo[38]
	pl	**nom**	blindái /blindɛ̄/	*blindē	*b^{h}lénd^{h}oi
		acc	blindans	*blindanz	*b^{h}lénd^{h}ons[α]
		gen	blindáizē /blindɛ̄zē/	*blindēzō^n	*b^{h}lend^{h}oisḗm
		dat	blindáim	*blindēmz	*b^{h}lend^{h}óimis

(α) These endings are those of the o- and ā-class nouns. The other endings are pronominal.

			Go	NWGmc	PIE
fem	**sg**	**nom**	blinda	*blindu	*bʰléndʰā$^{(\beta)}$
		acc	blinda	*blindō	*bʰléndʰām$^{(\beta)}$
		gen	blindáizōs	*blindēzōz	*bʰléndʰāisās
		dat	blindái	*blindē	*bʰléndʰāi$^{(\beta)}$
	pl	**nom**	blindōs	*blindōz	*bʰléndʰās$^{(\beta)}$
		acc	blindōs	*blindōnz	*bʰléndʰāns$^{(\beta)}$
		gen	blindáizō	*blindēzō^{n}	*bʰlendʰāisṓm
		dat	blindáim	*blindēmz	*bʰlendʰā́imis

		Go	NWGmc	PIE
neut$^{(\alpha)}$	**sg nom/acc**	blind	*blind	*bʰléndʰod
		blindata	*blindatō	*bʰléndʰod+ōm[37]
	pl nom/acc	blinda	*blindu	*bʰléndʰā$^{(\beta)}$

(α) Otherwise the neuter endings are those of the masculine.
(β) These endings are those of the o- and ā-class nouns. The other endings are pronominal.

2.1.2 jo- and jā-Class

These adjectives have historically the same endings as those of the o- and jā-class. In Gothic some of the endings differ from the o- and jā-class because of the effect of PIE 3.1.2f SIEVERS as well as 9h LOSS OF SIEVERS. E.g., the adjectives midjis 'mid, central' and wilþeis /wilθīs/ 'wild':

		Go	NWGmc	PIE
masc sg	**nom**	midjis	*miðjaz	*médʰjos[39]
		wilþeis	*wilðijaz	*wéltjos$^{(\alpha)}$[39]
	acc	midjana	*miðjanō	*médʰjom+ōm
		wilþjana	*wilðijanō	*wéltjom+ōm
	gen	midjis	*miðjes	*medʰjéso
		wilþeis	*wilðijes	*weltjéso

(α) The alternation of Go wilþeis with /θ/ vs. NWGmc *wilðijaz with /ð/ by 3 VERNER is the result of 4a GMC STRESS, which applied earlier in East Germanic than in NW Germanic, where the stress remained for a time on the endings of the oblique cases.

	Go	NWGmc	PIE
neut sg nom/acc	midi	*miðja	*médʰjod
	midjata	*miðjatō	*médʰjod+ōm
	wilþi	*wilðija	*wéltjod[(α)]
	wilþjata	*wilðijatō	*wéltjod+ōm

(α) The derivation is *wéltjod (PIE 3.1.2f SIEVERS applying synchronically) → *wéltijod (through 7b 1ST UMLAUT) > *wílθijat (8a MORA LOSS) > *wílθija (9h LOSS OF SIEVERS) > *wílθja (loss of word-final /a/ because the form is homophonous with the nominative/accusative plural neuter) > *wílθj > Go wilþi. Otherwise the Gothic stems are midj- and wilþj-; and the endings are those of the o- and ō-class.

2.1.3 i-Class

E.g., the adjective hráins /hrɛ̄ns/ 'pure':

			Go	NWGmc	PIE
sg	**nom**	**masc**	hráins	*hrainiz	*króinis
		fem	hráins	*hrainiz	*króinis
		neut	hráin	*hraini	*króini+od[40]
			hráinjata[41]	*hrainijatō	*króini+od+ōm
	gen	**masc**	hráinis	*hraines	*kroini+éso[42]
		fem	hráinjáizōs[41]	*hrainijēzōz	*króini+āisās
		neut	hráinis	*hraines	*kroini +éso[42]

Otherwise the Gothic stem is hrainj- plus the endings of the o-and ā-class.

2.1.4 u-class

E.g., the adjective hardus 'hard':

			Go	NWGmc	PIE
sg	**nom**	**masc**	hardus	*harðuz	*kórtus
		fem	hardus	*harðuz	*kórtus[(α)]
		neut	hardu	*harðu	*kórtu+d
			hardjata[(β)]	*harðjatō	*kórtu+od+ōm
	gen	**masc**	hardáus /hardɔ̄s/	*harðōz	*kórtous
		fem	hardjáizōs /hardjɛ̄zōs/	*harðijēzōz	*kórtu+āisās
		neut	hardáus	*harðōz	*kórtous

(α) The Germanic forms have [ð] by 3 VERNER from those cases with ending stress such as the gen pl fem *kort+j+āisṓm (ev) > Go hardjáizō [harðjɛ̄zō].

(β) The use of /j/ as a marker in most cases of this class occurred already in early Germanic times. It was imported from the jo/jā- and i-classes. Otherwise the Gothic stem is hardj- plus the endings of the o-and ā-class.

2.2 Weak Adjective Declension

These endings are those of the masculine, feminine and neut Vn-class nouns in 1.5.4 above. E.g., the following nominative singular forms of the adjective blinda 'blind':

	Go	NWGmc	PIE
masc	blinda	*blindō	*b^{h}lénd^h+ōn
fem	blindō[43]	*blindō	*b^{h}lénd^h+ōn
neut	blindō[43]	*blindō	*b^{h}lénd^h+ōn

Feminine weak adjectives in (a) the comparative in -iz-, (b) the comparative in –m- and (c) in the present participle have the endings of īn-class nouns such as háuhei /hɔ̄hī/'height' in 1.5.4 above. E.g., the following nominative singular forms:

		Go		NWGmc	PIE
(a)	**masc**	batiza	'better'	*batizō	*b^{h}ód+is+ōn
	fem	batizei		*batizī	*b^{h}ód+is+īn
(b)	**masc**	fruma	'former'	*frumō	*pr+ḿ̥ +ōn
	fem	frumei		*frumī	*pr+ḿ̥+īn
(c)	**masc**	nimanda	'taking'	*nemandō	*ném+ont+ōn
	fem	nimandei		*nemandī	*ném+ont+īn

The weak declension of the jo/jā-, i- and u-class adjectives has /j/ after the stem and before the inflectional endings. E.g., the following nominative singular masculine forms:

	Go		NWGmc	PIE
jo/jā-class	wilþja	'wild'	*wilðijō	*wélt+j+ōn
i-class	hráinja	'pure'	*hrainijō	*króin+j+ōn
u-class	hardja	'hard'	*harðijō	*kórt+j+ōn

2.3 Comparison

There are three types of comparison: (a) with the suffixes comparative -Vz- and superlative -Vst-, where V = /ō/ or /i/; (b) with the suffixes comparative -m- and superlative -mist-; and (c) by suppletion.

(a) This is the most frequent type of comparison. The following are nominative singular masculine forms of the positive, comparative, and superlative degrees:

	Go	**NWGmc**	**PIE**
pos	blinds 'blind'	*blindaz	*b^{h}lénd^h+os
	arms 'poor'	*armaz	*órb^{h}m+os
comp	blindiza[(α)]	*blindizō	*b^{h}lénd^h+is+ōn
	armōza[(α), 44]	*armōzō	*órb^{h}m+is+ōn
sup	blindists	*blindistaz	*b^{h}lénd^h+ist+os
	armōsts[44]	*armōstaz	*órb^{h}m+ist+os

(α) The comparative takes only the weak declension. The positive and superlative take both strong and weak declensions.

(b) This type of comparison is found with a few adjectives which indicate spatial or temporal location. They generally have no positive forms. E.g.,

	Go	**NWGmc**	**PIE**
pos	Ø	Ø	Ø
comp	aftuma 'second of two'	*aftumō	*apt+ḿ̥+ōn
	fruma 'former'	*frumō	*pr+ḿ̥+ōn
sup	aftmists 'next'	*aftumistaz	*apt+ḿ̥+ist+os
	frumists 'first'	*frumistaz	*pr+ḿ̥+ist+os

(c) This type of comparison is suppletion and occurs with only a few adjectives. E.g., the following nominative singular masculine forms:

	Go	**NWGmc**	**PIE**
pos	gōþs /gōθs/ 'good'	*ǥōðaz	*g^{h}ṓd^h+os
	mikils 'big'	*mikilaz	*mégil+os
comp	batiza 'better'	*batizō	*b^{h}ód+is+ōn
	máiza 'bigger'	*maizō	*má+is+ōn
sup	batists 'best'	*batistaz	*b^{h}ód+ist+os
	máists 'biggest'	*maistaz	*má+ist+os

3 Adverbs

There are two basic formations for deadjectival adverbs. One is (a) with –ē/ō onto the adjective stem. The other is (b) with the suffix -ba onto the adjective stem. E.g.,

	Go	NWGmc	PIE
(a)	swarē 'in vain'	*swarē	*sworḗd [(α)]
	galeikō 'likewise'	*ǥalīkō	*komlīgṓd
(b)	sunjaba 'truly'	*sunjaƀe/u	*sn̥jobʰḗ/ṓ [(β)]

(α) The PIE ending is an ablauting ablative singular. One derivation is *sworḗd (2 1ST SS) > *sworḗt (4a GMC STRESS) > *swórēt (6b o-TO-a) > *swárēt (8a MORA LOSS) > Go swarē.

(β) The PIE ending is an instrumental singular.

The comparative and superlative are formed with the suffixes -Vz and -Vst. There are no inflectional endings. E.g.,

	Go	NWGmc	PIE
comp	háuhis 'more highly'	*hauhiz	*kóuk+is
	sniumundōs 'faster'	*sneumundōz	*snéumn̥t+ōs
sup	frumist 'at first'	*frumist	*pr+ḿ̥+ist

4 Numerals

4.1 Cardinals

The cardinal numerals occur in three types of syntactic construction. For '1' through '3' (perhaps '4'), the numeral is an adjective agreeing in case, number and gender with its head noun. E.g., PIE nom sg masc *oinos *dʰógʰʷos '1 day' and nom pl *dwói *dʰógʰʷōses '2 days' (ev) > Gmc *ainaz *daǥaz and *twai *daǥōz (ev) > Go *áins dags and twái dagōs.

The numerals from '5' (perhaps '4') through '19' are generally uninflected. The head noun has its case as determined by its function in the sentence. E.g., PIE nom pl *pémpe *dʰógʰʷōs '5 days' (ev) > Gmc *fimf *daǥōz (ev) > Go fimf dagōs. However, sometimes these numerals can take i-class adjective inflection. E.g., PIE nom pl *pémpejes *dʰógʰʷōses '5 days' (ev) > Gmc *fimfīz *daǥōs (ev) > Go *fimfeis dagōs.

The numerals from '20' and beyond are nouns whose cases are determined by their function in the sentence. The semantically head nouns in these constructions are in the genitive plural. E.g., PIE nom pl neut *dwā *kn̥tā *dʰogʰʷōm '2 hundreds of days' (ev) > Gmc *twō *hundō *daǥōⁿ (ev) > Go twa hunda dagē.

'1'	Go	NWGmc	PIE
	áins /ɛ̄ns/	*ainaz	*óinos

The endings are those of the o- -and ā-class adjectives.

‘2’		Go	NWGmc	PIE
masc	nom	twái /twɛ̄/	*twai	*dw+ói
	gen	twaddjē	*twajōⁿ	*dwoi+ḗm[45]
fem	nom	twōs	*twōz	*dwā́+s[46]
	gen	*twaddjō	*twajōⁿ	*dwoi+ṓm[45]
neut	nom/acc	twa	*twu	*dw+ā[46]
	gen	twaddjē	*twajōⁿ	*dwoi+ḗm[45]

‘3’		Go	NWGmc	PIE
nom	masc / fem	*þreis /θrīs/	*θrīz	*trei+es[47]
	neut	*þrija	*θriju	*trei+ā

Otherwise the endings are those of the i-class strong adjectives

‘4’	Go	NWGmc	PIE
	fidwōr /fiðwōr/	fiðwōr	petwṓr
	Ø	feōr	pekʷṓr(α)

(α) While Go fidwōr is from PIE *petwṓr, other Germanic languages show reflexes of a PIE *pekʷṓr. Its derivation is *pekʷṓr (2 1ST SS, 3 VERNER, 4a GMC STRESS) > *féǥʷōr (5b LABIOVELARS) > *féwōr (ev) > OEng fēower and OHGerm feor.

	Go	NWGmc	PIE
‘5’	fimf	*fimf	*pémpe
‘6’	saíhs /sehs/	*sexs	*séks

The /h/ vs. /x/ in Gothic vs. NW Germanic results from the different versions of 5e x-TO-h.

‘7’	Go	NWGmc	PIE
	sibun /siƀun/	*seƀun	*sepń̥t

The derivation is *sepń̥t (2 1ST SS, 3 VERNER, 4a GMC STRESS) > *séƀn̥θ (6c SYL SON) >*séƀunθ (7b 1ST UMLAUT) > *síƀunθ (8a MORA LOSS) > Go sibun. The PIE antecedent usually cited is *septḿ̥. If this had been so in pre-Germanic PIE, then the derivation would have been *septḿ̥ (2 1ST SS, 4a GMC STRESS) > *séftm̥ (6c SYL SON, 7b 1ST UMLAUT, 7c NASAL LOSS) > Go **siftu. There was thus a restructuring of the pre-Germanic PIE *septḿ̥ to *sepń̥t. The suffix –n̥t was from *dékn̥t ‘10’ below.

	Go	NWGmc	PIE
'8'	ahtáu /ahtɔ̄/	*axtō	*oktṓu
'9'	niun	*neun	*neu+ń̥t

The derivation is *neuń̥t (PIE 3.1.2c i-j/u-w ALT applying as a synchronic rule) → *newń̥t (2 1ST SS, 4a GMC STRESS) > *néwn̥θ (6c SYL SON, 7b 1ST UMLAUT) > *níwunθ (8a MORA LOSS)> *níwun (the unusual sequence /iwu/ reformed to the normal diphthong /iu/) > Go niun. The PIE antecedent often cited is *newń̥. This, however, would have to result in Go **niu. The –ń̥t was added to *new- in pre-Gmc PIE from *dékn̥t '10'.

'10'	Go	NWGmc	PIE
	taíhun /tehun/	*tehun	*dékn̥t

A frequently cited PIE antecedent is *dékm̥. This, however, would have produced Go **taíhu.

'11'	Go	NWGmc	PIE
	áinlif /ɛ̄nlif/	*ainlif	*óin+ lìp
	Ø	*ainlifun	*óin+ lìp+n̥t
	Ø	*ainlifan	*óin+ lìp+ont

The meaning of the PIE construction is '1 remaining, i.e. after 10'. This is '1' plus some form of the verb *lip- 'remain'. There are at least three PIE antecedents for the Germanic forms. The first of those given above is *oin+lip with no suffix (ev) > Go áinlif. The second is with the suffix *-n̥t, possibly from '10', (ev) > OEng endlifun. The third is with the pres act. part. *-ont (ev) > OSax ellevan.

'12'	Go	NWGmc	PIE
	twalif	*twalif	*dwó+lìp

'13' through '19'

'13'	Go	NWGmc	PIE
	*þritaíhun	*θritehun	*trí+dékn̥t

These forms consist of the units numeral plus '10'.

'20' through '60'

'20'	Go	NWGmc	PIE
	twái tigjus [twɛ̄ tiǥjus]	*twai *tiǥjuz	*dwói *dekewes

These constructions consist of the units numeral followed by a u-class masc noun *dekewes '10-nesses' — in the plural and unstressed. A derivation is *dwói *dekewes '2 tennesses = 20' (2 1ST SS, 3 VERNER) > *twói *teǥewez (6b o-TO-a, 7b 1ST UMLAUT) > *twái *tiǥiwiz (8a MORA LOSS) > *twái *tiǥiwz (PIE 3.1.2c i-j/u-w ALT still in the grammar and applying as a persistent synchronic rule) > *twái *tiǥjuz (7a ai/au-MONOPH final stage 3, 9b CONT OBSTR DEVOICING) > Go twái tigjus. Later in the history of the

Germanic languages the noun *tiǥjuz was reinterpreted as a derivative suffix as in OEng twēn+tig '20'.

	Go	**NWGmc**	**PIE**
'70'	sibuntēhund	*siƀuntō^n *hunda	*sepn̥t+t+ṓm *kn̥tom
'80'	ahtáutēhund	*axtōtō^n *hunda	*oktōu+t+ṓm *kn̥tom
'90'	niuntēhund	*neuntō^n *hunda	*newn̥t+t+ṓm *kn̥tom

These three constructions are formed from the units numeral nominalized with the derivative suffix *-t. This results in an i-class feminine noun, which is in the genitive plural. (The problem of the Go gen pl -ē vs. *-ō^n in NW Germanic is discussed under the o-class nouns.) The second noun in the construction is an unstressed o-class neuter noun, *kn̥tom, which means 'a ten-fold, a 10-ness'. Hence PIE *sepn̥t+t+tṓm *kn̥tom means 'of 7's a ten-fold, i.e. 70'. The derivation is *sepn̥t+t+ṓm *kn̥tom (2 1ST SS, 3 VERNER) > *seƀn̥dtṓm *hundom (4a GMC STRESS, 6b o-TO-a, 6c SYL SON) > *séƀundtōm *hundam (7b 1ST UMLAUT, 7c NASAL LOSS) > *síƀundtō^n *hund (8a MORA LOSS, applying to *síƀund '7' and analogously to *síƀund+tō^n, ev) > Go sibuntē hund. This construction was probably formed in post-PIE Germanic times as opposed to pre-Germanic PIE. Otherwise one would expect the derivation *sepn̥t+t+ṓm (1e tt/ts-TO-ss) > *sepn̥ssṓm (ev) > Go **sibunsē hund.

'100'	**Go**	**NWGmc**	**PIE**
	taíhuntēhund /téhuntēhund/	*tehuntō^n *hunda	*dekn̥t+t+ṓm *kn̥tom

This construction is the same as that of '70', '80' and '90' above. Hence the original meaning was 'of 10's a ten-fold'. In other Germanic languages the form hund '100' occurs alone.

'200' through '900'

	Go	**NWGmc**	**PIE**
'200'	twa hunda	*twu *hundu	*dwā́ *kn̥tā
'300'	þrija hunda	*θriu *hundu	*triā́ *kn̥tā

These numerals consist of the units numeral plus the neuter plural of hund. The derivation of '200' is *dwā́ *kn̥tā (2 1ST SS) > *twā́ *xn̥θā (3 VERNER) > *twā́ *xn̥ðā (ev) > Go twa hunda. Hence we assume the Gmc *hund- '100' has its /d/ from an unstressed *kn̥t- by 3 VERNER.

	Go	**NWGmc**	**PIE**
'1000'	þūsundi	*θūshundiju	*tū́s *kn̥tjā
'2000'	twōs þūsundjōs	*twōz *θūsundijōz	*dwṓs *tū́s *kn̥tjōs

These forms develop from a PIE compound consisting of the adj. *tūs 'large' plus *kn̥tjā, itself a jā-class noun constructed of *kn̥t - '100' plus the jā-class endings.

4.2 Ordinals

These are adjectives of the o- and ā-class. We cite the nominative singular masculine forms.

	Go	NWGmc	PIE
'1st'	frumists	*frumistaz	*pr+ḿ̥+ist+os
'2nd'	anþar	*anθeraz	*ánter+os
'3rd'	þridja	*θriðjō	*tri+t+jṓn
'4th'	*fidwōrda[48]	*fiðwōrθō	*petwṓr+t+ōn
'5th'	fimfta[49]	*fimftō	*pémpe+t+ōn
'6th'	saíhsta	*sexstō	*séks+t+ōn
'7th'	*sibunda	*seƀundō	*sepń̥t+t+ōn
'8th'	ahtuda[48]	*axtuθō	*oktú+t+ōn

The Germanic ordinal suffixes can be -t, -ð, -d or -θ. All these are from PIE *-t.[50] The remaining attested Gothic ordinals are formed by affixing -d plus the o- and ā-class weak adjective endings to the cardinals.

5 Pronouns

These forms occurred both stressed and unstressed as enclitics.

5.1 First Person

		Go	NWGmc	PIE
sg	**nom**	ik 'I'	*eka	*egom
	acc	mik	*mek	*me+ge(α)
du	**nom**	wit 'we two'	*wit	*wid
	acc	ugkis [uŋkis](β)	*unkis	*n̥g+es
pl	**nom**	weis /wīs/ 'we'	*wīz	*wej+es
	acc	uns(γ)	*uns	*n̥s
		unsis	*unsiz	*ń̥s+es[51]

(α) The remaining singular forms begin with m-.
(β) The other dual forms begin with ugk- [uŋk-].
(γ) The other plural forms begin with uns-.

5.2 Second Person.

		Go	NWGmc	PIE
sg	nom	þu 'you'	*θu	*tu
	acc	þuk[α][β]	*θek	*te+ge
du	nom	*jut[α] 'you two'	*jit	*jid
	acc	*igqis [iŋk^{w}iz][γ]	*ink^{w}iz	*ing^w+es
pl	nom	jus[α]	*jiz	*jes
	acc	izwis[δ]	*izwiz	*isw+es

(α) The /u/ in the Gothic forms is from the nominative singular. The other Germanic languages have by regular change /e(:)/ or /i/ in these forms. E.g., earlier Gmc *θek (ev) > OEng þē and OHGerm dich.
(β) All singular forms begin with þ-.
(γ) The other dual forms begin with igk- [iŋk-].
(δ) The other plural forms begin with izw-

5.3 Third Person

Here we include one anaphoric pronoun meaning 'he, she, it, they' and two deictic pronouns meaning 'this, that, these, those'. The anaphoric pronoun is this:

			Go	NWGmc	PIE
masc	sg	nom	is 'he'	*(h)iz	*(k)i+s[52]
		acc	ina	*(h)inō	*(k)i+m+ōm[53]
		gen	is	*(h)is	*(k)i+so[54]
		dat	imma	*(h)immu	*(k)i+smō[55]
	pl	nom	eis /īs/	*(h)īz	*(k)ei+es[56]
		acc	ins	*(h)inz	*(k)i+ns
		gen	izē	*(h)izō^n	*(k)i+sēm
		dat	im	*(h)im	*(k)i+mis

			Go	NWGmc	PIE
fem	sg	nom	si 'she'	*siu	*si+ā[α]
		acc	ija	*(h)iō	*(k)i+ām[57]
		gen	izōs	*(h)izōz	*(k)i+sās
		dat	izái /izē/	*(h)izē	*(k)i+sāi
	pl	nom	ijōs	*(h)iōz	*(k)i+ās[57]
		acc	ijōs	*(h)iōnz	*(k)i+āns[β]
		gen	izō	*(h)izō^n	*(k)i+sōm
		dat	im	*(h)imz	*(k)i+mis

(α) Given the PIE antecedent *siā, one would expect Go **sija. The form si might have been influenced by the nominative singular feminine of jā-class nouns such as bandi 'bond'.
(β) The Gothic accusative plural is from the nominative plural.

			Go	NWGmc	PIE
neut	**sg**	**nom/acc**	ita 'it'	*(h)itō	*(k)i+d+ōm[53]
	pl	**nom/acc**	ija	*(h)iu	*(k)i+ā

Otherwise the neuter forms are like the masculine

The two deictics are as follows. The first is this:

			Go	NWGmc	PIE
masc	**sg**	**nom**	sa 'this'	*sa	*s+o
fem	**sg**	**nom**	sō	*sō	*s+ā
neut	**sg**	**nom/acc**	þata	*θatō	*t+od+ōm
neut	**pl**	**nom/acc**	þō	*θō	*t+ā
masc/ neut	**pl**	**dative**	þáim /θɛ̄m/	*θaimz	*t+oimis
fem	**pl**	**dative**	þáim /θɛ̄m/	*θaimz	*t+āimis

Otherwise the paradigm consists of þa- and þi- plus the endings of is 'he' above.[58]

The second deictic is this:

			Go	NWGmc	PIE
masc	**sg**	**nom**	sah 'this one'	*sah	*s+o+u+k^{w}e

This paradigm consists of sa 'this' given above plus the particle -uh 'and'. The synchronic derivation here is sa+uh (91 V-DELETION WITH ENCLITICS) → sah.

5.4 Reflexive

This pronoun is found only in the 3rd person oblique cases. The singular and plural forms are identical.

	Go	NWGmc	PIE
acc	sik 'oneself, themselves'	*sek	*sege
gen	seina /sīna/	*sīn-	*sīn/*sein (?+ō)
dat	sis	*siz/*sis	*sis

5.5 Possessive

These pronouns take the endings of o- and ā-class adjectives. The 3rd person possessives 'his, her, its, their' are the genitive forms of the anaphoric is 'he' above. We cite the nominative singular masculine forms below:

Go	NWGmc	PIE
meins /mīns/ 'my'	*mīnaz	*mei+n+os
þeins 'your (sg)'	*θīnaz	*tei+n+os
unsar 'our'	*unseraz	*n̥s+er+os[59]
izwar 'your (pl)'	*izweraz	*isw+er+os

5.6 Relative, Interrogative and Indefinite

The relative pronoun is formed from the deictic sa 'this' above plus the particle -ei /ī/. E.g., nominative singular masculine:

Go	NWGmc	PIE
saei /sa+ī/ 'he who'	*sa+ī	*so+ei

The interrogative has masculine, feminine and neuter forms. It occurs only in the singular.

		Go	NWGmc	PIE
masc	**nom**	ƕas /hʷas/ 'who?'	*hʷaz	*kʷos
	acc	ƕanō	*hʷanō	*kʷom+ōm
	gen	ƕis	*hʷis	*kʷiso
	dat	ƕamma	*hʷammu	*kʷosmō
fem	**nom**	ƕō	*hʷō	*kʷā
	acc	ƕō	*hʷō	*kʷā (α)
	gen	*ƕizōs	*hʷizōz	*kʷisās
	dat	ƕizái /hʷizɛ̄/	*hʷizē	*kʷisāi
neut(β)	**nom/acc**	ƕa 'what?'	*hʷat	*kʷod[60]
	instr.	ƕē	*hʷē	*kʷē

(α) The Gothic feminine accusative is from the PIE nominative.

(β) The remaining neuter forms of ƕa are like the masculine.

Other interrogatives are the following, which we cite in the nominative singular masculine. They are declined as adjectives of the jo- and jā-class and the o- and ā-class, respectively.

Go	NWGmc	PIE
ƕarjis 'who'	*h^warjaz	*k^worjos
ƕaþar 'who of two?'	*h^waθeraz	*k^woteros

Interrogative pronouns can also function as indefinite pronouns meaning 'someone,. something'. Other indefinites meaning 'whoever, whatever' are formed from the interrogatives ƕas, ƕarjis, and ƕaþar given above plus the enclitic -uh from PIE *-u+k^we. The change 9b CONT OBSTR DEVOICING cannot apply to these forms. Hence one has Go ƕazuh 'whoever', not **ƕasuh.

6 Verbs

The features of the Gothic verb are given in the following two tables. Table i contains the variable features—namely those which can change contingent upon the context. Table ii shows the lexical or inherent features—namely those that are idiosyncratic. They indicate the particular form-class of the verb.

(i) Variable Features

The first section of this table lists the purely verbal features. The second gives the features of deverbative adjectives and nouns.

Verbal Inflection

(a) Person	(b) Number	(c) Voice	(d) Mood
1. 1st	1. singular	1. active	1. indicative[61]
2. 2nd	2. dual	2. passive	2. subjunctive[(α)61]
3. 3rd	3. plural		3. imperative

(e) Tense Occurring in	Indicative	Subjunctive	Imperative
1. present	x	x	x
2. past	x	x	

(α) The subjunctive is often called the "optative" in historical grammars of Germanic since it develops from a PIE optative.

Adjectival and Nominal Inflection

(a) Person	(b) Number	(c) Voice	(d) Mood
Ø	1. singular	1. active	1. infinitive
	2. plural	2. passive	2. participle

(e) Tense Occurring in	Infinitive	Participle
1. present[62]	active	active
2. past[62]		passive

(ii) Inherent Features.

	Category of Verb	Number
1.	strong	7 classes
2.	weak	3 classes
3.	preterite present (pret-pres)	6 classes
4.	anomalous	5 items

In the above two tables the features in the columns are mutually exclusive. Not all the logical possibilities are realized: the notations in the (e) columns of Table i indicate which are.

6.1 Form Classes

As noted in table ii Inherent Features, there are four major classes of verbs. These are strong verbs, weak verbs, pret-pres verbs and anomalous verbs.

6.1.1 Strong Verbs

These verbs fall into seven classes. Each strong verb has four principal parts. These are the pres stem, the stem for the sg past ind, the stem for the remaining inflected past forms and finally, the stem for the pass part. Of the seven classes of strong verbs, the first six form their principal parts with ablaut. The seventh class forms its four principal parts with reduplication along with a few instances of concomitant ablaut. In PIE, Germanic and Gothic the membership of a particular strong verb in any one of the seven classes is determinable solely on the basis of the morpheme structure (morph str) of the verb root in the pres, i.e. the first principal part.

Examples of the morph str conditions of PIE and of Gothic are given in (i) and (ii) below. Under column (a) the verb class is listed, under (b) the particular morph str and under (c) the particular ablaut grade of the vowel of each of the four principal parts.

(i) The PIE Schema

(a) Class	(b) Morph Str	(c) V = Ablauting Vowel			
1	C_0ViC	V = e	o	Ø	Ø
2	C_0VuC	V = e	o	Ø	Ø
3	C_0V[C, +sonorant]C	V = e	o	Ø	Ø
4	C_0V[C, +sonorant]	V = e	o	ē	Ø
5	C_0V[C, –sonorant]	V = e	o	ē	e
6	C_0VC	V = o	ō	ō	o
7	None of the above. Morpheme structure reduplication. (See discussion below.)				

(ii) The Gothic Schema

(a) Class	(b) Morph Str	(c) V = Ablauting Vowel			
1	C₀V C	V = ī	ɛ̄	i/e	i/e(α)
2	C₀V C	V = iu	ɔ̄	u/o	u/o(α)
3	C₀V {C, +sonorant / +nasal} C	V = i	a	u	u(α)
	C₀V {C,+sonorant / –nasal} C	V = i/e	a	u/o	u/o(α)
4	C₀V [C, +sonorant]	V = i/e	a	ē	u/o(α)
5	C₀V [C, –sonorant]	V = i/e	a	ē	i/e(α)
6	C₀V C	V = a	ō	ō	a
7	None of the above. Morpheme structure reduplication. (See discussion below.)				

(α) The alternations /i/- /e/ and /u/- /o/ in these forms are the result of 7b 1ST UMLAUT, which differs in its Gothic and NW Germanic versions.

Examples of the four principal parts of a verb of each of the seven classes follow. As the first principal part we cite the 1 singular present indicative, the second is the 1 singular past indicative, the third the 1 plural past indicative and the fourth the nominative singular masculine of the past passive participle. The number on the left gives the verb class. The examples are the Proto-Indo-European, NW Germanic and Gothic forms, respectively.

Class		1 sg pres ind	1 sg past ind	1 pl past ind	nom sg masc past pass part
1	PIE	*gʰréibō 'seize'	*gʰróiba	*gʰribmé	*gʰribónos
	NW Gmc	*ǥrīpu	*ǥraip	*ǥripum	*ǥripanaz
	Go	greipa /grīpa/	gráip /grɛ̄p/	gripum	gripans
2	PIE	*néudō 'enjoy'	*nóuda	*nudmé	*nudónos
	NW Gmc	*neutu	*naut	*nutum	*notanaz(α)
	Go	niuta	náut /nɔ̄t/	nutum	nutans(α)

Class		1 sg pres ind	1 sg past ind	1 pl past ind	nom sg masc past pass part
3	PIE	*b^{h}énd^{h}ō 'tie'	*b^{h}ónd^{h}a	*b^{h}n̥d^{h}mé	*b^{h}n̥d^{h}ónos
	NW Gmc	*bindu	*band	*bundum	*bundanaz
	Go	binda	band	bundum	bundans
	PIE	*wértō 'turn'	*wórta	*wr̥tmé	*wr̥tónos
	NW Gmc	*werθu 'become'	*warθ$^{(\beta)}$	*wurðum$^{(\beta)}$	*worðanaz
	Go	waírþa /werθa/	warþ	waúrþum$^{(\beta)}$ /worθum/	waúrþans
4	PIE	*b^{h}érō 'carry'	*b^{h}óra	*b^{h}ērmé	*b^{h}r̥ónos
	NW Gmc	*beru	*bar	*bērum	*boranaz
	Go	baíra /bera/	bar	bērum	baúrans /borans/
5	PIE	*g^{h}éb^{h}ō 'give'	*g^{h}ób^{h}a	*g^{h}ēb^{h}mé	*g^{h}eb^{h}ónos
	NW Gmc	*ǥebu	*ǥaƀ	*ǥēƀum	*ǥeƀanaz
	Go	giba	gaf	gēbum	gibans
6	PIE	*pórō 'travel'	*pṓra	*pōrmé	*porónos
	NW Gmc	*faru	*fōr	*fōrum	*faranaz
	Go	fara	fōr	fōrum	farans

Class		1 sg pres ind	1 sg past ind	1 pl past ind	nom sg masc past pass part
7	PIE	*áugō 'increase'	*eáuga	*eaugmé	*augónos
		*lēdō 'let'	*lelṓda	*lelōdmé	*lēdónos
		*slḗbō 'sleep'	*seslḗba	*seslēbmé	*slēbónos
		*stald^{h}ō 'acquire'	*stestáld^{h}a	*stestald^{h}mé	*stald^{h}ónos
7	NW Gmc	*auku	*eáuk	*eáukum	*aukanaz
		*lētu	*lelṓt	*lelṓtum	*lētanaz
		*slēpu	*seslḗp	*seslḗpum	*slēpanaz
		*staldu	*stestáld	*stestáldum	*staldanaz
7	Go	áuka /ɔ̄ka/	aíáuk /eɔ̄k/	aíáukum /eɔ̄kum/	áukans /ɔ̄kans/
		lēta	laílōt /lelṓt/	laílōtum	lētans
		slēpa	saíslēp /seslḗp/	saíslēpum	slēpans
		stalda	staístald /stestáld/	staístaldum	staldans

(α) The alternations /i/- /e/ and /u/- /o/ in these forms are the result of 7b 1ST UMLAUT, which differs in its Gothic and NW Germanic versions.

(β) In the NW Germanic languages the third and fourth principal parts undergo 3 VERNER. This does not occur in Gothic because of the early East Germanic and as such Gothic stress-retraction onto the root by 4a GMC STRESS. As examples we cite the 1 singular past and 1 plural past forms of PIE *wórta 'turned, became' and *wr̥tmé (2 1ST SS) > *wórθa, *wr̥θmé (early application of 4a GMC STRESS in East Gmc) > *wórθa, East Gmc *wŕ̥θme vs. NW Gmc *wr̥θmé (3 VERNER) > *wórθa, East Gmc *wŕ̥θme vs. NW Gmc *wr̥ðmé (ev) > Go warþ, waúrþum vs. NW Gmc *warθ, *wurðum.

Morpheme Structure Reduplication

The PIE, early NW Germanic and Gothic reduplication rules applied to the 2nd and 3rd principal parts of class 7 strong verbs. The rule is this:

[C_0^n	V ... →	C_0^n	e	[C_0^n	V ...
verb				verb	
root				root	
1	2	1'	3	1	2

(where any recopied consonant cluster C_0^n over 1' does not contain a sonorant consonant.

That is, an initial consonant or consonant cluster in a verb root (1) is replicated (1') before /e/ 3, all of which is attached to the verb root. If the consonant cluster contains a sonorant consonant that consonant is not replicated. E.g., áuk 'increase' → past eáuk (since there is no consonant cluster to replicate), lḗt 'let' → past lelṓt (with ablaut), slḗp 'sleep' → past seslḗp (not **sleslēp), stáld 'acquire' → past stestáld.

Within Germanic the reduplicated past forms are best attested in Gothic. There are also a few remnants of the original reduplication in the NW Germanic languages such as OEng heht 'was called' from Gmc *heháit. Generally, however, the 2nd and 3rd principal parts of the verbs in the NW Germanic languages show an ablaut-like vowel change. As examples we cite the following Gothic past forms as opposed to the corresponding past forms in NW Germanic: note Go áuka 'increase' → aíáuk /eɔ̄́k/ and háitan 'be called' → haíháit /hehɛ̄́t/ vs. OIce áuka → past jók /jōk/ and OSax hētan /hɛ̄tan/ → past hiet from earlier *hēt.

There is disagreement on the history and development of the NW Germanic forms such as those cited above. We assume that the original past formative of these verbs was reduplication as in Gothic. Then later in the NW Germanic languages this original reduplication developed into the ablaut-like alternations as in the Old Icelandic and Old Saxon forms cited above.

We envisage this change into the NW Germanic languages as having proceeded as follows. Early Gmc 1 sg past *eáuk and *heh// áit (4a GMC STRESS, in the grammar as a synchronic rule, extends its domain to stress the first syllable, which is the reduplication syllable, of these forms) > *éauk, *héhait (7a ai/au-MONOPH, remaining for a time as a synchronic rule, applies to the now unstressed /au/ and /ai/) > *éōk, *héhēt (reinterpretation of /éō/ and /éhē/ not as reduplications, but rather as modifications of the vowel nucleus; loss of /h/ from /éhē/) > *éok, *héēt (replacement of the unusual vowel nuclei /éō/and /éē/ by the regularly occurring nearest equivalents, namely /éo/ and /ḗ/) > *éok, *hḗt (ev through regular changes in each language) > OIce jók and OSax hiet. (For more details, see Voyles 1980 and 1992: 66–69.)

6.1.2 Weak verbs

These verbs have as their salient morphological trait the formation of their past-tense and past-participle stem by means of a dental suffix. In Germanic there were three such: /d/ (= [ð] or [d] by 5d OBSTR-TO-STOP), /t/and occasionally /θ/. We assume the PIE antecedent to have been /t/. (This question has long been a subject of discussion in the literature. See Prokosch 1939: 194–9 and Tops 1974 for overviews of the various theories.)

The development of the Germanic suffixes was as follows. We cite the 1 singular past indicative of three PIE verbs *kousitṓm 'I heard', *tonktṓm 'I thought' and the preterite-present verb *gn̥tṓm 'I knew' (2 1ST SS, 4a GMC STRESS applying early in East Gmc) > *xóusiθōm, *θónxtōm, *kn̥̍θōm (3 VERNER) > *xóusiðōm, *θónxtōm, *kn̥̍θōm (ev) > Go háusida, þāhta, kunþa.

At some point in pre-Gothic it seems that the past formative *-dōm was associated with the Germanic verb *dōm 'I do' (from PIE dʰōmi in 6.1.4.1 below). Hence the Gothic past plural is háusidēdum from earlier Gmc *dēðum 'we did'.

There are three classes of weak verbs—the j-class, the ā-class and the oi-class. (As a result of changes 6a ā-TO-ō and 6b o-TO-a, the latter two classes are often referred to as the ō-class and the ai-class.) The rationale for this trichotomy is the fact that the present-tense paradigms of such verbs (and usually the past tense and past participle as well) have -j-, -ā- or -oi- between the root and the inflectional ending. Examples of a few forms follow. (Complete paradigms are under 6.2 below.)

6.1.2.1 j-Class

		Go	NWGmc	PIE
sg	1 pres	nasja 'save'	*nazju	*nosjṓ(α)
	1 past	nasida(β)	*naziðōⁿ	*nositṓm
past part		nasiþs(β)	*naziðaz	*nositós

(α) An /s/ occurs in Gothic vs. /z/ in NW Germanic (later /r/ as in OSax nerian 'save'). This is the result of the early stress retraction in East Germanic by 4a GMC STRESS. Hence 3 VERNER does not apply to the /s/ in the Gothic forms.

(β) The /i/ in the past forms is the reflex of /j/ in the present by the PIE rule 3.1.2c i-j/u-w Alt, which remains in the grammar to apply synchronically. Some j-class verbs do not carry the /i/ into the past. (We call these "i-less" verbs.) This characteristic seems to be lexically conditioned, i.e. idiosyncratic. As a result of regular phonological change, i-less weak verbs acquire irregular past forms in Germanic. E.g., PIE pres *tongjṓ 'I think' vs. past *tong+t+ṓm 'I thought' (1b OBSTR VOI/DEVOI) > *tongjṓ *tonktṓm (2 1ST SS, 4a GMC STRESS, 6b o-TO-a, 7c NASAL LOSS) > *θánkjō *θánxtō (8a MORA LOSS, 8b ŋ-DELETION) > Go þankja þāhta. But another j-class verb with a morpheme structure almost identical with the preceding retains the /i/ into the past. This is the PIE pres *dʰrongjṓ 'I make to drink, drench', past *dʰrongitṓm 'I made to drink' (ev) > Go drankja and drankida, not **drāhta from PIE **dʰrong+tōm.

Most j-class weak verbs are derived from adjectives, nouns or other verbs. In the latter instance they are usually causatives like Go drankjan 'make to drink'. E.g., Gothic infinitives gatamjan 'make tame' (Go tams) from PIE *domjonom, Go haúrnjan 'play a horn' (Go haúrn /horn/) from PIE *kr̥njónom and Go urráisjan /urrēsjan/'cause to rise, raise' (Go reisan /rīsan/) from PIE *ūs+roisjónom The deverbal causatives are always formed from the second principal part of any source strong verb of classes 1 through 6. A causative from a class 7 verb is from the first principal part. E.g., the class 5 strong verb Go sitan, sat 'sit' > Go satjan 'set, cause to sit'; but the class 7 strong verb Gmc *fallan, *fefall 'fall' > Gmc *falljan 'to cause to fall, fell', not **fefalljan.

6.1.2.2 ā-Class

		Go	NWGmc	PIE
sg	1 pres	salbō 'use salve'	*salƀōm	*salpā́mi(α)
	1 past	salbōda	*salƀōðōⁿ	*salpātṓm
past part		salbōþs	*salƀōðaz	*salpātós

(α) Verbs of this class originally formed the 1 singular present with the athematic ending *-mi, which still occurs in other Germanic languages such as in OHGerm salbōm 'I anoint'. In Gothic the -m was dropped, probably on analogy with the other Gothic weak verbs with no -m in the 1 singular present. (This ending also occurs in several of the anomalous verbs under 6.1.4 below.)

Several ā-class verbs occur derived from adjectives. They are formed with the derivative suffix -n- and mean 'be or become that adjective'. Such verbs in Gothic inflect as strong verbs in the present and as ā-class weak verbs in the past. E.g., Go 1 sg pres fralusna 'I become lost' (Gothic past part root lus- 'lost'), past fralusnōda.

6.1.2.3 oi-Class

		Go	NWGmc	PIE
sg	**1 pres**	haba 'have'	*haƀu	*kapṓ
	1 past	habáida [haƀɛ̄ða]	*haƀɛ̄ðō^{n}	*kapoitṓm
past part		habáiþs	*haƀɛ̄ðaz	*kapoitós

This class is defective in two respects. First, it contains comparatively few verbs. Second, oi-class verbs in many Germanic languages tend to take endings and undergo rules which are proper to other classes. Consequently most oi-class verbs tend in the later Germanic languages to pass into other classes.

The PIE antecedents of this class are disputed. (See on this Voyles 1992: 263.) Here we follow the account in Jasanoff 1973 in that we assume the origin of this class to have been a PIE middle ending *-oi (possible *-ai). Under this view an original PIE 3 sg mid *kap+oi 'one has for oneself or on one's own behalf' was later, say in pre-Germanic, reinterpreted as a weak verb adding the ending *-ti. The derivation was then *kapóiti (ev) > Go habáiþ /háƀɛ̄θ/.

6.1.3 Preterite-Present Verbs

These verbs have defective paradigms in that they usually lack the infinitive, imperative, and participial .forms. They are called "preterite-present" because their present-tense forms are derived historically from the past (i.e., preterite) forms of strong verbs.

Pret-pres verbs occur in six ablaut classes which correspond to the first six ablauting classes of strong verbs. In pret-pres verbs the present singular indicative root corresponds to the second principal part of strong verbs; the other present forms are constructed from a root corresponding to the third principal part of strong verbs; but to this root are added the weak verb endings of the i-less j-class.

Examples follow. The forms cited are the 1 singular present indicative, the 1 plural present indicative and the 1 singular past indicative, which is of the weak verb conjugation. The numbers on the left refer to the corresponding strong verb classes.

Class	Go	NWGmc	PIE
1	wáit /wɛ̄t/ 'know'	*wait	*wóida[(α)]
	witum	*witum	*widmé
	wissa	*wissō^{n}	*wid+t+ṓm[63]
2	dáug /dɔ̄x/ 'be valid'	*dauǥ	*d^{h}óug^{h}a
	*dugum	*duǥum	*d^{h}ug^{h}mé
	*daúhta /dohta/	*doxtō^{n}	*d^{h}ug^{h}+t+ṓm[64]

Class	Go	NW Gmc	PIE
3	kann 'can'	*kann	*gónna
	kunnum	*kunnum	*gn̥mé
	kunþa	*kunθō^n	*gń̥+t+ōm[65]
4	skal 'shall'	*skal	*skóla
	skulum	*skulum	*skl̥mé[β]
	skulda	*skulðō^n	*skl̥+t+ṓm[β]
5	mag /max/ 'be able'	*maǥ	*móg^{h}a
	magum	?*mēǥum	?*mēg^{h}mé[66]
	mahta	?*mēxtō^n	?*mēg^h+t+ṓm[66]
6	ōg /ōx/ 'fear'	*ōǥ	*ā́g^{h}a[67]
	*ōgum	*ōǥum	*āg^{h}mé
	ōhta	*ōxtō^n	*āg^h+t+ṓm

(α) This example illustrates the semantic development of pret-pres verbs. The meaning of PIE *wóida was 'I have seen'. Then 'have seen' came to mean 'now know'. A similar development in English is the change of "got" 'obtained' to 'now know' in a sentence like "I just now got it."

(β) The Gothic and NW Germanic forms with /u/ indicate a PIE antecedent *skl̥- with Ø-grade ablaut. However, strong verbs of the corresponding class have /ē/ in this principal part. Hence one would have expected Go **skēldum.

6.1.4 Anomalous Verbs

These are the verbs meaning 'be', 'do', 'go', 'stand' and 'will, wish, intend'. The first four are from PIE athematic verbs in their present paradigms. That is, there is no intermediate vowel between the root and the inflectional ending. (An example of this type of paradigm is in 6.3 below.) Aside from 'be', Gothic has replaced several paradigms of the other three athematic verbs with conventional weak or strong verbs. Hence for 'do', 'go' and 'stand' below we assume that the NW Germanic forms represent the earlier state and that the Gothic ones are innovations. The forms we cite are the 1 singular present indicative, the 1 plural past indicative and the past participle.

6.1.4.1 'do'

		Go	NWGmc	PIE
sg	**1 pres**	táuja[α][68] /tɔ̄ja/	*dōm	*d^{h}ṓ+mi
	1 past	tawida[α]	*deðō^n [69]	*d^{h}e+t+ṓm
past part		tawiþs[α] /tawiθs/	*dōnaz	*d^{h}ṓ+n+os

(α) The Gothic replacement of the original verb is a j-class weak verb. Its antecedent is PIE 1 sg pres *dōu+j+ṓ.

6.1.4.2 'go'

		Go	NWGmc	PIE
sg	**1 pres**	ganga[70]	*ǥēm	*g^{h}ḗ+mi
	1 past	iddja[71]	*ijiðō^{n}	*ei+i+tṓm
past part		gangans	*ǥanganaz	*g^{h}óng^{h}onos

6.1.4.3 'stand'

		Go	NWGmc	PIE
sg	**1 pres**	standa[72]	*stēm	*stḗ+mi
	1 past	stōþ	*stōð	*stā́+ta[73]
past part		standans	*standanaz	*stantónos[74]

6.1.4.4 'will, wish'

This verb has as its present indicative paradigm the endings of the past active subjunctive (6.2.2.2 below). The past tenses are those of an i-less j-class weak verb. The semantic development here is clear. The subjunctive meaning was 'I should like (if possible).' This came to mean simply 'I want.' Similar developments have occurred elsewhere as in ModGerm ich möchte 'I want' meaning originally 'I should like.' E.g.,

		Person	Go	NWGmc	PIE
sg	**pres**	1	wiljáu /wiljɔ̄/	*wiljō	*wél+ī+ō+u
		2	wileis /wilīs/	*wilīz	*wél+ī+s
		3	wili	*wili	*wél+ī+t
	past	1	wilda	*welðō^{n}	*wel+t+ṓm

6.2 Paradigms

We illustrate the inflectional endings with the fourth-class strong verb baíran /beran/ bar bērum baúrans /borans/ 'carry' and occasionally with the weak verbs nasjan nasida nasidēdum nasiþs /nasiθs/ 'save' and háusjan /hɔ̄sjan/ háusida háusidēdum háusiþs /hɔ̄siθs/'hear'.

6.2.1 Present

The present-tense endings of both strong and weak verbs are similar. However, the present-tense endings of the pret-pres verbs correspond to the past-tense endings of strong verbs in sections 6.2.2.1 and 6.2.2.2 below.

6.2.1.1 Present Active Indicative

	Person	Go	NWGmc	PIE
sg	1	baíra /bera/ 'carry'[75]	*beru	*b^{h}érō
	2	baíris	*biriz	*b^{h}éresi[76]
	3	baíriþ /beriθ/	*birið	*b^{h}éreti
du	1	baírōs	*berōz	*b^{h}érōwes[77]
	2	baírats	*berats	*b^{h}érotes[78]
pl	1	baíram	*beramz	*b^{h}éromes[79]
	2	baíriþ	*bereð	*b^{h}érete
	3	baírand	*berand	*b^{h}éronti

Historically, the PIE present endings of the weak verbs were essentially the same as those of the strong. However, the PIE stress was on the inflectional endings of weak verbs: *-ṓ, *-ési, *-éti; *-ṓwes, *-ótes; *-ómes, *-éte, *-ónti. This difference in stress resulted in slightly different endings in some Germanic languages. E.g., 3 sg strong *bʰéreti vs. weak *kousjéti 'hears' (2 1ST SS) > *béreθi, *housijéθi (3 VERNER) > *béreði, *houzijéθi (4a GMC STRESS) > *béreði, *hóuzijeθi (7b 1ST UMLAUT, NW Germanic version) > *bíriði, *hóuzijiθi (8a MORA LOSS, ev) > *bírið, *háuzīθ (ev) > OSax birid vs. hōrith /hɔ̄́riθ/.

A few lexically marked strong verbs add -n- and some others likewise lexically marked add -j- to the root in only the present paradigm. These verbs occur only in strong verb classes 5 and 6. Below we cite the 1 singular indicative present and past forms.

Class		Go	NWGmc	PIE
5	pres	bidja 'request'	*biðju	*bʰédʰ+j+ō
	past	baþ /baθ/	*bað	*bʰódʰ+a
	pres	fraíhna /frehna/ 'ask'	*frehnu	*prék+n+ō
	past	frah	*frax	*prók+a
6	pres	hafja 'lift'	*hafju	*káp+j+ō
	past	hōf	*hōf	*kṓp+a[80]

6.2.1.2 Present Active Subjunctive

Our example is that of a strong verb.

	Person	Go	NWGmc	PIE
sg	1	baíráu /berɔ̄/ 'carry'	*berō	*bʰérō+u[(α)] [81]
	2	baíráis /berɛ̄s/	*berēz	*bʰérois[(β)][82]
	3	baírái	*berē	*bʰéroit[82]
du	1	baíráiwa	*berēwe	*bʰéroiwē
	2	baíráits	*berēts	*bʰéroites
pl	1	baíráima	*berēmē	*bʰéroimē[83]
	2	baíráiþ /berɛ̄θ/	*berēð	*bʰéroite
	3	baíráina	*berēn	*bʰéroint[84]

(α) The PIE ending *-u is an enclitic particle attached to an original subj *bʰérō.

(β) The PIE *-oi- is an optative formative.

6.2.1.3 Present Active Imperative

	Person	Go	NWGmc	PIE
sg	2	baír /ber/ 'carry'	*ber	*bʰére[85]
		háusei /hɔ̄sī/ 'hear'	*hauzī	*kousjé[85]
	3	báiradáu [beraðɔ̄] 'he should carry'	*beraðō	*bʰéro+t+ō-u[86]
		háusjaðáu	*hauzjaðō	*kousjo+t+ṓ+u
du	2	Same as the present active indicative.		
pl	1/2/3			

6.2.1.4 Present Passive Indicative[(α)]

	Person	Go	NWGmc	PIE
sg	1/3	baírada [beraða] 'be carried'	*beraðe	*bʰérotai[87]
	2	baíraza	*beraze	*bʰérosai
pl	1/2/3	baíranda	*berande	*bʰérontai

(α) The passive endings occur only in the present paradigms. Otherwise the passive in other tenses is formed from verbs such as waírþan /werθan/ 'become' plus the past passive participle such as baúrans /borans/'carried'. Hence Gothic 3 sg past pass Warþ baúrans. 'He was carried'.

6.2.1.5 Present Passive Subjunctive

	Person	Go	NWGmc	PIE
sg	1/3	baíráidáu [berε̄ðɔ̄] 'be carried'	*berēðō	*bʰéroitai+u[88]
	2	baíráizáu	*berēzō	*bʰéroisai+u
pl	1/2/3	baíráindáu	*berēndō	*bʰérointai+u

6.2.2 Past

6.2.2.1 Past Active Indicative

The strong and weak endings differ. The strong paradigm, which derives from an PIE perfect, is as follows.

Strong Paradigm

	Person	Go	NWGmc	PIE
sg	1	bar	*bar	*bʰóra
	2	bart	*bar+t[(α)]	*bʰór+ta[(β)]
			*bēr+iz[(α)] [89]	*bʰḗr+es
	3	bar	*bar	*bʰóre
du	1	bēru	*bēru	*bʰērwé[(γ)90]
	2	bēruts	*bēruts	*bʰērtés
pl	1	bērum	*bērum	*bʰērmé
	2	bēruþ /bēruθ/	*bēruð	*bʰērté
	3	bērun	*bērun	*bʰērń̥̥t[(γ)90]

(α) This ending is *-t in Gothic and in North Germanic and *-iz in the West Germanic languages. The PIE antecedent *-es is a 2 singular aorist ending. In the West Germanic languages it was added to the third principal part of the strong verb.

(β) The PIE ending *-ta does not undergo 2 1ST SS. The reason for this may have been the influence of forms like *gʰóbʰ+ta (1b OBSTR VOI/DEVOI) > *gʰópta (2 1ST SS) > *gófta (6b o-TO-a, 8a MORA LOSS) > Go gaft, not **gafþ.

(γ) The /u/ in all dual and plural endings was analogized throughout the dual and plural from these forms where it occurred through regular phonological change.

The weak verb paradigm is this:

Weak Paradigm

	Person	Go	NWGmc	PIE
sg	1	nasida[α]	*naziðō^n [α]	*nositṓm
	2	nasidēs	*naziðēs	*nositḗs
	3	nasida[91]	*naziðē[91]	*nositḗt
du	1	nasidēdu[92]	*naziðu	*nositwé
	2	nasidēduts		
pl	1	nasidēdum	These are the strong verb endings: -uts, -um, -uþ, -un.[92]	
	2	nasidēduþ		
	3	nasidēdun		

(α) The /s/ in Go nasida vs. the /z/ in NW Gmc *nazidō^n is the result of 3 VERNER applying in NW Germanic and not in Gothic. VERNER did not apply to the Gothic form because of the early shift of stress to the root in East Germanic by 4a GMC STRESS.

6.2.2.2 Past Active Subjunctive

The endings are the same for strong and weak verbs. Weak verbs in Gothic affix these endings onto the long dual and plural stem in -idēd-, e.g., 1 sg nasidēdjáu /nasidēdjɔ̄/'I saved'. Strong verbs affix the endings onto their third principal part. A strong verb paradigm follows.

	Person	Go	NWGmc	PIE
sg	1	bērjáu /bērjɔ̄/ 'carry'	*bērī[93]	*b^{h}ērī́m[93]
	2	bēreis /bērīs/	*bērīs	*b^{h}ērī́s[α]
	3	bēri	*bērī	*b^{h}ērī́t[α]
du	1	bēreiwa	*bērīwe	*b^{h}ērī́wē[α]
	2	bēreits	*bērīts	*b^{h}ērī́tes[α]
pl	1	bēreima	*bērīme	*b^{h}ērī́mē[α]
	2	bēreiþ /bērīθ/	*bērīθ	*b^{h}ērī́te[α]
	3	bēreina	*bērīne	*b^{h}ērī́nt[α]

(α) These endings are those of the present subjunctive (6.2.1.2). The past subjunctive has the intermediate formative -ī-, spelled <ei>, while the pres has -ɛ̄́-, spelled <ái>. Both go back to an ablauting PIE optative marker *-oī- for the present vs. *-Øī- for the past. The *-oī- was probably restructured already in PIE times to *-oi- by the PIE rule 3.1.2b DIPH to bring it into line with the other diphthongs.

6.2.3 The Verbal Noun

The only verbal noun attested in the early Germanic languages is the present active infinitive. The antecedent formative is *-on-. The following examples are from Gothic and Old Saxon:

			NWGmc	PIE
Go		baíran /beran/ 'carry'	*berana	*bʰéronom[(α)]
OSax	**nom/acc**	beran	*berana	*bʰéronom[(α)]
	gen	berannies	*beranjes	*bʰeronjéso[(β)]
	dat	berannie	*beranjē	*bʰeronjṓi[(β)]

(α) The Gothic form occurs uninflected. It, as well as the Old Saxon nominative/accusative form, is an o-class neuter noun.

(β) In the West Germanic languages the infinitive occurs in the genitive and dative (singular only) as a jo-class neuter noun.

6.2.4 Verbal Adjectives

These adjectives are in the o- and ā-class, strong and weak declensions (2.1.1 and 2.2 above). Below we cite the nominative singular masculine strong ending.

6.2.4.1 Present Active Participle

Both strong and weak verbs use the same formative *-ont-.

Go	NWGmc	PIE
baírands /berands/'carrying'	*berandaz	*bʰérontos
háusjands /hɔ̄sjands/ 'hearing'	*hauzjandaz	*kousjontós

6.2.4.2 Past Passive Participle

This is usually referred to as the "perfect participle". The strong and weak formations differ.

Go	NWGmc	PIE
baúrans /borans/'carried'	*boranaz	*bʰr̥ónos
háusiþs /hɔ̄siθs/ 'heard'	*hauziðaz	*kousitós

6.3 The Verb 'be'

The verb occurs only in the active.

6.3.1 Present Indicative

	Person	Go	NWGmc	PIE
sg	**1**	im	*im	*és+mi[94]
	2	is	*is	*és+si
	3	ist	*ist	*és+ti
du	**1**	siju	*si+u	*s+wé[(α)]
	2	*sijuts	*si+uts	*s+tés[(α)]
pl	**1**	sijum	*si+um	*s+mé[(α)][95]
	2	sijuþ /sijuθ/	*si+uð	*s+té[(α)]
	3	sind	*si+nd	*s+entí[96]

(α) These endings are from the preterite-present paradigm (6.1.3). As such, they are past-tense endings (6.2.2.1). The stem *si- in Germanic and Gothic is from the 3 plural where it occurred regularly.

Other Germanic languages form the 'be' paradigm from a PIE *b^{h}V-. E.g., the following OHGerm singular forms.

Person	OHGerm	NWGmc	PIE
1	bim	*bim	*b^h+ésmi
2	bis	*bis	*b^h+éssi

6.3.2 Present Subjunctive

The Gothic forms consist of sij- (which develops as described above) plus the endings of the present active subjunctive in 6.2.1.2 above. E.g.,

	Person	Go	NWGmc	PIE
sg	1	sijáu /síjɔ̄/	*si+ō	*s+ṓ+u
	2	sijáis /síjɛ̄s/	*si+ēs	*s+óis[97]

6.3.3 Suppletive Paradigms

The infinitive, present participle and all past forms are those of a strong verb of class 5. E.g.,

		Go	NWGmc	PIE
infinitive		wisan	*wesan	*wésonom
pres	participle	wisands	*wesandaz	*wésontos
past	1 sg	was	*was	*wósa
	1 pl	wēsum	*wēzum	*wēsmé
	participle		Not attested.	

V Exercises

(1) Consider the following PIE forms and the changes which they underwent into Gothic. What is the Gothic form? Give the Gothic spelling and a phonemic or phonetic transcription. You may ignore the word stress since it is invariably on the first syllable by 4a GMC STRESS.

a. Nom sg *bhā́gā 'beech, (later) book' + 2 1ST SS, 6a ā-TO-ō, 8a MORA LOSS > Gothic?

b. 3 sg pres *b^{h}éreti 'carries' + 2 1ST SS, 3 VERNER, 5d OBSTR-TO-STOP, 7b 1ST UMLAUT, 8a MORA LOSS, 9b CONT OBSTR DEVOICING > Gothic?

c. 1 sg pres *b^{h}érō 'I carry' + 2 1ST SS, 5d OBSTR-TO-STOP, 8a MORA LOSS > Gothic?

d. 3 sg pres pass. *b^{h}érotai 'is carried' + 2 1ST SS, 3 VERNER, 5d OBSTR-TO-STOP, 6b o-TO-a, 7a ai/au-MONOPH, 8a MORA LOSS, 9c e-TO-a > Gothic?

e. Dat sg masc *b^{h}lend^{h}ósmō 'blind' + 2 1ST SS, 4a GMC STRESS stage 1, 3 VERNER, 5c MS CHANGES, 5d OBSTR-TO-STOP, 6b o-TO-a, 7b 1ST UMLAUT, 8a MORA LOSS > Gothic?

f. Nom sg *d^{h}úkter 'daughter' + 2 1ST SS, 5d OBSTR-TO-STOP, 5e x-TO-h, 7b 1ST UMLAUT, 9c e-TO-a > Gothic?

g. *dwói *dekewes '2 10's, i.e. 20' + 2 1ST SS, 3 VERNER, 6b o-TO-a, 7b 1ST UMLAUT, 8a MORA LOSS, PIE 3.1.2c i-j/u-w ALT applying as a persistent rule, 7a ai/au-MONOPH stage 3, 9b CONT OBSTR DEVOICING > Gothic ?

h. Gen pl masc *dwojḗm '2' + 2 1ST SS, 4a GMC STRESS, 6b o-TO-a, 7c NASAL LOSS, 9n *VERSCHÄRFUNG* > Gothic?

i. Nom sg jā-class *ékʷo+dn̥t+jā 'horse-tooth (a plant)' + 2 1ST SS, 3 VERNER, 5d OBSTR-TO-STOP, 5e x-TO-h, 6a ā-TO-ō, 6b o-TO-a, 6c SYL SON, 8a MORA LOSS > Gothic?

j. Dat pl *gʰortímis 'yards' + 2 1ST SS, 3 VERNER, 4a GMC STRESS, 5d OBSTR-TO-STOP, 6b o-TO-a, 8a MORA LOSS, 9i mz-TO-mm, 1a GEM C SIMP applying as a persistent rule > Gothic?

k. Nom sg *gŕ̥nom 'grain' + 2 1ST SS, 6c SYL SON, 7b 1ST UMLAUT, 7c NASAL LOSS, 8a MORA LOSS > Gothic?

l. Nom sg *gʷḿ̥+t+is 'arrival' + 2 1ST SS, 3 VERNER, 6c SYL SON, 8a MORA LOSS, 9b CONT OBSTR DEVOICING > Gothic?

m. 1 sg past *kapoitṓm 'I had' + 2 1ST SS, 3 VERNER, 4a GMC STRESS, 5e x-TO-h, 6b o-TO-a, 7a ai/au-MONOPH, 7c NASAL LOSS, 8a MORA LOSS > Gothic?

n. Nom sg *nízdos 'nest' + 2 1ST SS, 1b OBSTR VOI/DEVOI applying as a persistent rule, 3 VERNER, 6b o-TO-a, 8a MORA LOSS, 9b CONT OBSTR DEVOICING > Gothic?

o. Nom sg masc *nógʷodʰos 'naked' + 2 1ST SS, 3 VERNER, 6b o-TO-a, 8a MORA LOSS, 9b CONT OBSTR DEVOICING applying twice > Gothic?

p. Nom sg masc *ń̥seros 'our' + 3 VERNER, 6b o-TO-a, 6c SYL SON, 8a MORA LOSS, 9c e-TO-a, 9o z-DELETION > Gothic?

q. 1 sg pres *séngʰʷō 'I sing' + 2 1ST SS, 5d OBSTR-TO-STOP, 7b 1ST UMLAUT, 8a MORA LOSS > Gothic?

r. *sepń̥t '7' + 2 1ST SS, 3 VERNER, 4a GMC STRESS, 6c SYL SON, 7b 1ST UMLAUT, 8a MORA LOSS > Gothic?

s. Nom sg *snóigʰʷos 'snow' + 2 1ST SS, 3 VERNER, 5b LABIOVELARS, 6b o-TO-a, 8a MORA LOSS, 9b CONT OBSTR DEVOICING > Gothic?

t. Nom sg *ténkʷōn 'thunder' + 2 1ST SS, 5e x-TO-h, 7b 1ST UMLAUT, 7c NASAL LOSS, 8b ŋ-DELETION > Gothic?

u. Nom sg *wĺ̥pos 'wolf' + 2 1ST SS, 3 VERNER, 6b o-TO-a, 6c SYL SON, 8a MORA LOSS, 9b CONT OBSTR DEVOICING > Gothic?

v. Nom sg *wŕ̥g+stw+om 'work' + 1b OBSTR VOI/DEVOI, 2 1ST SS, 5e x-TO-h, 6b o-TO-a, 6c SYL SON, 7b 1ST UMLAUT, 7c NASAL LOSS, 8a MORA LOSS, 9e h-DELETION > Gothic?

w. Past part *wr̥tónos 'become' + 2 1ST SS, 4a GMC STRESS stage 1, 3 VERNER, 6b o-TO-a, 6c SYL SON, 7b 1ST UMLAUT, 8a MORA LOSS, 9b CONT OBSTR DEVOICING > Gothic?

(2) Given the following PIE forms, what will be the Gothic reflexes and what changes will they have undergone? Give the Gothic spelling and a phonemic or phonetic transcription. You may ignore the word stress since it is usually on the first syllable by 4a GMC STRESS.

a. Nom sg *áltis 'age'. (Assume the unstressed root *alt́- from the plural oblique cases was analogized throughout the paradigm.)

b. Nom sg masc adj *áltijos 'old'.

c. *apterṓd 'afterwards'.

d. 3 sg pres subj *bʰéroit 'carry'.

e. Nom sg *bʰrā́ter 'brother'.

f. *dékn̥t '10'.

g. Dat pl *dʰogʰʷómis 'days'.

h. 1 sg pres *ésmi 'I am'.

i. Inf *g^hréibonom 'seize'.
j. Nom sg *kléptus 'thief'.
k. Nom sg *kóupetom 'head'. (Assume the unstressed root *koupet́- from the plural oblique cases was analogized throughout the paradigm.)
l. 1 sg pres *léitō 'I go'.
m. Nom sg *mág^{hw}ilā 'maiden' and the same root in *mág^{hw}us 'boy'.
n. *oktōu '8'.
o. Gen pl *ouk^wōnḗm 'eyes'.
p. Nom sg *ózdos 'branch'.
q, Nom sg *pṓun 'fire'.
r. 1 sg past *se+slḗb+a 'I slept'.
s. Comp adv *snéumn̥tōs 'faster'.
t. Instr sg (later adv) *sworḗd 'in vain'.
u. 1 sg pres *tákō 'I am silent'.
v. 1 sg past *wid+t+ṓm 'I knew'.
w. Nom sg *wíros 'man'.

(3) What is a possible PIE antecedent for the following Gothic forms? (There may be more than one.)

a. 1 sg pres beida 'I await'. (The PIE ending is *-ō and the stress is on the root of this and the other strong verbs under b, d, e, g, and k below.)
b. 1 sg pres binda 'I tie'.
c. Nom sg fadar [faðar] 'father'.
d. 1 sg pres fāha [fā^{n}ha] 'I seize'.
e. 1 sg pres finþa 'I find'.
f. Nom sg o-class neut juk 'yoke'.
g. 1 sg pres saíƕa /seh^{w}a/ 'I see'.
h. Nom sg fem taíhswō 'right hand'. (The PIE ending is *-ōn.)
i. Nom sg tunþus 'tooth'.
j. 1 sg pres þankja 'I think'. (The PIE ending is *-jṓ.)
k. 1 sg pres waírþa 'I become'.

(4) The Late Latin root skrīƀ- 'write' was borrowed into early Germanic and treated as a strong verb. Given its present-tense morpheme structure, what strong-verb class will skrīƀ- automatically fall into? What will be its four principal parts in Gothic?

(5) Consider the alternation in the Gothic j-class i-less weak verb: 1 sg pres þankja 'I think' vs. 1 sg past þahta 'I thought'. The respective PIE endings are *-jṓ and *-tṓm. Both forms develop from a single PIE root with the vowel /o/. What is this root and what phonological changes account for the two different reflexes in Gothic? What are some weak verbs in Modern English which show similar alternations?

(6) The Gothic verb fāh-an 'take' and the noun figg-rs /fing-/ 'finger' derive from a single PIE root. The vowel of the root ablauts. (Recall that there are five ablaut possibilities: e(:), o(:) and Ø.) What is the PIE root; what are the ablauting vowels; what is the PIE stress on the two words; and what changes account for the different Gothic forms?

Similarly, the positive and comparative forms of 'young' are Go jugg-s /jung-s/ and jūh-iza, respectively. Both Gothic forms devolve from a single PIE root, *junk-. The PIE comparative suffix is *-is-. What is the stress on the PIE positive vs. comparative forms; and what changes account for their different reflexes in Gothic?

(7) What accounts for the alternation of the 3 singular present indicative endings in nasjiþ 'saves' vs. hauseiþ /hɔ̄́sīθ/ 'hears'? The PIE roots are *nos- and *kous- and the PIE ending is *-jeti.

(8) Consider the following different types of noun plurals in English: (a) child children, (b) day days, (c) goose geese, (d) ox oxen, (e) sheep sheep (originally a neuter noun). What might you guess are the corresponding Gothic plurals and as such the antecedent PIE classes?

(9) Consider the present infinitive forms (i.e., the first principal part) of the following eight Gothic strong verbs. Judging by the morpheme structure (morph str) of each verb, to which of the seven strong-verb classes will it belong; what are the other three principal parts of the Gothic verb; and what is the PIE root and the ablaut grade of each of these principal parts? The verbs are (a) dreiban 'drive', (b) finþan 'find', (c) hlaþan 'load', (d) hlifan 'steal', (e) saltan 'to salt', (f) stilan 'steal', (g) tiuhan 'pull', (h) waírpan /werpan/ 'throw'.

(10) Consider the glossed Gothic text in VI below. Give a smooth translation of this text.

VI A Gothic Text

The following is from Matthew 5:27-33. It is Wulfilian West Gothic from about 350 AD. Our version of the text is from Braune (1961: 139). We give here (a) the traditional romanization of Wulfila's original orthography, (b) a phonemic transcription (but phonetic in that we designate when /b, d, g/ are the continuants [ƀ, ð, ǥ]), (c) a gloss and (d) a grammatical description of each word in the text. We mark the word stress of those polysyllabic forms not having it on the first syllable. In compounds we mark primary and secondary stress. (A translation of the passage will be found at the end of the Key.)

1	**a**	háusidēduþ	þatei	qiþan	ist:	ni	hōrinōs.
	b	hɔ̄siðēðuθ	θátī̀	kʷíθan	ist	ni	hōrinōs
	c	*hear*	*that*	*say*	*be*	*not*	*fornicate*
	d	2 pl past ind j-class weak verb	conj	perf pass part nom sg neut, class 5 strong verb	3 sg pres ind verb	adv	2 sg pres act subj ā-class weak verb

2	**a**	aþþan	ik	qiþa	izwis	þatei	ƕazuh
	b	aθθan	ik	kʷiθa	izwis	θátī̀	hʷazuh
	c	*however*	*I*	*say*	*you*	*that*	*whoever*
	d	adv	nom sg	1 sg, pres act ind, class 5 strong verb	dat pl	conj	nom sg masc

3	**a**	saei	saíƕiþ	qinōn	du	lustōn	izōs
	b	sáī̀	sehʷiθ	kʷinōn	du	lustōn	izōs
	c	*who*	*see*	*woman*	*to*	*lust*	*she*
	d	rel pron, nom sg masc	3 sg, pres act ind, class 5 strong verb	acc sg fem Vn-class noun	prep	inf ā-class weak verb	gen sg

4	**a**	ju	gahōrinōda	izái	in	haírtin	seinamma
	b	ju	ǥahṓrinōð̌a	izɛ̄	in	hertin	sīnamma
	c	*already*	*commit adultery*	*she*	*in*	*heart*	*his*
	d	adverb	3 sg past ind ā-class weak verb	dat sg	prep	dat sg neut Vn-class noun	dat sg neut adj

5	**a**	iþ	jabái	áugō	þein	þata	taíhswō
	b	iθ	jaƀɛ̄	ɔ̄ǥō	θīn	θata	tehswō
	c	*but*	*if*	*eye*	*your*	*that*	*right*
	d	conj	conj	nom sg neut Vn-class noun	nom sg neut adj	nom sg neut adj	nom sg neut adj

6	**a**	marzjái	þuk	ūsstigg	ita	jah	waírp
	b	marzjɛ̄	θuk	ūssting	ita	jah	werp
	c	*offend*	*you*	*gouge out*	*it*	*and*	*throw*
	d	3 sg pres act subj j-class weak verb	acc sg	2 sg imp class 3 strong verb	acc sg neut	conj	2 sg imp class 3 strong verb

7	**a**	af	þus:	batizō	ist	áuk	þus	ei	fraqistnái
	b	af	θus	batizō	ist	ɔ̄k	θus	ī	frakʷístnɛ̄
	c	*from*	*you*	*good*	*is*	*also*	*you*	*that*	*perish*
	d	prep	dat sg	nom sg neut comp adj	3 sg pres ind verb	adv	dat sg	conj	pres act subj ā-class weak verb

8	**a**	áins	liþiwē	þeináizē	jah	ni	allata
	b	ɛ̄ns	liθiwē	θīnɛ̄zē	jah	ni	allata
	c	*one*	*member*	*your*	*and*	*not*	*all*
	d	nom sg masc	gen pl neut u-class	gen pl masc adj			nom sg neut adj

9	a	leik	þein	gadriusái	in	gaíaínnan
	b	līk̇	θīn	ǥadríusɛ̄	in	ǥeennan
	c	*body*	*your*	*fall*	*in*	*hell*
	d	nom sg neut	nom sg neut	3 sg pres act subj	prep	acc sg masc
		o-class	adj	class 2 strong		Vn-class

10	a	jah	jabái	taíhswō	þeina	handus	marzjái
	b	jah	jaƀɛ̄	tehswō	θīna	handus	marzjɛ̄
	c	*and*	*if*	*right*	*your*	*hand*	*offend*
	d	conj	conj	nom sg fem	nom sg fem	nom sg fem	3 sg pres act subj
				adj	adj	u-class noun	j-class weak verb

11	a	þuk,	afmáit	þō	jah	waírp	af
	b	θuk	áfmɛ̄̀t	θō	jah	werp	af
	c	*you*	*cut off*	*this*	*and*	*throw*	*from*
	d	acc sg	2 sg imp class 7	acc sg fem	conj	2 sg imp class 3	prep
			strong verb			strong verb	

12	a	þus …	qiþanuh	þan	ist	þatei
	b	θus	kʷiθanuh	θan	ist	θátī̀
	c	*you*	*say*	*then*	*is*	*that*
	d	dat sg	perf pass part nom sg neut, class 5 strong verb + enclitic	adv	3 sg pres ind verb	conj

13	a	ƕazuh	saei	aflētái	qēn	gibái
	b	hʷazuh	sáī̀	áflɛ̄̀tɛ̄	kʷēn	ǥiƀɛ̄
	c	*whoever*	*who*	*put aside*	*wife*	*give*
	d	nom sg	nom sg	3 sg, pres act subj,	acc sg fem	3 sg, pres act subj,
		masc	masc	class 7 strong verb	i-class noun	class 5 strong verb

14	a	izái	afstassáis	bōkōs	iþ	ik
	b	izɛ̄	afstassɛ̄s	bōkōs	iθ	ik
	c	*she*	*divorce*	*writ*	*but*	*I*
	d	dat sg fem	gen sg fem	acc pl fem	conj	nom sg
			i-class noun	ā-class noun		

15	a	qiþa	izwis	þatei	ƕazuh	saei	aflētiþ
	b	kʷiθa	izwis	θátī̀	hʷazuh	sáī̀	áflḕtiθ
	c	*say*	*you*	*that*	*whoever*	*who*	*put aside*
	d	1 sg, pres act ind, class 5 strong verb	dat pl	conj	nom sg masc	nom sg masc	3 sg, pres act ind, class 7 strong verb

16	a	qēn	seina	inuh	faírina	kalkinassáus
	b	kʷēn	sīna	inuh	ferina	kalkinassɔ̄s
	c	*wife*	*his*	*without*	*reason*	*adultery*
	d	acc sg fem i-class noun	acc sg fem adj	prep	acc sg fem ā-class noun	gen sg masc u-class noun

17	a	táujiþ	þō	hōrinōn	jah	sa
	b	tɔ̄jiθ	θō	hōrinōn	jah	sa
	c	*do*	*this*	*adultery*	*and*	*whoever*
	d	3 sg, pres act ind, j-class weak verb	acc sg fem	acc sg fem Vn-class noun	conj	nom sg masc

18	a	izē	afsatida	liugáiþ,	hōrinōþ.
	b	izē	áfsàtiða	liuǥɛ̄θ	hōrinōθ
	c	*they*	*set aside*	*marry*	*commit adultery*
	d	gen pl masc	perf pass part acc sg fem, j-class weak verb	3 sg, pres act ind, oi-class weak verb	3 sg, pres act ind, ā-class weak verb

VII Key

(1) The Gothic forms are these: (a.) bṓka /bōka/, (b.) baíriþ /beriθ/, (c.) baíra /bera/, (d.) baírada [beraða], (e.) blindamma /blindamma/, (f.) daúhtar /dohtar/, (g.) twái tigjus [twɛ̄ tiǥjus], (h.) twaddjḗ /twaddjḗ/, (i.) aíƕatundja /ehʷatundja/, (j.) gardim [ǥardim], (k.) kaúrn /korn/, (l.) qumþs /kʷumθs/, (m.) habáida [haƀɛ̄ða], (n.) nists /nists/, (o.) naqaþs /nakʷaθs/, (p.) unsar /unsar/, (q.) siggwa [singwa], (r.) sibun [siƀun], (s.) snáiws /snɛ̄ws/, (t.) þeiƕō /θīhʷō/ (perhaps /θīⁿhʷō/), (u.) wulfs /wulfs/, (v.) waúrstw /worstw/, (w.) waúrþans /worθans/.

(2) The Gothic forms and changes are these:

a. alds /alds/. The derivation is 2 1ST SS, 3 VERNER, 8a MORA LOSS, 9b CONT OBSTR DEVOICING.

b. alþeis /alθīs/. The derivation is 2 1ST SS, 3 VERNER, 8a MORA LOSS, 9b CONT OBSTR DEVOICING.

c. aftarō /aftarō/. The derivation is 2 1ST SS, 4a GMC STRESS, 8a MORA LOSS, 9c e-TO-a.
d. baírái /berɛ̄/. The derivation is 2 1ST SS, 3 VERNER, 6b o-TO-a, 7a ai/au-MONOPH, 8a MORA LOSS.
e. brōþar /brōθar/. The derivation is 2 1ST SS, 6a ā-TO-ō, 9c e -TO-a.
f. taíhun /tehun/. The derivation is 2 1ST SS, 3 VERNER, 6c SYL SON, 8a MORA LOSS.
g. dagam [daǥam]. The derivation is 2 1ST SS, 3 VERNER, 4a GMC STRESS, 6b o-TO-a, 8a MORA LOSS, 9i mz-TO-mm, la GEM C SIMP applying as a persistent rule.
h. im /im/. The derivation is lc s-z RULE, 5c MS CHANGES, 7b 1ST UMLAUT, 8a MORA LOSS, la GEM C SIMP applying as a persistent rule.
i. greipan [ǥrīpan]. The derivation is 2 1ST SS, 6b o-TO-a, 7b 1ST UMLAUT, 7c NASAL LOSS, 8a MORA LOSS.
j. hliftus /hliftus/. The derivation is 2 1ST SS, 3 VERNER, 5e x-TO-h, 7b 1ST UMLAUT, 9b CONT OBSTR DEVOICING.
k. háubiþ [hɔ̄ƀiθ]. The derivation is 2 1ST SS, 3 VERNER, 5e x-TO-h, 6b o-TO-a, 7b 1ST UMLAUT, 9b CONT OBSTR DEVOICING, 9g LATER ai/au-MONOPH.
l. leiþa /līθa/. The derivation is 2 1ST SS, 7b 1ST UMLAUT, 8a MORA LOSS.
m. mawila /mawila/ and magus [maǥus]. The derivation is 2 1ST SS, 3 VERNER, 5b LABIOVELARS, 6a ā-TO-ō, 8a MORA LOSS, 9b CONT OBSTR DEVOICING.
n. ahtáu /ahtɔ̄/. The derivation is 2 1ST SS, 4a GMC STRESS, 5a DIPH SHORTENING, 6b o-TO-a, 7a ai/au-MONOPH.
o. áugōnē [ɔ̄ǥōnē]. The derivation is 2 1ST SS, 3 VERNER, 4a GMC STRESS, 5b LABIOVELARS, 6b o-TO-a, 7c NASAL LOSS, 9g LATER ai/au-MONOPH.
p. asts /asts/. The derivation is 2 1ST SS, 1b OBSTR VOI/DEVOI applying as a persistent rule, 3 VERNER, 6b o-TO-a, 8a MORA LOSS, 9b CONT OBSTR DEVOICING.
q. fōn /fōn/. The derivation is 2 1ST SS, 9d ēi/ōu-TO-ē/ō.
r. saízlēp /sezlḗp/. The derivation is 2 1ST SS, 3 VERNER, 8a MORA LOSS.
s. sniumundōs /sniumundōs/. The derivation is 2 1ST SS, 3 VERNER, 5d OBSTR-TO-STOP, 7b 1ST UMLAUT, 9b CONT OBSTR DEVOICING.
t. swarē /swarē/. The derivation is 2 1ST SS, 4a GMC STRESS, 6b o-TO-a, 8a MORA LOSS.
u. þaha /θaha/. The derivation is 2 1ST SS, 5e x-TO-h, 8a MORA LOSS.
v. wissa /wissa/. The derivation is 1b OBSTR VOI/DEVOI, le tt/ts-TO-ss, 4a GMC STRESS, 7c NASAL LOSS, 8a MORA LOSS.
w. waír /wer/. The derivation is 3 VERNER, 6b o-TO-a, 7b 1ST UMLAUT, 9o z-DELETION.

(3) The possible PIE antecedents are these:
a. *bʰéidʰō or *bʰī́dʰō. It is the former.
b. *bʰéndʰō or *bʰíndʰō. It is the former.
c. *pádʰar, *pádʰer, *patár, *patér. It is the last.
d. *pánkō or *pónkō. It is the latter.
e. *péntō or *píntō. It is the former.
f. *júgom or *jugóm. It is probably the former.
g. *sékʷō or *síkʷō. It is the former.
h. *dékswōn, *díkswōn, *dekswṓn or *dikswṓn. It is probably the first.
i. *dn̥̍tus or *dúntus. It is the former.
j. *tangjṓ or *tongjṓ. It is the latter; its cognate occurs in Early Lat tongeō 'I think'.
k. *wértō or *wírtō. It is the former; its cognate occurs in Classical Lat vertō 'I turn'.

(4) Given the morpheme structure of /ī/ in the pres-tense root, the verb will have to go into class 1. The Gothic principal parts are skreiban [skrīƀan], skráif [skrɛ̄f], skriƀum [skriƀum], skribans [skriƀans].

(5) The PIE root is *tong-. The developments are 1 sg pres *tongjṓ (2 1ST SS, 4a GMC STRESS, 6b o-TO-a, 8a MORA LOSS) > Go þankja; and *tongtṓm (1b OBSTR VOI/DEVOI) > *tonktṓm (2 1ST SS, 4a GMC STRESS, 5e x-TO-h, 6b o-TO-a) > *þánhta (8b ŋ-DELETION) > Go þāhta (possibly [θā́ⁿhta]). Modern English verbs of this type are bring/brought, buy/bought, seek/sought, teach/taught and think/thought.

(6) The PIE root is *pVnk-, where V = the ablauting vowels /e,o/. The verb fāh(an) is from PIE *pónk- by 2 1ST SS, 6b o-TO-a, 5e x-TO-h and 8b ŋ-DELETION. The noun figg(rs) is from *penḱ- by 1ST SS, 3 VERNER, 5d OBSTR-TO-STOP and 7b 1ST UMLAUT. The derivation of *junk- is as follows: pos *junḱ- (2 1ST SS, 3 VERNER, 4a GMC STRESS, 5d OBSTR-TO-STOP) > Go jugg(s); comp *júnk- (2 1ST SS, 5e x-TO-h, 8b ŋ-DELETION) > Go jūh(iza).

(7) The alternation results from the application of 3.1.2f SIEVERS in PIE. Hence the synchronic derivation is *nosjéti vs. *kousjéti (3.1.2f SIEVERS) → *nosjéti vs. *kousijéti. The further derivation is *nosjéti *kousijéti (2 1ST SS) > *nosjéθi *xousijéθi (4a GMC STRESS applying early in East Germanic) > *nósjeθi *xóusijeθi (3 VERNER, 5e x-TO-h, 6b o-TO-a) > *násjeði *háusijeði (7b 1ST UMLAUT) > *násjiði *háusijiði (/iji/ interpreted as /ī/) > násjiði *háusīði (8a MORA LOSS, 9b CONT OBSTR DEVOICING, ev) > Go nasjiþ and háuseiþ.

(8) The corresponding Gothic pls and PIE classes are these:

a. The pl *kalƀ-iz-u 'calves' plus the pl haírt-ōn-a 'hearts'; hence the Vs-class (1.5.6) and the Vn-class (1.5.4).

b. The pl dag-ōs 'days'; hence the o-class (1.1).

c. The pl gast-eis /gast-īs/ 'guests'; hence the i-class (1.3).

d. The pl gum-ans 'men'; hence the Vn-class (1.5.4).

e. The pl waúrd-a 'words'; hence the o-class (1.1).

(9) The class, principal parts, PIE root and ablaut grades are these:

a. dreiban [drīƀan] 'drive' with the pres root morph str C_0īC- (where C_0 = no consonant, one consonant or a consonant cluster and C = a single consonant) must be class 1. The principal parts are dreiban dráif dribum dribans. The PIE root is *d^{h}rVib^h- in which the ablauting vowel V = e, o, Ø and Ø.

b. finþan 'find' with the present root morph str C_0i[C, +sononant]C- must be class 3. The principal parts are finþan fanþ funþum funþans. The PIE root is *pVnt- in which the ablauting V = e, o, Ø and Ø.

c. hlaþan 'load' with the present root morph str C_0aC- must be class 6. The principal parts are hlaþan hlōþ hlōþum hlaþans. The PIE root is *klVt- in which the ablauting V = o, ō, ō, o.

d. hlifan 'steal' with the present root morph str C_0i[C, –sonorant]- must be class 5. The principal parts are hlifan hlaf hlēfum hlifans. The PIE root is *klVp- in which the ablauting V = e, o, ē and e.

e. saltan 'salt' with the present root morph str C_0aCC-, which does not fit into any of the six ablauting classes, must fall into the reduplicating class 7. The principal parts are saltan saísalt /sesált/, saísaltum, saltans. The PIE root is *sald-, which reduplicates as *sesáld-.

f. stilan 'steal' with the present root morph str C_0i[C, +sonorant]- must be class 4. The principal parts are stilan stal stēlum stilans. The PIE root is *stVl- in which the ablauting V = e, o, ē and Ø.

g. tiuhan 'pull' with the present root morph str C_0iuC- must be class 2. The principal parts are tiuhan táuh /tɔ̄h/ taúhum /tohum/ taúhans /tohans/. The PIE root is *dVuk- in which the ablauting V = e, o, Ø and Ø.

h. waírpan /werpan/ 'throw' with the present root morph str C_0e [C, +sononant] C- must be class 3. The principal parts are waírpan warp waúrpum /worpum/ waúrpans. The PIE root is *wVrb- in which the ablauting V = e, o, Ø and Ø.

(10) The following is a translation of the text in section VI.

"You have heard that it is said, you should not fornicate. But I say to you that whoever sees a woman to lust after her has already committed adultery with her in his heart. But if your right eye should offend you, gouge it out and throw it from you: it is better for you that one of your bodily members should perish and not that your whole body should fall into hell. And if your right hand should offend you, cut it off and throw it from you... It is also said that whoever might put aside his wife should give her a writ of divorce. But I say to you that whoever puts aside his wife except for reasons of adultery commits adultery; and whoever of them marries a woman who has been so set aside also commits adultery."

VIII Notes

[1]Note in this derivation the necessary chronologies 4a GMC STRESS stage 3 > 7c NASAL LOSS stage 3 and NASAL LOSS stage 3 > 8a MORA LOSS.

[2] Note here the necessary chronology 5c MS CHANGES > am-TO-um.

[3] We assume that the phonemes /hʷ/ and /kʷ/ functioned as unary segments and not as sequences /h+w/ and /k+w/. One reason for assuming this is their behavior in the application of 9k THURNEYSEN. E.g., dative singular underlying ríkʷ+is+a 'darkness' (9k THURNEYSEN) → /ríkʷiza/. If the sequence had been underlying **ríkw+is+a (where /w/ is +voiced), then THURNEYSEN would not have applied and the result would have been **/ríkwisa/. Another reason for the same assumption is that/hʷ/ and /kʷ/ are represented in Gothic orthography by unary graphemes <ƕ> and <q>.

[4] The complementary distribution of the segments /b, ƀ/, /d, đ/, /g, ǥ/ is determined by 5d OBSTR-TO-STOP.

[5] The complementary distribution of /ǥ, x/ is determined by 9b CONT OBSTR DEVOICING. The same rule also accounts for the alternations /b/ = [ƀ] and /f/, /d/ = [đ] and /θ/, and /z/ and /s/.

[6] The voiceless stops /p, t, k, kʷ/ probably had aspirated and nonaspirated allophones /p⁼, pʰ/ etc. by the reflex of 2 1st SS.

[7] The alternation of the allophones /n, ŋ/ is determined by the reflex of the PIE rule 3.1.2d NASAL ASSIM, which remains in the Gothic grammar. E.g., inf /θankjan/ 'think' (NASAL ASSIM) → [θaŋkjan]. In such forms the allophone [ŋ] is often written as <g>. Hence both <þagkjan> and <þankjan> occur.

[8] The long vs. short vowels are often not indicated orthographically. Hence orthographic <ai> and <au> can represent both /e/ and /ɛ̄/ as well as /o/ and /ɔ̄/, respectively. In such instances we follow the usual editorial practice of writing the long vowels /ɛ̄, ɔ̄/ as <ái, áu> and the short /e, o/as <aí, aú>. Hence the Gothic forms such as the inf <baíran> 'carry' /beran/ vs. the nom sg masc <áins> 'one' /ɛ̄ns/' as well as the perf pass part <baúrans> 'carried' /borans/ vs. the nom sg masc adj. <háuhs> 'high' /hɔ̄hs/. The long vs. short /ī/ vs. /i/ is

indicated graphemically as <ei> vs. <i>. E.g. <seina> /sīna/ 'theirs' vs. <ins> /ins/ 'them'. But the other long vs. short vowels /ū, u/ and /ā, a/ are not indicated in the orthography.

[9] The long lax vowels /ɛ̄/ and /ɔ̄/ arise by 7a ai/au-MONOPH. Stage 3 of this change remains as a rule of Gothic and determines the alternations of /ɛ̄/ with /aj/ and /ɔ̄/ with /aw/ as in bái /bɛ̄/ vs. bajōþ /bajōθ/ 'both' and the inf táujan /tɔ̄jan/ 'make' vs. the past tawida /tawida/. These occurrences of [ɛ̄] and [ɔ̄] derive from underlying /ai/ and /au/. When 7a ai/au-MONOPH does not apply, /ai/ and /au/ are realized as [aj] and [aw] by the PIE rule 3.1.2c i-j/u-w ALT, still in the grammar. The /ɛ̄, ɔ̄/ in paradigms where there is no alternation with the diphthongs are underlying, e.g. áins 'one' /ɛ̄ns/ and háuhs 'high' /hɔ̄hs/.

[10] As a result of change 6a ā-TO-ō, the only long /ā/ in Gothic is in borrowings such as the Latin agent suffix -ār- in bōkāreis 'scribe'.

[11] The long nasal vowels arose by 8b ŋ-DELETION and can occur only under stress. They may have lost their nasality by Gothic times.

[12] The word-final voiceless continuant obstruents in inflectional endings generally come from voiced obstruents by 9b CONT OBSTR DEVOICING.

[13] The antecedent of NWGermanic *daǥē is a PIE dat sg in *-ṓi; that of Go daga is a PIE instrumental in *-ḗ or ablauting *-ṓ.

[14] The derivation of the long-stem forms (on which see 9h LOSS OF SIEVERS) is as follows: PIE *kérd^{h}jos (PIE rule 3.1.2f SIEVERS applying synchronically) → *kérd^{h}ijos (2 1st SS, 3 VERNER, 6b o-TO-a, 7b 1ST UMLAUT, ev) > *herdijaz (8a MORA LOSS) > *hérdijz = *herdīz (9b CONT OBSTR DEVOICING) > Go haírdeis.

[15] By a derivation analogous to the preceding one, one would expect Go **reikei **/rīkī/ instead of reiki. We assume the short /i/ in reiki came from the oblique cases as follows: PIE dat sg *rīgijē (ev through 9c e-TO-a) > *rīkija (9h LOSS OF SIEVERS) > *rīkja (transferral of /j/ to the nom sg) > nom sg *rīkj (PIE 3.1.2c i-j/u-w ALT, still applying as a synchronic rule) → Go nom sg reiki.

[16] The derivation is *g^{h}éb^{h}ā (2 1st SS) > *ǥéƀā (6a ā-TO-ō) > *ǥéƀō (7b 1ST UMLAUT) > NWGmc *ǥéƀō vs. East Gmc *ǥíƀō (8a MORA LOSS) > NWGmc *ǥéƀu vs. Go giba [gíƀa].

[17] The derivation is PIE *g^{h}éb^{h}ām (ev through 7b 1ST UMLAUT) > NWGmc *ǥéƀōm vs. East Gmc *ǥíƀōm (7c NASAL LOSS) > *ǥéƀōn vs. *ǥíƀō^n (8a MORA LOSS) > *ǥéƀōn vs. *ǥíƀō^n (7c NASAL LOSS reapplying synchronically) > *ǥéƀō vs. *ǥíƀō (word-final /o/ restructured to /a/ in East Germanic: see MORA LOSS) > NWGmc *ǥéƀō vs. Go giba.

[18] A possible derivation is *g^{h}éb^{h}āi (through 5a DIPH SHORTENING) > *ǥéƀai (7a ai/au MONOPH) > *ǥéƀɛ̄ (7b 1ST UMLAUT, 8a MORA LOSS for some reason not applying) > Go gibái.

[19] The derivation is *g^{h}eb^{h}ā́mis (2 1st SS, 3 VERNER, 4a GMC STRESS) > *ǥéƀāmiz (6a ā-TO-ō, 7b 1ST UMLAUT, 8a MORA LOSS) > *ǥíƀōmz (9i mz-TO-mm) > *ǥíƀōmm (la GEM C SIMP applying as a persistent synchronic rule) → Go gibōm.

[20] The derivation of these forms is PIE *b^{h}ónd^{h}jā vs. *b^{h}ánjā (PIE 3.1.2f SIEVERS applying synchronically) → *b^{h}ónd^{h}ijā *b^{h}ánjā (ev through 6b o-TO-a) > *bándijō *bánjō (an early application of 8a MORA LOSS to the word-final /ō/ in *bándijō since it is preceded by an unstressed syllable) > *bandijo *banjō (8a MORA LOSS reapplying) > *bándij *banja (9h LOSS OF SIEVERS) > *bandj *banja (PIE 3.1.2c i-j/u-w ALT still in the grammar) → Go bandi vs. banja.

[21] The PIE form consists of the e-grade ablaut of the stem *g^{h}ósteies plus the ending *-es. The derivation is *g^{h}ósteies (PIE 3.1.2c i-j/u-w ALT applying synchronically) → *g^{h}óstejes (through 6b o-TO-a) > *ǥástejez (7b 1ST UMLAUT) > *ǥástijiz (reinterpretation of /iji/ as /ī/) > *ǥástīz (9b CONT OBSTR DEVOICING) > Go gasteis.

[22] In NW Germanic the e-grade of these endings occurs, in Gothic the o-grade. A derivation is gen sg *g^{w}ḗneis (2 1st SS, 3 VERNER) > *k^{w}ḗneiz (7b 1ST UMLAUT) > *k^{w}ḗniiz = NWGmc *k^{w}ḗnīz.

[23] This form has o-grade ablaut in the stem.

[24] The Gothic form has the o-grade ablaut, the NWGermanic one the e-grade. The derivation of the latter is *súneu (7b 1ST UMLAUT) > *súniu (PIE 3.1.2c i-j/u-w ALT still in the grammar and applying synchronically) > NWGmc *sunju.

[25] These forms have the e-grade ablaut in the stem. Their derivation is *súneues and *súneuēm (PIE 3.1.2c i-j/u-w ALT applying synchronically) → *sunewes *sunewēm (3 VERNER, 4a GMC STRESS) > *súniwiz *súniwēm (7c NASAL LOSS, 8a MORA LOSS) > *stúniwz *súniwē (PIE 3.1.2c i-j/u-w ALT still in the grammar and applying synchronically) → *súniuz *súniwē (i-j/u-w ALT reapplying) → *súnjuz *súniwē (9b CONT OBSTR DEVOICING) > sunjus and suniwē.

[26] The plural is not attested. We reconstruct the stem as *pekeu- after *suneu-.

[27] The Germanic nominative singular in *-z seems to have been readded from other declensions such as the o-class *daga+z 'day'. Otherwise the derivation would be this: PIE *bʰŕ̥gʰs (1b OBSTR VOI/DEVOI) > *bʰŕ̥ks (2 1ST SS, 6c SYL SON) > *búrhs (7b 1ST UMLAUT) > Go **baúrhs instead of baúrgs.

[28] The derivation of these forms is *bʰŕ̥gʰes (2 1ST SS, 3 VERNER, 6c SYL SON) > *búrgez (7b 1ST UMLAUT, 8a MORA LOSS) > *bórgz (9b CONT OBSTR DEVOICING) > Go baúrgs [borxs].

[29] The derivation is *alút (2 1ST SS) > *alúθ (4a GMC STRESS) > *áluθ (8a MORA LOSS) > Go and NWGmc *alu.

[30] The derivation is *alútā (2 1ST SS, ev) > *alúθō (4a GMC STRESS stage 2 applying only in East Germanic) > EGmc *áluθō vs. NWGmc *alúθō (3 VERNER) > *áluða vs. NWGmc *áluθu.

[31] The alternation in the stem *pṓu- vs. *pú- is PIE ō-Ø ablaut. The derivation of Go fōn is PIE *pṓun (2 1ST SS) > *fṓun (9d ēi/ōu-TO-ē/ō) > Go fōn.

[32] These endings are from the o-class, probably added in Germanic times.

[33] The derivation is *bʰrā́ter (2 1ST SS) > *brā́θer (6a ā-TO-ō) > *brṓθer (9c e-TO-a) > Go brōþar.

[34] The /u/ in the Gothic stem vs. /o/ in NWGermanic is attributable to the differing East Germanic and NWGermanic versions of 7b 1ST UMLAUT.

[35] The derivation is not clear: PIE *gʰm̥onḿ̥is (2 1ST SS, 3 VERNER, 4a GMC STRESS , 6b o-TO-a, 6c SYL SON) > *gúmanumiz (possibly 8a MORA LOSS) > *gúmanmz (9i mz-TO-mm) > *gúmanmm (la GEM C SIMP applying as a synchronic rule) → *gúmanm (restructuring of the impossible word-final /nm/ to /m/) > Go gumam. Another possibility is that the dative plural is that of the o-class, *gʰm̥+ómis, which would also result in Go gumam.

[36] The dative plural ending may have been from the o-class.

[37] The accusative singular masculine occurred with the particle *-ōm. The derivation of PIE *bʰléndʰom+ōm to Go blindana is given under 7c NASAL LOSS. The same particle occurred optionally in the nominative/accusative singular neuter. This resulted in the occurrence of two optional forms in Gothic. Their derivation is as follows: PIE *bʰléndʰod vs. *bʰléndʰodōm (through 7b 1ST UMLAUT) > *blíndat vs. *blíndatōm (7c NASAL LOSS) > *blíndat vs. *blíndatō (8a MORA LOSS) > *blínda vs. *blíndata (loss of the word-final /a/ on *blínda because otherwise it would be homophonous with the neuter nominative/accusative plural form) > Go blind vs. blindata.

[38] The derivation is *bʰlendʰósmo (1c s-z RULE) > *bʰlendʰózmo (through 7b 1ST UMLAUT) > *blíndammō (8a MORA LOSS) > Go blindamma.

[39] The derivation of the long-stem form is *wéltjos (PIE 3.l.2f SIEVERS applying synchnonically) → *wéltijos (through 6b o-TO-a) > *wélθijaz (7b 1ST UMLAUT) > *wílθijaz (8a MORA LOSS) > *wílθijz, i.e. *wílθīz (9b CONT OBSTR DEVOICING) > Go wilþeis. The derivation of the short-stem form is *médʰjos (PIE 3.1.2f SIEVERS not applying, ev through 7b 1ST UMLAUT) > *míðjaz (8a MORA LOSS) > *míðjz, i.e. *míðiz (replacement of /i/ by the phonologically regular /ji/ from the gen sg *míðjiz, ev) > Go midjis.

[40] The development of hrain and hrainjata is analogous to that of blind and blindata 'blind' described above. The phonologically regular development of PIE *króini+od would be Go **hráini. The final /i/ was lost under the influence of neuter adjectives like blind.

[41] The use of /j/ as a marker in most cases of this class originated as follows: e.g., PIE *króini+āisās (PIE 3.1.2c i-j/u-w ALT applying synchronically) > *króinjāisās (ev) > Go hráinjáizōs.

[42] These endings are from the o-class.

[43] The regular development from PIE *bʰléndʰ+ōn is Go blinda. The feminine and neuter form blindō is from the oblique cases where the /ō/ did not occur word-finally.

[44] The -ōz- and -ōst- suffixes occur infrequently. The origin of the /ō/ is not clear. It may have come from the adverb ending.

[45] The derivational history of the masc gen *dwoiḗm is (PIE 3.1.2c i-j/u-w ALT applying synchronically) → *dwojḗm (2 1ST SS, 4a GMC STRESS) > *twójēm (6b o-TO-a, 7c Nasal Loss) > *twájē (9n *Verschärfung*) > Go twaddjē. The feminine genitive plural is not attested in Gothic.

[46] These endings were re-added in Germanic times from the o- and ā-class adjective declension. E.g., the derivation neut nom *dwā́ and the adj. *bʰlendʰā 'blind' (through 7b 1ST UMLAUT) > *twṓ and *blíndō (8a Mora Loss) > *twṓ and *blínda (replacement of the -ō by -a) > Go twa and blinda. Otherwise one would expect Go **twō.

[47] The derivation is *tréies (PIE 3.1.2c i-j/u-w ALT applying synchronically) → *tréjes (through 7b 1ST UMLAUT) > *θríjiz (/iji/ reinterpreted as /ī/) *θrī́z (9b CONT OBSTR DEVOICING) > Go *þreis.

[48] Although the suffix -θ existed in other Germanic languages, it may not have occurred in Gothic. The reason for the occurrence of -θ in other Germanic languages as opposed to -d in Gothic resides in the fact that the change 4a GMC STRESS applied earlier in East Germanic than in NWGermanic E.g., *oktútōn '8th' (2 1ST SS) > *oxtúθōn (4a GMC STRESS stage 1 applying early in East Germanic) > East Gmc *óxtuθōn vs. NWGmc *oxtúθōn (3 VERNER) > East Gmc *óxtuðōn vs. NWGmc *oxtúθōn (ev) > Go ahtuda [áhtuða] vs. NWGmc *áxtuθō.

[49] This form indicates that the ordinals were reformed in Germanic after the time of 8a MORA LOSS: PIE *pémpetōn '5th' (2 1ST SS, 3 VERNER) > *fémfeðōn (7b 1ST UMLAUT, 7c NASAL LOSS) > *fímfiðō (8a MORA LOSS) > *fímfiða (*fimfi- here replaced by *fimf '5') > *fímfða (the inadmissible sequence [fð] replaced by the normal [ft]) > Go fimfta.

[50] The derivations are these: a form like PIE *sékstōn '6th' retains the -t, to which neither 2 1ST SS nor 3 VERNER can apply, to result in Go saíhsta; the reflexes -ð and -d result from 3 VERNER. E.g., *tritjṓn '3rd' and *sepń̥t+t+ōn '7th' (through 3 VERNER) > *θriðjṓn and *seƀń̥θ+ð+ōn (ev) > *θríðjōn and *séƀunðōn (5d OBSTR-TO- STOP) > *θríðjōn and *séƀundōn (ev) > Go þridja [θríðja] and sibunda [síƀunda]. Regarding the suffix –θ, see the note to *fidwōrda and ahtuda above.

[51] The optionally occurring suffix *-es is probably from the nominative plural. The derivation is *ń̥ses (3 VERNER) > *ń̥sez (6c SYL SON) > *únsez (7b 1ST UMLAUT) > *únsiz (9b CONT OBSTR DEVOICING) > Go unsis.

[52] This pronoun had an optional initial *k- in PIE and consequently an optional initial *h- in Germanic. This optionality was variously sorted out later in the Germanic languages in that some of them took forms with initial /h/ and others without it. E.g., OEng dat sg masc him 'him' vs. Go imma.

[53] These forms have the PIE particle *-ōm, which also occurs in the strong adjective declension (2.1 above).

[54] This ending is from the genitive singular of o-class nouns.

[55] The derivation of the Gothic form is *ismō (lc s-z RULE) > *izmō (5c MS CHANGES) > *immō (8a MORA LOSS) > imma.

[56] The Gothic derivation is PIE *ei+es (PIE 3.1.2c i-j/u-w ALT applying synchronically) → *ejes (3 VERNER) > *ejez (7b 1ST UMLAUT) > *ijiz (/iji/ reinterpreted as /ī/) > *īz (9b CONT OBSTR DEVOICING) > īs.

[57] The derivations of these forms are similar. That of the nominative plural feminine is *i+ās (3 VERNER, 6a ā-TO- ō) > *iōz (9b CONT OBSTR DEVOICING) > *iōs (9f j-INSERTION) > Go ijōs.

[58] The PIE antecedents are *to– and *ti– respectively.

[59] The derivation is *ń̥seros (3 VERNER) > *ń̥seroz (6b o-TO- a, 6c SYL SON) > *únseraz (8a MORA LOSS) > *únserz (9c e -TO- a) > *únsarz (9o z-DELETION) > Go unsar.

[60] The derivation is *kʷod (2 1ST SS, 6b o-TO- a) > *hʷat (8a MORA LOSS applying to the unstressed neuter adjective ending *-at and resulting in *-a, which was transferred to *hʷ- in East Germanic, but not in NWGermanic) > Go ƕa, NWGmc *hʷat.

[61] The basic presupposition underlying the use of the subjunctive is that the truth value of the sentence is either doubtful or false. Hence a verb in the subjunctive can indicate (a) a wish, (b) a command, (c) possibility or doubt or

(d) outright falsehood in unreal conditional sentences, which are in the past subjunctive. Examples of each of these uses of the subjunctive follow, where for each we cite a contrasting indicative sentence.

(a)	**subj**	Nu fralētáis skalk þeinana. 'Now you should hopefully release your servant.'
	ind	Nu fralētis skalk þeina. 'Now you are releasing your servant.'
(b)	**subj**	Fraþjáiþ. 'You ought to understand.'
	ind	Fraþjiþ. 'You do understand.'
(c)	**subj**	ƕa sijái þata waúrd? 'What might that word be?'
	ind	ƕa ist þata waúrd? 'What is that word?'
(d)	**subj**	Jabái guþ atta izwar wēsi, friōdēdeiþ mik. 'If God were your father — which he is not — then you would love me — which you do not.'
	ind	Jabái guþ atta izwar ist, friōþ mik. 'Since God is your father, you love me.'

[62] The past can reflect either a perfected, completed past event or an imperfect and on-going one. While there is no formal future, this tense can be expressed by the present or by another verb such as waírþan 'become' plus the present infinitive.

[63] The derivation is *wid+t+ṓm (1b OBSTR VOI/DEVOI) > *wittṓm (le tt/ts-TO- ss) > *wissṓm (4a GMC STRESS , 7c NASAL LOSS, 8a MORA LOSS) > Go wissa.

[64] The derivation is *d^hug^h+t+ṓm (1b OBSTR VOI/DEVOI) > *d^huktṓm (2 1ST SS) > *duxtṓm (4a GMC STRESS) > *dúxtōm (5e x-TO- h in its NWGermanic and East Germanic versions) > NW Gmc *dúxtōm vs. East Gmc *dúhtōm (7b 1ST UMLAUT, 7c NASAL LOSS, 8a MORA LOSS) > NW Gmc *doxt$\bar{o}^n$ vs. Go *daúhta.

[65] In view of the Gothic form kunþa with /θ/ as well as that of NW Germanic also with /θ/ (it occurs in Modern English un-couth), the antecedent form had PIE root stress. Hence it did not undergo 3 VERNER.

[66] In Gothic and the other Germanic languages the second principal part *mag- has taken over the paradigm. Otherwise one would expect Go **mēgum.

[67] The vowel /ā/ does not regularly ablaut in PIE. Hence the Germanic form ōg- from PIE *āg^h- probably came into this ablauting class in Germanic times after the time of change 6a ā-TO- ō.

[68] Old Icelandic replaced the original verb with gørva 'do' from PIE *g^horw+j+ónom. Hence the original verb is retained only in the West Germanic languages.

[69] The past plural and past subjunctive forms derive from an ablauting PIE *d^hē+t+ weak verb endings. E.g., NW Gmc *dēðum 'we did'.

[70] The Gothic form is a class 7 strong verb.

[71] The PIE antecedent of this verb is not obvious. We posit the root *ei- plus a j-class weak verb past ending *-itṓm. The derivation is *ei+i+tṓm (PIE 3.1.2c i-j/u-w ALT applying synchronically) → *ejitṓm (3 VERNER) > *ejiðṓm (4a GMC STRESS, 7b 1ST UMLAUT) > *íjiðōm (7c NASAL LOSS, 8a MORA LOSS) > *íjiða (9n *VERSCHÄRFUNG*) > *íddjiða (? a dissimilatory dropping of [ið], particularly from forms like the 1 pl past ind. *iddjiðēðum) > Gothic sing iddja and pl iddjēdum.

[72] The Gothic verb is a 6th-class strong verb.

[73] The PIE antecedent is not clear. It may have been an ablauting root *stṓta. The NWGermanic form with [ð] may have come from a 1pl ind *stōtmé by 3 VERNER .

[74] The antecedent of Gmc *stand- is not clear. It may have been from an original PIE pres participle *sta+nt- 'standing' (3 VERNER) > Gmc *stand-. (See Voyles 1992: 269.)

[75] The 1 singular present indicative of ā-class verbs originally had the PIE athematic ending *-mi. E.g., PIE *salpā́mi 'I use salve' (ev) > Gmc *salƀōm (dropping of the /m/ in Gothic on the model of verbs like baíra above) > Go salbō.

[76] The derivation is *bʰéresi (2 1ST SS, 3 VERNER) > *bérezi (7b 1ST UMLAUT in East Germanic and NW Germanic versions) > NW Gmc *bírizi vs. East Gmc *bérizi (8a MORA LOSS) > *bíriz vs. *bériz (9b CONT OBSTR DEVOICING) > NW Gmc *bíriz vs. Go baíris.

[77] The derivation is *bʰérōwes (2 1ST SS, 3 VERNER) > *bérōwez (8a MORA LOSS) > *bérōwz (PIE 3.1.2c i-j/u-w ALT, replacement of the unusual sequence /ōu/ by the regular /ō/) > *bérōz (9b CONT OBSTR DEVOICING) > Go baírōs.

[78] The derivation is PIE *bʰérotes (2 1ST SS, 3 VERNER , 6b o-TO-a) > *béraðez (7b 1ST UMLAUT) > *béraðiz (8a MORA LOSS) > *béraðz (? 5d OBSTR-TO-STOP applying as a persistent synchronic rule) > *béradz (9b CONT OBSTR DEVOICING) > *bérads (1b OBSTR VOI/DEVOI applying as a persistent synchronic rule) → Go baírats /berats/.

[79] The derivation is *bʰéromes (2 1ST SS, 3 VERNER, 6b o-TO- a) > *béramez (8a MORA LOSS) > *béramz (9i mz-TO-mm) > Go baíram /beram/.

[80] This verb probably came into this class in Germanic times since a PIE /a/-/ō/ ablaut would be unusual.

[81] The derivation is *bʰérōu (2 1ST SS) > *bérōu (5a DIPH SHORTENING) > *bérou (6b o-TO- a) > *bérau (7a ai/au-MONOPH) > Go baíráu.

[82] The derivation of the two forms is *bʰérois and *bʰéroit (2 1ST SS, 3 VERNER) > *béroiz *béroið (6b o-TO- a) > *béraiz *béraið (7a ai/au-MONOPH) > *bérɛ̄z *bérɛ̄ð (8a MORA LOSS) > *bérɛ̄z *bérɛ̄ (9b CONT OBSTR DEVOICING) > Go baíráis and baírái /bérɛ̄/.

[83] The derivation is *bʰéroimē (2 1ST SS, 6b o-TO- a) > *béraimē. (7a ai/au-MONOPH, 8a MORA LOSS) > *bérɛ̄me (9c e -TO- a) > Go baíráima.

[84] The derivation is *bʰeroint (2 1ST SS, 3 VERNER , 6b o-TO- a, 7a ai/au-MONOPH) > *bérɛ̄nd (8a MORA LOSS) > *bérɛ̄n (-a added from the 1 plural) > Go baíráina.

[85] The PIE ending for both strong and weak verbs is *-e. Through regular phonological change the strong and weak endings differ in Gothic. The derivations are *bʰére and *kousjé (PIE 3.1.2f SIEVERS applying as a synchronic rule) → *bʰére *kousijé (2 1ST SS) > *bére *housijé (4a GMC STRESS applying early in East Germanic) > *bére *hóusije (6b o-TO- a, 7a ai/au-MONOPH) > *bére *hɔ̄́sije (8a MORA LOSS) > *bér *hɔ̄́sij (reinterpretation of /ij/ as /ī/) > Go baír and háusei.

[86] The PIE form consists of the stem *bʰero- plus the 3 singular ending *-t plus a common imperative ending *-ō plus the particle *-u.

[87] The derivation is *bʰérotai (2 1ST SS, 3 VERNER) > *béroðai (6b o-TO-a) > *béraðai (7a ai/au-MONOPH) > *béraðɛ̄ (8a MORA LOSS) > *béraðe (9c e -TO- a) > Go baírada [béraða].

[88] The particle *-u was probably added in later Germanic but pre-Gothic times. The derivation is *bʰéroitai (2 1ST SS, 3 VERNER) > *béroiðai (6b o-TO- a) > *béraiðai (7a ai/au-MONOPH) > *bérɛ̄ðɛ̄ (8a MORA LOSS) > *bérɛ̄ðe (9c e-TO-a) > *bérɛ̄ða (addition of the particle *-u) > *bérɛ̄ðau (7a ai/au-MONOPH applying as a persistent phon cond rule) > Go baíráidau [bérɛ̄ðɔ̄].

[89] The derivation of the Old High German form bāri 'you carried' is as follows: *bʰḗres (2 1ST SS, 3 VERNER) > *bḗrez (7b 1ST UMLAUT, NW Germanic version) > *bḗriz (NW Germanic changes of /ē/-TO- /ā/ and deletion of word-final /z/) > OHGerm bāri.

[90] The derivations are *bʰērwé and *bʰēr̥̥nt (2 1ST SS) > *bērwé *bēr̥nθ (4a GMC STRESS, 6c SYL SON) > *bḗrwe *bḗrunθ (8a MORA LOSS) > *bḗrw *bḗrun (PIE 3.1.2c i-j/u-w ALT applying as a persistent synchronic rule) > Go bēru and bērun.

[91] As a result of the early East Germanic stress shift of change 4a GMC STRESS, 8a MORA LOSS could apply at least twice word-finally to this form. Hence the derivation *nositḗt (2 1ST SS) > *nosiθḗθ (4a GMC STRESS applying early in East Germanic) > *nósiθēθ (3 VERNER) > *nósiðēð (6b o-TO- a) > *násiðēð (8a MORA LOSS applying early to a word-final segment in an unstressed syllable which itself is preceded by an unstressed syllable) > *násiðē (8a MORA LOSS reapplying for a time as a persistent rule) > *násiðe (9c e-TO-a) > Go nasida [násiða].

[92] In the other Germanic languages the forms consist of the root plus -ið- (not -iðēð- as in Gothic) plus the strong verb endings noted above. The Gothic conjugation may have been influenced by the verb *dēðum 'we did' in 6.1.4.1 above.

[93] The NW Germanic languages have the reflex of the ending *-ī without the Go -ɔ̄ as in OHGerm bāri 'I carried'. The Go -ɔ̄ was probably taken from the present subjunctive paradigm (6.2.1.2). If so, the derivation was *bʰērī́m (2 1ST SS) > *bērī́m (4a GMC STRESS applying early in East Germanic) > *bḗrīm (7c NASAL LOSS) > *bḗrī (8a MORA LOSS) > *bḗri (addition of 1sg subj *-au from earlier *-ōu) > *bḗriau (PIE 3.1.2c i-j/u-w ALT remaining in the grammar as a synchronic rule) → *bḗrjau (9g LATER ai/au-MONOPH) > Go bērjáu /bḗrjɔ̄/.

[94] The derivation is *ésmi (1c s-z RULE) > *ézmi (7b 1ST UMLAUT) > *ízmi (5c MS CHANGES) > *ímmi (8a MORA LOSS) > *ímm (1a GEM C SIMP, remaining in the grammar as a persistent phon cond rule) → Go im.

[95] The derivation is *s+mé (8a MORA LOSS, replacement of *s- by *si- and adjunction of the past ending *-um) > *sium (9f j-INSERTION) > Go sijum.

[96] The derivation is *sentí (3 VERNER) > *sendí (4a GMC STRESS) > *séndi (7b 1ST UMLAUT) > *síndi (8a MORA LOSS) > Go sind.

[97] The 2nd person forms are also used as imperatives.

Chapter 3

Latin

I Introduction

The stages usually posited in the development of Latin as in Kieckers (1960: 1: 8) or Safarewicz (1969: 272) are these:

450–100 BC:	Old Latin (OLat)
100 BC–0 AD	Classical Latin
0–100 AD:	"Silver" Latin
200 AD on:	Early Romance developing later into languages such as Italian, French, Spanish, Portuguese and Romanian.

In this chapter we consider the changes into the Classical Latin (which we refer to merely as "Latin") of ca. 0 AD. We assume the changes date from ca. 3000 BC when the pre-Italic dialect from which Latin eventually emerged began its separation from PIE.

Perhaps more than any of the other IE languages considered here (aside from Hittite), Latin accepted numerous lexical items from several other Indo-European and non-Indo-European languages. Italic languages which have contributed to the Latin lexicon are Faliscan (usually cited as the dialect closest to Latin), Sabine, Oscan and Umbrian. Non-Italic Indo-European languages contributing to the Latin lexicon are Celtic to the north and Greek to the south. A non-Indo-European community which affected the history and language of Latin was Etruscan located to the immediate north of Roman Latium.

In view of this history of Latin, Palmer (1954: 68) notes that these lexical borrowings into Latin from other languages—often referred to as "rustic" words when they come from Italic languages near to Rome—are analogous to those borrowings into English from the closely related Scandinavian languages. Examples are Scandinavian raid and skirt as opposed to the pure English cognates road and shirt. Analogous examples from Latin cited by Palmer (ibid.) are rustic rōbus 'red' vs. pure Latin ruber 'idem', both from IE *r(e)ud^{h}+os. (In our discussion of several changes such as 1 ASPIR STOPS and 2a LABIOVEL we cite rustic forms.)

Our transcription of Latin follows the usual conventions as described in the phonology (section III below) and exemplified in the Latin text (section VI). We usually do not mark the stress of Latin forms. It is fairly straightforward as described in 6c LATIN STRESS.

II The Changes from PIE into Latin

A Overview of the Changes and their Chronology

The stages are ordered. The changes within each stage may have been in any order or roughly simultaneous.

B The Changes

1 Changes in the Aspirate Stops (ASPIR STOPS)

These changes restructure various lexical items as well as the phonemic inventory of the language and then are dropped as rules from the grammar. They seem to have occurred in two stages: the first was perhaps common Italic, the second peculiar to Latin.

(1) b^h, d^h, g^h, g^{hw} → p^h, t^h, k^h, k^{hw} and then ev → f, θ, x, x^w

(2) f, θ, x, x^w change as follows:

(a)	f	→	b	/ [+segment] —
(b)	θ	→	f	/ ## ___ [+segment] (≠ l)
(c)	θ	→	b	/ (a) r ___
				(b) [+segment] ___ r
				(c) u(:) ___
				(d) [+segment] ___ u(:) or w
				(e) ___ l
(d)	θ	→	d	/ otherwise
(e)	x	→	f	/ ## ___ u(:), possibly also o(:)
(f)	x	→	h	/ ## or V ___ V (≠ u(:))
(g)	x	→	g	/ (a) ŋ ___
				(b) ## ___ l or r
(h)	x	→	w	/ [+segment] ___ u(:) otherwise

That is, (1) the PIE voiced aspirated stops eventually become the corresponding voiceless continuants. (2a) /f/ becomes /b/ word-internally; otherwise it remains /f/. (2b) /θ/ generally becomes /f/ word-initially except if followed by /l/. (2c) /θ/ becomes /d/ in the other instances noted. (2d) Otherwise, /θ/ becomes /d/. (2e) /x/ becomes /f/ word-initially before /u(:)/ or /o(:)/; (2f) it becomes /h/ word-initially or following a vowel and preceding any vowel except /u(:)/; (2g) it becomes /g/ after the nasal /ŋ/ or word-initially before /l/ or /r/. And (2h) word-internal /x/ becomes /w/ before /u(:)/. (The /x^w/resulting from ASPIR STOPS 1 is changed to /f/ and /g^w/ by 2a LABIOVEL below.)

E.g., (1) PIE 1sg *b^herō 'carry' > Lat ferō; (2a) PIE nom sg fem *neb^{h}ulā 'cloud' > Lat nebula; (2b) PIE nom sg masc *d^hūmos 'fume' (ASPIR STOPS) > *fūmos (4c UNSTRESSED V) > Lat fūmus; (2c) PIE 1sg *jud^{h}ējō 'command' (ASPIR STOPS) > *jubējō (7b j/w-CHANGES) > *jubēō (81 V̄V-TO-VV) > Lat jubeō, PIE nom sg neut *stad^{h}lom 'stable' (ASPIR STOPS, ev) > Lat stabulum. (2d) PIE nom sg masc adj *med^{h}jos 'central' (ASPIR STOPS) > *medjos (4c UNSTRESSED V) > *medjus (7b j/w-CHANGES) > Lat medius. (2e) PIE 1sg *g^hundō 'pour' > Lat fundō; also possibly PIE 1sg *g^howējō 'favor' (ev) > Lat foveō. (2f) PIE nom sg masc *g^homos 'earth' (ASPIR STOPS) > *homos (4c UNSTRESSED V) > *homus (7c o(:)-TO-u(:)) > Lat humus; PIE 1sg *weg^{h}ō 'travel' > Lat vehō /wéhō/. (2g) PIE 1sg pres *ling^{h}ō */ling^{h}ō/ 'lick' > Lat lingō, PIE 1sg deponent *g^hrad^{h}jō+r 'I step' (ASPIR STOPS) > *gradjōr (7b j/w-CHANGES) > *gradiōr (8f WORD-FINAL SHORT) > Lat gradior. (2h) PIE nom sg masc u-class (later i-class) adj *mreg^h+us 'short' (ASPIR STOPS) > *mrewus (2c PHONOTACTICS, ev) > Lat brevis /brewis/.

Palmer (1954: 229) notes the possibility that /h/ resulting from ASPIR STOPS may have in some instances been deleted word-internally during the 200's BC. E.g., PIE nom sg masc *ne+g^hemō 'no one' (ASPIR STOPS 1 and 2f) > *neemō = (nēmō in the same declension as the noun homō 'man') > Lat nēmō. Another example is PIE 1sg *dē+g^hab^{h}ējō 'un-have, owe' (ASPIR STOPS) > *dēhabējō (purported /h/-deletion) > *dēabējō (7b j/w-CHANGES) > *dēabēō (81 V̄V-TO-VV) > *dēabeō (6c LATIN STRESS, applying as a persistent synchronic rule) > *dḗabeō (8i V-CONTRACT) > Lat dēbeō. (Note here the necessary chronology ASPIR STOPS > 8i V-CONTRACT.) A similar example is PIE 1sg *dis+g^hab^{h}ējō 'sort out' (ASPIR STOPS) > *dis+habējō (purported /h/-Deletion) > *disabējō (3c ITALIC STRESS) > *dísabējō (3d s-TO-r: note the necessary chronology ASPIR STOPS > /h/-Deletion > 3d s-TO-r) > *dírabējō (4c UNSTRESSED V) > *díribējō (6c LATIN STRESS, 7b j/w-CHANGES, 81 V̄V-TO-VV) > Lat diribeō /diríbeō/. If /h/-Deletion did in fact occur, then graphemic <h> in a form like vehō 'travel' may have been retained only as a marker of a morpheme boundary.

There are numerous words in the Latin lexicon borrowed from the rustic dialects which have undergone their own particular versions of ASPIR STOPS 2. Examples are these: PIE nom sg fem *b^{h}ab^{h}ā 'bean' > Lat faba and borrowed haba; PIE nom sg masc *r(o)ud^{h}ros 'red' (ev) > Lat ruber and borrowed rūfus; PIE nom sg *g^{h}aidos 'goat' > Lat haedus and borrowed faedus; PIE nom sg neut *g^{h}r̥zd^{h}ejom 'barley' (ev) > Lat hordeum and borrowed fordeum; PIE nom sg *g^{h}asenā 'sand' Lat harena and Sabine fasena; and PIE nom sg masc i-class *g^{h}ostis 'enemy' > Lat hostis and Faliscan fostis. Another possible rustic borrowing is Lat anser 'goose' < PIE *g^{h}anser instead of the expected **hanser. (Kent 1940: 56 believes the word "...lost the *h* by the influence of *anas*, a similar bird name with initial vowel...")

Finally we note the following relative chronologies. (a) PIE nom sg masc *g^{h}lad^{h}ros 'bald, smooth' (ASPIR STOPS) > *glabros (4b SYNCOPE) > *glabers (2c PHONOTACTICS applying as a persistent synchronic rule) > Lat glaber. The sequence must be ASPIR STOPS > 4b SYNCOPE; otherwise the form would be Lat **glader. (b) PIE nom sg fem *wid^{h}ewā 'widow' (ASPIR STOPS) > *widewā (5a e-TO-o) > *widowā (6b ei/ou-CHANGES) > *widūā (81 V̄V-TO-VV) > Lat viduā /wíduā/. The sequences must be ASPIR STOPS > 5a e-TO-o and ASPIR STOPS > 6b ei/ou-CHANGES. Otherwise the form would be Lat **vibua **/wíbua/. (c) PIE nom sg masc *lond^{h}wos 'loin' (ASPIR STOPS) > *lonbwos (2c PHONOTACTICS lb Nasal assimilation) > *lombwos (7b j/w-CHANGES) > *lombos (7c o(:)-TO-u(:) > Lat lumbus. Here ASPIR STOPS must precede 7b j/w-CHANGES. Otherwise the Lat form would be **lundus.

2a Changes in the Labiovelar Consonants (LABIOVEL)

These changes restructure various lexical items and the phonemic inventory of the language and then are dropped as rules from the grammar.

(a)	k^w, g^w	→	k, g /___ [-vocalic]
(b)	k^w	→	k /___ u(:) and later ___ u(:), o(:)
(c)	g^w, x^w	→	w / V ___ V
	g^w, x^w	→	gw / ŋ ___
	g^w	→	w /## ___ V
	x^w	→	f /## ___
			/ ___ r

That is, (a) /k^w/ and /g^w/ lose their labiality before any nonvocalic segment. (b) /k^w/ becomes /k/ before /u(:)/ and later before /u(:)/ and /o(:)/ as well. This is a case of a rule persisting synchronically and then increasing its original domain of application. (Kent 1940: 122 notes that /k^w/ is first delabialized before /u(:)/ in Italic and then later in OLat before /o(:)/ as well.) (c) /g^w/ and /x^w/ become /w/ intervocalically and bisegmental /gw/ after /n/, i.e. [ŋ]/. /g^w/ becomes /w/ word-initially before a vowel; and /x^w/ becomes /f/ word-initially or if preceding an /r/.

E.g., (a) PIE nom sg *sok^{w}jos 'friend, follower' (LABIOVEL) > *sokjos (4c UNSTRESSED V) > *sokjus (7c j/w-CHANGES) > Lat socius /sókius/. The chronology must be LABIOVEL > 7c j/w-CHANGES; otherwise the Lat form would be **soquius **/sók^{w}ius/. PIE nom sg masc i-class adj *g^{w}rawis 'heavy' (LABIOVEL) > Lat gravis /gráwis/. PIE nom sg *ag^{w}nos 'lamb' (LABIOVEL) > *agnos (2c PHONOTACTICS (2b) Nasal clusters) > *aŋnos (4c UNSTRESSED V) > Lat agnus /áŋnus/.

(b) PIE adv *nē+kʷudʰi 'nowhere' (1 ASPIR STOPS) > nēkʷubi (LABIOVEL) > Lat nēcubi /nḗkubi/; PIE nom sg *kʷolos 'distaff' (ev) > Lat colus. The /kʷ/ was sometimes restored analogically as in Lat linquō /linkʷō/ 'I leave' < PIE *linkʷ+ō. Here one would expect Lat **lincō **/linkō/; however the /kʷ/ was restored from forms in the paradigm like the PIE 3sg pres *linkʷeti (ev) > Lat linquit /linkʷit/ where the /kʷ/ would have occurred.

(c) PIE 1sg *dʰeigʷō 'fasten' (1 ASPIR STOPS) > *feigʷō (LABIOVEL) > *feiwō (6b ei/ou-CHANGES) > OLat fīvō /fī́wō/, PIE acc sg *snigʰʷm̥ 'snow' (1 ASPIR STOPS) > *snixʷm̥ (LABIOVEL) > *sniwm̥ (2c PHONOTACTICS) *niwm̥ (2d SYL SON) > Lat nivem /níwem/. PIE nom sg masc adj *nogʷedos 'nude' (LABIOVEL) > *nowedos (4b SYNCOPE) > *nowdos (PIE 3.1.2c i-j/u-w ALT applying as a synchronic rule) → *noudos (4c UNSTRESSED V) > *noudus (6b ei/ou-CHANGES) > Lat nūdus. PIE nom sg Vn-class neut *ongʷen 'salve' = *[oŋgʷen] (LABIOVEL) > *ongwen (7c o(:)-TO-u(:)) > Lat unguen /úngwen/. PIE 1sg *gʷem+j+ō 'come' (LABIOVEL, ev) > Lat veniō /wéniō/. PIE nom sg masc adj *gʰʷormos 'warm' (1 ASPIR STOPS) > *xʷormos (LABIOVEL) > *formos (4c UNSTRESSED V) > Lat formus. PIE nom pl *negʰʷrōnes 'kidneys' (1 ASPIR STOPS) > *nexʷrōnes (LABIOVEL) > OLat nefrōnes.

Our formulation of the LABIOVEL change assumes the prior application of 1 ASPIR STOPS. We assume this chronology because 1 ASPIR STOPS is general Italic while LABIOVEL occurs in various versions in the various Italic dialects. E.g., Oscan kombened 'convened' vs. Lat convēnit, both from PIE *kom+gʷēm+et. There are also rustic borrowings in Lat from dialects which have undergone their own labiovelar changes which differ from 2a LABIOVEL, the Lat version. E.g., PIE nom sg *gʷōus 'cow' > Lat bōs instead of the expected **vōs **/wōs/. Another possible rustic borrowing is Lat lupus 'wolf'. One would expect **lucus from PIE *lukʷos.

2b Changes in the PIE Long Diphthongs (LONG DIPH)

This change restructures various lexical items and endings and then is dropped as a rule from the grammar.

$$\text{(a)}\quad \begin{bmatrix} \text{ēi, ēu} \\ \text{?ōi, ōu} \end{bmatrix} \rightarrow \begin{bmatrix} \text{ē} \\ \text{ō} \end{bmatrix} \;/\; \_\_ \begin{Bmatrix} \#\# \\ \text{m} \end{Bmatrix}$$

$$\text{(b)}\quad \text{Otherwise}\qquad \bar{\text{V}}\text{i, }\bar{\text{V}}\text{u} \rightarrow \text{Vi, Vu}$$

That is, (a) the long diphthongs /ēi, ēu/ and possibly /ōi/ and /ōu/ become /ē/ and /ō/ respectively if word-final or preceding an /m/. (b) Otherwise, the remaining PIE long diphthongs /āi, āu/ etc. are shortened.

E.g., (a) PIE nom sg fem *dʰēi+men+ā 'one who suckles, a woman' (1 ASPIR STOPS, Long Diph) > *fēmenā (4c UNSTRESSED V, ev) > Lat fēmina. PIE acc sg fem *rēim 'thing' > Lat rēm; PIE acc sg fem *gʷōu+m 'cow' (ev and under rustic borrowing) > Lat bōs. PIE *oktōu '8' > Lat octō. (b) PIE dat pl masc *wirōis 'men' (Long Diph) > *wirois (7a ai/oi-TO-ae/oe) > *wiroes (8h oe-CHANGES) > Lat virīs /wírīs/. PIE dat pl fem *terrāis 'lands' (Long Diph) > *terrais (4c UNSTRESSED V) > *terreis (6b ei/ou-CHANGES) > Lat terrīs. (Note the chronology LONG DIPH> 4c UNSTRESSED V, 6b ei/ou-CHANGES, 7a ai/oi-TO-ae/oe and 8h oe-CHANGES. The short diphthongs arising from the LONG DIPH change undergo these later changes just as the original short diphthongs do.) Also PIE nom sg masc adj *nāu+bʰr̥g+os 'shipwrecked' vs. nom sg fem i-class noun *nāu+is 'ship' (PIE 3.1.2c i-j/u-w ALT applying synchronically) → *nāubʰr̥gos and *nāwis (1 ASPIR STOPS) > *nāufr̥gos and *nāwis (Long Diph) > *naufr̥gos and *nāwos (2d SYL SON, 7c o(:)-TO-u(:)) > Lat naufragus and nāvis /nā́wis/. PIE nom sg masc *dʰēi+l+jos 'suckling, son' (1 ASPIR STOPS) > *fēiljos (Long Diph) > *feiljos (6b ei/ou-CHANGES) > *fīljos (7b j/w-CHANGES) > *fīlios (7c o(:)-TO-u(:)) > Lat fīlius.

2c Various Phonotactic Conditions (PHONOTACTICS)

A salient characteristic of Latin is the presence in the grammar of a number of phonotactic rules. We cite fifteen of these below. These rules restructure sequences of segments whenever they come into contact through prefixing, suffixing, compounding or through word-internal morpheme structure. The first four of them which we cite are inherited from PIE; the last eleven seem to be post-PIE innovations of Italic or of Latin. All of them, whether inherited or innovative, remain in the grammar as persistently applying morph cond or phon cond rules.

We give them in the following order.

(1) Rules inherited from PIE.
(1a) Geminate simplification (involving 2 segments).
(1b) Nasal assimilation (involving 2 segments).
(1c) Obstruent cluster voicing and devoicing (involving 2 segments).
(1d) "Osthoff's Law" (involving 3 segments).
(2) Innovations of Italic or Latin.
(2a) l-clusters (involving 2 segments).
(2b) Nasal clusters (involving 2 segments).
(2c) Obstruent assimilation (involving 2 segments).
(2d) r-clusters (involving 2 segments).
(2e) s-clusters (involving 2 segments).
(2f) t-clusters (involving 2 segments).
(2g) s-clusters (involving 3 segments).
(2h) Sonorant-initial clusters (involving 3 segments).
(2i) s-clusters (involving 4 segments).
(2j) l-final clusters (involving 5 segments).
(2k) s-clusters (involving 5 segments).

(1) Rules Inherited from PIE

(la) Geminate Simplification (Involving 2 Segments)

$$C_a\,C_a \rightarrow C \;/\; \left.\begin{matrix}\#\# \\ C\end{matrix}\right\} \;\_\_\; \text{or} \;\_\_\; \left\{\begin{matrix}\#\# \\ C\end{matrix}\right.$$

where $C_a\,C_a$ = two identical consonants.

That is, geminate consonants are simplified word-initially or if preceded by another consonant; or if word-final or followed by another consonant. E.g., PIE nom sg *pēd+s 'foot' (PHONOTACTICS 1c Obstruent cluster voicing and devoicing) > *pēts (PHONOTACTICS 2f t-clusters) > *pēss (PHONOTACTICS la Geminate simplification, reapplying as a synchronic rule) > Lat pēs.

While retaining the original geminate simplification change la as a persistent rule, later Latin tended to extend it to some additional environments such as these:

(a) $ss \rightarrow s \;/\; \bar{V}\,\_\_$

(b) $C_aC_a \rightarrow C_a \;/\; \_\_\; [V, +stress]$

where C_aC_a = mm, rr and occasionally other geminates as well.

That is, (a) /ss/ becomes /s/ after a long vowel; and (b) some geminates are simplified if preceding a stressed vowel.

E.g., PIE perf part *wid+tos (possibly *weid+tos) 'seen' and *kad+tos 'fallen' (PHONOTACTICS lc Obstruent cluster voicing and devoicing) > *wittos and *kattos (PHONOTACTICS 2f t-clusters) > *wissos and *kassos (7c o(:)-TO-u(:)) > *wissus and *kassus (8e LACHMANN) > *wīssus and *kāssus (PHONOTACTICS la Geminate simplification applying as a persistent rule) > Lat vīsus /wī́sus/ and cāsus /kā́sus/. Note that the chronology must be 3d s-TO-r > PHONOTACTICS la expansion: otherwise Lat **vīrus and **cārus would occur. Additional examples are the earlier forms *ob+míttō 'let go', *currūlis 'pertaining to a chariot', *offéllā 'morsel' and *opportū́nus 'opportune' (PHONOTACTICS lb Nasal assimilation) > *ommíttō, *currū́lis, *offéllā, *opportū́nus (PHONOTACTICS la Geminate simplification) > later Lat omittō, curūlis, ofella and oportūnus.

(1b) Nasal Assimilation (Involving 2 Segments)

[C, +nasal] [C, +obstruent, αfeatures] → [C, +nasal, αfeatures] same
1 2 1 3 2

That is, a nasal consonant has the same place of articulation as a following obstruent, provided no morpheme boundary intervenes between the two. E.g., Lat mandō 'entrust', ambō 'both' and quīnque [kʷīŋkʷe] '5' as opposed to forms like **mamdō, **anbo or **quīmque.

This rule, inherited from PIE, is extended in Latin to apply over at least one morpheme boundary, namely that between a prefix and a root. E.g., earlier *kom+stringō 'bind together', *en+bellis 'unwarlike' and *en+gnōtos 'unknown' (ev) > Lat constringō [konstríŋgō], imbellis and ignōtus [iŋnṓtus].

In some instances the nasal does not assimilate over certain morpheme boundaries. In such cases an appropriate obstruent is inserted to prevent the assimilation. E.g., the past part sūm+p+tus 'taken up' (pres sūm+ō) where the /m/ is retained and /p/ inserted; nom sg neut *eks+em+l+om 'example' (ev) > exemplum; and nom sg hiems 'winter' sometimes written hiemps (gen sg hiem+is).

(1c) Obstruent Cluster Voicing and Devoicing (Involving 2 Segments)

[C, +obstruent] [C, +obstruent, αvoiced] → [C, +obstruent, αvoiced] same
1 2 1 3 2

That is, consonants in obstruent clusters are uniformly voiced or voiceless depending on the final consonant in the cluster.

E.g., PIE nom sg *rēg+s 'king' > Lat rēx /rēks/; PIE nom sg *ni+sd+os 'a sit-in, nest' (PHONOTACTICS lc) > *nizdos (PHONOTACTICS 2g s-clusters) > *nīdos (7c o(:)-TO-u(:)) > Lat nīdus. By Latin times this rule can apply over prefix-root morpheme boundaries as in *dis+gerō 'separate' > *dizgerō > Lat dīgerō. Also PIE *ad+tendō 'attend' (PHONOTACTICS 1c) > Lat attendō. (Note that PHONOTACTICS 2f t-clusters does not apply to this form to produce **assendō. This indicates that PHONOTACTICS 1c continues to apply persistently after PHONOTACTICS 2f t-clusters has become morphologically conditioned.) Also PIE 1sg pres *apo+deukō 'remove' (4b SYNCOPE) > *ap+deukō (PHONOTACTICS 1c applying as a persistent rule) > *abdeukō (6b ei/ou-CHANGES) > Lat abdūcō /abdū́kō/. The prefix was then restructured to underlying /ab-/ as indicated in spellings like <absolvō> 'absolve'. Leumann (1977: 194) notes the occurrence of spellings like <apsolvō> instead of the more usual morphophonemic spelling <ab->.

(1d) "Osthoff's Law" (Involving 3 Segments)

[V, +long] → [-long] / ___ [C, +sonorant] [C, +obstruent]

That is, a long vowel is shortened if followed by a sonorant consonant /l, m, n or r/ followed in turn by an obstruent consonant. (This may or may not have been in PIE. See on this Sihler 1995: 58.) E.g., PIE nom sg masc adj *āridos 'arid' vs. nom sg masc noun *āridōs 'ardor' (4b SYNCOPE) > *āridos vs. *ārdōs (PHONOTACTICS 1d Osthoff's Law applying as a persistent synchronic rule) > *āridos vs. *ardōs (3d s-TO-r applying analogously from inflected forms) > *āridos vs. *ardōr (7c o(:)-TO-u(:), 8f WORD-FINAL SHORT) > Lat āridus vs. ardor. Another instance of the synchronic application of PHONOTACTICS 1d Osthoff's Law is the genitive singular of the pres act part /donā+nt+is/ 'giving' (PHONOTACTICS 1d) → Lat donantis.

The later Italic and Latin rules are as follows.

(2) Innovations of Italic or Latin

(2a) l-Clusters (Involving 2 Segments)

This rule has three parts.

(a)

l	C	or	C	l	→	l	l
1	2		1	2		1	2

for the sequences /ld, ln, lr, ls, dl, nl, rl/

(b)

k or t	l	→	k u l	/ [+segment] ___
b	l		b u l	
g	l		g u l	
1	2		1 3 2	

(c)

t or d	l	→	Ø l /	## ___
1	2		1 2	

That is, (2aa) the sequences /l/ plus the enumerated consonants or the consonants plus /l/ become/ll/. (2ab) The segments change word-internally as shown and a /u/ is inserted between the obstruent and /l/. (2ac) /tl/ and /dl/ become /l/ word-initially. E.g., (2aa) PIE 1sg pres *saldō 'I salt', *tol+n+ō 'I bear up' > Lat sallō, tollō; PIE inf *wel+si 'want' (ev) > Lat velle /wélle/, PIE 1sg dep *ad+labōr 'glide toward' (PHONOTACTICS) > *allabōr (8f WORD-FINAL SHORT) > Lat allabor, PIE nom sg *korōn+lā 'wreath' (ev) > Lat corōlla, PIE nom sg *puer+lā 'girl' (ev) > Lat puella. (2ab) PIE nom sg *pōt+l+om 'cup' > OLat pōclom as well as pōcolom (7c o(:)-TO-u(:)) > Lat pōculum; PIE nom sg *stad^h+l+om 'stable' (1 ASPIR STOPS) > *stablom (PHONOTACTICS) > *stabulom (ev) > Lat stabulum. Note here the relative chronology 1 ASPIR STOPS > 2c PHONOTACTICS 2a. Finally (2ac) PIE *tlatjom 'Latium' (PHONOTACTICS) > *latjom (7b j/w-CHANGES, 7c o(:)-TO-u(:)) > Lat Latium. Note the occurrence of the Umbrian gen sg Tlatie 'of Latium'. PIE nom sg masc *dlong^{h}os 'long' (ev) > Lat longus.

Consider the following derivations with regard to relative chronology. PIE nom pl *g^{h}rad^h+el+āi 'stilts' (1 ASPIR STOPS, 2b Long Diph) > *gradelai (4b SYNCOPE) > *gradlai (PHONOTACTICS 2ac applying as a persistent synchronic rule) > *grallai (7a ai/oi-TO-ae/oe) > Lat grallae. However, the form balinea 'baths' can appear as balnea by 4b SYNCOPE to which PHONOTACTICS 2a does not apply. This may indicate that PHONOTACTICS 2a applied optionally in some instances.

(2b) Nasal Clusters (Involving 2 Segments)

This rule consists of two parts.

(a)

[C, +obstruent , –continuant]	[C, +nasal]	→	[C, +sonorant, +nasal]	same
1	2		1 3	2

(b) $\begin{pmatrix} \text{n m} \\ \text{n n} \end{pmatrix} \rightarrow \begin{pmatrix} \text{m same} \\ \text{ŋ same} \end{pmatrix}$

1 2   1 2

That is, (a) an obstruent stop followed by a nasal consonant (generally) becomes a nasal retaining the place-of-articulation features of the original obstruent. (b) The sequences of nasal consonants are modified as shown.

E.g., (2ba) PIE nom sg *swepnos 'sleep' (PHONOTACTICS 2ba) > *swemnos (5a e-TO-o) > *swomnos (7b j/w-CHANGES) > *somnos (7c o(:)-TO-u(:)) > Lat somnus; PIE nom sg *atnos 'year' (ev) > Lat annus; PIE nom sg masc adj *deknos 'suitable' (PHONOTACTICS 2ba) > *deŋnos (7c o(:)-TO-u(:), 8c e-TO-i) > Lat dignus /diŋnus/; PIE nom sg masc adj *gnātos 'born' (ev) > Lat gnātus /ŋnātus/; PIE nom sg neut *sek+ment+om 'segment' (ev) > segmentum /seŋmentum/; and PIE nom sg neut *skab^hnom 'bench' (1 ASPIR STOPS) > *skabnom (PHONOTACTICS 2ba, ev) > Lat scamnum. On occasion PHONOTACTICS 2ba applies differently than expected, e.g. earlier nom sg fem *flag+mā 'flame' (ev) > Lat flamma instead of the expected **flagma **/flaŋma/. And often compounds which have undergone PHONOTACTICS 2ba are reformed. E.g., early inf *ab+negāre 'deny' (PHONOTACTICS 2ba) > later amnegāre, still later reformed to abnegāre again.

(2bb) Early nom sg masc i-class adjs *en+mortālis 'immortal' and *en+nōbilis 'ignoble' (PHONOTACTICS 2bb, ev) > Lat immortālis and ignōbilis /iŋnṓbilis/.

Finally, after long vowels and diphthongs, two-nasal sequences produced by PHONOTACTICS 2b tend to be simplified (probably by an extension of PHONOTACTICS rule la Geminate simplification, which remains in the grammar as a synchronic rule): e.g. PIE nom sg neut *leuk+mn̥ 'light' and *eks+āg+mn̥ 'a testing' (2d SYL SON) > *leukmen and *eksāgmen (PHONOTACTICS 2b) > *leuŋmen and *eksāŋmen (PHONOTACTICS la) > *leumen and *eksāmen (5a e-TO-a, 6b ei/ou-CHANGES) > Lat lūmen and exāmen.

(2c) Obstruent Assimilation (Involving 2 Segments)

[C, +obstruent] + [C, +obstruent, αfeatures] → [C, +obstruent, αfeatures] same same
1 2 3 1 4 2 3

where + (2) is a morpheme boundary between a prefix and a root and where the CC sequences are (assuming the prior application of PHONOTACTICS lc Obstruent cluster voicing and devoicing) the following: /bg, dg, tf, pk$^{(w)}$, tp, tk$^{(w)}$, pf, tf, sf/.

That is, the first obstruent assimilates to the second in the two-obstruent sequences listed above. E.g., PIE 1sg *sub+gesō 'put under' (PHONOTACTICS 2c) > *suggesō (3d s-TO-r) > Lat suggerō; *ad+gredjōr 'attack' (PHONOTACTICS 2c) > *aggredjōr (7b j/w-CHANGES) > *aggrediōr (8f WORD-FINAL SHORT) > Lat aggredior; early *ad+ferō 'carry to' (PHONOTACTICS lc Obstruent cluster voicing and devoicing) > *atferō (PHONOTACTICS 2c) > Lat afferō. Similar derivations involving PHONOTACTICS 1c are these: PIE 1sg *ob+kaidō 'kill' (PHONOTACTICS) > *okkaidō (3c ITALIC STRESS) > *ókkaidō (4c UNSTRESSED V) > *ókkīdō (6c LATIN STRESS) > Lat occīdō /okkī́dō/; PIE *tod+per 'speedily' (ev) > Lat topper; and the PIE 1sg forms *ad+kapjō 'receive', *sub+d^hakjō 'suffice', *ek+b^herō 'carry out', *dis+b^herō 'differ' (ev) > Lat accipiō, sufficiō, efferō and differō.

In classical and post-classical times PHONOTACTICS 2c expands its domain in two ways: (a) it can apply to other obstruent sequences; (b) it can apply over other types of morpheme boundary beside that between prefix and root. E.g., (a) Latin has the verb subcumbō /supkúmbō/ 'lie down' alongside later /sukkúmbō/; likewise PIE 1sg *sub+saljō 'jump up' (ev) > Lat subsiliō /supsíliō/ alongside later sussiliō. Also, Lat adverbium /adwerbium/ 'adverb' and later, Italian avverbio. (b) Lat 3sg perf scripsit

/skrip+s+it/ 'wrote', perf part conduc+t+us 'conducted' (ev by PHONOTACTICS 2c expanding to apply over the morpheme boundary between root and suffix) > Italian scrisse and condotto.

(2d) r-Clusters (Involving 2 Segments)

There are two parts to this rule.

(a)		rs	→	rr	/ [+segment] ___
		sr	→	br	"
		mr	→	rr	"
	optional	nr	→	rr	"
	optional	dr	→	rr	"
	optional	dr	→	tr	"
(b)		sr	→	fr	/ ## ___
		mr	→	br	"

That is, the sequences with /r/ are changed as described (a) word-internally and (b) word-initially.

E.g., (2da) PIE 1sg *torsējō 'burn' (PHONOTACTICS) > *torrējō (7b j/w-CHANGES) > *torrēō (81 V̄V-TO-VV) > Lat torreō; early nom sg masc i-class adj *funes+r+is 'funereal' > Lat funebris; PIE 1sg *kom+rumpō 'destroy' > Lat corrumpo; PIE 1sg *en+regō 'irrigate' (PHONOTACTICS) > *erregō (3c ITALIC STRESS) > *érregō (4c UNSTRESSED V) > *érrigō (8c e-TO-i) > Lat irrigō; PIE 1sg *ad+rogō 'misappropriate' > Lat arrogō as well as the later re-formed adrogō; PIE nom sg masc *taidros 'foul' (PHONOTACTICS) > *taitros (4b SYNCOPE: note the necessary chronology PHONOTACTICS 2d > 4b SYNCOPE in order for the correct form to be produced) > *taiter (7a ai/oi-TO-ae/oe) > Lat taeter. However, the /dr/-TO-/tr/ change does not occur in the derivation of earlier *k^{w}adrā+ginta '40' > Lat quadrāginta, not **quatrāginta.

(2db) PIE nom sg masc adj *srīgos 'cold' (ev) > Lat frīgus, PIE nom sg u-class (later i-class) adj *mreg^{h}us 'small' (ev) > Lat brevis /bréwis/.

Under certain circumstances the sequence /rs/ can occur in Lat: e.g., PIE 1sg perf *ard+s+ai 'burned' (PHONOTACTICS 1c Obstruent cluster voicing and devoicing) > *artsai (PHONOTACTICS 2f t-clusters) > *arssai (PHONOTACTICS la Geminate simplification applying as a persistent synchronic rule, ev) > Lat arsī, to which Phonotatics 2d r-clusters does not apply.

(2e) s-Clusters (Involving 2 Segments)

There are two parts to this rule.

(a)	[C, +obstruent]	s or t	→	Ø	same / ## ___
	1	2		1	2
(b)	s [C, +sonorant]		→	Ø	same / ## ___
	1 2			1	2

That is, (a) a word-initial obstruent followed by /s/ or /t/ is deleted; and (b) a word-initial /s/ followed by /l, m, n, r/ is deleted.

E.g., (2ea) PIE nom sg *psab^{h}ulom 'gravel', *ptiljā 'lime tree' (ev) > Lat sabulum, tilia. (2eb) PIE nom sg *snig^{hw}+s 'snow' and *sleimos 'slime' (ev) > Lat nix /niks/ and līmus. Borrowings from Greek do not undergo this change, e.g. the prefix pseudo- 'false'.

(2f) t-Clusters (Involving 2 Segments)

t	+	t or s	→	s	s
1		2		1	2

That is, the sequence /t/ plus a morpheme boundary (usually that between a root and a suffix) plus /t/ or /s/ changes to /ss/.

E.g., PIE perf part wid+tos (possibly *weid+tos) 'seen' (PHONOTACTICS) > *wissos (7c o(:)-TO-u(:)) > *wissus (8e LACHMANN, PHONOTACTICS la Geminate simplification applying as a persistent synchronic rule) > Lat vīsus /wī́sus/; PIE perf part *pat+tos 'suffered', nom sg *pēd+s 'foot' (ev) > Lat passus and pēs. Sometimes the derivational suffix –t is readded: e.g. PIE nom sg u-class masc *aid^{h}+t+us 'heat' (PHONOTACTICS) > *aissus (re-addition of -t, ev) > Lat aestus.

This change remains as a morph cond persistent rule in the grammar of Latin. It applies both diachronically and synchronically to the perfect participle and to the derivational ending shown above. However, it does not apply over the boundary between a prefix and a root. E.g., PIE 1sg *ad+tenējō 'hold to, keep' (PHONOTACTICS 1c Obstruent voicing and devoicing, but not PHONOTACTICS 2f, ev) > Lat attineō, not **assineō.

(2g) s-Clusters (Involving 3 Segments)

(a)

[C, +obstruent]	s	[C, +obstruent , –voiced]	→	Ø	same	same
1	2	3		1	2	3

(b)

V	s	[C, +voiced]	→	V̄	Ø	same
1	2	3		1	2	3

(c)

r	s	t	→	Ø	same	same
1	2	3		1	2	3

(d)

s	k	t	→	same	Ø	same
1	2	3		1	2	3

(e)

s	s	r	→	same	t	same
1	2	3		1	2	3

(f)

s	t	l	→	Ø	Ø	same / ## ___
1	2	3		1	2	3

The last one of these changes occurs only word-initially. (a) In a sequence of obstruent plus /s/ plus voiceless obstruent, the first obstruent is lost. (By PHONOTACTICS 1c Obstruent cluster voicing and devoicing, the first obstruent is also voiceless.) (b) In the sequence vowel plus /s/ plus any voiced consonant (where /s/ is realized as [z] by PHONOTACTICS 1c before a voiced obstruent), the /s/ is deleted and the vowel is lengthened. (c to f) The sequences change as described.

E.g., (2ga) PIE *sekskn̥toi '600' (ev) > Lat sescentī; PIE *sekstjos '6th' (ev) > Latin proper name Sestius (also occurring as Sextius); PIE 1sg pres *aps+portājō 'carry off', *ops+tendō 'show', *sups+kapjō 'take up' (ev) > Lat asportō, ostendō and suscipiō. However, PHONOTACTICS 2ga seems not to affect certain adjectives such as Lat obscūrus 'obscure', not **oscūrus, and obscēnus 'obscene', not **oscēnus.

(2gb) PIE nom sg masc *ni+sd+os 'in-sitting, nest', *k^{w}is+dam 'a certain one', nom sg adj *prismos 'first', 1sg pres *dis+rumpō 'shatter' (ev) > Lat nīdus, quīdam, prīmus and dīrumpō. Another possible example is PIE nom sg fem *pruswīnā 'frost' (PHONOTACTICS 2gb) > *prūwīnā = *prūīnā (81 V̄V-TO-VV, ev) > Lat pruīna. But PHONOTACTICS 2gb does not apply on occasion: e.g., earlier *satis+dō 'give enough, i.e. give bail' (ev) > Lat satisdō, not **satīdō.

(2gc) PIE perf part *tors+tos 'burned' (ev) > Lat tostus. (2gd) PIE perf part *pāsk+tos 'grazed' (ev) > Lat pāstus. (2ge) PIE nom sg neut *rad+trom 'rake' (PHONOTACTICS 1c and 2f) > *rassrom (PHONOTACTICS 2ge, ev) > Lat rastrum. (2gf) OLat stlocus 'place' > Lat locus.

Kent (1940: 126) has noted that our rule PHONOTACTICS 2g for s-clusters was frequently superseded in that "...new groups [of consonants] developed by recomposition...." For example, Lat sexcentī '60' occurs alongside sescentī, the former modeled after Lat sex 'six'. And for some reason Lat dexter /dekster/ 'right' occurs instead of **dester. This may result because of the following chronology: PIE *deksiteros (4b SYNCOPE) > *deksteros to which PHONOTACTICS 2g does not apply since it has already occurred (ev) > Lat dexter.

(2h) Sonorant-Initial Clusters (Involving 3 Segments)

[C, +sonorant]	C	C	→	same	Ø	same
1	2	3		1	2	3

That is, in a sequence of /l, m, n, r/ plus two other consonants, either obstruents or sonorants, the middle consonant is lost.

E.g., PIE nom sg *turb+mā 'troop' (ev) > Lat turma, *lampternā 'lamp' (PHONOTACTICS 2h) > *lamternā (PHONOTACTICS lb Nasal assimilation applying as a persistent synchronic rule, ev) > Lat lanterna, *urknā 'urn' (ev) > Lat urna, PIE perf part *ulk+t+os 'avenged' (ev) > Lat ultus. On occasion PHONOTACTICS 2h does not apply if the deleteable consonant occurs elsewhere in the paradigm, e.g. Lat perf part jūnctus 'joined' from underlying /jung+t+us/ as in the pres jungō 'I join', not **juntus.

(2i) s-Clusters (Involving 4 Segments)

V	C	s	[C, +voiced]	→	V̄	Ø	Ø	same
1	2	3	4		1	2	3	4

That is, in the sequence vowel plus consonant plus /s/ (which is realized as [z] by PHONOTACTICS lc Obstruent cluster voicing and devoicing) plus any voiced consonant, obstruent or sonorant, the vowel is lengthened, the second and third consonants are deleted, and the voiced consonant remains.

E.g., PIE nom pl *seks+wiroi 'committee of six men' (PHONOTACTICS 2i) > *sēwiroi (ev) > Lat sēvirī /sḗwirī/; PIE nom sg *akslā 'wing' (ev) > Lat āla; PIE 1sg *eks+deukō 'lead out', *trans+nō 'swim across' (ev) > Lat ēdūcō and trānō.

Note that PHONOTACTICS 2i is still in the grammar as a persistent rule after 4b SYNCOPE and after 6b ei/ou-CHANGES. PIE 1sg *subs+emō 'take up' (4b SYNCOPE) > *subsmō (PHONOTACTICS 2i) → Lat sūmō; and OLat iouxmentum 'ox' (6b ei/ou-CHANGES) > *jūksmentum (PHONOTACTICS 2i) → Lat jūmentum. Finally, PHONOTACTICS 2i can apply over some word boundaries, e.g. early *aps##deiwōd 'from a god' (ev) > Lat ā deō.

(2j) l-Final Clusters (Involving 5 Segments)

V	n	{s t / t s}		l	→	V̄	Ø	Ø	Ø	same
1	2	3	4	5		1	2	3	4	5

That is, in the sequences shown the initial vowel is lengthened and the next three segments are deleted, which results in the sequence /V̄l/. E.g., PIE nom pl fem *skand+sl+āi 'stairs, ladder' (PHONOTACTICS 1c Obstruent cluster voicing and devoicing) > *skantslāi (PHONOTACTICS 2j) > *skālāi (ev) > Lat scālae. This rule can on occasion apply over word boundaries: early *in##stlokō 'in that place' > Lat īloco.

(2k) s-Clusters (Involving 5 Segments)

s	[C_a, +obstruent]	V	s	[C_a, +obstruent]	→	same	same	same	Ø	same
1	2		3 4	5		1	2	3	4	5

where $C_a(2) = C_a(5)$.

That is, in a sequence /s/ plus obstruent plus vowel plus /s/ plus the same obstruent, the second /s/ is deleted. This rule appears to apply only to reduplicated perfect forms. E.g., PIE 1sg perf *spespondai 'promised' (PHONOTACTICS 2k) > *spepondai (4c UNSTRESSED V) > *spepondei (6b ei/ou-CHANGES) > Lat spepondī.

2d Changes in the Syllabic Sonorants (SYL SON)

These changes restructure various lexical items and endings and then are dropped from the grammar.

(a) l̥, r̥ → ol, or; sometimes al, ar, ra

(b) m̥, n̥ → em, en

That is, the PIE syllabic sonorant consonants leave the described reflexes. The forms in /al/ and /ar/ may be from rustic dialects. E.g.,

(a) PIE nom sg masc i-class adj *ml̥dwis 'gentle' (SYL SON) > *moldwis (2c PHONOTACTICS) > mollwis (7b j/w-CHANGES) > Lat mollis; PIE nom sg fem *pl̥+ejā 'chaff' (SYL SON) > *palejā (7b j/w-CHANGES, ev) > Lat palea; PIE nom sg *b[h]r̥+t+s 'fate' (ev) > Lat fors; PIE nom sg fem Vn-class *kr̥+ō 'meat' (ev) > Lat carō; and PIE nom sg masc adj *nāu+b[h]r̥g+os 'shipwrecked' (ev) > Lat naufragus. Sommer (1977: 45) considers some forms in /ar/ to be from PIE */r̥r/, e.g. purported PIE nom sg *wr̥ros (ev) > Lat varus /warus/ 'pimple'. Note the chronology in PIE *ml̥+jes 'weaker' (SYL SON) > *moljes (3d s-TO-r applying here analogously) > *moljer (7c o(:)-TO-u(:), which must apply after SYL SON, ev) > Lat mulier 'woman'.

(b) PIE *dekm̥ '10' > Lat decem, PIE perf part *tn̥+t+os 'held' (ev) > Lat tentus. PIE perf part *n̥+gnō+t+os 'unknown' (2d SYL SON) > *engnōtos (2c PHONOTACTICS 1b, 2b and la) > *eŋnōtos (8c e-TO-i, which must apply after SYL SON, ev) > Lat ignōtus /iŋnṓtus/.

Sometimes PIE long sonorant consonants are posited as antecedents for certain Latin forms. E.g., PIE nominative singular forms *wl̥̄n+ā 'wool', *gr̥̄n+om 'grain' and *wr̥̄dīk+s 'root' as well as the perf participles *str̥̄+tos 'strewn' and *gn̥̄+tos 'born' (ev) > Lat lāna, grānum, rādīx, strātus and gnātus. However, other antecedents are possible such as *wlānā, *grasnom, *wrādīks; and the perfect participles may have been *str+ā+t+os and *gn+ā+t+os as influenced by ā-class verbs. Sihler (1995: 103) posits an antecedent for grānum with a laryngeal, *gr̥h_2+nom.

3a Changes in Certain Consonants Followed by /j/ (C+j CHANGES).

These changes restructure various forms and then are dropped as rules from the grammar. They seem to have occurred in three chronological stages.

(1)	mj	→	nj	/ V	___
(2a)	d, g or s j 1 2	→	Ø same 1 2	/ ##	___
(2b)	V d, g or s j 1 2 3	→	?V̄ j j 1 2 3		
(3)	Cji	→	Ci		

That is, (1) word-internal /mj/ becomes /nj/. (2a) Word-initial /dj, gj, sj/ become /j/; and at about the same time (2b) word-internal and post-vocalic /dj, gj, sj/ become /jj/ and — possibly — the preceding vowel is lengthened. (3) The word-internal sequence /ji/ becomes /i/. E.g., (1) PIE 1sg pres *g^{w}em+j+ō 'come' (2a LABIOVEL) > *wemjō (C+j CHANGES) > *wenjō (7b j/w-CHANGES) > Lat veniō /wéniō/. Note here the chronology C+j CHANGES > 7b j/w-CHANGES. (2a) OLat gen sg Diovis /djowis/ 'Juppiter, Jove' > Lat Jovis /jowis/. (2b) PIE comp adj *ped+jos 'worse' and *mag+jos 'larger' (C+j CHANGES) > *pējjos, *mājjos (7c o(:)-TO-u(:)) > Lat pēius /pējjus/ and māius /mājjus/. Likewise PIE gen sg *k^{w}os+jos 'whose' (2a LABIOVEL) > *kosjos (C+j CHANGES) > *kōjjos (7c o(:)-TO-u(:)) > Lat cūius /kūjjus/. (3) Later PIE 2sg *kapjis 'seize' > Lat capis.

Leumann (1971: 126) maintains that Lat forms like maius 'more' and eius 'his' (from PIE *es+jos) were in fact pronounced /majjus/ and /ejjus/. If so, then the frequent spellings <mājus> and <ējus> may designate long syllables ending in the double consonant /jj/. Later post-Lat reflexes of these words indicate the possibility of Lat /jj/ in these forms: e.g., Italian peggiō /peǰo/ 'worse' < *pejjo.

3b The Change of /i, u/ to /e, o/ (i/u-TO-e/o)

This change restructures various forms and then is dropped from the grammar.

i, u → e, o / ___ z

That is, /i/ and /u/ are lowered to /e/ and /o/ before a /z/ (which can only arise after stage 1 and before stage 2 of 3d s-TO-r). E.g., PIE 1sg pres *si+sō 'sow' (3d s-TO-r stage 1) > *sizō (i/u-TO-e/o) > *sezō (3d s-TO-r stage 2) > Lat serō; PIE gen sg *kinises 'ash' (3d s-TO-r stage 1) > *kinizes (i/u-TO-e/o) > *kinezes (3d s-TO-r stage 2, 4c UNSTRESSED V) > Lat cineris; PIE 3sg imperf subj *b^{h}u+s+ēt 'will be' (1 ASPIR STOPS) > *fusēt (i/u-TO-e/o, 3d s-TO-r) > *forēt (8f WORD-FINAL SHORT) > foret.

This change seems to have occurred between stages 1 and 2 of 3d s-TO-r. It applies only before /z/, not before /s/ or /r/. E.g., PIE nom sg masc *wiros 'man' and *is 'he' (ev) > Lat vir /wir/ and is, not **ver or **es.

3c The Italic Word-Stress Rule (ITALIC STRESS)

This rule seems to have applied in Italic since it applies in Oscan, Umbrian and early Latin. It remained in the grammar of early Latin until it was replaced by 6c LATIN STRESS, the word-stress rule of classical Latin.

V → [+stress] / ##C_0 ___

That is, word-stress is on the vowel of the first syllable (and the earlier PIE stress was deleted). E.g., PIE 3sg pres *estí 'is' (ITALIC STRESS) > *ésti (4b SYNCOPE) > Lat est; PIE *oktṓu'8' ((2b) Long Diph) > *oktṓ (ITALIC STRESS) > Lat octō /óktō/; PIE 1sg pres *ob+kaidō 'kill' (2c PHONOTACTICS) > *okkaidō (ITALIC STRESS) > *ókkaidō (4c UNSTRESSED V) > *ókkeidō (6b ei/ou-CHANGES) > *ókkīdō (6c LATIN STRESS) > Lat occīdō /okkī́do/.

As noted in Palmer (1954: 212–13) and in Buck (1962: 165), changes like 4b SYNCOPE and 4c UNSTRESSED V presuppose first-syllable stress and as such the prior application of ITALIC STRESS and the later application of 6c LATIN STRESS. E.g., PIE nom sg masc adj *deksiteros 'right' (ITALIC STRESS) > *déksiteros (4b SYNCOPE, 4c UNSTRESSED V) > Lat dexter; early perf part *per+faktos 'perfect' (ITALIC STRESS) > *pérfaktos (4c UNSTRESSED V) > *pérfektos (6c LATIN STRESS, 7c o(:)-TO-u(:)) > Lat perfectus /perféktus/. Leumann (1977: 247) posits the ITALIC STRESS change as occurring during 500–400 BC.

3d The Change of /s/ to /r/ (s-TO-r)

This change remains in the grammar as a morph cond rule of Latin. It determines paradigmatic alternations such as genus and generis 'family' noted below. It occurred in two chronological stages. (See on this 3b i/u-TO-e/o.)

(1) s → z / V ___ V

(where /r/ does not occur elsewhere within the word)

(2) z → r / V ___ V (? or g)

That is, (1) intervocalic /s/ becomes /z/. Then, (2) intervocalic /z/ becomes /r/; and possibly the sequence /Vzg/ becomes /Vrg/.

E.g., PIE nom sg neut *genos 'family' vs. ablauting gen sg *genes+es (ev) > Lat genus, generis; PIE 3sg future es+eti as well as *es+k+eti 'will be' (ev) > Lat erit and escit. A possible instance of s-TO-r is in PIE 1sg *mes+gō 'merge' (2c PHONOTACTICS lc Obstruent cluster voicing and devoicing) > *mezgō (s-TO-r) > Lat mergō. (Otherwise one would expect Lat **mēgō by 2c PHONOTACTICS 2g s-clusters.)

Apparently s-TO-r often does not apply if the word already contains /r/. E.g., Lat rosa 'rose', miser 'wretched' and caesāriēs 'hair' instead of **rora, **mirer or **caerāriēs. Lat casa 'hut' instead of **cara may be a rustic borrowing. The s-TO-r change precedes 2c PHONOTACTICS la Geminate simplification (the later expansion): OLat caussa 'cause' (2a PHONOTACTICS, ev) > Lat causa, to which s-TO-r does not apply to produce **caura. Palmer (1954: 30) puts the s-TO-r change at about 350 BC.

4a The Change of Word-Initial /p/ to /kʷ/ (p-TO-kʷ)

This change restructures various lexical items and then is dropped from the grammar.

p → kʷ / ## ___ $[+\text{sonorant}]_1^n$ kʷ

That is, word-initial /p/ becomes /kʷ/ if followed by one or more sonorant segments followed in turn by /kʷ/. E.g., PIE 1sg *pekʷō 'cook' (p-TO-kʷ) > *kʷekʷō (5a e-TO-o) > *kʷokʷō (7b j/w-CHANGES) > Lat coquō /kokʷō/. Note here the necessary chronology p-TO-kʷ > 5a e-TO-o > 7b j/w-CHANGES. Also PIE *penkʷe '5' (ev) > Lat quīnque.

4b Syncope of Unstressed Short Vowels (SYNCOPE)

Several rules of short-vowel deletion were added at various stages in the development of PIE into Latin. They restructured various words and then were dropped from the grammar. In the following we sketch four such rules in the relative chronology of their addition to the grammar. In our formulations of the rules we use the notion of "syllable" (s). To determine what constitutes the Latin syllable, see the discussion under 6c LATIN STRESS. Kent (1940: 96) has noted that "...the conditions under which syncope occurred cannot be determined with absolute precision, and analogy to other forms and words often prevented it."

(1)
$$[\text{V, –long, –stress}] \rightarrow \emptyset \;/\; \underset{1}{[\text{+stress}]_{s}}\; \underset{2}{[\_\_\_]_{s}}\; \underset{3}{\left\{\begin{array}{l}[\text{heavy}]_{s}\\ s\\ s_2\end{array}\right.}$$

The stress here is that of 3c ITALIC STRESS. That is, a short unstressed vowel (over 2) is deleted if preceded by a stressed syllable (over 1) and if followed by a "heavy" syllable or at least two syllables (over 3). A heavy syllable is one containing a long vowel or diphthong or one ending in at least two consonants, i.e. $[\bar{\text{V}}]_s$, $[\text{VV}]_s$ or $[\ldots\text{C}_2]_s$.

Examples follow. (We cite them after the application of 3c ITALIC STRESS.)

PIE nom sg masc *déksiteros 'right' (SYNCOPE 1) > *déksteros (SYNCOPE 3) > Lat dexter; PIE nom sg *áwi+kap+s 'bird catcher' (SYNCOPE 1) > *áwkaps = *áukaps (4c UNSTRESSED V) > Lat auceps /aukeps/; early nom sg *fórmo+kaps 'hot-catcher, i.e. tongs or forceps' (SYNCOPE 1) > *fórmkaps (2c PHONOTACTICS 2h, applying as a persistent rule) > *fórkaps (4c UNSTRESSED V) > Lat forceps; early nom sg *fáklitās 'capacity' (SYNCOPE 1) > *fákltās (2c PHONOTACTICS 2aa) > Lat facultās; early *k^{w}énk^{w}edekem '15' (SYNCOPE 1) > *k^{w}énk^{w}dekem (2c PHONOTACTICS 2h) > *k^{w}éndekem (8c e-TO-i, 8j Vnk-TO-V̄nk, both applying to *k^{w}enk^{w}e '5' and analogously to '15', ev) > Lat quīndecim. PIE 1sg perf *ré+pe+pul+ai 'I repelled' (SYNCOPE 1) > *réppulai (ev) > Lat reppulī; and the 1sg pres forms *prái+dikō+r 'I beg' and *kóm+k^{w}atjō 'I shake' (SYNCOPE 1) > *práidkōr and *kómk^{w}tjō = *kómkutjō (2c PHONOTACTICS applying synchronically, ev) > Lat praedicor and concutiō. Note also the pair of early noun *ā́ridōs 'ardor' vs. the adj *ā́ridos 'dry' (SYNCOPE 1 applying to the first form but not to the second, ev) > Lat ārdor vs. āridus.

We note the following chronologies. Early 1sg pres áusi+kultō 'I give ear, listen to' (SYNCOPE 1) > Lat auscultō, to which 3d s-TO-r, at least its later stage 2, cannot apply since it has already occurred. Also the pres part *pró+widēns 'far-seeing, prudent' (SYNCOPE 1) > *prówdēns = *próudēns (6b ei/ou-CHANGES, which can only apply after SYNCOPE 1 has) > Lat prūdēns; early adv *ré+worsos 'back, again' (SYNCOPE 1) > *réursos (5a e-TO-o, 6b ei/ou-CHANGES, 7c o(:)-TO-u(:)) > Lat rūrsus. Note finally that our formulation of SYNCOPE 1 assumes the prior application of 3c ITALIC STRESS and the later application of 6c LATIN STRESS.

(2)
$$[\text{V, –long, –stress}] \rightarrow \emptyset \;/\; \underset{1}{[\text{+stress, heavy}]_{s}}\; \underset{2}{[\text{C}_0\,\_\_\_\,]_{s}}\; \underset{3}{s_1}$$

The stress here is that of 6c LATIN STRESS. That is, a vowel in an unstressed open (i.e., with no consonants in its coda) syllable (2) is deleted if preceded by a stressed heavy syllable (1) and if followed by at least one syllable (3) within the word. Since the stress here is that of 6c LATIN STRESS, we assume the relative chronology 3c ITALIC STRESS > SYNCOPE 2, 3 and 4. We cite our examples as they appeared after 6c LATIN STRESS: early adv *audā́kiter 'boldly' > Lat audācter, nom sg fem adj *sinístera 'left' > Lat sinistra, and the proper name *Falisinos (3b i/u-TO-e/o, 3d s-TO-r, SYNCOPE 2, ev) > Lat Falernus /falérnus/.

(3) This rule does not invariably apply to all forms.

(a)

e	r	[V, –long]	→	same	same	Ø
1	2	3		1	2	3

(b)

C	r	[V ,–long]	→	same	e	same	Ø
1	2	3		1	4	2	3

That is, (a) the sequence /e/ plus /r/ plus a short vowel loses the short vowel; and (b) the sequence consonant plus /r/ plus short vowel becomes consonant plus /e/ plus /r/. E.g., PIE nom sg masc adj *miseros 'wretched' (SYNCOPE 3) > *misers (2c PHONOTACTICS 2d r-clusters applying synchronically) > Lat miser; PIE nom sg *agros 'field' (ev) > Lat ager; PIE *tris '3 times' (ev) > Lat ter; PIE nom sg *agro+l+os 'small field' (SYNCOPE 3) > *agerlos (2c PHONOTACTICS 2a l-clusters, ev) > Lat agellus. Similarly, PIE nom sg *tri+st+is 'witness', *n̥+kritos 'uncertain', *akrib^{h}os 'sour' and *sakro+dōt+s 'priest' (ev) > Lat testis, incertus, acerbus and sacerdōs.

(4) These changes seem not to have applied invariably. They also seem to have occurred in the two consecutive stages noted below.

(a) [V ,–low , –long , –stress] → Ø / ___ ## C

(b) i → Ø / [heavy]$_s$ ___ /s/ ##

in the nom sg of certain i-class nouns.

Kent (1940: 97) describes SYNCOPE 4a as follows: "In final syllables, an absolutely final [short /e, i, o/] was often lost before words beginning with a consonant...; these losses seem to have been of different dates..." He further observes that "...the final short vowel was retained when it had value in identifying a grammatical form..." E.g., OLat 2sg imp dīce 'speak', OLat pres 3pl tremonti 'tremble' (ev) > Lat dīc and tremunt. But a form like the 2pl imp agite 'do' does not become *agit because it would then be identical with the 3rd singular present indicative form.

SYNCOPE 4b deletes /i/ after a heavy syllable (as defined above) in the nominative singular of some i-class nouns. E.g., PIE nom sg *mr̥tis 'death' and *sitis 'thirst' (2d SYL SON) > *mortis, *sitis (SYNCOPE 4b) > *morts, *sitis (2c PHONOTACTICS 2f t-clusters applying synchronically) > Lat mors and sitis.

4c Changes in Vowels in Unstressed Syllables (UNSTRESSED V)

These changes affect unstressed short vowels, both those occurring singly and those in diphthongs. They seem to have occurred in three chronological stages. The first two remain in restructured form in the grammar of Latin where they account for vowel alternations in verbs with and without prefixes such as /i/-/a/ in inter+ficiō 'I kill' vs. faciō 'I make', /ī/-/ae/ in oc+cīdō 'I kill' vs. caedō 'I cut', or in the examples below. The third change restructures various inflectional endings and vowels in other word-final syllables and then is dropped from the grammar.

For the first two stages the stress placement is that of 3c ITALIC STRESS. For stage 3 it is that of 6c LATIN STRESS. Thus we assume the chronology 3c ITALIC STRESS > 4c UNSTRESSED V 1 and 2 > 6c LATIN STRESS > 4c UNSTRESSED V 3. The changes are as follows.

(1) Stage 1

(a) a → e / $[\_\_, -\text{stress}]_s\ s_1$

(b) o, u → e / $[\_\_, -\text{stress}]_s\ [\text{X...}]_{s_1}$
(where X ≠ l)

(c) ai, au → ei, ou / [___, –stress]

(2) Stage 2

(a) e → i / X [___, –stress] CV
(where X ≠ i or j; and C ≠ r)

e → u (sporadic)/ X [___, –stress] [C, +bilabial] V
(where X ≠ i or j)

(b) ei, oi → ē / i [___, –stress] s_1

(3) Stage 3

(a) i, o → e / [___, –stress] ##

(b) a → e / [___, –stress] C_1##
(where if a single C, C ≠ r)

(c) e → i / [___, –stress] t or s##

(d) o → u / [___, –stress] C_1##

That is, at Stage 1 (a) an unstressed /a/ which is followed by at least one additional syllable in the word becomes /e/; (b) an unstressed /o/ or /u/ becomes /e/ if followed by at least one other syllable in the word, provided that the syllable does not begin with /l/; (c) unstressed /ai/ and /au/ become /ei/ and /ou/. (/ei/ and /ou/ later undergo 6b ei/ou-CHANGES.)

At Stage 2, (a) an unstressed /e/ followed by a single consonant can become /i/ unless preceded by /i/ or /j/ or if followed by /r/. And sometimes unstressed /e/ becomes /u/ if followed by a bilabial consonant /p, b, f or m/. This does not occur if the /e/ is preceded by /i/ or /j/. (b) The unstressed diphthongs /ei, oi/ in a non-word-final syllable, if preceded by /i/, become /ē/. (Otherwise /ei/ undergoes 6b ei/ou-CHANGES; and /oi/ undergoes 7a ai/oi-TO-ae/oe and 8h oe-CHANGES.)

At Stage 3, (a) unstressed /i/ or /o/ in absolute word-final position becomes /e/; (b) unstressed /a/ in a word-final closed syllable (which ends in at least one consonant) becomes /e/; (c) unstressed /e/ before word-final /t/ or /s/ becomes /i/. And (d) unstressed /o/ in a word-final closed syllable becomes /u/. (We have included this as an environment in 7c o(:)-TO-u(:). These probably represent one and the same change.) Palmer (1954: 221) and Sommer (1948: 144) assume that this change occurred during the 200's BC.

The examples we cite are forms as they occur after the application of 3c ITALIC STRESS. E.g., stage 1 (a) *pér+fakjō 'I complete' (UNSTRESSED V 1a) > *pér+fekjō (UNSTRESSED V 2a) > *pér+fikjō (7b j/w-CHANGES) > *pérfikiō (6c LATIN STRESS applying synchronically) > Lat perficiō /perfíkiō/. Perf part nom sg masc *per+fak+t+os (UNSTRESSED V 1a, but not 2a, ev) > Lat perfectus /perféktus/. Early *ád+tangō 'I touch' (UNSTRESSED V 1a, ev) > *áttengō (8c e-TO-i, ev) > attingō /attíŋgō/). Early *ín+saltō 'I jump at' (UNSTRESSED V 1a) > *inseltō (5a e-TO-o > *ínsoltō (7c o(:)-TO-u(:), ev) > Lat insultō /insúltō/. Also, the early inf. *ré+dida+si 'give back' (3d s-TO-r) > *rédidari (4b SYNCOPE) > *réddari (UNSTRESSED V 1a) > *rédderi (UNSTRESSED V 3) > Lat reddere. And nom sg masc *kón+tabern+āl+is 'one who shares the same tavern, comrade' (UNSTRESSED V 1a) > *kóntebernālis (UNSTRESSED V CHANGES 2a) > *kóntubernālis (6c LATIN STRESS) > Lat contubernālis /kontubernā́lis/. Examples of Stage 1b are early nom sg *néwo+tāt+s 'newness, novelty' and *sókjo+tāt+s 'society, friendship' (UNSTRESSED V 1b) > *néwetāts and *sókjetāts (UNSTRESSED V 2a applying only to the first form) > *néwitats and *sókjetāts (5a e-TO-o, 7b j/w-CHANGES, ev) > Lat novitās /nówitās/ and societās /sokíetās/. An example of /u/-reduction is nom sg *kórnu+kan 'horn-singer, trumpeter' (UNSTRESSED V 1b) > *kórnekan (UNSTRESSED V 2a) > *kórnikan (UNSTRESSED V 3b) > Lat cornicen /kórniken/.

Examples of Stage 1c are the early 1sg pres forms *áistimō 'think' vs. *éks+aistimō 'esteem' (UNSTRESSED V 1c) > áistimō vs. *ékseistimō (6b ei/ou-CHANGES, 7a ai/oi-TO-ae/oe, ev) > Lat aestimō /áestimō/ vs. exīstimō /eksī́stimo/; *kláudō 'close' vs. *ín+klaudō 'include' (UNSTRESSED V 1c) > *kláudō vs. *ínkloudō (6b ei/ou-CHANGES, 6c LATIN STRESS) > Lat claudō vs. inclūdō /inklū́dō/. Instances of diphthongs in word-final syllables are the 1sg perf *g^{w}ēmai 'I have come' (ev) > Lat vēnī /wḗnī/; and early abl pl *déiwīnōis 'gods' and *déiwīnāis 'goddesses' (2b LONG DIPH) > *déiwīnois and *déiwīnais (UNSTRESSED V 1c) > *déiwīnois and *déiwīneis (6b ei/ou-CHANGES) > *dī́wīnois and *dī́wīnīs (7a ai/oi-TO-ae/oe, 8h oe-CHANGES, ev) > Lat dīvīnīs /dīwī́nīs/ for both forms.

Examples of Stage 2 are (a) early gen sg *kápot+es 'head' (UNSTRESSED V 1b) > *kápetes (UNSTRESSED V 2a) > *kápites (UNSTRESSED V 3c) > Lat capitis /kápitis/. Examples of (b) are early nom sg masc adj *áli+oinos 'foreign' (UNSTRESSED V 2b) > *áliēnos (UNSTRESSED V 3d) > *áliēnus (6c LATIN STRESS) > aliēnus /aliḗnus/.

Examples of stage 3 are as follows: (a) 2sg pres dep *sék^{w}esō 'you follow' (3d s-TO-r) > *sék^{w}erō (UNSTRESSED V 3a) > Lat sequere, nom sg neut *mari 'sea'> Lat mare. (b) Nom sg *árti+fak+s 'artist' (UNSTRESSED V 3b) > Lat artifex. However, the /a/ is retained in Lat Caesar /káesar /, not **Caeser, because of the /r/. (c) 2sg pres *ágesi 'you drive' and 3sg pres *ágeti 'he drives' (4b SYNCOPE 4) >

*ages and *aget (UNSTRESSED V 3c) > Lat agis and agit. (d) OLat 3sg pres pass legontor 'they are read' (UNSTRESSED V 3d) > *legontur (7c o(:)-TO-u(:), ev) > Lat leguntur /legúntur/. Apparently the /s/ from /ts/ by 2c PHONOTACTICS does not trigger UNSTRESSED V 3c, e.g. early nom sg *mīlet+s 'soldier' (2c PHONOTACTICS 2f t-clusters) > Lat mīles, not **mīlis.

Often after UNSTRESSED V has applied, new compounds are formed having the original vowel. E.g., 1sg pres abigō 'drive away' < *ab+agō vs. peragō 'drive through' (not **perigō) and consecrō 'consecrate' < *kon+sakrō alongside consacrō; and the nom sg masc adjs inīquus 'unjust' < *in+aikʷos vs. later inaequālis 'unequal' (not **inīquālis).

There are some instances where UNSTRESSED V 1c and 2b (affecting diphthongs) encounter problems. E.g., early 1sg pres *ób+audiō 'obey' (ev) > Lat oboediō instead of the expected **obūdiō; and early nom sg neut *póst+moirjom 'wall space' (2c PHONOTACTICS 2i s-clusters) > *pṓmoirjom (UNSTRESSED V 2b applying for some reason, ev) > Lat pōmērium /pōmḗrium/ instead of the expected **pōmūrium by 7a ai/oi-TO-ae/oe and then 8h oe-CHANGES. Kent (1940: 104) considers such forms as instances of an "archaic spelling."

Finally, regarding relative chronology, it would seem that UNSTRESSED V Stages 1 and 2 preceded Stage 3. There are at least two reasons for assuming this chronology. First, there are numerous Old Latin forms attested which have not undergone UNSTRESSED V 3, while there are virtually no Old Latin attestations of forms which have not undergone Stages 1 and 2: e.g., OLat servos 'slave' > Lat servus. Second, UNSTRESSED V 1 and 2 must precede several other changes such as 5a e-TO-o, 7c o(:)-TO-u(:) and 8c e-TO-i. This is not true of UNSTRESSED V 3.

5a A Change of /e/ to /o/ (e-TO-o)

This change restructures various forms and is then generally dropped as a rule from the grammar (but see below).

e → o / (a) kʷ, w or u ___ or ___ w or u

(b) ___ l { [V, +back] | C_1^2 (where if a single C, then C ≠ l) | ## }

That is, /e/ becomes /o/ (a) if immediately preceded by /kʷ, w, or u/ or if immediately followed by /w or u/; and (b) if followed by /l/ followed by a back vowel /a(:), o(:), u(:)/, if followed by /l/ followed by one or two consonants (but not /ll/), or if followed by word-final /l/. (These environments may indicate a +back allophone of /l/ in these environments.) E.g.,

(a) 1sg pres *kʷekʷō 'cook' (e-TO-o) > *kʷokʷō (7b j/w-CHANGES) > Lat coquō, *deukō 'lead' (e-TO-o) > *doukō (OLat 3sg doucit 'leads' is attested, then 6b ei/ou-CHANGES) > Lat dūcō. Nom sg masc adj *newos 'new' (e-TO-o) >*nowos (7c o(:)-TO-u(:)) > Lat novus; nom sg masc *swepnos 'sleep' (2c PHONOTACTICS) > *swemnos (e-TO-o) > *swomnos (7b j/w-CHANGES with the necessary chronology e-TO-o > 7b) > *somnos (ev) > Lat somnus; early *newm̥ '9' (2d SYL SON, e-TO-o) > Lat novem.

(b) The early Greek borrowing *elaíwā 'olive' (3c ITALIC STRESS, e-TO-o) > *ólaiwā (4c UNSTRESSED V 1c applying as a persistent synchronic rule) → *óleiwā (6b ei/ou-CHANGES, 6c LATIN STRESS, ev) > Lat olīva /olī́wa/. Another Greek borrowing undergoing e-TO-o is telōneîon 'toll' (ev) > Lat tolōneum /tolṓneum/. Also 1 and 3sg pres ind *welō and *welt 'wish, will' (e-TO-o) > *wolō and *wolt (7c o(:)-TO-u(:)) > Lat volō and vult. Contrast the Lat 1sg pres subj velim < *welīm where neither e-TO-o nor 7c o(:)-TO-u(:) has applied. (One might argue on the basis of these alternations that both e-TO-o and 7c o(:)-TO-u(:) did in fact remain in the grammar of Latin as morph cond rules applying to a few forms.)

We may assume the e-TO-o change to have occurred fairly early since, according to Sommer (1948: 80), it also affects other Italic dialects such as Oscan and Umbrian. It also must have applied before 6b ei/ou-CHANGES: early nom sg fem *bréwi+mā 'shortest day' (4b SYNCOPE) > *brewmā = *breumā (e-TO-o) > *broumā (6b ei/ou-CHANGES, ev) > Lat brūma.

Part (a) of e-TO-o may have been more likely to apply if an /o/ was in the following syllable. E.g., early nom sg masc adj *dwénos 'good' vs. the adv *dwénēd 'well' (e-TO-o applying to the first form, but not to the second) > *dwónos vs. *dwénēd (6a d/t-CHANGES) > *dwónos vs. *dwénē (8b dw-CHANGES, ev) > Lat bonus vs. bene.

5b A Change of /u/ to /i/ (u-to-i)

This change restructures various lexical items and then is dropped from the grammar.

u → (? y) → i / l (V) ___ [C, +bilabial]

That is, /u/ becomes /i/ (possibly over an intermediate stage /y/) if preceded by /l/ and possibly an intervening vowel and if followed by a bilabial consonant /p, b, f or m/. E.g., early lubet 'is pleasing' > Lat libet, early clupeus 'shield' > Lat clipeus. PIE nom sg masc *leud^{h}ros 'free' (1 ASPIR STOPS) > *leubros (4b SYNCOPE 3) > *leuber (u-TO-i) > *leiber (6b ei/ou-CHANGES) > Lat līber. Note here the necessary chronology 1 ASPIR STOPS > u-TO-i > 6b ei/ou-CHANGES. Palmer (1954: 216) and Buck (1962: 80) state this change as occurring "between l and a labial." We include the intervening vowel to account for examples like līber. If u-TO-i had not applied here, the Latin form would be **lūber by 5a e-TO-o and 6b ei/ou-CHANGES.

5c A Change of /wo/ to /we/ (wo-TO-we).

This change restructures various lexical items and then is dropped from the grammar. It is approximately as follows:

wo → we / (a) ___ rC or sC
(b) ___ [C, ?–labial]
c) ? ## ___ i

That is, /wo/ becomes /we/ (a) if followed by /r/ or /s/ plus another consonant or (b) if followed by a non-labial consonant (namely any consonant except /p, b, f, m/); or (c) possibly, word-initial /woi/ becomes /wei/.

E.g., (a) OLat vortō 'I turn' and OLat voster 'your' > Lat vertō and vester. (b) OLat votō 'I forbid' > Lat vetō; PIE 1sg pres *wogējō 'stir up' (ev) > Lat vegeō. (c) Possible derivations are PIE 1sg perf *wóidai 'I saw' and nom sg *wóikos 'home, district' (4c UNSTRESSED V) > *wóidei, *woikos (wo-TO-we) > *wéidei, *wéikos (6b ei/ou-CHANGES) > *wī́dī, *wī́kos (7c o(:)-TO-u(:)) > Lat vīdī and vīcus. (Note here the necessary chronology wo-TO-we > 6b eu/ou-CHANGES.)

There are problems in the precise formulation of this change. One example is the early 1sg pres *wokō 'call'> Lat vocō instead of **vecō by wo-TO-we (b). Palmer (1954: 216) and Buck (1962: 84) place the wo-TO-we change at about 150 BC.

6a Changes in Word-Final /d/ and /t/ (d/t-CHANGES)

These changes restructure various lexical items and inflectional endings. They are retained in restructured form as a morph cond rule applying to a few nouns such as Lat lac 'milk' noted below. Otherwise the changes are dropped from the grammar. The changes occur in two chronological stages as given below. The first is early in that it occurs in other Italic languages besides Latin. The second is later and is assumed by Buck (1962: 157) to have occurred during the 200's BC.

(1) t	→	Ø	/	C ___ ##
	→	d	/	V ___ ##
(2) d	→	Ø	/	V̄ or C ___ ##
	→	l		(dialectically and sporadically)

That is, (1) /t/ is deleted word-finally after a consonant and becomes /d/ word-finally after a vowel. Then later, (2) a word-final /d/ is deleted if preceded by a long vowel or consonant. Word-internally or initially, it sometimes becomes /l/. E.g., PIE nom sg *lakt 'milk' vs. gen sg *laktes (d/t-CHANGES, ev) > Lat lac, lactis. PIE 3sg perf *dʰē+k+e+t 'made' (1 ASPIR STOPS) > *fēket (d/t-CHANGES) > OLat fēced /fḗked/. OLat abl sg sententiād 'opinion' > Lat sententiā (to which 8d IAMBIC SHORT does not apply: this may indicate that Stage 2 of d/t-CHANGES occurred after 8d IAMBIC SHORT). PIE nom sg *kr̥d vs. gen sg *kr̥des 'heart' (2d SYL SON) > *kord, *kordes (4c UNSTRESSED V, 6a d/t-CHANGES) > Lat cor, cordis. Note also OLat dingua 'language' > Lat lingua as well as the co-occurring doublets in Latin such as 1sg pres ol+eō 'smell' vs. nom sg od+or 'odor'; 1sg pres sed+eō 'sit' vs. nom sg sol+ium 'throne' < PIE ablauting *sod+jom.

6b Changes in /ei/ and /ou/ (ei/ou-CHANGES)

These changes restructure various morphemes (primarily lexical items and a few endings) and then are dropped from the grammar. The changes are basically as follows.

(a) ei	→	ē	/	___ j or w (usually)
	→	ī	/	(otherwise)
(b) ou	→	ō	/	___ ? n or t (often)
	→	ū	/	(otherwise)

That is, (a) /ei/ becomes /ē/ if immediately followed by /j/ or /w/; otherwise, /ei/ becomes /ī/. (b) /ou/ often becomes /ō/ if followed by /n/ or /t/ and otherwise becomes /ū/. E.g., (a) PIE gen sg *eis+jos 'his' (3a C+j CHANGES) > *eijjos (ei/ou-CHANGES) > *ējjos (7b j/w-CHANGES, 7c o(:)-TO-u(:)) > Lat ējus. PIE nom sg *deiwos 'god' (ei/ou-CHANGES) > *dēwos (7b j/w-CHANGES) > *dēos (7c o(:)-TO-u(:)) > *dēus (8l V̄V-TO-VV) > Lat deus. However, the adj dīvus 'divine' also occurs from the same source, PIE *deiwos, where /ī/ has resulted. Also PIE nom sg i-class adj *leiwis 'smooth' (ev) > Lat lēvis. But the more usual development is in OLat deicō 'I say' > Lat dīcō.

Examples of (b) are PIE 1sg *deukō 'lead' (5a e-TO-o) > OLat doucō (ei/ou-CHANGES) > Lat dūcō (with the necessary chronology 5a e-TO-o > ei/ou-CHANGES). Also the early nom sg masc adjs *nówenos '9th', perf part *mówitos 'moved',*pró+widēns 'fore-seeing, provident' (4b SYNCOPE) > *nównos, *mówtos, *prówdēns (PIE 3.1.2c i-j/u-w ALT, still applying synchronically) → *nóunos, *móutos, *próudēns (ei/ou-CHANGES) > *nṓnos, *mṓtos, *prū́dēns (7c o(:)-TO-u(:)) > Lat nōnus, mōtus and prūdēns. (Note the chronology 4b SYNCOPE > ei/ou-CHANGES.)

Regarding the absolute chronology of this change, Palmer (1954: 218) and Buck (1962: 89) estimate the change of /ou/ to /ū/ at about 200 BC; they (ibid., 217 and 86 respectively) estimate that of /ei/ to /ī/ at about 150 BC. ei/ou-CHANGES (a) and (b) seem to represent one and the same process: hence it may have begun by applying to /ou/ and then extended its domain to include /ei/.

6c The Word-Stress Rule of Classical Latin (LATIN STRESS)

This change remains in the grammar as a phon cond rule. It replaces 3c ITALIC STRESS.

$$V \rightarrow [+\text{stress}] \;/\; (1) \;\_\_\_ \begin{Bmatrix} V \\ C_2 \end{Bmatrix} \ldots V \ldots \#\#$$

where "..," contains no vowel and where

$C_2 \neq$ the sequence [C, –sonorant][C, +sonorant]

$$(2)\ \text{Otherwise: } [\_\_\_]_s\ s_2\ \#\#$$

That is, (1) the vowel nucleus in the penultimate syllable of a word is stressed if it is a long vowel or a diphthong (= VV) or if it is followed by at least two consonants (C_2), but not the sequence obstruent consonant plus sonorant consonant. (2) Otherwise, the vowel in the third-from-last syllable in a word is stressed.

As our examples of this change we shall cite instances of its application as a synchronic rule. We note first that the two-consonant (C_2) condition of part 1 of LATIN STRESS does not require that the two consonants be in the same syllable. Basing our algorithm of Latin syllable construction on the Roman grammarians' description (as outlined in Sommer 1977: 206-7), the first step is to locate the V nuclei in the word. Second, scan the –vocalic sequence to the left of the V nucleus: this constitutes the onset of the syllable and can only be those consonant sequences which can also occur word-initially. Third, the remaining consonants constitute the coda of the preceding syllable.Examples of the application of this algorithm are the following Latin forms: centum '100' → /ken+tum/ as opposed to **/ke+ntum/ since no word begins with /nt/, ambō 'both' → /am+bō/ as opposed to **/a+mbō/ since no word begins with /mb/, magnus 'large' → /ma+gnus/ since /gn/ = [ŋn] can begin a word such as gnārus 'knowledgeable', annus 'year' → /an+nus/. With this in mind, note the syllabification and the stress in the following forms: gen sg fem ca-la-mi-tā-tis 'calamity' and nom sg ca-la-mi-tās (LATIN STRESS) → calamitā́tis vs. calámitās; nom sg adj noc-tur-nus 'nocturnal' (LATIN STRESS) → noctúrnus (in which the stress-triggering C_2 sequence /r-n/ is heterosyllabic) and nō-te-scō 'become known' (LATIN WORD STRESS) → nōtéscō (in which the stress-triggering C_2 sequence /sk/ is in the onset of the following syllable). Finally, the sequence obstruent consonant plus sonorant consonant does not trigger stress: e.g., nom pl volucrēs 'birds' (LATIN STRESS 1 not applying, but by 2) → vólucrēs.

Two apparent exceptions to LATIN STRESS result as follows. First, from the application of the later change 4b SYNCOPE Stage 4: e.g., OLat 2sg imp addū́ce 'lead' (by LATIN STRESS, then later 4b SYNCOPE 4) > Lat addū́c. Second, from enclisis. Under enclisis a boundary is deleted between two words and the resulting construction is stressed as a single word. E.g., ##propter##mē## 'on account of me' (enclisis) → ##proptermē## (LATIN STRESS) → ##proptérmē##; and ##quibus##cum## 'with whom' (enclisis) → ##quibuscum## (LATIN STRESS) → ##quibúscum##.

Regarding the date of LATIN STRESS, Palmer (1954: 213) notes, "Plautine versification...implies that the earlier accentuation [our 3c ITALIC STRESS] still persisted in some words... In other respects Plautine prosody shows that the penultimate law [our 6c LATIN STRESS] was already operating in his time." (An example of what Palmer is referring to is Plautus' fácilius 'easier' as opposed to the later Latin facílius.) So during the time of Plautus (254–184 BC) both stress rules seem to have been operative, with LATIN STRESS eventually winning out. We assume then that the rule LATIN STRESS was added to the grammar shortly before about 200 BC.

Regarding the phonetic nature of Lat stress, Palmer (1954: 211-12) makes the following observation: "Scholars are...divided on the nature of the Latin accent... In grammatical studies as in much else, the Romans were slavish imitators of the Greeks. The very words *accentus, gravis*, and *acutus* are 'calques' [loan translations] of the Greek terms προσωδία, βαρεῖα, 'οξεῖα. So, it is suggested, we should be chary of accepting such descriptions of the Latin accent which are forced into a scientific terminology devised to describe a language of a different type. It is worth noting, too, that even the Greek grammarians continue to speak of 'οξεῖα and βαρεῖα long after the Greek accent had changed from pitch to stress."

In our considerations of Greek and OCSlavic stress, we note three phonetic components of what is called "stress" — pitch (frequency of vocal-chord vibration), amplitude (loudness, which is the extent of vocal-chord vibration) and length (duration of vocal-chord vibration). In the above quotation Palmer is referring to the fact that the terms used by ancient grammarians such as "altitudo" and "longitudo" to describe the Latin stress have led some to the view that the primary component of this stress was pitch. However, Palmer also notes that changes like 4b SYNCOPE and 4c UNSTRESSED V are probably indicative of a "dynamic" stress. To put this in our terms, we assume that both 3c ITALIC STRESS and 6c LATIN STRESS indicate a stress consisting of all three components — namely higher pitch, greater loudness and greater length of the stressed vowel.

7a The Change of /ai/ and /oi/ to /ae/ and /oe/ (ai/oi-TO-ae/oe)

This change restructures the respective diphthongs and then is dropped from the grammar.

ai, oi → ae, oe

That is, the second segment in the diphthongs /ai/ and /oi/ becomes –high /e/. E.g., PIE nom sg masc adj *laiwos 'left' (ev) > Lat laevus; PIE nom sg *b^{h}oid^{h}os 'agreement' (1 ASPIR STOPS) > *foidos (ai/oi-TO-ae/oe, ev) > Lat foedus. Most instances of /oe/ become /ū/ by 8h oe-CHANGES: e.g., PIE nom sg masc *oinos '1' (ai/oi-TO-ae/oe) > OLat oenos (8h oe-CHANGES, ev) > Lat ūnus.

We assume the change in /ai/ and that in /oi/ to represent one and the same process. Palmer (1954: 217) and Buck (1962: 88) consider the change of /ai/ to /ae/ to have begun around 200 BC. Sommer (1948: 74) notes that the first attested inscription with graphenic <oe> dates from about 112 BC. Hence ai/oi-TO-ae/oe may have begun around 200 BC affecting /ai/, then later spread to affect /oi/.

7b Changes in /j/ and /w/ (j/w-CHANGES)

The restructured reflexes of these changes remain in the grammar of Latin as phon cond rules. Below we first give the early version of the changes; then we give their synchronic reflexes as persistent rules in the grammar of Latin.

(1) The early changes.

(a) j	→	Ø	/	V ___ V
j	→	i	/	[+segment] ___ , otherwise.
(b) w	→	Ø	/	(a) [V, ±long, αfeatures] ___ [V, ±long, αfeatures]
				(b) ___ o(:), later ___ u(:) as well.
				(c) ## ___ C
				(d) C_2 ___
				(e) ? f, b or p ___
w	→	u	/	(f) [C_1 ___]$_S$

That is, (a) /j/ is deleted intervocalically and otherwise becomes /i/ word-internally. Word-initially /j/remains. (b) /w/ is deleted (ba) between two like vowels (which may differ in length), (bb) before /o(:)/ and later before /u(:)/ as well, (bc) word-initially when followed by a consonant, (bd) after a sequence of two or more consonants and (be) possibly, if following /f, b or p/. (bf) /w/ becomes /u/ whenever it is preceded by at least one consonant within a syllable; otherwise it remains /w/.

E.g., (a) PIE nom pl *trejes '3' (j/w-CHANGES) > *trees = Lat trēs, PIE nom sg masc *med^{h}jos 'mid' (j/w-CHANGES, ev) > Lat medius, not *medjus. (ba) Lat lavātrīna /lawātrī́na/ 'lavatory' (j/w-CHANGES) > lātrīna, both forms occurring. (bb) PIE nom sg *deiwos 'god' (6b ei/ou-CHANGES) > *dēwos (j/w-CHANGES) > *dēos (81 V̄V-TO-VV, ev) > Lat deus. (Note the necessary chronology 6b ei/ou-CHANGES > j/w-CHANGES > 81 V̄V-TO-VV.) PIE nom sg masc *swepnos 'sleep' (2c PHONOTACTICS) > *swemnos (5a e-TO-o) > *swomnos (j/w-CHANGES, ev) > Lat somnus. (Note the necessary chronology 5a e-TO-o > j/w-CHANGES.) Early nom sg masc *sek^{w}ondos 'following, second' (ev) > Lat secundus; PIE 1sg pres *pek^{w}ō cook (4a p-TO-k^w) > *k^{w}ek^{w}ō (5a e-TO-o) > *k^{w}ok^{w}ō (j/w-CHANGES) > *kokō (ev) > Lat coquō /kok^{w}ō/. The second /k/ has been reformed here to /k^w/ after those forms in the paradigm such as the 3sg pres *k^{w}ok^{w}eti where j/w-CHANGES would not apply to the second /k^w/. (Such analogies occur often: e.g., Lat quod 'what', not **cod, after forms such as quī 'who' where j/w-CHANGES would not apply.) Also PIE 1sg pres *wurgējō 'urge' (j/w-CHANGES, ev) > Lat urgeō.

(bc) PIE nom sg fem *wlānā 'wool' (j/w-CHANGES, ev) > Lat lāna. (bd) PIE nom sg masc adj *ml̥dwis 'gentle' (2d SYL SON) > *moldwis (2c PHONOTACTICS) > *mollwis (j/w-CHANGES) > Lat mollis. (be) PIE 1sg pres *b^{h}w+ī+ō 'become' (1 ASPIR STOPS) > *fwīō (j/w-CHANGES) > *fīō (81 V̄V-TO-VV) > Lat fiō. PIE 1sg pres *apo+werīō 'open' (4b SYNCOPE) > *apwerīō (j/w-CHANGES, ev) > Lat aperiō. (bf) PIE nom sg masc adj *swādwis 'sweet' (j/w-CHANGES) > *suādwis (8b dw-CHANGES) > Lat suavis /suāwis/.

(2) The synchronic reflex of the above changes is as follows:

(a) /j/ → [j] / ## ___ V
[i] / otherwise
(b) /w/ → [w] / [___ V...]
s
[u] / otherwise

That is, (a) of the possibilities [j] or [i], only [j] occurs word-initially before a vowel and [i] occurs word-internally and word-finally. (b) Of the possibilities [w] or [u], only [w] occurs in syllable-initial position (where it must be followed by a vowel); otherwise [u] occurs.

E.g., (a) Lat jubeō 'I command' and capiō /kapiō/ 'I seize' occur as opposed to **iubeō or **capjō. (b) Note the syllabic boundaries in the following words (as determined by the syllabification algorithm described above under 6c LATIN STRESS). E.g., Lat we-nj-ō 'I come', sil-wa 'forest', an-nw-ō 'I nod', ae-stw-ā-rj-um 'estuary', lae-wus 'left' (j/w-CHANGES applying synchronically) → veniō /weniō/, silva /silwa/, annuō /annuō/, aestuārium /aestuārium/, laevus /laewus/. (In the case of silva /silwa/ above the syllabification is apparently sil-wa instead of the expected **si-lu-a. Likewise with other /lw/ sequences, e.g. sol-wō 'I solve' → solvō /solwō/. The syllabification is often the same if an /r/ precedes: e.g. ser-wus 'servant' → servus /serwus/.)

In some Latin words /j/ can occur word-internally and intervocalically. E.g., PIE nom sg masc comp adj *magjōs 'larger' and PIE gen sg masc *eisjos 'his' (3a C+j CHANGES) > *mājjōs and *eijjos (j/w-CHANGES apparently not applying, ev) > Lat mājor and ējus, possibly /mājjor/ and /ējjus/. All such occurrences of orthographic intervocalic <j>, possibly phonemic /jj/, arise from 3a C+j CHANGES. Note here the necessary chronology 3a C+j CHANGES > j/w-CHANGES. Otherwise the derivation would be PIE *magjōs (no application of 3a C+j CHANGES, but by j/w-CHANGES, ev) > Lat **magior.

Buck (1962: 134 and 139) estimates the j/w-CHANGES as beginning about 400 BC in pre-literary times. Sommer (1977: 129) notes that the Latin pronunciation of graphemic <v> as /w/ is certain, given early spellings such as <jubentutis> 'youth' for /juwentūtis/. Kent (1940: 61) dates the later post-classical Latin change of /w/ to /v/ at about 200 AD.

7c The Changes of /o(:)/ to /u(:)/ (o(:)-TO-u(:))

These changes restructure various lexical items and endings and then are dropped from the grammar. They are as follows:

(a) o → u / { C (≠ w) | ## } ___ {
(a) ŋk or ŋgw
(b) mb, sometimes just m
(c) l { C (≠ l) | [V, +back] }
(d) C_2 (≠ ll, ng, ?others)
(e) C_1 ##
(f) rC (sporadically) }

(b) ō → ū (sporadically) / ## k^w ___ r or j

That is, (a) short /o/, stressed and unstressed, becomes /u/ if preceded by any consonant except /w/ or if word-initial and if followed by (aa) /ŋk/ or /ŋgw/, (ab) /mb/ or /m/, (ac) /l/ plus any consonant except /l/ or /l/ plus a back vowel, (ad) if followed by at least two consonants with some exceptions, (ae) if followed by one or more consonants in a word-final syllable or (af) sporadically if followed by /r/ plus a consonant. Further (b) /ō/ becomes /ū/ sporadically if preceded by word-initial /k^w/ and followed by /r/ or /j/.

E.g., (aa) OLat acc sg masc honc 'him' > Lat hunc, early nom sg *ongwis 'fingernail' > Lat unguis /uŋgwis/, but early nom sg masc *longos 'long' > Lat longus. (ab) PIE nom sg masc *omb^{h}ō 'boss on a shield' (ev) > Lat umbo, PIE nom sg masc *g^{h}omos 'earth' (ev) > Lat humus. (ac) OLat molcta 'fine' (2c PHONOTACTICS, o(:)-TO-u(:)) > Lat multa; OLat pōcolom 'cup' (ev) > Lat pōculum. PIE nom sg masc *d^{h}amel+os 'servant' vs. nom sg fem *d^{h}amel+jā 'household including servants, family' (1 ASPIR STOPS, 4c UNSTRESSED V, 5a e-TO-o) > *famolos vs. *fameljā (7b j/w-CHANGES, o(:)-TO-u(:), ev) > Lat famulus vs. familia. (ad and ae) OLat legontor 'they are read' (o(:)-TO-u(:)) > Lat leguntur; PIE nom sg masc adj *onostos 'burdened' and noun *orsos 'bear' (o(:)-TO-u(:)) > Lat onustus and ursus. Possibly also nom sg *m̥l̥+jes 'woman' (2d SYL SON) > *moljes (o(:)-TO-u(:)) > *muljes (ev) > Lat mulier. (af) Early nom sg *forn+āk+s 'oven' (ev) > Lat furnāx as well as fornāx. Examples of (b) are these: OLat quōr /k^{w}ōr/ 'why' > Lat cūr; PIE gen sg *k^{w}osjos 'whose' (3a C+j CHANGES) > *k^{w}ōjjos (o(:)-TO-u(:), ev) > Lat cūjus, possibly /kūjjus/.

Buck (1962: 83) notes that /o/ in these forms occurs until about 200 BC. We posit the onset of o(:)-TO-u(:) at about this time. By about 45 BC the o(:)-TO-u(:) change expands its domain in that the proviso "(≠ w)" in part (a) of the rule is dropped; so the rule then can apply to /o/ preceded by /w/. E.g., OLat equos 'horse', sequontor 'they follow' and servos 'slave' (ev) > Lat equus, sequuntur /sek^{w}untur/ and servus.

7d The Change of /ow/ to /aw/ (ow-TO-aw)

This change occurs sporadically and under unclear conditions. After applying, the rule restructures various lexical items and then is dropped from the grammar. Its basic form seems to be this:

ow → aw / ___ [V, +stress]

That is, /ow/ becomes /aw/ if the following vowel is stressed (by 6c LATIN STRESS: hence the relative chronology 6c LATIN STRESS > ow-TO-aw). This particular environment was suggested by Palmer (1959: 215) to account for cases like the early inf (*lowā́re 'wash' and *fowḗre 'favor'(ow-TO-aw) > Lat lavāre and favēre. Usually a stressed/ów/ does not change, but occasionally it can: e.g., early nom sg masc *kówos 'cave' vs. early *nówem '9' (ev) > Lat cavus /káwus/ vs. novem /nówem/. Finally, a possible change of PIE nom sg masc adj *oktōwos '8th' (ev) > Lat octāvus /oktā́wus/ may be a result of ow-TO-aw.

8a Various Dissimilatory Changes (DISSIMILATION)

These changes generally restructure lexical items and then are dropped from the grammar. At least one of the changes, namely (b) below, remains as a morph cond rule of Latin. The changes are as follows:

(a) l → r / ___ ... l

(b) l → r / l ... ___

(c) n → r / ___ ...n

(d) d → r / ___ ...d

(e) r → Ø / r... ___

where in all changes "..." does not contain a word boundary ##. That is, the segments /l, n, d, r/ tend to change as described whenever an identical segment occurs in the designated position within a word. E.g., PIE nom sg masc *kailoleos 'dark blue' (ev) > Lat caeruleus. (b) This change remains in the grammar and accounts for the allomorphic alternations of the adj suffix /-āl vs. -ār/: e.g., the synchronic derivation /mort+ālis/ 'mortal' and /lūn+ālis/ 'lunar' → Lat mortālis and lūnāris. Also the historical derivation of the early nom sg neut *lut+l+om 'profit' (2c PHONOTACTICS) > *lukulom (4b SYNCOPE) > *luklom (DISSIMILATION, ev) > Lat lucrum. (c) PIE nom sg neut *kan+men 'song' (DISSIMILATION) > Lat carmen; (d) early *medi+diē 'at noon' (DISSIMILATION) > Lat meridiē. (e) PIE nom sg masc adj *agros+tris 'rustic' (4c UNSTRESSED V) > *agrestris (DISSIMILATION) > Lat agrestis. In a similar case, Palmer (1954: 231) notes that an entire syllable may be lost as in nutrīx 'nurse' from an earlier *nutrī+trīx.

There are also changes in post-Classical Latin times which are reminiscent of our version of DISSIMILATION. E.g., Lat pelegrīnus 'pilgrim' (ev) > later peregrīnus and Lat cultellum 'knife' (ev) > later cuntellum.

8b Changes in the Sequence /dw/ (dw-CHANGES)

These changes restructure various lexical items and then are dropped from the grammar.

dw → (a) b / ## ___

(b) w / V ___

That is, (a) word-initial /dw/ becomes /b/; and word-internal /dw/ following a vowel loses the /d/ to become /w/.

E.g., (a) OLat nom sg duenos /dwenos/ 'good' (5a e-TO-o) > *dwonos (dw-CHANGES, ev) > Lat bonus. There is apparently the opposite chronology in the derivation of OLat duellum 'war' (dw-CHANGES) > Lat bellum, to which 5a e-TO-o has not applied. If 5a e-TO-o had consistently preceded dw-CHANGES, one would expect from the latter derivation **bollum instead of bellum. But we still assume dw-CHANGES to be a later rule since it fails to apply word-initially in OLat forms. (b) PIE nom sg masc adj *swādwis 'sweet' (7b j/w-CHANGES) > *suāduis (dw-CHANGES applying, which seems to indicate that it also applied to the sequence /duV/) > Lat suāvis /suāwis/.

8c The Change of Stressed /e/ to /i/ (e-TO-i)

This change restructures various lexical items and then is dropped from the grammar. All the conditioning factors of this rule are not obvious. Its basic form seems to be this:

[e, +stress] → i / (a) ___ ŋ

(b) optional ___ C_1[V, +high, ?-back] where $C_1 \neq$ w, z and perhaps some other consonants and consonant clusters.

(c) optional ___ mp and less frequently ___ mb

That is, stressed /e/ becomes /i/ (a) immediately before the velar nasal /ŋ/. This segment arises by the PIE rule 3.1.2d Nasal Assim before /k, k^{w}, g/ which is still in the Latin grammar as well as by 2c PHONOTACTICS 2b Nasal clusters. (b) Stressed /e/ becomes /i/ optionally if followed by a sequence of one or more consonants (with some restrictions) followed in turn by the high vowels /i(:)/ and possibly /u(:)/. (c) The change occurs optionally before /mp/ and /mb/. E.g.,

(a) PIE 1sg *tengō *[teŋgō] 'soak' > Lat tingō, PIE nom sg fem *dn̥g^{hw}ā 'tongue' (1 ASPIR STOPS, 2a LABIOVEL, 2d SYL SON, 6a d/t-CHANGES) > *lengwā (e-TO-i, ev) > Lat lingua. (Note here the relative chronology 2d SYL SON > e-TO-i.) PIE nom sg neut *legnom 'firewood'(2c PHONOTACTICS 2b Nasal clusters) > *leŋnom (e-TO-i, ev) > Lat lignum. (Note the relative chronology 2c PHONOTACTICS > e-TO-i.) PIE nom sg neut *n̥g^{hw}en 'groin' (1 ASPIR STOPS, 2a LABIOVEL, 2d SYL SON) > *engwen (e-TO-i) > Lat inguen; PIE nom sg *egnis 'fire' (2c PHONOTACTICS) > *eŋnis (e-TO-i) > Lat /iŋnis/ spelled <ignis>.

(b) Early dat sg *mehei 'to me' (6b ei/ou-CHANGES) > *mehī (e-TO-i) > *mihī (8d IAMBIC SHORT) > Lat mihi. (Note the chronology 6b ei/ou-CHANGES > e-TO-i.) Early nom sg masc Ø-class adj *wegil+s 'on the alert' (2c PHONOTACTICS 2a l-clusters, then la Geminate simplification) > *wegil (e-TO-i) > Lat vigil. PIE nom sg fem *d^{h}am+el+jā 'family' (1 ASPIR STOPS, 7b j/w-CHANGES) > *fameliā (e-TO-i, ev) > Lat familia. (Note the chronology 7b j/w-CHANGES> e-TO-i.) Instances where the consonants /w/ and /z/ inhibit the application of e-TO-i are these: early nom sg masc adj *brewis 'short' (ev) > Lat brevis, not **brivis; and PIE *g^{h}esi 'yesterday' (1 ASPIR STOPS) > *hesi (3d s-TO-r stage 1) > *hezi (e-TO-i not applying, then 3d s-TO-r stage 2: note here the necessary chronology 3d s-TO-r stage 1 > e-TO-i > 3d s-TO-r stage 2) > Lat heri. For some reason e-TO-i does not apply in the following derivation: PIE 1sg pres *g^{w}emjō 'come' (ev) > Lat veniō, not **viniō.

(c) PIE nom sg masc *m̥b^{h}ros 'rain' (1 ASPIR STOPS, 2d SYL SON) > *embros (4b SYNCOPE) > *ember (e-TO-i) > Lat imber; PIE nom sg masc adj *sem+plos 'simple' (e-TO-i, ev) > Lat simplus. But e-TO-i does not apply to early nom sg neut *templom 'temple' (ev) > Lat templum, not *timplum.

8d Iambic Shortening (IAMBIC SHORT)

This rule restructures certain inflectional endings. It may be considered as remaining in the grammar of Latin as a morph cond rule.

[V, +long] → [–long] / ## [C_0 [V , –long, +stress]] [C ___] ##
s1 s2

That is, a word-final vowel in a word-final syllable (s2) is shortened when following a word-initial syllable (s1) whose nucleus consists of a short stressed vowel with no consonants in the coda. (Varying formulations of this change are in Kent 1940: 107 and in Palmer 1954: 213.)

E.g., early *modō 'only' and *benē 'well' (IAMBIC SHORT) > Lat modo and bene. IAMBIC SHORT does not apply in a case like early *ok+tō '8' > Lat octō, not **octo, because s1 ends in a consonant. IAMBIC SHORT may be considered to apply as a synchronic rule in a few instances: e.g., Lat adv /benē/ 'well' and /rekt+ē/ 'justly' (IAMBIC SHORT applying synchronically) → Lat bene vs. rectē. IAMBIC SHORT does not apply in several paradigms in which the word-final long vowel is restored analogically: e.g. Lat 1sg pres amō 'love', not **amo, after forms like portō 'I carry', syllabic /por-tō/, to which IAMBIC SHORT would not apply.

8e Lachmann's Law (LACHMANN)

This change remains in the grammar as a morph cond rule. It has been the focus of attention in the literature because of its unusual nature.

V	→	V̄ /	{ perf pass part ___ }	{ C , –voiced by 2c PHONOTACTICS 1c Obstruent cluster voicing and devoicing }	+	t or s
			1	2	3	4

That is, a vowel in a perf pass part (over 1) is lengthened if followed by an obstruent consonant which has been devoiced by 2c PHONOTACTICS lc Obstruent cluster voicing and devoicing (over 2) followed by a morpheme boundary (over 3) followed by the /t, s/ perf pass part formative (over 4). Palmer (1954: 231) describes the change as follows: "In the passive participles when the final voiced consonant of the root becomes voiceless by assimilation [2c PHONOTACTICS lc Obstruent cluster voicing and devoicing] to the -t- of the suffix, the preceding vowel is lengthened."

E.g., PIE perf part *ag+t+os 'done', *leg+t+os 'read', *wid+t+os (possibly *weid+t+os) 'seen' (ev) > Lat āctus (inf agere), lēctus (inf legere) and vīsus (inf vidēre). However, LACHMANN does not apply to the perf part factus 'done' (inf facere), not **fāctus; nor does it apply to other parts of speech: e.g. nom sg *leg+s 'law' (ev) > Lat lex /leks/, not **lēx **/lēks/. LACHMANN also does not apply in at least two further instances. First, when the etymological connection with a form having a voiced consonant has become opaque: e.g., early nom sg masc *lad+t+os 'tired' (ev) > Lat lassus, not **lāsus (and there is no verb **ladere 'become tired'), nom sg *tud+t+is 'cough' (ev) > Lat tussis, not **tūsis. The form is related to tundere 'beat'; but the etymology is opaque. Similarly, the perf pass part *jud^h+t+os 'ordered' (ev) > Lat jussus, not **jūsus, since the etymological connection with the 1sg pres jubeō (from *jud^h+ējō) has been lost. Second, LACHMANN does not apply to the perf pass part form of verbs which have /n/ in the pres. E.g., 1sg pres stringō 'bind' and findō 'split' vs. perf pass part strictus and fissus as opposed to **strīctus and **fīsus.

For some reason Lachmann does not apply to the following forms in /d/: 1sg pres fodiō 'dig' and sedeō 'sit' vs. perf pass part fossus and sessus, not **fōsus or **sēsus. Finally in this connection, the fact that LACHMANN does not apply in the alternation of 1sg pres vehō 'travel' vs. perf pass part vectus, not **vēctus, is probably indicative of the relative chronology 1 ASPIR STOPS > 2c PHONOTACTICS > LACHMANN: PIE 1sg pres *weg^{h}ō and perf pass part *weg^h+t+os (1 ASPIR STOPS and 2c PHONOTACTICS) > *wehō and *wektos (LACHMANN not applying since /h/ is not +voiced) > Lat vehō and vectus.

The generally recognized problem with the formulation of Lachmann is the fact that it must "look back" in a derivation in order to apply: that is, it can lengthen vowels only before voiceless obstruent clusters whose first component has been devoiced by 2c PHONOTACTICS lc Obstruent cluster voicing and devoicing. Beekes (1995: 133) wants to give a phon cond environment for LACHMANN. His suggestion is that if one adopts a glottalic analysis of the PIE consonants, then instead of forms like PIE ag- 'do' cited above, one would reconstruct PIE *aḱ- with a glottalic /ḱ/. Then one has to posit a change of glottalic *aḱō 'I do' and *aḱtos 'done' to Lat agō and āctus.

8f Vowel Shortening in Certain Word-Final Syllables (WORD-FINAL SHORT)

This change remains as a phon cond rule in the grammar of Latin.

$$\bar{V} \rightarrow V \;/\; \text{(a)} \begin{pmatrix} -\text{stress} \\ \_\_ \end{pmatrix} \begin{Bmatrix} \text{m} \\ \text{nt} \\ \text{l} \\ \text{r} \\ \text{t} \end{Bmatrix} \#\#$$

$$\text{(b)} \begin{pmatrix} +\text{stress} \\ \_\_ \end{pmatrix} \begin{Bmatrix} \text{m} \\ \text{nt} \\ \text{t} \end{Bmatrix} \#\#$$

That is, in word-final syllables (a) unstressed vowels and (b) stressed vowels are shortened when followed by the consonants indicated.

E.g., (a) the synchronic derivations 1, 2, 3 pres subj dūk+ā+m 'lead', dūk+ā+s, dūk+ā+t, 1sg pres pass subj dūk+ā+r → dūcam, dūcās, dūcat, dūcar; 2sg port+ā+s and 3pl port+ā+nt → portās and portant. Nom sg animāl 'animal' and gen sg animālis → animal, animālis. (b) The synchronic derivations nom sg wī+s 'force' and acc sg wī+m → vīs and vim; pres subj 1sg sī+m 'be', 3sg sī+t, 3pl sī+nt→ sim, sit, sint vs. 2sg sīs. The change cannot apply to a form like sōl 'sun', not **sol. According to Palmer (1954: 221) WORD-FINAL SHORT occurs in later Latin times.

8g Restructuring of Certain "Long Sequences" (LONG SEQ RESTRUCT)

This change applies infrequently and sporadically. It restructures certain lexical items and then is dropped from the grammar.

$$\acute{\bar{V}}C_a \rightarrow \acute{V}C_aC_a$$

That is, a sequence consisting of a stressed long vowel followed by a single consonant becomes a sequence of the same vowel shortened plus the same consonant geminated.

E.g., OLat leitera 'letter' (6b ei/ou-CHANGES) > early Latin lītera (LONG SEQ RESTRUCT) > later Lat littera; early 1sg *meitō 'send' (6b ei/ou-CHANGES) > *mītō (LONG SEQ RESTRUCT) > Lat mittō. Note that 2c PHONOTACTICS 2f t-clusters does not apply here to produce **missō: hence the relative chronology 2c PHONOTACTICS 2f t-clusters > LONG SEQ RESTRUCT. Nom sg masc sūcus 'sap' (LONG SEQ RESTRUCT) > succus, both forms occurring. PIE nom sg *djeu+pater 'day-father' (3a C+j CHANGES) > *jeupater (3c ITALIC STRESS) > *jéupater (4c UNSTRESSED V) > *jéupiter (5a e-TO-o) > *jóupiter (6b ei/ou-CHANGES) > *jū́piter (LONG SEQ RESTRUCT, applying optionally) > Lat Jūpiter as well as Juppiter. (Note the chronology 6b ei/ou-CHANGES > LONG SEQ RESTRUCT.) A variation of LONG SEQ RESTRUCT may have applied in the derivation of early *k^{w}etwōr '4' (ev) > Lat quattuor.

8h Changes in /oe/ (oe-CHANGES)

This change restructures various lexical items and endings and then is dropped from the grammar.

oe → (a) ī / [–stressed, ___] C_0 ##
(b) ū / [+stressed, ___] (often)

That is, (a) unstressed /oe/ in a word-final syllable becomes /ī/; and (b) stressed /oe/ often becomes /ū/ and sometimes remains as /oe/. Note that by 5c wo-TO-we and 6b ei/ou-CHANGES, some potential occurrences of /oe/ have already become /ī/: e.g., nom sg masc *woikos 'district' (5c wo-TO-we) > *weikos (6b ei/ou-CHANGES, ev) > Lat vīcus /wīkus/.

E.g., (a) PIE nom pl *wiroi 'men' (oe-CHANGES) > Lat virī; PIE loc sg *domoi 'at home' (oe-CHANGES) > Lat domī. Note also the OLat nom pl poploi 'people' (ev) > Lat populī. (b) OLat oino as well as oenos '1', acc sg comoinem 'common' and the adv ploirume 'mostly' (ev) > Lat ūnus, commūnem and plūrimē.

The rule of oe-CHANGES does not apply over a morpheme boundary: e.g., early 1sg ko+apīō 'begin' (3c ITALIC STRESS) > *kó+apīō (4c UNSTRESSED V) > *kóepīō (oe-CHANGES not applying, ev) > Lat coepiō /koépiō/. There are also several other forms where oe-CHANGES (b) for some reason has not applied: e.g., PIE nom sg *bʰoidʰos 'treaty' (ev) > Lat foedus, not **fūdus; and nom sg *poinā 'penalty' (ev) > Lat poena, not **pūna, However, note the corresponding verb 1sg *poinīō 'I punish' (oe-CHANGES, ev) > Lat pūniō where oe-CHANGES has applied.

Buck (1962: 87) argues that the words to which oe-CHANGES (b) apparently did not apply represent archaisms retained from the language of the law. Kent (1940: 91) maintains that /oe/ remained after the bilabials /p, f, kʷ/. (But note the derivation of PIE nom sg *spoimā 'foam' to Lat spūma.) Buck (1962: 87) notes that the spelling <oe> in stressed syllables remains frequent until the 50's BC. We posit this time as the date of oe-CHANGES.

8i Vowel Contraction over a Word-Internal Morpheme Boundary (V-CONTRACT)

This change remains in the grammar of Lat as a phon cond rule. Its basic form is this:

V́(:)	+	V(:)	→	V̄́	∅	∅
1		2 3		1	2	3

with certain restrictions on the vowels V(:)1 and V(:)3 such as that they usually cannot be /e(:)/ + /o(:)/ and often not /i/ + /a(:)/, /i/ + /e(:)/ or /i/ + /o(:)/.

That is, in certain sequences consisting of (1) a stressed long or short vowel plus (2) a morpheme boundary plus (3) another long or short vowel, the stressed vowel is retained lengthened and the following vowel is deleted. E.g., early 2sg pres *plantājes 'you plant' (6c LATIN STRESS) > *plantā́jes (7b j/w-CHANGES) > *plantā́es (V-CONTRACT) > *plantā́s (6c LATIN STRESS applying as a persistent synchronic rule) > Lat plántās. (Note the necessary chronology 7b j/w-CHANGES > V-CONTRACT.) Possibly also OLat Māvors 'Mars' (?7b j/w-CHANGES) > *Māors (V-CONTRACT) > *Mārs (2c PHONOTACTICS ld Osthoff's Law applying as a persistent synchronic rule) > Lat Mars. Early 1sg *dḗ+agō 'pass time' > Lat dḗgō, *pró+emō 'bring forth' > Lat prōmō, *kó+agō 'bring forth' > Lat cōgō, but the 1sg perf *ko+ḗgī > Lat coēgī where V-CONTRACT has not applied because of the stress pattern. Also early nom sg masc *né+homō 'no+man, no one' (loss of /h/, which can occur sporadically) > *néomo (V-CONTRACT) > Lat nēmo; early nom pl *dwí+jugae 'two yokes, i.e. a span of horses' (7b j/w-CHANGES) > *dwíugae (8b dw-CHANGES) > *bíugae (V-CONTRACT) > Lat bīgae. V-CONTRACT can on occasion apply optionally, e.g. in the gen sg of jo-class nouns: /soki+ī/ 'friend' → Lat sociī or socī.

Sihler (1995: 83-4) maintains that a "reverse" application of V-CONTRACT occurs in a derivation like that of 1sg pres *portājō 'I carry' (7b j/w-CHANGES) > *portāō (ev) > Lat portō instead of **portā, which would have resulted from the application of V-CONTRACT. Sihler posits as the reason for the reverse application of V-CONTRACT the fact that otherwise the first singular would have been identical with the 2sg imp portā. Yet another reason for the retention of the 1st singular ending -ō is that it in any case would not have been deleted by V-CONTRACT in forms like habeō 'have' or capiō 'seize'.

8j Lengthening of a Vowel Before /n/ Plus /k/ Plus Obstruent (Vnk-TO-V̄nk)

This change remains as a phon cond rule in the Latin grammar.

V → V̄ / ___ nk [C, +obstruent]

That is, a vowel is lengthened when preceding the sequence /n/ plus /k/ plus an obstruent consonant, which turns out to be only /t/ or /s/. E.g., the early ordinal *kʷinkʷ+t+os '5th' (2a LABIOVEL) > *kʷinktos (Vnk-TO-V̄nk, ev) > *kʷīnktus (2c PHONOTACTICS 2h Sonorant-initial clusters applying as a persistent rule) > Lat quīntus, from which the cardinal quīnque '5' is reformed with a long /ī/. Note also the synchronic alternations between the following first singular present vs. perfect forms: jungō 'join' vs. part /jung+tus/ → jūnctus, lingō 'lick' vs. 1sg /ling+sī/ → līnxī, vinciō 'tie up' vs. part /wink+tus/ → vīnctus.

8k Changes in the Sequence /Vns/ (Vns-CHANGES)

These changes restructure various inflectional endings; a few may be considered to have remained as morph cond rules of Lat. Otherwise the changes drop from the grammar. The rules apply sporadically and usually to word-final syllables. Their basic structure is this:

(a)	[V, +stress]	n	s	→	[same, but +long]	same	same
	1	2	3		1	2	3
(b)	[V, –stress]	n	s	→	[same, but +long]	Ø	same
	1	2	3		1	2	3

That is, (a) in a sequence of a stressed vowel plus /n/ plus /s/, the stressed vowel is lengthened. (b) In a sequence of an unstressed vowel plus /n/ plus /s/, the vowel is lengthened and the /n/ is deleted. E.g., (a) early nom sg *front+s 'forehead' vs. gen sg *front+is (2c PHONOTACTICS 2f t-clusters) > *frons vs. *frontis (Vns-CHANGES) > Lat frōns vs. frontis. (Note here the chronology 2c PHONOTACTICS > Vns-CHANGES.) (b) Early acc pl forms *serwons 'servants', *mensāns 'tables', *rēgn̥s 'kings' (2d SYL SON) > *serwons, *mensāns, *rēgens (Vns-Changes) > Lat servōs, mensās and rēgēs. (Note here the chronology 2d SYL SON > Vns-CHANGES.)

Forms do occur with the /n/ retained in spite of Vns-CHANGES b: e.g., nom sg pres part amāns 'loving' and praesens 'present' as opposed to **amās and **praesēs. Kent (1940: 137) explains such occurrences as follows: "It is likely that writings with -ns were mainly analogical or pedantic..." A possible variation on Vns-CHANGES is indicated in certain OLat forms such as cosol 'consul' < earlier *kónsol in which the /n/ has been deleted after a stressed vowel.

8l Shortening of a Long Vowel Followed by Another Vowel (V̄V-TO-VV)

This change remains in the grammar as a sometimes optional phon cond rule.

V̄ → V / C ___ + V(:)

That is, a long vowel is shortened if preceded by a consonant and followed by a word-internal morpheme boundary plus a vowel, either long or short. E.g., early nom sg masc /pīus/ 'pious' → pius; early gen sg /diē+ī/ 'day' and /rē+ī/ 'thing' → diēī where V̄V-TO-VV has not applied vs. reī where it has. Early inf /dē+esse/ 'be lacking', 1sg pres /flē+ō/ 'weep' → deesse, fleō. Note also the following paradigmatic alternations: nom sg /sū+s/ 'pig' vs. gen sg /sū+is/ → sūs vs. suis; and 1sg pres /sū+ō/ 'sew', inf /sū+ere/, 1sg perf /sū+ī/ and perf part /sū+tus/→ suō, suere, suī, sūtus.

C. The Relative Chronology

The " > " means "must precede"; " > < " means "at approximately the same time as".

1 ASPIR STOPS > 2a LABIOVEL (see the discussion under 2a), > 2c PHONOTACTICS (see 2c and 8e LACHMANN), > 3d s-TO-r (see 1), > 4b SYNCOPE (see 1), > 5b u-TO-i (see 5b), > 6b ei/ou-CHANGES (see 1), > 7b j/w-CHANGES (see 1), > 8i V-CONTRACT (see 1).

2a LABIOVEL > 6b ei/ou-CHANGES (see 2a), > 7b j/w-CHANGES (see 2a).

2b LONG DIPH> 4c UNSTRESSED V (see 2b), > 6b ei/ou-CHANGES (see 2b), > 7a ai/oi-TO-ae/oe (see 2b).

2c PHONOTACTICS > 4c Syncope (see 2c), > 8c e-TO-i (see 8c), > 8e LACHMANN (see 8e), > 8g LONG SEQ RESTRUCT (see 8g), > 8k Vns-CHANGES (see 8k).

2d SYL SON > 7c o(:)-TO-u(:) (see 2d), > 8c e-TO-i (see 2d and 8c), > 8k Vns-CHANGES (see 8k).

3a C+j CHANGES > 7b j/w-CHANGES (see 3a and 7b), > 7c o(:)-TO-u(:) (see 3a).

3b i/u-TO-e/o > < 3d s-TO-r (see 3b).

3c ITALIC STRESS > 4b SYNCOPE (see 3c and 4b), > 4c UNSTRESSED V (see 3c and 4c), > 6c LATIN STRESS (see 3c).

3d s-TO-r > < 3b i/u-TO-e/o (see 3b).

4a p-TO-k^w > 5a e-TO-o (see 4a), > 7b j/w-Changes (see 4a).

4b Syncope > < 2c PHONOTACTICS (at least some parts, see 2c), > 3d s-TO-r (later part, see 4b), > 6b ei/ou-CHANGES (see 6b), > 6c LATIN STRESS (see 4b).

4c UNSTRESSED V > 5a e-TO-o (see 4c), > 6b ei/ou-CHANGES (see 4c), > 6c LATIN STRESS (see 4c), > 7c o(:)-TO-u(:) (see 4c), > 8c e-TO-i (see 4c).

5a e-TO-o > 6b ei/ou-CHANGES (see 5a and 6b), > 7b j/w-CHANGES (see 5a and 7b), > 7c o(:)-TO-u(:) (see 5a), > 8b dw-CHANGES (see 5a).

5b u-TO-i > 6b ei/ou-CHANGES (see 5b).

5c wo-TO-we > 6b ei/ou-CHANGES (see 5c).

6a d/t-CHANGES > Ø.

6b ei/ou-CHANGES > 7b j/w-CHANGES (see 7b), > 8c e-TO-i (see 8c), > 8g LONG SEQ RESTRUCT (see 8g), > 81 V̄V-TO-VV (see 1 ASPIR STOPS).

6c LATIN STRESS > 7d ow-TO-aw (see 7d), > 8i V-CONTRACT (see 8i).

7a ai/oi-TO-ae/oe > 8h oe-CHANGES (see 8h).

7b j/w-CHANGES > 8c e-TO-i (see 8c), > 8i V-CONTRACT (see 8i), > 81 V̄V-TO-VV (7b).

The following rules do not necessarily precede any other rules:

(7c) o(:)-TO-u(:) > Ø; (7d) ow-TO-aw > Ø; (8a) DISSIMILATION > Ø; (8b) dw-CHANGES > Ø; (8c) e-TO-i > Ø; (8d) IAMBIC SHORT > Ø; (8e) LACHMANN > Ø; (8f) WORD-FINAL SHORT > Ø; (8g) LONG SEQ RESTRUCT > Ø; (8h) oe-CHANGES > Ø; (8i) V-CONTRACT > Ø; (8j) Vnk-TO-V̄nk > Ø; (8k) Vns-CHANGES > Ø; (81) V̄V-TO-VV> Ø.

III Latin Phonology

After the changes described in the previous section, the inventory of segments in the phonology of Latin at about 0 AD was as follows.

Obstruent Consonants

labial	dental	alveolar	velar	labiovelar	glottal
p	t		k	k^w[1]	h
p^h	t^h		k^h[2]		
b	d		g		
f		s			

Sonorant Consonants

labial	dental	alveolar	velar
m	n		[ŋ][3]
	l		
	r		
[w	j][4]		

Vowels

i(:)				u(:)
	e(:)		o(:)	
		a(:)		

Diphthongs ae, au, oe; ei, eu, ui[5]

Latin Segments in Terms of Phonological Features: Consonants

	p	t	k	k^w	p^h	t^h	k^h	b	d	g	f	s	h	m	n	ŋ	l	r	w	j
consonantal	+	+	+	+	+	+	+	+	+	+	+	+		+	+	+	+	+	–	–
sonorant	–	–	–	–	–	–	–	–	–	–	–	–		+	+	+	+	+	+	+
vocalic	–	–	–	–	–	–	–	–	–	–	–	–		–	–	–	–	–	–	–
high	–	–	+	+	–	–	+	–	–	+	–	–		–	–	+	–	–	+	+
back	–	–	+	+	–	–	+	–	–	+	–	–		–	–	+	–	–	+	–
low	–	–	–	–	–	–	–	–	–	–	–	–		–	–	–	–	–	–	–
anterior	+	+	–	–	+	+	–	+	+	–	+	+		+	+	–	+	+	–	–
coronal	–	+	–	–	–	+	–	–	+	–	–	+		–	+	–	+	+	–	–
voiced	–	–	–	–	–	–	–	+	+	+	–	–	–	+	+	+	+	+	+	+
continuant	–	–	–	–	–	–	–	–	–	–	+	+	+	–	–	–	+	+	+	+
nasal	–	–	–	–	–	–	–	–	–	–	–	–		+	+	+	–	–	–	–
strident	–	–	–	–	–	–	–	–	–	–	–	+		–	–	–	–	–	–	–

	p	t	k	k^w	p^h	t^h	k^h	b	d	g	f	s	h	m	n	ŋ	l	r	w	j
delayed release	–	–	–	–	–	–	–	–	–	–	–	–		–	–	–	–	–	–	–
round	–	–	–	+	–	–	–	–	–	–	–	–		–	–	–	–	–	+	–
lateral	–	–	–	–	–	–	–	–	–	–	–	–		–	–	–	+	–	–	–
palatal	–	–	–	–	–	–	–	–	–	–	–	–		–	–	–	–	–	–	+
aspirated	–	–	–	–	+	+	+	–	–	–	–	–	+	–	–	–	–	–	–	–
stressed	–	–	–	–	–	–	–	–	–	–	–	–		–	–	–	–	–	–	–
long	–	–	–	–	–	–	–	–	–	–	–	–		–	–	–	–	–	–	–

Latin Segments in Terms of Phonological Features: Vowels

	a	e	i	o	u	ā	ē	ī	ō	ū
consonantal	–	–	–	–	–	–	–	–	–	–
sonorant	+	+	+	+	+	+	+	+	+	+
vocalic	+	+	+	+	+	+	+	+	+	+
high	–	–	+	–	+	–	–	+	–	+
back	+	–	–	+	+	+	–	–	+	+
low	+	–	–	–	–	+	–	–	–	–
continuant	+	+	+	+	+	+	+	+	+	+
nasal	–	–	–	–	–	–	–	–	–	–
round	–	–	–	+	+	–	–	–	+	+
tense	–	–	–	–	–	+	+	+	+	+
stressed	±	±	±	±	±	±	±	±	±	±
long	–	–	–	–	–	+	+	+	+	+

Certain of the changes have remained as rules in the grammar of Latin. Those below labeled "morph cond" are morphologically conditioned and apply either to lexically marked items or to morphosyntactically defined classes. Those marked "phon cond" are phonologically conditioned and apply more or less generally. The symbol "Ø" after a change means that it has restructured lexical items and/or changed the inventory of underlying segments and has then been dropped from the grammar. For those changes remaining as rules in the grammar we cite an illustrative derivation. Additional examples can be found in the discussions of the particular rules.

1 ASPIR STOPS: Ø.

2a LABIOVEL: Ø.

2b LONG DIPH: Ø.

2c PHONOTACTICS (morph cond and phon cond): nom sg /pēd+s/ 'foot' vs. gen sg /ped+is/ (PHONOTACTICS lc Obstruent cluster voicing and devoicing, PHONOTACTICS 2f t-clusters, PHONOTACTICS la Geminate simplification) → pēs vs. pedis.

2d SYL SON: Ø.

3a C+j CHANGES: Ø.

3b i/u-TO-e/o: Ø.

3c ITALIC STRESS (phon cond until replaced by 6c LATIN STRESS): Ø.

3d s-TO-r (morph cond): nom sg /genus/ 'family' vs. gen sg /genes+is/ (s-TO-r) → genus, generis.

4a p-TO-k^w: Ø.

4b SYNCOPE: Ø.

4c UNSTRESSED V (morph cond): 1sg pres /fakiō/ 'make' vs. /inter+fakiō/ 'kill' (UNSTRESSED V in its synchronic version) → faciō vs. interficiō.

5a e-TO-o (possibly morph cond): see 5a.

5b u-TO-i: Ø.

5c wo-TO-we: Ø.

6a d/t-CHANGES (morph cond): nom sg /lakt/ 'milk' vs. gen sg /lakt+is/ (d/t-CHANGES) → lac, lactis.

6b ei/ou-CHANGES: Ø.

6c LATIN STRESS (phon cond): nom sg /kalamitās/ 'calamity' vs. gen sg /kalamitātis/ (LATIN STRESS) → calamitās /kalámitās/ vs. calamitātis /kalamitā́tis /.

7a ai/oi-TO-ae/oe: Ø.

7b j/w-CHANGES (phon cond): 1sg pres /jubeō/ 'command' and /kapjō/ 'seize' (j/w-CHANGES) → jubeō and capiō.

7c o(:)-TO-u(:): Ø.

7d ow-TO-aw: Ø.

8a DISSIMILATION (morph cond): adj /lūn-āl+is/ 'lunar' (DISSIMILATION)→ lūnāris.

8b dw-CHANGES: Ø.

8c e-TO-i: Ø.

8d IAMBIC SHORT (morph cond): adv /ben+ē/ 'well' (IAMBIC SHORT) → bene.

8e LACHMANN (morph cond): perf pass part /ag+t+us/ 'done' (2c PHONOTACTICS 1c Obstruent cluster voicing and devoicing) → aktus (LACHMANN) → āctus.

8f WORD-FINAL SHORT (phon cond): pres sg subj 1 /dūk+ām/ 'lead' vs. 2 /dūk+ās/ (WORD-FINAL SHORT) → dūcam vs. dūcās.

8g LONG SEQ RESTRUCT: Ø.

8h oe-CHANGES: Ø.

8i V-CONTRACT (phon cond): 1sg pres /kó+agō/ 'bring forth' → cōgō /kṓgō/.

8j Vnk-TO-V̄nk (phon cond): perf pass part /wink+t+us/ 'tied up' (Vnk-TO-V̄nk)→ vīnctus.

8k Vns-CHANGES (morph cond): nom sg /front+s/ 'forehead' (2c PHONOTACTICS 2f t-clusters) → frons (Vns-CHANGES) → frōns.

8l V̄V-TO-VV (phon cond): inf /sū+ere/ 'sew' vs. perf pass part /sū+tus/ (V̄V-TO-VV) → suere vs. sūtus.

IV Historical Latin Morphology

A. Overview

B. Latin Morphology

In each paradigm below the Latin forms of ca. 0 AD are cited in the left-hand column. The forms on the right are the PIE antecedents.

1 Nouns

Nouns, like the other substantives and the verbs, are inflected for singular and plural. The cases are nominative, vocative, accusative, genitive, dative, ablative and a few remnants of a locative. In the plural the vocative forms are those of the nominative. In some paradigms the vocative is identical to the nominative in all forms, singular and plural. In such paradigms we cite only the nominative forms. In neuter substantives the nominative and accusative forms are identical.

In traditional grammars, Latin nouns are classified in five declensions. These are the first declension (our ā-class under 1.2 below), the second declension (our o-class 1.1), the third declension (our i-class 1.3 as well as several of the athematic forms under 1.5) and the fourth declension (our u-class 1.4). The fifth declension is of uncertain origin. We consider it an amalgam of o-class (1.1) forms and root-class athematic nouns (on which see 1.5.3).

1.1 o-Class (Masculine, Neuter, a few Feminine)

			Latin		**PIE**
masc	**sg**	**nom**	deus	'god'	*deiwos[6]
		voc	dee		*deiwe
		acc	deum		*deiwom
		gen	deī		*deiw+ī[7]
		dat	deō		*deiwōi[8]
		abl	deō		*deiwōd[9]
	pl	**nom**	deī		*deiw+oi[10]
		acc	deōs		*deiwons
		gen	deum, deōrum		*deiwo(:)m[11]
		dat	deīs		*deiwōis[12]
		abl	"		"

Some nouns of this class with stems ending in /r/ undergo a slightly different development in the nominative singular:

		Latin		PIE
masc sg	**nom**	ager	'field'	*agros[13]
	acc	agrum		*agrom

There are a few nouns in this class which are feminine. An example is Lat humus 'earth' from *g^{h}om+os from an original Vn-class *g^{h}om+ō (1.5.5).

Neuter o-Class nouns have the same endings as the masculine nouns except for the following:

		Latin		PIE
sg	**nom/acc**	jugum	'yoke'	*jugom
pl	**nom/acc**	juga		*jugā[14]

The jo-Class nouns have the same endings as Latin deus 'god' and jugum 'yoke' noted above. E.g.,

			Latin		PIE
masc	**sg**	**nom**	socius	'friend'	*sok^{w}jos[15]
neut		**nom**	imperium	'authority'	*imperjom
masc		**gen**	socī or sociī		*sok^{w}j+ī[16]
neut		**gen**	imperī or imperiī		*imperj+ī

1.2 ā-Class (Feminine, a few Masculine)

Sihler 1995: 266-75 refers to this class as the "eH$_2$" class. The /ā/ in the inflectional endings is considered derived from /e/ plus a laryngeal by a change like that which we formulate as Greek change 1a LARYNGEALS in Chapter 4. (See also on this 3.1.3.3 in Chapter 1.)

			Latin		PIE
fem	**sg**	**nom**	stella	'star'	*sterlā[17]
		voc	stella		*sterla[17]
		acc	stellam		*sterlām[17]
		gen	stellās		*sterlās[18]
			stellae		*sterlā+i[18]
		dat	stellae		*sterlāi
		abl	stellā		*sterlād[19]
		loc	viae	'on the way'	*wiāi[20]
	pl	**nom**	stellae		*sterlā+i;[21]
		acc	stellās		*sterlāns[22]
		gen	stellārum		*sterlā+som[23]
		dat	stellīs		*sterlāis[24]
		abl	"		"

There are a few masculine nouns of this class. One of them is agricola 'farmer'.

The jā-Class has the same endings as those of the ā-Class. There are many deadjectival nouns in this class such as the pres act part *sapjent- 'knowing' plus *-jā (7b j/w-CHANGES, ev) > Lat sapientia 'wisdom'.

1.3 i-Class (Masculine, Feminine, Neuter)

This class forms a a component of the Latin third declension as described above. The masculine and feminine nouns have the same endings. The following noun is masc.

			Latin		PIE
masc	**sg**	**nom**	ignis /iŋnis/	'fire'	*egni+s
		acc	ignem		*egni+m̥[25]
		gen	ignis		*egn+es[25]
		dat	ignī		*egn+ei[25]
		abl	ignī		*egn+īd[26]
			igne		*egn+ed
	pl	**nom**	ignēs		*egnei+es[27]
		acc	ignīs		*egni+ns[28]
			ignēs		
		gen	ignium		*egni+om
		dat	ignibus		*egni+bʰos
		abl	"		"

The neuter nouns of this class are like the masc and fem, forms except for the following:

sg	nom/acc	mare	'sea'	*mari[29]
pl	nom/acc	maria		*mari+ā

1.4 u-Class (Masculine, Feminine, Neuter)

The masc and fem nouns of this class have the same endings. The following is a masc. noun.

			Latin		PIE
masc	**sg**	**nom**	frūctus	'profit'	*bʰrūktus
		acc	frūctum		*bʰrūktum
		gen	frūctūs		*bʰrūktous[30]
		dat	frūctuī		*bʰrūkteuei[31]
			frūctū		*bʰrūktūd[32]
		abl	"		"
	pl	**nom**	frūctūs		*bʰrūkteues[33]
		acc	frūctūs		*bʰrūktuns[33]
		gen	frūctuum		*bʰrūktuom
		dat	frūctibus		*bʰrūktubʰos[34]
		abl	"		"

The neuter nouns have the same endings as frūctus above except for the following:

		Latin		PIE
sg	**nom/acc**	genū	'knee'	*genu[35]
pl	**nom/acc**	genua		*genuā

1.5 Athematic Classes

These classes along with the i-class under 1.3 above constitute the traditionally called Latin third declension.

1.5.1 Ø-Class (Masculine, Feminine, Neuter)

The masculine and feminine nouns have the same endings. An example of the masculine declension is the following:

			Latin		PIE
masc	**sg**	**nom**	rēx /rēks/	'king'	*rēg+s[36]
		acc	rēgem		*rēg+m̥
		gen	rēgis		*rēg+es
		dat	rēgī		*rēg+ei
		abl	rēge		*rēg+i[37]
	pl	**nom**	rēgēs		*rēg+es[38]
		acc	rēgēs		*rēg+n̥s[38]
		gen	rēgum		*rēg+om
		dat	rēgibus		*rēg+i+bʰos[39]
		abl	"		"

Neuter nouns of this class have the same endings as the masculine and feminine except for the following:

		Latin		PIE
nom/acc	**sg**	caput	'head'	*kapot[40]
	pl	capita		*kapotā[41]

1.5.2 r/n-Class (Neuter)

This class has the same endings as the neuter Ø-class:

		Latin		PIE
sg	**nom/acc**	iter	'journey'	*i+ter
	gen	itineris		*i+ten+er+es[42]

1.5.3 Root Class (Masculine, Feminine)

These are Ø-class athematic nouns whose roots end in a vowel or diphthong. The masculine and feminine nouns take the same endings. The following is a masculine noun.

		Latin		PIE
sg	**nom**	bōs	'ox'	*gʷōu+s[43]
	acc	bovem		*gʷou+m̥[44]
	gen	bovis		*gʷou+es
	dat	bovī		*gʷou+ei
	abl	bove		*gʷou+i

		Latin		PIE
pl	**nom**	bovēs	'oxen'	*g^{w}ou+es[45]
	acc	bovēs		*g^{w}ou+n̥s[45]
	gen	boum		*g^{w}ou+om[46]
	dat	bōbus		*g^{w}ōu+b^{h}os
	abl	"		"

A Latin spin-off of the root class is the so-called fifth declension. Nouns of this class are usually feminine, with one masculine noun. The masculine and feminine endings are identical. E.g., the following masculine noun:

		Latin		PIE
sg	**nom**	diēs	'day'	*diē(u)+s[47]
	acc	diem		*diē+m[47]
	gen	diēī		*diē+ī[47, 48, 49]
	dat	diēī		*diē+ei
	abl	diē		*diē+d[48]
pl	**nom**	diēs		*diē+es
	acc	diēs		*diē+n̥s
	gen	diērum		*diē+som[48]
	dat	diēbus		*diē+b^{h}os
	abl	"		"

An ablauting form of *diēu-, namely *dieu-, is the antecedent of the noun Juppiter, which is a (t)Vr-class noun in the nominative and vocative and is root class in the other cases. Derivations are nom sg *dieu+pater 'father of day, Juppiter' (PIE 3.1.2c i-j/u-w ALT applying synchronically) → *djeupater (3a C+j CHANGES) > *jeupater (3c ITALIC STRESS) > *jéupater (4c UNSTRESSED V) > *jéupiter (5a e-TO-o) > *jóupiter (6b ei/ou-CHANGES) > Lat Jūpiter (to which 8g LONG SEQ RESTRUCT can apply optionally) > Lat Juppiter as well; and gen sg *dieu+es (PIE 3.1.2c i-j/u-w ALT) → *djewes (3a C+j CHANGES) > *jewes (4c UNSTRESSED V) > *jewis (5a e-TO-o) > Lat Jovis /jowis/.

1.5.4 (t)Vr-Class (Masculine, Feminine)

Nouns of this class designate family members or human agents. The masculine and feminine nouns have the same endings, which are like those of the Ø-class above except that the nominative singular is in -Ø, not -s.

			Latin		PIE
sg	**nom**	**masc**	pater	'father'	*pater[50]
			auctor	'author'	*auktōr[51]
		fem	māter	'mother'	*māter[50]
			soror	'sister'	*swesōr[52]
	acc	**masc**	patrem		*patrm̥[50]
			auctōrem		*auktōrm̥
		fem	mātrem		*mātrm̥[50]
			sorōrem		*swesōrm̥
	gen	**masc**	patris		*patres
			auctōris		*auktōres
		fem	mātris		*mātres
			sorōris		*swesōres

1.5.5 Vn-Class (Masculine, Feminine, Neuter)

This class takes the same endings as the (t)Vr-class above. The masc and fem nouns have the same endings. E.g.,

			Latin		PIE
sg	**nom**	**masc**	homo	'man'	*g^{h}emō(n)[53]
			sermō	'sermon'	*sermō(n)[53]
		fem	nātio	'nation'	*nātjō(n)[53, 54]
			virgō		*wirgō(n)[53]
			carō	'meat'	*kr̥+ō(n)[53, 55]
	acc	**masc**	hominem		*g^{h}emenm̥[55]
			sermōnem		*sermōnm̥[55]
		fem	nātiōnem		*nātjōnm̥
			virginem		*wirgenm̥[55]
			carnem		*kr̥nm̥[55]

Neuter nouns of this class have the same endings as the masculine and feminine except for the following:

		Latin		PIE
nom/acc	**sg**	nomen	'name'	*nomen[56]
	pl	nomina		*nomenā[57]

1.5.6 Vs-Class (Masculine, Feminine, Neuter)

The masculine and feminine nouns of this class have the same endings. They are those of the Vn-class above. E.g.,

			Latin		PIE
sg	**nom**	**masc**	honōs	'honor'	*g^{h}on+ōs[58]
		fem	arbōs	'tree'	*ard^{h}+ōs[59]
			mulier	'woman'	*molj+es[59]
	acc	**masc**	honōrem		*g^{h}on+ōs+m̥[58]
		fem	arborem		*ard^{h}+os+m̥[59]
			mulierem		*molj+es+m̥[60]

A possible reflex of an -ēs suffix is the following feminine noun:

		Latin		PIE
sg	**nom**	nūbēs	'cloud'	*sneub^{h}+ēs
	acc	nūbem		*sneub^{h}+m̥[61]

The neuter nouns of this class have the same endings as the masculine and feminine except for the following:

		Latin		PIE
nom/acc	**sg**	genus	'race'	*gen+os
	pl	genera		*gen+es+ā[62]

2 Adjectives

2.1 o-Class and ā-Class

The endings of this class are those of the o-class nouns (1.1 above) for masculine and neuter adjectives and those of the ā-class nouns (1.2) for the feminine adjectives. E.g.,

			Latin		PIE
nom	**sg**	**masc**	bonus	'good'	*dwen+os
		neuter	bonum		*dwen+om
		fem	bona		*dwen+ā

The nominative singular masculine ending of adjectives ending in *-ros undergoes 4b SYNCOPE. E.g., nom sg masc *miseros 'wretched' > Lat miser.

Nine adjectives have some of their endings from the pronominal declension (5.3 below). These adjectives have pronominal-like meanings: e.g., alius 'other', neuter 'neither', nūllus 'no, none', sōlus 'alone, only', ūnus '1', uter 'which of two'. Most of these adjectives have only the genitive and dative singular pronominal endings; alius 'other' also has the pronominal ending of the nominative/accusative singular neuter. E.g.,

		Latin		PIE
sg	**gen**	alius	'other'	*ali+jos
	dat	alii		*ali+ei
	nom/acc neut	aliud		*ali+od

Finally, there also are jo- and jā-class adjectives which have the same endings as those of the o-and ā-classes. E.g.,

			Latin		PIE
nom	**sg**	**masc**	tertius	'3rd'	*tertj+os[63]
		fem	tertia		*tertj+ā
		neuter	tertium		*tertj+om

2.2 i-Class and Athematic Class

These adjectives divide into three subclasses: (1) those with three distinct nominative singular endings for masculine, feminine and neuter; (2) those with two nominative singular endings, masculine/feminine and neuter; and (3) those with one nominative singular ending for all genders. E.g., the following nominative singular forms:

		Latin		PIE
1	**masc**	ācer	'sharp'	*ākr+is[64]
	fem	ācris		*ākr+is[64]
	neuter	ācre		*ākr+i
2	**masc/fem**	levis	'light'	*leg^{hw}+is[65]
	neuter	leve		*leg^{hw}+i
3	**masc/fem/neuter**	atrōx	'fierce'	*atrōk+s[66]

Other adjectives of subclass (3) are these:

		Latin		PIE
sg	**nom**	vetus	'old'	*wet+os+s[67]
		pār	'equal'	*pār+s[68]
		praeceps	'headlong'	*prai+kapot+s[69]
	gen	veteris		*wet+os+es
		pāris		*pār+es
		praecipitis		*prai+kapot+es[69]

2.3 Comparison

The primary comparative and superlative formatives are as follows. (We cite nominative singular forms.)

		Latin		PIE
pos	**masc**	altus	'high'	*alt+os
comp	**masc/fem**	altior		*alt+jos+s[70]
	neuter	altius		*alt+jos+s[70]
sup	**masc**	altissimus		*alt+is+im+os[71]

Finally, a few common Lat adjs form their comparative and superlative by suppletion and on occasion with a superlative suffix other than the usual *-si+im-.
E.g.,

		Latin		PIE
a	**pos**	bonus	'good'	*dwenos
	comp	melior	'better'	*mel+jos
	sup	optimus	'best'	*opt+im+os
b	**pos**	malus	'bad'	*malos
	comp	pējor	'worse'	*ped+jos[72]
	sup	pessimus	'worst'	*ped+s+im+os[73]
c	**pos**	multus	'much'	*ml̥tos
	comp	plūs	'more'	*plē+jos[74]
	sup	plūrimus	'most'	*plē+s+im+os[75]

3 Adverbs

There are two basic formations for deadjectival adverbs.

	Latin		PIE
a	rēctē	'justly'	*reg+t+ēd[76,77]
	meritō	'deservedly'	*merit+ōd[76]
b	ācriter	'keenly'	*ākri+ter[78]

Some adverbs are formed from various case endings. E.g.,

		Latin		PIE
sg	**gen**	dius	'by day'	*diu+os[79]
	acc	facile	'easily'	*d^hakil+i[80]
		partim	'partly'	part+im[81]
		multum	'much'	*ml̥t+om[80]

The comparative of the adverb is the comparative neuter accusative of the corresponding adjective. The superlative adverb takes the ending -ē on the superlative stem of the adjective. E.g.,

	Latin		PIE
pos	rēctē	'justly'	*reg+t+ēd
comp	rēctius	'more justly'	*reg+t+jos
sup	rēctissimē	'most justly'	*reg+t+isimēd

4 Numerals

4.1 Cardinals

The cardinals '1, 2, 3', '200' through '900' and the thousands from '2000' on are inflected. The other cardinals are uninflected.

	Latin	PIE
'1'	ūnus	*oinos

The endings are those of o- and ā-class adjectives.

			Latin	PIE
'2'	**nom**	masc	duo	*duō(u)[82]
		fem	duae	*duāi
		neuter	duo	*duō(u)[82]
	acc	masc	duōs	*duōns[83]
		fem	duās	*duāns[83]
		neuter	duo	*duō(u)[82]
	gen	masc	duōrum	*duō+som[83]
		fem	duārum	*duā+som
		neuter	duōrum	*duō+som
	dat/abl	masc/neut	duōbus	*duōb^{h}os
		fem	duābus	*duāb^{h}os
'3'	**nom**	masc/fem	trēs	*trei+es[84,85,]
		neuter	tria	*tri+ā[86,85]

	Latin	PIE
'4'	quattuor	*k^{w}etwōr

The derivation is problematic. One would expect k^{w}etwōr (7b j/w-CHANGES) > *k^{w}etōr (8f WORD-FINAL SHORT) > Lat **quetor. Sihler (1995: 181) posits a change t → tt / __w. But even so, the /a/ in the Latin form is unexplained. Some have posited a PIE antecedent with schwa, namely *k^{w}ətwōr.

	Latin	PIE
'5'	quīnque	*penk^{w}e
'6'	sex	*seks
'7'	septem	*septm̥
'8'	octō	*oktōu

The derivation of '8' is *oktōu (2b LONG DIPH) > Lat octō.

	Latin	PIE
‘9’	novem	*newm̥

The derivation is *newm̥ (2d SYL SON) > *newem (5a e-TO-o) > Lat novem /nowem/. Some sources posit PIE *newn̥ on the basis of the ordinal nōnus ‘9th’ (see below). If so, then the dervation would be *newn̥ (ev) > Lat **noven **/nowen/. If this is correct, then the /m/ in Lat novem was from the Lat decem ‘10’ below.

	Latin	PIE
‘10’	decem	*dekm̥
‘11’	ūndecim	*oin+dekm̥

The origin of the ending /-im/ in ‘11’ instead of /-em/ is not clear. Kent (1946: 79) suggests that the form was influenced by the ordinal, where the development would have been regular: PIE *dekm̥+os ‘10th’ (2d SYL SON) > dekemos (3c ITALIC STRESS) > *dékemos (4c UNSTRESSED V) > *dékimos (7c o(:)-TO-u(:)) > Lat decimus.

	Latin	PIE
‘12’	duodecim	*duōdekm̥
‘13’	trēdecim	*trejes+dekm̥[87]
‘14’	quattuordecim	*k^wetwōr+dekm̥
‘15’	quīndecim	*penk^{w}e+dekm̥[87]
‘16’	sēdecim	*seks+dekm̥[87]
‘17’	septendecim	*septm̥+dekm̥[87]
‘18’	duodēvīgīntī	*duō+dē+’20’ = ‘2 from 20’
‘19’	ūndēvīgīntī	*oin+dē+’20’ = ‘1 from 20’
‘20’	vīgīntī	*wī+dkm̥+t+ī

The PIE antecedent of ‘20’ is not obvious. Kent (1946: 79) considers it a sequence consisting of *wī- ‘2’ plus *dkm̥- ‘10’ plus the derivative suffix *-t ‘-ness’ plus the dual ending -ī. Hence the construction means ‘2 ten-nesses’. Its derivation is not clear: *wī+dkm̥+t+ī (? an early assimilation) > *wīdgm̥tī (2c PHONOTACTICS 2c Obstruent assimilation) > *wīggm̥tī (2c PHONOTACTICS lb Nasal assimilation) > *wīggn̥tī (2d SYL SON) > *wīggentī (6c LATIN STRESS) > *wīggéntī (2c PHONOTACTICS la Geminate simplification applying as a persistent rule) > *wīgénti (8c e-TO-i) > Lat **vīgintī** /wīgíntī/.

	Latin	PIE
‘21’	vīgintī ūnus etc.	
‘30’	trīgintā	*trei+dkm̥+t+ā

The PIE antecedent of ‘30’ consists of *trei- ‘3’ plus the same abstract noun *dkm̥+t- ‘10-ness’ as in ‘20’ above plus the nominative plural neuter ending *-ā. The derivation is *treidkm̥tā (by the same changes as for ‘20’ above) > *treigintā (also 6b ei/ou-CHANGES) > Lat trīgintā.

	Latin	PIE
'40'	quadrāgintā	*kʷetwōr+ā+dkm̥tā[88]

The derivation here is not clear. From the purported antecedent one would expect Lat **quatuorāgintā.

	Latin	PIE
'50'	quīnquāgintā	*penkʷe+ā+dkm̥+t+ā[88]
'60'	sexagīntā	*seks+ā+dkm̥+t+ā[88]
'70'	septuāgintā	*septm+ā+dkm̥+t+ā[88]

The derivation of '70' is not clear. From the purported antecedent one would expect Lat **septmāgintā. The /u/ instead of /m/in the Lat septuāgintā may have been due to the influence of '50'.

	Latin	PIE
'80'	octōgintā	*oktōu+dkm̥+t+ā
'90'	nōnāgintā	*newn+ā+dkm̥+t+ā[88]
'100'	centum	*kn̥tom
'200'	ducentī	*du+kn̥t+oi[89]
'300'	trecentī	*tri+kn̥t+oi[89]
'400'	quadringentī	*kʷetwōr+kn̥t+oi[89,90]
'500'	quīngentī	*penkʷe+kn̥t+oi[89]
'600'	sescentī	*seks+kn̥t+oi[89]

The derivation of '600' is *sekskn̥toi (2c PHONOTACTICS 2g s-clusters) > *seskn̥toi (2d SYL SON) > *seskentoi (ev) > Lat sescentī.

	Latin	PIE
'700'	septingentī	*septm̥+kn̥t+oi[89]
'800'	octingentī	*oktōu+kn̥t+oi[89, 90]
'900'	nōngentī	*newn+kn̥t+oi[89]
'1000'	mīlle	*sm+i+gʰesl+i[91]
'2000'	duo mīlia	*duōu *sm+i+gʰesl+i+ā[91]

4.2 Ordinals

These forms are o- and ā-class adjectives. Below we cite the nominative singular masculine.

	Latin	PIE
'1st'	prīmus	*pri+is+m+os

This is an original superlative form. Its derivation is *pri+is+mos =*prīsmos (2c PHONOTACTICS 2g s-clusters) > *prīmos (7c o(:)-TO-u(:)) > Lat prīmus.

	Latin	**PIE**
'2nd'	alter	*al+ter+os[92]
	secundus	*sekʷ+ond+os[93]
'3rd'	tertius	*tri+t+jos

The endings of '3rd' are those of the jo- and jā- class adjectives described in 2.1 above.

	Latin	**PIE**
'4th'	quārtus	*kʷetwōr+t+os

The suffix -t- is used to form ordinals up to '7th'. E.g.,

	Latin	**PIE**
'5th'	quīntus	*penkʷe+t+os
'6th'	sextus	*seks+t+os
'7th'	septimus	*septm̥+os

The derivation of '7th' is*septm̥+os (2d SYL SON) > *septemos (3c ITALIC STRESS) > *séptemos (4c UNSTRESSED V) > *séptimos (7c o(:)-TO-u(:)) > Lat septimus. From '7th' to '20th' the o- and ā-class adjective ending is added directly to the ordinal. E.g.,

	Latin	**PIE**
'8th'	octāvus	*oktōu+os

The /ā/ in this form is unaccounted for. It may have been a result of 7d ow-TO-aw.

	Latin	**PIE**
'9th'	nōnus	*newn+os

The derivation is *newnos (PIE 3.1.2c i-j/u-w ALT applying as a synchronic rule) → *neunos (5a e-TO-o) > *nounos (6b ei/ou-CHANGES) > *nōnos (7c o(:)-TO-u(:)) > Lat nōnus.

	Latin	**PIE**
'10th'	decimus	*dekm̥+os
'20th'	vīcēsimus	*wī+dkm̥+t+sim+os

The antecedent consists of the cardinal *wī+dkm̥+t- plus the superlative ending *-simos. The derivation is *wīdkm̥tsimos (2c PHONOTACTICS: lb Nasal assimilation, lc Obstruent cluster voicing and devoicing and 2c Obstruent assimilation) > *wīkkn̥tsimos (2c PHONOTACTICS 2f t-clusters) > *wīkkn̥ssimos (2d SYL SON) >*wīkkenssimos (2c PHONOTACTICS la Geminate simplification reapplying as a persistent rule) > *wīkensimos (6c LATIN STRESS) > *wīkénsimos (7c o(:)-TO-u(:)) > *wīkénsimus (8k Vns-CHANGES in a possible variation) > Lat vīcēsimus /wīkḗsimus/. Notice the difference in the derivation of this form from that of the cardinal vīgintī '20' above. The ordinal vīgintī has a /g/, while the cardinal vīcēsimus has a /k/, which one would expect in the ordinal as well, given the change 2c PHONOTACTICS lc Obstruent cluster voicing and devoicing.

	Latin	PIE
'30th'	trīcēsimus	*trei+dkm̥+t+sim+os
'40th'	quādrāgēsimus	*kʷetwōr+dkm̥+t+sim+os
'1000th'	mīllēsimus	'1000'+dkm̥+t+sim+os

That is, the remaining Latin ordinals are formed from the cardinal plus the suffix -ēsimus.

4.3 Distributives

These mean '1 at a time', '2 at a time', etc. The are declined as plural o- and ā-class adjectives.

	Latin	PIE
'1 at a time'	singulī	*sem+gl+oi

The antecedent consists of *sem- '1' plus *-gl- plus the nominative plural masculine ending *-oi. The derivation is *semgloi (2c PHONOTACTICS lb Nasal assimilation) > *seŋgloi (2c PHONOTACTICS 2a l-clusters) > *seŋguloi (7a ai/oi-TO-ae/oe) > *seŋguloe (8c e-TO-i) > *siŋguloe (8h oe-CHANGES) > Lat singulī /siŋgulī/.

	Latin	PIE
'2 at a time'	bīnī	*dwis+n+oi

The derivation is *dwisnoi (2c PHONOTACTICS 2g s-clusters) >*dwīnoi (8b dw-CHANGES, ev) > Lat bīnī.

	Latin	PIE
'3 at a time'	ternī	*tris+n+oi

The derivation is *trisnoi (4b SYNCOPE having applied to the multiplicative *tris '3 times', now the form *ter is transferred to this paradigm, ev) > Lat terni.

The remaining distributives are formed from the multiplicative numeral plus -n- plus the adjective endings.

4.4 Multiplicatives

These numerals mean 'x times'. E.g.,

	Latin	PIE
'1 time, once'	semel	*sem+el+i

The antecedent consists of *sem- '1' plus a suffix *-el plus the neuter accusative singular i-class adjective ending *-i. The derivation is *sémeli (4b SYNCOPE) > Lat semel.

	Latin	PIE
'2 times'	bis	*dwi+s
'3 times'	ter	*tri+s

The derivation of ter is *tris (4b SYNCOPE, part 3) > *ters (2c PHONATACTICS, 2d r-clusters and la Geminate simplification applying as persistent synchronic rules) > Lat ter.

	Latin	PIE
'4 times'	quater	$*k^{w}$etwer+s
'5 times'	quīnquiēs	$*penk^{w}$+jn̥+s

Quīnquiēs and the remaining Latin multiplicatives are formed by adding the suffix -iēs to the ordinal. Its antecedent is the suffix *-jn̥t plus the adverb (genitive singular neuter) ending *-s. The derivation is $*penk^{w}$jn̥ts (2c PHONOTACTICS) > $*penk^{w}$jn̥s (3a C+j CHANGES) > $*penk^{w}$iens (4a p-TO-k^{w}) > $*k^{w}enk^{w}$iens (8c e-TO-i) > $*k^{w}ink^{w}$iens (8j Vnk-TO-V̄nk) > $*k^{w}īnk^{w}$iens (8k Vns-CHANGES) > Lat quīnquiēs.

5 Pronouns

5.1 First Person

		Latin		PIE
sg	nom	ego	'I'	*egō[94]
	acc	mē		*mēd[95,96]
pl	nom	nōs	'we'	*nōs[97]

5.2 Second Person

		Latin		PIE
nom	sg	tū	'you'	*tū[98]
	pl	vōs		*wōs[99]

5.3 Third Person

We include here four demonstrative pronouns and two so-called "emphatics". The first demonstrative is this:

			Latin		PIE
masc	sg	nom	is	'that'	*i+s[100]
		acc	eum		*ei+om[101]
		gen	ējus		*ei+s+jos[102]
		dat	eī		*ei+ei[103]
		abl	eō		*ei+ōd
	pl	nom	eī		*ei+oi
		acc	eōs		*ei+ons[104]
		gen	eum		*ei+om
			eōrum		*ei+ōs+om[105]
		dat/ abl	eīs		*ei+ōis[106]
fem	sg	nom	ea		*ei+ā[107]
		acc	eam		*ei+ām
		gen	ējus		*ei+s+jos
		dat	eī		*ei+āi[108]
		abl	eā		*ei+ād

			Latin		PIE
fem	**pl**	**nom**	eae	'that'	*ei+āi
		acc	eās		*ei+āns
		gen	eārum		*ei+āsom
		dat/ abl	eīs		*ei+āis
neut	**sg**	**nom/ acc**	id		*i+d[100]
	pl	**nom/ acc**	ea		*ei+ā[109]

The second demonstrative is this:

			Latin		PIE
sg	**masc**	**nom**	hic	'this'	*g^hi+ke[110]
		acc	hunc		*g^ho+m+ke[111]
		gen	hūjus		*g^ho+s+jos[112]
		dat	huic		*g^ho+ei+ke[113]
		abl	hōc		*g^hō+d+ke[114]
	fem	**nom**	haec		*g^hā+i+ke
		acc	hanc		*g^hā+m+ke[115]
		gen/ dat	same as masculine		
		abl	hāc		*g^hā+d+ke
	neut	**nom/ acc**	hoc		*g^ho+d+ke
		nom/ acc	haec		*g^hā+i+ke

The other forms of this paradigm lack the suffix -c and have the same endings as is/ea/id 'that' above: e.g. gen pl masc h+ōrum.

The third demonstrative is this:

			Latin		PIE
sg	**nom**	**masc**	iste	'that'	*is+to[116]
		fem	ista		*is+tā
		neut	istud		*is+tod[117]
	gen	**masc/ fem/ neut**	istīus		*is+t+ī+jos[118]

The other forms consist of ist- plus the endings of is 'that' above.

The fourth demonstrative is this:

			Latin		PIE
sg	**nom**	**masc**	ille	'that'	*ol+s+o
		fem	illa		*ol+s+ā
		neut	illud		*ol+s+od[119]

Otherwise the forms of this paradigm consist of the stem ill- plus the endings of is 'that' above.

There are two so-called "emphatic" pronouns. The first is this:

			Latin		PIE
sg	**nom**	**masc**	ipse	'self'	*is+p+s+o[120]
		fem	ipsa		*is+p+s+ā
		neut	ipsum		*is+p+s+om

Otherwise the forms of this paradigm consist of the stem ips- plus the endings of Latin is 'that' above.

The second emphatic pronoun is this:

			Latin		PIE
sg	**nom**	**masc**	īdem	'same'	*is+dem[121]
		fem	eādem		*ei+ā+dem
		neut	idem		*id+em[122]

That is, this paradigm consists of inflected is 'that' plus the suffix -dem.

5.4 Reflexive

This pronoun is found only in the 3rd person oblique cases. The singular and plural forms are identical.

	Latin		PIE
acc	sē	'oneself,	*sewe[123]
gen	suī	themselves'	*su+ī[124]
dat	sibi		*se+b^hei[125,126]
abl	sē		*se+ēd[125]

5.5 Possessive

These pronouns take the endings of o-and ā-class adjectives. We cite the nominative singular masculine forms.

Latin		PIE
meus	'my'	*mej+os
tuus	'your' (sg)	*tew+os[127]
suus	'his, her, its, their'	*sew+os[127]
noster	'our'	*nos+ter+os
vester	'your' (pl)	*wos+ter+os[128]

5.6 Relative, Interrogative and Indefinite

These pronouns have basically the same declension. The relative is as follows:

			Latin		PIE
masc	**sg**	**nom**	quī	'who'	*k^wo+i[129]
		acc	quem		*k^wi+m[130]
		gen	cūjus		*k^wo+s+jos
		dat	cui		*k^wo+ei[131]
		abl	quō		*k^wō+d

			Latin		PIE
	pl	dat/ abl	quibus	'who'	$^*k^wi+b^hos$
fem	sg	nom	quae		$^*k^w\bar{a}+i$
neut	sg	nom/ acc	quod	'what'	$^*k^wo+d$[132]
	pl	nom/ acc	quae		$^*k^w\bar{a}+i$

The interrogative pronoun is this:

			Latin		PIE
sg	nom	masc/fem	quis	'who?'	$^*k^wi+s$
		neuter	quid	'what?'	$^*k^wi+d$

Otherwise the forms of this paradigm are those of the relative pronoun immediately above.

The indefinite pronoun is this:

			Latin		PIE
sg	nom	masc/fem	quis	'whoever'	$^*k^wi+s$
		neuter	quid	'whatever'	$^*k^wi+d$

Most of the forms of this paradigm are like those of the interrogative.

6 Verbs

The features of the Latin verb are given in the following two tables. Table i contains the variable features — namely those which can change contingent upon the context. Table ii shows the lexical or inherent features — namely those that are idiosyncratic. They indicate the particular form-class of the verb.

(i) Variable Features

The first section of this table lists the purely verbal features. The second gives the features of deverbative adjectives and nouns.

(a) Person	(b) Number	(c) Voice	(d) Mood
1. 1st	1. singular	1. active	1. indicative[133]
2. 2nd	2. plural	2. passive	2. subjunctive[133]
3. 3rd			3. imperative

(e) Tense Occurring in	Indicative	Subjunctive	Imperative
1. present	x	x	x
2. imperfect[134]	x	x	
3. future	x		
4. present perfect[134]	x	x	
5. past perfect	x	x	
6. future perfect	x		

Adjectival and Nominal Inflection

(a) Person	(b) Number	(c) Voice	(d) Mood
Ø	1. singular	1. active	1. infinitive
	2. plural	2. passive	2. gerund[135]
			3. supine[135]
			4. participle

(e) Tense occurring in	Infinitive	Gerund	Supine	Participle
1. present	act/pass	active	active	active
2. imperfect				
3. future	act/pass			act/pass
4. present perfect	act/pass			passive
5. past perfect				
6. future perfect				

(ii) Inherent Features

(a) Inflectional type	(b) Class (conjugation)[136]		
1. deponent[137]	1. 1st conjugation or ā-class	dōnāre	'to give'
2. nondeponent[137]	2. 2nd conjugation or ē-class	vidēre	'to see'
	3. 3rd conjugation or Ø-class	dūcere	'to lead'
	4. 4th conjugation or ī-class	sāgīre	'to track'
	5. 3rd conjugation or io-class	capere	'to seize'
	and	capiō	'I seize'
	6. anomalous conjugations such as esse 'to be' vs. sum 'I am'		

In the above two tables the features in the columns are mutually exclusive. Not all the logical possibilities are realized: the notations in the (e) columns of table (i) indicate which are.

6.1 Present

6.1.1 Present Active Indicative

We cite the endings of the six conjugations.

(i) The 1st Conjugation or ā-Class

E.g.,

		Latin		PIE
sg	**1**	dōnō	'give'	*dōn+ā+j+ō[138]
	2	dōnās		*dōn+ā+j+esi[139]
	3	dōnat		*dōn+ā+j+eti[140]
pl	**1**	dōnāmus		*dōn+ā+j+omos
	2	dōnātis		*dōn+ā+j+etes[141]
	3	dōnant		*dōn+ā+j+onti

(ii) The 2nd Conjugation or ē-Class

E.g.,

		Latin		PIE
sg	1	videō	'see'	*wid+ē+j+ō[142]
	2	vidēs		*wid+ē+j+esi

Otherwise the endings are those of dōnō above, but with /e(:)/instead of /a(:)/.

(iii) The 3rd Conjugation or Ø-Class

The verbs of this class (as opposed to those of the other conjugations) have no intermediate -j- between the stem and the ending. E.g.,

		Latin		PIE
sg	1	dūcō	'lead'	*deuk+ō
	2	dūcis		*deuk+esi
	3	dūcit		*deuk+eti[143]
pl	1	dūcimus		*deuk+omos[144]
	2	dūcitis		*deuk+etes
	3	dūcunt		*deuk+onti[145]

The Ø-class verbs, which lacked the intermediate -j- in their antecedents, have three additional types of present, imperfect and future stem formations. In the following we cite the 1st singular present and perfect forms. The three formatives are these:

(a) Reduplication with /i/

E.g.,

	Latin		PIE
pres	gignō	'beget'	*gi+gn+ō[146]
perf	genuī		*gen+w+ai[146,147]
pres	sistō	'put'	*si+st+ō[146]
perf	stitī		*ste+st+ai[147]

(b) Infixal or Suffixal /n/

E.g.,

	Latin		PIE
pres	findō	'split'	*b^{h}id+n+ō[148]
perf	fīdī		*b^{h}eid+ai[149]
pres	rumpō	'break'	*rup+n+ō[148]
perf	rūpī		*reup+ai[149]
pres	tangō	'touch'	*tag+n+ō[148]
perf	tetigī		*te+tag+ai
pres	vincō	'conquer'	*wik+n+ō
perf	vīcī		*weik+ai[149]
pres	cernō	'separate'	*kri+n+ō[148,150]
perf	crēvī		*krei+w+ai[149,150]

	Latin		PIE
pres	sternō	'strew'	*ster+n+ō[148]
perf	strāvī		*str+ā+w+ai
pres	temnō	'shun'	*tem+n+ō[148]
perf	tempsī		*tem+s+ai
pres	tollō	'lift'	*tol+n+ō[148,151]
perf	(sus+)tulī		*tol+ai

(c) The Suffix /sk/

E.g.,

	Latin		PIE
pres	discō	'learn'	*dik+sk+ō[152]
perf	didicī		*de+dik+ai[153]
pres	gnōscō	'know'	*gnō+sk+ō
perf	gnōvī		*gnō+w+ai
pres	quiēscō	'rest'	*k^wiē+sk+ō
perf	quiēvī		*k^wiē+w+ai

(iv) The 4th Conjugation or ī-Class

E.g.,

		Latin		PIE
sg	**1**	sāgiō	'follow, track'	*sāg+j+ō[154,155]
	2	sāgīs		*sāg+j+esi[156,155]
	3	sāgit		*sāg+j+eti[157,155]
pl	**3**	sāgiunt		*sāg+j+onti
sg	**1**	sitiō	'be thirsty'	*siti+j+ō[154]

Otherwise the endings are those of dōnō above, but with /i(:)/ instead of /a(:)/.

(v) The 3rd io-Conjugation or io-Class

E.g.,

		Latin		PIE
sg	**1**	capiō	'seize'	*kap+j+ō[158]
	2	capis		*kap+j+esi
	3	capit		*kap+j+eti
pl	**3**	capiunt		*kap+j+onti

That is, the inflection of this class is like that of the Ø-class under iii above except for the 1st singular and 3rd plural.

(vi) Anomalous conjugations

The inflection of these verbs differs somewhat from that of the five other conjugations, primarily because of the retention of some of the original athematic endings. E.g.,

		Latin		PIE
sg	**1**	ferō	'carry'	*b^her+ō
	2	fers		*b^her+si
	3	fert		*b^her+ti

Other anomalous verbs are the infinitive esse 'be' < *es+si (see 6.9 below), and the 1st singular present forms volō 'want' < *wel+ō, eō 'go' < *ei+ō and dō 'give' < *d+ō.

6.1.2 Present Active Subjunctive

Examples of the formatives of the five main conjugations (aside from the anomalous conjugations) are as follows:

				Latin		PIE
(i)	ā-class	sg	1	dōnem	'give'	*dōn+ā+j+ē+mi[159]
			2	dōnēs		*dōn+ā+j+ē+si
(ii)	ē-class	sg	1	videam	'see'	*wid+ē+j+ā+mi[160]
			2	videās		*wid+ē+j+ā+si[160]
(iii)	Ø-class	sg	1	dūcam	'lead'	*deuk+ā+mi[160]
(iv)	ī-class	sg	1	sāgiam	'track'	*sāg+j+ā+mi[160]
(v)	io-class	sg	1	capiam	'seize'	*kap+j+ā+mi[160]

That is, the final segments of the pres subj endings are those of the present indicative except for the 1sg -m. In addition, the intermediate vowels differ from those of the present indicative: the ā-class has /e(:)/; the other classes have /a(:)/.

6.1.3 Present Active Imperative

				Latin		PIE
(i)	ā-class	sg	2	dōnā	'give'	*dōn+ā+j+e[161]
		pl	2	dōnāte		*dōn+ā+j+ete
(ii)	ē-class	sg	2	vidē	'see'	*wid+ē+j+e
		pl	2	vidēte		*wid+ē+j+ete
(iii)	Ø-class	sg	2	dūc	'lead'	*deuk+e[162]
		pl	2	dūcite		*deuk+ete[163]
(iv)	ī-class	sg	2	sāgī	'follow'	*sāg+j+e
		pl	2	sāgīte		*sāg+j+ete
(v)	io-class	sg	2	cape	'seize'	*kap+j+e[164]
		pl	2	capite		*kap+j+ete[164]

6.1.4 Present Passive Indicative

The present passive forms of all conjugations consist of the present active stem as given in 6.1.1 above plus the passive endings as given below.

				Latin		PIE
(i)	ā-class	sg	1	dōnor	'I am	*dōn+ā+j+ō+r[165]
			2	dōnāre (later dōnāris)	given'	*dōn+ā+j+eso[166]
			3	dōnātur		*dōn+ā+j+eto+r[167]

				Latin		PIE
(i)	ā-class	pl	1	dōnāmur	'I am given'	*dōn+ā+j+emo+r
			2	dōnāminī		*dōn+ā+j+omenoi[168]
			3	dōnantur		*dōn+ā+j+onto+r
(ii)	ē-class	sg	1	videor	'I am seen'	*wid+ē+j+ō+r
(iii)	Ø-class	sg	1	dūcor	'I am led'	*deuk+ō+r
(iv)	ī-class	sg	1	sāgior	'I am followed'	*sāg+j+ō+r
(v)	io-class	sg	1	capior	'I am taken'	*kap+j+ō+r

6.1.5 Present Passive Subjunctive

To form this paradigm the passive endings of 6.1.4 are added to the subjunctive stems of 6.1.2. E.g.,

				Latin		PIE
(i)	ā-class	sg	1	dōner	'I am given'	*dōn+ā+j+ē+r
			2	dōnēre		*dōn+ā+j+ē+so
(ii)	ē-class	sg	1	videar	'I am seen'	*wid+ē+j+ā+r
			2	videāre		*wid+ē+j+ā+so
(iii)	Ø-class	sg	1	dūcar	'I am led'	*deuk+ā+r
			2	dūcāre		*deuk+ā+so
(iv)	ī-class	sg	1	sāgiar	'I am followed'	*sāg+j+ā+r
			2	sāgiāre		*sāg+j+ā+so
(v)	io-class	sg	1	capiar	'I am seized'	*kap+j+ā+r
			2	capiāre		*kap+j+ā+so

6.1.6 Present Passive Imperative

To form this paradigm the passive endings of 6.1.4 are added to the present imperative stems of 6.1.3. E.g.,

				Latin		PIE
(i)	ā-class	2	sg	dōnāre	'be given'	*dōn+ā+j+eso
			pl	dōnāminī		*dōn+ā+j+omenoi
(ii)	ē-class	2	sg	vidēre	'be seen'	*wid+ē+j+eso
			pl	vidēminī		*wid+ē+j+omenoi

6.2 Imperfect

6.2.1 Imperfect Active Indicative

				Latin		PIE
(i)	ā-class	sg	1	dōnābam	'I gave'	*dōn+ā+bʰu+ā+m[169]
			2	dōnābās		*dōn+ā+bʰu+ā+s
			3	dōnābat		*dōn+ā+bʰu+ā+t[170]

				Latin		PIE
(i)	ā-class	pl	1	dōnābāmus	'I gave'	*dōn+ā+b^hu+ā+mos
			2	dōnābātis		*dōn+ā+b^hu+ā+tes[171]
			3	dōnābant		*dōn+ā+b^hu+ā+nt
(ii)	ē-class	sg	1	vidēbam	'I saw'	*wid+ē+b^hu+ā+m[169]
(iii)	Ø-class	sg	1	dūcēbam	'I led'	*deuk+es+b^hu+ā+m[172]
(iv)	ī-class	sg	1	sāgībam	'I followed'	*sāg+j+es+b^hu+ā+m[169,172]
(v)	io-class	sg	1	capiēbam	'I seized'	*kap+j+es+b^hu+ā+m[172]

6.2.2 Imperfect Active Subjunctive

This paradigm consists of what appears to be the infinitive stem plus active indicative endings under 6.2.1. E.g.,

				Latin		PIE
(i)	ā-class	sg	1	dōnārem	'I gave'	*dōnā+s+ē+m[173]
			2	dōnārēs		*dōnā+s+ē+s
(ii)	ē-class		1	vidērem	'I saw'	*widē+s+ē+m
(iii)	Ø-class		1	dūcerem	'I led'	*deuk+es+ēm
(iv)	ī-class		1	sāgīrem	'I followed'	*sāg+j+es+ē+m
(v)	io-class		1	caperem	'I seized'	*kap+j+es+ē+m

6.2.3 Imperfect Passive Indicative

This paradigm consists of the imperfect active indicative stem under 6.2.1 plus the passive endings endings under 6.1.4. E.g,

				Latin		PIE
(i)	ā-class	sg	1	dōnābar	'I was given'	*dōnā+b^hu+ā+r
			2	dōnābāre		*dōnā+b^hu+ā+so
(ii)	ē-class		1	vidēbar	'I was seen'	*widē+b^hu+ā+r
(iii)	Ø-class		1	dūcēbar	'I was led'	*deuk+es+b^hu+ā+r
(iv)	ī-class		1	sāgībar	'I was followed'	*sāg+j+es+b^hu+ā+r
(v)	io-class		1	capiēbar	'I was seized'	*kap+j+es+b^hu+ā+r

6.2.4 Imperfect Passive Subjunctive

This paradigm consists of the imperfect active subjunctive stem under 6.2.2 above plus the present passive subjunctive under 6.1.5. E.g.,

				Latin		PIE
(i)	ā-class	sg	1	dōnārer	'I was given'	*dōnā+s+ē+r
			2	dōnārēre		*dōnā+s+ē+so

				Latin		PIE
(ii)	ē-class	sg	1	vidērer	'I was seen'	*widē+s+ē+r
(iii)	Ø-class		1	dūcerer	'I was led'	*deuk+es+ē+r
(iv)	ī-class		1	sāgīrer	'I was followed'	*sāg+j+es+ē+r
(v)	io-class		1	caperer	'I was seized'	*kap+j+es+ē+r

6.3 Future

6.3.1 Future Active Indicative

For the ā- and ē-classes the paradigm consists of the stem plus -b- plus the present active indicative endings of 6.1.1. For the other classes the paradigm consists of the stem plus the 1sg -am and otherwise of the stem plus -e(:)- plus the present active indicative endings. E.g.,

				Latin		PIE
(i)	ā-class	sg	1	dōnābō	'I shall give'	*dōnā+bʰu+ō[174]
			2	dōnābis		*dōnā+bʰu+esi
(ii)	ē-class		1	vidēbō	'I shall see'	*widē+bʰu+ō
			2	vidēbis		*widē+bʰu+esi
(iii)	Ø-class		1	dūcam	'I shall lead'	*deuk+ā+mi[175,176]
			2	dūcēs		*deuk+ē+si
(iv)	ī-class		1	sāgiam	'I shall follow'	*sāg+j+ā+mi[175]
			2	sāgiēs		*sāg+j+ē+si
(v)	io-class		1	capiam	'I shall seize'	*kap+j+ā+mi[175]
			2	capiēs		*kap+j+ē+si

6.3.2 Future Active Imperative

This paradigm consists of the present active plural imperative, stems as given under 6.1.3 plus the endings given below. (We cite the complete paradigm of the ā-class only.)

				Latin		PIE
(i)	ā-class	sg	2	dōnātō	'give'	*dōnā+tōd[177]
			3	dōnātō		*dōnā+tōd
		pl	2	dōnātōte		*dōnā+tōd+te[178]
			3	dōnantō		*dōnānti+ōd[179]
(ii)	ē-class	sg	2	vidētō	'see'	*widē+tōd
(iii)	Ø-class	sg	2	dūcitō	'lead'	*deuk+e+tōd
(iv)	ī-class	sg	2	sāgītō	'follow'	*sāg+j+tōd
(v)	io-class	sg	2	capitō	'seize'	*kap+j+tōd

6.3.3 Future Passive Indicative

This paradigm consists of the future active stem under 6.3.1 plus the present passive indicative endings under 6.1.4. E.g.,

				Latin		PIE
(i)	ā-class	sg	1	dōnābor	'I will be given'	*dōnā+bʰu+ō+r
			2	dōnābere		*dōnā+bʰu+eso[180]
			3	dōnābitur		*dōnā+bʰu+eto+r[181]
(ii)	ē-class		1	vidēbor	'see'	*widē+bʰu+ō+r
(iii)	Ø-class		1	dūcar	'lead'	*deuk+ā+r
			2	dūcēre		*deuk+ē+so
(iv)	ī-class		1	sāgiar	'follow'	*sāgj+ā+r
(v)	io-class		1	capiar	'seize'	*kapj+ā+r

6.3.4 Future Passive Imperative

This paradigm consists of the future active imperative forms under 6.3.2 plus the passive ending -r. E.g.,

sg	2/3	dōnātor	'be given'	*dōnā+tōd+r[182]
pl	3	dōnantor		*dōnānti+tōd+r

6.4 Present Perfect

There are five types of perfect active formation. They are (i) the w-suffix, (ii) reduplication, (iii) the s-suffix, (iv) ABLAUT or some other vowel change in the root and (v) no change in the root, mere adjunction of the perfect endings. In general any of these five perfect formations may occur with any of the five conjugations given under 6 above. As examples we cite the 1st singular present perfect active forms.

(i) The w-Suffix

	Latin		PIE
ā-class	dōnāvī	'give'	*dōnā+w+ai[183]
	domuī	'subdue'	*dom+w+ai[183,184]
ē-class	dēlēvī	'destroy'	*dēlē+w+ai
Ø-class	aluī	'nourish'	*al+w+ai[184]
ī-class	audīvī	'hear'	*ausdʰī+w+ai
	saluī	'jump'	*sal+w+ai[184]
io-class	sapīvī	'be wise'	*sapī+w+ai

(ii) Reduplication

The PIE antecedent reduplication consisted of repeating the root-initial consonant or consonant cluster plus /e/. E.g.,

	Latin		PIE
ā-class	dedī	'give'	*de+d+ai
	stetī	'stand'	*ste+st+ai[185]
ē-class	momordī	'bite'	*me+mord+ai[186]
	spopondī	'promise'	*spe+spond+ai[185]
Ø-class	cecinī	'sing'	*ke+kan+ai[186,187]
	cucurrī	'run'	*ke+kurs+ai[188]
ī-class	repperī	'find'	*re+pe+per+ai[189]

(iii) The s-Suffix

The antecedent is a PIE aorist formative. E.g.,

	Latin		PIE
ē-class	ārsī	'burn'	*ārd+s+ai[190]
	mānsī	'wait'	*man+s+ai[191]
Ø-class	ānxī	'choke'	*ang+s+ai[192]
	rēxī	'rule'	*reg+s+ai[193]
ī-class	saepsī	'hedge in'	*saip+s+ai

(iv) ABLAUT or Some Other Vowel Change

In our examples we cite the 1st singular active indicative present and perfect forms. Instances of PIE ABLAUT are these:

		Latin		PIE
ē-class	**pres**	moveō	'move'	*mow+ējō
	perf	mōvī		*mōw+ai
	pres	sedeō	'sit'	*sed+ējō
	perf	sēdī		*sēd+ai[194]
	pres	videō	'see'	*wØid+ējō
	perf	vīdī		*weid+ai
Ø-class	**pres**	edō	'eat'	*ed+ō
	perf	ēdī		*ēd+ai
	pres	fundō	'pour'	*g^hØu(n)d+ō[195]
	perf	fūdī		*g^heud+ai[195]
	pres	linquō	'leave'	*lØi(n)k^w+ō[195]
	perf	līquī		*leik^w+ai[195,196]
ī-class	**pres**	fodiō	'dig'	*b^hod^h+jō
	perf	fōdī		*b^hōd^h+ai
	pres	veniō	'come'	*g^wem+jō[197]
	perf	vēnī		*g^wēm+ai
io-class	**pres**	fugiō	'flee'	*b^hØug^h+jō
	perf	fūgī		*b^heug^h+ai[198]

Instances of vowel change which is not PIE ABLAUT are these:

		Latin		PIE
ē-class	**pres**	faveō	'favor'	*g^haw+ējō
	perf	fāvī		*g^haw+ai[199]
Ø-class	**pres**	agō	'do'	*ag+ō
	perf	ēgī		*ag+ai[200]
	pres	frangō	'break	*b^hra(n)g+ō
	perf	frēgī		*b^hrag^h+ai[200]
	pres	scabō	'scratch'	*skab+ō
	perf	scābī		*skab+ai[199]
	pres	tollō	'lift'	*tol(n)+ō
	perf	(sus)tulī		*tol+ai[201]

		Latin		PIE
io-class	pres	capiō	'take'	*kap+jō
	perf	cēpī		*kap+ai[200]
	pres	faciō	'do'	*dʰak+jō
	perf	fēcī		*dʰak+ai[200]

(v) No Change in the Root

These perfect verbs are formed by the mere adjunction of the perfect endings onto the present-tense root. Such verbs are all of the Ø-class. E.g.,

	Latin		PIE
pres	eō	'go'	*ei+ō[202]
perf	iī		*ei+ai[203]
pres	luō	'wash'	*lu+ō
perf	luī		*lu+ai
pres	prehendō	'seize'	*pre+gʰe(n)d+ō
perf	prehendī		*pre+gʰe(n)d+ai[204]
pres	vertō	'turn'	*wert+ō
perf	vertī		*wert+ai

6.4.1 Present Perfect Active Indicative

We illustrate the endings with an ā-class paradigm.

		Latin		PIE
sg	1	dōnāvī	'I have given'	*dōnā+w+a+i[205]
	2	dōnāvistī		*dōnā+w+is+tai[206]
	3	dōnāvit		*dōnā+w+e+t[207]
pl	1	dōnāvimus		*dōnā+w+omos[208]
	2	dōnāvistis		*dōnā+w+is+te+s[209]
	3	dōnāvēre		*dōnā+w+ēr+i[210]

6.4.2 Present Perfect Active Subjunctive

This paradigm consists of the perfect stem plus -eri- plus the endings of the present active subjunctive (6.1.2 above). E.g.,

		Latin		PIE
sg	1	dōnāverim	'gave'	*dōnā+w+is+ī+mi[211]
	2	dōnāveris		*dōnā+w+is+ī+si
pl	3	dōnāverint		*dōnā+w+is+ī+nti

6.4.3 Present Perfect Passive Indicative

This paradigm consists of the perfect passive participle (6.8.4) plus the present indicative of 'be' (6.9.1).

		Latin		PIE
sg	1	dōnātus sum	'I have been given'	*dōnā+t+os *es+mi
pl	1	dōnātī sumus		*dōnā+t+oi *es+mos

6.4.4 Present Perfect Passive Subjunctive

This paradigm consists of the perfect passive participle (6.8.4) plus the present subjunctive of 'be' (6.9.2).

		Latin		PIE
sg	1	dōnātus sim	'I have been given'	*dōnā+t+os *s+īē+mi

6.5 Past Perfect

6.5.1 Past Perfect Active Indicative

This paradigm consists of the perfect stem plus -er- plus the endings of the imperfect active indicative (6.2.1). The antecedent consists of the perfect stem plus the aorist suffix *-is- plus the imperfect formative *-ā- plus the respective endings. E.g.,

		Latin		PIE
sg	1	dōnāveram	'I had given'	*dōnā+w+is+ā+m
	2	dōnāverās		*dōnā+w+is+ā+s

6.5.2 Past Perfect Active Subjunctive

This paradigm consists of the perfect stem plus the aorist suffix -is- plus the imperfect active subjunctive endings (6.2.2). E.g.,

		Latin		PIE
sg	1	dōnāvissem	'I had given'	*dōnā+w+is+sēm
	2	dōnāvissēs		*dōnā+w+is+sēs

6.5.3 Past Perfect Passive Indicative

This paradigm consists of the perfect passive participle (6.8.4) and the imperfect indicative of 'be' (6.9.4). E.g.,

		Latin		PIE
sg	1	dōnātus eram	'I had been given'	*dōnā+t+os *es+ā+m

6.5.4 Past Perfect Passive Subjunctive

This paradigm consists of the perfect passive participle (6.8.4) and the imperfect subjunctive of 'be' (6.9.5). E.g.,

		Latin		PIE
sg	1	dōnātus essem	'I had been given'	*dōnā+t+os *es+s+ēm

6.6 Future Perfect

6.6.1 Future Perfect Active Indicative

Aside from the 3rd plural, this paradigm consists of the perfect stem plus -er- plus the future active indicative endings of ā- or ē-class verbs (6.3.1). The antecedent paradigm consists of the perfect stem plus the aorist suffix *-is- plus the respective endings. (The future of 'be' under 6.9.6 may also have been a factor here.)

		Latin		PIE
sg	1	dōnāverō	'I shall have given'	*dōnā+w+is+ō
pl	3	dōnāverint		*dōnā+w+is+ī+nti[212]

6.6.2 Future Perfect Passive Indicative

This paradigm consists of the perfect passive participle (6.8.4) and the future indicative of 'be' (6.9.6). E.g.,

		Latin		PIE
sg	1	dōnātus erō	'I shall have been given'	*dōnā+t+os *es+ō

6.7 Verbal Nouns

6.7.1 Present Active Infinitive and Gerund

The infinitive is in effect the nominative case of the verbal noun; the oblique cases are the gerund forms, which take the endings of o-class neuter nouns (under 1.1 above). These forms occur only in the singular. E.g.,

	Latin		PIE
inf	dōnāre	'to give'	*dōnā+s+i[213]
ger	dōnandum		*dōnā+nd+om[214]

6.7.2 Present Passive Infinitive

	Latin		PIE
ā-class	dōnārī	'to be given'	*dōnā+s+ei[215,216]
ē-class	vidērī	'to be seen'	*widē+s+ei[215]
Ø-class	dūcī	'to be led'	*deuk+ei[215]
ī-class	sāgī	'to be followed'	*sāg+ei[215]
io-class	capī	'to be seized'	*kap+ei[215]

6.7.3 Future Active Infinitive

This construction consists of the o-class nominative singular neuter of the future active participle (6.8.2) and the present active infinitive of 'be' (6.9.13).

Latin		PIE
dōnātūrum esse	'to be going to give'	*dōnā+tūr+om *es+si[217]

6.7.4 Future Passive Infinitive

This construction consists of the supine (6.7.7) and the present passive infinitive (6.7.2) of the verb 'go'.

Latin		PIE
dōnātum īrī	'to be going to be given'	*dōnātum *ei+s+ei[218]

6.7.5 Perfect Active Infinitive

This construction consists of the perfect stem plus the suffix -isse.

Latin		PIE
dōnāvisse	'to have given'	*dōnā+w+is+si[219]

6.7.6 Perfect Passive Infinitive

This construction consists of the perfect passive participle (6.8.4) and the present infinitive of 'be' (6.9.13).

Latin		PIE
dōnātus esse	'to have been given'	*dōnā+t+os *es+si

6.7.7 Present Active Supine

This form consists of the perfect stem plus the endings of a u-class neuter noun (1.4) in either the accusative or ablative singular. The accusative expresses a goal or a purpose; the ablative, the relation 'with respect to'. E.g., acc 'Veniō dōnātum.' 'I come in order to give.' and ablative. 'Est facile factū.' 'It is easy with respect to doing, i.e. easy to do.'

		Latin		PIE
sg	**acc**	dōnātum	'to give'	*dōnā+t+um
	abl	dōnātū		*dōnā+t+ūd[220]

6.8 Verbal Adjectives

6.8.1 Present Active Participle

These forms consist of the present stem plus -nt- plus the endings of the athematic adjectives under 2.2 above. E.g.,

			Latin		PIE
ā-class	**sg**	**nom**	dōnāns	'giving'	*dōnā+nt+s[221]
		gem	dōnantis		*dōnā+nt+es[222]
Ø-class		**nom**	dūcēns	'leading'	*deuk+e+nt+s[223]
		gen	dūcentis		*deuk+e+nt+es

6.8.2 Future Active Participle

This paradigm consists of the stem of the future active infinitive (6.7.3) plus the o- and i-class adjective endings (2.1). E.g.,

			Latin		PIE
nom	**sg**	**masc**	dōnātūrus	'going to give'	*dōnā+tūr+os[224]

6.8.3 Future Passive Participle

These forms consist of the present stem plus the suffix -nd- (-end- for Ø-, ī- and io-class verbs) plus the o- and i-class adjective endings (2.1). E.g.,

			Latin		PIE
ā-class	**nom sg**	**masc**	dōnandus	'which will or should be given'	*dōnā+nd+os[225]
Ø-class			dūcendus	'which will or should be led'	*deuk+end+os

6.8.4 Perfect Passive Participle

There are two perfect passive formatives, -s- and the more frequently occurring -t-. The endings are those of the o- and i-class adjs (2.1). As our examples we cite the following nominative singular masculine forms:

	Latin		PIE
ā-class[226]	dōnātus	'given'	*dōn+ā+t+os
	domitus	'subdued'	*dom+i+t+os[227]
	sectus	'cut'	*sek+Ø+t+os
ē-class[226]	dēlētus	'deleted'	*dēl+ē+t+os
	monitus	'warned'	*mon+i+t+os[227]
	doctus	'taught'	*dok+Ø+t+os
	mulsus	'milked'	*melg+Ø+s+os[228,229]
	vīsus	'seen'	*weid+Ø+t+os[228]
Ø-class[226]	creditus	'believed'	*kred+i+t+os[227]
	coctus	'cooked'	*pek^w+Ø+t+os
	pulsus	'driven'	*pel+Ø+s+os[228]
ī-class[226]	audītus	'heard'	*ausd^h+ī+t+os[230]
	vīnctus	'tied'	*wink+Ø+t+os[231]
io-class[226]	raptus	'seized'	*rap+Ø+t+os

6.9 The Verb 'be'

The verb occurs only in the active.

6.9.1 Present Indicative

		Latin	PIE
sg	1	sum	*s+mi[232]
	2	es	*es+si
	3	est	*es+ti
pl	1	sumus	*s+omos[232]
	2	estis	*es+tes
	3	sunt	*s+onti[232]

6.9.2 Present Subjunctive

The antecedents consist of *s- plus the optative suffix *-īē- in the singular and the Ø-grade ablauting *-ī- in the plural plus the respective endings.

		Latin	PIE
sg	1	siem[233]	*s+īē+mi[234]
	2	siēs[233]	*s+īē+si[234]
	3	siet[233]	*s+īē+ti
pl	1	sīmus	*s+ī+mos
	2	sītis	*s+ī+tes
	3	sint	*s+ī+nti[235, 232]

6.9.3 Present Imperative

		Latin	PIE
sg	2	es	*es
pl	2	este	*es+te

6.9.4 Imperfect Indicative

These forms consist of er- plus the endings of the imperfect active indicative (6.2.1). E.g.,

		Latin	PIE
sg	1	eram	*es+ā+m[236]
	2	erās	*es+ā+s

6.9.5 Imperfect Subjunctive

There are two paradigms. One has the stem ess-, the other for-. Both take the imperfect active subjunctive endings (6.2.2). E.g.,

		Latin	PIE
sg	1	essem	*es+s+ēm
		forem	*b^hu+s+ēm[237,238]
	2	essēs	*es+s+ēs
		forēs	*b^hu+s+ēs[237]

6.9.6 Future Indicative

These forms consist of er- plus the endings of the future active indicative (6.3.1). E.g.,

		Latin	PIE
sg	1	erō	*es+ō
	2	eris	*es+esi

6.9.7 Future Imperative

The endings of this paradigm are those of the future active imperative (6.3.2).

		Latin		PIE
sg	2	estō	'you will have to be'	*es+tōd
	3	estō	'he will have to be'	*es+tōd
pl	2	estōte		*es+tōd+te
	3	suntō		*s+onti+ōd

6.9.8 Present Perfect Indicative

This paradigm consists of fu- plus the endings of the present perfect active indicative (6.4.1). E.g.,

		Latin	PIE
sg	1	fuī	*b^hu+ai[239]
	2	fuistī	*b^hu+istai

6.9.9 Present Perfect Subjunctive

These forms consist of fu- plus the endings of the present perfect active subjunctive (6.4.2). E.g.,

		Latin	PIE
sg	1	fuerim	*b^hu+is+ī+mi
	2	fueris	*b^hu+is+ī+si

6.9.10 Past Perfect Indicative

These forms consists of fu- plus the endings of the past perfect active indicative (6.5.1). E.g.,

		Latin	PIE
sg	1	fueram	*b^hu+is+ā+m
	2	fuerās	*b^hu+is+ā+s

6.9.11 Past Perfect Subjunctive

These forms consist of fu- plus the endings of the past perfect active subjunctive (6.5.2). E.g.,

		Latin	PIE
sg	1	fuissem	*b^hu+is+s+ē+m
	2	fuissēs	*b^hu+is+s+ē+s

6.9.12 Future Perfect Indicative

These forms consist of fu- plus the endings of the future perfect active indicative (6.6.1). E.g.,

		Latin	PIE
sg	1	fuerō	*b^hu+is+ō
	2	fueris	*b^hu+is+esi

6.9.13 Infinitives

These are present, future and perfect. They are formed like the present active (6.7.1), future active (6.7.3) and perfect active infinitives (6.7.5).

	Latin		PIE
pres	esse	'to be'	*es+s+i
future	futūrum esse	'to be going to be'	*b^hu+tūr+om *es+s+i
	fore		*b^hu+s+i
perf	fuisse	'to have been'	*b^hu+is+si

6.9.14 Participles

These are present and future; and they are formed like the present active (6.8.1) and future active participles. (6.8.2).

	Latin		PIE
pres	(ab)sēns	'absent'	*s+ent+s[240]
future	futūrus	'going to be'	*b^hu+tūr+os

V Exercises

(1) Consider the following PIE forms and the changes which they underwent into Latin. What is the Latin form? Give the Latin spelling and a phonemic transcription of the Latin word stress as determined by rule 6c LATIN STRESS.

a. Perf pass part *ag+t+os 'done' + 2c PHONOTACTICS 1c Obstruent cluster voicing and devoicing, 7c o(:)-TO-u(:), 8e LACHMANN > Latin?

b. Nom sg *ag^{w}nos 'lamb' + 2a LABIOVEL, 2c PHONOTACTICS 2b Nasal clusters, 7c o(:)-TO-u(:) > Latin?

c. Perf pass part *amb^h+kaid+s+os 'cut around' + 1 ASPIR STOPS, 2c PHONOTACTICS 1c Obstruent cluster voicing and devoicing & 2c Obstruent assimilation & 2f t-clusters & 1a Geminate simplification & 1b Nasal assimilation, 3c ITALIC STRESS, 4c UNSTRESSED V, 6b ei/ou-CHANGES, 6c LATIN STRESS, 7c o(:)-TO-u(:) > Latin?

d. 1sg perf *ausd^{h}īwai 'I heard' + 1 ASPIR STOPS, 2c PHONOTACTICS 2e s-clusters, 4c UNSTRESSED V, 6b ei/ou-CHANGES > Latin?

e. Dat sg *b^{h}rūkteuwi 'profit' + 1 ASPIR STOPS, 5a e-TO-o, 6b ei/ou-CHANGES, 8l V̄V-TO-VV > Latin?

f. 1sg imperf subj *b^{h}usēm 'I am' + 1 ASPIR STOPS, 3b i/u-TO-e/o, 3d s-TO-r, 8f WORD-FINAL SHORT > Latin?

g. Nom sg *deiwos 'god' + 6b ei/ou-CHANGES, 7b j/w-CHANGES , 7c o(:)-TO-u(:), 8l V̄V-TO-VV > Latin?

h. Nom sg masc *deksiteros 'right' + 3c ITALIC STRESS, 4b SYNCOPE stages 1 and 3 > Latin?

i. Nom sg *d^{h}amel+os 'servant' vs. *d^{h}amel+jā 'household' + 1 ASPIR STOPS, 4c UNSTRESSED V, 5a e-TO-o, 7b j/w-CHANGES, 7c o(:)-TO-u(:), shortening of the word-final /i/ > Latin? vs. ?

j. 1sg *d^{h}eig^{w}ō 'I fasten' + 1 ASPIR STOPS, 2a LABIOVEL, 6b ei/ou-CHANGES > Latin?

k. Nom sg *d^{h}ēi+l+jos 'son' + 1 ASPIR STOPS, 2b LONG DIPH, 6b ei/ou-changes , 7b j/w-CHANGES , 7c o(:)-TO-u(:) > Latin?

l. Nom sg *djeu+pater 'day-father, god' + 3a C+j CHANGES, 3c ITALIC STRESS, 4c UNSTRESSED V, 5a e-TO-o, 6b ei/ou-CHANGES, 8g LONG SEQ RESTRUCT applying optionally > Latin? or ?

m. 3sg *dōnājeti 'gives' + 6c LATIN STRESS,7b j/w-CHANGES, 4b SYNCOPE, 8i V-CONTRACT, 6c LATIN STRESS reapplying as a synchronic rule, 8f WORD-FINAL SHORT > Latin?

n. Nom pl *dwi+jugāi 'two yokes, i.e. a span of horses' + 7b j/w-CHANGES, 8b dw-CHANGES, 8i V-CONTRACT, and the ev change of /āi/ to /ae/> Latin?

o. Nom sg *egnis 'fire' + 2c PHONOTACTICS 2b Nasal clusters, 8c e-TO-i > Latin?

p. 1sg perf *ei+ai 'I went' + 3c ITALIC STRESS, 4c UNSTRESSED V, 6b ei/ou-CHANGES, 8l V̄V-TO-VV > Latin?

q. Nom sg masc *eud^{h}ros 'fruitful' + 1 ASPIR STOPS, 4b SYNCOPE stage 3, 5a e-TO-o, 6b ei/ou-CHANGES > Latin?

r. Nom sg masc *geib^{h}ros 'hunchbacked' + 1 ASPIR STOPS, 4b SYNCOPE stage 3, 6b ei/ou-CHANGES, 8g LONG SEQ RESTRUCT > Latin?

s. Nom sg masc *g^{hw}ormo+kap+s 'that which picks up hot material, i.e. tongs' + 1 ASPIR STOPS, 2a LABIOVEL, 4b SYNCOPE, 2c PHONOTACTICS 2h Sonorant-initial clusters applying as a persistent synchronic rule, 4c UNSTRESSED V > Latin?

t. Nom sg masc *kam+kr̥d+s 'of the same heart, i.e. in agreement' + 2c PHONOTACTICS lb Nasal assimilation & lc Obstruent cluster voicing and devoicing & 2f t-clusters & la Geminate simplification applying as a persistent synchronic rule, 2d SYL SON > Latin?

u. 1sg perf *man+s+ai 'I waited' + 4c UNSTRESSED V, 6b ei/ou-CHANGES, 8k Vns-changes > Latin?

v. 1sg *meitō 'I send' + 6b ei/ou-CHANGES, 8g LONG SEQ RESTRUCT > Latin?

w. Nom sg *ni+sd+os 'a sit-in, nest' + 2c PHONOTACTICS lc Obstruent cluster voicing and devoicing & 2g s-clusters, 7c o(:)-TO-u(:) > Latin?

x. Nom sg masc *n̥+gnō+t+os 'unknown' + 2d SYL SON, 2c PHONOTACTICS lb Nasal assimilation & la Geminate simplification all of which applying as persistent synchronic rules, 7c o(:)-TO-u(:), 8c e-TO-i > Latin?

y. 1sg *ob+kaidō 'I kill' + 2c PHONOTACTICS 1c Obstruent cluster voicing and devoicing & 2c Obstruent assimilation, 3c ITALIC STRESS, 4c UNSTRESSED V, 6c LATIN STRESS > Latin?

z. *penk^{w}e '5' + 4a p-TO-k^{w}, 8c e-TO-i, 8j Vnk-TO-V̄nk applying analogously > Latin?

aa. Perf pass part *per+d^{h}ak+t+os + 1 ASPIR STOPS, 3c ITALIC STRESS, 4c UNSTRESSED V, 6c LATIN STRESS, 7c o(:)-TO-u(:) > Latin?

bb. 2sg *plantājes 'you plant' + 6c LATIN STRESS, 7b j/w-CHANGES, 8i V-CONTRACT, 6c LATIN STRESS reapplying as a synchronic rule > Latin?

cc. Inf *re+dida+si 'to give back' + 3c ITALIC STRESS, 3d s-TO-r, 4b SYNCOPE, 4c UNSTRESSED V stages 1 and 3 > Latin?

dd. 1sg pres subj *s+īē+mi 'I am' + 4c SYNCOPE stage 4, 8f WORD-FINAL SHORT, 81 V̄V-TO-VV > Latin?

ee. Nom sg *sneub^{h}ēs 'cloud' + 1 ASPIR STOPS, 2c PHONOTACTICS 2e s-clusters, 5a e-TO-o, 6b ei/ou-CHANGES > Latin?

ff. Acc sg *snig^{hw}m̥ 'snow' + 1 ASPIR STOPS, 2a LABIOVEL, 2c PHONOTACTICS, 2d SYL SON > Latin?

gg. Acc sg *swoidōs+m̥ 'sweat' + 2d SYL SON, 3d s-TO-r, 7a ai/oi-TO-ae/oe, 7b j/w-CHANGES , 8h oe-CHANGES > Latin?

hh. Nom sg *swepnos 'sleep' + 2c PHONOTACTICS 2b Nasal clusters, 5a e-TO-o, 7b j/w-CHANGES, 7c o(:)-TO-u(:) > Latin?

ii. 1sg perf *te+tag+ai 'I touched' + 3c ITALIC STRESS, 4c UNSTRESSED V, 6b ei/ou-CHANGES > Latin?

jj. 1sg pres *weg^{hw}ējō 'I turn' + 1 ASPIRATE STOPS, 2a LABIOVEL, 5a e-TO-o, 7b j/w-CHANGES, 81 V̄V-TO-VV > Latin?

(2) Given the following PIE forms, what will be the Latin reflexes and what changes will they have undergone? Give the Latin spelling and a phonemic transcription with the Latin word stress as determined by rule 6c LATIN STRESS.

a. 1sg pres *agjō 'I speak'.
b. Nom sg *agros 'field'.
c. *aid^{h}ēs 'temple'.
d. *dekm̥ '10'.
e 1sg pres *d^{h}ingō 'I form'.
f. Nom sg *d^{h}ūmos 'fume'.
g. Pres pass inf *dōnā+s+ei 'to be given'.
h. Nom sg masc *dwenos 'good'.
i. Acc sg masc *ej+om 'him'.

j. Nom sg *g^{h}aidos 'goat'.
k. 1sg pres *g^{h}undō 'I pour'.
l. Nom sg masc *g^{hw}eros 'wild'.
m. Nom sg masc *g^{hw}ormos 'warm'.
n. 1sg pres *g^{w}em+j+ō 'I come'.
o. Gen sg *i+ten+er+es 'journey'.
p. 1sg pres *jud^{h}ējō 'I command'.
q. Nom sg *korōn+l+ā 'small crown, wreath'.
r. Nom sg *kr̥d 'heart' vs. gen sg *kr̥d+es.
s. Comp. adj *mag+jos 'larger'.
t. Acc pl *rēgn̥s 'kings'.
u. 2sg pres dep *sek^{w}eso 'you follow'.
v. Nom sg masc *septm̥+os '7th'.
w. Nom pl *skand+sl+āi 'stairs'.
x. Nom sg *stlokos 'place'.
y. Nom sg mase. *swādwis 'sweet'.
z. 1sg pres *torsējō 'I burn'.
aa. 1sg pres *trans+nō 'I swim across'.
bb. 1sg pres *weg^{h}ō 'I travel'.
cc. 1sg pres subj *wid+ē+j+ā+mi 'I see'.
dd. Nom sg *wid^{h}ewā 'widow'.
ee. Perf pass part *wid+t+os 'seen' (assume 8e LACHMANN).
ff. Perf pass part *wink-t+os 'tied'.

(3) The following Germanic verbs have Latin cognates. Construct the 1st singular present indicative form of the Latin verb as follows: (i)reconstruct the PIE form from the Germanic one in view of the consonantal changes in chapter 2. (ii) Put the PIE form through those Latin changes which apply to it. (iii) Put the verb into the Latin verb class as given.

a. *auk- 'increase' (English "eke out") in the Lat ē-class.
b. *bind- 'tie' in the Lat Ø-class. The vowel in the PIE root is /e/. The Latin verb occurs with the prefix of- from earlier ob-.
c. *get- 'get' in the Lat Ø-class. The Latin verb has the prefix pre- and has an /n/ infix in the present.
d. *k^{w}em- 'come' in the Lat ī-class. Posit the PIE 1sg pres ending *-jō.
e. *lik- 'lick' in the Lat Ø-class. The Latin verb has an /n/ infix in the present.
f. *seh^w- 'see' in the Lat Ø-class. The Latin verb is deponent.
g. *sōk- 'seek' in the Lat ī-class. The vowel in the PIE root is /ā/.
h. *skit- 'defecate' in the Lat Ø-class. The Latin verb has an /n/ infix in the present. It means 'cut off'.
i. *suk- 'suck' in the Lat Ø-class. The PIE root has e-grade ABLAUT /eu/ in the present.
j. *θink- 'think' in the Lat ē-class. The vowel in the PIE root is ablauting /o/.
k. *tug- 'lead, pull' (English "tug") in the Lat Ø-class. The Germanic form has undergone Gothic change 3 VERNER. The vowel nucleus in the PIE root is e-grade ablauting /eu/.

(4) Consider the 1sg present and perfect forms of the following verbs. Reconstruct the PIE antecedents of the perfect forms as follows: (i) Remove the nasal from the root. (ii) Note that the

perfect forms result from PIE ABLAUT. What types of ABLAUT would give the Latin forms? (iii) Recall that the PIE antecedent of the ending is *-ai.

a. findō 'split' vs. fīdī.
b. rumpō 'break' vs. rūpī.
c. vincō 'conquer' vs. vīcī.

(5) Consider the vowel alternations in the following forms. Which of them must be PIE ABLAUT and why? Which can be the result of ABLAUT or of some other change?

a. Sg nom frōns 'forehead' vs. gen frontis.
b. Sg nom pēs 'foot' vs. gen pedis.
c. Inf suere 'sew' vs. perf part sūtus.

(6) Consider the glossed Latin text in VI below. Give a smooth translation of this text.

VI A Latin Text

Our text is the opening passage of Cicero's *Dē nātūrā deōrum* 'On the nature of the gods' composed about 45 BC. Our version of the text is based on Rackham (1979: 2). In the text we give (a) the traditional Latin orthography, (b) a phonemic transcription, (c) a gloss and (d) a grammatical description of each word in the text.

1	**a**	Cum	multae	rēs	in	philosophiā	nēquāquam	satis
	b	kum	múltae	rēs	in	pʰilosópʰiā	nēkʷā́kʷam	sátis
	c	*since*	*many*	*things*	*in*	*philosophy*	*in no way*	*enough*
	d	conj	ā-class nom pl fem adj	fem root-class nom pl	prep	fem ā-class abl sg	adv	adv

2	**a**	adhūc	explicātae	sint,	tum	perdifficilis,	Brūte,	quod	tū
	b	adhū́k	eksplikā́tae	sint	tum	perdiffíkilis	brū́te	kʷod	tū
	c	*up to now*	*explain*	*be*	*then*	*very difficult*	*Brutus*	*which*	*you*
	d	adv	perf pass part nom pl fem	3 pl pres subj	adv	i-class nom sg fem adj	masc o-class voc sg	acc sg neut rel pron	nom sg

3	**a**	minimē	ignōras,	et	perobscūra	quaestio	est	dē
	b	mínimē	iŋnṓras	et	peropskū́ra	kʷáestio	est	dē
	c	*by no means*	*not know*	*and*	*very obscure*	*inquiry*	*be*	*about*
	d	adv	ā-class verb pres ind 2sg	conj	ā-class nom sg fem adj	fem Vn-class nom sg	3 sg pres ind	prep

4	**a**	nātūrā	deōrum,	quae	et	ad	cognitiōnem	animī
	b	nātū́rā	deṓrum	k^{w}ae	et	ad	koŋnitiṓnem	ánimī
	c	*nature*	*gods*	*which*	*and*	*for*	*knowledge*	*soul*
	d	fem ā-class	masc o-class	nom sg fem	conj	prep	fem Vn-class	masc o-class
		abl sg	gen pl	rel pron			acc sg	gen sg

5	**a**	pulcherrima	est	et	ad	moderandam	religiōnem	necessāria.	Dē
	b	pulk^{h}érrima	est	et	ad	moderándam	religiṓnem	nekessā́ria	dē
	c	*pertinent*	*be*	*and*	*for*	*guide*	*religion*	*necessary*	*about*
	d	ā-class nom	3sg	conj	prep	ā-class verb	fem Vn-class	jā-class nom	prep
		sg fem	pres ind			fut pass part	acc sg	sg fem adj	
		sup adj				acc sg fem			

6	**a**	quā	tam	variae	sunt	doctissimōrum	hominum	tamque
	b	k^{w}ā	tam	wáriae	sunt	doktissimṓrum	hóminum	támk^{w}e
	c	*which*	*so*	*various*	*be*	*wise, educated*	*man*	*so + and*
	d	abl sg fem	adv	jā-class nom	3 sg pres	o-class gen pl	masc Vn-class	adv + conj
		rel pron		sg fem adj	indic	masc sup adj	gen pl	

7	**a**	discrepantēs	sententiae,	ut	magnō	argumentō	esse	dēbeat
	b	diskrepántēs	senténtiae	ut	máŋnō	arguméntō	ésse	dḗbeat
	c	*disagree*	*opinion*	*that*	*great*	*argument*	*be*	*must*
	d	ā-class verb	fem jā-class	conj	o-class dat	neuter	pres inf	ē-class verb
		pres act part	nom pl		sg masc adj	o-class		3 sg
		nom pl fem				dat sg		pres subj

8	**a**	causam	et	principium	philosophiae	esse	inscientiam,	prūdenterque.
	b	káusam	et	priŋkípium	p^{h}ilosóp^{h}iae	ésse	inskiéntiam	prūdénterk^{w}e
	c	*cause*	*and*	*origin*	*philosophy*	*be*	*lack of knowledge*	*prudently + and*
	d	fem ā-class	conj	neut jo-class	fem jā-class	pres	fem jā-class	adv + conj
		acc sg		acc sg	gen sg	inf	acc sg	

9	a	Acadēmicōs	ā	rēbus	incertīs	adsensiōnum	cohibuisse:	quid
	b	akadḗmikōs	ā	rḗbus	iŋkértīs	atsensiṓnum	kohibuísse	k^{w}id
	c	*academician*	*from*	*affair*	*uncertain*	*assent, consent*	*hold back*	*what*
	d	masc o-class acc pl	prep	fem root- class abl pl	ā-class abl pl fem adj	fem Vn-class gen pl	ē-class verb perf act inf	nom sg neut inter pron

10	a	est	enim	temeritāte	turpius?	Aut	quid	tam	temerārium
	b	est	énim	temeritā́te	túrpius	aut	k^{w}id	tam	temerā́rium
	c	*be*	*indeed*	*rashness*	*bad*	*or*	*what*	*so*	*rash*
	d	3sg pres ind	adv	fem Ø-class abl sg	i-class nom sg neut comp adj	conj	nom sg neut inter pron	adv	jo-class nom sg neut adj

11	a	tamque	indignum	sapientis	gravitāte	atque	constantiā	quam	aut
	b	támk^{w}e	indíŋnum	sapiéntis	grawitā́te	átk^{w}e	konstántiā	k^{w}am	aut
	c	*so + and*	*unworthy*	*understand*	*importance*	*and*	*consistency*	*than*	*or*
	d	adv + conj	o-class nom sg neut adj	io-class verb pres act part gen sg masc	fem Ø-class abl sg	conj	fem jā-class abl sg	conj	conj

12	a	falsum	sentīre	aut	quod	nōn	satis	explōrātē	perceptum
	b	fálsum	sentī́re	aut	k^{w}od	nōn	sátis	eksplōrā́tē	perképtum
	c	*false*	*believe*	*or*	*what*	*not*	*enough*	*definitively*	*perceive*
	d	o-class nom sg neut adj	ī-class verb pres act inf	conj	acc sg neut rel pron	adv	adv	ā-class verb perf pass part adv	io-class verb perf pass part nom sg neut

13	a	sit	et	cognitum	sine	ullā	dubitātiōne	dēfendere?	Velut	in
	b	sit	et	kóŋnitum	síne	úllā	dubitātiṓne	dēféndere	wélut	in
	c	*be*	*and*	*know*	*without*	*any*	*hesitation*	*defend*	*while*	*in*
	d	3sg pres subj	conj	Ø-class verb perf pass part nom sg neut	prep	ā-class abl sg fem adj	fem Vn-class abl sg	Ø-class verb pres act inf	conj	prep

14	**a**	hāc	quaestiōne	plērīque	deōs	esse	dīxērunt,	dubitāre
	b	hāk	kʷaestiṓne	plḗrīkʷe	déōs	ésse	dīksḗrunt,	dubitā́re
	c	*this*	*question*	*many + and*	*god*	*be*	*say*	*doubt*
	d	abl sg	fem	o-class	o-class	pres inf	Ø-class	ā-class verb
		fem	Vn-class	nom pl masc	acc pl		verb 3pl	pres act inf
		dem pron	abl sg	adj + conj	masc		perf act	

15	**a**	sē	dīxit	Prōtagorās.
	b	sē	dī́ksit	prōtágorās
	c	*himself*	*say*	*Protagoras*
	d	acc sg	Ø-class verb	Greek noun
		masc refl	3sg perf act	nom sg masc
		pron		

VII Key

(1) The Latin forms are these: (a) āctus /āktus/, (b) agnus /áŋnus/, (c) ancīsus /aŋkī́sus/, (d) audīvī /audī́wī/, (e) frūctuī / frū́ktuī/, (f) forem /fórem/, (g) deus /déus/, (h) dexter /dékster/, (i) famulus /fámulus/ vs. familia /família/, (j) fīvō /fī́wō/, (k) fīlius /fī́lius/, (l) Jūpiter /jū́piter/ and Juppiter /júppiter/, (m) dōnāt /dṓnāt/ (n) bīgae /bī́gae/, (o) ignis /íŋnis/, (p) iī /íī/, (q) ūber /ū́ber/, (r) gibber /gíbber/, (s) forceps /fórkeps/, (t) concors /kóŋkors/, (u) mānsī /mā́nsī/, (v) mittō /míttō/, (w) nīdus /nī́dus/, (x) ignōtus /iŋnṓtus/, (y) occīdō /okkī́dō/, (z) quīnque /kʷī́ŋkʷe/, (aa) perfectus /perféktus/, (bb) plantās /plántās/, (cc) reddere /réddere/, (dd) siem /síem/, (ee) nūbēs /nū́bēs/, (ff) nivem /níwem/,/ (gg) sūdōrem /sūdṓrem/, (hh) somnus /sómnus/, (ii) tetigī /tétigī/, (jj) voveō /wóweō/.

(2) The Latin forms and changes are these:

a. ājō /ā́jjo/. The derivation is 3a C+j CHANGES.
b. ager /áger/. The derivation is 4b SYNCOPE stage 3.
c. aedēs /áedēs/. The derivation is 1 ASPIR STOPS, 7a ai/oi-TO-ae/oe.
d. decem /dékem/. The derivation is 2d SYL SON.
e. fingō /fíŋgō/. The derivation is 1 ASPIR STOPS.
f. fūmus /fū́mus/. The derivation is 1 ASPIR STOPS, 7c o(:)-TO-u(:).
g. dōnārī /dōnā́rī/. The derivation is 3d s-TO-r , 6b ei/ou-CHANGES.
h. bonus /bónus/. The derivation is 5a e-TO-o, 7c o(:)-TO-u(:), 8b dw-CHANGES.
i. eum /éum/. The derivation is 7b j/w-CHANGES , 7c o(:)-TO-u(:).
j. haedus /háedus/. The derivation is 1 ASPIR STOPS, 7a ai/oi-TO-ae/oe, 7c o(:)-TO-u(:).
k. fundō /fúndō/. The derivation is 1 ASPIR STOPS.

l. ferus /férus/. The derivation is 1 ASPIR STOPS, 2a LABIOVEL, 7c o(:)-TO-u(:).
m. formus /fórmus/. The derivation is 1 ASPIR STOPS, 2a LABIOVEL, 7c o(:)-TO-u(:).
n. veniō /wéniō/. The derivation is 2a LABIOVEL, 3a C+j CHANGES, 7b j/w-CHANGES .
o. itineris /itíneris/. The derivation is 3c ITALIC STRESS, 4c UNSTRESSED V, 6c LATIN STRESS.
p. jubeō /júbeō/. The derivation is 1 ASPIR STOPS, 7b j/w-CHANGES , 8l V̄V-TO-VV,
q. corolla /koróllа/. The derivation is 2c PHONOTACTICS 2a l-clusters, shortening of /ā/.
r. cor /kor/ and cordis /kórdis/. The derivation is 2d SYL SON, 6a d/t-CHANGES, 8c e-TO-i.
s. mājus /mā́jjus/. The derivation is 3a C+j CHANGES,7c o(:)-TO-u(:).
t. rēgēs /rḗgēs/. The derivation is 2d SYL SON, 8k Vns-CHANGES.
u. sequere /sék^{w}ere/. The derivation is 3d s-TO-r, 4c UNSTRESSED V stage 3.
v. septimus /séptimus/. The derivation is 2d SYL SON, 3c ITALIC STRESS, 4c UNSTRESSED V, 7c o(:)-TO-u(:).
w. scālae /skā́lae/. The derivation is 2b LONG DIPH, 2c PHONOTACTICS 2j l-final clusters, 7a ai/oi-TO-ae/oe.
x. locus /lókus/. The derivation is 2c PHONOTACTICS 2g s-clusters, 7c o(:)-TO-u(:).
y. suāvis /suā́wis/. The derivation is 7b j/w-CHANGES, 8b dw-CHANGES.
z. torreō /tórreō/. The derivation is 2c PHONOTACTICS 2d r-clusters, 7b j/w-CHANGES , 8l V̄V-TO-VV.
aa. trānō /trā́nō/. The derivation is 2c PHONOTACTICS 2i s-clusters.
bb. vehō /wéhō/. The derivation is 1 ASPIR STOPS.
cc. videam /wídeam/. The derivation is 4b Syncope, 7b j/w-CHANGES , 8f WORD-FINAL SHORT, 8l V̄V-TO-VV.
dd. vidua /wídua/. The derivation is 1 ASPIR STOPS, 5a e-TO-o, 6b ei/ou-CHANGES, 8l V̄V-TO-VV, shortening of the word-final /ā/.
ee. vīsus /wī́sus/. The derivation is 2c PHONOTACTICS 1c Obstruent cluster voicing and devoicing, 7c o(:)-TO-u(:), 8e LACHMANN, 2c PHONOTACTICS 1a Geminate simplification reapplying as a persistent synchronic rule.
ff. vīnctus /wī́ŋktus/. The derivation is 7c o(:)-TO-u(:), 8j Vnk-TO-V̄nk.

(3) We give the 1st singular present PIE and Latin forms as well as the rules from PIE to Latin.

a. PIE *aug+ē+j+ō, Lat augeō. The derivation is 7b j/w-CHANGES, 8l V̄V-TO-VV.
b. PIE *b^{h}end^{h}+ō, Lat (of)fendō. The derivation is 1 ASPIR STOPS.
c. PIE *g^{h}end+ō, Lat (pre)hendō. The derivation is 1 ASPIR STOPS.
d. PIE *g^{w}em+j+ō, Lat veniō. The derivation is 2a LABIOVEL, 3a C+j CHANGES, 7b j/w-CHANGES.
e. PIE *ling+ō, Lat lingō. The PIE-to-Latin derivation is Ø.
f. PIE *sek^{w}+ō+r, Lat sequor. The derivation is 8f WORD-FINAL SHORT.
g. PIE *sāg+ī+ō, Lat sāgiō. The PIE-to-Latin derivation is 8l V̄V-TO-VV.
h. PIE *skind+ō, Lat scindō. The PIE-to-Latin derivation is Ø.
i. PIE *seug+ō, Lat sūgō. The derivation is 5a e-TO-o, 6b ei/ou-CHANGES.
j. PIE *tong+ē+j+ō, Lat tongeō. The derivation is 7b j/w-CHANGES , 8l V̄V-TO-VV.
k. PIE *deuk+ō, Lat dūcō. The derivation is 5a e-TO-o, 6b ei/ou-CHANGES.

(4) The PIE 1st singular perfect forms are these:

a. *b^heidai.
b. *reupai or *roupai.
c. *weikai.

The derivations include the changes 4c UNSTRESSED V, 5a e-TO-o, 6b ei/ou-CHANGES.

(5) The alternations result as follows:

a. Nom sg *b^hrōnt+s vs. gen sg *b^hront+es byABLAUT; or non-ablauting nom sg *b^hront+s (1 ASPIR STOPS) > *fronts (2c PHONOTACTICS) > *frons (8k Vns-CHANGES) > Lat frōns.
b. Nom sg *pēd+s vs. gen sg *ped+es must be PIE ABLAUT .
c. One possibility is ABLAUT as inf *su+es+i vs. perf part *seu+t+os or *sou+t+os. Another is the non-ablauting root *sū-. The derivation of the inf *sū+es+i is (3d s-TO-r) > *sūeri (4c UNSTRESSED V) > *sūere (81 V̄V-TO-VV) > Lat suere.

(6) The following is a translation of the text in section VI.

"Since many things in philosophy remain up to now insufficiently explained — as you well know, Brutus — the inquiry into the nature of the gods is both very difficult and very obscure. This same inquiry is also very pertinent for attaining knowledge of the human soul and is also necessary for guiding religion. The various opinions on this question held by wise men are at such variance that this very fact must be considered a cogent argument that lack of knowledge is in point of fact the impetus for and origin of philosophy. This same fact must also be considered the reason that the academicians have prudently withheld any unanimous consensus on such uncertain matters. For, indeed, what is worse than rashness? And what is so rash or so unworthy of the gravity and the consistency of any thinking person than to believe something false or to defend without hesitation something which is not sufficiently perceived or known? While on this question of gods many have said that they exist, Protagaras has said that he doubts it."

VIII Notes

[1] We assume that the only Lat labiovelar remaining from PIE was /k^w/. By 2a LABIOVEL PIE /g^w/ was bisegmentalized to /gw/, which occurred only after [ŋ]. Then by 7b j/w-CHANGES /ngw/ becomes /ngu/.

[2] The aspirated voiceless stops occur mainly in Greek borrowings such as philosophia 'philosophy', thermae 'hot baths' and chaos /k^haos/ 'chaos'. According to Sommer (1948: 199), Roman writers began recording the aspiration about 150 BC. Aspirated stops also occur for some reason in a few native Latin words such as pulcher 'beautiful'.

[3] The segment [ŋ] occurs as a predictable variant of /n/ by 2c PHONOTACTICS lb Nasal assimilation and of /g/ and /k/ by 2c PHONOTACTICS 2b Nasal clusters.

[4] The segments /w-u/ and /j-i/ are in complementary distribution by 7b j/w-CHANGES, which remains as a phon cond rule of Latin.

[5] The last three sequences may in fact not constitute Latin diphthongs. The /ei/ in deinde 'then' may be /de+inde/ with an intervening morpheme boundary. Similarly, the /eu/ in Lat neuter 'neuter' may be morphemic /ne+uter/; and the /ui/ in fluitō 'flow' may be considered morphemic /flu+it+ō/. Elsewhere /eu/ does occur in Greek borrowings such as Eurōpa 'Europe'.

[6] We usually do not mark the stress on the Lat forms since it can easily be supplied by following rule 6c LATIN STRESS. We usually do not mark the stress on the PIE forms; however we assume it was reflected in the patterns of Greek and Sanskrit. The derivation of this form (including the original stress) was *deiwós (3c ITALIC STRESS) > *déiwos (6b ei/ou-CHANGES) > *dḗwos (6c LATIN STRESS, here applying vacuously) > *dḗwos (7b j/w-CHANGES) > *dḗos (7c o(:)-TO-u(:)) > dḗus (81 V̄V-TO-VV) > Lat deus /déus/.

[7] The origin of the ending /ī/, which also occurs in Old Irish, is not clear. The earlier PIE form was probably *deiw+osjo.

[8] The derivation is *deiwōi (2b LONG DIPH) > *deiwō (ev) > Lat deō.

[9] The PIE ending *-ōd is posited in several sources including Kieckers (1960: part 2, page 4). Sihler (1995: 258) posits *-ōt. In either event the Latin reflex would be the same.

[10] The earlier nominative plural was probably *deiwōs. The ending *-oi is from the nom pl masc pronoun *ei+oi 'those' (see 5.3).

[11] The earliest Latin genitive plural ending is -um. Its PIE antecedent is often considered to have been *-ōm. If so, its derivation after 7b j/w-CHANGES would be *dēōm (8f WORD-FINAL SHORT) > *dēom (7c o(:)-TO-u(:), perhaps applying for a time as a persistent rule) > *dēum (81 V̄V-TO-VV) > deum. Another possibility is that the PIE ending had the ablauting short vowel *-om. The later genitive plural in -ōrum first occurs about 200 BC and was formed on the model of the ā-class gen pl -ārum discussed under 1.2 below.

[12] The dative and ablative plural are from a PIE instrumental ending. The derivation is *deiwōis (2b LONG DIPH) > *deiwois (6b ei/ou-CHANGES) > *dēwois (7b j/w-CHANGES) > *dēois (7a ai/oi-TO-ae/oe) > dēoes (8h oe-CHANGES) > *dēīs (81 V̄V-TO-VV) > Lat deīs.

[13] The derivation is *agros (4b SYNCOPE part 3) > Lat ager.

[14] The derivation is *jugā (8d IAMBIC SHORT) > Lat juga. The ending short -a was then transferred to all neuters such as bella 'wars' where 8d IAMBIC SHORT did not apply.

[15] The derivation is *sok^{w}jos (2a LABIOVEL) > *sokjos (7b j/w-CHANGES) > *sokios (7c o(:)-TO-u(:)) > Lat socius.

[16] The derivation is like the preceding except that 8i V-CONTRACT applies as an optional synchronic rule. Hence /sokiī/ (8i V-CONTRACT applying optionally) → socī or sociī.

[17] The derivation of the accusative singular is *sterlām (2c PHONOTACTICS 2a l-clusters) > *stellām (8f WORD-FINAL SHORT) > Lat stellam. The derivation of a nominative singular like Lat rosa 'rose' is *rosā (8d IAMBIC SHORT) > Lat rosa. And the vocative singular probably ended in short /a/. Hence short /a/was transferred to a root like /stell-/ (where 8d IAMBIC SHORT did not apply) to result in the nom sg stella, not **stellā.

[18] The earlier ending was -ās, the later -ae. The antecedent of the latter ending, namely *-ī, was imported from the o-Class. The derivation after 2c PHONOTACTICS is *stellāī (2b LONG DIPH) > *stellaī (restructuring of /aī/ to the actually occurring diphthong /ai/) > *stellai (7a ai/oi-TO-ae/oe) > Lat stellae.

[19] The derivation after 2c PHONOTACTICS is *stellād (6a d/t-CHANGES) Lat stellā.

[20] The locative is attested in only a few words.

[21] The *-i, like that of the o-class nominative plural, was taken from the pronominal declension. The later derivation was *stellā+i (2b LONG DIPH applying for a time as a persistent synchronic rule) > *stellai (7a ai/oi-TO-ae/oe) > Lat stellae. Note that the addition of *-i to the ā-Class nouns, unlike the case of o-Class nouns, must have occurred after the time of 4c UNSTRESSED V at about 250 BC. Otherwise the derivation would be *stellai (4c UNSTRESSED V) > Lat **stellī instead of stellae.

[22] The derivation is *sterlāns (8k Vns-CHANGES, ev) > Lat stellās.

[23] This ending is from the pronominal declension as in the gen pl *ei-āsom 'those' in 5.3 below. The later derivation is *stellāsom (3d s-TO-r) > *stellārom (7c o(:)-TO-u(:)) > Lat stellārum.

[24] The derivation is *sterlāis (2b LONG DIPH, 2c PHONOTACTICS) > *stellais (4c UNSTRESSED V) > *stelleis (6b ei/ou-Changes) > Lat stellīs.

[25] These endings are from the athematic class. The derivation of the accusative singular is *egnm̥ (2c PHONOTACTICS 2b Nasal clusters) > *eŋnm̥ (2d SYL SON) > *eŋnem (8c e-TO-i) > ignem /iŋnem/.

[26] The ending *-īd was probably formed in post-PIE Italic times on the model of the o-Class ablative singular ending *-ōd.

[27] The derivation is *egneies (PIE 3.1.2c i-j/u-w ALT applying synchronically) → *egnejes (2c PHONOTACTICS) > *eŋnejes (7b j/w-CHANGES) > *eŋnees = *eŋnēs (8c e-TO-i) > Lat ignēs /iŋnēs/.

[28] The derivation is *egnins (ev) > *iŋnins (8k Vns-CHANGES) > Lat ignīs. The acc pl ignēs is from the nominative plural and occurs later.

[29] The derivation is *mari (4c UNSTRESSED V, Stage 3a) > Lat mare. The ending is the same on the polysyllabic noun *sedīli 'seat' (ev) > Lat sedīle. Some polysyllabic neuter nouns have their nominative /accusative singular in -Ø instead of -e. The reason for this is not clear; perhaps it is the influence of the athematic neuter nouns under 1.5 below. One example is the sg nom *animāl 'animal' vs. gen *animāles (4c UNSTRESSED V) > *animāl vs. animālis (8f WORD-FINAL SHORT) > Lat animal vs. animālis.

[30] The derivation is *bʰrūktous (1 ASPIR STOPS) > *frūktous (6b ei/ou-CHANGES) > Lat frūctūs. The endings in *-Vu- are ablauting variants of *-u-. Another variant could be *-eus, which by e-TO-o and 6b ei/ou-CHANGES would also result in Lat -ūs.

[31] The derivation is *bʰrūkteuei (1 ASPIR STOPS) > *frūkteuei (5a e-TO-o) > *frūktouei (6b ei/ou-CHANGES) > *frūktūī (8l V̄V-TO-VV) > Lat frūctuī.

[32] The ablative ending was formed in post-PIE Italic times on the model of the o-Class abl *-ōd.

[33] The derivation of the accusative plural is *bʰrūktuns (1 ASPIR STOPS, 8k Vns-CHANGES) > Lat frūctūs. The Latin nominative plural is probably from the accusative. Otherwise one would expect Lat **frūctuis.

[34] The /i/ in the Latin ending is from the i-Class (1.3 above).

[35] The antecedent of the long /ū/ in the Latin ending is not clear. Sihler (1995: 323) suggests a PIE dual ending *-ū. Another possibility is an ablauting ending *gen(e/o)u (5a e-TO-o) > *genou (6b ei/ou-CHANGES) > Lat genū.

[36] The derivation is *rēgs (2c PHONOTACTICS 1c Obstruent cluster voicing and devoicing) > Lat rēx /rēks/. Other nouns of this class also undergo 2c PHONOTACTICS: nom sg /aetāt+s/ 'age' (2c PHONOTACTICS 2f t-clusters and 2c PHONOTACTICS la Geminate simplification) → aetās; and nom sg /sōl+s/ 'sun' (2c PHONOTACTICS 2a l-clusters) → sōl.

[37] The derivation is *rēgi (4c UNSTRESSED V) > Lat rēge.

[38] The derivation of the accusative plural is *rēgn̥s (2d SYL SON) > *rēgens (8k Vns-CHANGES) > Lat rēgēs. This form took over for the nominative plural as well; otherwise one would expect a Lat nom pl **rēgis.

[39] The /i/ in this ending is from the i-class. Otherwise one would expect **rēgbus.

[40] The derivation is *kapot (7c o(:)-TO-u(:)) > Lat caput.

[41] The derivation is *kapotā (4c UNSTRESSED V, ev) > capita. It is possible that the vowel alternation in this stem reflects PIE ABLAUT, *kapot- and *kapet- respectively.

[42] All cases except the nominative and accusative singular have the stem itiner-. The earlier oblique case stem was probably *iten- to which *-er was added in pre-Latin times. The derivation of the genitive singular is *iteneres (3c ITALIC STRESS) > *íteneres (4c UNSTRESSED V, which does not apply to /er/) > *ítineris (6c LATIN STRESS) > Lat /itíneris/.

[43] The derivation is not clear: *gʷōus (2a LABIOVEL) > *wōus (? borrowed from a rustic dialect) > *bōus (? 2b LONG DIPH, applying regularly to a vocative form *bōu > *bō, the /ō/ then replacing /ōu/ in the other forms) > Lat bōs.

[44] The derivation is *gʷou+m̥ (PIE 3.1.2c i-j/u-w ALT applying synchronically) → *gʷowm̥ (2d SYL SON, ev) > Lat bovem /bowem/. Some forms seem to have come from a nonsyllabic *-m. E.g., the feminine noun nom sg *wī+s 'force' vs. acc sg *wī+m (8f WORD-FINAL SHORT) > Lat vīs vs. vim. We have assumed an ablaut of /ō/-/o/ in this paradigm. Sihler (1995: 334) assumes ablauting /e/ where we posit /o/. If so, then 5a e-TO-o has applied in the derivations.

[45] The Latin nominative plural is from an earlier accusative plural.

[46] The derivation is *gʷou+om (ev) > *bowom (7b j/w-CHANGES) > *boom (7c o(:)-to-u(:)) > Lat boum.

[47] It is generally agreed that the antecedent was *diēu+endings. The derivation of a form like the genitive singular where the ending began with a vowel is *diēu+ī (PIE 3.1.2c i-j/u-w ALT applying as a persistent synchronic rule) > *diēwī (7b j/w-CHANGES) > Lat diēī. The diē- without the /u/ was then extended throughout the paradigm.

[48]These endings are from the o- and ā-classes.

[49]Another noun of this class is the fem rēs 'thing'. The derivation of the genitive singular is *rē+ī (81 V̄V-TO-VV) > Lat reī. Notice that 81 V̄V-TO-VV cannot apply to diēī.

[50] The nominative singular has -ter; the other cases -tr-. This is PIE ABLAUT.

[51]The derivation is *auktōr (8f WORD-FINAL SHORT) > Lat auctor.

[52] The antecedent of this noun seems to have had /s/ instead of /t/. The derivation is *swesōr (3d s-TO-r) > *swerōr (5a e-TO-o) > *sworōr (7b j/w-CHANGES) > *sorōr (8f WORD-FINAL SHORT) > Lat soror.

[53]It is questionable whether the nominative singular forms originally had word-final /n/. If so, given our rules, one would expect Lat **homōn, **sermōn, etc. The derivation of Lat homo is *gʰemō (1 ASPIR STOPS) > *hemō (possibly 5a e-TO-o) > *homō (8d IAMBIC SHORT, applying here optionally) > Lat homo as well as homō. But note that 8d IAMBIC SHORT cannot apply to a form like *sermō > Lat sermō.

[54] The derivation is *nātjō (7b j/w-CHANGES) > *nātiō (8d IAMBIC SHORT applying analogously) > Lat nātio.

[55] The alternations in the suffixes –ōn- , –en- and -n- reflect PIE ABLAUT.

[56] The PIE antecedent may have been the Ø-grade ablauting *nom̥n̥. Then the derivation is *nomn̥ (2d SYL SON) > Lat nomen.

[57] The derivation is *nomenā (4c UNSTRESSED V) > *nominā (replacement of /ā/ by /a/ from the neuter o-class) > Lat nomina.

[58] The derivation of the accusative singular is *gʰonōsm̥ (1 ASPIR STOPS) > *honōsm̥ (2d SYL SON) > *honōsem (3d s-TO-r) > Lat honōrem. In later Latin the form with /r/ took over the nominative singular. Its derivation is *honōr (8f WORD-FINAL SHORT) > Lat honor.

[59] These forms have PIE ABLAUT /ō–o–e/ in the -Vs suffix.

[60] The derivation is *moljesm̥ (2d SYL SON) > *moljesem (3d s-TO-r) > *moljerem (7b j/w-CHANGES) > *molierem (possibly 7c o(:)-TO-u(:)) > Lat mulierem.

[61] The other singular forms add the Ø-class endings to the root nūb-; the plural forms add the i-class endings to the same root. The derivation of the accusative singular is *sneubʰm̥ (1 ASPIR STOPS) > *sneubm̥ (2c PHONOTACTICS 2e s-clusters) > *neubʰm̥ (2d SYL SON) > *neubem (5a e-TO-o, 6b ei/ou-CHANGES) > Lat nūbem.

[62] The other forms of the paradigm have the /e/ grade of the ablauting -Vs suffix. Some neuter nouns keep *-os throughout the paradigm: e.g., nom sg *korp+os 'body' vs. nom pl *korp+os+ā (ev) > Lat corpus, corpora.

[63] The derivation is *tertjos (7b j/w-CHANGES) > *tertios (7c o(:)-TO-u(:)) > Lat tertius.

[64] It is the application of 4b SYNCOPE part 3 which produces the different masculine and feminine endings of this class. Hence all such adjectives have roots ending in /r/as masc alacer 'swift', fem alacris and neut alacre. For some reason 4b SYNCOPE applies only to the nom sg masc *ākris 'sharp' and not to the homophonous feminine form: *ākris (4b SYNCOPE) > masc ācer but fem ācris.

[65] The derivation is *legʰʷis (1 ASPIR STOPS) > *lexʷis (2a LABIOVEL) > Lat levis /lewis/.

[66] The neuter nominative accusative singular takes the ending -s like the nominative singular masculine and feminine. Otherwise the endings are those of ignis 'fire' and mare 'sea' noted earlier.

[67] The derivation is *wetoss (2c PHONOTACTICS la Geminate simplification) > *wetos (7c o(:)-TO-u(:)) > Lat vetus.

[68] The derivation is *pārs (2c PHONOTACTICS 2d r-clusters) > *pārr (2c PHONOTACTICS la Geminate simplification, applying as a persistent synchronic rule) → Lat pār.

[69] The derivations are *praikapots and *praikapotes (2c PHONOTACTICS) >*praikapos and *praikapotes (3c ITALIC STRESS) > *práikapos and *práikapotes (the nom sg -os, which now looks like an o-class ending, is then replaced by the athematic ending -s) > *práikaps and *práikapotes (4c UNSTRESSED V) > *práikeps and *práikipitis (6c LATIN STRESS, 7a ai/oi-TO-ae/oe) > Lat praeceps /práekeps/ and praecipitis /praekípitis/.

[70] The comparative endings are those of vetus 'old' in 2.2 above. The nominative and accusative singular have the short /o/ ablaut grade in the suffix. All other forms have the long /ō/such as the gen sg altiōris. The derivation of the neuter comparative is *altjoss (2c PHONOTACTICS) > *altjos (4c UNSTRESSED V) > *altjus (7b j/w-CHANGES) > Lat altius. The derivation of the masc/fem form is similar, except that after the application of 2c PHONOTACTICS, the development is *altjos (replacement of the ending -os by -ōr from the oblique cases) > *altjōr (7b j/w-CHANGES) > *altiōr (8f WORD-FINAL SHORT) > Lat altior.

[71] The PIE antecedents of the superlative forms are not clear. The derivation here is *alt+is+im+os (3c ITALIC STRESS) > *áltisimos (3d s-TO-r) > *áltirimos (4b SYNCOPE, parts 1 and 3) > *áltermos (7c o(:)-TO-u(:), ev) > Lat **altermus instead of altissimus. An explanation of the occurrence of altissimus instead of **altermus may reside in derivations like these: PIE *miser+isimos 'most wretched' and *dʰakil+isimos 'easiest' (1 ASPIR STOPS, 3c ITALIC STRESS, ev) > *míserisimos and *fákilisimos (3d s-TO-r applying to the second form but not to the first one because of the /r/ already within the word) > *míserisimos and *fákilirimos (4b SYNCOPE) > *mísersimos and *fákilrimos (2c PHONOTACTICS: 2a l-clusters and 2d r-clusters, applying as persistent rules) > *míserrimos and *fákillimos (7c o(:)-TO-u(:), ev) > Lat miserrimus and facillimus. It is possible that these double consonants /rr/ and /ll/ in the superlative forms may somehow have occasioned the double /ss/ in superlative forms like Lat altissimus 'highest' noted above. Sihler (1995: 367) hypothesizes that the /ss/ in forms like altissimus is the result of so-called "expressive lengthening". If so, then a form like Lat clārissimus 'clearest' may have developed as follows: *klār+is+im+os (to which 3d s-TO-r does not apply because of the /r/ occurring within the root) > *klārisimos (then the /s/ is geminated to /ss/ on the model of miserrimus and facillimus cited above) > Lat clārissimus.

[72] The derivation is *pedjos (3a C+j CHANGES) > *pējjos (ev) > Lat pējor.

[73] The derivation is *pedsimos (2c PHONOTACTICS) > *pessimos (7c o(:)-TO-u(:)) > Lat pessimus.

[74] The suppletive stem *plē- also occurs in the Lat adj plēnus 'full'. The derivation is not totally clear: *plējos (7b j/w-CHANGES) > *plēos (7c o(:)-TO-u(:)) > *plēus (the unusual diphthong /ēu/ replaced by the more usual /eu/) > *pleus (5a e-TO-o, applying for a time as a persistent rule) > OLat plous (6b ei/ou-CHANGES) > Lat plūs.

[75] The Latin form was influenced by the comparative. Otherwise one would expect Lat **plērimus.

[76] Adjectives of the o- and ā-class form their adverbs with -ē or the ablauting -ō. The PIE antecedent was originally an ablative ending.

[77] The derivation is *reg+t+ēd (2c PHONOTACTICS) > *rektēd (6a d/t-CHANGES) > *rektē (8e LACHMANN) > Lat rēctē.

[78] Adjectives of the i- and athematic class form their adverbs with the suffix -ter, the antecedent of which is not clear.

[79] The derivation is *diuos (PIE 3.1.2c i-j/u-w ALT applying as a synchronic rule) → *diwos (7b j/w-CHANGES) > *dios (7c o(:)-TO-u(:)) > Lat dius.

[80] These are neuter endings.

[81] This is a feminine ending.

[82] The antecedents of these endings are according to Kent (1946: 76) PIE duals. If so, the derivation is *duōu (2b LONG DIPH) > *duō (8d IAMBIC SHORT) > Lat duo.

[83] These forms are the plural endings of o- and ā-class adjectives.

[84] The derivation is *treies (PIE 3.1.2c i-j/u-w ALT applying synchronically) → *trejes (7b j/w-CHANGES) > *trees = Lat trēs.

[85] The declension is that of an i- and athematic class adjective.

[86] This root has the Ø ablaut grade. The derivation is *triā (8d IAMBIC SHORT) > Lat tria.

[87] Rule 2c PHONOTACTICS applied in the derivation of these forms: part 2g s-clusters in '13' and '16'; and part 2h Sonorant-initial clusters in '14' and '17'.

[88] In these compounds both the first and second constituents take the nominative plural neuter ending.

[89] These forms take o- and ā-class plural adjective endings. All Latin reflexes of *kn̥t- if preceded by an /n/ become /gent-/. The reason for this is not clear.

[90] The sequence /in/ in these forms probably results from the influence of the forms for '500', '700' and '900'.

[91] By Latin times mīlle is an indeclinable adjective. It was probably originally an i-class neuter noun, as is the plural mīlia. The antecedent and derivation of the forms are not clear. A possible antecedent is a compound *sm+i 'one' plus *g^hesl+i '1000', both constituents having the i-class marker -i. The derivation of the plural would then be *smig^hesliā (1 ASPIR STOPS) > *smihesliā (? early loss of /h/) > *smiesliā (? replacement of the unusual diphthong /ie/ by /ī/) > *smīsliā (2c PHONOTACTICS 2e and 2g s-clusters) > *mīliā (8d IAMBIC SHORT applying analogously) > Lat mīlia. It is not clear why the singular form mīlle has two /ll/'s. One would expect Lat **mīle.

[92] The PIE antecedent is a comparative of *al- 'other'.

[93] The PIE antecedent was the future passive participle of the deponent verb sequor 'follow'.

[94] The derivation is *egō (8d IAMBIC SHORT) > Lat ego.

[95] The derivation is *mēd (6a d/t-CHANGES) > Lat mē.

[96] The other singular forms begin with m-.

[97] The other plural forms begin with n-.

[98] The other singular forms begin with /t/.

[99] The other plural forms begin with <v> /w/.

[100] These forms show the Ø-grade of the ablauting root *(e)i-.

[101] The derivation is *eiom (PIE 3.1.2c i-j/u-w ALT) > *ejom (7b j/w-CHANGES) > *eom (7c o(:)-TO-u(:)) > Lat eum.

[102] The derivation is *eisjos (3a C+j CHANGES) > *eijjos (6b ei/ou-CHANGES) > *ējjos (7c o(:)-TO-u(:)) > Lat ējus /ējjus/.

[103] The derivation is *eiei (PIE 3.1.2c i-j/u-w ALT) > *ejei (6b ei/ou-CHANGES) > *ejī (7b j/w-CHANGES) > Lat eī.

[104] The derivation is *eions (PIE 3.1.2c i-j/u-w ALT) >*ejons (7b j/w-CHANGES) > *eons (8k Vns-CHANGES) > Lat eōs.

[105] The later masc/neut gen pl eorum was formed in imitation of the fem gen pl eārum.

[106] The derivation is *eiōis (PIE 3.1.2c i-j/u-w ALT) > *ejōis (2b LONG DIPH) > *ejois (7a ai/oi-TO-ae/oe, 7b j/w-CHANGES) > *eoes (8h oe-CHANGES) > Lat eīs.

[107] The derivation is *eiā (ev) > *ejā (7b j/w-CHANGES) > *eā (8d IAMBIC SHORT) > Lat ea.

[108] The Latin form has been taken from the masculine/neuter dative singular. Otherwise one would expect Lat **eae.

[109] The remaining neuter forms are the same as the masculine ones.

[110] The antecedent forms of this paradigm consist of the root *g^hV- plus (occasionally) the deictic particle *-i plus (occasionally) the enclitic *-ke (possibly *-ki) 'this here'. The derivation of the nominative singular masculine is *g^hike (1 ASPIR STOPS) > *hike (4b SYNCOPE part 4) > Lat hic.

[111] The derivation is *g^homke (1 ASPIR STOPS) > *homke (2c PHONOTACTICS lb Nasal assimilation) > *hoŋke (4b SYNCOPE) > *hoŋk (7c o(:)-TO-u(:) > Lat hunc.

[112] The derivation is *g^hosjos (3a C+j CHANGES, ev) > *hōjjos (7c o(:)-TO-u(:) applying to/o/ and apparently to /i/ as well) > Lat hūjus /hūjjus/. The application of 7c o(:)-TO-u(:) to the long /i/ is not certain: the /ū/ may have been imported from the genitive singular of the relative pronoun cūjus 'whose' in 5.6 below where it would have occurred regularly by 7c o(:)-TO-u(:).

[113] The derivation is not clear. A possibility is *g^hoeike (1 ASPIR STOPS) > *hoeike (4b SYNCOPE) > *hoeik (4c UNSTRESSED V applying when the form is unstressed) > *hueik (6b ei/ou-CHANGES) > *huīk (possibly 8d IAMBIC SHORT applying to a form *huī without the enclitic *-k) > Lat huic.

[114] The derivation is *g^hōdke (2c PHONOTACTICS 2c Obstruent assimilation, ev) > *hōkke (4b SYNCOPE) > *hōkk (2c PHONOTACTICS la Geminate simplification applying as a persistent rule) > Lat hōc.

[115] The derivation is *g^hāmke (2c PHONOTACTICS lb Nasal assimilation and 1d Osthoff's Law, ev) > *haŋke (4b SYNCOPE) > Lat hanc.

[116] The antecedents consist of the demonstratives *is- plus *t-. The derivation is *isto (4c UNSTRESSED V) > Lat iste.

[117] The derivation is *istod (4c UNSTRESSED V Stage 3d) > Lat istud.

[118] The antecedent consists of the demonstratives *is+t- plus the nominal genitive singular ending *-ī plus the pronominal genitive singular ending *-jos. The derivation is *istījos (7b j/w-CHANGES) > *istīos (7c o(:)-TO-u(:)) > Lat istīus.

[119] The antecedent consists of the demonstratives *ol- and *s- plus the endings. The derivation is *olsod (2c PHONOTACTICS 2a l-clusters) > *ollod (7c o(:)-TO-u(:)) > *ollud (replacement of /o/ by /i/ from the iste paradigm) > Lat illud.

[120] The antecedent is not clear. It may have consisted of the demonstrative *is- plus /p/ plus the demonstrative *s- plus the endings. A possible derivation is *ispso (2c PHONOTACTICS 2g s-clusters) > *ipso (4c UNSTRESSED V) > Lat ipse. Palmer (1954: 257) suggests that the /p/ was inserted in these forms because of derivations like this one: accusative singular masculine consisting of the demonstrative *ei- plus the ending *-om plus the demonstrative *s- plus the ending *-om again, namely *eiomsom (PIE 3.1.2c i-j/u-w ALT) > *ejomsom (in which the /m/ is retained, resulting in the application of 2c PHONOTACTICS lb Nasal assimilation, by which /p/ is inserted after the first /m/) > *ejompsom (ev) > OLat eumpsum. The /p/ was then inserted throughout the paradigm.

[121] The derivation is *isdem (2c PHONOTACTICS 2g s-clusters) > Lat īdem.

[122] The original antecedent consisted of the neuter pronoun *id- plus the enclitic *-em. It was later reanalyzed as *i+dem; and the new suffix *-dem was then added to the various forms of *is.

[123] The derivation is *sewe (7b j/w-CHANGES) >*see = Lat sē.

[124] This form may represent the Ø-grade ABLAUT of *sew-. The derivation is *sw+ī (7b j/w-CHANGES) > Lat suī.

[125] These forms may have been influenced by the accusative singular where the /w/ was regularly lost.

[126] The derivation is *sebʰei (1 ASPIR STOPS) > *sebei (6b ei/ou-CHANGES) >*sebī (8c e-TO-i) > *sibī (8d IAMBIC SHORT) > Lat sibi.

[127] The antecedents of these forms may have been the Ø-grade ablauting *tw- and *sw- (ev) > *tu- and *su-. If in the e-grade, then the derivation is *tewos (5a e-TO-o) > *towos (7b j/w-CHANGES) > *toos (7c o(:)-TO-u(:) applying to both /o/'s when unstressed) > Lat tuus.

[128] The derivation is *wosteros (4b SYNCOPE part 3, ev) > *woster (5c wo-TO-we) > Lat vester /wester/.

[129] The derivation is *kʷoi (7a ai/ai-TO-ae/oe) > kʷoe (8h oe-CHANGES) > Lat quī.

[130] The expected Latin form is **quim. The ending on quem is from the accusative singular masculine/feminine of the athematic class (1.5 above).

[131] The derivation is problematic. A possibility is *kʷoei (6b ei/ou-CHANGES) > *kʷoī (replacement of the diphthong /oī/ > by the more usual /oi/) > OLat quoi /kʷoi/. This occurs later as Lat cui /kui/. Here the earlier /kʷ/ may have been delabialized to /k/ by the persistent application of 2a LABIOVEL; and the /u/ may have been inserted under the influence of the gen sg /kūjjus/.

[132] In some forms of this paradigm the /kʷ/ was restored, taken from those many forms in the paradigm where it would not have been affected by 2a LABIOVEL. Hence this form is not Lat **cod, which one might expect.

[133] The basic presupposition underlying the Latin subjunctive is that the speaker assumes that the truth value of the sentence is either in doubt or false. Examples of the subjunctive-indicative dichotomy are the following:

(a)	**subj**	Eāmus. 'Let us go; we should go.'
	ind	Īmus. 'We're going.'
(b)	**subj**	Sit fūr. 'Maybe he's a thief.'
	ind	Est fūr. 'He's a thief.'
(c)	**subj**	Vīvat. 'May he live!'
	ind	Vīvit. 'He's living.'

(d) **subj** Quid agat? 'What may, can or should he do?'
ind Quid agit? 'What is he doing?'

(e) **perfect subj** Forsitan id fēcerit. 'Maybe he did it.'
perfect ind Id fēcit. 'He did it.'

(f) **imperfect subj** Sī vīveret, eum audīrētis.
'If he were alive (which he is not), you'd be hearing him (which you are not).'

imperfect ind Sī vīvit, eum audītis.
'If (or since) he's living, you're hearing him.'

[134] The imperfect is a past tense that denotes a continued action or state. The perfect is a past tense that denotes a completed action or a state of brief duration. E.g., imperfect: Hunc audiēbant. 'They used to hear a lot about him.' Perfect: Hunc audiēvērunt. 'They have heard about him (perhaps once).'

[135] Possibly unfamiliar terms such as gerund and supine will be defined in their respective sections below.

[136] Latin verbs are traditionally considered to have four principal parts. E.g., the 1st conjugation ā-class (i) 1sg pres dōnō 'I give', (ii) pres inf dōnāre, (iii) 1sg pres perf dōnāvī and (iv) perf pass part dōnātus. The stem of parts i and ii occurs in all present, imperfect and future tenses; the stem of part iii occurs in all perfect tenses; and the stem of part iv forms the perfect passive participle and the supine.

The structure and history of the six conjugations are described in our consideration of the present active indicative under 6.1.1 below. Membership in one or the other of these classes determines only the present, imperfect or future tense forms. The perfect may be formed variously.

[137] The term deponent designates a verb which takes passive inflection but has an active meaning. E.g., PIE *sekʷō+r 'I follow' (ev) > Lat sequor, not **sequō.

[138] The expected derivation is *dōnājō (7b j/w-CHANGES) > *dōnāō (8i V-CONTRACT) > Lat **dōnā instead of dōnō. The -ō was probably added from 3rd conjugation or Ø-class verbs like dūcō 'lead' described below.

[139] The expected derivation is *dōnājesi (3d s-TO-r) > *dōnājeri (4b SYNCOPE) > *dōnājer (7b j/w-CHANGES) > *dōnāer (8i V-CONTRACT) > *dōnār (8f WORD-FINAL SHORT) > Lat **dōnar instead of dōnās. The -s may have been taken from secondary paradigms such as the imperfect active indicative in 6.2.1 below.

[140] The derivation is *dōnājeti (6c LATIN STRESS) > *dōnā́jeti (7b j/w-CHANGES) > *dōnā́eti (4b SYNCOPE later stage 4 applying after 6a d/t-CHANGES) > *dōnā́et (8i V-CONTRACT) > *dōnā́t (6c LATIN STRESS applying as a persistent synchronic rule) > *dṓnāt (8f WORD-FINAL SHORT) > Lat dōnat /dṓnat/.

[141] Sihler (1995: 465) assumes the ending -s is an original dual ending. The derivation is *dōnājetes (4c UNSTRESSED V Stage 3) > *dōnājetis (ev) > Lat dōnātis.

[142] The derivation is *widējō (7b j/w-CHANGES) > *widēō (81 V̄V-TO-VV) > Lat videō /wideō/.

[143] The derivation is *deuketi (4c UNSTRESSED V) > *deukiti (4b SYNCOPE later stage 4 applying after 6a d/t-CHANGES) > *deukit (5a e-TO-o) > *doukit (6b ei/ou-CHANGES) > Lat dūcit.

[144] The derivation is *deukomos (4c UNSTRESSED V stage 2) > *deukimos (4c UNSTRESSED V stage 3) > *deukimus (5a e-TO-o) > *doukimus (6b ei/ou-CHANGES) > Lat dūcimus.

[145] The derivation is *deukonti (4b SYNCOPE stage 4) >*deukont (4c UNSTRESSED V stage 3) > *deukunt (ev) > Lat dūcunt.

[146] The reduplication of the present (as opposed to that of the perfect described under 6.5 below) consists of the word-initial consonant plus /i/. The alternation of the stems *gn- and *gen- is PIE ablaut.

[147] The derivations of these forms are under 6.4 below.

[148] The nasal occurs within the verb root only if it ends in an obstruent consonant; otherwise the nasal /n/ is suffixed onto the root. We assume that /n/ was originally suffixed to all roots, then metathesized after an obstruent. The derivation would then be *rupnō 'break' (metathesis) >*runpō (2c PHONOTACTICS lb Nasal assimilation applying as a persistent synchronic rule) > Lat rumpō.

[149] These perfect forms show e-grade ABLAUT.

[150] The present derivation is *krinō (4b SYNCOPE part 3b) > Lat cernō; the perfect derivation is *kreiwai (4c UNSTRESSED V) > *kreiwei (6b ei/ou-CHANGES) > Lat crēvī /krēwī/.

[151] The derivation is *tolnō (2c PHONOTACTICS 2a l-clusters) > Lat tollō.

[152] The derivation is *didskō (2c PHONOTACTICS 2g s-clusters) > Lat discō.

[153] The derivation is *dedikai (3c ITALIC STRESS) > *dédikai (4c UNSTRESSED V) > *dédikei (6b ei/ou-CHANGES) > *dédikī (8c e-TO-i) > Lat didicī /dídikī/.

[154] The antecedent formation of this class, like that of the 3rd io-conjugation described below, consists of the stem plus *-j- plus the inflectional endings. The development of /-i-/ in these forms resulted from two causes. The first is instantiated in the following derivation: *sāgjo (PIE 3.1.2f SIEVERS applying synchronically) → *sāgijō (/ij/ reinterpreted as /ī/) > *sāgīō (81 V̄V-TO-VV) > Lat sāgiō. The second source of /-i-/ in this paradigm is from deverbal i-class nouns such as *siti+s 'thirst'. The derivation is *siti+j+ō (reinterpretation of /ij/ as /ī/) > *sitīō (81 V̄V-TO-VV) > Lat sitiō.

[155] An indication that PIE 3.l.2f SIEVERS has applied here is the fact that most 4th-conjugation verbs have long stems, which are necessary to trigger SIEVERS: e.g., Lat aper+iō 'cover', sent+iō 'feel' and stabil+iō 'fasten down'.

[156] The derivation is *sāgjesi (PIE 3.l.2f SIEVERS) → *sāgijesi (reinterpretation of /ij/ as /ī/) > *sāgīesi (4b SYNCOPE stage 4) > *sāgīis (8i V-CONTRACT) > Lat sāgīs.

[157] The derivation is *sāgjeti (same changes as in the preceding derivation) > *sāgīt (8f WORD-FINAL SHORT) > Lat sāgit.

[158] The antecedent endings of this class are the same as those of the ī-class under iv above. However, the resulting forms differ because PIE 3.1.2f SIEVERS cannot apply to io-class verbs since all of them have short stem. Hence the derivation here is *kapjō (SIEVERS not applying, but by 7b j/w-CHANGES) > Lat capiō.

[159] The subjunctive marker /e(:)/ occurring in the ā-class is problematical. Its antecedent may have been a PIE optative marker *-jē- (possibly originally *-ī+ē-). Even if so, the derivation is still problematic: *dōnājēmi (4b SYNCOPE) > *dōnājēm (7b j/w-CHANGES) > *dōnāēm (ev) > Lat **dōnaem instead of dōnem.

[160] The antecedent *-ā- as a subjunctive marker is attested elsewhere in PIE and is not problematical. A derivation is *widējāmi (4b SYNCOPE stage 4) > *widējām (7b j/w-CHANGES) > *widēām (8f WORD-FINAL SHORT) > *widēam (81 V̄V-TO-VV) > Lat videam /wídeam/

[161] The derivation is *dōnāje (6c LATIN STRESS) > *dōnā́je (7b j/w-CHANGES) > *dōnā́e (8i V-CONTRACT) > *dōnā́ (6c LATIN STRESS reapplying as a persistent synchronic rule) > Lat dōnā /dṓnā/.

[162] The derivation is *deuke (4b SYNCOPE stage 4) > *deuk (ev) > Lat dūc. The change 4b SYNCOPE stage 4 does not apply invariably to all forms, e.g. *age 'drive'> Lat age, not **ag.

[163] The derivation is *deukete (4c UNSTRESSED V) > *deukite (5a e-TO-o, 6b ei/ou-CHANGES) > Lat dūcite.

[164] These derivations are not totally clear. A possibility for the singular is *kapje (4b SYNCOPE stage 4) > *kapj (PIE 3.l.2c i-j/u-w ALT applying as a synchronic rule) > *kapi (4c UNSTRESSED V stage 3) > Lat cape. As for the plural, given our rules, one would expect Lat **capiete as opposed to capite. The Lat capite was perhaps influenced by the Ø-class form dūcite.

[165] The derivation is *dōnājōr (7b j/w-CHANGES) > *dōnāōr (8i V-CONTRACT, but somewhat problematical: see the derivation of dōnō under 6.1.1 above) > *dōnōr (8f WORD-FINAL SHORT) > Lat dōnor.

[166] The derivation is *dōnājeso (3d s-TO-r) > *dinājero (4c UNSTRESSED V stage 3) >*dōnājere (7b j/w-CHANGES) >*dōnāere (8i V-CONTRACT) > Lat dōnāre. The -is on the later occurring Lat dōnāris may be from the Ø-class 2nd singular active indicative under 6.1.1 above.

167 The derivation is *dōnājetor (7b j/w-CHANGES) > *dōnāetor (7c o(:)-TO-u(:)) > *dōnāetur (8i V-CONTRACT) > Lat dōnātur.

168 The antecedent of the Latin ending -minī is not clear. Sommer (1948: 495) assumes an infinitive ending *-menai used as an imperative. Another possibility is that the antecedent ending was the nominative plural masculine of the middle participle *-menoi. In the latter event, the derivation is *dōnājomenoi (3c ITALIC STRESS) > *dṓnājomenoi (4c UNSTRESSED V stages 1 and 2) > *dṓnājiminoi (6c LATIN STRESS) > *dōnājī́minoi (7a ai/oi-TO-ae/oe) > *dōnājī́minoe (7b j/w-CHANGES) > *dōnāī́minoe (possibly 8i V-CONTRACT) > *dōnā́minoe (8h oe-CHANGES) > Lat dōnāminī /dōnā́minī/.

169 To form these paradigms the imperfect endings in -ba(:)- are added to the present active indicative stems in 6.1.1 above. The antecedent of the -ba(:)- suffix is not clear. It may have been *-bʰu(:)- 'be' plus *-ā- of unclear provenience plus the inflectional endings. If so, the derivation of the ā-class 1st singular is *dōnābʰuām (PIE 3.1.2c i-j/u-w ALT applying as a synchronic rule) > *dōnābʰwām (1 ASPIR STOPS) > *dōnābwām (7b j/w-CHANGES) > *dōnābām (8f WORD-FINAL SHORT) > Lat dōnābam.

170 The -t in this ending is from the 3rd singular present active in *-ti. Otherwise one would expect Lat **dōnābā by 6a d/t-CHANGES.

171 This ending is from the 2pl pres ind *-tes.

172 The antecedents of these forms may have consisted of the infinitive stem plus the *-bʰa(:)- formative. If so, the derivation of the Ø-class 1st singular is *deuk+es+bʰu+ā+m (PIE 3.1.2c i-j/u-w ALT) > *deukesbʰwām (1 ASPIR STOPS) > *deukesbwām (2c PHONOTACTICS 2g s-clusters) > *deukēbwām (5a e-TO-o, 6b ei/au-CHANGES) > *dūkēbwām (7b j/w-CHANGES) > *dūkēbām (8f WORD-FINAL SHORT) >Lat dūcēbam. The derivation of the ī- and io-class is similar. The ī-class has the alternative imperfect form sāgiēbam.

173 The derivation is *dōnāsēm (3d s-TO-r) > dōnārēm (8f WORD-FINAL SHORT) > Lat dōnārem. The *-s- in the antecedent form may have been the infinitive marker or according to Kent (1946: 102) a PIE aorist formative.

174 The derivation is *dōnābʰuō (PIE 3.1.2c i-j/u-w ALT applying as as a synchronic rule) > *dōnābʰwō (1 ASPIR STOPS) > *dōnābwō (7b j/w-CHANGES) > LAT dōnābō. The antecedent *-bʰu- is 'be'.

175 The antecedent formatives *-ā- and *-ē- may have originally been subjunctive markers.

176 There are traces in OLatin of a future formative in -s-, which was restricted to a few Ø-class verbs. E.g.,

		Latin		PIE
sg	1	faxō	'I shall do'	*dʰak+sō
	1	dīxō	'I shall say'	*deik+s+ō

177 The derivation is *dōnātōd (6a d/t-CHANGES) > Lat dōnātō.

178 The derivation is the same as the preceding to *dōnātō, to which the 2pl pres act imp *-te under 6.1.3 above is added producing Lat dōnātōte. Thus the form must have been created sometime after 6a d/t-CHANGES at about 200 BC: if the construction had been formed earlier, one would expect the derivation *dōnātōdte (2c PHONOTACTICS 1c Obstruent cluster voicing and devoicing) > *dōnātōtte (2c PHONOTACTICS 2f t-Clusters) > *dōnātōsse (2c PHONOTACTICS 1a Geminate simplification, applying as a persistent synchronic rule) > Lat **dōnātōse.

179 The derivation is the same as that of the 3pl pres ind dōnant down to the time of 4b SYNCOPE later stage 4 at about 200 BC by which the word-final /-i/ was deleted. At this time the /-ō/ from the other forms of the paradigm was added. If this had occurred before the time of 4b SYNCOPE, one would expect Lat **dōnantiō.

180 The derivation is *dōnābʰueso (PIE 3.1.2c i-j/u-w ALT applying synchronically) > *dōnābʰweso (1 ASPIR STOPS) > *dōnābweso (3d s-TO-r) > *dōnābwero (4c UNSTRESSED V stage 3) > *dōnābwere (7b j/w-CHANGES) > Lat dōnābere.

181 The derivation is similar to the preceding one up to *dōnābwetor (4c UNSTRESSED V stage 2) > *dōnābwitor (7b j/w-CHANGES) > *dōnābitor (7c o(:)-TO-u(:)) > dōnābitur.

[182] The derivation after 6a d/t-CHANGES is *dōnātō+r (8f WORD-FINAL SHORT) > Lat dōnātor. Hence the -r was added after the time of 6a d/t-CHANGES and before the time of 8f WORD-FINAL SHORT, i.e. sometime between 200 and 100 BC.

[183] The origin of -w- is not clear. It may have resulted from a reanalysis of an early perfect form of 'be' such as 1sg perf *b^{h}ū+ai = [b^{h}uuai] (PIE 3.1.2c i-j/u-w ALT applying synchronically) → *b^{h}uwai, from which the endings *-w+ai, *-w+istai, etc. were derived.

[184] The *-w- can be added either to the bare root as with *dom- and *sal- or to the root plus the class marker as with *don+ā- and *ausd^{h}ī-. The derivation of Lat domuī is *domwai (ev) > *domwī (7b j/w-CHANGES) > Lat domuī.

[185] The derivation is *stestai (2c PHONOTACTICS 2k s-clusters) > *stetai (ev) > Lat stetī. (The same rule 2c PHONOTACTICS applies in the derivation of Lat spopondī from *spespondai.) There is another perfect form from the same root as Lat stetī 'stand', namely stitī meaning 'stop'. Its derivation is *stestai (ev) > *stetī (8c e-TO-i, which can apply optionally) > Lat stitī.

[186] The reduplicating vowel was originally /e/; and the OLatin forms memordī and cecurrī occur. In later Latin the vowel of the reduplicating syllable, particularly when unstressed, was generally replaced by the vowel of the root. Hence the derivations *memordai and *kekanai (ev through 6b ei/ou-CHANGES) > *memordī and *kekinī (6c LATIN STRESS) > *memórdi and *kékini (replacement of the unstressed reduplicating /e/ by the root vowel) > Lat momórdī vs. cécinī.

[187] The derivation is *kekanai (3c ITALIC STRESS) > *kékanai (4c UNSTRESSED V stages 1 and 2) > *kékinei (6b ei/ou-CHANGES) > *kékinī (6c LATIN STRESS applying vacuously) > Lat cecinī /kékinī/.

[188] The derivation is *kekursai (2c PHONOTACTICS 2d r-clusters) > *kekurrai (ev through 6c LATIN STRESS) > *kekúrrī (replacement of unstressed /e/ by /u/) > Lat cucurrī /kukúrrī/.

[189] The derivation is*re+pe+perai in which *re- is a verbal prefix and *pe- the perfect reduplication (3c ITALIC STRESS) > *répeperai (4b SYNCOPE stage 1) > *répperai (ev) > Lat repperī /répperī/.

[190] The derivation is *ārdsai (2c PHONOTACTICS 1c Obstruent cluster voicing and devoicing, 2f t-clusters and 1a Geminate simplification applying as a persistent synchronic rule) > *ārsai (ev) > Lat ārsī.

[191] The derivation is *mansai (ev) > *mansī (8k Vns-CHANGES) > Lat mānsī.

[192] The derivation is *angsai (2c PHONOTACTICS, ev) > *anksī (8j Vnk-TO-V̄nk) > Lat ānxī /ānksī/.

[193] The derivation is *regsai (ev) > *reksī (8e LACHMANN) > Lat rēxī /rēksī/.

[194] Another possible source of the perfect is reduplication and Ø-grade ABLAUT of the root. If so, the derivation would be *se+sd+ai (2c Phonotactics 2g s-clusters) > *sēdai (ev) > Lat sēdī.

[195] These Ø-class verbs take /n/ in the present-tense forms as described under 6.1.1 above.

[196] The derivation is *leik^{w}ai (4c UNSTRESSED V) > *leik^{w}ei (6b ei/ou-CHANGES) > Lat līquī.

[197] The derivation of these forms is *g^{w}emjō and *g^{w}ēmai (2a LABIOVEL) > *wemjō and *wēmai (3a C+j-CHANGES) > *wenjō and *wēmai (transfer of the /n/ to the perfect form) > *wenjō and *wēnai (7b j/w-CHANGES, ev) > Lat veniō and vēnī.

[198] The derivation is *b^{h}eug^{h}ai (1 ASPIR STOPS) > *feugai (4c UNSTRESSED V) > *feugei (5a e-TO-o) > *fougei (6b ei/ou-CHANGES) > Lat fūgī.

[199] These verbs form their perfect by lengthening the root vowel /a/. This is probably the result of analogy on PIE ABLAUT, by which various short vs. long alternations arose between present and perfect forms. E.g., /o-ō/, /e-ē/, /i-ī/ and /u-ū/ in the preceding paradigm. This was then transferred to /a-ā/.

[200] The antecedents of these perfect forms are not clear. Sihler (1995: 581) suggests the /ē/ may have resulted from an original reduplicating syllable. If so, the derivation was *e+ag+ai (with the nonexistent diphthong /ea/ mapped onto /ē/) > *ēgai (ev) > Lat ēgī. The /ē/ was then used as a perfect formative for other verbs with the present-tense root vowel /a/. Another possibility is that since verbs with the present-tense root vowel /a/ could not ablaut , the /a/ was either lengthened to /ā/ to form the perfect, or the phonetically close and regularly ablauting /ē/ was used.

[201] The vowel alternation /o-u/ to form the perfect is not clear. Given the usual changes, one would expect the derivation *tolai (4c UNSTRESSED V) > *tolei (6b ei/ou-CHANGES) > *tolī (to which 7c o(:)-TO-u(:) cannot apply because /ī/ is a –back vowel) > Lat **tolī instead of tulī. There are at least three explanations for the occurrence of Lat tulī. One is that somehow 7c o(:)-TO-u(:) applied before 4c UNSTRESSED V while the form was still *tolai and the /l/ was followed by a +back vowel. But this is odd since otherwise 4c UNSTRESSED V must precede 7c o(:)-TO-u(:). A second possibility suggested by Sihler (1995: 534) is that the antecedent was a root ending in a laryngeal, namely *tl̥H_2-. The derivation would then be *tl̥H_2ai (2d SYL SON) > *tolH_2ai (4c UNSTRESSED V) > *tolH_2ei (6b ei/ou-CHANGES) > *tolH_2ī (7c o(:)-TO-u(:) in environment (ad) where C_2 = /lH_2/) > *tulH_2ī (ev loss of the laryngeal) > Lat tulī. A third possibility is suggested by an observation in Kieckers (1960: 2, 261). He notes the occurrence of an OLat perf feruī 'carried, lifted' < PIE *b^{h}er+w+ai as a suppletive perfect of the verb tollō 'lift'. If we then assume that somewhat later the perfect formative -w- was added to the present root *tol-, then the derivation might have been this: *tol+w+ī (7b j/w-CHANGES) > *toluī (7c o(:)-TO-u(:) in environment (ac) now applying) > *tuluī (reassignment of the perfect formation to the class with only changes in the root vowel and thus the consequent removal of the suffix -u-) > Lat tulī.

[202] The derivation is *eiō (PIE 3.1.2c i-j/u-w ALT applying synchronically) > *ejō (7b j/w-CHANGES) > Lat eō.

[203] The antecedent may be either *ei+ai or the Ø-grade ABLAUT *i+ai. The respective derivations are *ei+ai (perhaps PIE 3.1.2c i-j/u-w ALT not applying, but 4c UNSTRESSED V) > *eiei (6b ei/ou-CHANGES) > *īī (81 V̄V-TO-VV) > Lat iī. The other derivation is *i+ai (4c UNSTRESSED V) > *iei (6b ei/ou-CHANGES) > Lat iī.

[204] This verb retains its n-present root in the perfect.

[205] The *-i was added to the original perfect ending *-a from the present paradigm. The derivation is *dōnāwai (3c ITALIC STRESS) > *dṓnāwai (4c UNSTRESSED V) > *dōnāwei (6b ei/ou-CHANGES) > *dṓnāwī (6c LATIN STRESS) > Lat dōnāvī /dōnā́wī/.

[206] The composition of the ending after *dōnāw- may have been as follows: -is- (possibly an aorist ending) plus *-t- (the 2nd singular perfect ending) plus *-ai (from the 1st singular).

[207] This ending underwent 6a d/t-CHANGES and appears in early sources as -d, e.g. OLat fēced 'made' vs. later Lat fēcit. The later -t is from the 3rd singular present.

[208] This ending is from the present.

[209] The earlier ending was *-ete. The endings *-is and *-s are from the 2nd singular. The derivation is *dōnāwistes (4c UNSTRESSED V) > Lat dōnāvistis.

[210] The antecedent ending consists of the perfect ending *-ēr plus *-i from the present. Later the perfect dōnāvērunt occurs with -unt from the 3rd plural present.

[211] The antecedent consists of the perfect stem *dōnāw- plus the aorist suffix *-is- plus the optional marker -ī- plus the respective endings. The derivation is *dōnāwisīmi (3b i/u-TO-e/a and 3d s-TO-r) > *dōnāwerīmi (4b SYNCOPE stage 4) > *dōnāwerīm (8f WORD-FINAL SHORT) > Lat dōnāverim. (The short /i/ then spread throughout the paradigm.)

[212] This ending is probably in origin an optative ending. Otherwise the 3rd plural future perfect active indicative would be homophonous with the 3pl pres perf act ind dōnāvērunt under 6.4.1 above.

[213] The antecedent of this form may have been the dative singular of a neuter Vs-class noun (1.5.6). The derivation would then be *dōnāsi (3d s-TO-r) > *dōnāri (4c UNSTRESSED V) > Lat dōnāre.

[214] The antecedent is not clear; it may have been *-nd^h-. It may also have been the same as that of the future passive participle (6.8.3). On this see Sihler (1995: 627).

[215] The ā- and ē-class verbs add the -ī to the infinitive stem; the other classes add the -ī- directly to the root.

[216] An alternate and probably somewhat later form occurs such as OLat dōnārier. It was constructed from the original passive infinitive plus the passive ending *-er. The derivation is *dōnārī+er (81 V̄V-TO-VV) > Lat dōnārier.

[217] In later Latin the participle began taking additional inflection such as the masc dōnātūrum esse.

[218] The derivation is *eisei (3d s-TO-r) > *eirei (6b ei/ou-CHANGES) > Lat īrī.

219 The antecedent consists of the perfect stem plus the aorist suffix *-is- plus the present active infinitive ending (6.7.1) *-si. The derivation is *dōnāwissi (4c UNSTRESSED V) > Lat dōnāvisse.

220 The derivation is *dōnātūd (6a d/t-CHANGES) > Lat dōnātū. Another possible antecedent may have been a dative/locative form *dōnāteu. The derivation is then *dōnāteu (5a e-TO-o) > *dōnātou (6b ei/ou-CHANGES) > Lat dōnātū.

221 The derivation is *dōnānts (2c PHONOTACTICS 1d Osthoff's Law) > *dōnants (2c PHONOTACTICS 2f t-clusters) >*dōnanss (2c PHONOTACTICS la Geminate simplification applying as a persistent synchronic rule) > *dōnans (8k Vns-CHANGES) > *dōnās (the /n/ reinserted from the oblique case forms which could not undergo 8k Vns-CHANGES) > Lat dōnāns.

222 The derivation is *dōnāntes (2c PHONOTACTICS ld Osthoff's Law) > *dōnantes (4c UNSTRESSED V stage 3) > Lat dōnantis.

223 The Ø-class verbs have an ablauting /e/ between the root and the -nt- formative. The derivation of dūcēns is analogous to that of dōnāns described above.

224 Kent (1946: 131) posits as the origin of the future active participle the sequence supine (6.7.7) in the locative singular plus a neuter infinitive form *esom 'be'. A derivation would then be *dōnātū+*esom 'to be at or in the act of giving' (3d s-TO-r) > *dōnātūerom (4b SYNCOPE stage 2) > *dōnātūrom (7c o(:)-TO-u(:)) > Lat dōnātūrum. This form, originally invariable, was later reinterpreted as an adjective.

225 The antecedent is not obvious. It may be the same as that of the present active gerund (6.7.1). Kent (1946: 135) suggests the antecedent may have been a compound consisting of a noun in the accusative plus a verbal adj *d+os meaning 'giving'. Hence a derivation would be *dōnām+d+os 'gift-giving, (ev) that which will be given' (2c PHONOTACTICS lb Nasal assimilation) > *dōnāndos (2c Phonotactics ld Osthoff's Law) > *dōnandos (7c o(:)-TO-u(:)) > Lat dōnandus.

226 The following basic generalizations obtain for the intermediate segment occurring between the verbal root and the perfect passive formative -t- or -s-: ā-class verbs have -ā-,-i- or -Ø-; ē-class verbs have -ē-, - i- or -Ø-; Ø-class verbs have -i- or -Ø-; ī-class verbs have -ī- or -Ø-; and io-class verbs have -Ø-.

227 The intermediate -i- in these forms is the reflex of the -j- which occurred in the present paradigms. (It may have been intrusive in the Ø-class.) Hence the perf pass part *dom+j+tos 'subdued' (7b j/w-CHANGES) > *domitos (ev) > Lat domitus.

228 The -s- formative has two sources. First, its antecedent was the PIE aorist formative *-s-, imported into the perfect passive participle from the various perfect forms (see 6.4iii). Second, it arose from *-t- through regular change as in the derivation *weid+t+os 'seen' (possible *wid+t+os) (2c PHONOTACTICS 1c Obstruent cluster voicing and devoicing and 2f t-clusters) > *weissos (6b ei/ou-CHANGES) > *wīssos (2c PHONOTACTICS la Geminate simplification applying as a persistent synchronic rule) > *wīsos (7c o(:)-TO-u(:)) > Lat **vīsus**.

229 The derivation is *melg+Ø+s+os (2c PHONOTACTICS 2h Sonorant-initial clusters) > *melsos (5a e-TO-o) > *molsos (7c o(:)-TO-u(:)) > Lat mulsus.

230 The derivation is *ausd^{h}ītos (1 ASPIR STOPS) > *ausdītos (2c PHONOTACTICS 2g s-clusters) > *audītos (7c o(:)-TO-u(:)) > Lat audītus.

231 The derivation is *winktos (7c o(:)-TO-u(:)) > *winktus (8j Vnk-TO-V̄nk) > Lat vīnctus.

232 The precise antecedents of these forms are not clear. We have assumed the Ø-ABLAUT grade of the verb *es. Sihler (1995: 549) assumes most of these verbs are from original enclitics, i.e. suffixal forms. Hence the derivation of the 1st plural might have been from such sequences as *##wirai##esomos## 'we are men' (encliticization, i.e. treating two words as one) > *##wiroiesomos## (3c ITALIC STRESS) > *##wíraiesomos## (4b SYNCOPE stage 1) > *##wíroisomos## (7a ai/oe-TO-ae/oe) > *##wíroesumus## (7c o(:)-TO-u(:) > *##wíroesumus## (8h oe-CHANGES) > Lat virī sumus. Then the /u/ in sumus was inserted into other forms of the paradigm such as sum and sunt (instead of **sont).

233 The later singular forms are sim, sīs and sit. They took the /i(:)/ from the plural. The derivation of the 1st singular is siem (replacement with /ī/) > *sīm (8f WORD-FINAL SHORT) > Lat sim.

[234] The derivations are *sīēmi and *sīēsi (4b SYNCOPE stage 4) > *sīēm and *sīēs (8f WORD-FINAL SHORT) > *sīem and * sīēs (81 V̄V-TO-VV) > Lat siem and siēs.

[235] The derivation is *sīnti (4b SYNCOPE stage 4) > *sīnt (8f WORD-FINAL SHORT) > Lat sint.

[236] The derivation is *esām (3d s-TO-r) > *erām (8f WORD-FINAL SHORT) > Lat eram.

[237] It is sometimes assumed that the antecedent root was *b^{h}ū. If so, one would expect Lat **fūrem and **fūrēs.

[238] The derivation is *b^{h}usēm (1 ASPIR STOPS) >*fusēm (3b i/u-TO-e/o, 3d s-TO-r) > *forēm (8f WORD-FINAL SHORT) > Lat forem.

[239] The antecedent may have been *b^{h}ū-. If so, the derivation was *b^{h}ū+ai (1 ASPIR STOPS) > *fūai (3c ITALIC STRESS) > *fū́ai (4c UNSTRESSED V) > *fū́ei (6b ei/ou-CHANGES) > *fū́ī (81 V̄V-TO-VV) > Lat fuī. Similarly in the present and past perfect paradigms cited below, the antecedent may have been *b^{h}ū- as opposed to *b^{h}u-.

[240] The present participle occurs only in compounds in earlier Latin: hence ab+sēns meant 'being away, absent'. The derivation is *sents (2c PHONOTACTICS 2f t-clusters) > *senss (2c PHONOTACTICS la Geminate simplification applying as a persistent synchronic rule) > *sens (8k Vns-CHANGES) > Lat (ab)sēns.

Chapter 4

Ancient Greek

I Introduction

The earliest attestations of Greek are generally assumed to date from about 1300 BC with the Mycenaean inscriptions of Linear B. The earliest extensive attestations are from about 800 BC with the first Greek literature, namely the Iliad and the Odyssey. The Ancient Greek dialects have been variously classified in sources such as Atkinson (1952: 165), Buck (1962: 3), Chantraine (1961: 17-21), Hirt (1912: passim), Meillet (1948: 7) and Pedersen (1952: 84-5).

Here we assume the following classification: (1) Eastern Greek, which includes Attic and Ionic, the latter the language of the Iliad and the Odyssey. (2) Western Greek, which includes Doric (also called Laconian), the dialect of Sparta. (3) Northern Greek, which includes Aeolic in Thessaly, Boeotian to the north of Athens and Lesbic on the island of Lesbos off northern Asia Minor. And (4) Southern Greek, which includes the Arcadian area of the Peloponnesus and Cyprus.

Although we shall occasionally cite forms from other dialects, our main focus here will be the Attic dialect of Ancient Greek at about 200 BC. We shall designate this dialect simply as "Greek". It is the dialect usually cited in traditional grammars. Here we shall cite Greek forms in a romanized version of the Greek alphabet. Our transcriptional conventions are described in III Greek Phonology below. On occasion we shall include our romanized forms within brackets < … > and their phonemic transcription within slashes /…/. In some derivations we assume the application of rule 2f GREEK STRESS without noting it explicitly, particularly when the Greek stress reflects that of PIE.

As may be seen from the chronology of the changes in the next section, we assume that the developments from PIE to Greek began around 3000 BC; we trace these changes into the Greek of about 200 BC. During this time Greek had contact with and was influenced by other languages: Atkinson (1952: 26) estimates that about 10% of the vocabulary of Greek is of non-PIE origin.

II The Changes from PIE into Greek.

A. Overview of the Changes and their Chronology

The stages are ordered. The changes within each stage may have been in any order or roughly simultaneous.

STAGE 1 (ca. 3000 BC)

STAGE 2

B. The Changes

1a Purported Reflexes of Laryngeals (LARYNGEALS)

The rules for these changes, which are posited in several sources, restructured the phonemic inventory of Greek and then were dropped from the grammar. Below we give in outline a common version of the laryngeal changes as they affected Greek. (Our account is based on Sihler 1995:165–8 et passim and Beekes 1969: 138 et passim.)

Under this account, the PIE of this stage had only short vowels, namely /i, e, o, u/. The phonemic inventory also included three laryngeal segments of uncertain phonetic content. We label them h_1, h_2, h_3; and the symbol h designates any of these laryngeals.

The changes are as follows:

(a)
$$\begin{bmatrix} h_1 \\ h_2 \\ h_3 \end{bmatrix} \text{e} \rightarrow \emptyset \begin{bmatrix} \text{e} \\ \text{a} \\ \text{o} \end{bmatrix}$$
$$\quad 1 \;\; 2 \qquad\quad 1 \;\; 2$$

(b) $$e \begin{bmatrix} h_1 \\ h_2 \\ h_3 \end{bmatrix} \rightarrow \begin{bmatrix} \bar{e} \\ \bar{a} \\ \bar{o} \end{bmatrix} \emptyset$$
1 2 → 1 2

(c) Syllabic $\underset{\circ}{h}_1$, $\underset{\circ}{h}_2$, $\underset{\circ}{h}_3$ → e, a, o

(d) ih, uh → ī, ū

(e) ph, th, kh → p^h, t^h, k^h

That is, (a) the sequences /h_1e, h_2e, h_3e/ become /e, a, o/ respectively. (b) The sequences /eh_1, eh_2, eh_3/ become long /ē, ā, ō/ respectively. (c) The syllabic laryngeals /$\underset{\circ}{h}_1$, $\underset{\circ}{h}_2$, $\underset{\circ}{h}_3$/ become /e, a, o/ respectively. Under this account it is assumed that the laryngeals underwent a synchronic rule of PIE like that of PIE 3.1.2g SYL SON in Chapter 1 whereby they became +vocalic /$\underset{\circ}{h}$/ in a nonvocalic environment. (d) The short vowels /i, u/ followed by any laryngeal are lengthened to /ī, ū/ and the laryngeal is lost. (e) The sequences /p, t, k/ plus a laryngeal become the Greek unary segments /p^h, t^h, k^h/. (Most occurrences of Gk /p^h, t^h, k^h/ are from PIE /b^h, d^h, g^h/ by 2a ASPIR DEVOI.) E.g.,

(a) PIE 1sg pres *$h_1$esmi 'I am' (LARYNGEALS) >*esmi (3e s-h-Ø) > Gk eimí /ēmí/. (We often record the word stress only on the Greek forms. In such cases it may be assumed that the Greek stress reflects that of PIE. See on this 2f GREEK STRESS below.) PIE 1sg pres *$h_2$egō 'drive' (LARYNGEALS) > *agō (2b ē/ō-TO-ɛ̄/ɔ̄) > Gk ágɔ̄. PIE 1sg pres *$h_2$eid^{h}ō 'kindle, light' (LARYNGEALS) > *aid^{h}ō (2a ASPIR DEVOI, 2b ē/ō-TO-ɛ̄/ɔ̄) > Gk aít^{h}ɔ̄; PIE nom sg *$h_3$ek^{w}m̥t 'eye' (LARYNGEALS) > *ok^{w}m̥t (2d SYL SON) > *ok^{w}mat (2e WF STOP DELE) > *ok^{w}ma (5a LABIOVEL) > *opma (6b C-Cl CHANGES) > Gk ómma.

(b) PIE 1sg pres *d^{h}i+d^{h}eh_1+mi 'put' (LARYNGEALS) > *d^{h}id^{h}ēmi (2a ASPIR DEVOI) > *t^{h}it^{h}ēmi (2b ē/ō-TO-ɛ̄/ɔ̄) > *t^{h}it^{h}ɛ̄mi (7b GRASSMANN) > Gk tít^{h}ɛ̄mi. PIE 1sg pres *si+steh_2+mi 'stand' (LARYNGEALS) > *sistāmi (3e s-h-Ø) >*histāmi (6a ā-TO-ɛ̄) > Gk hístɛ̄mi. Also the nom sg of the ā-class noun *moleh_2 'mill' (LARYNGEALS) > *molā (2c o-TO-u) > *mulā (6a ā-TO-ɛ̄) > *mulɛ̄ (6d u(:)-TO-y(:)) > Gk mýlɛ̄. PIE nom sg adj *gneh_3+t+os 'known' (LARYNGEALS) > *gnōtos (2b ē/ō-TO-ɛ̄/ɔ̄) > Gk gnɔ̄tós.

(c) PIE nom sg adj *$\underset{\circ}{h}_1$urus 'broad' (LARYNGEALS) > *eurus (6d u(:)-TO-y(:)) > Gk eurýs. PIE nom sg *p$\underset{\circ}{h}_2$tēr 'father' (LARYNGEALS) > *patēr (2b ē/ō-TO-ɛ̄/ɔ̄) Gk patɛ́r. PIE nom sg *$\underset{\circ}{h}_3$nog^{hw}+s 'nail' (LARYNGEALS) > *onog^{hw}s (2a ASPIR DEVOI) > *onok^{hw}s (2c o-TO-u) > *onuk^{hw}s (5a LABIOVEL) > *onuk^{w}s (6b C-Cl CHANGES) > *onuks (6d u(:)-TO-y(:)) > Gk ónyks. (Another derivation of this form minus LARYNGEALS is to assume that the word-initial /o/ resulted from change 4a PROTHESIS.) Also in this connection note the derivations PIE nom sg masc adj *d^h$\underset{\circ}{h}_1$+tos 'placed', nom sg fem noun *st$\underset{\circ}{h}_2$+tis 'act of standing', nom sg masc adj *d$\underset{\circ}{h}_3$+tos 'given' (LARYNGEALS) > *d^{h}etos, *statis, *dotos (ev) > Gk t^{h}etós, stásis, dotós.

(d) PIE nom sg *wih+s 'force' and *muh+s 'mouse' (LARYNGEALS, ev) > Gk ī́s and mŷs.

(e) PIE nom sg fem jā-class *sp$h_2$erja 'ball' (LARYNGEALS) > *sp^{h}arja (3c j/w-MET) > Gk sp^{h}aîra.

Note that it is also possible to posit other PIE antecedents for these forms without laryngeals. However, if laryngeals are posited, then the changes given here must have occurred early since they have to precede all of the other vowel changes from PIE into Greek.

lb Shortening of a Vowel Before Sonorant Consonant Plus Obstruent ($\bar{V}$+SON SHORT)

This change applied early in the history of Greek and was then dropped as a rule from the grammar. It is sometimes posited as a rule of PIE and is termed in this context "Osthoff's Law". The rule is this:

$\bar{V}$ → V / — [C, +sonorant] [C, –sonorant]

That is, a long vowel occurring before a sonorant consonant /l, m, n, r/ plus an obstruent consonant is shortened. E.g., PIE 3pl aorist *e+gnō+nt 'they knew' ($\bar{V}$+SON SHORT) >*egnont (2e WF STOP DELE) > Gk égnon (Note that $\bar{V}$+SON SHORT in our formulation must precede 2e WF STOP DELE.) PIE nom sg *ptērsnā 'heel' ($\bar{V}$+SON SHORT) > *ptersnā (3e s-h-Ø, 6a ā-TO-ɛ̄) > Gk ptérnɛ̄.

By attested Greek times $\bar{V}$+SON SHORT no longer applies as a rule in the grammar. Hence the form occurs 3pl mid subjunctive pʰérɔ̄ntai 'carry', not **pʰérontai. And $\bar{V}$+SON SHORT does not apply after 5c V-CONTRACT: PIE nom pl pres part *tīmā+ontes 'honoring' (2f GREEK STRESS) > *tīmā́ontes (5c V-CONTRACT) > Gk tīmɔ̄̂ntes, not **tī́montes.

2a Devoicing of Voiced Aspirated Consonants (ASPIR DEVOI)

The rules for these two changes restructured the phonemic inventory of the language and were then dropped from the grammar. The first of these changes occurred in pre-historic times; the second at ca. 300 AD.

(1) b^h, d^h, g^h, g^{hw} → p^h, t^h, k^h, k^{hw}

(2) p^h, t^h, k^h → f, θ, x

That is, (1) the voiced aspirated stops become voiceless.Then later (2) the voiceless aspirated stops became continuants. (By this time the labiovelar /k^{hw}/ had disappeared as a result of 5a LABIOVEL.)

E.g., PIE 1sg pres *bʰuō 'produce', *bʰerō 'carry' (ASPIR DEVOI 1) > *pʰuō, *pʰerō (2b ē/ō-TO-ɛ̄/ɔ̄ 6d u(:)-TO-y(:)) > Gk pʰýɔ̄, pʰérɔ̄ (ASPIR DEVOI 2) > later Gk fýɔ̄, férɔ̄. PIE nom sg *dʰūmos 'smoke', 1sg pres *steigʰō 'climb' (ASPIR DEVOI 1) > Gk tʰūmós, steíkʰɔ̄ (ASPIR DEVOI 2, ev) > later θȳmós, steíxɔ̄ /stḗxɔ̄/.

Atkinson (1953: 43 notes, "The Greek aspirated stops maintained their [original] character till the early centuries of the Christian era." Sturtevant (1940: 85) believes the continuant pronunciation may have begun by 100 AD. Sturtevant also notes that "standard pronunciation treated φ, θ, χ as aspirates in Hellenistic and Byzantine Greek until the ninth century A.D." Hirt (1912: 87) notes that there is orthographic evidence that the change ASPIR DEVOI 2 began with the change of /t^h/ to /θ/.

2b The Change /ē, ō/ to /ɛ̄, ɔ̄/ (ē/ō-TO-ɛ̄/ɔ̄)

It is generally assumed that PIE closed (+tense) /ē, ō/ become in Greek the more open (–tense) /ɛ̄, ɔ̄/. (See Atkinson 1952: 31.) After this change, the phonemic inventory of the language is slightly changed and the rule was dropped from the grammar. The change is this:

ē, ō → ɛ̄, ɔ̄

That is, tense /ē, ō/ become lax /ɛ̄, ɔ̄/. E.g., PIE 1sg pres *dʰi+dʰē+mi 'put' and *bʰerō 'carry' (ev) > Gk títʰɛ̄mi and pʰérɔ̄.

2c A Change of /o/ to /u/ (o-TO-u)

This change is sometimes called "Cowgill's Law". Its exact environment is not clear. After applying, the rule for the change restructures certain lexical items and then is dropped from the grammar. Its approximate formulation is this:

$$o \rightarrow u \;/\; \left.\begin{matrix}[C, +\text{sonorant}] \\ [C, +\text{labial}]\end{matrix}\right\} \;\_\_\; \left\{\begin{matrix}[C, +\text{labial}] \\ [C, +\text{sonorant}]\end{matrix}\right.$$

That is, the change of /o/ to /u/ occurs, as formulated in Sihler (1995: 45), "between a labial [consonant] and a sonorant [consonant]."

E.g., PIE nom sg *nok^{w}t+s 'night' (o-TO-u) > *nuk^{w}ts (5a LABIOVEL) > *nukts (6b C-Cl CHANGES) > *nuks (6d u(:)-TO-y(:)) > Gk nýks; PIE nom sg *b^{h}oljom 'leaf' (2a ASPIR DEVOI) > *p^{h}oljom (o-TO-u, 3a C+j CHANGES) > *p^{h}ullom (3d m-TO-n) > *p^{h}ullon (6d u(:)-TO-y(:)) > Gk p^{h}ýllon; PIE nom sg *molā 'mill' (o-TO-u) > *mulā (6a ā-TO-ɛ̄) > *mulɛ̄ (6d u(:)-TO-y(:)) > Gk mýlɛ̄; PIE nom sg *nog^{hw}+s 'nail' (2a ASPIR DEVOI) > *nok^{hw}s (o-TO-u) > *nuk^{hw}s (4a PROTHESIS) > *onuk^{hw}s (5a LABIOVEL) > *onuk^{h}s (6b C-Cl CHANGES) > *onuks (6d u(:)-TO-y(:)) > Gk ónyks.

Two chronological observations are to be made here. First, given our formulation of the o-TO-u change, it must apply before 5a LABIOVEL in order for forms like Gk nýks < PIE *nok^{w}ts to be derived. Second, the o-TO-u change has to have occurred before 6d u(:)-TO-y(:) since the latter change applied to those /u/'s derived by o-TO-u.

2d Changes in the Syllabic Sonorant Consonants (SYL SON)

After occurring, these changes restructure certain lexical items and inflectional endings and then are dropped as rules from the grammar. The rules are these:

(a) m̥ , n̥ → { am, an / ___ V or j ; a / ___ C, w or ## }

(b) l̥, r̥ → { al, ar ; la, ra }

That is, (a) syllabic /m̥, n̥/ occur as Greek /am, an/ if preceding a vowel or /j/. Syllabic /m̥, n̥/ occur as Greek /a/ if preceding a consonant, /w/, or if word-final. (b) Syllabic /l̥, r̥/ become Greek /al, ar/ or /la, ra/ apparently unpredictably. E.g.,

(a) PIE 1sg pres *g^{w}m̥+j+ō 'come' (2b ē/ō-TO-ɛ̄/ɔ̄) > *g^{w}m̥jɔ̄ (SYL SON) > *g^{w}amjɔ̄ (3a C+j CHANGES) > *g^{w}anjɔ̄ (3c j/w-MET) > *g^{w}ainɔ̄ (5a LABIOVEL) > Gk baínɔ̄. (Note the necessary chronology 3a C+j CHANGES > 3c j/w-MET.) The same root also occurs in the nom sg noun *g^{w}m̥+t+is 'step' (SYL SON) > *g^{w}atis (4b t-TO-s) > *g^{w}asis (5a LABIOVEL) > Gk básis. Also PIE *sm̥+paks 'once' as well as the same root in sm̥+ōs 'somehow' (SYL SON, ev) >*sapaks, *samɔ̄s (3e s-h-Ø) > Gk hápaks, hámɔ̄s. PIE nom sg *nomn̥t 'name' (SYL SON) > *nomat (2e WF STOP DELE) > *noma (4a PROTHESIS) > Gk ónoma. Note also the different reflexes of the PIE negative prefix *n̥- in the nom sg masc adjectives n̥+osteos 'no-boned, boneless' and *n̥+logos 'speechless' (SYL SON) > Gk anósteos and álogos. Notice also in this connection the negative adj *n̥+woikos 'no-home, homeless' (SYL SON) > *awoikos (7c w-DELE) > Gk áoikos. (Here the chronology must be SYL SON > 7c w-DELE: otherwise the Greek reflex would be **ánoikos.)

(b) PIE nom sg masc adj *ml̥dus 'soft' (SYL SON) >*mladus (6b C-Cl CHANGES) > *bladus (6d u(:)-TO-y(:)) > Gk bladýs. Compare in this connection the PIE nom sg masc adj *ml̥d^{h}akos 'soft' (2a ASPIR DEVOI) > *ml̥t^{h}akos (SYL SON) > Gk malt^{h}akós. PIE nom sg *kr̥d+i+ā 'heart' (SYL SON) > Gk kardíā. Note also the occurrence from the same PIE source of Homeric (Ionic) Gk kradíɛ̄ 'heart'.Some sources such as Buck (1962: 106) posit PIE long sonorant consonants, e.g., PIE nom sg masc adj *str̥̄tos 'strewn' (ev) > Gk strɔ̄tós. The derivation would be *str̥̄tos (SYL SON) > *strōtos (2b ē/ō-TO-ɛ̄/ɔ̄) > Gk strɔ̄tós. Another possible PIE antecedent is *strōtos.

2e Loss of Word-Final Obstruent Stops (WF STOP DELE)

The rule for this change remains in the grammar. It is phon cond.

$$\begin{bmatrix} \text{C, –sonorant} \\ \text{–continuant} \end{bmatrix}_1^2 \rightarrow \emptyset \;/\; \_\_\_ \;\#\#$$

That is, one or two obstruent stops occurring in absolute word-final position are deleted.

E.g., PIE voc sg *pawid 'boy', *gunaik 'woman', *wanakt 'prince' (WF STOP DELE) > *pawi, *gunai, *wana (6d u(:)-TO-y(:), 7c W-DELE) > Gk paî, gýnai, ána. Note in this connection the respective genitive singular forms, with the ending -os, to which WF STOP DELE cannot apply: Gk paidós, gynaikós and anaktós. Note also the derivation of the nom sg *wanakt+s 'prince' (to which WF STOP DELE cannot apply because there is no word-final obstruent stop, but 6b C-Cl CHANGES does apply) > *wanaks (7c W-DELE) > Gk ánaks. Also PIE 3pl imperfect *e+b^{h}er+ont 'carried' (2a ASPIR DEVOI) > *ep^{h}eront (WF STOP DELE) > Gk ép^{h}eron. And the PIE nom sg neuter *tod 'that' (WF STOP DELE) > Gk tó.

In the application of WF STOP DELE, the word-final stops of so-called "proclitics" are unaffected. Proclitics are words which attach themselves to a following word to form a single stress component (see on this 2f GREEK STRESS below). E.g., the synchronic derivation /ék##potamoû/ 'from the river' (2f4 GREEK STRESS: PHRASAL STRESS) → /ekpotamoû/, where WF STOP DELE does not apply because the /k/ in /ek/ is in effect no longer word-final.

2f The Word–Stress Rules (GREEK STRESS)

There are four ordered rules of Greek word stress. We assume they were added chronologically as given below. They all remain in the grammar of Greek in the same synchronic ordering.The rules are (2f1 MORPH COND STRESS) the original PIE morphologically conditioned stress rule (MORPH COND STRESS), (2f2) the recessive stress rule (RECESSIVE STRESS), (2f3) the acute stress rule (ACUTE STRESS) and (2f4) the phrasal stress rule (PHRASAL STRESS). The first of these seems to have been retained in great part (except for verb stress) from PIE. The second, third and fourth rules are Greek innovations.

We shall give these four rules below. As a preliminary we note that according to numerous traditional sources such as Atkinson (1952: 53), "The accent of the ancient Greek language was a pitch accent." Atkinson then continues (ibid.: 62), "In Hellenistic times the Greek pitch accent changed to a stress incident upon the same syllable as that on which the pitch had previously been. Indications that this change of accent had begun as early as the third century B.C. come to us from papyri and inscriptions." Sturtevant (1940: 104) believes that the Greek "pitch" accent became one of "stress" as late as during the 300's AD.

Here we do not make these assumptions. Rather, we assume the following. First, we assume that a "stressed" vowel may consist of one or more of three phonetic characteristics: (a) It may occur at a higher pitch (frequency of vibration of the vocal chords). (b) It may occur at a greater degree of loudness (amplitude of vibration of the vocal chords). (c) It may be longer than other vowels (duration of vibration of the vocal chords). Second, we assume that a stressed vowel in PIE as well as in Greek evinced at least two and perhaps all three of these characteristics. Third, we shall assume that in Greek the difference between the acute accent which can occur over a short vowel, a long vowel or diphthong and the circumflex which occurs only over a long vowel or a diphthong was not one of pitch, but rather one of different stress placement. Hence the acute V́ is /VV́/; and the circumflex V̂ is /V́V/. (In our phonemic transcriptions we shall generally mark the latter sequences as /V̂/.) Our position is not unlike that of Horrocks (1997:4) who notes that ". . . the ancient 'pitch' accent was in reality a contonation involving either a monosyllabic rise-fall on a single long vowel or diphthong (marked ^), or a rise (marked ´) on one syllable followed by a fall (unmarked) on the next; in certain circumstances ... the rise was neutralized in some way (marked `)."

(2f1) The Morphologically Conditioned Stress Rule (MORPH COND STRESS)

We give here only the basic structure of this early rule. Details and more examples may be found in sources such as Smyth (1959) and in section IV Historical Greek Morphology below. (Note also the similarity of this rule to the Sanskrit stress rule 11 SANSKRIT STRESS.)

MORPH COND STRESS occurs in five basic configurations:

(I) On the first syllable of a word: ## [C_0 ___]$_s$

(II) On the second syllable of a word: ## s [C_0 ___]$_s$

(III) On a derivative suffix in a word: [C_0, derivative suffix ___]$_s$

(IV) On an inflectional ending (always its first syllable): [C_0, inflectional suffix ___]$_s$ s_o ##

(V) Alternating in a paradigm between the first syllable (of the root) and the inflectional ending (i.e., I and IV above):

##[C_0 ___]$_s$ or [C_0, inflectional suffix ___]$_s$$s_o$ ##

Exactly which of these five stress patterns accrues to a word is determined by one of three possible parameters:

(A) a particular derivative suffix,
(B) a particular marked lexical item, or
(C) a particular combination of syntactic and morphological features such as case, number or particular form class.

(I) First-Syllable Stress

(A) As Determined by a Particular Derivative Suffix

E.g., (i) comparative and superlative suffixes: pos kakós 'bad', comp /kak+iɔ̄n/ (2f1 MORPH COND STRESS) → /kákiɔ̄n/ (2f2 RECESSIVE STRESS) → kakíɔ̄n, sup /kak+ist+os/ (2f1 MORPH COND STRESS) → kákistos. Also pos isk^{h}ȳrós 'strong', comp /isk^{h}ȳr+oteros/ (2f1 MORPH COND STRESS) → ísk^{h}ȳroteros (2f2 RECESSIVE STRESS) → isk^{h}ȳróteros. Likewise, sup isk^{h}ȳrótatos.

(B) As Determined by a Particular Lexical Item

E.g., (i) ánt^{h}rɔ̄pos 'man' o-class masc.
(ii) t^{h}álatta 'sea' ā-class fem.
(iii) léɔ̄n 'lion' Vnt-class masc.
(iv) The adj áksios 'worthy'.
(v) Certain pronouns such as hóde 'this' and állos 'other'.
(vi) The numerals '1' through '6' and (with the exception of '100') from '10' on. E.g., pénte '5' vs. heptá '7'.

(C) As Determined by Particular Syntactic and Morphological Features

E.g., (i) in certain nouns the voc sg has first-syllable stress, regardless of the stress placement of the other cases. Such nouns occur in all classes but are particularly numerous in the athematic class. E.g., o-class nom sg adelp^{h}ós 'brother' vs. voc sg ádelp^{h}e; athematic tVr-class nom sg patɛ̄́r 'father' vs. voc sg páter. There are no adjectives of this type. Hence nom sg masc agat^{h}ós 'good', voc sg agat^{h}é, not **ágat^{h}e.
(ii) In some compounds. E.g., lytós 'dissoluable' vs. álytos 'indissoluable'.

(iii) In virtually all verb forms except certain participles and so-called "enclitic" verbs which we describe below. E.g., 1sg indicative lȳ́ɔ̄ 'loose', tít^{h}ɛ̄mi 'put, place'. (See IV Historical Greek morphology for other examples.) The so-called "contract" verbs as described in section 6 of IV Historical Greek morphology are only apparent counterexamples to 2f1 MORPH COND STRESS. Hence the 1sg indicative tīmɔ̄̂ 'I honor' instead of **tī́mɔ̄ is derived as *tīmā+ɔ̄ (2f1 MORPH COND STRESS) > tī́māɔ̄ (2f2 RECESSIVE STRESS) > *tīmā́ɔ̄ (5c V-CONTRACT) > tīmɔ̄̂. Hence we assume the chonological sequence 2f GREEK STRESS > 5c V-CONTRACT

(II) Second-Syllable Stress

(A) As Determined by a Particular Derivative Suffix: Ø

(I.e., no such parameter exists to condition second-syllable stress.)

(B) As Determined by a Particular Lexical Item

(i) o-class masc karkínos 'crab'.
(ii) ā-class fem hɛ̄méra 'day', where the nom pl is hɛ̄mérai, not **hɛ̄́merai.
(iii) u-class masc nom sg ik^{h}t^{h}ȳ́s 'fish', gen sg ik^{h}t^{h}ýos.
(iv) tVr-class masc nom sg patɛ̄́r 'father', gen sg patrós.
(v) Ø-class nom sg *katɛ̄́lip+s 'attic', gen sg *katɛ̄́lip+os (2f3 ACUTE STRESS) > katɛ̄̂lips, katɛ̄́lipos
(vi) A few adjectives such as nom sg masc hɛ̄dýs 'sweet', gen sg hɛ̄déos.

(C) As Determined by Particular Syntactic and Morphological Features: Ø

(III) Derivative-Suffix Stress

(A) As Determined by a Particular Derivative Suffix

E.g., (i) in nouns and adjectives of all classes. E.g., o-class paid+í+on 'small child'; Ø-class noun nom sg p^{h}yll+ád+s 'foliage', gen sg *p^{h}yll+ád+os (ev) > p^{h}yllás, p^{h}ylládos; Vn-class nom sg algɛ̄+dɔ̄́n 'pain', gen sg algɛ̄+dón+os. An adjective is the nom sg masc andr+eî+os 'manly'.

(ii) In certain verbal participles. E.g., the nom sg masc forms of the perf mid lely+mén+os 'having loosed', perf act lely+k+ɔ̄́+s 'idem', aorist act bal+ɔ̄́+n 'having thrown', pres act, of mi-class verbs such as did+oú+s 'giving'; and the "obligational" verbal adjective such as ly+t+é+os 'that which must be loosed'.

(B) As Determined by a Particular Lexical Item: Ø

(C) As Determined by Particular Syntactic and Morphological Features: Ø

(IV) Inflectional-Ending Stress

(A) As Determined by a Particular Derivative Suffix

E.g., (i) -k- in adjectives such as paidi+k+ós 'of a boy'.
(ii) -on- in nouns such as kall+on+ɛ̄́ 'beauty'.
(iii) -t- in deverbal adjectives such as ly+t+ós 'dissoluble'.
(iv) -tr- in neuter nouns such as loe+tr+ón 'bath'.

(B) As Determined by a Particular Lexical Item

E.g., (i) o-class nom sg zygós 'yoke'.

(ii) ā-class nom sg oropʰɛ̄́ 'roof'.

(iii) The adj agatʰós 'good'.

(C) As Determined by Particular Syntactic and Morphological Features

E.g., (i) in the personal pronouns such as nom egɔ̄́ 'I', gen emoû, dat emoí.

(ii) In the intensive pron autós 'oneself'.

(iii) In the 2nd singular aorist imperative of some verbs such as eipé 'speak'.

(iv) In the pres indicative paradigm of at least two verbs which are marked as "clitics". These are eimí 'I am' and pʰɛ̄mí 'I say'.

(v) In all prepositions and in most coordinating conjunctions the final syllable (usually historically an inflectional ending) is stressed. E.g., epí 'upon', hypér 'over', allá 'but'.

(V) Stress Alternating Between the Root and the Inflectional Ending

(A) As Determined by a Particular Derivative Suffix: Ø □

(B) As Determined by a Particular Lexical Item

In a few lexically marked u-class nouns, root–stress occurs in the nominative and accusative; and ending stress is on the inflectional ending in the genitive and dative. E.g., nom sg góny 'knee', gen sg gounós /gōnós/.

(C) As Determined by Particular Syntactic and Morphological Features

In all monosyllabic Ø-class nouns there is root stress in the nominative and accusative — and ending stress in the genitive and dative. E.g., nom sg gȳ́ps 'vulture', gen gȳpós, acc gȳ̂pa. The derivation of the nominative and accusative forms is /gyyp/(i.e. /gȳp/) /+s/ and /+a/respectively (2f1 MORPH COND STRESS) → gýyps and gýypa (2f3 ACUTE STRESS) → gyýps (= gȳ́ps) and/gýypa/ (gȳ̂pa). Some polysyllabic tVr-class nouns have a similar stress pattern, but with the root stress often on the second syllable. E.g., nom sg mɛ̄́tɛ̄r 'mother', gen sg mɛ̄trós, acc sg mɛ̄téra. Finally, a single Ø-class adjective follows this stress pattern in its singular paradigm, masculine and neuter. E.g., nom sg masc pâ̄s /páas/ 'all' vs. gen sg pantós.

(2f2) The Recessive Stress Rule (RECESSIVE STRESS)

This change is basically phonologically conditioned, is a Greek innovation and remains in the grammar as a rule. RECESSIVE STRESS functions as a type of filter: it prescribes that word stress can occur only so far from the end of a word. Accordingly, when the stress assigned by 2f1 MORPH COND STRESS is placed too far to the left, it is moved to the right. The rule is this:

```
## ... [V, +stress] ... [V, –stress]  ⎧ (a) [VV(V)] ## →  ##... [V, –stress] ... [V, +stress] same
      s                 s              ⎨      s                  s               s
                                       ⎩ (b) s[V]##
                                               s

        1                  2                   3                  1                2            3
```

That is, a stressed vowel in a syllable (1) too far to the left in a word is moved rightwards onto a vowel in a syllable (2) which is either (a) penult (next-to-last) if the word-final syllable contains a long vowel (V̄ = VV), a diphthong (VV) or a long diphthong (V̄V = VVV). Or (b), the stress is moved to the antepenultimate syllable (third-to-last) if the word-final syllable contains only a short vowel (V).

E.g., nom sg /antʰrɔ̄pos/, i.e. /antʰrɔɔpos/ 'man' vs. gen sg /antʰrɔɔpō / (2f1 MORPH COND STRESS) → ántʰrɔɔpos and ántʰrɔɔpō (2f2 RECESSIVE STRESS) → ántʰrɔɔpos and antʰrɔ́ɔpō (2f3) ACUTE STRESS) → Gk ántʰrɔ̄pos /ántʰrɔɔpos/ and antʰrɔ̄́pou = /antʰrɔɔ́pō/. (The historical development reflects the synchronic derivation.) Likewise nom sg masc adj *aksios 'worthy' vs. dat sg *aksiɔ̄i (morpheme and as such syllable boundaries) → *aks+i+os and *aks+i+ɔ̄i (2f1 MORPH COND STRESS) > *áks+i+os and *áks+i+ɔ̄i (2f2 RECESSIVE STRESS) > Gk áksios vs. aksíɔ̄i. Finally, for the purposes of this rule the word-final diphthongs /ai/ and /oi/, particularly when occurring as nominative plural endings, are for some reason considered the metric equivalents of a short vowel. Hence the nom pl /antʰrɔ̄poi/ 'men' (2f1 MORPH COND STRESS) → ántʰrɔ̄poi (to which 2f2 RECESSIVE STRESS does not apply).

It would seem that the development of the stress rules in the other early IE languages may have paralleled that of Greek in the addition of a rule like 2f2 RECESSIVE STRESS to the rule inherited from PIE. That is, for a time — as in Attic Greek — both rules were operative. In most IE languages the phon cond rule (here 2f2 RECESSIVE STRESS) eventually became the dominant and sole rule of word stress. This in fact did occur in the Greek dialect of Lesbos. Here the MORPH COND STRESS rule was almost totally lost (except for prepositions and conjunctions, which retained their word-final stress); and the RECESSIVE STRESS rule applied to all other forms. Hence Attic agatʰós 'good' is Lesbic ágatʰos.

(2f3) The Acute Stress Rule (ACUTE STRESS)

As noted earlier, long vowels and diphthongs in Greek admitted of two kinds of stress, circumflex or falling (V̂ = V́V = V́V̀) and acute or rising (V̄́ = VV́ = V̀V́). E.g., gen pl andrɔ̄̂n /andrɔ́ɔn/ 'men' vs. gen sg antʰrɔ̄́pou /antʰrɔɔ́pō/'man'. (We shall occasionally transcribe long vowels such as /ɛ̄, ɔ̄/ as /ɛɛ/ and /ɔɔ/. Long tense /ē, ō/ may be written /ee/ and /oo/. The short and lax vowels are written /e/ and /o/.)

Languages like Ancient Greek which have these two stress configurations are sometimes called "polytonous". A language like English in which a stressed long vowel or a diphthong has the ictus only on the first mora is called "monotonous". Hence a word like English tide can be stressed only as /táid/ and not **/taíd/.

We assume that PIE stress was monotonous in this sense since most of the PIE daughter languages have this type of stress. If this was in fact the case, then the innovation of Greek was not — as is often implicitly assumed — the development of the circumflex accent V̂ (= V́V), but rather the development of the acute V̄́ (VV́). The rule for deriving the acute VV́ from the earlier circumflex V́V is this:

V́(V)V → V(V)V́ / (a) ___ { $[VV(V)]_s$ ## / s_2 ## }

(b) $[\_\_\_]_s$ ## in nouns, adjectives and some pronouns in the nominative, vocative or accusative cases; and in nonadjectival adverbs.

That is, acute stress develops from an earlier falling stress on long vowels (V́V), diphthongs (V́V) or long diphthongs (V́VV) (which then become VV́ or VVV́) in either (a) a penultimate syllable followed by a syllable containing a long vowel, diphthong or long diphthong; or in an antepenultimate (third-to-last) syllable. Or (b) in a word-final syllable under the morph cond environment described.

As our examples we cite synchronic derivations which reflect the historical chronology.

(a) Sg gen antʰrɔ̄pou /antʰrɔɔpoo/ 'man' and dat antʰrɔ̄pɔ̄i /antʰrɔɔpɔɔi/ (2f1 MORPH COND

STRESS) → ántʰrɔɔpoo and ántʰrɔɔpɔɔi (2f2 RECESSIVE STRESS) → antʰrɔ́ɔpoo and antʰrɔ́ɔpɔɔi (2f3 ACUTE STRESS) → antʰrɔ̄́pou /antʰrɔɔ́poo/ and antʰrɔ̄́pɔ̄i /antʰrɔɔ́pɔɔi/. 1sg future deiksɔ̄ /deeksɔ̄/ 'show' vs. 2sg aorist imp deikson /deekson/ (2f1 MORPH COND STRESS) → déeksɔ̄ and déekson (2f3 ACUTE STRESS) → deíksɔ̄ /deéksɔ̄/ and deîkson /déekson/.

(b) Nom sg /pʰygɛɛ/ 'flight' vs. gen sg /pʰygɛɛs/ and nom pl /pʰygai/ vs. gen pl /pʰygɔɔn/ (2f1 MORPH COND STRESS) → pʰygɛ́ɛ, pʰygɛ́ɛs, pʰygái, pʰygɔ́ɔn (2f3 ACUTE STRESS) → pʰygɛ̄́ /pʰygɛɛ́/, pʰygɛ̄̂s /pʰygɛ́ɛs/, pʰygaí and pʰygɔ̄̂n /pʰygɔ́ɔn/. Similar examples are nom sg masc alɛ̄tʰɛ̄́s /alɛɛtʰɛɛ́s/ 'true' vs. gen sg alɛ̄tʰoûs /alɛɛtʰóos/; nom sg anɛ̄́r 'man' vs. gen pl andrɔ̄̂n. Also, note the nom sg pron egɔ̄́ 'I', not **egɔ̄̂; and the adverb pɔ̄́ 'yet', not **pɔ̄̂.

Part (a) of 2f3 ACUTE STRESS may in fact be a mere recapitulation of 2f2 RECESSIVE STRESS: if one interprets RECESSIVE STRESS as moving the stress onto that mora *immediately* preceding

(i) [VV(V)] ##   or   (ii) s[V] ##,
  s   s

then this automatically results in acute stress in these environments. Hence gen pl antʰrɔɔpɔɔn 'men' (2f1 MORPH COND STRESS) → ántʰrɔɔpɔɔn (2f2 RECESSIVE STRESS under this interpretation) → antʰrɔ̄́pɔ̄n /antʰrɔɔ́pɔɔn/. Thus at least part (a) of 2f3 ACUTE STRESS above may have arisen in this way. Then later acute stress was also introduced into word-final syllables under the morph cond environment given in part (b).

(2f4) The Phrasal Stress Rules (PHRASAL STRESS)

These rules apply over a word boundary to form a phrasal unit. They often involve "proclitics" and "enclitics" — the former type of word forming a stress unit with an immediately following word and the latter, with an immediately preceding word. In basic outline the PHRASAL STRESS rules are these:

(1) (V)V́ → (V)V̀ / (a) [___] ## ... [V, +stress] ... ##
                          s
                    (b) optional [___ , proclitic or enclitic]

(2) V → V́ / (a) [...V, –stress...][C ___] ## ... [V, –stress, enclitic] ... ##
                   s   s
             (b) [...V, –stress...] ## s[___, enclitic] ##
                   s   s

That is, (1) an acute stress on a long or short vowel is reduced (or possibly entirely removed) (a) in a word-final syllable if the immediately following word is stressed and (b) optionally in a proclitic or enclitic word. And (2) an unstressed short vowel is stressed if (a) in a word-final syllable, preceded by an unstressed vowel and followed by an unstressed enclitic or if (b) in the second syllable of an enclitic and preceded by a word whose final syllable is unstressed. (Note that our formulation of 2f4 PHRASAL STRESS assumes the prior application of the other stress rules.)

E.g., (la) kalɛ̄́ partʰénos 'beautiful girl' → kalɛ̄̀ partʰénos; (ib) hós ántʰrɔ̄pos 'the man' → hòs ántʰrɔ̄pos, dós moí 'give me' → dós moì. (2a) sɔ̄̂son /sɔ́ɔson/ me 'save me' → sɔ̄̂són me. However, the rule cannot apply to a sequence like kʰɔ̄́rā /kʰɔɔ́rā/ tis 'a certain land' because the stress configuration is /ɔɔ́/ instead of either /ɔ́ɔ/ or unstressed /ɔɔ/. (2b) paîdes tines 'certain children' → paîdes tinés.

3a Changes of a Consonant Followed by /j/ (C+j CHANGES)

For the most part these changes restructure various lexical items and then are dropped as rules from the grammar. A restructured version of parts (b, c, d) of the change remains as a morph cond rule applying to verbs (examples below). The changes are basically these:

(a)	t or t^h	+ j	→	s(s)	/	{[+sonorant], ##} ___
(b)	p or p^h	+ j		pt		
(c)	k$^{(w)}$ or k$^{(w)h}$	+ j		s(s)		
(d)	g$^{(w)}$ or d	+ j		dz		
(e)	l	+ j		ll		
(f)	m	+ j		nj		

That is, the sequences of consonants if preceded by a sonorant consonant or a vowel or if word-initial change as shown. (The geminate /ss/ later becomes /s/.) Sihler (1995: 189–96) considers part (a) of the rule to have occurred first. He also assumes that the changes underwent various intermediate stages such as kj > čč > ss > s. E.g.,

(a) PIE nom sg masc *jotjos 'that much' (C+j CHANGES) > *jossos (3e s-h-Ø) > *hossos (6b C-Cl CHANGES) > Attic hósos vs. Ionic (and as such Homeric) hóssos, PIE nom sg masc adj *med^{h}jos 'middle' (2a ASPIR DEVOI) >*met^{h}jos (C+j CHANGES) > Gk mésos, PIE 1sg pres *platjō 'mould' (2b ē/ō-TO-ɛ̄/ɔ̄) > *platjɔ̄ (C+j CHANGES) > Gk plássɔ̄. Possibly PIE 1sg pres *tjeg^{w}omai 'worship' (C+j CHANGES) > *seg^{w}omai (5a LABIOVEL) > Gk sébomai.

(b) PIE 1sg pres *skepjomai 'look at' (C+j CHANGES) > Gk sképtomai. (Note the future sképsomai < *skep+s+omai to which C+j has not applied. Hence a morph cond reflex of C+j CHANGES is the alternation /pt/-/p/ in the present vs. the future paradigm.) PIE 1sg pres *pjuō 'spit' (2b ē/ō-TO-ɛ̄/ɔ̄) > *pjuɔ̄ (C+j CHANGES) > *ptuɔ̄ (6d u(:)-TO-y(:)) > Gk ptýɔ̄. PIE 1sg pres *d^{h}ab^{h}jō 'honor' (2a ASPIR DEVOI, ev) > *t^{h}ap^{h}jɔ̄ (C+j CHANGES) > Gk t^{h}áptɔ̄. C+j CHANGES must precede 7b GRASSMANN. If the order were reversed, the Greek form would be **taptɔ̄.

(c) PIE 1sg pres *b^{h}ulakjō 'guard' (C+j CHANGES, ev) → Gk p^{h}ylássɔ̄. (Note the future p^{h}yláksɔ̄ < *b^{h}ulak+s+ō to which C+j CHANGES has not applied. Hence a morph cond reflex of C+j CHANGES is the alternation /ss/-/ks/ in the pres vs. future paradigms.) PIE comp adj *d^{h}ŋ̥g^h+jōn 'faster' (2a ASPIR DEVOI, 2b ē/ō-TO-ɛ̄/ɔ̄, 2d SYL SON) > *t^{h}ak^{h}jɔ̄n (C+j CHANGES) > Gk t^{h}ā́ssɔ̄n (the cause of the long /ā/ is not known). Compare the pos *d^{h}ŋ̥g^{h}us 'fast' (2a ASPIR DEVOI, 2d SYL SON, 6d u(:)-TO-y(:)) > *t^{h}ak^{h}ys (7b GRASSMANN) > Gk tak^{h}ýs. Also PIE 1sg pres *pek^{w}jō 'cook' (ev) > Gk péssɔ̄.

(d) PIE 1sg pres *jagjomai 'revere' (C+j CHANGES) > *jadzomai (3b j-CHANGES) > Gk házomai. (In the following we will transcribe /dz/ as graphemic <z>.) Likewise PIE 1sg pres *nig^{w}jō 'wash' (C+j CHANGES, ev) > Gk nízɔ̄. (Note the future nípsɔ̄ < *nig^w+s+ō to which C+j CHANGES has not applied. Hence a morph cond reflex of C+j CHANGES is the alternation /dz/-/p/ in some present vs. future paradigms.) Also the PIE adv *pedjos 'on foot' (ev) > Gk pézos and PIE nom sg *djeus 'god' (ev) > Gk Zeús.

(e) PIE adj *aljos 'another' (C+j CHANGES) > Gk állos. Note that this derivation assumes the relative chronology C+j CHANGES > 3c j/w-MET: otherwise the Greek form would be **aîlos. Also PIE 1sg *steljō 'put' (ev) > Gk stéllɔ̄.

(f) PIE 1sg pres *gʷm̥jō 'come' (2b ē/ō-TO-ɛ̄/ɔ̄, 2d SYL SON) > *gʷamjɔ̄ (C+j CHANGES) > *gʷanjɔ̄ (3c j/w-MET) > *gʷainɔ̄ (5a LABIOVEL) > Gk baínɔ̄.

Given the above derivations it would seem that C+j CHANGES must precede 3c j/w-MET. However, consider the following derivation: PIE comp adj *meg+jōn 'larger' (2b ē/ō-TO-ɛ̄/ɔ̄) >*megjɔ̄n (C+j CHANGES) > *medzɔ̄n (? 3c j/w-MET) > Gk meízɔ̄n /meédzɔ̄n/. If the order is reversed, then C+j CHANGES cannot apply: *megjɔ̄n (3c j-MET) > Gk **meígɔ̄n. A possible scenario is that C+j CHANGES and 3c j/w-MET were approximately simultaneous. The derivation would then be *megjɔ̄n (3c j/w-MET first copying the /j/ into the root and leaving the /j/ in the ending) > *mejgjɔ̄n (by the PIE rule 3.1.2c i-j/u-w ALT, still in the grammar and applying synchronically) → *meigjɔ̄n (3a C+j CHANGES) > *meidzjɔ̄n (3c j/w-MET then completing the change by deleting the /j/) > Gk meízɔ̄n /meédzɔ̄n/.

Another chronology is indicated by the derivation of mésos 'middle' above. Here we assumed in the derivation 2a ASPIR DEVOI > C+j CHANGES. If this sequence were reversed, the Greek form would probably have been **mézos **/médzos/.

Finally, in some instances it is not clear why C+j CHANGES has not applied. E.g., the PIE adj *jag+j+os 'holy' (ev) > Gk hágios as opposed to **hádzos. (The C+j CHANGES rule has applied in the derivation of the corresponding verb hádzomai under (d) above.) A possible reason for the retention of /g/ in the adjective may be that the PIE adj *jagjos 'holy' was affected by the PIE rule 3.1.2f Sievers on the analogy of long-stemmed forms. The derivation would then be PIE *jagjos 'holy' (PIE 3.1.2f Sievers applying as a synchronic rule) → *jagijos (3b j-CHANGES) > Gk hágios.

3b Changes in /j/ (j-CHANGES)

These changes restructure various lexical items and are then dropped as rules from the grammar. They seem to have occurred in the following chronological sequence:

(1) j → h and sometimes dz / ## ___

(2) j → Ø / V ___ V

That is, (1) word-initial /j/ becomes /h/ and occasionally /dz/. (2) Between vowels /j/ is deleted. E.g., (1) PIE nom sg masc *jos 'who', *jōros 'year' (ev) > Gk hós, hɔ̂ros. But also PIE nom sg neuter *jugom 'yoke' and 1sg pres *jesō 'seethe' (ev) > Gk zygón and zéɔ̄. It is not clear under what circumstances /dz/ occurs. A possible derivation of the first form is the PIE demonstrative and noun *tód##jugóm 'this yoke' (encliticization) → *todjugóm (3a C+j CHANGES) > *tod zugóm (ev) > Gk tò zygón 'the yoke'. (2) PIE nom sg neuter *dwejos 'fear' (j-CHANGES) > *dweos (7c w-DELE) > Gk déos.

Note the necessary chronology 2b ē/ō-TO-ɛ̄/ɔ̄ > 3b j-CHANGES in this derivation: PIE nom pl *polejes (j-CHANGES) > Gk pólees = pólɛ̄s 'cities', spelled <póleis>, to which 2b ē/ō-TO-ɛ̄/ɔ̄ cannot apply to produce Gk **polɛ̄s. Judging from the Linear B evidence, j-CHANGES 2 seems to have been a later change than j-CHANGES 1. (See on this Ventris and Chadwick 1953.)

3c Metathesis of /j/ and /w/ (j/w-MET)

For the most part this change restructures various lexical items. (There are many more instances of j-MET than of w-MET.) It also remains in a restructured version as a morph cond rule describing certain vowel alternations in some verb paradigms (examples below). The early form of the change is this:

V C j or w → V j or w C (ev) → V i or u C
1 2 3   1 3   2   1 3   2

That is, the sequence vowel plus single consonant (including <z> = /dz/) plus /j/ or /w/ becomes vowel plus /j/ or /w/ plus consonant. Then the /j/ and /w/ are realized as /i/ and /u/ by the rule PIE 3.1.2c i-j/u-w ALT, which is still in the grammar from PIE times.

E.g., PIE nom sg *morja 'part' (j/w-MET) > Gk moîra. PIE 1sg pres *b^{h}anjō 'appear' and *ktenjō 'kill' (j/w-MET, ev) > Gk p^{h}aínɔ̄ and kteínɔ̄. Contrast here the corresponding future forms p^{h}anɔ̂ and ktenɔ̂ < PIE *b^{h}anes+ō and *ktenes+ō to which j/w-MET does not apply. Hence the synchronic alternations /ai/-/a/ and /ē/ <ei>-/e/ result from j/w-MET. Note also PIE u-class gen sg *gonu+os 'knee' (PIE 3.1.2c i-j/u-w ALT applying synchronically) → *genwos (j/w-MET) > *gounos (7a ei/ou-TO-ē/ō) > Gk gounós /gōnós/ vs. PIE nom sg *gonu+s (ev) > Gk gónys.

Whenever j/w-MET produced vowel nuclei which did not otherwise occur in Greek, such nuclei are then usually realized as vowel sequences phonetically close to already existant ones. E.g., PIE 1sg pres *klinjō 'I lean' (j/w-MET, ev) > kliinɔ̄ (ev) > Gk klī́nɔ̄; likewise PIE 1sg pres *otrunjō 'encourage' (j/w-MET, ev) > *otruinɔ̄ (6d u(:)-TO-y(:)) > otryinɔ̄ (ev) > Gk otrȳ́nɔ̄. But without such restructuring, PIE nom sg *musja 'house fly' (j/w-MET) > *muisa (3e s-h-Ø) > Gk myîa /mýia/.

There are forms such as Gk sop^{h}íā 'wisdom', where for some reason j/w-MET does not apply to produce Gk **soíp^{h}ɛ̄. A possible derivation is PIE ? *twob^{h}jā (PIE 3.1.2f SIEVERS applying as a synchronic rule) → *twob^{h}ijā (2a ASPIR DEVOI, 2f GREEK STRESS) > *twop^{h}íjā (3a j-CHANGES, 4b t-TO-s, 7c w-DELE) > Gk sop^{h}íā.

3d The Change of Word-Final /m/ to /n/ (m-TO-n)

This change restructures various morphemes, primarily inflectional suffixes, and then is dropped from the grammar.

m → n / ___ ##

That is, word-final /m/ becomes /n/. E.g., PIE acc sg masc *tom *gomb^{h}om 'the, that bolt' (ev) > Gk tòn gómp^{h}on.

3e The Change of /s/ to /h/ and its Eventual Conditioned Disappearance (s-h-Ø)

The change consists of two chronologically ordered rules. After restructuring various lexical items, the rules for this change are dropped from the grammar.

(1) s → h / (a) ## ___ [+sonorant]

(b) {+sonorant, –nasal} ___ [+sonorant]

(2) h → Ø / (a) ## ___ [C, +sonorant] (? ≠ /r/)

(b) [+sonorant]$_1$ ___ [+sonorant]$_2$

(where if sonorant 1 = a vowel and sonorant 2 = a consonant, then segment 1 is lengthened).

That is, (1) /s/ becomes /h/ (a) word-initially if followed by any sonorant (i.e., a vowel or /l, m, n, r/) or (b) between two sonorants, the first of which cannot be /m/ or /n/ (see on this change 5b NASAL+s). (2) The resulting /h/ is deleted (a) word-initially if followed by a sonorant consonant /l, m, n/ — with the possible exception of /r/ (see on this 8a h-ADD). (b) The /h/ is also deleted between two sonorant segments (and if the first segment is a vowel, that vowel is lengthened).

E.g., PIE 1sg pres *seg^{h}ō 'get, have' (2a ASPIR DEVOI, ev) > *sek^{h}ɔ̄ (s-h-∅) > *hek^{h}ɔ̄ (7b GRASSMANN: note the necessary chronology s-h-∅ > 7b GRASSMANN) > Gk ék^{h}ɔ̄. PIE 1sg pres *srewō 'flow' (s-h-∅, ev) > *hrewɔ̄ (7c w-DELE) > Gk hréɔ̄. PIE 3sg pres *sneig^{hw}eti 'it snows' (2a ASPIR DEVOI) > *sneik^{hw}eti (s-h-∅) > *neik^{hw}eti (5a LABIOVEL, applying analogously after endings beginning with a back vowel) > *neip^{h}eti (7a ei/ou-TO-ē/ō) > *nēp^{h}eti (ev, see on this the morphology 6.1.1 below, note 167) > Gk neíp^{h}ei /nḗp^{h}ē/. PIE nom sg masc *sem+s 'one' as well as ablauting PIE nom sg fem *sm+ja 'one' (s-h-∅ 1) > *hems and *hmja (s-h-∅ 2) > *hems, *mja (5b NASAL+s, ev) > Gk heîs /hê̄s/ and mía. PIE 1sg pres *eusō 'singe' and *esmi 'I am' (ev) > Gk eúɔ̄ and eimí. PIE nom sg fem *kswelasnā 'moon' (s-h-∅ 2, ev) > Gk selɛ́̄nɛ̄.

Many Greek words beginning with /s/ are borrowings, e.g. Sábbaton 'Sabbath'. Some word-initial /s/'s are from other sources, e.g. PIE *twn̥jō 'fawn' (2b ē/ō-TO-ɛ̄/ɔ̄, 2d SYL SON) > *twanjɔ̄ (3c j/w-MET) > *twainɔ̄ (4b t-TO-s) > *swainɔ̄ (7c W-DELE) > Gk saínɔ̄. In some instances the rule appears not to apply. Sometimes this is the result of dialectal borrowing, e.g. hŷs and sŷs 'swine' < PIE *sūs. Sometimes the /s/ may be restored on the analogy of forms where s-h-∅ would not have applied, e.g. the future t^{h}ɛ́̄sɔ̄ 'I shall set' with the /s/ restored on the model of verbs like p^{h}yláksɔ̄ 'I shall guard'.

Note the necessary chronology 2b ē/ō-TO-ɛ̄/ɔ̄ > s-h-∅ in the following derivation: PIE 1sg pres *esmi 'I am' (s-h-∅) > Gk /ēmí/ <eimí>, to which 2b ē/ō-TO-ɛ̄/ɔ̄ > cannot apply to produce Gk **/ɛ̄mí/. The chronology s-h-∅ > t-TO-s is also necessary: PIE 3sg pres *b^{h}eronti 'carry' (ev) > *p^{h}eronti (4b t-TO-s) > *p^{h}eronsi (to which s-h-∅ cannot apply since it has already occurred, then 5b NASAL+s, which must apply after t-TO-s, ev) > Gk p^{h}érousi /p^{h}érōsi/.

4a Insertion of Word-Initial "Prothetic" Vowels (PROTHESIS)

This change restructures various lexical items and then is dropped from the grammar. The exact formulation of the rule is not clear.

optional ∅ → a, e or o / ##___ (r, l, m, n or w) V

That is, /a, e or o/ is inserted — perhaps for a time optionally — word-initially before /r, l, m, n or w/ followed by a vowel. Which of these three vowels is inserted seems to be unpredictable. A tendency is for /e/ to occur before /r/ or /l/ plus a back vowel and for /o/ to occur before /r/ or /l/ plus a front vowel.

E.g., PIE 1sg *melgō 'milk' (ev) > Gk amélgɔ̄, PIE nom sg *nār 'man' (ev) > Gk anɛ́̄r, PIE nom sg masc *rud^{h}ros 'red' (ev) > Gk eryt^{h}rós, PIE nom sg neuter *reg^{w}os 'darkness' (PROTHESIS) > *ereg^{w}os (5a LABIOVEL) > Gk érebos, PIE nom sg masc *ln̥g^{h}us 'small' (2a ASPIR DEVOI, 2d SYL SON) > *lak^{h}us (PROTHESIS, ev) > elak^{h}ýs, PIE *wikonti '20' (PROTHESIS) > *ewikonti (4b t-TO-s) > *ewikonsi (5b NASAL+s) > *ewikosi (7c w-DELE) > Gk eíkosi. PIE nom sg neuter *nomn̥t 'name' (2d SYL SON) > *nomat (2e WF STOP DELE) > *noma (PROTHESIS) > Gk ónoma. PROTHESIS does not apply in all instances, e.g. PIE 1sg pres *legō 'gather' (ev) > Gk légɔ̄, not **olégɔ̄ or the like.

In some sources a laryngeal is assumed instead of the application of PROTHESIS as in Sihler (1995: 42). Here the PIE antecedent of ónyks 'nail' is assumed to be *h̥$_3$nog^{hw}+s where /h̥$_3$/ is a laryngeal which results in /o/ by change la LARYNGEALS above.

Finally, note that in the derivation of eíkosi '20', PROTHESIS in our formulation must precede 7c w-DELE. Another chronology is indicated by the fact that PROTHESIS does not apply before original word-initial /j/. Since PROTHESIS does apply before all other sonorant consonants, this would seem to indicate that /j/ had already been deleted by 3b j-CHANGES by the time PROTHESIS applied.

4b The Change of /t/ to /s/ (t-TO-s)

This change restructures various morphemes and then is dropped as a rule from the grammar. The rule seems to admit of numerous exceptions.

$$\text{t} \rightarrow \text{s} \;/\; \begin{array}{l} \text{(a) [+segment](not /s/) \_\_\_ [V, +high]} \\ \text{(b) \#\# \_\_\_ w} \end{array}$$

That is, /t/ becomes /s/ (a) if word-internal and preceded by any segment except /s/ and if followed by a high vowel, namely /i(:), u(:)/. And (b) the same change occurs if the if the /t/ is word-initial and followed by /w/ (which is later deleted by 7c W-DELE). E.g.,

(a) PIE nom sg *g^{w}m̥tis 'a step' (2d SYL SON) > *g^{w}atis (t-TO-s) > *g^{w}asis (5a LABIOVEL) > Gk básis, PIE *tu 'you' (ev) > Gk sý, PIE 3pl pres *b^{h}eronti 'carry' (2a ASPIR DEVOI) > *p^{h}eronti (t-TO-s) > *p^{h}eronsi (5b NASAL+s) > Gk p^{h}érousi /p^{h}érōsi/. (Note here the necessary chronology t-TO-s > 5b NASAL+s.) PIE nom sg masc adj *n̥+mbrot+os 'immortal' vs. nom sg fem noun *n̥+mbrot+ijā 'ambrosia, drink of the immortals' (2d SYL SON, ev) > ambrotos and *ambrotijā (3b j-CHANGES) > *ambrotos and *ambrotiā (t-TO-s, ev) > Gk ámbrotos and ambrosíā.

(b) PIE nom sg *twakos 'sack' (t-TO-s) > *swakos (7c W-DELE) > Gk sákos. There are also some apparent exceptions to t-TO-s, e.g. PIE *anti 'against' (ev) > Gk antí, not **ɛ̄sí or the like.

Finally, note the necessary chronology 4b t-TO-s > 5a LABIOVEL: t-TO-s does not apply to those /t/'s derived from /k^w/ by 5a LABIOVEL. Hence PIE nom sg k^{w}is 'who?' (5a LABIOVEL) > Gk tís, not **sís.

5a Changes in the Labiovelar Obstruents (LABIOVEL)

This change restructures various lexical items and then is dropped as a rule from the grammar. Although some of the data illustrating this change are contradictory, probably because of interdialectal borrowings, the basic form of the rule for Attic Greek is this:

$$\left\{\begin{array}{c} k^w \\ k^{hw} \\ g^w \end{array}\right\} \rightarrow \begin{array}{l} \text{(a)} \left\{\begin{array}{c} t \\ t^h \\ d \end{array}\right\} \;/\; \_\_\_ \;\text{[V, –back] (= e(:), i(:))} \\[2ex] \text{(b)} \left\{\begin{array}{c} p \\ p^h \\ b \end{array}\right\} \;/\; \_\_\_ \left\{\begin{array}{l} \text{[V, +back, –high] (= a(:), o(:))} \\ \text{[C, +nasal]} \end{array}\right. \\[2ex] \text{(c)} \left\{\begin{array}{c} k \\ k^h \\ g \end{array}\right\} \;/\; \_\_\_ \left\{\begin{array}{l} \text{[V, +back, +high] (= u(:))} \\ \text{[C, –nasal]} \end{array}\right. \end{array}$$

That is, the changes described occur (a) before front vowels, (b) before nonhigh back vowels and possibly before the nasal consonants /m, n/ and (c) before /u(:)/ and possibly before any nonnasal consonant. (Given our formulation of LABIOVEL, we assume it applied after 2a ASPIR DEVOI and before 6d u(:)-TO-y(:).) E.g.,

(a) PIE *k^{w}is 'who?' (ev) > Gk tís, PIE *g^{hw}ermos 'warm' (2a ASPIR DEVOI) > *k^{hw}ermos (LABIOVEL) > Gk t^{h}ermós, PIE *g^{w}elb^{h}us 'womb' (ev) > Gk delp^{h}ýs, PIE *penk^{w}e '5' (ev) > Gk pénte.

(b) PIE 1sg pres *sek^{w}omai 'I follow' (3e s-h-Ø) > *hek^{w}omai (LABIOVEL) > Gk hépomai, PIE nom sg *g^{hw}onos 'a slaying' (ev) > Gk p^{h}ónos vs. the ablauting verbal form PIE 1sg pres *g^{hw}enjō 'I slay' (2a ASPIR DEVOI, 2b ē/ō-TO-ɛ̄/ɔ̄, 3c j/w-MET) > *k^{hw}einɔ̄ (LABIOVEL) > Gk t^{h}eínɔ̄. PIE 1sg *g^{w}m̥jō 'go' (2d SYL SON) > *g^{w}amjō (2b ē/ō-TO-ɛ̄/ɔ̄, 3a C+j CHANGES, 3c j/w-MET) > *g^{w}ainɔ̄ (LABIOVEL) > Gk baínɔ̄. PIE *k^{w}ou 'where' (ev) > Gk poû /póo/. PIE nom sg *g^{w}ōu+s 'ox' (ev) > Gk boûs, PIE *ag^{w}nos 'lamb' (LABIOVEL) > *abnos (6b C-Cl CHANGES) > Gk ámnos. PIE nom sg neuter *ok^{w}mn̥t 'eye' (2d SYL SON) > *ok^{w}mat (2e WF-DELE) > *ok^{w}ma (LABIOVEL) > *opma (6b C-Cl CHANGES) > Gk ómma.

(c) PIE nom sg *l̥ng^{hw}us 'small' (2a ASPIR DEVOI) > *l̥nk^{hw}us (2d SYL SON) > *lak^{hw}us (4a PROTHESIS) > elak^{hw}us (LABIOVEL) > *elak^{h}us (6d u(:)-TO-y(:)) > Gk elak^{h}ýs, PIE nom sg *k^{w}uk^{w}los 'wheel' (ev) > Gk kýklos. A possible derivation is PIE nom sg nok^{w}t+s 'night' (2c o-TO-u) >*nuk^{w}ts (LABIOVEL) > *nukts (6b C-Cl CHANGES) > *nuks (6d u(:)-TO-y(:)) > Gk nýks.

There are forms for which our version of LABIOVEL does not account. These may be instances of dialect borrowing. E.g., PIE nom sg *wlok^{w}os 'wolf' and *g^{w}iwos 'life' (ev) > Gk lýkos and bíos, not **lýpos or **díos. Also PIE 3sg pres *sneig^{h}eti 'it snows' (ev) > Gk neíp^{h}ei, not **neít^{h}ei. (This form may have been influenced by the acc sg of the noun PIE *snig^{hw}m̥ 'snow' (2a ASPIR DEVOI) > *snik^{hw}m̥ (2d SYL SON) > *snik^{hw}a (LABIOVEL) > *snip^{h}a (6b C-Cl CHANGES) > Gk níp^{h}a.)

A similar problem is in the derivation of Gk híppos 'horse' from PIE *ek^{w}os. The expected derivation would be *ek^{w}os (LABIOVEL) > Gk **épos. Given our rules, the Greek form híppos would go back to something like PIE *sippos or *wippos.

Given our formulation of LABIOVEL we assume it follows 2d SYL SON: PIE nom sg masc *g^{w}r̥us 'heavy' (2d SYL SON) > *g^{w}arus (LABIOVEL, ev) > Gk barýs. LABIOVEL must also precede 6a ā-TO-ɛ̄: PIE nom sg fem *song^{hw}ā 'song, voice, oracle' (2a ASPIR DEVOI) > *sonk^{hw}ā (3e s-h-Ø) > honk^{hw}ā (5a LABIOVEL and concomitantly PIE 3.1.2d Nasal Assim, still functioning as a persistent synchronic rule) > *homp^{h}ā (6a ā-TO-ɛ̄) > *homp^{h}ɛ̄ (7b GRASSMANN) > Gk omp^{h}ɛ̄́. Note that in this derivation if the sequence had been 6a ā-TO-ɛ̄ > LABIOVEL, the Greek form would have been **ont^{h}ɛ̄́.

5b Changes in the Sequence Nasal Consonant Plus /s/ (NASAL+s)

These changes for the most part restructured various lexical items and inflectional endings and then dropped from the grammar. In a few paradigms described below, change 2 remains as a morph cond rule. There are two chronologically ordered changes:

(1) Vns → (a) V̄s / ___ ##
(b) Vs / ___ C
(c) V̄n / ___ V

(2) Vns → V̄s / ___ { ## , [+sonorant] }

That is, first (1) the sequence Vns becomes (a) V̄s word finally, (b) Vs if a consonant follows and (c) V̄n if a vowel follows. Second (2) the sequence Vns becomes V̄s if word-final or if followed by a sonorant segment.

E.g., (la) PIE acc pl masc *tons 'those, the' (NASAL+s) > Gk toús /tɔ̄́s/. (lb) PIE nom sg fem *ksun+statis 'composition' (4b t-TO-s) > *ksunstasis (NASAL+s) > *ksustasis (6b C-Cl CHANGES) > *sustasis (6d u(:)-TO-y(:)) >Gk sýstasis. (lc) PIE 1sg aorist *e+b^{h}an+sa 'appeared' (2a ASPIR DEVOI) > *ep^{h}ansa (NASAL+s) > *ep^{h}āna (6a ā-TO-ɛ̄) > Gk ép^{h}ɛ̄na. (Note the necessary chronology 5b

NASAL+s 1 > 6a ā-TO-ɛ̄.)

(2) PIE nom sg masc *pant+s 'all' (6b C-Cl CHANGES) > *pans (NASAL+s 2 applying later) > Gk pâ̄s. Also PIE nom sg fem *pantja 'all' (3a C+j CHANGES) > *pansa (NASAL+s 2) > Gk pâ̄sa. (Note that 6a ā-TO-ɛ̄ does not apply here; hence the chronology 6a ā-TO-ɛ̄ > NASAL+s 2.) Also PIE acc pl fem *bʰugans 'flights' (2a ASPIR DEVOI) > *pʰugans (NASAL+s 2, ev) > Gk pʰygā́s to which 6a ā-TO-ɛ̄ does not apply.

Note also the following additional chronological observations. First, as seen above, change 6a ā-TO-ɛ̄ applies to part 1 of NASAL+s but not to part 2. This indicates a chronology 5b NASAL+s 1 > 6a ā-TO-ɛ̄ > 5b NASAL+s 2. Second, the derivation of Greek toús above indicates the chronology 2b ē/ō-TO-ɛ̄/ɔ̄ > NASAL-s. Otherwise one would expect Gk acc pl masc **tɔ̄́s instead of toús /toós/. Note also that much of NASAL+s 2 may well represent an expansion of a persistent rule, namely NASAL-s 1, which remained in the grammar.

Finally, NASAL+s 2 remains in a restructured form as a morph cond rule to apply to various Vnt-class noun and adj paradigms (see sections 1.5.5 and 2.3.5 in the morphology). E.g., nom sg masc pâ̄s 'all' < *pants vs. gen sg masc pantós < *pant+os.

5c Vowel Contraction (V-CONTRACT)

This rule remains in the grammar as a morph cond rule. The change is optional on occasion; and it varies dialectally. Here in basic outline is the Attic version:

V(V)	+	V(V)(V)	→	VV(V)
1	2	3		4

That is, a sequence consisting of (1) a short vowel, a long vowel or a diphthong plus (2) a word-internal morpheme boundary plus (3) a short vowel, a long vowel, a diphthong or a long diphthong becomes a long vowel, a diphthong or a long diphthong. Various sequences of vowel nuclei are realized differently. Below we outline the conditions in the order of their precedence:

(la) If V1 = any vowel and V3 = /i/ or /u/, then V4 = the same diphthong /Vi/ or /Vu/.

(1b) If V1 = V3, then V4 = the same long vowel.

(2) If either V1 or V3 = /o, ɔ̄, ō/, then V4 = /ɔ̄, ō/.

(3a) If V1 = /a(:)/ and V3 ≠ /o, ɔ̄, ō/, then V4 = /ā/.

(3b) If V1 = /e, ɛ̄/ or /ā/ and V3 ≠ /o, ɔ̄, ō/, then V4 = /ā/ or /ɛ̄/.

E.g., (la) earlier dat sg kéraï 'horn' (where the dieresis indicates two separate syllables) (V-CONTRACT) > > later kérai, earlier eü 'well' (V-CONTRACT) > later eû. (1b) Earlier nom sg lâ̄as /láaas/ 'stone' (V-CONTRACT) > later lâ̄s /láas/, earlier 2pl pres subjunctive pʰanɛ̄́ɛ̄te 'show' (V-CONTRACT) > later pʰanɛ̂̄te /pʰanɛ́ɛte/, earlier adj kʰíios 'of the island of Chios' (V-CONTRACT) > kʰî̄os /kʰíios/.

(2) Earlier 1pl pres in tīmáomen 'honor' (V-CONTRACT) > tīmɔ̂̄men /tīmɔ́ɔmen/, earlier 1sg pres opt tīmaoíɛ̄n 'honor' (V-CONTRACT) > tīmɔ̄íɛ̄n, earlier 2pl pres opt. pʰiléoite 'love' (V-CONTRACT) > later pʰiloîte, earlier 3sg imperfect edɛ̄́loe 'made manifest' (V-CONTRACT) > edɛ̄́lou /edɛ̄́lō/ (3a) Earlier 2pl pres subjunctive tīmáɛ̄te 'honor' (V-CONTRACT) > tīmâ̄te. (3b) Earlier gen sg masc of the pres act part. tīmɛ̄́entos 'honoring' (V-CONTRACT) > tīmɛ̂̄ntos, earlier 2sg pres act indicative tīmɛ̄́eis /tīmɛ̄́ēs/ (V-CONTRACT) > later tīmɛ̂̄s /tīmɛ́ɛs/. Also earlier nom sg fem adj hapléa 'simple' (V-CONTRACT, ev) > haplɛ̂̄.

Note the chronology 3b j-CHANGES > V-CONTRACT > 7c w-DELE: V-CONTRACT can apply to the output of 3b j-CHANGES but not to that of 7c w-DELE. E.g., PIE 1sg pres *dejō 'I bind' vs. *dewō 'I lack'

(3b j-CHANGES, ev) > *deɔ̄ vs.*dewɔ̄ (V-CONTRACT) > *dɔ̄ vs. *dewɔ̄ (7c w-DELE, ev) > dɔ̄̂ vs. déɔ̄. Note also the chronologies 2d SYL SON > V-CONTRACT and 3e s-h-Ø > V-CONTRACT: PIE gen sg *ousn̥tos 'ear' (2d SYL SON) > *ousatos (3e s-h-Ø) > *ouatos (V-CONTRACT) > ɔ̄tós.

6a The Change of /ā/ to /ɛ̄/ (ā-TO-ɛ̄)

This change restructures various lexical items and endings and then is dropped from the grammar. The change occurs in Attic and Ionic, but not in Doric. The change is as follows:

ā → ɛ̄ / everywhere except: e(:), i(:), r ___

That is, the change of /ā/ to /ɛ̄/ occurs everywhere except if /ā/ is preceded by /e(:)/, /i(:)/ or /r/. It is possible that the change occurred in two chronological stages:

(1) ā → ɛ̄

(2) ɛ̄ → ā / e(:), i(:), r ___

E.g., PIE *mātēr 'mother' (2b ē/ō-TO-ɛ̄/ɔ̄) > *mātɛ̄r (ā-TO-ɛ̄) > Attic mɛ̄́tɛ̄r vs. Doric mā́tɛ̄r. But ā-TO-ɛ̄ does not apply in forms like PIE nom sg fem *geneā 'race', *kr̥diā 'heart', *g^hōrā 'place' (ev) > Gk geneā́, kardíā, k^hɔ̄́rā (not **geneɛ̄́, **kardíɛ̄ or **k^hɔ̄́rɛ̄). Another possible constraint on the change may be that it did not apply to /ā/ in the diphthong /āu/. Hence PIE *nāus 'ship' (ev) > Gk naûs /náus/. Another possibility is that 6c DIPH SHORT preceded ā-TO-ɛ̄: PIE *nāus (6c DIPH SHORT) > Gk naûs, to which ā-TO-ɛ̄ cannot apply.

According to Atkinson (1952: 28), the ā-TO-ɛ̄ change occurred sometime before the 300's BC. It was at about this time that Attic became the dominant Greek dialect. Sihler (1995: 51) says, ". . . it is clear that *ā did not merge with *ē [our /ɛ̄/] in Attic until the end of the 5th century BC." Hence we assume the ā-TO-ɛ̄ change occurred sometime between 400 and 300 BC.

Note the following chronology: PIE nom sg *korwā 'maiden' (ā-TO-ɛ̄) > *korwɛ̄ (7c w-DELE) > Gk korɛ̄́. If the order had been 7c w-DELE > ā-TO-ɛ̄, then the Greek form would be **korā́ since /ā/ is retained after a preceding /r/.

6b Changes in Consonant Clusters (C-Cl CHANGES)

We give here only the principal changes. Some of them remain as phon cond or morph cond rules in the grammar. Others restructure various lexical items and then are dropped from the grammar. We cite the changes in two chronological stages.

(1) The following rule is inherited from PIE and remains as a phon cond rule of Greek.

[C, +obstruent] → [αvoiced] / ___ [C, +obstruent, αvoiced]

That is, obstruent clusters are either voiced or voiceless contingent upon the final obstruent.

(2) The following are Greek innovations or Greek modifications of early PIE rules. We list first those that remain as phon cond rules in the grammar — namely (a) through (e). Then those changes follow which restructure various forms and then are dropped as rules from the grammar. These are changes (f) through (i).

(a) [C, +obstruent] → [αaspirated] / — [C, +obstruent, αaspirated]

That is, obstruent consonant clusters are either aspirated or plain depending on the final consonant.

(b) tt$^{(h)}$ → st$^{(h)}$

The sequences /tt/ or /tt^{h}/ become /st/ and /st^{h}/, respectively.

(c) ts → ss (ev) → s

(d) ksk → sk

(e) b, p$^{(h)}$ + $\begin{bmatrix} \text{m} \\ \text{n} \end{bmatrix}$ → m $\begin{bmatrix} \text{m} \\ \text{n} \end{bmatrix}$

g, k$^{(h)}$ + m → ŋ m

(f) sn → n / ## __

(g) optional ks → s / ## __

(h) $\begin{bmatrix} \text{m} \\ \text{n} \end{bmatrix}$ + r → $\begin{bmatrix} \text{mbr} \\ \text{ndr} \end{bmatrix}$ (ev) → $\begin{bmatrix} \text{br} \\ \text{dr} \end{bmatrix}$ / ## __

m + l → mbl → bl

(i) d, n + l → ll

As our examples we cite both synchronic and diachronic derivations. E.g., (1) 1sg pres trīb+ō 'rub' vs. 3sg perf mid tetrib+tai (C-Cl CHANGES 1) → trī́bō and tétriptai, 1sg pres *krup+jō 'hide' (ev) > krýptō vs. adv *krup+dēn (C-Cl CHANGES 1, ev) > krýbdēn 'secretly'. 1sg pres légō 'gather' vs. 3sg perf mid *leleg+tai (C-Cl CHANGES 1) > lélektai. 1 sg pres plékō 'weave' vs. adverb plek+dēn 'confusedly' (C-Cl CHANGES 1) → plégdēn. Finally the construction noun + suffix At^{h}ēnas+de 'to Athens' (C-Cl CHANGES 1) → /at^{h}ḗnazde/, spelled <At^{h}ḗnaze>. (Note that the grapheme <z> usually stands for /dz/.)

Examples of (2) are these: (a) 1sg pres pémpō 'lead' vs. 1sg aorist pass pemp+t^{h}ēn (C-Cl CHANGES 2a) → pémp^{h}t^{h}ēn, 1sg pres gráp^{h}ō 'write' vs. 3sg perf mid gegrap^{h}+tai (C-Cl CHANGES 2a) → gégraptai, 1sg pres plékō 'weave' vs. 1sg aorist pass eplek+t^{h}ēn (C-Cl CHANGES 2a) → eplék^{h}t^{h}ēn. Finally, note that for the purposes of this rule, /s/ must be considered –aspirated. Hence 1sg pres grap^{h}ō 'write' vs. 1sg future grap^{h}+s+ō (C-Cl CHANGES 2a) → grápsō. Also nom sg *t^{h}rik^{h}+s 'hair' (C-Cl CHANGES 2a) > Gk t^{h}ríks. Contrast the gen sg *t^{h}rik^{h}+os (to which C-Cl CHANGES 2a cannot apply, but the later rule 7b GRASSMANN does) > trik^{h}ós.

(b) 1sg pres anýtō 'accomplish' vs. the adj anyt+tos 'accomplishable' (C-Cl CHANGES 2b) → anystós. Also the 1sg aorist pass anyt+t^{h}ēn (C-Cl CHANGES 2b) → anýst^{h}ēn.

(c) Dat pl of pres part *b^{h}eront+si 'carrying' (2a ASPIR DEVOI) > *p^{h}erontsi (C-Cl CHANGES 2c) > p^{h}eronsi (5b NASAL+s: later rule 2) > p^{h}érousi /p^{h}érōsi/. Nom sg t^{h}emist+s 'law' vs. gen sg t^{h}emist+os (C-Cl CHANGES 2b) → t^{h}émis vs. t^{h}émistos.

(d) 1sg pres *di+dak+sk+ō 'I teach' (C-Cl CHANGES 2d, ev) > didáskō. (e) 1sg pres gráp^{h}ō 'write' vs. 1sg perf mid ge+grap^{h}+mai (C-Cl CHANGES 2e) → gégrammai. Note the necessary chronology 5a LABIOVEL > C-Cl CHANGES 2e in the following: PIE nom sg neuter *ok^{w}+mn̥t 'eye' and masc *ag^{hw}+nos 'lamb' (ev through 5a LABIOVEL) > *opma and *ap^{h}nos (C-Cl CHANGES 2e) > ómma and ámnos. Also 1sg pres plékɔ̄ 'weave' vs. 1sg perf mid pe+plek+mai (C-Cl CHANGES 2e, ev) → péplegmai /pépleŋmai/. This part of C-Cl CHANGES 2e seems to have become morph cond in that it often applies in verb paradigms, but less often elsewhere — e.g., the Greek noun akmɛ̄́ 'point, apex' not **agmɛ̄́ **/aŋmɛ̄́/.

(f) PIE acc sg *snig^{hw}m̥ 'snow' (ev) > Gk níp^{h}a. (g) PIE *ksun 'with' (ev) > Gk sýn as well as ksýn. (h) PIE nom sg masc *n̥+mrotos 'not dying, immortal' (2d SYL SON) > *amrotos (C-Cl CHANGES 2h) > Gk ámbrotos vs. the non-negative form of the same adj PIE *mrotos 'mortal' (ev) > Gk brótos. Also nom sg anɛ̄́r 'man' vs. ablauting gen sg anr+os (C-Cl CHANGES 2h, apparently applying here as a synchronic rule) → andrós. (i) PIE nom sg fem sed+lā 'seat' (ev) > Doric Gk héllā, PIE nom sg masc *ksun+log+os 'assembly'(ev) > sýllogos.

6c Shortening of Certain Long Diphthongs (DIPH SHORT)

These changes restructure various lexical items and then are dropped from the grammar. The PIE long diphthongs are shortened according to the following rules:

(a) V̄u → Vu / everywhere

(b) V̄i → Vi / ___ [+segment]

That is, (a) all long diphthongs ending in /u/ are shortened and (b) word-internal (as opposed to word-final) diphthongs ending in /i/ are shortened.

E.g., (a) PIE nom sg *nāus 'ship' (ev) > naûs, *g^{w}ōus 'ox' (ev) > boûs, *djēus 'Zeus' (ev) > Zeús /dzeús/. (b) PIE nom sg *āi+ōn 'lifetime' (ev) > aíɔ̄n. (Note that 6a ā-TO-ɛ̄ has not applied in this derivation, either because the chronology was 6c DIPH SHORT > 6a ā-TO-ɛ̄ or because 6a ā-TO-ɛ̄ did not apply to the diphthong /āi/.) PIE 1sg aorist e+lēib+s+a 'I poured' (6b C-Cl CHANGES) > *elēipsa (DIPH SHORT) >*eleipsa (7a ei/ou-TO-ē/ō) > Gk éleipsa /élēpsa/. However, DIPH SHORT does not apply to the word-final /V̄i/ diphthongs: e.g., PIE dat sg o-class *ek^{w}ōi 'horse', ā-class *g^{h}ōrāi 'place', *k^{w}īmāi 'honor' (ev) > Gk híppɔ̄i, k^{h}ɔ̄́rāi and tī́mɛ̄i. (Note that 6a ā-TO-ɛ̄ has applied in the derivation of tī́mɛ̄i.) These long diphthongs in /i/ are written in the Greek alphabet with so-called "iota subscripts": <ᾳ> = /āi/, <ῃ> = /ēi/ and <ῳ> = /ɔ̄i/.

A possible derivation which entails a chronology somewhat different from the one posited here is the following: PIE nom sg *klāw+id+s 'key' (6a ā-TO-ɛ̄) > *klɛ̄wids (6b C-Cl CHANGES) > *klɛ̄wis (7c w-DELE) > *klɛ̄is (6c DIPH SHORT, perhaps applying for a time as a persistent synchronic rule) > *kleis (7a ei/ou-TO-ē/ō) > Gk kleís /klēs/.

Sturtevant (1940: 56-58) notes that Attic inscriptions of the early fourth century BC have <ει> = /ei/ optionally alongside <ηι> = /ɛ̄i/. This seems to indicate that DIPH SHORT occurred during the later 300's BC.

Finally, we note that after the occurrence of DIPH SHORT, principally as the result of reduplicating or lengthening of word-initial vowels in aorist forms (see on this 6.5 in the morphology below), new long diphthongs do arise after the time of DIPH SHORT: e.g., 1sg pres aitéɔ̄ 'ask' vs. 1sg aorist *āitē+s+a (6a ā-TO-ɛ̄) > ɛ̄ítɛ̄sa; 1sg pres oikéɔ̄ 'inhabit' vs. 1sg aorist *ɔ̄ikē+s+a (2b ē/ō-TO-ɛ̄/ɔ̄) > Gk ɔ̄íkɛ̄sa; and 1sg pres auksánɔ̄ 'increase' vs. 1sg aorist *āuksē+s+a (2b ē/ō-TO-ɛ̄/ɔ̄) > Gk ɛ̄úksɛ̄sa.

6d The Change of /u(:)-to-y(:)/ (u(:)-TO-y(:))

This change restructures the phonemic inventory of the language and then is dropped from the grammar. It is as follows:

u(:) → y(:) / C or ##___

That is, the +back /u(:)/ becomes –back /y(:)/ everywhere except if occurring after a +vocalic segment, namely if occurring in a diphthong such as /au, eu, ou/.

E.g., PIE nom sg neuter jugom 'yoke' (3b J-CHANGES) > *dzugom (3d m-TO-n) > *dzugon (u(:)-TO-y(:)) > Gk zygón /dzygón/. PIE nom sg masc *dʰūmos 'spirit' (2a ASPIR DEVOI) > *tʰūmos (u(:)-TO-y(:)) > Gk tʰȳmós. Also PIE *upo 'below' (u(:)-TO-y(:)) > *ypo (8a h-ADD) > Gk hypó, PIE nom sg *sūs 'pig' (3e s-h-Ø) > *ūs (u(:)-TO-y(:)) > *ȳs (8a h-ADD) > Gk hȳ̂s. But u(:)-TO-y(:) does not apply to PIE 1sg pres *auksō 'I increase', nom sg masc *eurus 'broad' and nom sg fem *spoudā 'speed' (ev) > Gk aúksɔ̄ (not **aýksɔ̄), eurýs (not **eyrýs) and spoudɛ̄́ /spōdɛ̄́/ (not **spoydɛ̄́).

According to Atkinson (1952: 29) the u(:)-TO-y(:) change occurred sometime during the 400's BC. Further, on the basis of the following observations in Sturtevant (1940: 53, 54 and 56 respectively), we assume that the /u/ if preceded by a vowel remained and did not undergo u(:)-TO-y(:). First, (p. 53) "In various dialects the final member of a diphthong is occasionally written with F [i.e., <w>] ...as in 'αFtós [/autós/ 'he']..." We assume the graphemic <w> here does not represent /y/, since <w> is not used in other environments for that purpose. Second, (p. 54) "While the Romans borrowed Gk υ [<y>] for use in loan-words, they were nevertheless content to write *au* and *eu* for αυ and ευ." Hence Gk /au/ and /eu/ were not **/ay/ or **/ey/. Finally in this connection, (p. 56) "The use of *yi* in Latin to represent [Greek <υι>] (e.g. *Ilithyia*) shows that in Hellenistic as in Ionic and early Attic the prior element of [graphemic <υι>] was the front rounded vowel [y]." Hence /u/ if not preceded by a vowel underwent u(:)-TO-y(:).

7a The Change of /ei, ou/ to /ē, ō/ (ei/ou-TO-ē/ō)

This change restructures the phonemic inventory of the language and then is dropped from the grammar. The rules is this:

ei, ou → ē, ō (and later) → ī, ū

That is, the diphthongs /ei/ and /ou/ became (probably during the 400's BC) /ē/ and /ō/. These in turn later (probably around 200 BC) become /ī/ and /ū/. (Sturtevant 1940: 46 estimates the change of /ō/ to /ū/ as early as around 350 BC.)

E.g., PIE nom sg *gʰeimōn 'winter' (2a ASPIR DEVOI, 2b ē/ō-TO-ɛ̄/ɔ̄) > *kʰeimɔ̄n (ei/ou-TO-ē/ō) > Gk /kʰēmɔ̄́n/, spelled <kʰeimɔ̄́n>. Also PIE nom sg *spoudā 'speed' (ev) > Gk /spōdɛ̄́/, spelled <spoudɛ̄́>. Later the forms are /kʰīmɔ̄́n/ and /spūdɛ̄́/.

The phonemes /ē/ and /ō/ from other sources are also written <ei> and <ou> and are sometimes called "spurious diphthongs" in the literature. E.g., PIE nom pl *trejes '3' (3b j-CHANGES) > Gk /trées/ = /trē̂s/ <treîs>. PIE 1sg pres *esmi 'I am' (3e s-h-Ø) > Gk eimí /ēmí/; PIE gen sg *andʰrōposjo 'man' as well as acc pl *andʰrōpons (2a ASPIR DEVOI, 2b ē/ō-TO-ɛ̄/ɔ̄, 3e s-h-Ø) > *antʰrɔ̄pojo, *antʰrɔ̄pons (3b j-CHANGES, 5b NASAL+s) > Gk antʰrɔ̄́pou /antʰrɔ̄́pō/ and antʰrɔ̄́pous /antʰrɔ̄́pōs/.

Note the necessary chronology 2b ē/ō-TO-ɛ̄/ɔ̄ > ei/ou-TO-ē/ō. Otherwise all the forms above with /ē, ō/ would have /ɛ̄, ɔ̄/, e.g. Gk **<kʰɛ̄mɔ̄́n> 'winter' instead of <kʰeimɔ̄́n> /kʰēmɔ̄́n /.

7b grassmann's law (GRASSMANN)

This change remains in the grammar as a phon cond rule. It is as follows:

[C, –sonorant, +aspirated] → [–aspirated]

/ ___ [+sonorant]$_1$ [C, +obstruent, +aspirated, –continuant]

That is, the aspirated voiceless obstruents /p^h, t^h, k^h, h/ become unaspirated /p, t, k/ and /h/ disappears. This occurs if the /p^h, t^h, k^h or h/ precedes a sequence consisting of one or more sonorants (namely a vowel, diphthong or vowel plus /l, m, n or r/) and some other aspirated stop.

E.g., PIE 1sg pres *b^heid^{h}ō 'persuade' and *d^hub^{h}ō 'smoke' (2a ASPIR DEVOI, 2b ē/ō-TO-ɛ̄/ɔ̄) > *p^heit^{h}ɔ̄,*t^hup^{h}ɔ̄ (GRASSMANN, which must apply after 2a ASPIR DEVOI) > *peit^{h}ɔ̄,*tup^{h}ɔ̄ (6d u(:)-TO-y(:), 7a ei/ou-TO-ē/ō) > Gk peít^{h}ɔ̄ and týp^{h}ɔ̄. PIE nom sg *sm̥+log^h+os 'same-bed person, i.e. spouse' (2a ASPIR DEVOI, 2d SYL SON) > *salok^{h}os (3e s-h-Ø) > *halok^{h}os (GRASSMANN applying over the sonorant sequence /alo/) > Gk álok^{h}os. (Note the necessary chronology 3e s-h-Ø > GRASSMANN.) The same prefix occurs in the PIE nom sg masc *sm̥+pl+os 'one-fold, simple' (ev) > Gk háplos, to which GRASSMANN has not applied. Finally, in the formulation of GRASSMANN the specification -continuant prevents the rule from being triggered by the (presumably) +aspirated /s/ in a Greek form like hístɛ̄mi 'stand' from PIE 1sg pres *sistēmi, not Gk **ístɛ̄mi.

GRASSMANN remains in the grammar as a phon cond rule and applies in such paradigms as Gk nom sg t^hríks 'hair', gen sg trik^{h}ós. The derivation is PIE nom sg *d^hríg^h+s vs. gen sg *d^hrig^h+ós (PIE antecedent of 6b C-Cl applying as a synchronic rule) → *d^hríks and *d^hrig^{h}ós (2a ASPIR DEVOI) > *t^hríks, *t^hrik^{h}ós (GRASSMANN) > Gk t^hríks, trik^{h}ós.

7c Deletion of /w/ (w-DELE)

This change restructures various lexical items as well as the phonemic inventory of the language. Then the change is dropped as a rule from the grammar. Buck (1962: 136) posits this change in the following chronology:

(1) w → Ø / ___C or C___

(2) w → Ø / V___V

(3) w → h or Ø (under unclear conditions) / ##___V

That is, (1) /w/ is deleted word-internally before or after a consonant, then (2) word-internally between vowels and (3) finally, /w/ becomes /h/ or is deleted word-initially before a following vowel.

E.g., (1) PIE nom sg fem *kswelasnā 'moon' (3e s-h-Ø) > *kswelānā (6a ā-TO-ɛ̄) > kswelɛ̄nɛ̄ (6b C+Cl CHANGES) > *swelɛ̄nɛ̄ (w-DELE) > Gk selɛ̄́nɛ̄; PIE nom sg masc *monwos 'single, alone' (w-DELE) > Gk mónos. (2) PIE nom sg masc adj *newos 'new' and nom sg neuter noun *klewos 'glory' (w-DELE) > Gk néos and kléos. (3) PIE nom sg masc *wid+tōr 'one who knows' (2b ē/ō-TO-ɛ̄/ɔ̄, 6b C-Cl CHANGES) >*wistɔ̄r (w-Deletion) > Gk hístɔ̄r. However, note the derivation of the same root in the PIE inf wid+esen 'see' (3e s-h-Ø) > *wideen = *widēn (w-DELE) > Gk ídein, not **hidein. Also PIE nom sg fem *wesperā 'evening' and nom sg neuter *wek^{w}os 'word' (ev) > Gk hespérā (not **espérā), but épos (not **hépos).

An argument can be made that a reflex of this change is still present as a morph cond rule in the grammar in view of alternations like Gk hier+eú+s 'priest' vs. hiér+ei+a 'priestess' < earlier *hier+ew+ia.

According to Atkinson (1952: 34) w-DELE occurred "early" in Attic Greek, while in other Greek dialects the /w/ remained until the 300's BC. We therefore assume that w-DELE occurred in Attic Greek before the 300's BC. Finally, we assume that the alternation of word-initial /h/ vs. its absence in other forms is attributable to dialect mixture.

8a Addition of /h/ Word-Initially (h-ADD)

This change restructures various lexical items and then is dropped as a rule from the grammar.

Ø → h / ##___ r or y(:)

That is, /h/ is inserted word-initially before /r/ or /y(:)/.

E.g., PIE nom sg *rapus 'turnip' (ev) > Gk hrápys, PIE 1sg pres *regjō 'perform' (2b ē/ō-TO-ɛ̄/ɔ̄, 3a C+j CHANGES) > *redzɔ̄ (h-ADD) > Gk hrézɔ̄. The ## in the environmental statement includes the boundary between a prefix and a verb: PIE *apo##regjō 'offer' (ev) > Gk /apo##hrédzɔ̄/, spelled <aporrézɔ̄>. Also PIE nom sg *udōr 'water' (2b ē/ō-TO-ɛ̄/ɔ̄, 6d u(:)-TO-y(:)) > *ydɔ̄r (h-ADD) > Gk hýdɔ̄r, PIE *uper (possibly *super) 'above' (ev) > Gk hypér.

h-ADD may have been triggered by 3e s-h-Ø and by 7c w-DELE. Both of these changes could leave /h/ before word-initial /r/ or /y(:)/. E.g., PIE 1sg pres *sreō 'flow' (2b ē/ō-TO-ɛ̄/ɔ̄, 3e s-h-Ø) > Gk hréɔ̄. PIE 1sg pres *wr̥pidjō 'strike' (2b ē/ō-TO-ɛ̄/ɔ̄, 2d SYL SON) > *wrapidjɔ̄ (3a C+j CHANGES) > *wrapizɔ̄ (possibly 7c w-DELE) > Gk hrapízɔ̄. Also PIE nom sg *sūs 'pig' (3e s-h-Ø, 6d u(:)-TO-y(:)) > Gk hȳ̂s. If h-ADD was in fact triggered by 3e s-h-Ø and 7c w-DELE, this would indicate the relative chronology 3e s-h-Ø and 7c w-DELE > h-ADD.

8b Vowel Shortening and "Quantitative Metathesis" (V-SHORT/Q-MET)

Both these changes remain as phon cond rules of Greek grammar. Neither of them applies obligatorily: on occasion a form may choose between the one or the other of them.

(a) VOWEL SHORTENING

V̄ → V / ___ + V(:)

That is, a long vowel is shortened if followed by a word-internal morpheme boundary (+) and another vowel, short or long.

(b) QUANTITATIVE METATHESIS

[V, +long]	+	[V, –long]	→	[V, –long]	+	[V, +long]
1		2		1		2

That is, a long vowel (1) followed by a word-internal morpheme boundary (+) followed in turn by a short vowel (2) becomes (1) a short vowel followed by (2) the corresponding long vowel. (Both rules apply most frequently to an e(:)-o(:) sequence, i.e. (a) to /ɛ̄/ + /o(:), ɔ̄/ and (b) to /ɛ̄/ + /o/.)

As our first examples we cite synchronic derivations. (a) Gen pl basilɛ̄́+ɔ̄n 'king' (V-SHORT, ev) → basiléɔ̄n; (b) Gen sg nɛ̄+ós 'ship' (Q-MET, ev) → neɔ̄́s. (The stress on this word remains acute, /neɔɔ́s/, as it was on the short vowel and not circumflex, **neɔ̄̂s **/neɔ́ɔs/, as one would expect. We take this to indicate the relative chronology 2f GREEK STRESS > V-SHORT/Q-MET.)

Examples of "choosing" between (a) V-SHORT and (b) Q-MET are the following historical derivations. PIE gen sg masc u-class adj *swādēwos 'sweet' vs. gen sg masc u-class *b^{h}āg^{h}ēwos 'cubit' (2a ASPIR DEVOI, 2b ē/ō-TO-ɛ̄/ɔ̄, 2f GREEK STRESS) > *swādɛ̄́wos, *p^{h}āk^{h}ɛ̄́wos (3e s-h-Ø, 6a ā-TO-ɛ̄) > *hwɛ̄dɛ̄́wos, *p^{h}ɛ̄k^{h}ɛ̄́wos (7b GRASSMANN) > *hwɛ̄dɛ̄́wos,*pɛ̄k^{h}ɛ̄́wos (7c w-DELE) > *hɛ̄dɛ̄́os, *pɛ̄k^{h}ɛ̄́os (V-SHORT applying to the first form, Q-MET to the second) > Gk hɛ̄déos and pɛ̄k^{h}éɔ̄s. (Note that in the derivation of these forms the chronology must be 7c w-DELE > V-SHORT/Q-MET.)

C. The Relative Chronology

The “>“ means “must precede”; and “> <“ means “at approximately the same time as”.

la Laryngeals > all other changes (see the discussion under la).

lb V̄+SON SHORT > 2e WF STOP DELE (see 1b), > 5b NASAL+s (see lb), > 5c V-CONTRACT (see 1b).

2a ASPIR DEVOI > 3a C+j CHANGES (see 3a) > 7b GRASSMANN (see 7b).

2b ē/ō-TO-ɛ̄/ɔ̄ > 3b j-CHANGES (see 3b), > 3e s-h-Ø (see 3e), > 5b NASAL+s (see 5b), > 7a ei/ou-TO-ē/ō (see 7a).

2c o-TO-u > 5a LABIOVEL (see 2c), > 6d u(:)-TO-y(:) (see 2c).

2d SYL SON > 5a LABIOVEL (see 5a), > 5c V-CONTRACT (see 5c), > 6b C-CL CHANGES (see 6b), > 7c w-DELE (see 2d).

2e WF STOP DELE > Ø.

2f GREEK STRESS > 3c j/w-MET (see 3c), > 4a PROTHESIS (see 2f), > 5c V-CONTRACT (see 2f), > 8b V-SHORT/Q-MET (see 8b).

3a C+j CHANGES >< 3c j/w-MET (see 2d and 3a),> 5b NASAL+s (see 5b),> 7b GRASSMANN (see 3a).

3b j-CHANGES > 4a PROTHESIS (see 4a), > 5c V-CONTRACT (see 5c).

3c j/w-MET > Ø.

3d m-TO-n > Ø.

3e s-h-Ø > 4b t-TO-s (see 3e), > 5c V-CONTRACT (see 5c), > 7b GRASSMANN (see 3e and 7b), > 8a h-ADD (see 8a).

4a PROTHESIS > 7c w-DELE (see 4a).

4b t-TO-s > 5a LABIOVEL (see 4b), > 5b NASAL+s (see 3e and 4b), > 7c w-DELE (see 4b).

5a LABIOVEL > 6a ā-TO-ɛ̄ (see 5a), > 6b C-Cl CHANGES (see 6b), > 6d u(:)-TO-y(:) (see 5a).

5b NASAL+s > 6a ā-TO-ɛ̄ (see 5b).

5c V-CONTRACT > 7c w-DELE (see 5c).

6a ā-TO-ɛ̄ > 5b NASAL+s 2 (see 5b), > 7c w-DELE (see 6a).

6b C-Cl CHANGES > 5b NASAL+s 2 (see 5b), > 7b GRASSMANN (see 6b).

6c DIPH SHORT > 7a ei/ou-TO-ē/ō (see 6c).

6d u(:)-TO-y(:) > Ø.

7a ei/ou-TO-ē/ō > Ø.

7b GRASSMANN > Ø.

7c w-DELE > 8a h-ADD (see 8a), > 8b V-SHORT/Q-MET (see 8b).

8a h-ADD > Ø.

8b V-SHORT/Q-MET > Ø.

III Greek Phonology

After the changes described in the previous section, the inventory of segments in the phonology of Attic Greek at about 200 BC was as follows.

Obstruent Consonants

labial	dental	alveolar	velar	glottal
p	t		k	
p^h	t^h		k^h	
b	d		g	
		s[1]		h
		z[1, 2]		
		dz		

Sonorant Consonants

m n ŋ[3]

l

r[4]

Vowels

Short

i, y u[5]

e o

a

Vowels

Long

ī, ȳ

ē ō

ɛ̄ ɔ̄

ā

Diphthongs ai, au, eu, oi

āi, āu, ɛ̄i, ɛ̄u, ɔ̄i, ɔ̄u[6]

Greek Segments in Terms of Phonological Features: Consonants

	p	t	k	p^h	t^h	k^h	b	d	g	s	z	dz	h	m	n	ŋ	l	r
consonantal	+	+	+	+	+	+	+	+	+	+	+	+		+	+	+	+	+
sonorant	–	–	–	–	–	–	–	–	–	–	–	–		+	+	+	+	+
vocalic	–	–	–	–	–	–	–	–	–	–	–	–		–	–	–	–	–
high	–	–	+	–	–	+	–	–	+	–	–	–		–	–	+	–	–
back	–	–	+	–	–	+	–	–	+	–	–	–		–	–	+	–	–
low	–	–	–	–	–	–	–	–	–	–	–	–		–	–	–	–	–
anterior	+	+	–	+	+	–	+	+	–	+	+	+		+	+	–	+	+
coronal	–	+	–	–	+	–	–	+	–	+	+	+		–	+	–	+	+
voiced	–	–	–	–	–	–	+	+	+	–	+	+		+	+	+	+	+
continuant	–	–	–	–	–	–	–	–	–	+	+	–	+	–	–	–	+	+
nasal	–	–	–	–	–	–	–	–	–	–	–	–		+	+	+	–	–
strident	–	–	–	–	–	–	–	–	–	+	+	+		–	–	–	–	–
delayed release	–	–	–	–	–	–	–	–	–	–	–	+		–	–	–	–	–
round	–	–	–	–	–	–	–	–		–	–	–		–	–	–	–	–
lateral	–	–	–	–	–	–	–	–	–	–	–	–		–	–	–	+	–
palatal	–	–	–	–	–	–	–	–	–	–	–	–		–	–	–	–	–
aspirated	–	–	–	+	+	+	–	–	–	–	–	–	+	–	–	–	–	–
stressed	–	–	–	–	–	–	–	–	–	–	–	–		–	–	–	–	–
long	–	–	–	–	–	–	–	–	–	–	–	–		–	–	–	–	–

Greek Segments in Terms of Phonological Features: Vowels

	i	y	e	a	o	u	ī	ȳ	ē	ɛ̄	ā	ɔ̄	ō
consonantal	−	−	−	−	−	−	−	−	−	−	−	−	−
sonorant	+	+	+	+	+	+	+	+	+	+	+	+	+
vocalic	+	+	+	+	+	+	+	+	+	+	+	+	+
high	+	+	−	−	−	+	+	+	−	−	−	−	−
back	−	−	−	+	+	+	−	−	−	−	+	+	+
low	−	−	−	+	−	−	−	−	−	−	+	−	−
voiced	+	+	+	+	+	+	+	+	+	+	+	+	+
continuant	+	+	+	+	+	+	+	+	+	+	+	+	+
nasal	−	−	−	−	−	−	−	−	−	−	−	−	−
round	−	+	−	−	+	+	−	+	−	−	−	+	+
tense	−	−	−	−	−	−	+	+	+	−	+	−	+
stressed	±	±	±	±	±	±	±	±	±	±	±	±	±
long	−	−	−	−	−	−	+	+	+	+	+	+	+

One generalization about the rules of Greek phonology is that after the occurrence of 2e WF STOP DELE and 3d m-TO-n, the only possible word-final consonants were /n, r, l, s/. In addition, a number of the changes which Greek has undergone from PIE have remained in the Greek grammar. Those given below labeled "morph cond" are morphologically conditioned and apply either to lexically marked items or to morphosyntactically marked classes. Those marked "phon cond" are phonologically conditioned and apply more or less generally. The symbol "Ø" after a change means that it has restructured lexical items and/or changed the inventory of underlying segments and has then been dropped from the grammar.

For those changes remaining as rules in the grammar we cite an illustrative example. Additional examples can be found in the discussions of the particular rules.

1a Laryngeals: Ø.

1b V̄+SON SHORT: Ø.

2a ASPIR DEVOI: Ø.

2b ē/ō-TO-ɛ̄/ɔ̄: Ø.

2c o-TO-u: Ø.

2d SYL SON: Ø.

2e WF STOP DELE (phon cond): voc sg /ánakt/ 'prince', gen sg /anaktós/ (WF STOP DELE) → ána and anaktós.

2f GREEK STRESS (morph cond and phon cond): nom sg /patɛ̄r/ 'father' vs. voc sg /pater/ (GREEK STRESS) → patɛ̄́r vs. páter.

3a C+j CHANGES (Ø for most forms, but a morph cond rule in some verb paradigms): 1sg pres /p^hylak+ɔ̄/ 'guard' vs. 1sg future /p^hylak+s+ɔ̄/ (C+j CHANGES) → p^hylássɔ̄ vs. p^hyláksɔ̄.

3b j-Changes: Ø.

3c j/w-MET (morph cond): 1sg pres /p^han+ɔ̄/ 'appear' vs. 1sg future /p^han+ɔ̄/ (morph cond version of j/w-MET) → p^haínɔ̄ vs. p^hanɔ̂.

3d m-TO-n: Ø.

3e s-h-Ø: Ø.

4a PROTHESIS: Ø.

4b t-TO-s: Ø.

5a LABIOVEL: Ø.

5b NASAL+s (morph cond): nom sg masc /pant+s/ ‘all’ vs. gen sg /pant+os/ (NASAL+s) → pâ̄s vs. pantós.

5c V-CONTRACT (morph cond): 2sg pres /tīmɛ̄+ēs/ ‘honor’ (GREEK STRESS applying as a synchronic rule) → tīmɛ̄́+ēs (V-CONTRACT) → tīmê̄s.

6a ā-TO-ɛ̄: Ø.

6b C-Cl CHANGES (phon cond and morph cond): 1sg pres /trīb+ɔ̄/ ‘rub’ vs. 3sg perf mid /te+trib+tai/ (C-Cl CHANGES) → trī́bɔ̄ and tétriptai.

6c DIPH SHORT: Ø.

6d u(:)-TO-y(:): Ø.

7a ei/ou-TO-ē/ō: Ø.

7b GRASSMANN (phon cond): gen sg /t^{h}rik^{h}+ós/ ‘hair’ (GRASSMANN) → trik^{h}ós.

7c w-DELE: Ø.

8a h-ADD: Ø.

8b V-SHORT/Q-MET (phon cond): gen pl /basilɛ̄́+ɔ̄n/ ‘king’ (V-SHORT/Q-MET) → basiléɔ̄n.

IV Historical Greek Morphology

A. Overview

B. Greek Morphology

We shall usually indicate both the PIE and Greek stress. Recall from our discussion of 2f GREEK STRESS that what we mark as PIE "V̄́" over long vowels or diphthongs corresponds to the Greek circumflex "V̂". And the Greek acute "V̄́" over long vowels represents /VV́/ — an innovation from PIE.

1 Nouns

In most traditional sources such as Smyth (1959) only three main noun classes are posited for Greek — the o-class, the ā-class and the so-called "third declension", which includes the i-, u- and athematic classes as given in the following. The cases of the noun and adjectives are the nominative, vocative, accusative, genitive, and dative with traces of a locative and instrumental case from PIE. There are singular, dual and plural numbers. In the paradigms below we do not list the vocative dual or plural since they are invariably the same as the respective nominative forms.

1.1 o-Class (Masculine, Feminine, Neuter)

			Greek		PIE
masc	**sg**	**nom**	lýkos	'wolf'	*wlók^{w}os[7]
		voc	lýke		*wlók^{w}e
		acc	lýkon		*wlók^{w}om
		gen	lýkou /lýkō/		*wlók^{w}osjo[8]
		dat	lýkɔ̄i		*wlók^{w}ɔ̄i
		loc	oíkoi	'at home'	*wóik+oi[9]
	du	**nom**	lýkɔ̄		*wlók^{w}ɔ̄
		acc	"		"
		gen	lýkoin		*wlók^{w}oin[10]
		dat	"		"
	pl	**nom**	lýkoi		*wlók^{w}oi[11]
		acc	lýkous /lýkōs/		*wlók^{w}ons[12]
		gen	lýkɔ̄n		*wlók^{w}ɔ̄m
		dat	lýkois		*wlók^{w}ois(i)[13]
		instr	t^{h}eóp^{h}in	'from god(s)'	*d^{h}weó+b^{h}in[9]

There are a few feminine o-class nouns. They decline like masculine nouns; however any modifying adjectives or articles are feminine ā-class. E.g., Gk hɛ̄̀ agat^{h}ɛ̄̀ hódos 'the good road' < PIE *sā́ agad^{h}ā́ *sódos.

Neuter o-class nouns have the endings of the masculine except for the following:

		Greek	PIE
nom/voc/acc	**sg**	zygón /dzygón/ 'yoke'	*jugóm
	pl	zygá	*jugá[14]

As a result of the various changes affecting /j/ such as 3a C+j CHANGES, 3b j-CHANGES and 3c j/w-MET, nouns in the original jo-class have tended to pass into the o-class. One of the few remaining jo-class nouns is paidíon 'small child'. Its derivation may have been as follows: PIE nom sg neuter *paid+í+om (to which the /j/-changes cannot apply, but by 3d m-TO-n) > Gk paidíon.

Some o-class nouns are not easily identifiable as such, either because they have undergone 5c V-CONTRACT or 8b V-SHORT/Q-MET. E.g.,

		Greek		PIE
sg	**nom**	noûs /nō̂s/	'mind'	*nó+os[15]
		neɔ̄́s	'temple'	*nasw+ós[16]

1.2 ā-Class (Feminine, Masculine)

There are only a few masculine nouns in this class. Sihler (1995: esp. 266-75) calls our ā-class the "eH_2" class. He considers the /ā/ to have been derived from /eh_2/ by a rule like la LARYNGEALS.

			Greek		PIE
fem	**sg**	**nom**	p^{h}ygɛ̄́	'flight'	*b^{h}ugā́[17]
			sp^{h}aîra	'sphere'	*sb^{h}ŕ̥ja[18]
		voc	= nom		
		acc	p^{h}ygɛ̄́n		*b^{h}ugā́m[17]
			sp^{h}aîran		*sb^{h}ŕ̥jam[18]
		gen	p^{h}ygɛ̄̂s		*b^{h}ugā́s[17]
		dat	p^{h}ygɛ̄̂i		*b^{h}ugā́i
	du	**nom**	p^{h}ygā́		*b^{h}ug+ā́[17]
		acc	"		*b^{h}ug+ā́+e[19]
		gen	p^{h}ygaîn		*b^{h}ugáin
		dat	"		"
	pl	**nom**	p^{h}ygaí		*b^{h}ugái[17, 20]
		acc	p^{h}ygā́s		*b^{h}ugā́ns[17, 21]
		gen	p^{h}ygō̂n		*b^{h}ugā́+ōm[22]
		dat	p^{h}ygaîs		*b^{h}ugā́+is(i)[23]

The masc ā-class nouns seem to be a Greek innovation. Their endings are those of the feminine ā-class except for the following:

			Greek		PIE
masc	**sg**	**nom**	kritɛ̄́s	'judge'	*kritā́+s[24]
		voc	kritá		*kríta[25]
		gen	kritoû		*kritā́+sjo

There also exist in the ā-class so-called contracted forms which have undergone 5c V-CONTRACT: e.g. PIE nom sg *sūké+ā 'fig' (5c V-CONTRACT) > *sūkā̂ = */sūkáa/ (6a ā-TO-ɛ̄, 6d u(:)-TO-y(:)) > sȳkɛ̄̂ = /sȳkɛ́ɛ/.

Nouns which are clearly jā-class occur infrequently since the /j/ was removed by changes such as 3a C+j CHANGES, 3b j-CHANGES or 3c j/w-MET. However, in a few instances a reflex of /j/ remains as Gk /i/. This usually occurs after a long stem, probably as a result of the application of the PIE rule 3.1.2f SIEVERS. E.g., PIE jā-class nom sg *wóikjā 'house' (PIE 3.1.2f SIEVERS applying as a persistent synchronic rule) → PIE *wóikijā (2f GREEK STRESS) > *woikíjā (3b j-CHANGES) > *woikíā (7c w-DELE) > Gk oikíā. Gk pótnia 'mistress' < PIE *pótnija underwent a similar derivation.

1.3 i-Class (Masculine, Feminine)

The masculine and feminine nouns of this class have identical endings.

			Greek		PIE
fem	**sg**	**nom**	pólis	'city'	*póli+s[26]
		voc	póli		*póli
		acc	pólin		*póli+m
		gen	póleɔ̄s		*pólēi+os[26]
		dat	pólɛ̄i		*pólēi+i
	du	**nom**	pólei		*pólei+e[26]
		acc	"		"
		gen	poléoin		*pólei+oin[27]
		dat	"		"
	pl	**nom**	póleis		*pólei+es[28]
		acc	"		"
		gen	póleɔ̄n		*pólei+ōm[29]
		dat	pólesi(n)		*pólei+si(n)[30]

1.4 u-Class (Masculine, Neuter)

			Greek		PIE
masc	**sg**	**nom**	pɛ̄̂kʰys	'elbow,	*bʰā́gʰu+s[31]
		voc	pɛ̄̂kʰy	cubit'	*bʰā́gʰu
		acc	pɛ̄̂kʰyn		*bʰā́gʰu+m
		gen	pɛ̄́kʰeɔ̄s		*bʰā́gʰēu+os[31, 32]
		dat	pɛ̄́kʰɛ̄i		*bʰā́gʰēu+i

			Greek		PIE
masc	du	nom	pɛ́́kʰei	'elbow, cubit'	*bʰā́gʰeu+e[31, 33]
		acc	"		"
		gen	pɛ̄kʰéoin		*bʰā́gʰeu+oin
		dat	"		"
	pl	nom	pɛ́́kʰeis		*bʰā́gʰeu+es
		acc	"		"
		gen	pɛ́́kʰeɔ̄n		*bʰā́gʰeu+ōm[34]
		dat	pɛ́́kʰesi(n)		*bʰā́gʰeu+si(n)[35]

The neuter nouns of this class have the same endings as the masculine ones except for the following:

		Greek		PIE
nom/voc/acc	sg	ásty	'city'	*wástu
	pl	ástɛ̄		*wásteu+a[36]

1.5 Athematic Classes

The masculine and feminine nouns of these classes have the same endings.

1.5.1 Ø-Class (Masculine, Feminine, Neuter)

			Greek		PIE
masc	sg	nom	poús /poós/	'foot'	*pṓds[37]
		voc	"		"
		acc	póda		*pódm̥[38]
		gen	podós		*podós
		dat	podí		*podí
	du	nom	póde		*póde
		acc	"		"
		gen	podoîn /podóin/		*podóin
		dat	"		"
	pl	nom	pódes		*pódes
		acc	pódas		*pódn̥s
		gen	podȭn		*podṓm
		dat	posí(n)		*podsí(n)

The fem nouns of this class usually have the same endings as the masc ones. However, some feminine nouns may possibly have not had the antecedent PIE ending *-s. E.g., PIE nom sg fem *gʰésr > Gk kʰeír 'hand' = /kʰeér/. One derivation is PIE *gʰésr (2a ASPIR DEVOI) > *kʰésr (3e s-h-Ø) > *kʰḗr (2f3 GREEK STRESS: ACUTE STRESS, applying as a synchronic rule) → Gk kʰḗr = /kʰeér/, spelled <kʰeír>. Another possible derivation positing an PIE antecedent with *-s is PIE *gʰesr+s (2a ASPIR DEVOI) > *kʰesrs (? 2e WF STOP DELE, applying to the word-final sequence /rs/ and possibly also /ns/) > *kʰesr

(3e s-h-Ø) > *kʰēr (2f3 GREEK STRESS: ACUTE STRESS) → Gk kʰḗr = /kʰeér/.

In the other athematic classes of the masculine and feminine we shall note several stems ending in /n/ or /r/ where a nominative singular in *-s seems to be lacking. In all these instances it is not clear whether this reflects a morphological fact of PIE or a later phonological change of Greek, possibly caused by 2e WF STOP DELE.

Neuter nouns of this class have the same endings as the masculine except for these:

		Greek		PIE
neuter nom/acc	**sg**	pŷr /pýyr/	'fire'	*pū́r
	pl	pyrá		*pūrá[39]

Some Ø-class nouns are affected by change 2e WF STOP DELE.

			Greek		PIE
sg	**fem**	**nom**	gynḗ	'woman'	*gwnáik (? –s)[40]
		acc	gynaîka		*gwnáikm̥[41]
sg	**neuter nom/acc**		gála	'milk'	*gálakt
			gálaktos		*gálaktos

1.5.2 Root Class (Masculine, Feminine)

			Greek		PIE
masc	**sg**	**nom**	boûs /bóos/	'cow'	*gʷṓu+s[42]
		voc	boû		*gʷṓu
		acc	boûn		*gʷṓu+m̥[43]
		gen	boós		*gʷou+ós[42, 44]
		dat	boí		*gʷou+í
	du	**nom**	bóe		*gʷóu+e
		acc	"		"
		gen	booîn /boóin/		*gʷou+óin
		dat	"		"
	pl	**nom**	bóes		*gʷóu+es
		acc	boûs /bóos/		*gʷóu+n̥s[45]
		gen	boɔ̂n /boɔ́ɔn/		*gʷou+ṓm
		dat	bousí(n) /bōsín/		*gʷou+sí(n)

Another masculine noun of this class, the name 'Zeus', has /ē/- Ø ablaut in its paradigm:

		Greek	PIE
sg	**nom**	Zeús /dzeús/	*diēú+s[46]
	voc	Zeû /dzéu/	*diḗu[47]
	acc	Zɛ̂n or Día	*diḗu+m̥[48] *díu+m̥[48]
	gen	Diós	*diu+ós[49]
	dat	Dií	*diu+í

There are also nouns of this class which are polysyllabic. One example is the word for 'king' with the agentive derivative suffix -ḗu-. It is a masculine noun, e.g.:

		Greek		PIE
sg	**nom**	basileús	'king'	*gʷm̥tilḗu+s[50]
	voc	basileû		*gʷm̥tilḗu[50]
	acc	basiléā		*gʷm̥tilḗu+m̥[51]
	gen	basiléɔ̄s		*gʷm̥tilḗu+os
	dat	basileî		*gʷm̥tilḗu+i
du	**nom**	basilɛ̄̂		*gʷm̥tilḗu+e
	acc	"		"
	gen	basiléoin		*gʷm̥tilḗu+oin
	dat	"		"
pl	**nom**	basilɛ̄̂s		*gʷm̥tilḗu+es
	acc	basiléās		*gʷm̥tilḗu+n̥s[52]
	gen	basiléɔ̄n		*gʷm̥tilḗu+ōm
	dat	basileûsi(n)		*gʷm̥tilḗu+si(n)

Other root-class nouns have stems ending in /ī, ū, ɔ̄ and ɔ̄i/. E.g.,

			Greek		PIE
masc	**sg**	**nom**	kîs	'worm'	*kī́+s
		acc	kîn		*kī+m[53]
		gen	kīós		*kī+ós
fem	**sg**	**nom**	sȳ̂s	'sow'	*sū́+s
		voc	sȳ̂		*sū́
		acc	sȳ̂n		*sū́+m[53]
		gen	syós		*sū+ós[54]
masc	**sg**	**nom**	hɛ̄́rɔ̄s	'hero'	*sḗrwō+s[55]
		gen	hɛ̄́rɔ̄s		*sḗrwō+os
fem	**sg**	**nom**	peitʰɔ̄í	'persuasion'	*bʰeidʰṓi[56]
		voc	peitʰoî		*bʰéidʰoi
		acc	peitʰɔ̄́		*bʰeidʰṓi+m̥[57]
		gen	peitʰoûs		*bʰeidʰói+os[58]
		dat	peitʰoî		*bʰeidʰói+i[58]

The other endings are those of boûs 'cow' above.

1.5.3 tVr-Class (Masculine, Feminine)

This class contains nouns of family relationship such as patḗr 'father' and mḗtēr 'mother'as well as agent nouns like dotḗr 'giver' and ístōr 'one who knows' from PIE *do-tḗr and *wíd+t+ōr. As with the other athematic nouns, the masculine and feminine endings are the same. Below we cite a masculine noun.

			Greek		PIE
masc	**sg**	**nom**	patḗr	'father'	*patḗr[59, 60]
		voc	páter		*páter
		acc	patéra		*patérm̥
		gen	patrós		*patrós
		dat	patrí		*patrí
	du	**nom**	patére		*patére
		acc	"		"
		gen	patéroin		*patéroin
		dat	"		"
	pl	**nom**	patéres		*patéres
		acc	patéras		*patérn̥s
		gen	patérōn		*patérōm
		dat	patrási(n)		*patŕ̥+si(n)[61]

1.5.4 Vn-Class (Masculine, Feminine)

As with the other athematic class nouns, the feminine nouns of this class such as algēdṓn 'pain' have the same endings as the masculine nouns such as the one below:

		Greek		PIE
sg	**nom**	poimḗn	'shepherd'	*poimḗn[62]
	voc	"		"
	acc	poiména		*poiménm̥
	gen	poiménos		*poiménos
	dat	poiméni		*poiméni
du	**nom**	poiméne		*poiméne
	acc	"		"
	gen	poiménois		*poiménois
	dat	"		"
pl	**nom**	poiménes		*poiménes
	acc	poiménas		*poiménn̥s
	gen	poiménōn		*poiménōm
	dat	poimési(n)		*poimén+si(n)[63]

Some Vn-class nouns have ablauting /ō-o/ in the stem, e.g. masc nom sg daímōn vs. acc sg daímona < PIE *dáimōn vs. *dáimonm̥. And some Vn-class nouns do not ablaut in their paradigms. E.g., nom sg Héllēn 'Hellene', leimṓn 'meadow' vs. acc sg Héllēna, leimȭna.

Those neuter nouns which were originally in the Vn-class have passed into the Vnt-class below. The earlier Vn-class declension was probably as follows:

		Greek		PIE
sg	**nom**	ónoma	'name'	*nóm+n̥
	gen	*onómanos		*nóm+n̥+os

The derivation of these forms would be *nómn̥ and *nómn̥os (2d SYL SON) > *nóma and *nómanos (4a PROTHESIS and 2f GREEK STRESS applying synchronically) > Gk ónoma and *onómanos. After the the transition into the Vnt-class, the genitive singular is Gk onómatos.

1.5.5 Vnt-Class (Masculine, Neuter)

			Greek		PIE
masc	**sg**	**nom**	odoús /odoós/	'tooth'	*odónt+s[64]
		voc	"		"
		acc	odónta		*odónt+m̥
		gen	odóntos		*odóntos
		dat	odónti		*odónti
	du	**nom**	odónte		*odónte
		acc	"		"
		gen	odóntoin		*odóntoin
		dat	"		"
	pl	**nom**	odóntes		*odóntes
		acc	odóntas		*odóntn̥s
		gen	odóntɔ̄n		*odóntōm
		dat	odoûsi(n)		*odónt+si(n)

The neuter nouns of this class have the same endings as the masc except for the nominative/accusative singular and plural. Many neuter nouns originally in other classes tend to come into the Vnt-class. E.g.,

		Greek		PIE
sg	**nom/acc**	ónoma	'name'	*nóm+n̥t[65]
	gen	onómatos		*nóm+n̥t+os
pl	**nom/acc**	onómata		*nóm+n̥t+a
	dat	onómasi(n)		*nóm+n̥t+si(n)

The above noun was probably originally of the PIE Vn-class. Other neuter nouns were attracted into the Greek Vnt-class from the u-class, the r/n-class (cited for other languages such as Latin in Chapter 3 morphology section 1.5.2) and the Vs-class. Respective examples are these.

		Greek		PIE
sg	nom/acc	góny	'knee'	*gónu
	gen	gónatos		*gón+n̥t+os
	nom/acc	hýdɔ̄r	'water'	*ẃdɔ̄r[66]
	gen	hýdatos		*ẃd+n̥t+os
	nom/acc	hɛ̄̂par	'liver'	*jɛ̄́kʷr̥t[67]
	gen	hɛ̄́patos		*jɛ̄́kʷ+n̥t+os
	nom/acc	kéras	'horn'	*kér+as[68]
	gen	krātós		*kr̥+n̥t+ós[68]

Finally, one neuter noun, probably originally of the athematic Ø-class, passed into the Vnt-class and underwent such developments as to make it almost appear as a suppletive root:

		Greek		PIE
sg	nom/acc	oûs /óos/	'ear'	*óus[69]
	gen	ɔ̄tós		*ous+n̥t+ós[70]

1.5.6 Vs-Class (Masculine, Feminine, Neuter)

Most nouns of this are neuter such as the following.

		Greek		PIE
sg	nom/acc	génos	'race'	*gén+os[71]
	voc	"		"
	gen	génous		*gén+es+os[71]
	dat	génei		*gén+es+i[72]
du	nom/acc	génei		*gén+es+e[73]
	gen	génoin		*gén+es+oin
	dat	"		"
pl	nom/acc	génɛ̄		*gén+es+a[74]
	gen	genɔ̄̂n		*gén+es+ōm[75]
	dat	génesi		*gén+es+si(n)

The masculine nouns of this class consist of a few proper names:

		Greek		PIE
sg	nom	Sɔ̄krátɛ̄s	'Socrates'	*sɔ̄́kratɛ̄s[76]
	voc	Sɔ̄́krates		*sɔ̄́krates[77]
	acc	Sɔ̄krátɛ̄		*sɔ̄́
	gen	Sɔ̄krátous		*sɔ̄́
	dat	Sɔ̄krátei		*sɔ̄́krates+i

The masculine/feminine plural may be illustrated by the adjective sap^{h}ɛ̂s 'clear'.

□		Greek	PIE
pl	nom	sapʰeîs	*sabʰés+es
	acc	"	"

Otherwise the dual and pl endings are like those of the neuter as given above.

There are a few feminine Vs-class nouns:

		Greek		PIE
sg	no	aidɔ̄́s	'shame'	*aidṓs[79]
	acc	aidɔ̄́		*aidósm̥[79]
	gen	aidoûs		*aidósos
	dat	aidoî		*aidósi

2 Adjectives

The adjectives form basically the same classes as nouns. However, there are no i-class adjectives.

2.1 o- and ā-Class

The masculine and neuter forms have the o-class noun endings; and the feminine forms are of the ā-class.

			Greek		PIE
nom	sg	masc	agatʰós	'good'	*agadʰós
		fem	agatʰɛ̄́		*agadʰā́[80]
		neuter	agatʰón		*agadʰóm

Some o- and ā-class adjs undergo 5c V-CONTRACT; and some undergo 8b V-SHORT/Q-MET. E.g.,

			Greek		PIE
nom	sg	masc	kʰrȳsoûs	'golden'	*kʰrūsé+os[81]
			hī́leɔ̄s	'kindly'	*síslā+os[82]

2.2 u-Class

The masculine and neuter adjectives of this class have the same endings as the corresponding u-class nouns cited under 1.4 above. E.g.,

			Greek		PIE
sg	masc	nom	hɛ̄dýs	'sweet'	*swādú+s[83]
		acc	hɛ̄dý		*swādú+m
		gen	hɛ̄déos		*swādéu+os[84]
	neuter	nom	hɛ̄dý		*swādú
		gen	hɛ̄déos		*swādéu+os
pl		nom	hɛ̄déa		*swādéu+a

Since there are no feminine u-class nouns, the feminine u-class adjectives were formed through the addition of jā-class endings such as those for the noun spʰaîra 'sphere' given under 1.2 above. E.g.,

			Greek		PIE
fem	sg	nom	hɛ̄deîa	'sweet'	*swādéu+ja[85]
		acc	hɛ̄deîan		*swādéu+jam
	du	nom	hɛ̄deíā		*swādéu+jā
	pl	gen	hɛ̄deiɔ̂̄n		*swādéu+jā+ōm[86]

The declension of the u-class adj polýs 'much, many' is somewhat irregular in that the nominative and accusative masculine and neuter stem is pol-, while the other forms are poll-, which is possibly of the jo- and jā-classes. E.g.,

			Greek		PIE
sg	masc	nom	polýs	'much, many'	*polú+s
		acc	polýn		*polú+m
	neuter	nom/acc	polý		*polú
	masc	gen	polloû		*pol+j+ósjo[87]
	fem	nom	pollɛ̄́		*pol+j+ā[88]
pl	masc	nom	polloí		*pol+j+ói

2.3 Athematic Classes

These adjectives fall generally into the corresponding athematic noun classes.

2.3.1 Ø-Class

One example of this is that original i-class nouns employed adjectivally pass into the Ø-class. E.g.,

			Greek		PIE
sg	nom	masc/fem	ápolis	'without a city'	*ń̥+polid+s[89]
		neuter	ápoli		*ń̥+polid[90]
	acc	masc/fem	apólida		*ń̥+polid+m̥

2.3.2 Root Class

There seems to be a remnant of at least one root-class adjective. (Recall that these forms consist of a stem which ends in a vowel.) This remnant is in the following forms of the adj 'large'.

			Greek		PIE
sg	masc	nom	mégas	'large'	*mégn̥+s
		acc	mégan		*mégn̥+m
	neuter	nom/acc	méga		*mégn̥

Otherwise the adjective stem is még+al-, which takes o- and ā-class endings: e.g., gen sg masc megálou < PIE *még+al+osjo.

2.3.3 tVr-Class

E.g.,

			Greek		PIE
sg	masc/fem	nom	apátɔ̄r	'fatherless'	*n̥+pátōr
		acc	apátora		*n̥pátorm̥
	neuter	nom/acc	apátor		*n̥pátor

2.3.4 Vn-Class

The masculine and feminine adjectives of this class have the endings of poimɛ́n 'shepherd' under 1.5.4 above. E.g.,

			Greek		PIE
sg	masc/fem	nom	mnɛ́mɔ̄n	'mindful of'	*mnḗmōn[91,92]
		acc	mnɛ́mona		*mnḗmonm̥[91]
	neuter	nom/acc	mnɛ̂mon		*mnḗmon[92]
pl	neuter	nom/acc	mnɛ́mona		*mnḗmona

2.3.5 Vnt-Class

There are numerous participles in this class. The masculine and neuter adjectives have the endings of the Vnt-class nouns. The feminine adjectives have the endings of the jā-class (1.2 above). E.g.,

			Greek		PIE
sg	masc	nom	kʰaríeis	'graceful'	*gʰŕ̥wents[93]
	neuter	nom	kʰaríen		*gʰŕ̥went[94]
		gen	kʰaríentos		*gʰŕ̥wentos
	fem	nom	kʰaríessa		*gʰŕ̥wentja[95]
		acc	kʰaríessan		*gʰŕ̥wentjam
		gen	kʰariéssɛ̄s		*gʰŕ̥wentjās

Active participles (except for the perfect act) and the aorist passive participle are in the Vnt-class. Most such adjectives have the endings of kʰaríeis 'graceful' above. However, the nominative singular masculine on most participles is -Ø. E.g.,

			Greek		PIE
sg	masc	nom	lȳ́ɔ̄n	'loosing'	*lū́+ōnt[96,97]
		gen	lȳ́ontos		*lū́+ont+os[96]
	fem	nom	lȳ́ousa		*lū́+ont+ja
	neuter	nom	lȳ̂on		*lū́+ont

The adjective pâs 'all' is in this class and has historically the same endings as kʰaríeis 'graceful' above. E.g.,

			Greek		PIE
sg	masc	nom	pâs	'all'	*pánt+s[98]
		acc	pánta		*pánt+m̥
		gen	pantós		*pant+ós
	fem	nom	pâsa		*pánt+ja[99]
		gen	pā́sɛ̄s		*pánt+jās
	neuter	nom/acc	pân		*pánt[100]

2.3.6 Vs-Class

These adjectives have the same endings as the Vs-class nouns under 1.5.6 above. E.g.,

			Greek		PIE
sg	masc/fem	nom	alɛ̄tʰɛ̄́s	'true'	*n̥+lādʰ+ḗs[101]
		acc	alɛ̄tʰɛ̂		*n̥+lādʰ+és+m̥[102]
	neuter	nom/acc	alɛ̄tʰés		*n̥+lādʰ+és

The perfect active participle seems to have consisted of an amalgam of the Vs-class and the Ø-class. The respective suffixes are *-wVs and *-wVt. E.g.,

			Greek		PIE
sg	masc	nom	lelykɔ̄́s	'having loosed'	*lelu+k+wṓs[103]
		acc	lelykóta		*lelu+k+wót+m̥[103]
		gen	lelykótos		*lelu+k+wót+os
	neuter	nom	lelykós		*lelu+k+wós
	fem	nom	lelykyîa		*lelu+k+ẃs+ja[103, 104]
		acc	lelykyîan		*lelu+k+ẃs+jam
pl	fem	acc	lelykyíās		*lelu+k+ẃs+jāns
		gen	lelykiɔ̂n		*lelu+k+ẃs+jā+ōm[105]

2.4 Comparison

There are two main types of comparative and superlative formation: comp -īɔn, sup -istos; and comp -teros, sup -tatos. Adjectives are lexically marked for the one or the other type of formation. Recall that by 2f2 GREEK STRESS: RECESSIVE STRESS, all comparative and superlative forms have RECESSIVE STRESS. The forms cited below are nominative singular masculine.

Examples of -īɔn/-istos comparison are these:

	Greek		PIE
pos	hɛ̄dýs	'sweet'	*swādús
comp	hɛ̄dī́ɔn		*swā́d+is+ōn[106, 107]
sup	hɛ̄́distos		*swā́d+is+t+os[106]

The comparative of some of these adjectives is formed from the ablauting antecedent suffix *-ios. E.g.,

	Greek		PIE
pos	mégas	'large'	*még+n̥+s
comp	meízɔ̄n		*még+ios+ōn[108]
sup	mégistos		*még+is+t+os

Examples of -teros/-tatos comparison are these:

	Greek		PIE
pos	mīkrós	'small'	*mīkrós
comp	mīkróteros		*mī́kro+ter+os[109]
sup	mīkrótatos		*mī́kro+tm̥+t+os[110]

A spin-off of the -teros/-tatos type of comparison is that of the -esteros/-estatos class. The source of these endings is the comparative and superlative of Vs-class adjectives.
E.g.,

	Greek		PIE
pos	alɛ̄tʰɛ̄́s	'true'	*n̥+lādʰ+ɛ̄́s
comp	alɛ̄tʰésteros		*ń̥+lādʰ+es+teros
sup	alɛ̄tʰéstatos		*ń̥+lādʰ+es+tm̥tos

These comparative and superlative suffixes may also be added to other than Vs-class adjectives, e.g. pos eudaímɔ̄n 'happy' (Vn-class), comp eudaiméstero s, sup eudaiméstatos.

Finally, as in most IE languages a number of frequently occurring adjectives with meanings such as 'good', 'bad', 'much, many', 'few', etc. are suppletive. E.g.,

	Greek		PIE
pos	agatʰós	'good'	*agadʰós
comp	beltī́ɔ̄n	'better'	*bélt+is+ōn
sup	béltistos	'best'	*bélt+ist+os

3 Adverbs

These can be formed from nouns or adjectives in any case in the singular. E.g.,

	Greek		PIE
nom	hápaks	'once'	*sḿ̥+pn̥k+s
acc	dɛ̄rón	'long-lasting'	*dwār+óm
gen	hespérās	'during evening'	*wésper+ās
dat	koinɛ̄̂i	'in common'	*kom+j+ā́i[111]
abl	kalɔ̂s	'well'	*kal+ɔ̄́d+s[112]
loc	oíkoi	'at home'	*wóik+oi
instr	ánɔ̄	'above'	*án+ō

Adverbs in the comparative and superlative are the neuter accusative singularand plural, respectively:

	Greek		**PIE**
pos	kalɔ̂	'well'	*kalɔ̄́d
comp	kállīon	'better'	*kálj+is+om[113]
sup	kállista	'best'	*kálj+ist+a

4 Numerals

4.1 Cardinals

The cardinals from '1' through '4' are declined and agree in case, number and gender with the head noun in the construction. Likewise for the numerals from '200' through '1000'. The other cardinals are uninflected.

'1' The nominative singular forms are these:

	Greek	**PIE**
masc	heîs	*sém+s[114]
fem	mía	*sm+já[115]
neuter	hén	*sém

The endings are those of the Ø-class athematic adjectives for the masculine and neuter forms; they are of the jā-class for the feminine paradigm.

'2' The following forms are for all genders. The declension is that of the dual.

	Greek	**PIE**
nom/acc	dýo	*dú+ō[116]
gen/dat	dyoîn	*du+ṓin[116]

'3' The declension is that of the athematic root class. E.g.,

		Greek	**PIE**
masc/fem	**nom**	treîs	*tréi+es[117, 118]
	gen	tríɔ̄n	*tri+ṓm[117]
neuter	**nom/acc**	tría	*trí+a

'4' The declension is that of the athematic Ø-class. E.g.,

	Greek	**PIE**
masc/fem	téttares	*kʷétwor+es[119]
neuter	téttara	*kʷétwor+a

	Greek	PIE
'5'	pénte	*pénk^{w}e
'6'	héks	*swéks[120]
'7'	heptá	*septḿ̥
'8'	oktɔ̄́	*oktṓ
'9'	ennéa	*néwm̥

The derivation of ennéa is *néwm̥ (2d SYL SON) > néwa (4a PROTHESIS) > *enéwa (7c w-DELE) > **enéa. The cause of the geminate /nn/ in ennéa is not clear. Buck (1962: 231) assumes an PIE ablauting alternative *nwm̥ (2d SYL SON, 4a PROTHESIS) > *enwa; and *newm̥ (ev) > *newa. Then by some sort of contamination *en(wa) + *newa > *ennewa (ev) > ennéa.

	Greek	PIE
'10'	déka	*dékm̥
'11'	héndeka	*sém+*dekm̥
'12'	dɔ̄́deka	*dwṓ +*dekm̥
'13'	treîs kai deka	*tréjes *kai *dekm̥

Etc. down to '20'.

	Greek	PIE
'20'	eíkosi	*wíkomti

The derivation is *wíkomti (PIE 3.1.2d NASAL ASSIM applying synchronically) → *wíkonti (4a PROTHESIS) > *ewíkonti (4b t-TO-s) > ewíkonsi (5b NASAL+s, but with short /o/ retained from the other decades like triā́konta '30' below) > *ewíkosi (7c w-DELE) > Gk eíkosi.

	Greek	PIE
'30'	triā́konta	*tria+*(d)komta

The /a/ in the antecedent form may have been the neuter plural ending. Sihler (1995: 418) assumes that the second constituent was originally *dkomt- meaning something like 'a ten-ness'. Hence *tria *dkonta meant '3 ten-nesses, i.e. 30'. The purported derivation was then PIE *tría+dkonta (? loss of /d/ and lengthening of the preceding vowel) > *tríākonta (2f GREEK STRESS) > Gk triā́konta.

	Greek	PIE
'40'	tettarákonta	*k^{w}étwor+(d)komta
'50'	pentɛ̄́konta	*pénta+(d)komta
'60'	heksɛ̄́konta	*swéksa+(d)komta
'70'	hebdomɛ̄́konta	*séptoma+(d)komta[121]
'80'	ogdoɛ̄́konta	*óktowa+(d)komta[121]
'90'	enenɛ̄́konta	*néwm̥+(d)komta
'100'	hekatón	*sem+km̥tóm

The derivation of hekatón may be PIE *sem+km̥tóm as well as Ø-grade ablauting *sm̥+km̥tóm 'one hundred' (2d SYL SON) > *semkatóm and *sakatóm (3d m-TO-n, 3e s-h-Ø) > *hemkatón and *sakatón (? some sort of contamination) > Gk hekatón.

	Greek	PIE
'200'	diākósioi	*duō+(d)kḿ̥tjoi[122, 123]
'300'	triākósioi	*tria+(d)kḿ̥tjoi[123]
'400'	tetrakósioi	*kʷetr̥+(d)kḿ̥tjoi
'500'	pentakósioi	*penta+(d)kḿ̥tjoi
'600'	heksakósioi	*seksa+(d)kḿ̥tjoi
'700'	heptakósioi	*septm̥+(d)kḿ̥tjoi
'800'	oktakósioi	*okta+(d)kḿ̥tjoi
'900'	enakósioi	*na+(d) kḿ̥tjoi [124]
'1000'	kʰī́lioi	*gʰésljoi[125]

4.2 Ordinals

These forms are o- and ā-class adjectives.

	Greek	PIE
'1st'	prɔ̂tos	*prṓ+t+os
'2nd'	deúteros	*déu+ter+os

The *deu- in deúteros is not from *duō '2'. Rather, it is from the verb deú-omai 'be inferior to'. The *-ter is the comparative suffix.

	Greek	PIE
'3rd'	trítos	*trí+t+os
'4th'	tétartos	*kʷétr̥+t+os

The remaining forms are constructed with the suffix *-t up to these:

	Greek	PIE
'7th'	hébdomos	*sépt+m+os[126]
'8th'	ógdoos	*óktou+os[126]
'9th'	énatos	*nwḿ̥+t+os

The antecedent root of énatos might have been the Ø-grade ablaut of *newm̥ above. If so, then the derivation is *nwḿ̥tos (2d SYL SON) > *nwátos (4a PROTHESIS and 2f GREEK STRESS applying as a synchronic rule) > *énwatos (7c w-DELE) > Gk énatos.

	Greek	PIE
'10'	dékatos	*dékm̥+t+os

The remaining forms are constructed with the suffix *-t up to

	Greek	PIE
'20'	eikostós	*wikom+stós

And the remaining forms are constructed with the suffix *-st, e.g.

	Greek	PIE
‘1000th’	kʰīlistós	*gʰesli+stós

4.3 Numerical Adverbs

These forms mean ‘x number of times’.

	Greek	PIE
‘once’	hápaks	*sḿ̥+pn̥ks

The meaning of the antecedent may have been ‘one alone’.

	Greek	PIE
‘twice’	dís	*d+ís
‘3 times’	trís	*tr+ís
‘4 times’	tetrákis	*kʷetr+ń̥kis

The remaining forms have the suffix -akis.

5 Pronouns

5.1 First Person

		Greek		PIE
sg	**nom**	egɔ̄́	‘I’	*egṓ[127]
	acc	(e)mé		*mé[128]
du	**nom/acc**	nɔ̄́	‘we two’	*nṓ[127]
	gen/dat	nɔ̄̂in		*nṓ+in
pl	**nom**	hɛ̄meîs	‘we’	*n̥sm+éjes[129]

5.2 Second Person

		Greek		PIE
sg	**nom**	sý	‘you’	*tú
	acc	sé		*tu+é[130]
du	**nom/acc**	spʰɔ̄́	‘you two’	*t+bʰṓ[131]
	gen/dat	spʰɔ̄̂in		*t+bʰṓ+in
pl	**nom**	hȳmeîs	‘you’	*wsm+éjes[132]

5.3 Third Person

Some, such as Chantraine (1961: 138), assume there was no 3rd person pronoun in PIE. If so, then these 3rd person pronouns in Greek were all originally demonstratives. The 3rd person forms cited for Greek include a non-nominative masculine/feminine/neuter form from an PIE *s- (e.g., acc sg he ‘him, her, it’ < PIE *se) as well as the following plural forms. (There is no dual.)

	Greek		PIE
nom	sp^heîs	'they'	*s+b^h+éjes
acc	sp^hâ̄s		*s+b^h+áns
gen	sp^hɔ̂̄n		*s+b^h+ṓm
dat	sp^hísi(n)		*s+b^h+ísi(n)

5.4 Demonstrative

There are four types of these pronouns. The first, meaning 'this, these' becomes the definite article 'the' in later Greek:

			Greek		PIE
nom	**sg**	**masc**	ho[133]	'this, these'	*só
		fem	hɛ̄[133]		*sā́
		neuter	tó[133]		*tód
	du	**masc/fem/neut**	tɔ̄́		*tṓ
	pl	**masc**	hoi[133]		*sói
		fem	hai[133]		*sái
		neuter	tá		*tá[134]

The second demonstrative is like the preceding, but with the addition of the suffix -de. The forms are all stressed, e.g. nom sg masc hóde < PIE *só+de.

The third demonstrative is this:

			Greek		PIE
nom	**sg**	**masc**	hoûtos	'this, these'	*só+u+t+os[135]
		fem	haútɛ̄		*sā́+u+t+ā[136]
		neuter	toûto		*tód+u+t+od[137]
	pl	**masc**	hoûtoi		*só+u+t+oi
		fem	haûtai		*sā́+u+t+ai
		neuter	taûta		*tá+u+t+a

Otherwise the masculine and neuter singular, all dual and all genitive plural forms have the stem tout-; the feminine stem is taut-. The endings are those of the o- and ā-class adjectives. (2.1 above).

The fourth demonstrative is Gk ekeînos 'that'. It has the same endings as hoûtos above. E.g.,

			Greek		PIE
nom	**sg**	**masc**	ekeînos	'that'	*e+ké+en+os[138]

5.5 Reflexive

There are three main reflexive formations. The first consists of a pronoun such as the PIE *se (under 5.3 above) plus *aut- plus the o- and ā-class endings. E.g., 3 sg héautos 'oneself' < PIE *sé+autos.

The second reflexive is a 3rd person plural in sp^h-. It is basically the same as the 3rd person acc pl sp^hâ̄s 'themselves' under 5.3 above.

The third reflexive is the so-called reciprocal pronoun. It means 'one another, each other' and is not found in the nominative nor in the singular. The endings are those of the o- and ā-class adjectives. E.g.,

		Greek		PIE
gen	**du**	allḗloin	'one another'	*álja+al+oin[139]
	pl	allḗlōn		*ála+al+ōm

5.6 Possessive

These pronouns take the endings of o- and ā-class adjectives. E.g.,

	Greek	PIE
'my'	emós	*m+ós[140]
'your' sg	sós	*tu+ós
'his, her, its'	toû, hê̄s, toû[141]	
'our'	hēméteros	*ń̥sm+eter+os[142]
'your' pl	hȳméteros	*ẃsm+eter+os
'their own'	sp^héteros	*s+b^h+éter+os

5.7 Interrogative and Indefinite

The main interrogative pronoun is this:

			Greek		PIE
sg	**masc/fem**	**nom**	tís	'who'	*k^wís[143]
		acc	tína		*k^wím+m̥[144]
	neuter	**nom**	tí		*k^wíd

Otherwise the stem is tin- with the endings of the masc and neuter athematic adjective classes (2.3 above). Other interrogatives are these. They take the endings of o- and ā-class adjectives. We cite the nominative singular masculine forms.

Greek		PIE
póteros	'which of two?'	*k^wóteros[145]
pósos	'how much?'	*k^wót+j+os[146]
poîos	'of what kind?'	*k^wói+os

The indefinite tìs 'whoever' is like the interrogative except that nom sg tìs, gen sg tinòs undergoes 2f4 GREEK STRESS: PHRASAL STRESS and has syllable-final and enclitic stress. Another indefinite is formed with the relative pronoun hós plus tìs > hóstis 'whoever'.

5.8 Relative

These pronouns generally have the endings of o- and ā-class adjectives. E.g.,

			Greek	PIE
nom	**sg**	**masc**	hós	*j+ós
		fem	hḗ /hɛέ/	*j+ā́[147]
		neuter	hó	*j+ód[148]
	du	**masc/fem/neut**	hṓ /hɔɔ́/	*j+ṓ[147]

			Greek	PIE
	pl	masc	hoí	*j+ói[147]
		fem	haí	*j+ái[147]
		neuter	há	*j+á
gen	sg	masc	hoû	*j+ósjo
		fem	hɛ̂s /hɛ́ɛs/	*j+ā́s[147]

6 Verbs

The features of the Greek verb are given in the following two tables. Table i contains the variable features — namely those which can change contingent upon the context. Table ii gives the lexical or inherent features — namely those that are idiosyncratic. They indicate the particular form-class of the verb.

(i) Variable Features

The first section of this table lists the purely verbal features. The second gives the features of deverbative adjectives and nouns.

(a) Person	(b) Number	(c) Voice	(d) Mood
1. 1st	1. singular	1. active[149]	1. indicative[150]
2. 2nd	2. dual	2. middle[149]	2. subjunctive[150]
3. 3rd	3. plural	3. passive[149]	3. imperative[151]
			4. optative[152]

(e) Tense Occurring in	Indicative	Subjunctive	Imperative	Optative
1. present[153]	x	x	x	x
2. imperfect[154, 155]	x			
3. perfect[156]	x	x	x	x
4. pluperfect[157]	x			
5. aorist[158, 155]	x	x	x	x
6. future[153]	x			x
6. future perfect[157]	x			x

Adjectival and Nominal Inflection

(a) Person	(b) Number	(c) Voice	(d) Mood
Ø	1. singular	1. active	1. infinitive
	2. dual	2. middle	2. participle[159]
	3. plural	3. passive	3. adjective[159]

(e) Tense occurring in	Infinitive	Participle	Adjective
1. present	act/mid	act/mid/pass	
2. imperfect			
3. perfect	act/pass	act/mid	pass
4. pluperfect			
5. aorist	act/mid/pass	act/mid/pass	
6. future	act/mid/pass	act/mid/pass	
7. future perfect	act/mid/pass		

(ii) Inherent Features.

(a) Inflectional type	(b) Class (conjugation)
1. deponent	1. thematic (ɔ̄-class)
2. nondeponent	2. athematic (mi-class)

(c) Class (conjugation)

1. j-class (thematic)	nízɔ̄	'I wash'	<*níg^{w}+j+ō[160]
2. n-class (thematic)	témnɔ̄	'I cut'	<*tém+n+ō[161]
3. sk-class (thematic)	gignɔ̄́skɔ̄	'I know'	<*gígnō+sk+ō[162]
4. root-class (thematic)	leípɔ̄	'I leave'	<*léik^{w}+ō[163]
5. nV-class (athematic)	pérnɛ̄mi	'I import'	<*pér+nā+mi[164]
6. reduplicating class (athematic)	dídɔ̄mi	'I give'	<*dí+dō+mi
7. root-class (athematic)	eîmi	'I go'	<*éi+mi

In Tables i and ii the features in the columns are mutually exclusive. Not all the logical possibilities are realized: the notations in the (e) columns of Table i indicate which are.

Regarding the endings noted below, the so-called "primary endings" usually occur with the present and future indicative (and occasionally subjunctive) forms. The "secondary endings" occur in the imperfect and aorist tenses, in the optative mood and occasionally in the subjunctive. The perfect, pluperfect and imperative forms have their own particular sets of endings. Note also that the difference between thematic and athematic endings occurs only in the present and imperfect tenses. Finally, since no single Greek verb is attested in all its possible forms, we cite various verbs in our paradigms.

6.1 Present

These forms differ in their thematic and athematic paradigms. We shall cite both.

6.1.1 Present Active Indicative

The thematic paradigm is as follows:

		Greek		PIE
sg	**1**	leípɔ̄	'leave'	*léik^{w}+ō[165]
	2	leípeis		*léik^{w}+esi[166]
	3	leípei		*léik^{w}+eti[167]
du	**2/3**	leípeton		*léik^{w}+etom[168]
pl	**1**	leípomen		*léik^{w}+omes[169]
	2	leípete		*léik^{w}+ete
	3	leípousi		*léik^{w}+onti[170]

The athematic paradigm is this:

		Greek		PIE
sg	**1**	tít^{h}ɛ̄mi	'set'	*d^{h}í+d^{h}ē+mi[171]
	2	tít^{h}ɛ̄s		*d^{h}í+d^{h}ē+s(i)[171, 172]
	3	tít^{h}ɛ̄si		*d^{h}í+d^{h}ē+ti
du	**2/3**	tít^{h}eton		*d^{h}í+d^{h}e+tom[171]

		Greek		PIE
pl	1	tít^{h}emen	'set'	*d^{h}í+d^{h}e+me(n)[171]
	2	tít^{h}ete		*d^{h}í+d^{h}e+te
	3	tit^{h}éāsi		*d^{h}í+d^{h}e+n̥ti[173]

6.1.2 Present Active Subjunctive

These endings are basically the same for both thematic and athematic paradigms. The endings are those of the present active indicative except that the vowels of the endings are lengthened. The thematic paradigm is this:

		Greek		PIE
sg	1	leípɔ̄	'leave'	*léik^w+ō
	2	leípɛ̄is		*léik^w+ēsi[174]
	3	leípɛ̄i		*léik^w+ēti[175]
du	2/3	leípɛ̄ton		*léik^w+ētom
pl	1	leípɔ̄men		*léik^w+ōmen
	2	leípɛ̄te		*léik^w+ēte
	3	leípɔ̄si		*léik^w+ōnti[176]

The athematic paradigm is this:

		Greek		PIE
sg	1	tit^{h}ɔ̄̂	'set'	*d^{h}í+d^{h}e+ō[177]
	2	tit^{h}ɛ̄̂is		*d^{h}í+d^{h}e+ēsi
	3	tit^{h}ɛ̄̂i		*d^{h}í+d^{h}e+ēti
du	2/3	tit^{h}ɛ̄̂ton		*d^{h}í+d^{h}e+ētom
pl	1	tit^{h}ɔ̄̂men		*d^{h}í+d^{h}e+ōmen
	2	tit^{h}ɛ̄̂te		*d^{h}í+d^{h}e+ēte
	3	tit^{h}ɔ̄̂si		*d^{h}í+d^{h}e+ōnti

6.1.3 Present Active Imperative

The thematic and athematic paradigms have historically the same endings. The thematic paradigm is this:

		Greek		PIE
sg	2	leîpe	'leave'	*léik^w+e
	3	leipétɔ̄		*léik^w+etōt[178]
du	2	leípeton		*léik^w+etom
	3	leipétɔ̄n		*léik^w+etōn
pl	2	leípete		*léik^w+ete
	3	leipóntɔ̄n		*léik^w+ontōn

The athematic imp uses the same endings (minus the thematic vowel) added to the athematic stem. E.g.,

		Greek		PIE
sg	**2**	tít^{h}ei /tít^{h}ē/	'set'	*d^{h}í+d^{h}e+e[179]
	3	tit^{h}étɔ̄		*d^{h}í+d^{h}e+tōt

6.1.4 Present Active Optative

The thematic paradigm is this:

		Greek		PIE
sg	**1**	leípoimi	'leave'	*léik^w+oi+mi[180, 181]
	2	leípois		*léik^w+oi+s
	3	leípoi		*léik^w+oi+t
du	**2**	leípoiton		*léik^w+oi+tom
	3	leipoítɛ̄n		*léik^w+oi+tām
pl	**1**	leípoimen		*léik^w+oi+men
	2	leípoite		*léik^w+oi+te
	3	leípoien		*léik^w+oi+ent

The athematic paradigm is this:

		Greek		PIE
sg	**1**	tit^{h}eíɛ̄n	'set'	*d^{h}í+d^{h}e+īē+m[180,181]
	2	tit^{h}eíɛ̄s		*d^{h}í+d^{h}e+īē+s
	3	tit^{h}eíɛ̄		*d^{h}í+d^{h}e+īē+t
du	**2**	tit^{h}eîton		*d^{h}í+d^{h}e+ī+tom
	3	tit^{h}eítɛ̄n		*d^{h}í+d^{h}e+ī+tām
pl	**1**	tit^{h}eîmen		*d^{h}í+d^{h}e+ī+men
	2	tit^{h}eîte		*d^{h}í+d^{h}e+ī+te
	3	tit^{h}eîen		*d^{h}í+d^{h}e+ī+ent

6.1.5 Present Mediopassive Indicative

The thematic and athematic paradigms take the same endings. The thematic paradigm is as follows:

		Greek		PIE
sg	**1**	leípomai	'leave'	*léik^w+o+mai
	2	leípɛ̄i		*léik^w+e+sai[182]
	3	leípetai		*léik^w+e+tai
du	**2/3**	leípest^{h}on		*léik^w+e+sd^{h}om[183]
pl	**1**	leipómet^{h}a		*léik^w+o+med^{h}a[184]
	2	leípest^{h}e		*léik^w+e+sd^{h}e[183]
	3	leípontai		*léik^w+o+ntai

The athematic paradigm had historically the same endings, but without the thematic vowel. E.g.,

		Greek		PIE
sg	1	tít^{h}emai	'set'	*d^{h}í+d^{h}e+mai
	2	tít^{h}esai		*d^{h}í+d^{h}e+sai[185]
	3	tít^{h}etai		*d^{h}í+d^{h}e+tai

6.1.6 Present Mediopassive Subjunctive

The endings of the thematic and athematic classes are the same. They are like those of the indicative, except that the thematic vowels are long.
E.g., the thematic paradigm:

		Greek		PIE
sg	1	leípɔ̄mai	'leave'	*léik^w+ō+mai
	2	leipɛ̄̂i		*léik^w+ē+sai
	3	leipɛ̄̂tai		*léik^w+ē+tai

Examples of the athematic paradigm are these:

		Greek		PIE
sg	1	tit^{h}ɔ̄̂mai	'set'	*d^{h}í+d^{h}e+ō+mai[186]
	2	tit^{h}ɛ̄̂i		*d^{h}í+d^{h}e+ē+sai
	3	tit^{h}ɛ̄̂tai		*d^{h}í+d^{h}e+ē+tai

6.1.7 Present Mediopassive Imperative

The thematic and athematic paradigms have the same endings historically.
The thematic paradigm is this:

		Greek		PIE
sg	2	leípou /leépɔ̄/	'leave'	*léik^w+e+so[187]
	3	leipést^{h}ɔ̄		*léik^w+e+sd^{h}ōt
du	2	leípest^{h}on		*léik^w+e+sd^{h}om
	3	leipést^{h}ɔ̄n		*léik^w+e+sd^{h}ōn
pl	2	leípest^{h}e		*léik^w+e+sd^{h}e
	3	leipést^{h}ɔ̄n		*léik^w+e+sd^{h}ōn

Examples of the athematic paradigm are these:

		Greek		PIE
sg	2	tít^{h}eso	'set'	*d^{h}í+d^{h}e+so[187]
	3	tit^{h}ést^{h}ɔ̄		*d^{h}í+d^{h}e+sd^{h}ōt

6.1.8 Present Mediopassive Optative

The thematic paradigm is as follows:

		Greek		PIE
sg	1	leipoímɛ̄n	'leave'	*léik^w+oi+mām[188]
	2	leípoio		*léik^w+oi+so
	3	leípoito		*léik^w+oi+to
du	2	leípoist^{h}on		*léik^w+oi+sd^{h}om
	3	leipoíst^{h}ɛ̄n		*léik^w+oi+sd^{h}ām
pl	1	leipoímet^{h}a		*léik^w+oi+med^{h}a
	2	leípoist^{h}e		*léik^w+oi+sd^{h}e
	3	leípointo		*léik^w+oi+nto

The athematic endings are historically the same. The intermediate optative formative is *-ī-. E.g.,

		Greek		PIE
sg	1	tit^{h}eímɛ̄n	'set'	*d^{h}í+d^{h}e+ī+mām[188]
	2	tit^{h}eîo		*d^{h}í+d^{h}e+ī+so[189]

6.2 Imperfect

6.2.1 Imperfect Active Indicative

The thematic paradigm is this:

		Greek		PIE
sg	1	éleipon	'leave'	*é+leik^w+om[190]
	2	éleipes		*é+leik^w+es
	3	éleipe		*é+leik^w+et
du	2	eleípeton		*é+leik^w+etom
	3	eleipétɛ̄n		*é+leik^w+etām
pl	1	eleípomen		*é+leik^w+ome+n[191]
	2	eleípete		*é+leik^w+ete
	3	éleipon		*é+leik^w+ont

The athematic paradigm is as follows:

		Greek		PIE
sg	1	etít^{h}ɛ̄n	'set'	*é+d^{h}i+d^{h}ē+m[192]
	2	etít^{h}eis		*é+d^{h}i+d^{h}e+es[193]
	3	etít^{h}ei		*é+d^{h}i+d^{h}e+et[193]
du	2	etít^{h}eton		*é+d^{h}i+d^{h}e+tom
	3	etit^{h}étɛ̄n		*é+d^{h}i+d^{h}e+tām
pl	1	etít^{h}emen		*é+d^{h}i+d^{h}e+men
	2	etít^{h}ete		*é+d^{h}i+d^{h}e+te
	3	etít^{h}esan		*é+d^{h}i+d^{h}e+n̥t[194]

6.2.2 Imperfect Mediopassive Indicative

The forms of the thematic paradigm consist of the augment plus the stem plus the thematic vowel of the present mediopassive indicative (6.1.5 above) plus the secondary endings of the present mediopassive optative (6.1.8). E.g.,

		Greek		PIE
sg	1	eleipómēn	'leave'	*é+leik^w+o+mām
	2	eleípou		*é+leik^w+e+so

The athematic paradigm has historically the same endings as those of the thematic class. The endings are added directly to the stem without the thematic vowel, e.g.

		Greek		PIE
sg	1	etit^{h}émēn	'set'	*é+d^{h}i+d^{h}e+mām
	2	etít^{h}eso		*é+d^{h}i+d^{h}e+so[195]

6.3 Perfect

There are two main types of perfect formation. The so-called "first perfect" is formed by reduplication of the root and addition of the suffix -k- plus the perfect endings. The "second perfect" is also formed with reduplication, but without the suffix -k-. Reduplication usually consists of repeating the root-initial consonant followed by /e/. The first perfect is found only with verbs whose roots end in a vowel. (It seems to be a later formation.) The second perfect is usually found with verbs whose roots end in consonants and sometimes with verb roots ending in vowels.

6.3.1 Perfect Active Indicative

The first perfect paradigm is as follows:

		Greek		PIE
sg	1	lélyka	'loose'	*lé+lu+k+a[196, 197]
	2	lélykas		*lé+lu+k+as
	3	lélyke		*lé+lu+k+e[197]
du	2/3	lelýkaton		*lé+lu+k+atom
pl	1	lelýkamen		*lé+lu+k+amen
	2	lelýkate		*lé+lu+k+ate
	3	lelýkāsi		*lé+lu+k+a+n̥ti[198]

The second perfect paradigm has the endings of the first perfect without -k-. E.g.,

		Greek		PIE
sg	1	léloipa	‘leave’	*lé+loik^w+a[199]
	2	tétrip^{h}a	‘rub’	*té+trib^h+a[200]

The reflex of an early, non-reduplicating but ablauting perfect paradigm also occurs:

		Greek		PIE
sg	1	oîda[201]	‘know’	*wóid+a ‘have seen’ [201]
	2	oîst^{h}a		*wóid+t^{h}a[202]
	3	oîde		*wóid+e
du	2/3	íston		*wíd+tom[203, 204]
pl	1	ísmen		*wíd+men[204]
	2	íste		*wíd+te[204]
	3	ísāsi		*wíd+a+n̥ti[204, 205]

6.3.2 Perfect Active Subjunctive

There are two of these formations. The first of them consists of the perfect stem plus the present active subjunctive endings (as in 6.1.2 above). The second consists of the perfect active participle (6.9.3 below) plus the present subjunctive of the verb ‘be’ (6.10.2). E.g.,

		Greek		PIE
sg	1	lelýkɔ̄	‘loose’	*lé+lu+k+ō
		lelykɔ̄̀s ɔ̄̂		*le+lu+k+wṓs *ésō[206]

6.3.3 Perfect Active Imperative

There are two of these formations: the first is constructed of the perfect stem plus the thematic present active imperative endings (6.1.3). The second consists of the perfect act part (6.9.3) plus the present imperative of ‘be’ (6.10.3). E.g.,

		Greek		PIE
sg	2	lélyke	‘loose’	*lé+lu+k+e
		lelykɔ̄̀s íst^{h}e		*le+lu+k+wṓs *és+d^{h}i

6.3.4 Perfect Active Optative

This paradigm is formed in two ways. The first is the perfect stem plus the present active optative endings (6.1.4), either thematic or athematic in free variation. The second consists of the perfect active participle (6.9.3) plus the present optative of the verb ‘be’ (6.10.4). E.g.,

		Greek		PIE
sg	1	lelýkoimi	‘loose’	*lé+lu+k+oi+mi[207]
		lelykoíɛ̄n		*lé+lu+k+oi+ēm[207]
		lelykɔ̄̀s eíɛ̄n		*le+lu+k+wṓs *és+ī̆ē+m

6.3.5 Perfect Mediopassive Indicative

This paradigm is formed from the perfect stem plus the athematic present mediopassive indicative endings (6.1.5 above). E.g.,

		Greek		PIE
sg	1	lélymai	'loose'	*lé+lu+mai[208]
		léleimmai	'leave'	*lé+leik^w+mai[209]
		gégrammai	'write'	*gé+grab^h+mai[209]
		tét^heimai	'set'	*d^hé+d^hē+mai[210]

6.3.6 Perfect Mediopassive Subjunctive

This paradigm consists of the perfect mediopassive participle (6.9.4) and the present subjunctive of 'be' (6.10.2). E.g.,

		Greek		PIE
sg	1	lelyménos ɔ̂	'loose'	*le+lu+mén+os *és+ō
pl	3	lelyménoi ɔ̂si		*le+lu+mén+oi *és+ōnti

6.3.7 Perfect Mediopassive Imperative

This paradigm is constructed of the perfect stem (without -k- for first perfects) plus the present athematic mediopassive imperative endings (6.1.7). E.g.,

		Greek		PIE
sg	2	lélyso	'loose'	*lé+lu+so[211]
		léleipso	'leave'	*lé+leik^w+so
	3	lelýst^hɔ̄		*lé+lu+sd^hōt
		leleí$p^h$$t^h$ɔ̄		*lé+leik^w+d^hōt[212]

6.3.8 Perfect Mediopassive Optative

This paradigm consists of the perfect mediopassive participle (6.9.4) and the present optative of 'be' (6.10.4). E.g.,

		Greek		PIE
sg	1	lelyménos eíɛ̄n	'loose'	*le+lu+mén+os *és+īē+m
pl	1	lelyménoi eíɛ̄men		*le+lu+mén+oi *és+īē+men

6.4 Pluperfect

According to Sihler (1995: 578), this tense was not in PIE but represents a wholly Greek innovation.

6.4.1 Pluperfect Active Indicative

The forms of this paradigm consist of the augment e- plus the reduplicated perfect root (with -k- for first perfect forms) plus an -e- of unknown origin plus the endings of the perfect act indicative (6.3.1). The first perfect paradigm is this:

		Greek		PIE
sg	1	elelýkē̆	'loose'	*é+le+lu+k+e+a[213]
	2	elelýkē̆s		*é+le+lu+k+e+as
	3	elelýkei /elelýkē/		*é+le+lu+k+e+e[214]
du	2	elelýketon		*é+le+lu+k+e+t+om
	3	elelykétē̆n		*é+le+lu+k+e+tām
pl	1	elelýkemen		*é+le+lu+k+e+men
	2	elelýkete		*é+le+lu+k+e+te
	3	elelýkesan		*é+le+lu+k+e+sn̥t[215]

The second perfect has the same endings, e.g.

		Greek		PIE
sg	1	eleloípē̆	'leave'	*é+le+loik^w+e+a

6.4.2 Pluperfect Mediopassive Indicative

The forms of this paradigm are constructed from the pluperfect stem described above plus the endings of the athematic imperfect mediopassive indicative (6.2.2). E.g.,

		Greek		PIE
sg	1	elelýmē̆n	'loose'	*é+le+lu+mām[216]
		eleleímmē̆n	'leave'	*é+le+leik^w+mām
	2	elélyso		*é+le+lu+so
		eléleipso		*é+le+leik^w+so

6.5 Aorist

There are two types of aorist formation. The so-called "first aorist" adds to the stem the suffix -s- plus the endings given below. The "second aorist" adds to the stem the endings of the imperfect (6.2 above). The aorist indicative forms prefix an augment e-. In the aorist paradigms below the middle endings differ from those of the passive. Few generalizations can be made about whether a verb takes first aorist or second aorist endings. One generalization is that only "primitive" verbs (i.e., those which are not derived from adjectives or nouns) are second aorist. However, some verbs occur with both aorists. E.g., first aorist élȳsa 'loosed' vs. second aorist élȳon 'idem' and first aorist éleipsa 'left' vs. ablauting second aorist élipon 'idem'.

6.5.1 Aorist Active Indicative

The first aorist paradigm is as follows.

		Greek		PIE
sg	1	égrapsa	'write'	*é+grab^h+s+m̥[217]
	2	égrapsas		*é+grab^h+s+Vs[218]
	3	égrapse		*é+grab^h+s+et[218]
du	2	egrápsaton		*é+grab^h+s+Vtom[218]
	3	egrapsátɛ̄n		*é+grab^h+s+Vtām[218]
pl	1	egrápsamen		*é+grab^h+s+Vmen[218]
	2	egrápsate		*é+grab^h+s+Vte[218]
	3	égrapsan		*é+grab^h+s+n̥t[219]

An example of the second aorist is this:

		Greek		PIE
sg	1	élipon	'leave'	*é+lik^w+om[220]
	2	élipes		*é+lik^w+es

Some athematic verbs have a combination of first and second aorist endings. E.g.,

		Greek		PIE
sg	1	éstɛ̄n	'stand'	*é+stā+m
	2	éstɛ̄s		*é+stā+Vs
	3	éstɛ̄		*é+stā+et
du	2	éstɛ̄ton		*é+stā+tom
	3	estɛ̄́tɛ̄n		*é+stā+tām
pl	1	éstɛ̄men		*é+stā+men
	2	éstɛ̄te		*é+stā+te
	3	éstɛ̄san		*é+stā+s+n̥t

And some athematic verbs take a -k- in the aorist singular. E.g.,

		Greek		PIE
sg	1	ét^{h}ɛ̄ka	'set'	*é+d^{h}ē+k+m̥
	2	ét^{h}ɛ̄kas		*é+d^{h}ē+k+Vs
	3	ét^{h}ɛ̄ke		*é+d^{h}ē+k+et
du	2	ét^{h}eton		*é+d^{h}e+tom[221]

6.5.2 Aorist Active Subjunctive

The first aorist paradigm consists of the unaugmented aorist stem plus the thematic present active subjunctive endings (6.1.2). The second aorist paradigm has the same endings. E.g.,

		Greek		PIE
sg	1	grápsɔ̄	'write'	*gráb^h+s+ō
		lípɔ̄	'leave'	*lík^w+ō

Some athematic verbs add the second aorist endings to a stem ending in a vowel, e.g.

		Greek		PIE
sg	1	t^{h}ɔ̂	'set'	*d^{h}é+ō[222]

6.5.3 Aorist Active Imperative

The first aorist paradigm is as follows.

		Greek		PIE
sg	2	grápson	'write'	*gráb^h+s+om[223]
	3	grapsátɔ̄		*gráb^h+sa+tōt[224]

The second aorist paradigm takes the thematic present active imperative endings (6.1.3). E.g.,

		Greek		PIE
sg	2	lípe	'leave'	*lík^{w}e
	3	lipétɔ̄		*lík^w+etōt

Athematic verbs are generally like lípe. There are a few exceptions, e.g.

		Greek		PIE
sg	2	t^{h}és	'set'	*d^{h}é+s
		stɛ̂ t^{h}i	'stand'	*stā́+d^{h}i
		gnɔ̂t^{h}i	'know'	*gnṓ+d^{h}i

6.5.4 Aorist Active Optative

The first aorist paradigm is as follows.

		Greek		PIE
sg	1	grápsaimi	'write'	*gráb^h+sa+ī+mi[225]
	2	grápsais		*gráb^h+sa+ī+s

The second aorist has the endings of the present active, optative thematic paradigm (6.1.4). E.g.,

		Greek		PIE
sg	1	lípoimi	'leave'	*lík^w+oi+mi
	2	lípois		*lík^w+oi+s.

6.5.5 Aorist Middle Indicative

Both the first aorist and second aorist paradigms consist of the augmented aorist stem plus the endings of the imperfect mediopassive indicative (6.2.2). E.g.,

		Greek		PIE
sg	1	egrapsámɛ̄n	'write'	*é+grab^h+sa+mām
		elipómɛ̄n	'leave'	*é+lik^w+o+mām
	2	egrápsɔ̄		*é+grab^h+sa+so[226]
		elípou		*é+lik^w+o+so[227]

6.5.6 Aorist Middle Subjunctive

Both the first and second aorist paradigms are formed with the unaugmented aorist stem plus the endings of present mediopassive subjunctive (6.1.6). E.g.,

		Greek		PIE
sg	1	grápsɔ̄mai	'write'	*gráb^h+s+ō+mai
		lípɔ̄mai	'leave'	*lík^w+ō+mai
		t^{h}ɔ̂mai	'set'	*d^{h}é+ō+mai[228]

6.5.7 Aorist Middle Imperative

Aside from the 2nd singular of the first aorist, these forms consist of the unaugmented aorist stem plus the endings of the athematic present mediopassive imperative (6.1.7) for the first aorist and the corresponding thematic endings for the second aorist. E.g.,

		Greek		PIE
sg	2	grápsai	'write'	*gráb^h+sa+i[229]
		lípou	'leave'	*lík^w+e+so
		t^{h}oû	'set'	*d^{h}é+so[230]
	3	grapsást^{h}ɔ̄		*gráb^h+sa+sd^{h}ōt
		lipést^{h}ɔ̄		*lík^w+e+sd^{h}ōt
		t^{h}ést^{h}ɔ̄		*d^{h}é+sd^{h}ōt[230]

6.5.8 Aorist Middle Optative

The first aorist forms consist of the unaugmented aorist stem ending in /s/ plus the aorist active optative (6.5.4) formative -ai- plus the athematic endings of the present mediopassive optative (6.1.8). The second aorist forms consist of the unaugmented aorist root plus the aorist active optative (6.5.4) formative -oi- plus the athematic endings of the present mediopassive optative (6.1.8). E.g.,

		Greek		PIE
sg	1	grapsaímɛ̄n	'write'	*gráb^h+sa+ī+mām
		lipoímɛ̄n	'leave'	*lík^w+oi+mām

6.5.9 Aorist Passive Indicative

In the aorist passive there is no distinction made in first-aorist and second-aorist formations. There is also no -s added to aorist stems. Rather, these forms consist of the aorist root (augmented only in the indicative) plus the aorist passive formative -t^{h}ɛ̄- plus the respective endings. The passive indicative has the endings of the athematic imperfect active indicative (6.2.1).

		Greek		PIE
sg	1	egráp^{h}t^{h}ɛ̄n	'write'	*é+grab^h+d^{h}ē+m[231]
		elíp^{h}t^{h}ɛ̄n	'leave'	*é+lik^w+d^{h}ē+m[232]
		elýt^{h}ɛ̄n	'loose'	*é+lu+d^{h}ē+m
	2	egráp^{h}t^{h}ɛ̄s		*é+grab^h+d^{h}ē+s
	3	egráp^{h}t^{h}ɛ̄		*é+grab^h+d^{h}ē+t
du	2	egráp^{h}t^{h}ɛ̄ton		*é+grab^h+d^{h}ē+tom
	3	egrap^{h}t^{h}ɛ̄́tɛ̄n		*é+grab^h+d^{h}ē+tām
pl	1	egráp^{h}t^{h}ɛ̄men		*é+grab^h+d^{h}ē+men
	2	egráp^{h}t^{h}ɛ̄te		*é+grab^h+d^{h}ē+te
	3	egráp^{h}t^{h}ɛ̄san		*é+grab^h+d^{h}ē+n̥t[233]

6.5.10 Aorist Passive Subjunctive

This paradigm is formed with the unaugmented aorist passive stem in -t^h- plus the present active subjunctive endings (6.1.2). E.g.,

		Greek		PIE
sg	1	gráp^{h}t^{h}ɔ̄	'write'	*gráb^h+d^h+ō[234]
	2	líp^{h}t^{h}ɔ̄	'leave'	*lík^w+d^h+ō
	3	lýt^{h}ɔ̄	'loose'	*lú+d^h+ō

6.5.11 Aorist Passive Imperative

Aside from the following forms, this paradigm consists of the unaugmented aorist stem ending in -t^{h}ɛ̄- plus the endings of the athematic present mediopassive imperative (6.1.7).

		Greek		PIE
sg	2	lýt^{h}ɛ̄ti	'loose'	*lú+d^{h}ē+t+i[235]
	3	lyt^{h}ɛ̄́tɔ̄		*lú+d^{h}ē+tōt
du	2	lýt^{h}ɛ̄st^{h}on		*lú+d^{h}ē+sd^{h}om[236]

6.5.12 Aorist Passive Optative

The forms of this paradigm consist of the unaugmented aorist root plus the formant -t^{h}ei- = /-t^{h}ē-/ plus the endings of the aorist passive indicative (6.5.9). E.g.,

		Greek		PIE
sg	1	lyt^{h}eíɛ̄n	'loose'	*lú+d^{h}e+ī̆ē+m[237]

6.6 Future

The future is formed from the bare verb root (minus the present/imperfect class formatives described under 6 above in Table ii, column c) plus -s- or the ablauting -es- plus the respective endings. The future occurs only in the indicative and the optative. However, like the aorist, the future has separate paradigms for the middle and the passive.

6.6.1 Future Active Indicative

This paradigm is formed with the future stem in *-(e)s- plus the thematic present active indicative endings (6.1.1). E.g.,

		Greek		PIE
sg	1	leípsɔ̄	'leave'	*léikʷ+s+ō[238]
		tʰɛ́sɔ̄	'set'	*dʰé̄+s+ō[238]
		nīkɛ́sɔ̄	'be victorious'	*nī́ka+es+ō[239]
		stelɔ̂	'place'	*stél+es+ō[240]

6.6.2 Future Active Optative

This paradigm is formed from the future stem with -s- plus the thematic present active optative endings (6.1.4). E.g.,

		Greek		PIE
sg	1	leípsoimi	'leave'	*léikʷ+s+oi+mi
		tʰɛ́soimi	'set'	*dʰé̄+s+oi+mi

6.6.3 Future Middle Indicative

This paradigm is formed from the future stem with -s- plus the thematic present mediopassive indicative endings (6.1.5). E.g.,

		Greek		PIE
sg	1	leípsomai	'leave'	*léikʷ+s+oi+mai
		tʰɛ̄soímai	'set'	*dʰé̄+s+oi+mai

6.6.4 Future Middle Optative

This paradigm is formed from the future stem with -s- plus the thematic present mediopassive optative endings (6.1.8). E.g.,

		Greek		PIE
sg	1	leipsoímɛ̄n	'leave'	*léikʷ+s+oi+mām
		tʰɛ̄soímɛ̄n	'set'	*dʰé̄+s+oi+mām

6.6.5 Future Passive Indicative

This paradigm consists of the root plus the suffix -tʰɛ̄- plus the future marker -s- plus the thematic present mediopassive indicative endings (6.1.5). E.g.,

		Greek		PIE
sg	1	leipʰtʰɛ̂somai	'leave'	*léikʷ+dʰē+s+omai[241]
		dotʰɛ̂somai	'give'	*dó+dʰē+s+omai

6.6.6 Future Passive Optative

This paradigm consists of the root plus the suffix -tʰɛ̄- plus the future marker -s- plus the thematic present mediopassive optative endings (6.1.8). E.g.,

		Greek		PIE
sg	1	leipʰtʰɛ̄soímɛ̄n	'leave'	*léikʷ+dʰē+s+oi+mām
		tetʰɛ̄soímɛ̄n	'set'	*dʰé+dʰē+s+oi+mām

6.7 Future Perfect

These paradigms are probably Greek innovations. The forms are constructed from the perfect stem plus the future formative -s- plus the respective endings. Like the future, the future perfect occurs only in the indicative and optative; but it has separate paradigms for the middle and passive.

6.7.1 Future Perfect Active Indicative

The endings are those of the future active indicative (6.6.1). E.g.,

		Greek		PIE
sg	1	leleípsɔ̄	'leave'	*lé+leikʷ+s+ō
		hestɛ̄́kɔ̄	'stand'	*sé+stā+k+ō

6.7.2 Future Perfect Active Optative

The endings are those of the future active optative (6.6.2). E.g.,

		Greek		PIE
sg	1	leleípsoimi	'leave'	*lé+leikʷ+s+oi+mi

6.7.3 Future Perfect Middle Indicative

The endings are those of the future middle indicative (6.6.3). E.g.,

		Greek		PIE
sg	1	leleípsomai	'leave'	*lé+leikʷ+s+oi+mai

6.7.4 Future Perfect Middle Optative

The endings are those of the future middle optative (6.6.4). E.g.,

		Greek		PIE
sg	1	leleipsoímɛ̄n	'leave'	*lé+leikʷ+s+oi+mām

6.7.5 Future Perfect Passive Indicative

The endings are those of the future passive indicative (6.6.5). E.g.,

		Greek		PIE
sg	1	leleip^{h}t^{h}ɛ̂somai	'leave'	*lé+leik^w+d^{h}ē+s+omai

6.7.6 Future Perfect Passive Optative

The endings are those of the future passive optative (6.6.6). E.g.,

		Greek		PIE
sg	1	leleip^{h}t^{h}ɛ̄soímɛ̄n	'leave'	*lé+leik^w+d^{h}ē+s+omām

6.8 Infinitives

6.8.1 Present Active

The thematic and athematic infinitives are these:

Greek		PIE
leípein	'to leave'	*léik^w+es+en[242]
tit^{h}énai	'to set'	*d^{h}í+d^{h}e+n+ai[243]

6.8.2 Present Mediopassive

Greek		PIE
leípest^{h}ai	'to be left'	*léik^w+es+d^{h}ai

6.8.3 Perfect Active

Greek		PIE
leloipénai	'to have left'	*lé+loik^w+enai

6.8.4 Perfect Mediopassive

Greek		PIE
leloipést^{h}ai	'to have been left'	*lé+loik^w+es+d^{h}ai

6.8.5 Aorist Active

The first and second aorist infinitives are as follows.

Greek		PIE
lŷ̄sai	'to have loosed'	*lú+s+ai[244]
lípein	'to have left'	*lík^w+es+en

6.8.6 Aorist Middle

Greek		PIE
lípest^{h}ai	'to have left'	*lík^w+es+d^{h}ai

6.8.7 Aorist Passive

Greek		PIE
lyt^{h}ɛ̂nai	'to have been loosed'	*lú+d^{h}ē+nai

6.8.8 Future Active

Greek		PIE
leípsein	'to be going to leave'	*léik^{w}+s+es+en

6.8.9 Future Middle

Greek		PIE
leípsest^{h}ai	'to be going to leave'	*léik^{w}+s+es+d^{h}ai

6.8.10 Future passive

Greek		PIE
lut^{h}ɛ́sest^{h}ai	'to be going to be loosed'	*lú+d^{h}ē+s+es+d^{h}ai

6.8.11 Future Perfect Active

Greek		PIE
leleípsein	'to be going to have left'	*lé+leik^{w}+s+es+en

6.8.12 Future Perfect Mediopassive

Greek		PIE
leleípsest^{h}ai	'to be going to have been left'	*lé+leik^{w}+s+d^{h}ai

6.9 Participles and Verbal Adjectives

We cite the nominative singular masculine form.

6.9.1 Present Active Participle

The thematic and athematic forms follow. Both these participles are Vnt-class adjectives.

Greek		PIE
lȳ́ɔ̄n	'loosing'	*lū́+ōnt[245]
tit^{h}eîs	'setting'	*d^{h}i+d^{h}é+nt+s[246]

6.9.2 Present Mediopassive Participle

This is an o/ā-class adjective.

Greek		PIE
lȳómenos	'being loosed'	*lú+o+men+os

6.9.3 Perfect Active Participle

This is a Vs-class adjective.

	Greek		PIE
masc sg nom	lelykɔ̄́s	'having loosed	*le+lu+k+wṓs[247]
	lelykóta		*le+lu+k+wót+m̥[247]

6.9.4 Perfect Mediopassive Participle

This is an o/ā-class adjective.

Greek		PIE
lelyménos	'having been loosed'	*le+lu+mén+os

6.9.5 Aorist Active Participle

The first and second aorist forms are as follows. They are both Vnt-class adjectives.

Greek		PIE
lȳ́sās	'having loosed'	*lú+sa+nt+s[248]
lipɔ̄̂n	'having left'	*likʷ+ṓnt[249]

6.9.6 Aorist Middle Participle

These are o/ā-class adjectives. The first and second aorist forms are as follows.

Greek		PIE
lȳsámenos	'having loosed'	*lú+sa+men+os
lipómenos	'having left'	*líkʷ+o+menos

6.9.7 Aorist Passive Participle

This is a Vnt-class adjective.

Greek		PIE
lytʰeís	'having been loosed'	*lu+dʰé+nt+s[250]

6.9.8 Future Active Participle

This is a Vnt-class adjective.

Greek		PIE
lȳ́sɔ̄n	'going to loose'	*lū́+s+ōnt

6.9.9 Future Middle Participle

This is an o/ā-class adjective

Greek		PIE
lȳsómenos	'going to loose'	*lū́+s+o+men+os

6.9.10 Future Passive Participle

This is an o/ā-class adjective.

Greek		PIE
lyt^{h}ɛ̄sómenos	'going to be loosed'	*lú+d^{h}ē+s+o+men+os

6.9.11 Future Perfect Active Participle

This is a Vnt-class adjective.

Greek		PIE
lelȳ́sɔ̄n	'going to have loosed'	*lé+lu+s+ōnt

6.9.12 Future Perfect Mediopassive Participle

This is an o/ā-class adjective.

Greek		PIE
lelȳsómenos	'going to have been loosed'	*lé+lu+s+o+men+os

6.9.13 Verbal Adjectives

There are two such constructions. The first has the meaning of a perfect passive participle; the second indicates obligation or necessity. Both are o/ā-class adjectives. E.g.,

Greek		PIE
lytós	'loosed'	*lu+t+ós
lytéos	'which should or ought to be loosed'	*lu+téw+os

6.10 The Verb 'be'

6.10.1 Present Indicative

		Greek	PIE
sg	**1**	eimí	*és+mi[251]
	2	eî	*és+si[252]
	3	estí	*és+ti
du	**2/3**	estón	*es+tóm
pl	**1**	esmén	*es+mén[253]
	2	esté	*es+té
	3	eisí	*es+entí[254]

6.10.2 Present Subjunctive

The forms of this paradigm devolve from *es- plus the endings of the present active subjunctive (6.1.2). E.g.,

		Greek	PIE
sg	1	ɔ̂	*és+ō[255]
	2	ɛ̂is	*és+ēsi
	3	ɛ̂i	*és+ēti

6.10.3 Present Imperative

Aside from the 2nd singular form, the endings are those of the present active imperative (6.1.3). E.g.,

		Greek	PIE
sg	2	ístʰi	*és+dʰi[256]
	3	éstɔ̄	*és+tōt

6.10.4 Present Optative

The antecedents of this paradigm consist of *es- plus the athematic present active optative endings (6.1.4). E.g.,

		Greek	PIE
sg	1	eíɛ̄n	*és+ī̆ē+m[257]

6.10.5 Imperfect Indicative

The antecedent forms of this paradigm consist of the augment *e- plus *es- plus (for the most part) athematic imperfect active indicative endings (6.2.1).

		Greek	PIE
sg	1	ɛ̂n	*é+es+m̥[258]
	2	ɛ̂stʰa	*é+est+tʰa[259]
	3	ɛ̂n	*?[260]
du	2	ɛ̂ston	*é+es+tom
	3	ɛ́stɛ̄n	*é+es+tām
pl	1	ɛ̂men	*é+es+men
	2	ɛ̂te	*é+es+te[261]
	3	ɛ̂san	*é+es+n̥t[262]

6.10.6 Future Indicative

The endings of this paradigm are those of the future middle indicative (6.6.3). E.g.,

		Greek	PIE
sg	1	ésomai	*és+s+omai[263]

6.10.7 Perfect Indicative

Hirt (1912: 503) cites the following perfect forms:

		Greek	PIE
sg	1	ɛ̄̂ a	*é+es+a[264]
	2	ɛ̄̂ stʰa	*é+es+tʰa
	3	ɛ̄̂ e	*é+es+e

V Exercises

(1) In the following the PIE forms and the changes into Greek are given. (Assume in all instances the application of 2f GREEK STRESS.) What are the Greek forms? Give them in our romanization of the traditional orthography <...> as well as the phonemic transcription /.../ when the two differ.

a. Acc sg *bʰeidʰṓj+m̥ 'persuasion' + 2a ASPIR DEVOI, 2b ē/ō-TO-ɛ̄/ɔ̄, 2d SYL SON, 2f3 GREEK STRESS: ACUTE STRESS, 3b j-CHANGES, 5c V-CONTRACT, 7a ei/ou-TO-ē/ō, 7b GRASSMANN > Greek ?

b. 1sg pres *dʰábʰ+j+ō 'honor' + 2a ASPIR DEVOI, 2b ē/ō-TO-ɛ̄/ɔ̄, 3a C+j CHANGES > Greek?

c. 1sg pres *dʰídʰēmi 'place, set'+2a ASPIR DEVOI, 2b ē/ō-TO-ɛ̄/ɔ̄, 7b GRASSMANN > Greek?

d. *dʰwr̥+j+ós 'door-mover, i.e. hinge' + 2a ASPIR DEVOI, 2d SYL SON, 3c j/w-MET, 7c w-DELE > Greek?

e. 1sg pres subj *és+ō 'be' + 2b ē/ō-TO-ɛ̄/ɔ̄, 3e s-h-Ø, 5c V-CONTRACT > Greek?

f. *gʰebʰalā́ 'head' + 2a ASPIR DEVOI, 6a ā-TO-ɛ̄, 7b GRASSMANN > Greek?

g. Nom sg masc *gʰr̥+íwents 'graceful' + 2a ASPIR DEVOI, 2d SYL SON, 6b C-Cl CHANGES (early rules), 5b NASAL+s (late rules), 7c w-DELE > Greek?

h. 1sg pres *gʷj+ɛ̄́+j+ō 'live' + 2b ē/ō-TO-ɛ̄/ɔ̄, 3a C+j CHANGES, 3b j-Changes, 5c V-CONTRACT > Greek?

i. 1sg pres *gʷĺ̥+j+ō 'throw' + 2b ē/ō-TO-ɛ̄/ɔ̄, 2d SYL SON, 3a C+j CHANGES, 5a LABIOVEL > Greek?

j. *gʷm̥tilḗus 'king' + 2d SYL SON, 2f3 GREEK STRESS: ACUTE STRESS, 4b t-TO-s, 5a LABIOVEL, 6c DIPH SHORT > Greek?

k. komjāi 'in common' + 3a C+j CHANGES, 3c j/w-MET, 6a ā-TO-ɛ̄ > Greek?

l. *nḗr 'man' + 2b ē/ō-TO-ɛ̄/ɔ̄, 2f3 GREEK STRESS: ACUTE STRESS, 4a PROTHESIS > Greek?

m. Nom sg *nokt+s 'night' + 2c o-TO-u, 6b C-Cl CHANGES, 6d u(:)-TO-y(:) > Greek?

n. Nom sg *nóm+n̥t 'name' + 2d SYL SON, 2e WF STOP DELE, 4a PROTHESIS, 2f2 GREEK STRESS: RECESSIVE STRESS (applying as a persistent synchronic rule) > Greek?

o. *ń̥+satos 'insatiable' + 2d SYL SON, 3e s-h-Ø > Greek?

p. Nom sg *ókʷ+mn̥t 'eye' + 2d SYL SON, 2e WF STOP DELE, 5a LABIOVEL, 6b C-Cl CHANGES > Greek?

q. *sā́welios 'sun' + 3e s-h-Ø, 6a ā-TO-ɛ̄, 7c w-DELE, 5c V-CONTRACT (applying as a persistent synchronic rule) > Greek?

r. Future perf 1sg *sé+stā+k+ō 'I shall have stood' + 2b ē/ō-TO-ɛ̄/ɔ̄, 2f GREEK STRESS, 3e s-h-Ø, 6a ā-TO-ɛ̄ > Greek?

s. *sḿ̥+logʰ+os 'same-bed person, spouse' + 2a ASPIR DEVOI, 2d SYL SON, 3e s-h-Ø, 7b GRASSMANN > Greek?

t. Acc sg *snígʰʷm̥ 'snow' + 2a ASPIR DEVOI, 2d SYL SON, 3e s-h-Ø, 5a LABIOVEL > Greek?

u. *stéig^{h}ō 'go' + 2a ASPIR DEVOI, 2b ē/ō-TO-ɛ̄/ɔ̄, 2f2 GREEK STRESS: RECESSIVE STRESS, 7a ei/ou-TO-ē/ō > Greek?
v. *wérgom 'work' + 3d m-TO-n, 7c w-DELE > Greek?

(2) Given the following PIE forms, what will be the Greek reflexes and what changes will they have undergone? Give them in the romanized traditional orthography <...> as well as the phonemic transcription /.. . / when the two differ.

a. *ag^{hw}nós 'lamb'.
b. *b^{h}ā́g^{h}us 'arm'.
c. *b^{h}éid^{h}ō 'persuade'.
d. *b^{h}úō 'produce'.
e. *dámadjō 'overpower'.
f. *d^{h}éig^{h}os 'wall'.
g. *d^{h}urā́ 'door'.
h. *éng^{h}elus 'eel'.
i. *g^{hw}ermós 'hot'.
j. *g^{w}ṓus cow
k. *klépjō 'steal'.
l. *kswelásnā 'moon'.
m. Nom sg masc adj *mrotós 'mortal'.
n. *pédja 'edge'.
o. Nom sg *sáld+s 'salt'.
p. *sédjomai 'sit'.
q. *sék^{w}omai 'follow'.
r. *sélesen 'to seize'.
s. Nom sg *sermēn+eú+s 'interpreter'.
t. 1sg pres *sí+sd+ō 'sit down'.
u. státis 'stance'.
v. Nom sg masc adj *swādús 'sweet'.
w. *wék^{w}os 'word'.

(3) Consider the following Greek forms under (a). Match them with their correct PIE antecedents under (b) and give the changes which they have undergone.

(a) Greek forms. (i) akoúɔ̄ 'hear', (ii) baínɔ̄ 'go', (iii) barýs 'heavy', (iv) déka 'ten', (v) eíkosi '20', (vi) eleút^{h}eros 'free', (vii) érebos 'hell', (viii) ereút^{h}ɔ̄ 'make red', (ix) hállomai 'jump', (x) haplóos 'simple', (xi) hédos 'seat', (xii) hɛ̄géomai 'lead', (xiii) hístɛ̄mi 'put', (xiv) leípɔ̄ 'leave', (xv) nom sg masc adj mésos 'mid', (xvi) mýlɛ̄ 'mill', (xvii) omp^{h}ɛ̄́ 'voice, oracle', (xviii) p^{h}érɔ̄ 'carry' (xix) sɔ̂ma 'body', (xx) t^{h}ɛ̄lɛ̄́ 'breast', (xxi) typ^{h}lós 'blind'.

(b) PIE antecedents. (i') *ákousō, (ii') *b^{h}érō, (iii') *dékm̥, (iv') *d^{h}ēlā́, (v') *d^{h}ub^{h}lós, (vi') *g^{w}ḿ̥+j+o, (vii') *g^{w}r̥+ús, (viii') *léik^{w}ō, (ix') *léud^{h}eros, (x') méd^{h}jos, (xi') *mólā, (xii') *rég^{w}os, (xiii') *réud^{h}ō, (xiv') *sáljomai, (xv') *sédos, (xvi') *sḗgejomai, (xvii') *sístāmi, (xviii') *sm̥+pló+os, (xix') *song^{hw}ā́, (xx') *twṓm+n̥t, (xxi') *wíkonti.

(4) Consider the following Greek paradigmatic alternations.

(a)	sg	**masc**	heîs /hɛ̂ s/ = /hées/	'1'
		fem	mía	
		neuter	hén	

(b)	tís	'who?'
	póteros	'which of 2?'

The antecedents of the forms under (a) are ablaut variations of PIE *sVm. The respective endings are *-s, *-ija and *-Ø. What changes account for the Greek forms? The PIE antecedents of the forms under (b) begin with the interrogative segment *k^w-. What change accounts for the Greek forms?

(5) Consider the following Greek paradigmatic alternations.

(a)	sg	**voc**	ána	'prince'
		nom	ánaks	
		gen	anaktós	
(b)	sg	**nom**	génos	'race'
	pl		génɛ̄	
(c)	sg	**nom**	odoús /odoós/	'tooth'
		gen	odóntos	
(d)	sg	**nom**	oûs /óos/	'ear'
		gen	ɔ̄tós	
(e)	sg	**nom**	t^hríks	'hair'
		gen	trik^{h}ós	
(f)	sg	**nom**	Zeús	'Zeus'
		gen	Diós	

The antecedents are as follows:

(a) *wanakt- plus the endings.
(b) This is a Vs-class noun. The plural antecedent is *génes+ā.
(c) The nominative singular is *odónt+s.
(d) These are Vnt-class neuter nouns, *óus and *ous+n̥t+ós.
(e) The antecedent root is *d^hrig^h- plus the endings *-s and *-os.
(f) The antecedents are *diVú+s and *diVu+ós, where V = an ablauting vowel. (The PIE rule 3.1.2c i-j/u-w ALT applies in this derivation.)

Given these facts, what changes and rules account for the alternations in the Greek forms?

(6) Consider the following alternations in verbs.

(a)	**pres**	p^haínɔ̄	'appear'
	future	p^hanɔ̂	
(b)	**pres**	klī́nɔ̄	'lean'
	aorist	ékline	
(c)	**pres**	ék^{h}ɔ̄	'have'
	future	héksɔ̄	
(d)	**pres**	sképtomai	'look at'
	future	sképsomai	
(e)	**pres**	stéllɔ̄	'place'
	future	stelɔ̂	

Note also the following:

(a) This is a j-class verb. The future formative was *-es+ō.
(b) This is a j-class verb.
(c) The future formative was *-s+ō.
(d) This is a j-class verb. The future formative was *-s+ō.
(e) This a j-class verb. The future formative was *es+ō.

Given these facts, what are the PIE antecedents and what changes and rules account for the alternations in the Greek forms?

(7) Consider the following alternations.

(a)	**pos**	mégas	'big'
	comp	meízɔ̄n	'bigger'
	sup	mégistos	'biggest'
(b)	**noun**	p^hónos	'act of slaying'
	verb	t^heínɔ̄	'I slay'

In (a), what is the PIE root and what changes explain the form of méizɔ̄n? (Hint: consider the PIE comparative ending to be *-jis+ōn.) The forms in (b) devolve from a single PIE root which ablauts. The verb is j-class. What is the PIE antecedent and what changes did it undergo to derive the Greek forms?

(8) See the glossed Greek text in VI below. Give a smooth translation of this text.

VI A Greek Text

The following are the opening paragraphs of Xenophon's *Memorabilia*, written ca. 380 BC in the Attic dialect. The Greek text is from Marchant (1953: 2). In our transcription of the text, we give (a) the romanization of the Greek original, (b) a phonemic transcription, (c) a gloss and (d) a grammatical description of each word. Stressed long vowels are written as two segments with the stress on the first or second mora indicated.

		Lines a–d		
TITLE	1	a	Ksenop^{h}ɔ̄̂ntos	Apomnɛ̄moneúmata
TITLE		b	ksenop^{h}ɔ́ɔntos	apomnɛ̄moneúmata
TITLE		c	*Xenophon*	*memoir*
TITLE		d	Vnt-class	Vnt-class neuter
TITLE			masc gen sg	nom pl

		Word 1	Word 2	Word 3	Word 4	Word 5	Word 6
2	a	Pollákis	et^{h}aúmasa,	tísi	potè	lógois	At^{h}ɛ̄naíous
	b	pollákis	et^{h}aúmasa	tísi	potè	lógois	at^{h}ɛ̄naíɔ̄s
	c	*often*	*be astonished as*	*that*	*when*	*reason*	*Athenians*
	d	adv	1sg aorist	indef pron	adv	o-class	o-class
				dat pl		masc dat pl	masc acc pl
3	a	épeisan	hoi	grapsámenoi	Sɔ̄krátɛ̄n,	hɔ̄s	áksios
	b	épēsan	hoi	grapsámenoi	sɔ̄krátɛ̄n	hɔ̄s	áksios
	c	*persuade*	*they*	*accuse*	*Socrates*	*that*	*worthy*
	d	3pl aorist	dem pron	aorist mid part	Vs-class	conj	o/ā-class
		act ind	nom pl masc	nom pl masc	masc sg acc		adj
4	a	eíɛ̄	t^{h}anátou	tɛ̄̂i	pólei.	Hɛ̄	mèn
	b	eéɛ̄	t^{h}anátō	tɛ́ɛi	pólē	hɛ̄	mèn
	c	*be*	*death*	*the*	*city*	*the*	*so*
	d	3 sg	o-class	dem pron	i-class	dem pron	particle
		pres opt	masc gen sg	dat sg	fem dat sg	nom sg fem	
5	a	gàr	grap^{h}ɛ̄̀	kat'	autoû	toiā́de	tis
	b	gàr	grap^{h}ɛɛ̀	kat	autóo	toiaáde	tis
	c	*for*	*write*	*against*	*him*	*such*	*something*
	d	conj	ā-class	prep + gen	3 pers pron	pron	indef pron
			fem nom sg		gen sg masc	nom sg fem	nom sg fem

6	**a**	ɛ̄̂n:	Adikeî	Sɔ̄krátɛ̄s	hoùs	mèn	hɛ̄
	b	ɛ́ɛn:	adikée	sɔ̄krátɛ̄s	hoòs	mèn	hɛ̄
	c	*be*	*do wrong*	*Socrates*	*which*	*so*	*the*
	d	3sg	3sg pres	Vs-class	rel pron	particle	dem pron
		imperf ind	ind	masc nom sg	acc pl masc		nom sg fem

7	**a**	pólis	nomízei	t^{h}eoùs	ou	nomízɔ̄n,	hétera
	b	pólis	nomídzɛ̄	t^{h}eoòs	ō	nomídzɔ̄n	hétera
	c	*city*	*acknowledge*	*god*	*not*	*acknowledge*	*other*
	d	i-class	3sg	o-class	adv	pres act part	o/ā-class adj
		fem nom sg	pres ind	masc acc pl		nom sg masc	acc pl neuter

8	**a**	dè	kainà	daimónia	eisp^{h}érɔ̄n.	Adikeî	dè
	b	dè	kainà	daimónia	ēsp^{h}érɔ̄n	adikée	dè
	c	*but*	*new*	*deity*	*import*	*do wrong*	*and*
	d	conj	o/ā-class adj	o-class neuter	pres act	3sg pres	conj
			acc pl neuter	acc pl	nom sg masc	ind	

9	**a**	kaì	toùs	néous	diap^{h}t^{h}eírɔ̄n.	Prɔ̄̂ton	mèn
	b	kaì	toòs	néōs	diap^{h}t^{h}eérɔ̄n	prɔ́ɔton	mèn
	c	*and*	*the*	*young*	*corrupt*	*first*	*so*
	d	conj	dem pron	o/ā-class adj	pres act part	adv	particle
			acc pl masc	acc pl masc	nom sg masc		

10	**a**	oûn,	hɔ̄s	ouk	enozímen	hoùs	hɛ̄
	b	óon	hɔ̄s	ōk	enodzímen	hoòs	hɛ̄
	c	*now*	*that*	*not*	*acknowledge*	*which*	*the*
	d	particle	conj	adv	3sg imperf	rel pron	dem pron
					ind	acc pl masc	nom sg fem

11	**a**	pólis	nomízei	t^{h}eoús,	poíɔ̄i	pot'	ek^{h}rɛ̄́santo
	b	pólis	nomídzɛ̄	t^{h}eoós	poíɔ̄i	pot	ek^{h}rɛɛ́santo
	c	*city*	*acknowledge*	*god*	*what sort of*	*ever*	*furnish*
	d	i-class	3sg pres	o-class	o/ā-class adj	adv	3pl aorist
		fem nom sg	ind	masc	dat sg neuter		mid ind

12	**a**	tekmɛ̄ríɔ̄i?	T^{h}ýɔ̄n	te	gàr	p^{h}anerós	ɛ̂n
	b	tekmɛ̄ríɔ̄i	t^{h}ýɔ̄n	te	gàr	p^{h}anerós	ɛ́ɛn
	c	*proof*	*sacrifice*	*and*	*and*	*visible*	*be*
	d	o-class neuter	pres act part	conj	conj	o/ā-class adj	3sg
		dat sg	nom sg masc			nom sg masc	imperf ind

13	**a**	pollákis	mèn	oíkoi,	pollákis	dè	kaì
	b	pollákis	mèn	oíkoi	pollákis	dè	kaì
	c	*often*	*so*	*at home*	*often*	*and*	*and*
	d	adv	particle	adv	adv	conj	conj

14	**a**	epì	tɔ̂n	koinɔ̂n	tɛ̂s	póleɔ̄s	bɔ̄mɔ̂n
	b	epì	tɔ́ɔn	koinɔ́ɔn	tɛ́ɛs	póleɔ̄s	bɔ̄mɔ́ɔn
	c	*in*	*the*	*public*	*the*	*city*	*altar*
	d	prep + gen	dem pron	o/ā-class adj	dem pron	i-class	o-class
			gen pl masc	gen pl masc	gen sg fem	fem gen sg	masc gen pl

15	**a**	kaì	mantikɛ̂i	k^{h}rɔ̄́menos	ouk	ap^{h}anɛ̂s	ɛ̂n:
	b	kaì	mantikɛ́ɛi	k^{h}rɔɔ́menos	ɔ̄k	ap^{h}anɛɛ̀s	ɛ́ɛn
	c	*and*	*divination*	*use*	*not*	*unseen*	*be*
	d	conj	ā-class	pres mid part	adv	Vs-class adj	3sg ind
			fem dat sg	nom sg masc		nom sg masc	

16	**a**	dietet^{h}rȳ́lɛ̄to	gár,	hɔ̄s	p^{h}aíɛ̄	Sɔ̄krátɛ̄s	tò
	b	dietet^{h}ryýlɛ̄to	gár	hɔ̄s	p^{h}aíɛ̄	sɔ̄krátɛ̄s	tò
	c	*report*	*for*	*that*	*say*	*Socrates*	*the*
	d	3sg mediopass	conj	conj	3sg	Vs-class	dem pron
		pass perf			pres act opt	masc nom sg	acc sg neuter

17	**a**	daimónion	heautɔ̂i	sɛ̄maínein;	hót^{h}en	dɛ̂	kaì
	b	daimónion	heautɔ́ɔi	sɛ̄maínɛ̄n	hót^{h}en	dɛɛ̀	kaì
	c	*deity*	*he*	*give a sign to*	*therefore*	*indeed*	*and*
	d	o-class	dat sg masc	pres act inf	adv	adv	conj
		neuter acc sg					

18						
a	málistá	moi	dokoûsin	autòn	aitiástʰai	kainà
b	málistá	moi	dokóosin	autòn	aitiástʰai	kainà
c	*especially*	*I*	*seem*	*he*	*accuse*	*new*
d	adv	dat sg	3pl pres act ind	acc sg masc	aorist mid inf	o/ā-class acc pl neuter

19		
a	daimónia	eispʰérein.
b	daimónia	ēspʰérēn
c	*deity*	*introduce*
d	o-class neuter acc pl	pres act inf

VII Key

(1) The Greek forms are these: (a) <peitʰɔ̃́> /pētʰɔɔ́/, (b) tʰáptɔ̄, (c) títʰɛmi, (d) tʰairós, (e) <ɔ̂> = /ɔ́ɔ/, (f) <kepʰalɛ̃́> = /kepʰalɛɛ́/, (g) <kʰaríeis> = /kʰaríēs/, (h) <zɔ̂> = /dzɔ́ɔ/, (i) bállɔ̄, (j) basileús, (k) <koinɛ̂i> = /koinɛ́ɛi/, (l) <anɛ̃́r> = /anɛɛ́r/, (m) nýks, (n) ónoma, (o) áatos, (p) ómma, (q) <hɛ̃́lios> = /hɛɛ́lios, (r) <hestɛ̃́ɔ̄> = /hestɛɛ́ɔ̄/, (s) álokʰos, (t) nípʰa, (u) <steíkʰɔ̄> = /steékʰɔ̄/, (v) érgon.

(2) The Greek forms and changes are these:

- (a) amnós. The derivation is 2a ASPIR DEVOI, 5a LABIOVEL, 6b C-Cl CHANGES.
- (b) <pɛ̂kʰys> = /pɛ́ɛkys/. The derivation is 2a ASPIR DEVOI, 6a ā-TO-ɛ̄, 6d u(:)-TO-y(:), 7b GRASSMANN.
- (c) <peítʰɔ̄> = /peétʰɔ̄/. The derivation is 2a ASPIR DEVOI, 2b ē/ō-TO-ɛ̄/ɔ̄, 7a ei/ou-TO-ē/ō, 7b GRASSMANN.
- (d) pʰýɔ̄. The derivation is 2a ASPIR DEVOI, 2b ē/ō-TO-ɛ̄/ɔ̄, 6d u(:)-TO-y(:).
- (e) <damázɔ̄> = /damádzɔ̄/. 2b ē/ō-TO-ɛ̄/ɔ̄, 2f2 GREEK STRESS: RECESSIVE STRESS, 3a C+j CHANGES.
- (f) <teîkʰos> = /téekʰos/. 2a ASPIR DEVOI, 7a ei/ou-TO-ē/ō, 7b GRASSMANN.
- (g) <tʰyrā̃́> = /tʰyraá/. 2a ASPIR DEVOI, 2f3 GREEK STRESS: ACUTE STRESS, 6d u(:)-TO-y(:).
- (h) <égkʰelys> = /éŋkʰelys/. 2a ASPIR DEVOI, 6d u(:)-TO-y(:).
- (i) tʰermós. 2a ASPIR DEVOI, 5a LABIOVEL.
- (j) <boûs> = /bóos/. 5a LABIOVEL, 6c DIPH SHORT, 7a ei/ou-TO-ē/ō.
- (k) kléptɔ̄. 2b ē/ō-TO-ɛ̄/ɔ̄, 3a C+j CHANGES.
- (l) <selɛ̃́nɛ̄> = /selɛɛ́nɛ̄/. 2f3 GREEK STRESS: ACUTE STRESS, 3e s-h-Ø, 6a ā-TO-ɛ̄, 6b C-Cl CHANGES, 7c w-DELE.
- (m) brotós. 6b C-Cl CHANGES.
- (n) <péza> = /pédza/. 3a C+j CHANGES.
- (o) háls. 3e s-h-Ø, 6b C-Cl CHANGES.

(p) <hézomai> /hédzomai/. 3a C+j CHANGES, 3e s-h-Ø.
(q) hépomai. 3e s-h-Ø, 5a LABIOVEL.
(r) <hélein> = /hélēn/. 3e s-h-Ø.
(s) hermɛ̄neús. 2b ē/ō-TO-ɛ̄/ɔ̄, 3e s-h-Ø.
(t) <hízɔ̄> = /hídzɔ̄/ (perhaps /hízdɔ̄/). 2b ē/ō-TO-ɛ̄/ɔ̄, 3e s-h-Ø.
(u) stásis. 4b t-TO-s.
(v) hɛ̄dýs. 3e s-h-Ø, 6a ā-TO-ɛ̄, 6d u(:)-TO-y(:), 7c w-DELE.
(w) épos. 5a LABIOVEL, 7c w-DELE.

(3) The PIE antecedents and changes are as follows.

(i) PIE i', *ákousō. The derivation is 2b ē/ō-TO-ɛ̄/ɔ̄, 2f GREEK STRESS, 3e s-h-Ø.
(ii) PIE vi', *g^{w}ḿ̥+j+ō. The derivation 2b ē/ō-TO-ɛ̄/ɔ̄, 2d SYL SON, 3a C+j CHANGES, 3c j/w-MET, 5a LABIOVEL.
(iii) PIE vii', *g^{w}r̥+ús. 2d SYL SON, 5a LABIOVEL, 6d u(:)-TO-y(:).
(iv) PIE iii', *dékm̥. 2d SYL SON.
(v) PIE xxi', *wíkonti. 4a PROTHESIS, 4b t-TO-s, 5b NASAL+s (minus the vowel-lengthening), 7c w-DELE.
(vi) PIE ix', *léud^{h}eros. 2a ASPIR DEVOI, 2f2 GREEK STRESS: RECESSIVE STRESS, 4a PROTHESIS.
(vii) PIE xii', *rég^{w}os. 4a PROTHESIS, 2f2 GREEK STRESS: RECESSIVE STRESS (applying as a synchronic rule), 5a LABIOVEL.
(viii) PIE xiii', *réud^{h}ō. 2a ASPIR DEVOI, 2b ē/ō-TO-ɛ̄/ɔ̄, 2f2 GREEK STRESS: RECESSIVE STRESS, 4a PROTHESIS.
(ix) PIE xiv', *sáljomai. 3a C+j CHANGES, 3e s-h-Ø.
(x) PIE xviii', *sm̥+pló+os. 2d SYL SON, 3e s-h-Ø.
(xi) PIE xv', *sédos. 3e s-h-Ø.
(xii) PIE xvi', *sɛ̄́gejomai. 2b ē/ō-TO-ɛ̄/ɔ̄, 2f GREEK STRESS, 3b j-CHANGES, 3e s-h-Ø.
(xiii) PIE xvii', *sístāmi. 3e s-h-Ø, 6a ā-TO-ɛ̄.
(xiv) PIE viii', *léik^{w}ō. 2b ē/ō-TO-ɛ̄/ɔ̄, 2f GREEK STRESS, 5a LABIOVEL.
(xv) PIE x', *méd^{h}jos. 2a ASPIR DEVOI, 3a C+j CHANGES.
(xvi) PIE xi', *mólā. 2c o-TO-u, 6a ā-TO-ɛ̄, 6d u(:)-TO-y(:).
(xvii) PIE xix', *song^{hw}ā́. 2a ASPIR DEVOI, 2f3 GREEK STRESS: ACUTE STRESS, 5a LABIOVEL and then PIE 3.1.2d NASAL ASSIM (applying as a persistent synchronic rule), 6a ā-TO-ɛ̄, 7b GRASSMANN.
(xviii) PIE ii', *b^{h}érō. 2a ASPIR DEVOI, 2b ē/ō-TO-ɛ̄/ɔ̄.
(xix) PIE xx', twɔ̄́m+n̥t. 2b ē/ō-TO-ɛ̄/ɔ̄, 2d SYL SON, 2e WF STOP DELE, 4b t-TO-s, 7c w-DELE.
(xx) PIE iv', *d^{h}ēlā́. 2a ASPIR DEVOI, 2b ē/ō-TO-ɛ̄/ɔ̄, 2f3 GREEK STRESS: ACUTE STRESS, 6a ā-TO-ɛ̄.
(xxi) PIE v', *d^{h}ub^{h}lós. 2a ASPIR DEVOI, 6d u(:)-TO-y(:), 7b GRASSMANN.

(4) (a) The PIE antecedents are *séms, *smíja and *sém. The changes are PIE 3.1.2d NASAL ASSIM, 3d m-TO-n, 3e s-h-Ø, 5b NASAL+s.
(b) The change is 5a LABIOVEL.

(5) (a) The changes are 2e WF-STOP DELE, 6b C-Cl CHANGES, 7c w-DELE.
(b) The changes are 3e s-h-Ø and 5c V-CONTRACT.

(c) The changes are 6b2 C-Cl CHANGES applying early to /ts/, 5b2 NASAL+s applying late to word-final /ns/, 2f3 GREEK STRESS: ACUTE STRESS applying as a persistent synchronic rule.

(d) The changes are 2d SYL SON, 3e s-h-∅, 7a ei/ou-TO-ē/ō, 5c V-CONTRACT applying as a persistent synchronic rule.

(e) The changes are 2a ASPIR DEVOI, 6b C-Cl CHANGES, 7b GRASSMANN.

(f) The PIE antecedents are ablauting *diēú+s and *diu+ós (PIE 3.1.2c i-j/u-w ALT applying synchronically) → *djḗus and *diwós. The changes then are 3a C+j CHANGES, 6c DIPH SHORT, 7c w-DELE.

(6) (a) The PIE antecedents are *b^{h}án+jō and *b^{h}án+esō. The changes are 2a ASPIR DEVOI, 2b ē/ō-TO-ɛ̄/ɔ̄, 2f GREEK STRESS, 3c j/w-MET, 3e s-h-∅ and 5c V-CONTRACT.

(b) The PIE antecedents are *klínjō and *ékline. The changes are 2b ē/ō-TO-ɛ̄/ɔ̄ and 3c j/w-MET (by which *klínjɔ̄ > *klíjnɔ̄ = klī́nɔ̄).

(c) The PIE antecedents are *ség^{h}+ō and *ség^{h}+s+ō. The changes are 2a ASPIR DEVOI, 2b ē/ō-TO-ɛ̄/ɔ̄, 3e s-h-∅, 6b2 C-Cl CHANGES (whereby *hék^{h}sɔ̄ > héksɔ̄), 7b GRASSMANN (whereby *hék^{h}ɔ̄ > ék^{h}ɔ̄).

(d) The PIE antecedents are *skép+j+omai and *skép+s+omai. The change is 3a C+j CHANGES.

(e) The PIE antecedents are *stél+j+ō and *stél+es+ō. The changes are 2b ē/ō-TO-ɛ̄/ɔ̄, 2f GREEK STRESS, 3a C+j CHANGES, 3e s-h-∅, 5c V-CONTRACT.

(7) (a) The PIE antecedent root is *meg-. The derivation of the comparative is *még+jos+ōn (2b ē/ō-TO-ɛ̄/ɔ̄ > *mégjosɔ̄n (3a C+j CHANGES) > *médzjosɔ̄n (3c j/w-MET) > *méjdzosɔ̄n = *méidzosɔ̄n (3e s-h-∅) > *méidzoɔ̄n (5c V-CONTRACT) > *méidzɔ̄n (2f GREEK STRESS applying as a persistent synchronic rule) >*meídzɔ̄n (7a ei/ou-TO-ē/ō) > /meédzɔ̄n/, written <meízɔ̄n>.

(b) The PIE ablauting root is *g^{hw}ón+os and *g^{hw}én+jō. The derivation is *g^{hw}ónos and *g^{hw}énjō (2a ASPIR DEVOI) > *k^{hw}ónos *k^{hw}énjō (2b ē/ō-TO-ɛ̄/ɔ̄) > *k^{hw}ónos *k^{hw}énjɔ̄ (3c j/w-MET) > *k^{hw}ónos *k^{hw}éjnɔ̄ = *k^{hw}éinɔ̄ (2f GREEK STRESS applying as a persistent synchronic rule) > *k^{hw}ónos *k^{hw}éinɔ̄ (5b LABIOVEL) > p^{h}ónos and t^{h}éinɔ̄.

(8) The following is a translation of the text in section VI.

"Title: *Xenophon's Memoirs*.

"I have often been astonished by what reasons those who accused Socrates persuaded the Athenians that he was worthy of death from the city. The writ against him was this: Socrates does wrong in that he does not acknowledge those gods which the city acknowledges and he imports foreign deities. He also does wrong in that he corrupts the youth.

"First, that he did not acknowledge the gods which the city acknowledges, by what kind of proof did they furnish this evidence? Socrates was often seen sacrificing at home and at public altars of the city. He was also not unseen to use divination: in fact, it had been reported that Socrates said that the deity had given signs to him. So for this reason it seems to me that they accused Socrates of introducing new deities."

VIII Notes

[1] Both [s] and [z] may have been dental.

[2] The /dz/, which may be considered either a single affricate [dᶻ] or a sequence of two segments [dz], arises from 3a C+j CHANGES and 3b j-CHANGES. The [z] can arise as an allophone of /s/ by 6b C-Cl CHANGES 1 as in the sequence /atʰɛ̄nās+de/ 'to Athens' (encliticization) → /atʰɛ̄nāsde/ (6b C-Cl CHANGES 1) → [atʰɛ̄nāzde], spelled <Atʰɛ̄nāze>.

[3] The segment [ŋ] occurs before the velar stops /k, kʰ, g / by the PIE NASAL ASSIM rule 3.1.2d in Chapter 1, which remains in the phonology of Greek. As such, [ŋ] may be considered an allophone of /n/. It also occurs by 6b C-Cl CHANGES as an alternate for /k, g/ before /m/. Hence /km, gm/ → [ŋm]. As such, [ŋ] may also be considered an allophone of /k/ and /g/. In all its occurrences [ŋ] is written in traditional Greek orthography with <g>, e.g., <aggelos> 'messenger'. We transcribe this form as phonemic /ángelos/, phonetic [áŋgelos].

[4] According to Hirt (1912: 85) the /r/ has been described by ancient grammarians as tongue-tip. The /r/ as well as the other segments which we have labeled "dental" may have been alveolar.

[5] After the changes 6c DIPH SHORT and 7a ei/ou-TO-ē/ō, short /u/ occurs only as the second segment in diphthongs.

[6] After the occurrence of 6c DIPH SHORT and 7a ei/ou-TO-ē/ō, these are the remaining diphthongs. (On the creation of the new long diphthongs, see 6c.) We follow the traditional orthographic practice and record /ē, ō/ in Greek forms as <ei, ou>.

[7] The usual PIE form posited is *wĺ̥kʷos. If so, the expected Greek form would be **lákos by 2d SYL SON. We assume the o-grade ablaut form. The derivation is *wlókʷos (2c o-TO-u) > *wlúkʷos (5a LABIOVEL) > *wlúkos (6d u(:)-TO-y(:), 7c w-DELE) > lýkos. (One might expect by 5a LABIOVEL **lýpos; lýkos is perhaps a dialect form.)

[8] The derivation is *wlókʷosjo (2c o-TO-u) > *wlúkʷosjo (3e s-h-Ø, then 3b j-CHANGES) > *wlukʷoo = *wlúkʷō (5a LABIOVEL, 6d u(:)-TO-y(:), 7c w-DELE) > /lýkō/ = <lýkou>.

[9] The locative and instrumental endings are attested only as remnants. The instrumental ending -pʰi(n) is found either as a singular or a plural, e.g. naûpʰi 'from ships'. Note that 7b GRASSMANN has not applied here to produce Gk **teópʰin instead of tʰeópʰin. This probably means that the sequence was considered as two separate words, /tʰeó##pʰin/.

[10] The PIE antecedent is not clear.

[11] This ending is from the nominative plural masculine of the pronominal declension *s+oi 'these' (see 5.4 below).

[12] The derivation is *wlókʷons (2c o-TO-u, 5a LABIOVEL) > *wlúkons (5b NASAL+s) > *wlúkōs (6d u(:)-TO-y(:), 7c w-DELE) > /lýkōs/ = <lýkous>.

[13] The optionally occurring -i in this ending may be from the dative or locative singular. The ending -ois may be from an PIE locative or instrumental plural. The /s/ is retained in the ending instead of being lost by 3e s-h-Ø. The reason for this may be the occurrence of /s/ in Ø-class athematic nouns such as PIE *aig+s+ín 'goat' (ev) > aiksín where the /s/ could not have been deleted.

[14] The ending -a instead of **-ā may have come from the athematic class (1.5). Some sources such as Brandenstein (1959: 23) consider the PIE antecedent ending to have been *-ə.

[15] The derivation is *nó+os (5c V-CONTRACT) > /nō̂s/ <noûs>.

[16] The derivation is *naswós (3e s-h-Ø) > *nāwós (6a ā-TO-ɛ̄) > *nɛ̄wós (7c w-DELE) > *nɛ̄ós (8b V-SHORT/Q-MET) > neɔ̄́s /neɔɔ́s/.

[17] The stress changes in the nominative and accusative endings as follows: PIE nom sg *bʰugā́ = */bʰugáa/ (2a ASPIR DEVOI) > *pʰugáa (2f3 GREEK STRESS: ACUTE STRESS) > pʰugaá (6a ā-TO-ɛ̄, 6d u(:)-TO-y(:)) > Gk pʰygɛ̄́ = /pʰygɛɛ́/. The rule 2f3 GREEK STRESS does not apply in cases other than the nom or acc: PIE gen sg *bʰugā́s */bʰugáas/ (ev) > Gk pʰygɛ̂s = /pʰygɛ́ɛs/.

[18] The PIE nom, voc and acc endings for *sbʰr̥j- differ from those of *bʰug- in that the *-a(m) is short. Brandenstein (1959: 25) derives these endings in short /a/ from the jā-class (or ja-class according to Brandenstein). The derivation of the nominative singular is PIE *sbʰŕ̥ja (2a ASPIR DEVOI, 2d SYL SON) > *spʰárja (3c j/w-MET) > Gk

spʰaîra = /spʰáira/. Another possible source of short /a/, which can occur in plain ā-class nouns as well as jā-class ones, is an PIE vocative singular, e.g.

		Greek		PIE
sg	**voc**	nýmpʰa	‘bride’	*snúmbʰa
	nom	nýmpʰɛ̄		*snúmbʰā

[19] Hirt (1912: 336) assumes that the dual in –ā was formed in later Greek on the model of the o-class dual in –ɔ̄ < PIE *-ō. If so, then the -ā must have been formed after the time of 6a ā-TO-ɛ̄. Otherwise one would expect Gk **pʰygɛ̄́ instead of pʰygā́. Sihler (1995: 272) assumes the antecedent was *-a+e from the athematic class. If so, then this ending must also have been formed after the time of 6a ā-TO-ɛ̄. The derivation would then be PIE *bʰugá (ev after 6d u(:)-TO-y(:)) > *pʰygá+e (2f3 GREEK STRESS: ACUTE STRESS and 5c V-CONTRACT applying as persistent synchronic rules) → pʰygā́ = /pʰygaá/.

[20] The ending is from the demonstrative pronoun in 5.4 below.

[21] The derivation is PIE *bʰugā́ns (ev through 5b2 NASAL+s Changes, the later rule applying after 6a ā-TO-ɛ̄) > *pʰugā́s = */pʰugaás/ (6d u(:)-TO-y(:)) > pʰygā́s.

[22] The derivation is *bʰugā́+ōm (2a ASPIR DEVOI, 2b ē/ō-TO-ɛ̄/ɔ̄, 3d m-TO-n) > *pʰugā́ɔ̄n (5c V-CONTRACT, 6d u(:)-TO-y(:)) > pʰygɔ̂̄n = /pʰygɔ́ɔn/.

[23] The derivation is *bʰugā́is (ev after 6c DIPH SHORT) > pʰygaîs = /pʰygáis/.

[24] These endings are from the o-class. The derivation of the genitive singular is *kritā́sjo (3b j-CHANGES, 3e s-h-Ø) > *kritā́o (5c V-CONTRACT) > kritoû = /kritɔ̄̂/ /kritóo/.

[25] The vocative is ā-class. We assume the early PIE stress was word-initial in vocative forms.

[26] The alternation in the roots *poli-, *polēi-, *polei- is PIE ablaut. The derivation of the gen sg is *pólēi+os (PIE 3.1.2c i-j/u-w ALT applying as a synchronic rule) → *pólējos (2b ē/ō-TO-ɛ̄/ɔ̄) > *pólɛ̄jos (3b j-CHANGES) > *pólɛ̄os (V-SHORT/Q-MET) > póleɔ̄s. Change 2f GREEK STRESS has occurred earlier and does not apply to produce Gk **poléɔ̄s. The derivation of the nom dual is *pólei+e (PIE 3.1.2c i-j/u-w ALT applying synchronically) → *póleje (3b j-CHANGES) > Gk pólee = /pólē/, written <pólei>.

[27] The derivation is PIE *pólei+oin (PIE 3.1.2c i-j/u-w ALT) → *pólejoin (2f2 GREEK STRESS: RECESSIVE STRESS) > *poléjoin (3b j-CHANGES) > poléoin.

[28] The accusative plural must have devolved from a PIE nominative plural. Otherwise the derivation would have been PIE acc pl *póli+ns (5b NASAL+s Changes) > Gk **pólīs.

[29] Given the PIE antecedent, one would expect here the Greek genitive plural form **poléɔ̄n. However, the stress remained on the first syllable, Gk póleɔ̄n, perhaps on the analogy of the other plural forms.

[30] From the PIE antecedent one would expect the derivation PIE *póleisi(n) (7a ē/ō-TO-ɛ̄/ɔ̄) > Gk **pólēsi(n) **<póleisi(n)>. The attested form pólesi(n) with /e/ is probably from the other dual and plural forms of the paradigm.

[31] The alternation in the roots *bʰāgʰu-, *bʰāgʰeu- and *bʰāgʰēu- results from PIE ablaut. The derivation of the nominative singular is PIE *bʰā́gʰus (2a ASPIR DEVOI) > *pʰā́kʰus (6a ā-TO-ɛ̄) > *pʰɛ̄́kʰus (6d u(:)-TO-y(:)) > *pʰɛ̄́kʰys (7b GRASSMANN)> pɛ̄̂kʰys = /pɛ́ɛkʰys/.

[32] The derivation is PIE *bʰā́gʰēu+os (PIE 3.1.2c i-j/u-w ALT applying synchronically) → *bʰā́gʰēwos = *bʰáagʰēwos (ev through 2f2 GREEK STRESS: RECESSIVE STRESS) > *bʰaágʰēwos (ev through 7c w-DELE) > *pɛɛ́kʰeɔ̄s (8b V-SHORT/Q-MET) > pɛ̄́kʰeɔ̄s /pɛɛ́kʰeɔ̄s/.

[33] The derivation is PIE *bʰáagʰewe (ev through 7c w-DELE) > pɛɛ́kʰē = pɛ̄́kʰē, spelled < pɛ̄́kʰei>.

[34] According to 2f GREEK STRESS, one would expect Gk **pɛ̄kʰéɔ̄n. The stress remained on the first syllable, probably on the analogy of the other plural forms.

[35] From the PIE antecedent, one would expect Gk **pḗ kʰeusi(n). The attested form pḗ kʰesi(n) has its /e/ from the other dual and plural cases.

[36] The derivation is PIE *wásteu+a (PIE 3.1.2c i-j/u-w ALT applying as a synchronic rule) → *wástewa (7c w-DELE) > *ástea (5c V-CONTRACT) > Gk ástē.

[37] One would expect the derivation *pṓds = */póods/ (2b ē/ō-TO-ɛ̄/ɔ̄, 2f GREEK STRESS) > *pɔ̄́ds = /pɔɔ́ds/ (6b C-Cl CHANGES) > Gk pɔ̄́s = /pɔɔ́s/, which does occur in Doric. The Attic form is poús = /poós/.

[38] The alternation in the roots *pōd- and *pod- is PIE ablaut.

[39] The stress pattern here is not clear. One would expect nom/acc pl **pȳ̂ ra = */pýyra/. Another mystery is that in those cases where this noun has endings, the root vowel is short /y/ instead of long /ȳ/: e.g., nom pl pyrá (not **pȳrá) or gen sg pyrós (not **pȳrós). A possible rationale for the alternation is that it occurred on the analogy of root-class words such as nom sg sȳ̂ s 'pig' vs. gen sg syós where the /ȳ/-/y/ alternation occurred regularly (see the derivation of syós in 1.5.2 below).

[40] This form either may or may not have had the nominative singular ending *-s. In any event, the derivation would be *gwnáik(s) (PIE 3.1.2c i-j/u-w ALT applying synchronically) →*gunáik(s) (2e WF STOP DELE) > *gunái (possible interpretation of this form as an ā-class nominative plural: hence the addition of the nominative singular feminine ending -ā) > *gunā́ (6a ā-TO-ɛ̄, 6d u(:)-TO-y(:)) > Gk gynɛ̄́.

[41]The derivation is PIE *gwnáikm̥ = *gunáikm̥ (2d SYL SON) > gunáika (6d u(:)-TO-y(:)) > Gk gynaîka =/gynáika/.

[42] The alternation of /ō/ and /o/ in the root is due to PIE ablaut. The derivation is PIE *gʷṓus (5a LABIOVEL, 6c DIPH SHORT) > *bóus (7a ei/ou-TO-ē/ō) > Gk boûs = /bȏs/ = /bóos/.

[43] The word-final /n/ in the Greek form is from the thematic class. Otherwise the derivation would be PIE *gʷṓu+m̥ (ev) > Gk **bóa. (The form bóa does occur in some dialects.)

[44] The derivation is PIE *gʷou+ós (PIE 3.1.2c i-j/u-w ALT applying as a synchronic rule) → *gʷowós (5a LABIOVEL) > *bowós (7c w-DELE) > boós.

[45] The derivation is PIE *gʷóu+n̥s (PIE 3.1.2c i-j/u-w ALT) → *gʷówn̥s (2d SYL SON) > *gʷówas (5a LABIOVEL, 7c w-DELE) > bóas (5c V-CONTRACT applying as a persistent synchronic rule) > boûs /bóos/.

[46] The derivation is PIE *diēú+s (PIE 3.1.2c i-j/u-w ALT) → *djēús (3a C+j CHANGES) > *dzēús (6c DIPH SHORT) > Zeús /dzeús/.

[47] The derivation is analogous to the preceding. The stress in the two forms differs.

[48] The derivation of both these forms is this: diḗu+m̥ vs.*díu+m̥ (PIE 3.1.2c i-j/u-w ALT) → *djḗwm̥ vs. *díwm̥ (2b ē/ō-TO-ɛ̄/ɔ̄) > *djɛ̄́ wm̥ vs. *díwm̥ (2d SYL SON) > *djɛ̄́ wa vs. *díwa (3a C+j CHANGES) > *dzɛ̄́wa vs. *díwa (7c w-DELE) > *dzɛ̄́ a vs. *día (5c V-CONTRACT, applying as a persistent synchronic rule, and the addition of the accusative ending /-n/ from the thematic class — both these changes applying to the first form) > Gk Zɛ̄̂ n /dzɛ́ɛn/ vs. Día.

[49] The derivation is PIE *diu+ós (PIE 3.1.2c i-j/u-w ALT) → *diwós (7c w-DELE) > Gk Diós.

[50] The derivation is nom sg *gʷm̥tiléus (2b ē/ō-TO-ɛ̄/ɔ̄) > *gʷm̥tilɛ̄́ u+s (2d SYL SON) > *gʷatilɛ̄́ u+s (2f3 GREEK STRESS: ACUTE STRESS) > *gʷatilɛ̄ús (4b t-TO-s) > *gʷasilɛ̄ús (5a LABIOVEL) > *basilɛ̄ús (8b V-SHORT/Q-MET) > basileús. The derivation of the vocative singular is like that of the nominative singular except that the stress does not change, hence Gk basileû = /basiléu/.

[51] The derivation is PIE *gʷm̥tiléu+m̥ (PIE 3.1.2c i-j/u-w ALT, applying as a synchronic rule) → *gʷm̥tiléwm̥ (2b ē/ō-TO-ɛ̄/ɔ̄, 2d SYL SON) > *gʷatilɛ̄́ wa (4b t-TO-s, 5a LABIOVEL) > *basilɛ̄́ wa (7c w-DELE) > *basilɛ̄́ a (8b V-SHORT/Q-MET) > basiléā.

[52] The derivation is analogous to the immediately preceding one.

[53] These endings are from the thematic classes. Otherwise one would expect **kī̂a and **sýa respectively.

[54] The derivation is PIE *sū+ós (6d u(:)-TO-y(:)) > *sȳós (8b V-SHORT/Q-MET) > syós. One might have also expected **hyós by 3e s-h-Ø. (The word sȳ̂ s may represent a dialectal form.)

[55] The derivation is PIE *sḗrwōs = */séerwōs/ (2b ē/ō-TO-ɛ̄/ɔ̄) > *sɛ̄́rwɔ̄s (2f3 GREEK STRESS: ACUTE STRESS) > *sɛɛ́rwɔ̄s (3e s-h-Ø) > *hɛɛ́rwɔ̄s > (7c w-DELE) > hɛ̄́rɔ̄s = /hɛɛ́rɔ̄s/.

[56] The derivation is PIE *b^{h}eid^{h}ṓi (2a ASPIR DEVOI, 2b ē/ō-TO-ɛ̄/ɔ̄) > *p^{h}eit^{h}ɔ̄́i (2f3 GREEK STRESS: ACUTE STRESS) > *p^{h}eit^{h}ɔ̄í (7a ei/ou-TO-ē/ō) > *p^{h}ēt^{h}ɔ̄í (7b GRASSMANN) > Gk /pēt^{h}ɔ̄í/, written <peit^{h}ɔ̄í>.

[57] The derivation is PIE *b^{h}eid^{h}ṓi+m̥ (PIE 3.1.2c i-j/u-w ALT applying synchronically) → *b^{h}eid^{h}ṓjm̥ (2a ASPIR DEVOI) > *p^{h}eit^{h}ṓjm̥ (2b ē/ō-TO-ɛ̄/ɔ̄, 2d SYL SON) > *p^{h}eit^{h}ɔ̄́ja (2f3 GREEK STRESS: ACUTE STRESS) > *p^{h}eit^{h}ɔ̄já (3b j-CHANGES) > *p^{h}eit^{h}ɔ̄á (5c V-CONTRACT) > *p^{h}eit^{h}ɔ̄́ = */p^{h}eit^{h}ɔɔ́/ (7a ei/ou-TO-ē/ō , 7b GRASSMANN) > Gk /pēt^{h}ɔɔ́/, spelled <peit^{h}ɔ̄́ >.

[58] We assume the short-/o/ grade ablaut in these forms. The derivation of the genitive singular is *b^{h}eid^{h}ói+os (PIE 3.1.2c i-j/u-w ALT applying synchronically) → *b^{h}eid^{h}ój+os (2a ASPIR DEVOI) > *p^{h}eit^{h}ójos (3b j-CHANGES) > *p^{h}eit^{h}óos (7a ei/ou-TO-ē/ō, 7b GRASSMANN) > Gk /pēt^{h}óo/, spelled <peit^{h}oû>. If the antecedent had been PIE **b^{h}eid^{h}ōi+os, one would expect Gk **peit^{h}ɔ̄̂s = **/pēt^{h}ɔ́ɔs/. The derivation of the dative singular is similar. If the antecedent had been PIE **b^{h}eid^{h}ṓi+i, one would expect Gk **peit^{h}ɔ̄̂i = **/pēt^{h}ɔ́ɔi/.

[59] The alternations of the vowel in the nom sg *patḗr, acc sg *patérm̥ and gen sg *patrós result from PIE ablaut. Aside from the vocative singular, the stress on this word is by 2f1 GREEK STRESS: MORPH COND STRESS always on the second syllable, whether or not that syllable is part of the stem (patɛ̄́r) or in the inflectional ending (patrós).

[60] The antecedent ending may have had *-s. In either event the derivation is PIE *patḗr(s) or possibly *pətḗr(s) (2b ē/ō-TO-ɛ̄/ɔ̄) > *patɛ̄́r(s) (? 2e WF STOP DELE) > *patɛ̄́r = */patɛɛ́r/ (2f3 GREEK STRESS: ACUTE STRESS) > Gk patɛ̄́r = /patɛɛ́r/.

[61] The derivation is PIE Ø-grade *patr+si(n) (PIE 3.1.2g SYL SON rule applying synchronically) → *patr̥si(n) (2d SYL SON) > patrasi(n) (2f GREEK STRESS) > *patrási(n) (3e s-h-Ø not applying here for the reasons discussed under 1.1 note 13) > Gk patrási(n).

[62] Some Vn-class nouns have an -s in the nominative singular. For example, PIE nom sg fem *n̥ktī́+n+s 'beam of light' (2d SYL SON) > aktī̂ns (5b NASAL+s) > aktī́s. The accusative singular is aktī̂na < PIE *n̥ktīn+m̥. Sihler (1995: 290) considers the absence of /-s/ in the nominative singular the result of an early PIE phonological process whereby rs > r. Hirt (1912: 368) maintains that the reason for nom sg -s vs. -Ø in the nominative singular of this class is not known. The problem of the nominative singular in *-s is the same as that discussed in 1.5.3, note 60 above. It is also possible that the /s/ in these forms was introduced from the thematic classes.

[63] One would expect the derivation PIE *poiménsi(n) (5b NASAL+s) > Gk **poimeîsi(n) = **/poimē̂si(n)/. We assume the short /e/ in poimési(n) is from the other cases.

[64] The derivation is PIE *odónt+s (6b2 C-Cl CHANGES applying early to the sequence /ts/) > *odóns (5b2 NASAL+s applying later to word-final /ns/) > *odóos (2f3 GREEK STRESS: ACUTE STRESS applying as a synchronic persistent rule) > Gk odoús = /odoós/. Some masculine Vnt-class nouns possibly do not devolve from forms with -s in the nominative singular. E.g., Gk nom sg gérɔ̄n 'old man' and acc sg géronta from PIE *gérɔ̄nt and *gérontm̥, respectively. If the PIE antecedent had been nom sg **gérɔ̄nt+s, the Greek reflex would be **gérɔ̄s.

[65] This noun was originally Vn-class. The derivation of this form is PIE *nómn̥t (2d SYL SON) > *nómat (2e WF STOP DELE) > *nóma (4a PROTHESIS) > *onóma (2f2 GREEK STRESS: RECESSIVE STRESS applying as a persistent synchronic rule) > ónoma.

[66] This is the Ø ablaut grade of a noun found also as PIE *wódōr. The derivation is PIE *ẃØdōr (PIE 3.1.2c i-j/u-w ALT applying synchronically) → *údōr (2b ē/ō-TO-ɛ̄/ɔ̄) > *údɔ̄r (6d u(:)-TO-y(:), 8a h-ADD) > Gk hýdɔ̄r.

[67] The derivation is PIE *jḗk^{w}r̥t (2b ē/ō-TO-ɛ̄/ɔ̄) > *jɛ̄́k^{w}r̥t (2d SYL SON) > *jɛ̄́k^{w}art (2e WF STOP DELE) > *jɛ̄́k^{w}ar (3b j-CHANGES) > *hɛ̄́k^{w}ar (5a LABIOVEL) > Gk hɛ̄̂par = /hɛ́ɛpar/.

[68] The alternation of PIE *ker- vs. *kr̥- results from PIE ablaut. The derivation of the gen sg is PIE *kr̥+n̥t+ós (2d SYL SON) > kra+at+ós = *krātós (to which 6a ā-TO-ɛ̄ cannot apply because of the /r/) > Gk krātós.

[69] The derivation is *óus (7a ei/ou-TO-ē/ō) > Gk oûs = /ō̂s/ = /óos/.

[70] The derivation is *ous+n̥t+ós (2d SYL SON) > *ousatós (3e s-h-Ø) > *ouatós (7a ei/ou-TO-ē/ō) > *ōatós (5c V-CONTRACT, applying synchronically as a persistent rule) > Gk ɔ̄tós.

[71] The alternation -es- vs. -os- in the derivative suffix is PIE ablaut.

[72] The derivation is PIE dat sg.*génesi (3e s-h-Ø) > *génei (7a ei/ou-TO-ē/ō) > Gk génei = /génē/.

[73] The derivation is PIE *génese (3e s-h-Ø) > génee = /génē/, spelled <génei>.

[74] The derivation is PIE *genesa (3e s-h-Ø) > *génea (5c V-CONTRACT) > Gk génɛ̄.

[75] The derivation is PIE *genesōm (2b ē/ō-TO-ɛ̄/ɔ̄) > *génesɔ̄m (2f2 GREEK STRESS: RECESSIVE STRESS) > *genésɔ̄m (3d m-TO-n, 3e s-h-Ø) > *genéɔ̄n (5c V-CONTRACT) > Gk genɔ̄̂n = /genɔ́ɔn/.

[76] This name very likely does not date from PIE times. We cite it as illustrative of the endings.

[77] The alternation -ēs/-es is PIE ablaut.

[78] The derivation is *sṓkratesm̥ (2b ē/ō-TO-ɛ̄/ɔ̄, 2d SYL SON) > *sɔ̄́kratesa (2f2 GREEK STRESS: RECESSIVE STRESS) > *sɔ̄krátesa (3e s-h-Ø) > *sɔ̄krátea (5c V-CONTRACT) > Gk Sɔ̄krátɛ̄.

[79] The alternation -ōs/-os is PIE ablaut. The stress in the PIE nominative singular is *aidṓs = */audóos/; the stress in the Greek reflex is aidɔ̄́s = /aidɔɔ́s/ by 2f3 GREEK STRESS: ACUTE STRESS.

[80] The derivation is PIE *agadʰā́ (2a ASPIR DEVOI) > *agatʰā́ = */agatʰáa/ (2f3 GREEK STRESS: ACUTE STRESS) > */agatʰaá/ (6a ā-TO-ɛ̄) > Gk agatʰɛ̄́ = /agatʰɛɛ́/. Some adjectives escape the triggering environment of 6a ā-TO-ɛ̄, e.g. Gk nom sg fem makrā́ = /makraá/ 'long'. Some feminine adjectives do not take the i-class endings, but rather those of the masc o-class. E.g., nom sg masc and fem álogos 'without speech' vs. neuter álogon.

[81] This is an early non-PIE borrowing, apparently adopted after the time of 3e s-h-Ø. The derivation is *kʰrūséos (5c V-CONTRACT, 6d u(:)-TO-y(:)) > Gk kʰrȳsoûs = /kʰrȳsóos/.

[82] The derivation is *síslā+os (3e s-h-Ø) > *hī́lāos (6a ā-TO-ɛ̄) > *hī́lɛ̄os (8b V-SHORT/Q-MET) > Gk hī́leɔ̄s.

[83] The alternation of *swādu- vs. *swādeu- in the paradigm is PIE ablaut. The derivation of the nominative singular masculine is PIE *swādús (3e s-h-Ø) > *hwādús (6a ā-TO-ɛ̄) > *hwɛ̄dús (6d u(:)-TO-y(:)) > *hwɛ̄dýs (7c w-DELE) > Gk hɛ̄dýs.

[84] The ablauting vowel could also be long /ē/. If so, the derivation would be *swādḗu+os (PIE 3.1.2c i-j/u-w ALT applying synchronically) → *swādḗwos (ev through 6a ā-TO-ɛ̄) > hwɛ̄dɛ̄́wos (7c w-DELE) > hɛ̄dɛ̄́os (8b V-SHORT/Q-MET) > Gk hɛ̄déos. The derivation for *swādéwos is similar, but without 8b V-SHORT/Q-MET.

[85] The derivations are PIE sg *swādéu+ja and dual *swādéu+jā (PIE 3.1.2c i-j/u-w ALT and 3.1.2f SIEVERS applying as synchronic rules) → *swādéwija and *swādéwijā (2f2 GREEK STRESS: RECESSIVE STRESS) > *swādéwija and *swādewíja (3b j-CHANGES) > *swādéwia and *swādewíā (3e s-h-Ø) > *hwādéwia and *hwādewíā (6a ā-TO-ɛ̄) > *hwɛ̄déwia and *hwɛ̄dewíā (7c w-DELE and 7a ei/ou-TO-ē/ō, the latter applying for a time as a synchronic rule) > Gk hɛ̄deîa = /hɛ̄déea/ and hɛ̄deíā = /hɛ̄deéā/.

[86] The derivation of this form is similar to that of the preceding. After the application of 3e s-h-Ø, the derivation is *hwādewiā́ɔ̄n (5c V-CONTRACT) > *hwādewiɔ́ɔn (6a ā-TO-ɛ̄, 7c w-DELE) > Gk hɛ̄deiɔ̄̂n = /hɛ̄dēɔ́ɔn/.

[87] The derivation is PIE *poljósjo (3a C+j CHANGES) > *pollósjo (3e s-h-Ø and 3b j-CHANGES) > Gk pollóo spelled <polloû>= /pollóo/.

[88] The derivation is PIE *poljā (2f3 GREEK STRESS: ACUTE STRESS) > *poljaá (3a C+j CHANGES) > *pollaá (6a ā-TO-ɛ̄) > Gk pollɛ̄́ = /pollɛɛ́/.

[89] The derivation is PIE *ń̥+ *polids (2d SYL SON) > ápolids (6b C-Cl CHANGES) > Gk ápolis.

[90] The derivation is PIE *ń̥polid (2d SYL SON, 2e WF STOP DELE) > Gk ápoli.

[91] The /ō-o/ alternation is ablaut.

[92] The/derivations of the masculine/feminine and neuter nominative are PIE *mnḗmōn and *mnḗmon (2b ē/ō-TO-ɛ̄/ɔ̄) > *mnḗmɔ̄n and *mnɛ̄́mon (2f3 GREEK STRESS: ACUTE STRESS) > Gk mnɛ̄́mɔ̄n /mnɛɛ́mɔɔn/ vs. mnɛ̄̂mon /mnɛ́ɛmon/.

[93] The derivation is PIE *gʰr̥íwents (2a ASPIR DEVOI, 2d SYL SON) > *kʰaríwents (6b C-Cl CHANGES, early rules) > *kʰaríwens (5b NASAL+s, later rules) > *kʰaríwēs (7c w-DELE) > Gk kʰaríeis = /kʰaríēs/.

[94] The derivation of PIE *gʰr̥íwent is like the preceding example except that 2e WF STOP DELE applies to produce Gk kʰaríen.

[95] The derivation is after 2d SYL SON *kʰaríwentja (3a C+j CHANGES) > *kʰaríwenssa (5b NASAL+s) > *kʰaríwessa (7c w-DELE) > Gk kʰaríessa.

[96] The /ō-o/ alternation is PIE ablaut.

[97] The derivation is PIE *lū́+ōnt (2b ē/ō-TO-ɛ̄/ɔ̄, 2e WF STOP DELE) >*lū́ɔ̄n (6d u(:)-TO-y(:)) > lȳ́ɔ̄n. If the PIE antecedent had been **lū́ōnt+s, the Greek form would be **lȳ́ɔ̄s.

[98] The derivation is *pánts (6b C-Cl CHANGES, an early version) > *páns (5b NASAL+s, later stage 2) > Gk pā̂s = /páas/.

[99] The derivation is PIE *pántja (3a C+j CHANGES) > *pánsa (5b NASAL+s, later stage 2 which applies after 6a ā-TO-ɛ̄, which therefore does not apply) > Gk pā̂sa.

[100] The expected developments of this form would be PIE *pánt (2e WF STOP DELE) > Gk **pán. The actually occurring pā̂n = /páan/ probably has its long /ā/ from the nominative singular masculine and feminine forms.

[101] The PIE antecedent was a compound: *n̥- 'not' plus *lādʰ- 'hidden'.

[102] The derivation is *n̥lādʰésm̥ (2a ASPIR DEVOI) > *n̥lātʰésm̥ (2d SYL SON) > *alātʰésa (3e s-h-Ø) > *alātʰéa (5c V-CONTRACT) > *alātʰā́ (6a ā-TO-ɛ̄) > alɛ̄tʰɛ̄̂ = /alɛ̄tʰɛ́ɛ/.

[103] The alternation /ō-o-Ø/ in these forms is PIE ablaut. The occurrence of short /u/ in *lu-k as opposed to long /ū/ in the pres part *lū+ont cited above is not clear. A possibility is that the original PIE word was *lū- which in some forms, possibly before a vocalic ending, was realized as PIE *luw-, say in the 1sg pres *luwō. Then after 7c w-DELE, two forms *lu- and original *lū- arose.

[104] The derivation is PIE *leluk+ẃs+ja (PIE 3.1.2c i-j/u-w ALT applying synchronically) → *lelukúsja (PIE 3.1.2f SIEVERS applying synchronically) → *lelukúsija (3b j-CHANGES) > *lelukúsia (3e s-h-Ø) > *lelukúia (6d u(:)-TO-y(:)) > Gk lelykŷ̂a = /lelykýia/.

[105] The derivation is *lelukẃsjāōm (PIE 3.1.2c i/u-TO-e/o and 3.1.2f SIEVERS applying synchronically) → *lelukúsijā́ōm (2b ē/ō-TO-ɛ̄/ɔ̄) > *lelukúsijā́ɔ̄m (2f GREEK STRESS) > *lelukusijā́ɔ̄m (3b j-CHANGES) > *lelukusiā́ɔ̄m (3d m-TO-n) > *lelukusiā́ɔ̄n (3e s-h-Ø) > *lelukuiā́ɔ̄n (5c V-CONTRACT) > *lelukuiɔ̄̂n (6d u(:)-TO-y(:)) > Gk lelykyiɔ̄̂n = /lelykyiɔ́ɔn/.

[106] The comparative takes the endings of 2.3.4 Vn-class; the superlative, those of 2.1 o- and ā-class.

[107] The derivation is *swā́disōn (2b ē/ō-TO-ɛ̄/ɔ̄) > *swā́disɔ̄n (2f GREEK STRESS) > *swādísɔ̄n (3e s-h-Ø) > *hwādíɔ̄n (6a ā-TO-ɛ̄) > *hwɛ̄díɔ̄n (7c w-DELE) > Gk hɛ̄díɔ̄n.

[108] The derivation is *még+ios+ōn (PIE 3.1.2c i-j/u-w ALT applying synchronically) → *mégjosōn (2b ē/ō-TO-ɛ̄/ɔ̄) > *mégjosɔ̄n (2f2 GREEK STRESS: RECESSIVE STRESS) > *megjósɔ̄n (3a C+j CHANGES and 3c j/w-MET) > *meidzōsɔ̄n (3e s-h-Ø) > *meidzóɔ̄n (5c V-CONTRACT) > *meidzɔ̄́n (2f2 GREEK STRESS: RECESSIVE STRESS, reapplying as a persistent synchronic rule) → Gk meízɔ̄n = /meédzɔ̄n/.

[109] The derivation is *mī́kroteros (2f2 GREEK STRESS: RECESSIVE STRESS) > Gk mīkróteros.

[110] The derivation is *mī́kro+tm̥+t (from the -is+t ending) + os (2d SYL SON) > *mī́krotatos (2f2 GREEK STRESS: RECESSIVE STRESS) > Gk mīkrótatos.

[111] The derivation is PIE *komjā́i (3a C+j CHANGES) > *konjā́i (3c j/w-MET) > *koinā́i (6a ā-TO-ɛ̄) > Gk koinɛ̄̂i.

[112] This is the most frequent adverb formative. A possible derivation is PIE abl sg *kalṓd (2b ē/ō-TO-ɛ̄/ɔ̄) > *kalɔ̄́d (2e WF STOP DELE) > *kalɔ̄́. At this point -s was added, possibly from a genitive singular ending. Hence *kalɔ̄́+s > kalɔ̄̂s =//kalɔ́ɔs/.

[113] The source of the geminate /ll/ in the Greek form is not clear. It might have been in the comparative and superlative, a jo-/jā-class adjective. The derivation would be *káljisom (3a C+j CHANGES) > *kállisom (3d m-TO-n, 3e s-h-Ø) > kállīon.

[114] The derivation is PIE *séms (3e s-h-Ø) >*héms (5b NASAL+s, applying to /ms/, which was at this time possibly /ns/ by PIE 3.1.2d NASAL ASSIM) > Gk heîs = /hées/.

[115] The PIE antecedent has the Ø-grade ablaut of *sVm-. The derivation is *smjá (PIE 3.1.2f SIEVERS applying synchronically) → *smijá (2fa GREEK STRESS: RECESSIVE STRESS) > *smíja (3b j-CHANGES) > *smía (3e s-h-Ø) > Gk mía.

[116] The derivation is *duṓin (6c DIPH SHORT) > *duóin (6d u(:)-TO-y(:)) > Gk dyoîn = /dyóin/. The short /o/ in the nominative/accusative is from the genitive/dative.

[117] The e-grade ablaut *trei- occurs only in the masculine/feminine nominative/accusative. Otherwise the Ø-grade *tri- occurs.

[118] The derivation is PIE *tréi+es (PIE 3.1.2c i-j/u-w ALT applying synchronically) → *tréjes (3b j-CHANGES) > Gk treîs = /trées/.

[119] The expected derivation of this form would be *k^{w}étwores (5a LABIOVEL) > *tétwores (7c w-DELE) > Gk tétores, which form does in fact occur in Doric. The Attic form may be from a Ø-grade ablauting antecedent *k^{w}étwr̥-. If so, one would expect Attic **tétar+es. The geminate /tt/ is unexplained.

[120] The Attic form héks could be from either *séks or *swéks. Sihler (1995: 413) records the occurrence of dialectal weks '6'. Its derivation would have to be *sweks (3e s-h-Ø)> weks (which must have occurred before the time of 7c w-DELE).

[121] The cardinals for '70' and '80' seem to have been influenced by the ordinals for '7th' and '8th' as described under 4.2 below.

[122] The numerals from '200' through '1000' are jo- and jā-class adjectives.

[123] The derivation of '300' is *tria+(d)kḿ̥tjoi (PIE 3.1.2f SIEVERS applying synchronically) → *tria+(d)kḿ̥tijoi (possible loss of /d/ and lengthening of the preceding vowel) > *triākḿ̥tijoi (2d SYL SON) > *triākátijoi (the /a/ replaced by /o/ from the decades in -konta; or the antecedent may have had the o-grade *-kontjoi from the beginning) > *triākótijoi (3b j-CHANGES) > *triākótioi (4b t-TO-s) > Gk triākósioi. The diā- in '200' is probably modeled after triā- in '300'. Otherwise one would expect Gk **dyɔ̄kósioi.

[124] The antecedent *na- for '9' is not certain.

[125] The /ī/ in k^{h}ī́lioi is unexpected. The expected derivation would be *g^{h}ésljoi (PIE 3.1.2f SIEVERS applying synchronically) → *g^{h}éslijoi (2a ASPIR DEVOI) > *k^{h}éslijoi (3b j-CHANGES) > *k^{h}éslioi (3e s-h-Ø) > Gk **k^{h}ɛ̄́lioi, spelled **<k^{h}eílioi> as opposed to the actually occurring k^{h}ī́lioi.

[126] The reason for the occurrence of the voiced clusters /bd/ and /gd/ in these forms is not clear. A possible derivation could be PIE *séptmos and *óktouos (PIE 3.1.2c i-j/u-w ALT applying synchronically) → *séptmos, *óktowos (3e s-h-Ø) > *héptmos, *óktowos (? a proviso of 6b C-Cl CHANGES) > *hébdmos, *óktowos (? some mutual influence, '7' taking the intermediate /o/ from '8' and '8' forming a voiced cluster like '7') > *hébdomos, *ogdowos (7c w-DELE) > Gk hébdomos and ógdɔ̄s.

[127] The derivation is PIE *egṓ */egóo/ (2b ē/ō-TO-ɛ̄/ɔ̄) > *egɔ̄́ (2f3 GREEK STRESS: ACUTE STRESS) > Gk egɔ̄́ = /egɔɔ́/. The derivation of Gk nɔ̄́ is similar.

[128] The other singular forms have (e)m- < *m-. The forms with initial e- arise by 4a PROTHESIS. Those without e- are enclitic pronouns.

[129] The PIE antecedent seems to have been constructed from the non-nom pl *n̥s plus the non-nom sg *m plus the i-class noun plural ending *-ejes. The derivation is PIE *n̥sméjes (2d SYL SON) >*asméjes (3b j-CHANGES) > *asmées = *asmɛ̄́s (3e s-h-Ø) > *āmɛ̄́s (6a ā-TO-ɛ̄) > *ɛ̄mɛ̄́s (addition of /h/ from the 2nd plural; see the derivation under 5.2 below) > Gk /hɛ̄mɛ̄́s/, spelled <hɛ̄meîs>.

[130] The derivation of the accusative singular is *tu+é (PIE 3.1.2c i-j/u-w ALT) → *twé (4b t-TO-s) > *swé (7c w-DELE) > Gk sé. The nominative singular and the other singular forms adopted the /s/.

[131] The antecedent of the dual forms is not clear. The *b^{h}ō may be the form meaning 'both'. Brandenstein (1959: 71) posits PIE *s+b^{h}-. Another possibility is PIE *t+b^{h}ṓ (2a ASPIR DEVOI) > *t+p^{h}ṓ (after 4b t-TO-s, substitution of *t- by *s- from the singular) > Gk sp^{h}ɔ̄́.

[132] The form is constructed from the Ø-grade of the plural *ws- plus the singular *m plus the i-class pl *-ejes. The derivation is *wsméjes (PIE 3.1.2c i-j/u-w ALT)→ *usméjes (3b j-CHANGES) > *usmées = *usmḗs (3e s-h-Ø) > *ūmḗs (6d u(:)-TO-y(:)) > *ȳmḗs (8a h-ADD) > Gk hȳmeîs = /hȳmées/. Brandenstein (1959: 71) derives Gk hȳmeîs from a PIE *jūsm-.

[133] For some reason these forms are usually recorded in Greek without stress. Otherwise the stress is recorded, as in the nominative singular neuter.

[134] For the other forms of this paradigm, the stem is *t- and the endings are those of the o- and ā-class adjectives under 2.1 above. E.g., gen sg fem tɛ̂s < PIE *t+ā́s.

[135] The constitution of this form is not clear. It may have resulted from a combination of the demonstrative *só- plus a deictic *-u- plus the demonstrative *t+os.

[136] The derivation is *sā́utā (2f3 GREEK STRESS: ACUTE STRESS) > *sāútā (3e s-h-Ø) > *hāútā (6a ā-TO-ɛ̄ and 6c DIPH SHORT, perhaps applying in reverse order) > Gk haútɛ̄.

[137] The derivation is PIE *tód 'this' (2e WF STOP DELE) > *tó (addition of the other constituents in this construction) > *tó+u+to (7a ei/ou-TO-ē/ō) > /tṓto/ = /tóoto/, spelled <toûto>.

[138] The antecedent may have consisted of a particle *e- plus the demonstratives *ké- and *en- plus the endings. The derivation is *ekéenos = *ekḗnos (to which 2b ē/ō-TO-ɛ̄/ɔ̄ does not apply, which probably means that the construction was formed after that time) > Gk /ekē̂nos/ = /ekéenos/, spelled <ekeînos>.

[139] The exact antecedents are not clear. The derivation is *álja+al+oin = *áljāloin (2f2 GREEK STRESS: RECESSIVE STRESS) > *aljā́loin (3a C+j CHANGES) > *allā́loin (6a ā-TO-ɛ̄) > Gk allɛ̄́loin.

[140] The derivation is *mós (4a PROTHESIS) > emós.

[141] These forms are the genitive singular of the demonstrative (5.4 above).

[142] The *-eter ending is probably from the comparative adjective. See the derivation under 2.4.

[143] The masculine form took over the nominative singular. Otherwise one might have expected a nom sg fem interrogative **tin-ja (ev) > Gk **tîna. An Attic gen sg toû 'of whom?' and dat sg tɔ̂i 'to whom' are attested. Their antecedents are *kʷ+ósjo and *kʷ+ṓi, respectively.

[144] The derivation is *kʷím (3d m-TO-n) > *kʷín (5a LABIOVEL) > *tín (addition of the acc sg *-a < PIE *-m̥) > Gk tína.

[145] The derivation is *kʷóteros (5a LABIOVEL) > póteros.

[146] The derivation is *kʷótjos (3a C+j CHANGES) > *kʷóssos (5a LABIOVEL, 6b C-Cl CHANGES) > pósos.

[147] The nominative forms all undergo 2f3 GREEK STRESS: ACUTE STRESS. The genitive singular does not. The derivations are PIE nom sg fem *jā́ /jáa/ vs. gen sg fem *jā́s */jáas/ (3b j-CHANGES) > *hā́ and *hā́s (2f3 GREEK STRESS: ACUTE STRESS) > *haá and *háas (6a ā-TO-ɛ̄) > Gk hɛ̄́ and hɛ̂s.

[148] The antecedent ending is not o- and ā-class adjectives, but the neuter pronominal.

[149] The middle and passive forms are usually identical. We shall sometimes call such forms "mediopassive". There are distinct middle and passive forms only in the aorist, future and future perfect. The notions "active" and "passive" are familiar. E.g., "I see." vs. "I am seen." The middle voice denotes an action performed to, for or on behalf of the subject. E.g.,the following infinitives.

act pʰyláttein 'to guard something'
mid pʰyláttestʰai 'to guard oneself against something'

act gameîn 'to marry someone'
mid gameîstʰai 'to get married'

act paúein 'to stop something'
mid pauéstʰai 'to stop oneself from doing, cease doing'.

As noted in Table ii, some verbs have the inherent feature +deponent. This means that they take mediopassive inflection without a middle or passive meaning. E.g., the inf. pétest^{h}ai 'to fly' or the 1sg future ésomai 'I shall be'. Nondeponent verbs have the active endings.

[150] The indicative is the unmarked mood used to express a simple assertion. The subjunctive is used in a sentence or clause when the speaker presupposes that its truth value (i.e., whether it is true or false) is in doubt or unknown. E.g.,

(a) nŷn íɔ̄men.
'Now we go (subjunctive).' = 'Now we may or should go.'

(b) mɛ̄́ ouk ɛ̂i didaktón aretɛ̄́.
'Perhaps not is (subjunctive) teachable virtue.' = 'Perhaps virtue is not teachable.'

(c) eípɔ̄men ɛ̄̀ sīgɔ̂men.
'We speak (subjunctive) or remain silent (subjunctive)' = 'Should we speak or not?'

(d) toíous oudè ídɔ̄mai.
'Such (men) not I see (subjunctive)' = 'I shall probably not see such men.'

[151] The imperative expresses a command. E.g.,

(a) ágete. 'You (pl) get moving.'

(b) mɛ̄̀ grap^{h}étɔ̄. 'Not he write (imperative).' = 'He should not write.'

[152] The optative is used in a sentence or clause for which the speaker presupposes, first, that its truth value is in doubt and second, that the hope is that it should be true. E.g.,

(a) génoio patròs eutyk^{h}ésteros 'You become (opt) than father more fortunate.' = 'May you become more fortunate than your father.'

(b) K^{h}eirísop^{h}os hɛ̄goîto 'Chirisophos lead (opt)' = 'Chirisophos should lead.'

[153] The present and future are like those of English. E.g., pres gráp^{h}ɔ̄ 'I write', future grápsɔ̄ 'I shall write'.

[154] The imperfect denotes an action in the past which was in progress over some time. E.g., égrap^{h}on 'I was writing, I used to write'.

[155] In contrary-to-fact conditional sentences, the imperfect indicative denotes present contrary to fact and the aorist indicative, past contrary to fact. E.g., ei taûta epoíeis, kalɔ̂s àn epoíeis 'If these things you did (imperfect), well you did (imperfect).' = 'If you were doing these things now, you would be doing well.' And past contrary-to-fact, ei taûta epoíɛ̄sas, kalɔ̂s àn epoíɛ̄sas 'If these things you did (aorist), well you did (aorist).' = 'If you had done these things, you would have done well.'

[156] The perfect denotes a past action which has been completed. E.g., gégrap^{h}a 'I have written and finished.' It also denotes completed past actions whose effects remain into the present. E.g., tā̂s póleis autoɔ̂n parɛ̄írɛ̄tai 'Their cities he has taken (and still holds).'

[157] The pluperfect and future perfect tense are translatable as follows: pluperf egegráp^{h}ɛ̄ 'I had written (and finished)' and the future perf pass gegrápsetai 'it shall have been written (and finished).'

[158] The aorist expresses the occurrence of an action in the past without reference to the length of time it may have taken. E.g., édoksen tɛ̂i boulɛ̂i 'It seemed good to the senate (whether for a long or short time is undetermined).'

[159] The participles are more numerous than those of English. Their meanings are translatable into English as relative clauses (see section 6.9 below).

[160] The types of class formatives noted here occur only in the present and imperfect tenses and are lacking in the other tenses. Furthermore, which formatives occur for other tenses (such as the two types of aorist formations noted in 6.5 below) is independent of what the present/imperfect class formatives are. Thus there are no "conjugations" in Greek such as exist in Latin or Gothic. E.g., the j-class pres nízɔ̄ 'I wash' < *níg^{w}+j+ō vs. the future nípsɔ̄ < *níg^{w}+s+ō without -j-. Likewise, the pres stéllɔ̄ 'I place' < *stél+j+ō and the imperfect éstellon < *é+stel+j+om with -j- vs. the perf éstalka < Ø-grade ablauting *e+stl̥+k+a without -j-. Some j-class verbs have stems ending in a vowel. E.g., *k^{w}imá+j+ō 'I honor' (2b ē/ō-TO-ɛ̄/ɔ̄, 2f GREEK STRESS) > *k^{w}imájɔ̄ (3b j-CHANGES) > *k^{w}imáɔ̄

(5a LABIOVEL) > *timáɔ̄ (5c V-CONTRACT) > timɔ̂ = /timɔ́ɔ/. Such verbs are called "contract" verbs. Their stress pattem indicates that 5c V-CONTRACT has applied as in timɔ̂, not **tímɔ̄.

[161] The n-class takes /n/ either as a suffix or an infix. E.g., the suffix in pres témnɔ̄ 'cut' < *tém+n+ō vs. aorist étemon < *é+tem+om without /n/; and the infix and suffix in pres lankʰánɔ̄ 'get' < *lá+n+gʰ+an+ō vs. aorist élakʰon < *é+lagʰ+om. In some n-class verbs ablaut can occur, e.g. pres tynkʰánɔ̄ 'meet with' < *tú+n+gʰ+an+ō vs. future teúksomai < *téugʰ+s+omai.

[162] The aorist of this form is égnɔ̄n < *é+gnō+m without -isk-.

[163] The root class can contain denominal verbs such as dakrýɔ̄ 'I weep' < the u-class noun *dákru+ō. Ablaut in the e-, o- or Ø-grade can occur sporadically in some root-class verbs. E.g., pres keútʰɔ̄ 'I hide' and perf kékeutʰa < *kéudʰ+ō and *ké+keudʰ+a respectively vs. aorist ékʰytʰon < Ø-grade ablauting *é+kudʰ+om. Also pres trépʰɔ̄ 'I feed', aorist étrapʰon and perf tétropʰa < ablauting e-grade *dʰrébʰ+ō, Ø-grade é+dʰr̥bʰ+om and o-grade dʰé+dʰrobʰ+a.

[164] The nV-class verbs add the reflexes of *-nu(:)- or *-na(:)-. The long vowels appear in the singular and the short ones in the dual and plural. E.g., 1sg zeúgnȳmi 'join' vs. pl zeúgnymen < *jéug+nū+mi vs. *jéug+nu+men; and 1sg pérnēmi 'export' vs. pl pérnamen < *pér+nā+mi vs. pér+na+men. According to Brandenstein (1959: 171) the antecedent of the suffix *-nu(:)- is an ablauting *-n(e/Ø)u-. Sihler (1995: 500) posits *-n(e/o)h$_2$- as the antecedent of *-na(:)-. Another possibility is that the PIE antecedents were simply *-nu and *-na-. Then the vowels were lengthened in the singular on the analogy of the regular type of ablaut found in verbs like 1sg títʰɛ̄mi 'I set' vs. 1pl títʰemen noted in 6.1.1 below.

[165] Sihler (1995: passim) considers the ending to have been originally *-oh$_2$ with a laryngeal. In our view, the derivation is *léikʷō (2b ē/ō-TO-ɛ̄/ɔ̄) > *léikʷɔ̄ (2f GREEK STRESS) > *leíkʷɔ̄ (5a Labiovelar) > Gk leípɔ̄.

[166] The derivation is *léikʷesi (3e s-h-Ø, ev) > *leíkʷei (possibly, addition of the 2sg imperfect *-s, which would not have been affected by 3e s-h-Ø) > *leíkʷeis (7a ei/ou-TO-ē/ō, ev) > Gk leípeis = /lḗpēs/.

[167] The derivation here is not clear. From the PIE antecedent one would expect *léikʷeti (4b t-TO-s, ev) > Gk **leípesi. The form leípei may have arisen on the analogy of the 2nd vs. 3rd sg imperfect forms (see 6.2.1 below). I.e., imperfect sg 2 éleipes: sg 3 éleipe = pres sg 2 leípeis: sg 3 leípei.

[168] The dual occurs only in the 2nd and 3rd persons. The ending is from the secondary paradigm.

[169] The source of the word-final /n/ is not clear.

[170] The derivation is *léikʷonti (2f GREEK STRESS) > *leíkʷonti (4b t-TO-s) > *léikʷonsi > *léikʷōsi (5a LABIOVEL) > *leípōsi (7a ei/ou-TO-ē/ō) > Gk /lḗpōsi/, written <leípousi>.

[171] The alternation ē-e in the sg *dʰē- vs. the dual/pl *dʰe- is PIE ablaut. Note that the athematic endings are like the thematic ones without the intermediate vowel: e.g., 2sg thematic *léikʷ+e+si vs. athematic *dʰí+dʰē+s(i). Sihler (1995: passim) posits a laryngeal for this root, namely sg *dʰeh$_1$- vs. dual/pl *dʰh$_1$- (1a LARYNGEALS, ev) > Gk tʰɛ̄- vs. tʰe-. The derivation of the 1st singular is *dʰídʰēmi (2a ASPIR DEVOI) > *tʰítʰēmi (2b ē/ō-TO-ɛ̄/ɔ̄) > *tʰítʰɛ̄mi (7b GRASSMANN) > títʰɛ̄mi.

[172] The antecedent must have been *dʰídʰēs with a secondary ending *-s as opposed to a primary *-si. Otherwise one would expect the derivation *dʰídʰēsi (3e s-h-Ø, ev) > Gk **títʰɛ̄i.

[173] The derivation is *dʰídʰen̥ti (2a ASPIR DEVOI) > *tʰítʰen̥ti (2d SYL SON) > *tʰítʰeati (readdition of /n/ from other paradigms such as *léikʷonti 'they leave') > *tʰítʰeanti (2f GREEK STRESS) > *tʰitʰéanti (4b t-TO-s) > *tʰitʰéansi (5b NASAL+s) > *tʰitʰéāsi (7b GRASSMANN) > titʰéāsi.

[174] The derivation is *léikʷēsi (2b ē/ō-TO-ɛ̄/ɔ̄, 2f GREEK STRESS) > *leíkʷɛ̄si (3e s-h-Ø) > *leíkʷɛ̄i (readdition of *-s from the 2nd singular imperfect) > *leíkʷɛ̄is (5a LABIOVEL, with /p/ instead of /t/ after those endings beginning with /ō/) > leípɛ̄is.

[175] This form may have been modeled after the 2nd vs. 3rd singular imperfect forms (see 6.2.1 below).

[176] The derivation is *léikʷōnti (2b ē/ō-TO-ɛ̄/ɔ̄, 2f GREEK STRESS, 4b t-TO-s) > *leíkʷɔ̄nsi (5a LABIOVEL, 5b NASAL+s) > leípɔ̄si.

[177] The derivation is *d^{h}íd^{h}eō (2a ASPIR DEVOI) > *t^{h}ít^{h}eō (2b ē/ō-TO-ɛ̄/ɔ̄) > *t^{h}ít^{h}eɔ̄ (2f GREEK STRESS) > *t^{h}it^{h}éɔ̄ (5c V-CONTRACT) > *t^{h}it^{h}ɔ̄̂ = /*t^{h}it^{h}ɔ́ɔ/ (7b GRASSMANN) > tit^{h}ɔ̄̂.

[178] The imperative forms occur only in the 2nd and 3rd persons. The 3rd person means 'he, she, it should leave'. The derivation here is *léik^{w}etōt (2b ē/ō-TO-ɛ̄/ɔ̄) > *léik^{w}etɔ̄t (2e WF STOP DELE, 2f GREEK STRESS) > *leik^{w}étɔ̄ (5a LABIOVEL applying analogously from those forms with endings beginning in /o(:)/) > leipétɔ̄.

[179] The original athematic ending was probably -Ø. The *-e was taken from the thematic paradigm. The derivation is *d^{h}íd^{h}e (2a ASPIR DEVOI) > *t^{h}ít^{h}e (addition of thematic ending *-e, 7b GRASSMANN) > *tít^{h}ee = /tít^{h}ē/ written <tít^{h}ei>. The *-e must have been added sometime after 2b ē/ō-TO-ɛ̄/ɔ̄. Otherwise the Greek form would be **tít^{h}ɛ̄.

[180] Hirt (1912: 583) posits as the PIE optative formatives the ablauting suffixes *-ejē-, *-jē- and *-ī-. Brandenstein (1959: 107) and Buck (1962: 299) posit *-jē- and *-ī-. Chantraine (1961: 362) posits *-jē- and an ablauting *-jə- (ev) > *-ī-. Sihler (1995: 595) assumes ablauting *jeh$_1$- vs. *-ih$_1$-, which by 1a LARYNGEALS would produce *-jē- and *-ī-. Finally we posit the PIE optative formatives as *-ī+ē- vs. ablauting *-ī-. The first of these occurs in the singular of the athematic paradigm. The Ø-grade ablauting *-ī- occurs elsewhere, namely in all forms of the thematic paradigm as well as in the dual and plural of the athematic one. The thematic formative -oi- resulted from the combination of the thematic vowel /o/ plus *-ī-. This gave rise to the aberrant diphthong /oī/, which was regularized to the acceptable diphthong /oi/ by the PIE rule 3.1.2b DIPH. Similarly, the Greek athematic formative in -ei- resulted from the combination of /e/ plus *-ī-, which produced the aberrant diphthong /eī/ which was similarly regularized to /ei/. The derivation of the athematic 1sg is *d^{h}íd^{h}eīēm (regularization of the diphthong) > *d^{h}íd^{h}eiēm (2a ASPIR DEVOI, 2b ē/ō-TO-ɛ̄/ɔ̄) > *t^{h}ít^{h}eiɛ̄m (2f GREEK STRESS) > *t^{h}it^{h}eíɛ̄m (3d m-TO-n) > *t^{h}it^{h}eíɛ̄n (7b GRASSMANN) > tit^{h}eíɛ̄n.

[181] Most optative endings are secondary, i.e. those of the imperfect. However, the 1st singular thematic leípoimi has a primary ending.

[182] The derivation is *léik^{w}esai (2f GREEK STRESS) > *leík^{w}esai (3e s-h-Ø) > *leík^{w}eai (5a LABIOVEL analogized according to a following /o/) > *leípeai (5c V-CONTRACT) > leípɛ̄i.

[183] The source of the /s/ in these forms is unclear.

[184] Hirt (1912: 484) posits a PIE 1 dual ending *-met^{h}on or possibly *-met^{h}om. Sihler (1995: 471) considers the PIE ending to have been *-med^{h}h$_2$. This would result in Gk -met^{h}a by 1a LARYNGEALS and 2a ASPIR DEVOI.

[185] The /s/ in the Greek form was probably reintroduced from the secondary endings such as the imperfect -s. Otherwise the derivation would be *d^{h}íd^{h}esai (ev) > Gk **tít^{h}ɛ̄i.

[186] The derivation is *d^{h}íd^{h}eōmai (2a ASPIR DEVOI, 2b ē/ō-TO-ɛ̄/ɔ̄) > *t^{h}ít^{h}eɔ̄mai (2f GREEK STRESS) > *t^{h}it^{h}éɔ̄mai (5c V-CONTRACT) > *t^{h}it^{h}ɔ̄̂mai (7b GRASSMANN) > tit^{h}ɔ̄̂mai.

[187] The derivation of the thematic form is *léik^{w}eso (2f GREEK STRESS) > *leík^{w}eso (3e s-h-Ø) > *leík^{w}eo (5a LABIOVEL, applying analogously after forms with /o/) > *leípeo (5c V-CONTRACT) > *leípō (7a ei/ou-TO-ē/ō) > leépō = /lḗpō/, spelled <leípou>. In the derivation of the athematic form one would expect 3e s-h-Ø to apply to result in Gk **tít^{h}ou. The intervocalic /s/ was retained here, probably from secondary endings such as in the 2nd singular imperfect active indicative (6.2.1).

[188] The antecedent of this ending is not clear. Hirt (1912: 491) posits the secondary ending *-m plus a particle *-ām. The derivation would be *léik^{w}oimām (2f GREEK STRESS) > *leik^{w}oímām (3d m-TO-n) > *leik^{w}oímān (5a LABIOVEL) > *leipoímān (6a ā-TO-ɛ̄) > leipoímɛ̄n.

[189] The derivation is *d^{h}íd^{h}eīso (2a ASPIR DEVOI) > *t^{h}ít^{h}eīso (2f GREEK STRESS) > *t^{h}it^{h}éīso (reformation to an acceptable diphthong) > *t^{h}it^{h}éiso (3e s-h-Ø) > *t^{h}it^{h}éio (7a ei/ou-TO-ē/ō) > *t^{h}it^{h}ḗo = *t^{h}it^{h}éeo (7b GRASSMANN) > tit^{h}eîo = /tit^{h}éeo/.

[190] The *é- is the so-called "augment", which is added to imperfect and aorist indicative forms. If the verb root begins with a vowel, the Greek reflex of augment plus vowel is a lengthened vowel. E.g., pres *ágō 'drive' > Gk ágɔ̄ vs. imperfect *é+ag+om (3d m-TO-n) > *éagon (5c V-CONTRACT) > ɛ̄̂gon; pres *ódjō 'smell' > Gk ózɔ̄ vs.

imperfect *é+odj+om (3a C+j CHANGES, 3d m-TO-n) > *éodzon (5c V-CONTRACT) > /ɔ́ɔdzon/ = /ɔ̂dzon/, written <ɔ̂zon>. Another peculiarity of the augment occurs with verbs beginning with /h/. E.g., pres *sérpō 'crawl' vs. imperfect *é+serpom (3d m-TO-n, 3e s-h-Ø, ev) > *hérpɔ̄ vs. *éerpon (addition of /h/ onto the imperfect form) > hérpɔ̄ vs. /héerpon/, written <heîrpon>.

[191] The source of the final -n is unknown.

[192] The 1st singular in *dʰē- vs. the other forms in *dʰe- is ē-e ablaut.

[193] These are thematic endings. Otherwise one would expect Gk **étitʰes and **étitʰe. These endings must have been added after the time of 2b ē/ō-TO-ɛ̄/ɔ̄. Otherwise the Greek forms would be **étitʰɛ̄s and **etítʰɛ̄. The derivation of the 2nd singular is *é+dʰi+dʰe+s (2a ASPIR DEVOI) > *étʰitʰes (addition of thematic ending) > *étʰitʰe+es (2f GREEK STRESS) > *etʰítʰēs (7b GRASSMANN) > /etítʰēs/, written <etítʰeis>.

[194] The expected derivation from the PIE antecedent would be *é+dʰi+dʰe+n̥t (2a ASPIR DEVOI) > *étʰitʰen̥t (2d SYL SON) > *étʰitʰeat (2e WF STOP DELE) > *étʰitʰea (2f GREEK STRESS) > *etʰítʰea (5c V-CONTRACT) > *etʰítʰɛ̄ (7b GRASSMANN) > Gk **etítʰɛ̄ instead of the actually occurring etítʰesan. Brandenstein (1959: 155) assumes that the ending -san was from the 3rd plural imperfect of 'be', ɛ̄́san (in 6.10.5 below). Another possible source is the -san from the 1st aorist active indicative (in 6.5.1 below).

[195] The /s/ is retained here instead of undergoing 3e s-h-Ø. It may have been taken from the imperfect active paradigm.

[196] An athematic verb with a first perfect is tétʰɛ̄ka 'I set' < *dʰé+dʰē+k+a. According to Brandenstein (1959: 123), reduplication in early Greek repeated only the first consonant of a cluster: e.g., pres kleíɔ̄ 'close' vs. perf kékleika, not **klékleika. In later Greek the consonant cluster was not repeated at all; only the e- was affixed. E.g., pres gi+gnɔ̄́+sk+ɔ̄ 'know' vs. perf é+gnɔ̄+ka. Likewise mid pres zeúg+nȳ+mi 'yoke' vs. mid perf é+zeug+mai = /édzeugmai/ in which graphemic <z> represents the consonant cluster /dz/. Finally, if a verb root begins with (h)V-, then the vowel is lengthened in the perfect. E.g., pres ágɔ̄ 'drive' vs. the so-called "aspirated" perf ɛ̄̂kʰa. The derivation of the perfect is *é+ag+a (aspiration of some second-perfect verbs, the reasons for which are obscure; see Sihler 1995: 575) > *égʰa (2a ASPIR DEVOI) > *éakʰa (5c V-CONTRACT) > ɛ̄̂kʰa = /ɛ́ɛkʰa/.

[197] These are probably the only original PIE perfect endings in the paradigm. The other endings with /a/ were probably influenced by the aorist active indicative (see 6.5.1 below).

[198] The *-n̥ti is the athematic present active indicative ending (see 6.1.1). Its derivation is *lé+lu+k+a+n̥ti (2d SYL SON) > *lé+lu+k+a+ati (2f GREEK STRESS) > *lelúka+ati (4b t-TO-s) > *lelúka+asi (realization of /a+a/ as /ā/, which must have happened after 6a ā-TO-ɛ̄) > *lelúkāsi (6d u(:)-TO-y(:)) > lelýkāsi.

[199] This is an ablauting form of *leikʷ- noted earlier.

[200] This is an instance of an aspirated perfect referred to in note 196 above. The present is tríbɔ̄.

[201] The semantic development is 'have seen' > 'now know'. A similar development can be seen in the Gothic preterite-present verb wáit /wɛ̄t/ 'know'.

[202] The derivation is *wóid+tʰa (6b C-Cl CHANGES) > *wóistʰa (7c w-DELE) > oîstʰa = /óistʰa/.

[203] The dual and plural forms of this paradigm show Ø-grade ablaut.

[204] The derivation of the dual forms and the 2nd plural is analogous to that of oîstʰa with */dt/ resulting in /st/ by 6b C+j CHANGES: DELETION. This produced the stem *wis- (7c w-DELE) > is-, which then was analogized throughout the plural paradigm.

[205] The derivation of the ending on this form is analogous to that of lelýkāsi described above.

[206] The derivation is *lelukwṓs *ésō (2b ē/ō-TO-ɛ̄/ɔ̄) > *lelukwɔ̄́s *ésɔ̄ (2f4 GREEK STRESS: PHRASAL STRESS) > *lelukwɔɔ̀s *ésɔ̄ (3e s-h-Ø) > *lelukwɔɔ̀s *éɔ̄ (5c V-CONTRACT) > *lelukwɔɔ̀s *ɔ́ɔ (6d u(:)-TO-y(:), 7c w-DELE) > lelykɔ̄̀s ɔ̄̂ = / lelukɔɔ̀s ɔ́ɔ/.

[207] The two endings here are the thematic and athematic ones, respectively.

[208] The -k- formative is lacking in this form. If the antecedent had been **lélukmai, the Greek form would be **lélygmai **/lélyŋmai/ by 6b C-Cl CHANGES.

[209] The derivation of these forms includes 6b C-Cl CHANGES. E.g., *léleikʷmai 'leave' (5a LABIOVEL applying analogously to forms in /kʷ+o/) > *léleipmai (6b C-Cl CHANGES) > Gk léleimmai.

[210] The /ē/ in tétʰeimai /tétʰēmai/ is unexplained. The expected derivation would be *dʰédʰēmai (2a ASPIR DEVOI, 2b ē/ō-TO-ɛ̄/ɔ̄) > *tʰétʰɛ̄mai (7b GRASSMANN) > **tétʰɛ̄mai.

[211] The /s/ is retained here instead of being deleted by 3e s-h-Ø. This was probably on the analogy of forms like *le+leikʷ+so where 3e s-h-Ø could not apply.

[212] The second perfect has the same endings as those of the first perfect except that /s/ is lacking in all endings except the 2nd singular. The derivation is *léleikʷdʰōt (2a ASPIR DEVOI, 2b ē/ō-TO-ɛ̄/ɔ̄) > *léleikʷtʰɔ̄t (2e WF STOP DELE) > *léleikʷtʰɔ̄ (2f GREEK STRESS) > *leleíkʷtʰɔ̄ (5a LABIOVEL) > *leleíptʰɔ̄ (6b C-Cl CHANGES) > leleípʰtʰɔ̄.

[213] The derivation is *élelukea (2f GREEK STRESS) > *elelúkea (5c V-CONTRACT) > *elelúkɛ̄ (6d u(:)-TO-y(:)) > elelýkɛ̄.

[214] The ending -ei /-ē/ seems to indicate that the form was constructed after the time of 2b ē/ō-TO-ɛ̄/ɔ̄. Otherwise one would expect the derivation *éleluke+e = *élelukē (2b ē/ō-TO-ɛ̄/ɔ̄, ev) > **elelýkɛ̄ instead of elelýkei.

[215] The ending -san may have been taken from the athematic 3rd plural imperfect active indicative (6.2.1).

[216] The -k- is lacking in first perfect verbs in this paradigm.

[217] The derivation is *égrabʰsm̥ (2a ASPIR DEVOI) > *égrapʰsm̥ (2d SYL SON) > *égrapʰsa (6b C-Cl CHANGES)> égrapsa. Notice that the -s- in these forms cannot undergo 3e s-h-Ø. Hence this -s- was analogized into other paradigms such as élȳsa 'loose'.

[218] The original vowel V in these forms is not clear. It seems to have been replaced by /a/ from the 1st singular and 3rd plural endings.

[219] The derivation is *égrabʰsn̥t (2a ASPIR DEVOI, 2d SYL SON) > *égrapʰsat (2e WF STOP DELE) > *égrapʰsa (-n readded from 3rd plural imperfect act indicative 6.2.1) > *égrapʰsan (6b C-Cl CHANGES) > égrapsan.

[220] That is, the endings are those of the imperf act ind éleipon 'leave' in 6.2.1 above. Often the ablaut grade of the aorist form differs from that of the imperfect as in the present example with an e-Ø alternation.

[221] Otherwise the dual and plural endings are those of éstɛ̄n noted above added onto the e-grade ablauting root *dʰe-.

[222] The derivation is *dʰéō (2a ASPIR DEVOI, 2b ē/ō-TO-ɛ̄/ɔ̄) > *tʰéɔ̄ (5c V-CONTRACT) > tʰɔ̄̂ = /tʰɔ́ɔ/.

[223] The source of this ending is not known. Brandenstein (1959: 110) posits an original infinitive ending.

[224] This form and the others in the paradigm consist of the aorist stem in -sa plus the athematic present active imperative endings (6.1.3).

[225] The rest of the paradigm consists of the aorist stem ending in -s- plus -ai- plus the endings of the present active optative (6.1.4). The derivation is *grábʰsaīmi (where the -ī- is from the present active optative athematic paradigm, then replacement of the aberrant diphthong /aī/ by /ai/) > *grábʰsaimi (ev) > grápsaimi.

[226] The derivation is *égrabʰsaso (through 2f GREEK STRESS) > *egrápʰsaso (3e s-h-Ø) > *egrápʰsao (5c V-CONTRACT) > *egrápʰsɔ̄ (6b C-Cl CHANGES) > egrápsɔ̄.

[227] The derivation *élikʷoso (2f GREEK STRESS) > *elíkʷoso (3e s-h-Ø) > *elíkʷoo (where /oo/ = /ō/, to which 2b ē/ō-TO-ɛ̄/ɔ̄ cannot apply since it has already occurred) > *elíkʷō (5a LABIOVEL) > elípou = / elípō/.

[228] This verb, like lípɔ̄mai, is second aorist. Its derivation is *dʰé+ō+mai (2a ASPIR DEVOI, 2b ē/ō-TO-ɛ̄/ɔ̄) > *tʰéɔ̄mai (5c V-CONTRACT) > tʰɔ̄̂mai = /tʰɔ́ɔmai/.

[229] The source of the -i is not clear.

[230] This verb is a second aorist with an athematic ending.

[231] The source of the *-dʰē- antecedent is not clear. Sometimes the formative -ɛ̄- is added instead of -tʰɛ̄-. Hence the 1sg egrápʰɛ̄n can occur alongside egrápʰtʰɛ̄n.

[232] The derivation is *élikʷdʰēm (2a ASPIR DEVOI, 2b ē/ō-TO-ɛ̄/ɔ̄) > *élikʷtʰɛ̄m (2f GREEK STRESS) > *elíkʷtʰɛ̄m (3d m-TO-n) > *elíkʷtʰɛ̄n (5a LABIOVEL) > *elíptʰɛ̄n (6b2a C-Cl CHANGES) > *elípʰtʰɛ̄n.

[233] See the discussion of this ending under 6.2.1, athematic paradigm note 194.

[234] We assume the antecedent -dʰ- is the Ø-grade ablaut variant of the *-dʰē- suffix above.

235 This form may have been constructed in later times, at least after the time of t-TO-s. Otherwise one would expect **lýt^{h}ɛ̄si.

236 This and the other forms of the paradigm have the endings in 6.1.7.

237 The antecedent consists of the stem *lu- plus the e-grade ablauting *-d^{h}e- plus the athematic present active optative formative *īē- (see 6.1.4) plus the ending. The derivation of *lúd^{h}eīēm to lyt^{h}eíɛ̄n /lyt^{h}ɛ̄́ɛ̄n/ is analogous to that of *d^{h}íd^{h}eīēm 'set' to tit^{h}eíɛ̄n described in 6.1.4.

238 The /s/ would have been deleted by 3e s-h-Ø in d^{h}ḗsō; however, it was retained in *léik^{w}sō and transferred analogically to *d^{h}ḗ+ō.

239 The present form is *nī́ka+j+ō (2b ē/ō-TO-ɛ̄/ɔ̄, 2e WF STOP DELE, 2f GREEK STRESS) > *nīkájɔ̄ (3b j-CHANGES) > nīkáɔ̄. The derivation of the 1st singular future is nī́ka+es+ō (2b ē/ō-TO-ɛ̄/ɔ̄, 2f GREEK STRESS) > *nīkaésɔ̄ (the intervocalic /s/ is retained for the reasons given immediately above, but by 5c V-CONTRACT) > *nīkā́sɔ̄ (6a ā-TO-ɛ̄) > nīkɛ̄́sɔ̄.

240 However, in contrast to the immediately preceding derivation, some *-es- future forms do undergo 3e s-h-Ø in their derivations. E.g., 1sg pres *stél+j+ō (ev) > stéllɔ̄. And 1sg future *stél+es+ō (2b ē/ō-TO-ɛ̄/ɔ̄, 2f GREEK STRESS) > *stelésɔ̄ (3e s-h-Ø) > *steléɔ̄ (5c V-CONTRACT) > stelɔ̄̂ = /stelɔ́ɔ/. In some verbs the optional rule 5c V-CONTRACT applies to the future paradigm but not to the present. E.g. 1sg pres *kále+j+ō 'call' vs. future *kále+s+ō (2b ē/ō-TO-ɛ̄/ɔ̄, 2f GREEK STRESS, 3b j-CHANGES, 3e s-h-Ø) > *kaléɔ̄ for both forms (6a V-CONTRACT applying only to the future form) > pres kaléɔ̄ vs. future kalɔ̄̂. This type of construction is sometimes called the "Attic future".

241 The derivation is *léik^{w}d^{h}ēsomai (2a ASPIR DEVOI, 2b ē/ō-TO-ɛ̄/ɔ̄, 2f GREEK STRESS, 5a LABIOVEL) > *leipt^{h}ɛ̄̂somai (6b C-Cl CHANGES) > leip^{h}t^{h}ɛ̄̂somai.

242 Sihler (1995: 608) suggests the PIE antecedent was "an n-stem locative." It may have been combined with a Vs-class noun ending. The derivation is *léik^{w}esen (2f GREEK STRESS, 3e s-h-Ø) > *leík^{w}een = *leík^{w}ēn (5a LABIOVEL) > *leípēn (7a ei/ou-TO-ē/ō) > leípein = /lḗpēn/.

243 The antecedent of this ending is not clear. Hirt (1912: 600) assumes it may have been a dative singular ending.

244 The reason for the lengthening of /u/ to /ū/ (ev /ȳ/) is not clear. It occurred perhaps on the analogy of regular ablauting short-long vowel alternations such as in 1sg tít^{h}ēmi 'I set' vs. 1pl tít^{h}emen from *d^{h}ē- and *d^{h}e-, respectively.

245 The derivation is *lúōnt (2b ē/ō-TO-ɛ̄/ɔ̄, ablaut-like lengthening of /u/ to /ū/) > *lū́ōnt (2e WF STOP DELE, 6d u(:)-TO-y(:)) > lȳ́ɔ̄n.

246 The derivation is *d^{h}id^{h}énts (2a ASPIR DEVOI, early part of 6b C-Cl CHANGES) > t^{h}it^{h}éns (5b2 the later version of NASAL+s) > *t^{h}it^{h}ḗs (7b GRASSMANN) > tit^{h}eîs = /tit^{h}ē̂s/.

247 See the derivation in 2.3.6 above.

248 The derivation is *lúsants (lengthening of /u/ to /ū/) > *lū́sants (early participle of 6b C-Cl CHANGES) > *lū́sans (later participle of 5b NASAL+s) > *lū́sās (6a ā-TO-ɛ̄ not applying, but 6d u(:)-TO-y(:)) > lȳ́sās.

249 See the derivation in 2.3.5 above.

250 The derivation is analogous to that of tit^{h}eîs under 6.9.1 above.

251 We assume the PIE stress as shown. Word-final stress then was set throughout the paradigm except for the 2nd singular by 2f1 GREEK STRESS: MORPH COND STRESS.

252 From PIE *és+si one would expect Gk **ési. Brandenstein (1959: 163) assumes an early PIE development of *éssi to *ési. The derivation would then be *ési (3e s-h-Ø) > *éi (7a ei/ou-TO-ē/ō) > eî = /ē̂/ = /ée/.

253 One would expect the /s/ in this form to be deleted by 3e s-h-Ø. It was restored because of other forms in the paradigm such as 2pl esté where /s/ would have remained.

254 Buck (1962: 243), erroneously in our view, posits as the antecedents of the plural forms the Ø-grade ablauting stem *s+endings. The derivation of our 3pl *esentí (3e s-h-Ø) > *eentí = *ēntí (4b t-TO-s) > *ēnsí (5b NASAL+s) > ēsí, written <eisí>.

[255] The derivation is *ésō (2b ē/ō-TO-ɛ̄/ɔ̄) > *ésɔ̄ (3e s-h-Ø) > *éɔ̄ (5c V-CONTRACT) > ɔ̂ = /ɔ́ɔ/. For the history of these endings see 6.1.1 and 6.1.2.

[256] Given the antecedent, one would expect Gk **ést^hi instead of íst^hi.

[257] The derivation is *ésīēm (2b ē/ō-TO-ɛ̄/ɔ̄) > *ésīɛ̄m (2f GREEK STRESS) > *esī́ɛ̄m (3d m-TO-n) > *esī́ɛ̄n (3e s-h-Ø) > eī́ɛ̄n (replacement of the unusual diphthong /eī/ by the usual /ei/) > *eíɛ̄n (7a ei/ou-TO-ē/ō) > eíɛ̄n = /ḗɛ̄n/ = /eéɛ̄n/.

[258] The derivation is *é+es+m̥ = *ḗsm̥ (2b ē/ō-TO-ɛ̄/ɔ̄) > *ɛ̄́sm̥ (2d SYL SON) > *ɛ̄́sa (readdition of -m from the imperfect active indicative 6.2.1) > *ɛ̄́sam (3d m-TO-n, 3e s-h-Ø) > *ɛ̄́an (5c V-CONTRACT) > ɛ̂n = /ɛ́ɛn/.

[259] This ending seems to be from an early perfect paradigm such as in oîst^ha 'know' cited in 6.3.1 above.

[260] The antecedent of this form is totally obscure.

[261] The /s/ is deleted from this form analogously to the other plural forms.

[262] The derivation is *é+es+n̥t = *ḗsn̥t (2b ē/ō-TO-ɛ̄/ɔ̄)> *ɛ̄sn̥t (2d SYL SON > *ɛ̄́sat (2e WF STOP DELE) > *ɛ̄́a (3e s-h-Ø) > *ɛ̄́a (/s/ replaced from other forms of the paradigm, word-final /n/ added from the thematic 3rd plural imperfect active indicative 6.2.1) > ɛ̂san.

[263] The derivation is *éssomai (3e s-h-Ø not applying, but later by 6b C-Cl CHANGES) > ésomai.

[264] The derivation is *é+es+a = *ḗsa (2b ē/ō-TO-ɛ̄/ɔ̄) > *ɛ̄́sa (3e s-h-Ø) > ɛ̂a = /ɛ́ɛa/.

Chapter 5

Old Irish

I Introduction

The earliest amply attested Celtic language is Old Irish (OIr). Its situation within the Celtic language family is described by McCone (1996: 3) as follows: "Documentation of the Celtic languages extends more or less continuously from about [500 BC] right down to the present. The first part of this long period is primarily represented by the meagre but growing corpus of Continental Celtic epigraphic material down to the third or fourth century A.D. and then by short fifth- and sixth-century Irish Ogam inscriptions. The emergence of the manuscript record in the seventh and eighth centuries A.D. marks the beginning of the by and large adequate attestation of Irish [i.e., OIr] and British Celtic thereafter." (The Ogam system of writing was in McCone's opinion based on the Roman alphabet.)

Although various dates have been posited for the Old Irish period (Rockel 1989: 26 notes six), we assume with Thurneysen (1909: 8) that the Old Irish period extended from ca. 700 to ca. 1000 AD. Our description of the language is intended to be early from ca. 700 AD. We record the Old Irish forms in terms of the traditional orthography as well as in a phonemic transcription, which we describe in section III Old Irish Phonology below.

II The Changes from PIE into Old Irish

A. Overview of the Changes and their Chronology

The stages below are ordered. Changes listed within a single stage can occur in any order within that stage or may be approximately simultaneous. We give some approximate dates for the changes which have been found in the literature.

STAGE 1 (ca. 3000-800 BC)

STAGE 2 (ca. 800 BC – 500 AD)

STAGE 3 (ca. 800 BC – 500 AD)

B. The Changes

1a Deaspiration of Voiced Obstruents (DEASP)

This change restructures the phonemic inventory of the language and then is dropped from the grammar.

$$\begin{pmatrix} \text{C, –sonorant} \\ \text{+voiced} \\ \text{+aspirated} \end{pmatrix} \rightarrow [\text{–aspirated}]$$

That is, the PIE voiced aspirates /b^h, d^h, g^h, g^{hw}/ become /b, d, g, g^w/.

E.g., PIE 3sg pres *b^{h}ereti 'carry' (DEASP) > *bereti (2b LEN) > *bereði (6a i-e/u-o ALT) > *beriði (6b INFEC) > *berið'i (8b W-F SEG DELE) > OIr berid /berið'/. PIE u-class nom sg neuter *d^{h}orestum 'door' (DEASP) > *dorestum (2c m-TO-n, 6b INFEC) > *dorest^{u}un (8a LATER C CL) > *dores^{u}un (8b W-F SEG DELE) > OIr dorus /dores^u/. PIE nom sg masc *g^{h}ortos 'garden' (DEASP) > *gortos (ev) > OIr gort. PIE nom sg neuter *g^{hW}onim 'act of killing' (DEASP) > *g^{w}onim (2a g^w-CHANGES, 2c m-TO-n) > *gonin (6a i/u-TO-e/o) > *gunin (6b INFEC) > *gun'in (8b W-F SEG DELE) > OIr guin /gun'/.

lb Change of /ē/ to /ī/ (ē-TO-ī)

This change restructures the phonemic inventory of the language and is then dropped from the grammar. Lewis and Pedersen (1937: 7) consider this change as occurring “very early”.

$$\bar{e} \quad \rightarrow \quad \bar{\imath} \quad / \quad \_\_ \left\{ \begin{array}{l} [-\text{vocalic}] \\ \#\# \end{array} \right.$$

That is, stressed or unstressed /ē/ becomes /ī/ unless occurring in the long diphthongs /ēi, ēu/.

E.g., PIE nom sg masc adj *wēros ‘true’ (ē-TO-ī) >*wīros (7c w-CHANGES, 8b W-F SEG DELE) > OIr fír /fīr/. PIE nom sg *patēr ‘father’ (ē-TO-ī) > *patīr (1d p-CHANGES) > *atīr (2b LEN) > *aθīr (6b INFEC) > aθ'īr (9c LATER UNSTR-V) > OIr aithir /aθ'ir/.

lc Early Conditions on Consonant Clusters (EARLY C CL)

The following changes are early and are chronologically ordered as shown. The first was already a rule in PIE and remains as a phon cond rule of Old Irish. The second was a somewhat later change in early Celtic. It restructured various lexical items and was then dropped as a rule from the grammar.

(1) $$\begin{bmatrix} C, -\text{sonorant} \\ \alpha\text{voiced} \end{bmatrix} \quad \rightarrow \quad [\beta\text{voiced}] \quad / \quad \_\_ \begin{bmatrix} C, -\text{sonorant} \\ \beta\text{voiced} \end{bmatrix}$$

(2) tt → ss

That is, (1) an obstruent cluster must be voiced if its final segment is voiced and voiceless if its final segment is voiceless. (2) The sequence /tt/ becomes /ss/.

E.g., PIE u-class nom sg *wid+t+us ‘state of knowing, knowledge’ (EARLY C CL 1) > *wittus (EARLY C CL 2) > *wissus (2b LEN not applying to the geminate /ss/, but 6b INFEC) > *wiss^{u}us (7c w-CHANGES) > *fiss^{u}us (8a LATER C CL) > *fis^{u}us (8b W-F SEG DELE) > OIr fius /fis^{u}/. Also PIE o-class nom sg *ni+sd+os ‘an in-sitting, a nest’ (EARLY C CL 1) > *nizdos (2b LEN cannot apply to the /d/, but 5 EARLY UNSTR-V) > *nizdas (6a i-e/u-o ALT) > *nezdas (8a LATER C CL) > *nedas (8b W-F SEG DELE) > OIr net /ned/. Note in both these derivations the necessary chronology 2b LEN > 8a LATER C CL. If the order were reversed, the Old Irish forms would be **fí **/fī/ and **ned **/neð/.

ld Changes in /p/ (p-CHANGES)

This change restructures various lexical items as well as the phonemic inventory of the language and then is dropped from the grammar. It seems to have occurred in two chronological stages:

(1) $$p \quad \rightarrow \quad f \quad / \quad \left. \begin{array}{l} \#\# \\ V \end{array} \right\} \_\_$$

(2) $$f \quad \rightarrow \quad \begin{array}{l} x \quad / \quad \_\_ [C, -\text{sonorant}] \\ \varnothing \quad / \text{ elsewhere} \end{array}$$

That is, (1) /p/ becomes /f/ if word-initial or if preceded by a vowel. (2) The resulting /f/ becomes /x/ if followed by an obstruent consonant; otherwise any remaining /f/’s are lost. (Our formulation follows that of Thurneysen 1909: 136-7.)

E.g., PIE *septōm ‘7’ (p-CHANGES) > *sextōm (ev through 8b W-F SEG DELE) > OIr secht /sext/.

PIE nom sg *kaptos 'slave, servant' (p-CHANGES) > *kaxtos (ev) > OIr cacht /kaxt/. Examples of the complete disappearance of /p/ are PIE nom sg *patēr 'father' (lb ē-TO-ī) > *patīr (p-CHANGES) > *atīr (2b LEN, 6b INFEC) > *aθ'īr (9c LATER UNSTR-V) > OIr aithir /aθ'ir/. Also PIE nom sg masc i-class adj *pilis 'much, many' (p-CHANGES) > *ilis (2b LEN, 6b INFEC) > *il'is (8b W-F SEG DELE) > OIr hil /il'/. (Words beginning with vowels are often written in Old Irish with word-initial <h>.)

Also the PIE Ø-class nom sg *kaper+āk+s 'sheep' (1d p-CHANGES) > *kaerāks (8b W-F SEG DELE) > *kaerā (9c LATER UNSTR-V) > OIr caera /kaera/. And PIE nom sg *sopnos 'sleep' (p-CHANGES) > *sōnos or possibly *sounos (where the loss of /p/ either lengthened the preceding vowel to /ō/ or perhaps resulted in the diphthong /ou/, then 8b W-F SEG DELE) > *sōn or *soun (9a DIPH CHANGES applying in either case) > OIr suan. (Note the necessary chronology p-CHANGES > 9a DIPH CHANGES.)

When second member of a consonant cluster, /p/ remains: e.g., PIE jā-class nom sg fem *spenjā 'breast' (p-CHANGES not applying, but 2b LEN, 6a i-e/u-o ALT, 6b INFEC) > *spin'jā (8a LATER C CL) > *sin'jā (9b j-Dele) > *sin'ā (9c LATER UNSTR-V) > OIr sine /sin'e/.

Later borrowings into Old Irish retain /p/ because p-CHANGES has by this time dropped from the grammar. E.g., Latin apostolus 'apostle' (1f IRISH STRESS applying as a synchronic rule) > *ápostolus (8b W-F SEG DELE, l0b SYNCOPE) > OIr apstol, not **astol. The p-CHANGES rule may represent the first stage of 2b LEN. If so, then the relative chronology is p-CHANGES > 2b LEN. This is the view of Pedersen (1909: 437), who gives a possible date for p-CHANGES at about 800 BC.

le Syllabic Sonorant Changes (SYL SON)

This change restructures various morphemes — lexical and inflectional —and then is dropped as a rule from the grammar. The precise conditions of these changes are not clear. Our description of them follows mainly those of Lewis and Pedersen (1937: 4) and of Pokorny (1969: 23–4).

l̥, r̥ → (a) {li, ri / la, ra} / ___ {[C, –sonorant, –continuant][1] / [C, +sonorant][1]}

(b) {la, ra / al, ar} / ___ {[C, –sonorant, +continuant][1] / C_2 / V / ##}

m̥, n̥ → (c) am, an / ___ {[C, –sonorant, +continuant][1] / [m, j or w] V / V}

(d) em, en / otherwise

That is, (a) the reflexes of PIE syllabic /l̥, r̥/ are either (unpredictably) /li/ or /la/ and /ri/ or /ra/, respectively, if followed by a single obstruent stop or a single sonorant consonant. (b) The reflexes of /l̥, r̥/ are /la/ or /al/ and /ra/ or /ar/, respectively, if followed by a single obstruent continuant consonant, a consonant cluster of at least two segments, a vowel, or if word-final. (c) PIE /m̥, n̥/ become /am, an/ if followed by a single obstruent consonant or by /m, j, or w/ followed by a vowel, or if followed immediately by a vowel. Otherwise, (d) PIE /m̥, n̥/ become /em, en/.

E.g., (a) PIE nom sg *wl̥tis 'rulership' (SYL SON) > *wlatis (2b LEN: note the necessary chronology SYL SON > 2b LEN) > *wLaθis (6b INFEC) > *wLaθ'is (7c w-CHANGES) > *fLaθ'is (8b W-F SEG DELE) > OIr flaith /fLaθ'/. Also PIE nom sg *bʰr̥tos 'act of bearing' (la DEASP) > *br̥tos (SYL SON) > *britos (2b LEN, 5 EARLY UNSTR-V) >*bRiθas (6a i-e/u-o ALT : note here the chronology SYL SON > 6a i-e/u-o ALT) > *bReθas (8b W-F SEG DELE) > OIr breth /bReθ/.

(b) PIE nom sg *tr̥stos 'thirst' (SYL SON) > *tarstos (ev through 8a LATER C CL) > OIr tart.

(c and d) PIE nom sg neuter *n̥m+n̥ 'name' (SYL SON) > *anmen (2b LEN) > *anMen (6b INFEC) > *anM'en (8b W-F SEG DELE) > OIr ainmm /anM'/. (Note the necessary chronology SYL SON > 6b INFEC.) PIE *kn̥tom '100' (SYL SON) > *kentom (ev through 7b VnC-TO-VC) > *kētan (8b W-F SEG DELE) > OIr cét /kēt/. PIE nom sg masc *n̥+gnō+t+os 'unknown, unusual' (SYL SON) > *engnōtos (2b LEN) > *eNgNōθos (3b ō-CHANGES, 5 EARLY UNSTR-V) > *eNgNāθas (6a i-e/u-o ALT applying to other adjectives with *en-) > *iNgNāθas (8b W-F SEG DELE) > OIr ingnáth /iNgNāθ/.

1f Word-Stress Rule (IRISH STRESS)

This change was added to the post-PIE and pre-Old Irish grammar. It remained as a morph cond rule in Old Irish.

[V, –pronoun, –conjunction] → [+stress] / (1) ## C_0 {(a) [____, +imperative]
{(b) [____, –verb prefix]

(2) Otherwise: ## $_s$[___]

The stress rule does not assign stress to pronouns (including the article) nor to conjunctions. The parts of the rule are ordered: (1) The first syllable is stressed (a) in all imperative forms of verbs and (b) in all other stressable parts of speech (i.e., nouns, adjectives, adverbs, numerals and verbs) except on a verbal prefix. (2) Otherwise, the second syllable of a word is stressed, whether in a verbal prefix or not.

E.g., (1) PIE 2sg imp *eks+b^{h}ere say (1a DEASP) >*eks+bere (IRISH STRESS) > *éks+bere (5 EARLY UNSTR-V) > *éks+beri (6a i-e/u-o ALT : note the necessary chronology 5 > 6a) > *éks+biri (6b INFEC) > *éks+bir'i (8b W-F SEG DELE: note the necessary chronology 6b > 8b) > *é+bir', i.e. OIr epir /ébir'/. PIE nom sg neuter *d^{h}orestum 'door' (1a DEASP) > *dorestum (IRISH STRESS) > *dórestum (6b INFEC, ev) > *dórest^{u}un (8b W-F SEG DELE) > OIr dorus /dóres^u/. PIE nom sg Vn-class fem *do+mentjō 'opinion' (a noun formed with a prefix, but since it is not a verb prefix, IRISH STRESS 1 applies) > *dómentjō (2b LEN applying only to /m/, 3b ō-CHANGES) > *dómeNtjū (6b INFEC) > *dómeNt'jū (7b VnC-TO-VC) > *dómet'jū (9b j-DELE, 9c LATER UNSTR-V) > *dómet'u (10b SYNCOPE) > OIr toimtu /dómt'u/.

(2) PIE 3sg pres conj *do+b^{h}eret 'carries' (1 DEASP) > *do+beret (IRISH STRESS 1 does not apply because *do- is a verbal prefix, but IRISH STRESS 2 does) > *do+béret (6b INFEC, 8b W-F SEG DELE) > OIr dobeir /do+bér'/. Note also this example of a verb with two prefixes: PIE 3sg pres pass *do+upor+mag+or 'is increased' (1d p-CHANGES) > *do+uor+mag+or (PIE 3.1.2c i-j/u-w ALT, still applying as a synchronic rule) → *do+wor+mag+or (IRISH STRESS 2) > *do+wór+mag+or (2b LEN, 7c w-CHANGES) > *do+fór+maǥ+or (9c LATER UNSTR-V) > OIr doformagar /do+fór+maǥ+ar/.

In compounds the stress is often on the second constituent. PIE nom sg masc *ala##aljos 'other' (IRISH STRESS) > *ala##áljos (restructuring of /a##á/ to /ā́/, 5 EARLY UNSTR-V) > *alā́ljas (6b INFEC) > *alā́l'jas (8b W-F SEG DELE) > *alā́l'ja (9b j-DELE) > *alā́l'as (9c LATER UNSTR-V) > OIr aláile /alā́l'e/.

Our derivations here give a somewhat false impression in that we do not mark the pre-Old Irish or PIE stress, so it would seem that the IRISH STRESS rule assigned stress for the first time. This is of course erroneous: the pre-Old Irish word stress was that of PIE, which we have outlined in Chapter 1 in the PIE rule 3.1.2h WORD STRESS. In view of their formulation, the following changes must follow WORD STRESS: 2c m-TO-n, 2d V̄+NASAL SHORT, 5 EARLY UNSTR-V, 6a i-e/u-o ALT, 8b W-F SEG DELE, 9a DIPH CHANGES, 9c LATER UNSTR-V, 9d STR-V LENG, 10b SYNCOPE.

2a Changes in /g^w/ (g^w-CHANGES)

This change may be assumed to have occurred early since it seems to be the same for all Celtic languages. It restructured the phonemic inventory as well as various lexical items and then was dropped from the grammar. It seems to have occurred in two chronological stages.

(1) g^w → b / (a) ##___V (≠ u(:))
(b) ##___[C, +nasal] (and later bn → mn)
(c) C___V

(2) g^w → g elsewhere, namely:
/ (a) ##___u(:)
(b) V___V
(c) ___C

That is, (1) /g^w/ becomes /b/ word-initially if followed by (a) any vowel except /u(:)/ or (b) word-initially if followed by a nasal consonant. (Later the word-initial sequence /bn/ becomes /mn/.) Also /g^w/ becomes /b/ (c) after a consonant and before a following vowel. (2) Otherwise, /g^w/ becomes /g/, namely (a) word-initially before /u(:)/, (b) between vowels or (c) if followed by a consonant.

E.g., (la and 1b) PIE ā-class fem nom sg *g^wenā 'woman' vs. the Ø-grade ablauting gen sg *g^wnās (g^w-CHANGES) > *benā, *mnās (8b W-F SEG DELE) > OIr ben /ben/ and mná /mNā/. (1c) PIE Vn-class neuter nom sg *n̥g^{hw}n̥ 'butter' (la DEASP) > *n̥g^wn̥ (1e SYL SON) > *eng^{w}en (g^w-CHANGES, also PIE 3.1.2d NASAL ASSIM still applying synchronically) > *emben (5 EARLY UNSTR-V) > *embin (6a i-e/u-o ALT) > *imbin (8b W-F SEG DELE) > OIr imb.

(2a) This example is somewhat problematic. PIE nom sg *g^{hw}n+is 'to kill, act of killing' (perhaps realized as *g^hun+is, la DEASP, g^w-CHANGES, 2b LEN, 6b INFEC, 8b W-F SEG DELE) > OIr guin /gun'/. (2b) PIE 3sg pres *snig^{hw}eti 'it snows' (la DEASP, g^w-CHANGES) > *snigeti (2b LEN) > *sNigeði (6a i-e/u-o ALT) > *sNigiði (6b INFEC) > *sNigið'i (8b W-F SEG DELE) > OIr snigit /sNigið'/. (2c) PIE nom sg *ag^{w}nos 'lamb' (g^w-CHANGES) > *agnos (2b LEN, and apparently further development of /g/ to /u/) > *auNos (5 EARLY UNSTR-V) > *auNas (8b W-F SEG DELE) > *auN (9a DIPH CHANGES) > OIr uan.

There are problems in our formulation of this change in that some words undergo part la while others under apparently the same conditions undergo 2a. E.g., PIE nom sg *g^wōus 'cow' vs. 3sg pres *g^{hw}od^{h}eti 'asks' (la DEASP) > *g^wōus, *g^wodeti (g^w-CHANGES la applying to the first form, 2a to the second) > *bōus, *godeti (2b LEN, 4 DIPH SHORT) > *bous, *goðeði (6a i-e/u-o ALT) > *bous, *guðiði (6b INFEC) > *bous, *guðið'i (8b W-F SEG DELE) > *bo, *guðið' (9d STR-V LENG) > OIr bó /bō/ and guidid /guðið'/. (It is also possible that instead of g^w-CHANGES 2a, g^w-CHANGES 2b applied to the verb if preceded by a prefix such as *do-.)

2b So-Called "Lenition" Changes on Consonants (LEN)

The term "aspiration" is also found in the literature to describe these changes. The rules for the changes remain in the grammar of Old Irish as morph cond rules. Intuitively, one can say in some sense that the changes involve a weakening of the affected consonants. The LEN changes are in basic outline as follows:

(a) [C, –sonorant, –continuant] → [+continuant]
(b) [C, +sonorant] → [+continuant, –tense]
(c) s → h (and soon h → Ø)
} / V (##) ___ [+sonorant]

(and additionally Vkt → Vxt)

That is, the following changes occur if the segment is preceded by a vowel (with the possibility of an intervening word boundary) and is followed by any sonorant segment — i.e., any vowel or /l, m, n, r, j, w/. (In addition /kt/ becomes lenited /xt/.) The changes are (a) /p, t, k, b, d, g/ → /f, θ, x, ƀ, ð, ǥ/. (b) The sonorants /l, m, n, r/ are "lenited". This means that they become continuants and require less muscular effort and as such less oral constriction. Given their usual environments, most of the sonorant segments are lenited. Hence we adopt a practice often found in the literature of designating only the unlenited sonorants, which we do by writing them in capitals: /L, M, N, R/. We designate the lenited sonorants as /l, m, n, r/. Such lenited sonorants are pronounced with less muscular effort and with less oral constriction. (We denote this in the environment (b) with the designation "–tense".) In some sources lenited /m/ is designated graphemically as <w̃>, which is a nasalized [w^n]. Analogously, we may assume that lenited /n/ may have been a nasalized [j^n] and that lenited /l/ and /r/ may also have been glides of some sort. (c) The segment /s/ becomes /h/ and eventually disappears.

E.g., (a) PIE nom sg *patēr 'father' (1b ē-TO-ī) > *patīr (1d p-CHANGES) > *atīr (LEN) > *aθīr (6b INFEC) > *aθ'īr (9c LATER UNSTR-V) > OIr aithir /aθ'ir/. (Note here the necessary chronology 1d p-CHANGES > LEN. Otherwise the OIr 'father' would be **faithir instead of aithir.) PIE *dekm̥ '10' (1e SYL SON) > *dekem (LEN, 2c m-TO-n) > *dexen (6b INFEC) > *dex'en (ev through 8b W-F SEG DELE) > OIr deich /dex'/. PIE *oktōm '8' (LEN, ev) > *oxtōn (2d V̄+NASAL SHORT) > *oxton (8b W-F SEG DELE) > OIr ocht /oxt/. PIE dat pl *teutā$b^h$is 'people' (1a DEASP) > *teutābis (LEN) > *teuθāƀis (6b INFEC) > *teuθāƀ'is (8b W-F SEG DELE) > *teuθāƀ' (9a DIPH CHANGES) > *tuaθāƀ' (9c LATER UNSTR-V) > OIr tuathaib /tuaθaƀ'/. PIE nom sg *sodjom 'seat' (LEN, 2c m-TO-n) > *soðjon (5 EARLY UNSTR-V, 6a i-e/u-o ALT) > *suðjan (6b INFEC) > *suð'jan (8b W-F SEG DELE) > *suð'ja (9b j-DELE) > *suð'a (9c LATER UNSTR-V) > OIr suide /suð'e/. PIE nom sg fem *enigenā 'daughter' (LEN) > *eniǥenā (6a i-e/u-o ALT , 6b INFEC) > *iniǥ'enā (8b W-F SEG DELE) > *iniǥ'en (10b SYNCOPE) > OIr ingen/inǥ'en/. (Note here the necessary chronology LEN > 10b SYNCOPE.)

(b) Virtually all occurrences of /l, m, n, r/ are subject to LEN; but a few word-internal sonorants consistently elude it. We transcribe them as /L, M, N, R/. They are often written as geminates in Old Irish texts. E.g., PIE 1sg pres *es+mi 'I am' (LEN applying to the /s/, not to /m/) > *eMi (8b W-F SEG DELE) > *eM (9c LATER UNSTR-V) > OIr amm /aM/.

(c) PIE Vs-class gen sg neuter *teg+es+os 'house' (LEN) > *teǥeos (ev through 6b INFEC) > *teǥ'eos (8b W-F SEG DELE) > OIr tige /teǥ'e/.

MacAulay (1992: 93) dates LEN as occurring during the 400's AD. Later during attested Old Irish times at ca. 600 AD the lenited voiceless obstruents underwent the following change, which remained as an optional rule in Old Irish:

f, θ, x → ƀ, ð, ǥ / [V, –stress] ___ { [V, –stress] / ## }

That is, / f, θ, x / (as well as /f', f^u; θ', $θ^u$; x', x^u/ produced by 6b INFEC) are voiced to /ƀ, ð, ǥ/ if preceded by an unstressed vowel and followed by an unstressed vowel or in word-final position. E.g., the later Old Irish borrowings from Latin such as 3sg pres oirdnithe or oirdnide 'one gives orders' for /oRdNiθ'/ and /oRdNið'/; and nom sg peccath or peccad 'sin' for /pekaθ/ and /pekað/.

Note the following two chronologies. First, PIE Vnt-class neuter nom sg *dentom 'tooth' (LEN not applying, but 2c m-TO-n, 5 EARLY UNSTR-V and 7b VnC-TO-VC) > *dētan (8b W-F SEG DELE) > OIr dét /dēt/. (The sequence must be LEN > 7b VnC-TO-VC. Otherwise the Old Irish form would be **déth **/dēθ/.) Second, PIE *k^wonk^{w}e *teutās '5 nations' (LEN) > *k^wonk^{w}e *θeuθās (6b INFEC) > *k^wonk^w'e *θeuθās (7a k^w-TO-k) > *konk'e *θeuθās (7b VnC-TO-VC) > *kōk'e *θeuθās (8b W-F SEG DELE) > *kōk' *θeuθā (9a DIPH CHANGES) > *kōk' *θuaθā (9c LATER UNSTR-V) > OIr cóic thuatha /kōk' θuaθa/. (The chronology must be LEN > 8b W-F SEG DELE. Otherwise the Old Irish forms would be **cóic **tuatha

**/kōk' tuaθa/.) Contrast the preceding with the sequence PIE *seks *teutās '6 nations' (LEN applying only to the word-internal /t/) > *seks *teuθās (8b W-F SEG DELE) > *se *teuθā (9a DIPH CHANGES) > *se *tuaθā (9c LATER UNSTR-V) > *se *tuaθa (9d STR-V LENG) > OIr sé tuatha /sē tuaθa/. (Here too the chronology must be LEN > 8b W-F SEG DELE. Otherwise the Old Irish forms would be **sé **thuatha **/sē θuaθa/.)

As illustrated by the preceding derivations, after the change 8b W-F SEG DELE and by the time of attested Old Irish, the LEN change is a morph cond rule of Old Irish phonology. It applies to word-initial consonants in the following morph cond environments, namely if the preceding words belong to any of the following categories.

(a) An ā-class fem noun or adj in the nom sg (< PIE *-ā). E.g., nom sg fem /sen tuaθ/ 'old nation' (LEN) → OIr sen thuath /sen θuaθ/.

(b) An o-class masculine noun, adjective or article in the nominative plural (< PIE *-oi). E.g., nom pl /ind pRekeptōr'/ 'the preachers' (LEN) → OIr ind phreceptóri /ind fRekeptōr'/. (The word is a later borrowing from Latin.)

(c) An o-class masculine or neuter noun or adjective in the genitive singular (< PIE *-ī). E.g., masc /sin' karat/ 'of an old friend' (LEN) → OIr sin charat /sin' xarat/.

(d) An ā-class fem or o-class masc or neuter in the dat sg (< PIE *-āi and *-ōi respectively). E.g., dat sg masc /sin^{u} karat'/ 'to an old friend' (LEN) → OIr siun charait /sin^{u} xarat'/.

(e) Those few monosyllabic words which retained their word-final vowels from PIE. One example is the PIE voc particle *ō > OIr á /ā/. E.g., /ā tuaθ/ 'ō people!' (LEN) → OIr á thuath /ā θuaθ/.

Here and elsewhere in the literature those forms which trigger morph cond LEN are marked with a superscript "l", e.g. coic^{l} /kōk'/^{l} '5' which triggers LEN vs. sé /sē/ '6' which does not.

The fact that LEN was retained as a morph cond rule of Old Irish phonology has been remarked on variously in the literature. Lewis and Pedersen (1937: 129) put the following interpretation: "[OIr] p-, which [as a result of 1d p-CHANGES] occurs in borrowings only and so was introduced after the period of lenition, was lenited to f-... by analogy with k-: /x-/, t:/þ-/..."

The reference here is to alternations like preceptóri 'preacher' vs. lenited phreceptóri noted under (b) above. Note also in this connection that later Latin borrowings with /s/ also undergo LEN. E.g., nom sg fem Lat syllaba 'syllable' (ev) > OIr /ind^{l} sillab/ 'the syllable' (LEN)→ int hillab /ind iLab/.

The so-called "analogy" to which Lewis and Pedersen refer is certainly not analogy in any obvious sense. Rather, what has clearly occurred is not analogy, but rather that LEN remained as a rule of Old Irish phonology and affected the new borrowings with word-initial /p/ and /s/. Lewis and Pedersen (1937: 148) also take note of the Old Irish orthographic convention whereby "...every non-len[ited] sound can be represented by a double cons[onant]..." Old Irish examples are i-ccach lucc 'in every place' for /i kax luk/ and do-lleicet 'they leave' for /do-Lḗket/ (where in accordance with our practice /L/ represents the unlenited /l/). If these examples had been written **i-cach luc or **do-leicet, the tendency would have been to pronounce them **/igax lug/ and **/do-lḗket/.

Some sources such as Lehmann and Lehmann (1975: 38-9) believe there was a gemination change which occurred with unlenited consonants. Although this is possible, it is more likely that most instances of what is misleadingly labeled Old Irish "gemination" are in fact merely orthographic devices to designate unlenited consonants.

Finally, we note that there are a few problematic derivations such as the PIE o-class acc pl masc *mak^{w}ōns 'sons' (3b ō-CHANGES) > *mak^{w}ūns (LEN for some reason not applying, but perhaps some sort of "expressive" or hypocoristic gemination) > *mak^{w}k^{w}ūns (7a k^{w}-TO-k) > *makkūns (8b W-F SEG DELE) > *makkū (9c LATER UNSTR-V) > OIr maccu /makku/ (perhaps /maku/). If LEN had applied, one would have OIr **machu **/maxu/.

2c Change of /m/ to /n/ (m-TO-n)

After occurring, this change drops as a rule from the grammar. Its indirect manifestation is in rule 3a ECLIP below.

m → n / [V, ?–stress] ___##

That is, a word-final /m/ after a vowel (which probably has to be unstressed) becomes /n/.

E.g., PIE nom pl masc *septom *pateres '7 fathers' (1d p-CHANGES) > *sextōm *ateres (2b LEN) > *sextōm *aθeres (m-TO-n) > *sextōn *aθeres (2d V̄+NASAL SHORT) > *sexton *aθeres (3a ECLIP) > *sexton *naθeres (5 EARLY UNSTR-V) > *sextan *naθiris (6b INFEC) > *sextan *naθ'ir'is (8b W-F SEG DELE) > OIr secht naithir /sext naθ'ir'/. (The usual nominative plural is aithir /aθ'ir'/ 'fathers'.) Note in this derivation the necessary chronology 1d p-CHANGES > m-TO-n > 3a ECLIP > 8b W-F SEG DELE.

Also PIE o-class masc acc sg *wirom 'man' (m-TO-n) > *wiron (3a ECLIP, which copies a reflex of the word-final /n/ onto the following word) > *wiron##n (5 EARLY UNSTR-V) > *wiran##n (6a i-e/u-o ALT) > *weran##n (7c w-CHANGES) *feran##n (8b W-F SEG DELE) > OIr fer##n. The accusative singular triggers the OIr synchronic reflex of 3a ECLIP. Following a common practice, we shall usually write such forms with a superscript $^{\text{“n”}}$, e.g. acc sg fer^{n} 'man', secht^{n} '7', etc. (See 3a ECLIP below.)

2d Vowel Shortening Before a Word-Final Nasal Consonant (V̄+NASAL SHORT)

After being added to the grammar as a rule, this change restructures some inflectional endings and then is dropped from the grammar.

[V, ?–stressed, +long] → [–long] / ___ [C, +nasal] ##

That is, a long (probably unstressed) vowel in a word-final syllable which ends in a nasal consonant /n/ (or /m/ if 2c m-TO-n has not yet applied) becomes short.

E.g., PIE 1sg subj conj *-b^{h}erām 'carry' (la DEASP) > *-berām (1f IRISH STRESS) > *-bérām (2c m-TO-n) > *-bérān (V̄+NASAL SHORT) > *-béran (8b W-F SEG DELE) > OIr -ber. Similarly PIE gen pl *wirōm 'man' (2c m-TO-n) > *wirōn (V̄+NASAL SHORT) > *wiron (5 EARLY UNSTR-V) > *wiran (6a i-e/u-o ALT) > *weran (6b INFEC not applying here, then 7c w-CHANGES) > *feran (8b W-F SEG DELE) > OIr fer.

Note the following three chronologies. First, V̄+NASAL SHORT > 5 EARLY UNSTR-V > 6b INFEC. If the sequence were 5 EARLY UNSTR-V > V̄+NASAL SHORT, the derivation would be *wirōn (5 EARLY UNSTR-V not applying, then V̄+NASAL SHORT) > *wiron (6a i-e/u-o ALT) > *weron (6b INFEC now applying) > *wer^{u}on (7c w-CHANGES, 8b W-F SEG DELE) > OIr **feur **/fer^{u}/ instead of /fer/.

Second, V̄+NASAL SHORT must precede 8b W-F SEG DELE. Given our formulation of 8b, if the vowel before the word-final nasal were not short by this time, the Old Irish forms -ber 'carry' and fer 'man' cited above would be **-bera and **fera.

Finally, the sequence must be V̄+NASAL SHORT > 3b ō-CHANGES. If this sequence were reversed, the OIr gen pl fer 'men' < PIE *wirōm cited above would be OIr **fiur **/fir^{u}/.

3a Effects of /n/ in Word-Final Position (ECLIP)

These changes remain in Old Irish as morph cond rules. The term for them used in the literature is "eclipsis".

(a) p, t, k → b, d, g
(b) b, d, g → mb, nd, ŋg (later → m, n, ŋ)
(c) Ø → n
} / n ## ___ [V, +stress]

That is, when the preceding word ends in /n/, (a) word-initial /p, t, k/ followed by a stressed vowel become /b, d, g/; and (b) word-initial /b, d, g/ if followed by a stressed vowel become /mb, nd, ŋg/

and later /m, n, ŋ/, respectively. Finally, (c) a word beginning with a stressed vowel takes the final /n/ from the preceding word. (Note that by the time of ECLIP, rule 2c m-TO-n had already applied, so the only possible word-final nasal was /n/.)

E.g., (a) PIE nom pl neuter *septōm *tegesā '7 houses' (1d p-CHANGES) > *sextōm *tegesā (2b LEN) > *sextōm *teǥeā (2c m-TO-n) > *sextōn *teǥeā (2d V̄+NASAL SHORT) > *sexton *teǥeā (ECLIP) > *sexton *deǥeā (5 EARLY UNSTR-V) > *sextan *deǥea (6b INFEC) > *sextan *deǥ'ea (8b W-F SEG DELE) > OIr secht dige /sext deǥ'e/. Otherwise the nom pl is OIr tige /teǥ'e/. (Note the necessary chronology ECLIP > 8b W-F SEG DELE.)

(b) PIE nom pl neuter *septōm *dʰorestjā '7 doors' (la DEASP, ld p-CHANGES, 2c m-TO-n, 2d V̄ +NASAL SHORT > *sexton *dorestjā (ECLIP) > *sextan *ndorestjā (5 EARLY UNSTR-V, 6b INFEC) > *sextan *ndor'est'jā (8b W-F SEG DELE) > *sext *ndor'est'jā (9b j-DELE) > *sext *ndor'est'ā (9c LATER UNSTR-V) > *sext *ndor'est'e (10b SYNCOPE) > *sext *ndors'e (to which the neuter pl *-a from the article was readded) > OIr secht ndoirsea /sext ndors'ea/. Otherwise the nominative plural is OIr doirsea /dors'ea/.

(c) PIE nom pl *septōm *pateres '7 fathers' (ev) > OIr secht naithir /sext naθ'ir'/. (See the derivation under 2c m-TO-n above.) The usual nominative plural is OIr aithir /aθ'ir'/. Note the necessary chronology 1d p-CHANGES > ECLIP.

As noted earlier, ECLIP remains as a rule of Old Irish. After the time of 8b W-F SEG DELE, ECLIP is morph cond. These are among several of its morph cond environments:

(a) After all substantives — namely nouns, adjectives, pronouns and those numerals which inflect — in the accusative singular or genitive plural (< PIE *-V(:)m). E.g., acc sg masc /fer/ 'man' + gen sg neuter /teg'e/ 'house' = 'man of the house' (ECLIP) → OIr fer dige /fer deǥ'e/. And gen pl masc /fer/ 'men' + gen sg neuter /teǥ'e/ 'house' = 'men of the house' (ECLIP)→ OIr fer dige /fer deǥ'e/ again. The usual genitive singular is tige /teg'e/.

(b) After all substantives in the nom or acc sg neuter (< PIE *-Vm). E.g., nom sg neuter /doresᵘ/ 'door' + gen sg neuter /teǥ'e/ 'house' = 'door of the house' (ECLIP) → OIr dorus dige /doresᵘ deg'e/.

(c) After the numerals secht '7' /sext/, ocht '8' /oxt/, noi '9' /noi/ and deich '10' /dex'/ (< PIE numerals ending in*-V(:)m). E.g., nom pl /dex' aθ'ir/ '10 fathers' (ECLIP) → OIr deich naithir /dex' naθ'ir'/.

Frequently in the literature as well as here those forms which trigger ECLIP are marked with a superscript "n": e.g., sechtⁿ /sext/ⁿ '7', ochtⁿ /oxt/ⁿ, but sé /sē/ '6'.

3b Changes in /ō/ (ō-Changes)

These changes restructure various lexical items and inflectional endings and are then dropped from the grammar. They seem to have occurred in the following chronology.

(1) (a) ō → ū / ___ C_o^n ##
(b) ōi → ū / ___ ##
(2) ō → ā / otherwise

That is, (la) /ō/ becomes /ū/ in a word-final syllable. (1b) Word-final /ōi/ becomes /ū/. (2) Otherwise /ō/ becomes /ā/.

E.g., (la) PIE Vn-class nom sg masc *kʷō 'dog' (ō-CHANGES) > *kʷū (7a kʷ-TO-k) > OIr cú /kū/. PIE o-class acc pl masc *wirōns 'men' (ō-CHANGES) > *wirūns (7c w-CHANGES) > *firūns (8b W-F SEG DELE) > OIr firu. PIE comp adj *senjōs 'older' (ō-CHANGES) > *senjūs (6a i-e/u-o ALT) > *sinjūs (6b INFEC) > *sin'jūs (8b W-F SEG DELE) > *sin'jū (9b j-DELE) > *sin'ū (9c LATER UNSTR-V) > OIr siniu /sin'u/.

(1b) PIE o-class dat sg masc *wirōi 'man' (ō-CHANGES) > *wirū (6b INFEC) > *wir^{u}ū (7c w-CHANGES) > *fir^{u}ū (8b W-F SEG DELE) > OIr fiur /fir^{u}/.

(2) PIE o-class nom sg masc *b^{h}lōtos 'flower' and nom sg neuter *dōnom 'gift' (1a DEASP) > *blōtos, *dōnom (2b LEN) > *bLōθos, *dōnom (2c m-TO-n) > *bLōθos, *dōnon (ō-CHANGES) > *bLāθos, *dānon (5 EARLY UNSTR-V) > *bLāθas, *dānan (8b W-F SEG DELE) > OIr bláth /bLāθ/ and dán /dān/.

4 Shortening of Long Diphthongs (DIPH SHORT)

This change restructures various underlying forms and then is dropped as a rule from the grammar.

[V, +long] → [–long] / ___ [V, +high]

That is, the PIE long diphthongs /āi, ēi, ōi, āu, ēu, ōu/ become /ai, ei, oi, au, eu, ou/.

E.g., PIE ā-class nom sg fem *nāu+ā 'ship' (DIPH SHORT) > *nau+ā (8b W-F SEG DELE) > OIr nau. PIE *dwōu '2' (3b ō-CHANGES) > *dwāu (DIPH SHORT) > *dwau (7c w-CHANGES, 9a DIPH CHANGES, 9c LATER UNSTR-V) > OIr da.

Note the necessary chronology 3b ō-CHANGES > DIPH SHORT in the following derivation: PIE o-class dat sg masc *wirōi 'man' (3b ō-CHANGES) > *wirū (DIPH SHORT not applying, 6b INFEC) > *wir^{u}ū (7c w-CHANGES) > *fir^{u}u (8b W-F SEG DELE) > OIr fiur /fir^{u}/. If the sequence were DIPH SHORT > 3b ō-CHANGES , the derivation would be *wirōi (DIPH SHORT) > *wiroi (3b ō-CHANGES not applying, but by 5 EARLY UNSTR-V) > *wirī (6b INFEC) > *wir'ī (7c w-CHANGES) > *fir'ī (8b W-F SEG DELE) > OIr **fir **/fir'/ instead of fiur /fir^{u}/.

5 Early Changes in Unstressed Vowels (EARLY UNSTR-V)

These changes are added as rules to the grammar, restructure certain morphemes (primarily inflectional suffixes) and then are dropped from the grammar. They are as follows:

(a) e → i / [–stressed ___] C_0 ##

(b) o → a / [–stressed ___] $\begin{Bmatrix} C_0 \\ u \end{Bmatrix}$ ##

(c) ai, oi → ī / [–stressed ___] ##

That is, (a) unstressed /e/ becomes /i/ in a word-final syllable which may have none, one or more consonants in its coda. (b) Unstressed /o/ becomes /a/ under the same circumstances. In addition, unstressed /o/ in a word-final diphthong /ou/ becomes /a/. (c) Unstressed /ai, oi/ if absolutely word-final become /ī/.

E.g., (a) PIE voc sg *wire 'man' (EARLY UNSTR-V) > *wiri (6b INFEC) > *wir'i (7c w-CHANGES) > *fir'i (8b W-F SEG DELE) > OIr fir /fir'/.

(b) PIE nom sg *wiros 'man' (EARLY UNSTR-V) > *wiras (6a i-e/u-o ALT) > *weras (no 6b INFEC, ev) > OIr fer. Notice here that EARLY UNSTR-V must precede 6b INFEC. Otherwise the derivation would be PIE *wiros (6a i-e/u-o ALT) > *weros (6b INFEC) > *wer^{u}os (EARLY UNSTR-V) > *wer^{u}as (7c w-CHANGES, 8b W-F SEG DELE) > OIr **feur **/fer^{u}/ instead of fer. Note also the PIE o-class dual gen *wirou (EARLY UNSTR-V) > *wirau (ev) > OIr fer.

(c) PIE nom pl *wiroi 'men' (EARLY UNSTR-V) > *wirī (6b INFEC) > *wir'ī (7c w-CHANGES, 8b W-F SEG DELE) > OIr fir /fir'/. Note in this derivation the necessary chronology EARLY UNSTR-V > 6a i-e/u-o ALT. Otherwise the Old Irish form would be **fer.

6a Alternations of /i/-/e/ and /u/-/o/ (i-e/u-o ALT)

This change remains as a morph cond rule in the phonology of Old Irish. Its early version is this:

(a) i, u → e, o/ [+stress or +post-tonic ___] C_1^n [V, –high]
where $C_1^n \neq$ nd or nt

(b) e, o → i, u/ [+stress or +post-tonic ___] C_1^n [V, +high] or j

That is, (a) /i/ and /u/, if stressed or if following the stressed syllable in a word, become /e/ and /o/, respectively, if followed by at least one consonant or a consonant cluster (but not /nd/ or /nt/) and by a nonhigh vowel /a(:), e(:), o(:)/. (b) Under the same stress conditions and if followed by a single consonant or a consonant cluster followed in turn by a high vowel /i(:), u(:)/ or by /j/, /e/ and /o/ become /i/ and /u/, respectively.

E.g., (a) PIE u-class nom sg masc *wid^{h}us 'wood' vs. gen sg *wid^{h}ous (la DEASP) > *widus, *widous (2b LEN) > *wiðus, *wiðous (i-e/u-o ALT) > *wiðus, *weðous (? 6b INFEC) > *wið^{u}us, *weð^{u}ous (7c w-CHANGES) > *fið^{u}us, *feð^{u}ous (8b W-F SEG DELE) > *fið^u, *feð^{u}ou (9a DIPH CHANGES) > *fið^u, *feð^{u}ō (9c LATER UNSTR-V) > OIr fid /fið/ and fedo /feðo/. (If 6b INFEC did in fact apply in this derivation, one would expect OIr **fiud **/fið^u/ and **feudo **/feð^{u}o/.) Likewise, PIE u-class nom sg masc *srutus 'stream' vs. gen sg *srutous (ev) > OIr sruth /sruθ^u/ and srotho /sroθ^{u}o/. The i-e/u-o ALT change does not apply to the PIE nom sg masc adj *windos 'white' (ev) > OIr find, not **fend. But i-e/u-o ALT does apply over other nasal clusters. E.g., the 3sg pres subj of the ī-class weak verb 'leave' *link^{w}āti (2b LEN) > *link^{w}āði (5 EARLY UNSTR-V) > *link^{w}aði (i-e/u-o ALT) > *lenk^{w}aði (6b INFEC applying analogously to /k^w/ from other forms in the paradigm) > *lenk^w'að'i (7a k^w-TO-k) > *lenk'að'i (7b VnC-TO-VC) > *lēk'að'i (8b W-F SEG DELE) > OIr (presumable but unattested) léica(i)d /lēk'að'/. (Note the necessary chronology i-e/u-o ALT > 7b VnC-TO-VC.)

(b) PIE 1sg pres conj *eks+b^{h}erō 'I say' vs. 3sg pres conj *eks+b^{h}eret 'he says' (la DEASP) > *eks+berō, *eks+beret (1f IRISH STRESS) > *eks+bérō, *eks+béret (3b ō-CHANGES) > *eks+bérū, *eks+béret (i-e/u-o ALT applying only to the first form) > *eks+bírū, *eks+béret (6b INFEC) > *eks+bír^{u}ū, *eks+bér'et (8a LATER C CL) > *es+bír^{u}ū, *es+bér'et (8b W-F SEG DELE) > *es+bír^u, *es+bér' (9c LATER UNSTR-V) > OIr asbiur /as+bír^u/ and asbeir /as+ber'/. (Note the necessary chronology 3b ō-CHANGES > i-e/u-o ALT > 8b W-F SEG DELE.) Also PIE nom sg jo-class neuter *sodjom 'seat' (2b LEN) > *soðjom (2c m-TO-n, 5 EARLY UNSTR-V) > *soðjan (i-e/u-o ALT) > *suðjan (6b INFEC) > *suð'jan (8b W-F SEG DELE) > *suð'ja (9b j-DELE) > *suð'a (9c LATER UNSTR-V) > OIr suide /suð'e/.

The i-e/u-o ALT change must precede 10b SYNCOPE: PIE nom sg masc Ø-class *seno-tūt+s 'old age' (1f IRISH STRESS) > *sénotūts (2b LEN) > *sénoθūts (i-e/u-o ALT not applying, but 8b W-F SEG DELE does) > *sénoθū (9c LATER UNSTR-V) > *sénoθu (10b SYNCOPE) > *sénθu (? restructuring of the consonant cluster /nθ/ — which after 7b VnC-TO-VC was phonotactically impossible — to /nt/) > OIr sentu. If the chronology had been 10b SYNCOPE > i-e/u-o ALT, the Old Irish form would be **sintu.

The i-e/u-o ALT change remains as a morph cond rule of Old Irish and accounts for several paradigmatic alternations such as the nom sg o-class masc fer /fer/ 'man' vs. the gen sg fir /fir'/. The morph cond rule differs substantially from the originally phon cond one. Lewis and Pedersen (1937: 104) note that "Anal[ogical] formations are very frequent." In general, i-e/u-o ALT applies more often in post-tonic syllables than in stressed ones.

6b Rounding or Palatalization of Consonants (INFEC)

This change is often referred to in the literature as "infection". It remains in the Old Irish grammar as a partly phon cond and partly morph cond rule. It consisted originally of two phon cond changes:

C_1^n → (a) [+palatal] / ___ [V, –back] or j
(b) [+round] / ___ [V, +round] or w

The rule applies to all consonants, obstruent or sonorant. A consonant or consonant cluster is palatalized (a) if immmediately followed by /e(:), i(:)/ or /j/ and is rounded (b) if immediately followed by /o(:), u(:)/ or /w/. In the literature the palatalized consonants are often called "slender" and the others "broad". The term "broad" also includes those consonants unaffected by INFEC, namely those followed by /a(:)/ or ##. E.g., PIE gen sg *wirī 'man' vs. the dat sg *wirōi (3b ō-CHANGES) > *wirī, *wirū (INFEC) > *wir'ī, *wir^{u}ū. Here we designate the palatal consonant with the prime (C') and the rounded one with the superscript (C^u). The derivation continues: *wir'ī, *wir^{u}ū (7c w-CHANGES) > *fir'ī, *fir^{u}ū (8b W-F SEG DELE) > OIr fir /fir'/ and fiur /fir^u /. Note here the necessary chronology INFEC > 8b W-F SEG DELE. Note also the necessary chronology INFEC > 9b j-DELE in this derivation: PIE comp adj *sen+jōs 'older' (3b ō-CHANGES) > *senjūs (6a i-e/u-o ALT) > *sinjūs (INFEC) > *sin'jūs (8b W-F SEG DELE) > *sin'jū (9b j-DELE, 9c LATER UNSTR-V) > OIr siniu /sin'u/.

Other examples are PIE nom sg i-class masc *wātis 'prophet, seer' (2b LEN) > *wāθis (INFEC) > *wāθ'is (7c w-CHANGES, 8b W-F SEG DELE) > OIr fáith /fāθ'/. Likewise, note the derivation under 6a i-e/u-o ALT above of PIE 1sg pres conj *eks+b^{h}erō 'I say' vs. 3sg pres conj *eks+b^{h}eret into OIr asbiur /as+bír^u/ and asbeir /as+bér'/.

After the application of 8b W-F SEG DELE, INFEC is in part morph cond. So, for instance, as in the immediately preceding examples in word-final position both /r^u/ and /r'/ can occur. It will be our usual practice to mark palatalized and rounded consonants only in those instances where the following vowel has been deleted. Otherwise the palatalization or the rounding is predictable from the following vowel as indicated in the INFEC rule. Hence we shall transcribe OIr asbiur and asbeir noted in the previous paragraph as /as+bir^u/ and /as+ber'/, not as **/as+b'ir^u/ and **/as+b'er'/.

Similarly, in the case of consonant clusters — all members of which are uniformly either palatalized or rounded or neither — we shall mark only the final consonant in the cluster. E.g., PIE dat sg ā-class fem *sterkāi 'love' (4 DIPH SHORT, ev) > *steRkai (5 EARLY UNSTR-V) > *steRkī (INFEC) > *st'eRk'ī (8a LATER C CL) > *s'eRk'ī (8b W-F SEG DELE) > OIr seirc which is phonetically [s'eR'k'] and which we shall transcribe /seRk'/. (Note here the necessary chronology 4 DIPH SHORT > 5 EARLY UNSTR-V > INFEC.)

An instance where INFEC does not apply is the PIE o-class nom sg masc *wiros 'man' (5 EARLY UNSTR-V) > *wiras (6a i-e/u-o ALT) > *weras (INFEC not applying, but 8b W-F SEG DELE, ev) > OIr fer. Note here the necessary chronology 5 EARLY UNSTR-V > INFEC.

The OIr dat sg fiur 'man' and the nom sg fáith 'seer' cited above were in our view pronounced /fir^u/ and /fāθ'/; and the orthographic <iu> and <ái> indicated only that the following consonants were rounded and palatalized, respectively. However, it is sometimes assumed that such forms were in fact pronounced /fiur^u/ and /fāiθ'/. If this should have been the case, then there would have existed a (possibly optional) phonetic rule of Old Irish, which would have applied after INFEC:

(a) Ø → i / [V, +back] ___ [C, +palatal]
[C, +palatal] ___ [V, +back]

(b) Ø → u / [V, –back] ___ [C, +round]
? [C, +round] ___ [V, –back]

That is, (a) /i/ is inserted between a back vowel /a(:), o(:), u(:)/ and a palatal consonant (C') or between a palatal consonant and a back vowel. (b) And /u/ is inserted between a front vowel /e(:), i(:)/ and a rounded consonant (C^u) or between a rounded consonant and a front vowel.

E.g., the Old Irish synchronic derivations nom sg /fāθ'/ 'seer' → [fāiθ'], dat pl /feraƀ'/ 'men' → [feraiƀ'] — the latter written either <ferab> or <feraib>. Also the 1 sg pres conj <-biur> /-bir^u/ 'I carry' → [–biur^u].

7a Change of Original /k^w/ to /k/ (k^w-TO-k)

This change restructured the phonemic inventory of the language and was then dropped as a rule from the grammar.

k^w, k^{w}', k^{wu}, x^w, x^{w}', x^{wu} → k, k', k^u, x, x', x^u

That is, the labiovelar consonants lose their labial element. (If one assumes, as we do, that this change applies after 2b LEN and after 6b INFEC, then the k^w-TO-k change also delabializes the lenited and/or slender or rounded velars as well.)

E.g., PIE *k^wetwores '4' (2b LEN, 6b INFEC) > *k^w'eθwor'es (k^w-TO-k) > *k'eθwor'es (7c W-CHANGES) > *k'eθor'es (8b W-F SEG DELE) > *k'eθor' (9c LATER UNSTR-V) > OIr ceth(a)ir /k'eθar'/. Also PIE 1sg pres dep *sek^{w}ōr 'I follow' (2b LEN) > *sex^{w}ōr (3b ō-CHANGES) > *sex^{w}ūr (k^w-TO-k) > *sexūr (9c LATER UNSTR-V) > OIr sechur /sexur/.

We assume that 2a g^w-CHANGES occurs before k^w-TO-k since g^w-CHANGES affects all Celtic languages similarly. However, the k^w-TO-k change is peculiar to Old Irish; and different /k^w/-changes occur elsewhere within Celtic. E.g., Welsh pedwar '4' < PIE *k^wetwores, where /k^w/ has become Welsh /p/.

Lewis and Pedersen (1937: 43-44) note that /k^w/ seems to be preserved in the Ogam monuments of Old Irish from ca. 400–600 AD. Hence we assume that k^w-TO-k occurred shortly after 600 AD.

7b Changes in the Sequence Vowel+Nasal+Voiceless Obstruent (VnC-TO-VC)

After applying as an obligatory rule, this change restructures various lexical items and then is dropped as a rule from the grammar. Its precise form is not clear. Here we follow mainly the version in Thurneysen (1909: 1, 124):

$$\underset{1}{\begin{Bmatrix}\text{(a) i, o, u}\\ \text{(b) a, e}\end{Bmatrix}}\quad \underset{2}{\text{n}}\quad \underset{3}{\begin{bmatrix}\text{C, –sonorant}\\ \text{–voiced}\end{bmatrix}} \quad\rightarrow\quad \underset{1}{\begin{Bmatrix}\text{(a) same}\\ \text{(b) ē}\end{Bmatrix}}\quad \underset{2}{\emptyset}\quad \underset{3}{\text{same}}$$

That is, (a) a sequence consisting of /i, o or u/ plus /n/ plus a voiceless obstruent /p, t, k, possibly k^w/ and /s/) loses the /n/. (b) If the vowel is /a/ or /e/, the same change occurs and the vowel becomes /ē/.

E.g., PIE u-class nom sg masc *sentus 'way' (6b INFEC) > *sent^{u}us (VnC-TO-VC) > *sēt^{u}us (8b W-F SEG DELE) > OIr sét /sēt^u/. PIE o-class nom sg neuter *tonkatom 'happiness' (2b LEN, 2c m-TO-n, ev) > *tonkaðan (VnC-TO-VC) > *tokaðan (8b W-F SEG DELE) > OIr tocad /tokað/. PIE i-class nom sg fem *g^hansis 'swan' (1a DEASP) > *gansis (6b INFEC) > *gans'is (VnC-TO-VC) > *gēs'is (8b W-F SEG DELE) > OIr géis /gēs'/. Note also the derivation of the PIE Vn-class masc acc pl *k^won+n̥s 'dogs' (le SYL SON) > *k^wonans (1f IRISH STRESS) > *k^wónans (7a k^w-TO-k) > *kónans (VnC-TO-VC) > *kónēs (8b W-F SEG DELE) > *kónē (9c LATER UNSTR-V) > OIr cona /kóna/.

In some instances short /o/ seems to have been lengthened: PIE *k^wonk^{w}e '5' (6b INFEC) > *k^wonk^w'e (7a k^w-TO-k) > *konk'e (VnC-TO-VC) > *kōk'e (8b W-F SEG DELE) > OIr cóic /kōk'/. And in some forms, short /a/ seem to have become long /ā/, at least temporarily. E.g., PIE nom pl *karantes 'friends' (ev) > OIr karait /karat'/, not **careit **/karet'/. (See the complete derivation under 8b W-F SEG DELE below.)

7c Changes of /w/ (w-CHANGES)

These changes restructure the phonemic inventory (adding /f/) as well as various lexical items and then are dropped as rules from the grammar. They are basically as follows and seem to have occurred in the relative chronology given below.

(1) (a) w → f / ## ___

(b) w → Ø / (a) {## / C} C ___

(b) θ or x ___

(c) V ___ {## / V}

(2) w → ƀ otherwise

That is, (1)(a) /w/ becomes /f/ word-initially; (b) /w/ disappears (a) after a word-initial consonant or after two consonants, (b) after /θ/ or /x/ and (c) word-finally after a vowel or between two vowels. (2) Otherwise, /w/ becomes /ƀ/.

E.g., (1a) PIE nom sg masc adj *wēros 'true' (1b ē-TO-ī) > *wīros (5 EARLY UNSTR-V) > *wīras (w-CHANGES) > *fīras (8b W-F SEG DELE) > OIr fír /fīr/. (1ba) PIE nom dual neuter *dw+ā '2' (w-CHANGES, ev) > OIr da /da/. (1bb) PIE nom pl masc *k^{w}etwores '4' (2b LEN, ev) > *k^{w}eθworis (6b INFEC) > *k^{w}eθwor'is (7a k^w-TO-k) > *keθwor'is (w-CHANGES) > *keθor'is (8b W-F SEG DELE) > *keθor' (9c LATER UNSTR-V) > OIr cethair /keθar'/. (1bc) PIE gerundive *kl̥+teu+āi 'which should be hidden' (PIE 3.1.2c i-j/u-w ALT applying synchronically) > *kl̥tewāi (1e SYL SON) > *klitewāi (2b LEN) > *kLiθewāi (4 DIPH SHORT) > *kLiθewai (5 EARLY UNSTR-V) > *kLiθewī (6a i-e/u-o ALT) > *kLeθewī (6b INFEC) > *kLeθ'iwī (w-CHANGES) > *kLeθ'i-ī (8b W-F SEG DELE) > OIr clethe /kLeθi/. (2) PIE nom sg fem *wid^{h}wā 'widow' (1a DEASP) > *widwā (2b LEN) > *wiðwā (6a i-e/u-o ALT) > *weðwā (w-CHANGES) > *feðƀā (8b W-F SEG DELE) > OIr fedb /feðƀ/.

Finally, we note that at least the latter stages of w-CHANGES may have occurred during the 600's AD.

8a Later Conditions on Consonant Clusters (LATER C CL)

Some aspects of these changes are not clear; hence our formulations of them are somewhat approximative. The changes restructured various lexical items and then were dropped as rules from the grammar. The changes appear to occur in at least two chronological stages.

(1) The first change involves conditions on consonant clusters:

(a) s p r → s Ø r
s t r → s Ø r
1 2 3 → 1 2 3

s p → s Ø
s t → s Ø (sometimes Ø t)
1 2 → 1 2 (1 2) / ## ___

(b) l or r s [C, −sonorant] → same Ø same / [+segment] —
1 2 3 → 1 2 3

(c) ? h (< s) { C, +nasal / α features } → { C, +nasal / α features } same / [+segment] ___
1 2 1 2

(d) { C, –sonorant / –continuant / α features } { C, –sonorant / β features } → { C, –sonorant / β features } same / [+segment] ___
1 2 1 2

(e) s t → s s / [+segment] ___
z d d d
1 2 1 2

(f) l or ? h (< s) l → l l
r r r

l p or s → l l / [+segment] ___
r r r

l n → l l
1 2 1 2

That is, (a) word-initially, consonant clusters beginning with /s/ change as shown. The other parts of this rule apply only word-internally: (b) A sequence consisting of /l/ or /r/ plus /s/ plus /p, t, k/ loses the /s/. (The sonorant /n/ does not occur in this environment since it has already been deleted by 7b VnC-TO-VC.) (c) Possibly, the sequence /h/ (from /s/ by 2b LEN) plus /m/ or /n/ becomes /mm/ and /nn/, respectively. (d) A sequence of two different obstruents, the first of which must be a stop, becomes geminates according to the second obstruent. (The two consonants already agree in voicing because of 1c EARLY C CL, which is still in the grammar applying synchronically.) So sequences like /tk, dg, ts/ become /kk, gg, ss/. (e) The sequences /st/ and /zd/ become /ss/ and /dd/ respectively. (f) The sequences shown (including possibly /h/ from /s/ by 2b LEN) containing /l/ or /r/ all become /ll/ or /rr/, respectively.

The next LATER C CL change simplifies geminate consonants:

(2) [C, αfeatures][C, αfeatures] → [C, αfeatures]

That is, all geminate consonants become single. (This happens only word-internally or word-finally since no geminates occur word-initially.)

E.g., (1a) PIE nom sg *stratos 'valley' (2b LEN, 5 EARLY UNSTR-V) > *stRaθas (LATER C CL) > *sRaθas (8b W-F SEG DELE) > OIr srath /sRaθ/. PIE 1sg pres *steig^{h}ō 'go' (la DEASP, 2b LEN, 3b ō-CHANGES) > *steiḡū (LATER C CL, 9a DIPH CHANGES, 9c LATER UNSTR-V) > OIr tiagu /tiaḡu/. But a somewhat different derivation is PIE nom sg *steros 'star' (LATER C CL, ev) > OIr ser, not **ter.

(1b) PIE nom sg neuter *tarstom 'thirst' (ev) > OIr tart /taRt/. Here /R/ is unlenited.

(1c) PIE nom sg masc adj *plusmos 'bare' (1d p-CHANGES) > *lusmos (2b LEN) > *luhMos (5 EARLY UNSTR-V) > *luhMas (6a i-e/u-o ALT) > *lohMas (LATER C CL 1c) > *loMMas (LATER C CL 2) > *loMas (8b W-F SEG DELE) > OIr lomm /loM/. An alternative account is to assume that there was in fact no change LATER C CL 1c. In such an event the derivation is PIE *plusmos (1d p-CHANGES, 2b LEN) > *luhMos (ev) > OIr lomm /loM/. Here there was in fact no gemination of /M/. Rather, orthographic <mm> is used to indicate unlenited /M/.

(1d) PIE loc pl *pēd+su 'at the feet of = under' (1b ē-TO-ī) > *pīdsu (1c EARLY C CL) > *pītsu (1d p-CHANGES) > *ītsu (6b INFEC apparently not applying here, perhaps because the prep 'under' was usually unstressed, but 8b W-F SEG DELE) > *īts (LATER C CL 1d and 2) > OIr ís /īs/ 'under'. PIE 3sg pres conj *-ek+b^{h}eret 'bring forth' (later 'say') (la DEASP, lc EARLY C CL) > *-egberet (2b LEN, 5 EARLY UNSTR-V) > *-egberit (6a i-e/u-o ALT, 6b INFEC) > *-egbir'it (LATER C CL 1d and 2) > *-ebir'it (8b W-F SEG DELE) > OIr -epir /-ebir'/. Note that if this word had been spelled **<-ebir>, the tendency would have been to pronounce it **/-eƀir'/.

(1e) PIE nom sg masc o-class *ni+sd+os 'an in-sitting, a nest' (lc EARLY C CL) > *nizdos (2b LEN not applying, but 5 EARLY UNSTR-V, 6a i-e/u-o ALT) > *nezdas (8a LATER C CL 1d and 2) > *nedas (8b W-F SEG DELE) > OIr net /ned/. If this word had been spelled **<ned>, the pronunciation would have been **/neð/. In both the preceding derivations, 2b LEN must precede LATER C CL. If the order had been reversed, the Old Irish forms would be **/-eƀir'/ and **/neð/. (See also the derivation of PIE *justjos 'just' > OIr huisse /us'e/ under 9b j-DELE below.)

(1f) PIE nom sg masc *koslos 'hazel tree' (2b LEN, 5 EARLY UNSTR-V) > *kohLas (LATER C CL) > *koLas (8b W-F SEG DELE) > OIr coll /koL/, where graphemic <ll> represents unlenited /L/. And PIE nom sg fem *sirpā 'sickle' (no 2b LEN, but 6a i-e/u-o ALT) > *seRpā (LATER C CL) > *seRā (8b W-F SEG DELE) > OIr serr /seR/.

8b Deletion of Certain Word-Final Segments (W-F SEG DELE)

These changes have to our knowledge not been explicitly stated in the literature. Our version follows somewhat that of Thurneysen (1909: 52–6 and 106–8). According to Pedersen (1909: 1, 243), the W-F SEG DELE changes occurred during the 500's AD. The changes seem to occur in three chronological stages, of which only the second remains as a morph cond rule in Old Irish. The first of these changes is this:

(1) $[\text{V}, -\text{stress}]_1^2 \quad \rightarrow \quad \emptyset$ / C ___ ## (where C = any –vocalic segment except /j/)

That is, any word-final vocalic segments — whether a short vowel, a long vowel or a diphthong — are deleted. The vocalic segments must be preceded by any –vocalic segment except /j/, in which case the rule does not apply. (The –stress configuration is that of Old Irish, not PIE. Hence the chronology is 1f IRISH STRESS > W-F SEG DELE.) E.g., PIE dat sg *wirōi 'man' (3b ō-CHANGES) > *wirū (6b INFEC) > *wir^{u}ū (7c w-CHANGES) > *fir^{u}ū (W-F SEG DELE) > OIr /fir^u/. PIE gen dual *wirou 'man' (5 EARLY UNSTR-V) > *wirau (6a i-e/u-o ALT) > *werau (7c w-CHANGES) > *ferau (W-F SEG DELE) > OIr fer. PIE 2sg imp *karā 'love' (ev) > OIr car /kar/. PIE nom sg fem jo/jā-class adj *aljā 'other' (6b INFEC) > *al'jā (W-F SEG DELE not applying because of the /j/, but 9b j-DELE) > *al'ā (9c LATER UNSTR-V) > OIr aile /al'e/. (Note here the necessary chronology W-F SEG DELE > 9b j-DELE.) Finally, there are instances — particularly in abs (absolute) verb forms — where W-F SEG DELE appears to have to apply, but does not. E.g., PIE 1sg pres ind *b^{h}erō 'carry' (la DEASP) > *berō (3b ō-CHANGES) > *berū (6a i-e/u-o ALT) > *birū (to which W-F SEG DELE does not apply, perhaps because of the occasional presence of an enclitic pronoun such as /-m/ 'I'; but 9c LATER UNSTR-V does apply) > OIr biru, not **bir.

The next change, and the one which remains as a morph cond rule of OIr, is this:

(2) $C_1^n \quad \rightarrow \quad \emptyset$ / ___##

(where $C_1^n \neq$ /l/ or /r/ or certain other consonant clusters as well, particularly those containing /l/ or /r/)

That is, various word-final consonants and consonant clusters are deleted, irrespective of whether the immediately preceding vowel is stressed or not.

E.g., PIE Ø-class nom sg masc *rēg+s 'king' (lb ē-TO-ī) > *rīgs (1c EARLY C CL) > *rīks (W-F SEG DELE) > OIr rí /rī/. Contrast here the PIE gen sg *rēgos (lb ē-TO-ī, 2b LEN, 5 EARLY UNSTR-V) >

*rīgas (W-F SEG DELE 2 and 3) > OIr ríg /rīg/. In such paradigms as this with its alternation of the nom sing rí with the gen sg ríg, W-F SEG DELE continues to function as a morph cond rule.

Other derivations are the PIE o-class acc pl masc *wir+ōns 'men', the ā-class acc pl fem *teut+ās 'peoples' and the Vn-class acc pl masc *kʷon+n̥s 'dogs' (ev up to W-F SEG DELE) > *firūns, *teuθās, *konēs (W-F SEG DELE 2) > *firū, *teuθā, *konē (9a DIPH CHANGES, 9c LATER UNSTR-V) > OIr firu, tuatha /tuaθa/, cona /kona/.

Note also the chronology in the following derivation: PIE nom sg neuter *tod 'this' (ev coming to mean 'thus, yes') (1f IRISH STRESS) > *tód (W-F SEG DELE) > *tó (9d STR-V LENG) > OIr tó /tō/. Here the chronology must be W-F SEG DELE > 9d STR-V LENG.

The final change in the W-F SEG DELE series is this:

(3) [V, –long, –stress] → Ø / C ___ ## (where C = any –vocalic segment except /j/)

That is, an unstressed short vowel occurring after any –vocalic segment (as defined under W-F SEG DELE 1 above) and in word-final position is deleted. (Note that a long vowel in this environment is retained.)

E.g., PIE 3sg pres conj *-bʰeret 'carry' (1a DEASP) > *-beret (6b INFEC) > *-ber'et (W-F SEG DELE 2) > *ber'e (W-F SEG DELE 3) > OIr –beir /-ber'/. PIE nom sg masc *wiros 'man' (5 EARLY UNSTR-V) > *wiras (6a i-e/u-o ALT) > *weras (7c w-CHANGES) > *feras (W-F SEG DELE) > OIr fer. (Note in this derivation the necessary chronology 5 EARLY UNSTR-V > 6a i-e/u-o ALT > W-F SEG DELE.) PIE gen pl *wirōm 'men' (2c m-TO-n, 2d V̄+NASAL SHORT) > *wiron (5 EARLY UNSTR-V) > *wiran (6a i-e/u-o ALT) > *weran (7c w-CHANGES) > *feran (W-F SEG DELE) > OIr fer. (Note here the necessary chronology 2d V̄+NASAL SHORT > W-F SEG DELE.)

Note also the Vnt-class masc nom sg *karant+s 'loving one, friend' vs. the pl *karantes (5 EARLY UNSTR-V) > *karants, *karantis (6b INFEC) > *karants, *karant'is (7b VnC-TO-VC) > *karāts, *karāt'is (W-F SEG DELE 2) > *karā, *karāt'i (W-F SEG DELE 3) > *karā, *karāt' (9c LATER UNSTR-V) > OIr carae /kare/ and carait /karat'/. (Note that in the derivation of the nominative singular, the chronology must be 7b VnC-TO-VC > W-F SEG DELE. Otherwise the Old Irish form would be **car **/kar/.)

In some instances certain word-final consonants are resistant to W-F SEG DELE: e.g., PIE nom sg *patēr 'father' (ev) > OIr aithir /aθ'ir/, not OIr **aithi **/aθ'i/ by W-F SEG DELE. In other instances consonants are retained for reasons which are not clear. E.g., PIE 3sg pres ind *bʰeronti 'carry' (1a DEASP) > *beronti (6b INFEC) > *beront'i (7b VnC-TO-VC) > *berōt'i (only W-F SEG DELE 1 applying, not 2) > *berōt' (9c LATER UNSTR-V) > OIr berait /berat'/. Why W-F SEG DELE 2 does not apply here is not clear. Perhaps it was because of the presence of affixed enclitic pronouns.

9a Changes in Diphthongs (DIPH CHANGES)

After change 4 DIPH SHORT, the pre-Old Irish diphthongs were /ai, au, ei, eu, oi, ou/. Probably during the 600's AD, the following three DIPH CHANGES occur in the order given. The first restructures various lexical items and then is dropped from the grammar. The second remains in the grammar as a morph cond rule. The third also remains in the grammar, but as a phon cond rule.

(1) (a) au, eu, ou → ō
(b) ei → ē
(c) ai and oi remain.

(2) (a) [ō, +stress] → ua / ___ [+segment]

(b) [ē, +stress] → ia / { ## , [C, +palatal] }

(3) See below.

That is, (1) the diphthongs monophthongize as shown; /ai, oi/ remain. (2)(a) The resultant stressed /ō/ becomes /ua/ unless word-final; (b) stressed /ē/ becomes /ia/ if word-final or if followed by any consonant except one which has been palatalized (C') by 6b INFEC. The stress referred to is that of Old Irish. Hence we assume that 1f IRISH STRESS as well as 6b INFEC precedes DIPH CHANGES.

E.g., (la and 2a) PIE nom sg masc adj *roudʰos 'red' (ev through 8b W-F SEG DELE) > *rouð (DIPH CHANGES) > OIr ruad /ruað/. Also PIE nom sg fem *teuta 'people' (2b LEN) > *teuθā (8b W-F SEG DELE) > *teuθ (DIPH CHANGES) > OIr tuath /tuaθ/.

(la, but not 2a) PIE u-class gen sg masc *srutous 'stream' (2b LEN) > *sRuθous (6a i-e/u-o ALT) > *sRoθous (6b INFEC) > *sRoθᵘous (8b W-F SEG DELE) > *sRoθᵘou (DIPH CHANGES la applying, but not DIPH CHANGES 2a because /ou/ is not stressed) > *sRoθᵘō (9c LATER UNSTR-V) > OIr srotho /sRoθo/ = [sRoθᵘo] Here is an instance where DIPH CHANGES may have applied optionally over a morpheme boundary: PIE 1sg pres conj *-stā+ō 'I stand, am' (3b ō-CHANGES) > *-stāū (8a LATER C CL) > *-tāū (? reformation of /āū/ to the usual diphthong /au/, then DIPH CHANGES applying optionally as a temporarily synchronic rule) > *-tō or *-tau = OIr –tó as well as –táu (the latter perhaps /-tāu/).

(lb and 2b) PIE 1sg pres *steigʰō 'I go' vs. 2sg *steigʰesi 'you go' (1a DEASP, 2b LEN) > *steiǥō, *steiǥehi (3b ō-CHANGES) > *steiǥū, *steiǥehi (6a i-e/u-o ALT) > *steiǥū, *steiǥihi > *steiǥii = *steiǥī (6b INFEC) > *steiǥᵘū, *steig'ī (8a LATER C CL) > *teiǥᵘū, *teig'ī (DIPH CHANGES 1b) > *tēǥᵘū, *tēg'ī (DIPH CHANGES 2b) > *tiaǥᵘū, *tēg'ī (9c LATER UNSTR-V) > OIr tiagu /tiaǥu/ and tégi /tēǥi/. Also PIE nom sg *deiwos 'god' vs. dat pl *deiwobʰis (ev through 7c w-CHANGES) > *deias, *deioƀ'is (8b W-F SEG DELE) > *dei, *deioƀ' (9a DIPH CHANGES) > *dia, *dēoƀ' (9c LATER UNSTR-V) > OIr dia, déib /dēaƀ'/. (In this derivation 7c w-CHANGES and 8b W-F SEG DELE must precede DIPH CHANGES.)

Note that DIPH CHANGES does not affect /ē/ resulting from 7b VnC-TO-VC: e.g., PIE *sentus 'way' (ev) > OIr sét /sētᵘ/, not **siat. Now it appears that 7b does not follow DIPH CHANGES since the sequence seems to be 7b VnC-TO-VC > 8b W-F SEG DELE > DIPH CHANGES (see section C, The Relative Chronology below). Therefore we assume that by the time of DIPH CHANGES, the long vowels produced by 7b VnC-TO-VC were still slightly nasalized and DIPH CHANGES did not apply to them.

After the application of DIPH CHANGES 1 and 2, the sole remaining original diphthongs are /ai/ and /oi/. These seem to alternate in Old Irish according to the following optionally applying phon cond rule:

(3) ai } → ae, ai, oe or oi
oi }

That is, both /ai/ and /oi/ may be realized in any of the four ways shown. Hence the OIr word /ais/ 'age' may be written <aes, ais, oes, ois> as noted in Thurneysen (1909: 1, 41). Here we shall transcribe these diphthongs as either /ai/ or /oi/ contingent upon their etymologies: e.g., OIr caich /kaix/ 'blind' < PIE *kaikos and OIr oin /oin/ '1' < PIE *oinos.

9b Deletion of /j/ (j-DELE)

After applying as an obligatory rule, this change restructures various lexical items and then is dropped from the grammar.

j → Ø

That is, /j/ is deleted in all environments.

E.g., PIE nom sg masc jo-class adj *justjos 'just' (ev through 6b INFEC) > *just'jas (8a LATER C CL) > *jus'jas (8b W-F SEG DELE) > *jus'ja (j-DELE) > *us'a (9c LATER UNSTR-V) > OIr huisse /us'e/. (Note the necessary chronology 6b INFEC > j-DELE.) A possible derivation is PIE 1sg pres conj *-stājō 'I stand, am' (ev) > OIr -táu or –tó. (However, the antecedent form may have lacked the /j/.)

9c Later Changes in Unstressed Vowels (LATER UNSTR-V)

These changes occur in two chronological stages. Both changes remain as phon cond rules of Old Irish. The second rule may well have been for the most part optional.

(1)		[V, –stress]	→	[–long]		
(2) optional	(a)	[a, –stress]	→	e	/ usually ___ ##	
optional	(b)	[e, –stress]	→	a	/ usually ___ [+segment]	
optional	(c)	[o, –stress]	→	a	/ usually ___ [+segment]	

That is, (1) unstressed vowels are short. (2)(a) Unstressed and word-final /a/ may become /e/; (b and c) unstressed and word-internal /e/ and /o/ may also become /a/. (Rule 2 may in fact reflect a tendency for all nonhigh short unstressed vowels to become schwas, /ə/.)

E.g., (1) PIE 1sg pres dep *sek^{w}ōr 'I follow' (2b LEN) > *sex^{w}ōr (3b ō-CHANGES) > *sex^{w}ūr (7a k^{w}-TO-k) >*sexūr (LATER UNSTR-V) > OIr sechur /sexur/. PIE nom pl *karantes 'friends' (ev through 8b W-F SEG DELE: see the derivation under 8b) > *karāt' (LATER UNSTR-V) > OIr carait /karat'/.

(2a) PIE nom sg *karants 'friend' (ev through 8b W-F SEG DELE) > *karā (LATER UNSTR-V 1 and 2a) > OIr carae /kare/. (Given our formulation, LATER UNSTR-V must follow 8b W-F SEG DELE.) Also, the PIE jo-class masc nom sg *b^{h}aljos 'place' and dual *b^{h}aljā (ev through 5 EARLY UNSTR-V) > *baljas, *baljā (6b INFEC) > *bal'jas, *bal'jā (8b W-F SEG DELE) > *bal'ja, *bal'jā (9b j-DELE) > *bal'a, *bal'ā (LATER UNSTR-V 1 and 2a) > OIr baile /bal'e/ for both forms.

(2b) PIE 1sg pres *esmi 'I am' (2b LEN applying to the /s/, but not the /m/) > *ehMi (ev) > *eMi (8b W-F SEG DELE) > *eM (LATER UNSTR-V: the word was usually unstressed) > OIr amm /aM/ (possibly /aM'/ if 6b INFEC applied). Also PIE 3sg pres conj *eks+b^{h}eret 'says' (1a DEASP) > *eks+beret (1f IRISH STRESS) > *eks+béret (5 EARLY UNSTR-V) > *eks+bérit (? 6a i-e/u-o ALT not applying or perhaps the /e/ was retained from other forms in the paradigm, but 6b INFEC) > *eks+bér'it (8a LATER C CL) > es+bér'it (8b W-F SEG DELE) > *es+bér' (LATER UNSTR-V) > OIr asbeir /as+bér'/.

(2c) PIE nom pl masc *k^{w}etwores '4' (ev through 7c w-CHANGES, under which see the complete derivation) > *keθor' (LATER UNSTR-V) > OIr cethair /keθar'/.

9d Lengthening of Word-Final Stressed Vowels (STR-V LENG)

This change remains as a phon cond rule in Old Irish.

[V, +stress] → [+long] / ___ ##

That is, a stressed vowel in word-final position is lengthened.

E.g., PIE u-class nom sg masc *krow+us 'blood' (1f IRISH STRESS) > *krówus (6a i-e/u-o ALT) > *krúwus (7c w-CHANGES)/> *krúus (8b W-F SEG DELE, where the morpheme boundaryin *krú+us acts as a C) > *krú (STR-V LENG) > OIr crú /krū́/. (Note in this derivation that all the changes must precede STR-V LENG.) Also PIE acc sg neuter *tód 'this' (8b W-F SEG DELE) > *tó (STR-V LENG) > OIr tó /tṓ/ 'thus, yes'.

10a Deletion of Obstruents Before Sonorant Consonants (OBSTR+SON DELE)

This change, some details of which are unclear in that it seems not to apply in some instances, restructures certain lexical items and then is dropped from the grammar. Its basic structure is as follows:

V	[C, –sonorant]	[C, +sonorant]	→	V̄	Ø	same
1	2	3		1	2	3

That is, in a sequence of vowel plus obstruent plus a sonorant consonant /l, m, n, r/, the obstruent is deleted and the vowel is lengthened.

E.g., PIE nom sg o-class neuter *sk^{w}etlom 'story', ā-class fem *agrā 'massacre' and i-class fem *agnis 'act of going' (2b LEN) > *sk^{w}eθLom, *aǥRā, *aǥNis (2c m-TO-n, 5 EARLY UNSTR-V) > *sk^{w}eθLan, *aǥRā, *aǥNis (6b INFEC) > *sk^{w}eθLan, *aǥRā, *aǥN'is (7a k^{w}-TO-k, 8b W-F SEG DELE) *skeθL, *aǥR, *aǥN' (OBSTR+SON DELE) > OIr scél /skēL/, ár /āR/, áin /āN'/ (where /L, R, N/ are unlenited).

Note that in the derivation of OIr scél above the sequence must be 9a DIPH CHANGES > OBSTR+SON DELE. Otherwise the Old Irish form would be **scial instead of scél. We also assume that OBSTR+SON DELE occurred after 2b LEN since the deletion of a continuant obstruent in such an environment is more likely than that of a stop. This change seems to be later Celtic in that it affects only Old Irish.

10b Vowel Syncope (SYNCOPE)

This change remains as a phon cond rule of Old Irish

```
[V, –stress]   →   Ø  /  ## s   s      s  (s          s)
                                |          |
                               [__]       [_____]
                             1  2      3   4          5
```

That is, in words of at least three syllables, the vowel of the unstressed second syllable is deleted; and in words of at least five syllables, the vowel of the unstressed second syllable and that of the unstressed fourth syllable are deleted.

E.g., PIE u-class masc sg nom *k^{w}ent+tōt+us 'suffering' vs. gen *k^{w}ent+tōt+ous (1c EARLY C CL, 1f IRISH STRESS) > *k^{w}énssōtus, *k^{w}énssōtous (2b LEN) > *k^{w}énssōđus, *k^{w}énssōđous (7a k^{w}-TO-k) > *kénssōđus, *kénssōđous (7b VnC-TO-VC) > *kḗssōđus, *kḗssōđous (8a LATER C CL) > *kḗsōđus, *kḗsōđous (8b W-F SEG DELE) > *kḗsōđ, *kḗsōđou (9a DIPH CHANGES) > *kḗsōđ, *kḗsōđō (9c LATER UNSTR-V) > *kḗsađ, *kḗsađo (SYNCOPE) > *kēsađ, *kēsđo (replacement of the nonoccurring consonant cluster/sđ/ by the phonetically closest existing one /st/) > OIr nom sg césad /kḗsađ/ and gen sg césto /kḗsto/. Note also the borrowing from Latin apostolus 'apostle' > pre-OIr *ápostol (SYNCOPE) > OIr apstol.

SYNCOPE would seem to have applied after 9c LATER UNSTR-V since it is more natural that short unstressed vowels rather than long ones would be deleted. SYNCOPE must also follow 8a LATER C CL in view of the following derivation: PIE neuter u-class nom pl *d^{h}or+est+jā 'doors' (1a DEASP) > *dorestjā (1f IRISH STRESS) > *dórestjā (6b INFEC, 8a LATER C CL) > *dóres'jā (9b j-DELE) > *dóres'ā (9c LATER UNSTR-V) > *dóres'a (SYNCOPE) > OIr doirsea /dors'a/. Another reason for assuming the sequence 8a LATER C CL > SYNCOPE is that otherwise OIr apstol 'apostle' cited above would have become **astol.

On occasion SYNCOPE does not apply — particularly if its application would result in an unwieldy consonant cluster. E.g., PIE jo-class nom sg neuter *kom+akt+jom 'might, power' (ev) > OIr cumachte /kúmaxte/, not **cumchte **/kumxte/.

C. The Relative Chronology

The " > " means "must precede".

1a DEASP > Ø.

1b ē-TO-ī > Ø.

1c EARLY C CL > Ø.

1d p-CHANGES > 2b LEN (see 1d, 2b), > 2c m-TO-n (see 2c), > 9a DIPH CHANGES (see 1d).
1e SYL SON > 2a g^w-CHANGES (see 2a), > 2b LEN (see 2b), > 6a i-e/u-o ALT (see 1e), > 6b INFEC (see 1e).
1f IRISH STRESS > 2c m-TO-n (see 1f), > 2d V̄+NASAL SHORT (see 1f), > 5 EARLY UNSTR-V (see 1f), > 6a i-e/u-o ALT (see 1f), > 7b VnC-TO-VC (see 7b), > 8b W-F SEG DELE (see 1f, 8b), > 9a DIPH CHANGES (see 1f, 9a), > 9c LATER UNSTR-V (see 1f), > 9d STR-V LENG (see 1f, 9d), >10b SYNCOPE (see 1f).
2a g^w-CHANGES > 7a k^w-TO-k (see 7a), > 8b W-F SEG DELE (see 2a).
2b LEN > 7b VnC-TO-VC (see 2b), > 8a LATER C CL (see 1c, 8a), > 8b W-F SEG DELE (see 2b), > 10a OBSTR+SON DELE (see 10a), > 10b SYNCOPE (see 2b).
2c m-TO-n > 3a ECLIP (see 2c, 3a).
2d V̄+NASAL SHORT > 3b ō-CHANGES (see 2d), > 5 EARLY UNSTR-V (see 2d), > 8b W-F SEG DELE (see 2d, 8b).
3a ECLIP > 8b W-F SEG DELE (see 2c, 3a).
3b ō-CHANGES > 4 DIPH SHORT (see 4), > 6a i-e/u-o ALT (see 6a), > 6b INFEC (see 3b).
4 DIPH SHORT > 5 EARLY UNSTR-V (see 4).
5 EARLY UNSTR-V > 6a i-e/u-o ALT (see 1f, 5, 8b), > 6b INFEC (see 2d, 5).
6a i-e/u-o ALT > 7b VnC-TO-VC (see 6a), > 8b W-F SEG DELE (see 6a, 8b), > 9d STR-V LENG (see 9d), > 10b SYNCOPE (see 6a).
6b INFEC > 8b W-F SEG DELE (see 1f, 6b), > 9a DIPH CHANGES (see 9a), > 9b j-DELE (see 6b, 9b).
7a k^w-TO-k > Ø.
7b VnC-TO-VC > 8a LATER C CL (see 8a), > 8b W-F SEG DELE (see 8b).
7c w-CHANGES > 9a DIPH CHANGES (see 9a), > 9d STR-V LENG (see 9d).
8a LATER C CL > 10b SYNCOPE (see 10b).
8b W-F SEG DELE > 9a DIPH CHANGES (see 9a), > 9b j-DELE (see 8b), > 9c LATER UNSTR-V (see 9c), > 9d STR-V LENG (see 8b, 9d).
9a DIPH CHANGES > 7b VnC-TO-VC (see 9a), > 10a OBSTR+SON DELE (see 10a).
9b j-DELE > Ø.
9c LATER UNSTR-V > 10b SYNCOPE (see 10b).
9d STR-V LENG > Ø.
10a OBSTR+SON DELE > Ø.
10b SYNCOPE > Ø.

III Old Irish Phonology

After the changes described in the previous section, the inventory of segments in the phonology of Old Irish at about 700 AD was as follows.

Obstruent Consonants

	labial	dental	alveolar	velar	glottal
Plain (neutral)[1]					
–lenited[2]	p	t		k	
+lenited[2]	f	θ		x	
–lenited	b	d		g	
+lenited	ƀ[3]	ð		ǥ	
–lenited			s		
+lenited					h

Obstruent Consonants

	labial	dental	alveolar	velar	glottal
Palatal (slender)[1]					
–lenited	p'	t'		k'	
+lenited	f'	θ'		x'	
–lenited	b'	d'		g'	
+lenited	ƀ'[3]	ð'		ǥ'	
–lenited			s'		
+lenited					?h'[4]
Rounded (broad)					
–lenited	p^{u}	t^{u}		k^{u}	
+lenited	f^{u}	θ^{u}		x^{u}	
–lenited	b^{u}	d^{u}		g^{u}	
+lenited	ƀ^{u}[3]	ð^{u}		ǥ^{u}	
–lenited			s^{u}		
+lenited					?h^{u}[4]

Sonorant Consonants

	labial	dental	alveolar	velar
Plain (neutral)				
–lenited	M	N		[ŋ][5]
+lenited	m	n		
–lenited		L		
+lenited		l		
–lenited		R		
+lenited		r		
Palatal (slender)[1]				
–lenited	M'	N'		[ŋ'][5]
+lenited	m'	n'		
–lenited		L'		
+lenited		l'		
–lenited		R'		
+lenited		r'		
Rounded (broad)				
–lenited	M^{u}	N^{u}		[ŋ^{u}][5]
+lenited	m^{u}	n^{u}		
–lenited		L^{u}		
+lenited		l^{u}		
–lenited		R^{u}		
+lenited		r^{u}		

Vowels

i u ī ū

e o ē ō

a ā

Diphthongs: ai, oi, ia, ua[6]

Old Irish Segments in Terms of Phonological Features: Consonants

	p	t	k	f	θ	x	b	d	g	ƀ	ð	ǥ	s	h[7]	M	N	ŋ	L	R	m	n	l	r[8]
consonantal	+	+	+	+	+	+	+	+	+	+	+	+	+		+	+	+	+	+	+	+	+	+
sonorant	–	–	–	–	–	–	–	–	–	–	–	–	–		+	+	+	+	+	+	+	+	+
vocalic	–	–	–	–	–	–	–	–	–	–	–	–	–		–	–	–	–	–	–	–	–	–
high	–	–	+	–	–	+	–	–	+	–	–	+	–		–	–	+	–	–	–	–	–	–
back	–	–	+	–	–	+	–	–	+	–	–	+	–		–	–	+	–	–	–	–	–	–
low	–	–	–	–	–	–	–	–	–	–	–	–	–		–	–	–	–	–	–	–	–	–
anterior	+	+	–	+	+	–	+	+	–	+	+	+	+		+	+	–	+	+	+	+	+	+
coronal	–	+	–	–	+	–	–	+	–	–	+	–	+		–	+	–	+	+	–	+	+	+
voiced	–	–	–	–	–	–	+	+	+	+	+	+	–	–	+	+	+	+	+	+	+	+	+
continuant	–	–	–	+	+	+	–	–	–	+	+	+	+	+	–	–	–	+	+	–	–	+	+
nasal	–	–	–	–	–	–	–	–	–	–	–	–	–		+	+	+	–	–	+	+	–	–
strident	–	–	–	–	–	–	–	–	–	–	–	–	+		–	–	–	–	–	–	–	–	–
delayed –release	–	–	–	–	–	–	–	–	–	–	–	–	–		–	–	–	–	–	–	–	–	–
round	–	–	–	–	–	–	–	–	–	–	–	–	–		–	–	–	–	–	–	–	–	–
lateral	–	–	–	–	–	–	–	–	–	–	–	–	–		–	–	–	+	–	–	–	+	–
palatal	–	–	–	–	–	–	–	–	–	–	–	–	–		–	–	–	–	–	–	–	–	–
tense															+	+	+	+	+	–	–	–	–
aspirated	–	–	–	–	–	–	–	–	–	–	–	–	–	+	–	–	–	–	–	–	–	–	–
long	–	–	–	–	–	–	–	–	–	–	–	–	–		+[9]	+	+	+	+	–	–	–	–

Old Irish Segments in Terms of Phonological Features: Vowels

	a	e	i	o	u	ā	ē	ī	ō	ū
consonantal	–	–	–	–	–	–	–	–	–	–
sonorant	+	+	+	+	+	+	+	+	+	+
vocalic	+	+	+	+	+	+	+	+	+	+
high	–	–	+	–	+	–	–	+	–	+
back	+	–	–	+	+	+	–	–	+	+
low	+	–	–	–	–	+	–	–	–	–
voiced	+	+	+	+	+	+	+	+	+	+
continuant	+	+	+	+	+	+	+	+	+	+
nasal	–	–	–	–	–	–	–	–	–	–
round	–	–	–	+	+	–	–	–	+	+
tense	–	–	–	–	–	+	+	+	+	+
stressed	±	±	±	±	±	+	+	+	+	+[10]
long	–	–	–	–	–	+	+	+	+	+

Some of the changes from PIE into Old Irish described in section B above remain as rules in the Old Irish grammar. Others are lost as rules after restructuring lexical items and/or adding new segments to the phonemic inventory. Below we note those changes which have remained as rules in the grammar. We label them as phon cond and/or morph cond and usually cite an illustrative example of their application. (Additional examples can be found under the respective rule as well as in the morphology section IV.) The symbol "Ø" marks those changes which have restructured lexical items and/or changed the inventory of underlying segments and then have been dropped from the grammar.

1a DEASP: Ø.

1b ē-TO-ī: Ø.

1c EARLY C CL (phon cond): the rule states that obstruent clusters must be uniformly voiced or voiceless, contingent upon the last obstruent in the cluster.

1d p-CHANGES: Ø.

1e SYL SON: Ø.

1f IRISH STRESS (morph cond): 3sg pres /do+ber'/ 'carries', nom sg /dores^{u}/ 'door' (IRISH STRESS) → [dobér'] and [dóres^{u}].

2a g^{w}-CHANGES: Ø.

2b LEN (morph cond): /di^{l} tuaθa/ '2 nations' (where the superscript "^{l}" indicates that the form triggers LEN) vs. /sē tuaθa/ '6 nations' (LEN) → [di θuaθa] vs. [sē tuaθa].

2c m-TO-n: Ø.

2d V̄+NASAL SHORT: Ø.

3a ECLIP (morph cond): /sext^{n} teǥe/ '7 houses' (where the superscript "^{n}" indicates that the form triggers ECLIP) vs. /sē teǥe/ '6 houses' (ECLIP) → [sext ndeǥe] vs. [sē teǥe].

3b ō-CHANGES : Ø.

4 DIPH SHORT: Ø.

5 EARLY UNSTR-V: Ø.

6a i-e/u-o ALT (morph cond): 1sg pres conj /as+bér^{u}/ 'say' vs. 3sg pres conj /as+bér'/ (i-e/u-o ALT) → [as-bír^{u}] vs. [as+bér'].

6b INFEC (phon cond and morph cond): /sin+u/ 'older' (INFEC applying to the /s/ in a phon cond environment and to the /n/ in a morph cond one) → [s'in'u].

7a k^{w}-TO-k: Ø.

7b VnC-TO-VC: Ø.

7c w-CHANGES: Ø.

8a LATER C CL: Ø.

8b W-F SEG DELE (morph cond): nom sg /rīǥ/ 'king' vs. gen sg /rīǥ/ (W-F SEG DELE) → [rī] vs. [rīǥ].

9a DIPH CHANGES (morph cond and phon cond): nom sg /dē/ 'god' vs. dat pl /dē+aƀ'/ (DIPH CHANGES) → [dia] vs. [dēaƀ'].

9b j-DELE: Ø.

9c LATER UNSTR-V (phon cond): possibly nom sg /kara/ 'friend' (LATER UNSTR-V) → [kara] or [kare].

9d STR-V LENG (phon cond): the rule states that a stressed word-final vowel must be long.

10a OBSTR+SON DELE: Ø.

10b SYNCOPE (phon cond): nom sg /kēsað/ 'suffering' vs. gen sg /kēsaðo/ (SYNCOPE) → [kēsað] vs. [kēsto].

IV Historical Old Irish Morphology

A. Overview

B. Old Irish Morphology

In each paradigm below the forms in the left-hand column are those of Old Irish at about 700 AD, while those on the right are the PIE antecedents of 3000 BC or somewhat later. We cite the Old Irish forms in the traditional Old Irish orthography. Where the orthography is not perspicuous, we give a phonemic transcription of the form. We usually do not mark the Old Irish stress when it falls on the first syllable. Parentheses in the spelling of a form like the dat pl fer(a)ib 'men' mean that the orthography is either <feraib> or <ferib>. We mark those forms which trigger the synchronic versions of 2b LEN and 3a ECLIP in the following word. We do this with the respective superscripts $^{-l}$ and $^{-n}$. E.g., the gen sg fir^{l} 'man' and the acc sg fer^{n}. (Interestingly, no verb form triggers ECLIP in a following word; and only one triggers LEN — namely the conjunct of the copulative 'be' in 6.8.2.1 below.)

1 Nouns

The substantives inflect for five cases — nominative, vocative, accusative, genitive and dative — and three genders — masculine, feminine and neuter. Nouns inflect for singular, dual and plural. The other substantives and the verbs inflect for only singular and plural. Unless otherwise indicated the vocative has the same form as the nominative.

1.1 o- and jo-Class (Masculine, Neuter)

			Old Irish		PIE
masc	**sg**	**nom**	fer /fer/	'man'	*wiros
		voc	fir^{l} /fir'/		*wire[11]
		acc	fer^{n} /fer/		*wirom[12]
		gen	fir^{l} /fir'/		*wirī[13]
		dat	fiur^{l} /fir^{u}/		*wirō (? +i)[14]
	du	**nom**	fer^{l} /fer/		*wir-ā or -ōu[15]
		acc	" "		"
		gen	" "		*wirou
		dat	fer(a)ib /feraƀ'/		*wirob^{h}im
	pl	**nom**	fir^{l} /fir'/		*wiroi[16]
		voc	firu		*wirōs[17]
		acc	"		*wirōns[17]
		gen	fer^{n}		*wirōm[18]
		dat	fer(a)ib /feraƀ'/		*wirob^{h}is[19]

The o-class neuter nouns have the same endings as the masc ones except for the following:

		Old Irish		PIE
nom/voc/acc	**sg**	scél^{n} /skēL/	'story'	*sk^{w}etlom
	pl	scél^{l} or scéla^{l}		*sk^{w}etlā[20, 21]

Historically the jo-class had the same endings as the o-class. But because of the conditions on change 8b W-F SEG DELE, the endings differ by Old Irish times:

			Old Irish		PIE
masc	**sg**	**nom**	ba(i)le /bal'e/	'place'	*b^haljos[22]
		voc	ba(i)li /bal'i/		*b^halje
		acc	ba(i)le^n		*b^haljom
		gen	ba(i)li^l		*b^haljī
		dat	ba(i)liu^l /bal'u/		*b^haljō(i)
	du	**nom**	ba(i)le^l		*b^halj-ā or -ōu
		acc	"		" "
		gen	"		*b^haljou
		dat	ba(i)lib /bal'aƀ'/		*b^haljob^{h}im
	pl	**nom**	ba(i)li^l		*b^haljoi
		voc	ba(i)liu /bal'u/		*b^haljōs
		acc	" "		*b^haljōns
		gen	ba(i)le^n		*b^haljōm
		dat	ba(i)lib /bal'aƀ'/		*b^haljob^{h}is

The neuter jo-class nouns have the same endings as the masc ones except for the following:

		Old Irish		PIE
nom/voc/acc	**sg**	kride^n /kRiðe/	'heart'	*kr̥djom[23]
	pl	kride^l		*kr̥djā[23]

1.2 ā- and jā-Class (Feminine)

			Old Irish		PIE
masc	**sg**	**nom**	tuath /tuaθ/	'people'	*teutā
		voc	" "		*teuta
		acc	tuaith^n /tuaθ'/		*teutāi[24]
		gen	tuaithe /tuaθ'e/		*teutjās[25]
		dat	tuaith^l /tuaθ'/		*teutāi[24]
	du	**nom**	tuaith^l		*teutai
		acc	"		"
		gen	tuath^l		*teutou
		dat	tuath(a)ib /tuaθaƀ'/		*teutāb^{h}im
	pl	**nom**	tuatha		*teutās
		voc	"		"
		acc	"		*teutāns
		gen	tuath^n		*teutōm
		dat	tuath(a)ib /tuaθaƀ'/		*teutab^{h}is

The following paradigm is of interest in that many of the endings are preserved since they occurred under stress.

			Old Irish		PIE
masc	**sg**	**nom**	ben^{l}	'woman'	*g^{w}enā[26]
		acc	mnái^{n}		*g^{w}nāi[26]
		gen	mná /mNā/		*g^{w}njās
		dat	mnái^{l}		*g^{w}nāi
	du	**nom**	mnái^{l}		*g^{w}nai
		acc	"		"
		gen	ban^{l} ?/ben/		*g^{w}enou[27]
		dat	mnáib /mNāƀ'/		*g^{w}nāb^{h}im
	pl	**nom**	mná /mNā/		*g^{w}nās
		acc	" "		*g^{w}nāns
		gen	ban^{n} ?/ben/		*g^{w}enōm[27]
		dat	mnáib /mNāƀ'/		*g^{w}nāb^{h}is

The jā-nouns had historically the same endings as the ā-class. But, as with the jo-class above, because of the conditions on change 8b W-F SEG DELE, the endings differ by Old Irish times:

			Old Irish		PIE
masc	**sg**	**nom**	insce /ínsk'e/	'speech'	*enisk^{w}jā[28]
		voc	" "		*enisk^{w}ja
		acc	insci^{n}		*enisk^{w}jāi
		gen	insce		*enisk^{w}jās
		dat	insci^{l}		*enisk^{w}jāi
	du	**nom**	insci^{l}		*enisk^{w}jāi
		acc	"		"
		gen	insce^{l}		*enisk^{w}ou
		dat	inscib /ínsk'iƀ'/		*enisk^{w}jāb^{h}im[29,30]
	pl	**nom**	insci /ínsk'i/		*enisk^{w}jās[30]
		voc	" "		"
		acc	" "		*enisk^{w}jāns[30]
		gen	insce^{n}		*enisk^{w}jōm
		dat	inscib /insk'iƀ'/		*enisk^{w}jāb^{h}is[29,30]

In at least two instances, -ā and jā-class nouns seem to have been influenced by forms originally of the root class (1.5.2 below). In the first instance, a few ā-class nouns seem to have had a nominative singular ending from PIE *-ū. E.g.,

		Old Irish		PIE
nom/voc/acc	**sg**	mucc^{l} /muk/	'pig'	*muk^{w}+ū[31]
	pl	muicc^{l}		*muk^{w}+āi[32]

In the second instance, all polysyllabic-stem jā-class nouns have the nominative/vocative singular and nominative/accusative dual ending -Ø. This seems to derive from an PIE ending *-ī:

		Old Irish		PIE
sg	nom	sétig^{l} /sḗt'i$\bar{g}$'/	'wife'	*sentik+ī[33]
	gen	séitche /sḗtx'e/		*sentik+jās[34]
du	nom	sétig^{l}		*sentik+ī[33]
	acc	"		"
pl	nom	séitchi /sḗtx'i/		*sentik+jās

1.3 i-Class (Masculine, Feminine, Neuter)

Most of the nouns of this class are masculine or feminine. The neuters are rare. E.g.,

			Old Irish		PIE
masc	sg	nom	fáith /fāθ'/	'prophet'	*wātis
		voc	fáith^{l} "		"[35]
		acc	fáith^{n} "		*wātim
		gen	fátho^{l} /fāθo/		*wātous[36]
		dat	fáith^{l} /fāθ'/		*wātei
	du	nom	fáith^{l} /fāθ'/		*wātī
		acc	" "		"
		gen	fátho^{l} /fāθo/		*wātous[36]
		dat	fáithib /fāθ'iƀ'/		*wātib^{h}im
	pl	nom	fá(i)thi /fāθ'i/		*wātejes[37]
		acc	" "		"[38]
		gen	fá(i)the^{n} /fāθ'e/		*wāti+ōm[39]
		dat	fá(i)thib /fāθ'iƀ'/		*wātib^{h}is

Feminine nouns of this class such as flaith /fLaθ'/ 'rule, power' < PIE *wlatis have the same endings as fáith cited above.The few neuter nouns of this class have the same endings as fáith except for the following:

		Old Irish		PIE
nom/voc/acc	sg	muir^{n} /mur'/	'sea'	*mori+m[40]
	pl	muire^{l}		*mori+ā[41]

1.4 u-Class (Masculine, Neuter)

			Old Irish		PIE
masc	sg	nom	giun /gin^{u}/	'mouth'	*genus
		voc	giun^{l} "		"[42]
		acc	giun^{n} "		*genum
		gen	geno /geno/		*genous[43]
		dat	giun^{l}		*genū[44]

		Old Irish		PIE
du	**nom**	giun^{l}	'mouth'	*genū
	acc	"		"
	gen	geno^{l}		*genous[43]
	dat	gen(a)ib /genaƀ'/		*geneub^{h}im[43, 45]
pl	**nom**	gen(a)i /geni/		*gen+ejes[46]
	acc	" "		"[46]
	gen	gen(a)e^{n} /gene/		*gen+jōm[46]
	dat	gen(a)ib /genaƀ'/		*geneub^{h}is[43, 45]

The neuter u-class nouns have the same endings as the masculine except for the nominative/accusative singular and plural. An example paradigm is this:

			Old Irish		PIE
neuter	**sg**	**nom**	dorus^{n} /dores^{u}/	'door'	*d^{h}wor+est+u+m[47]
		acc	" "		"
		gen	doirseo /dors'o/		*d^{h}wor+est+jous[48]
		dat	dorus^{l} /dores^{u}/		*d^{h}wor+est+ū
	du	**nom**	" "		"
		acc	" "		"
		gen	doirseo^{l} /dors'o/		*d^{h}wor+est+jou[48]
		dat	doirsib /dors'iƀ'/		*d^{h}wor+est+ib^{h}im[48]
	pl	**nom**	dorus^{l} /dores^{u}/		*d^{h}wor+est+u+ā[49]
			doirsea^{l} /dors'a/		*d^{h}wor+est+j+ā[48,49]
		acc	same as nom pl		
		gen	doirse^{n} /dors'e/		*d^{h}wor+est+j+ōm[48]
		dat	doirsib /dors'iƀ'/		*d^{h}wor+est+ib^{h}is[48]

1.5 Athematic Classes

These are referred to as "konsonantische Stämme" in Thurneysen (1909: 1, 192).

1.5.1 Ø-Class (Masculine, Feminine)

			Old Irish		PIE
masc	**sg**	**nom**	rí /rī/	'king'	*rēg+s[50]
		voc	rí^{l} "		*rēg+e
		acc	ríg^{n} /rīǥ'/		*rēg+m̥[51]
		gen	ríg /rīǥ/		*rēg+os[52]
		dat	ríg^{l} /rīǥ'/		*rēg+i[53]
	du	**nom**	ríg^{l} /rīǥ'/		*rēg+ī[53]
		acc	" "		"
		gen	ríg^{l} /rīǥ/		*rēg+ous
		dat	ríg(a)ib /rīǥaƀ'/		*rēg+ob^{h}im

		Old Irish		PIE
pl	nom	ríg /rīǥ'/	'king'	*rēg+es[54]
	voc	ríga /rīǥa/		*rēg+n̥s[55]
	acc	″ ″		″
	gen	ríg^{n} /rīǥ/		*rēg+ōm
	dat	ríg(a)ib /rīǥaƀ'/		*rēg+ob^{h}is

The feminine nouns of this class have the same endings as the masculine ones. In addition, polysyllabic nouns of both genders evince a paradigm like this:

			Old Irish		PIE
fem	sg	nom	traig /tRaǥ'/	'foot'	*trag^{h}et+s[56]
		voc	traig^{l} ″		*trag^{h}et[56]
		acc	traigid^{n} /tRaǥ'eð'/		*trag^{h}etm̥[57]
		gen	traiged /tRaǥ'eð/		*trag^{h}etos[57]
		dat	traigid^{l} /tRaǥ'eð'/		*trag^{h}eti[57]
	du	nom	traigid /tRaǥ'eð'/		*trag^{h}etī[57]
		acc	″ ″		″
		gen	traiged^{l} /tRaǥ'eð/		*trag^{h}etou[57]
		dat	traigthib /tRaǥð'aƀ'/		*trag^{h}etob^{h}im[58]
	pl	nom	traigid /tRaǥ'eð'/		*trag^{h}etes[57]
		voc	traigthea /tRaǥð'a/		*trag^{h}etn̥s[58]
		acc	″ ″		″
		gen	traiged^{n} /tRaǥ'eð/		*trag^{h}etōm[57]
		dat	traigthib /tRaǥð'aƀ'/		*trag^{h}etob^{h}is

1.5.2 Root Class (Feminine)

These nouns had stems ending in a vowel. They all tend to pass into other classes. Examples are the following:

		Old Irish		PIE
sg	nom	bó /bō/	'cow'	*g^{w}ōu+s[59]
		mucc /muk/	'pig'	*muk^{w}ū+s[60]
		na(i)thir /naθ'ir'/	'snake'	*naterī+s[60]

1.5.3 (t)Vr-Class (Masculine, Feminine)

This class contains only masculine and feminine nouns denoting family members.

			Old Irish		PIE
masc	sg	nom	ath(a)ir /aθar'/	'father'	*patēr[61]
		voc	ath(a)ir^{l} ″		*patēr+e
		acc	ath(a)ir^{n}		*pater+m̥
		gen	athar /aθar/		*patr̥+os[61]
		dat	ath(a)ir^{l} /aθar'/		*patr̥+i[61]

		Old Irish		PIE
du	nom	a(i)thir /aθ'ar'/	'father'	*paterī[62]
	acc	" "		"
	gen	athar^{l} /aθar/		*patr̥+ou
	dat	athr(a)ib /aθraƀ'/		*patr̥+ob^{h}im
pl	nom	a(i)thir /aθ'ir'/		*pateres
	voc	aithrea /aθr'a/		*patern̥s
	acc	" "		"
	gen	athra(e)^{n} /aθre/		*patr̥+jōm[63]
	dat	aithr(a)ib /aθr'aƀ'/		*paterob^{h}is

The fem nouns of this class have the same endings as the masculine ones. E.g., nom sg fem máth(a)ir /māθar'/ 'mother' < PIE *mātēr. One feminine noun of this class has the same inflectional endings, but a different derivational suffix:

		Old Irish		PIE
sg	nom	siur /siur/	'sister'	*swe+sōr[64]
	gen	sethar /seθar/		*swe+tr̥+os[65]

1.5.4 Vn-Class (Masculine, Feminine, Neuter).

An example of a masculine noun is the following:

		Old Irish		PIE
sg	nom	cú /kū/	'dog'	*k^{w}ō (?+n)[66]
	voc	" "		"
	acc	coin^{n} /kon'/		*k^{w}on+m̥[67]
	gen	con /kon/		*k^{w}on+os
	dat	coin^{l} /kon'/		*k^{w}on+i[67]
du	nom	coin^{l} /kon'/		*k^{w}on+ī[67]
	acc	" "		"
	gen	con^{l} /kon/		*k^{w}on+ou
	dat	con(a)ib /konaƀ'/		*k^{w}on+ob^{h}im
pl	nom	coin /kon'/		*k^{w}on+es[67]
	acc	cona /kona/		*k^{w}on+n̥s[68]
	gen	con^{n} /kon/		*k^{w}on+ōm
	dat	con(a)ib /konaƀ'/		*k^{w}on+ob^{h}is

Masc nouns of this class with stems of more than one syllable have the same endings as cú /kū/ 'dog' above; but change 6a i-e/u-o ALT can apply in their derivations to the *-on- suffix. E.g.,

		Old Irish		PIE
sg	nom	brithem /bRiθ'em/	'judge'	*b^{h}r̥tem+o(:)n[69]
	acc	brithem(u)in^{n} /bRiθ'emun'/		*b^{h}r̥tem+on+m̥[70]
	gen	brithemon /bRiθ'emon/		*b^{h}r̥tem+on+os
	dat	brithem(u)in^{l} /bRiθ'emun'/		*b^{h}r̥tem+on+i
pl	dat	brithemn(a)ib /bRiθ'emnaƀ'/		*b^{h}r̥tem+on+ob^{h}is[71]

The fem nouns of this class have the same endings as the masculine ones. However, for some feminine nouns in all cases except the nominative singular, the PIE *-Vn- suffix seems to appear in the e-grade ablaut. E.g., the following jVn-class noun:

			Old Irish		PIE
fem	**sg**	**nom**	toimtiu /domt'u/	'opinion'	*do+ment+jō[72]
		acc	toimtin^{n} /domt'in'/		*do+ment+jen+m̥[73]
		gen	toimten /domt'en/		*do+ment+jen+os[73]

The neuter nouns of this class show the following paradigm:

		Old Irish		PIE
sg	**nom**	ainm(m)^{n} /anM'/	'name'	*n̥m+n̥[74]
	acc	" "		"
	gen	anm(a)e /anMe/		*n̥m+on+s[75]
	dat	ainm^{l} /anM'/		*n̥m+i[76]
		ainm(a)im(m)^{l} /anMam'/		? *n̥m+n̥m+i
du	**nom**	ainm^{l} /anM'/		? = nom sg form
	acc	" "		" " "
	gen	anman(n) /anMaN/		*n̥m+on+ou
	dat	anman(n)aib /anManaƀ'/		*n̥m+on+ob^{h}im[77]
pl	**nom**	anman(n)^{l} /anMaN/		*n̥m+on+ā
	acc	" "		"
	gen	anman(n)^{n}		*n̥m+on+ōm
	dat	anman(n)aib /anManaƀ'/		*n̥m+on+ob^{h}is[77]

1.5.5 Vnt-Class (Masculine, Neuter)

The masculine nouns of this class have historically the same endings as rí 'king' in 1.5.1 above.

			Old Irish		PIE
masc	**sg**	**nom**	car(a)e /kare/	'friend'	*kar+ant+s[78]
		voc	car(a)e^{l} /kare/		*kar+ant
		acc	car(a)it^{n} /karat'/		*kar+ant+m̥[79]
		gen	carat /karat/		*kar+ant+os
		dat	car(a)it /karat'/		*kar+ant+i
	du	**nom**	" "		*kar+ant+ī
		acc	" "		"
		gen	carat /karat/		*kar+ant+ou
		dat	cairtib /kart'iƀ'/		*kar+ant+ib^{h}im[80]
	pl	**nom**	car(a)it /karat'/		*kar+ant+es
		voc	cairtea /kart'a/		*kar+ant+n̥s
		acc	" "		"
		gen	carat^{n} /karat/		*kar+ant+ōm
		dat	cairtib /kart'iƀ'/		*kar+ant+ib^{h}is[80]

The neuter nouns of this class have the same endings as the masculine above except for the following forms:

		Old Irish		PIE
nom/acc	sg	détⁿ /dēt/	'tooth'	*dent+om[81]
	du	" "		? = nom/acc sg
	pl	détˡ /dēt/		*dentā

1.5.6 Vs-Class (Neuter)

		Old Irish		PIE
sg	nom	tegⁿ /teg/	'house'	*teg+os[82]
	acc	" "		"
	gen	tige /teg'e/		*teg+es+os[83]
	dat	tigˡ /teg'/		*teg+es+i
du	nom	tegˡ /teg/		? = nom/acc sg
	acc	" "		" " "
	gen	tige /teg'e/		*teg+es+ou
	dat	tigib /teg'iƀ'/		*teg+es+ibʰim[84]
pl	nom	tigeˡ /teg'e/		*teg+es+ā
	acc	" "		"
	gen	tigeⁿ "		*teg+es+ōm
	dat	tigib /teg'iƀ'/		*teg+es+ibʰis[84]

2 Adjectives

The adjectives inflect for only singular and plural without a dual. The inflection of the adjectives corresponds approximately to that of the corresponding noun classes. They are as follows.

2.1 o-Class and ā-Class

These adjectives have the endings of the o-class (1.1) for masc and neuter and those of the ā-class (1.2) for feminine. E.g.,

			Old Irish		PIE
sg	nom	masc	sen	'old'	*senos
		fem	senˡ		*senā
		neuter	senⁿ		*senom

2.2 jo-Class and jā-Class

These adjectives also have the endings of the o-class (1.1) for masculine and neuter and of the ā-class (1.2) for feminine E.g.,

			Old Irish		PIE
sg	nom	masc	uile /ul'e/	'every'	*poljos[85]
		fem	uileˡ "		*poljā[85]
		neuter	uileⁿ "		*poljom[85]

2.3 i-Class

These adjectives follow generally the declension of the i-class nouns (1.3 above). In some instances, these adjectives tend to pass into the o- and ā-class. E.g.,

			Old Irish		PIE
sg	nom	masc	maith /maθ'/	'good'	*matis[86]
		fem	" "		
		neuter	maith^{n} "		*matim[86]

2.4 u-Class

These adjectives generally follow the declension of the u-class nouns (1.4 above). The feminine nouns follow the masculine declension. As is the case with the i-class adjectives above, in some instances these adjectives are moving into the o- and ā-class . E.g.,

			Old Irish		PIE
sg	nom	masc	dub /duƀ^{u}/	'black'	*d^{h}ub^{h}us[87]
		fem	" "		"
		neuter	dub^{n}		*d^{h}ub^{h}um[87]

2.5 Athematic class.

These few adjectives follow the declension of the Vnt-class athematic nouns (1.5.5). The feminine adjective endings are the same as the masculine. E.g.,

			Old Irish		PIE
sg	nom	masc	té /tē/	'hot'	*tepents[88]
		fem	" "		"
		neuter	" "		*tepent[88]
pl		masc	téit /tēt'/		*tepentes[89]
		fem	" "		"
		neuter	tét /tēt/		*tepentā[90]

2.6 Comparison

There are three degrees of comparison: the so-called "equative", the usual comparative and the usual superlative. The meaning of the equative is 'as + adj + as', e.g., 'as good as, as bad as' etc. The comparative and superlative adjectives have their usual meanings of 'more + adjective + than' and 'most + adjective + of all'. These forms do not take inflectional endings.

The equative is as follows:

Old Irish		PIE
déinithir /dēn'iθr'/	'just as fast as'	*dein+itris[91]

Historically there are two comparative formations. The suffix is the same, but in the ō- and Ø-ablaut grades. E.g.,

	Old Irish		PIE
	(a) siniu /sin'u/	'older'	*sen+jōs[92]
	(b) sia /sia/	'longer'	*sē+is[93]

That is, (a) the Old Irish comparative is formed with the usual adjective stem plus the suffix /-u/, which by 6b INFEC triggers palatalization of the stem-final consonant. (b) And in some forms the suffix of the positive is lost and the stem vowel changes. (See note 93 below.)

The superlative is as follows:

Old Irish		PIE
sinem /sin'em/	'oldest'	*sen+is+m̥+ending[94]

Some adjectives form their comparative and superlative forms by suppletion.E.g.,

		Old Irish		PIE
(a)	**pos**	becc /bek/	'small'	? *bekk+ending
	comp	lugu /luǥ'u/		*lug^{h}+jōs[95]
	sup	lugam /luǥam/		*lug^{h}+m̥+ending
(b)	**pos**	maith /maθ'/	'good'	*mat+i+class ending
	comp	ferr ?/feR/	'better'	? *wer[95]
	sup	dech /dex/	'best'	*dek+ending[96]
(c)	**pos**	olc /olk/	'bad'	*ulk+ending
	comp	messa /mesa/	'worse'	*med^{h}+s+?ending[95]
	sup	messam /mesam/	'worst'	*med^{h}+s+m̥+ending[97]

3 Adverbs

The most common adverb formation is the dative singular neuter of the definite article (5.2 below) followed by the same form of the adjective. E.g.,

Old Irish		PIE
ind maith^{l} /ind maθ'/	'well'	*sem+dō *matei[98]

Another adverb formation is with the preposition co^{n} "to' followed by the accusative singular neuter of the adjective. E.g.,

Old Irish		PIE
commaith /koMaθ'/	'well'	*kom matim[99]

The comparative and superlative of the adverb are formed with the dative singular neuter. E.g.,

	Old Irish		PIE
pos	commaith /koMaθ'/	'well'	*kom matim
comp	ind fer /ind fer/	'better'	*sem+dō *wer
sup	ind dech /ind dex/	'best'	*sem+dō *dek+ending

4 Numerals

4.1 Cardinals

The numeral '1' is uninflected and forms the first constituent in a compound. The numerals '2', '3' and '4' are inflected as shown below. The other numerals up to '20' are uninflected. The numerals '20' through '90' are Vnt-class masculine nouns; '100' is an o-class neuter noun; and '1000' is a borrowing from Latin and a jā-class feminine noun. When the numerals are nouns, the following nouns are in the genitive plural, e.g. fiche 'a score' fer 'of men' = '20 men'.

	Old Irish	PIE
'1'	oin	*oin(+os)

			Old Irish	PIE
'2'	**masc**	**nom**	da^{l}	*dwōu[100]
		acc		"
		gen	"	"
		dat	dib^{n} /diƀ'/	*dwib^{h}im[101]
	fem	**nom**	di^{l}	dwai[102]
		acc	"	"
		gen	same as masc	
		dat	" " "	
	neuter	**nom**	da^{n}	*dwā+?m[103]
		acc	"	"
		gen	"	*dwā+ōm
		dat	same as masc	

The endings here are by and large those of the dual o- and i-class nouns.

			Old Irish	PIE
'3'	**masc**	**nom**	tri	*tri+es[104]
		acc	"	*tri+ns[104]
		gen	tri^{n}	*tri+ōm[104]
		dat	trib /tRiƀ'/	*tri+b^{h}is[104]
	fem	**nom**	téoir /tēor'/	*t+eisores[105]
		acc	téoir /tēor'/	*t+eisorn̥s[105]
		gen	téoira^{n} /tēora/	*t+eisorōm[105]
		dat	téor(a)ib /tēoraƀ'/	*t+eisorāb^{h}is
	neuter	**nom**	tri^{l}	*tri+ā[104]
		acc	"	"

Otherwise the same as masc.

'4' The genitive and dative of the masculine and neuter are not attested. The attested forms are as follows.

		Old Irish	**PIE**
masc	**nom**	ceth(a)ir /keθar'/	*k^wetwores
	acc	ce(i)thri /keθr'i/	*k^wetworins[106]
fem	**nom**	cethéoir /keθēor'/	? *k^wetweisores[107]
	acc	cethéora /keθēora/	*k^wetweisorn̥s[107]
	gen	cethéora^n "	*k^wetweisorjōm[108]
	dat	cethéor(a)ib /keθēoraƀ'/	*k^wetworob^{h}is
neuter	**nom**	cethé(a)ir^l /keθar/	*k^wetworā[109]
	acc	" "	"

	Old Irish	**PIE**
'5'	cóic /kōk'/	*k^wonk^{w}e[110,111]
'6'	sé /sē/	*seks[112,113]
'7'	secht^n /sext/	*septōm[114]
'8'	ocht^n /oct/	*oktōm[114]
'9'	noi^n /noi/	*noi(?+ō)m[114]
'10'	deich^n /dex'/	*dekm̥[114,115]
'20'	fiche /fix'e/	*wi+kn̥t+s[116,117]
'30'	tricha /tRixa/	*tri+kont+s[116,118]
'40'	cethorcha /keθorxa/	*k^wetwor+kont+s[116]
'50'	cóica /kōk'a/	*k^wonk^{w}e+kont+s[116,119]
'60'	sesca /seska/	*seks+kont+s [116,120]
'70'	sechtmoga /sextmoǥa/	*septōmo+kont+s[116,121]
'80'	ochtmoga /oxtmoǥa/	*oktōmo+kont+s[116]
'90'	nócha /nōxa/	*new+kont+s[121]
'100'	cét /kēt/	*kentom
'1000'	míle /mīle/	*mīl+jā

4.2 Ordinals

The adjectives for '1st' and '2nd' are jo- and jā-class. The adj '3rd' is uninflected. The other ordinals are o- and ā-class adjectives. The */t/ and */m/ in the antecedent forms are used in other PIE languages to form superlative adjective forms.

	Old Irish	**PIE**
'1st'	cétn(a)e /kētNe/	*kent+no+jos[122]
'2nd'	tán(a)ise /tānas'e/	? *tānos+t+jos
'3rd'	triss /tris/	*tris+t[123]
'4th'	cethramad /keθramað/	*k^wetwor+omo+tos[124]
'5th'	cóiced /kōk'eð/	*k^wonk^{w}e+tos
'6th'	seissed /ses'eð/	*seks+etos
'7th'	sechtmad /sextmað/	*septōm+ot+os[125]

The remaining ordinals are jo- and jā-class adjectives. They are formed with the Old Irish suffix –mad /-mað/ from PIE *-mo+t+o/ā-class adjective endings.

5 Pronouns

5.1 Personal Pronouns

The original PIE case morphology has largely been lost. Instead, these pronouns occur in three constructions: (1) as independent (indep) constituents, (2) as infixes after prefixes and before roots in verbal constructions and (3) as suffixes after verbs or after prepositions. E.g., (1) OIr is mé /is mē/ 'it is I', (2) OIr ro+m+gab = prefix + pronoun + verb 'he seized me' and (3) OIr do+m = preposition + pronoun 'to me'.

5.1.1 First Person

		Old Irish	PIE
sg	indep	mé	*med[126]
	infix	-m^{l}-	*mē[127]
	suffix	-m	*mē
pl	indep	sní /sNī/	*n̥s+oi[128]
	infix	-nn- /N/	*n̥s[129]
	suffix	-nn /N/	*n̥s

5.1.2 Second Person

		Old Irish	PIE
sg	indep	tú /tū/	*tū
	infix	-t^{l}-	" [130]
	suffix	-t	"
pl	indep	sí /sī/	?*s+w+oi[131]
	infix	-b- /ƀ/	? *wVs[132]
	suffix	-b /ƀ/	" [132]

5.1.3 Third Person

The plural forms of this paradigm do not differ as to gender.

			Old Irish		PIE
sg	masc	indep	hé /ē/	'he'	*ei+s[133]
		infix	-a^{n}- /a/		*ei+m[134]
			-Ø^{n}-		"
		suffix	-i(d) /i(ð)/		*i+d+ā[135]
	fem	indep	sí /sī/	'she'	*s+ī
		infix	-s^{n}-		*s+ī+m
		suffix	(verb +) -s		"
			(dat prep +) –i		*j+āi
	neuter	indep	hed /eð/	'it'	*id
		infix	-a^{l}-		*(id)+ā[135]
			-Ø^{l}-		"
		suffix	same as masc		

		Old Irish		PIE
pl	indep	hé /ē/	'they'	*j+ei
	infix	-sⁿ-		*s+ōns[136]
	suffix	(verb+) –s /sᵘ/		*s+ōns[137]
		(dat prep+) –ib /iƀ'/		*s+ibʰis[137]
		(acc prep+) –hu /u/		*s+ōns[137]

5.1.4 Emphatic

The independent forms of all personal pronouns have additional "emphatic" versions. E.g.,

		Old Irish			PIE
sg	1	meisse	/mēs'e/	'I myself'	*mē##sēm
	2	tusse	/tuse/	'you yourself'	*tu##som
	3	hésom	/ēsom/	'he himself'	*eis##somos
		héside	/ēs'iðe/	'he himself'	*eis##sidʰos

5.1.5 Possessive

These consist of pronouns and adjectives. The possessive adjectives are unstressed forms of the pronouns.

			Old Irish			PIE
sg	1	pron	muí	/muī/	'my'	*mu+ī[138]
		adj	muˡ	/mu/		*mu
	2	pron	tuí	/tuī/	'your'	*tu+ī[138]
		adj	tuˡ	/tu/		*tu
	3	pron	aí	/aī/	'his'	*esjo+ī[138,139]
		adj	aˡ	/a/		*esjo
pl	1	pron	athar	/aθar/	'our'	? *esjo+tar
		adj	arⁿ	/ar/		*esjo+tar+ōm[140]
	2	pron	sethar	/seθar/	'your'	*swe+tar
		adj	farⁿ			*swe+tar+ōm[140]
	3	pron	aí	/aī/	'their'	*esjo+ī[139]
		adj	aⁿ	/a/		*esjo+ōm[140]

5.2 Demonstrative

These forms generally have the endings of o-class nouns for the masculine and neuter and those of the ā-class for the feminine. The meanings here are 'this, that, the'.

			Old Irish		PIE
sg	masc	nom	in(t)	/iN(d)/	*sem+d+os[141]
		acc	inⁿ	/in/	*sem+Ø+om[142]
		gen	indˡ	/iNd/	*sem+d+ī
		dat	"	"	*sem+d+ōi
	fem	nom	"	"	*sem+d+ā
		acc	inⁿ	/in/	*sem+Ø+ām[142]
		gen	inna	/iNa/	*sem+Ø+jās[142]
		dat	indˡ	/iNd/	*sem+d+āi
	neuter	nom	aⁿ		? *sem
		acc	"		"

			Old Irish		PIE
du	all forms		in[l]	/in/	*sem+ā or -ōu
pl	masc	nom	ind[l]		*sem+d+oi
	fem		inna	/iNa/	*sem+Ø+ās[142,143]
	neuter		"	"	? "
	all forms	acc	"	"	? "
		gen	inna[n]	/iNa/	? "
		dat	(prep+)–naib	/naƀ'/	*n+ob^{h}is

5.3 Relative

There is no single Old Irish relative pronoun or formation. Rather, relative constructions are formed by several means. Here are five frequently occurring types.

(1) No overt marking. E.g., OIr bruden roboi inhérinn = 'hostels' + 'it was' + 'in' + 'Ireland' = 'hostels which were in Ireland'.

(2) A particle like /-s/ suffixed to the verb. E.g., OIr beres 'he who carries'. The derivation is *b^{h}eret 'carries' + *esti 'is' (ev) > *bereðesti (8b W-F SEG DELE) > *bereðes (? 10b SYNCOPE of the last vowel) > *bereðs (? 8a LATER C CL still applying synchronically) → OIr beres.

(3) The neuter nominative/accusative singular demonstrative a[n] /a/ (see 5.2 above) used as a general relative pronoun. E.g., OIr dí+a[n] 'from which or whom' < PIE *dē+sem.

(4) The synchronic version of 3a ECLIP applying within a verb stem and generally after the first prefix. E.g., OIr cech irnigdo do+n+gneid 'each prayer (which) you (pl.) make', where the verb do+n+gneid = /do+n+gneð'/ = prefix + application of 3a ECLIP + 2pl indicative of verb.

(5) Insertion of the Old Irish infix -d- (< PIE *id^{h}e 'there') after the first prefix within a verb. E.g., OIr fo+fera /fo+féra/ 'it affects' vs. the relative /fo+d+féra/ 'that which affects' (8a LATER C CL applying synchronically) → OIr fodera /fodéra/.

5.4 Interrogative

The following are the independent forms as opposed to those occurring within verbs or after prepositions.

			Old Irish			PIE
sg	nom	masc	cia	/kia/	'who'	*k^{w}ei+s[144]
		fem	"	"		"
		neuter	cid	/kið/	'what'	*k^{w}i+d+ā[145]
	acc		"	"		"
	gen	all genders	coich	/kox'/		*k^{w}o+k^{w}ī[146]
pl	nom		cit	/kid'/		*k^{w}i##d+oi[147]

6 Verbs

The features of the Old Irish verb are given in the following two tables. Table i contains the variable features — namely those which can change contingent upon the context. Table ii shows the lexical or inherent features — namely those which are idiosyncratic. They indicate the particular form-class for the verb.

(i) Variable Features

The first section of this table lists the purely verbal features. The second gives the features of deverbative adjectives and nouns.

Verbal Inflection

(a) Person	(b) Number	(c) Voice	(d) Mood
1. 1st	1. singular	1. active	1. indicative
2. 2nd	2. plural[148]	2. passive[149]	2. subjunctive[150]
3. 3rd			3. imperative
			4. conditional[151]

(e) Tense occurring in	Indicative	Subjunctive	Imperative	Conditional
1. present	x	x	x	x
2. imperfect[152]	x	x		
3. preterite	x			
4. perfect	x			
5. future	x			

Adjectival and Nominal Inflection

(a) Person	(b) Number	(c) Voice	(d) Mood
Ø	1. singular	1. active	1. noun[153]
	2. plural	2. passive	2. participle

(e) Tense Occurring in	Noun	Participle
1. present	active	passive[154]
2. imperfect		
3. preterite		passive
4. perfect		
5. future		

(ii) Inherent Features.

(a) Inflectional type

1. nondeponent[155]
2. deponent

(b) Syntactic type

1. absolute[156]
2. conjunct[156]
3. relative[156]

(c) Class[157]

1. weak ā-class, e.g. móraid /mōrað'/ 'magnifies' < PIE *mōr+ā+ti
2. weak ī-class, e.g. lécid /lēkið'/ 'leaves' < PIE *link^w+ī+ti
3. strong e-class, e.g. berid /berið'/ 'carries' < PIE *b^her+e+ti
4. strong je-class, e.g. midithir /miðiðar'/ 'judges' < PIE *med+je+torai
5. strong n-class, e.g. bongid /boNgið'/ 'breaks' < PIE *b^ho+n+g+eti
6. strong nV-class, e.g. benaid /benað'/ 'strikes' < PIE *b^he+nā+ti

In the Tables i and ii, the features in the columns are mutually exclusive. Not all the logical possibilities are realized: the notations in the (e) columns of Table i indicate which are.

6.1 Present

6.1.1 Present Active Indicative

As examples we cite first a strong e-class and then a weak ā-class verb.

			Old Irish			PIE
abs	**sg**	**1**	biru		'carry'	*b^her+ō[158]
		2	beri			*b^her+esi[159]
		3	berid	/berið'/		*b^her+eti[160]
	pl	**1**	berm(a)i	/berMi/		*b^her+omos[161]
		2	ber(i)rthe	/berθ'e/		*b^her+ete[162]
		3	ber(a)it	/berat'/		*b^her+onti[163]
conj	**sg**	**1**	-biur	/-bir^u/		*b^her+ō[158,164]
		2	-bir	/-bir'/		*b^her+es[165]
		3	-beir	/-ber'/		*b^her+et[165]
	pl	**1**	-beram	/-beram/		*b^her+omos[166]
		2	-berid	/-berið'/		*b^her+ete[167]
		3	-berat			*b^her+ont[167]

			Old Irish			PIE
abs	**sg**	**1**	mór(a)im(m)	/mōraM'/	'magnify'	*mōr+ā+mi[168]
		2	mór(a)i	/mōri/		*mōr+ā+si[169]
		3	mór(a)id	/mōrað'/		*mōr+ā+ti

			Old Irish			PIE
	pl	1	mór(a)im(m)	/mōrMi/	'magnify'	*mōr+ā+mos[170]
		2	mórth(a)e	/mōrθ'e/		*mōr+ā+te[170]
		3	mór(a)it	/mōrat'/		*mōr+ā+nti[171]
conj	sg	1	mór(a)im(m)	/mōraM'/		*mōr+ā+m[168]
		2	mór(a)i	/mōri/		*mōr+ā+s[172]
		3	móra	/mōra/		*mōr+ā+t
	pl	1	móram	/mōram/		*mōr+ā+mos[173]
		2	mór(a)id	/mōrað'/		*mōr+ā+te
		3	mórat	/mōrat/		*mōr+ā+nt[171]

6.1.2 Present Active Subjunctive

There are two types of subjunctive formation. These are (a) the ā-subjunctive and (b) the s-subjunctive. The s-subjunctive is used with strong verbs whose stem-final consonant is a +dental or +velar obstruent, i.e. /t, θ, d, ð; t', θ', d' etc./ as well as /k, x, g, ǥ; k', x', g' etc./. The s-subjunctive is also used with strong verbs whose stem-final consonant is the unlenited dental nasal /N/. The ā-subjunctive occurs elsewhere, namely with weak verbs and with strong verbs not conforming to the phonotactical conditions just described.

(a) ā-Subjunctive

			Old Irish			PIE
abs	sg	1	bera		'carry'	*b^{h}er+ā+mi
		2	ber(a)i	/beri/		*b^{h}er+ā+si
		3	ber(a)id	/berað'/		*b^{h}er+ā+ti
	pl	1	berm(a)i	/berMi/		*b^{h}er+ā+mos
		2	berth(a)e	/berθ'e/		*b^{h}er+ā+te
		3	ber(a)it	/berat'/		*b^{h}er+ā+nti
conj	sg	1	-ber			*b^{h}er+ā+m
		2	-ber(a)i	/-beri/		*b^{h}er+ā+s
		3	-bera			*b^{h}er+ā+t
	pl	1	-beram			*b^{h}er+ā+mos
		2	-ber(a)id	/-berað'/		*b^{h}er+ā+te
		3	-berat			*b^{h}er+ā+nt

			Old Irish			PIE
abs	sg	1	tiasu		'go'	*steig^h+s+ō[174]
		2	tési	/tēs'i/		*steig^h+s+si[175]
		3	téis	/tēs'/		*steig^h+s+ti[176]
	pl	1	tiasmi	/tiasMi/		*steig^h+s+ā+mos[177]
		2	téste	/tēste/		*steig^h+s+ete
		3	tias(a)it	/tiasat'/		*steig^h+s+ā+nti[177]

			Old Irish			PIE
conj	sg	1	-tias		'go'	*steig^h+s+ō
		2	-téis	/-tēs'/		*steig^h+s+s[178]
		3	-téi	/-tē/		*steig^h+s+t
	pl	1	-tiasam			*steig^h+s+ā+mos
		2	-tésid	/tēs'ið'/		*steig^h+s+ete
		3	-tiasat			*steig^h+s+ā+nt

6.1.3 Present Active Imperative

Most imperatives are in the absolute form. We cite first a strong and then a weak verb.

		Old Irish			PIE
sg	2	beir	/ber'/	'carry'	*b^{h}ere
	3	bered	/bereð/		*b^{h}ereto[179]
pl	1	beram	/beraM/		*b^{h}eromos[180]
	2	bered	/bereð'/		*b^{h}erete[180]
	3	berat	/berat/		*b^{h}eront[180]
sg	2	mór	/mōr/	'magnify'	*mōr+ā[180]
	3	mórad	/mōrað/		*mōr+ā+to[180]
pl	1	móram	/mōram/		*mōr+ā+mos[180]
	2	mórad	/mōrað'/		*mōr+ā+te[180]
	3	mórat	/mōrat/		*mōr+ā+nt[180]

6.1.4 Present Active Conditional

This paradigm is constructed from the future stem of the verb plus the imperfect subjunctive endings. The future stems are described under 6.5 below; the endings of the imperfect subjunctive under 6.2.2. Since the endings are those of the imperfect subjunctive these verbs occur only in the conjunct E.g.,

	Old Irish		PIE
(a) f-future 3sg	-léicfinn /-lēkf'aN'/	'would leave'	*link^w+ī+b^h+onn+[V, -back][181]
(b) s-future	-gigsinn /-giǥsaN'/	'would ask'	*g^{hw}i+g^{hw}od+s+onn+[V, -back]
(c) ¡-future	-bérinn /-bēraN'/	'would carry'	*b^{h}er+ā+onn+[V, -back]

6.1.5 Present Deponent and Passive Indicative

Our example of a deponent verb is from the weak ī-class.

			Old Irish			PIE
abs	sg	1	suidigur	/suð'aǥ'ur/	'set'	*sodj+ag+ī+ō+r[182]
		2	suidigther	/suð'aǥð'er/		*sodj+ag+ī+te+r[183]
		3	suidigider	/suð'aǥiðar'/		*sodj+ag+ī+to+r+ai[184]
	pl	1	suidigmmir	/suð'aǥMar'/		*sodj+ag+ī+mor+ai[184,185]
		2	suidigthe	/suð'aǥð'e/		*sodj+ag+ī+te
		3	suidigitir	/suð'aǥitar'/		*sodj+ag+ī+nto+r+ai[184]

			Old Irish			PIE
conj	sg	1	-suidigur	/suð'ag'ur/	'set'	same as absolute
		2	-suidigther	/suð'agð'er/		" " "
		3	-suidigedar	/suð'agð'er/		*sodj+ag+ī+to+r
	pl	1	-suidigmar	/suð'agMar/		*sodj+ag+ī+mor
		2	-suidigid	/suð'agið'/		same as absolute
		3	-suidigetar	/suð'ag'itar/		*sodj+ag+ī+nto+r

The passive forms occur only in the 3rd person. E.g.,

			Old Irish			PIE
abs	sg	3	ber(a)ir	/berar'/	'be carried'	*b^h^er+o+r+ai
	pl	3	bert(a)ir	/bertar'/		*b^h^er+oto+r+ai[186]
conj	sg	3	-berar			*b^h^er+o+r
	pl	3	-bertar			*b^h^er+onto+r[186]

6.1.6 Present Deponent and Passive Subjunctive

The absolute and conjunct forms are usually identical.

(a) ā-Subjunctive

We cite two examples.

			Old Irish			PIE
abs	sg	1	suidiger	/suð'ag'ar/	'set'	*sodj+ag+ī+ā+r
		2	suidigther	/suð'agð'er/		*sodj+ag+ī+ā+te+r

That is, aside from the 1st singular, the subjunctive and indicative forms are identical. This results from historical development. Hence, PIE 2sg ind *sodjagīater (by the derivation in 6.1.5 above) > OIr suidigther /suð'agð'er/; and PIE 2sg subj *sodj+ag+ī-ā-te-r (PIE 3.1.2c i-j/u-w ALT applying synchronically) → *sodjagjāter (2b LEN, 6a i-e/u-o ALT) > *suðjagjāðer (6b INFEC, 9b j-DELE) > *suð'ag'āð'er (10b SYNCOPE) > OIr suidigther /suð'agð'er/, which is homophonous with the 2nd singular indicative.

(b) s-Subjunctive

			Old Irish			PIE
conj	sg	1	-messur	/-mesur/	'judge'	*med+s+ō+r
		2	-messer	/-meser/		*med+s+ā+te+r[187]
		3	-mestar	/-mestar/		*med+s+ā+to+r
	pl	1	-messamar	/-mesaMar/		*med+s+ā+mo+r
		2	-messid	/-mesað'/		*med+s+ā+te
		3	-messatar	/-mesatar/		*med+s+ā+nto+r

6.1.7 Present Deponent and Passive Imperative

The imperative occurs only in the absolute. The deponent endings of weak and strong verbs are basically the same. E.g., the ī-class weak verb 'set':

			Old Irish			PIE
conj	sg	2	suidigthe	/suð'g̶ð'e/	'set'	*sodj+ag+ī+te[188]
		3	suidigid	/suð'g̶ð'ið/		*sodj+ag+ī+to[189]
	pl	1	suidigem	/suð'ag̶'eM/		*sodj+ag+ī+mos[189]
		2	suidigid	/suð'ag̶'ið'/		*sodj+ag+ī+te[189]
		3	suidigetar	/suð'ag̶'etar/		*sodj+ag+ī+nto+r[188]

The passive imperative forms occur only in the 3rd person, e.g.:

	Old Irish		PIE
sg	berar	'carry'	*b^her+or
pl	bertar		*b^her+ont+or[190]

6.2 Imperfect

These paradigms occur only in the active and only in the conjunct. Even a verb otherwise without a prefix must then take the "empty" prefix no- < PIE *nu- 'now'.

6.2.1 Imperfect Active Indicative

The endings are basically the same for strong and weak verbs. We cite the strong verb 'carry' and one form of the weak verb 'magnify'. The antecedent forms are not clear.

		Old Irish			PIE
sg	1	-ber(a)inn	/-beraN'/	'carry'	*b^her+o+nn+[V, –back]
	2	-beirthea	/-berð'a/		*b^her+e+t+[V, –back] + [V, +back] ?
	3	-berad	/-berað'/		*b^her+o+t+[V, –back]
pl	1	-bermis	/-berMas'/		*b^her+o+mos+s+[V, –back]
	2	-beirthe	/-berð'e/		*b^her+e+te+syllable (?)
	3	-beirtis	/-bert'as'/		*b^her+o+nt+[V, –back]+ss+[V, +back]
sg	1	-mór(a)inn	/-mōraN'/	'magnify'	*mōr+ā+nn+[V, -back]

6.2.2 Imperfect Active Subjunctive

This paradigm is formed from the ā- on s-present active subjunctive stem (6.1.2) to which we added the imperfect active indicative endings (6.2.1). The resultant forms are often homophonous with those of the imperfect active indicative (6.2.1) because of historical changes. E.g.,

	Old Irish		PIE
(a) ā-subjunctive			
1sg	-ber(a)inn /-beraN'/	'carry'	*b^her+ā+nn+[V, –back][191]
(b) s-subjunctive			
1sg	-tésinn /-tēsiN'/	'go'	*steig^h+s+e+nn+[V, –back]

6.3 Preterite

These forms occur only in the indicative; there are both active and deponent passive forms. There are three types of preterite formation: (a) the s-preterite which applies to all weak verbs; (b) the t-preterite which applies to those strong verbs whose stems end in /l, r/ and optionally to those strong verbs with stems ending in /m/; and (c) the asuffixal preterite which applies to those strong verbs to which the t-preterite does not apply. Some t-preterite verbs reduplicate.

6.3.1 Preterite Active Indicative

(a) s-Preterite[192]

			Old Irish			PIE
abs	sg	1	carsu		'love'	*kar+ā+s+ō[193]
		2	cars(a)i	/karsi/		*kar+ā+s+si[194]
		3	cars(a)is	/karsas'/		*kar+ā+s+ti[194]
	pl	1	cars(a)immi	/karsaM'i/		*kar+ā+s+omos
		2	cars(a)id	/karsað'/		*kar+ā+s+ete
		3	cars(a)it	/karsat'/		*kar+ā+s+onti
conj	sg	1	-carus	/-kars^u/		*kar+ā+s+ō[193]
		2	-cars(a)is	/-karsas'/		*kar+ā+s+s
		3	-car			*kar+ā+s+t
	pl	1	-carsam			*kar+ā+s+omos
		2	-cars(a)id	/-karsað'/		*kar+ā+s+ete
		3	-carsat	/-karsat/		*kar+ā+s+ont

(b) t-Preterite

This paradigm is only sparsely attested. E.g.,

			Old Irish			PIE
abs	sg	3	birt	/biRt'/	'carry'	*b^{h}er+t+i[195]
conj	sg	1	-biurt			*b^{h}er+t+o
		2	-birt	/-biRt'/		*b^{h}er+t+es[196]
		3	-bert			*b^{h}er+t[197]
	pl	1	-bertammar	/-beRtaMar/		*b^{h}er+t+omor[198]
		2	-bert(a)id	/-beRtað'/		*b^{h}er+t+ote
		3	-bertar or			*b^{h}er+t+or
			-bertatar			*b^{h}er+t+o+tor

(c) Asuffixal Preterite

This paradigm does not add a derivational suffix. Rather, the endings, which are from the PIE perfect paradigm, are added directly to the verb stem. Some of these verbs reduplicate and others change the root vowel in an ablaut-like alternation. Below is an example of a reduplicating preterite.

			Old Irish			PIE
abs	**sg**	**1**	cechan	/kéxan/	'sang'	*kekan+a
		2	"	"		*kekan+ta
		3	cechain	/kéxan'/		*kekan+e
			cechuin	/kéxun'/		? *kekon+e[199]
	pl	**1**	cechn(a)immir	/kéxnaM'ar'/		*kekan+omor[200]
		2	cechn(a)id	/kéxnað'/		*kekan+ote[201]
		3	cechn(a)itir	/kéxnat'ar'/		*kekan+ont+or[200]
conj	**sg**	**1**	-cechan	/-kéxan/		Same antecedents as
		2	"	"		the corresponding
		3	-cechain	/-kéxan'/		absolute forms above.
	pl	**1**	-cechnammar	/-kéxnaMar/		
		2	-cechn(a)id			
		3	-cechnatar	/-kéxnatar/		

Below we cite some nonreduplicating asuffixal preterites. Several of these have present-vs.-preterite ablaut. E.g.,

□		Old Irish			PIE
3sg	**pres**	guidid	/guðið'/	'ask'	$*g^{hw}$od+eti
	pret	gád	/gāð'/		$*g^{hw}$ōd+e[202]
	pres	techid	/texið'/	'flee'	$*tek^{w}$+eti
	pret	tách	/tāx'/		$*tōk^{w}$+e[202]

Some nonreduplicating asuffixal preterites show vowel alternations that cannot be ascribed to PIE ablaut. E.g.,

		Old Irish			PIE
3sg	**pres**	fichid	/fixið'/	'fight'	*wik+eti
	pret	fích	/fīx'/		? *wīk+e[203]

6.3.2 Preterite Deponent and Passive Indicative

The preterite deponent and passive forms differ.

6.3.2.1 Preterite Deponent Indicative

This paradigm is constructed from the respective active preterite forms to which -r is added (except for the 2nd plural which has the same active and deponent form). E.g., the s-preterite verb 'set':

	Old Irish			PIE
1sg	suidigsiur	/suð'ags'ur/	'set'	*sodj+ag+ī+s+ō+r
2sg	suidigser	/suð'ags'er/		*sodj+ag+ī+s+si+r[204]

When the preterite is asuffixal, the antecedent is likewise constructed of the active form plus *-r. E.g.,

	Old Irish		PIE
1sg	doménar /do+mē̃nar/	'think'	*do+men+a+r[205]

6.3.2.2 Preterite Passive Indicative

These forms occur only in the 3rd singular and plural. E.g.,

		Old Irish			PIE
abs	**3sg**	brethe	/breθ'e/	'was carried'	*bʰr̥+t+jos[206]
	3pl	brethae	/breθe/	'were carried'	*bʰr̥+t+jā[207]
conj	**3sg**	-breth	/-breθ/		*bʰr̥+t+os[206]
	3pl	-bretha	/-breθa/		*bʰr̥+t+ā[207]

6.4 Perfect

These paradigms are the same as those of the preterite immediately above. However, the perfect is usually distinguished from the preterite by the addition of a prefix, usually ro- < *pro-. E.g., the following 1st singular active absolute forms:

		Old Irish		PIE
pret	**3sg**	cechlad /kéxLað/	'dug'	*keklad+a
perf		rocechlad /rokéxLað/	'have dug'	*pro+keklad+a

6.5 Future

There are three types of future: (a) the f-future, (b) the s-future and (c) the ā-future.

(a) f-Future

This future is constructed from the weak-verb stem plus -f- (-b if word-final) plus the endings. Except for the 1st singular active conjunct, the endings of both the active and deponent passive future are those of the pres ā-class subjunctive (6.1.2 and 6.1.6).

Examples of active forms are the following:

			Old Irish			PIE
abs	**sg**	**1**	léicf(e)a	/lēkf'a/	'leave'	*linkʷ+ī+bʰ+āmi[208]
		2	léicf(a)i	/lēkfi/		*linkʷ+ī+bʰ+āsi
conj	**sg**	**1**	-léiciub	/-lēk'iƀᵘ/		*linkʷ+ī+bʰ+ō[209]
		2	-léicf(a)i	/-lēkfi/		*linkʷ+ī+bʰ+ās

Deponent and passive forms have the same endings as those of the ā-subjunctive in 6.1.6. E.g.,

		Old Irish			PIE
pres subj	**1sg**	suidiger	/suð'aǥ'ar/	'set'	*sodj+ag+ī+ā+r
future ind		suidigfer	/suð'aǥf'ar/		*sodj+ag+ī+bʰ+ā+r

(b) s-Future

This future is usually found with the same verbs as the s-subjunctive (6.1.2 and 6.1.6), namely strong verbs whose stem-final consonant is a dental or velar obstruent (/t, θ, d, ð; t', θ' etc./ or /k, x, g, ɡ, k', x' etc./) or if the stem-final consonant is the unlenited dental nasal /N/. Aside from the active 1st singular absolute and conjunct, the endings are those of the s-subjunctive. The s-future is usually formed by reduplication with the vowel /i/. Examples of active forms are these:

			Old Irish			PIE
abs	**sg**	**1**	gigsea	/giɡsa/	'ask'	$*g^{hw}i+g^{hw}od+s+\bar{a}+mi$[210]
		2	gigsi	/giɡs'i/		$*g^{hw}i+g^{hw}od+s+si$[211]
		3	gigis	/giɡs'/		$*g^{hw}i+g^{hw}od+s+ti$[212]
conj	**sg**	**1**	-gigius	$/\text{-giɡis}^u/$		$*g^{hw}i+g^{hw}od+s+\bar{o}$[213]
		2	-gigis	/-giɡas'/		$*g^{hw}i+g^{hw}od+s+s$[214]
		3	-gig	/-giɡ'/		$*g^{hw}i+g^{hw}od+s+t$[215]

(c) ā-Future

Those strong verbs which do not fulfill the conditions for membership in the s-future paradigm immediately above are in this paradigm. The ā-future is a reduplicated form of the ā-subjunctive (6.1.2 and 6.1.6 above). The usual reduplicating vowel is /i/, less often /e/. Both are from an antecedent */i/. E.g.,

			Old Irish			PIE
3sg	**abs**	**dep**	gignither	/gíɡnaθer/	'will be born'	*gi+gen+ā+to+r
	conj	**act**	-cechna	/-kéxna/	'will sing'	*ki+kan+ā+t[216]
	abs	**act**	cél(a)id	/kḗlað'/	'will conceal'	*ki+kl+ā+ti[217]

6.6 Verbal Nouns

These are often referred to as "infinitives". This designation for the Old Irish verbal noun is perhaps somewhat misleading since these "infinitives", unlike those in other IE languages, are not so directly connected with the verb syntactically: e.g., they cannot take accusative objects.

There are three formations for verbal nouns. These are as follows. In each of these examples we cite first the 3rd singular present indicative of the verb followed by the corresponding noun.

(a) With Suppletion

These verbal nouns are formed with different lexical items from those of the corresponding verbs. E.g.,

		Old Irish			PIE
verb	**weak ā-class**	car(a)id	/karað'/	'loves'	*kar+ā+ti
noun	**fem ā-class**	serc	/serk/	'love'	*sterk+ā

(b) With the Verb Root Alone

E.g.,

		Old Irish			PIE
verb	**strong je-class**	-cuirethar	/-kureθar/	'throws'	*kor+je+tor[218]
noun	**neuter o-class**	cor	/kor/	'throw'	*kor+om
verb	**strong e-class**	sa(i)did	/saðið'/	'sits'	? *sod+eti[219]
noun	**neuter jo-class**	suide	/suð'e/	'act of sitting'	*sod+jom

(c) With a Derivative Suffix

There are several of these. The following three are the most frequently occurring.

(i) The Derivative Suffix /-m-/. E.g.,

		Old Irish			PIE
verb	**strong n-class**	cingid	/kiNgið'/	'walks'	*ke+n+g+eti[220]
noun	**neuter Vn-class**	céimm	/kēM'/	'a walk'	*keg+m+n̥[221]
verb	**strong e-class**	gníid	/gNīið'/	'acts'	*gnē+eti
noun	**masc u-class**	gním	?/gNīm^u/	'an act'	*gnē+m+us[222]
verb	**weak ī-class**	sechither	/sexiθar'/	'follows'	*sek^w+ī+tor+ai
noun	**fem ā-class**	sechem	/sexem/	'a following'	*sek^w+em+ā[223]

(ii) The Derivative Suffix /-n-/. E.g.,

		Old Irish			PIE
verb	**weak ā-class**	org(a)id	/oRgað'/	'slays'	*porg+ā+ti
noun	**fem ā-class**	orgon		'slaughter'	*porg+on+ā[224]
verb	**strong e-class**	a(i)gid	/aḡið'/	'drives'	*ag+eti
noun	**fem i-class**	áin	/āN'/	'act of driving'	*ag+n+is[225]

(iii) The Derivative Suffix /-t-/ E.g.,

		Old Irish			PIE
verb	**strong e-class**	berid	/berið'/	'carries'	*b^{h}er+eti
noun	**fem ā-class**	breth	/bReθ/	'act of carrying'	*b^{h}r̥+t+ā[226]
noun	**fem i-class**	brith	/bRiθ'/	'idem'	*b^{h}r̥+t+is[226]
verb	**strong je-class**	domoinethar	/do+món'eθar/	'thinks'	*do+mon+je+tor[227]
noun	**fem Vn-class**	toimtiu	/dómt'u/	'opinion'	*do+men+t+jō
verb	**strong e-class**	(ro)-fitir	/-fitar'/	'knows'	*wid+s+tor+ai[228]
noun	**masc u-class**	fius	/fis^u/	'knowledge'	*wid+t+us
verb	**strong n-class**	mairnid	/marN'ið'/	'betrays'	*mr̥+n+eti[229]
noun	**neuter o-class**	mrath	/mRaθ/	'betrayal'	*mr̥+t+om[229]

6.7 Verbal Adjectives

There are two of these: (a) the preterite (or perfect) passive participle and (b) the present passive participle. The meaning of the former is like that of the corresponding perfect passive participle. in English, namely 'that which or one who has been Verb-ed'. The present passive participle. (b) is referred to as the "gerundive" or "participle of necessity". Its meaning is 'that which or one who should be Verb-ed'. The inflection of (a) the preterite passive participle is that of the jo-/jā-class adjective (2.2). The present passive participle (b) is not inflected. E.g.,

(a) Preterite Passive Participle

			Old Irish			PIE
masc	**sg**	**nom**	céte	/kēte/	'sung'	*kan+t+jos
			clithe	/kLiθ'e/	'hidden'	*kl̥+t+jos[230]
			suidigthe	/suð'agð'e/	'placed, set'	*sodj+ag+ī+t+jos

(b) Gerundive Participle

Old Irish			PIE
clethi	/kleθ'i/	'that should be hidden'	*kl̥+teu+āi[231]

6.8 The Verb 'be'

This verb has two versions. One is called the "substantive be" and means 'be present, exist'. The other is the "copulative be" and links a subject with a predicate. Both verbs are suppletive in that their paradigms consist of at least two different lexical items. The major 'be' paradigms follow.

6.8.1 Substantive 'be'

6.8.1.1 Present Active Indicative

There are two paradigms here, the non-habitual present and the habitual, iterative or consuetudinal present. The latter is distinguished from the former in that it means 'be often, usually or habitually'. Both habitual and non-habitual present paradigms occur in absolute and conjunct forms. The habitual conjunct occurs only with the prefix ro- < *pro-. The habitual/non-habitual distinction occurs only in the present indicative, active and passive.

The Habitual Paradigm

			Old Irish		PIE
abs	**sg**	**1**	bíuu	/bīu/	*bʰē+ō[232]
		2	bíi	/bīi/	*bʰē+eso
		3	bíith		*bʰē+eti
	pl	**1**	bímmi	/bīMi/	*bʰē+omos
		2	bíid		*bʰē+ete
		3	bíit	/bīat'/	*bʰē+onti

The Non-Habitual Paradigm

			Old Irish		PIE
conj	**sg**	**1**	-táu	/-tāu/	*stā+ō[233]
		2	-tái	/-tāi/	*stā+es
		3	-tá		*stā+et
	pl	**1**	-táam	/-tāaM/	*stā+omos
		2	-tá(a)id	/-tāað'/	*stā+ete
		3	-táat	/-tāat/	*stā+ont

6.8.1.2 Present Active Subjunctive

The endings are those of the s-subjunctive (see 6.1.2). E.g.,

			Old Irish		PIE
abs	**sg**	**1**	beu		*b^{h}e+ō[234]
		2	bee	/bee/	*b^{h}e+si
		3	beid	/beð'/	*b^{h}e+ti
	pl	**1**	be(i)mmi	/beMi/	*b^{h}e+mos
		2	be(i)the	/beθ'e/	*b^{h}e+te
		3	beit	/beat'/	*b^{h}e+ānti
conj	**sg**	**3**	bé		*b^{h}e+t[235]

6.8.1.3 Present Active Imperative

All imperatives are in the absolute form. The endings are those of 6.1.3 above.

		Old Irish	PIE
sg	**2**	bí /bī/	*b^{h}ē+e
	3	bíth /bīθ/	*b^{h}ē+eto
pl	**2**	bíid /bīð'/	*b^{h}ē+ete
	3	bíat /bīat/	*b^{h}ē+ont

6.8.1.4 Present Passive Indicative

This is the so-called impersonal form of 'be'. Its basic meaning "There is a ... ", where the "..." is a noun or pronoun. This paradigm occurs only in the 3rd singular, absolute and conjunct. We give first the habitual form, then the non-habitual one:

□	Old Irish	PIE
3sg	-bíthir /-bīθar'/	*b^{h}ē+tor+ai
	-táthar /-tāθar/	*stā+tor

6.8.1.5 Imperfect Active Indicative

These forms occur only as conjunct. They consist of the Old Irish root bí- /bī-/ plus the imperfect endings of 6.2 above. E.g.,

	Old Irish	PIE
1sg	-bíinn /-bīaN'/	*b^{h}ē+onn+[V, –back]

6.8.1.6 Preterite Active Indicative

The endings are those of the asuffixal preterite cechan /kéxan/ 'sang' in 6.3.1 above. E.g., the following conjunct forms:

		Old Irish		PIE
sg	1	-bá	/-bā́/	*bʰ+a[236]
	2	-bá	/-bā́/	? *bʰ+ta[237]
	3	-bái	/-bā́i/	*bʰ+a+e[238]
pl	1	-bámmar	/-bā́Mar/	*bʰ+a+mor[238,239]
	2	-báid	/-bā́ð'/	*bʰ+a+te[238]
	3	-bátar	/-bā́tar/	*bʰ+a+nt+or[238]

6.8.1.7 Future Active Indicative

This paradigm is that of a nonreduplicated ā-future as described under 6.5. The endings are those of the present active subjunctive under 6.1.2. E.g.,

			Old Irish		PIE
abs	sg	1	bía	/bīa/	*bʰē+ā+mi
		2	bíae	/bīe/	*bʰē+ā+si
		3	bíe(i)d	/bīeð'/	*bʰē+ā+ti

6.8.2 Copulative 'be'

6.8.2.1 Present Active Indicative

			Old Irish		PIE
abs	sg	1	am	/aM/	*es+mi[240]
		2	at		*es(+si)+tu[241]
		3	is		*es+ti[242]
	pl	1	ammi	/aMi/	*es+mos[240]
		2	adib	/aðiƀ/	*es+ete+2pl pron[243]
		3	it	/at'/	*es+onti[244]

The conjunct forms are cited with the negative prefix ni-.

conj	sg	1	ni-tá	/nitā́/	*ni+stā+m[245]
		2	"		*ni+stā+s[245]
		3	ní	/nī́/	*ni+Ø (?)[246]
	pl	1	ní-tamˡ	/nitáM/	*ni+stā+mos[245]
		2	nitadˡ	/nitáð'/	*ni+stā+te[245]
		3	ni-tat		*ni+stā+nt

6.8.2.2 Present Active Subjunctive

We cite here absolute forms. These have the ā-subjunctive endings (6.1.2) in the singular and the same endings minus the /ā/ in the plural. The roots *b^{h}- and *b^{h}e- are ablaut alternates.

		Old Irish		PIE
sg	1	bá	/bā́/	*b^{h}+ā+mi
	2	"	"	*b^{h}+ā+si
	3	"	"	*b^{h}+ā+ti
pl	1	bem		*b^{h}e+mos
	2	bede	/beðe/	*b^{h}e+te
	3	bet	/bet'/	*b^{h}e+nti

V Exercises

(1) Consider the following PIE forms and the changes which they undergo into Old Irish. Give the Old Irish forms, both in the conventional orthography < ... > as well as in phonemic transcription /.../. (We note 1f IRISH STRESS in our derivations only when the stress is not word-initial.)

a. Nom sg *agnis 'act of going' + 2b LEN, 6b INFEC, 8b W-F SEG DELE, 10a OBSTR+SON DELE > Old Irish?

b. Nom sg *b^{h}aljos 'place' + 1a DEASP, 2b LEN, 6b INFEC, 8b W-F SEG DELE, 9b j-DELE, 9c LATER UNSTR-V > Old Irish?

c. 3sg pass abs *b^{h}er+o+r+ai 'is carried' + 1a DEASP, 2b LEN, 5 EARLY UNSTR-V, 6b INFEC, 8b W-F SEG DELE > Old Irish?

d. Nom sg *b^{h}lōtos 'flower' + 1a DEASP, 2b LEN, 3b ō-CHANGES, 5 EARLY UNSTR-V, 8b W-F SEG DELE > Old Irish?

e. Nom sg *deiwos 'god' + 7c w-CHANGES, 8b W-F SEG DELE, 9a DIPH CHANGES > Old Irish?

f. *dekm̥ '10' + 1e SYL SON, 2b LEN, 2c m-TO-n, 6b INFEC, 8b W-F SEG DELE > Old Irish?

g. Nom sg *d^{h}worestum 'door' + 1a DEASP, 3a ECLIP, 6b INFEC, 7c w-CHANGES, 8a LATER C CL, 8b W-F SEG DELE > Old Irish?

h. Nom sg *dn̥tom 'tooth' + 2c m-TO-n, 3a ECLIP, 7b VnC-TO-VC, 8b W-F SEG DELE > Old Irish?

i. 3sg pres conj *eks+beret 'he says' + 1a DEASP, 1f IRISH STRESS, 2b LEN, 6b INFEC, 8a LATER C CL, 8b W-F SEG DELE, 9c LATER UNSTR-V > Old Irish?

j. 1sg pres *esmi 'I am' + absence of 1f IRISH STRESS, 2b LEN, 6b INFEC, 8b W-F SEG DELE, 9c LATER UNSTR-V > Old Irish?

k. Nom sg masc *justjos 'just' + 5 EARLY UNSTR-V, 6b INFEC, 8a LATER C CL, 8b W-F SEG DELE, 9b j-DELE, 9c LATER UNSTR-V > Old Irish?

l. 1sg pret abs *kar+ā+s+ō 'I loved' + absence of 2b LEN on /s/ because of analogy with other forms but its application to /r/, 3b ō-CHANGES, 9c LATER UNSTR-V, 10b SYNCOPE > Old Irish?

m. Nom sg neuter *keg+m+n̥ 'a walk' + 1e SYL SON, 2b LEN, 6b INFEC, 8b W-F SEG DELE, 10a OBSTR+SON DELE > Old Irish?

n. *kentom '100' + 5 EARLY UNSTR-V, 7b VnC-TO-VC, 8b W-F SEG DELE > Old Irish?

o. 3sg future *ki+kl+āti 'will hide' + 2b LEN, 6a i-e/u-o ALT, 6b INFEC, 10a OBSTR+SON DELE > Old Irish?

p. Nom sg *krow+us 'blood' + 6a i-e/u-o ALT, 7c w-CHANGES, 8b W-F SEG DELE, 9d STR-V LENG > Old Irish?
q. Nom sg interrogative pron *k^wei+s 'who?' + 7a k^w-TO-k, 8b W-F SEG DELE, 9a DIPH CHANGES > Old Irish?
r. 3sg pres *ml̥geti 'milks' + 1e SYL SON, 2b LEN, 6a i-e/u-o ALT, 6b INFEC, 8b W-F SEG DELE > Old Irish?
s. Nom sg *morim 'sea' + 2b LEN, 6a i-e/u-o ALT, 6b INFEC, 8b W-F SEG DELE > Old Irish?
t. Nom sg neuter *n̥g^{hw}n̥ 'butter' + 1a DEASP, 1e SYL SON, 2a g^w-CHANGES, PIE 3.1.2d NASAL ASSIM applying synchronically, 8b W-F SEG DELE) > Old Irish?
u. Nom sg *ni+sd+os 'a sit-in, a nest' + 1c EARLY C CL, 5 EARLY UNSTR-V, 6a i-e/u-o ALT, 8a LATER C CL, 8b W-F SEG DELE > Old Irish?
v. Nom sg neuter *n̥m+n̥ 'name' + 1e SYL SON, 2b LEN, 6b INFEC, 8b W-F SEG DELE > Old Irish?
w. 3sg pres *porgāti 'slays' + 1d p-CHANGES, 2b LEN, 6b INFEC, 8b W-F SEG DELE > Old Irish?
x. 1sg pres dep *sek^{w}ōr 'I follow' + 2b LEN, 3b ō-CHANGES, 7a k^w-TO-k, 9c LATER UNSTR-V > Old Irish?
y. comp *sen+jōs 'older' + 2b LEN, 3b ō-CHANGES, 6a i-e/u-o ALT, 6b INFEC, 8b W-F SEG DELE, 9b j-DELE, 9c LATER UNSTR-V > Old Irish?
z. Nom sg *sk^{w}etlom 'story' + 2b LEN, 2c m-TO-n, 5 EARLY UNSTR-V, 7a k^w-TO-k, 8b W-F SEG DELE, 10a OBSTR+SON DELE > Old Irish?
aa. Nom sg *stratos 'valley' + 2b LEN, 5 EARLY UNSTR-V, 8a LATER C CL, 8b W-F SEG DELE > Old Irish?
bb. *s(w)eks '6' + ? 7c w-CHANGES, 8b W-F SEG DELE, 9d STR-V LENG > Old Irish?
cc. Nom pl *teutās 'peoples' + 2b LEN, 8b W-F SEG DELE, 9a DIPH CHANGES, 9c LATER UNSTR-V > Old Irish?
dd. Nom sg neuter *tod 'this, thus, yes' + 8b W-F SEG DELE, 9d STR-V LENG > Old Irish?
ee. Nom pl *wātejes 'prophets' + 2b LEN, 5 EARLY UNSTR-V, 6a i-e/u-o ALT, 6b INFEC, 7c w-CHANGES, 8b W-F SEG DELE, 9c LATER UNSTR-V > Old Irish?
ff. Nom sg *wid+t+us 'knowledge' + 1c EARLY C CL, 6b INFEC, 7c w-CHANGES, 8a LATER C CL, 8b W-F SEG DELE > Old Irish?
gg. *wi+kn̥ts '20' + 1e SYL SON, 2b LEN, 6b INFEC, 7b VnC-TO-VC, 7c w-CHANGES, 8b W-F SEG DELE > Old Irish?

(2) Given the following PIE forms, what will be the Old Irish reflexes and what changes will they have undergone? Give the Old Irish forms in the traditional orthography <...> and in phonemic transcription /.../.

a. 2sg pres act imp *b^here 'carry'.
b. 1sg pres conj *b^herō 'I carry'.
c. Nom sg *dōnom 'gift'.
d. Nom sg *enigenā 'daughter'.
e. Nom sg *enisk^{w}jā 'speech'.
f. Nom sg *genus 'mouth'.
g. Non. sg *g^hansis 'goose'.
h. Nom sg *g^hortos 'garden'.
i. Nom sg *g^{hw}onim 'act of killing'.
j. Nom sg masc *kaikos 'blind'.
k. Nom sg *kaper+āk+s 'sheep'.
l. 1sg pret. *ke+klad+a 'I dug'.
m. Nom sg masc *kl̥+t+jos 'hidden'.

n. Nom pl neuter *kr̥djā ‘hearts’.
o. Nom pl *k^{w}etwores ‘4’.
p. *k^{w}onk^{w}e ‘5’.
q. Nom sg *koslos ‘hazel tree’.
r. Nom sg masc Ø-class *mēns ‘month’.
s. Nom sg *patēr ‘father’.
t. Instr pl *pēd+su ‘at the feet of, (later) under’.
u. Nom sg masc *plusmos ‘bare’.
v. Nom sg masc *poljos ‘every’.
w. Nom sg *sentus ‘way’.
x. Nom sg *smerus ‘marrow’.
y. 3sg pres *snig^{hw}eti ‘it snows’.
z. Nom sg *srutus ‘stream’.
aa. 1sg pres conj *steig^{h}ō ‘I go’ (NB: 8b W-F SEG DELE does not apply.).
bb. Nom sg *sterk+ā ‘love’.
cc. Gen sg neuter Vs-class *teg+es+os ‘house’.
dd. Nom sg *tr̥stos ‘thirst’.
ee. Nom sg *weg^{h}nos ‘wagon’.
ff. Gen sg u-class *wid^{h}ous ‘wood’.
gg. Nom sg *wid^{h}wā ‘widow’.
hh. Nom sg *wl̥tis ‘rulership’ (NB: the output of le SYL SON is /la/.).

(3) The Latin nouns apostolus ‘apostle’ and philosophia /filosofja/ ‘philosophy’ are borrowed into Old Irish. The first becomes an o-class masculine noun; the second, a jā-class feminine noun. The first undergoes the following synchronic rules in this sequence: 1f IRISH STRESS, 10b SYNCOPE, 8b W-F SEG DELE. The second undergoes these synchronic rules in this sequence: 1f IRISH STRESS, 10b SYNCOPE, 2b LEN on word-internal /f/, 9b j-DELE, 9c LATER UNSTR-V. What are the resultant Old Irish forms, both in the traditional orthography and in phonemic transcription?

(4) Consider the PIE antecedents of the verb ‘carry’: 3sg conj *b^{h}eret, 3pl conj *b^{h}eront and 3pl abs *b^{h}eronti. What are the corresponding forms in the Old Irish paradigm? Give them in the traditional Old Irish orthography and in phonemic transcription.

(5) The PIE ā-class paradigm for ‘woman’ shows ablaut: nom sg *g^{w}enā, gen sg *g^{w}njās. What are the corresponding forms of the Old Irish paradigm? (Hint: the rules which apply are 1f IRISH STRESS, 2a g^{w}-CHANGES, 8b W-F SEG DELE, 9b j-DELE.)

(6) The PIE paradigm for ‘friend’ has the following forms: nom pl *karantes, gen pl *karantōm, dat pl *karantib^{h}is. What are the corresponding Old Irish forms? Give them in the traditional orthography and in phonemic transcription.

(7) The PIE adjective paradigm for the athematic adjective ‘hot’ has the following forms: nom sg *tepents, nom pl *tepentes. What are the corresponding Old Irish forms? Give them in the traditional orthography and in phonemic transcription.

(8) The PIE masc o-class paradigm for ‘man’ has the following forms: non. sg *wiros, voc sg *wire, dat sg *wirōi, nom pl *wiroi, gen pl *wirōm, dat pl *wirob^{h}is. What are the corresponding Old Irish forms? Give them in the traditional orthography and in phonemic transcription.

(9) Consider the two PIE sequences nom pl *septōm pateres ‘7 fathers’ and *seks pateres ‘6 fathers’. What will be the corresponding Old Irish sequences? Give them in the traditional orthography and in phonemic transcription.

(10) The Old Irish word for ‘sister’ is siur from PIE *swesōr. What is the derivation of the Old Irish word from the PIE form? Provide another derivation in which 2b LEN has applied to the word-initial /s/. What is the resultant Old Irish lenited form?

(11) Consider the glossed Old Irish text in VI below. Give a smooth translation of this text.

VI An Old Irish Text

The following is an excerpt from an Old Irish epic, the *Scéla Mucce Meic Dathó* ‘Stories of MacDatho’s pig’. The story may date from ca. 100 AD. The language is that of the Old Irish of ca. 600-700 AD.

Our textual description is based on but does not in all respects follow that of Lehmann and Lehmann (1975: 3-5 and 11-13). In the passage below we give (a) the traditional Old Irish orthography and (b) a phonemic transcription. Here we mark the stress only when it is not on the first syllable of a word: unmarked words may be assumed to have stress on their first syllables. We mark those forms which trigger 2b LEN or 3a ECLIP with the superscripts “^{l}”and “^{n}”, respectively. We note unlenited sonorants, both word-initial and word-internal, as /L, M, N, R/. Finally, we mark consonants which have undergone 6b INFEC only where the context is unrevealing: hence we write /Laǥniƀ'/ ‘Leinstermen’, not **/Laǥn'iƀ'/. Under (c) below we give a gloss. And under (d) we give a grammatical description of each form.

1	**a**	1. Boí	rí	amrae	for	Laignib,	Mac
	b	bāi	Rī	amre	for	Laǥniƀ'	Mak
	c	*be*	*king*	*famous*	*over*	*Leinstermen*	*son*
	d	3sg pret abs	nom sg masc	nom sg masc	prep + dat	dat pl masc	nom sg masc

2	**a**	Dathó	a	ainm.	2. Boí	cú	occo.
	b	daθō	a	anM'	bāi	kū	ogo
	c	*Datho*	*his*	*name*	*be*	*dog*	*to him*
	d	nom sg masc	poss pron	nom sg neut	3sg pres abs	nom sg masc	prep + dat sg masc

3	**a**	3. Imdíched	in	cú	Laigniu	huili.	4. Ailbe
	b	iM+dīxeð	iN	kū	Laǥn'u	uli	alƀe
	c	*protect*	*the*	*dog*	*Leinstermen*	*all*	*Ailbe*
	d	3sg imperf conj	nom sg masc	nom sg masc	acc pl masc	acc pl masc	nom sg masc

4	**a**	ainm	in	chon,	ocus	ba	lán
	b	anM'	iNd^{l}	xon	ogus^{l}	ƀa	Lān
	c	*name*	*the*	*dog*	*and*	*be*	*full*
	d	nom sg neut	gen sg masc	gen sg masc	conj	3sg pret conj	nom sg fem

5	**a**	Hériu	dia	airdircus	in	chon.	5. Doeth
	b	ēr'u	dia	aRdiRkes^{u}	iNd^{l}	xon	do+éθ
	c	*Ireland*	*of it*	*fame*	*the*	*dog*	*come*
	d	nom sg fem	prep + gen sg masc	dat sg masc	gen sg masc	gen sg masc	3sg pret pass subj

6	**a**	ó	Ailill	ocus	ó	Meidb	do
	b	ō^{l}	aliL'	ogus^{l}	ō^{l}	meðƀ'	do^{l}
	c	*from*	*Ailill*	*and*	*from*	*Medb*	*to*
	d	prep + dat	dat sg masc	conj	prep + dat	dat sg fem	prep + inf dat

7	**a**	chungid	in	chon.	6. Immalle	dano	? tancatar[247]
	b	xungið'	iNd^{l}	xon	iMalé	danó	? dāngatar[247]
	c	*seek*	*the*	*dog*	*at the same time*	*then*	*?come*[247]
	d	inf. dat sg fem	gen sg masc	gen sg masc	prep phrase	adv	3pl pret

8	**a**	ocus	techta	Ulad	ocus	Conchobair	do
	b	ogus^{l}	θexta[248]	ulað	ogus^{l}	xonxoƀar'[248]	do^{l}
	c	*and*	*messengers*	*Ulstermen*	*and*	*Conchobor*	*to*
	d	conj	nom pl fem	gen pl masc	conj	gen sg masc	prep + inf dat

9	**a**	chungid	in	chon	chétna.	7. Roferad	fáilte
	b	xungið'	iNd^{l}	xon^{l} [249]	xēdNa	Ro+férað	fāLte
	c	*seek*	*the*	*dog*	*same*	*pour*	*welcome*
	d	inf dat sg fem	gen sg masc	gen sg masc	uninflected pron	3sg pret pass conj	nom sg fem

10	**a**	friu	huili,	ocus	ructha	cuci	sium
	b	fr'u	uli	ogus^{l}	rukθa	kugi	s'um
	c	*to them*	*all*	*and*	*take*	*to him*	*himself*
	d	prep + 3pl pron acc	acc pl masc	conj	3pl perf pass conj	prep + acc sg masc	acc sg masc

11	**a**	isin	mbrudin.	8. Is	sí	sin	in
	b	i+sin^{n}	mbRuðin'	is	sī	siNd^{l}	iNd^{l}
	c	*into the*	*hostel*	*be*	*it*	*this*	*the*
	d	prep + acc sg fem art	acc sg fem	3sg pres	nom sg fem	nom sg fem	nom sg fem

12	**a**	chóiced	bruden	roboí	i	nHérinn	isind
	b	xōkeð^{l}	ƀRuðen	roƀāi	i^{n}	nēriN'	isiNd'
	c	*fifth*	*hostel*	*be*	*in*	*Ireland*	*in the*
	d	nom sg fem	nom sg fem	3sg pret conj relative clause form	prep +dat	dat sg fem	prep + dat sg fem article

13	**a**	aimsir	sin,	ocus	bruden	Da-Derg	i
	b	amsir'	siNd'	ogus^{l}	ƀRuðen	da^{l}ðéRg	i^{n}
	c	*time*	*that*	*and*	*hostel*	*Da Derga*	*in*
	d	dat sg fem	dat sg fem	conj	nom sg fem	gen sg	prep +dat

14	**a**	crích	Cúalann	ocus	bruden	Forgaill	Manaich
	b	ngRīx'^{l}	xūalaN	ogus^{l}	ƀRuðen	foRǥaL'^{l}	manax'
	c	*district*	*Cualu*	*and*	*hostel*	*Forgall*	*Manach*
	d	dat sg fem	gen sg masc	conj	nom sg fem	gen sg masc	gen sg masc

15	**a**	ocus	bruden	Meic	Da-Réo	i	mBréfni
	b	ogus^{l}	ƀRuðen	mek'^{l}	ða^{l}rḗo	i^{n}	mbRēfni^{l}
	c	*and*	*hostel*	*son*	*DaReo*	*in*	*Brefne*
	d	conj	nom sg fem	gen sg masc	gen sg masc	prep + dat	dat sg fem

16						
a	ocus	bruden	Da-Choca	i	niarthur	Midi.
b	ogus^{l}	ƀruðen	da^{l}xoga	i^{n}	niaRθar^{ul}	miði^{l}
c	*and*	*hostel*	*Da Choca*	*in*	*western part*	*Meath*
d	conj	nom sg fem	gen sg masc	prep + dat	dat sg neuter	gen sg fem

VII Key

(1) The Old Irish forms are these: (a) <áin> /āN'/, (b) <baile> /bal'e/, (c) <ber(a)ir> /berar'/, (d) <bláth> /bLāθ/, (e) <dia> /dia/, (f) <deich> /dex'/, (g) <dorus> /dores^{u}/, (h) <dét> /dēt/, (i) <asbeir> /as+ber'/, (j) <a(i)mm> /aM'/, (k) <huisse> /us'e/, (l) <carsu> /karsu/, (m) <céimm> /kēM'/, (n) <cét> /kēt/, (o) <cel(a)id> /kēLað'/, (p) <crú> /kRū/, (q) <cia> /kia/, (r) <mligid> /mLiǥið'/, (s) <muir> /mur'/, (t) <imb> /iMb/, (u) <net> /ned/, (v) <ainm(m)> /anM'/, (w) <org(a)id> /oRgað'/, (x) <sechur> /sexur/, (y) <siniu> /sin'u/, (z) <scél> /skēL/, (aa) <srath> /sRaθ/, (bb) <sé> /sē/, (cc) <thuatha> /θuaθa/, (dd) <tó> /tō/, (ee) <fáithi> /fāθ'i/, (ff) <fius> /fis^{u}/, (gg) <fiche> /fix'e/.

(2) The Old Irish forms and changes are these:

a. <beir> /ber'/. The derivation is 1a DEASP, 2b LEN, 6b INFEC, 8b W-F SEG DELE.
b. <-biur> /-bir^{u}/. The derivation is 1a DEASP, 2b LEN, 6a i-e/u-o ALT, 6b INFEC, 8b W-F SEG DELE.
c. <dán> /dān/. The derivation is 2b LEN, 3b ō-CHANGES, 5 EARLY UNSTR-V, 8b W-F SEG DELE.
d. <ingen> /inǥen/. The derivation is 2b LEN, 6a i-e/u-o ALT, 8b W-F SEG DELE, 10b SYNCOPE.
e. <insce> /inske/. The derivation is 2b LEN, 6a i-e/u-o ALT, 6b INFEC, 7a k^{w}-TO-k, 9b j-DELE, 9c LATER UNSTR-V.
f. <giun> /gin^{u}/. The derivation is 2b LEN, 6a i-e/u-o ALT, 6b INFEC, 8b W-F SEG DELE.
g. <géis> /gēs'/. The derivation is 1a DEASP, 6b INFEC, 7b VnC-TO-VC, 8b W-F SEG DELE.
h. <gort> , /goRt/. The derivation is 5 EARLY UNSTR-V, 8b W-F SEG DELE.
i. <guin> /gun'/. The derivation is 1a DEASP, 2a g^{w}-CHANGES, 2b LEN, 6a i-e/u-o ALT, 6b INFEC, 8b W-F SEG DELE.
j. <caich> /kaix/. The derivation is 2b LEN, 8b W-F SEG DELE.
k. <caera> /kaera/. The derivation is 1d p-CHANGES, 2b LEN, 8b W-F SEG DELE, 9c LATER UNSTR-V.
l. <cechlad> /kéxLað/. The derivation is 1f IRISH STRESS, 2b LEN, 8b W-F SEG DELE, 10b SYNCOPE.
m. <clithe> /kLiθ'e/. The derivation is 1e SYL SON, 2b LEN, 5 EARLY UNSTR-V, 6b INFEC, 8b W-F SEG DELE, 9b j-DELE.
n. <kride> /kRið'e/. The derivation is 1e SYL SON, 2b LEN, 6b INFEC, 9b j-DELE, 9c LATER UNSTR-V.
o. <ceth(a)ir> /keθar'/. The derivation is 2b LEN, 5 EARLY UNSTR-V, 6b INFEC, 7a k^{w}-TO-k, 7c w-CHANGES, 8b W-F SEG DELE, 9c LATER UNSTR-V.
p. <cóic> /kōk'/. The derivation is 6b INFEC, 7a k^{w}-TO-k, 7b VnC-TO-VC.
q. <coll> /koL/. The derivation is *koslos (2b LEN) > *kohLos (ev) > *koLos, then 5 EARLY UNSTR-V, 8b W-F SEG DELE.

r. <mí> /mī/. The derivation is 1b ē-TO-ī, 8b W-F SEG DELE.

s. <aithir> /aθ'ir/. The derivation is 1b ē-TO-ī, 1d p-CHANGES, 2b LEN, 6b INFEC, 9c LATER UNSTR-V.

t. <ís> /īs/. The derivation is 1b ē-TO-ī, 1c EARLY C CL, 1d p-CHANGES, 8a LATER C CL, 8b W-F SEG DELE.

u. <lomm> /loM/. The derivation is *plusmos (1d p-CHANGES) > *lusmos (2b LEN) > *luhMos (ev) > *luMos, then 5 EARLY UNSTR-V, 6a i-e/u-o ALT, 8b W-F SEG DELE.

v. <uile> /ul'e/. The derivation is 1d p-CHANGES, 2b LEN, 6a i-e/u-o ALT, 6b INFEC, 8b W-F SEG DELE, 9b j-DELE, 9c LATER UNSTR-V.

w. <sét> /sēt/. The derivation is 6b INFEC, 7b VnC-TO-VC, 8b W-F SEG DELE.

x. <smiur> /sMir^{u}/. The derivation is 2b LEN (of /r/), 6a i-e/u-o ALT, 6b INFEC, 8b W-F SEG DELE.

y. <snigid> /sNiǥið'/. The derivation is 1a DEASP, 2a g^{w}-CHANGES, 2b LEN, 6a i-e/u-o ALT, 6b INFEC, 8b W-F SEG DELE.

z. <sruth> /sRuθ^{u}/. The derivation is 2b LEN, 6b INFEC, 8b W-F SEG DELE.

aa. <tiagu> /tiaǥu/. The derivation is 1a DEASP, 2b LEN, 3b ō-CHANGES, 8a LATER C CL, 9a DIPH CHANGES, 9c LATER UNSTR-V.

bb. <serc> /seRk/. The derivation is 8a LATER C CL, 8b W-F SEG DELE.

cc. <tige> /teǥ'e/. The derivation is *teg+es+os (2b LEN) > *teǥehos (ev) > *teǥos (5 EARLY UNSTR-V) > *teǥeas (6b INFEC) > *teǥ'eas (8b W-F SEG DELE) > OIr teǥ'e.

dd. <tart> /taRt/. The derivation is 1e SYL SON, 5 EARLY UNSTR-V, 8b W-F SEG DELE.

ee. <fén> /fēN/. The derivation is *weg^{h}nos (1a DEASP) > *wegnos (2b LEN) > *weǥNos, then 5 EARLY UNSTR-V, 8b W-F SEG DELE, 10a OBSTR+SON DELE.

ff. <fedo> /feðo/. The derivation is 1a DEASP, 2b LEN, 5 EARLY UNSTR-V, 6a i-e/u-o ALT, 7c w-CHANGES, 8b W-F SEG DELE, 9a DIPH CHANGES, 9c LATER UNSTR-V.

gg. <fedb> /feðƀ/. The derivation is 1a DEASP, 2b LEN, 6a i-e/u-o ALT, 7c w-CHANGES, 8b W-F SEG DELE.

hh. <flaith> /fLaθ'/. The derivation is 1e SYL SON, 2b LEN, 6b INFEC, 7c w-CHANGES, 8b W-F SEG DELE.

(3) The resultant forms are <apstol> /apstol/ and <fellsube> /féLsuƀ'e/, respectively.

(4) The Old Irish forms are 3sg conj <-beir> /-ber'/, 3 pl conj <-berat> /-berat/, 3pl abs <ber(a)it> /berat'/.

(5) The Old Irish forms are nom sg <ben> /ben/, gen sg <mná> /mNā/.

(6) The Old Irish forms are nom pl <car(a)it > /karat'/, gen pl <carat> /karat/, dat pl <cairtib> /kart'iƀ'/.

(7) The Old Irish forms are nom sg <té> /tē/, nom pl <téit> /tēt'/.

(8) The Old Irish forms are nom sg <fer> /fer/, voc sg <fir> /fir'/, dat sg <fiur> /fir^{u}/, nom pl <fir> /fir'/, gen pl <fer> /fer/, dat pl <fer(a)ib> /feraƀ'/.

(9) The Old Irish sequences are <secht^{n} naithir> /sext naθ'ir'/ and <sé aithir> /sē aθ'ir'/.

(10) The derivation is PIE *swesōr (2b LEN) > *sweōr (3b ō-CHANGES) > *sweūr (6a i-e/u-o ALT) > *swiūr (7c w-CHANGES)> *siūr (9c LATER UNSTR-V) > OIr siur. If 2b LEN applies to word-initial /s/, the derivation is PIE *swesōr (2b LEN) > *weōr (3b ō-CHANGES, 6a i-e/u-o ALT) > *wiūr (7c w-CHANGES) > *fiūr (9c LATER UNSTR-V) > OIr fiur. Hence the lenited form of OIr /siur/ is /fiur/.

(11) The following is a translation of the text in Section VI.

"1. There was a famous king over Leinster; MacDatho was his name. 2. He had a dog. 3. The dog protected all Leinster. 4. Ailbe was the name of the dog; and Ireland was full of the fame of the dog. 5. There was a coming, i.e. many came from Ailill and Medb to seek the dog. 6. At this same time messengers of Ulster and of Conchobor also came to seek the same dog. 7. A welcome was poured, i.e. prepared, for them all; and they were taken into the hostel to the dog himself. 8. It is the fifth hostel which was in Ireland at that time; and there were also the hostel Da Derag in the district of Cualu and the hostel Forgall of Manach and the hostel of the son of Da Reo in Brefne and the hostel Da Choca in the western part of Meath."

VIII Notes

[1] The alternations among plain, palatal and rounded consonants are ascribable to the rule 6b INFEC, which remains in the grammar. It is in part morph cond and in part phon cond.

[2] The alternation –lenited vs. +lenited is ascribable to the action of the morph cond rule 2b LEN.

[3] These segments may have been /v, v'/ and /v^{u}/, respectively.

[4] According to Lewis and Pedersen (1937: 16), OIr /h/ does not have palatal or rounded variants, i.e., no **/h'/ or **/h^{u}/.

[5] The velar nasal [ŋ] occurs only as an allophone of /n/ by PIE 3.1.2d NASAL ASSIM, which remains in the grammar; [ŋ] occurs only before velar obstruents. As such it cannot undergo 2b LEN. It can however undergo 6b INFEC.

[6] The diphthongs /ai/ and /oi/ alternate optionally with /ae/ and /oe/ by 9a DIPH CHANGES; /ia/ and /ua/ alternate with /ē/ and /ō/ by the same change, which remains as a morph cond rule of Old Irish. Some sources posit additional diphthongs such as /āi/ in fáith 'seer' (which we consider to have been /fāθ'/) and /iu/ in the dat sg fiur 'man' (which we consider to have been /fir^{u}/). See on this 6b INFEC. There is a possible diphthong /iu/ in the word /siur/ 'sister' (see on this section 1.5.3 of the morphology). However, one could also analyze this word as consisting of two morphemes, namely /si+ur/.

[7] All the obstruents except possibly /h/ have palatal and rounded variants by 6b INFEC. The palatal obstruents have the same features as the plain obstruents cited above except for the feature +palatal. The rounded obstruents are also like those given in the chart except for the feature +round.

[8] Likewise, the sonorant consonants also have palatal and rounded variants which differ from those cited in the chart in the features +palatal and +round.

[9] It is possible that the unlenited sonorants /M N L R/ were somewhat longer than the lenited /m n l r/. On this, see 2b LEN. Hence in our chart we have considered the lenited sonorant consonant segments as –tense and –long; and the unlenited: ones as +tense and +long.

[10] By 9c LATER UNSTR-V, long vowels occur only under stress.

[11] The derivation is *wire (5 EARLY UNSTR-V) > *wiri (6b INFEC) > *wir'i (7c w-CHANGES, 8b W-F SEG DELE) > OIr fir /fir'/.

[12] The derivation is *wirom (2c m-TO-n, 5 EARLY UNSTR-V) > *wiran (6a i-e/u-o ALT) > *weran (6b INFEC not applying, 7c w-CHANGES, 8b W-F SEG DELE) > OIr fer.

[13] Pokorny (1969: 35), upon which we base many of the PIE reconstructions cited here, posits the PIE antecedent *-ī as originally an adverb ending.

[14] The antecedent could be either *wirō or *wirōi. The derivation is*wirō or *wirōi (3b ō-CHANGES) > *wirū in both instances (6b INFEC) > *wir^{u}ū (7c w-CHANGES, 8b W-F SEG DELE) > fiur /fir^u/.

[15] Pokorny (1969: 36) posits the antecedent ending *-ā which comes from the numeral da /dā/ '2'. Another possibility suggested in Lewis and Pedersen (1937: 167) is *-ōu. In either event, the outcome would be the same: *wirā, *wirōu (3b ō-CHANGES) > *wirā, *wirāu (4 DIPH SHORT) > *wirā, *wirau (6a i-e/u-o ALT) > *werā, *werau (7c w-CHANGES) > *ferā, *ferau (8b W-F SEG DELE) > OIr fer.

[16] The ending *-oi is from the pronominal declension. (See 5.2 below.) The derivation is *wiroi (5 EARLY UNSTR-V) > *wirī (6b INFEC, 7c w-CHANGES, 8b W-F SEG DELE) > OIr fir /fir'/.

[17] The dual and plural vocative is usually like the nominative. Here the vocative plural is either from the original nom pl *wirōs (before the addition of *-oi) or from the acc pl *wirōns. In either event the Old Irish reflex is the same: *wirōs, *wirōns (3b ō-CHANGES) > *wirūs, *wirūns (7c w-CHANGES) > *firūs, *firūns (8b W-F SEG DELE) > *firū for both forms (9c LATER UNSTR-V) > OIr firu.

[18] The derivation is *wirōm (2c m-TO-n) > *wirōn (2d V̄+NASAL SHORT) > *wiron (5 EARLY UNSTR-V) > *wiran (6a i-e/u-o ALT , but no 6b INFEC) > *weran (7c w-CHANGES, 8b W-F SEG DELE) > OIr fer.

[19] The derivation is *wirob^{h}is (1a DEASP) > *wirobis (2b LEN) > *wiroƀis (6a i-e/u-o ALT) > *weroƀis (6b INFEC) > *weroƀ'is (7c w-CHANGES, 8b W-F SEG DELE) > *feroƀ' (9c LATER UNSTR-V) > OIr feraib /feraƀ'/.

[20] Pokorny (9: 36) assumes the Old Irish ending –a was readded from the demonstrative pronoun (see 5.2 below). Otherwise the derivation is *sk^{w}etlā (2b LEN) > *sk^{w}eθLā (7a k^w-TO-k) > *skeθLā (8b W-F SEG DELE) > *skeθL (10a OBSTR+SON DELE) > OIr scél /skēL/.

[21] The other forms of this class have the same endings as the masculine paradigm. They can show the effects of 6b INFEC: e.g., gen sg scéuil /skēL'/; and dat sg scéul /skēL^u/ < *sk^{w}etlō(i).

[22] The derivation is *b^{h}aljos (la DEASP, 2b LEN) > *baljos (5 EARLY UNSTR-V) > *baljas (6b INFEC) > *bal'jas (8b W-F SEG DELE applying only to the /s/, but not to the preceding /a/ because of the presence of /j/) > *bal'ja (9b j-DELE) > *bal'a (9c LATER UNSTR-V) > OIr ba(i)le /bal'e/. The other forms are derived similarly with 8b W-F SEG DELE not applying to the vowels because of the preceding /j/.

[23] The derivation of both forms is *kr̥djom and *kr̥djā (le SYL SON) > *kridjom, *kridjā (2b LEN, 2c m-TO-n, 5 EARLY UNSTR-V) > *kRiðjan, *kRiðjā (6b INFEC) > *kRið'jan, *kRiðjā (8b W-F SEG DELE) > *kRið'ja, *kRið'jā (9b j-DELE) > *kRið'a, *kRið'a (9c LATER UNSTR-V) > OIr kride /kRið'e/ for both forms.

[24] The derivation of the dative singular is *teutāi (2b LEN) > *teuθāi (4 DIPH SHORT) > *teuθai (5 EARLY UNSTR-V) > *teuθī (6b INFEC) > *teuθ'ī (8b W-F SEG DELE) > *teuθ' (9a DIPH CHANGES) > OIr tuaith /tuaθ'/. The accusative singular is generally assumed to be from the dative singular since it is also /tuaθ'/ and has undergone 6b INFEC. However, the accusative singular does trigger 3a ECLIP, which would have been the case if the PIE ending had been *-m, or if 3a ECLIP been triggered analogously from other accusative singular forms.

[25] The ending is generally considered to devolve from the jā-class genitive ending. The respective derivations would be as follows: jā-class gen sg *teutjās vs. ā-class gen sg *teutās (2b LEN) > *teuθjās, *teuθās (6b INFEC) > *teuθ'jās, *teuθās (8b W-F SEG DELE) > *teuθ'jā, *teuθā (9a DIPH CHANGES) > *tuaθ'jā, *tuaθā (9b j-DELE, 9c LATER UNSTR-V) > OIr tuaithe /tuaθ'e/ as opposed to **tuathe **/tuaθe/.

[26] The vowel alternation e-Ø is PIE ablaut. The derivation of these two forms is *g^{w}enā, *g^{w}nā (1f IRISH STRESS) > *g^{w}énā, *g^{w}nā́i (2a g^w-CHANGES, ev) > *bénā, *Mnā́i (4 DIPH SHORT) > *bénā, *Mnái (8b W-F SEG DELE) > OIr ben and mnái.

[27] The spelling <ban> may have been for /ben/with orthographic <a> used to indicate that the final /n/ is "plain",

i.e. is neither palatalized nor rounded by 6b INFEC. The derivation of the forms is *g^{w}enou, *g^{w}enōm (2a g^w-CHANGES) > *benou, *benōm (2c m-TO-n, 2d V̄+NASAL SHORT) > *benou,*benon (5 EARLY UNSTR-V) > *benau, *benan (no 6b INFEC, but 8b W-F SEG DELE) > OIr ban /ben/ for both forms.

[28] The derivation is *enisk^{w}jā (1f IRISH STRESS) > *énisk^{w}jā (6a i-e/u-o ALT) > *ínisk^{w}jā (6b INFEC) > *ínisk^w'jā (7a k^w-TO-k) > *ínisk'ja (9b j-DELE) > *ínisk'ā (9c LATER UNSTR-V) > *ínisk'e (10b SYNCOPE) > OIr insce /ínsk'e/.

[29] The orthography here may represent OIr /insk'aƀ'/.

[30] The forms /insk'i/ and /insk'iƀ'/, if they had developed normally into Old Irish, would be expected as **/insk'a/ **<insc(e)a> and **/insk'aƀ'/ **<insca(i)b>, respectively. The endings here may have been those of the i-class (1.3 below).

[31] The derivation is *muk^{w}ū (2b LEN not applying: see the discussion under 2b LEN; but 7a k^w-TO-k does apply) > *mukū (8b W-F SEG DELE) > OIr mucc /muk/.

[32] The derivation is *muk^{w}āi (no 2b LEN, but 4 DIPH SHORT) > *muk^{w}ai (5 EARLY UNSTR-V) > *muk^{w}ī (6b INFEC) > *muk^w'ī (7a k^w-TO-k, 8b W-F SEG DELE) > OIr muicc /muk'/.

[33] The derivation is *sentikī (1f IRISH STRESS) > *séntikī (2b LEN) > *séntiǥī (6b INFEC) > *sént'iǥ'ī (7b VnC-TO-VC) > *sḗt'iǥ'ī (8b W-F SEG DELE) > OIr sétig /sḗt'iǥ'/. If the nominative singular had had the jā-class ending, the derivation would have been *sentikjā (ev) > OIr nom sg **séitche **/sḗtx'e/.

[34] The derivation is *sentikjās (if IRISH STRESS) > *séntikjas (2b LEN, 6b INFEC) > *sént'iǥ'jās (7b VnC-TO-VC) > *sḗt'iǥ'jās (8b W-F SEG DELE) > *sḗt'iǥ'jā (9b j-DELE) > *sḗt'iǥ'ā (9c LATER UNSTR-V) > *sḗt'iǥ'e (10b SYNCOPE) > *sḗt'ǥ'e = *sḗtǥ'e (reformation of the unacceptable consonant cluster /tǥ'/ to /tx'/) > OIr séitche /sḗtx'e/.

[35] The vocative singular is probably from the nominative singular. If it were from an original PIE voc sg *wāti, the Old Irish form would be **fá **/fā/ by 8b W-F SEG DELE.

[36] These forms are probably from the u-class. The derivation is *wātous (2b LEN) > *wāθous (5 EARLY UNSTR-V) > *wāθaus (7c w-CHANGES) > *fāθaus (8b W-F SEG DELE) > *fāθau (9a DIPH CHANGES) > *fāθō (9c LATER UNSTR-V) > OIr fátho /fāθo/. One would not expect this form to trigger 2b LEN in the following word as it does: fátho^l. LEN is triggered on the analogy of other gen sg forms such as fir^l /fir'/ 'man' above < PIE *wirī, which triggers 2b LEN naturally.

[37] The derivation is PIE *wātei+es (PIE 3.i.2c i-j/u-w ALT applying as a synchronic rule) → *wātejes (2b LEN, 5 EARLY UNSTR-V) > *wāθejis (6a i-e/u-o ALT) > *wāθijis = *wāθīs (6b INFEC, 7c w-CHANGES) > *fāθ'is (8b W-F SEG DELE) > *fāθ'ī (9c LATER UNSTR-V) > OIr fáithi /fāθ'i/.

[38] The PIE antecedent here is probably the nominative plural. The original acc pl *wātins would have resulted in OIr **fáith **/fāθ'/.

[39] The derivation is *wāti+ōm (PIE 3.1.2c i-j/u-w ALT) → *wātjōm (2b LEN, 2c m-TO-n, 2d V̄+NASAL SHORT) > *wāθjon (5 EARLY UNSTR-V, 6b INFEC) > *wāθ'jan (7c w-CHANGES, 8b W-F SEG DELE) > *fāθ'ja (9b j-DELE, 9c LATER UNSTR-V) > OIr fáithe /fāθ'e/.

[40] The PIE antecedent may have been without the *-m. In either event the Old Irish form would be muir /mur'/.

[41] The derivation is *mori-ā (PIE 3.1.2c i-j/u-w ALT applying synchronically) → *morjā (6a i-e/u-o ALT) > *murjā (6b INFEC) > *mur'jā (8b W-F SEG DELE not applying because of the presence of /j/, then 9b j-DELE) > *mur'ā (9c LATER UNSTR-V) > OIr muire /mur'e/.

[42] The Old Irish vocative is probably from the PIE nominative. The derivation is *genus (6a i-e/u-o ALT) > *ginus (6b INFEC >) *gin^{u}us (8b W-F SEG DELE) > OIr giun /gin^u/. If the antecedent were the PIE voc *genu, the ev Old Irish would be **gí **/gī/.

[43] These forms show ablaut in the ending preceding the stem vowel. The ablauting vowel could be either /e/ or /o/; in either event the Old Irish forms would be the same.

[44] This is the ending posited in Pokorny (1969: 39). It could also have been *-ō from the o-class: *gen+ō (3b ō-CHANGES) > *genū (6a i-e/u-o ALT) > *ginū (6b INFEC) > *gin^{u}ū (8b W-F SEG DELE) > OIr giun /gin^u/.

[45] The dative dual and plural may have the PIE antecedents as given; or they may have their endings from the o-class. In either instance the result in Old Irish is the same. The derivation of the dative plural is *geneub[h]im or o-class *genob[h]is (la DEASP) >*geneubim, *genobis (2b LEN) > *geneuƀim, *genoƀis (6b INFEC) > *geneuƀ'im, *genoƀ'is (8b W-F SEG DELE) > *geneuƀ', *genoƀ' (9a DIPH CHANGES) > *genōƀ', *genoƀ' (9c LATER UNSTR-V) > OIr gena(i)b /genaƀ'/ for both forms.
[46] These endings are from the i-class. (See the derivation of *wātejes 'seers' to *fāθī to OIr fáithi /fāθ'i/ in 1.3 above.) Notice that neither 6a i-e/u-o ALT nor 6b INFEC has applied here. Otherwise the nominative plural would be **gini **/gin'i/ instead of gen(a)i /geni/. Hence the i-class endings must have been added after the time of 6a i-e/u-o ALT and 6b INFEC, i.e. after about 500 AD.
[47] The PIE antecedent *d[h]worestum is that of Pokorny (1969: 33). The *-m may or may not have been present. The derivation is *d[h]worestu (la DEASP) > *dworestu (lf IRISH STRESS) *dwórestu (6b INFEC) > *dwórest[u]u (7c w-CHANGES) > *dórest[u]u (8a LATER C CL) > *dóres[u]u (8b W-F SEG DELE) > OIr dórus /dores[u]/.
[48] These endings seem to be from the i-class. The derivation of the genitive singular is *d[h]worestjous (1a DEASP, 1f IRISH STRESS) > *dwórestjous (6b INFEC) > *dwórest'jous (8a LATER C CL, 8b W-F SEG DELE) > *dóres'jou (9a DIPH CHANGES) > *dóres'jo (9b j-DELE) > *dóres'ō (9c LATER UNSTR-V) > *dóres'o (10b SYNCOPE) > OIr doirseo /dórs'o/.
[49] There seem to be two antecedents for the nominative/accusative plural. The first is u-class. Its derivation is *d[h]worestu+ā (PIE 3.1.2c i-j/u-w ALT, applying synchronically) → *d[h]worestwā (la DEASP, 1f IRISH STRESS, 6b INFEC) > *dworest[u]wā (7c w-CHANGES) > *dorest[u]ā (8a LATER C CL) > *dores[u]ā (8b W-F SEG DELE) > OIr dorus /dores[u]/. The second of these forms is from the i-class. Its derivation is *d[h]worestjā (through 6b INFEC) > *dworest'jā (7c w-CHANGES, 8a LATER C CL) > *dores'jā (no 8b W-F SEG DELE, but 9b j-DELE) > *dores'ā (9c LATER UNSTR-V) > *dóres'a (10b SYNCOPE) > OIr doirsea /dórs'a/.
[50] The derivation is *rēg+s (lb ē-TO-ī) > *rīgs (1c EARLY C CL) > *rīks (1f IRISH STRESS) > *rī́ks (8b W-F SEG DELE > OIr rí /rī́/.
[51] The derivation is *rēgm̥ (lb ē-TO-ī) > *rīgm̥ (1e SYL SON) > *rīgem (2b LEN) > *rīɡem (2c m-TO-n) > *rīɡen (5 EARLY UNSTR-V) > *rīɡin (6b INFEC) > *rīɡ'in (8b W-F SEG DELE) > OIr ríg /rīɡ'/.
[52] The derivation is *rēɡos (lb ē-TO-ī, 2b LEN, 5 EARLY UNSTR-V) > *rīɡas (no 6b INFEC, but 8b W-F SEG DELE) > OIr ríg /rīɡ/.
[53] Given our formulation of 8b W-F SEG DELE, one would expect these forms to be OIr **rí **/rī/. The /ɡ'/ was probably readded from the oblique cases.
[54] The derivation is *rēges (ev through 5 EARLY UNSTR-V) > *rīɡis (6b INFEC, 8b W-F SEG DELE) > OIr ríg /rīɡ'/.
[55] The derivation is *rēgn̥s (lb ē-TO-ī, le SYL SON) > *rīgans (2b LEN) > *rīɡans (6b INFEC not applying, but 7b VnC-TO-VC) > *rīɡēs (8b W-F SEG DELE) > *rīɡē (9c LATER UNSTR-V) > OIr ríga /rīɡa/.
[56] The derivations of these forms are similar. E.g., nom sg *trag[h]ets (la DEASP, 2b LEN) > *tRaɡets (6b INFEC) > *tRaɡ'ets (8b W-F SEG DELE) > OIr traig /tRaɡ'/.
[57] The derivations of these forms are similar. E.g., acc sg *trag[h]etm̥ and gen sg *trag[h]etos (1a DEASP, 1e SYL SON) > *tragetem, *tragetos (2b LEN) > *tRaɡeðem, *tRaɡeðos (5 EARLY UNSTR-V) > *tRaɡeðim, *tRaɡeðas (6a i-e/u-o ALT, 6b INFEC) > *tRaɡ'ið'im, *tRaɡ'eðas (8b W-F SEG DELE) > OIr traigid /tRaɡ'ið'/ and traiged /tRaɡ'eð/.
[58] These derivations are similar. E.g., dat dual *trag[h]etob[h]im (1a DEASP) > *tragetobim (2b LEN, 2c m-TO-n) > *tRaɡeðoƀin (6b INFEC) > *tRaɡ'eð[u]oƀ'in (8b W-F SEG DELE) > *tRaɡ'eð[u]oƀ' (9c LATER UNSTR-V and concomitant unrounding of /ð[u]/) > *tRaɡ'eðaƀ' (10b SYNCOPE) > OIr traigthib /tRaɡð'aƀ'/.
[59] The derivation is *g[w]ōus (2a g[w]-CHANGES) > *bōus (4 DIPH SHORT) > *bous (8b W-F SEG DELE) > *bou (9a DIPH CHANGES) > OIr bó /bō/. This word tends to go into the Vn-class (1.5.4 below): e.g. dat sing boin /bon'/ < *g[w]o+n+i.
[60] These words tend to pass into ā- and jā-class (see 1.2 above).

[61] The historically regular alternations of /θ/ vs. /θ'/ and /r/ vs. /r'/ within this paradigm are sometimes analogized out. E.g., from the PIE nom sg *patēr one would expect OIr **aithir **/aθ'ir/ instead of /aθar'/. The /θ/here comes from a form like the gen sg, the /r'/ from one like the dative singular. The respective derivations are *patr̥+os and *patr̥+i (ld p-CHANGES) > *atr̥os, *atr̥i (1e SYL SON) >*ataros, *atari (2b LEN) > *aθaros, *aθari (5 EARLY UNSTR-V) > *aθaras, *aθari (6b INFEC) > *aθaras, *aθar'i (8b W-F SEG DELE) > OIr athar /aθar/ and ath(a)ir /aθar'/.

[62] The derivation is *paterī (through 2b LEN) > *aθerī (6a i-e/u-o ALT) > *aθirī (6b INFEC) > *aθ'ir'ī (8b W-F SEG DELE) > OIr a(i)thir /aθ'ir'/.

[63] The ending here is possibly from the i-class. The derivation is *patr̥+jōm (through 2b LEN) > *aθarjōm (2c m-TO-n, 2d V̄+NASAL SHORT, 5 EARLY UNSTR-V) > *aθarjan (6b INFEC) > *aθar'jan (8b W-F SEG DELE) > *aθar'ja (9b j-DELE) > *aθar'a (9c LATER UNSTR-V) > *aθar'e (10b SYNCOPE) > *aθr'e (reformation of the consonant cluster to unpalatalized /θr/ because of unpalatalized /θ/) > OIr athra(e) /aθre/.

[64] The derivation is *swesōr (2b LEN) > *swehōr (3b ō-CHANGES) > *swehūr (6a i-e/u-o ALT) > *swihūr (7c w-CHANGES) > *sihūr (ev later loss of /h/ also by 2b LEN, 9c LATER UNSTR-V) > OIr siur.

[65] The /θar/ suffix was probably added later from other (t)Vr-class forms such as gen sg athar /aθar/ 'father'.

[66] This form has /ō/-grade ablaut vs. short /o/ in the other forms. It may or may not have had final *-n in PIE. In either case, the Old Irish would be cú /kū/.

[67] Note that in the derivation of these forms change 6a i-e/u-o ALT apparently does not apply: otherwise one would have OIr dat sg **cuin **/kun'/ instead of coin /kon'/. The forms in */ku-/ were probably analogized out on the basis of forms like the gen sg *kʷonos > OIr con where 6a i-e/u-o ALT would not have applied.

[68] The derivation is *kʷon+n̥s (1e SYL SON) > *kʷonans (7a kʷ-TO-k) > *konans (7b VnC-TO-VC) > *konēs (8b W-F SEG DELE) > *konē (9c LATER UNSTR-V) > OIr cona /kona/.

[69] The antecedent ending here may be either *-on or *-ōn. If the latter, the derivation is *bʰr̥temōn (la DEASP) > *br̥temōn (1e SYL SON) > *britemōn (lf IRISH STRESS) > * brítemōn (2b LEN) > *bRíθemōn (2d V̄+NASAL SHORT) > *bRríθemon (5 EARLY UNSTR-V) > *bRríθeman (6b INFEC) > *bRríθ'eman (8b W-F SEG DELE) > OIr brithem /bRíθ'em/.

[70] The derivations of these forms are similar to the preceding one, except that 6a i-e/u-o ALT applies to the *-on-suffix. E.g., acc sg *bʰr̥temonm̥ and gen sg *bʰr̥temonos (1a DEASP, 1e SYL SON, 2b LEN, 2c m-TO-n, 5 EARLY UNSTR-V) > *bRiθ'emonin, *bRiθ'emonas (6a i-e/u-o ALT) > *bRiθ'emunin,*bRiθ'emonas (6b INFEC) > *bRiθ'emun'in, *bRiθ'emonas (8b W-F SEG DELE) > OIr brithem(u)in /bRiθ'emun'/ and brithemon /bRiθ'emon/.

[71] The derivation is *bʰr̥temonobʰis (similar to the above, ev through 8b W-F SEG DELE) > *bRiθ'emonoƀ' (9c LATER UNSTR-V) > *bRiθ'emanaƀ' (? 10b SYNCOPE, but applying here to the third syllable) > OIr brithemn(a)ib /bRiθ'emnaƀ'/.

[72] In view of the Old Irish reflex, the PIE antecedent must have been *domentjō with no *-n on the ending. (If there had been an *-n, the Old Irish reflex would be **toimte **/domt'e/ by 2d V̄+NASAL SHORT.) Given the Old Irish form, the derivation is *domentjō (lf IRISH STRESS) > *dómentjō (3b ō-CHANGES) > *dómentjū (6b INFEC) > *dóment'jū (7b VnC-TO-VC) > *dómēt'jū (no 8b W-F SEG DELE applying here because of the /j/, then 9b j-DELE) > *dómēt'ū (9c LATER UNSTR-V) > *dómet'u (10b SYNCOPE) > OIr toimtiu /dómt'u/. (The orthography here is unusual: one would expect OIr **<doimtiu>.)

[73] The derivation of these forms is acc sg *domentjenm̥ and gen sg *domentjenos (ev through 7b VnC-TO-VC) > *dómēt'jin'in, *dómēt'jenas (8b W-F SEG DELE) > *dómēt'jin', *dómēt'jen (9b j-DELE) > *dómēt'in', *dómēt'en (10b SYNCOPE) > OIr toimtin /dómt'in'/ and toimten /dómt'en/.

[74] The antecedent forms which we posit are based mainly on those in Pokorny (1969: 43), except that where he posits the suffix *-en-, we posit *-on-. The derivation of the nominative singular is *n̥mn̥ (1e SYL SON) > *anmen (2b LEN, not applying to the /m/) > *anMen (6b INFEC) > *anM'en (8b W-F SEG DELE) > OIr ainm(m) /anM'/.

[75] The derivation is *n̥mons (le SYL SON) > *anmons (2b LEN) > *anMons (7b VnC-TO-VC) > *anMōs (8b W-F SEG DELE) > *anMō (9c LATER UNSTR-V) > OIr anm(a)e /anMe/.

[76] The derivation of the first form is nonproblematic. The second one seems to have been later and possibly the result of some sort of spontaneous reduplication to differentiate it from the nominative singular.

[77] The derivation of these two forms is identical. E.g., dat pl *n̥monob^{h}is (1a DEASP, 1e SYL SON) > *anmonobis (2b LEN, for some reason not applying to the second /n/, perhaps because of the preceding unlenited /m/) > *anMoNoƀis (ev through 8b W-F SEG DELE) > *anMoNoƀ (9c LATER UNSTR-V, but not 10b SYNCOPE, perhaps because of the phonotactically difficult consonant cluster **/nMN/) > OIr anman(n)aib /anMaNaƀ'/.

[78] This word was originally a present participle meaning 'loving (one)'. It is very possible that the intermediate /a/ was in fact long, e.g. nom sg *kar+ā+nt+s. The derivation of the nominative singular is *karants (7b VnC-TO-VC) >*karēts (8b W-F SEG DELE) > *karē (9c LATER UNSTR-V) > OIr car(a)e /kare/.

[79] The derivation is *karantm̥ (1e SYL SON) > *karantem (2c m-TO-n, 5 EARLY UNSTR-V) > *karantin (6b INFEC) > *karant'in (7b VnC-TO-VC) > *karēt'in (8b W-F SEG DELE) > *karēt' (9c LATER UNSTR-V) > OIr car(a)it /karat'/.

[80] These endings are from the i-class. The derivation of the dative plural is *karantib^{h}is (1a DEASP, 2b LEN) > *karantiƀis (6b INFEC) > *karant'iƀ'is (7b V̄+NASAL SHORT, 8b W-F SEG DELE) > *karēt'iƀ' (10b SYNCOPE) > OIr cairtib /kart'iƀ'/.

[81] The derivation is *dentom (2c m-TO-n, 5 EARLY UNSTR-V) > *dentan (7b VnC-TO-VC) > *dētan (8b W-F SEG DELE) > OIr dét /dēt/. It is possible that the PIE antecedent was *dent. But if so, one would expect OIr **dé **/dē/, unless the /dēt/ was reintroduced from other forms in the paradigm.

[82] This form has the o-grade of the Vs-suffix; the other forms, the e-grade. The derivation is *tegos (2b LEN) > *teǥos (5 EARLY UNSTR-V) > *teǥas (8b W-F SEG DELE) > OIr teg /teǥ/. This form triggers synchronic 3a ECLIP on the analogy of those neuter forms of other declensions ending in *-om.

[83] We assume the orthographic <i> indicates the palatalization of the following /-ǥ'/. The derivation is *tegesos (2b LEN) > *teǥehos (5 EARLY UNSTR-V) > *teǥehas (6b INFEC) > *teǥ'ehas (later reflex of 2b LEN: loss of /h/, 8b W-F SEG DELE) > OIr tige /teǥ'e/.

[84] These endings are from the i-class. The derivation of the dative plural is *tegesib^{h}'is (1a DEASP, 1f IRISH STRESS, 2b LEN) > *téǥihiƀis (6b INFEC) > *téǥ'ihiƀ'is (8b W-F SEG DELE) > *téǥ'ihiƀ' (later reflex of 2b LEN: loss of /h/, 10b SYNCOPE) > OIr tigib /téǥ'iƀ'/.

[85] The derivation of these forms is *poljos, *poljā, *poljom (1d p-CHANGES) > *oljos, *oljā, *oljom (2c m-TO-n, 5 EARLY UNSTR-V) > *oljas, *oljā, *oljan (6a i-e/u-o ALT) > *uljas, *uljā, *uljan (6b INFEC) > *ul'jas, *ul'jā,*ul'jan (8b W-F SEG DELE, which does not delete the vowels because of the presence of /j/) > *ul'ja, *ul'jā, *ul'jan (9b j-DELE) > *ul'a, *ul'ā, *ul'a (9c LATER UNSTR-V) > OIr uile /ul'e/ for all forms.

[86] The derivation of these forms is *matis, *matim (2b LEN) > *maθis, *maθim (ev through 6b INFEC) > *maθ'is, *maθ'in (8b W-F SEG DELE) > OIr maith /maθ'/ for all forms.

[87] The derivation of these forms is *d^{h}ub^{h}us, *d^{h}ub^{h}um (1a DEASP) > *dubus, *dubum (2b LEN) > *duƀus, *duƀum (2c m-TO-n, 6b INFEC) > *duƀ^{u}us, *duƀ^{u}un (8b W-F SEG DELE) > OIr dub /duƀ^{u}/ for all three forms.

[88] The derivation of these two forms is *tepent(s) (1d p-CHANGES) > *teent(s) = *tēnt(s) (7b VnC-TO-VC) > *tēt(s) (8b W-F SEG DELE) > OIr té /tē/.

[89] The derivation is *tepentes (1d p-CHANGES) > *tēntes (5 EARLY UNSTR-V, 6b INFEC) > *tēnt'is (7b VnC-TO-VC, 8b W-F SEG DELE) > OIr téit /tēt'/.

[90] This form is posited, not attested. Its derivation is like that of the immediately preceding except that 6b INFEC cannot apply.

[91] The noun following the equative adjective is in the accusative. The derivation is *deinitris (2b LEN) > *deiniθris (6b INFEC) > *dein'iθr'is (8b W-F SEG DELE) > *dein'iθr' (9a DIPH CHANGES) > OIr déinithir /dēn'iθr'/.

[92] The derivation is *senjōs (3b ō-CHANGES) >*senjūs (6a i-e/u-o ALT) > *sinjūs (6b INFEC) > *sin'jūs (8b W-F SEG DELE) > *sin'jū (9b j-DELE) > *sin'ū (9c LATER UNSTR-V) > OIr siniu /sin'u/.

93 The positive form of this adjective is OIr sír /sīr/ 'long' < PIE *sē+r+os. In the formation of the comparative, the /-r-/ suffix is deleted. Its derivation is *sēis (lb ē-TO-ī not applying since the /i/ follows the /ē/, but by 4 DIPH SHORT) > *seis (8b W-F SEG DELE) > *sei (9a DIPH CHANGES) > OIr sia.

94 In view of the changes 2c m-TO-n and 8b W-F SEG DELE, there must have been some sort of ending on the earlier form which protected the word-final /m/ in Old Irish. The derivation is something like this: *senism̥+ending (le SYL SON) > *senisam+ending (2b LEN) > *seniam+ending (PIE 3.1.2c i-j/u-w ALT, still applying synchronically) → *senjam+ending (6a i-e/u-o ALT) > *sinjam+ending (6b INFEC) > *sin'jam+ending (8b W-F SEG DELE) > *sin'jam (9b j-DELE) > *sin'am (9c LATER UNSTR-V) > OIr sinem /sin'em/.

95 It appears that the comparative forms did not have endings, with the possible exception of messa 'worse'. The derivation of ferr might be PIE *wer (2b LEN not applying to the /r/ because it is word-final, hence) > *weR (7c w-CHANGES) > OIr ferr /feR/.

96 The PIE antecedent must have had an ending since 2b LEN, which has to apply here, would not apply otherwise.

97 The derivation is *med^h+s+m̥+ending (la DEASP, 1c EARLY C CL) > *metsm̥+ending (le SYL SON) > *metsam+ending (8a LATER C CL) > *mesam+ending (8b W-F SEG DELE) > OIr messam /mesam/.

98 The derivation of the definite article is given under 5.2 below. That of *matei under the i-class in 1.3 above.

99 The derivation is *kom *matim (2b LEN applying to /t/, but not to the word-initial /m/) > *kom *Maθim (2c m-TO-n) > *kon *Maθin (6b INFEC) > *kon *Maθ'in (8b W-F SEG DELE) > OIr commaith /ko+Maθ'/.

100 The derivation is *dwōu (4 DIPH SHORT) > *dwou (7c w-CHANGES) > *dou (9a DIPH CHANGES) > *dō (and since this form was often unstressed, 9c LATER UNSTR-V applies) > OIr da /da/. However, when the noun does not follow the numeral, the latter can be stressed. If so, then the Old Irish forms dau /dau/ and dó /dō/ occur, where 9c LATER UNSTR-V has not applied. Occasionally the originally unstressed forms /da/ and /di/ can occur under stress. When this happens, then the phon cond synchronic version of 9d STR-V LENG applies. This produces the Old Irish forms dá /dā/ and dí /dī/.

101 The ending *-ib^{h}im seems to be from the i-class.

102 The derivation is *dwai (5 EARLY UNSTR-V applying to the unstressed dual noun ending *-ai and producing *-ī, which is then transferred to the numeral) > *dwī (7c w-CHANGES) > *dī (9c LATER UNSTR-V applying in those instances where the numeral is unstressed) > OIr di.

103 The derivation of this form is analogous to that of *d^{w}ōu as described in note 100 above. The fact that the nominative/accusative triggers 3a ECLIP in an immediately following word may be ascribable to analogy with the singular neuter forms rather than to the presence of a word-final *-m in the PIE antecedent.

104 These endings are those of the i-class.

105 The antecedent of the feminine forms is not clear, in particular with regard to the antecedent suffix *-eisor, which also occurs in '4' below. The derivation of the nominative plural is *teisores (2b LEN) > *teiores (5 EARLY UNSTR-V, 6b INFEC) > *teior'is (8b W-F SEG DELE) > *teior' (9a DIPH CHANGES)/> OIr téoir /tēor'/.

106 The masculine and feminine endings seem to be generally those of the i-class. The derivation is *k^{w}etworins (2b LEN) > *k^{w}eθworins (6b INFEC) > *k^{w}eθwor'ins (7a k^w-TO-k) >*keθwor'ins (7b VnC-TO-VC) > *keθwor'īs (7c w-CHANGES) > *keθor'īs (8b W-F SEG DELE) > *keθor'ī (9c LATER UNSTR-V) > *keθar'i (10b SYNCOPE) > OIr ce(i)thri /keθr'i/.

107 The origin of the suffix *-eisor is not clear. The derivation of the two forms is *k^{w}etweisores and *k^{w}etweisorn̥s (1e SYL SON) > *k^{w}etweisores, *k^{w}etweisorans (2b LEN) > *k^{w}eθweiores, *k^{w}eθweiorans (6b INFEC) > *k^{w}eθweior'es, *k^{w}eθweiorans (7a k^w-TO-k, 7b VnC-TO-VC) > *keθweior'es, *keweiorās (7c w-CHANGES, 8b W-F SEG DELE) > *keθeior', *keθeiorā (9a DIPH CHANGES) > *keθēor', *keθēorā (9c LATER UNSTR-V) > OIr cethéoir /keθēor'/ and cethéora /keθēora/. The occurrence of the long vowel /ē/ in the second syllable of the feminine forms may mean that these forms were stressed on that syllable, /keθḗor'/. Otherwise one would expect OIr **cetheoir **/kéθeor'/ by 9c LATER UNSTR-V.

108 The derivation of this form is *k^{w}etweisorjōm (ev through 7c W-CHANGES) > *keθeior'jan (8b W-F SEG DELE, 9a DIPH CHANGES) > *keθēor'ja (9b j-DELE, possibly depalatalization of /r'/ to /r/ after other forms in the paradigm) > OIr cethéora /keθēora/.

109 The derivation is not clear. From the PIE antecedent *k^{w}etworā, one would expect OIr **cethar^l **/keθar/ as opposed to ceth(a)ir^l /keθar'/. The palatalized /r'/ may have come from the masculine and feminine plural.

110 The derivation is *k^{w}onk^{w}e (6b INFEC) > *k^{w}onk'e (7a k^w-TO-k) > *konk'e (7b VnC-TO-VC) > *kōk'e (8b W-F SEG DELE) > OIr cóik /kōk'/.

111 When the head noun in the construction was in the genitive, the numerals ‘5’ and ‘6’ trigger 3a ECLIP: cóic^n ‘5’ and sé^n ‘6’.

112 The derivation is *séks (8b W-F SEG DELE) > *sé (9d STR-V LENG) > OIr sé /sḗ/.

113 See note 111 above.

114 These numerals trigger 3a ECLIP. The antecedent suffix of ‘7’, ‘8’ and perhaps ‘9’ seems to have been *-ōm, which probably represents a conflation of the suffixes on earlier *okt-ō and *sept-m̥. The pre-Old Irish form was not *septm̥: if it had been, the Old Irish form would be **seicht^n **/sext'/ instead of secht^n /sext/. The derivation of ‘7’ is *septōm (1d p-CHANGES) > *sextōm (2c m-TO-n, 2d V̄+NASAL SHORT) > *sexton (5 EARLY UNSTR-V) > *sextan (to which 6b INFEC cannot apply, but 8b W-F SEG DELE) > OIr secht^n /sext/. The derivation of ‘10’ is analogous: *dekm̥ (le SYL SON) > *dekem (2b LEN) > *dexem (ev through 6b INFEC) > *dex'in (8b W-F SEG DELE) > OIr deich^n /dex'/.

115 There is a genitive of ‘10’ attested: it is déec /dḗek/. Its derivation seems to be *dwei ‘2’ plus an early form of ‘5’ in the dual genitive *penk^{w}ou ‘2 fives’ = ‘10’ (considered as a single word) > *dweipenk^{w}ou (1d p-CHANGES, 1f IRISH STRESS) > *dwéienk^{w}ou (5 EARLY UNSTR-V, 7a k^w-TO-k) > *dwéienkau (7b VnC-TO-VC) > *dwéiēkau (7c W-CHANGES, 8b W-F SEG DELE) > *déiēk (9a DIPH CHANGES) > *dḗēk (9c LATER UNSTR-V) > OIr déec /dḗek/.

116 These forms are all Vnt-class masculine nouns. The numeral ‘20’ has the Ø-grade of the *-kVnt suffix; the other numerals have the o-grade.

117 The derivation is *wikn̥ts (1e SYL SON) > *wikents (2b LEN) > *wixents (6b INFEC) > *wix'ents (7b VnC-TO-VC) > *wix'ēts (7c W-CHANGES) > *fix'ēts (8b W-F SEG DELE) > *fix'ē (9c LATER UNSTR-V) > OIr fiche /fix'e/.

118 The derivation is *trikonts (generally the same rules as above, ev through 7b VnC-TO-VC) > *tRixōts (8b W-F SEG DELE, 9c LATER UNSTR-V) > OIr tricha /tRixa/.

119 The derivation is *k^{w}onk^{w}ekonts (ev through 7b VnC-TO-VC) > *kōk'exōts (8b W-F SEG DELE) > *kōk'exo (9c LATER UNSTR-V) > *kōk'exa (10b SYNCOPE) > *kōk'xa (restructuring of /k'x/ to the phonotactically regular /k'/) > OIr cóica /kōk'a/.

120 The derivation is *seskonts (7b VnC-TO-VC) > *sekskōts (8a LATER C CL) > *seskōts (8b W-F SEG DELE) > *seskō (9c LATER UNSTR-V) > OIr sesca /seska/.

121 The derivation of these two forms is *septōmokonts and *neukonts (ld p-CHANGES, 1f IRISH STRESS) > *séxtōmokonts, *néukonts (2b LEN, which also voices the /x/ from /k/ in the first form since it is preceded by an unstressed vowel) > *séxtōmog̱onts, *néuxonts (7b VnC-TO-VC) > *séxtōmog̱ōts, *néuxōts (8b W-F SEG DELE) > *séxtōmog̱ō, *neuxō (9a DIPH CHANGES 1, but 2 not applying possibly because the numeral was not under primary stress) > *séxtōmog̱ō, *nṓxō (9c LATER UNSTR-V) > *séxtomog̱a, *nṓxa (10b SYNCOPE) > OIr sechtmoga /séxtmog̱a/ and nócha /nṓxa/.

122 Since the /tN/ sequence does not palatalize by 6b INFEC, we assume that the following vowel in the PIE antecedent was +back. The derivation is *kentnojos (2b LEN not applying, ev through 7b VnC-TO-VC) > *kētNojas (8b W-F SEG DELE) > *kētNoja (9b j-DELE) > *kētNoa (9c LATER UNSTR-V) > *kētNoe (10b SYNCOPE) > OIr cétn(a)e /kētNe/.

123 The derivation is *trist (8a LATER C CL) > OIr triss /tris/.

124 The derivation is *k^{w}etworomotos (2b LEN) > *k^{w}eθworomoðos (5 EARLY UNSTR-V, 7a k^w-TO-k, 7c W-CHANGES) > *keθoromoðas (8b W-F SEG DELE, 9c LATER UNSTR-V) > *keθaramað (10b SYNCOPE) > OIr cethramad /keθramað/.

[125] The derivation is *septōmotos (1d p-CHANGES, 2b LEN) > *sextōmoðos (8b W-F SEG DELE, 9c LATER UNSTR-V) > *sextamað (10b SYNCOPE) > OIr sechtmad /sextmað/.

[126] The derivation is *med (1f IRISH STRESS) > *méd (8b W-F SEG DELE) > *mé (9d STR-V LENG) > OIr mé /mē/.

[127] This form triggers 2b LEN in the following morpheme. E.g., OIr ni+m+charat = 'not' + 'me'+ 'they like' = 'they do not like me' in which lenited charat/xarat/ occurs instead of the usual carat /karat/. The derivation is *ni##mē##karānt (2b LEN) > *ni##mē##xarānt (7b VnC-TO-VC) > *ni##mē##xarāt (8b W-F SEG DELE applying to *mē from those instances where it occurred as a word-final suffix as in *do+mē 'to me', restructuring of the sequence as a single word) > *nimxarāt (9c LATER UNSTR-V) > OIr nimcharat /nimxarat/.

[128] The antecedent is not clear. A possible derivation is *n̥s+oi = oblique plural of 'us' + nominative plural masculine ending (1e SYL SON) > *ansoi (no 2b LEN, but 5 EARLY UNSTR-V) > *aNsī (? loss of /a/, possibly from infix or suffix forms) > *Nsī (restructuring of word-initial /Ns/ to the phonotactically acceptable /sN/) > OIr sní /sNī/.

[129] The antecedent is not clear. A possibility is that the independent form *sN described above was used as an infix and a suffix. The derivation is *V+sN (2b LEN applying as a synchronic rule to /s/ but not to /N/) → OIr -nn- /-N-/.

[130] The derivation of this form is analogous to that of *mē described above.

[131] The antecedent is not clear. A possible derivation is *s+w+oi = demonstrative + 'you' + nominative plural masculine (5 EARLY UNSTR-V) > *swī (7c w-CHANGES) > OIr sí /sī/.

[132] The antecedent is not clear: it may have been the PIE 2nd pl pronoun *wVs. A possible derivation of the suffix is *-V##wVs## (7c w-CHANGES) > *-V##fVs## (restructuring of the sequence as a single word) > *-VfVs (? voicing of the now intervocalic /f/, which otherwise does not occur between vowels) > *-VƀVs (8b W-F SEG DELE) > OIr -b/ƀ/. The suffix form was then used as an infix.

[133] The antecedent seems to be the e-grade ablaut of the PIE demonstrative *i-. The derivation is *eis (8b W-F SEG DELE) > *ei (9a DIPH CHANGES, part 1 applying, but not part 2, perhaps because the form was often unstressed) > OIr hé /ē/.

[134] The Old Irish infix can be either /a/ or Ø. In either event, 3a ECLIP applies to the following segment in the word. E.g., OIr niagarat = /ni+a+garat/ as well as nigarat /ni-i-garat/ 'they do not like him'. The usual form of the verb is karat /karat/ 'they like'. The derivation is *-C##eim##C- (2c m-TO-n) > *-C##ein##C- (3a ECLIP) > *-C##ein^{n}##C- (8b W-F SEG DELE) > *-C##ei^{n}##C- (9a DIPH CHANGES) > *-C##ē^{n}##C- (restructuring of the sequence as a single word) > *-Cē^{n}C- (9c LATER UNSTR-V) > OIr –a^{n}-. The OIr –Ø^{n}- infix may have arisen after a preceding vowel, i.e. in the environment *-V##eim##C-.

[135] The antecedent of both these forms seems to have been the neuter pronoun *id plus a particle *-ā. The neuter infix -a- or -Ø- may have arisen from *-ā without *id. Both -a- and -Ø- trigger 2b LEN. E.g., OIr niacharat or nicharat 'they do not like it' vs. carat 'they like'.

[136] The infix -s- triggers 3a ECLIP. If the antecedent was in fact *sōns, one would not expect ECLIP to apply. The fact that it applies may result from analogy with the masculine and feminine singular infixes, which do trigger ECLIP through regular historical development.

[137] Respective examples of these suffixes are OIr beirthius /berð'is^{u}/ 'he carries them', OIr díib /dīiƀ'/ 'from them' and OIr etarru /etaRu/ 'between them'. Their respective derivations are as follows: *b^{h}ereti##sōns 'he carries them' (1a DEASP, 1f IRISH STRESS) > *béreti##sōns (2b LEN) > *béreði##sōns (3b ō-CHANGES) > *béreði##sūns (restructuring of the sequence as a single word, then 6b INFEC) > *béreð'is^{u}ūns (8b W-F SEG DELE) > *béreð'is^{u}ū (10b SYNCOPE) > *bérð'is^{u}ū (? loss of word-final /u/) > OIr beirthius /bérð'is^{u}/. Also *dē##sib^{h}is 'from them' (1a DEASP, 1b ē-TO-ī, restructuring of the sequence as a single word) > *dīsiƀis (2b LEN, 6b INFEC) > *díiƀ'is (8b W-F SEG DELE) > OIr díib /dīiƀ'/. Finally, *entr̥##sōns 'between them' (1e SYL SON) >*entar##sōns (2b LEN affecting word-initial /s/ on analogy with those instances where a vowel precedes, then deletion of the word boundary) > *entaRōns (3b ō-CHANGES , 7b VnC-TO-VC) > *etaRūs (8b W-F SEG DELE) > *etaRū (9c LATER UNSTR-V) > OIr etarru /etaRu/.

138 The /u/ in /mu(ī)/ is possibly from *tu. The *-ī in the sg forms is the o-class genitive singular ending.
139 The derivation is *esjo (2b LEN) > *ejo (5 EARLY UNSTR-V) > *eja (9b j-DELE) > *ea (? assimilation) > *aa =*ā (9c LATER UNSTR-V) > OIr a, to which the genitive singular ending *-ī could be added, producing aí /aī/.
140 The *-ōm in these forms is the genitive plural ending.
141 The derivation is *sem+d+os (PIE 3.1.2d NASAL ASSIM applying synchronically) → *sendos (2b LEN applying to word-initial /s/) > *eNdos (6a i-e/u-o ALT applying where the ending has a +high vowel, ev) > *iNdas (8b W-F SEG DELE) > OIr in(t) /iNd/.
142 The forms with lenited /n/may have had antecedents without *d, which inhibited the application of 2b LEN.
143 The unlenited /N/ in these forms may have been introduced from the forms with /d/.
144 The derivation is *k^weis (7a k^w-TO-k) > *keis (8b W-F SEG DELE) > *kei (9a DIPH CHANGES) > OIr cia /kia/.
145 The antecedent consists of the stem *k^wi- plus the neuter ending *-d plus the particle *-ā.
146 The derivation is *k^wok^wī (2b LEN) > *k^wox^wī (6b INFEC) > *k^wox^{w}'ī (7a k^w-TO-k) > *kox'ī (8b W-F SEG DELE) > OIr coich /kox'/.
147 The antecedent consists of the stem *k^wi- plus the demonstrative *d- plus the nom pl masc *-oi. The derivation is *k^wi##doi (2b LEN not applying since the /d/ is at this stage word-initial, but the sequence is then restructured as a single word) > *k^widoi (5 EARLY UNSTR-V) > *k^widī (6b INFEC, 7a k^w-TO-k) > *kid'ī (8b W-F SEG DELE) > OIr cit /kid'/.
148 There are only a singular and plural in verb inflection. Nouns in the dual take plural verb endings.
149 The passive occurs only in the 3rd person singular and plural The other persons are expressed by a verbal prefix plus the respective personal pronoun plus the 3rd person singular passive ending. E.g., OIr pres pass no+m+berar 'I am carried' = the particle 'now' plus 'me' plus 3sg pres pass 'is carried' < PIE *nu+mē+b^her+or.
150 The subjunctive is used in sentences expressing wishes such as "Long live the king." It is also used in sentences expressing propositions whose truth values are uncertain, often with the adv. bés /bēs/ 'perhaps'.
151 The conditional is sometimes called "secondary future". It is usually used in contrary-to-fact if-then sentences like "If I were rich, I'd travel."
152 The imperfect, preterite and perfect are past tenses. The imperfect denotes a repetitive event or action; the preterite, an action that is one-time. E.g., the imperfect "He used to eat fish." vs. the preterite "He ate fish once." The perfect forms are those of the preterite plus the addition of a prefix, usually ro- < PIE *pro-. There are only minor differences between the preterite and the perfect such as that the preterite rather than the perfect tends to be used in indirect speech.
153 The verbal nouns are sometimes referred to as "infinitives". They are formed variously (see 6.6).
154 The present passive participle is called the "participle of necessity" or the "gerundive".
155 Deponent (dep) verbs have passive inflections but active meanings. (See 6.1.5 below.)
156 Verbs occur in absolute (abs) and conjunct (conj) forms. The conjunct occurs when the verb has one or more adverb or pronominal prefixes; the absolute form occurs alone. Here we shall designate conjunct forms with a preceding hyphen. E.g., abs 3sg pres berid /berið'/ 'carries' < *b^hereti vs. conj -beir in as-beir /as-bér'/ 'says' < *eks-b^heret. Some verbs have special forms for relative clauses. This form is usually the conjunct or the conjunct plus a particle. E.g., beres 'he who carries' < 3sg conj *b^heret plus the relative suffix –s (see 5.3). We shall not cite the relative forms.
157 The principal classification here is weak vs. strong verb. Weak verbs are for the most part denominal or deadjectival. (E.g., the ā-class móraid 'magnifies' cited above is derived from the adj mór 'large'.) Morphologically, weak verbs are either ā-class or ī-class contingent upon the occurrence of -ā- or –ī- between the root and the inflectional ending of the antecedent form. Similarly, strong verbs are also classified according to the intermediate morpheme occurring between the verb stem and the ending. These six verb types are used to form the present indicative, imperfect indicative and present imperative paradigms. Finally, the fact that a verb belongs to one of these six classes usually says nothing about how it forms its other tenses. Thus the Old Irish verb does not have a consistent conjugational system.

158 The derivation of the absolute and conjunct forms is. *b^{h}erō (1a DEASP) > *berō (3b ō-CHANGES) > *berū (6a i-e/u-o ALT) > *birū (6b INFEC) > *bir^{u}ū (8b W-F SEG DELE which applies only to the conjunct form, perhaps because of the presence on the absolute form of enclitic pronouns such as *mē 'I', hence *birū-mē) > abs *birū vs. conj *bir^u (9c LATER UNSTR-V) > OIr abs biru vs. conj –biur /-bir^u/.

159 The derivation is *b^{h}eresi (1a DEASP) > *beresi (2b LEN) > *berehi (6a i-e/u-o ALT) > *berihi (ev loss of /h/) > *berii = *berī (retention of word-final /ī/ from forms with pronominal suffixes, 9c LATER UNSTR-V) > OIr beri.

160 The derivation is *b^{h}ereti (1a DEASP, 2b LEN) > *bereði (6a i-e/u-o ALT, 8b W-F SEG DELE) > OIr berid /berið'/.

161 The derivation is not clear. A possibility is *b^{h}eromos (1a DEASP) > *beromos (8b W-F SEG DELE) > *berom (possible addition of the 1pl suffix /-N/ plus the ending /ī/ from the indep pl /sNī/ as described in 5.1.1 above) > *beromNī (? assimilation of /mN/ to /MM/) > *beroMMī (8a LATER C CL) > *beroMī (9c LATER UNSTR-V) > *beroMi (10b SYNCOPE) > OIr berm(a)i /berMi/. Another possibility for the origin of the unlenited /M/ in this form is the 1pl present active indicative of the copulative 'be' ammi /aMi/ < *es+mos (6.8.2.1 below).

162 The derivation is *b^{h}erete (1a DEASP, 2b LEN) > *bereθe (6b INFEC) > *ber'eθ'e (8b W-F SEG DELE not applying, perhaps because of the presence of a pronominal suffix, 10b SYNCOPE) > OIr be(i)rthe /berθ'e/.

163 The derivation is *b^{h}eronti (1a DEASP) > *beronti (6b INFEC) > *beront'i (7b VnC-TO-VC) > *berot'i (8b W-F SEG DELE, 9c LATER UNSTR-V) > OIr ber(a)it /berat'/.

164 The PIE antecedents of the conjunct forms were formerly thought to have been secondary or past-tense endings. However, it is more likely that the PIE antecedents were the unmarked forms of the so-called "injunctive". (See the Sanskrit morphology 6.1.5 Present Active Injunctive.)

165 The derivation of the 2nd singular is *b^{h}eres (1a DEASP) > *beres (5 EARLY UNSTR-V) > *beris (6a i-e/u-o ALT , 6b INFEC) > *bir'is (8b W-F SEG DELE) > OIr –bir /bir'/. The 3sg /ber'/ with /e/ instead of /i/ may have been influenced by the absolute form.

166 The derivation is *b^{h}eromos (1a DEASP, 8b W-F SEG DELE) > *berom (9c LATER UNSTR-V) > OIr -beram.

167 The Old Irish forms may have been influenced by the absolute. Otherwise one would expect for 2nd and 3rd plural OIr **ber.

168 The PIE *-mi is from the athematic conjugation. The Old Irish unlenited /-M'/ instead of **/-m'/ is unexpected here. It may have been from the 1sg pres ind am /aM/ < PIE *es+mi 'am' (see 6.8.2.1 below). The derivation is *mōrāmi (2b LEN, but the lenited /m/ replaced by /M/ from *esmi 'am') > *mōrāMi (6b INFEC) > *mōrāM'i (8b W-F SEG DELE) > *mōrāM' (9c LATER UNSTR-V) > OIr mór(a)im(m) /mōraM'/.

169 A possible derivation is *mōrāsi (2b LEN) > *mōrāi (4 DIPH SHORT) > *mōrai (5 EARLY UNSTR-V) > *mōrī (6b INFEC not applying, perhaps on analogy of those forms in the paradigm where /ā/ followed /r/; 8b W-F SEG DELE not applying, possibly because of the presence of suffixed pronouns; 9c LATER UNSTR-V) > OIr móri /mōri/.

170 The derivation of these forms is like that of berm(a)i and ber(i)the 'carry' described above.

171 The derivations are abs *mōrānti vs. conj *mōrānt (6b INFEC) > *mōrānt'i vs. *mōrānt (8b W-F SEG DELE) > *mōrānt' vs. *mōrānt (7b VnC-TO-VC) > *mōrāt' vs. *mōrāt (9c LATER UNSTR-V) > OIr abs mór(a)it /mōrat'/ vs. conj –mórat /-mōrat/.

172 This form was influenced by the 2sg abs mór(a)i described above. Otherwise one would expect OIr 2sg conj **-móra.

173 The derivation is *mōrāmos (2b LEN, 8b W-F SEG DELE) > mōrām (9c LATER UNSTR-V) > OIr -móram.

174 The derivation is *steig^h+s-ō (1c EARLY C CL) > *steiksō (3b ō-CHANGES) > *steiksū (8b W-F SEG DELE not applying because of the presence of suffixed pronouns; 8a LATER C CL) > *teisū (9a DIPH CHANGES) > *tiasū (9c LATER UNSTR-V) > OIr tiasu.

175 The derivation is analogous to the preceding one. The word-final /i/ is from the present active indicative 2nd singular in 6.1.1 above.

[176] The derivation is *steig^h+s+ti (1c EARLY C CL) > *steiksti (6b INFEC) > *steikst'i (8a LATER C CL la) > *teikst'i (8a LATER C CL 1d) > *teisst'i (8a LATER C CL 2) > *teist'i (8b W-F SEG DELE) > *teis' (9a DIPH CHANGES) > OIr téis /tēs'/.

[177] The antecedents of these forms seem to have taken /ā/ from the ā-subjunctive.

[178] The palatalized /s'/ may have come from the absolute paradigm.

[179] The derivation is *b^{h}ereto (la DEASP) > *bereto (2b LEN) > *bereðo (5 EARLY UNSTR-V) > *bereða (8b W-F SEG DELE) > OIr bered /bereð/.

[180] The plural imperative forms are those of the present active indicative conjunct forms under 6.1.1 above.

[181] Regarding the long /ē/, see the derivations in footnote 217 of the ā-future in 6.5 below.

[182] The derivation is *sodj+ag+ī+ō+r (PIE 3.1.2c i-j/u-w ALT applying synchronically) → *sodjagjōr (2b LEN) > *soðjagjōr (3b ō-CHANGES) > *soðjagjūr (6a i-e/u-o ALT) > *suðjagjūr (6b INFEC) > *suð'jag'jūr (9b j-DELE) > *suð'ag'ūr (9c LATER UNSTR-V) > OIr suidigur /suð'ag'ur/.

[183] The derivation is *sodjagīter (like the preceding through 9b j-DELE) > *suð'ag'īð'er (10b SYNCOPE applying to /ī/, perhaps on the model of the derivation of the 1st singular) > OIr suidigther /suð'agð'er/.

[184] These forms ended in a palatalized /r'/. This may have arisen from an PIE mediopassive ending *-ai. E.g., 3sg *sodjagītorai (2b LEN) >*soðjagīðorai (5 EARLY UNSTR-V) > *soðjagīdorī (6a i-e/u-o ALT, 6b INFEC) > *suð'jag'īðor'ī (8b W-F SEG DELE) > *suð'jag'īðor' (9b j-DELE, 9c LATER UNSTR-V) > OIr suidigider /suð'agiðar'/. Where we have posited an PIE *-or antecedent, one might also posit PIE *-r̥.

[185] The unlenited /M/ is from the present active indicative paradigm (see 6.1.1).

[186] The absolute forms derive from forms with the mediopassive suffix *-ai. The derivation of the 3rd plural absolute is *b^{h}erontorai (la DEASP) > *berontonai (2b LEN not applying to /t/, but 5 EARLY UNSTR-V) > *berontorī (6b INFEC, 7b VnC-TO-VC)> *berotor'ī (8b W-F SEG DELE) > *berotor' (9c LATER UNSTR-V) > *berotar' (10b SYNCOPE) > OIr bert(a)ir /bertar'/.

[187] The derivation is *med+s+ā+te+r (1c EARLY C CL) > *messāter (2b LEN) > *messāðer (8a LATER C CL) > *mesāðer (10b SYNCOPE) > *mesðer (? change of the phonotactically unusual /sð/ to /s/) > OIr –messer /-meser/.

[188] These are the only deponent pass endings in this paradigm. The others are those of the present active imperative (6.1.3). The derivation of the 2nd singular is not clear: since the word-final /e/ is retained, it may have been followed by a pronominal suffix.

[189] These are present active imperative forms.

[190] The derivation is *b^{h}erontor (la DEASP) > *berontor (5 EARLY UNSTR-V) > *berontar (7b VnC-TO-VC) > *berotar (10b SYNCOPE) > OIr bertar.

[191] The derivation of the subjunctive form and that of the corresponding indicative one result in a homophonous Old Irish form: subj *b^{h}er+ā+nn+V vs. ind *b^{h}er+o+nn+V (la DEASP) > *berānnV vs. *beronnV (2b LEN) > *berāNV vs. *beroNV (6b INFEC, 8b W-F SEG DELE) > *beraN' vs. *beroN' (9c LATER UNSTR-V) > OIr ber(a)inn /beraN'/ for both forms.

[192] The -s- is probably from a PIE aorist.

[193] The derivation is *kar+ā+s+ō (2b LEN deleting /s/, which is replaced from the 2 and 3 person forms where 2b LEN would not apply, 3b ō-CHANGES > *karāsū (6b INFEC) > *karās^{u}ū (8b W-F SEG DELE applying only to the conjunct form; the absolute form had word-final pronominal suffixes which inhibited W-F SEG DELE) > abs *karās^{u}ū vs. conj *karas^u (9c LATER UNSTR-V) > abs *karas^{u}u vs. conj *karas^u (10b SYNCOPE applying to the absolute form and analogically to the conjunct) > OIr abs carsu /karsu/ and conj –carus /-kars^u/.

[194] The derivation of the 3sg is *kari-ā+si-ti (6b INFEC) > *karāst'i (8a LATER C CL) > *karās'i (8b W-F SEG DELE) > *karas' (9c LATER UNSTR-V) > OIr car(a)is /karas'/. The derivation of the 2nd singular is analogous. The final /-ī/ is from the present active indicative (6.1.1).

[195] This preterite may be from the PIE 3rd singular asigmatic aorist, i.e. *b^{h}er+t. The -t was then re-interpreted as a preterite marker and introduced throughout the paradigm. The derivation of the absolute 3rd singular is the stem

*b[h]er- plus the preterite marker *-t- plus the *-i from the present active indicative (la DEASP) > *berti (6a i-e/u-o ALT, ev) > *biRti (6b INFEC) > *biRt'i (8b W-F SEG DELE) > OIr birt /biRt'/.

[196] The derivation is *b[h]ertes (1a DEASP, 5 EARLY UNSTR-V, ev) > *beRtis (6a i-e/u-o ALT) > *biRtis (6b INFEC) > *biRt'is (8b W-F SEG DELE) > OIr birt /biRt'/.

[197] The antecedent of this form may have been the original PIE 3rd singular asigmatic aorist *b[h]er+t.

[198] The unlenited /M/ in the Old Irish is from the present active indicative (6.1.1).

[199] The derivation is *kekone (1f IRISH STRESS) > *kékone (2b LEN) > *kéxone (5 EARLY UNSTR-V) > *kéxoni (6a i-e/u-o ALT) > *kéxuni (6b INFEC) > *kéxun'i (8b W-F SEG DELE) > OIr cechuin /kéxun'/.

[200] The palatalized consonants /M', r', t'/ in the absolute forms are ahistorical. It seems likely that on the basis of a paradigm like that of the present deponent and passive indicative (6.1.5), palatalization by 6b INFEC came to be a morph cond marker of absolute as opposed to conjunct forms.

[201] The derivation is *kekanote (1f IRISH STRESS) >*kékanote (2b LEN) > *kéxanoðe (5 EARLY UNSTR-V, 6b INFEC) > *kéxanoð'i (8b W-F SEG DELE, 9c LATER UNSTR-V) > *kéxanað' (10b SYNCOPE applying to the second syllable, which is why we assume that it was unstressed and that the stress was on the reduplicating first syllable) > OIr cechn(a)id /kéxnað'/.

[202] The ablauts here are the usual o-ō and e-ō. The derivation of OIr gád is *g[hW]ōde (1 DEASP, 2a g[w]-CHANGES > *gōde (2b LEN) > *gōðe (3b ō-CHANGES) > *gāðe (5 EARLY UNSTR-V, 6b INFEC) > *gāð'i (8b W-F SEG DELE) > OIr gád /gāð'/.

[203] The vowel alternation here cannot be PIE ablaut such as pres *wik- vs. pret. *weik-. The latter form would result in OIr **feich **/fēx'/ by 9a DIPH CHANGES. Rather, the Old Irish alternation of /i/ - /ī/ probably arose by analogy of the early short-long alternation of forms like *g[hW]od vs. *g[hW]ōd noted above. If so, the /i/ - /ī/ alternation was probably formed before the time of 3b ō-CHANGES , i.e. before about 500 AD.

[204] The derivation is *sodj+ag+ī+s+si+r (2b LEN, 6a i-e/u-o ALT) > *suðjaǥīssir (6b INFEC) > *suð'jaǥ'īss'ir (8a LATER C CL, 9b j-DELE) > *suð'ag'īs'ir (9c LATER UNSTR-V) > *suð'ag'īs'er (10b SYNCOPE, applying to the third syllable instead of the more usual second one) > OIr suidigser /suð'aǥs'er/.

[205] The derivation is *do+men+a+r (1f IRISH STRESS) > *doménar (vowel-lengthening by pseudo-ablaut of the kind described at the end of 6.3.1 above) > OIr doménar /domḗnar/. Note that if the PIE antecedent had been ablauting **do+mēn+a+r, the Old Irish would be **domínar **/domīnar/. Note also that the ending *-a, otherwise lost by 8b W-F SEG DELE, is protected by the *-r and is retained.

[206] The absolute forms were jo-/jā-class adjectives; the conjunct forms were o-/ā-class. The *-t- was the PIE perfect participle marker. The respective derivations are *b[h]r̥+t+jos and *b[h]r̥+t+os (la DEASP, le SYL SON) > *britjos, *britos (2b LEN) >*bRiθjos, *bRiθos (5 EARLY UNSTR-V) > *bRiθjas, *bRiθas (6a i-e/u-o ALT applying to the second form and analogously to the first) > *bReθjas, *bReθas (6b INFEC) > *bReθ'jas,*bReθas (8b W-F SEG DELE) > *bReθ'ja, *bReθ (9b j-DELE)> *bReθ'a, *bReθ (9c LATER UNSTR-V) > OIr brethe /bReθ'e/ and -breth /-bReθ/.

[207] The antecedent endings are either the neuter nom pl o-class *-ā or the fem nom pl ā-class *-ās. The absolute plural should be OIr **breithe **/bReθ'e/ by 6b INFEC. The nonpalatal /θ/ in brethae /bReθe/ was probably influenced by the conjunct plural form –bretha /-bReθa/ where 6b INFEC would not have applied.

[208] The origin of the OIr /f/ and /ƀ/ future marker is not clear. If it is from an PIE *-b[h]-, the derivation of this form is *link[w]+ī+b[h]+āmi (la DEASP) > *link[w]ībāmi (2b LEN) > *link[w]īƀāmi > (6a i-e/u-o ALT applying perhaps because of other paradigmatic forms) > *lenk[w]īƀāmi (6b INFEC) > *lenk[w]'īƀām'i (7a k[w]-TO-k) > *lenk'īƀām'i (7b VnC-TO-VC) > *lēk'īƀām'i (8b W-F SEG DELE) > *lēk'īƀā (9c LATER UNSTR-V) > *lēk'īƀa (10b SYNCOPE) > *lēk'ƀa > (assimilation of –voiced and +palatal from the /k'/ to the /ƀ/, which then becomes /f'/) > OIr léicfea /lēkf'a/.

[209] The derivation is *link[w]+ī+b[h]+ō (la DEASP, 2b LEN) > *link[w]īƀō (3b ō-CHANGES) > *link[w]+ī+b[h]ū (6a i-e/u-o ALT, 6b INFEC) > *lenk[w]'īƀ[u]ū (7a k[w]-TO-k, 7b VnC-TO-VC) > *lēk'īƀ[u]ū (8b W-F SEG DELE) > *lēk[w]'īƀ[u] (9c LATER UNSTR-V, but 10b SYNCOPE not applying) > OIr léiciub /lēkiƀ[u]/.

210 The derivation is *g^{hw}i+g^{hw}od+s+ā+mi (la DEASP) > *g^{w}ig^{w}odsāmi (1c EARLY C CL) > *g^{w}ig^{w}ossāmi (1f IRISH STRESS, 2a g^{w}-CHANGES) > *gígossāmi (2b LEN) > *gígossāmi (8a LATER C CL, 8b W-F SEG DELE) > *gígosā (9c LATER UNSTR-V, 10b SYNCOPE) > OIr gigsea /gígsa/, or possibly /gíg'sa/ with /-gs'/ palatalized on the model of the 2nd or 3rd singular where palatalization occurred historically by 6b INFEC.

211 The derivation is like the preceding one. The Old Irish ending /-i/ is taken from the 2nd singular present indicative (6.1.1).

212 The derivation is *g^{hw}i+g^{hw}od+s+ti (la DEASP, 1c EARLY C CL, 1f IRISH STRESS) > *g^{w}íg^{w}osti (2a g^{w}-CHANGES, 2b LEN, 6b INFEC) > *gígost'i (8a LATER C CL) > *gígos'i (8b W-F SEG DELE) > *gígos' (10b SYNCOPE, deleting the /o/ in other forms in the paradigm and applying analogously here) > OIr gigis /gígs'/.

213 The derivation is *g^{hw}i+g^{hw}od+s+ō (la DEASP, 1c EarlyC Cl, 1f IRISH STRESS, 2a g^{w}-CHANGES) > *gígossō (2b LEN, 3b ō-CHANGES) > *gígossū (6a i-e/u-o ALT) > *gígussū (? replacement of /u/ by /i/ because of the word-initial stressed /i/) > *gígissū (6b INFEC) > *gígiss^{u}ū (8a LATER C CL, 8b W-F SEG DELE) > OIr –gigius /-gígis^{u}/.

214 The derivation is *g^{hw}i+g^{hw}od+s+s (1a DEASP, 1c EARLY C CL, 1f IRISH STRESS, 2a g^{w}-CHANGES) > *gígosss (2b LEN, 5 EARLY UNSTR-V) > *gígasss (8b W-F SEG DELE possibly applying only to /ss/ here) > *gígas (ev) > OIr -gigis /-gígas'/. The palatalized word-final /s'/ may have arisen on analogy with the absolute forms.

215 The derivation is *g^{hw}i+g^{hw}od+s+t (1a DEASP, 1c EARLY C CL, 1f IRISH STRESS, 2a g^{w}-CHANGES) > *gígost (2b LEN, 5 EARLY UNSTR-V) > *gígast (8b W-F SEG DELE) > *gig (? palatalization of the word-final consonant on analogy with the absolute form) > OIr -gig /-gíg'/.

216 The reduplications in /e/ are from earlier /i/. The derivation of this form is *ki+kan+ā+t (1f IRISH STRESS, 2b LEN) > *kíxanāt (6a i-e/u-o ALT) > *kéxanāt (8b W-F SEG DELE) > *kéxanā (9c LATER UNSTR-V) > *kéxana (10b SYNCOPE) > OIr –cechna /-kéxna/.

217 We cite in this connection the 3sg pres ind celid /kelið'/ 'hides'. Its derivation is *kel+eti (ev) > OIr celid. The antecedent of the 3rd singular future is the reduplicated Ø-grade ablaut of the root. The derivation is *ki+kl+ā+ti (1f IRISH STRESS, 2b LEN) > *kíxlāði (6a i-e/u-o ALT) > *kéxlāði (6b INFEC) > *kéxlāð'i (8b W-F SEG DELE) > *kexlāð' (9c LATER UNSTR-V) > *kéxlað' (l0a OBSTR+SON DELE) > OIr cél(a)id /kḗlað'/. On occasion the new root vowel /ē/ becomes a marker for ā-future verbs where it did not occur historically. E.g., OIr ā-future 3sg abs béraid /bērað'/ 'will carry' < PIE *b^{h}er+āti. (The pres 3sg ind is berid < PIE *b^{h}er+eti.)

218 This is a deponent verb in the conjunct form. Its derivation is *kor+je+tor (2b LEN) > *korjeθor (5 EARLY UNSTR-V) > *korjeθar (6a i-e/u-o ALT) > *kurjeθar (9b j-DELE) > OIr -cuirethar /-kureθar/.

219 From the antecedent *sod+eti one would expect OIr **so(i)did **/soðið'/, not sa(i)did, presumably for /saðið'/. The reason for the root in /a/ is not clear.

220 The derivation is *kengi-eti (2b LEN) >*keNgeði (6a i-e/u-o ALT) > *kiNgiði (6b INFEC) > *kiNg'ið'i (8b W-F SEG DELE) > OIr cingid /kiNgið'/.

221 The derivation is *keg+m+n̥ (le SYL SON) > *kegmen (2b LEN)> *kegMen (6b INFEC) > *kegM'en (8b W-F SEG DELE) > *kegM' (l0a OBSTR+SON DELE) > OIr céimm /kēM'/.

222 The OIr gním may have represented /gNīm^{u}/ with rounded /m^{u}/ by 6b INFEC. One would also expect orthographic **<gníum>.

223 The derivation is *sek^{w}+em+ā (2b LEN) > *sex^{w}emā (7a k^{w}-TO-k) > sexemā (8b W-F SEG DELE with the /m/ retained, probably on analogy with the oblique cases) > OIr sechem / sexem/.

224 The derivation is *porg+on+ā (ld p-CHANGES) > *orgonā (2b LEN) > *oRgonā (8b W-F SEG DELE, with the /n/ retained from the oblique cases) > OIr /oRgon/.

225 The derivation is *ag+n+is (2b LEN) > *agNis (6b INFEC) > *agN'is (8b W-F SEG DELE) > *agN' (10a OBSTR+SON DELE) > áin /āN'/.

226 The derivation of these forms is *b^{h}r̥+t+ā and *b^{h}r̥+t+is (la DEASP, le SYL SON) > *britā, *britis (2b LEN, 6a i-e/u-o ALT) > bReθa, *bRiθis (6b INFEC) > *bReθa,*bRiθ'is (8b W-F SEG DELE) > OIr breth /bReθ/ and brith /bRiθ'/.

[227] The derivation of the verb is *do+mon+je+tor (1f IRISH STRESS) > *domónjetor (2b LEN, 6b INFEC, 9b j-DELE) > *domón'eθor (9c LATER UNSTR-V) > OIr domoinethar /do+món'eθar/. The derivation of the noun is similar, except that 1f IRISH STRESS accents the first syllable to produce *dómentjō to which 10b SYNCOPE eventually applies to produce OIr toimtiu /dómt'u/. (See the derivation under1.5.4.)

[228] This verb is a perfect conjunct with the prefix ro- < *pro-. It meant originally 'has seen' and then came to mean 'now knows'. It is constructed from the root plus the s-preterite morpheme plus the present indicative deponent ending *-torai. The derivation is *wid+s+tor+ai (1c EARLY C CL) > *witstorai (5 EARLY UNSTR-V) > *witstorī (6b INFEC) > *witstor'ī (7c w-CHANGES) > *fitstor'ī (8a LATER C CL: ld, whereby /tst/ > /ttt/, then 8a LATER C CL: 2, whereby /ttt/ > /t/) > *fitor'ī (8b W-F SEG DELE) >*fitor' (9c LATER UNSTR-V) > OIr -fitir /-fitar'/.

[229] The derivations are *mr̥+n+eti and *mr̥+t+om (le SYL SON, for some reason producing both /ar/ and /ra/) > *marneti, *mratom (2b LEN, 2c m-TO-n) > *marNeði, *mRaθon (5 EARLY UNSTR-V, 6a i-e/u-o ALT) > *marNiði, *mRaθan (6b INFEC, 8b W-F SEG DELE) > OIr mairnid /marN'ið'/ and mrath /mRaθ/.

[230] The derivation is *kl̥+t+jos (le SYL SON) >*klitjos (2b LEN, 5 EARLY UNSTR-V) > *kLiθjas (6b INFEC, 8b W-F SEG DELE) > *kLiθ'ja (9b j-DELE) > *kLiθ'a (9c LATER UNSTR-V) > OIr clithe /kLiθ'e/. The antecedent *-t- in these forms is a PIE perfect passive participle formative.

[231] The antecedent *-āi may have been an ā-class dative singular feminine ending (see 1.2 above). The derivation of this form is *kl̥+teu+āi (3.1.2c PIE i-j/u-w ALT) → *kl̥tewāi (le SYL SON, 2b LEN) > *kLiθewāi (4 DIPH SHORT, 5 EARLY UNSTR-V) > *kLiθewī (6a i-e/u-o ALT) > *kLeθewī (6b INFEC) > *kLeθ'ewī (7c w-CHANGES) > * kLeθ'e+i (9c LATER UNSTR-V) > *kLeθ'e+i (10b SYNCOPE) > OIr clethi /kLeθ'i/.

[232] The derivation is *b^{h}ē+ō (la DEASP, lb ē-TO-ī-)> *bīō (3b ō-CHANGES) > *bīū (9c LATER UNSTR-V) > OIr bíuu /bīu/. The derivations of the endings in this paradigm are like those of the present active in 6.1 above.

[233] The two derivations are first *stā+ō (3b ō-CHANGES) > *stāū (8a LATER C CL) > *tāū (9c LATER UNSTR-V) > OIr -táu /-tāu/. The second derivation is *stā+ō (3b ō-CHANGES) > *stāū (4 DIPH SHORT) > *staū (? adjustment of the unusual diphthong /āu/ to /au/) > *stau (8a LATER C CL) > *tau (9a DIPH CHANGES)> OIr -tó /-tō/.

[234] The origin of the short /e/ (as well as the long /ē/ > OIr /ī/) in the antecedent forms is not clear. This antecedent /e(:)/ may have been from the PIE root *e(:)s 'be' (which occurs in the copulative 'be' in 6.8.2 below).

[235] The conjunct forms are constructed from the root *b^{h}e- plus the subjunctive conjunct endings in 6.1.2 above. The derivation of this form is *b^{h}e+t (la DEASP, 1f IRISH STRESS) > *bét (8b W-F SEG DELE) > *bé (9d STR-V LENG) > OIr bé /bē/.

[236] The preterite endings seem to have been added directly to the root *b^{h}-. The derivation of this form is *b^{h}+a (1a DEASP, 1f IRISH STRESS) > *bá (9d STR-V LENG) > OIr -bá /-bā/.

[237] The derivation is unclear. It may have been as follows: *b^{h}+ta (? deletion of /t/ from the phonotactically impossible consonant cluster) > *b^{h}a (ev as in the preceding derivation) > OIr –bá /-bā́/.

[238] In the derivation of these forms, the basic root may have been considered *bā́-, to which the respective endings were added.

[239] The unlenited /M/ here is probably from the present active indicative as derived in 6.l.1 above plus the preterite ending /-ar/ as in –cechnammar 'sang' /-kexnaMar/ in 6.3.1.

[240] The derivation of these forms is *es+mi and *es+mos (2b LEN) > *eMi, *eMos (ev with the 1st plural ending derived from a suffixed pronoun as described under 6.1.1 above) > *eM, *eMi (9c LATER UNSTR-V) > OIr am /aM/ and ammi /aMi/.

[241] The /t/ in the Old Irish form is from the pronoun *tu.

[242] The derivation is *es+ti (6a i-e/u-o ALT) > *isti (8b W-F SEG DELE) > OIr is.

[243] The derivation is *es+ete (2b LEN) > *eeðe =*ēðe (5 EARLY UNSTR-V) > *ēði (addition of the 2nd plural pronoun /ƀ/ under 5.1.2) > *ēðiƀ (since the form was usually unstressed, 9c LATER UNSTR-V 1 applies) > *eðiƀ (9c LATER UNSTR-V 2) > OIr adib /aðiƀ/.

[244] The antecedent may have been the ablaut variant *s+onti. In either event the /s/ was lost by 2b LEN. The remaining derivation is like that of OIr ber(a)it /berat'/ 'carry' under 6.1.1.

[245] The copulative 'be' is the only verb which can trigger 2b LEN in a following word. The only triggers for it are the indicated conjunct forms. Exactly why these forms cause LEN is not clear.

[246] The antecedent of this form seems to have lacked the expected verb *stāt. Otherwise one would expect OIr **nitá. Hence the derivation may have been *ni (9d STR-V LENG) > OIr ní /nī́/.

[247] The verb here is not clear. The ending is a 3rd plural preterite. Lehmann and Lehmann (1975: 5) consider it a form of the verb < do+icc > 'comes'.

[248] The spelling of these forms does not reflect the application of 2b LEN. Although we transcribe them in their lenited forms, it is possible that the rule applied on occasion optionally.

[249] Historically the Vn-class genitive singular did not trigger 2b LEN. Here it is triggered in the following word /xēdNa/ (usually /kēdNa/) on the analogy of the genitive singular of other nouns such as those of the o-class.

Chapter 6

Old Church Slavic

I Introduction

The earliest attested language of the Balto-Slavic group is the South Slavic language Old Church Slavic (OCSlav), which is sometimes referred to as Old Bulgarian in the literature. The earliest home of the Slavic peoples seems to have been somewhere east of the Carpathian mountains and west of the Pripet Marshes. The Slavs then appear in the area of the Balkan peninsula. Before and during their advent in the Balkans, the Slavs had linguistic contact with and received numerous borrowings from other linguistic communities such as Iranian, Baltic, Greek, Latin and in particular Germanic (especially Gothic).

The Old Church Slavic language was first recorded by the brother clerics Constantine (usually known as Cyril) and Methodius at around 850 AD. These two missionaries had set out from Byzantium and proceeded into Moravia and Slovakia, where they translated portions of the New Testament into Old Church Slavic. These Old Church Slavic literary monuments were written in two alphabets, the glagolitic and the cyrillic. Here we have transliterated the Old Church Slavic language in what is for the most part the usual romanization, which we describe in our treatment of Old Church Slavic phonology in section III of this chapter.

II The Changes from PIE into Old Church Slavic

A. Overview of the Changes and their Chronology

The stages below are ordered. The changes within each stage may have been in any order or roughly simultaneous. The dates are approximate and are based on those in Shevelov (1965: 633–4). The designation "areal" means that the change spread over the Slavic area — perhaps in slightly varying versions — after the initial differentiation of the dialects.

B. The Changes

1a Deaspiration of Voiced Stops (DEASP)

Shevelov (1965: 32) considers this the first change from PIE into Slavic. It restructures the phonemic inventory and then is dropped from the grammar.

$$\begin{pmatrix} \text{C, –sonorant} \\ \text{+voiced} \\ \text{+aspirated} \end{pmatrix} \rightarrow \text{[–aspirated]}$$

That is, /b^h, d^h, g^h, g^{hw}/ → /b, d, g, g^w/

E.g., PIE 1sg pres *b^{h}erṓm ‘I carry’ (DEASP) > *berṓm (ev) > OCSlav berǫ ‘gather’; PIE nom sg *méd^{h}us ‘honey’ (ev) > OCSlav médʊ. PIE nom sg *g^{h}rómos ‘thunder’ (DEASP) > *grómos (ev) > OCSlav grómʊ; and PIE nom sg *snóigh^{w}os ‘snow’ (DEASP) > *snóig^{w}os (1f W-F SYL) > *snóig^{w}us (2b DELAB) > *snóigus (4c W-F C DELE) > *snóigu (5a e(:)/o(:)-LOW, 7b MON) > *snǣ́gu (10 V-SHORT) > OCSlav snḗgʊ.

1b Shortening of Long Diphthongs (DIPH SHORT)

This change occurs chronologically before monophthongization (7b MON) since long and short diphthongs develop identically — and quite possibly before all other Slavic vowel changes as well. DIPH SHORT restructured the morpheme structure conditions for diphthongs in the language and was then dropped from the grammar. The change is this:

[V, +long] → [–long] / ___ [V, +high]

That is, the PIE long diphthongs /āi, ēi, ōi, āu, ēu, ōu/ are shortened to /ai, ei, oi, au, eu, ou/. Note in this connection the PIE root *sēi- 'sow, sift'. It can occur either in the *sḗi+ātei 'to sow' or in the neuter noun *sḗi+tom 'sieve'. The derivations are *sḗi+ātei and *sḗi+tom (the former undergoing PIE 3.1.2c i-j/u-w ALT as a synchronic rule) > *sḗjātei and *sḗitom (DIPH SHORT) > *sḗjātei and *séitom (5 a e(:)/o(:)-LOW, 7b MON, ev) > *sǽjātī, *sī́ta (10 V-SHORT) > OCSlav sḗjati, síto.

lc The Earliest Palatalization of Velar Consonants (EARLIEST PAL)

This change restructured the phonemic inventory of the language and then dropped from the grammar. The change is very likely the same as the Sanskrit change 2a 1ST PAL, "first palatalization". In the context of Slavic we designate this change as "earliest palatalization" because in all the literature EARLIEST PAL has been ignored and the term "first palatalization" has been used to designate the later change 5b 1ST PAL given below.

EARLIEST PAL seems to have occurred in at least two stages:

(1) $\begin{pmatrix} \text{C, –sonorant} \\ \text{+back} \\ \text{–round} \end{pmatrix} \rightarrow \begin{pmatrix} \text{–back} \\ \text{+palatal} \end{pmatrix}$ / (not /s/) ___ [+sonorant]

That is, the PIE back unrounded obstruents /k, g^h, g/ — except for /k/ in /sk/ and probably /g/ in /zg/ — before any sonorant segment become the front palatal obstruents /k', g^{h}', g'/. (The PIE /g^h/ may well have been /g/ by this time by la DEASP. In the following we shall assume that la DEASP has indeed applied.)

After EARLIEST PAL 1, the following change occurs:

(2) $\begin{bmatrix} \text{k'} \\ \text{g'} \end{bmatrix} \rightarrow \begin{bmatrix} \text{s} \\ \text{z} \end{bmatrix}$

That is, the segments /k', g'/ palatalized by EARLIEST PAL 1 now become — perhaps over some intermediate stages — /s/ and /z/, respectively.

E.g., PIE nom sg fem *klṓwā 'glory' (EARLIEST PAL) > *slṓwā (ev) > OCSlav sláva; PIE nom sg fem *g^heimā́ 'winter' (la DEASP, EARLIEST PAL) > *zeimā́ (7b MON, 10 V-SHORT) > OCSlav zimá; PIE 1sg pres *weg^{h}ṓm 'I travel' (ev) > OCSlav vezǫ́; PIE *gnṓtei 'to know' (EARLIEST PAL) > *znṓtei (ev) > OCSlav znáti; PIE nom sg masc *gómb^{h}os 'tooth' (la DEASP, EARLIEST PAL) > *zómbos (1f W-F SYL, 4c W-F C DELE, 7c NASAL V, ev) > zǫ́bʊ. The EARLIEST PAL change cannot apply to the PIE nom singular feminine i-class noun *nóktis 'night' (but by 4c W-F C DELE, 8a JOTA, ev) > OCSlav nóštɪ; nor can EARLIEST PAL apply to the PIE 1sg pres *skoubṓm 'rip' (ev) > OCSlav skubǫ́.

There are numerous forms where EARLIEST PAL could have, but did not apply. E.g., PIE *klonéitei 'lean' (ev) > OCSlav kloníti (not **sloníti); PIE nom sg masc *ángulos 'corner, angle' (ev) > OCSlav *ǫ́gʊlʊ (not **ǫ́zʊlʊ); PIE nom sg fem *g^{h}ánsis 'goose' (ev) > OCSlav gǫ́sɪ (not **zǫ́sɪ). These apparent exceptions to EARLIEST PAL occur because of borrowings at various times from several IE languages (such as Germanic) which did not undergo EARLIEST PAL. We note in this connection that within the Balto-Slavic language community, pairs of cognates often occur, one of which has not undergone EARLIEST PAL (and is thus a borrowing) while the other has (and so is a native Baltic or Slavic form). For example, OCSlav kloníti 'lean' cited above has a Russian cognate sloníť' from the same PIE source which has undergone EARLIEST PAL. Similarly, OCSlav gǫ́sɪ 'goose' has a Baltic cognate in Lithuanian žąsìs which has in fact undergone EARLIEST PAL. (Hereafter whenever EARLIEST PAL does not apply in an otherwise possible derivation, we shall assume that we are dealing with an early borrowing.)

1d Syllabic Sonorant Change (SYL SON)

This change restructures various morphemes — lexical items and affixes —and then drops from the grammar.

l̥, m̥, n̥, r̥ → il, im, in, ir

E.g., PIE nom sg masc *wĺ̥k^{w}os 'wolf' (SYL SON, 2b DELAB) > *wílkos (1f W-F SYL, 4c W-F C DELE) > *wílku (9a MET, 9c w-TO-**v**) > ***v**líku (10 V-SHORT) > OCSlav **v**lɪ́kʊ. PIE *mn̥+ḗtei 'think' (SYL SON) > *minḗtei (5a e(:)/o(:)-LOW, 7b MON) > *minǣ́ti (10 V-SHORT) > OCSlav mɪnḗti. The same PIE root occurs in the i-class feminine noun *pō+mn̥+t+ís 'memory' (SYL SON) > *pōmintís (4c W-F C DELE, 5a e(:)/o(:)-LOW) >*pāmintí (7c NASAL V) > *pāmę̄tí (10 V-SHORT) > OCSlav pamętɪ́. PIE nom sg i-class *dékm̥+t+is '10' (1c EARLIEST PAL) > *désm̥tis (SYL SON) > *désimtis (4c W-F C DELE, 7c NASAL V, ev) > OCSlav désętɪ. PIE *wr̥t+ḗtei 'turn' (SYL SON) > *wirtḗtei (5a e(:)/o(:)-LOW) > *wirtǣ́tæi (7b MON) > *wirtǣ́tī (9a MET) > *writǣ́tī (9c w-TO-**v**) > ***v**ritǣ́tī (10 V-SHORT) > OCSlav **v**rɪtḗti.

In view of the above derivations, SYL SON must precede 7c NASAL V and 9a MET. A few Old Church Slavic forms occur in which SYL SON seems to have produced /u/ instead of /i/. E.g., PIE *kn̥tóm '100' (ev) > OCSlav sʊtó, where one would expect OCSlav **sętó. According to Bräuer (1961: 1, 95) this word may have been an early borrowing from Iranian.

le The Word-Stress Rule (OCS STRESS)

The nature of Proto-Slavic and Old Church Slavic word stress is disputed. For reasons which we will give directly, we assume that the earliest Proto-Slavic and Old Church Slavic word stress was a morph cond rule which was inherited in a modified version from the PIE word-stress rule. This Slavic rule remained in the grammar of Old Church Slavic as a morph cond rule. We further assume that the earlier PIE word-stress rule (3.1.2h PIE WORD STRESS in Chapter 1) is best preserved in Sanskrit and in part in Ancient Greek. In traditional terms the early Slavic morph cond rule has been described as incorporating three types of paradigmatic stress patterns. First, there are those paradigms where the stress falls consistently on the stem (Stem-stress). Second, there are those paradigms where the stress is consistently on the inflectional ending (End-stress). Third and finally, there are paradigms in which the stress alternates in morph cond environments between the stem (Stem-stress) and the inflectional ending (End-stress). This is called alternating stress (Alt-Stress).

We give the OCSlav rule below. It is morph cond: we list the environments as first (a) Nouns, Stem-stress with examples, End-stress with examples and Alt-stress with examples. (b) Adjectives, Stem-stress with examples, End-stress with examples and Alt-stress with examples. (c) Verbs, Stem-stress with examples, End-stress examples and Alt-stress with examples. Finally, (d) a brief consideration of the stress of other paradigms such as adverbs, numerals and pronouns.

V → [+stress] / in the following environments:

(a) **Nouns**

Stem-Stress

Nouns with Stem-stress seem to be lexically marked as such and do not occur in any particular gender or form class. E.g.,

(i) o-class masc sg nom PIE *b^{h}rā́tr+os 'brother', gen *b^{h}rā́tr+ōd (ev) > OCSlav brátrъ and brátra. (Note that the stress we record on our PIE antecedents is that of later, pre-Slavic PIE and reflects the stress of Old Church Slavic.)

(ii) o-class neuter sg nom PIE *móistom 'place', gen *móistōd (ev) > OCSlav mě́sto, mě́sta.

(iii) ā-class fem sg nom PIE *séilā 'strength', pl acc *séilās (ev) > OCSlav síla, síly.

(iv) Vn-class neuter sg nom PIE *sḗment 'seed', gen *sḗmen+es (ev) > OCSlav sě́mę, sě́mene. Bisyllabic stems with Stem-stress are lexically marked as taking their stress on either the first or second syllable. An example of the former is the immediately preceding. An example of the latter is the Greek borrowing korábion 'ship', which came into Slavic as the i-class masc sg nom *korábl+is (ev) > OCSlav koráblь.

End-Stress

Nouns with End-stress are lexically marked as such. E.g.,

(i) o-class masc sg nom PIE *stolós 'chair', gen *stolṓd (ev) > OCSlav stolъ́ and stolá.

(ii) o-class neuter sg nom PIE *b^{h}agistwóm 'divinity', gen *b^{h}agistwṓd (ev) > OCSlav božьstvó and božьstvá.

(iii) jā-class fem sg nom PIE *g^{h}ospodjā́ 'mistress', acc *g^{h}ospodjā́m (ev) > OCSlav gospoždá and gospoždǫ́.

(iv) i-class masc sg nom PIE *mekís 'sword', gen *mekéis (ev) > OCSlav mečí and mečí.

Alt-Stress

These nouns are lexically marked as such. The principal case configurations triggering Alt-stress (i.e., Stem-stress and End-stress) are the following five. (Here the designation "plural" includes the dual.)

(i) Stem-stress in singular, End-stress in plural. E.g., o-class masc nom sg PIE *wékeros 'evening', pl *wekerói (ev) > OCSlav véčeru and večerí. jo-class neuter nom sg *márjom 'sea', pl *marjā́ (ev) > OCSlav mórje and morjá.

(ii) Stem-stress in plural, End-stress in singular. E.g., o-class masc nom pl PIE *léistoi 'leaf', sg *leistós (ev) > OCSlav lísti and listъ́. ā-class fem nom pl PIE *g^{h}wóigzd^{h}ās 'star', sg *g^{h}woigzdā́ (ev) > OCSlav zvě́zdy and zvězdá. Vn-class neuter nom pl PIE *péikmenā 'letter', sg *peikmént (ev) > OCSlav písmena and pismę́.

(iii) Stem-stress in nom plural, End-stress otherwise. E.g., masc i-class nom pl PIE *g^{h}wózd^{h}ejes 'nail', sg *g^{h}wozdís (ev) > OCSlav gvózdьje and gvozdí. Fem ā-class nom pl PIE *klígās 'tear', sg *kligā́ (ev) > OCSlav slízy and slьzá.

(iv) Stem-stress in all singular forms and the nominative plural, End-stress otherwise. E.g., o-class masc nom sg PIE *wĺ̥k^{w}os 'wolf', nom pl *wĺ̥k^{w}oi, gen pl *wl̥k^{w}óm (ev) > OCSlav vlíkʊ, vlíki and vlɪkʊ́. i-class fem nom sg PIE *nóktis 'night', nom pl *nóktejes, acc pl *noktíns (ev) > OCSlav nóštɪ, nóštɪje and noští. Vs-class neuter nom sg PIE *ók^{w}os 'eye' , nom pl *ók^{w}esā, gen pl *ok^{w}esóm (ev) > OCSlav óko, óčesa and očesʊ́.

(v) Stem-stress in the accusative singular and nominative plural, End-stress otherwise. E.g., fem ā-class sing acc PIE *wrónkām 'hand', nom sg *wronkā́ (ev) > OCSlav rǫ́kǫ and rǫká.

(b) Adjectives

Stem-Stress

Adjectives with this stress are usually (as in (i) below) marked lexically. A few instances (as in (ii) and (iii)) of adjective Stem-stress are morphosyntactically conditioned. E.g.,

(1) Nominative sg masc PIE *prṓwos 'right', fem *prṓwā, neuter *prṓwom (ev) > OCSlav právʊ, práva, právo.

(ii) Adjectives formed with the Old Church Slavic derivative suffix -ɪsk- seem all to have had Stem-stress. An example is the nom sg masc PIE *g^{h}órd^h+isk+os 'of a city, urban' (ev) > OCSlav grádɪskʊ.

(iii) A morphosyntactic Stem-stress condition on adjectives is for the comparative and superlative forms. (According to Kiparsky 1962: 277, this was originally the case in Russian.) An example is the nom sg masc comp PIE *stā́rējis 'older' > OCSlav stárěi.

End-Stress

These adjectives are lexically marked as such. E.g., nom sg mase. PIE *kr̥nós 'black', fem *kr̥nā́ neuter *kr̥nóm, pl masc *kr̥nói (ev) > OCSlav črɪnʊ́, črɪná, črɪnó and črɪní.

Alt-Stress

These adjectives are lexically marked as such. The principal case configurations triggering Alt-stress (i.e., Stem-stress and End-stress) are these two:

(i) Stem-stress in all masculine forms, all neuter forms and in all plural short-declension forms. End-stress elsewhere. E.g., long-declension sg nom PIE *d^{h}rṓg+os+jos 'dear', short-declension masculine plural PIE *d^{h}rṓg+oi vs. short and long-declension fem sg nom *d^{h}rōg+ā́ and *d^{h}rōg+ā́+jā (ev) > OCSlav drágyi, drági vs.dragá and dragája.

(ii) Stem-stress in long-declension forms. End-stress in short-declension forms. E.g., long-declension nom sg masc PIE *wésel+os+jos 'happy' vs. short declension PIE *wesel+ós (ev) > OCSlav véselyi and veselʊ́.

(c) Verbs

Stem-Stress

Most such verbs are lexically marked. A generalization is that all 2nd-class and several 4th-class verbs have Stem-stress. (See Kiparsky 1962: 286 and 288.)

E.g., the following 2nd-class verb:

			OCS		PIE
sg	pres	1	dvígnǫ	'move'	*dwéig+n+ōm
		3	dvígnetʊ		*dwéig+n+etu
	perf	masc	dvíglʊ		*dwéig+l+os
		fem	dvígla		*dwéig+l+ā
		neuter	dvíglo		*dwéig+l+om

End-Stress

One generalization is that most 1st-class, 4th-class and 5th-class verbs take End-stress (Kiparsky 1962: passim). Many other verbs with End-stress are lexically marked.

			OCS		PIE
sg	pres	1	vezǫ́	'travel'	*weg^{h}+ṓm
		3	vezétʊ		*weg^{h}+étu
	perf	masc	vezlʊ́		*weg^{h}+l+ós
		fem	vezlá		*weg^{h}+l+ā́
		neuter	vezló		*weg^{h}+l+óm
pl		masc	vezlí		*weg^{h}+l+ói

Alt-Stress

Halle (1973: 326) notes only seven such verbs in Russian. Kiparsky (1962: 289) records several more. In any event, they are lexically marked and fairly rare in Russian. Hence, as we shall discuss in more detail directly, we assume they were also lexically marked and similarly infrequent in Proto-Slavic and in Old Church Slavic. The principal parameter for Alt-stress is End-stress in the 1st singular present indicative vs. Stem-stress otherwise. E.g.,

				OCS		PIE
Class 1	pres	sg	1	mogǫ́	'be able'	*mag^{h}+ṓm
			3	móžetʊ		*mág^{h}+etu
Class 4			1	gonǫ́	'drive'	*g^{hw}on+ṓm
			3	gónetʊ		*g^{hw}ón+etu

The perfect forms, which are formed from adjectives, take Stem-stress, End-stress or Alt-stress contingent upon their lexical specifications. E.g., nom sg masc moglʊ́ 'be able' is consistently End-stress while gónilʊ 'drive' is an Alt-stress adjective inflecting as follows:

		OCS		PIE
perf sg	masc	gónilʊ	'drive'	*g^{hw}ón+ei+l+os
	fem	gonilá		*g^{hw}on+ei+l+ā́
	neuter	gónilo		*g^{hw}ón+ei+l+om
pl	masc	gónili		*g^{hw}ón+ei+l+oi

(d) Other Paradigms

Adverbs take the stress of the corresponding nouns or adjectives from which they are derived. E.g., the comp adv PIE *óusn+jes 'better' (with Stem-stress as an adjective under b-iii above, ev) > OCSlav únje; and the genitive singular of the noun PIE *wikerṓd 'yesterday' (ev) > OCSlav vɪčerá. The stress on numerals is given in Section 4 of the morphology; and that on pronouns in Section 5. (Most of the latter had End-stress.)

Our rationale for positing the preceding early Slavic and Old Church Slavic word-stress rule is as follows. The evidence of the attested Slavic languages is this. First, some Slavic languages have phon cond stress: Czech has its word stress on the first syllable; Macedonian has it on the antepenult; and Polish has its word stress on the penult. Second, some Slavic languages have morph cond stress. Examples are Russian, Ukrainian, Bulgarian and Serbo-Croatian. Third, some few Slavic languages such as the Štokavian dialect of Serbo-Croatian have morph cond stress combined with a pitch configuration. The question arising from these data is what constituted the nature of Proto-Slavic and Old Church Slavic word stress.

We assume first that Proto-Slavic and OCSlav word stress was as given above, namely morph cond: it would seem to be a more natural development in the later Slavic languages for the phon cond stress to have replaced the morph cond stress than the other way around. The question then remains as to whether the morph cond stress of early Slavic was like that of Russian etc. or like that of Štokavian with a pitch configuration.

We begin our consideration of this matter with the observation that a stressed syllable generally evinces three phonetic traits: (a) a higher pitch, (b) a slight lengthening of the stressed vowel and (c) an increase in the loudness or amplitude of the stressed syllable. With this in mind, the first of the Slavic data which we shall turn to is the Štokavian morph cond-cum-pitch stress. The phonetics of Štokavian pitch stress have been described by Vaillant (1950: 1, 235). There are basically two kinds of pitch stress. These are rising and falling. A stressed syllable in Štokavian may have either a rising or a falling pitch.

What this means is illustrated by the following examples as cited by Vaillant:

(a)	long rising:	nom sg rúka	'hand'	[rú^{uka}]
	long falling:	acc sg rûku		[rú$_{uku}$]
(b)	short rising:	nom sg sèlo	'village'	[sé^{lo}]
	short falling:	nom pl sȅla		[sé$_{la}$]

The diacritics in the above forms are those conventionally used in the literature to describe the respective pitch configurations. Thus "ú" designates a stressed long vowel with rising or high pitch on its second mora and also on the following syllable if there is one, hence [ú^{uka}]. The "û" indicates a stressed long vowel with falling or low pitch on its second mora and also on the following syllable if there is one, hence [ú$_{uku}$]. The "è" indicates a stressed short vowel with high pitch on the following syllable [é^{lo}]; and the "ȅ" means a stressed short vowel with a low pitch on the following syllable [é$_{la}$]. Sources such as Stang (1957: 5), Tornow (1984: 72) and Carlton (1991: 186) posit the Štokavian type of stress-pitch configuration as Proto-Slavic — and as such possibly Old Church Slavic. We consider this unlikely. Rather, we take a view like that expressed in Halle (1997: 276) that the Štokavian stress-cum-pitch configuration represents a later development and did not occur in Proto-Slavic, Old Church Slavic — and certainly not in PIE .

Given our version of the Proto-Slavic and Old Church Slavic le OCS STRESS rule formulated above, we assume that the stress-cum-pitch rule of Štokavian arose from the earlier le OCS STRESS rule by a stress-retraction rule like this:

$$\underset{1}{V} \quad \underset{2}{C_0^3 \begin{pmatrix} V & \\ +\text{stress} = & \text{(a) high pitch} \\ & \text{(b) length} \\ & \text{(c) loudness} \end{pmatrix}} \rightarrow$$

$$\underset{1}{\begin{pmatrix} V & \\ +\text{stress} = & \text{(a) high pitch} \\ & \text{(b) length} \\ & \text{(c) loudness} \end{pmatrix}} \quad C_0^3 \underset{2}{\begin{pmatrix} V & \\ -\text{stress} = & \text{(a) high pitch} \\ & \text{(b) } \emptyset \\ & \text{(c) } \emptyset \end{pmatrix}}$$

That is, in the change of the three-parametrical stress consisting of (a) high pitch, (b) a lengthening of the vowel and (c) an increase in loudness or amplitude of vocal-chord vibration — the stress is retracted to the immediately preceding syllable. However, the high pitch was retained in the following syllable where the original stress had been. E.g., the following derivation of the PIE nom sg *wronkā 'hand' and acc sg *wronkām (as stressed by OCS STRESS) > later pre-Slavic PIE *wronkā́ and *wrónkām (ev) > OCSlav rǫká and rǫ́kǫ as well as the corresponding Russian forms ruká and rúku. And the same *wronkā́ and *wrónkām (by the stress retraction rule cited immediately above, ev) > Štokavian rúka and rûky.

The following correspondence thus holds between Štokavian and Russian (and presumably Old Church Slavic) cognates: whenever a Štokavian word occurs with falling stress, the Russian (and Old Church Slavic) cognate has the stress on that syllable; and whenever a Štokavian word has rising stress, the Russian (and Old Church Slavic) word retains the original stress on the following syllable.

Later PIE		**OCS**	**Russian**	**Štokavian**
(a) *wronkā́	'hand'	rǫká	ruká	rúka
*wrónkām		rǫ́kǫ	rúku	rûku
(b) *selóm	'village'	seló	seló	sèlo
*sélā		séla	séla	sȅla

We emphasize that the OCSlav words are not attested with marked stress. We have considered as the pre-Slavic later PIE, Proto-Slavic and Old Church Slavic word stress that which is for the most part still reflected in Russian, Bulgarian and the other Slavic languages which have morph cond word stress.

1f Changes in Word-Final Syllables (W-F SYL)

There are two such chronologically ordered changes. The first restructures various word-final syllables and then is dropped from the grammar. The second remains as a morph cond rule, the application of which we illustrate below.

(1) o → u / ___ { m / n(t)s / s } ##

ō → ū / ___ n ##

(2) in(t)s → īs / ___ ##

un(t)s → ūs

That is, (1) short /o/ becomes /u/ in word-final syllables ending in /m/, /ns/, /nts/ or /s/. And long /ō/ becomes /ū/ in a word-final syllable ending in /n/. (2) Word-final /ins/ or /ints/ and /uns/ or /unts/ become /īs/ and /ūs/ respectively.

E.g., PIE acc sg masc *wĺ̥kʷom 'wolf' (1d SYL SON) > *wílkʷom (1f W-F SYL) > *wílkʷum (2b DELAB, 4c W-F C DELE) > *wílku (9a MET, 9c w-TO-v, 10 V-SHORT) > OCSlav vlíkʊ. The nominative singular is PIE *wĺ̥kʷos (ev) > OCSlav vlíkʊ. (In this derivation either the W-F SYL change applied before /s/, or the Old Church Slavic form was taken from the accusative singular.) PIE acc pl *wl̥kʷóns (1d SYL SON, 2b DELAB) > *wilkóns (W-F SYL 1) > *wilkúns (W-F SYL 2) > *wilkū́s (4c W-F C DELE) > *wilkū́ (9a MET) > *wlikū́ (9b ū-TO-ȳ, 9c w-TO-v) > *vlikȳ́ (10 V-SHORT) > OCSlav vlɪký. PIE nom sg *ákmōn 'stone' (W-F SYL 1) > *ákmūn (4c W-F C DELE) > *ákmū (9a MET) > *kā́mū (9b ū-TO-ȳ) > *kā́mȳ (10 V-SHORT) > OCSlav kámy. PIE nom sg masc pres act part *bʰer+ónt+s 'carrying' (la DEASP) >*herónts (W-F SYL 1) > *berúnts (W-F SYL 2) > *berū́s (4c W-F C DELE) > *berū́ (9b ū-TO-ȳ) > *berȳ́ (10 V-SHORT) > OCSlav berý.

W-F SYL must precede 5a e(:)/o(:)-LOW since the latter change does not affect those /o/'s which have already been changed to /u/ by W-F SYL. Furthermore, in view of the above derivations, W-F SYL must also precede 4c W-F C DELE, 7c NASAL V and 9a ū-TO-ȳ.

A restructured version of W-F SYL 2 remains as a morph cond rule in the Old Church Slavic grammar. It applies in the synchronic derivation of the present active participle. E.g., the following masculine forms:

		OCS		**PIE**
sg	nom	berý	'gathering'	*bʰerónt+s
	acc	berǫ́štɪ		*bʰerónt+m̥

(The derivation of the latter form is given in 6.9.1 Present active participle in the morphology below.)

2a Consonant-Cluster Conditions (C-CL)

The following rules are ordered as shown. The first was already in PIE. The rules under (2) are Slavic innovations. The changes C-CL 1, C-CL 2a and possibly C-CL 2d remain in the Old Church Slavic grammar as phon cond rules. The other C-CL rules, after restructuring various lexical items, are dropped from the grammar.

(1) [C, –sonorant / αvoiced] → [βvoiced] / ___ [C, –sonorant / βvoiced]

(2a) tt → st

(2b) sr → str

zr → zdr

(2c) w → Ø / (a) ## ___ l or r
(b) b ___

(2d) ts → ss

That is, (1) an obstruent cluster must be voiced if its final segment is voiced and voiceless if its final segment is voiceless. (2a, 2b, 2d) The consonant clusters are modified as indicated. (2c) /w/ is deleted (a) word-initially if followed by /l/ or /r/ and (b) if preceded by /b/.

E.g., (1) PIE nom sg fem *misdʰā́ 'reward' (la DEASP)/ > *misdā́ (C-CL 1) > *mizdā́ (10 V-SHORT) > OCSlav mɪzdá.

(2a) PIE *met+téi 'throw' vs. 1sg pres *met+ṓm (C-CL 2a applying only to the first form) > *mestéi and *metṓm (5a e(:)/o(:)-LOW) > *mæstǽi and *mætā́m (7b MON) > *mæstī́ and *mætā́m (7c NASAL V) > *mæstī́ and *mætǭ́ (10 V-SHORT) > OCSlav mestí and metǫ́. (1 and 2a) PIE *wedʰ+téi 'lead' vs. 1sg pres *wedʰ +ṓm (la DEASP) > *wedtéi and wedṓm (C-CL 1) > *wettéi and *wedṓm (C-CL 2a) > *westéi and *wedṓm (5a e(:)/o(:)-LOW, 7b MON, 7c NASAL V, 9c w-TO-v, 10 V-SHORT) > OCSlav vestí and vedǫ́.

(2b) PIE masc sg adj *ákros 'sharp' (1c EARLIEST PAL) > *ásros (1f W-F SYL) > *ásrus (C-CL 2b) > *ástrus (4c W-F C DELE) > *ástru (10 V-SHORT) > OCSlav óstrʊ. Note in this derivation the necessary sequence 1c EARLIEST PAL > C-CL.

(2c) PIE nom sg fem *wronkā́ 'hand' (C-CL 2c) > *ronkā́ (5a e(:)/o(:)-LOW) > *rankā́ (7c NASAL V) > *rǭkā́ (10 V-SHORT) > OCSlav rǫká. PIE *obʰ+wortéitei 'turn' (1a DEASP) > *obwortéitei (C-CL 2c) > obortéitei (5a e(:)/o(:)-LOW) > *abartǽitæi (7b MON) > *abartī́tī (9a MET) > *abrātī́tī (10 V-SHORT) > OCSlav obratíti.

(2d) This part of 2a C-CL may also have been the result of 4a C-CL SIMP. E.g., PIE *mū́dʰ+sl+eitei 'think' (la DEASP) > *mū́dsleitei (C-CL 1) > *mū́ssleitei (4a C-CL SIMP 2g allowing no geminate consonants) > *mū́sleitei (5a e(:)/o(:)-LOW, 7b MON) > OCSlav mýsliti.

As the result of later changes, the sequences /sr/, /wl/ (later /vl/) and /wr/ (later /vr/) — which were eliminated by C-CL — can in fact occur in Old Church Slavic. E.g., PIE nom sg fem *kerd+ā́ 'heart' (1c EARLIEST PAL) > *serdā́ (5a e(:)/o(:)-LOW) > *særdā́ (9a MET) > *srǣdā́ (to which C-CL does not apply: hence it must precede 9a MET, then 10 V-SHORT) > OCSlav srědá 'center'. PIE 1sg pres *waldṓm 'I rule'(5a e(:)/o(:)-LOW) > *waldā́m (7c NASAL V) > *waldǭ́ (9a MET) > *wlādǭ́ (to which C-CL does not apply since it has already occurred, but 9c w-TO-v does) > *vlādǭ́ (10 V-SHORT) > OCSlav vladǫ́.

2b Delabialization of Labiovelars (DELAB)

This change restructures the phonemic inventory of the language; and then the rule for it drops from the grammar.

k^w, g^w → k, g

That is, assuming that la DEASP had already applied, the PIE /$k^{(h)w}$/ and /$g^{(h)w}$/ become /k/ and /g/. E.g., PIE Vs-class nom sg neuter *kʷolós 'wheel' > *kolós (4c W-F C DELE) > OCSlav koló. (See the analogous derivation of OCSlav slóvo 'word' in the morphology under 1.5.6 below.) PIE nom sg masc *snóigʰʷos 'snow' (1a DEASP, 1f W-F SYL) > *snóigʷus (DELAB) > *snóigus (4c W-F C DELE) > *snóigu (5a e(:)/o(:)-LOW, 7b MON) > *snǣ́gu (10 V-SHORT) > OCSlav snégʊ. PIE *bʰḗgʷātei 'flee' (la DEASP) > *bḗgʷātei (DELAB) > *bḗgātei (5a e(:)/o(:)-LOW) > *bǣ́gātæi (7b MON) > *bǣ́gātī (10 V-SHORT) > OCSlav bě́gati.

DELAB must follow 1c EARLIEST PAL and must precede 5b 1ST PAL . This is evident in the following derivation: PIE nom sg fem *gʷenā́ 'woman' (to which 1c EARLIEST PAL cannot apply, but by DELAB) >

*genā́ (to which 5b 1ST PAL can now apply) > *ženā́ (10 V-SHORT) > OCSlav žená. If 1c EARLIEST PAL had applied in this derivation, the Old Church Slavic form would be **zená.

3 The "ruki" Change (RUKI)

The main Old Church Slavic reflex of this change is the addition of /x/ to the phonemic inventory of the language. Another Old Church Slavic reflex is a morph cond alternation between /x/ and /s/ in some verb paradigms. (See on this section 6.3 of the morphology.) The early form of this change is this:

s → x / k, r, i(:), u(:) ___ V

That is, /s/ becomes /x/ if immediately preceded by any of the segments /k/, /r/, /i(:)/, or /u(:)/ (hence the name for the change) and if followed by a vowel. Shevelov (1965: 127) suggests that the historical sequence of this change may have been /s/ > /š/ > /x/. This change is similar to the Sanskrit change 4a Retroflex (RETRO).

E.g., PIE 1sg aorist *rḗk+s+om 'I said' (1f W-F SYL) > *rḗksum (RUKI) > *rḗkxum (4a C-CL SIMP) > *rḗxum (4c W-F C DELE, 10 V-SHORT) > OCSlav rě́xʊ. (Note in this derivation the necessary chronology RUKI > 4a C-CL SIMP.) PIE nom sg masc *pórsos 'dust' (1f W-F SYL) > *pórsus (RUKI) > *pórxus (4c W-F C DELE) > *pórxu (5a e(:)/o(:)-LOW) > *párxu (9a MET) > *prā́xu (10 V-SHORT) > OCSlav práxʊ. (Note here the necessary chronology RUKI > 9a MET.) PIE nom sg masc *snáisos 'laughter' (1f W-F SYL) > *snáisus (RUKI) > *snáixus (4c W-F C DELE) > *snáixu (5a e(:)/o(:)-LOW, 7b MON) >*snǣ́xu (10 V-SHORT) > OCSlav sně́xʊ. (Note here the necessarychronology RUKI > 7b MON.) PIE nom sg fem *mū́sis 'mouse' (RUKI) > *mū́xis (4c W-F C DELE) > *mū́xi (5b 1ST PAL) > *mū́ši (9b ū-TO-ȳ) > *mȳ́ši (10 V-SHORT) > OCSlav mýšɪ. (Note here the necessary chronology RUKI > 5b 1ST PAL .)

RUKI does not apply to PIE nom sg masc *déksnos 'right-handed' (1f W-F SYL) > *déksnus (4a C-CL SIMP) > *désnu (10 V-SHORT) > OCSlav désnʊ. RUKI does not apply to the /s/ here to produce OCSlav **déxnʊ because the /s/ is followed by /n/, not a vowel. RUKI also does not apply in the derivation of OCSlav ósʊ 'axis'. The antecedent is *áksos, so one would expect the derivation *áksos (1f W-F SYL) > *áksus (RUKI) > *ákxus (4a C-CL SIMP) > *áxus (4c W-F C DELE) > *áxu (10 V-SHORT) > OCSlav **óxʊ, which does not occur. Rather, it seems likely that a form like *aks+os was borrowed from Greek or Latin after the time of RUKI. Hence the derivation was from borrowed *áks+us (after the RUKI change, but by 4a C-CL SIMP) > *ásus (4c W-F C DELE) > *ásu (10 V-SHORT) > OCSlav ósʊ.

As noted above, RUKI must precede 4a C-CL SIMP, 5b 1ST PAL, 7b MON and 9a MET. RUKI must also precede the second stage of 1c EARLIEST PAL. E.g., in the derivation of the PIE *pikā́tei 'mark, write' (1c EARLIEST PAL stage1) > *pik'ā́tei (3 RUKI, which cannot affect this form) > *pikā́tei (1c EARLIEST PAL stage 2) > *pisā́tei (to which RUKI having already occurred does not apply, but 7b MON) >*pisā́tī (10 V-SHORT) > OCSlav pɪsáti. If RUKI had applied, the form would be OCSlav **pɪxáti.

RUKI was no longer operative at the time various borrowings came into Slavic from Germanic. This was at about 200-300 AD. E.g., Gmc (probably Go) *kaus- 'test' occurring in the inf *káus+eitei (7b MON) > *kū́sītī (10 V-SHORT) > OCSlav kúsiti, not OCSlav **kúxiti.

The segment /x/ arising from RUKI usually occurs word-internally. But there are at least two sources for Old Church Slavic word-initial /x/. First, verbs can occur with prefixes having vowels which can trigger RUKI. E.g., the PIE *prei+sodéitei 'to come' (RUKI) > *preixodéitei (5a e(:)/o(:)-LOW, 7b MON) > *prīxadī́tī (10 V-SHORT) > OCSlav prixodíti. The same verb can also occur without the prefix as xodíti 'go'.

Second, there are Germanic borrowings in Old Church Slavic in which the Germanic word-initial /h/ is rendered as /x/. E.g., Gmc *húlm- 'hill' > *xúlm+os (1f W-F SYL, 4c W-F C DELE) > *xúlmu (10 V-SHORT) > OCSlav xʊ́lmʊ.

4a Simplification of Consonant Clusters (C-CL SIMP)

The precise conditions for C-CL SIMP are not clear. This change remains in the grammar of Old Church Slavic as a morph cond rule. In our formulation of the rule we follow the presentation of Carlton (1991: 100–8). Carlton gives the first two sets listed below of permissable word-internal consonantal (i.e., -vocalic) clusters for Proto-Slavic. (Given change 9c W-TO-v, the conditions also apply to Old Church Slavic.) We have added condition (3). These three sets may be considered ordered filters as we shall explain below.

(1) Three-segment clusters

	1	2	3
(a)	s	p	r
	z	b	r
(b)	s	t	r, w
	z	d	r, w
(c)	s	k	r, w, l
	z	g	r, w, l

(2) Two-segment clusters.

(a)	s	l, w, m, n, p, t, k
	z	l, w, m, n, b, d, g
(b)	x	r, l, w
(c)	p, b	r, l
(d)	t, d	r, l, w
(e)	k, g	r, l, w, n
(f)	l, m, n, r	any –vocalic segment
(g)	C_α	$\neq C_\alpha$ (i.e., no geminate consonants)

(3) One-segment clusters. Any single consonantal segment can occur word-internally.

That is, the above three conditions act as filters as follows: If a 3-consonant cluster does not fit condition (1), one of its segments is deleted so that it fits condition (2). If a 2-consonant cluster does not fit condition (2), the first consonant is usually deleted. Hence it will fit condition (3). (There are no 4-consonant clusters.)

E.g., (1) for inadmissible 3-consonant sequences, PIE neuter Vn-class *wértment 'turn, time' (C-CL SIMP 1 deleting /t/ since the resulting sequence /rm/ is permissible by C-CL SIMP 2) > *wérment (4c W-F C DELE) > *wérmen (5a e(:)/o(:)-LOW) > *wǽrmæn (7c NASAL V) > *wǽrmę̄ (9a MET) > *wrǣ́mę̄ (9c W-TO-v) > *vrǣ́mę̄ (10 V-SHORT) > OCSlav vrě́mę. PIE nom sg neuter *kʷeit+sl+óm 'number' (2b DELAB) > *keitslóm (C-CL SIMP 1 deleting /t/ since by C-CL 2 /sl/ is permissible, while **/tl/ or **/ts/ would not be) > *keislóm (4c W-F C DELE, 5a e(:)/o(:)-LOW) > *kæislá (5b 1ST PAL) > *čæislá (7b MON) > *čīslá (10 V-SHORT) > OCSlav čisló. PIE nom sg masc *trónktos 'guard' (1f W-F SYL) > *trónktus (C-CL SIMP 1 deleting /k/ since C-CL 2 allows /nt/) > *tróntus (4c W-F C DELE) > *tróntu (5a e(:)/o(:)-LOW, 7c NASAL V) > *trǭ́tu (10 V-SHORT) > OCSlav trǫ́tʊ. Finally nom sg fem PIE *louksnā́ 'moon' (3 RUKI) > *loukxnā́ (C-CL SIMP 1 deleting /k/, then C-CL SIMP 2 deleting /x/) > *lounā́ (5a e(:)/o(:)-LOW) > *launā́ (7b MON) > *lūnā́ (10 V-SHORT) > OCSlav luná.

(2) For inadmissible 2-consonant sequences, PIE *sups+ā́+tei 'suck' (C-CL SIMP 2) > *susā́tei (to which 3 RUKI does not apply since it has already occurred, but by 5a e(:)/o(:)-LOW and 7b MON) > *susā́tī (10 V-SHORT) > OCSlav sʊsáti. PIE nom sg masc *súpnos 'sleep' (1f W-F SYL) > *súpnus (C-CL SIMP 2) > *súnus (4c W-F C DELE) > *súnu (10 V-SHORT) > OCSlav sʊ́nʊ. PIE nom sg neuter *ū́dʰment 'udder' (la DEASP) > *ū́dment (C-CL SIMP 2) > *ū́ment (4b PROTHESIS) > *wū́ment (4c W-F C DELE, 5a e(:)/o(:)-LOW) > *wū́mæn (7c NASAL V) > *wū́mę̄ (9b ū-TO-ȳ, 9c w-TO-v) > *vȳ́mę̄ (10 V-SHORT) > OCSlav výmę. PIE *kwít+nān+tei 'shine' (lc EARLIEST PAL) > *swítnāntei (C-CL SIMP 2) > *swínāntei (7b MON) > *swínāntī (7c NASAL V) > *swínǭtī (9c w-TO-v) > *svínǭtī (10 V-SHORT) > OCSlav svínǫti.

C-CL SIMP 2 also deletes one of the consonants in a geminate cluster. E.g., the Germanic (possibly Gothic) borrowing *smakk- 'fig' > Slavic Vn-class fem *smákkōn (1f W-F SYL) > *smákkūn (C-CL SIMP 2) > *smákūn (4c W-F C DELE, 9b ū-TO-ȳ) > *smákȳ (10 V-SHORT) > OCSlav smóky. A similar development is the Germanic borrowing *skatt- 'cattle, money' > Slavic nom sg masc *skátt+us (C-CL SIMP) > *skátus (4c W-F C DELE)) *skátu (10 V-SHORT) > OCSlav skótʊ. The derivation of this form indicates that 2a C-CL CHANGES must have preceded and been dropped by the time of C-CL SIMP. Otherwise there would have been no /tt/ sequence for C-CL SIMP 2 to apply to and the Old Church Slavic form would have been **skóstʊ.

As we noted earlier, the C-CL SIMP change remains as a morph cond rule in the phonology of Old Church Slavic. It accounts for alternations such as OCSlav 1sg pres grebǫ́ 'dig' vs. the /greb+tí/ (C-CL SIMP applying synchronically) → gretí. Occasionally C-CL SIMP can apply optionally: e.g. the OCSlav /gýb+nǫti/ 'perish' → gýnǫti and gýbnǫti. Later in Old Church Slavic the C-CL SIMP rule expands its domain to exclude the clusters /dl/ and /tl/. E.g., PIE *modʰl+éitei 'ask, pray' (ev) > OCSlav molíti, but Polish modlić with the /d/ retained. The C-CL SIMP change functions with certain other changes to create open syllables, namely those with the structure C_1^nV (where C_1^n is a sequence of one or more –vocalic segments). The process of creating open syllables is an early Slavic tendency: other changes having the same effect are 4b PROTHESIS, 4c W-F C DELE, 7c NASAL V, 8a JOTA and 9a MET. (The creation of open syllables as a general Proto-Slavic tendency has been noted in several sources, e.g. Carlton 1991. It is disputed in Shevelov 1965: 203.)

The algorithm for setting syllable boundaries is this: (1) Mark the word's +vocalic segments. (2) Mark any –vocalic segment(s) which occur to the left of the +vocalic segment and which can also occur word- or morpheme-initially. These segments constitute the onset of the syllable. (3) Finally, any remaining unmarked –vocalic segments to the right of a +vocalic segment constitute the syllable-final consonants. These are in the coda of the syllable; the rime consists of the +vocalic segment(s) — which is called the syllabic nucleus — plus any syllable-final consonants.

As examples we cite the following Old Church Slavic words, the inf mestí 'throw'and the Greek borrowing tálantʊ 'talent, i.e. a sum of money'. Applying the algorithm described above, we can segment the syllables as follows. OCSlav mestí (step 1) → m[e]st[í] (step 2 applies in that both /m/ and /st/ can occur word-initially) → [me][stí]. OCSlav tálantʊ (step 1)→ t[á]l[a]nt[ʊ] (step 2, but /nt/ cannot occur word- or morpheme-initially while /t/ and /l/ can) → [tá][la]n[tʊ] (step 3) → [tá][lan][tʊ]. This word does not typify Old Church Slavic syllabification because of the occurrence of the closed syllable [lan]. The word was borrowed into OCSlav after the time of 7c NASAL V , which would have made this an open syllable and into an Old Church Slavic form **tálǫtʊ.

4b Development of "Prothetic" Consonants (PROTHESIS).

This change remains in the grammar of OCSlav as a phon cond rule. It is probably best described as a tendency or a permanently optional rule in that there are numerous exceptions to it.

$$\#\# \quad \begin{Bmatrix} [V, -round] \\ [V, +round] \end{Bmatrix} \quad \rightarrow \quad \#\# \quad \begin{Bmatrix} j & [V, -round] \\ w & [V, +round] \end{Bmatrix}$$

$$1 \quad 2 \qquad\qquad\qquad 1 \quad 3 \quad 2$$

That is, /j/ is prefixed word-initially if the word begins with a nonround vowel /a(:), e(:), i(:)/; and /w/ is prefixed before the round vowels /o(:), u(:)/.

E.g., the PIE infs *em+téi 'take' and *up+eitéi 'cry out' (PROTHESIS) > *jemtéi and *wupeitéi (5a e(:)/o(:)-LOW, 7b MON) > *jæmtī́ and *wupītī́ (7c NASAL V , 9c w-TO-v) St > *ję̄tī́ and *vupītī́ (10 V-SHORT) > OCSlav ję̨tí and vʊpití.

Some chronological considerations are these. First, PROTHESIS precedes 9c w-TO-v. We assume that our formulation of PROTHESIS is a more natural change if the prefixed segment is a +round /w/ before +round vowels as opposed to /v/, which is –round. Second, given our formulation of PROTHESIS , it must precede 5a e(:)/o(:)-LOW since by the latter change +round /o(:)/ became –round /a(:)/. Third, PROTHESIS precedes 9a MET in view of this derivation: the early Germanic borrowing *órtigard+os 'garden' as in Go aúrtigards 'orchard'(1f W-F SYL) > *órtigardus (PROTHESIS) > *wórtigardus (4c W-F C DELE) > *wórtigardu (5a e(:)/o(:)-LOW) > *wártigardu (? some sort of vowel exchange whereby á–i in the word becomes í-a) > *wírtagardu (9a MET) > *wrítagrādu (9c w-TO-v) > *vrítagrādu (10 V-SHORT) > OCSlav vrítogradʊ. In this derivation if 9a MET had applied before PROTHESIS, PROTHESIS could not have applied and the Old Church Slavic form would have been **rítogradʊ.

Fourth, the derivation is the PIE inf *ēd+téi 'eat' (2a C-CL) > *ēstéi (PROTHESIS) > *jēstéi (5a e(:)/o(:)-LOW) > *jǣstǽi (6a ǣ-TO-ā) > *jāstǽi (7b MON) > *jāstī́ (10 V-SHORT) > OCSlav jastí. In this derivation PROTHESIS must precede 6a ǣ-TO-ā since the latter change is triggered by the /j/ inserted by PROTHESIS.

Fifth, PIE nom sg neuter *áutrom 'morning' (PROTHESIS) > *jáutrom (4c W-F C DELE) > *jáutro (5a e(:)/o(:)-LOW) > *jáutra (7b MON) > *jū́tra (10 V-SHORT) > OCSlav jútro. Here PROTHESIS must apply before 7b MON. Otherwise the Old Church Slavic form would be **vútro. Sixth and finally, we cite the derivation of the PIE 1sg pres *m̥+ṓm 'I take' (1d SYL SON) > *imṓm (PROTHESIS) > *jimṓm (5a e(:)/o(:)-LOW) > *jimā́m (6b V-FRONT) > *īmā́m (7c NASAL V) > *īmǭ́ (10 V-SHORT) > Old Church Slavic imǫ́. In this derivation the chronology must be 1d SYL SON > PROTHESIS > 6b V-FRONT.

As noted above, PROTHESIS remains as a phon cond rule in the phonology of Old Church Slavic. It determines such alternations as the OCSlav ję̨tí 'take' vs. the OCSlav 1sg pres ind imǫ́ 'I take' noted above. PROTHESIS as a synchronic rule can sometimes apply optionally, as in PIE *ése 'behold' (ev) > OCSlav ése or jése. Interestingly, there seem to be no Old Church Slavic words with a word-initial /v/-Ø alternation.

4c Word-Final Consonant Deletion (W-F C DELE)

After this rule applies, various words and particularly inflectional endings are restructured. Then the rule drops from the Old Church Slavic grammar. The rule for the change is this:

C → Ø / ___ ## (but not the /m/ in V̄m##)

That is, any word-final obstruent or sonorant consonant (except for /m/ preceded by a long vowel) is deleted. E.g., PIE nom sg masc *wl̥kʷos 'wolf' (1d SYL SON, 1f W-F SYL, 2b DELAB) > *wílkus (W-F C DELE) > *wílku (9a MET, 9c w-TO-v) > *vlíku (10 V-SHORT) > OCSlav vlíkʊ. Note here the necessary chronology 1f W-F SYL > W-F C DELE. The derivation of the PIE abl sg masc (later gen sg) is *wl̥kʷōd 'wolf' (1d SYL SON, 2b DELAB) > *wílkōd (W-F C DELE) > *wílkō (5a e(:)/o(:)-LOW, 9a MET, 9c w-TO-v) > *vlíkā (10 V-SHORT) > OCSlav vlí ka.

Oddly, W-F C DELE does not apply to word-final /m/ when preceded by a long vowel. Two examples are these. First, PIE acc sg *gʷenā́m 'woman' (2d DELAB) > *genā́m (W-F C DELE not applying, but 5a e(:)/o(:)-LOW does) > *gænā́m (5b 1ST PAL) > *žænā́m (7c NASAL V) > *žænǭ́ (10 V-SHORT) > OCSlav ženǫ́. Second, the PIE 1sg pres *wegʰṓm 'I travel' (1a DEASP) > *wegṓm (1c EARLIEST PAL) > *wezṓm (W-F C DELE not applying, but 5a e(:)/o(:)-LOW does) > *wæzā́m (7c NASAL V) > *wæzǭ́ (9c w-TO-v) > væzǭ́ (10 V-SHORT) > OCSlav vezǫ́. If W-F C DELE had applied in these derivations, then the OCSlav forms would be **žená and **vezá. But consider the derivation of the PIE acc sg masc *wl̥kʷom (1a DEASP, 1d SYL SON) > *wílkom (1f W-F SYL) > *wílkum (W-F C DELE) > *wílku (9a MET) > *wlíku (9c w-TO-v) > *vlíku (10 V-SHORT) > OCSlav vlíkʊ. In this derivation W-F C DELE does apply while 7c NASAL V does not. This fact indicates the chronology W-F C DELE > 7c NASAL V.

W-F C DELE does not apply in instances of so-called enclisis. This occurs when a word (usually a preposition) attaches itself to a following word and the intervening word boundary is lost. E.g., PIE *bʰes##*bʰrā́trōd 'without a brother' (removal of the word boundary ## through enclisis) > *bʰesbʰrā́trōd (1a DEASP) > *besbrā́trōd (2a C-CL part 1) > *bezbrā́trōd (W-F C DELE) > *bezbrā́trō (5a e(:)/o(:)-LOW) > *bæzbrā́trā (10 V-SHORT) > OCSlav bez brátra.

Shevelov (1965: 224) suggests that W-F C DELE occurred in successive expansions:

(1) Before 100 BC, [C, +sonorant] → Ø / ___ ##

(2) Ca. 0 AD, [C, –sonorant, –continuant] → Ø / ___ ##

(3) Ca. 500 AD, x or s → Ø / ___ ##

5a Lowering of e(:) and o(:) (e(:)/o(:)-LOW)

This change restructured the Proto-Slavic vowel system and then dropped from the grammar.

[V, –high] → [+low, –round]

That is,

$$\begin{Bmatrix} \text{e(:)} \\ \text{o(:)} \end{Bmatrix} \rightarrow \begin{Bmatrix} \text{æ(:)} \\ \text{a(:)} \end{Bmatrix}$$

E.g., PIE nom sg masc *wétusos 'old' (1f W-F SYL) > *wétusus (3 RUKI) > *wétuxus (4c W-F C DELE) > *wétuxu (e(:)/o(:)-LOW) > *wǽtuxu (9c w-TO-v) > *vǽtuxu (10 V-SHORT) > OCSlav vétʊxʊ. PIE inf *dʰḗtei 'put' (1a DEASP) > *dḗtei (e(:)/o(:)-LOW) > *dǣ́tæi (7b MON) > *dǣ́tī (10 V-SHORT) > OCSlav dě́ti. Examples of o(:)-lowering are these: PIE Vs-class neuter nom sg *ókʷos 'eye' (2b DELAB, 4c W-F C DELE) > *óko (e(:)/o(:)-LOW) > *áka (10 V-SHORT) > OCSlav óko. PIE o-class masc nom sg *dómos 'house' (1f W-F SYL, 4c W-F C DELE) > *dómu (e(:)/o(:)-LOW) > *dámu (10 V-SHORT) > OCSlav dómʊ. PIE inf *dō+téi 'give' (e(:)/o(:)-LOW) > *dātǽi (7b MON) > *dātī́ (10 V-SHORT) > OCSlav datí.

Some sources consider /e(:)/-lowering and /o(:)/-lowering separate changes. We consider them as results of one and the same rule or process. The change may have begun as e(:)-lowering and then expanded its domain to lower /o(:)/ as well. Shevelov (1965: 157 and 164) considers e(:)-lowering and o(:)-lowering as separate but contemporaneous changes occurring around 100-0 BC.

The change e(:)/o(:)-LOW restructured the Proto-Slavic vowel system to the following:

i	u	ī	ū
æ	a	ǣ	ā
ai	au	æi	æu

5b The So-Called "First" Palatalization (1ST PAL)

This change remains as a morph cond rule in the grammar of Old Church Slavic. Although 1ST PAL is not in point of historical fact the first palatalization in Slavic (the first palatalization is 1c EARLIEST PAL), we label it "first palatalization" because that is what it is called in all the literature. The original version of the change was probably this:

$$\begin{Bmatrix} \text{C, –sonorant} \\ \text{+velar} \end{Bmatrix} \rightarrow \begin{Bmatrix} \text{–velar} \\ \text{+palatal} \end{Bmatrix} / \ \_\_\_ \ [\text{V, –back}]$$

That is, the velar obstruents /k, g, x/ (the last by 3 RUKI) are palatalized to /k', g', x'/ when followed by a front vowel /i(:), e(:)/ (or /i(:), æ(:)/ if 5a e(:)/o(:)-LOW had already applied).

The later version of the change at the time it was incorporated as a morph cond rule of Old Church Slavic was this:

$$\begin{Bmatrix} \text{k'} \\ \text{g'} \\ \text{x'} \\ \text{sk'} \\ \text{zg'} \end{Bmatrix} \rightarrow \begin{Bmatrix} \text{č} \\ \text{ž} \\ \text{š} \\ \text{št'} \\ \text{žd'} \end{Bmatrix}$$

That is, the palatalized velar obstruents /k', g', x'/ occurring singly as well as when occurring in the clusters /k'/ after /s/ and /g'/ after /z/ become /č, ž, š, št' and žd'/, respectively. (We shall write the latter two clusters as /št/ and /žd/.)

E.g., PIE nom sg fem *kerd^{h}ā́ 'herd' (la DEASP) >*kerdā́ (to which EARLIEST PAL does not apply, in our view because the word is an early borrowing from Western PIE, but 1ST PAL does apply) > *čerdā́ (9a MET, ev) > *črǣdā́ (10 V-SHORT) > OCSlav črědá. (The chronology in this derivation must be 1ST PAL > 9a MET. If the order of these two changes were reversed, 1ST PAL could not apply.) PIE inf *kreikḗtei 'scream' (5a e(:)/o(:)-LOW) > *kræikǣ́tæi (1ST PAL) > *kræičǣ́tæi (6a ǣ-TO-ā) > *kræičā́tæi (7b MON) > *krīčā́tī (10 V-SHORT) > OCSlav kričáti. (The chronology must be 1ST PAL > 6a ǣ-TO-ā. If the sequence were reversed, neither 1ST PAL nor 6a ǣ-TO-ā could apply.) The same chronology is in the derivation of PIE inf *legḗtei 'lie, recline' (5a e(:)/o(:)-LOW) > *lægǣ́tæi (1ST PAL) > *læžǣ́tæi (6a ǣ-TO-ā > *læžā́tæi (7b MON) > *læžā́tī (10 V-SHORT) > OCSlav ležáti. PIE nom sg masc *g^{w}ī́wos 'alive' (1f W-F SYL) > *g^{w}ī́wus (2b DELAB) > *gī́wus (4c W-F C DELE) > *gī́wu (1ST PAL) > *žī́wu

(9c W-TO-v) > *žī́vu (10 V-SHORT) > OCSlav žívʊ. (In this derivation 2b DELAB must precede 1ST PAL.) PIE inf *róuseitei 'destroy' (3 RUKI) > *róuxeitei (5a e(:)/o(:)-LOW) > *ráuxæitæi (1ST PAL) > *ráušæitæi (7b MON) > *rū́šītī (10 V-SHORT) > OCSlav rúšiti. (Here 3 RUKI must precede 1ST PAL.) PIE 1sg pres *aiskōm 'seek' vs. 3sg pres *aiskétu (5a e(:)/o(:)-LOW) > *aiskā́m and *aiskǽtu (1ST PAL applying to the second form) > *aiskā́m and *aištǽtu (7b MON) > *īskā́m and *īštǽtu (7c NASAL V) > *īskǫ́ and *īštǽtu (10 V-SHORT) > OCSlav iskǫ́ and ištétʊ. The PIE noun *mózg+os 'brain' vs. the nom sg masc adj *mózg+ēn+os 'of the brain' (1f W-F SYL) > *mózgus and *mózgēnus (4c W-F C DELE) > *mózgu and *mózgēnu (5a e(:)/o(:)-LOW) > *mázgu and *mázgǣnu (5b 1ST PAL) > *mázgu and *mážd́ǣnu (10 V-SHORT) > OCSlav mózgʊ and móžděnʊ.

As a morph cond rule in the phonology of Old Church Slavic, 1ST PAL accounts for the alternations /k, č/, /g, ž/, /x, š/, /sk, št/ and /zg, žd/ which occur in many paradigms. E.g., the OCSlav nom sg bógʊ 'god' vs. the voc sg bóže; and the alternations in the verb paradigm iskǫ́ 'I seek' vs. ištétʊ 'he seeks' cited earlier. (See also the examples in the morphology in IV below.)

6a Change of /ǣ/ to /ā/ (ǣ-TO-ā)

This change remains as a morph cond rule in the grammar of Old Church Slavic. Its early version is this:

ǣ → ā / č, ž, š or j ___

That is, /ǣ/ becomes /ā/ if preceded by /j/ or any consonant palatalized by 5b 1ST PAL.

E.g., PIE inf *klū́s+j+ētei 'hear' (1c EARLIEST PAL) > *slū́sjētei (3 RUKI) > *slū́xjētei (5a e(:)/o(:)-LOW) > *slū́xjǣtæi (ǣ-TO-ā) > *slū́xjātæi (7b MON) > *slū́xjātī (8a JOTA) > *slū́šātī (9b ū-TO-ȳ) > *slȳ́šātī (10 V-SHORT) > OCSlav slýšati. (In this derivation 5a e(:)/o(:)-LOW must precede ǣ-TO-ā; and ǣ-TO-ā must precede 10 V-SHORT.) PIE inf *leg[h]+ḗtei 'lie down' (1c EARLIEST PAL not applying, perhaps because the word is an early borrowing, but by 1a DEASP) > *legḗtei (5a e(:)/o(:)-LOW, 5b 1ST PAL) > *læžǣ́tæi (ǣ-TO-ā) > *læžā́tæi (7b MON, 10 V-SHORT) > OCSlav ležáti. (Note here the necessary chronology 5b 1ST PAL > ǣ-TO-ā. If the order were reversed, 1ST PAL could not apply.) PIE nom sg *k[w]ḗsos 'period of time' (1f W-F SYL, 2b DELAB) > *kḗsus (4c W-F C DELE, 5a e(:)/o(:)-LOW) > *kǣ́su (5b 1ST PAL) > *čǣ́su (ǣ-TO-ā) > *čā́su (10 V-SHORT) > OCSlav čásʊ. PIE *ḗd+tei 'eat' (2a C-CL) > *ḗstei (4b PROTHESIS) > *jḗstei (5a e(:)/o(:)-LOW) > *jǣ́stæi (ǣ-TO-ā) >*jā́stæi (7b MON) > *jā́stī (10 V-SHORT) > OCSlav jásti. (In this derivation a necessary chronology is 4b PROTHESIS > ǣ-TO-ā. If the order were reversed, ǣ-TO-ā could not apply.)

6b Fronting of Short Vowels (V-FRONT)

V-FRONT remains in restructured form as a morph cond rule of Old Church Slavic. The original change consists of two chronologically ordered rules. The first is Proto-Slavic; the second is restricted to Old Church Slavic.

$$(1)\quad \begin{bmatrix} \text{V}, +\text{back} \\ -\text{long} \end{bmatrix} \rightarrow \begin{bmatrix} -\text{back} \\ -\text{round} \end{bmatrix} \;/\; \begin{bmatrix} -\text{vocalic} \\ -\text{back} \\ +\text{palatal} \end{bmatrix} \_\_$$

$$(2)\quad \text{jí (:)} \rightarrow \text{ī} \;/\; \#\#C_0 \_\_$$

That is, (1) given that by this time 5a e(:)/o(:)-LOW had applied, the short back vowels /a, u/ became /æ, i/ if immediately preceded by any nonvocalic palatal, i.e. by /č, š, ž or j,/. (2) Later, stressed /ji/ or /jī/ in a word-initial syllable becomes /ī/.

E.g., (1) PIE nom sg neuter *póljom 'field' (4c W-F C DELE, 5a e(:)/o(:)-LOW) > *pálja (6b V-

FRONT) > *pálјæ (10 V-SHORT) > OCSlav pólje. PIE nom sg masc *dúzdjus 'bad day, i.e. rain' (4c W-F C DELE) > *dúzdju (V-FRONT) > *dúzdji (8a JOTA) > *duždi (10 V-SHORT) > OCSlav dʊ́ždɪ. PIE voc sg *d^h^óusja 'soul' vs. nom sg *d^h^ousjā́ (la DEASP) > *dóusja and *dousjā́ (3 RUKI) > *dóuxja and *douxjā́ (5a e(:)/o(:)-LOW) > *dáuxja and *dauxjā́ (V-FRONT) > *dáuxjæ and *dauxjā́ (7b MON) > *dū́xjæ and *dūxjā́ (8a JOTA) > *dū́šæ and *dūšā́ (10 V-SHORT) > OCSlav dúše and dušá.

(2) PIE nom sg neuter *júgom 'yoke' (4c W-F C DELE, 5a e(:)/o(:)-LOW) > *júga (V-FRONT 1) > *jíga (V-FRONT 2) > *ī́ga (10 V-SHORT) > OCSlav ígo. The chronology 1d SYL SON > 4b PROTHESIS > V-FRONT 2 is indicated by the following derivation: PIE 1sg pres *ḿ̥+ōm 'I take' (1d SYL SON) > *ímōm (4b PROTHESIS) > *jímōm (5a e(:)/o(:)-LOW) > *jímām (V-FRONT 2) > *ī́mām (7c NASAL V) > *ī́mǭ (10 V-SHORT) > OCSlav ímǫ.

The following derivation of two PIE infinitives made from one root with two different suffixes indicates the relative chronology 7b MON > 8a JOTA. PIE infs *péu+nān+tei 'to spit' as well as *peu+ā́ +tei 'idem' (5a e(:)/o(:)-LOW) > *pǽunāntæi and *pæuā́tæi (7b MON) > *pjū́nāntī and *pjūā́tī (? V-FRONT 1, here applying to a long vowel, /ū/) > *pjī́nāntī and *pjīā́tī (? a glide-insertion rule) > *pjī́nāntī and *pjīwā́tī (7c NASAL V) > *pjī́nǭtī and *pjīvā́tī (8a JOTA) > *pljī́nǭtī and *pljīwā́tī (9c w-TO-v, 10 V-SHORT) > OCSlav pljínǫti and pljiváti. In this somewhat problematic derivation, V-FRONT seems to have applied — perhaps as as persistent synchronic rule in the grammar with a somewhat expanded environment — after 8a JOTA and to a long vowel /ū/.

The following derivation indicates that V-FRONT must precede 7c NASAL V : PIE gen sg masc pres act part *mód^h^l+j+ont+jōd 'asking' (la DEASP, 4a C-CL SIMP) > *móljontjōd (4c W-F C DELE) > *móljontjō (5a e(:)/o(:)-LOW) > *máljantjā (V-FRONT) > *máljæntjā (7c NASAL V) > *málję̄tjā (8a JOTA) > *málję̄štā (10 V-SHORT) > OCSlav mólję̄šta. (1f 7c NASAL V had preceded V-FRONT, V-FRONT could not apply since it affects only –long vowels.)

As noted above, V-FRONT remains in restructured form as a morph cond rule in the phonology of Old Church Slavic. It accounts for differing endings in -o- vs. -jo- and -ā- vs. -jā- paradigms. E.g., OCSlav nom sg neuter seló 'village' vs. pólje 'field' and voc sg fem žéno 'woman' vs. dúše 'soul' from PIE *selóm, *póljom, *g^w^éna and *d^h^óusja, respectively.

7a Change of /æw/ to /aw/ (æw-TO-aw)

This change restructures a few forms and then is dropped from the grammar of Old Church Slavic.

æ → a / ___ w [V, +back]

That is, /æ/ is backed to /a/ if followed by /w/ plus a back vowel (at this stage /a(:)/ or /u(:)/).

E.g., PIE nom sg masc *néwos 'new' (1f W-F SYL, 4c W-F C DELE) > *néwu (5a e(:)/o(:)-LOW) > *nǽwu (æw-TO-aw) > *nawu (9c w-TO-v, 10 V-SHORT) > OCSlav nóvʊ. We assume the chronologies æw-TO-aw > 9c w-TO-v and æw-TO-aw > 10 V-SHORT. Regarding the former chronology, a change of /æ/ to /a/ seems more natural if occurring before a /w/ than before a /v/. Regarding the latter chronology, if the sequence were reversed, the OCSlav form would be **névʊ.

7b Monophthongization of Diphthongs (MON)

The principal Old Church Slavic reflex of this change is the presence of restructured lexical items. Another minor reflex is a morph cond rule which accounts for a few paradigmatic alternations, an example of which we cite below. The change seems to occur in two chronological stages. Assuming that it occurs after 5a e(:)/o(:)-LOW and before 10 V-SHORT, the two stages of MON are these:

(1) Diphthongs ending in /i/

(a) æi → ī

(b) ? ai → ī / [–stress ___] ##

(c) ai → ǣ / otherwise

(2) Diphthongs ending in /u/

(a) au → ū

(b) æu → jū

That is, (1) (a) /aei/ becomes /ī/, (b) unstressed and word-final /ai/ becomes /ī/ and (c) /ai/ otherwise becomes /ǣ/. (2) (a) /au/ becomes /ū/ and (b) /æu/ becomes /jū/. (The PIE antecedents of these diphthongs are /æi/ < PIE /e(:)i/ or /a(:)i, o(:)i/ by 6b V-FRONT; /ai/ < PIE /a(:)i, o(:)i/; /au/ < PIE /a(:)u, o(:)u/; /æu/ < PIE /e(:)u/ or /a(:)u, o(:)u/ by 6b V-FRONT .)

E.g., (1) (a) PIE inf *péi+tei 'drink' (5a e(:)/o(:)-LOW) > *pǽitæi (MON 1a) > *pī́tī (10 V-SHORT) > OCSlav píti. (b) PIE o-class nom pl masc *g^{h}órd^{h}oi 'cities' (perhaps a later borrowing *gard- from Germanic, but for the sake of the exposition we posit it as PIE, 1c EARLIEST PAL not applying, but by la DEASP) > *górdoi (5a e(:)/o(:)-LOW) > *gárdai (MON 1b) > *gárdī (9a MET) > *grā́dī (10 V-SHORT) > OCSlav grádi. (c) PIE nom sg masc *láiwos 'left' (1f W-F SYL, 4c W-F C DELE) > *láiwu (MON 1c) > *lǣ́wu (9c w-TO-v) > *lǣ́vu (10 V-SHORT) > OCSlav lě́vʊ.

(2) (a) PIE inf *plóu+tei 'swim' (5a e(:)/o(:)-LOW) > *pláutæi (MON lb) > *pláutī (MON 2a) > *plū́tī (10 V-SHORT) > OCSlav plúti. (b) PIE nom sg masc adj *leub^{h}ós 'dear, desired' (1a DEASP, 1f W-F SYL) > *leubús (4c W-F C DELE, 5a e(:)/o(:)-LOW) > *læubú (MON 2b) > *ljūbú (8a JOTA) > *l'jūbú (10 V-SHORT) > OCSlav ljubʊ́. Note in this derivation the necessary chronology MON > 8a JOTA.

MON 1 affecting diphthongs ending in /i/ precedes MON 2 affecting /au/ and /æu/. The latter change must follow 9b ū-TO-ȳ, as in the following derivation: Germanic borrowing as an inf *káup+eitei 'buy' (MON 1) > *káupītī (9b ū-TO-ȳ occurring, but not affecting this form, then MON 2) > *kū́pītī (10 V-SHORT) > OCSlav kúpiti, not **ký piti.

The chronology 5b 1ST PAL > MON is evident in this derivation: PIE nom sg neuter *kéudos 'wonder' (4c W-F C DELE, 5a e(:)/o(:)-LOW) > *kǽuda (5b 1ST PAL) > *čǽuda (MON) > *čjū́da = *čū́da (10 V-SHORT) > OCSlav čúdo.

The chronology 6b V-FRONT > MON > 10 V-SHORT is indicated in this derivation. PIE dat sg fem jā-class *d^{h}ousjā́i 'soul' (la DEASP, lb DIPH SHORT) > *dousjái (3 RUKI) > *douxjái (5a e(:)/o(:)-LOW) > *dauxjái (6b V-FRONT) > *dauxjǽi (MON) > *dūxjī́ (8a JOTA) > *dūšī́ (10 V-SHORT) > OCSlav duší.

The questionable change under (1b) whereby unstressed and word-final /ai/ becomes /ī/ seems to apply only in two instances, namely in the nominative plural masculine of nouns, adjectives and some pronouns as well as in the 2nd singular imperative. E.g., PIE nom pl masc *néwoi 'new' (5a e(:)/o(:)-LOW) > *nǽwai (7a æw-TO-aw) > *náwai (MON 1b) > *náwī (9c w-TO-v) > *návī (10 V-SHORT) > OCSlav nóvi. PIE 2nd sg imp *b^{h}érois 'carry, gather' vs. 2nd pl imp *b^{h}eroite (1a DEASP, 4c W-F C DELE) > *béroi and *béroite (5a e(:)/o(:)-LOW) > *bǽrai and *bǽraitæ (MON lb and 1c respectively) > *bǽrī and *bǽrǣtæ (10 V-SHORT) > OCSlav béri and bérěte. Note that for the derivation of OCSlav béri, 4c W-F C DELE must precede MON in order for the latter to apply. MON can apply only if the diphthong is followed by a –vocalic segment or is word-final. If followed by a vowel, the inherited PIE rule 3.1.2c i-j/u-w ALT applies and MON cannot. E.g., the PIE inf *plóu+tei 'to swim' vs. 1sg pres *plóu+ōm 'I swim' (PIE 3.1.2c i-j/u-w ALT applying synchronically) → *plóutei and *plówōm (5a e(:)/o(:)-LOW) > *pláutæi and *pláwām (MON) > *plū́tī and *pláwām (7c NASAL V) > *plū́tī and *pláwǭ (9c w-TO-v) > *plū́tī and *plávǭ (10 V-SHORT) > OCSlav plúti and plóvǫ. (The /u/-/ov/ alternation in this paradigm is the morph cond restructured reflex of MON in the Old Church Slavic grammar.)

7c Nasalization of Vowels (NASAL V)

The main reflex of this change is the restructuring of lexical items and endings and the concomitant addition of the new nasal segments /ę̄/ and /ǭ/ (later OCSlav /ę/ and /ǫ/) to the phonemic inventory of the language. Another reflex is a minor morph cond rule governing a few verb alternations, an example of which we cite below.

The rule is this:

$$\underset{1\quad 2}{\mathrm{V}\begin{pmatrix}\mathrm{C}\\ +\text{nasal}\end{pmatrix}} \rightarrow \underset{1}{\begin{pmatrix}\mathrm{V}, +\text{long}\\ +\text{nasal}\\ -\text{high}\\ -\text{low}\end{pmatrix}}\quad \underset{2}{\varnothing} \quad / \; \_\_ \begin{Bmatrix}[-\text{vocalic}]\\ \#\#\end{Bmatrix}$$

It may also be formalized as follows:

$$\underset{1}{\begin{pmatrix}\text{æ}(:) & \text{or} & \mathrm{i}(:)\\ \mathrm{a}(:) & \text{or} & \mathrm{u}(:)\end{pmatrix}} \quad \underset{2}{\begin{Bmatrix}\mathrm{m}\\ \mathrm{n}\\ \text{ŋ}\end{Bmatrix}} \rightarrow \underset{1}{\begin{pmatrix}\bar{\mathrm{e}}^{\mathrm{n}}\\ \bar{\mathrm{o}}^{\mathrm{n}}\end{pmatrix}} \quad \underset{2}{\varnothing} \quad / \; \_\_ \begin{Bmatrix}[-\text{vocalic}]\\ \#\#\end{Bmatrix}$$

That is, the sequence vowel plus nasal consonant becomes the indicated long nasal vowel and the nasal consonant is deleted. This occurs before any nonvocalic segment or word-finally. (In the following we shall designate the nasalized vowels /$\bar{\mathrm{e}}^{\mathrm{n}}$/ and /$\bar{\mathrm{o}}^{\mathrm{n}}$/ with the conventional symbols /ę̄/ and /ǭ/, later shortened to /ę/ and /ǫ/.)

E.g., PIE acc sg fem *wrónkām 'hand' (2a C-CL) > *rónkām (5a e(:)/o(:)-LOW) > *ránkām (NASAL V) > *rǭ́kǭ (10 V-SHORT) > OCSlav rǫ́kǫ. PIE inf *em+téi 'to take' vs. the ablauting Ø-grade PIE 1sg pres *ḿ̥+ōm 'I take' (1d SYL SON) > *emtéi and *ímōm (4b PROTHESIS) > *jemtéi and *jímōm (5a e(:)/o(:)-LOW) > *jæmtǽi and *jímām (6b V-FRONT) > *jæmtǽi and *ī́mām (7b MON) > *jæmtī́ and *ī́mām (NASAL V) > *ję̄tī́ and *ī́mǭ (10 V-SHORT) > OCSlav jętí and ímǫ. (The morph cond reflex of NASAL V in Old Church Slavic accounts for alternations such as /ję-/ vs. /im-/ in the two forms just cited.) Another example is the Gothic borrowing *kínt+ā 'coin' (NASAL V) > *kę̄́tā (8b 2ND PAL) > *cę̄́tā (10 V-SHORT) > OCSlav cę́ta. The following derivation indicates that NASAL V must apply after 4c W-F C DELE: PIE acc sg masc *g^{h}óstim 'guest' (la DEASP) > *góstim (4c W-F C DELE) > *gósti (5a e(:)/o(:)-LOW) > *gásti (10 V-SHORT) > OCSlav góstɪ. If NASAL V had preceded 4c W-F C DELE, the Old Church Slavic form would be **góstę.

8a Jotation of Consonants (JOTA)

This change remains as a morph cond rule of Old Church Slavic. It accounts for several paradigmatic alternations cited below. It also restructured some lexical items such as OCSlav nóštɪ 'night' in which /št/ occurs throughout the paradigm. The change has been so termed because its triggering environments are "iotas", namely /j/ and occasionally /i(:)/. JOTA may have been an areal change which spread over the Slavic area after the initial differentiation of the dialects: its reflexes can vary slightly from language to language. We base our description of the Old Church Slavic version on Carlton (1991: 113) and on Schmalstieg (1983: 32-36).

(i) Bisegmental sequences.

(a) xj, sj → š
(b) gj, zj → ž
(c) kj → č
(d) tj → št
(e) dj → žd

(ii) Trisegmental sequences.

(f) stj, skj → št
(g) zdj, zgj → žd
(h) slj, snj → šlj, šnj
(i) zlj, znj → žlj, žnj

(iii) Insertion of /l/

(j) pj → plj
(k) bj → blj
(1) mj → mlj
(m) wj → wlj

(iv) Jotation triggered by /i(:)/ or /j/

(n) kt → št / ___ /i(:)/ or /j/

(v) Jotation of sonorant consonants

(o) nj, lj, rj → n', l', r'

That is, the sequences change as shown. The clusters /št/ and /žd/ are probably phonetically [št'] and [žd']. We shall designate the palatalized sonorants /n', l', r'/ as /nj, lj, rj/.

E.g., (a) PIE jā-class noun *sáusjā 'dryness' (3 RUKI) > *sáuxjā (7b MON) > *sū́xjā (JOTA) > *sū́šā (10 V-SHORT) > OCSlav súša. PIE inf *pik+ā́tei 'write, paint' vs. the ablauting 1sg pres *peik+jṓm (1c EARLIEST PAL) > *pisā́tei and *peisjṓm (5a e(:)/o(:)-LOW) > *pisā́tæi and *pæisjā́m (7b MON) > *pisā́tī and *pīsjā́m (7c NASAL V) > *pisā́tī and *pīsjǭ́ (JOTA) > *pisā́tī and *pīšǭ́ (10 V-SHORT) > OCSlav pɪsáti and pišǫ́. The alternation of /s/ and /š/ in these two forms is the Old Church Slavic reflex of JOTA as a morph cond rule. In this derivation the chronology must be lc EARLIEST PAL > JOTA in order for JOTA to apply.

(b) PIE nom sg fem *lúg^hjā 'a lie' (la DEASP) > *lúgjā (1c EARLIEST PAL) > *lúzjā (JOTA) > *lúžā (10 V-SHORT) > OCSlav lʊ́ža.

(c) PIE inf *plā́kātei 'weep' vs. 1sg pres *plā́kjōm (no 1c EARLIEST PAL, but by 5a e(:)/o(:)-LOW) > *plā́kātæi and *plā́kjām (7b MON, 7c NASAL V) > *plā́kātī and *plā́kjǭ (JOTA) > *plā́kātī and *plā́čǭ (10 V-SHORT) > OCSlav plákati and pláčǫ. Also PIE nom sg neuter *kéudos 'wonder' (4c W-F C DELE, 5a e(:)/o(:)-LOW) > *kǽuda (7b MON) > *kjū́da (JOTA) > *čū́da (10 V-SHORT) > OCSlav čúdo.

(d) PIE nom sg fem *kwoitjā́ 'light' (1c EARLIEST PAL) > *swoitjā́ (5a e(:)/o(:)-LOW, 7b MON) >

*swǣtjā́ (JOTA) > *swǣštā́ (9c w-TO-v, 10 V-SHORT) > OCSlav svěštá.

(e) PIE nom sg fem *medʰjā́ 'middle' (1a DEASP, ev) > *mædjā́ (JOTA) > *mæždā́ (10 V-SHORT) > OCSlav meždá 'middle, border'.

(f) PIE inf *paust+éitei 'let go' vs. 1sg pres *paust+jṓm (5a e(:)/o(:)-LOW) > *paustǽitæi and *paustjā́m (7b MON) > *pūstī́tī and *pūstjā́m (7c NASAL V) > *pūstī́tī and *pūstjǭ́ (JOTA) > *pūstī́tī and *pūštǭ́ (10 V-SHORT) > OCSlav pustíti and puštǫ́.

(g) PIE nom sg masc *dús+djus 'bad sky, i.e. rain' (2a C-CL) > *dúzdjus (4c W-F C DELE) > *dúzdju (6b V-FRONT) > *dúzdji (JOTA) > *dúždi (10 V-SHORT) > OCSlav dы́ždɪ.

(h) PIE inf *mūdʰ+sl+éitei 'think' vs. 1sg pres *mūdʰ+sl+jṓm (la DEASP, 2a C-CL) > mūtsléitei and *mūtsljṓm (4a C-CL SIMP) > *mūsléitei and *mūsljṓm (5a e(:)/o(:)-LOW) > *mūslǽitæi and *mūsljā́m (7b MON) > *mūslī́tī and *mūsljā́m (7c NASAL V) > *mūslī́tī and *mūsljǭ́ (JOTA) > *mūslī́ti and *mūšljǭ́ (9b ū-TO-ȳ) > *mȳslī́ti and *mȳšljǭ́ (10 V-SHORT) > OCSlav myslíti and myšljǫ́.

(k) PIE *leubʰ+éitei 'love' vs. 1sg pres *leubʰ+jṓm (la DEASP, 5a e(:)/o(:)-LOW) > *læubǽitæi and *læubjā́m (7b MON) > *ljūbī́tī and *ljūbjā́m (7c NASAL V) > *ljūbī́tī and *ljūbjǭ́ (JOTA (o) applying to the first form and JOTA (o) and (k) applying to the second) > *l'jūbī́tī and *l'jūbljǭ́ (10 V-SHORT) > OCSlav ljubíti and ljubljǫ́.

(n) PIE nom sg fem *nóktis 'night' (to which neither 1c EARLIEST PAL nor 5b 1ST PAL can apply, but 4c W-F C DELE and 5a e(:)/o(:)-LOW) > *nákti (JOTA) > *nášti (10 V-SHORT) > OCSlav nóštɪ.

(o) PIE nom sg neuter *mórjom 'ocean' (4c W-F C DELE, 5a e(:)/o(:)-LOW) > *márja (6b V-FRONT) > *márjæ (JOTA) > *már'jæ (10 V-SHORT) > OCSlav mórje.

In part iii of JOTA, the rule applies to bilabial segments. Hence we assume at this time /w/ was still bilabial and had not yet become /v/ by 9c w-TO-v.

As noted earlier, JOTA remains as a morph cond synchronic rule of Old Church Slavic and accounts for the paradigmatic alternations of the infinitives vs. the 1st singular present forms noted above. In some instances Old Church Slavic JOTA seems to have applied optionally, e.g. the OCSlav nom sg fem zemjá 'earth' as well as zemljá from PIE *gʰemjā́.

8b The "Second" Palatalization (2ND PAL)

This change remains as a morph cond rule in Old Church Slavic. It is in fact the third palatalization, following as it does 1c EARLIEST PAL and 5b 1ST PAL . The change is probably areal: its reflexes differ somewhat over the Slavic area.

The following is the Old Church Slavic version of the change:

(a)	k	→	c
(b)	g	→	dz (ev) → z
(c)	x	→	s
(d)	sk	→	sc (ev) → st
(e)	zg	→	zdz (ev) → zd / ___ (w) [V, –back]

That is, the segments change as indicated when followed by a –back vowel (i.e., /æ(:)/ or /i(:)/ with the possibility of an intervening /w/. (Here /c/ = /ts/ and /sc/ = /sts/.) During attested Old Church Slavic times /dz/ becomes /z/, /sc/ becomes /st/ and /zdz/ becomes /zd/.

E.g., (a) PIE nom sg fem *kʷoinā́ 'price' (2b DELAB) > *koinā́ (5a e(:)/o(:)-LOW) > *kainā́ (7b MON)

> *kǣnā́ (2ND PAL) > *cǣnā́ (10 V-SHORT) > OCSlav cěná. Note in this derivation the necessary chronology 7b MON > 2ND PAL.

(b) PIE *g^{h}óilom 'very' (la DEASP) > *góilom (4c W-F C DELE, 5a e(:)/o(:)-LOW) > *gáila (7b MON) > *gǣ́la (2ND PAL) > *dzǣ́la (10 V-SHORT) > OCSlav dzě́lo and later zě́lo. PIE nom sg fem *gwoizdā́ 'star' (5a e(:)/o(:)-LOW, 7b MON) > *gwǣzdā́ (2ND PAL) > *dzwǣzdā́ (9c W-TO-v, 10 V-SHORT) > OCSlav zvězdá. (An instance of a dialectal variant of 2ND PAL is that in Polish it has not applied over /w/. Hence the cognate Polish word is gwiázda 'star'.)

(c) PIE adj masc nom sg *sausós 'dry' vs. pl *sausói (1f W-F SYL) > *sausós and *sausói (3 RUKI) > *sauxús and *sauxói (4c W-F C DELE, 5a e(:)/o(:)-LOW) > *sauxú and *sauxái (7b MON) > *sūxú and *sūxī́ (2ND PAL) > *sūxú and *sūsī́ (10 V-SHORT) > OCSlav suxʊ́ and susí.

(d) PIE adj masc nom sg *léud^{h}iskos 'of people' vs. pl *léud^{h}iskoi (la DEASP, 1f W-F SYL) > *léudiskus and *léudiskoi (4c W-F C DELE, 5a e(:)/o(:)-LOW) > *lǽudisku and *lǽudiskai (7b MON) > *ljū́disku and *ljū́diskī (2ND PAL) > *ljū́disku and *ljū́discī (10 V-SHORT) > OCSlav ljúdɪskʊ and ljúdɪsci (later ljúdɪsti).

(e) PIE nom sg fem *drenzgā́ 'forest' vs. dat sg *drenzgā́i (lb DIPH SHORT) > *drenzgā́ and *drenzgái (5e e(:)/o(:)-LOW) > *drænzgā́ and *drænzgái (7b MON) > *drænzgā́ and *drænzgǣ́ (7c NASAL V) > *drę̄zgā́ and *drę̄zgǣ́ (2ND PAL) > *drę̄zgā́ and *drę̄zdǣ́ (10 V-SHORT) > OCSlav dręzgá and dręzdě́.

As noted above, the 2ND PAL change remains as a morph cond rule in Old Church Slavic. It accounts for numerous alternations involving /k-c/, /g-z/, /x-s/, /sk-st/ and /zg-zd/ in noun, adjective and verb paradigms. E.g., OCSlav nom sg rǫká 'hand' vs. dat sg rǫ́cě from PIE *wronkā́ and *wrónkāi; and OCSlav nom sg nogá 'foot' vs. dat sg nózě from PIE *nog^{h}ā́ and *nóg^{h}āi. Note also the alternations cited above of OCSlav suxʊ́ and susí 'dry', ljúdɪskʊ and ljúdɪsti 'of the people', and dręzgá and dręzdě́ 'forest'. In some instances 2ND PAL has restructured a word and there is no paradigmatic alternation as in OCSlav cě́sarɪ 'emperor' from Go *káisar 'Caesar'.

9a Metathesis (MET)

This change restructured numerous Old Church Slavic words. It also remained as a morph cond rule in the Old Church Slavic grammar. The change is areal: hence its reflexes differ in the various Slavic languages. Below is the Old Church Slavic version.

$$\underset{1}{V}\ \underset{2}{\begin{pmatrix}\text{C}\\ +\text{sonorant}\end{pmatrix}} \rightarrow \underset{2}{\begin{pmatrix}\text{C}\\ +\text{sonorant}\end{pmatrix}}\ \underset{1}{\begin{pmatrix}\text{V, +long}\\ (\text{if} -\text{high})\end{pmatrix}} \ / \ \begin{Bmatrix}\#\#\\ [-\text{vocalic}]\end{Bmatrix} \ \_\_\_ \ [-\text{vocalic}]$$

That is, the sequence of vowel plus sonorant consonant (at this time only /l/ or /r/) is permuted to sonorant consonant plus vowel. If the vowel is –high (i.e., /æ, a/), it is lengthened. MET occurs when the vowel plus sonorant sequence occurs either word-initially and followed by a –vocalic segment or word-internally if preceded and followed by a –vocalic segment. (The second -vocalic segment here does not include /j/. This probably means that 8a JOTA has preceded MET. The nasal sonorant consonants /m, n, ŋ/ do not undergo MET. We assume this means that 7c NASAL V also preceded MET.)

E.g., PIE inf *ord+téi 'grow' (2a C-CL) > *orstéi (5a e(:)/o(:)-LOW) >*arstǽi (7b MON) > *arstī́ (MET) > *rāstī́ (10 V-SHORT) > OCSlav rastí. PIE inf *mel+téi 'grind' vs. 1sg pres *mel+jṓm (5a e(:)/o(:)-LOW) > *mæltǽi and *mæljā́m (7b MON) > *mæltī́ and *mæljā́m (7c NASAL V) > *mæltī́ and *mæljǭ́ (MET) > *mlǣtī́ and *mæljǭ́ (10 V-SHORT) > OCSlav mlětí and meljǫ́. The early Germanic borrowing, the inf *gelt+téi 'to pay off' (2a C-CL) > *gelstéi (5a e(:)/o(:)-LOW) > *gælstǽi (5b 1ST PAL) > *žælstǽi (7b MON) > *žælstī́ (MET) > *žlæstī́ (10 V-SHORT) > OCSlav žlestí. Note that the chronology here must be 5b 1ST PAL > MET. Otherwise 1ST PAL could not apply. PIE nom sg *wald^h

+t+is 'power' (1a DEASP, 2a C-CL) > *wálstis (4c W-F C DELE) > *wálsti (MET) > *wlā́sti (9c w-TO-v) > *vlā́sti (10 V-SHORT) > OCSlav vlástɪ. The early Germanic borrowing *kírk+ū 'church' (8b 2ND PAL) > *církū (MET) > *crī́kū (9b ū-TO-ȳ) > *crī́kȳ (10 V-SHORT) > OCSlav críky. In this derivation the chronology must be 8b 2ND PAL > MET. Otherwise 2ND PAL would not apply. Finally, MET may have applied, albeit under somewhat different circumstances, in this derivation: PIE nom sg *ákmōn 'stone' (1f W-F SYL) > *ákmūn (4c W-F C DELE) > *ákmū (9a MET) > *kā́mū (9b ū-TO-ȳ) > *kā́mȳ (10 V-SHORT) > OCSlav kámy. Some sources such as Shevelov (1965: 391) and Carlton (1991: 144-8) consider word-initial metathesis (## ___ [–vocalic]) to have been a different process from that which occurred word-internally ([–vocalic] ____ [–vocalic]). As a morph cond rule remaining in the Old Church Slavic grammar, MET accounts for several paradigmatic alternations, particularly in 1st class verbs such as mlětí 'to grind' vs. meljǫ́ 'I grind' noted above.

9b Change of /ū/ to /ȳ/ (ū-TO-ȳ)

This change restructures the phonemic inventory of the language to include /ȳ/ and then is dropped from the grammar.

[ū, +round] → [ȳ, –round]

That is, +round /ū/ becomes –round /ȳ/ while retaining its other features such as +back, +long, +high, etc.

E.g., the PIE inf *bʰū+téi 'be' (1a DEASP, 5a e(:)/o(:)-LOW) > *būtǽi (7b MON) > *būtī́ (ū-TO-ȳ) > *bȳtī́ (10 V-SHORT) > OCSlav bytí.

9c Change of /w/ to /v/ (w-TO-v)

This change restructures the phonemic inventory of the language to include /v/ and then is dropped from the grammar.

w → v

That is, all occurrences of /w/ become /v/.

E.g., PIE nom sg fem *widʰowā́ 'widow' (la DEASP) > *widowā́ (5a e(:)/o(:)-LOW) > *widawā́ (w-TO-v) > *vidavā́ (10 V-SHORT) > OCSlav vɪdová.

9d The "Third" Palatalization (3RD PAL)

This change is in fact the fourth palatalization in the history of Old Church Slavic, following as it does 1c EARLIEST PAL, 5b 1ST PAL and 8b 2ND PAL. The change remains in the Old Church Slavic grammar as a morph cond rule, examples of whose application will be cited below. The change is areal. The Old Church Slavic version, for which we follow the formulation of Bräuer (1961: 1, 193), is this:

(a)	k	→	c	/	V, –back	V
(b)	g	→	dz (ev) → z		–stress	—— –round
(c)	x	→	s			

That is, the velar consonants change as indicated (where /c/ is /ts/) if preceded by an unstressed front vowel /æ(:), i(:), ę̄/ and if followed by any unrounded vowel, namely /æ(:), i(:), ę̄, a(:)/ as opposed to /u(:)/ or /ǭ/.

E.g., (a) PIE nom sg fem *owikā́ 'sheep' (5a e(:)/o(:)-LOW) > *awikā́ (3RD PAL) > *awicā́ (9c w-TO-v, 10 V-SHORT) > OCSlav ovɪcá. (b) PIE iterative verb inf dweig+ā́+tei 'move often' (7b MON) > *dwīgā́tī (3RD PAL) > *dwīdzā́tī (9c w-TO-v, 10 V-SHORT) > OCSlav dvizáti. (c) PIE nom sg fem *wisā́ 'every, all' (3 RUKI) > *wixā́ (9c w-TO-v) > *vixā́ (3RD PAL) > *visā́ (10 V-SHORT) > OCSlav vɪsá.

The 3RD PAL change may represent an expansion in the application of 8b 2ND PAL, which had remained as a rule in the Old Church Slavic grammar. Carlton (1991: 133) notes that 3RD PAL is "very irregular in its operation." Shevelov (1965: 350) attributes this irregularity to the fact that the change was unusually susceptible to morphological restructuring. However this may have been, 3RD PAL remains in the Old Church Slavic grammar as a morph cond rule. As such it accounts for Old Church Slavic alternations like the following: the infinitives dvíg+nǫti 'to move' vs. the iterative dviz+áti 'to move often'; and the nouns účenica 'female student'vs. účenikʊ 'male student' to which 3RD PAL could not have applied. The respective PIE antecedents are PIE *óukenīkā and *óukenīkos.

The change 7c NASAL V must precede 3RD PAL in view of the following derivation: Germanic borrowing put into the i-class nom sg *kúning+is 'king' (4c W-F C DELE) > *kúningi (7c NASAL V) > *kúnę̄gi (3RD PAL) > *kúnę̄zi (10 V-SHORT) > OCSlav kʊ́nęzɪ. If 7c NASAL V had not applied, the /g/ would have been preceded by the consonant /n/ instead of the vowel /ę̄́/ and 3RD PAL could not have applied. Hence the Old Church Slavic form would have been **kʊ́nęgɪ.

Several Germanic borrowing were taken into Slavic after the time of 8b 2ND PAL and before the time of 3RD PAL. (This is an indication of the relative chronology 8b 2ND PAL > 3RD PAL.) E.g., nom sg i-class *káup+ik+i 'merchant' (7b MON) > *kū́piki (3RD PAL) > *kū́pici (10 V-SHORT) > OCSlav kúpɪcɪ. If 2ND PAL had applied in this derivation, the Old Church Slavic form would be **kúpɪčɪ.

10 Shortening of Vowels (V-SHORT)

This change restructured the phonemic inventory of Old Church Slavic and then was dropped from the grammar. The change seems to have been rather late and as such spread over Slavic territory as an areal change. The change is this:

V → [–long]

That is, all vowels become short. However, the formerly long vowels retained their feature +tense, which was now the sole feature which distinguished the former [+long, +tense] vowels from the [–long, –tense] ones.The change applied as follows. After the changes 5a e(:)/o(:)-LOW, 7b MON, 7c NASAL V and 9b ū-TO-ȳ, the vowel inventory of Proto-Slavic was this:

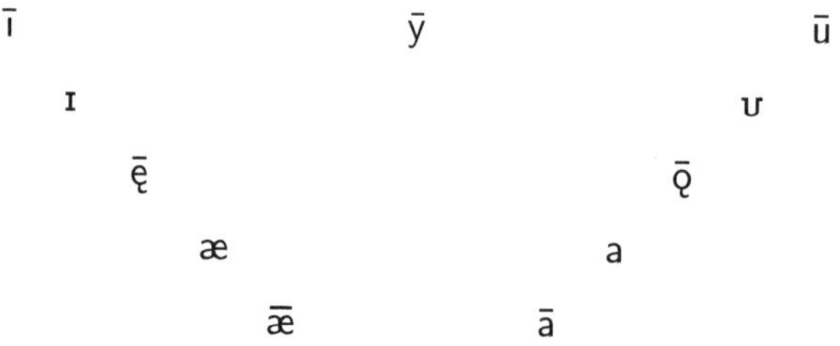

In this system short and long vowels differ not only in length, but also the feature of tenseness. Long vowels are +tense; and short vowels are lax (–tense). Tense vowels are pronounced with more muscular effort and are formed more toward the periphery of the vowel triangle than their lax counterparts are. The /ę̄/ and /ǭ/ are the long, tense, nasal vowels arising from 7c NASAL V. They have no short lax counterparts.

After V-SHORT occurred, the resulting Old Church Slavic vowel system was this:

i (+tense) y (+tense) u (+tense)
ɪ (–tense) ʊ (–tense)
ę (+tense) ǫ (+tense)
e (–tense) o (–tense)
ě (+tense) a (+tense)

Here we use the conventional romanization of the Old Church Slavic cyrillic alphabet to designate the Old Church Slavic phonemes. Hence <ě> is +tense /æ/ from earlier /ǣ/; <e> is –tense /ɛ/ from earlier /æ/; <a> is +tense /a/ from earlier /ā/; <o> is -tense /ɔ/ from earlier /a/ (which may have acquired some concomitant rounding); and <y> is +tense /y/ from earlier /ȳ/. The lax <ɪ> and <ʊ> from earlier /i/ and /u/ are cyrillic < ь > and < ъ >, respectively, and are referred to as "jers" in the literature. The tense <i> and <u> are from earlier /ī/ and /ū/.

In the following examples of V-SHORT the antecedent forms are those of pre-Old Church Slavic and immediately pre-V-SHORT. E.g., nom pl *līstī́ 'leaves' > OCSlav listí, nom pl *lístī 'deceptions' > OCSlav lɪ́sti; inf *plūtī́ 'to navigate' > OCSlav plutí, gen sg *plútī 'flesh' > OCSlav plʊ́ti; gen pl *nāsú 'of us' > OCSlav nasʊ́, nom sg *násu 'nose' > OCSlav nósʊ; 1sg aorist *nǣ́su 'I carried' > OCSlav ně́sʊ, past act part *næsú 'having carried' > OCSlav nesʊ́; inf *bȳtī́ 'be' > OCSlav bytí.

Shevelov (1965: 433) notes that in most of the Slavic languages after Old Church Slavic "the *jers* did not last long." Bräuer (1961: 1, 123) notes the presence of an optional rule in Old Church Slavic:

(a) ʊ → ɪ / ___ C [V, –back]

(b) ɪ → ʊ / ___ C [V, +back]

That is, (a) /ʊ/ may become /ɪ/ if the following syllable contains a –back vowel and (b) vice versa.

E.g., (a) OCSlav loc sg /sʊně́/ 'sleep' → [sʊně́] and [sɪně́]; and (b) OCSlav inf /sʊbɪráti/ 'gather' → [sʊbɪráti] and [sʊbʊráti].

C. The Relative Chronology

In the following " > " means "must precede".

1a DEASP > Ø.

1b DIPH SHORT > 7b MON (see the discussion under 7b).

1c EARLIEST PAL > 2a C-CL (see 2a), > 2b DELAB (see 2b), > 8a JOTA (see 8a).

1d SYL SON > 4b PROTHESIS (see 4b and 6b V-FRONT), > 6b V-FRONT (see 6b), > 7c NASAL V (see 1d), > 9a MET (see 1d).

1e OCS STRESS > Ø.

1f W-F SYL > 4c W-F C DELE (see 1f and 4c), > 5a e(:)/o(:)-LOW (see 1f), > 7c NASAL V (see 1f), > 9b ū-TO-ȳ (see 1f).

2a C-CL > 2a C-CL > 4a C-CL SIMP (see 4a), > 9a MET (see 2a).

2b DELAB > 5b 1ST PAL (see 2b).

3 RUKI > 1c EARLIEST PAL (part 2, see 3 RUKI), 4a C-CL SIMP (see 3 and 4a) > 5b 1ST PAL (see 3), > 7b MON (see 3), > 9a MET (see 3).

4a C-CL SIMP > Ø.

4b PROTHESIS > 5a e(:)/o(:)-LOW (see 4b), > 6a ǣ-TO-ā (see 4b), > 6b V-FRONT (see 4b and 6b), > 7b MON (see 4b), 9a MET (see 4b), > 9c w-TO-**v** (see 4b).

4c W-F C DELE > 7b MON (see 7b), 7c NASAL V (see 4c and 7c).

5a e(:)/o(:)-LOW > 6a ǣ-TO-ā (see 6a), > 6b V-FRONT (see 6b), > 7b MON (see 7b), > 10 V-SHORT (see 5a and 10).

5b 1ST PAL > 6a ǣ-TO-ā (see 5b), 7b MON (see 7b), > 9a MET (see 5b and 9a).

6a ǣ-TO-ā > 10 V-SHORT (see 6a).

6b V-FRONT > 7b MON (see 7b), > 7c NASAL V (see 6b).

7a æw-TO-aw > 9c w-TO-**v** (see 7a), > 10 V-SHORT (see 7a).

7b MON > 5a JOTA (see 6b V-FRONT and 7b), > 8b 2ND PAL (see 8b), > 10 V-SHORT (see 7b).

7c NASAL V > 9a MET (see 9a), > 9d 3RD PAL (see 9d).

8a JOTA > 9a MET (see 9a), > 9c w-TO-**v** (see 8a).

8b 2ND PAL > 9a MET (see 9a), > 9d 3RD PAL (see 9d).

9a MET > Ø.

9b ū-TO-ȳ > 7b MON (part 2, see 7b).

9c w-TO-**v** > Ø.

9d 3RD PAL > Ø.

10 V-SHORT > Ø.

III Old Church Slavic Phonology

After the changes described in the previous section, the inventory of segments in the phonology of Old Church Slavic at about 850 AD was as follows.

Obstruent Consonants

labial	dental	alveopalatal	palatal	velar
p	t		t'[1]	k
b	d		d'[1]	g
f[2]	s	š[3]		x
v	z	ž[3]		
	c[4]	č[3]		
	dz[4]			

Sonorant Consonants

labial	dental	alveopalatal	palatal	velar
m	n		nj[1]	ŋ[5]
	r		rj[1]	
	l		lj[1]	
			j	

Vowels[6]

Lax

ɪ[7] ʊ[7]

e o

Tense

i y u

ě a

Tense and Nasal

ę ǫ

Old Church Slavic Segments in Terms of Phonological Features: Obstruents

	p	t	t'	k	b	d	d'	g	f	s	š	x	v	z	ž	c	č	dz
consonantal	+	+	+	+	+	+	+	+	+	+	+	+	+	+	+	+	+	+
sonorant	–	–	–	–	–	–	–	–	–	–	–	–	–	–	–	–	–	–
vocalic	–	–	–	–	–	–	–	–	–	–	–	–	–	–	–	–	–	–
high	–	–	–	+	–	–	–	+	–	–	–	+	–	–	+	–	+	–
back	–	–	–	+	–	–	–	+	–	–	–	+	–	–	–	–	–	–
low	–	–	–	–	–	–	–	–	–	–	–	–	–	–	–	–	–	–
anterior	+	+	+	–	+	+	+	–	+	+	–	–	+	+	–	+	–	+
coronal	–	+	–	–	–	+	–	–	–	+	–	–	–	+	–	+	–	+
voiced	–	–	–	–	+	+	+	+	–	–	–	–	+	+	+	–	–	+
continuant	–	–	–	–	–	–	–	–	+	+	+	+	+	+	+	–	–	–
nasal	–	–	–	–	–	–	–	–	–	–	–	–	–	–	–	–	–	–
strident	–	–	–	–	–	–	–	–	–	+	+	–	–	+	+	+	+	+
delayed release	–	–	–	–	–	–	–	–	–	–	–	–	–	–	–	+	+	+
round	–	–	–	–	–	–	–	–	–	–	–	–	–	–	–	–	–	–
lateral	–	–	–	–	–	–	–	–	–	–	–	–	–	–	–	–	–	–
palatal	–	–	+	–	–	–	+	–	–	–	+	–	–	–	+	+	+	–
long	–	–	–	–	–	–	–	–	–	–	–	–	–	–	–	–	–	–

Old Church Slavic Segments in Terms of Phonological Features: Sonorants

	m	n	nj	ŋ	r	rj	l	lj	j	ɪ	e	o	ʊ	i	ě	a	u	y	ę	ǫ
consonantal	+	+	+	+	+	+	+	+	−	−	−	−	−	−	−	−	−	−	−	−
sonorant	+	+	+	+	+	+	+	+	+	+	+	+	+	+	+	+	+	+	+	+
vocalic	−	−	−	−	−	−	−	−	−	+	+	+	+	+	+	+	+	+	+	+
high	−	−	−	+	−	+	−	+	+	+	−	−	+	+	−	−	+	+	−	−
back	−	−	−	+	−	−	−	−	−	−	−	+	+	−	−	+	+	+	−	+
low	−	−	−	−	−	−	−	−	−	−	−	−	−	−	+	+	−	−	−	−
anterior	+	+	−	−	+	−	+	−	−	−	−	−	−	−	−	−	−	−	−	−
coronal	−	+	−	−	+	−	+	−	−	−	−	−	−	−	−	−	−	−	−	−
voiced	+	+	+	+	+	+	+	+	+	+	+	+	+	+	+	+	+	+	+	+
continuant	−	−	−	−	+	+	+	+	+	+	+	+	+	+	+	+	+	+	+	+
nasal	+	+	+	+	−	−	−	−	−	−	−	−	−	−	−	−	−	−	+	+
strident	−	−	−	−	−	−	−	−	−	−	−	−	−	−	−	−	−	−	−	−
round	−	−	−	−	−	−	−	−	−	−	−	+	+	−	−	−	+	+	−	+
lateral	−	−	−	−	−	−	+	+	−	−	−	−	−	−	−	−	−	−	−	−
palatal	−	−	+	−	−	+	−	+	+	−	−	−	−	−	−	−	−	−	−	−
tense	−	−	−	−	−	−	−	−	−	−	−	−	−	+	+	+	+	+	+	+
stressed	−	−	−	−	−	−	−	−	−	±	±	±	±	±	±	±	±	±	±	±
long	−	−	−	−	−	−	−	−	−	−	−	−	−	−	−	−	−	−	−	−

Several of the changes which Old Church Slavic has undergone from PIE have remained as rules in the Old Church Slavic grammar. Those given below labeled "morph cond" are morphologically conditioned and apply either to lexically marked items or to morphosyntactically marked classes. Those marked "phon cond" are phonologically conditioned and apply more or less generally. The symbol "Ø" after a change means that it has restructured lexical items and/or changed the inventory of underlying segments and has then been dropped from the grammar.

For those changes remaining as rules in the grammar we cite an illustrative example. Additional examples can be found in the discussions of the particular rules.

1a DEASP: Ø.

1b DIPH SHORT: Ø.

1c EARLIEST PAL: Ø.

1d SYL SON: Ø.

1e OCS STRESS (morph cond): nom sg /večerʊ/ 'evening' vs. nom pl /večeri/ (OCS STRESS) → véčerʊ and večerí.

1f W-F SYL (morph cond): note the alternation of the pres part nom sg masc berý 'carrying' vs. the acc sg berǫ́štɪ.

2a C-CL (phon cond): inf /met+tí/ 'throw' vs. 1sg pres /met+ǫ́/ (C-CL) → mestí and metǫ́.

2b DELAB: Ø.

3 RUKI (morph cond): 1 pl aorist /bɪ́ras+omʊ/ 'we gathered' vs. 2 pl aorist /bɪ́ras+te/ 'you gathered' (RUKI) → bɪ́raxomʊ and bɪ́raste.

4a C-CL SIMP (morph cond): /greb+tí/ 'dig' vs. 1sg pres /greb+ǫ́/ (C-CL SIMP) → gretí and grebǫ́.

4b PROTHESIS (phon cond): the adv particle /ése/ 'behold' (PROTHESIS applying optionally) → ése or jése.

4c W-F C DELE: ∅.

5a e(:)/o(:)-LOW: ∅.

5b 1ST PAL (morph cond: nom sg /bóg+ʊ/ 'God' vs. voc sg /bóg+e/ (1ST PAL) → bógʊ vs. bóže.

6a ǣ-TO-ā (morph cond): the class 3 verbs, inf /mɪn+ě́ti/ 'to mean' vs. /lež+ě́ti/ 'to lie' (ǣ-TO-ā) → mɪně́ti and ležáti.

6b V-FRONT (morph cond): nom sg o-class neuter /sel+ó/ 'village' vs. nom sg jo-class /pól+jo/ 'field' (V-FRONT) → seló vs. pólje.

7a æw-TO-aw : ∅.

7b MON (morph cond): note the alternation of the inf plúti 'to swim' vs. the 1sg pres plóvǫ 'I swim'.

7c NASAL V (morph cond): inf /jem+tí/ 'to take' vs. 1sg pres /jím+ǫ/ 'I take' (NASAL V , ev)→ jętí vs. ī́mǫ.

8a JOTA (morph cond): inf /pɪs+áti/ 'to write' vs. 1sg pres /pis+jǫ́/ 'I write' (JOTA) → pɪsáti vs. pišǫ́.

8b 2ND PAL (morph cond): nom sg /rǫk+á/ 'hand' vs. dat sg /rǫ́k+ě/ (2ND PAL) → rǫká vs. rǫcě́.

9a MET (morph cond): inf /mel+tí/ 'grind' vs. 1sg pres /mel+jǫ́/ (MET) → mlětí vs. meljǫ́.

9b ū-TO-ȳ: ∅.

9c w-TO-v: ∅.

9d 3RD PAL (morph cond): inf /dvíg+nǫti/ 'to move' vs. /dvig+áti/ 'move often' (3RD PAL) → dvígnǫti vs. dvizáti.

10 V-SHORT: ∅.

IV Historical Old Church Slavic Morphology

A. Overview

B. Old Church Slavic Morphology

The substantives and verbs inflect for singular, dual and plural. The forms in the left-hand column are those of Old Church Slavic at ca. 850 AD. The forms on the right are the PIE antecedents. As noted under change 1e OCS STRESS, we have reconstructed the Old Church Slavic and PIE word stress along the lines of the morph cond in languages such as Russian and Bulgarian.

1 Nouns

The genders are masculine, feminine and neuter; cases are nominative, vocative, accusative, genitive, locative and and instrumental. In the dual and plural, the nominative and vocative are identical.

1.1 o- and jo-Class (Masculine, Neuter)

The following is a masculine noun.

		OCS		PIE
sg	**nom**	vlíkʊ	'wolf'	*wĺ̥kʷos[8]
	voc	vlíče		*wĺ̥kʷe[9]
	acc	vlíkʊ		*wĺ̥kʷom
	gen	vlíka		*wĺ̥kʷōd[10]
	loc	vlícě		*wĺ̥kʷoi[9]
	dat	vlíku		*wĺ̥kʷōu[11]
	instr	vlíkomɪ		*wĺ̥kʷo+mi[12]
du	**nom**	vlíka		*wĺ̥kʷō
	acc	"		"
	gen	vlɪkú		*wl̥kʷóus
	loc	"		"
	dat	vlɪkóma		*wl̥kʷómō
	instr	"		"
pl	**nom**	vlíci		*wĺ̥kʷoi[13]
	acc	vlíky		*wĺ̥kʷons[14]
	gen	vlɪkʊ́		*wl̥kʷóm
	loc	vlɪcě́xʊ		*wl̥kʷóisu[15]
	dat	vlɪkómʊ		*wl̥kʷómus
	instr	vlɪký		*wl̥kʷṓis[16]

The o-class neuter nouns have the same endings as the masculine ones except for the following:

		OCS		PIE
nom/voc/acc	**sg**	mě́sto	'place'	*móistom[17]
	du	městě́		*moistói
	pl	městá		*moistā́

In PIE the jo-class had the same endings as those of the o-class. However, after the PIE-to-Old Church Slavic changes, the OCSlav jo- and o-class endings differ. E.g., the following jo-class masculine noun:

			OCS		PIE
masc	**sg**	**nom**	mǫ́žɪ	'man'	*mángjos[18]
		voc	mǫ́žu		*mángjou[19]
		acc	mǫžá		*mangjṓd[20]
		gen	mǫžá		*mangjṓd
		loc	mǫží		*mangjói
		dat	mǫžú		*mangjṓu
		instr	mǫžémɪ		*mangjómi

		OCS		PIE
du	nom	mǫžá	'man'	*mangjṓ
	acc	"		"
	gen	mǫžú		*mangjóus
	loc	"		"
	dat	mǫžéma		*mangjómō
	instr	"		"
pl	nom	mǫží		*mangjói
	acc	mǫžę́		*mangjóns[21]
	gen	mǫžĭ́		*mangjóm
	loc	mǫžíxʊ		*mangjóisu
	dat	mǫžémʊ		*mangjómus
	instr	mǫží		*mangjṓis[22]

The neuter jo-class nouns have the same endings as the masculine ones except for the following:

		OCS		PIE
nom/voc/acc	sg	pólje	'field'	*póljom[23]
	du	poljí		*poljói
	pl	poljá		*poljā́

Some jo-class neuter nouns end in OCSlav -ije. These have long stems and reflect the operation of the PIE rule 3.1.2f SIEVERS . E.g., the nom sg jo-class neuter *gnṓ+n+jom 'knowledge' (3.1.2f SIEVERS applying synchronically) → *gnṓnijom (1c EARLIEST PAL) > *znṓnijom (4c W-F C DELE) > *znṓnijo (5a e(:)/o(:)-LOW> *znā́nija (6b V-FRONT) > *znā́nijæ (10 V-SHORT) > OCSlav znánije. (Change 10 V-SHORT treats the sequence /ij/ as a long vowel: hence the OCSlav form is znánije, not **znánɪje.)

1.2 ā- and jā-Class (Feminine, Masculine)

The great majority of these nouns are feminine, while a few are semantically masculine agent nouns such as OCSlav slugá 'servant' from PIE *slougā́ 'service, help'. The following is a feminine noun.

		OCS		PIE
sg	nom	žená	'woman'	*gʷenā́
	voc	žéno		*gʷéna[24]
	acc	ženǫ́		*gʷenā́m
	gen	žený		*gʷenā́s[25]
	loc	ženě́		*gʷenā́i
	dat	"		"
	instr	ženójǫ		*gʷenā́i+ām[26]
du	nom	ženě́		*gʷenái
	acc	"		"
	gen	ženú		*gʷenóus
	loc	"		"
	dat	ženáma		*gʷenā́mō
	instr	"		"

		OCS		PIE
pl	**nom**	žený	'woman'	*gʷenā́s[25]
	acc	"		"
	gen	ženú̆		*gʷenóm
	loc	ženáxʊ		*gʷenā́su[27]
	dat	ženámʊ		*gʷenā́mus
	instr	ženámi		*gʷenā́mīs[28]

The jā-class nouns originally had the same endings as the ā-class. However, by Old Church Slavic times some of the endings came to differ as a result of phonological change:

		OCS		PIE
sg	**nom**	dušá	'soul'	*dʰousjā́[29]
	voc	dúše		*dʰóusja[29]
	acc	dúšǫ		*dʰóusjām
	gen	dušę́		*dʰousjā́s[30]
	loc	duší		*dʰousjā́i[31]
	dat	"		"
	instr	dušéjǫ		*dʰousjā́i+ām
du	**nom**	dúši		*dʰóusjai
	acc	"		"
	gen	dušú		*dʰousjóus
	loc	"		"
	dat	dušáma		*dʰousjā́mō
	instr	"		"
pl	**nom**	dúšę		*dʰóusjās[30]
	acc	"		"
	gen	dušı́		*dʰousjóm
	loc	dušáxʊ		*dʰousjā́su
	dat	dušámʊ		*dʰousjā́mus
	instr	dušámi		*dʰousjā́mīs

Some jā-class nouns differ from dušá 'soul' above in the following cases:

		OCS		PIE
sg	nom	ladıjí	'boat'	*aldʰjā́[32]
pl	nom	"		*aldʰjā́s[33]
	acc	"		"

1.3 i-Class (Masculine, Feminine)

The following Old Church Slavic masculine noun góstɪ from PIE *gʰóstis does not undergo 1c EARLIEST PAL to become OCSlav **zóstɪ. Hence we assume it was a borrowing from Germanic after the time of 1c EARLIEST PAL.

			OCS		PIE
masc	sg	nom	góstɪ	'guest'	*gʰóstis
		voc	gósti		*gʰóstei[34]
		acc	góstɪ		*gʰóstim
		gen	gósti		*gʰósteis[34]
		loc	gósti		*gʰóstei[34]
		dat	"		"
		instr	góstɪmɪ		*gʰóstimi
	du	nom	gósti		*gʰóstī
		acc	"		"
		gen	gostíju		*gʰostí+ous[35]
		loc	"		"
		dat	gostíma		*gʰostí+mō
		instr	"		"
	pl	nom	góstɪje		*gʰósti+es[35]
		acc	gósti		*gʰósti+ns[36]
		gen	gostíjɪ		*gʰostí+om[37]
		loc	gostíxʊ		*gʰostí+su
		dat	gostímʊ		*gʰostí+mus
		instr	gostími		*gʰostí+mīs

Feminine i-class nouns have the same endings as the masc paradigm above except for the following:

		OCS		PIE
sg	instr	kóstɪjǫ	'bone'	*kósti+ām[38]
pl	nom	kósti		*kósti+ns[39]

1.4 u-Class (Masculine)

By Old Church Slavic times the nouns of this class are tending to pass into the o-class. The original u-class paradigm is the following.

		OCS		PIE
sg	nom	sýnʊ	'son'	*sū́nu+s[40]
	voc	sýnu		*sū́nou[40]
	acc	sýnʊ		*sū́nu+m
	gen	sýnu		*sū́nou+s
	loc	sýnu		*sū́nou
	dat	sýnovi		*sū́nou+ei[41]
	instr	sýnʊmɪ		*sū́nu+mi

		OCS		PIE
du	**nom**	syný	'son'	*sūnū́
	acc	"		"
	gen	synovú		*sūnou+óus
	loc	"		"
	dat	synʊmá		*sūnu+mṓ
	instr	"		"
pl	**nom**	synové		*sūnou+és[42]
	acc	syný		*sūnú+ns
	gen	synovʊ́		*sūnou+óm
	loc	synʊxʊ́		*sūnu+sú
	dat	synʊmʊ́		*sūnu+mús
	instr	synʊmí		*sūnu+mī́s

1.5 Athematic Classes

Nouns in these classes are sometimes called "consonant-stem nouns" in the literature, as in Schmalstieg (1983: 96). Some of the athematic classes are sparsely attested: the nouns which formerly constituted them tend to pass into other classes, usually the i-class . (Our examples of complex athematic paradigms are those of the tVr-class and the Vn-class below.)

1.5.1 Ø-Class (Masculine)

This class has for the most part disappeared. A remnant is the Old Church Slavic noun lákʊtɪ 'elbow', which has most of its endings from the i-class. However, one form has retained the original Ø-class ending:

		OCS		PIE
pl	**gen**	lákʊtʊ	'elbow'	*ṓlkutom[43]

Other instances of Ø-class nouns are referred to in the literature as tel-class and r-class. By OCSlav times these nouns had for the most part gone into the jo-class. In a few instances they retain the original Ø-class endings (which we give in toto under 1.5.4 below).

		OCS		PIE
nom	**sg**	děláteljɪ	'worker'	*dʰēlṓtel+jos[44]
		mýtarjɪ	'toll-taker'	*mū́tār+jos[45]
	pl	dělátele		*dʰēlṓtel+es
		mýtare		*mū́tār+es

1.5.2 Root Class (Feminine)

The stems of these nouns originally ended in /ī/ or /ū/. There is only one remaining reflex of such a noun in Old Church Slavic. It is OCSlav crʊ́kʊv- 'church', which aside from the forms cited below takes the endings of the tVr-class (and in a few plural cases, those of the ā-class).

		OCS		PIE
sg	**nom**	crʊ́ky	'church'	*kírk+ū+s[46]
	voc	"		"
	acc	crʊ́kʊvɪ		*kírk+ū+m̥[47]

1.5.3 tVr-Class (Feminine)

The masculine nouns originally in this class have all passed into other classes. E.g., PIE *b^{h}rā́tr- 'brother' (ev) > OCSlav o-class brátrʊ. There are apparently only two Old Church Slavic feminine nouns in this class, máti 'mother' and dʊ́šti 'daughter'. The declension is this:

			OCS		PIE
masc	**sg**	**nom**	máti	'mother'	*mā́t(er)+ī[48]
		voc	"		"
		acc	máterɪ		*mā́term̥
		gen	mátere		*mā́teres
		loc	"		*mā́tere
		dat	máteri		*mā́terei
		instr	máterɪjǫ		*mā́ter+i+ām[49]
	du	**nom**	máteri		*mā́terī
		acc	"		"
		gen	máteru		*mā́terous
		loc	"		"
		dat	máterɪma		*mā́ter+imō[49]
		instr	"		"
	pl	**nom**	máteri		*mā́ter+n̥s[50]
		acc	"		"
		gen	máterʊ		*mā́terom
		loc	máterɪxʊ		*mā́ter+isu[49]
		dat	máterɪmʊ		*mā́ter+imus[49]
		instr	máterɪmi		*mā́ter+imīs[49]

1.5.4 Vn-Class (Masculine, Neuter)

The following is a masculine noun.

		OCS		PIE
sg	**nom**	kámy	'stone'	*ákmōn[51,52]
	voc	"		"
	acc	kámenɪ		*ákmenm̥[52]
	gen	kámene		*ákmenes
	loc	"		*ákmene
	dat	kámeni		*ákmenei
	instr	kámenɪmɪ		*ákmen+imi[53]
du	**nom**	kámeni		*ákmenī
	acc	"		"
	gen	kamenú		*akmenóus
	loc	"		"
	dat	kamenɪ́ma		*akmen+ímō[53]
	instr	"		"

		OCS		PIE
pl	nom	kámene	'stone'	*ákmenes
	acc	kámeni		*ákmenn̥s[54]
	gen	kamenʊ́		*akmenóm
	loc	kamenɪ́xʊ		*akmen+ísu[53]
	dat	kamenɪ́mʊ		*akmen+ímus[53]
	instr	kamenɪ́mi		*akmen+ímīs[53]

Some Vn-class masculine nouns act like o-class nouns, aside from a few plural endings which are Vn-class. E.g.,

		OCS		PIE
nom	sg	graždanínʊ	'citizen'	*gard+jān+ī́n+os[55]
	pl	graždaníne		*gard+jān+ī́n+es[55]

The neuter nouns of this class have the same endings as the masculine except for the following.

		OCS		PIE
sg	nom	sě́mę	'seed'	*sē̗ment[56]
	voc	"		"
	acc	"		"
du	nom	sě́meně		*sē̗menoi
	acc	"		"
pl	nom	sě́mena		*sē̗menā
	acc	"		"
	instr	sě́meny		*sē̗men+ois[57]

1.5.5 Vnt-Class (Neuter)

These nouns denote small animals and children. The endings are those of the Vn-class immediately above. E.g.,

		OCS		PIE
sg	nom	ágnę	'lamb'	*ṓg^{hw}nent
	gen	ágnęte		*ṓg^{hw}nentes[58]

1.5.6 Vs-Class (Neuter)

The endings are those of sě́mę 'seed' in 1.5.4 above. E.g.,

		OCS		PIE
nom	sg	slóvo	'word'	*klówos[59]
	du	slovesě́		*klowesói
	pl	slovesá		*klowesā́

2 Adjectives

Old Church Slavic masculine and neuter adjectives take o- or jo- class endings; and feminine adjectives take ā- or jā-class endings. Slavic developed a so-called "definite" or long adjective declension alongside the original "indefinite" or short declension. The long declension is formed from short forms to which the respective 3rd person anaphoric pronouns (as in 5.3 below) have been added.

Nandriş (1959: 113) describes the syntactic and semantic differences between the definite and indefinite declensions: "The original syntactical function of the pronominal, definite adjective is attributive; the short, indefinite adjective was used predicatively. So, [Old Church Slavic] člověkʊ dobrʊ = a good man, man is good; člověkʊ dobryi = the man who is good. The last construction can be said to contain a relative clause which defines the noun. There is a difference in meaning between the two constructions: the first has a general, indefinite meaning; the second refers to a certain, definite category: the good man."

This Slavic distinction is analogous to that in Germanic between the strong (indefinite) and weak (definite) declensions. (See Chapter 2 Gothic, Historical Gothic morphology, sections 2.1 Strong Adjective Declension and 2.2 Weak Adjective Declension.)

2.1 Indefinite or Short Declension

An example of an o/ā-class adjective follows. The endings are those of the masc o-class (1.1 vlɪ́kʊ 'wolf'), the fem ā-class (1.2 žená 'woman') and the neuter o-class (1.1 mě́sto 'place'). E.g.,

			OCS		PIE
nom	**sg**	**masc**	slábʊ	'weak'	*slṓb+os
		fem	slába		*slṓb+ā
		neuter	slábo		*slṓb+om

An example of a jo-/jā-class adjective follows. The endings are those of the masc jo-class (1.1 mǫ́žɪ 'man'), the fem jā-class (1.2 dušá 'soul') and the neuter jo-class (1.1 pólje 'field'). E.g.,

			OCS		PIE
nom	**sg**	**masc**	lʊ́žɪ	'lying, mendacious'	*lúg^{h}+jos[60]
		fem	lʊ́ža		*lúg^{h}+jā
		neuter	lʊ́že		*lúg^{h}+jom

2.2 Definite or Long Declension

These forms are constructed from those of the short declension in 2.1 above plus the respective anaphoric pronouns i 'he, she, it, they', jego etc. as described under 5.3 below. In the following paradigm the forms in both columns are Old Church Slavic: those on the left are the long-declension forms; those on the right are the antecedent short forms followed by the respective anaphoric pronouns.

			Long-Forms		Short-Forms+Pron
masc	**sg**	**nom**	slábyi	'weak'	slábʊ́+i[61]
		acc	"		"
		gen	slábajego		slába+jego
		loc	slábějemɪ́		slábě+jemɪ́
		dat	slábujemu		slábu+jemu
		instr	slábyimɪ́		slábu+imɪ́ [61,62]

			Long-Forms		Short-Forms+Pron
masc	**du**	**nom**	slábaja	‘weak’	slába+ja
		acc	"		"
		gen	slábuju		slábu+(je)ju[63]
		loc	"		"
		dat	slábyima		slábŭ́+ima[61,62]
		instr	"		"
	pl	**nom**	slábii		slábi+i
		acc	slábyję		sláby+ję
		gen	slábyixŭ́		slábŭ́+ixŭ́[61]
		loc	"		" [61,62]
		dat	slábyimŭ́		slábŭ́+imŭ́[61,62]
		instr	slábyimi		slábŭ́+imi
fem	**sg**	**nom**	slábaja		slába+ja
		acc	slábǫjǫ		slábǫ+jǫ
		gen	slábyję		sláby+(je)ję[63]
		loc	sláběi		slábě+(je)i[63]
		dat	"		"
		instr	slábǫjǫ		slábǫjǫ+(jeję)[63]
	du	**nom**	sláběi		slábě+i
		acc	"		"
		gen	slábuju		slábu+(je)ju[63]
		loc	"		"
		dat	slábyima		slábŭ́+ima[61,62]
		instr	"		"
	pl	**nom**	slábyje		sláby+ję
		acc	"		"
		gen	slábyixŭ́		slábŭ́+ixŭ́[61]
		loc	"		" [61,62]
		dat	slábyimŭ́		slábŭ́+imŭ́[61,62]
		instr	slábyimi		slábŭ́+imi[61,62]
neut	**sg**	**nom**	sláboje		slábo+je[64]
		acc	"		"
	du	**nom**	sláběi		slábě+i[64]
		acc	"		"
	pl	**nom**	slábaja		slába+ja[64]
		acc	"		"

The jo/jā-class long declension is formed like the preceding o-/ā-class long paradigm above. E.g., the following masculine singular forms:

			Long-Forms		Short-Forms+Pron
masc	sg	nom	lŭžii	'mendacious'	lŭžĭ+i
		gen	lŭžajego		lŭža+jego
		loc	lŭžijemĭ		lŭži+jemĭ
		dat	lŭžujemu		lŭžu+jemu
		instr	lŭžiimĭ		lŭži+imĭ

2.3 Comparison

The adjective has only a comparative degree, but no superlative. The comparative endings are jo/jā-class adjectives. As noted in our description of change 1e OCS STRESS, the stress was on the first syllable of comparative adjectives.

The Old Church Slavic comparative formative develops from two PIE antecedent suffixes, *-jis- (possibly *-jes- in the nominative/accusative singular neuter) and *-ē+jis-. The former suffix is usually found with suppletive adjectives such as OCSlav nom sg masc mĭnjii 'smaller' from the pos málŭ 'small'. The latter suffix occurs more frequently on non-suppletive comparative adjectives like the nom sg masc stárěi 'older' from the pos stárŭ 'old'.

Examples of comparative adjectives, generally in the short declension, follow. The forms are singular.

		OCS		PIE
nom	masc	mĭnjii	'smaller'	*mín+jis[65]
		stárěi	'older'	*stā́r+ē+jis[65,66]
		úbožai	'poorer'	*áubag+ē+jis[65,67]
	fem	mĭnjĭši		*mín+jis+jā[68]
		stárěiši		*stā́r+ē+jis+jā
		úbožaiši		*áubag+ē+jis+jā
	neuter	mĭnje		*mín+jes[69]
		stárěje		*stā́r+ē+jes
		úbožaje		*áubag+ē+jes
gen	masc/neut	mĭnjĭša		*mín+jis+jōd
		stárěša		*stā́r+ē+jis+jōd
		úbožaiša		*áubag+ē+jis+jōd
	fem	mĭnjĭšę		*mín+jis+jās[70]
		stárěišę		*stā́r+ē+jis+jās
		úbožaišę		*áubag+ē+jis+jās

3 Adverbs

Old Church Slavic has no specific adverb paradigm. Rather, adverbial constructions are formed with a preposition plus a substantive or — more usually — with a bare noun or neuter adjective in any non-nominative case.

Examples of this type of formation are these:

				OCS		PIE
adj	**neuter**	**sg**	**acc**	górɪko	'bitterly'	*gʰʷórik+om
				takó	'thus'	*tōk+óm
				únje	'better'	*óusn+jes
			loc	dóbrě	'well'	*dʰóbr+oi
				právɪ	'rightly'	*prṓw+i
		pl	**instr**	právy	'rightly'	*prṓw+ōis
noun	**masc**	**sg**	**gen**	vɪčerá	'yesterday'	*wiker+ṓd
			instr	núdɪma	'necessarily'	*nóud+imō

4 Numerals

4.1 Cardinals

The numerals from 1 through 4 are adjectives which agree in case with the head noun of the construction: nom sg jedinứ vlíkʊ '1 wolf', nom dual dʊvá vlíka '2 wolves'. From 5 through 10 the numeral is an i-class noun which takes the case determined by the context. The head noun is in the genitive plural. E.g., pętɪ vlɪkứ 'a 5-ness of wolves, i.e. 5 wolves'. From 11 through 14, the construction is a prepositional phrase; and as is the case with 1 through 4, the first numeral is an adjective which agrees with the head noun. E.g., jedinứ ná désęte vlíkʊ '1 wolf on a 10-ness, i.e. 11 wolves' and dʊvá ná désęte vlíka '2 wolves (dual) on a 10-ness, i.e. 12 wolves'. From 15 on the numerals are nouns taking the case determined by the context; and the head noun is in the genitive plural. E.g., dứvá désęti vlɪkứ '2 10-nesses (dual) of wolves, i.e. 20 wolves', sʊtó vlɪkứ 'a 100-ness of wolves, i.e. 100 wolves'. (The stress on 1, 2, 100 and 10,000 is End-stress. That on 1,000 is first-syllable Stem-stress. The stress on the other numerals is Alt-stress — Stem-stress in the nominative/accusative and End-stress in the other cases.)

'1' The endings are those of the demonstrative tứ 'that' in 5.3 below. E.g., the nominative singular masculine form:

	OCS	PIE
'1'	jedinứ	*ed+oin+ós[71]

'2' The endings are the dual endings of the o/ā-class adjectives.

			OCS	PIE
'2'	**dual**	**masc**	dʊvá	*duwṓ
		fem	dʊvě́	*duwói
		neuter	duvě́	*duwái

'3' The endings are those of an i-i-class noun in the plural.

			OCS	PIE
'3'	**pl**	**masc**	trɪjé	*trijés
		fem/neuter	trí	*tríns[72]

'4' The endings are those of the athematic class — namely those of the masculine Vn-Vn-class (1.5.4) and those of the feminine and neuter tVrclass (1.5.3).

			OCS	PIE
'4'	**nom**	**masc**	četýre	*kʷetū́res
		fem/neuter	četýri	*kʷetū́rn̥s[73]
	gen	**all genders**	četyrú̆	*kʷetūróm[74]

	OCS	PIE
'5'	pę́tɪ	*péntis
'6'	šéstɪ	*ksékstis

The derivation of '5' is *péntis (4c W-F C DELE) > *pénti (7c NASAL V) > *pḗ̜ti (10 V-SHORT) > OCSlav pę́tɪ́. The word-initial /k/ in the PIE antecedent of '6' is posited so that 3 RUKI can apply. The derivation is *ksékstis (3 RUKI, which can apply only to the first /s/ in the word) > *kxékstis (4a C-CL CHANGES SIMP) > *xéstis (4c W-F C DELE) > *xésti (5b 1ST PAL) > *šésti (10 V-SHORT) > OCSlav šéstɪ́.

	OCS	PIE
'7'	sédmɪ	*séptm+is

The derivation here is not clear. The original PIE numeral may have been *septḿ̥. Then the ending *-is was added, so that by PIE 3.1.2g SYL SON the form became *septmis. Then le OCS STRESS (Stem-stress) applied resulting in *séptmis. The subsequent derivation was then *séptmis (? 4a C-CL CHANGES SIMP 1) > *sétmis (? 4a C-CL CHANGES SIMP 2) > *sédmis (4c W-F C DELE, 10 V-SHORT) > OCSlav sédmɪ́.

	OCS	PIE
'8'	ósmɪ́	*ókt+mis

The derivation is not clear. A possibility is PIE *oktṓu (addition of *-mis from '7' to the perceived root *okt- and addition of the stress from '7' as well) > *óktmis (? early application of 4a C-CL CHANGES SIMP) > *ókmis (lc EARLIEST PAL) > *ósmis (4c W-F C DELE) > *ósmi (10 V-SHORT) > OCSlav ósmɪ́.

	OCS	PIE
'9'	dévętɪ́	*néwm̥+tis

The derivation is *néwm̥ (addition of *-tis from '10' below) > *néwm̥tis (PIE 3.1.2d NASAL ASSIM applying synchronically) → *newn̥tis (replacement of word-initial /n/ by /d/ from '10') > *déwn̥tis (1d SYL SON) > *déwintis (4c W-F C DELE) > *déwinti (7c NASAL V) > *déwḗ̜ti (9c W-TO-V-v) > *dévḗ̜ti (10 V-SHORT) > OCSlav dévętɪ́.

	OCS	PIE
'10'	désętɪ	*dékn̥+t+is

The PIE antecedent consists of the numeral plus a derivative suffix plus the i-i-class nominative singular ending.

'11' through '19'
jedinú na désęte '1 on 10 = 11', etc.

These constructions consist of the numeral plus na 'on' plus désęte '10' in the locative singular of the athematic class.

'20' through '90'
duvá désęti '2 10's = 20'[75]
trɪjé désęti '3 10's = 30'[76]
pę́ti désętu '5 10's = 50', etc.[77]

	OCS	PIE
'100'	sutó	*kn̥tóm

The Old Church Slavic form is an o-class neuter noun. The expected derivation from the PIE antecedent would be *kn̥tóm (1c EARLIEST PAL) > *sn̥tóm (1d SYL SON) > *sintóm (4c W-F C DELE) > *sintó (7c NASAL V) > *sę̄tó (10 V-SHORT) > OCSlav **sętó instead of the actually occurring sutó. The form sutó may have been an early borrowing from another IE language, possibly Indo-Iranian.

'200' to '900'
duvě̋ sutě̋ '200'[78]
pę́tɪ sutú '500', etc.[79]

	OCS	PIE
'1000'	týsǫšti	*tū̋sunt+jī

This form may well have been a borrowing from the Old High German dialect of Germanic. In Slavic the form was put into the jā-class feminine class like ladíjí 'boat'. The derivation is *tū̋sunt+jī (3 RUKI not applying to the /s/, which indicates that the Old High German borrowing occurred after 500 AD, but 7c NASAL V does apply) > *tū̋sǭtjī (8a JOTA) > *tū̋sǭštī (9b ū-TO-ȳ) > *tȳ̋sǭštī (10 V-SHORT) > OCSlav týsǫšti.

	OCS	PIE
'10,000'	tumá	*tumā̋

This form is an ā-class feminine noun.

4.2 Ordinals

These forms are adjectives, for the most part of the o/ā-class except for '3rd', which is jo/jā-class. All are of the long declension (2.2 above) since they have "definite" meanings.

Examples are these:

	OCS	PIE	
'1st'	prívyi	*príw	+endings[80]
'2nd'	vʊtorýi	*wutor	"
'3rd'	trétii	*tré+t	" [80]
'4th'	četvrítyi	*kʷetūŕ̥+t	" [81]
'5th'	pę́tyi	*pént	"
'6th'	šestýi	*kseks+t	"
'7th'	semýi	*septm	"

5 Pronouns

The pronouns may have had stress on the word-final syllable. When occurring enclitically, they were probably unstressed. Here we shall not mark their stress.

5.1 First Person

		OCS		PIE
sg	**nom**	azʊ́	'I'	*ēgom[82]
	acc	mę		*m+ēm[83]
du	**nom**	vě	'we two'	*w+ē
	acc	na		*n+ō[83]
pl	**nom**	my	'we'	*m+ū
	acc	ně		*n+ē[83]

5.2 Second Person

		OCS		PIE
sg	**nom**	ty	'you'	*tū
	acc	tę		*t+ēm[84]
du	**nom**	va	'you two'	*w+ō
	acc	"		"
pl	**nom**	vy̅		*w+ū
	acc	"		" [84]

5.3 Third Person

There are two types of declension — the "soft" declension and the "hard" declension. Forms of the soft declension have /j/ in the paradigm and tend to undergo 6b V-FRONT . Forms of the hard declension have not undergone this change.

We begin with an example of the soft declension. This is the anaphoric pronoun i, ja, je, i 'he, she, it, they'.

			OCS	PIE
masc	**sg**	**nom**	i	*j+os[85,86]
		acc	i	*j+om[85,86]
		gen	jego	*j+og^{w}o[86,87]
		loc	jemĭ	*j+omi[86]
		dat	jemu	*j+omōu[86]
		instr	imĭ	*j+oimi[86,88]
	du	**nom**	ja	*j+ō[89]
		acc	"	"
		gen	jeju	*j+oi+ous[90]
		loc	"	"
		dat	ima	*j+oi+mō[86]
		instr	"	"
	pl	**nom**	i	*j+oi[86]
		acc	ję	*j+ons[86]
		gen	ixŭ	*j+oi+som[86,91]
		loc	"	"
		dat	imŭ	*j+oi+mus[86]
		instr	imi	*j+oi+mīs[86]
fem	**sg**	**nom**	ja	*j+ā
		acc	ją	*j+ām
		gen	jeję	*j+a+jans[86,92]
		loc	jei	*j+a+āi[86,93]
		dat	"	"
		instr	jeję	*j+a+jans[86,92]
	du	**nom**	i	*j+ai[86]
		acc	i	"
		gen	jeju	*j+ai+ous[86,94]
		loc	"	"
		dat	ima	*j+ai+mō[86]
		instr	"	"
	pl	**nom**	ję	*j+āns[86]
		acc	"	"
		gen	ixŭ	*j+ai+som[86]
		loc	"	"
		dat	imŭ	*j+ai+mus[86]
		instr	imi	*j+ai+mīs[86]
neut	**sg**	**nom**	je	*j+od[86,95]
		acc	"	"
	du	**nom**	i	*j+oi[86]
		acc	"	"
	pl	**nom**	j+a	*j+ā
		acc	"	"[96]

Other pronouns of the soft declension are these, cited in the nominative singular masculine.

OCS		PIE
moi	'my'	*mo+jos
naší	'our'	*nōs+jos[97]
síjí	'this'	*ki+jos
vísi	'all'	*wis+jos

The anaphoric and relative pronouns, when preceded by a preposition, prefix an /n/. E.g., OCSlav /sứ imí/ 'with him' → sứn imí.

The historical background of this construction may be illustrated in the following derivation: PIE *sun##joimi 'with him' (enclisis in a prepositional phrase with a pronoun such that the word boundary is lost and the phrase is treated as a single word) > *sunjoimi (4c W-F C DELE applying to *sun followed by a noun, but not in the prepositional phrase) > *su vs. *sunjoimi (ev) > OCSlav sứ vs. sứnimí = sứ nimí. This /n/ was then added after other prepositions where it had not occurred historically such as OCSlav na njemí 'on him' from PIE *nō jomi.

Pronouns in the hard declensicn are OCSlav onứ 'that one' from PIE *on+os, inứ 'another' from PIE *ein+os, takứ 'such a' from PIE $*tōk^w$+os and the deictic tứ 'that one over there' which we cite below.

			OCS		PIE
masc	**sg**	**nom**	tứ	'that'	*t+os
		acc	togo		$*t+og^wo$
		gen	"		"
		loc	tomí		*t+omi
		dat	tomu		*t+omōu
		instr	těmí		*t+oimi[98]
	du	**nom**	ta		*t+ō
		acc	"		"
		gen	toju		*t+oi+ous[99]
		loc	"		"
		dat	těma		*t+oi+mō
		instr	"		"
	pl	**nom**	ti		*t+oi
		acc	ty		*t+ons
		gen	těxứ		*t+oi+som
		loc	"		"
		dat	těmứ		*t+oi+mus
		instr	těmi		*t+oi+mīs
fem	**sg**	**nom**	ta		*t+ā
		acc	tǫ		*t+ām
		gen	toję		*t+a+jans
		loc	toi		*t+a+āi
		dat	"		"
		instr	toję		*t+a+jans

			OCS		PIE
fem	**du**	**nom**	tě	'that'	*t+ai
		acc	"		"
		gen	toju		*t+ai+ous
		loc	"		"
		dat	těma		*t+ai+mō
		instr	"		"
	pl	**nom**	ty		*t+āns
		acc	"		"
		gen	těxʊ		*t+ai+som
		loc	"		"
		dat	těmʊ		*t+ai+mus
		instr	těmi		*t+ai+mīs
neut	**sg**	**nom**	to		*t+od
		acc	"		"
	du	**nom**	tě		*t+oi
		acc	"		"
	pl	**nom**	ta		*t+ā
		acc	"		"

5.4 Reflexive

This pronoun occurs only in the singular and in all cases except the nominative and vocative.

		OCS		PIE
sg	**acc**	sebe, sę	'oneself, themselves'	*sebʰe, *sem
	gen	" "		" "
	loc	sebě		*sebʰoi
	dat	sebě, si		*sebʰoi, *sei
	instr	sobojǫ		*sobʰo+jām[100]

5.5 Relative

The Old Church Slavic relative pronoun consists of the anaphoric i under 5.3 above plus the Old Church Slavic particle -že from PIE *-gʰʷe. E.g., the following masculine forms:

		OCS		PIE
sg	**nom**	iže	'who, which, that'	*jos+gʰʷe
	gen	jegože		*jogʷo+gʰʷe

5.6 Interrogative

The masculine and feminine forms are identical. The forms occur only in the singular.

		OCS		PIE
masc	**nom**	kʊto	'who'	*kʷos##tod[101]
	acc	kogo		*kʷ+ogʷo
	gen	"		"
	dat	komu		*kʷ+omōu
	instr	čěmɪ		*kʷ+oimi[102]

		OCS		PIE
neut	nom	čɪto	'what'	$*k^w$+i+tod[101]
	acc	"		"
	gen	česo		$*k^w$+eso
	loc	čemɪ		$*k^w$+emi
	dat	česomu		$*k^w$+es+omōu
	instr	čimɪ		$*k^w$+oimi[102]

An interrogative adj OCSlav koi 'which one(s)?' is derived from PIE $*k^w$o- and takes the endings of i 'he' in 5.3 above. E.g., the following nominative singular forms:

	OCS		PIE
masc	koi	'which one'	$*k^w$o+jos
fem	kaja		$*k^w$ā+jā
neuter	koje		$*k^w$o+jod

6 Verbs

The features of the Old Church Slavic verb are given in the following two tables. Table i contains the variable features — namely those which can change contingent upon the context. Table ii shows the lexical or inherent features — namely those that are idiosyncratic. They indicate the particular form-class of the verb.

(i) Variable Features

The first section of this table lists the purely verbal features. The second gives the features of deverbative adjectives and nouns.

Verbal Inflection

(a) Person	(b) Number	(c) Voice	(d) Tense + Mood[103]
1. 1st	1. singular	1. active	1. present
2. 2nd	2. dual	2. passive[104]	2. imperfect (past)[105]
3. 3rd	3. plural		3. aorist (past)[105]
			4. perfect tenses (past)[106]
			5. imperative
			6. future
			7. conditional [107]

Adjectival and Nominal Inflection

(a) Person	(b) Number	(c) Voice	(d) Tense and Mood
Ø	1. singular	1. active	1. present
	2. dual	2. passive	2–4. (past, as above)
	3. plural		6. future

(i) Variable Features (cont.)

(e) Mood Occurring in	Present	Past	Future
1. departicipial noun	active		
2. infinitive	active		
3. supine	active		
4. participal	active/passive	active/passive	active/passive

(ii) Inherent Features.

(a) Type	(b) Class[108]
1. perfective[109,110]	1st singular or e-class, e.g. nes+é+tъ 'carries'
2. imperfective[109,110]	2nd or ne-class, e.g. dvíg+ne+tъ 'moves'
	3rd or je-class, e.g. zná+je+tъ 'knows'
	4th or i-class , e.g. sed+í+tъ 'sits'
	5th athematic or Ø-class, e.g. dás+tъ 'gives'

In Tables i and ii above the features in the columns are mutually exclusive. Not all the logical possibilities are realized: the notations in the (e) columns of table (i) indicate which are.

6.1 Present

There are two kinds of present endings, so-called thematic for classes 1 through 4 and athematic for class 5. Classes 1, 3 and 4 each admit of two different types of infinitive formation. (See 6.8.2 below.) The 1st class had PIE -e- or -o(:)- between the root and the ending. E.g.,

		OCS		PIE
sg	1	berǫ́	'carry together, collect'	*bʰer+ṓ+m[111]
	2	beréši		*bʰer+é+si+ai[112]
	3	berétъ		*bʰer+é+ti[113]
du	1	berévě		*bʰer+é+wēs
	2	beréta		*bʰer+é+tō[114]
	3	beréte		*bʰer+é+te
pl	1	berémъ		*bʰer+é+mos
	2	beréte		*bʰer+é+te
	3	berǫ́tъ		*bʰer+ó+nti[113]

The other thematic classes 2, 3 and 4 have the same endings as berǫ́, but with different intermediate morphemes.

		OCS		PIE
		The 2nd class had –n(e)–. E.g.,		
sg	1	dvígnǫ	'move'	*dwéig+n+ōm
	2	dvígneši		*dwéig+ne+si+ai
	3	dvígnetъ		*dwéig+ne+ti
pl		dvígnǫtъ		*dwéig+n+onti
		The 3rd class had –j(e)–. E.g.,		
sg	1	znájǫ	'know'	*gnṓ+j+ōm
	2	znáješi		*gnṓ+j+esi+ai
	3	znájetъ		*gnṓ+j+eti
pl		znájǫtъ		*gnṓ+j+onti[115]
		The 4th class had –i–.[116] E.g.,		
sg	1	sěždǫ́	'sit'	*sēd+j+ṓm[117]
	2	sědíši		*sēd+éj+si+ai[118]
	3	sědítъ		*sēd+éj+ti
pl		sědętъ		*sēd+j+ónti[115]

The 5th class has no intermediate vowel between the stem and the ending. It is called the athematic or Ø-class. There are four verbs in this class. They are OCSlav 3 sg jéstъ 'be', dástъ 'give', véstъ 'know' and jástu 'eat'. E.g., the present forms of 'be' and 'give'.

		OCS		PIE
sg	1	jésmь	'be'	*és+mi[119]
		dámь	'give'	*dṓd+mi[120]
	2	jési		*és+sai[121]
		dási		*dṓd+sai
	3	jéstъ		*és+ti
		dátъ		*dṓd+ti
du	1	jesvě́		*es+wḗs[119,122]
		davě́		*dōd+wḗs[122]
	2	jestá		*es+tṓ
		dastá		*dōd+tṓ[123]
	3	jesté		*es+tés
		dasté		*dōd+tés
pl	1	jesmú		*es+mós
		damú		*dōd+mós
	2	jesté		*es+tés
		dasté		*dōd+tés
	3	sǫtú		*s+n̥tí[124]
		dadętú		*dōd+n̥tí[124]

6.2 Imperfect

This paradigm is formed with the intermediate suffixes –V́ax- and -ě́ax- plus the personal endings. The intermediate suffixes are added to the stems of verbs (on which see 6.8.2 below). The suffix -V́ax- is added to stems ending in vowels and -ě́ax- to those ending in consonants. Examples of the two intermediate suffixes are the 1st class 1sg imperf bɪráaxʊ 'collect' vs. 2nd class dvigně́axʊ 'move'. An example of the imperfect paradigm is the following:

		OCS		PIE
sg	**1**	bɪráaxʊ	'collect'	*b^hr̥+ā́##ēs+om[125,126]
	2	bɪráaše		*b^hr̥+ā́##ēs+es[127]
	3	bɪráaše		*b^hr̥+ā́##ēs+et
du	**1**	bɪráaxově		*b^hr̥+ā́##ēs+owēs
	2	bɪráašeta		*b^hr̥+ā́##ēs+etō
	3	bɪráašete		*b^hr̥+ā́##ēs+etes
pl	**1**	bɪráaxomʊ		*b^hr̥+ā́##ēs+omos
	2	bɪráašete		*b^hr̥+ā́##ēs+ete
	3	bɪráaxǫ		*b^hr̥+ā́##ēs+ont[128]

6.3 Aorist

There are three aorist formations. These are (i) the so-called "simple" or "asigmatic" aorist, (ii) the sigmatic or s-aorist and (iii) the so-called "enlarged" sigmatic aorist, a later formation.

None of these formations is restricted to any one of the five verb classes: any one of the three aorist formations can occur with a verb of any of the five classes. On occasion a verb can take more than one aorist formation. E.g., the 1st class verb nestí 'to carry' can take either the simple aorist (PIE *ně́kom > OCSlav ně́sʊ 'I carried') or the enlarged sigmatic aorist (PIE *nekósom > OCSlav nesóxʊ 'idem').

The Proto-Slavic and Old Church Slavic stress on verbs in the aorist is not clear. One possibility is that the stress was on the first syllable, as was probably the case in PIE with the original stress on the augment. (See on this the stress rules of Ancient Greek and of Sanskrit.) Here, however, we shall place the stress on Proto-Slavic and Old Church Slavic in accordance with the views of Vaillant (1966: 3, 530-4).

(i) The Simple Aorist

The following is a 1st class verb.

		OCS		PIE
sg	**1**	mogʊ́	'was able'	*mog^h+óm
	2	možé		*mog^h+és[129]
	3	možé		*mog^h+ét[129]
du	**1**	mogóvě		*mog^h+ówēs
	2	možéta		*mog^h+étō
	3	možéte		*mog^h+étes
pl	**1**	mogómʊ		*mog^h+ómos
	2	možéte		*mog^h+éte
	3	mogǫ́		*mog^h+ónt[130]

(ii) The Sigmatic or s-Aorist

The following is a 1st class verb.

		OCS		PIE
sg	**1**	bɪráxʊ	'gathered'	*bʰr̥+ā́+s+om[131]
	2	bɪrá		*bʰr̥+ā́+s+s[132]
	3	bɪrá		*bʰr̥+ā́+s+t[132]
du	**1**	bɪráxově		*bʰr̥+ā́+s+owēs
	2	bɪrásta		*bʰr̥+ā́+s+tō[133]
	3	bɪráste		*bʰr̥+ā́+s+tes[133]
pl	**1**	bɪráxomʊ		*bʰr̥+ā́+s+omos
	2	bɪráste		*bʰr̥+ā́+s+te[133]
	3	bɪrášę		*bʰr̥+ā́+s+n̥t[134]

(iii) The Enlarged Sigmatic Aorist

The following is a 1st class verb.

		OCS		PIE
sg	**1**	nesóxʊ	'carried'	*nek+ós+om[135]
	2	nesé		*nek+és[135]
	3	nesé		*nek+ét[135]
du	**1**	nesóxově		*nek+ós+owēs
	2	nesósta		*nek+ós+tō
	3	nesóste		*nek+ós+tes
pl	**1**	nesóxomʊ		*nek+ós+omos
	2	nesóste		*nek+ós+te
	3	nesóšę		*nek+ós+n̥t[136]

Finally, two general observations on the aorist. First, some verbs with monosyllabic stems which end in consonants form their aorist i or aorist ii paradigms with e-ē, o-o or Øi-ei ablaut. E.g.,

				OCS		PIE
(a)	**1**	**sg**	**pres**	nesǫ́	'carry'	*nek+ṓm
			aorist	nḗsʊ		*nḗk+om
	2			nése		*nék+es[137]
(b)	**1**	**sg**	**pres**	bodǫ́	'sting'	*bʰod+ṓm
			aorist	básʊ		*bʰṓd+s+om[138]
	2			bóde		*bʰód+es[137]
(c)	**1**	**sg**	**pres**	čɪtǫ́	'read'	*kʷit+ṓm
			aorist	čísʊ		*kʷéit+s+om[139]

Second, a few 2nd and 3rd person singular aorists add -tʊ alongside the usual endings cited above. E.g., the following aorist forms:

		OCS		PIE
sg	**2**	dá	'gave'	*dṓ+s+s
		dátʊ		*dṓ+tu
	3	dá		*dṓ+s+t
		dátʊ		*dṓ+tu

6.4 Perfect Tenses

The only original PIE perfect form remaining in Old Church Slavic is the following:

	OCS		PIE
1sg	vě̌dě	'I know'	*wóid+ai[140]

Otherwise the perfect tenses are constructed from the past active participle (described in 6.9.3 below) and the respective present, past and future forms of the Old Church Slavic verb bytí 'be'. E.g.,

1sg	**masc**	**perf**	**pres**	jésmɪ neslʊ́	'I have carried'[141]
			past	bě̆axʊ́ neslʊ́	'I had carried'[142]
			future	bǫdǫ́ neslʊ́	'I shall have carried'[143]

6.5 Imperative

There are three classes of imperative endings.

(i) The endings of 1st and 2nd class verbs are as follows.
The verb is of the 1st class.

		OCS		PIE
sg	**2**	berí	'gather'	$*b^her+ói+s$[144]
	3	berí		$*b^her+ói+t$
du	**1**	berě̌vě		$*b^her+ói+wēs$[144]
	2	berě̌ta		$*b^her+ói+tō$
pl	**1**	berě̌mʊ		$*b^her+ói+mos$
	2	berě̌te		$*b^her+ói+te$

The imperative of 'be' is formed from the future stem bǫd- given under 6.6 below. The endings are those of berí. E.g.,

		OCS		PIE
sg	**2**	bǫdí	'be'	$*b^h+ont+d+óis$
	3	bǫdí		$*b^h+ont+d+óit$

(ii) Verbs of classes 3 and 4 have the marker -i- throughout the paradigm.
The following is a 3rd class verb.

		OCS		PIE
sg	2	znáji	'know'	*gnṓ+j+oi+s
	3	znáji		*gnṓ+j+oi+t
du	1	znájivě		*gnṓ+j+oi+wēs[145]
	2	znájita		*gnṓ+j+oi+tō
pl	1	znájimʊ		*gnṓ+j+oi+mos
	2	znájite		*gnṓ+j+oi+te

(iii) Verbs of class 5 inflect as follows.

		OCS		PIE
sg	2	daždí	'give'	*dōd+ī́+s[146]
	3	daždí		*dōd+ī́+t
du	1	dadívě		*dōd+ī́+wēs
	2	dadíta		*dōd+ī́+tō
pl	1	dadímʊ		*dōd+ī́+mos
	2	dadíte		*dōd+ī́+te

6.6 Future

This tense can be expressed by the present of a perfective verb or by a verb such as xotě́ti 'to will' plus the infinitive. E.g., OCSlav pridǫ́ 'I shall arrive' from PIE *pri+eidṓm; and OCSlav xotě́ti ití 'to be going to go'.

The only verb to have a special future paradigm is bytí 'to be'. In this paradigm the endings of the present tense under 6.1 above are added to the Old Church Slavic stem bǫd-. E.g.,

		OCS		PIE
sg	1	bǫdǫ́	'I will be'	*b^h+ont+d+ṓm[147]
	2	bǫdéši		*b^h+ont+d+ési+ai

6.7 Conditional

This paradigm is constructed of the conditional forms of 'be' plus the present active participle as given under 6.9.1 below. E.g., OCSlav bimɪ́ neslʊ 'I (masc) would carry or would have carried'. The conditional forms of 'be' are these.

		OCS		PIE
sg	1	bimɪ́	'would be or would have been'	*b^h+ī+mí[148]
	2	bí		*b^h+ī́+s
	3	bí		*b^h+ī́+t

		OCS		PIE
du	1	bivě́	'would be or would have been'	*bʰ+ī+wḗs
	2	bistá		*bʰ+ī+s+tṓ
	3	bisté		*bʰ+ī́+s+tés[149]
pl	1	bimŭ́		*bʰ+ī+mós
	2	bisté		*bʰ+ī+s+té[149]
	3	bǫ́ or		*bʰ+ónt[150]
		bišę́		*bʰ+ī+s+ń̥t[149,150]

6.8 Verbal Nouns

There are three of these: departicipial nouns, infinitive and the supine.

6.8.1 Departicipial Nouns

These are constructed of the past passive participle described under 6.9.4 below plus jo-class neuter noun endings as described under 1.1 above. E.g., the following nominative singular forms:

OCS		PIE
znánije	'knowledge'	*gnṓ+n+j+om[151]
začętije	'child conception'	*gʰō+kén+t+j+om

6.8.2 Infinitives

The Old Church Slavic suffix is -ti. Its antecedent was the noun suffix *-t- plus the dative or perhaps locative singular ending of an i-class noun as described under 1.3 above.

The five verb classes form their infinitives as follows:

Class 1 verbs have intermediate -Ø- or -a-:

OCS		PIE
nestí	'to carry'	*nek+Ø+t+éi[152]
leští	'to lie down'	*leg+Ø+t+éi[153]
bɪráti	'to gather'	*bʰr̥+ā́+t+ei

Class 2 verbs have only intermediate –nǫ-:

OCS		PIE
dvígnǫti	'to move'	*dwéig+nān+t+ei[154]

Class 3 verbs have intermediate -Ø-, -a-, or -ova-:

OCS		PIE
znáti	'to know'	*gnṓ+Ø+t+ei
pɪsáti	'to write'	*pik+ā́+t+ei
kupováti	'to buy'	*kaup+ou+ā́+t+ei[155]

Class 4 verbs have intermediate -e- or -i-:

OCS		PIE
sědě́ti	'to sit'	*sēd+ḗ+t+ei
molíti	'to request'	*mod^{h}l+éi+t+ei[156]

Class 5 verbs have intermediate -Ø-:

OCS		PIE
jastí	'to eat'	*ēd+Ø+t+éi[152,157]

6.8.3 Supine

According to Nandriş (1959: 154), "[t]he supine has the meaning of a verbal noun with a final sense..." That is, the supine occurs after verbs of motion and can be translated 'in order to'. E.g., OCSlav pridé vidě́tʊ (supine) gróba 'she came in order to see (supine) the grave'.

For all verbs, the supine stem is that of the infinitive; and the ending is a u-class accusative singular. E.g., OCSlav inf bɪráti 'to gather' vs. the supine bɪrátʊ 'in order to gather' from PIE *b^{h}r̥+ā́+tum.

6.9 Verbal Adjectives

These participial adjectives, like those described under 2.1 and 2.2 above, can occur in both short- and long-declension forms. Below we shall generally cite short-declension forms.

6.9.1 Present Active Participle

The antecedent suffix for these forms was PIE *-ont-. Aside from the masculine nominative/accusative and neuter nominative singular forms, the endings are those of the jo-/jā-class adjectives. E.g., the following singular forms.

		OCS		PIE
masc	**nom**	berý	'gathering'	*b^{h}er+ónt+s[158]
	gen	berǫ́šta		*b^{h}er+ónt+j+ōd[159]
	acc	berǫ́štɪ		*b^{h}er+ónt+m̥[160]
fem	**nom**	berǫ́šti		*b^{h}er+ónt+j+ī[161]
	acc	berǫ́štǫ		*b^{h}er+ónt+j+ām
neuter	**nom**	berý		*b^{h}er+ónt[162]
	acc	berǫ́šte		*b^{h}er+ónt+j+om[163]

Verbs of the 3rd and 4th classes have an intermediate /j/ in the Old Church Slavic and the PIE paradigm. Since this is so, the present active participles of these verbs can differ through regular changes from the forms of OCSlav berý cited above. E.g., the following masculine singular forms:

			OCS		PIE
class	**3**	**nom**	znáję	'knowing'	*gnṓ+j+ont+s[164]
		gen	znájǫšta		*gnṓ+j+ont+j+ōd[165]
	4	**nom**	mólję	'asking'	*módʰl+j+ont+s[164]
		gen	móljęšta		*módʰl+j+ont+j+ōd[166]

6.9.2 Present Passive Participle

In this formation the intermediate suffix -m- is added to the present stem. The adjective endings are those of the masculine/neuter o-class and the feminine ā-class. E.g., the following nominative singular forms:

	OCS		PIE
masc	berómʊ	'being gathered'	*bʰeró+m+os
fem	beróma		*bʰeró+m+ā
neuter	berómo		*bʰeró+m+om

6.9.3 Past Active Participle

There are two of these formations. The first and probably earlier form is from PIE *-wVs-, where V = an ablauting vowel, in the Ø grade in Old Church Slavic. The second is from PIE *-l-. Both formations can occur with a verb of any class; on occasion both types of formation occur with one and the same verb. One restriction is that the l-formative occurs with compound verbs which are verbs formed with a prefix.

Examples of the *-wVs- formation are the following nominative singular forms. The endings are those of o- and i-class adjectives.

	OCS		PIE
masc/neuter	nesʊ́	'having carried'	*nek+ús[167]
fem	nesʊ́ši		*nek+ús+jī[168]
masc/neuter	bɪrávʊ	'having gathered'	*bʰr̥+ā́+us[167]
fem	bɪrávʊši		*bʰr̥+ā́+us+jī

Examples of the *-l- formation are the following nom singular forms. The endings are those of o- and i-class adjectives.

	OCS		PIE
masc	neslʊ́	'having carried'	*nek+l+ós
fem	neslá		*nek+l+ā́
neuter	nesló		*nek+l+óm
masc	bɪrálʊ	'having gathered'	*bʰr̥+ā́+l+os
fem	bɪrála		*bʰr̥+ā́+l+ā
neuter	bɪrálo		*bʰr̥+ā́+l+om

6.9.4 Past Passive Participle

There are two types of this formation. The first and most frequently occurring is from PIE *-Vn-, where V is an ablauting vowel. The second is from PIE *-t- and occurs with all verbs whose stems end in OCSlav /ę/ as well as sporadically elsewhere. And some verbs can take either ending. E.g., the following nominative singular masculine forms.

OCS		PIE
bɪránʊ	'gathered'	*b^{h}r̥+ā́+n+os
nesénʊ	'carried'	*nek+én+os
jętʊ́	'seized'	*em+t+ós[169]
strítʊ or	'extended'	*stŕ̥+t+os[170]
stírenʊ		*stŕ̥+en+os[170]

6.9.5 Future Active Participle

Nandriş (1959: 153) considers this a later formation. It occurs only with the verb 'be'. E.g., the following nominative singular feminine form:

OCS		PIE
byšę́šti	'going to be'	*b^{h}ū+s+ń̥t+j+ī[171]

V Exercises

(1) Consider the following PIE forms and the changes which they underwent into Old Church Slavic. What is the Old Church Slavic form?

a. Nom sg masc *ákros 'sharp' + 1c EARLIEST PAL, 1f W-F SYL, 2a C-CL , 4c W-F C DELE, 5a e(:)/o(:)-LOW, 10 V-SHORT > OCSlav?

b. Nom sg *ángulos 'corner, angle' + no 1c EARLIEST PAL (hence a borrowing), 1f W-F SYL, 4c W-F C DELE, 7c NASAL V, 10 V-SHORT > OCSlav?

c. Pres act part nom sg masc *b^{h}erónts 'gathering' + 1a DEASP, 1f W-F SYL, 4c W-F C DELE, 9b ū-TO-ȳ, 10 V-SHORT > OCSlav? Also the gen sg masc *b^{h}eróntjōd la DEASP, 5a e(:)/o(:)-LOW, 7c NASAL V, 8a JOTA, 10 V-SHORT > OCSlav?

d. 3 pl cond *b^h+ī+s+ń̥t 'they would be' + la DEASP, 1d SYL SON, 3 RUKI, 4c W-F C DELE, 5b 1ST PAL, 7c NASAL V, 10 V-SHORT > OCSlav?

e. Nom sg masc *ed+oin+ós '1' + 1f W-F SYL, 4b PROTHESIS , 4c W-F C DELE, 5a e(:)/o(:)-LOW, 7b MON, 10 V-SHORT > OCSlav?

f. Inf *ēd+t+éi 'to eat' + 2a C-CL , 4b PROTHESIS , 5a e(:)/o(:)-LOW, 6a ǣ-TO-ā, 7b MON, 10 V-SHORT > OCSlav?

g. Nom sg masc *dékm̥tos '10th' + 1c EARLIEST PAL, 1d SYL SON, 1f W-F SYL, 4c W-F C DELE, 7c NASAL V , 10 V-SHORT > OCSlav?

h. Nom sg *dús+djus 'bad day; rain' + 2a C-CL, 4c W-F C DELE, 6b V-FRONT, 8a JOTA, 10 V-SHORT > OCSlav?

i. Nom sg *d^{h}úkt+ī 'daughter' + 1a DEASP, 8a JOTA, 10 V-SHORT > OCSlav?

j. Nom sg *gʰánsis 'goose' + 1a DEASP, no 1c EARLIEST PAL, 4c W-F C DELE, 7c NASAL V, 10 V-SHORT > OCSlav?
k. Nom sg *gʰemjā́ 'earth' + la DEASP, 1c EARLIEST PAL, 8a JOTA, 10 V-SHORT > OCSlav?
l. Nom sg *gʰwois+dā́ 'star' + 1a DEASP, 1c EARLIEST PAL, 2a C-CL , 5a e(:)/o(:)-LOW, 7b MON, 9c w-TO-**v**, 10 V-SHORT > OCSlav?
m. Nom sg *kŕ̥d+ik+jom 'heart' + 1c EARLIEST PAL applying to the first /k/ only (which probably means the suffix was an early borrowing), 1d SYL SON, 1f W-F SYL, 4c W-F C DELE, 5a e(:)/o(:)-LOW, 6b V-FRONT, 9a MET, 9d 3RD PAL > OCSlav?
n. Acc pl fem *kʷetū́r+n̥s '4' + 1d SYL SON, 1f W-F SYL part 2, 2b DELAB, 4c W-F C DELE, 5b 1ST PAL, 9b ū-TO-ȳ, 10 V-SHORT > OCSlav?
o. Nom sg masc *leubʰós 'dear' + 1a DEASP, 1f W-F SYL, 4c W-F C DELE, 5a e(:)/o(:)-LOW, 7b MON, 8a JOTA, 10 V-SHORT > OCSlav?
p. Nom sg masc adj *lúgʰjos 'lying, mendacious' + 1a DEASP, 1f W-F SYL, 4c W-F C DELE, 6b V-SHORT, 8a JOTA, 10 V-SHORT > OCSlav?
q. Nom sg *medʰjā́ 'middle' + la DEASP, 8a JOTA, 10 V-SHORT > OCSlav?
r. Inf *met+t+éi 'throw' + 2a C-CL , 5a e(:)/o(:)-LOW, 7b MON, 10 V-SHORT > OCSlav?
s. Nom sg *mórjom 'ocean' + 4c W-F C DELE, 5a e(:)/o(:)-LOW, 6b V-FRONT , 8a JOTA, 10 V-SHORT > OCSlav?
t. Nom sg *mū́sis 'mouse' + 3 RUKI, 4c W-F C DELE, 5b 1ST PAL, 9b ū-TO-ȳ, 10 V-SHORT > OCSlav?
u. Nom sg masc *néwos 'new' + 1f W-F SYL, 4c W-F C DELE, 5a e(:)/o(:)-LOW, 7a æw-TO-aw, 9c w-TO-**v**, 10 V-SHORT > OCSlav?
v. Inf *obʰ+wortéitei 'turn' + 1a DEASP, 2a C-CL , 5a e(:)/o(:)-LOW, 7b MON, 9a MET, 10 V-SHORT > OCSlav?
w. Gen sg neuter *ṓgʰʷnentes 'lamb' + 1a DEASP, 2b DELAB, 4c W-F C DELE, 5a e(:)/o(:)-LOW, 7c NASAL V, 10 V-SHORT > OCSlav?
x. Gen pl *ṓlkutom 'elbows' + 1f W-F SYL, 4c W-F C DELE, 5a e(:)/o(:)-LOW, 9a MET, 10 V-SHORT > OCSlav?
y. Nom sg masc *óus+n+jes 'better' + 4a C-CL SIMP, 4c W-F C DELE, 5a e(:)/o(:)-LOW, 7b MON, 8a JOTA, 10 V-SHORT > OCSlav?
z. Nom sg *pō+mn̥+t+ís 'memory' + 1d SYL SON, 4c W-F C DELE, 5a e(:)/o(:)-LOW, 7c NASAL V, 10 V-SHORT > OCSlav?
aa. 1sg aorist *rḗk+s+om 'I said' + 1f W-F SYL, 3 RUKI, 4a C-CL SIMP, 4c W-F C DELE, 10 V-SHORT > OCSlav?
bb. Nom sg *ū́dʰ+ment 'udder' + la DEASP, 4a C-CL SIMP, 4b PROTHESIS , 4c W-F C DELE, 5a e(:)/o(:)-LOW, 7c NASAL V, 9b ū-TO-ȳ, 9c w-TO-**v**, 10 V-SHORT > OCSlav?
cc. 1sg pres *wegʰṓm 'travel' + 1a DEASP, 1c EARLIEST PAL, 5a e(:)/o(:)-LOW, 7c NASAL V , 9c w-TO-**v**, 10 V-SHORT > OCSlav?
dd. Loc pl *wl̥kʷóisu 'wolves' + ld SYL SON, 2b DELAB, 3 RUKI, 5a e(:)/o(:)-LOW, 7b MON, 8b 2ND PAL, 9a MET, 9c w-TO-**v**, 10 V-SHORT > OCSlav?
ee. Acc sg *wrónkām 'hand' + 4a C-CL SIMP, 5a e(:)/o(:)-LOW, 7c NASAL V, 9c w-TO-**v**, 10 V-SHORT > OCSlav?

(2) Given the following PIE forms, what will be the Old Church Slavic reflexes and what changes will they have undergone?

a. Nom sg *áusi+ring+i 'ear ring', borrowed from Germanic after the time of 5b 1ST PAL.
b. Nom sg *bʰrā́tr+os 'brother'.

c. Nom sg masc *déksnos 'right'.
d. Nom sg *dʰousjā́ 'soul' vs. voc sg *dʰóusja.
e. Inf *ém+t+ei 'to take'.
f. Inf *gnṓ+t+ei 'to know'.
g. Nom sg *gómbʰos 'tooth'.
h. Nom sg *gr̥nóm 'grain'.
i. Nom sg *gʰeimā́ 'winter'.
j. Nom sg *gʰóltom 'gold'.
k. Nom sg *gʷenā́ 'woman'.
l. Nom sg masc *gʷīwós 'alive'.
m. Nom sg *júgom 'yoke'. (No 1c EARLIEST PAL in this derivation.)
n. Nom sg *káisar+is 'emperor', borrowed after the time of 3 RUKI.
o. Nom sg *klṓwa 'glory'.
p. *ksékstis '6'.
q. Nom sg *kúningi 'king, ruler', borrowed from Germanic after 5b 1ST PAL.
r. Nom sg Vs-class neuter *kʷolós 'wheel'.
s. Nom sg *lóikʷos 'remainder'.
t. Nom sg *maksinā́ 'pouch'.
u. Nom sg *mángjos 'man'.
v. Nom sg *nóktis 'night'.
w. Nom sg masc *nogʷós 'naked'.
x. Nom sg *owi+kʷā́ 'sheep'.
y. Nom sg *pórsos 'dust'.
z. Nom sg masc *sáusos 'dry'.
aa. Nom sg *snóigʰʷos 'snow'.
bb. Nom sg *táuros 'steer, ox'.
cc. *tū́suntjī '1000', borrowed from Germanic after 3 RUKI.
dd. Nom sg *wáldʰ+tis power
ee. Nom sg *wértment 'a turning, time'.
ff. Nom sg *widʰewā́ 'widow'.

(3) Give at least one possible PIE antecedent for each of the following Old Church Slavic forms.
a. 1sg pres bljudǫ́ 'I protect'.
b. Masc o-class búgʊ 'armband', borrowed from Germanic after the time of 1a DEASP and 1c EARLIEST PAL.
c. Masc o-class dólʊ 'valley'.
d. Masc i-class góstɪ 'guest', borrowed after 1c EARLIEST PAL.
e. Nom sg masc lě́vʊ 'left'.
f. Masc o-class ljúdʊ 'people'.
g. Masculine o-class ósʊ 'axis', borrowed after 3 RUKI.
h. Feminine ā-class pě́na 'foam'.
i. Neuter o-class rámo 'shoulder'.
j. Neuter Vnt-class sě́mę 'seed'.
k. Masculine o-class skǫ́dʊlʊ 'tile'.
l. Masculine o-class sʊ́nʊ 'sleep'.
m. Masculine u-class sýnʊ 'son'.
n. Inf šibáti 'whip'. The antecedent of the infinitive ending is PIE *-ātei.

o. Neuter Vs-class úxo ‘ear’.
p. 3 sg pres vezétʊ ‘goes’.
q. Inf vrɪtě́ti ‘to turn’. The antecedent of the infinitive ending is PIE *-ḗtei. The root is in a PIE ablaut grade; decide which one.
r. vy ‘you’.

(4) Consider the following alternations in the Old Church Slavic verb paradigm between the 1st singular present and infinitive forms:

a. grebǫ́ ‘dig’ vs. gretí.
b. koljǫ́ ‘stab’ vs. klatí.
c. mɪrǫ́ ‘die’ vs. mrětí.
d. pletǫ́ ‘weave’ vs. plestí.
e. slovǫ́ ‘be called’ vs. slutí.
f. vrɪgǫ́ ‘throw’ vs. vreští.

What are the proto-forms (take into account PIE ablaut) and what changes account for these alternations? The 1st singular present ending is PIE *-ṓm and the infinitive is *-téi.

(5) Consider the following singular forms of the OCSlav o-class noun ‘wolf’ and the PIE antecedents:

	OCS	PIE
nom	vlɪ́kʊ	*wĺ̥kʷos
voc	vlɪ́če	*wĺ̥kʷe
loc	vlɪ́cě	*wĺ̥kʷoi

Aside from the change 2b DELAB, what changes account for the occurrence of /k/, /č/ and /c/ in this paradigm?

(6) The following alternations result from PIE roots with /e(:), o(:), Ø/ ablaut. Given the Old Church Slavic forms, what are the ablaut grades of the PIE antecedents?

	OCS		PIE
1sg pres	berǫ́	‘gather’	*bʰ_rṓm
inf	bɪráti	‘gather’	*bʰ_rā́tei
1sg pres	bljudǫ́	‘protect’	*bʰ_udṓm
inf	budíti	‘awaken’	*bʰ_udī́tei
inf	bʊdě́ti	‘be awake’	*bʰ_udḗtei
1sg pres	móriti	‘kill’	*m_́rītei
inf	mrě́ti	‘die’	*m_rḗtei
1sg pres	pišǫ́	‘write’	*p_ikjṓm
inf	pɪsáti	‘write’	*p_ikā́tei
1sg pres	sadíti	‘set’	*s_dī́tei
inf	sědě́ti	‘sit’	*s_dḗtei

(7) Consider the glossed Old Church Slavic text in VI below. Give a smooth translation of this text.

VI An Old Church Slavic Text

The following is the Old Church Slavic translation of the book of Matthew 5: 1-12. It is from the *Codex Zographensis*, dates from sometime during the 900's AD and ranks among the earliest Old Church Slavic texts. (See on this Baldi 1983: 118, Diels 1934: 6 and Schmalstieg 1983:196.)

In the passage below we give (a) a romanization of the Old Church Slavic cyrillic text with what we posit as the Old Church Slavic word stress (unmarked for monosyllabic words), (b) a gloss and (c) a grammatical description of each word.

1	**a**	(1) uzɪrě́vʊ	že	naródy	vʊzíde	na	górǫ.
	b	*see*	*indeed*	*people*	*go up*	*on*	*mountain*
	c	past act part nom sg masc	particle	acc pl masc	3sg aorist	prep + acc	acc sg fem

2	**a**	i	ěkó	sě́de	prístǫpiše	kʊ	njemú
	b	*and*	*when*	*sit down*	*approach*	*to*	*he*
	c	conj	adv	3sg aorist	3pl aorist	prep + dat	dat sg masc

3	**a**	učeníci	egó.	(2) i	otvrízʊ	ustá	svoě́
	b	*disciple*	*he*	*and*	*open*	*lip*	*one's own*
	c	nom pl masc	gen sg masc	conj	past act part nom sg masc	acc pl neuter	reflex. acc dual neuter

4	**a**	učáaše	ję	glagólję:	(3) blažéni	níštii	duxómɪ.
	b	*teach*	*they*	*say*	*bless*	*poor*	*spirit*
	c	3sg imperf	acc pl	pres act part nom sg masc	past pass part nom pl masc	nom pl masc	instr sg masc

5	**a**	ěkó	těxʊ́	éstʊ	cěsarɪstvó	nébesɪskoe.	(4) blažéni
	b	*for*	*these*	*be*	*kingdom*	*heavenly*	*bless*
	c	conj	gen pl masc	3sg pres	nom sg neuter	nom sg neuter	past pass part nom pl masc

6	**a**	pláčǫštii.	ěkó	ti	utěšę́tʊ	sę.	(5) blažéni
	b	*mourn*	*for*	*these*	*comfort*	*themselves*	*bless*
	c	pres act part nom pl masc	conj	nom pl masc	3pl pres	reflexive acc pl masc	past pass part nom pl masc

7	**a**	krótɪci.	ěkó	ti	naslě́dętʊ	zémljǫ.	(6) blažéni
	b	*meek*	*for*	*these*	*inherit*	*earth*	*bless*
	c	nom pl masc	conj	nom pl masc	3pl pres	acc sg fem	past pass part
							nom pl masc

8	**a**	álʊčǫštii	i	žę́ždǫštii	právɪdy	radí.	ěkó
	b	*be hungry*	*and*	*thirst*	*truth*	*after*	*for*
	c	pres act part	conj	pres act part	gen sg fem	prep + gen	conj
		nom pl masc		nom pl masc			

9	**a**	ti	nasytę́tʊ	sę.	(7) blažéni	mílostivii.	ěkó
	b	*these*	*satisfy*	*themselves*	*bless*	*merciful*	*for*
	c	nom pl masc	3pl pres	acc pl	past pass part	nom pl masc	conj
				reflexive	nom pl masc		

10	**a**	ti	pomílovani	bǫdǫ́tʊ.	(8) blažéni	čístii	srídɪcemɪ.
	b	*these*	*show mercy*	*be*	*bless*	*pure*	*heart*
	c	nom pl masc	past pass part	3pl future	past pass part	nom pl masc	instr sg neuter
			nom pl masc		nom pl masc		

11	**a**	ěkó	ti	bóga	uzɪrę́tʊ.	(9) blažéni	sii
	b	*for*	*these*	*God*	*see*	*bless*	*these*
	c	conj	nom pl masc	acc sg masc	3pl pres	3pl pres	nom pl masc

12	**a**	mirě́jǫštii.	ěkó	ti	synové	bóžii	narekǫ́tʊ
	b	*make peace*	*for*	*these*	*son*	*of God*	*call*
	c	pres act part	conj	nom pl masc	nom pl masc	nom pl masc	3pl pres
		nom pl masc				adj	

13	**a**	sę.	(10) blažéni	izgʊnáni	právɪdy	radí.	ěkó
	b	*themselves*	*bless*	*persecute*	*truth*	*for the sake of*	*for*
	c	acc pl	past pass part	past pass part	gen sg fem	prep + gen	conj
		reflexive	nom pl masc	nom pl masc			

14	**a**	těxʊ́	éstʊ	cěsarɪstvó	nébesɪskoe.	(11) blažéni	esté
	b	*these*	*be*	*kingdom*	*of heaven*	*bless*	*be*
	c	gen pl masc	3sg pres	nom sg neuter	nom sg neuter adj	past pass part nom pl masc	2pl pres

15	**a**	egdá	ponosę́tʊ	vamʊ́	i	iždenǫ́tʊ	vy
	b	*whenever*	*insult*	*you*	*and*	*persecute*	*you*
	c	adv	3pl pres	dat pl	conj	3pl pres	acc pl

16	**a**	i	rekǫ́tʊ	vɪsákʊ	zʊlʊ́	glagóljǫtʊ	na
	b	*and*	*say*	*every*	*evil*	*say*	*against*
	c	conj	3pl pres	acc sg masc	acc sg masc	3pl pres	prep + acc

17	**a**	vy	lužǫ́šte	mené	radí.
	b	*you*	*lie*	*I*	*about*
	c	acc pl	pres act part nom pl masc	gen sg	prep + gen

VII Key

(1) The Old Church Slavic forms are these: (a) óstrʊ, (b) ǫ́gʊlʊ, (c) berý and berǫ́šta respectively, (d) bišę́, (e) jedinʊ́, (f) jastí, (g) désętʊ, (h) dʊ́ždɪ, (i) dʊ́šti, (j) gǫ́sɪ, (k) zemljá, (l) zvězdá, (m) srídɪce, (n) četýri, (o) ljubʊ́, (p) lʊ́ži, (q) meždá, (r) mestí, (s) mórje, (t) mýšɪ, (u) nóvʊ, (v) obratíti, (w) ágnęte, (x) lákʊtʊ, (y) únje, (z) pamętí, (aa) rě́xʊ, (bb) výmę, (cc) vezǫ́, (dd) vlɪcě́xʊ, (ee) rǫ́kǫ.

(2) The Old Church Slavic forms and changes are these:

a. úsɪręzɪ. The derivation is 7b MON, 7c NASAL V , 8b 2ND PAL, 10 V-SHORT.

b. brátrʊ. The derivation is la DEASP, 1f W-F SYL, 4c W-F C DELE, 10 V-SHORT.

c. désnʊ. The derivation is 1f W-F SYL, 4a C-CL SIMP, 4c W-F C DELE, 10 V-SHORT.

d. The forms are dušá and dúše, respectively. The first derivation is la DEASP, 3 RUKI, 5a e(:)/o(:)-LOW, 5b 1ST PAL, 7b MON, 8a JOTA, 10 V-SHORT. The second derivation is the same except that it includes 6b V-FRONT because the /a/ in the voc sg *d^{h}óusja is short.

e. ję́ti. The derivation is 4b PROTHESIS, 7b MON, 7c NASAL V , 10 V-SHORT.

f. znáti. The derivation is 1c EARLIEST PAL, 5a e(:)/o(:)-LOW, 7b MON, 10 V-SHORT.

g. zǫ́bʊ. The derivation is la DEASP, lc EARLIEST PAL, 4c W-F C DELE, 7c NASAL V , 10 V-SHORT.

h. zrɪnó. The derivation is 1c EARLIEST PAL, 1d SYL SON, 4c W-F C DELE, 9a MET.

i. zimá. The derivation is la DEASP, 1c EARLIEST PAL, 7b MON, 10 V-SHORT.

j. zláto. The derivation is la DEASP, lc EARLIEST PAL, 4c W-F C DELE, 5a e(:)/o(:)-LOW, 9a MET, 10 V-SHORT.

k. žená. The derivation is 2b DELAB, 5b 1ST PAL , 10 V-SHORT.

l. živʊ́. The derivation is 1f W-F SYL , 2b DELAB, 4c W-F C DELE, 5b 1ST PAL, 9c w-TO-**v**, 10 V-SHORT.

m. ígo. The derivation is 4c W-F C DELE, 6b V-FRONT, 10 V-SHORT.

n. cě́sarɪ. The derivation is 4c W-F C DELE, 7b MON, 8b 2ND PAL, 10 V-SHORT.

o. sláva. The derivation is 1c EARLIEST PAL, 5a e(:)/o(:)-LOW, 9c w-TO-**v**, 10 V-SHORT.

p. šéstɪ. The derivation is 3 RUKI, 4a C-CL SIMP, 4c W-F C DELE, 5b 1ST PAL, 10 V-SHORT.

q. kʊ́nęzɪ. The derivation is 7c NASAL V , 8b 2ND PAL, 10 V-SHORT.

r. koló. The derivation is 2b DELAB, 4c W-F C DELE.

s. lě́kʊ. The derivation is 1f W-F SYL, 2b DELAB, 4c W-F C DELE, 5a e(:)/o(:)-LOW, 7b MON, 10 V-SHORT.

t. mošɪná. The derivation is 3 RUKI, 4a C-CL SIMP, 5b 1ST PAL.

u. mǫ́žɪ. The derivation is 1c EARLIEST PAL, 1f W-F SYL, 4c W-F C DELE, 6b V-FRONT , 7c NASAL V, 8a JOTA, 10 V-SHORT.

v. nóštɪ. The derivation is 4c W-F C DELE, 8a JOTA, 10 V-SHORT.

w. nagʊ́. The derivation is 1f W-F SYL, 2b DELAB, 4c W-F C DELE, 5a e(:)/o(:)-LOW, 10 V-SHORT.

x. ovɪcá. The derivation is 2b DELAB, 9c w-TO-**v**, 9d 3RD PAL, 10 V-SHORT.

y. práxʊ. The derivatian is 1f W-F SYL , 3 RUKI, 4c W-F C DELE, 5a e(:)/o(:)-LOW, 9a MET, 10 V-SHORT.

z. súxʊ. The derivation is 1f W-F SYL, 3 RUKI, 7b MON, 10 V-SHORT.

aa. sně́gʊ. The derivation is 1a DEASP, 1f W-F SYL, 2b DELAB, 4c W-F C DELE, 7b MON, 10 V-SHORT.

bb. túrʊ. The derivation is 1f W-F SYL, 4c W-F C DELE, 7b MON, 10 V-SHORT.

cc. týsǫšti. The derivation is 7c NASAL V , 8a JOTA, 9b ū-TO-ȳ, 10 V-SHORT.

dd. vlástɪ. The derivation is 1a DEASP, 2a C-CL , 4c W-F C DELE, 9a MET, 9c w-TO-**v**, 10 V-SHORT.

ee. vrě́mę. The derivatian is 4a C-CL SIMP, 4c W-F C DELE, 7c NASAL V, 9a MET, 9c w-TO-**v**, 10 V-SHORT.

ff. vɪdová. The derivation is 1a DEASP, 5a e(:)/o(:)-LOW, 7a æw-TO-aw , 9c w-TO-**v**, 10 V-SHORT.

(3) The possible PIE antecedents as well as the actual antecedent are as follows.

a. The possible antecedents are *b$^{(h)}$(l)eud$^{(h)}$ṓm. The actual antecedent is *b^{h}eud^{h}ṓm.

b. The possible antecedents are *b(áu/óu)gos. The actual antecedent is the Germanic borrowing *báug+os.

c. The possible antecedents are *d$^{(h)}$(á/ó)los. The actual antecedent is the Germanic borrowing *dál+os.

d. The possible antecedents are *g$^{(h)}$(á/ó)stis. The actual antecedent is *g^{h}óstis.

e. The possible antecedents are *l(ái/ói/ḗ)wos. The actual antecedent is *láiwos.

f. The possible antecedents are *léud$^{(h)}$os. The actual antecedent is *léud^{h}os.

g. The possible antecedents are *(á/ó)C_0sos. The actual antecedent is *áksos.
h. The possible antecedents are *p(ái/ói/ḗ)C_0nā. The actual antecedent is *póinā.
i. The possible antecedents are *r(ā́/ṓ)mom and *(á/ó)rmom. The actual antecedent is *ármom.
j. The possible antecedents are *s(ái/ói/ḗ)ment. The actual antecedent is *sḗment.
k. The possible antecedents are *sk(á/ó)nd$^{(h)}$ulos. The actual antecedent is the Latin borrowing *skándulus.
l. The possible antecedents are *súC_0nos. The actual antecedent is *súpnos.
m. The antecedent is *sū́nus.
n. The possible antecedents are *(k/r)s(ei/ī)b$^{(h)}$ā́tei. The actual antecedent is *kseibā́tei.
o. The possible antecedents are *(á/ó)usos. The actual antecedent is *óusos.
p. The possible antecedents are *weg$^{(h)}$étu. The actual antecedent is *weg^{h}étu.
q. The antecedent is *wr̥tḗtei with the root in the Ø-grade ablaut.
r. The possible antecedents are *(w)ūC_0^1 . The actual antecedent is *ūs.

(4) The respective PIE forms are (a) *g^{h}reb^{h}ṓm and *g^{h}reb^{h}téi, (b) *koljṓm and *koltéi, (c) *mr̥ṓm and *mertéi, (d) *pletṓm and *plettéi, (e) *klouṓm and *kloutéi and (f) *wr̥gṓm and wergtéi. The changes involved are 1a DEASP, 1c EARLIEST PAL, 1d SYL SON, 2a C-CL, 4c W-F C DELE, 5a e(:)/o(:)-LOW, 7b MON, 7c NASAL V , 8a JOTA, 9a MET, 9c w-TO-v and 10 V-SHORT. Some of the derivations are in note 152 in Section 6.8.2 Infinitives in the morphology.

(5) The derivations are these:

nom *wĺ̥kos (1d SYL SON, 1f W-F SYL, 4c W-F C DELE, 9a MET, 9c w-TO-v) > OCSlav vlíkъ. Voc *wĺ̥ke (ld SYL SON, 5b 1ST PAL, 9a MET, 9c w-TO-v) > OCSlav vlíče. Loc *wĺ̥koi (1d SYL SON, 7b MON, 8b 2ND PAL, 9a MET, 9c w-TO-v, 10 V-SHORT) > OCSlav vlícě.

(6) The ablauting grades are these:

(a) *b^{h}erṓm, *b^{h}Ør̥ā́tei.
(b) *b^{h}eudṓm, *b^{h}oudī́tei, *b^{h}Øudḗtei.
(c) *mórītei, *mØrḗtei.
(d) *peikjṓm, *pØikā́tei.
(e) *sōdī́tei, *sēdḗtei.

(7) The following is a translation of the text in Section VI.

"(1) Having seen the people he went up onto a mountain. and when he sat down his disciples approached him. (2) And having opened his lips he taught them saying, (3) 'Blessed (are the) poor in spirit. For theirs is the heavenly kingdom. (4) Blessed (are those) mourning. For they comfort themselves (will be comforted). (5) Blessed (are the) meek. For they inherit the earth. (6) Blessed (are those) being hungry and thirsting for truth. For they satisfy themselves (= will be satisfied). (7) Blessed (are the) merciful. For they will be shown mercy. (8) Blessed (are the) pure in heart. For they (will) see God. (9) Blessed are those making peace. For they call themselves (will be called) God's sons. (10) Blessed (are those) persecuted far the sake of truth. For theirs is the heavenly kingdom. (11) Blessed are you whenever they insult you and persecute you and may say every evil (and) talk against you (when they are) lying about me.'"

VIII Notes

[1] The palatal obstruents occurred solely in the clusters [št'] and [žd'] by 8a JOTA. We write them as /št/ and /žd/. The palatal sonorants /nj, rj, lj/ also resulted from 8a JOTA and are sometimes written /n', r', l'/.

[2] This phoneme occurs only in Greek borrowings such as filósofʊ 'philosopher'.

[3] Our analysis of the obstruents generally follows that of Schmalstieg (1983: 23-4) except that we consider Schmalstieg's "retracted" obstruents to be alveopalatal.

[4] These segments arise from 8b 2ND PAL and 9d 3RD PAL. The /dz/ soon becomes /z/. The /c/ and /dz/ may be considered either affricates [t^s, d^z], or as bisegmental sequences [ts, dz].

[5] After the application of 7c NASAL V, there would have been no instances of [ŋ] in Slavic words since [ŋ] would have occurred only before /k, g/. After 7c NASAL V and in Old Church Slavic, [ŋ] occurs only in borrowings such as ángelʊ 'angel' from Greek. We assume this to have been phonetic [áŋgelʊ].

[6] The Old Church Slavic vowel inventory follows from the vowel changes, in particular 5a e(:)/o(:)-LOW, 7c NASAL V, 9b ū-TO-ȳ and 10 V-SHORT. Our analysis of the vowels follows that of Schmalstieg (1983: 15–16). He gives these pronunciation hints for the Old Church Slavic vowels: /i/ as in feet, /ɪ/ as in sit, /e/ as in bed, /ĕ/ as in bad, /u/ as in food, /ʊ/as in put, /o/ as in his pronunciation of caught (i.e., /kɔt/), /a/ as in father, /y/ as the Russian /y/ (which is +back and –round), /ę/ as in French fin and /ǫ/ as in French monde or bon.

[7] In romanizing the Old Church Slavic cyrillic alphabet we usually follow the traditional transcriptional conventions. We depart from these conventions in our transcription of the high lax vowels /ɪ, ʊ/ — the so-called "jers". Their conventional transcriptions are < ь > and < ъ >, respectively.

[8] The derivation is *wĺ̥k^{w}os (1d SYL SON) > *wílk^{w}os (1f W-F SYL) > *wílk^{w}us (2b DELAB) > *wílkus (4c W-F C DELE) > *wílku (9a MET) > *wlíku (9c w-TO-v, 10 V-SHORT) > OCSlav vlíkʊ.

[9] The respective derivations are voc sg *wĺ̥k^{w}e and loc sg *wĺ̥k^{w}oi (1d SYL SON, 2b DELAB) > *wílke and *wílkoi (5a e(:)/o(:)-LOW) > *wílkæ and *wílkai (5b 1ST PAL) > *wílčæ and *wílkai (7b MON) > *wílčæ and *wílkǣ (8b 2ND PAL) > *wílčæ and *wílcǣ (9a MET) > *wlíčæ and *wlícǣ (9c w-TO-v, 10 V-SHORT) > OCSlav vlíče and vlícě.

[10] The PIE abl sg *-ōd is the antecedent of the OCSlav gen sg -a.

[11] The usual PIE dat sg ending is *-ōi, from which one would expect the Old Church Slavic ending **-ě. Schmalstieg (1983: 73) suggests the pre-Old Church Slavic antecedent was *-ōu with the same suffix as in OCSlav tu 'here' from earlier *t+ōu. The derivation would then be *-ōu (lb DIPH SHORT) > *-ou (5a e(:)/o(:)-LOW) > *-au (7b MON) > *-ū (10 V-SHORT) > OCSlav -u.

[12] The instr sg in –mɪ is apparently a Balto-Slavic innovation. Its origin is obscure.

[13] The ending *-oi is from the PIE nom pl masc pron. *t+oi 'these'. (See 5.3 below.)

[14] The derivation is *wĺ̥k^{w}ons (1d SYL SON, 1f W-F SYL) > *wílk^{w}ūs (2b DELAB) > *wílkūs (4c W-F C DELE) > *wílkū (9a MET) > *wlíkū (9b ū-TO-ȳ) > *wlíkȳ (9c w-TO-v, 10 V-SHORT) > OCSlav vlíky.

[15] The derivation is *wl̥k^{w}óisu (ld SYL SON, 2b DELAB) >*wilkóisu (3 RUKI) > *wilkóixu (5a e(:)/o(:)-LOW) > *wilkáixu (7b MON) > *wilkǣ́xu (8b 2ND PAL) > *wilcǣ́xu (9a MET, 9c w-TO-v) > *vlicǣ́xu (10 V-SHORT) > OCSlav vlɪcě́xʊ.

[16] The expected Old Church Slavic form from the posited PIE antecedent would be **vlɪcě́. Schmalstieg (1983: 78) posits an early conflation of dative plural and instrumental plural endings into something like *wĺ̥k^w+om+s (PIE 3.1.2d NASAL ASSIM) → *wĺ̥k^{w}ons (ev) > OCSlav vlíky in a derivation like that under note 14 above.

[17] The expected derivation of this form would be *móistom (1f W-F SYL) > *móistum (4c W-F C DELE) > *móistu (5a e(:)/o(:)-LOW) > *máistu (7b MON) > *mǣ́stu (10 V-SHORT) > OCSlav **mě́stʊ instead of mě́sto. The occurrence of word-final -o here instead of -ʊ may have been the influence of the OCSlav neuter dem pron to 'this, that', which developed regularly from PIE *tod (see 5.3 below).

[18] The derivation is *mángjos (1c EARLIEST PAL) > *mánzjos (1f W-F SYL) > *mánzjus (4c W-F C DELE) > *mánzjus (6b V-FRONT) > *mánzji (7c NASAL V) > *mǫ́zji (8a JOTA) > *mǫ́ži (10 V-SHORT) > OCSlav mǫ́žɪ.

[19] The voc ending is from the u-class. The respective derivations are voc *mángjou and dat *mangjṓu (lb DIPH SHORT) > *mángjou and *mangjóu (1c EARLIEST PAL, 5a e(:)/o(:)-LOW) >*mánzjau and *manzjáu (6b V-FRONT) > *mánzjæu and *manzjǽu (7c NASAL V, 8a JOTA) > *mǭ́žæu and *mǭžǽu (7b MON, later stage 2) > *mǭ́žū and *mǭžū́ (10 V-SHORT) > OCSlav mǫ́žu and mǫžú.

[20] In Old Church Slavic, animate nouns often take the gen sg ending as an accusative singular. The derivation is *mangjṓd (1c EARLIEST PAL, 4c W-F C DELE) > *manzjṓ (5a e(:)/o(:)-LOW) > *manzjā́ (no 6b V-FRONT applying since the /ā́/ is long; but 7c NASAL V and 8a JOTA do) > *mǭžā́ (10 V-SHORT) > OCSlav mǫžá.

[21] The derivation is not clear in that only part 1 of change 1f W-F SYL applies: mangjóns (1c EARLIEST PAL, 1f W-F SYL, part 1) > *manzjúns (4c W-F C DELE) > *manzjún (6b V-FRONT) > *manzjín (7c NASAL V) > *mǭzję̄́ (8a JOTA) > *mǭžę̄́ (10 V-SHORT) > OCSlav mǫžę́.

[22] The derivation is *mangjóis (lb DIPH SHORT, 1c EARLIEST PAL) > *manzóis (4c W-F C DELE, 5a e(:)/o(:)-LOW) > *manzái (6b V-FRONT) > *manzjǽi (7b MON) > *manzjī́ (7c NASAL V) > *mǭzjī́ (8a JOTA) > *mǭžī́ (10 V-SHORT) > OCSlav mǫží.

[23] The derivation is *póljom (4c W-F C DELE: see the derivation of mě́sto 'place' above) > *póljo (5a e(:)/o(:)-LOW) > *pálja (6b V-FRONT) > *páljæ (8a JOTA, 10 V-SHORT) > OCSlav pólje.

[24] The vocative singular in PIE and very likely in Old Church Slavic had the stress on the first syllable. The derivation here is *g^{w}éna (2b DELAB) > *géna (5a e(:)/o(:)-LOW) > *gǽna (5b 1ST PAL) > *žǽna (10 V-SHORT) > OCSlav žéno.

[25] The derivation of these forms is not clear. From the posited PIE antecedent one would expect OCSlav **zená. Schmalstieg (1983: 89) suggests that the acc pl *g^{w}enā́ns may have replaced the nominative plural and the genitive singular. Then the derivation would be *g^{w}enā́ns (? possibly 1f W-F SYL) > *g^{w}enū́s (2b DELAB, 4c W-F C DELE) > *genū́ (5a e(:)/o(:)-LOW, 5b 1ST PAL) > *žænū́ (9b ū-TO-ȳ, 10 V-SHORT) > OCSlav žený.

[26] The Old Church Slavic ending may have arisen from an original dat sg *-āi to which an instr sg *-ām was added. Its derivation would be *-āi (lb DIPH SHORT) > *-ai (addition of * -ām) > *-aiām (PIE 3.1.2c i-j/u-w ALT, still applying) → *-ajām (7c NASAL V) > *-ajǭ (10 V-SHORT) > OCSlav –ojǫ.

[27] One would expect from *g^{w}enā́su OCSlav **ženásʊ. The form ženáxʊ with /x/ instead of /s/ is from the o-class vlɪcě́xʊ 'wolf' which has undergone 3 RUKI. Its derivation is described in 1.1 above.

[28] Schmalstieg (1983: 92) posits the PIE instr pl *-mī. Bräuer (1969: 2, 107) posits *-mīs. In either event the same Old Church Slavic form is derived: *g^{w}enā́mī(s) (2b DELAB, 4c W-F C DELE) > *genā́mī (5a e(:)/o(:)-LOW) > *gænā́ml (5b 1ST PAL) > *žænā́mī (10 V-SHORT) > OCSlav ženámi.

[29] The respective derivations of these two forms are *d^{h}ousjā́ and *d^{h}óusja (la DEASP) > *dousjā́ and *dóusja (3 RUKI) > *douxjā́ and *dóuxja (5a e(:)/o(:)-LOW) > *dauxjā́ and *dáuxja (6b V-FRONT applying to the latter form only) > *dauxjā́ and *dáuxjæ (7b MON) > *dūxjā́ and *dū́xjæ (8a JOTA) > *dūšā́ and *dū́šæ (10 V-SHORT) > OCSlav dušá and dúše.

[30] The derivation from a PIE *d^{h}ousjā́s is problematic: one would expect OCSlav **dušá. However, 1f one posits a PIE acc pl *d^{h}ousjáns, the derivation is (1a DEASP) > *dousjáns (3 RUKI, 4c W-F C DELE) > *douxján (5a e(:)/o(:)-LOW) > *dauxján (6b V-FRONT) > *dauxjǽn (7b MON) > *dūxjǽn (7c NASAL V) > *dūxję̄́ (8a JOTA) > *dūšę̄́ (10 V-SHORT) > OCSlav dušę́.

[31] The derivation is *d^{h}ousjā́i (la DEASP, lb DIPH SHORT) > *dousjái (3 RUKI) > *douxjái (5a e(:)/o(:)-LOW) > *dauxjái (6b V-FRONT) > *dauxjǽi (7b MON) > *dūxjī́ (8a JOTA) > *dūšī́ (10 V-SHORT) > OCSlav duší.

[32] The form ladɪjí instead of **ladɪjá is attested. It would seem that the PIE rule 3.l.2f SIEVERS was involved in the derivation of these forms. Thus the stems of these nouns, like that of OCSlav jo-class znánije 'knowledge' described in 1.1 above, were invariably long. The derivation may have been this: PIE *ald^{h}jā́ (PIE 3.1.2f SIEVERS applying synchronically) → *ald^{h}ijā́ (la DEASP) > *aldijā́ (9a MET) > *lādijā́ (replacement of word-final /ā/ by /ī/, perhaps taken from the root-class nouns described in 1.5.2 below) > *lādijī́ (10 V-SHORT) > OCSlav ladɪjí.

[33] Otherwise the endings of this noun are those of dušá 'soul' given above, e.g. acc sg ladɪjǫ́.

[34] These forms have e-grade ablaut between the root *g^{h}ost- and the class marker *-i-. The other forms of this paradigm have Ø-grade ablaut in the class marker.

[35]The derivation of these forms is this: *g^{h}ostí+ous and *g^{h}ósti+es (PIE 3.1.2c i-j/u-w ALT applying synchronically) → *g^{h}ostjóus and *g^{h}óstjes (PIE 3.1.2f SIEVERS applying synchronically) → *g^{h}ostijóus and *g^{h}óstijes (la DEASP) > *gostijóus and *góstijes (4c W-F C DELE) > *gostijóu and *góstije (5a e(:)/o(:)-LOW) > *gástija and *gastíjæ (6b V-FRONT) > *gastíjæu and *gástijæ (7b MON) > *gastíjū and *gástijæ (10 V-SHORT) > OCSlav gostíju and góstɪje.

[36] The derivation is *g^{h}óstins (la DEASP, 1f W-F SYL part 2) > *góstīs (4c W-F C DELE) > *góstī (5a e(:)/o(:)-LOW, 10 V-SHORT) > OCSlav gósti.

[37] The derivation is *g^{h}ostí+om (PIE 3.1.2c i-j/u-w ALT and PIE 3.1.2f SIEVERS applying synchronically) → *g^{h}ostíjom (la DEASP, 1f W-F SYL) > *gostíjum (4c W-F C DELE) > *gostíju (6b V-FRONT) > *gostíji (ev) > OCSlav gostíjɪ.

[38] The *-ām is from the ā-class. The derivation is is *kósti+ām (PIE 3.l.2c i-j/u-w ALT and 3.1.2f SIEVERS applying synchronically) → *kóstijām (5a e(:)/o(:)-LOW, 7c NASAL V) > *kástijǭ (10 V-SHORT) > OCSlav kóstɪję.

[39] This form is an original accusative plural ending.

[40] The alternations of *sūnu- vs. *sūnou- are instances of PIE Ø-o ablaut.

[41] The derivation is *sū́nou+ei (PIE 3.1.2c i-j/u-w ALT applying synchronically) → *sū́nowei (5a e(:)/o(:)-LOW) > *sū́nawæi (7b MON) > *sū́nawī (9b ū-TO-ȳ) > *sȳ́nawī (9c w-TO-v, 10 V-SHORT) > OCSlav sýnovi.

[42] Bräuer (1969: 2, 147) posits the PIE nominative plural as *sūnewes on the basis of Go sunjus, which was clearly from PIE *sūneu+es However, this antecedent would have resulted in OCSlav **synevé. Hence we assume that the pre-Old Church Slavic PIE u-class paradigm had only o-Ø ablaut. The derivation is *sūnou+és (PIE 3.1.2c i-j/u-w ALT applying synchronically) → *sūnowés (4c W-F C DELE) > *sūnowé (5a e(:)/o(:)-LOW) > *sūnawǽ (9b ū-TO-ȳ, 9c w-TO-v) > *sȳ navǽ (10 V-SHORT) > OCSlav synové.

[43] The derivation is *ṓlkutom (1f W-F SYL) > *ṓlkutum (4c W-F C DELE) > *ṓlkutu (5a e(:)/o(:)-LOW) > *ā́lkutu (9a MET) > *lā́kutu (10 V-SHORT) > OCSlav lákʊtʊ.

[44] The change 8a JOTA can affect only the singular forms because of the jo-class endings. Hence /lj/ and /rj/ occur in the nominative singular vs. /l/ and /r/ in the nominative plural.

[45] This word is a later borrowing from Germanic. Its derivation is *mū́tār+jos (1f W-F SYL) > *mū́tārjus (4c W-F C DELE) > *mū́tārju (6b V-FRONT) > *mū́tārji (8a JOTA, 9b ū-TO-ȳ) > *mȳ́tārji (10 V-SHORT) > OCSlav mýtarjɪ.

[46] The word is a borrowing from Germanic. The derivation is *kírkūs (8b 2ND PAL) > *církūs > (4c W-F C DELE, continuing to apply as a morpheme-structure rule) > *církū (9a MET) > *críkū (9b ū-TO-ȳ) > *críkȳ (10 V-SHORT, including the later i-TO-u change) > OCSlav crʊ́ky.

[47] The derivation is *kírkū (plus the reflex of the ending *-m̥, which by 1d SYL SON and 4c W-F C DELE would be *-i) > *kírkū+i (where /ūi/ > /uui/, which by PIE 3.1.2c i-j/u-w ALT applying synchronically) > *kírkuwi (8b 2ND PAL) > *církuwi (9a MET) > *críkuwi (9c w-TO-v) > *críkuvi (10 V-SHORT including the later ɪ-TO-ʊ change) > OCSlav crʊ́kʊvɪ.

[48] The derivations of this form is not obvious. Schmalstieg (1983: 97) posits a PIE sandhi or morph cond alternation of *mā́ter vs. *mā́tē and a subsequent change into Slavic whereby *mā́tē (ev) > OCSlav máti. Another possibility is that the Old Church Slavic word-final -i may have come from the root class (1.5.2 above).

[49]These endings are from the i-class.

[50] The nominative plural may have come from an original accusative plural ending. The derivation is *mā́tern̥s (1d SYL SON) > *mā́terins (1f W-F SYL) > *mā́terīs (4c W-F C DELE) > *mā́terī (5a e(:)/o(:)-LOW, 10 V-SHORT) > OCSlav máteri.

[51] The derivation is *ákmōn (1f W-F SYL) > *ákmūn (4c W-F C DELE) > *akmū (9a MET) > *kā́mū (9b ū-TO-ȳ) > *kā́mȳ (10 V-SHORT) > OCSlav kámy.

[52] Note the ō-e ablaut in the -Vn suffix. The derivation of the accusative singular is *ákmenm̥ (1d SYL SON) > *ákmenim (4c W-F C DELE) > *ákmeni (9a MET, 10 V-SHORT) > OCSlav kámenɪ.

[53] These endings are from the i-class.

[54] The derivation is analogous to that of the OCSlav acc pl máterı under 1.5.3 above.

[55] The nominative singular is o-class; the nominative plural, Vn-class athematic. The root is a borrowing from Germanic. The respective derivations are *gard+jān+ī́n+os and *gard+jān+ī́n+es (1f W-F SYL) > *gardjānī́nus and *gardjānī́nes (4c W-F C DELE) > *gardjānī́nu and *gardjānī́ne (8a JOTA) > *garždānī́nu and *garždānī́ne (9a MET) > *grāždānī́nu and *grāždānī́ne (10 V-SHORT) > OCSlav graždanínʊ and graždaníne.

[56] These forms added -t from the Vnt-class under 1.5.5 below. The derivation is *sē̍ment (4c W-F C DELE) > *sē̍men (7c NASAL V) > *sē̍mę̄ (10 V-SHORT) > OCSlav sē̍mę.

[57] This ending is from the o-class. The derivation is problematical.

[58] The derivation is *ṓg^hw^nentes (la DEASP, 2b DELAB) > *ṓgnentes (4c W-F C DELE) > *ṓgnente (5a e(:)/o(:)-LOW) > *ā́gnæntæ (7c NASAL V) > *ā́gnętæ (10 V-SHORT) > OCSlav ágnęte.

[59] The nominative/vocative/accusative singular has the o-grade ablaut in the -Vs suffix; otherwise the e-grade occurs. The derivation is *klówos (lc EARLIEST PAL) > *slówos (? 1f W-F SYL) > *slówus (4c W-F C DELE) > *slówu (? replacement of -u by -o from the neuter pron to 'this' described under 5.3 below) > *slówo (5a e(:)/o(:)-LOW) > *slā́wa (9c w-TO-v) > *sláva (10 V-SHORT) > OCSlav slóvo.

[60] This, like many other jo-/jā-class adjectives, undergoes 5b 1ST PAL and/or 8a JOTA. The derivation here is *lúg^h+jos (la DEASP, 1f W-F SYL) > *lúgjus (4c W-F C DELE) > *lúgju (6b V-FRONT) > *lúgji (8a JOTA) > *lúži (10 V-SHORT) > OCSlav lʊ́žı. Adjectives like this one are often called "soft stems" in the literature; those like slábʊ 'weak' above which undergo neither 5b 1ST PAL nor 8a JOTA are called "hard stems".

[61] In these forms a sequence /ʊ+i/ has resulted in /yi/. This fact may indicate a time-frame for the creation of the long declension. First, the affixed nom sg masc pron -i derives from earlier *-ī (ultimately PIE *-ijos) by 6b V-FRONT. Hence 6b V-FRONT had applied by the time the long declension arose. This would be sometime after 500-600 AD. Second, the further derivation seems to have been *slā́bu+ī (? assimilation of length to /u/) > *slā́būī (9b ū-TO-ȳ) > *slā́bȳī (10 V-SHORT) > OCSlav slábyi. This derivation indicates that the long declension was formed before the time of 9b ū-TO-ȳ (ca. 700-800 AD). Therefore the long declension may have been formed sometime between 500 and 800 AD.

[62] In the construction of these long forms slábʊ- seems to have replaced the original short-declension forms. These are the masc/neuter instr sg slábomı, the dual dat/instr sláboma, the pl loc sláběxʊ and the dat pl slábomʊ.

[63] When a polysyllabic pronoun is affixed to a short form, the first syllable of the pronoun is deleted. In the case of the instr sg fem slábǫjǫ+(jeję) the entire pronoun is deleted.

[64] The other neuter endings are the same as those of the masculine declension.

[65] The nominative singular masculine forms are always in the long declension. The derivation here is *minjis (4c W-F C DELE, 8a JOTA) > *mínji (addition of the nominative singular masculine long-declension ending -i) > *minjiī (10 V-SHORT) > *mínjıi, which we, following the usual practice, write as OCSlav mínjii.

[66] The derivation is PIE *stā́rējis (4c W-F C DELE) > *stā́rēji (10 V-SHORT) > *stárějı = OCSlav stárěi.

[67] The derivation is *áubagējis (4c W-F C DELE) > *áubagēji (5a e(:)/o(:)-LOW) > *áubagǣji (5b 1ST PAL) > *áubažǣji (6a ǣ-TO-ā) > *áubalāji (7b MON) > *ū́bažāji (10 V-SHORT) > *úbožajı = OCSlav úbožai.

[68] The derivation is *mínjisjā (the ending -ā replaced by -ī, probably on the model of the jā-class noun ladijí 'boat' under 1.2 above) > *mínjisjī (3 RUKI) > *mínjixjī (8a JOTA) > *mínjišī (10 V-SHORT) > OCSlav mínjıši.

[69] Instead of assuming *-jes as the antecedent of the nominative/accusative singular neuter, one might posit the following derivation: *minjis (4c W-F C DELE) > *mínji (replacement of -i by the nominative/accusative neuter pronominal ending -o in Slavic *to from PIE *tod) > *mínjo (5a e(:)/o(:)-LOW) > *mínja (6b V-FRONT) > *mínjæ (10 V-SHORT) > OCSlav mínje.

[70] The derivation of the ending is problematic. See the derivation of the jā-class gen sg dušę 'soul' under 1.2 above.

[71] The derivation is *edoinós (1f W-F SYL) > *edoinús (4b PROTHESIS) > *jedoinús (4c W-F C DELE) > *jedoinú (5a e(:)/o(:)-LOW) > *jædainú (7b MON, but applying somewhat irregularly) > *jædīnú (10 V-SHORT) > OCSlav jedinʊ́.

[72] The antecedent may have been the PIE masculine/feminine accusative plural. The derivation is *tríns (1f W-F SYL) > *trī́s (4c W-F C DELE) > *trī́ (10 V-SHORT) > OCSlav trí.

[73] The derivation is *k^{w}etűr̥ns (1d SYL SON) > *k^{w}etűrins (1f W-F SYL) > *k^{w}etűrīs (2b DELAB) > *ketűrīs (4c W-F C DELE) > *ketűrī (5a e(:)/o(:)-LOW) > *kætűrī (5b 1ST PAL) > *čætűrī (9b ū-TO-ȳ) > *čætȳ́rī (10 V-SHORT) > OCSlav četýri.

[74] The stress is on the endings in the oblique cases.

[75] This construction consists of the dual nominative of both forms.

[76] This construction consists of the nominative plural endings of the athematic class.

[77] This construction consists of the nominative singular of '5' plus the genitive plural of '10'.

[78] These are o-class neuter dual endings.

[79] This construction consists of the i-class nominative singular form plus the genitive plural of the o-class neuter sʊtó.

[80] These and the remaining ordinals are formed either by adding the ending directly to the cardinal numeral or by adding an intermediate suffix -t- between the root and the ending.

[81] The derivation is *k^{w}etūŕ̥+t (1d SYL SON) > *k^{w}etūírt (PIE 3.1.2c i-j/u-w ALT applying synchronically) → *k^{w}etwírt- (2b DELAB) > *ketwírt- (5a e(:)/o(:)-LOW) > *kætwírt- (5b 1ST PAL) > *čætwírt- (9a MET) > *čætwrít- (9c w-TO-v) > *čætvrít- (10 V-SHOR T as well as the addition of the adjective endings) > OCSlav četvrítyi.

[82] The derivation is *ēgom (1c EARLIEST PAL) > *ēzom (1f W-F SYL) > *ēzum (4b PROTHESIS, either applying sporadically or applying only to the stressed form) > *jēzum as well as *ēzum (4c W-F C DELE) > *jēzu and *ēzu (5a e(:)/o(:)-LOW) > *jǣzu and *ǣzu (6a ǣ-TO-ā) > *jāzu and *ǣzu (/ā/ replacing /ǣ/ in the latter form) > *jāzu and *āzu (loss of *jāzu from pre-Old Church Slavic, then 10 V-SHORT) > OCSlav azʊ.

[83] The remaining forms of the singular begin with /m/. Those of the dual and plural begin with /n/.

[84] The remaining forms of the singular begin with /t/. Those of the dual and plural begin with by /v/.

[85] The derivation of these forms is nom sg masc *jos and acc sg masc *jom (1f W-F SYL) > *jus and *jum (4c W-F C DELE) > *ju for both forms (6b V-FRONT 1) > *ji (6b V-FRONT 2) > OCSlav i. The earliest PIE forms were *i+os and *i+om (PIE 3.1.2c i-j/u-w ALT applying synchrcnically) → *j+os and *j+om.

[86] These endings are historically the same as these of the Old Church Slavic demonstrative tʊ 'this, that' given below. The OCSlav i- and tʊ- paradigms differ because the former has undergone 6b V-FRONT . E.g., gen sg masc *tog^{w}o 'this' vs. *jog^{w}o 'he' (2b DELAB) > *togo and *jogo (5a e(:)/o(:)-LOW) > *taga and *jaga (6b V-FRONT) > *taga and *jæga (10 V-SHORT) > OCSlav togo and jego.

[87] The PIE antecedent of this ending is not clear.

[88] The derivation is *joimi (5a e(:)/o(:)-LOW) > *jaimi (6b V-FRONT 1) > *jæimi (7b MON) > *jīmi (6b V-FRONT 2) > *īmi (10 V-SHORT) > OCSlav imɪ.

[89] The derivation is *jō (5a e(:)/o(:)-LOW) > *jā (6a V-FRONT not applying to a long /ā/, but by 10 V-SHORT) > ja.

[90] The derivation is *joi+ous (PIE 3.1.2c i-j/u-w ALT applying synchronically) → *jojous (4c W-F C DELE) > *jojou (5a e(:)/o(:)-LOW) > *jajau (6b V-FRONT) > *jæjæu (7b MON) > *jæjū (10 V-SHORT) > OCSlav jeju.

[91] The derivation is *joisom (1f W-F SYL) > *joisum (3 RUKI) > *joixum (4c W-F C DELE) > joixu (5a e(:)/o(:)-LOW) > *jaixu (6b V-FRONT 1) > *jæixu (7b MON) > *jīxu (6b V-FRONT 2) > *īxu (10 V-SHORT) > OCSlav ixʊ.

[92] The ending of the PIE antecedent is not clear. See on this the derivation of the jā-class gen sg dušę 'soul' under 1.2 above.

[93] The derivation is *ja+āi (lb DIPH SHORT) > *jaai (6b V-FRONT) > *jæai (7b MON) > jæī (10 V-SHORT) > OCSlav jei.

[94] The derivation is analogous to that of the dual masculine genitive given above.

[95] The derivation is *jod (4c W-F C DELE) > *jo (5a e(:)/o(:)-LOW) > *ja (6b V-FRONT) > *jæ (10 V-SHORT) > OCSlav je.

[96] The other neuter forms are the same as the masculine.

[97] All possessive adjectives are in this declension.

[98] The derivation is *toimi (5a e(:)/o(:)-LOW) > *taimi (7b MON) > *tǣmi (10 V-SHORT) > OCSlav těmɪ.

[99] The derivation is *toi+ous (PIE 3.1.2c i-j/u-w ALT applying synchronically) → *tojous (4c W-F C DELE) > *tojou (5a e(:)/o(:)-LOW) > *tajau (6b V-FRONT) > *tajæu (7b MON) > *tajū (10 V-SHORT) > OCSlav toju.

[100] The ending may be that of the ā-class ženíjǫ under 1.2 above. The derivation is *sobʰojām (1a DEASP) > *sobojām (5a e(:)/o(:)-LOW) > *sabajām (7c NASAL V) > *sabajǭ (10 V-SHORT) > OCSlav sobojǫ.

[101] The derivation of these forms is *kʷos##tod and *kʷ+i+tod in which *tod is the neuter deictic of Old Church Slavic to as given in 5.3 above (1f W-F SYL) > *kʷus##tod and *kʷitod (2b DELAB) > *kus##tod and *kitod (4c W-F C DELE) > *kuto and *kito (5a e(:)/o(:)-LOW) > *kuta and *kita (5b 1ST PAL) > *kuta and *čita (10 V-SHORT) > OCSlav kʊto and čɪto.

[102] The derivation of these forms is the masc instr *kʷoimi and the neuter instr *kʷoimi (2b DELAB) > *koimi and *koimi (5a e(:)/o(:)-LOW) > *kaimi and *kaimi (replacement of /k/ by /č/ in the neuter form after the other forms in the neuter paradigm which had undergone 5b 1ST PAL) > *kaimi and čaimi (6b V-FRONT) > *kaimi and *čæimi (7b MON) > *kǣmi and *čīmi (8b 2ND PAL) > *čǣmi and *čīmi (10 V-SHORT) > OCSlav masc instr čěmɪ and neuter instr čimɪ. In this derivation the replacement of /k/ by /č/ in the neuter form must have occurred before the time of 6b V-FRONT , i.e. before about 500-600 AD.

[103] The features in this column are in fact mutually exclusive. Thus there is in Old Church Slavic no contrast between a present indicative and subjunctive. A present subjunctive or optative meaning can be expressed by an Old Church Slavic present form combined with an adverbial particle. E.g., OCSlav da slýšitʊ 'indeed, yes he hears = may he hear, let him hear' (Schmalstieg 1983: 153).

[104] The passive has no special endings. Passive paradigms are constructed either with a reflexive verb such as OCSlav krɪstíti sę 'to baptize oneself, i.e. to be baptized'; or they are formed with one of the passive participles (6.9.2 and 6.9.4 below) plus an auxiliary form of bytí 'to be'. E.g., OCSlav izgʊnánʊ bytí 'to be cast out'.

[105] The imperfect and the aorist are both past tenses. The difference between them is that the aorist indicates only that an action took place in the past, while the imperfect indicates a past action with the added information of duration or repetition of the event as well. E.g., aorist oní...ídošę "They departed, i.e., went out once" vs. imperf zvězdá íděaše prédʊ nimí "The star went continually and for some time before them" (Schmalstieg 1983: 154).

[106] The perfect is a past tense which denotes a present state which is the result of a past event. E.g., aorist dʊ́šti tvoě umrě́tʊ "Your daughter died" vs. perf ně́stʊ umrʊlá, nʊ sʊpítʊ "Your daughter has not died, i.e. is still alive, but she is sleeping" (Schmalstieg 1983: 156).

[107] The conditional is most frequently used to express contrary-to-fact statements in either the present or past. E.g., á̆šte bi bylʊ́ sɪ́de, ne bi brátrʊ moi umrʊlʊ́ "If you had been there, my brother would not have died" or "If you were there, my brother would not now be dying."

[108] The assignment of verbs into five classes is the practice followed in most sources such as Nandriş (1959) and Schmalstieg (1983). (1t is not followed in Diels 1932.) The classification is based on the intermediate morpheme which occurs in present-tense forms between the stem and the inflectional ending. Examples follow.

[109] Verbs may be either perfective or imperfective. A perfective verb describes an event as occurring without indicating the manner of its occurrence. The event began and then stopped. On the other hand, an imperfective verb describes an event as occurring over some time and not necessarily being completed. E.g., the following imperfective vs. perfective infinitives: ití 'to go' vs. pr+ití 'to go and then stop going, i.e. to arrive' and nestí 'to carry' vs. pre+nestí 'to carry to completion, to bring'. Perfective verbs generally do not occur in the imperfect. And imperfective verbs generally do not occur in the aorist or perfect.

[110] The differentiation of imperfective vs. perfective is realized in three main ways. (a) First, some perfective verbs are formed from imperfectives by means of a prefix such as the perfective pr+ití 'to arrive' vs. the imperfective ití 'to go'. (b) Second, some perfective and imperfective verbs devolve from the same root, but in different verb classes. E.g., the perfective 2nd class tlě́nǫti 'to push once, to knock' from PIE *télk+nān+tei vs. the imperfective 1st class tlěští 'to push continually' from PIE *telk+téi. (c) Third, for some verbs the difference between

perfective and imperfective is suppletive in that the two verbs are different lexical items. E.g., the perfective 1st class inf rešti 'to say' vs. the imperfective 3rd class glagoláti 'to say continually, to talk'.

[111] The antecedent of this form is not clear. A possibility is *bʰer+ṓ (the thematic 1st person ending) + m (from the imperfect or aorist). The derivation is *bʰerṓm (1a DEASP) > *berṓm (5a e(:)/o(:)-LOW) > *bærā́m (7c NASAL V) > *bærǫ́ (10 V-SHORT) > OCSlav berǫ́.

[112] The origin of the final vowel is not clear. If the ending had been the usual PIE *-si, the Old Church Slavic form would be **berésɪ. We posit that the PIE middle ending *-ai was added to the form. The derivation is then *bʰerési+ai (PIE 3.1.2c i-j/u-w ALT applying synchronically) → *bʰerésjai (1a DEASP, 5a e(:)/o(:)-LOW) > *bærǽsjai (6b V-FRONT) > *bærǽsjæi (7b MON) > *bærǽsjī (8a JOTA) > *bærǽšī (10 V-SHORT) > OCSlav beréši.

[113] The source of the final -ʊ in these forms is not clear. From the PIE antecedents one would expect OCSlav **berétɪ and **berǫ́tɪ. The -ʊ may be from the nominative singular masculine adjective ending. (See 2.1.)

[114] The PIE antecedent may have been the masculine dual nominative ending *-ō. On occasion another dual 2nd person ending is attested, namely berétě. This may have come from the feminine dual nominative ending. *-ai.

[115] The derivation of sědę́tʊ is *sēdjónti (5a e(:)/o(:)-LOW) > *sǣdjánti (6b V-FRONT) > *sǣdjǽnti (7c NASAL V) > *sǣdję́ti (8a JOTA) > *sǣždę́ti (/žd/ replaced by /d/ from elsewhere in the paradigm, replacement of word-final -i by -u) > *sǣdę́tu (10 V-SHORT) > OCSlav sědę́tʊ. The derivation of the PIE 3rd class 3pl *gnṓjonti to OCSlav znájǫtʊ is similar to the preceding, except that one would expect OCSlav **znáję́tʊ. The /ǫ/ in znájǫtʊ comes from the -ǫtʊ ending of the 1st and 2nd classes.

[116] There are at least three possible PIE antecedents for this intermediate morpheme. They are *-ī-, *-ij- or *-ej-. The *-ij- may have arisen from *-j- by the PIE rule 3.1.2f SIEVERS applying after long-syllable verb stems. The -ej- was an ablauting variant of the 3rd class suffix *-j-.

[117] The derivation is *sēdjṓm (5a e(:)/o(:)-LOW) > *sǣdjā́m (7c NASAL V) > *sǣdjǫ́ (8a JOTA) > *sǣždǫ́ (10 V-SHORT) > OCSlav sěždǫ.

[118] The derivation is *sēdéjsiai (PIE 3.1.2c i-j/u-w ALT applying synchronically) → *sēdéisjai (3 RUKI) > *sēdéixjai (5a e(:)/o(:)-LOW) > *sǣdǽixjai (6b V-FRONT) > *sǣdǽixjæi (7b MON) > *sǣdī́xjī (8a JOTA) > *sǣdī́šī (10 V-SHORT) > OCSlav sědíši.

[119] The 5th-class verbs are generally assumed to have taken End-stress throughout their present paradigms. (See on this le OCS STRESS.) However, it is also possible that pre-Slavic PIE, early Slavic and Old Church Slavic as well had the word stress of early PIE. This would have been Stem-stress in the sg and End-stress in the dual and plural.

[120] The derivation is *dṓdmi (4a C-CL SIMP) > *dṓmi (5a e(:)/o(:)-LOW) > *dā́mi (10 V-SHORT) > OCSlav dámɪ.

[121] PIE *-sai is a middle ending. The derivation is *éssai (4a C-CL SIMP) > *ésai (4b PROTHESIS) > *jésai (5a e(:)/o(:)-LOW) > *jǽsai (7b MON) > *jǽsī (10 V-SHORT) > OCSlav jési.

[122] The derivation is *dōdwḗs (4a C-CL SIMP) > *dōwḗs (4c W-F C DELE) > *dōwḗ (5a e(:)/o(:)-LOW) > *dāwǣ́ (9c W-TO-V) > *dāvǣ́ (10 V-SHORT) > OCSlav davě́. Note that change 4a C-CL SIMP does not apply in the derivation of OCSlav jesvě́.

[123] The derivation is *dōdtṓ (2a C-CL) > *dōstṓ (5a e(:)/o(:)-LOW) > *dāstā́ (10 V-SHORT) > OCSlav dastá.

[124] The derivation is *dōdn̥tí (1d SYL SON) > *dōdintí (5a e(:)/o(:)-LOW) > *dādintí (7c NASAL V) > *dādę́tí (10 V-SHORT, substitution of -u for word-final -i) > OCSlav dadętʊ́. As for OCSlav sǫtʊ́, one would expect by a similar derivation **sętʊ́. However, the ending –ǫtʊ came from the 3rd plural ending of classes 1, 2 and 3 above.

[125] We assume that the stress on the Proto-Slavic and Old Church Slavic imperfect was that of early Russian. This was on the thematic vowel of the stem (i.e., Stem-stress). (See on this Vaillant 1966: 3, 527-8.)

[126] The PIE antecedents of the Old Church Slavic imperfect are not clear. One possibility is that the PIE antecedent of the ending was the imperfect of 'be' *es-. If formed with an aorist augment, the result would have been *e+es- = *ēs-. The 1st singular aorist would have been *ēsom. Then the derivation of the 1st singular imperfect would be from a form consisting of two forms, the stem plus the imperfect of 'be'. E.g., *bʰr̥+ā́##ēsom (1a DEASP, 1d SYL SON) > *birā́##ēsom (1f W-F SYL) > *birā́##ēsum (3 RUKI applying to aorist forms like *péi+s+um 'I drank' > *péixum cited in 6.3 below; then this /x/ replaces the imperfect with /s/) > *birā́#ēxum (4b PROTHESIS) >

*birā́#jēxum (4c W-F C DELE) > *birā́##jēxu (5a e(:)/o(:)-LOW) > *birā́##jǣxu (6a ǣ-TO-ā) > *birā́##jāxu (? reinterpretation of the two words as one) > *birā́jāxu (? deletion of /j/ since it otherwise does not occur word-internally) > *birā́āxu (10 V-SHORT) > OCSlav bъráaxъ.

[127] The derivation is *bʰr̥ā́##ēses (1a DEASP, 1d SYL SON) > *birā́##ēses (3 RUKI applying analogously as in the immediately preceding derivation, 4b PROTHESIS, 4c W-F C DELE) > *birā́##jēxe (5a e(:)/o(:)-LOW) > *birā́##jǣxæ (5b 1ST PAL) > *birā́##jǣšæ (6a ǣ-TO-ā) > *birā́##jāšæ (removal of word boundary and /j/, 10 V-SHORT) > OCSlav bъráaše.

[128] The derivation is *bʰr̥ā́##ēsont (la DEASP, ld SYL SON, 3 RUKI applying analogously) > *birā́##ēxont (4b PROTHESIS , 4c W-F C DELE) > *birā́##jēxon (5a e(:)/o(:)-LOW) > *birā́##jǣxan (6a ǣ-TO-ā) > *birā́##jāxan (7c NASAL V , removal of word boundary and /j/) > *birā́āxǭ (10 V-SHORT) > OCSlav bъráaxǫ.

[129] The derivation of these forms is *mogʰés and *mogʰét (la DEASP) > *mogés and *mogét (no 1c EARLIEST PAL, which means that the verb was a later borrowing, then 4c W-F C DELE applies) > *mogé (5a e(:)/o(:)-LOW) > *magǽ (5b 1ST PAL) > *mažǽ (10 V-SHORT) > OCSlav možé.

[130] The derivation is *mogʰónt (la DEASP, no 1c EARLIEST PAL for the reason given above) > *mogónt (4c W-F C DELE) > *mogón (5a e(:)/o(:)-LOW) > *magán (7c NASAL V) > *magǭ́ (10 V-SHORT) > OCSlav mogǫ́.

[131] The derivation is *bʰr̥+ā́+som alongside another 1sg aorist *péi+s+om 'I drank' (la DEASP, 1d SYL SON, 1f W-F SYL) > *birā́sum and *péisum (3 RUKI) > *birā́sum and *péixum (replacement of /s/ by /x/ in those forms where RUKI had not applied) > *birā́xum and *péixum (4c W-F C DELE, 5a e(:)/o(:)-LOW) > *birā́xu and *pǽixu (7b MON) > *birā́xu and *pī́xu (10 V-SHORT) > OCSlav bъráxъ and píxъ. For some reason, the aorist -s- is preserved in verbs whose roots originally ended in a nasal. E.g., 1sg aorist *émsom 'I took' (1f W-F SYL) > *émsum (4b PROTHESIS) > *jémsum (4c W-F C DELE) > *jémsu (7c NASAL V) > *ję̄́su (10 V-SHORT) > OCSlav ję́sъ.

[132] The derivation of these forms is *bʰr̥+ā́+s+s and *bʰr̥+ā́+s+t (1a DEASP, 1d SYL SON) > *birā́ss and *birā́st (4a C-CL SIMP) > *birā́s and *birā́st (4c W-F C DELE) > *birā́ and *birā́s (the latter form then losing the word-final /s/, possibly because it was considered a 2nd singular marker) > *birā́ for both forms (10 V-SHORT) > OCSlav bъrá.

[133] Change 3 RUKI cannot apply in the derivation of these forms because the /s/ is followed by an obstruent. Hence 1sg aorist *péi+s+om 'I drank' vs. 2 dual *péi+s+tō (ev) > OCSlav píxъ vs. písta.

[134] This ending is the Ø-grade ablaut which occurs in the o-grade in the simple aorist under (i) above. The derivation is *bʰr̥+ā́+s+n̥t (la DEASP, 1d SYL SON) > *birā́sint (3 RUKI not applying here, but the /x/ resulting by RUKI in other forms such as *peisom 'I drank' immediately above) > *birā́xint (4c W-F C DELE) > *birā́xin (5b 1ST PAL) > *birā́šin (7c NASAL V) > *birā́šę̄ (10 V-SHORT) > OCSlav bъrášę.

[135] This aorist seems to have been a later formation dating from post-PIE times. The 2nd and 3rd singular forms are those of formation (i) the simple aorist.

[136] The derivation is *nekósn̥t (1c EARLIEST PAL) > *nesósn̥t (ld SYL SON) > *nesósint (3 RUKI applying analogously) > *nesóxint (4c W-F C DELE) > *nesóxin (5b 1ST PAL) > *nesóšin (7c NASAL V) > *nesóšę̄ (10 V-SHORT) > OCSlav nesóšę.

[137] The ablaut does not occur in the 2nd or 3rd persons singular aorist.

[138] The derivation is *bʰṓd+s+om (la DEASP) > *bṓdsom (1f W-F SYL) > *bṓdsum (2a C-CL) > *bṓtsum (4a C-CL SIMP) > *bṓsum (4c W-F C DELE) > *bṓsu (5a e(:)/o(:)-LOW) > *bā́su (10 V-SHORT) > OCSlav básъ.

[139] The derivation is *kʷeitsom (1f W-F SYL) > *kʷéitsum (2a C-CL) > *kʷéissum (2b DELAB) > *kéissum (4a C-CL SIMP) > *kéisum (4c W-F C DELE) > *kéisu (5a e(:)/o(:)-LOW) > *kǽisu (5b 1ST PAL) > *čǽisu (7b MON) > *čī́su (10 V-SHORT) > OCSlav čísъ.

[140] The PIE ending was a 1st singular mediopassive. The meaning of the PIE form was 'I have seen'. The derivation is *wóidai (5a e(:)/o(:)-LOW) > *wáidai (7b MON) > *wǣ́dǣ (9c w-TO-v) > *vǣ́dǣ (10 V-SHORT) > OCSlav vě́dě.

[141] The literal translation is 'I am a having carried one'. The inflected verb is the 5th-class present of bytí 'be' as given under 6.1 above.

[142] The literal translation is 'I was a having carried one'. The inflected verb is the 5th-class imperfect of bytí 'be' as given under 6.2 above.

[143] The literal translation is 'I shall be a having carried one'. The inflected verb is the future of bytí 'be' as given under 6.6 below.

[144] The PIE antecedent *-oi- is the optative marker. The derivation of the two forms is *b^{h}eróis and *b^{h}eróiwēs (1a DEASP) > *beróis and *beróiwēs (4c W-F C DELE) > *berói and *beróiwē (5a e(:)/o(:)-LOW) > *bærái and *bæráiwǣ (7b MON) > *bærī́ and *bærǣwǣ (9c W-TO-v, 10 V-SHORT) > OCSlav berí and berě̌vě.

[145] The OCSlav -i- occurs throughout the paradigm from PIE *-oi- as the result of derivations like this one. (Note that /j/occurs stem-finally in every form.) The derivation is *gnṓ+j+oi+wēs (1c EARLIEST PAL) > *znṓjoiwēs (4c W-F C DELE) > *znṓjoiwē (5a e(:)/o(:)-LOW) > *znā́jaiwǣ (6b V-FRONT) > *znā́jæiwǣ (7b MON) > *znā́jīwǣ (9c W-TO-v) > *znā́jīvǣ (10 V-SHORT) > OCSlav znájivě. A few Old Church Slavic verbs of this class have /a/ instead of /i/ in their imperative forms. This seems to have occurred as in the following derivation of a 1 dual form: *gálgal+j+oi+wēs 'let us speak' (4c W-F C DELE, 5a e(:)/o(:)-LOW) > *gálgaljaiwǣ (6b V-FRONT) > *gálgaljæiwǣ (7b MON) > *gálgaljīwǣ (replacement of the ending *-īwǣ by *-ǣwǣ from paradigms like that of berí 'gather' above) > *gálgaljǣwǣ (6a ǣ-TO-ā, still applying as a persistent rule) > *gálgaljāwǣ (9a MET) > *glā́galjāwǣ (9c W-TO-v, 10 V-SHORT) > OCSlav glágoljavě.

[146] The intermediate morpheme *-ī- is perhaps the Ø-grade ablaut of *-oi- (originally *-oī-). From the PIE 2nd singular antecedent *dōdī́s one would expect OCSlav **dadí. A possible derivation of OCSlav daždí is PIE *dōd+ī́+s (4c W-F C DELE) > *dōdī́ (? word-final /ī/ reinterpreted as /ji/) > *dōdjí (5a e(:)/o(:)-LOW) > *dādjí (8a JOTA) > *dāždí (10 V-SHORT) > OCSlav daždí.

[147] The origin of OCSlav bǫd- is not clear. According to Nandriş (1959: 197), it may have begun as an athematic verb. The 1st singular form may have been 'be' plus the present participle ending plus /d/ which all Old Church Slavic athematic verbs seem to have added to their roots plus the 1st singular present ending, i.e. *b^{h}+ont+d+ṓm. The derivation is *b^{h}ontdṓm (1a DEASP) > *bontdṓm (2a C-CL) > *bonddṓm (4a C-CL SIMP) > *bondṓm (5a e(:)/o(:)-LOW) > *bandā́m (7c NASAL V) > *bǭdǭ́ (10 V-SHORT) > OCSlav bǫdǫ́.

[148] The intermediate *-ī- in the PIE antecedents is probably the same morpheme as that occurring in the imperative of class 5 verbs described in 6.5 above.

[149] The antecedent of the -s- in these forms is not clear. It may have been the future marker found in the future active participle described in 6.9.5 below.

[150] The ending *-ont is the thematic 3rd plural and *-n̥t is the athematic one. The derivation of the latter form is *b^{h}+ī+s+ń̥t (1a DEASP) > *bīsń̥t (1d SYL SON) > *bīsínt (3 RUKI) > *bīxínt (4c W-F C DELE) > *bīxín (5b 1ST PAL) > *bīšín (7c NASAL V) > *bīšę̄́ (10 V-SHORT) > OCSlav bišę́.

[151] The derivation is *gnṓ+n+j+om (PIE 3.1.2f SIEVERS applying as a synchronic rule) → *gnṓnijom (1c EARLIEST PAL) > *znṓnijom (4c W-F C DELE) > *znṓnijo (5a e(:)/o(:)-LOW) > *znā́nija (6b V-FRONT) > *znā́nijæ (10 V-SHORT) > OCSlav znánije.

[152] A number of verbs with intermediate -Ø- show historically predictable alternations between the infinitive and the present paradigm. Consider for example the following 1st singular present and infinitive forms:

	OCS		PIE
(a)	grebǫ́	'dig'	*g^{h}reb^{h}+ṓm
	gretí		*g^{h}reb^{h}+t+éi
(b)	koljǫ́	'stab'	*kol+j+ṓm
	klatí		*kol+t+éi
(c)	mırǫ́	'die'	*mr̥+ṓm
	mrětí		*mer+t+éi
(d)	pletǫ́	'weave'	*plet+ṓm
	plestí		*plet+t+éi

(e)	slovǫ́	'be called'	*klou+ṓm
	slutí		*klou+t+éi
(f)	vrɪgǫ́	'throw'	*wr̥g+ṓm
	vrěští		*werg+t+éi

Some derivations are these: (a) PIE inf *g^{h}reb^{h}+téi (a DEASP, 2a C-CL) > *greptéi (4a C-CL SIMP) > *gretéi (ev) > OCSlav gretí. (b) PIE inf *koltéi (5a e(:)/o(:)-LOW, 7b MON) > *kaltī́ (91 MET) > *klātī́ (10 V-SHORT) > OCSlav klatí. (c) This paradigm shows ablaut: PIE 1sg *mr̥ṓm vs. inf *mertéi (1d SYL SON) > *mirṓm and *mertéi (5a e(:)/o(:)-LOW, 7b MON) > *mirā́m and *mærtī́ (7c NASAL V) > *mirǭ́ and *mærtī́ (9a MET) > *mirǭ́ and *mrǣtī́ (10 V-SHORT) > OCSlav mɪrǫ́ and mrětí. (d) PIE inf *plet+téi (2a C-CL) > *plestéi (ev) > OCSlav plestí. (e) PIE 1sg *klou+ṓm vs. *klou+téi (PIE 3.1.2c i-j/u-w ALT applying synchronically) → *klowṓm and *kloutéi (lc EARLIEST PAL) > *slowṓm and *sloutéi (5a e(:)/o(:)-LOW, 7b MON) > *slawā́m and *slūtī́ (7c NASAL V) > *slawǭ́ and *slūtī́ (9c w-TO-v, 10 V-SHORT) > OCSlav slovǫ́ and slutí. (f) This paradigm shows Ø-e ablaut. PIE 1sg *wr̥g+ṓm vs. inf *werg+téi (1d SYL SON) > *wirgṓm and *wergtéi (2a C-CL) > *wirgṓm and *werktéi (5a e(:)/o(:)-LOW) > *wirgā́m and *wærktǽi (7b MON , 7c NASAL V) > *wirgǭ́ and *wærktī́ (8a JOTA) > *wirgǭ́ and *wærštī́ (9a MET) > *wrigǭ́ and *wrǣštī́ (9c w-TO-v, 10 V-SHORT) > OCSlav vrɪgǫ́ and vrěští.

[153] Some 1st class verbs have a nasal vowel throughout the present paradigm, but not in the infinitive. E.g., PIE 1sg pres *le+n+g^{h}+ṓm 'I lie down' vs. *leg^{h}+t+éi (la DEASP, 2a C-CL) > *lengṓm and *lektéi (5a e(:)/o(:)-LOW, 7b MON) > *længā́m and *læktī́ (7c NASAL V) > *lęgǭ́ and *læktī́ (8a JOTA) > *lęgǭ́ and *læštī́ (10 V-SHORT) > OCSlav lęgǫ́ and lešti.

[154] The PIE antecedents could be either *dwéig+nān+tei or *dwéig+non+tei.

[155] This verb is a borrowing from Germanic. Its derivation is *kaup+ou+ā́+tei 'to buy' (PIE 3.1.2c i-j/u-w ALT still applying synchronically) → *kaupowā́tei (5a e(:)/o(:)-LOW) > *kaupawā́tæi (7b MON) > *kūpawā́tī (9c w-TO-v, 10 V-SHORT) > OCSlav kupováti.

[156] The derivation is *mod^{h}l+éi+t+ei 'to request' (la DEASP) > *modléitei (4a C-CL SIMP) > *moléitei (5a e(:)/o(:)-LOW) > *malǽitæi (7b MON) > *malī́tī (10 V-SHORT) > OCSlav molíti.

[157] The derivation is PIE *ēd+t+éi (2a C-CL) > *ēstéi (4b PROTHESIS) > *jēstéi (5a e(:)/o(:)-LOW) > *jǣstǽi (6a ǣ-TO-ā) > *jāstǽi (7b MON) > *jāstī́ (10 V-SHORT) > OCSlav jastí.

[158] The corresponding long-declension form is OCSlav berýi. The derivation of the short form is *b^{h}er+ónts (la DEASP) > *beróntsْ (1f W-F SYL) > *berū́s (4c W-F C DELE, 5a e(:)/o(:)-LOW) > *bærū́ (9b ū-TO-ȳ) > *bærȳ́ (10 V-SHORT) > OCSlav berý.

[159] The corresponding long-declension form is OCSlav berǫ́štajego. The derivation of the short form is *b^{h}er+ónt+j+ōd (la DEASP) > *beróntjōd (4c W-F C DELE) > *beróntjō (5a e(:)/o(:)-LOW) > *bærántjā (7c NASAL V) > *bærǭ́tjā (8a JOTA) > *bærǭ́štā (10 V-SHORT) > OCSlav berǫ́šta.

[160] The derivation is *b^{h}eróntm̥ (la DEASP) > *beróntm̥ (ld SYL SON) > *beróntim (1f W-F SYL) > *berónti (5a e(:)/o(:)-LOW, 7c NASAL V) > *bærǫ́ti (8a JOTA applying analogously since it applies to other forms in the paradigm) > *bærǫ́šti (10 V-SHORT) > OCSlav berǫ́štɪ.

[161] This ending is probably that of the OCSlav jā-class ladijí 'boat' cited under 1.2 above.

[162] The expected derivation is *b^{h}erónt (la DEASP, 4c W-F C DELE, 5a e(:)/o(:)-LOW) > *bærán (7c NASAL V , 10 V-SHORT) > OCSlav berǫ́. The form berý probably came from the nominative singular masculine.

[163] The derivation is *b^{h}eróntjom (la DEASP) > *beróntjom (4c W-F C DELE, 5a e(:)/o(:)-LOW) > *bærántja (6b V-FRONT) > *bærántjæ (7c NASAL V) > *bærǭ́tjæ (8a JOTA) > *bærǭ́štæ (10 V-SHORT) > OCSlav berǫ́šte.

[164] The expected derivation of these forms is *gnṓ+j+ont+s and *mód^{h}l+j+ont+s (la DEASP, lc EARLIEST PAL, 1f W-F SYL) > *znṓjūs and *módljūs (4a C-CL SIMP, 4c W-F C DELE) > *znṓjū and *móljū (5a e(:)/o(:)-LOW) > *znā́jū and *máljū (9b ū-TO-ȳ, 10 V-SHORT) > OCSlav **znájy and **móljy. The /ę/in the Old Church Slavic forms znáję and mólję is from the oblique cases of these forms, where the /ę/ occurred through regular change such as described

in note 166 below.

[165] The expected derivation is *gnṓjontjōd (1c EARLIEST PAL) > *znṓjontjōd (4c W-F C DELE) > *znṓjontjō (5a e(:)/o(:)-LOW) > *znā́jantjā (6b V-FRONT) > *znā́jæntjā (7c NASAL V) > znā́ję́tjā (8a JOTA) > *znā́ję̄štā (10 V-SHORT) > OCSlav **znáję̄šta instead of znájǫšta. The /ǫ/ in the latter form is from a form like berǫ́šta 'gathering' noted above.

[166] The derivation is *módʰl+j+ont+j+ōd (1a DEASP, 4a C-CL SIMP) > *móljontōd (4c W-F C DELE, 5a e(:)/o(:)-LOW) > *máljantjā (6b V-FRONT) > *máljæntjā (7c NASAL V) > *máljętjā (8a JOTA) > *máljęštā > (10 V-SHORT) > OCSlav móljęšta.

[167] The *-us is the Ø grade of *-wVs-. The derivation of these forms is *nekẃs and *bʰr̥+ā́+ws (PIE 3.1.2c i-j/u-w ALT applying synchronically) → *nekús and *bʰr̥ā́us (? insertion of a glide /w/) > *nekús and *bʰr̥ā́wus (la DEASP, 1c EARLIEST PAL, 1d SYL SON) > *nesús and *birā́wus (4c W-F C DELE) > *nesú and *birā́wu (9c W-TO-V) > *nesú and *birā́vu (10 V-SHORT) > OCSlav nesʊ́ and bɪrávʊ. Hence when the Old Church Slavic verb stem ends in a vowel, the suffix is -vʊ, not-ʊ.

[168] The ending *-jī is probably that of the OCSlav jā-class ladijí 'boat' cited under 1.2 above. The derivation of this form is PIE *nek+ús+jī (1c EARLIEST PAL) > *nesúsjī (3 RUKI) > *nesúxjī (5a e(:)/o(:)-LOW) > *næsúxjī (8a JOTA) > *næsúšī (10 V-SHORT) > OCSlav nesʊ́ši.

[169] The derivation is *emtós (1f W-F SYL) > *emtús (4b PROTHESIS) > *jemtús (4c W-F C DELE) > *jemtú (5a e(:)/o(:)-LOW) > *jæmtú (7c NASAL V) > jętú (10 V-SHORT) > OCSlav jętʊ́.

[170] The derivations are *stŕ̥̥tos and *stŕ̥̥enos (1d SYL SON) > *stírtos and *stírenos (1f W-F SYL) > *stírtus and *stírenus (4c W-F C DELE) > *stírtu and *stírenu (5a e(:)/o(:)-LOW, 9a MET) > *strítu and *stíræenu (10 V-SHORT) > OCSlav strítʊ and stɪ́renʊ.

[171] The *-s- in the antecedent form is the PIE future marker. The derivation is *bʰū+s+ń̥t+j+ī (la DEASP, 1d SYL SON) > *būsíntjī (3 RUKI) > *būxíntjī (5b 1ST PAL) > *būšíntjī (7c NASAL V) > *būšę́tjī (8a JOTA) > *būšę́štī (9b ū-TO-ȳ) > *bȳšę́štjī (10 V-SHORT) > OCSlav byšę́šti. The PIE antecedent may also have been *bʰū+s+ént+j+ī with e-grade ablaut in the derivational suffix. In this case the same form would result in Old Church Slavic, but without the change 1d SYL SON in its derivation.

Chapter 7

Sanskrit

I Introduction

One of the earliest attested languages in the Indo-Iranian group is Sanskrit. Sanskrit is usually considered as consisting of two main stages. The first stage and the earliest literary material consist of the collection of hymns known as the *Rig-Veda*. Its origin has been variously dated from 2000 to 1000 BC. (The extant manuscripts, however, date from much later.) This early stage of the language is referred to as Vedic Sanskrit.

The next stage is called classical Sanskrit. Classical Sanskrit, which is in fact very close to Vedic Sanskrit, was codified during the 400's BC by the grammarian Pāṇini. Classical Sanskrit literature consists of various poetic works, narratives and histories — most of which are in metrical form. Most of the literature of the classical period was written well after the time of Pāṇini except for two epics, the *Mahābhārata* (an excerpt from which constitutes our reading selection in VI below) and the *Rāmāyana*. Both of these epics may have been composed around Pāṇini's time.

During its later period from around 500 BC on, Sanskrit took numerous lexical items from various other Indic dialects on the subcontinent. These dialects and this stage are often referred to as "Middle Indic". In addition to these borrowings, other words came into Sanskrit from several non-Indo-European languages on the Indian subcontinent, in particular Dravidian.

Sanskrit is written in a syllabary called the "dēvānāgari". Romanizations of the dēvānāgari can vary slightly. The one we use here is described in III Sanskrit Phonology below. Note in this connection that our PIE /j/ is romanized as Skt <y>; and Skt <j> represents the palatalized voiced affricate /ɟ/. E.g., PIE 3sg pres mid *jugetai 'yoke' (ev) > Skt yujatē /juɟatē/ 'join'.

A salient characteristic of Sanskrit is the fact that many of the changes that it underwent in its development from PIE remained in the grammar as phon cond or morph cond phonological rules. The aggregate of these rules has been traditionally referred to by the Sanskrit grammarians as "sandhi". (This word is a Skt i-class masc noun saṁdhís /sa^{n}d^{h}ís/, which means 'combination'.) In view of the many sandhi rules of Sanskrit, a particular word (especially its final segment) can vary considerably depending upon its environment. (E.g., the nom sg saṁdhís 'combination' cited above can also occur as saṁdhíḥ or saṁdhír.) For this reason Sanskrit words are often cited without any particular inflectional ending. That is, Sanskrit forms are often cited as roots and as such written with a hyphen. E.g., the masc sg nom dēvás 'god' may also be written as dēvá-; and the 3sg pres ájati 'drives' is written as a root as áj-.

In most Sanskrit forms we mark the stress as assigned by the morph cond rule 11 SKT STRESS 1 below. But for some words this morph cond stress is not indicated since the form does not occur in any source with its stress marked. For example, the o-class masc noun plāvas 'bath' has unknown stress while dēvás 'god' occurs frequently with its stress marked. In such instances where we have not given the morph cond stress, the word may be stressed according to the later phon cond rule 11 SKT STRESS 2. Hence plāvas 'bath' (11 SKT STRESS 2) → plā́vas.

II The Changes from PIE into Sanskrit

A. Overview of the Changes and their Chronology

The stages are ordered. The changes within each stage may have been in any order or roughly simultaneous.

B. The Changes

1a Putative Changes Involving Laryngeals (LARYNGEALS)

The existence of these changes, like that of the laryngeals themselves, is disputed. If they did in fact occur, they were very early and left reflexes in all IE languages. They would have restructured various lexical items as well as the phonemic inventory and then, like the laryngeals themselves, would have been dropped from the grammar. The following changes have been assumed for the history of Sanskrit in sources such as Burrow (1959: 84-88) and in Mayrhofer (1965: 18-20). After the changes given under (1) below, the laryngeals are assumed to have been lost, as noted under (2). In our account we shall use /h/ to designate any laryngeal and /h_1, h_2, h_3/ to differentiate among various types of laryngeals.

(1) The reflexes of the laryngeals. There are four of these often cited.

(i) The PIE schwa /ə/ interpreted as an original laryngeal.

h → hi / [C, –sonorant] __ [C, –sonorant]

That is, a laryngeal, /h/ between two obstruent consonants inserts a following /i/. E.g., PIE *dʰughtŕ̥- 'daughter' (LARYNGEALS 1i) > *dʰughitŕ̥- (LARYNGEALS 1ii) > *dʰugʰhitŕ̥- (LARYNGEALS 2) > *dʰugʰitŕ̥- (2a 1ST PAL) > *dʰuɟʰitŕ̥- (2b GRASSMANN, which must in this derivation follow LARYNGEALS 2) > *duɟʰitŕ̥- (8a ɟʰ-TO-h) > Skt duhitŕ̥-. Contrast the development into Greek: PIE ablauting *dʰughtēr (the Greek change 1a LARYNGEALS, ev) > Greek tʰugátēr. Also PIE *phtŕ̥- 'father' (instead of *pətŕ̥-) (LARYNGEALS 1i) > *phitŕ̥- (ev) > Skt pitŕ̥-. (If one posits the change LARYNGEALS 1iii below, it is not clear why the Sanskrit form would not be **phitŕ̥-.)

(ii) The syllabic sonorant consonants followed by a laryngeal.

(a)	r̥ h	→	ī	or ū	r	h		/ __ C
	l̥ h	→	ī	or ū	l	h		
	m̥h	→	ā		n	h		
	n̥ h	→	ā		Ø	h		
	1 2		3		1	2		
(b)	r̥ h	→	i	or u	r	h		/ __ V
	l̥ h	→	i	or u	l	h		
	1 2		3		1	2		

That is, (a) the syllabic sonorant consonants /r̥, l̥, m̥, n̥/ when followed by a laryngeal and a consonant leave the vowels as described over 3. (b) The syllabic sonorants /r̥, l̥/ when followed by a laryngeal and a vowel leave the vowels as described over 3. In both cases the syllabic sonorants are now nonsyllabic. (The occurrence of /i(:)/ vs. /u(:)/ before /r/ and /l/ may have been conditioned by a preceding consonant and/or a following vowel.)

E.g., PIE *kr̥hs+én 'head' (LARYNGEALS 1ii-a) > *kīrhsén (LARYNGEALS 2) > *kīrsén- (2a 1ST PAL) > *šīrsén- (4a RETRO) > *šīrṣén- (5a e(:)/o(:)-TO-a(:)) > Skt masc Vn-class śīrṣán-; vs. the same ablauting PIE root *kŕ̥hes- 'head' (LARYNGEALS 1ii-b) > *kírhes- (LARYNGEALS 2) > *kíres- (2a 1ST PAL) > *šíres- (5a e(:)/o(:)-TO-a(:)) > Skt neuter Vs-class śíras-.

Also PIE *dom̥h+tó- 'tamed' (LARYNGEALS 1ii-a) > *doānhtó- (LARYNGEALS 2) > *doāntó- (5a e(:)/o(:)-TO-a(:)) > *daāntá- (re-interpretation of the unusual sequence /aā/ as /ā/) > Skt perf pass part dāntá-. PIE *g^{w}r̥hú- 'heavy' (LARYNGEALS ii-b and 2) > *g^{w}urú- (3 DELAB) > Skt u-class adj gurú-. PIE *pl̥hnó- 'full' (LARYNGEALS 1ii-a and 2) > *pūlnó- (5a e(:)/o(:)-TO-a(:)) > *pūlná- (9b l/r ALT) > Skt o- and ā-class adj pūrṇá-. PIE *sn̥h+tó- 'won' (LARYNGEALS 1ii-a and 2) > *sātó- (5a e(:)/o(:)-TO-a(:)) > Skt perf pass part sātá-.

(iii) The obstruent stops followed by a laryngeal.

[C, –sonorant, –continuant, ?–voiced]	h	→	[same C, except +aspirated]	h
1	2		1	2

That is, the voiceless obstruent stops /p, t, k, k^{w}/ (and perhaps voiced ones /b, d, g, g^{w}/ as well) if immediately followed by a laryngeal become aspirated /p^{h}, b^{h}/ etc.

E.g., PIE *phoinó- 'foam' (LARYNGEALS 1iii) > *p^{h}hoinó- (LARYNGEALS 2) > *p^{h}oinó (5a e(:)/o(:)-TO-a(:)) > *p^{h}ainá (7a MON) > Skt phēná-. PIE 3sg pres *sphr̥héti 'throb' (LARYNGEALS 1ii-b) > *sphurhéti (LARYNGEALS 1iii) > *sp^{h}hurhéti (LARYNGEALS 2) > *sp^{h}uréti (5a e(:)/o(:)-TO-a(:)) > Skt sphuráti. (This word may be related to Greek spaírō 'I gasp', which under a laryngeal interpretation would be from PIE *sphŕ̥h+j+ō.) PIE 3sg pres *sphŕ̥hgeti 'resound' (LARYNGEALS 1ii-a) > *sphū́rhgeti (LARYNGEALS 1iii) > *sp^{h}hū́rhgeti (LARYNGEALS 2) > *sp^{h}ū́rgeti (2a 1ST PAL) > *sp^{h}ū́rǰeti (5a e(:)/o(:)-TO-a(:)) > Skt sphū́rjati. (A cognate may be Greek spargéomai 'I sputter'.) Finally, PIE 2sg perf *wóid+tha 'you knew' (LARYNGEALS 1iii and 2) > *wóidt^{h}a (1b OBSTR CL 2) > *wóittha (5a e(:)/o(:)-TO-a(:), 7a MON, 10 w-TO-v) > Skt vḗttha.

(iv) Vowels resulting from laryngeals.

As we noted in Chapter 1, according to one view there were originally in PIE three different laryngeals /h_1, h_2, h_3/ and one vowel /e/. According to this theory, the development of the other PIE vowels proceeded as follows:

(a)	h_1 e	→	h_1 e	(b)	e h_1	→	ē h_1
	h_2 e		h_2 a		e h_2		ā h_2
	h_3 e		h_3 o		e h_3		ō h_3
	1 2		1 2		1 2		1 2

That is, (a) if the respective laryngeal precedes /e/, the short vowels /e, a, o/ are produced; and (b) if the laryngeal follows /e/, the long vowels /ē, ā, ō/ result. (LARYNGEALS 2 then applies to delete the laryngeals.)

E.g., PIE *h$_2$énti 'in front of' (LARYNGEALS liv-a) > *h$_2$ánti (LARYNGEALS 2) > Skt ánti; and PIE nominative singular of the ā-class feminine noun *séineh$_2$ 'army' (LARYNGEALS liv-b) > *séināh$_2$ (LARYNGEALS 2) > *séinā (5a e(:)/o(:)-TO-a(:), 7a MON) > Skt sḗnā. Also the PIE root *sth$_2$- 'stand' alongside ablauting *steh$_2$- (LARYNGEALS 1i) > *st^{h}h$_2$ and *steh$_2$- (LARYNGEALS liv) > *st^{h}h$_2$- and *stāh$_2$- (LARYNGEALS 2) > *st^h- and *stā-, both forms combined into the Skt root sthā-.

Some possible Sanskrit cognates occurring in other PIE languages are these: PIE *egh$_3$(+ém) 'I' vs. ablauting *egéh$_3$ (LARYNGEALS liii and LARYNGEALS liv, respectively) > *eg^{h}h$_3$óm and *egṓh$_3$ (LARYNGEALS 2) > *eg^{h}óm and *egṓ (2a 1ST PAL) > *eɟ^{h}óm (5a (e(:)/o(:)-TO-a(:)) > *aɟ^{h}ám (8a ɟ^h-TO-h) > Skt ahám vs. Gk egṓ. PIE *meg^h+ént- 'large' vs. ablauting *mégeh- (LARYNGEALS liii) > *meg^{h}hént- (LARYNGEALS 2) > *meg^{h}ént- (2a 1ST PAL) > meɟ^{h}ént- (5a e(:)/o(:)-TO-a(:)) > *maɟ^{h}ánt- (8a ɟ^h-TO-h) Skt mahánt- vs. Gk méga. Also PIE *róth$_2$e- 'wagon' (LARYNGEALS liii) > *rót^{h}h$_2$e- (LARYNGEALS liv-a) > *rót^{h}h$_2$a- (LARYNGEALS 2) > *rót^{h}a- (5a e(:)/o(:)-TO-a(:)) > Skt rátha- vs. ablauting *roteh$_2$ (LARYNGEALS liv-b) > *rotāh$_2$ (LARYNGEALS 2, ev) > Lat rota 'wheel'.

(2) The laryngeals are deleted after having effected the above changes:

$$\text{h} \rightarrow \emptyset$$

lb Changes in Obstruent Clusters (OBSTR CL)

The following three changes are early, the first two probably PIE. They are ordered as shown; and all remain as phon cond rules of sandhi in the Sanskrit grammar.

$$(1)\quad \underset{1}{\begin{pmatrix}\text{C, –sonorant}\\ \text{+voiced}\\ \text{+aspirated}\end{pmatrix}} \underset{2}{\begin{pmatrix}\text{C, –sonorant}\\ \text{–continuant}\\ \text{–voiced}\end{pmatrix}} \rightarrow \underset{1}{\begin{pmatrix}\text{same C, but}\\ \text{–aspirated}\\ \end{pmatrix}} \underset{2}{\begin{pmatrix}\text{same C, but}\\ \text{+voiced}\\ \text{+aspirated}\end{pmatrix}}$$

That is, when through morpheme concatenation a voiced aspirated consonant (1) comes into contact with a voiceless stop (2), the first segment loses the aspiration and the second one becomes voiced and aspirated. (This process is sometimes referred to as "Bartholomae's Law".) E.g., the PIE perf pass participles *lab^h+tó- 'taken' (OBSTR CL 1) > *labd^{h}ó- (5a e(:)/o(:)-TO-a(:)) > Skt labdhá-; *b^{h}ud^h+tó- 'understood' (OBSTR CL 1) > *b^{h}udd^{h}ó- (2b GRASSMANN) > *budd^{h}ó- (5a e(:)/o(:)-TO-a(:)) > Skt buddhá-; *d^{h}eg^{hw}+tó- 'burnt' (OBSTR CL 1) > *d^{h}eg^{w}d^{h}ó- (2b GRASSMANN) > *deg^{w}d^{h}ó- (3 DELAB) > *degd^{h}ó- (5a e(:)/o(:)-TO-a(:)) > Skt dagdhá-.

$$(2)\quad \begin{pmatrix}\text{C, –sonorant}\\ \alpha\text{voiced}\end{pmatrix} \rightarrow [\beta\text{voiced}] \;/\; \_\_\_ \;[\text{C, –sonorant, }\beta\text{voiced}]$$

That is, an obstruent cluster is voiced if its final segment is voiced and voiceless if its final segment is voiceless. (Recall that OBSTR CL 1 has already applied; so there are no longer sequences such as /b^h+t/ in which the first segment was aspirated.) E.g., PIE u-class masc noun *éd+t+um 'act of eating, to eat' (OBSTR CL 2) > *éttum (5a e(:)/o(:)-TO-a(:)) > Skt áttum; PIE loc pl *ped+sú 'feet' (OBSTR CL 2) >

*petsú (ev) > Skt patsú; PIE perf pass part *jug+tó- 'joined' (OBSTR CL 2) > *juktó- (5a e(:)/o(:)-TO-a(:)) > Skt yaktá-. Further examples, but of voicing and not devoicing, are these: PIE o-class masc noun *upo+pd+ó- 'act of trampling' in which *pd- is the Ø-ablaut grade of *ped- 'foot' (OBSTR CL 2) > *upobdó- (5a e(:)/o(:)-TO-a(:)) > Skt upabdá-; PIE o- and ā-class compound adj *ap- 'water' + *gn̥- 'born', i.e. 'born in water' (OBSTR CL 2) > *abgn̥- (2a 1ST PAL) > *abɟn̥- (2c SYL NAS) > Skt abja-; PIE instr pl *dn̥t+b^{h}ís 'teeth' (OBSTR CL 2) > *dn̥db^{h}ís (2c SYL NAS) > Skt dadbhís; PIE *wōk+b^{h}ís 'words' (OBSTR CL 2) > *wōgb^{h}ís (5a e(:)/o(:)-TO-a(:), 10 w-TO-v) > Skt vāgbhís.

(3) The following "cluster simplification" rule is probably exclusively Sanskrit and as such not common PIE.

[C, –sonorant]	s	t	→	same	Ø	t
1	2	3		1	2	3

That is, the sequence obstruent consonant plus /s/ plus /t/ loses the /s/. E.g., PIE 1pl aorist *é+tēud+s+me 'push' and 2pl aorist *é+tēud+s+te (OBSTR CL 2) > *étēutsme and *étēutste (OBSTR CL 3) > *étēutsme and *étēutte (5a e(:)/o(:)-TO-a(:)) > Skt átāutsma and átāutta; similarly PIE 1pl aorist *é+jēug+s+me 'bind, yoke' and 2pl aorist *é+jēug+s+te (OBSTR CL 2) > *éjēuksme and *éjēukste (OBSTR CL 3) > *éjēuksme and *éjēukte (4a RETRO) > *éjēukṣme and *éjēukte (5a e(:)/o(:)-TO-a(:)) > Skt áyāukṣma and áyāukta.

2a The First Palatalization (1ST PAL)

This change remains in the Sanskrit grammar as a morph cond rule. It occurred in two stages.

(1) $$\begin{pmatrix} \text{C, –sonorant} \\ \text{+back} \\ \text{–round} \end{pmatrix} \rightarrow \begin{pmatrix} \text{–back} \\ \text{+palatal} \end{pmatrix} \; / \; \text{(not /s/)} \_\_ \text{[+sonorant]}$$

That is, the PIE back obstruents /k, g^h, g/ (but not the +round /k^w, g^{hw}, g^w/) become the front palatal stops /k', g$^{h'}$, g'/. The change occurs only if the velars /k, g^h, g/ are followed by a sonorant segment — i.e., neither followed by an obstruent nor in word-final position. The /k/ in the sequence /sk/ also eludes the change.

We assume this change occurred in two stages as follows:

k, g^h, g → k', g$^{h'}$, g' → č, ɟ^h, ɟ

That is, /k, g^h, g/ first became palatal, then became affricates (+delayed release) /č, ɟ^h, ɟ/. Then after 1ST PAL 1 and before 4b 2ND PAL, the following change occurred:

(2) č → š

That is, the affricate /č/ becomes the Skt continuant /š/. (In our romanization of Sanskrit the segment is written <ś>; other sources such as Whitney 1960 use the grapheme <ç>.)

E.g., PIE *kn̥tóm '100' (1ST PAL 1) > *čn̥tóm (1ST PAL 2) >*šn̥tóm (2c SYL NAS, 5a e(:)/o(:)-TO-a(:)) > Skt śatám. PIE Vn-class masc *kwón- 'dog' (1ST PAL 1 and 2) > *šwón (5a e(:)/o(:)-TO-a(:), 10 w-TO-v) > Skt śván-. PIE perf pass part *klu+tó- 'heard' (1ST PAL, 5a e(:)/o(:)-TO-a(:)) > *šlutá- (9b l/r ALT) > Skt śrutá-. PIE o-class masc *g^{h}imó- (1ST PAL) > *ɟ^{h}imó- (5a e(:)/o(:)-TO-a(:)) > *ɟ^{h}imá- (8a ɟ^h-TO-h) > Skt himá- 'snow, frost'. PIE Vs-class neuter *áng^{h}os- 'narrowness, pinch, pain' (1ST PAL) > *ánɟ^{h}os- (5a e(:)/o(:)-TO-a(:), 8a ɟ^h-TO-h) > *ánhas- (9d NASAL DELE) > Skt /ã^{n}has-/ written <áṁhas->. Finally, the PIE u-class neuter *gḗnu- 'knee' (1ST PAL, 5a e(:)/o(:)-TO-a(:)) > Skt jā́nu-; and the PIE 3sg pres act ind *ágeti 'drives' (1ST PAL, 5a e(:)/o(:)-TO-a(:)) > Skt ájati. The 1ST PAL change does not apply to velars followed by an obstruent consonant or in word-final position. Hence the following derivations: PIE i-class fem *nókti- 'night' (1ST PAL not applying, but by 5a e(:)/o(:)-TO-a(:)) > Skt nákti-. If 1ST PAL had applied here, one would have the derivation *nókti- (1ST PAL) > *nóšti- (4a RETRO, 5a e(:)/o(:)-TO-a(:)) > Skt **násṭi-. Likewise, the PIE nom sg fem Ø-class *dík+s 'direction' (1ST PAL not applying, but by 5c WF CL) > Skt dík, not **díś. Under our formulation of 1ST PAL, PIE *oktṓu '8' should result in Skt **aktā́u instead of the actually occurring aṣṭā́u. The Sanskrit form was influenced by the word for '80', PIE *ok+ītís, and developed as follows: PIE *oktṓu '8' and *ok+ītís '80' (1ST PAL) > *oktṓu and *ošītís (substitution of *oš- for *ok- in '8') > *oštṓu and *ošītis (4a RETRO) > *oṣṭṓu and *ošītís (5a e(:)/o(:)-TO-a(:)) > Skt aṣṭā́u and aśītís.

The 1ST PAL change remains in the Sanskrit grammar as a morph cond rule. E.g., the PIE fem Ø-class noun paradigm nom sg *dík+s 'direction' (no 1ST PAL, but 5c WF CL) > Skt dík; acc sg *dík+m̥ (1ST PAL) > *díšm̥ (2c SYL NAS) > Skt díśam; dat pl *dik+b^{h}jós (lb OBSTR CL, but no 1ST PAL) > *digb^{h}jós (5a e(:)/o(:)-TO-a(:)) > Skt digbhyás; loc pl *dik+sú (neither lb OBSTR CL nor 1ST PAL, but by 4a RETRO) > Skt dikṣú. An example of 1ST PAL as a sandhi rule within a verb paradigm is the following: PIE 3sg pres ind *ju+n+g+eti 'joins' (1ST PAL, 5a e(:)/o(:)-TO-a(:), 7b NASAL ASSIM) > Skt yuñjati, vs. perf pass part *ju+g+tó- 'joined' (lb OBSTR CL, but not 1ST PAL, 5a e(:)/o(:)-TO-a(:)) > Skt yuktá-.

2b Grassmann's Law (GRASSMANN)

This change remains as a phon cond rule in the Sanskrit grammar.

$$\begin{pmatrix} \text{C, }-\text{sonorant} \\ -\text{continuant} \\ +\text{aspirated} \end{pmatrix} \rightarrow [-\text{aspirated}] \;/\; \_\_\_ \; [+\text{vocalic}] \; C_0 \begin{pmatrix} \text{C, }-\text{sonorant} \\ -\text{continuant} \\ +\text{aspirated} \end{pmatrix}$$

That is, an aspirated stop /b^h, d^h etc./ is deaspirated to /b, d etc./ if followed by a vowel, an optional consonantal segment (either obstruent or sonorant) and another aspirated stop consonant.

E.g., PIE 1sg perf *g^{hw}e+g^{hw}ṓn+a 'I have killed' (GRASSMANN) > *g^{w}eg^{hw}ṓna (3 DELAB) > *geg^{h}ṓna (4b 2ND PAL) > *ɟeg^{h}ṓna (5a e(:)/o(:)-TO-a(:)) > Skt jaghā́na. But the 3rd singular present of the same verb is the ablauting PIE *g^{hw}én+ti 'kills' (3 DELAB, 4b 2ND PAL) > *ɟ^{h}énti (5a e(:)/o(:)-TO-a(:)) > *ɟ^{h}ánti (8a ɟ^h-TO-h) > Skt hánti. In the 1st singular perfect cited first, 8a ɟ^h-TO-h cannot apply because GRASSMANN has applied first. If the chronology had been 8a ɟ^h-TO-h > GRASSMANN, then the Skt 1st singular perfect would have been **haghā́na.

Additional examples are the PIE 1st singular perfect forms *b^{h}eb^{h}ága 'share' and *d^{h}ed^{h}ḗu 'put' (2a 1ST PAL) > *b^{h}eb^{h}áɟa and *d^{h}ed^{h}ḗu (GRASSMANN) > *beb^{h}áɟa and *ded^{h}ḗu (5a e(:)/o(:)-TO-a(:)) > Skt babhája and dadhā́u. Also the PIE perf pass part *b^{h}ud^h+tó- 'enlightened' (lb OBSTR CL) > *b^{h}udd^{h}ó- (GRASSMANN) > *budd^{h}ó- (ev) > Skt buddhá-. Note the 3sg pres *b^{h}n̥d^h+nā́+ti 'binds' (GRASSMANN) > *bn̥d^{h}nā́ti (2c SYL NAS) > Skt badhnā́ti, as opposed to the ablauting 3rd singular future *b^{h}end^h+s+j+eti (lb OBSTR CL) > *b^{h}entsjeti (where GRASSMANN does not apply, but 5a e(:)/o(:)-TO-a(:) does) > Skt bhantsyati. (Note here the necessary chronology lb OBSTR CL > GRASSMANN.)

An example of GRASSMANN applying to a voiceless aspirate is PIE (or perhaps an early borrowing) 1sg perf *kʰe+kʰā́d+a 'bite' (to which 2a 1ST PAL has not applied, perhaps because the word was borrowed after that time, but by GRASSMANN) > *kekʰā́da (4b 2ND PAL) > *čekʰā́da (5a e(:)/o(:)-TO-a(:)) > Skt cakhā́da.

2c Changes in the Syllabic Nasals (SYL NAS)

This change does not remain as a rule in the grammar, but rather restructures various morphemes and then drops from the language.

[C, +nasal / +vocalic] → a

That is, the PIE syllabic nasals [m̥, n̥, ŋ̥] become [a].

E.g., the PIE perf pass participles *mn̥+tó- 'considered', *ŋ̥gʷ+tó- 'anointed' and *ń̥+gnō+to- 'unknown' (lb OBSTR CL) > *mn̥tó-, *ŋ̥kʷtó-, *ń̥gnoto- (2a 1ST PAL) > *mn̥tó-, *ŋ̥kʷtó-, *ń̥ɟnōto- (SYL NAS) > *mató, *akʷtó-, *áɟnōto- (3 DELAB , 5a e(:)/o(:)-TO-a(:), 7b NASAL ASSIM) > Skt matá-, aktá- (but otherwise the Sanskrit root is añj- from ablauting PIE *oŋ̥gʷ-) and ájñāta-. PIE masc i-class *gʷḿ̥+ti- 'act of going' (2c SYL NAS) > *gʷáti- (3 DELAB) > Skt gáti-. SYL NAS must precede 7a MON in view of this derivation: PIE *dékm̥ *idʰi '10 here' (2a 1ST PAL, SYL NAS) > *déša *idʰi (5a e(:)/o(:)-TO-a(:)) > *dáša *idʰi (7a MON) > *dášēdʰi (9a bʰ/dʰ-TO-h) > Skt dáśēhi.

3 Delabialization of the Labiovelars (DELAB)

This change does not remain as a rule in the grammar; rather, it creates the new segments /k, gʰ, g/ in the pre-Sanskrit phoneme inventory.

[C, –sonorant / +back / +round] → [–round]

That is, the PIE rounded velar obstruents /kʷ, gʰʷ, gʷ/ become unrounded to /k, gʰ, g/.

E.g., PIE nom sg masc interrogative *kʷos 'who?' (DELAB) > *kos (ev) > Skt kas. PIE masc o-class *gʰʷormó- 'heat' (DELAB) > *gʰormó- (5a e(:)/o(:)-TO-a(:)) > Skt gharmá-. PIE u-class adj *legʰʷú- 'light, swift' (DELAB, ev) > Skt laghú-. PIE root-class nom sg fem *gʷṓus 'cow' (DELAB) > *gṓus (ev) > Skt gā́us; PIE ā-class nom sg fem *gʷn+ā 'woman, wife' (DELAB) > Skt gnā.

DELAB must follow 2a 1ST PAL: otherwise 1ST PAL would apply to the output of DELAB and produce incorrect forms. E.g., PIE *kʷos 'who?' (DELAB) > *kos (2a 1ST PAL) > **šos (ev) > Skt **śas instead of kas.

4a Changes Producing Retroflex Consonants (RETRO)

Such consonants are often referred to as "cerebrals". There are two chronologically ordered changes which remain in the Sanskrit grammar as morph cond and phon cond rules, respectively.

(1) s, z → ṣ, ẓ / k, r, r̥(:), i(:) or u(:) ___ [+segment] (≠ r or r̥(:))

That is, the coronal consonants /s, z/ become -coronal and retroflex /ṣ, ẓ/ if preceded by the segments indicated and if followed by any segment except /r/ or vocalic /r̥(:)/. Hence RETRO 1 does not apply to word-final /s, z/. It also does not apply over some morpheme boundaries such as that between a prefix and a root: e.g., Skt anusvāra (grammatical term for 9d NASAL DELE), consisting of /anu#svāra/, not Skt **anuṣvāra.

Because of its rather unusual environment this change is sometimes referred to as the "ruki rule". It is reminiscent of the Old Church Slavic change 3 RUKI. (The /z/ which undergoes RETRO arises by lb OBSTR CL 2; and both /z/ and /ẓ/ are lost in pre-Sanskrit by 5b (VzC-TO-V̄C.)

E.g., PIE 1sg aorist *é+lik^w+s+om 'I left' (3 DELAB) > *éliksom (RETRO) > *élikṣom (5a e(:)/o(:)-TO-a(:)) > *álikṣam (9b l/r ALT) > Skt árikṣam. (Note in this derivation the necessary chronology 3 DELAB > RETRO.) PIE Vn-class neuter *wórs+men- 'summit' (RETRO) > *wórṣmen- (5a e(:)/o(:)-TO-a(:)) > *wárṣman- (10 w-TO-v) > Skt várṣman-. PIE 3sg pres act ind *d^{h}r̥s+néu+ti 'dare' (RETRO 1) > *d^{h}r̥ṣnéuti (RETRO 2) > *d^{h}r̥ṣṇéuti (5a e(:)/o(:)-TO-a(:), 7a MON) > Skt dhr̥ṣṇṓti. PIE loc pl *tri+sú '3' (RETRO) > Skt triṣú. PIE loc pl *ékwoisu 'horses' (2a 1ST PAL) > *éšwoisu (RETRO) > *éšwoiṣu (5a e(:)/o(:)-TO-a(:)) > *ášwaiṣu (7a MON) > *ášwēṣu (10 w-TO-v) > Skt áśvēṣu. (Note here the necessary chronology RETRO > 7a MON.) PIE fem Ø-class *mūs- 'mouse' (RETRO) > Skt mūṣ-; and PIE masc o-class *nisdó- 'nest' (lb OBSTR CL 2) > *nizdó- (RETRO 1) > *niẓdó- (RETRO 2) > *niẓḍó- (5a e(:)/o(:)-TO-a(:)) > *niẓḍá- (5b VzC-TO-V̄C) > Skt nīḍá-. (Note here the necessary chronology RETRO > 5b VzC-TO-V̄C.)

(2) After RETRO 1, the following changes occurred creating additional retroflex consonants.

(a) t$^{(h)}$, d$^{(h)}$ → ṭ$^{(h)}$, ḍ$^{(h)}$/ ṣ, ẓ or š ___
and a resulting šṭ → ṣṭ

(b) (ṣ or š)$_1$ s$_2$ → ṭ$_1$ ṣ$_2$ (often) and k$_1$ ṣ$_2$ (sometimes)

(c) n → ṇ / r̥ (:), r or ṣ … ___ [+sonorant]
where "…" contains only labials (/p/ etc.), velars (/k/ etc.), the glottal /h/ or vowels.

That is, (a) the second segments in these consonant sequences beginning with /ṣ, ẓ or š/ become the retroflex consonants /ṭ(h), ḍ(h)/; and the sequence /šṭ/ becomes /ṣṭ/. The/ṣ, ẓ/ arise through RETRO 1. The source of /š/ is 2a 1ST PAL: hence the chronology 2a 1ST PAL > RETRO. (b) The sequences /ṣs/ and /šs/ can become either /ṭṣ/ or /kṣ/, the first more often than the second. (The cluster-initial /ṣ/ and /š/ arise from RETRO 1 and 2a 1ST PAL, respectively.) (c) The coronal nasal /n/ becomes the noncoronal retroflex /ṇ/ when preceded (not necessarily immediately) by /r̥(:)/, /r/ or /ṣ/. The /n/ must be followed by a sonorant segment. (It cannot be word-final or be followed by an obstruent: in the latter case 7b NASAL ASSIM applies.) Between the triggering segments /r̥(:)/, /r/ or /ṣ/ and the /n/ ("…" in the rule) there can occur only bilabials such as /p, b/, velars such as /k, g/, the glottal /h/ or vowels. Segments which cannot occur here are the dentals like /t, d/, retroflexes like /ṭ, ḍ/ or palatals such as /š, č, ǰ/, i.e. Skt <ś, c, j>.

E.g., (a) PIE i-class fem *wr̥s+tí- 'rain' (RETRO 1) > *wr̥ṣtí- (RETRO 2) > *wr̥ṣṭí- (10 w-TO-v) > Skt vr̥ṣṭí-. PIE *ok+ītís '80' (2a 1ST PAL) > *ošītís (the *oš- then replaces the *ok- in *oktṓu '8') > (RETRO 2) > *oṣṭṓu (5a e(:)/o(:)-TO-a(:)) > Skt aṣṭā́u. (b) PIE Ø-class nom sg fem *dwís+s 'hatred' (RETRO 1) > *dwíṣs (RETRO 2) > *dwíṭṣ (5c WF CL) > *dwíṭ (10 w-TO-v) > Skt dvíṭ. The derivation of the accusative singular of this same noun is *dwís+m̥ (2c SYL NAS) > *dwísa (RETRO 1) > *dwíṣa (10 w-TO-v and replacement of -m from other paradigms) > Skt dvíṣam. An ablauting form of the same root occurs in the PIE 2sg pres *dwéis+si 'hate' (RETRO 1) > *dwéiṣsi (RETRO 2) > *dwéikṣi (5a e(:)/o(:)-TO-a(:), 7a MON) > *dwḗkṣi (10 w-TO-v) > Skt dvḗkṣi. And the PIE fem Ø-class nom sg *wík+s 'house' vs. acc sg *wík+m̥ (2a 1ST PAL) > *wíks and *wíšm̥ (2c SYL NAS and addition of -m from other paradigms) > *wíks and *wíšam (RETRO 2) > *wíṭs and *wíšam (5c WF CL) > *wíṭ and *wíšam (10 w-TO-v) > Skt víṭ and víśam.

(c) IE 3sg pres *mus+nāti 'steal' (RETRO 1) > *muṣnāti (RETRO 2) > Skt muṣṇāti. The PIE o- and ā-class adjs *k^{w}ōro+no- 'making' and *sréwo+no- 'flowing' (3 DELAB) > *kōrono- and *sréwono- (RETRO 2) > *kōroṇo- and *sréwoṇo- (5a e(:)/o(:)-TO-a(:), 10 w-TO-v) > Skt kāraṇa- and srávaṇa-. Contrast the PIE o- and ā-class adj *dérko+no- 'seeing' (2a 1ST PAL) > *déršono- (RETRO 2 not applying because /š/ intervenes between /n/ and the trigger /r/, but 5a e(:)/o(:)-TO-a(:)) > Skt dárśana-.

The RETRO changes remain as rules of Sanskrit sandhi. They account for such alternations as the instrumental pl in –ṣu or -su. E.g., Skt áśvēṣu 'horses' and rā́jasu 'kings' from PIE *ékwoisu and *rḗgn̥su. RETRO also results in alternations in paradigms such as the nom sg víṭ 'house' vs. acc sg víśam noted above. By the time of attested Sanskrit, RETRO had been restructured by later changes such as 5a e(:)/o(:)-TO-a(:) and 7a MON. Hence the synchronic version of RETRO is usually stated as something like "s → ṣ after any vowel except /a(:)/" — i.e. after /i(:), u(:)/ or /ē, ō/, the latter two from the diphthongs Vi and Vu.

The RETRO changes provided the usual avenue by which the retroflex consonants came into Sanskrit. Some of them, however, came from other sources. For example, the Sanskrit o-class masculine noun naṭa- 'actor' comes from a Middle Indic dialect which changed the PIE antecedent *nr̥t- 'dance' by its own rules. (A Sanskrit verb nr̥̄́tyati 'dances' occurs from the same source.) There are also Sanskrit borrowings with retroflex consonants from Dravidian dialects such as the o- and ā-class adj kuṭila- 'crooked'. (See on this Burrow 1959: 95-97.)

4b The Second Palatalization (2ND PAL)

This change remains in the Sanskrit grammar as a morph cond rule. We assume three chronological stages involving 2ND PAL.

$$(1)\quad \begin{bmatrix} \text{C, –sonorant} \\ \text{+back} \end{bmatrix} \rightarrow \begin{bmatrix} \text{–back} \\ \text{+palatal} \\ \text{+delayed release} \end{bmatrix} \;/\; \underline{\quad} \begin{Bmatrix} \text{[+vocalic, –back]} \\ \text{j} \end{Bmatrix}$$

That is, the velar obstruents /k, g^{h}, g/ become the front affricates (+delayed release) /č, ɟ^{h}, ɟ/ (written in romanized Skt as <c, jh, j>) if followed by a -back vowel /e(:) or i(:)/ or by /j/ (written as Skt <y>). The only source of /k, g^{h}, g/ is from earlier /k^{w}, g^{hw}, g^{w}/ by 3 DELAB: hence the relative chronology 3 DELAB > 2ND PAL. After 2a 1ST PAL and 2ND PAL, Skt <jh> and <j> can arise through either change. But <ś> arises only from 2a 1ST PAL and <c> from 2ND PAL .

E.g., nom sg masc interrogative *k^{w}os 'who?' vs. the conj *k^{w}e 'and' (3 DELAB) > *kos and *ke (2ND PAL) > *kos and *če (5a e(:)/o(:)-TO-a(:)) > Skt kas and ca. (Note here the necessary chronology 2ND PAL > 5a e(:)/o(:)-TO-a(:).) PIE 3sg pres mid *sék^{w}etai follows (3 DELAB) > *séketai (2ND PAL) > *séčetai (5a e(:)/o(:)-TO-a(:)) > *sáčatai (7a MON) > Skt sácatē. PIE 3sg mid *k^{w}jéwetai 'move' (3 DELAB) > *kjéwetai (2ND PAL) > *čjéwetai (ev) > Skt cyávatē. PIE 3sg pres *g^{hw}én+ti 'slays' vs. the ablauting 3pl pres g^{hw}n+ónti 'they slay (3 DELAB) > *g^{h}énti and *g^{h}nónti (2ND PAL) > *ɟ^{h}énti and *g^{h}nónti (5a e(:)/o(:)-TO-a(:)) > *ɟ^{h}ánti and *g^{h}nánti (8a ɟ^{h}-TO-h) > Skt hánti and ghnánti. PIE 3sg pres *álg^{hw}+eti 'is worth' vs. the o-class masc noun *alg^{hw}+ó- 'price' (3 DELAB, 2ND PAL) > *álɟ^{h}eti and *alg^{h}ó- (5a e(:)/o(:)-TO-a(:), 8a ɟ^h-TO-h, 9b l/r ALT) > Skt árhati and arghá-. PIE o- and ā-class adj *g^{w}īwó- 'alive' (3 DELAB , 2ND PAL , 5a e(:)/o(:)-TO-a(:), 10 w-TO-v) > Skt jīvá-. PIE i-class fem *g^{w}ēni- 'wife' (3 DELAB) > *gēni- (2ND PAL) > *ɟēni- (5a e(:)/o(:)-TO-a(:)) > Skt jāni-.

(2) At the next stage the following change occurs:

sč → čč^h, written <cch>.

That is, 2ND PAL 1 above can apply to the sequence /sk/ to produce /sč/, which then by 2ND PAL 2 becomes /čč^h/. E.g., PIE 3sg pres *skind+éti 'cut off' vs. *skánd+eti 'jump' (2ND PAL 1) > *sčindéti vs. *skándeti (2ND PAL 2) > *čč^{h}indéti vs. *skándeti (5a e(:)/o(:)-TO-a(:)) > Skt cchindáti vs. skándati. Also PIE 3sg pres *g^{w}ḿ̥+sk+eti 'goes' (2c SYL NAS) > *g^{w}ásketi (3 DELAB) > *gásketi (2ND PAL 1 and 2) > *gáčč^{h}eti (5a e(:)/o(:)-TO-a(:)) > Skt gácchati.

(3) The above change which produced the sequence /čč^h/was followed by this change:

$$\check{c}\check{c}^h \rightarrow \check{c}^h \;/\; \left.\begin{matrix}[V, +long] \\ C\end{matrix}\right\} (\#\#) \_\_\_$$

That is, the cluster /čč^h/ is simplified to /č^h/ if preceded by a long vowel or consonant — either within a word or over a word boundary (##). E.g., Skt cchindáti 'cut off' noted above can also occur as chindáti.

The 2ND PAL changes remain in the Sanskrit grammar as rules of sandhi. They account for paradigmatic alternations such as 3sg hánti 'slays' vs. the 3pl ghánti 'slay' cited above as well as for the reduplicating consonants in some verbs such as the 1sg perf jagama 'I came' from PIE *g^{w}e+g^{w}oma instead of Skt **gagama.

Since both 2a 1ST PAL and 2ND PAL remain as morph cond rules of Sanskrit phonology, restructurings can occur such that a /k/ occurring in a paradigm is associated ahistorically with a 2ND PAL /č/ instead of the original 1ST PAL reflex /š/. Examples of historically accurate alternations are Skt nom sg dík 'direction' and acc sg díśam from PIE *dík+s and *dík+m̥ by 2a 1ST PAL; and Skt 3sg pres mid sácatē 'follows' vs. 3sg aorist mid ásakṣata from PIE *sék^{w}etai and *ések^{w}seto by 2ND PAL. But there are also alternations like the Ø-class nom sg fem vā́k 'word' vs. the acc sg vā́cam from PIE *wṓk+s and *wṓk+m̥. Here one would expect Skt vā́k, but **vā́śam by 2a 1ST PAL. However, the latter form has been restructured to vā́cam on the model of paradigms like that of sácatē and ásakṣata noted above.

By the time of attested Sanskrit, both 2a 1ST PAL and 2ND PAL were not phon cond, but morph cond. Hence back velar obstruents can at this time occur before front vowels. An example is the nom/acc interrogative pron kim 'what' from PIE *k^{w}im instead of Skt **cim **/čim/. The /k/ in this form of the paradigm arises from other forms where /k/ would have occurred regularly such as the nom sg masc kas 'who?' from PIE *k^{w}os.

Still other Sanskrit words with velar obstruents before front vowels are Middle Indic borrowings into Sanskrit. E.g., the o-class neuter noun kiṭṭa- 'dirt' is according to Uhlenbeck (1973: 53) a later, Middle Indic borrowing and from a dialect which did not undergo either 1ST PAL or 2ND PAL .

In view of several apparent exceptions to 1ST PAL and 2ND PAL, some sources assume what Burrow (1955: 75-6) terms a "pure velar" series for PIE. The postulation of this series was intended to account for those Sanskrit forms which seem to elude both 1ST PAL and 2ND PAL . We cite below three examples of such cognate sets.

(i) The Skt masc o-class kákṣa- 'armpit' and the ablauting Latin cōxa /kōksa/ 'hip bone'. If one posits PIE *k^{w}ó(:)ks-, then by 3 DELAB, 4a RETRO and 5a e(:)/o(:)-TO-a(:) one has Skt kákṣa-. But under this reconstruction one would expect Latin **quōxa **/k^{w}ōksa/. And if one posited PIE *kó(:)ks-, the correct Latin form would result. But the Sanskrit derivation would be *kóks- (2a 1ST PAL, 4a RETRO, 5a e(:)/o(:)-TO-a(:)) > **śákṣa-. The same problem arises with two o-class masculine nouns, namely Skt lōká- 'place' and Latin lūcus 'clearing in a forest'. If the PIE antecedent is *louk^{w}ó-, the Skt derivation is *louk^{w}ó- (3 DELAB) > *loukó- (5a e(:)/o(:)-TO-a(:), 7a MON) > Skt lōká-; but the Latin form would be the incorrect **lūquus. If the antecedent is PIE *loukó-, the Latin form is fine; but the Sanskrit form would be **lōśá-.

(ii) The Skt 3sg pres stighnōti 'mount' and the ablauting Go inf steigan /stīgan/ 'to ascend'. If the PIE antecedent is *st(e)ig^{h}- the Go form is fine; but the Sanskrit derivation would be *stig^{h}neuti (2a 1ST PAL) > *stiɟ^{h}neuti (5a e(:)/o(:)-TO-a(:), 7a MON) > **stiɟ^{h}nōti (8a ɟ^{h}-TO-h) > Skt **stihnōti. If the PIE form is *st(e)ig^{hw}-, the Sanskrit derivation is fine; but the Gothic form would be **steiwan **/stīwan/ by Gothic change 5b LABIOVELARS.

(iii) The Skt 3sg pres sthagati 'covers' and the Greek 1sg pres stégō 'I cover'. If the PIE antecedent was *stheg-, the Sanskrit derivation would be *sthegeti (la LARYNGEALS) > *st^{h}egeti (2a 1ST PAL) > *st^{h}eɟeti (5a e(:)/o(:)-TO-a(:)) > Skt **sthajati. If the antecedent was *stheg^{w}-, then the Skt sthagati could be derived; but then the Greek form would be by the Greek change 5a LABIOVEL **stébō or possibly **stédō.

To account for the comparatively few cognate sets like those just given, some scholars have posited a set of PIE back obstruents like this:

k'	k	k^{w}
g$^{h'}$	g^{h}	g^{hw}
g'	g	g^{w}
1	2	3

Here the velars over 1 can undergo 2a 1ST PAL; those over 3 can undergo 3 DELAB and 4b 2ND PAL; and those over 2 are "pure velars" which do not undergo 2a 1ST PAL nor 4b 2ND PAL. Given this interpretation, for cognate set (i) above one would posit PIE *kó(:)kso- 'armpit' and *loukó- 'place', neither of which would undergo 1ST PAL or 2ND PAL , as opposed to a form like PIE *k'n̥tóm '100' which would undergo 1ST PAL to become Skt śatám. For cognate set (ii) one would posit PIE *st(e)ig^{h}- 'ascend' as opposed to a form like the o-class noun *g$^{h'}$imó- 'snow' (2a 1ST PAL, 5a e(:)/o(:)-TO-a(:), 8a ɟ^{h}-TO-h) > Skt himá-. And for set (iii) one would posit PIE *stheg- as opposed to a form like PIE 3sg pres *ág'eti 'drives' (2a 1ST PAL, 5a e(:)/o(:)-TO-a(:)) > Skt ájati.

Our alternative to positing three sets of velars for PIE is to assume that there were only two:

k	k^{w}
g^{h}	g^{hw}
g	g^{w}
1	2

The velars over 1 undergo 2a 1ST PAL; those over 2 undergo 3 DELAB and can undergo 2ND PAL .

The comparatively few forms which do not undergo either 1ST PAL or 2ND PAL we consider to have been early borrowings into Sanskrit from PIE dialects which did not undergo these changes. As such these words are analogous to Modern English forms like skirt or brig. These forms are borrowed into English from closely related Germanic languages (often Norse). The native English words are shirt and bridge, both of which underwent a rule of English palatalization such that earlier *skirt > širt and *brig > briǰ. The borrowings entered the language after the time of the palatalization.

5a The Change of /e, o/, /ē, ō/ to /a/, /ā/, respectively (e(:)/o(:)-TO-a(:))

This change restructures the underlying phonemic inventory of the language and then is dropped as a rule from the grammar. The change is this:

$$\begin{bmatrix} +\text{vocalic} \\ -\text{high} \end{bmatrix} \rightarrow \begin{bmatrix} +\text{low} \\ -\text{round} \end{bmatrix}$$

That is, the -high vowels /e, ē, o, ō/ whether alone or in the diphthongs /ei, ēi, oi, ōi, eu, ēu, ou, ōu/ become /a/ and /ā/. (The original PIE /a(:)/ remains.)

E.g., PIE 3sg pres *b^{h}éreti 'carry' (e(:)/o(:)-TO-a(:)) > Skt bhárati; PIE nom sg *ékwos 'horse' (2a 1ST PAL) > *éšwos (e(:)/o(:)-TO-a(:)) > *ášwas (10 w-TO-v) > Skt áśvas. PIE nom sg *ówis 'sheep' (ev) > Skt ávis. PIE Vn-class nom sg *rḗgō 'king' (2a 1ST PAL) > *rḗǰō (e(:)/o(:)-TO-a(:)) > Skt rā́jā. PIE nom sg *wōk+s 'word' (e(:)/o(:)-TO-a(:)) > *wāks (5c WF CL) > *wāk (10 w-TO-v) > Skt vāk. PIE 3sg pres *éiti 'goes' (e(:)/o(:)-TO-a(:)) > *áiti (7a MON) > Skt ḗti. PIE 1sg pres *wóida 'I have seen, i.e. know' (e(:)/o(:)-TO-a(:)) > *wáida (7a MON, 10 w-TO-v) > Skt vḗda. PIE o-class nom sg neuter *kléu+mn̥t+om 'act of hearing, blessing' (2a 1ST PAL, 2c SYL NAS) > *šléumatam (e(:)/o(:)-TO-a(:)) > *šláumatam (7a MON) > *šlṓmatam (9b l/r ALT) > Skt śrṓmatam. The following words have long diphthongs: PIE 1sg aorist *é+lēik^{w}+s+om 'I left' (3 DELAB) > *élēiksom (4a RETRO) > *élēikṣom (e(:)/o(:)-TO-a(:)) > *álāikṣam (9b l/r ALT) > Skt árāiksam. PIE o-class instr pl masc *deiwṓis 'gods' (e(:)/o(:)-TO-a(:)) > *daiwā́is (7a MON, 10 w-TO-v) > Skt dēvā́is. And the PIE root-class nom sg masc *djḗu+s 'god' (e(:)/o(:)-TO-a(:)) > Skt dyā́us.

5b The Change of VzC to V̄C (VzC-TO-V̄C)

This change does not remain as a rule of Sanskrit sandhi, but rather restructures various lexical items and then drops from the grammar.

$$\begin{array}{cc} V & z/ẓ \\ 1 & 2 \end{array} \rightarrow \begin{array}{cc} \bar{V} & \emptyset \\ 1 & 2 \end{array} / \;\_\_\_ \begin{bmatrix} C, -\text{sonorant} \\ -\text{continuant} \\ +\text{voiced} \end{bmatrix}$$

That is, the sequence of a vowel plus /z/ or /ẓ/ (the latter by 4a RETRO) plus a voiced obstruent stop becomes a long vowel and the /z/ or /ẓ/ is deleted. The voiced obstruent stop consonant remains.

E.g., the PIE o-class masc nouns *nizdó- 'nest' and *mizd^{h}ó- 'reward' (4a RETRO) > *niẓḍó- and *miẓḍ^{h}ó- (5a e(:)/o(:)-TO-a(:)) > *niẓḍá- and *miẓḍ^{h}á- (VzC-TO-V̄C) > Skt nīḍá- and mīḍ^{h}á-. Note here the relative chronology 4a RETRO > VzC-TO-V̄C.

5c Reduction of Word-Final Consonant Clusters (WF CL)

This change remains as a phon cond rule in the Sanskrit grammar. Its basic structure is this:

$$\begin{array}{ccccccc} C_1 & +n & \rightarrow & C_1 & +\emptyset & / \; \_\_ & \#\#C \\ 1 & 2 & & 1 & 2 & & 3 \end{array}$$

where C_1 $_{+n}$ ≠ rp, rt, rṭ, rk and C_1 $_{+n}$ ≠ ns if the next word begins with a consonant (C over 3 above) which is a voiceless dental, retroflex or palatal: i.e., if C over 3 = /t, tʰ, s; ṭ, ṭʰ, ṣ; č, čʰ, š/.

That is, a word-final consonant cluster loses all its consonants except the first one, namely C_1 over 1. There are restrictions: the consonantal clusters /rp, rt, rt, rk/ are not affected. Further, word-final /ns/ is not affected if the following word begins with /t, ṭ or č/.

E.g., PIE nom sg *pōd+s 'foot' (lb OBSTR CL) > *pōts (5a e(:)/o(:)-TO-a(:)) > *pāts (WF CL) > Skt pāt. PIE nom sg masc pres participle *bʰéront+s 'carrying' (5a e(:)/o(:)-TO-a(:)) > *bʰárants (WF CL) > Skt bháran; but the accusative singular form is PIE *bʰérontm̥ (2c SYL SON and addition of -m from other paradigms) > *bʰérontam (5e e(:)/o(:)-TO-a(:), but WF CL not applying) > Skt bhárantam. Note the PIE sequence in the acc pl *deiwṓns totra 'the gods here' (5a e(:)/o(:)-TO-a(:)) > *daiwā́ns tatra (to which WF CL cannot apply because C over 3 = t, but 7a MON does apply) > *dēwā́ns tatra (9d NASAL DELE) > *dēwā́ⁿs tatra (10 w-TO-v) > Skt devā́ṁs tatra. (Other retained word-final /s/'s undergo 7c s-ASSIM, which we assume follows WF CL.)

6 Conflation of Vowels over a Word Boundary (V##V-TO-V̄)

This change remains in the grammar as a phon cond rule of sandhi.

$$\underset{1}{\begin{pmatrix} \text{V}, \pm\text{long} \\ \alpha\text{features} \end{pmatrix}} \;\underset{2}{\#\#}\; \underset{3}{\begin{pmatrix} \text{V}, \pm\text{long} \\ \alpha\text{features} \end{pmatrix}} \rightarrow \underset{4}{\begin{pmatrix} \text{V}, +\text{long} \\ \alpha\text{features} \end{pmatrix}} \; / \; [-\text{vocalic}] \; \_\_$$

That is, (1) a long or short vowel (not the second member of a diphthong) plus (2) a word boundary plus (3) the same vowel, long or short, is conflated into (4) the same vowel, long.

E.g., PIE *ne esti 'is not' (5a e(:)/o(:)-TO-a(:)) > *na asti (V##V-TO-V̄) > Skt nāsti; PIE 3sg pres mid *ne ḗstai 'he does not sit' (5a e(:)/o(:)-TO-a(:)) > *na *ā́stai (V##V-TO-V̄) > *nā́stai (7a MON) > Skt nā́stē. Synchronic derivations by the sandhi rule are /nadī iva/ 'like a river' and /sadhu uktam/ 'well said' → nadīva and sadhūktam.

The following derivations are illustrative of relative chronology. PIE *edjo oiwe 'today + up to' = 'up to today' (5a e(:)/o(:)-TO-a(:)) > *adja aiwa (V##V-TO-V̄) > *adjāiwa (10 w-TO-v) > Skt adyāiva. Note that 7a MON does not apply in this derivation because the diphthong is long /āi/. In isolation the form is PIE *oiwe (5a e(:)/o(:)-TO-a(:)) > *aiwa (7a MON) > *ēwa (10 w-TO-v) > Skt ēva. (Hence V##V-TO-V̄ must apply before 7a MON.) A similar derivation is PIE *tosjo 'his' plus the neuter Vs-class noun *augos 'strength' (2a 1ST PAL) > *tosjo auɟos (5a e(:)/o(:)-TO-a(:)) > *tasja auɟas (V##V-TO-V̄) > Skt tasyāujas. In isolation the noun is Skt ōjas. Also PIE *ne ageti 'he does not drive' (2a 1ST PAL) > *ne aɟeti (5a e(:)/o(:)-TO-a(:)) > *na aɟati (V##V-TO-V̄) > Skt nājati. (Note that in the preceding two derivations the chronology must be 5a e(:)/o(:)-TO-a(:) > V##V-TO-V̄.)

7a Monophthongization of /ai/ and /au/ (MON)

This change has two facets, both of which remain as phon cond rules of sandhi.

$$\text{(a)}\quad \begin{bmatrix} \text{ai} \\ \text{au} \end{bmatrix} \rightarrow \begin{bmatrix} \bar{\text{e}} \\ \bar{\text{o}} \end{bmatrix}$$

$$\text{(b)}\quad \begin{pmatrix} \text{a(:) \#\# i(:)} \\ \text{a(:) \#\# u(:)} \end{pmatrix} \rightarrow \begin{bmatrix} \bar{\text{e}} \\ \bar{\text{o}} \end{bmatrix}$$

That is, (a) word-internally the short diphthongs /ai/ and /au/ become /ē/ and /ō/. In most romanizations of Sanskrit these vowels are written without the macron <e, o>. Similarly, the long diphthongs are often written without the macron. Hence what we write as Skt dāiśika- 'regional' and tāulin- 'weigher' can also be found as <daiśika-> and <taulin->. And (b) over a word boundary the sequences /āi/, /aī/, /āī/, /ai/ and /āu/, /aū/, /āū/, /au/ become /ē/ and /ō/ respectively.

E.g., (a) PIE 3sg athematic pres *éi+ti 'goes' vs. the corresponding thematic pres 3sg *éi+eti 'idem' (PIE 3.1.2c i-j/u-w ALT applying as a synchronic rule) → *éiti and *éjeti (5a e(:)/o(:)-TO-a(:)) > *áiti and *ájati (MON) > Skt ḗti and áyati. A similar alternation is PIE instr pl *g^{w}ou+b^{h}ís 'cows' and the gen pl *g^{w}ou+ṓm (PIE 3.1.2c i-j/u-w ALT) → *g^{w}oub^{h}ís and *g^{w}owṓm (3 DELAB) > *goub^{h}ís and *gowṓm (5a e(:)/o(:)-TO-a(:)) > *gaub^{h}ís and *gawā́m (MON, 10 w-TO-v) > Skt gōbhís and gavā́m.

(b) PIE *k^{w}e##id^{h}i 'and here' (3 DELAB) > *ke##id^{h}i (4b 2ND PAL) > *če##id^{h}i (5a e(:)/o(:)-TO-a(:)) > *ča##id^{h}i (7a MON b) > *čēd^{h}i (9a b^{h}/d^{h}-TO-h) > Skt cēhi. PIE *k^{w}e##uwṓke 'and he spoke' (2a 1ST PAL) > *k^{w}e##uwṓše (3 DELAB) > *ke##uwṓše (4b 2ND PAL) > *če##uwṓše (5a e(:)/o(:)-TO-a(:)) > *ča##uwā́ša (MON) > *čōwā́ša (restructuring of the verb to have /č/ as if by 2a 1ST PAL, 10 w-TO-v) > Skt cōvā́ca. Examples of the synchronic application of MON b are the derivations /vinā##īrṣyayā/ 'without envy' → vinērṣyayā and /sā##uvā́ca/ 'she spoke' → sōvā́ca. MON b cannot apply to the output of 6 V##V-TO-V̄, which must precede it: *edjo##oiwe 'up to today' (5a e(:)/o(:)-TO-a(:)) > *adja##aiwa (6 V##V-TO-V̄) > *adjāiwa (MON b not applying since there is no word boundary ##, but 10 w-TO-v) > Skt adyāiva, not **adyēva.

We make two additional chronological observations. First, we assume that a more natural statement of MON entails the prior application of 5a e(:)/o(:)-TO-a(:). That is, the change is /ai/ > /ē/ and /au/ > /ō/; not /ei, /oi/ > /ē/ or /eu/, /ou/ > /ō/. Second, we note the derivation PIE *dékm̥##id^{h}i '10 here' (2a 1ST PAL) > *déšm̥##id^{h}i (2c SYL NAS) > *déša##id^{h}i (5a e(:)/o(:)-TO-a(:)) > *dáša##id^{h}i (MON b) > *dášēd^{h}i (9a b^{h}/d^{h}-TO-h) > Skt dáśēhi. Here 2c SYL NAS must precede MON.

The changes 5a e(:)/o(:)-TO-a(:) and MON caused a restructuring of the original PIE ablaut system. Recall that in that system under morph cond circumstances the vowel nucleus (V) of a morpheme could occur in five possible versions: V = e, ē, o, ō, Ø. In the literature these alternations are often referred to as the null grade for Ø, the normal grade for short /e, o/ and the lengthened grade for /ē, ō/. The Sanskrit grammarians termed the e/o-grade "guṇa" and the ē/ō-grade "vr̥ddhi".

Examples of the Sanskrit alternations are the following:

	Ø-grade	e/o-grade	ē/ō-grade
(a)	Ø	a	ā
(b)	i(:)	ē	āi
(c)	u(:)	ō	āu
(d)	r̥	ar	ār
(e)	l̥	al	āl

(In the following examples it is often impossible from the Sanskrit forms to determine whether the PIE antecedent had /e(:)/ as opposed to /o(:)/. Unless the evidence clearly indicates otherwise, we shall posit PIE /e(:)/.)

E.g., (a) PIE 1pl perf *pe+pØt+ime 'fly, fall', 3sg pres *pét+eti 'idem', 3sg pres *pēt+éjeti 'cause to fall' (5a e(:)/o(:)-TO-a(:)) > Skt paptima, pátati, pātáyati.

(b) PIE Ø-class noun *dØik- 'region', o-class noun *deiko- 'idem', adj *dēikik^{w}o- 'regional' (2a 1ST PAL) > *diš-, *deišo-, *dēišik^{w}o- (3 DELAB) > *diš-, *deišo-, *dēišiko- (5a e(:)/o(:)-TO-a(:)) > *diš-, *daiša-, *dāišika- (MON) > Skt diś-, dēśa-, dāiśika-.

(c) PIE ā-class fem *tØulā- 'scales', neuter o-class *teulono- 'act of weighing', masc Vn-class *tēulin- 'weigher' (5a e(:)/o(:)-TO-a(:)) > *tulā-, *taulana-, *tāulin- (MON) > Skt tulā-, tōlana-, tāulin-.

(d) PIE perf pass participle *k^{w}Ør+tó- 'made', masc tVr-class noun *k^{w}or+tŕ̥- 'maker', neuter jo-class *k^{w}or+jó- 'intent' (PIE 3.1.2g SYL SON applying as a synchronic rule) → *k^{w}r̥tó-, *k^{w}ortŕ̥-, *k^{w}ōrjó- (3 DELAB) > *kr̥tó-, *kortŕ̥-, *kōrjó- (5a e(:)/o(:)-TO-a(:)) > Skt kr̥tá-, kartŕ̥-, kārjá-.

(e) PIE perf pass participle *k^{w}Ølp+tó- 'adapted', 3sg pres mid *k^{w}ólp+etai 'adapts' (PIE 3.1.2g SYL SON applying synchronically) → *k^{w}l̥ptó- and *k^{w}ólpetai (3 DELAB) > *kl̥ptó- and *kólpetai (5a e(:)/o(:)-TO-a(:)) >*kl̥ptá- and *kálpatai (MON) > Skt kl̥ptá- and kálpatē.

(b and c) The ablaut alternations with long /ī/ and /ū/ arise as follows. PIE perf pass participle *nØī+tó- 'led', the masc tVr-class noun *neī+tŕ̥- 'leader' and the 3sg pres *nḗī+eti 'leads' (the PIE rule 3.1.2b DIPH applying synchronically to the impossible sequences /eī/ and /ēī/ to produce acceptable diphthongs) → *nītó-, *neitŕ̥-, *nḗieti (PIE 3.1.2c i-j/u-w ALT also applying synchronically) → *nītó-, *neitŕ̥-, *nḗjeti (5a e(:)/o(:)-TO-a(:)) > *nītá-, *naitŕ̥-, *nā́jati (MON) > Skt nītá-, nētŕ̥-, nā́yati. Similarly, PIE perf pass participle *pØū+tó- 'cleansed' and the 3sg pres mid *péū+etai 'cleanses' (PIE 3.1.2b DIPH) → *pūtó- and *péuetai (PIE 3.1.2c i-j/u-w ALT) → *pūtó- and *péweti (5a e(:)/o(:)-TO-a(:)) > *pūtá- and *páwati (10 w-TO-v) > Skt pūtá- and pávati.

7b Assimilation of Nasal Consonants (NASAL ASSIM)

These changes occurred in at least two stages. They remain as phon cond rules of sandhi.

(1) The first stage is the inherited PIE rule 3.1.2d NASAL ASSIM:

[C, +nasal] → [αfeatures] / ___ [C, –sonorant, αfeatures]

where no morpheme boundary intervenes between the nasal and the obstruent consonant.

That is, a nasal consonant takes the place features of a following obstruent within the same morpheme.

E.g., PIE */pénk^{w}e/ '5' → *[péŋk^{w}e].

NASAL ASSIM 1 remains in the grammar of Sanskrit to apply as a phon cond rule. Hence the following derivations: PIE (3 DELAB) > *péŋke (4b 2ND PAL) > *péŋče (NASAL ASSIM 1 applying synchronically) → *péñče (5a e(:)/o(:)-TO-a(:)) > Skt pañca. PIE nom sg masc Ø-class adj */prōnk^{w}+s/ 'forward-looking, eastern' (NASAL ASSIM 1) → *[prōŋk^{w}s] (3 DELAB) > *prōŋks (5a e(:)/o(:)-TO-a(:)) > *prāŋks (5c WF CL) > Skt prāŋ). (Hence NASAL ASSIM 1 must have been in the grammar before 5c WF CL . occurred.)

(2) Later the following additional NASAL ASSIM rules are added to the grammar. The first is clearly an expansion of NASAL ASSIM 1 to apply over a word boundary and to be triggered by other consonants beside obstruents.

(a) n → ñ / ___##ɟ$^{(h)}$ or š
ṇ / ___##[C, +retroflex]
l^{n} / ___##l

(b) n → ñ / ɟ ___

That is, (a) word-final /n/ becomes palatal /ñ/, retroflex /ṇ/ or the nasalized /l/ (/l^{n}/) over a word boundary when the following word begins with the consonants shown. (b) /n/ becomes /ñ/ after a palatalized /ɟ/.

E.g., (a) PIE acc pl o-class masc *tōns génōns 'those people', *tōns ḍambarōns 'those voices' (probably a non-IE borrowing) and *tōns loukṓns 'those worlds' (2a 1ST PAL) > *tōns ɟénōns, *tōns ḍambarōns, *tōns loukṓns (5a e(:)/o(:)-TO-a(:)) > *tāns ɟánāns, *tāns ḍambarāns, *tāns laukā́ns (5c WF CL) > *tān ɟánān, *tān ḍambarān, *tān laukā́n (7a MON) > *tān ɟánān, *tān ḍambarān, *tān lōkā́n (NASAL ASSIM 2) > Skt tāñ jánān, tāṇ ḍambarān, tāl^{n} lōkā́n. Note in this derivation the necessary chronologies 2a 1ST PAL (as well as 4b 2ND PAL) > NASAL ASSIM and 5c WF CL > NASAL ASSIM. (b) PIE *gnō- 'know' (2a 1ST PAL) > *ɟnō- (5a e(:)/o(:)-TO-a(:)) > *ɟnā- (NASAL ASSIM) > Skt jñā-.

7c Assimilation of /s/ (s-ASSIM)

The first of these changes remains as a phon cond rule of sandhi. The second restructures certain lexical items and then is dropped from the grammar.

(a) s → š / ___ ## [C, –sonorant, –voiced, +palatal]
ṣ / ___ ## [C, –sonorant, –voiced, +retroflex]

(b) s → š / ##___ [+sonorant]$_{1}^{n}$ [C, –sonorant, –voiced, +palatal]
ṣ / ##___ [+sonorant]$_{1}^{n}$ [C, –sonorant, –voiced, +retroflex]

That is, (a) word-final /s/ becomes a palatal /š/ if the following word begins with a voiceless palatal obstruent /č, č^{h}, š/ and a retroflex /ṣ/ if the following word begins with a voiceless retroflex obstruent /ṭ, ṭ^{h}, ṣ/. (b) Word-initial /s/ is assimilated to /š/ or /ṣ/ over any number of sonorant segments if the following obstruent consonant is a voiceless obstruent, palatal or retroflex respectively.

E.g., (a) PIE *deiwós k^{w}e 'and a god' (3 DELAB) > *deiwós ke (4b 2ND PAL) > *deiwós če (5a e(:)/o(:)-TO-a(:)) > *daiwás ča (7a MON) > *dēwás ča (s-ASSIM) > *dēwáš ča (10 w-TO-v) >Skt dēváś ca. PIE *deiwós kak^{w}néuti 'a god helps' (2a 1ST PAL, 3 DELAB) > *deiwós šaknéuti (5a e(:)/o(:)-TO-a(:), 7a MON) > *dēwás šaknṓti (s-ASSIM) > *dēwáš šaknṓti (10 w-TO-v) > Skt dēváś śaknṓti. And early acc pl *tons ṭankōns 'those chisels' (the noun an early borrowing, 5a e(:)/o(:)-TO-a(:)) > *tāns ṭankāns (5c WF CL applying only to the noun, not to *tāns because the following word begins with /ṭ/) > *tāns ṭankān (s-ASSIM) > *tānṣ ṭankān (9d NASAL DELE) > Skt tāṁṣ /tā^{n}ṣ/ ṭankān. Note that in these derivations s-ASSIM must follow 2a 1ST PAL, 4a RETRO, 4b 2ND PAL and 5c WF CL.

(b) PIE o-class *swékuro- 'father-in-law' (2a 1ST PAL) > *swéšuro- (5a e(:)/o(:)-TO-a(:)) >

*swášura- (s-ASSIM) > *šwášura- (10 w-TO-v) > Skt śváśura-. PIE *seks '6' (4a RETRO) > *sekṣ (restructuring of the cluster /kṣ/ to /ṭṣ/ from the numerals for '7' and '8') > *seṭṣ (5a e(:)/o(:)-TO-a(:)) > *saṭṣ (5c WF CL) > *saṭ (s-ASSIM) > Skt ṣaṭ. Note here the necessary chronology 4a RETRO > 5c WF CL.

The s-ASSIM (a) change remains as a rule of Sanskrit phonology. Notice in this connection that the previously applying rule 5c WF CL does not delete the /s/ in word-final /ns/ if the following word begins with a voiceless obstruent — dental, retroflex or palatal, namely /t, t^{h}, s; ṭ, ṭ^{h}, ṣ; č, č^{h}, š/. Hence when s-ASSIM applies as a synchronic rule, it has been restructured to insert /s, ṣ, š/ after a word-final /n/ if the following word begins with the respective dental, retroflex or palatal consonants.

A synchronic derivation is underlying /vŕ̥kān ca/ 'and wolves' (s-ASSIM) → *vŕ̥kānś ca (9d NASAL DELE, also applying synchronically) → vŕ̥kaṁś ca. The historical derivation is PIE acc pl *wĺ̥k^{w}ōns k^{w}e (3 DELAB) > *wĺ̥kōns ke (4b 2ND PAL) > *wĺ̥kōns če (5a e(:)/o(:)-TO-a(:)) > *wĺ̥kāns ča (9b l/r ALT) > *wŕ̥kāns ča (9d NASAL DELE) > *wŕ̥kā^{n}š ča (10 w-TO-v) > Skt vŕ̥kāṁś ca.

Sometimes the synchronic version of s-ASSIM applies ahistorically and inserts /s, ṣ, š/ where they had not occurred previously. E.g., PIE 3pl imperf *éb^{h}eront totro 'they carried there' (5a e(:)/o(:)-TO-a(:)) > *áb^{h}arant tatra (5c WF CL) > *áb^{h}aran tatra. One would thus expect Skt **ábharan tatra. However, the synchronic versions of s-ASSIM and 9d NASAL DELE apply to produce Skt ábharaṁs tatra.

7d Assimilation of Obstruent Stops (STOP ASSIM)

This change consists of three rules, all of which remain as phon cond rules in the Sanskrit grammar. The rules are these:

(a) $\begin{bmatrix} \text{C, –sonorant} \\ \text{–continuant} \end{bmatrix} \rightarrow [\alpha\text{voiced}] \ / \ \_\_\#\#[\alpha\text{voiced}]$

$[\quad " \quad] \rightarrow [+\text{nasal}] \ / \ \_\_\#\#[+\text{nasal}]$

(b) $\begin{bmatrix} \text{C, –sonorant} \\ \text{–continuant} \\ \text{+dental} \end{bmatrix} \rightarrow [+\text{palatal}] \ / \ \_\_\#\#[+\text{palatal}]$

$[\quad " \quad] \rightarrow [+\text{retroflex}] \ / \ \_\_\#\#[+\text{retroflex}]$

$[\quad " \quad] \rightarrow \text{l} \ / \ \_\_\#\#\,\text{l}$

(c) $\text{d} \rightarrow \text{n} \ / \ \_\_ +\text{n}$

That is, (a) any word-final obstruent stop becomes voiced or voiceless if the following word begins with a voiced or voiceless segment. And a word-final obstruent stop becomes the corresponding nasal consonant if the following word begins with a nasal consonant. (b) The word-final dental consonants /t, t^{h}, d^{h}, d, s/ become the palatals /č, č^{h}, ɟ^{h}, ɟ, š/ if the following word begins with a palatal consonant; these same consonants become the retroflex /ṭ, ṭ^{h}, ḍ^{h}, ḍ, ṣ/ if the following word begins with a retroflex consonant; and they become /l/ if the following word begins with /l/. (c) Finally, /d/ becomes /n/ word-internally if followed by a morpheme beginning with /n/.

E.g., (a) PIE 3sg imperf *éb^{h}eret ékwōns 'he brought horses' (2a 1ST PAL, 5a e(:)/o(:)-TO-a(:)) > *áb^{h}arat ášwāns (5c WF CL) > *áb^{h}arat ášwān (STOP ASSIM) > *áb^{h}arad ášwān (10 w-TO-v) > Skt ábharad áśvān. PIE *wōks g^{h}i 'the word indeed' (2a 1ST PAL, 5a e(:)/o(:)-TO-a(:)) > *wāks ɟ^{h}i (5c WF CL) > *wāk ɟ^{h}i (STOP ASSIM) > *wāg ɟ^{h}i (to which 8a ɟ^{h}-TO-h cannot apply because of the preceding

/g/ and a possible change of /ɟʰ/ to /gʰ/, 10 w-TO-v) > Skt vāg ghi. PIE *tod meme 'that which is mine' (5a e(:)/o(:)-TO-a(:)) > *tad mama (STOP ASSIM) > Skt tan mama. PIE nom sg *wōks moi 'my speech' (5a e(:)/o(:)-TO-a(:), 5c WF CL) > *wāk mai (7a MON) > *wāk mē (STOP ASSIM) > *wāŋ mē (10 w-TO-v) > Skt vāŋ mē. Note in the previous examples the necessary chronology 5c WF CL > STOP ASSIM > 8a ɟʰ-TO-h.

(b) IE *tod kʷe 'and this' (3 DELAB , 4b 2ND PAL, 5a e(:)/o(:)-TO-a(:)) > *tad ca (STOP ASSIM a) > *tat ča (STOP ASSIM b) > Skt tac ca. The PIE gerund *tod klutwō 'having heard this' (2a 1ST PAL, 5a e(:)/o(:)-TO-a(:)) > *tad šlutwā (STOP ASSIM) > *tač šlutwā (possibly by 4b 2ND PAL 2, applying as a synchronic rule) → *tač čʰlutwā (9b l/r ALT, 10 w-TO-v) > Skt tac chrutvā. PIE *tod génom 'that race', *tod ḍalam 'that branch' (a non-IE borrowing), *tod laksóm 'that sign' (2a 1ST PAL, 4a RETRO) > *tod ɟénom, *tod ḍalam, *tod lakṣóm (5a e(:)/o(:)-TO-a(:)) > *tad ɟánam, *tad ḍalam, *tad lakṣám (STOP ASSIM a and b) > Skt taj jánam, taḍ ḍalam, tal lakṣám.

(c) PIE perf participle *sed+no- 'having sat' (5a e(:)/o(:)-TO-a(:)) > *sadna- (STOP ASSIM c) > Skt sanna-.

8a The Change of /ɟʰ/ to /h/ (ɟʰ-TO-h)

This change remains as a morph cond rule of Sanskrit sandhi.

ɟʰ → h

That is, /ɟʰ/ which has arisen by either 2a 1ST PAL or 4b 2ND PAL, becomes /h/. There is also a morph cond environmental condition that /ɟʰ/ will not change if word-initial and if the preceding word ends in a velar obstruent. (In such cases the /ɟʰ/ may have been de-palatalized to /gʰ/. See the derivation of Skt vāg ghi 'the word indeed' under 7d STOP ASSIM above.)

E.g., PIE Vnt-class adj *megʰő̄nt- 'large' (2a 1ST PAL) > *meɟʰő̄nt- (5a e(:)/o(:)-TO-a(:)) > *maɟʰā́nt- (ɟʰ-TO-h) > Skt mahā́nt-. PIE 3sg pres *gʰʷén+ti 'kills' vs. the ablauting 1sg perf *gʰʷe+gʰʷő̄n+a 'I have killed' (2b GRASSMANN) > *gʰʷénti vs. *gʷegʰʷő̄na (3 DELAB) > *gʰénti vs. *gegʰő̄na (4b 2ND PAL) > *ɟʰénti vs. *ɟegʰő̄na (5a e(:)/o(:)-TO-a(:)) > *ɟʰánti vs. *ɟagʰā́na (ɟʰ-TO-h) > Skt hánti vs. jaghā́na. Notice in these derivations that ɟʰ-TO-h must follow 2a 1ST PAL, 2b GRASSMANN, 4b 2ND PAL and 7d STOP ASSIM.

8b The Changes of /s, ṣ/ and /r/ (s/r CHANGES)

These changes remain as phon cond rules of sandhi. We give the principal ones in outline below. They apply in mutually exclusive environments and are not ordered.

(a) as → ō / ___ { (a) + [C, –sonorant, +voiced] ; (b) ## [C, +voiced] }

where + is a word-internal morpheme boundary and ## a word boundary.

(b) as → a / ___## [+vocalic, –low]

(c) ās → ā / ___## [+vocalic]

(d) s or ṣ → r / [V, –low] ___ { (a) + [C, –sonorant, +voiced] ; (b) ## [+voiced] }

$$\text{(e) s, ṣ or r} \;\rightarrow\; \text{h} \,/\, \_\_\_ \begin{cases} \text{(a) + [C −voiced]} \\ \text{(b) \#\# } \begin{bmatrix} \text{C, −voiced} \\ \text{+labial or +velar} \end{bmatrix} \\ \text{(c) \#\#\#\#} \end{cases}$$

where #### is a sentence-final boundary.

That is, (a) /ās/ becomes /ō/ (aa) over a word-internal morpheme boundary if the following morpheme begins with a voiced obstruent and (ab) over a word boundary if the following segment is any voiced consonant — obstruent or sonorant. (b) Word-final /as/ becomes /a/ if the next word begins with any vowel except /a(:)/. (c) Word-final /ās/ becomes /ā/ if the following word begins with any voiced segment, consonant or vowel. (d) /s/ or /ṣ/ becomes /r/ if preceded by any vowel except /a(:)/ and (da) over a word-internal morpheme boundary if the following morpheme begins with a voiced obstruent consonant; or (db) over a word boundary if the following word begins with any voiced segment, vowel or consonant. (e) /s, ṣ/ or /r/ becomes /h/ (ea) over a word-internal morpheme boundary if the following morpheme begins with any voiceless consonant, (eb) over a word boundary if the following word begins with /p, p^{h}, k, k^{h}/, or (ec) if in sentence-final position.

E.g., (a) PIE Vs-class dat pl neuter *mén+os+b^{h}jos 'mind' (5a e(:)/o(:)-TO-a(:)) > *mánasb^{h}jas (s/r CHANGES aa) > Skt mánōbhyas. Underlying Skt /áśvas váhati/ 'the horse travels' (s/r CHANGES ab applying synchronically) → áśvō váhati.

(b) Underlying Skt /nr̥pas uvaca/ 'the king spoke' (s/r CHANGES b applying synchronically) → nr̥pa uvaca. Note that 7a MON does not apply here to produce Skt **nr̥pōvaca. Hence the relative chronology is 7a MON > s/r CHANGES. (c) Underlying Skt /nr̥pās jayanti/ 'the kings win' (s/r CHANGES c) → nr̥pā jayanti.

(d) PIE pl *g^{h}ewís+bhjos 'oblations' (2a 1ST PAL) > *$ɟ^{h}$ewísb^{h}jos (4a RETRO) > *$ɟ^{h}$ewíṣb^{h}jos (5a e(:)/o(:)-TO-a(:)) > *$ɟ^{h}$awíṣb^{h}jas (8a $ɟ^{h}$-TO-h) > *hawíṣb^{h}jas (s/r CHANGES da) > *hawírb^{h}jas (10 w-TO-v) > Skt havírbhyas. Underlying Skt /agnís dáhati/ 'a fire is burning' and /nāus váhati/ 'a ship is moving' (s/r CHANGES db applying synchronically) → agnír dáhati and nāur váhati.

(e) IE Vs-class loc pl neuter *mén+os+su 'minds' (5a e(:)/o(:)-TO-a(:)) > *mán+as+su (s/r CHANGES ea) > Skt mánaḥsu. PIE *deiwós k^{w}oréuti 'a god does it' vs. *deiwós totro 'a god there' (3 DELAB, 5a e(:)/o(:)-TO-a(:)) > *daiwás karáuti vs. *daiwás tatra (7a MON) > *dēwás karṓti vs. *dēwás tatra (s/r CHANGES eb) > *dēwáḥ karṓti vs. *dēwás tatra (10 w-TO-v) > Skt dēváḥ karṓti vs. dēvás tatra. Also Sanskrit underlying /punar punar/ 'again and again' (s/r CHANGES e applying as a synchronic rule) → punaḥ punaḥ vs. underlying /punar tatra/ 'again there' (to which s/r CHANGES cannot apply) → punar tatra.

The /h/ which results from s/r CHANGES e is called "visarga" by the Sanskrit grammarians. The visarga /h/ is distinguished orthographically from the /h/ which arises by other changes such as 8a $ɟ^{h}$-TO-h. In the usual romanization of Sanskrit, <ḥ> is used for the visarga, <h> for the other /h/. (The dēvanāgarī script also distinguishes the two.) Here we have assumed they were phonemically the same and were differentiated orthographically only to show their different synchronic underlying sources. This view is not universally accepted: Mayerhofer (1965: 16) considers visarga <ḥ> –voiced, the other <h> +voiced.

8c Alternations of Vowels with Nonvocalic Sonorants (V-SON ALT)

These changes remain as phon cond rules of sandhi.

(a) $\begin{Bmatrix} \text{i(:)} \\ \text{u(:)} \\ \text{r̥(:)} \end{Bmatrix} \rightarrow \begin{Bmatrix} \text{j} \\ \text{w} \\ \text{r} \end{Bmatrix}$ / ___ ## [+vocalic]

where the +vocalic segment cannot be i(:), u(:) or r̥(:) respectively.

(b) $\begin{Bmatrix} \bar{\text{ı}} \\ \bar{\text{u}} \end{Bmatrix} \rightarrow \begin{Bmatrix} \text{ij} \\ \text{uw} \end{Bmatrix}$ / ___+ [+vocalic]

where + is a word-internal morpheme boundary.

That is, (a) the word-final vocalic segments, long or short, become the corresponding nonvocalic segments if the following word begins with a vowel. (The vowels will not be the same since by this time the change 6 V##V-TO-V̄ has already applied.) (b) Word-internal /ī, ū/ become /ij, uw/ if followed by a morpheme boundary plus a vowel.

E.g., the following synchronic derivations: (a) underlying /yadi ētat/ 'if this', /astu ētat/ 'this should be' and /kartr̥ asti/ 'he is the creator' (V-SON ALT) → yady ētat, astv ētat and kartr asti. (By this time the synchronic version of V-SON ALT has been restructured by the later application of 10 w-TO-v to produce /v/ instead of /w/.) (b) Underlying root class nom sg /dhī+s/ 'understanding' and /bhū+s/ 'earth' vs. loc sg /dhī+i / and /bhū+i/ (V-SON ALT) → dhīs and bhūs vs. dhiyi and bhuvi.

In the following derivation 7a MON must precede V-SON ALT : PIE loc sg *deiwei esti 'he is with a god' (5a e(:)/o(:)-TO-a(:)) > *daiwai asti (7a MON) > *dēwē asti (to which V-SON ALT cannot apply, but by 9c LATER V##) > *dēwē 'sti (10 w-TO-v) > Skt dēvē 'sti. If the sequence had been V-SON ALT > 7a MON, the Sanskrit form would be **dēvay asti.

9a The Change of /bʰ/ and /dʰ/ to /h/ (bʰ/dʰ-TO-h)

The forms which undergo this "change", if it did indeed occur, may have been in fact borrowings into Sanskrit from various Middle Indic dialects. The change restructures various lexical items and then is dropped from the grammar. Its environment is not clear; and it often applies optionally.

bʰ, dʰ → h / in certain instances.

E.g., PIE 3sg pres *gʰr̥bʰ+nā́+ti 'seizes' (2b GRASSMANN) > *gr̥bʰnā́ti (bʰ/dʰ-TO-h, perhaps applying optionally) > Skt gr̥hnā́ti as well as gr̥bhnā́ti. PIE o- and ā-class adjs *róudʰito- 'red' as well as the ablauting *rudʰiró- 'idem' (5a e(:)/o(:)-TO-a(:)) > *ráudʰita- and *rudʰirá- (7a MON) > *rṓdʰita- and *rudʰirá- (bʰ/dʰ-TO-h applying only to the first form) > Skt rṓhita- vs. rudhirá-.

As noted above, it is not clear that the change bʰ/dʰ-TO-h actually occurred. There are, however, derivations like these: PIE verb endings 1dual and 1pl mid -wodʰai and *-medʰai (ev) > Skt -vahē and -mahē, where bʰ/dʰ-TO-h has clearly applied. Since such endings are unlikely to have been borrowings, this change may have occurred in certain restricted environments. If the time of the change and that of the Middle Indic borrowings were approximately contemporaneous, then bʰ/dʰ-TO-h may have occurred shortly after 500 BC.

9b Alternation of /l/ and /r/ (l/r ALT)

Like the preceding one, this "change" may be a mere reflection of various Middle Indic borrowings into Sanskrit. It restructures various lexical items and then is dropped from the grammar. The basic form of the change is this:

(a) l → r / in some forms (possibly from eastern Middle Indic dialects).

(b) r → l / in fewer forms (possibly from western Middle Indic dialects).

E.g., (a) 3sg pres *li+né+k^{w}+ti 'leaves' (3 DELAB) > *linékti (4a RETRO) > *liṇékti (5a e(:)/o(:)-TO-a(:)) > *liṇákti (l/r ALT) > Skt riṇákti. PIE Vs-class neuter noun *selpís- 'butter' (4a RETRO, 5a e(:)/o(:)-TO-a(:)) > *salpíṣ- (l/r ALT) > Skt sarpíṣ-. PIE o-class masc noun *k^{w}ek^{w}ló- 'wheel' (3 DELAB) > *kekló- (4b 2ND PAL) > *čekló- (5a e(:)/o(:)-TO-a(:)) > *čaklá- (l/r ALT) > Skt cakrá-. But PIE 3sg pres *lúb^{h}jeti 'covets' (5a e(:)/o(:)-TO-a(:)) > *lúb^{h}jati (l/r ALT not applying) > Skt lúbhyati. (b) PIE o- and ā-class adj *róud^{h}ito- 'red' (5a e(:)/o(:)-TO-a(:), 7a MON) > *rṓd^{h}ita- (9a b^{h}/d^{h}-TO-h) > *rṓhita- (l/r ALT applying optionally) > Skt lṓhita- as well as rṓhita-.

9c Later Changes in Vowels over a Word Boundary (LATER V##)

These changes remain as phon cond rules of sandhi in the grammar. Recall that ## in the following designates a word boundary.

(a) a → Ø / ē or ō ## ___

(b) ē or ō → a / ___ ## [+vocalic] (≠ /a/)

(c) āi (and sometimes āu) → ā / ___ ## [+vocalic]

That is, (a) word-initial /a/ is deleted if the preceding word ends in /ē/ or /ō/; (b) word-final /ē/ or /ō/ becomes /a/ if the next word begins with any vowel except /a/. (c) Word-final /āi/ and occasionally /āu/ become /ā/ if the following word begins with any vowel whatsoever. (At the time of LATER V##, 8c V-SON ALT had probably already applied, so the input here would have been /āj/ and /āw/.)

E.g., (a) PIE nom pl masc *toi opi 'these also' (5a e(:)/o(:)-TO-a(:)) > *tai api (7a MON) > *tē api (LATER V##) > Skt tē 'pi. Note here the necessary chronology 7a MON > LATER V##. Also PIE *deiwós opi 'a god also' (5a e(:)/o(:)-TO-a(:) and 7a MON) > *dēwás api (8b s/r CHANGES) > *dēwṓ api (LATER V##) > *dēwṓ 'pi (10 w-TO-v) > Skt dēvṓ 'pi. Note here the necessary chronology 8b s/r CHANGES > LATER V##.

(b) PIE nom pl masc *toi id^{h}i 'those here' (5a e(:)/o(:)-TO-a(:), 7a MON) > *tē id^{h}i (9a b^{h}/d^{h}-TO-h) > *tē ihi (LATER V##) > Skt ta ihi. Note that in this derivation the sequence is 7a MON > LATER V##.

(c) PIE ī-class fem dat sg *deiwjā́i id^{h}i 'for a goddess here' (5a e(:)/o(:)-TO-a(:), 7a MON) > *dēwjā́i id^{h}i (9a b^{h}/d^{h}-TO-h) > *dēwjā́i ihi (LATER V##) > *dēwjā́ ihi (10 w-TO-v) > Skt dēvyā́ ihi. LATER V## usually does not apply to the diphthong /āu/. E.g., underlying dual nom /tāu ihi/ 'these 2 here' (LATER V## not applying, but 10 w-TO-v applying synchronically) → tāv ihi.

9d Deletion of a Nasal Consonant (NASAL DELE)

These two rules, which are manifestations of one and the same change, remain as phon cond rules of sandhi in the Sanskrit grammar. The process is referred to by Sanskrit grammarians as "anusvāra".

(a) [+vocalic] [C, +nasal] → [+vocalic, +nasal] Ø / ___ [C, –voiced, +continuant]
1 2 1 2

(b) [+vocalic] m → [+vocalic, +nasal] Ø / ___ ## [–vocalic]
1 2 1 2

where ## is a word or prefix boundary.

That is, (a) the sequence vowel plus any nasal consonant plus a voiceless continuant consonant (which can only be /s, ṣ, š or h/) becomes a nasalized vowel and the nasal consonant is lost. (b) The sequence vowel plus /m/ in word-final or prefix-final position if the next word begins with a nonvocalic segment becomes a nasalized vowel and the /m/ is dropped.

E.g., (a) PIE o-class masc noun *ánso- 'shoulder' (5a e(:)/o(:)-TO-a(:)) > ánsa- (NASAL DELE) > Skt /á^{n}sa-/, in the usual romanization written <áṁsa->. The PIE u-class adj *ang^{h}ú- 'narrow' (2a 1ST PAL) > *anɟ^{h}ú- (8a ɟ^h-TO-h) > *anhú- (NASAL DELE) > Skt aṁhú- /a^{n}hú-/. Note in this derivation the necessary chronology 8a ɟ^h-TO-h > NASAL DELE. If one assumes this sequence, then the environment of NASAL DELE becomes a natural one in that it now applies before all voiceless continuant consonants including /h/ by 8a ɟ^h-TO-h.

(b) PIE acc sg o-class masc *deiwóm k^{w}e 'and a god' (3 DELAB) > *deiwóm ke (4b 2ND PAL) > *deiwóm če (5a e(:)/o(:)-TO-a(:), 7a MON) > *dēwám ča (NASAL DELE) > *dēwá^n ča (10 w-TO-v) > Skt dēváṁ ca. PIE 3pl pres *som##g^{w}m̥skonti 'they come together' (2c SYL NAS, 3 DELAB) > *somgaskonti (4b 2ND PAL applying analogously after those forms in the paradigm which have /e/ in the ending) > *somgačč^{h}onti (5a e(:)/o(:)-TO-a(:)) > *samgačč^{h}anti (NASAL DELE) > Skt saṁgacchanti. PIE o-class masc noun *som##jougo- 'union' (5a e(:)/o(:)-TO-a(:), 7a MON) > *samjōga- (NASAL DELE) > Skt saṁyōga-.

10 The Change of /w/ to /v/ (w-TO-v)

This change restructures the phonemic inventory of the language and then is dropped from the grammar:

w → v

E.g., PIE nom sg *deiwós 'god' (5a e(:)/o(:)-TO-a(:), 7a MON) > *dēwás (w-TO-v) > Skt dēvás. PIE loc sg *b^{h}ū+i 'on the earth' (8c V-SON ALT) > *b^{h}uwi (w-TO-v) > Skt bhuvi. Note in this derivation the necessary chronology 8c V-SON ALT > w-TO-v .

11 The Earlier and Later Word-Stress Rules (SKT STRESS)

Until about 700 AD, Sanskrit had a morph cond word-stress rule similar to that of Greek. We assume that this rule reflects in large part that of the PIE rule 3.1.2h WORD STRESS. After 700 AD, the earlier morph cond stress rule was replaced by a later phon cond stress rule. In the following we give first a basic outline of the earlier morph cond stress rule. Then we give the phon cond rule which replaced it. Burrow (1959: 113) and Whitney (1960: 28) assume that the stress was primarily tonal.

(11.1) The Morph Cond Stress Rule (11.1 SKT STRESS)

This stress is marked only in manuscripts of the older Sanskrit literature such as the Vedic texts. Here as in other works forms are often cited without any indication of stress since no source attests to their morph cond stress. Here we give only the basic structure of this early rule.

SKT STRESS occurs in six basic configurations:

(I) On the first syllable of a word: ## [C_0 ___]
s

(II) On the second syllable of a word: ## s [C_0 ___]
s

(III) On a derivative suffix in a word: [C_0, derivative suffix ___]
s

(IV) On an inflectional ending (always its first syllable): [C_0, inflectional suffix ___] s_o ##
s

(V) Alternating in a paradigm between the root (usually its first syllable) and the inflectional ending (i.e., I and IV above):

##[C_0 ___] or [C_0, inflectional suffix ___]s_o ##
s s

(VI) Alternating in a paradigm between the derivative suffix and the inflectional ending (i.e. III and IV above):

[C_0, derivative suffix ___] or [C_0, inflectional suffix ___]s_o ##
s s

Exactly which of these six stress patterns accrues to a word is determined by one of three parameters:

(A) a particular derivative suffix,
(B) a particular marked lexical item,
(C) a particular combination of syntactic and morphological features such as case, number or particular form class (such as class 1 verbs).

In the following we first give the stress rule as it applies to substantives (nouns, adjectives, numerals and pronouns). Next we give the rule as it applies to verbs.

(11.la) Substantives

(I) First-Syllable Stress

(A) As Determined by a Particular Derivative Suffix

E.g., (i) comparative and superlative suffixes: pos gurú- 'heavy', comp /gar+īyaṁs-/ (SKT STRESS 1) → gárīyaṁs-, sup /gar+iṣṭha-/ (SKT STRESS 1) → gáriṣṭha-.

(ii) -t- in the inf: /ē+t+um/ 'to go' (SKT STRESS 1) → ḗtum.

(iii) -(t)ya in the gerund: /kīr+ya/ 'making' (SKT STRESS 1) →kī́rya.

(B) As Determined by a Particular Lexical Item

E.g., (i) káma- 'love' o-class masc.
(ii) vā́ri- 'water' i-class fem.
(iii) rā́jan- 'king' Vn-class masc (vs. another Vn-class masculine noun like ātmán- 'soul').
(iv) Certain pronouns such as the dat sg masc demonstrative tásmāi 'that'.

(C) As Determined by Particular Syntactic and Morphological Features

E.g., (i) in nouns of all classes the voc sg — and usually the voc dual and pl as well — take first-syllable stress. Nom sg masc o-class dēvás 'god' vs. voc sg dḗva.

(II) Second-Syllable Stress

(A) As Determined by a Particular Derivative Suffix: Ø

(I.e., no such parameter exists to condition second-syllable stress.)

(B) As Determined by a Particular Lexical Item

E.g.,(i) root class fem nom sg nadī́s 'stream' and acc sg nadíam.
(ii) tVr-class nom sg pitā́ 'father', acc sg pitáram, dat sg pitrḗ.
(iii) Nom pl masc catvā́ras '4' and instr pl catúrbhis.

(C) As Determined by Particular Syntactic and Morphological Features: Ø

(III) Derivative-Suffix Stress

(A) As Determined by a Particular Derivative Suffix

E.g.(i) -ay- in the inf /pīt+ay+ē/ 'to drink' (SKT STRESS 1) → pītáyē.
(ii) -tvā- in the gerund: /śru+tvā+i/ 'hearing' → śrutvā́i.
(iii) -v(V(:))ns- in the perf act participle: nom sg masc vidvā́n 'having known', acc sg vidvā́ṁsam, instr sg vidúṣa.

(B) As Determined by a Particular Lexical Item: Ø

(C) As Determined by Particular Syntactic and Morphological Features: Ø

(IV) Inflectional-Ending Stress

(A) As Determined by a Particular Derivative Suffix

E.g.(i) -m- in ordinal adjectives: pañca+m+á- '5th', sapta+m+á- '7th'.
(ii) -n- and -t- in perfect passive participles: kīr+n+á- 'scattered', ga+t+á- 'gone'.

(B) As Determined by a Particular Lexical Item

E.g. (i) o-class nom sg dēvás 'god', instr sg dēvḗna, but voc sg dḗva by SKT STRESS 11.la-I-C-i above.
(ii) i-class masc sg agnís 'fire', dat pl agníbhyam, but voc sg ágnē.
(iii) Nom pl aṣṭā́u '8', instr pl aṣṭābhís.

(C) As Determined by Particular Syntactic and Morphological Features: Ø

(V) Stress Alternating between the Root and the Inflectional Ending

(A) **As Determined by a Particular Derivative Suffix: Ø**

(B) **As Determined by a Particular Lexical Item: Ø**

(C) **As Determined by Particular Syntactic and Morphological Features**

E.g., (i) monosyllabic-root nouns of any of the athematic classes (1.5 in the Morphology) have root stress in the nominative, vocative and accusative and otherwise on the inflectional ending. Masc Ø-class acc sg pā́dam 'foot' vs. instr sg padā́. Fem root class acc sg bhúvam 'earth' vs. instr sg bhuvā́. Also nom pl masc tráyas '3' vs. instr pl tribhís.

(11.lb) Verbs

The rather strange condition obtains that verbs in main clauses are stressed only when sentence-initial. They are stressed in all positions in subordinate clauses.

(I) First-Syllable Stress

(A) **As Determined by a Particular Derivative Suffix**

E.g., (i) -y- in all present forms of class 4 verbs: 3sg pres act kúp+y+ati 'is angry'.

(B) **As Determined by a Particular Lexical Item: Ø**

(C) **As Determined by Particular Syntactic and Morphological Features**

E.g., (i) in all augmented verbs, which is to say all aorist, imperfect and conditional forms: 3sg aorist á+dik+ṣ+at 'point to', 3sg imperf á+diṣ+at 'idem' and 3sg cond á+dik+ṣ+yat 'idem'.

(ii) In the present of class 1 verbs and desideratives: class l 3sg pres bhávati 'be' and desiderative 3sg pres jíjīviṣati 'want to live'.

(II) Second-Syllable Stress: Ø

(III) Derivative-Suffix Stress

(A) **As Determined by a Particular Derivative Suffix**

E.g., (i) -ay- in the present of class 10 verbs and of causatives: class 10 3sg pres cint+áy+ati 'think' and causative 3sg pres dhār+áy+ati 'cause to hold'.

(B) **As Determined by a Particular Lexical Item: Ø**

(C) **As Determined by Particular Syntactic and Morphological Features: Ø**

(IV) Inflectional-Ending Stress

(A) **As Determined by a Particular Derivative Suffix**

E.g. (i) -y- in the s-future and in the present passive of all verbs. 3sg s-future dā+s+y+áti 'will give' and pres pass 3sg yug+y+átē 'is yoked'.

(B) **As Determined by a Particular Lexical Item: Ø**

(C) **As Determined by Particular Syntactic and Morphological Features**

E.g., (i) in the present of class 6 verbs: 3sg pres viṣáti 'enter'.

(ii) In the present middle indicative of athematic verbs: 3sg pres mid sunutḗ 'push out'.

(V) Stress Alternating between the Root and the Inflectional Ending

Verbs take the stress on the root in the singular and on the ending in the dual and plural.

(A) **As Determined by a Particular Derivative Suffix**: Ø

(B) **As Determined by a Particular Lexical Item: Ø**

(C) **As Determined by Particular Syntactic and Morphological Feature**

E.g., (i) in most athematic verbs in the present active indicative: class 3 reduplicating verb 1sg juhṓmi 'sacrifice' vs. 1pl juhumás. Occasionally the root stress is on the reduplicated syllable as in 1sg bíbharmi 'carry' vs. 1pl bibhr̥más.

(ii) In the present perfect of all verbs: 1sg bubṓdha 'know' vs. 1pl bubudhimá.

(iii) In the present of intensive verbs: 1sg vḗvēdmi 'know well' vs. 1pl vēvidmás.

(VI) Stress Alternating between the Derivative Suffix and the Inflectional Ending

Verbs take the stress on the derivative suffix in the singular and on the ending in the dual and plural.

(A) **As Determined by a Particular Derivative Suffix**

These are all suffixes which form the present-tense paradigms of athematic verbs.

E.g., (i) -n(V)- in verbs of classes 7 and 9: class 7 1sg ruṇádhmi 'obstruct' vs. 1pl rundhmás.

(ii) -(n)Vu- in verbs of classes 5 and 8: class 5 1sg sunṓmi 'press' vs. 1pl sunumás.

(B) **As Determined by a Particular Lexical Item: Ø**

(C) **As Determined by Particular Syntactic and Morphological Feature: Ø**

(11.2) The Later Phonologically Conditioned Stress Rule (11.2 SKT STRESS)

This rule replaced 11.1 morph cond SKT STRESS outlined above. The environments of phon cond 11.2. SKT STRESS are ordered. The rule is this:

$$V \rightarrow [+\text{stress}] \;/\; (1)\ \_\_ \begin{Bmatrix} V \\ C_2 \end{Bmatrix}\ s\ \#\#$$

$$(2)\ \text{"}\qquad \text{"}\ ss\ \#\#$$

$$(3)\ \_\_\ sss\ \#\#$$

That is, the vowel is stressed in a long sequence, namely a long vowel or diphthong (VV) or a vowel followed by at least two consonants (VC_2) if occurring in (1) the next-to-last syllable in a word. (2) If these conditions are not fulfilled for the penult, the antepenult is similarly scanned and if possible stressed. (3) Otherwise, the fourth-to-last syllable is stressed, whether or not it contains a long sequence.

As examples we cite pairs of forms, the first as stressed by 11.1 SKT STRESS, the second stressed by 11.2 SKT STRESS. Pos adj gurú- 'heavy' > gúru-. Comp gárīyaṁs- 'heavier' > garī́yaṁs-. Sup gáriṣṭha- 'heaviest' > garíṣṭha-. Acc sg nadíam 'river' > nádiam. Ordinal saptamá- '7th' > sáptama-. 3sg pres desiderative jíjīviṣati 'want to live' > jijī́viṣati. And 1pl perf act bubudhimá 'we knew' > búbudhima.

C. The Relative Chronology

In the following ">" means "must precede".

la LARYNGEALS > 2b GRASSMANN (see the discussion under la), > all other changes (see la).

1b OBSTR CL > 2b GRASSMANN (see 2b), > all other changes (see lb).

2a 1ST PAL > 3 DELAB (see 3), > 4a RETRO (see 4a), > 4b 2ND PAL (see 2a), > 7b NASAL ASSIM (see 7b).

2b GRASSMANN > 8a ɟ^h-TO-h (see 2b and 8a).

2c SYL NAS > 7a MON (see 2c and 7a).

3 DELAB > 4a RETRO (see 4a), > 4b 2ND PAL (see 4b).

4a RETRO > 5b VzC-TO-V̄C (see 4a and 5b), > 5c WF CL (see 7c), > 7a MON (see 4a), > 7c s-ASSIM (see 7c).

4b 2ND PAL > 5a e(:)/o(:)-TO-a(:) (see 4b), > 7b NASAL ASSIM (see 7b), > 7c s-ASSIM (see 7c), > 7d STOP ASSIM (see 7d), > 8a ɟ^h-TO-h (see 8a).

5a e(:)/o(:)-TO-a(:) > 6 V##V-TO-V̄ (see 6), > 7a MON (see 7a), 8b s/r CHANGES (see 8b).

5b VzC-TO-V̄C > Ø.

5c WF CL > 7b NASAL ASSIM (see 7b), > 7c s-ASSIM (see 5c), > 7d STOP ASSIM (see 7d).

6 V##V-TO-V̄ > 7a MON (see 6), > 8c V-SON ALT (see 8c).

7a MON > 8b s/r CHANGES (see 8b), > 8c V-SON ALT (see 8c), > 9c LATER V## (see 9c).

7b NASAL ASSIM > Ø.

7c s-ASSIM > Ø.

7d STOP ASSIM > 8a ɟ^h-TO-h (see 7d and 8a).

8a ɟ^h-TO-h > 9d NASAL DELE (see 9d).

8b s/r CHANGES > 9c LATER V## (see 9c).

8c V-SON ALT > 9c LATER V## (see 8c), > 10 w-TO-v (see 8c and 10).

9a b^h/d^h-TO-h > Ø.

9b l/r ALT > Ø.

9c LATER V## > Ø.

9d NASAL DELE > Ø.

10 w-TO-v > Ø.

11 SKT STRESS > Ø.

III Sanskrit Phonology

After the changes described in the previous section, the inventory of segments in the phonology of Sanskrit at about 400 BC (the time of the grammarian Pāṇini) was as follows.

Obstruent Consonants

labial	dental	retroflex	palatal	velar	glottal
p	t	ṭ	c	k[1]	
ph	th	ṭh	ch	kh[1]	
bh	dh	ḍh	jh	gh[1]	
b	d	ḍ	j	g[1]	
	s	ṣ	ś[1]		h[2]
v					

Sonorant Consonants

labial	dental	retroflex	palatal	velar
m	n	ṇ	ñ	ŋ[1]
	r			
	[l, l^{n}][3]			
			y	

Vowels

i	u		ī		ū
	a[4]		ē[5]	ō[5]	
				ā	
r̥, l̥[6]			r̥̄[6]		

Nasal Vowels All the above except r̥ (:) and l̥[7].

Diphthongs āi, āu[8]

Sanskrit Segments in Terms of Phonological Features: Obstruents

	p	t	ṭ	c	k	ph	th	ṭh	ch	kh	bh	dh	ḍh	jh	gh	b	d	ḍ	j	g	v	s	ṣ	ś	h
consonantal	+	+	+	+	+	+	+	+	+	+	+	+	+	+	+	+	+	+	+	+	+	+	+	+	
sonorant	–	–	–	–	–	–	–	–	–	–	–	–	–	–	–	–	–	–	–	–	–	–	–	–	
vocalic	–	–	–	–	–	–	–	–	–	–	–	–	–	–	–	–	–	–	–	–	–	–	–	–	
high	–	–	–	+	+	–	–	–	+	+	–	–	–	+	+	–	–	–	+	+	–	–	–	+	
back	–	–	–	–	+	–	–	–	–	+	–	–	–	–	+	–	–	–	–	+	–	–	–	–	
low	–	–	–	–	–	–	–	–	–	–	–	–	–	–	–	–	–	–	–	–	–	–	–	–	
anterior	+	+	+	–	–	+	+	+	–	–	+	+	+	–	–	+	+	+	–	–	+	+	+	–	
coronal	–	+	+	+	–	–	+	+	+	–	–	+	+	+	–	–	+	+	+	–	–	+	+	–	
voiced	–	–	–	–	–	–	–	–	–	–	+	+	+	+	+	+	+	+	+	+	+	–	–	–	–
continuant	–	–	–	–	–	–	–	–	–	–	–	–	–	–	–	–	–	–	–	–	+	+	+	+	+
strident	–	–	–	+	–	–	–	–	+	–	–	–	–	+	–	–	–	–	+	–	–	+	+	+	
delayed rel.	–	–	–	+	–	–	–	–	+	–	–	–	–	+	–	–	–	–	+	–	–	–	–	–	
aspirated	–	–	–	–	–	+	+	+	+	+	+	+	+	+	+	–	–	–	–	–	–	–	–	–	+
palatal	–	–	–	+	–	–	–	–	+	–	–	–	–	+	–	–	–	–	+	–	–	–	–	+	

Sanskrit Segments in Terms of Phonological Features: Resonants

	m	n	ṇ	ñ	ŋ	r	l	l^n	y
consonantal	+	+	+	+	+	+	+	+	–
sonorant	+	+	+	+	+	+	+	+	+
vocalic	–	–	–	–	–	–	–	–	–
high	–	–	–	+	+	–	–	–	+
back	–	–	–	–	+	–	–	–	–
low	–	–	–	–	–	–	–	–	–
anterior	+	+	+	–	–	+	+	+	–
coronal	–	+	+	+	–	+	+	+	–
voiced	+	+	+	+	+	+	+	+	+
continuant	–	–	–	–	–	+	+	+	+
nasal	+	+	+	+	+	–	–	+	–
lateral	–	–	–	–	–	–	+	+	–
palatal	–	–	–	+	–	–	–	–	+
stressed	–	–	–	–	–	–	–	–	–
long	–	–	–	–	–	–	–	–	–

Sanskrit Segments in Terms of Phonological Features: Vowels

	i	a	u	ī	ē	ā	ō	ū	i^n	a^n	u^n	$ī^n$	$ē^n$	$ā^n$	$ō^n$	$ū^n$	r̥	r̥̄	l̥
consonantal	−	−	−	−	−	−	−	−	−	−	−	−	−	−	−	−	−	−	−
sonorant	+	+	+	+	+	+	+	+	+	+	+	+	+	+	+	+	+	+	+
vocalic	+	+	+	+	+	+	+	+	+	+	+	+	+	+	+	+	+	+	+
high	+	−	+	+	−	−	−	+	+	−	+	+	−	−	−	+	−	−	−
back	−	+	+	−	−	+	+	+	−	+	+	−	−	+	+	+	−	−	−
low	−	+	−	−	−	+	−	−	−	+	−	−	−	+	−	−	−	−	−
anterior	−	−	−	−	−	−	−	−	−	−	−	−	−	−	−	−	+	+	+
coronal	−	−	−	−	−	−	−	−	−	−	−	−	−	−	−	−	+	+	+
voiced	+	+	+	+	+	+	+	+	+	+	+	+	+	+	+	+	+	+	+
continuant	+	+	+	+	+	+	+	+	+	+	+	+	+	+	+	+	+	+	+
nasal	−	−	−	−	−	−	−	−	+	+	+	+	+	+	+	+	−	−	−
lateral	−	−	−	−	−	−	−	−	−	−	−	−	−	−	−	−	−	−	+
stressed	±	±	±	±	±	±	±	±	±	±	±	±	±	±	±	±	±	±	±
long	−	−	−	+	+	+	+	+	−	−	−	+	+	+	+	+	−	+	−

A salient characteristic of Sanskrit phonology is that most of the changes it has undergone from PIE have remained in the grammar as synchronic rules of sandhi. Those below labeled "morph cond" are morphologically conditioned and apply either to lexically marked items or to morphosyntactically defined classes. Those marked "phon cond" are phonologically conditioned and apply more or less generally. The symbol "Ø" after a change means that it has restructured lexical items and/or changed the inventory of underlying segments and has then been dropped from the grammar.

For those changes remaining as rules in the grammar we cite an illustrative derivation. Additional examples can be found in the discussions of the particular rules.

1a LARYNGEALS: Ø.

1b OBSTR CL (phon cond): perf pass part /labh+tá-/ 'taken' (OBSTR CL) → labdhá-.

2a 1ST PAL (morph cond): acc sg /dík+am/ 'direction' vs. instr pl /dik+sú-/ (1ST PAL) → díśam vs. diksú (4a RETRO) → díśam vs. dikṣú.

2b GRASSMANN (phon cond): 3sg pres /bhadh+nā́+ti/ 'binds' (GRASSMANN) → badhnā́ti.

2c SYL NAS: Ø.

3 DELAB : Ø.

4a RETRO (morph cond and phon cond): instr pl /dik+sú/ 'directions' (RETRO) → dikṣú.

4b 2ND PAL (morph cond): 3sg pres mid /sák+atē/ 'follow' vs. 3sg aorist mid /á+sak+s+ata/ 'idem' (4a RETRO) → sákatē vs. ásakṣata (4b 2ND PAL) → sácatē vs. ásakṣata.

5a e(:)/o(:)-TO-a(:) : Ø.

5b VzC-TO-V̄C: Ø.

5c WF CL (phon cond): masc sg pres part nom /bhárant+s/ 'carrying' vs. acc /bhárant+am/ (WF-CL) → bháran vs. bhárantam.

6 V##V-TO-V̄ (phon cond): 3sg pres mid /na##ā́stē/ 'he does not sit' (V##V-TO-V̄) → nā́stē.

7a MON (phon cond): /dáśa##ihi/ '10 here' (MON) → dáśēhi.

7b NASAL ASSIM (phon cond): /pánca/ '5' (NASAL ASSIM) → pañca.

7c s-ASSIM (phon cond): /dēvás ca/ 'and a god' (s-ASSIM) → dēváś ca.

7d STOP ASSIM (phon cond): 3sg imperf /ábharat aśvam/ 'he brought a horse' (STOP ASSIM) → ábharad aśvam.

8a ɟʰ-TO-h (morph cond and applying rarely): /vāk ghi/ 'the word indeed' vs. /ghi/ 'indeed' standing alone (7d STOP ASSIM) → vāg ghi vs. ghi (ɟʰ-TO-h applying only to the latter form) → vāg ghi vs. hi.

8b s/r CHANGES (phon cond): /dēvás karṓti/ 'a god does it' (s/r CHANGES) → dēváh karṓti.

8c V-SON ALT (phon cond): /yadi ētat/ 'if this' (V-SON ALT) → yadyētat.

9a bʰ/dʰ-TO-h: Ø.

9b l/r ALT: Ø.

9c LATER V## (phon cond): /tē api/ 'these also' (LATER V##) → tē 'pi.

9d NASAL DELE (phon cond): acc sg /dēvám ca/ 'and a god' (NASAL DELE) → dēváṁ ca.

10 w-TO-v : Ø.

11.1 SKT STRESS (morph cond): nom sg /dēvas/ 'god' and voc sg /dēva/ (SKT STRESS) → devás and dḗva.

11.2 SKT STRESS (phon cond): nom sg /dēvas/ and voc sg /dēva/ (SKT STRESS) → dḗvas and dḗva.

IV Historical Sanskrit Morphology

A. Overview

B. Sanskrit Morphology

In each paradigm below the Sanskrit forms of ca. 400 BC are cited in the left-hand column and the PIE forms of perhaps 3000 BC in the right-hand column. The Sanskrit forms are those before the advent of phon cond stress, i.e. before the time of change 11.2 SKT STRESS. We assume morph cond stress, i.e. 11.1 SKT STRESS, reflects the stress of PIE.

1 Nouns

Nouns, like all inflected froms of Sanskrit, are inflected for singular, dual and plural. The cases of the substantives are nominative, vocative, accusative, genitive, locative, dative, ablative and instrumental. In the dual and plural the vocative forms are those of the nominative.

1.1 o-Class (Masculine, Neuter)

This class is the largest in the language. In most Sanskrit grammars it is called the a-class.

			Sanskrit		PIE
masc	**sg**	**nom**	dēvā́s	'god'[9]	*deiwós
		voc	dḗva		*déiwe
		acc	dēvám		*deiwóm
		gen	dēvásya		*deiwésjo[10]
		loc	dēvḗ		*deiwéi[10]
		dat	dēvā́ya		*deiwṓi+a[11]
		abl	dēvā́d		*deiwṓd
		instr	dēvḗna		*deiw+óino[12]
	du	**nom**	dēvā́u		*deiwṓu
		acc	"		"
		gen	dēváyōs		*deiw+ój+ous[13]
		loc	"		"
		dat	dēvā́bhyām		*deiwṓb^hjōm
		abl	"		"
		instr	"		"
	pl	**nom**	dēvā́s		*deiwṓs
		acc	dēvā́n		*deiwṓns[14]
		gen	dēvā́nām		*deiwṓnōm[15]
		loc	dēvḗṣu		*deiwóisu[16]
		dat	dēvḗbhyas		*deiwóib^hjos
		abl	"		"
		instr	dēvā́is		*deiwṓis[16]

The o-class neuter nouns have the same endings as the masculine except for the following:

		Sanskrit		PIE
nom/voc/acc	**sg**	yugám	'yoke'	*jugóm
	du	yugḗ		*jugói
	pl	yugā́		*jugā́[17]

The jo-class nouns have the same endings as those of the o-class. E.g., nom sg neuter ā́syam 'mouth' < PIE *ṓs+j+om.

1.2 ā-Class and Derivatively ī / ū-Class (Feminine)

		Sanskrit		PIE
sg	nom	sḗnā	'army'	*séinā
	voc	sḗnē		*séina+i[18]
	acc	sḗnām		*séinām
	gen	sḗnāyās		*séinā+jā+s[19]
	loc	sḗnāyām		*séinā+jā+m[20]
	dat	sḗnāyāi		*séinā+jā+i
	abl	sḗnāyās		*séinā+jā+s
	instr	sḗnāyā		*séinā+jā
du	nom	sḗnē		*séina+i[18]
	acc	"		"
	gen	sḗnayōs		*séina+i+ous[18]
	loc	"		"
	dat	sḗnābhyām		*séinābʰjōm
	abl	"		"
	instr	"		"
pl	nom	sḗnās		*séinās
	acc	"		*séināns[21]
	gen	sḗnānām		*séinā+n+ōm[22]
	loc	sḗnāsu		*séināsu
	dat	sḗnābhyas		*séinābʰjos
	abl	"		"
	instr	sḗnābhis		*séinābʰis

The jā-class nouns have the same endings as the ā-class. E.g.,

		Sanskrit		PIE
sg	nom	kanyā́	'girl'	*konjā́
	gen	kanyā́yās		*konjā́jās

The ā-class served as a model for the creation of the ī- and ū-class feminine nouns in Sanskrit. Their development seems to have occurred as follows: in PIE there were root-class nouns as described in 1.5.2 below whose stems ended in /ī/ or /ū/: PIE *dʰī+s 'understanding'and PIE *bʰū+s 'earth' > Skt dhīs and bhūs. Then in post-PIE but pre-Sanskrit times some of these nouns were influenced by the ā-class declension in that the /ī, ū/ was equated with the /ā/. E.g., the following ī-class noun. Here we mark ā-class endings with superscript (note) 23 and root-class endings with superscript 24.

		Sanskrit		PIE
sg	nom	dēvī́	'goddess'	*deiw+ī́[23]
	voc	dḗvi		*déiw+i[23]
	acc	dēvī́m		*deiw+ī́m[23]
	gen	dēvyā́s		*deiw+ī+ā́s[23,24]
	loc	dēvyā́m		*deiw+ī+ā́m[23,24]
	dat	dēvyā́i		*deiw+ī+ā́i
	abl	dēvyā́s		*deiw+ī+ā́s[23,24]
	instr	dēvyā́		*deiw+ī+ā́[23,24]
du	nom	dēvyā́u		*deiw+ī+ṓu[25]
	acc	"		"
	gen	dēvyṓs		*deiw+ī+óus[25]
	loc	"		"
	dat	dēvī́b^{h}yām		*deiw+ī́+b^{h}jōm[25]
	abl	"		"
pl	nom	dēvyā́s		*deiw+ī+ā́s[23,24]
	acc	dēvī́s		*deiw+ī́+s[23]
	gen	dēvī́nām		*deiw+ī́+nōm[25]
	loc	dēvī́ṣu		*deiw+ī́+su[25]
	dat	dēvī́b^{h}yas		*deiw+ī́+b^{h}jos[25]
	abl	"		"
	instr	dēvī́b^{h}is		*deiw+ī́+b^{h}is[25]

The fem ū-class paradigm is formed in the same way as the ī-class in that /u(:)/ replaces /a(:)/. The endings are those of the ī-class except for the nominative singular which comes from the root class, not the ā-class. E.g.,

		Sanskrit		PIE
sg	nom	vadhū́s	'woman'	*wed^{h}ū́+s[26]
	voc	vádhu		*wéd^{h}u[27]
	acc	vadhū́m		*wed^{h}ū́+m[27]
	gen	vadhvā́s		*wed^{h}ū+ā́s[27,28]

Burrow (1959: 252) considers the endings of ā-, ī- and ū-class nouns as deriving from PIE short vowels plus a laryngeal. E.g., PIE nom sg *séinah 'army', *deiwíh 'goddess' and *wed^{h}úhs 'woman' (ev) > Skt sḗnā, dēvī́ and vadhū́s.

1.3 i-Class (Masculine, Feminine, Neuter)

The following is a masc noun.

			Sanskrit		PIE
masc	sg	nom	agnís	'fire'	*egnís[29]
		voc	ágnē		*égnei[29]
		acc	agním		*egním
		gen	agnḗs		*egnéis
		loc	agnā́u		*egnḗu[30]
		dat	agnáyē		*egnéi+ei[31]
		abl	agnḗs		*egnéis
		instr	agnínā		*egnínē/ō[29]
	du	nom	agnī́		*egnī́[32]
		acc	"		"
		gen	agnyṓs		*egni+óus
		loc	"		"
		dat	agníbhyām		*egníb^{h}jōm
		abl	"		"
		instr	"		"
	pl	nom	agnáyas		*egnéi+es
		acc	agnī́n		*egnī́+ns[32]
		gen	agnīnā́m		*egnī+n+ṓm[32,33]
		loc	agníṣu		*egnísu
		dat	agníbhyas		*egníb^{h}jos
		abl	"		"
		instr	agníbhis		*egníb^{h}is

The fem i-class nouns have the same endings as the masc agnís except that the oblique singular endings may optionally be those of the ā-class. E.g.,

		Sanskrit		PIE
sg	gen	gátyās	'act of going'	*g^{w}ḿ̥ti+ās[34,35]
	loc	gátyām		*g^{w}ḿ̥ti+ām[34]
	dat	gátyāi		*g^{w}ḿ̥ti+āi[34]
	abl	gátyās		*g^{w}ḿ̥ti+ās[34]
	instr	gátyā		*g^{w}ḿ̥ti+ā

The neuter i-class nouns have essentially the endings

		Sanskrit		PIE
sg	nom	vā́ri	'water'	*wṓri[36]
	acc	"		"
	gen	vā́riṇas		*wṓri+n+es[37]
	loc	vā́riṇi		*wṓri+n+i
du	nom	vā́riṇī		*wṓri+n+ī
pl	nom	vā́rīṇi		*wṓri+n+ə[38]
	acc	"		"

Some i-class neuter nouns do not carry the -i(:)n- throughout the paradigm, but rather for some cases follow the paradigm of nā́ma 'name', which has the Ø-grade ablaut of -Vn- in various cases. E.g.,

		Sanskrit		PIE
sg	**nom**	ákṣi	'eye'	*ókʷsi
	gen	ákṣṇas		*ókʷs+n+es[39]

1.4 u-Class (Masculine, Feminine, Neuter)

The u-class endings are historically the same as those of the i-class except where the i-class paradigm has endings in /i(:)/, the u-class has /u(:)/. The feminine nouns — like those of the i-class — generally have the same endings as the masculine nouns except that the oblique sg endings may optionally be those of the ā-class. E.g.,

			Sanskrit		PIE
masc	**sg**	**nom**	śátrus	'enemy'	*kótrus[40]
		voc	śátrō		*kótreu
		acc	śátrum		*kótrum
		gen	śátrōs		*kótreus
		loc	śátrāu		*kótrēu
		dat	śátravē		*kótreu+ei[41]
masc	**sg**	**nom**	dhēnús	'cow'	*dʰeinús
		voc	dhḗnō		*dʰéineu
		acc	dhēnúm		*dʰeinúm
		gen	dhēnvā́s		*dʰeinu+ā́s[42]
		loc	dhēnvā́m		*dʰeinu+ā́m[43]

The neuter u-class nouns — like those of the i-class — have essentially the endings of the Vn-class neuter nā́ma 'name' under 1.5.4 below. E.g.,

		Sanskrit		PIE
sg	**nom**	mádhu	'honey'	*médʰu
	acc	"		"
	gen	mádhunas		*médʰu+n+es
	loc	mádhuni		*médʰu+n+i
du	**nom**	mádhunī		*médʰu+n+ī
pl		mádhuni		*médʰu+n+ə

The declension of u-class mádhu is totally analogous to that of i-class vā́ri 'water' in 1.3 above.

1.5 Athematic Classes

The masculine and feminine nouns of these classes have the same endings.

1.5.1 Ø-Class (Masculine, Feminine, Neuter)

The following is a masculine noun.

			Sanskrit		PIE
masc	**sg**	**nom**	pā́t	'foot'	*pḗd+s[44]
		voc	pā́d		*pḗd[44]
		acc	pádam		*pédm̥[45]
		gen	padás		*pedés[46]
		loc	padí		*pedí
		dat	padé̄		*pedéi
		abl	padás		*pedés
		instr	padā́		*pedḗ
	du	**nom**	pā́dāu		*pḗdōu
		acc	"		"
		gen	padṓs		*pedóus
		loc	"		"
		dat	padbhyā́m		*pedb^{h}jṓm
		abl	"		"
		instr	"		"
	pl	**nom**	pā́das		*pḗdes
		acc	padás		*pedń̥s[47]
		gen	padā́m		*pedṓm
		loc	patsú		*ped+sú
		dat	padbhyás		*pedb^{h}jós
		abl	"		"
		instr	padbhís		*pedb^{h}ís

Feminine nouns have the same endings as masculine ones. E.g.,

		Sanskrit		PIE
sg	**nom**	vā́k	'voice'	*wṓk+s[48]
du	**acc**	vā́cam		*wṓk+m̥
pl	**gen**	vācás		*wōk+és[48]

The few neuter nouns of this class have the same endings as the masculine and feminine except for the following cases:

		Sanskrit		PIE
sg	**nom/acc**	jágat	'world'	*g^{w}ég^{w}n̥t[49]
du		jágatī		*g^{w}ég^{w}n̥tī
pl		jáganti		*g^{w}ég^{w}ontə[49,50]

1.5.2 Root Class (Masculine, Feminine)

These nouns have roots ending in long vowels or diphthongs. Most of these roots are monosyllabic. The nouns take the athematic endings of the Ø-class in 1.5.1. (We take the term "root" noun from Whitney 1960: 124.) E.g., the following feminine noun:

		Sanskrit		PIE
sg	nom	bhū́s	'earth'	*b^{h}ū́+s[51,52]
	voc	"		"[51]
	acc	bhúvam		*b^{h}ū́+m̥
	gen	bhuvás		*b^{h}ū+és[52,53]
	loc	bhuví		*b^{h}ū+í[53]
	dat	bhuvḗ		*b^{h}ū+éi[53]
du	dat	bhūbhyā́m		*b^{h}ū+b^{h}jṓm
pl	loc	bhūṣú		*b^{h}ū+sú[54]

Roots ending in diphthongs have the endings of bhū́s 'earth' cited above. E.g., the following fem noun:

		Sanskrit		PIE
sg	nom	nā́us	'ship'	*nā́u+s
	voc	"		"
	acc	nā́vam		*nā́u+m̥
	gen	nāvás		*nāu+és[55]

Ablaut occurs in two nouns of this class, the masc dyā́us 'day', the fem gā́us 'cow'. E.g.,

			Sanskrit		PIE
masc	sg	nom	dyā́us	'day'	*diḗu+s[56]
		acc	dívam		*díØu+m̥
		gen	divás		*diØu+és[57]
	pl	dat	dyúbhyas		*diØú+b^{h}jos[58]
fem	sg	nom	gā́us	'cow'	*g^{w}ṓu+s
		acc	gā́m		*g^{w}ṓu+m̥[59]
		loc	gávi		*g^{w}ou+í[60]
	pl	nom	gāvás		*g^{w}ṓu+és

Some root-class nouns are bisyllabic. Their stems end in /i(:)/ and /u(:)/; and these segments are stressed throughout the paradigm. E.g., the following feminine nouns:

			Sanskrit		PIE
fem	sg	nom	nadī́s	'river'	*ned+ī́+s[61]
			tanū́s	'body'	*ten+ū́+s[61]
		gen	nadías		*ned+ī́+es[61]
			tanúas		*ten+ū́+es[61]

1.5.3 tVr-Class (Masculine, Feminine, Neuter)

Nouns of this class denote family members such as 'father, mother' or agent nouns such as 'doer, giver'. The masculine and feminine nouns have the same endings, namely those of the Ø-class under 1.5.1. (It is possible that the nom singular masculine and fem of this class did not have the *-s ending in the pre-Sanskrit antecedent.) The neuter is rare and usually occurs adjectivally as in Skt dātṛ́ 'that which gives'. The vowel in the –tVr suffix can appear in all three ablaut grades: Ø; normal /e, o/; or lengthened /ē, ō/. E.g., the following masculine noun:

		Sanskrit		PIE
sg	nom	pitā́	'father'	*pətḗr+s[62]
	voc	pítar		*pə́ter
	acc	pitáram		*pətér+m̥
	gen	pitúr		*pətŗ́+es[63]
pl	nom	pitáras		*pətér+es
	acc	pitṝ́n		*pətṛ́+ns[64]
	gen	pitṝṇā́m		*pətṛ+n+ṓm[64]
	loc	pitṛ́ṣu		*pətṛ́+su[65]

The agent nouns such as the masculine dātā́ 'giver' can have ablaut grades in the -tVr suffix which can differ from those of pitā́ 'father'. E.g.,

		Sanskrit		PIE
sg	acc	dātā́ram	'giver'	*dōtḗrm̥
		pitáram	'father'	*pətérm̥

The neuter endings differ from those of the masculine and feminine only in the following nominative/accusative case forms:

	Sanskrit		PIE
sg	dātṛ́	'that which gives'	*dōtṛ́
du	dātṛ́ṇī		*dōtṛ́+n+ī[66]
pl	dātṛ́ṇi		*dōtṛ́+n+ə[67]

1.5.4 Vn-Class (Masculine, Feminine, Neuter)

The endings of this class are those of the other athematic nouns, but without *-s in the nominative singular antecedent. The vowel in the –Vn suffix can occur in Ø-, ē/ō-grade ablaut. E.g., the following masculine noun:

		Sanskrit		PIE
sg	nom	rā́jā	'king'	*rḗgōn[68]
	voc	rā́jan		*rḗgon
	acc	rā́jānam		*rḗgēn+m̥[69]
	gen	rā́jñas		*rḗgn+es[70]
	loc	rā́jñi		*rḗgn+i
		rā́jani		*rḗgen+i

		Sanskrit		PIE
pl	nom	rā́janas	'kings'	*rḗgon+es
	acc	rā́jñas		*rḗgn+n̥s[71]
	dat	rā́jabhyas		*rḗgn̥+bʰjos

The neuter nouns have the same endings as rā́jā except for the following cases:

		Sanskrit		PIE
nom/acc	sg	nā́ma	'name'	*nṓm+n̥[72]
	du	nā́mnī		*nṓm+n+ī
	pl	nā́māni		*nṓm+ēn+ə[73]

There are also j+Vn-class nouns. Since the ablaut grade of the Vn-suffix is Ø, the Sanskrit version appears as -in. The endings are those of the other Vn-class nouns. E.g., the following masculine noun:

		Sanskrit		PIE
sg	nom	hastī́	'elephant'[74]	*gʰestj+V́n[75]
	voc	hástin		*gʰéstj+n[75]
	acc	hastínam		*gʰestj́+n+m̥
	gen	hastínas		*gʰestj́+n+es
pl	dat	hastíbhyas		*gʰestj́+n+bʰjos[76]

1.5.5 Vnt-Class (Masculine, Feminine, Neuter)

This class consists of adjectives, including present active participles. The masculine and neuter endings are those of the Ø-class under 1.5.1. The feminine adjectives take the ī-class endings under 1.2. E.g.,

			Sanskrit		PIE
sg	masc	nom	bháran	'carrying'	*bʰéront+s[77]
		acc	bhárantam		*bʰéront+m̥
		gen	bháratas		*bʰérn̥t+es[78]
	neute	nom	bhárat		*bʰérn̥t[79]
	fem	nom	bhárantī		*bʰéront+ī[80]

1.5.6 Vs-Class (Masculine, Feminine, Neuter)

The masculine and feminine members of this class are for the most part adjectives. The endings are those of the other masculine and feminine athematic nouns, but with -Ø instead of -s in the nominative singular. The neuter endings are those of the other athematic neuter nouns.

An example of the masculine/feminine declension is the following adjective.

		Sanskrit		PIE
sg	nom	sumánās	'well-disposed'	*su+mén+ōs[81]
	acc	sumánasam		*su+mén+os+m̥

Examples of the neuter declension are the following nouns.

		Sanskrit		PIE
sg	**nom**	mánas	'mind'	*mén+os[82]
		havís	'oblation'	*g^{h}ew+ís[82]
		cákṣus	'eye'	*k^{w}éks+us[82]
	gen	mánasas		*mén+os+es
		havíṣas		*g^{h}ew+ís+es[83]
		cákṣuṣas		*k^{w}éks+us+es
pl	**nom**	mánāṁsi		*mén+ōns+ə[84]
		havī́ṁṣi		*g^{h}ew+ī́ns+ə[84,85]
		cákṣūṁṣi		*k^{w}éks+ūns+ə[84,85]
	dat	mánōbhyas		*mén+os+b^{h}jos[86]
		havírbhyas		*g^{h}ew+ís+b^{h}jos[87]
		cákṣurbhyas		*k^{w}éks+us+b^{h}jos
	loc	mánahsu		*mén+os+su[88]
		havíhṣu		*g^{h}ew+ís+su[89]
		cákṣuhṣu		*k^{w}éks+us+su

2 Adjectives

There is no difference between adjective and noun declension. The adjectives occur in the same declensional classes and with the same endings as the nouns. Examples follow.

2.1 o- and ā-Class

The o-class is masculine and neuter; the ā-class (and optionally ī-class) is feminine.

			Sanskrit		PIE
nom	**sg**	**masc**	pāpás	'evil'	*pēpós
		fem	pāpā́ or pāpī́		*pēpā́ or *pēpī́
		neuter	pāpám		*pēpóm

2.2 i-Class

			Sanskrit		PIE
nom	**sg**	**masc**	śúcis	'pure'	*kú$k^{w}$is
		fem	"		"
		neuter	śúci		*kúk^{w}i

2.3 u-Class

			Sanskrit		PIE
nom	**sg**	**masc**	tanús	'thin'	*tenús
		fem	"		"
		neuter	tanú		*tenú

2.4 Ø-Class

			Sanskrit		PIE
nom	**sg**	**masc**	cátuṣpat	'4-footed'	*k^{w}étus+pod+s[90]
		fem	cátuṣpadī		*k^{w}étus+pod+ī[91]
		neuter	cátuṣpad		*k^{w}étus+pod+Ø[92]

2.5 tVr-Class

			Sanskrit		PIE
nom	**sg**	**masc**	dhātā́	'founding'	*dʰō+tḗr+s[93]
		fem	dhātrī́		*dʰō+tr+ī́
		neuter	dhātŕ̥̥		*dʰō+tŕ̥[94]

2.6 Vn-Class

			Sanskrit		PIE
nom	**sg**	**masc**	balī́	'strong'	*belj́+Vn[95]
		fem	balī́nī		*belj́+n+ī[96]
		neuter	balí		*belj́+Ø[97]

2.7 Vnt-Class

See the paradigm of bháran 'carrying' under 1.5.5 above.

2.8 Vs-class

See the paradigm of sumánās 'well-disposed' under 1.5.6 above.

2.9 Comparison

There are two types of comparative and superlative formation. Adjectives are lexically marked as taking the one type or the other. (Unless otherwise marked, the adjectives cited below are the nominative singular masculine forms.)

2.9.1 -tar- and -tam-

This is the more frequent type. E.g.,

	Sanskrit		PIE
pos	priyás	'dear'	*prijós[98]
comp	príyataras	'dearer'	*príjo+ter+os[99]
sup	príyatamas	'dearest'	*príjo+tem+os[99]
pos	mahā́n	'large'	*megʰ+ṓnt+s[100]
comp	máhattaras	'larger'	*mégʰ+n̥t+ter+os[99,101]
sup	máhattamas	'largest'	*mégʰ+n̥t+tem+os[99]

2.9.2 -īyāṁs- and -ṣṭh-

This is the less frequent type of comparative and superlative formation. E.g.,

		Sanskrit		PIE
pos		mr̥dús	'soft'	*ml̥dús[102]
com	**nom**	mrádīyān		*mléd+ījōns+s[103]
	acc	mrádīyāṁ		*mléd+ījōns+m̥[104]
	gen	mrádīyasas		*mléd+ījn̥s+es[105]
sup	**nom**	mrádīṣṭhas		*mléd+isth+os[106]

3 Adverbs

There are no specific suffixes for forming deadjeetival or denominal adverbs. Rather, various case endings are used.

		Sanskrit		PIE
sg	acc	satyám	'truly'	*sn̥t+j+óm[107]
	abl	kásmād	'why, from what'	*kʷósm+ōd[108]
	instr	divā́	'by day'	*diw+ḗ
pl	instr	śánakāis	'slowly'	*kónekʷ+ōis[109]

4 Numerals

4.1 Cardinals

The cardinal numerals from 1 through 19 are in the main used adjectivally and agree in case (and sometimes in gender) with their head nouns. From 20 on they are usually considered nouns. They either take the head noun as a dependent genitive; or they may be in the singular and take the same case as the head noun. (In our examples below we cite unless otherwise noted the nominative masculine forms.)

	Sanskrit	PIE
'1'	ḗkas	*óikʷ+os

The endings are those of the o- and ā-class adjectives.

	Sanskrit	PIE
'2'	dvā́u	*dw+ṓu

The endings are those of the dual of o- and ā-class adjectives.

			Sanskrit	PIE
'3'	masc	nom	tráyas	*tréj+es[110]
	fem		tisrás	*tisr+és[111]
'4'	masc	nom	catvā́ras	*kʷetwṓres[112]
		acc	catúras	*kʷetúr+n̥s[113]
	neuter	nom	catvā́ri	*kʷetwṓr+ə[112]
	fem	nom	cátasras	*kʷétosr+es[114]
'5'	masc	nom	páñca	*pénkʷe
		instr	pañcábhis	*penkʷé+bʰis[115]
'6'	masc	nom	ṣaṭ	*seks[116]
		instr	ṣaḍbhís	*seks+bʰís[117]
'7'	masc	nom	saptá	*septḿ̥

			Sanskrit	PIE
'8'	masc	nom	aṣṭáu	*oktṓu[118]
		instr	aṣṭābhís	*oktōb^{h}ís[119]
	neuter	instr	aṣṭabhís	*oktob^{h}ís[119]
'9'	masc	nom	náva	*nówm̥
'10'			dáśa	*dékm̥
'11'			ḗkādaśa	*óik^{w}ō+dekm̥[120]
'12'			dvā́daśa	*dwṓ+dekm̥[120]
'20'			viṁśatís	*wi+n+km̥+t+ís[121]
'30'			triṁśátis	*tri+n+kḿ̥+t+is
'40'			catvāriṁśátis	*k^{w}etwōr+n+kḿ̥+t+is
'50'			pañcāśátis	*penk^{w}ē+kḿ̥+t+is
'60'			ṣaṣṭís	*seks+t+ís

The numerals from '60' through '90' are i-class nouns, but formed without the *-km̥- constituent.

			Sanskrit	PIE
'70'	masc	nom	septatís	*septm̥+t+ís
'80'			aśītís	*ok+ī+t+ís[122]
'90'			navatís	*nowm̥+t+ís
'100'			śatám	*kn̥tóm[123]
'1000'			sahásram	*sm̥+g^{h}éslom[124]

4.2 Ordinals

These are o- and ā-class adjectives. We cite the nominative singular masculine form.

	Sanskrit	PIE
'1st'	prathamás	*pro+them+ós[125]
'2nd'	dvitī́yas	*dwi+tī́j+os
'3rd'	tr̥tī́yas	*tr̥+tī́j+os
'4th'	caturthás	*k^{w}etur+th+ós[126]
'5th'	pañcamás	*penk^{w}e+m+ós[127]
'11th'	ēkādaśás	*oik^{w}ōdekm̥+ós[128]
'20th'	viṁśás or viṁśatitamás	*wink+ós[129] or *winkm̥+ti+tem+ós[129]

5 Pronouns

5.1 First Person

		Sanskrit		PIE
sg	**nom**	ahám	'I'	*egʰóm[130]
	acc	mā́m		*mḗ+m[131]
du	**nom**	āvā́m	'we two'	*ēwḗ+m[132]
	acc	"		"
pl	**nom**	vayám	'we'	*wei+óm[133]
	acc	asmā́n		*n̥s+m+ṓns[134]

3.2 Second Person

		Sanskrit		PIE
sg	**nom**	tvám	'you'	*tu+óm[135]
	acc	"		"
du	**nom**	yuvā́m	'you two'	*juw+ṓm[136]
	acc	"		"
pl	**nom**	yūyám	'you'	*jū+j+óm
	acc	yuṣmā́n		*jus+m+ṓns[137]

5.3 Third Person

There are four demonstrative pronouns meaning 'this, that, these, those'. These are tad-, idam-, adas- and the unstressed defective form *ēnam. They are as follows.

The tad-declension consists of the roots s- in the nominative singular masculine and feminine and t- elsewhere. Most of the endings are those of the o- and ā-class nouns. E.g.,

			Sanskrit		PIE
masc	**sg**	**nom**	sás	'this, that'	*s+ós[138]
		acc	tám		*t+óm[138]
		gen	tásya		*t+ésjo[138]
		loc	tásmin		*t+ésmin[139]
		dat	tásmāi		*t+ésmōi[139]
		abl	tásmād		*t+ésmōd[139]
		instr	tḗna		*t+óino[138]
	du	**nom**	tā́u		*t+ṓu[138]
		acc	"		"
		gen	táyōs		*t+ójous[138]
		loc	"		"
		dat	tā́bhyām		*t+ṓbʰjōm[138]
		abl	"		"
		instr	"		"

			Sanskrit		PIE
masc	pl	nom	tḗ	'this, that'	*t+ói[139]
		acc	tā́n		*t+ṓns[138,140]
		gen	tḗṣām		*t+óisōm[139,141]
		loc	tḗṣu		*t+óisu[138]
		dat	tḗbhyas		*t+óibʰjos
		abl	"		"
		instr	tā́is		*t+ṓis
fem	sg	nom	sā́		*s+ā́[142]
		acc	tā́m		*t+ā́m[142]
		gen	tásyās		*t+ésjās
		loc	tásyām		*t+ésjām[139]
		dat	tásyāi		*t+ésjāi
		abl	tásyās		*t+ésjās
		instr	táyā		*t+ájā[142]
	du	nom	tḗ		*t+ái[142,143]
		acc	"		"
	pl	nom	tā́s		*t+ā́s[142]
		acc	"		"
		gen	tā́sām		*t+ā́sōm[139]
		dat	tā́bhyas		*t+ā́bʰjos[142]
		abl	"		"
		instr	tā́bhis		*t+ā́bʰis[142]
neut	sg	nom	tád		*t+ód[139]
		acc	"		"
	du	nom	tḗ		*t+ói[138]
		acc	"		"
	pl	nom	tā́ni		*t+ā́nə[139,144]
		acc	"		"

The deictic idam- 'this, that' generally takes the same endings as tad- above. Some five different types of roots participate in the paradigm. Their antecedents are *ei-, *im-, *Ø-, *en- and *id-. E.g.,

			Sanskrit		PIE
masc	sg	nom	ayám	'this, that'	*ei+óm[145,146]
		acc	imám		*im+óm[147]
		gen	asyá		*Ø+esjó[148]
		instr	anḗna		*en+óino
	pl	instr	ēbhís		*ei+bʰís[146]
fem	sg	acc	iyā́m		*i+ā́m
neuter	sg	nom	idám		*id+óm[149]
		acc	"		"

The deictic adas- 'that, those' has generally the same endings as tad- above. There are four different roots: *es(ō/ā)-, *emī-, *emu(:)- and *edos-. E.g.,

			Sanskrit		PIE
masc	**sg**	**nom**	asā́u	'that, those'	*esṓ+u
		acc	amúm		*emú+m
	pl	**nom**	amī́		*emī́
		acc	amū́n		*emū́+ns
fem	**sg**	**nom**	asā́u		*esā́+u
		acc	amū́m		*emū́+m
	pl	**nom**	amū́s		*emū́+s
		acc	"		"
neuter	**sg**	**nom**	adás		*edós
		acc	"		"
	pl	**nom**	amū́ni		*emū́+nə
		acc	"		"

Finally, the unstressed defective deictic ēnam 'this, that' occurs only in the accusative, genitive, locative, and instrumental cases. The endings are those of tad- above. E.g.,

			Sanskrit		PIE
masc	**acc**	**sg**	ēnam	'that, those'	*oin+om
		pl	ēnān		*oin+ōns

5.4 Reflexive

There are two reflexive pronouns. The Vn-class masculine noun ātmán- 'soul' < PIE *ātmén- occurs in the singular and less frequently in the dual and plural. And the o- and ā-class adj sva- 'self, one's own' < PIE *swo- also occurs.

5.5 Relative

The stem is ya-, which is declined like tad- in 5.3 above. E.g.,

			Sanskrit		PIE
masc	**nom**	**sg**	yás	'who, that'	*i+ós[150]
		du	yā́u		*i+ṓu
		pl	yḗ		*i+ói

5.6 Interrogative and Indefinite

Except for the nominative/accusative singular neuter, the declension is that of tad- above. The interrogative is also used as an indefinite meaning 'whoever, whatever'. E.g.,

			Sanskrit		PIE
masc	**sg**	**nom**	kás	'whoever, whatever'	$*k^w$+ós
		acc	kám		$*k^w$+óm
fem	**sg**	**nom**	kā́		$*k^w$+ā́
		acc	kā́m		$*k^w$+ā́m
neuter	**nom/acc**	**sg**	kím		$*k^w$+ím[151]
		dual	kḗ		$*k^w$+ói
		pl	kā́ni		$*k^w$+ānə

6 Verbs

The features of the Sanskrit verb are given in the following two tables. Table i contains the variable features— namely those which can change contingent upon the context. Table ii gives the lexical or inherent features — namely those that are idiosyncratic. They indicate the particular form-class of the verb.

(i) Variable Features

The first section of this table lists the purely verbal features. The second gives the features of deverbative adjectives and nouns.

(a) Person	(b) Number	(c) Voice	(d) Mood
1. 1st	1. singular	1. active	1. indicative
2. 2nd	2. dual	2. middle[152]	2. subjunctive[153]
3. 3rd	3. plural	3. passive[154]	3. imperative[153]
			4. optative[153]
			5. injunctive[155]
			6. conditional[156]

(e) Tense Occurring in	Indicative	Subjunctive	Imperative	Optative	Injunctive	Conditional
1. present	x	x	x	x	x	
2. imperfect[157]	x					
3. perfect[157]	x	(x	x	x) [158]		
4. pluperfect	x					
5. aorist[157]	x	(x	x	x)		
6. future	x	(x	x	x)		x

(f) "Secondary" conjugations

1. intensive
2. desiderative
3. causative
4. denominative

Adjectival and Nominal Inflection

(a) Person	(b) Number	(c) Voice	(d) Mood
Ø	1. singular	1. active	1. infinitive
	2. dual	2. middle	2. participle
	3. plural	3. passive	3. gerund

(e) Tense occurring in	Infinitive	Participle	Gerund
1. present	act	act/mid	act
2. imperfect			
3. perfect		act/mid/pass	
4. pluperfect			
5. aorist			
6. future		act/mid/pass	

(ii) Inherent Features.

(a) Type	(b) Class for Present and Imperfect Formations[159]			
1. thematic[160]	1st	thematic	bhárati	'carries'
2. athematic	2nd	athematic	dvḗṣṭi	'hates'
	3rd	athematic	juhṓti	'sacrifices'
	4th	thematic	náhyati	'ties'
	5th	athematic	sunṓti	'presses out'
	6th	thematic	tudáti	'pushes'
	7th	athematic	yunákti	'joins'
	8th	athematic	tanṓti	'stretches'
	9th	athematic	badhnā́ti	'ties'
	10th	thematic	cōráyati	'steals'

In the above Tables i and ii the features in the columns are mutually exclusive. Not all the logical possibilities are realized: the notations in the (e) columns of Table i indicate which are.

The verbal endings fall into four main classes: (i) the primary endings, which occur in the present indicative and future indicative paradigms (6.1.1, 6.1.6 and 6.6 below); (ii) the secondary endings, which occur in the injunctive, imperfect, pluperfect, aorist and optative (6.1.5, 6.2, 6.4, 6.5, 6.1.4 and 6.1.9); (iii) the perfect endings (6.3); and (iv) the imperative endings (6.1.3 and 6.1.8). The subjunctive paradigms may take either primary or secondary endings in free variation.

6.1 Present

6.1.1 Present Active Indicative

As our example we cite a 1st class thematic verb.

		Sanskrit		PIE
sg	**1**	bhárāmi	'carry'	*b^{h}ér+ō+mi[161]
	2	bhárasi		*b^{h}ér+e+si
	3	bhárati		*b^{h}ér+e+ti
du	**1**	bhárāvas		*b^{h}ér+ō+wes
	2	bhárathas		*b^{h}ér+e+thes[162]
	3	bháratas		*b^{h}ér+e+tes
pl	**1**	bhárāmas		*b^{h}ér+ō+mes
	2	bháratha		*b^{h}ér+e+the[162]
	3	bháranti		*b^{h}ér+o+nti

In the following we give the defining traits of each of the ten classes of verbs cited above.

6.1.1.1 1st Class Thematic

E.g., bhárati 'carry'. The root is stressed and is usually in the normal grade (/e, o/-grade) of ablaut.

6.1.1.2 2nd Class Athematic.

E.g., dveṣṭi 'hate'. The endings are added directly to the root without the intermediate thematic vowel. The root in the singular has e/o-grade ablaut; in the dual and plural, it has Ø-grade ablaut. The stress in the singular is on the root; in the dual and plural the stress is on the ending. E.g.,

		Sanskrit		PIE
sg	**1**	dvḗṣmi	'hate'	*dwéis+mi
	3	dvḗṣṭi		*dwéis+ti[163]
du	**1**	dviṣvás		*dwis+wés
pl	**1**	dviṣmás		*dwis+més
	3	dviṣánti		*dwis+ónti[164]

6.1.1.3 3rd Class Athematic

E.g., juhṓti 'sacrifice'. The singular has e/o-grade ablaut; the dual and plural have the Ø-grade. The stress in the singular is on the root; that in the dual and plural is on the ending. These forms reduplicate the word-initial consonant plus the next vowel. E.g.,

		Sanskrit		PIE
sg	**1**	juhṓmi	'sacrifice'	*g^{h}u+g^{h}éu+mi[165]
du	**1**	juhuvás		*g^{h}u+g^{h}u+wés
pl	**1**	juhumás		*g^{h}u+g^{h}u+més

6.1.1.4 4th Class Thematic

E.g., náhyati 'tie'. These forms add -y- to the root. The endings are thematic; and the root is stressed. E.g.,

		Sanskrit		PIE
sg	**1**	náhyāmi	'tie'	*néd^h+j+ō+mi[166]
du	**1**	náhyāvas		*néd^h+j+ō+wes
pl	**1**	náhyāmas		*néd^h+j+ō+mes

6.1.1.5 5th Class Athematic

E.g., sunṓti 'press out'. These forms add the suffix *-n(e)u- plus the athematic endings to the root. The e/o-grade ablaut occurs in the suffix in the singular; the Ø-grade occurs in the dual and plural. The stress is on the suffix in the singular and on the ending in the dual and plural. E.g.,

		Sanskrit		PIE
sg	**1**	sunṓmi	'press out'	*su+néu+mi
du	**1**	sunuvás		*su+nu+wés
pl	**1**	sunumás		*su+nu+més

6.1.1.6 6th Class Thematic

E.g., tudáti 'push'. The thematic vowel and the endings are added directly to the root. The stress is on the thematic vowel throughout the paradigm. E.g.,

		Sanskrit		PIE
sg	**1**	tudā́mi	'push'	*tud+ṓ+mi
	2	tudā́si		*tud+ḗ+si
du	**1**	tudā́vas		*tud+ṓ+wes
pl	**1**	tudā́mas		*tud+ṓ+mes

6.1.1.7 7th Class Athematic

E.g., yunákti 'join'. The ablauting infix *-n(e)- is inserted within the root before its final consonant. The e/o-grade ablaut occurs in the infix in the singular; otherwise the Ø-grade occurs in the infix. The stress is on the infix in the singular and on the ending otherwise. E.g.,

		Sanskrit		PIE
sg	**1**	yunájmi	'join'	*ju+né+g+mi[167]
	2	yunákṣi		*ju+né+g+si[168]
du	**1**	yuñjvás		*ju+n+g+wés[169]
pl	**1**	yuñjmás		*ju+n+g+més

6.1.1.8 8th Class Athematic

E.g., tanṓti 'stretch'. This class is historically the same and has basically the same endings as the 5th class sunṓti 'press out' above. E.g.,

		Sanskrit		PIE
sg	1	tanṓmi	'stretch'	*tn̥+néu+mi[170]
du	1	tanuvás		*tn̥+nu+wés[171]
pl	1	tanumás		*tn̥+nu+més

6.1.1.9 9th Class Athematic

E.g., badhnā́ti 'tie'. The stressed suffix -nā́- is added to the root in the singular; in the dual and plural the suffix is -n(ī)- and the stress is on the ending. E.g.,

		Sanskrit		PIE
sg	1	badhnā́mi	'tie'	*bʰn̥dʰ+nā́+mi[172]
du	1	badhnīvás		*bʰn̥dʰ+nī+wés[173]
pl	3	badhnánti		*bʰn̥dʰ+n+ónti

6.1.1.10 10th Class Thematic

E.g., cōráyati 'steal'. The stressed suffix -áy- is added to the root. The root is usually in the e/o-ablaut grade. E.g.,

		Sanskrit		PIE
sg	1	cōráyāmi	'steal'	*kʷeur+éj+ō+mi[174]
du	1	cōráyāvas		*kʷeur+éj+ō+wes
pl	1	cōráyāmas		*kʷeur+éj+ō+mes

6.1.2 Present Active Subjunctive

The formation of the subjunctive consists of lengthening the indicative thematic vowel in thematic verbs and of inserting a thematic vowel in the indicative forms of athematic verbs. The stress is that of the present singular indicative of the respective verb. Here and in the following paradigms we shall generally cite one thematic and one athematic paradigm.

Thematic Conjugation

		Sanskrit		PIE
sg	1	bhárāni	'carry'	*bʰér+ō+ni[175]
	2	bhárās(i)		*bʰér+ē+s(i)[175]
	3	bhárāt(i)		*bʰér+ē+t(i)[175]
du	1	bhárāva		*bʰér+ō+we
	2	bhárāthas		*bʰér+ē+thes
	3	bhárātas		*bʰér+ē+tes
pl	1	bhárāma		*bʰér+ō+me
	2	bhárātha		*bʰér+ē+the
	3	bhárān		*bʰér+ō+nt[176]

Athematic Conjugation

The athematic conjugation has the long thematic vowel in all 1st person endings. Otherwise it has the corresponding short vowel of the thematic conjugation. E.g.,

		Sanskrit		PIE
sg	1	dvḗṣāni	'hate'	*dwéis+ō+ni
	2	dvḗṣas(i)		*dwéis+e+s(i)
	3	dvḗṣat(i)		*dwéis+e+t(i)

6.1.3 Present Active Imperative

Thematic Conjugation

		Sanskrit		PIE
sg	1	bhárāni	'carry'	$*b^hér+ō+ni$[177]
	2	bhára		$*b^hér+e$
	3	bháratu		$*b^hér+e+t+u$
du	1	bhárāva		$*b^hér+ō+we$[177]
	2	bháratam		$*b^hér+e+tom$
	3	bháratām		$*b^hér+e+tām$
pl	1	bhárāma		$*b^hér+ō+me$[177]
	2	bhárata		$*b^hér+e+te$
	3	bhárantu		$*b^hér+o+nt+u$

Athematic Conjugation

The athematic conjugation is similar. Aside from the 1st person forms, which are subjunctives, the endings lack a thematic vowel. E.g.,

		Sanskrit		PIE
sg	1	dvḗṣāni	'hate'	*dwéis+ō+ni
	2	dviḍḍhí		$*dwis+d^hí$[178]
	3	dvḗṣṭu		*dwéis+t+u

6.1.4 Present Active Optative

Thematic Conjugation

		Sanskrit		PIE
sg	1	bhárēyam	'carry'	$*b^hér+oi+om$[179]
	2	bhárēs		$*b^hér+oi+s$[180]
	3	bhárēt		$*b^hér+oi+t$

		Sanskrit		PIE
du	1	bhárēva	'carry'	*bʰér+oi+we
	2	bhárētam		*bʰér+oi+tom
	3	bhárētām		*bʰér+oi+tām
pl	1	bhárēma		*bʰér+oi+me
	2	bhárēta		*bʰér+oi+te
	3	bhárēyur		*bʰér+oi+ur [179.181]

Athematic Conjugation

The athematic conjugation has the same endings as the thematic. However, the athematic optative marker is –yā́-, not the thematic -ē-. E.g.,

		Sanskrit		PIE
sg	1	dviṣyā́m	'hate'	*dwis+jḗ+m [182]
	2	dviṣyā́s		*dwis+jḗ+s

6.1.5 Present Active Injunctive

These forms occur rarely by classical times. Although we have designated the injunctive as "present active", it is often used in a negative imperative or as an atemporal form denoting an action or state of being without specifying its exact time. The forms are those of the imperfect active (6.2.1 below), but without the augment. E.g.,

		Sanskrit		PIE
sg	1	bharam	'carry'	*bʰer+om

6.1.6 Present Middle Indicative

Thematic Conjugation

		Sanskrit		PIE
sg	1	bhárē	'carry'	*bʰér+ai
	2	bhárasē		*bʰér+e+s+ai [183]
	3	bháratē		*bʰér+e+tai
du	1	bhárāvahē		*bʰér+ō+wodʰ+ai [184]
	2	bhárēthē		*bʰér+ai+th+ai
	3	bhárētē		*bʰér+ai+t+ai
pl	1	bhárāmahē		*bʰér+ō+medʰ+ai
	2	bháradhvē		*bʰér+e+dʰw+ai
	3	bhárantē		*bʰér+o+nt+ai

Athematic Conjugation

		Sanskrit		PIE
sg	1	dviṣḗ	'hate'	*dwis+ái
	2	dvikṣḗ		*dwis+s+ái[185]
	3	dviṣṭḗ		*dwis+t+ái[186]
du	1	dviṣváhē		*dwis+wód^h+ai
	2	dviṣā́thē		*dwis+ḗ+th+ai
	3	dviṣā́tē		*dwis+ḗ+t+ai
pl	1	dviṣmáhē		*dwis+méd^h+ai
	2	dviḍḍhvḗ		*dwis+d^{h}w+ái[187]
	3	dviṣatḗ		*dwis+n̥t+ái

6.1.7 Present Middle Subjunctive

Thematic Conjugation

		Sanskrit		PIE
sg	1	bhárāi	'carry'	*b^{h}ér+āi
	2	bhárāsē/sāi		*b^{h}ér+ēs+a(:)i[188]
	3	bhárātē/tāi		*b^{h}ér+et+a(:)i[188]
du	1	bhárāvahāi		*b^{h}ér+ō+wod^h+āi
	2	bhárāithē		*b^{h}ér+āi+th+ai
	3	bhárāitē		*b^{h}ér+āi+t+ai
pl	1	bhárāmahāi		*b^{h}ér+ō+med^h+āi
	2	bhárādhvāi		*b^{h}ér+ē+d^{h}w+āi
	3	bhárāntāi		*b^{h}ér+ō+nt+āi

Athematic Conjugation

		Sanskrit		PIE
sg	1	dviṣā́i	'hate'	*dwis+ā́i
	2	dviṣásē		*dwis+és+ai
	3	dviṣā́itē		*dwis+ā́i+t+ai
du	1	dviṣávahē/hāi		*dwis+ó+wod^h+a(:)i
	2	dviṣā́ithē		*dwis+ā́ith+ai
	3	dviṣā́itē		*dwis+ā́it+ai
pl	1	dviṣā́mahē/hāi		*dwis+ṓ+med^h+a(:)i
	2	dviṣádhvē/vāi		*dwis+é+d^{h}w+a(:)i
	3	dviṣántē/tāi		*dwis+ó+nt+a(:)i

6.1.8 Present Middle Imperative

Thematic Conjugation

		Sanskrit		PIE
sg	1	bhárāi	'carry'	*b^hér+āi
	2	bhárasva		*b^hér+es+we
	3	bháratām		*b^hér+et+ām
du	1	bhárāvahāi		*b^hér+ōwed^h+āi
	2	bhárēthām		*b^hér+aith+ām
	3	bhárētām		*b^hér+ait+ām
pl	1	bhárāmahāi		*b^hér+ōmed^h+āi
	2	bháradhvam		*b^hér+ed^hw+om
	3	bhárantām		*b^hér+ont+ām

Athematic Conjugation

The athematic verbs have basically the same endings as those of the thematic class, but without the thematic vowel. E.g.,

		Sanskrit		PIE
sg	3	dviṣṭā́m	'hate'	*dwis+t+ā́m

6.1.9 Present Middle Optative

Thematic Conjugation

		Sanskrit		PIE
sg	1	bhárēya	'carry'	*b^hér+oi+a[189]
	2	bhárēthās		*b^hér+oi+thēs
	3	bhárēta		*b^hér+oi+te
du	1	bhárēvahi		*b^hér+oi+wod^hi
	2	bhárēyāthām		*b^hér+oi+ēthām[189]
	3	bhárēyātām		*b^hér+oi+ētām[189]
pl	1	bhárēmahi		*b^hér+oi+med^hi
	2	bhárēdhvam		*b^hér+oi+d^hwem
	3	bhárēran		*b^hér+oi+r+ont

Athematic Conjugation

The athematic conjugation has the same endings as the thematic. However, the opt marker is -ī- , not -ē- . E.g.,

		Sanskrit		PIE
sg	1	dviṣīyá	'hate'	*dwis+ī+á[190]
	2	dviṣīthā́s		*dwis+ī+thḗs

6.1.10 Present Passive

The present passive in all moods is formed by suffixing -yV- to the Ø-grade ablaut of the root. The endings are those of the middle. (In traditional Sanskrit grammars the passive is usually considered one of the "secondary" conjugations as described in 6.7 below.) E.g.,

		Sanskrit		PIE
3sg	ind	badhyátē	'be tied'	*b^{h}n̥d^h+j+étai
	subj	badhyā́tē		*b^{h}n̥d^h+j+ḗtai
	imp	badhyátām		*b^{h}n̥d^h+j+étām
	opt	badhyḗta		*b^{h}n̥d^h+j+óite

6.2 Imperfect

This tense is formed by prefixing an augment vowel, which is always stressed, and then by suffixing to the root the "secondary" endings (as defined under 6 above). The imperfect occurs only in the indicative.

6.2.1 Imperfect Active Indicative

Thematic Conjugation

		Sanskrit		PIE
sg	1	ábharam	'carry'	*é+b^{h}er+o+m
	2	ábharas		*é+b^{h}er+e+s
	3	ábharat		*é+b^{h}er+e+t
du	1	ábharāva		*é+b^{h}er+ō+we
	2	ábharatam		*é+b^{h}er+e+tom
	3	ábharatām		*é+b^{h}er+e+tām
pl	1	ábharāma		*é+b^{h}er+ō+me
	2	ábharata		*é+b^{h}er+e+te
	3	ábharan		*é+b^{h}er+o+nt

Athematic Conjugation

The athematic conjugation has the same endings as the thematic, but lacks the thematic vowel in the 2nd /3rd singular, all dual forms and the 1st /2nd plural E.g.,

		Sanskrit		PIE
sg	1	ádvēṣam	'hate'	*é+dweis+o+m[191]
	2	ádvēṭ		*é+dweis+s[192]
	3	ádvēṭ		*é+dweis+t[192]
du	1	ádviṣva		*é+dwis+we[193]
pl	1	ádviṣma		*é+dwis+me[193]
	3	ádviṣan		*é+dwis+o+nt[191,193]

6.2.2 Imperfect Middle Indicative

Thematic Conjugation

		Sanskrit		PIE
sg	1	ábharē	'carry'	*é+b^{h}er+ai
	2	ábharathās		*é+b^{h}er+e+thās
	3	ábharata		*é+b^{h}er+e+to
du	1	ábharāvahi		*é+b^{h}er+ō+wod^{h}i
	2	ábharēthām		*é+b^{h}er+ai+thām
	3	ábharētām		*é+b^{h}er+ai+tām
pl	1	ábharāmahi		*é+b^{h}er+ō+med^{h}i
	2	ábharadhvam		*é+b^{h}er+e+d^{h}wom
	3	ábharanta		*é+b^{h}er+o+nto

Athematic Conjugation

The athematic conjugation is similar, but generally lacks the thematic vowels. E.g.,

		Sanskrit		PIE
sg	1	ádviṣi	'hate'	*é+dwis+i
	3	ádviṣṭa		*é+dwis+to
du	2	ádviṣāthām		*é+dwis+ē+thām[194]
	3	ádviṣātām		*é+dwis+ē+tām[194]
pl	3	ádviṣata		*é+dwis+n̥to

6.2.3 Imperfect Passive Indicative

The imperfect pass is formed like the present passive as described under 6.1.10. That is, the middle endings are added to the augmented imperfect stem. E.g.,

	Sanskrit		PIE
3sg	ábadhyātē	'was tied'	*é+b^{h}n̥d^h+jetai

6.3 Perfect (PERFECT)

The perfect is formed in the same way for any verb regardless of its particular class. The antecedent PIE rule for perfect formation is in basic outline this:

$$\#\#\ [C_o^n\ V\ \ldots]\ \rightarrow\ \#\#\ C_o^n\ V\ \text{or}\ e\ [C_o^n\ V\ \ldots]$$

##	[C_o^n V ...]	→	## C_o^n V	or e	[C_o^n V ...]
	verb root				verb root
1	2 3		1 2' 3'		2 3

That is, any root-initial consonant cluster C_o^n is reduplicated word-initially (over 2') and followed by either the root vowel or /e/ (over 3'). The stress is on the root in the perfect active singular and on the ending otherwise. In the perfect active singular the root usually has normal /e, o/ or lengthened /ē, ō/ ablaut; in the other forms the root has Ø-grade ablaut. The former are labled "strong forms"; the latter are "weak forms".

Some examples of 1st singular perfect formations are these:

(a) PIE *tud- 'push' (the perfect rule, PERFECT, applying synchronically) → *tu+téud+a (5a e(:)/o(:)-TO-a(:) and 7a MON) > Skt tutṓda.

(b) PIE *gʷom- 'go' (PERFECT) → *gʷe+gʷóm+a (3 DELAB) > *gegóma (4b 2ND PAL) > *ɟegóma (5a e(:)/o(:)-TO-a(:)) > Skt jagáma.

(c) PIE *bʰū- 'be' (PERFECT) → *bʰe+bʰū́+a, phonetically *bʰebʰū́wa (2b GRASSMANN) > *bebʰū́wa (5a e(:)/o(:)-TO-a(:)) > *babʰū́wa (10 w-TO-v) > Skt babhū́va.

Roots beginning with vowels reduplicate with either /e/ or the root vowel. E.g.,

(d) IE *ed- 'eat' (PERFECT) → *e+éd+a, phonetically *ḗda (5a e(:)/o(:)-TO-a(:)) > Skt ā́da.

(e) PIE *is- 'wish' (PERFECT and ablaut) → *i+óis+a, phonetically *ijóisa (4a RETRO, 5a e(:)/o(:)-TO-a(:), 7a MON) > Skt iyḗṣa. The 1st plural is PIE *i+is+imé, phonetically *īsimé (4a RETRO, 5a e(:)/o(:)-TO-a(:)) > Skt īṣimá.

(f) PIE *us- 'burn' (PERFECT) → 1st singular *u+óus+a, phonetically *uwóusa, and 1st plural *u+us+imé, phonetically *ūsimé (4a RETRO) > *uwóuṣa and *ūṣimé (5a e(:)/o(:)-TO-a(:) and 7a MON) > *uwṓuṣa and *ūṣimá (10 w-TO-v) > Skt uvṓṣa and īṣimá.

Some Sanskrit roots beginning with /v/ seem to have reduplicated without the usual vowel. E.g.,

(g) PIE *wōk- 'speak' (PERFECT) → 1sg perf *w+wṓk+a (PIE 3.1.2c i-j/u-w ALT applying synchronically) → *uwṓka (2a 1ST PAL) > *uwṓša (5a e(:)/o(:)-TO-a(:)) > *uwā́ša (restructuring of /š/ to /č/, on which see 4b 2ND PAL) > *uwā́ča (10 w-TO-v) > Skt uvā́ca.

At least one perfect beginning with Skt /v/ has no reduplication: i.e.,

(h) PIE 1sg *wóid+a 'have seen, know' (ev) > Skt vḗda.

In classical Sanskrit the perfect occurs only in the indicative. In the earlier Vedic the perfect can sometimes occur in other moods beside the indicative. Such forms are constructed from the perfect stem plus the respective athematic endings. E.g., PIE 2sg perf act subj *bʰu+bʰóud+es 'know' where *-es is the present active subjunctive ending under 6.1.2 above (ev) > Skt bubṓdhas.

6.3.1 Perfect Active Indicative

		Sanskrit		PIE
sg	1	tutṓda	'push'	*tu+téud+a[195]
	2	tutṓditha		*tu+téud+(i)tha[196]
	3	tutṓda		*tu+téud+e
du	1	tutudivá		*tu+tud+(i)wé
	2	tutudáthur[197]		*tu+tud+éthur
	3	tutudátur		*tu+tud+étur
pl	1	tutudimá		*tu+tud+(i)mé
	2	tutudá		*tu+tud+é
	3	tutudúr		*tu+tud+úr

6.3.2 Perfect Middle Indicative

		Sanskrit		PIE
sg	**1**	tutudḗ	'push'	*tu+tud+ái
	2	tutudiṣḗ		*tu+tud+(i)sái[198]
	3	tutudḗ		*tu+tud+ái
du	**1**	tutudiváhē		*tu+tud+(i)wód^{h}ai[198]
	2	tutudā́thē		*tu+tud+ḗthai
	3	tutudā́tē		*tu+tud+ḗtai
pl	**1**	tutudimáhē		*tu+tud+(i)méd^{h}ai[198]
	2	tutudidhḗ		*tu+tud+(i)d^{h}ái[198]
	3	tutudirḗ		*tu+tud+(i)rái[198]

6.4 Pluperfect

These forms occur rarely in early Sanskrit. They are constructed from the imperfect augment plus the reduplicated perfect stem plus the usually thematic endings of the imperfect as given under 6.2.1 above. E.g., the following 1st singular pluperfect indicative form:

	Sanskrit		PIE
1sg	ájagrabham	'had seized'	*é+g^{h}e+g^{h}rob^h+om[199]

6.5 Aorist

There are seven types of aorist formation. None of them is determined by any of the ten verb classes cited under 6 above. All aorist paradigms are constructed as follows: the stressed augment Skt á- plus the verb root in various degrees of ablaut plus one of the seven aorist formations noted below plus the respective thematic or athematic endings which we cite under 6.5.2 and 6.5.3 below. The following examples are 3rd singular indicative forms.

6.5.1 Aorist Formations

6.5.1.1 Root Aorist (Athematic)

This paradigm consists of the augment plus the root plus the athematic ending. E.g.,

	Sanskrit		PIE
3sg	ádāt	'give'	*é+dōt

6.5.1.2 a-Aorist (Thematic)

This paradigm consists of the augment plus the root plus the thematic vowel plus the ending. E.g.,

	Sanskrit		PIE
3sg	ágamat	'go'	*é+g^{w}om+e+t

6.5.1.3 Reduplicated Aorist (Thematic)

This paradigm consists of the augment plus the reduplicative syllable plus the root plus the ending. E.g.,

	Sanskrit		PIE
3sg	ápaptat	'fall'	*é+pe+pt+et

6.5.1.4 Sigmatic s-Aorist (Athematic)

This paradigm consists of the augment plus the root plus the -sV- formative plus the ending. E.g.,

	Sanskrit		PIE
3sg	átāutsīt	'push'	*é+tēud+sī+t

6.5.1.5 Sigmatic i(:)s-Aorist (Athematic)

This paradigm consists of the augment plus the root plus the -i(:)s- formative plus the ending. E.g.,

		Sanskrit		PIE
sg	**1**	ábōdhiṣam	'awaken'	*é+b^heud^h+is+om[200]
	3	ábōdhīt		*é+b^heud^h+īs+t[200,201]

6.5.1.6 Sigmatic sis-Aorist (Athematic)

This paradigm consists of the augment plus the root plus the ending. E.g.,

	Sanskrit		PIE
3sg	áyāsit	'go'	*é+jē+sis+t[202]

6.5.1.7 Sigmatic sa-Aorist (Thematic)

This paradigm consists of the augment plus the root plus the -s- formative plus the ending. E.g.,

	Sanskrit		PIE
3sg	ádikṣat	'point out'	*é+dik+s+et

6.5.1.8 Additional Aorist Formatives

The aorist generally occurs in the indicative. The rare subjunctive, imperative or optative aorists consist of the unaugmented aorist stem plus the present endings of the subjunctive, imperative or optative. E.g., the following 1st singular forms:

	Sanskrit		PIE
subj	dikṣāni	'point out'	*dik+s+ōni
opt	dikṣyām		*dik+s+jē+m

A so-called "precative" mood occurs in later Sanskrit and is derived from the aorist. It means "May it happen that..." or "It should happen that..." It consists of the unaugmented Ø-grade verb root plus –yā- plus -s- plus signatic s-aorist endings (6.5.1.4 above). E.g.,

		Sanskrit		PIE
sg	**1**	bhūyā́sam	'should be'	*b^{h}ū+jḗ+s+om
	2	bhūyā́s		*b^{h}ū+jḗ+s+s[203]
	3	bhūyā́t		*b^{h}ū+jḗ+s+t[203]

6.5.2 Aorist Active Indicative

E.g., the thematic a-aorist (6.5.1.2 above):

		Sanskrit		PIE
sg	**1**	ágamam	'go'	*é+g^{w}om+o+m
	2	ágamas		*é+g^{w}om+e+s
	3	ágamat		*é+g^{w}om+e+t

The endings are those of the imperfect active indicative (6.2.1).

E.g., the athematic sigmatic s-aorist (6.5.1.4 above):

		Sanskrit		PIE
sg	**1**	átāutsam	'push'	*é+tēud+s+om[204]
	2	átāutsīs		*é+tēud+sī+s
	3	átāutsīt		*é+tēud+sī+t
du	**1**	átāutsva		*é+tēud+s+we
	2	átāuttam		*é+tēud+s+tom[205]
	3	átāuttām		*é+tēud+s+tām
pl	**1**	átāutsma		*é+tēud+s+me
	2	átāutta		*é+tēud+s+te
	3	átāutsur		*é+tēud+s+ur[206]

6.5.3 Aorist Middle Indicative

E.g., the thematic a-aorist (6.5.1.2):

	Sanskrit		PIE
1sg	ágamē	'come'	*é+g^{w}om+ai[207]

E.g., the athematic sigmatic s-aorist (6.5.1.4):

		Sanskrit		PIE
sg	1	átōtsi	'push'	*é+teud+s+i[208]
	2	átōtthās		*é+teud+s+thās[209]

6.6 Future and Conditional

The future and the conditional are formed similarly.

6.6.1 Future

There are two ways of forming the future. The chronologically earlier one is the so-called "s-future"; the later is the "periphrastic future". Both types of future take the present-tense endings of 6.1 above.

The s-future consists of the root, usually in the normal e/o-grade, plus -(i)s- plus the -j- formative plus the stressed present active indicative thematic endings (6.1.1). E.g.,

		Sanskrit		PIE
sg	1	bhariṣyā́mi	'carry'	*bʰer+is+j+ṓmi
		dāsyā́mi	'give'	*dō+s+j+ṓmi

The periphrastic future consists of the nominative of a tVr-class (1.5.3) agent noun plus the Ø-grade of the class 2 athematic verb as- 'be' plus the present-tense athematic endings. E.g.,

		Sanskrit		PIE
sg	1	dātā́smi	'give'	*dōtṓ+s+mi
	2	dātā́si		*dōtṓ+s+si[210]
	3	dātā́		*dōtṓ[211]
du	3	dātā́rāu		*dōtṓrōu[211]
pl	3	dātā́ras		*dōtṓres[211]

The future usually occurs only in the indicative. To form the subjunctive, imperative or optative of the future, the respective thematic present endings could be added to the s-future. E.g., the following 1st singular forms:

	Sanskrit		PIE
subj	dāsyā́ni	'give'	*dō+s+j+ṓni
imp	"		"
opt	dāsyḗyam		*dō+s+j+ói+om

6.6.2 Conditional

This construction consists of the stressed augment á- plus the s-future stem plus the endings of the imperfect indicative (6.2.1 and 6.2.2 above). E.g., the following 1st singular forms:

	Sanskrit		PIE
1sg	ábhariṣyam	'carry'	*é+bher+is+j+om[212]
	ádāsyam	'give'	*é+dō+s+j+om[212]

6.7 Derived or Secondary Conjugations

These conjugations are the intensive, the desiderative, the causative and the denominative. In many Sanskrit grammars the passive (in 6.1.10 above) is also considered a derived conjugation.

6.7.1 Intensive

This conjugation indicates the repetition or intensification of the action denoted by the unmarked verb. The forms consist of a stressed reduplicated syllable constructed on the model of the perfect as described under 6.3 above — but with either the normal /e, o/-grade or the lengthened /ē,ō/-grade ablaut in the reduplicated syllable plus the verb stem plus the endings. The verbs transformed into intensives are usually of class 3. E.g., the following 3rd singular present indicative forms:

	Sanskrit		PIE
unmarked	dī́pyatē	'shine'	*dī́p+j+etai
	pátati	'fall'	*pét+eti
	vḗtti	'know'	*wéid+ti
intensive	dḗdīpyatē	'shine a lot'	*déī+dīp+j+etai[213]
	pā́patati	'fall a lot'	*pḗ+pet+eti
	vḗvētti	'know well'	*wéi+weid+ti[214]

6.7.2 Desiderative

These verbs designate a desire or wish for the action or state as denoted by the unmarked verb. The forms consist of a stressed reduplicated syllable constructed on the model of the perfect as described under 6.3 above plus the root plus the suffix -(i)s- plus the thematic endings. E.g., the following 3rd singular present indicative forms:

	Sanskrit		PIE
unmarked	jī́vati	'live'	*gʷī́w+eti
	márati	'die'	*mér+eti
desiderative	jíjīviṣati	'want to live'	*gʷí+gʷīw+is+eti[215]
	múmūrṣati	'want to die'	*mú+mūr+s+eti[216]

`6.7.3 Causative

The meaning of these verbs is to cause or bring about the action or state as denoted by the unmarked verb. The forms consist of the verb root, usually in normal /e,o/-grade or lengthened /ē, ō/-grade ablaut, plus the stressed suffix -áy- plus the thematic endings. E.g., the following 3rd singular present indicative forms:

	Sanskrit		PIE
unmarked	pátati	'fall'	*pét+eti
causative	pātáyati	'cause to fall'	*pēt+éj+eti

6.7.4 Denominative

These verbs have various meanings and are derived from nouns. The forms consist of the noun stem plus -y- plus the stressed thematic endings. E.g., the following nominative singular and 3rd singular present indicative forms:

	Sanskrit		PIE
noun	dēvás	'god'	*deiw+ós
verb	dēvayáti	'cultivate the gods, be pious'	*deiwo+j+éti

6.8 Verbal Noun

This is the infinitive. It is formed in two ways: (a) by the addition to the verb root of the suffix -(i)t- plus the u-class accusative singular masculine ending; or (b) by the addition directly to the root of a neuter singular case ending. E.g., the following singular forms:

	Sanskrit		PIE
acc	bhávitum	'to be'	*b^héū+it+um[217]
	kártum	'to do'	*k^wór+t+um[217]
dat	dr̥śḗ	'to see'	*dr̥k+éi[218]
abl	ētṓs	'to go'	*ei+t+éus[217]

6.9 Verbal Adjectives.

6.9.1 Present Active Participle

The suffixes are -ant- and -at- plus the endings of the Vnt-class as described in 1.5.5 above. E.g.,

		Sanskrit		PIE
nom	**masc**	bhávant-	'being'	*b^héū+ont-[219]
	neuter	júhvat-	'sacrificing'	*g^hú+g^hu+n̥t-[220]

6.9.2 Present Middle Participle

These forms are constructed with the suffix -mān- for thematic verbs and -ān- for athematic ones. The endings are those of the o- and ā-class adjectives under 2.1 above. E.g.,

	Sanskrit		PIE
thematic	bháramāṇa-	'carrying for oneself'	*bʰéro+mēn+o-[221]
athematic	bʰindāná-	'splitting for oneself'	*bʰind+ēn+ó-

6.9.3 Perfect Active Participle

These forms consist of the reduplicated perfect verb stem — usually in Ø-grade ablaut — plus the stressed suffix –vV́(:)(n)(t or s)- plus the athematic Ø-class adjective endings (see 2.4 above). Contingent upon the case, gender and number of the adjective, the Sanskrit suffix appears as -vān-, -vāṁs- /vā^{n}s/, -uṣ-, -vad- or -vat-. The earliest PIE antecedent was probably *-wVs- in which the V = ablauting /ō/or Ø. In Sanskrit this suffix was conflated with the present active participle *-Vnt- in all cases except where –uṣ- occurs. E.g.,

			Sanskrit		PIE
masc/fem	**sg**	**nom**	cakr̥vā́n	'having made'	*kʷekʷr̥+wṓns+s[222]
		acc	cakr̥vā́ṁsam		*kʷekʷr̥+wṓns+m̥[223]
		gen	cakrúṣas		*kʷekʷr̥+ẃs+es[224]
	pl	**nom**	cakr̥vā́ṁsas		*kʷekʷr̥+wṓns+es
		dat	cakr̥vádbhyas		*kʷekʷr̥+wń̥t+bʰjos[225]
neuter	**sg**	**nom**	cakr̥vát		*kʷekʷr̥+wń̥t

A second type of perfect active part consists of the stem of the perfect passive participle (6.9.5 below) plus the suffix -va(:)nt- plus the endings of the athematic Vnt-class adjectives. (2.7 above). E.g., the following nominative singular masculine form:

Sanskrit		PIE
kr̥távān	'having made'	*kʷr̥+tó+wōnt+s[226]

6.9.4 Perfect Middle Participle

These forms consist of the perfect stem plus the suffix -ān- plus the o- and ā-class adjective endings (2.1 above), which are stressed. E.g.,

Sanskrit		PIE
tutudāná-	'having pushed for onself'	*tu+tud+ēn+ó-

6.9.5 Perfect Passive Participle

These forms consist of the bare verb root plus the suffixes -(i)t- or less frequently -n- plus the o- and ā-class adjective endings (2.1 above), which are stressed. E.g.,

Sanskrit		PIE
bhūtá-	'been'	*b^{h}ū+t+ó-
kr̥tá-	'done'	*k^{w}r̥+t+ó-
patitá-	'fallen'	*pet+it+ó-
kīrná-	'scattered'	*k^{w}īl+n+ó-[227]

6.9.6 Future Active Participle

This form consists of the future stem (6.6 above) plus -ya- plus the present active part suffix plus the respective endings (6.9.1). E.g.,

Sanskrit		PIE
bhaviṣyánt-	'going to be'	*b^{h}eū+is+jó+nt-

6.9.7 Future Middle Participle

This form consists of the future stem (6.6 above) plus -yá- plus the present middle participle suffix plus the respective endings (6.9.2). E.g.,

Sanskrit		PIE
bhaviṣyámāna-	'going to be for oneself'	*b^{h}eū+is+jó+mēno-

6.9.8 Future Passive Participle

This construction is also called a "gerundive". The meaning is 'that which will be done or ought to be done'. It consists of the verb root plus any one of three possible suffixes plus the o- and ā-class adjective endings (2.1 above). E.g.,

Sanskrit		PIE
kā́rya-	'to be done'	*k^{w}ṓr+jo-
kartavyá-		*k^{w}or+tewjó-
karaṇīyá-		*k^{w}or+enījó-[228]

6.9.9 Gerund

This construction is a tenseless and indeclinable active participle. It usually modifies the subject of a sentence; it denotes an action either accompanying or preceding that of the main verb of the sentence. There are four such constructions. E.g.,

Sanskrit		PIE
kr̥tvā́[229]	'doing'	*k^{w}r̥+twṓ[230]
nipátya	'falling down'	*ni+pét+jo
abhidrútya	'running up'	*eb^{h}i+drú+tjo
kāram	'doing'	*k^{w}ōr+om[231]

V Exercises

(1) Consider the following PIE forms and the changes which they underwent into Sanskrit. What is the Sanskrit form? Give the Sanskrit in our romanization. In some instances we cite only the stem, which is written with a hyphen. The stress is that of 11 SKT STRESS 1, the early PIE stress rule.

a. Adjective stem *ang- 'narrow' + 2a 1ST PAL, 8a ɟ^{h}-TO-h, 9d NASAL DELE > Sanskrit?

b. Pres act part sg nom *b^{h}ér+ont+s 'carrying' and gen *b^{h}ér+n̥t+es + 2c SYL NAS, 5a e(:)/o(:)-TO-a(:), 5c WF CL > Sanskrit? and?

c. Perf pass part *b^{h}ud^{h}+tó- 'understood' + 1b OBSTR CL 1 ("Bartholomae's Law"), 2b GRASSMANN, 5a e(:)/o(:)-TO-a(:) > Sanskrit?

d, deiwós kak^{w}néuti 'a god helps' + 2a 1ST PAL, 3 DELAB , 5a e(:)/o(:)-TO-a(:), 7a MON, 7c s-ASSIM, 10 w-TO-v > Sanskrit?

e. Adjective stems *dérko+no- 'seeing' and *k^{w}ōro+no- 'making' + 2a 1ST PAL, 3 DELAB , 4a RETRO, 5a e(:)/o(:)-TO-a(:) > Sanskrit? and?

f. *éb^{h}eret ékwōns 'he brought horses' + 2a 1ST PAL, 5a e(:)/o(:)-TO-a(:), 5c WF CL, 7d STOP ASSIM, 10 w-TO-v > Sanskrit?

g. 1sg pluperf *é+g^{h}e+g^{h}rob^{h}+om 'I had seized' + 2b GRASSMANN applying twice and from left to right, 4b 2ND PAL , 5a e(:)/o(:)-TO-a(:) > Sanskrit?

h. 3sg athematic pres *éi+ti 'go' and the same verb in a thematic conjugation *éi+eti + PIE 3.1.2c i-j/u-w ALT applying synchronically, 5a e(:)/o(:)-TO-a(:), 7a MON > Sanskrit? and ?

i. *ékwos wég^{h}eti 'the horse travels' + 2a 1ST PAL, 5a e(:)/o(:)-TO-a(:), 8a ɟ^{h}-TO-h, 8b s/r CHANGES, 10 w-TO-v > Sanskrit?

j. 1sg aorist *é+lēik^{w}+s+om 'leave' + 3 DELAB , 4a RETRO, 5a e(:)/o(:)-TO-a(:), 9b l/r ALT > Sanskrit?

k. Nom sg masc *g^{h}r̥d^{h}ós 'house' + 2b GRASSMANN, 5a e(:)/o(:)-TO-a(:), 9a b^{h}/d^{h}-TO-h > Sanskrit?

l. Noun stem *g^{hw}ómb^{h}on- 'depth' + 2b GRASSMANN, 3 DELAB, 5a e(:)/o(:)-TO-a(:) > Sanskrit?

m. 3sg pres *g^{w}ḿ̥+sk+eti 'go' + 2c SYL NAS, 3 DELAB, 4b 2ND PAL , 5a e(:)/o(:)-TO-a(:) > Sanskrit?

n. Instr pl *g^{w}ou+b^{h}ís 'cow' vs. gen pl *g^{w}ou+ṓm + PIE 3.1.2c i-j/u-w ALT applying synchronically, 3 DELAB , 5a e(:)/o(:)-TO-a(:), 7a MON, 10 w-TO-v > Sanskrit? and?

o. 2sg pres *ju+né+g+si 'join' vs. 1pl pres *ju+n+g+més + 1b OBSTR CL, 2a 1ST PAL, 4a RETRO, 5a e(:)/o(:)-TO-a(:), 7b NASAL ASSIM > Sanskrit? and?

p. Nom sg neuter *kléu+mn̥t+om 'act of hearing' + 2a 1ST PAL, 2c SYL NAS, 5a e(:)/o(:)-TO-a(:), 7a MON, 9b l/r ALT > Sanskrit?

q. Nom sg masc *k^{w}ek^{w}lós 'wheel' + 3 DELAB, 4b 2ND PAL , 5a e(:)/o(:)-TO-a(:), 9b l/r ALT > Sanskrit?

r. Nom sg masc of perfect act participle *k^{w}e+k^{w}r̥+wṓns+s 'having made' + 3 DELAB , 4b 2ND PAL, 5a e(:)/o(:)-TO-a(:), 5c WF CL, 10 w-TO-v > Sanskrit?

s. Dat pl *mén+os+b^{h}yos 'mind' + 5a e(:)/o(:)-TO-a(:), 8b s/r CHANGES > Sanskrit?

t. *ne ageti 'he does not drive' + 2a 1ST PAL, 5a e(:)/o(:)-TO-a(:), 6 V##V-TO-V̄ > Sanskrit?

u. Perf pass participle stem *ń̥+gnō+to- 'unknown' + 2a 1ST PAL, 2c SYL NAS, 5a e(:)/o(:)-TO-a(:), 7b NASAL ASSIM > Sanskrit?

v. Nom sg masc *ni+sd+ós 'sit-in, nest' + 1b OBSTR CL, 4a RETRO, 5a e(:)/o(:)-TO-a(:), 5b VzC-TO-V̄C > Sanskrit?

w. Gen sg *ókʷs+n+es 'eye' + 3 DELAB, 4a RETRO, 5a e(:)/o(:)-TO-a(:) > Sanskrit?

x. Nom sg masc adj *prōnkʷ+s 'forward-looking, eastern' + 7b NASAL ASSIM 1 applying as a synchronic rule of PIE, 3 DELAB , 5c WF CL > Sanskrit?

y. Adj stem *róudʰito- 'red' + 5a e(:)/o(:)-TO-a(:), 7a MON, 9a bʰ/dʰ-TO-h, 9b l/r ALT applying optionally > Sanskrit? and?

z. Nom sg *séineh$_2$ 'army' + 1a LARYNGEALS, 5a e(:)/o(:)-TO-a(:), 7a MON > Sanskrit?

aa. 3sg pres mid *sékʷ+etai 'follow' vs. 3sg aorist mid *é+sekʷ+s+eto 'idem' +3 DELAB, 4a RETRO, 4b 2ND PAL , 5a e(:)/o(:)-TO-a(:), 7a MON > Sanskrit? and?

bb. *sm̥+gʰéslom '1000' + 2a 1ST PAL, 2c SYL NAS, 5a e(:)/o(:)-TO-a(:), 8a ɟʰ-TO-h, 9b l/r ALT > Sanskrit?

cc. Noun stem *swékuro- 'brother-in-law' + 2a 1ST PAL, 5a e(:)/o(:)-TO-a(:), 7c s-ASSIM, 10 w-TO-v > Sanskrit?

dd. *tod génom 'that race' vs. *tod laksóm 'that sign' + 2a 1ST PAL, 4a RETRO, 5a e(:)/o(:)-TO-a(:), 7d STOP ASSIM > Sanskrit? and?

ee. Nom sg masc *upo+pd+ós 'act of trampling' + 1b OBSTR CL, 5a e(:)/o(:)-TO-a(:) > Sanskrit?

ff. Acc pl *wĺ̥kʷōns kʷe 'and wolves' + 3 DELAB , 4b 2ND PAL , 5a e(:)/o(:)-TO-a(:), 7c s-ASSIM, 9b l/r ALT, 9d NASAL DELE, 10 w-TO-v > Sanskrit?

gg. *wōks moi 'my speech' + 5a e(:)/o(:)-TO-a(:), 5c WF CL, 7a MON, 7d STOP ASSIM, 10 w-TO-v > Sanskrit?

(2) Given the following PIE forms, what will be the Sanskrit reflexes and what changes will they have undergone? Give the Sanskrit forms in our romanization.

a. 2sg pres opt *bʰérois 'carry'.
b. 1sg pres *bʰn̥dʰ+nā́+mi 'tie'.
c. dékm̥ '10'.
d. 3sg pres *dʰr̥s+néu+ti 'dare'.
e. Stem *dʰugʰitŕ̥- 'daughter'.
f. Instr pl *dn̥t+bʰís 'teeth'.
g. 3sg pres *dwéis+ti 'hate'.
h. 3pl pres mid *dwis+n̥t+ái 'hate'.
i. 1pl aorist *é+jēug+s+me 'yoke' and 2pl aorist *é+jēug+s+te 'idem'.
j. Loc pl *ékwoisu 'horses'.
k. 3sg pres *géuseti 'taste'.
l. Stem *gʰansó- 'goose'.
m. Nom sg masc *gʰimós 'snow, frost'.
n. 1sg pres *gʰu+gʰéu+mi 'sacrifice'.
o. Nom sg neuter *gʷégʷn̥t 'world'.
p. 3sg pres *ju+n+g+eti 'join'.
q. Perf pass participle stem *klu+tó- 'heard'.
r. *kʷe 'and' and nom sg masc *kʷos 'who?'.
s. Nom sg neuter *kʷéks+us 'eye' and gen sg *kʷéks+us+es.
t. Nom sg masc adj *kʷétus+ped+s '4-footed'.
u. 1sg pres *kʷeur+éj+ōmi 'steal'.

v. Nom sg masc adj *mégʰ+n̥t+temos ‘largest’.
w. Adjective stem *ōkú- ‘fast’.
x. 3sg pres *óuseti ‘burn’.
y. *pénkʷe ‘5’.
z. Noun stem *phoinó- ‘foam’. (Assume here the laryngeal /h/.)
aa. Gen sg *rḗgn+es ‘king’.
bb. 3sg pres mid *ségʰetai ‘prevail’.
cc. *wi+n+km̥+t+ís ‘20’.

(3) Give a possible PIE antecedent for each of the following Sanskrit forms. In every case there are more than a single possibility. The Sanskrit forms with /a(:)/ can devolve from PIE /e(:)/, /o(:)/ or /a(:)/. In such cases reconstruct the PIE antecedent with “[V, -high]”, long or short.

a. 3sg ájati ‘drive’.
b. Neuter Vs-class noun stem ṓjas ‘power’.
c. 3sg pres kr̥nṓti ‘make’.
d. Neuter o-class noun stem garbhá- ‘child’.
e. 3sg pres gŕ̥dhyati ‘be greedy’.
f. Fem ā-class noun stem gnā- ‘divine woman’ and fem i-class noun stem jáni- ‘woman’. The root is one and the same; posit the PIE ablaut involved.
g. Stem catvā́ra- ‘4’.
h. Masc o-class noun stem gharmá- ‘heat’
i. Masc o-class noun stem jámbha- ‘tooth’.
j. Neuter Vn-class noun nom sg nā́ma ‘name’.
k. 3sg pres mid vártatē ‘turn’.

(4) Consider the Sanskrit root gr̥bh- ‘seize’. Its cognate is Eng grab. Given that English like Gothic underwent the Gothic change 2 1ST SS, what must be the PIE antecedent? What rule must apply in deriving the Sanskrit form? (Ignore in the Sanskrit derivation rule 2a 1ST PAL.)

(5) Consider the following two forms of the root-class noun dyāus ‘god’:

sg nom dyā́us, gen divás.

The two forms show ablaut. What are the PIE antecedents and what rules apply in the derivation of the Sanskrit forms?

(6) The following Sanskrit forms have the earlier morph cond stress of 11 SKT STRESS 1. What is their later phon cond stress by 11 SKT STRESS 2? gurú- ‘heavy’, comp gárīyaṁs- ‘heavier’, sup gáriṣṭha- ‘heaviest’; 3sg pres jíjīviṣati ‘want to live’.

(7) Consider the following Sanskrit verb alternations. Posit a plausible PIE ablauting root and indicate the changes it must have undergone to result in the Sanskrit form.

a. 3sg pres badhnā́ti ‘tie’ vs. 3sg future bhantsyáti. The PIE pres suffix is *-nā́-; the future suffix is *-sj-. The 3rd singular ending is *-(e)ti.

b. The verb root añj- ‘anoint’ vs. the perfect passive participle stem aktá-. The participle is formed with the PIE suffix *-tó-.

c. The verb root hu- ‘sacrifice’ is a class 3 athematic reduplicating verb. Consider the 1sg pres juhṓmi vs. the 1pl juhumás. The ablaut in the PIE antecedents is /e/ and Ø; the PIE endings are -mi and *-mes.

d. 3sg pres hánti 'slay' vs. 3pl pres ghnánti vs. 3sg perf jaghā́na. The respective PIE endings are *-ti, *-onti and *-e. The 3pl pres root has the Ø-grade ablaut. The other two ablaut grades are unambiguous. How so?

(8) Consider the glossed Sanskrit text in VI below. Give a smooth translation of this text.

VI A Sanskrit Text

The following is the so-called Nala episode from the *Great Bhārata Story*, an epic poem whose exact date is unknown. According to Lanman (1959: 297), it "...may well have existed several centuries before our era..." We have generally followed Lanman's romanization of the Sanskrit dēvānāgari. We depart from Lanman in some respects: we mark length on /ē/ and /ō/; we write <ś> for Lanman's <ç>; we write <h> for Lanman's visarga <ḥ> which occurs word-finally by 8b s/r CHANGES; we have marked the stress according to the earlier morph cond stress rule 11 SKT STRESS 1 in those words for which the stress is known; and finally we have capitalized sentence-initial words and proper nouns.

We give here (a) our romanization of the text, which represents in effect a phonemic transcription; (b) the underlying forms to which the rules of sandhi apply, some of which are described in the notes; (c) a gloss; and (d) a grammatical description of each word in the text. In those instances where the underlying and derived forms coincide, we mark the (b)-level with a ditto. The accompanying notes indicate some of the synchronic word-external sandhi derivations.

1	**a**	Átha	Nalōpākhyānam.[232]	Bŕ̥hadasva	uvāca.	Ā́sīd	rā́ja
	b	"	Nala+upa+akhyānam	Bŕ̥hadasvas	"	ā́sīt	"
	c	*then*	*Nala episode*	*Bŕ̥hadasva*	*speak*	*be*	*king*
	d	adv	compound, o-class neuter nom sg	o-class masc nom sg	perf 3sg act class 2/3	3sg imperf act class 3	Vn-class masc nom sg

2	**a**	Nalō	nā́ma	vīrasēnasutō	balī́,	upapannṓ[233]	guṇā́ir
	b	Nalas	"	vīrasēnasutas	"	upa+pad+n+ás	guṇā́is
	c	*Nala*	*name*	*son of Vīrasēna*	*mighty*	*endow*	*quality*
	d	o-class masc nom sg	Vn-class neut acc sg	compound, o-class masc nom sg	Vn-class masc nom sg	perf pass part o-class masc nom sg	o-class masc instr pl

3	**a**	iṣṭā́ir	rūpavān,	aśvakōvidah.	Átiṣthan	manujēndrāṇām	mūrdhni
	b	iṣṭā́is	rūpavānts	aśvakōvidas	Átiṣthat	"	"
	c	*desire*	*handsome*	*skilled in horses*	*stand*	*prince*	*head*
	d	perf pass part o-class instr pl	Vnt-class masc nom sg	compound, o-class masc nom sg	3sg imperf act class 3	compound, o-class masc gen pl	Vn-class masc loc sg

4	a	dēvapatir	yátha,	upáry[234]	upári	sárvēṣām	ādityá
	b	dēvapatis	"	upari	"	"	ādityás
	c	*lord of the gods*	*just as*	*above*	*above*	*all*	*sun-god*
	d	compound, i-class masc sg nom	adv	adv	adv	o-class masc gen pl	o-class masc nom sg

5	a	iva	tḗjasā;	brahmaṇyṓ	vēdavíc,	chū́rō,[235]	Niṣadhēṣu
	b	"	"	brahmaṇyás	vēdavíts	śū́ras	"
	c	*as, like*	*splendor*	*pious*	*Veda-knowing*	*bold*	*people of Niṣadha*
	d	adv	Vs-class neut nom instr sg	o-class masc nom sg	Ø-class masc nom sg	o-class masc nom sg	o-class masc loc pl

6	a	mahīpatih,	akṣapriyah,	satyavādī́	mahā́n	akṣāuhiṇīpatih;	īpsitṓ
	b	mahīpatis	akṣapriyas	"	mahā́nts	akṣāuhiṇīpatis	īpsitás
	c	*king*	*lucky at gambling*	*truth-speaking*	*great*	*army-chief*	*admire*
	d	i-class masc nom sg	o-class masc nom sg	Vn-class masc nom sg	Vnt-class masc nom sg	i-class masc nom sg	perf pass part o-class masc nom sg

7	a	naranārīṇām,	udārah,	sáṁyatēndriyah,	rakṣitā,	dhanvināṁ	śrḗṣṭhah,
	b	"	udāras	sáṁyatēndriyas	"	dhanvinām	śrḗṣṭhas
	c	*man and woman*	*excellent*	*self-controlled*	*protector*	*bowman*	*best*
	d	compound, i-class fem gen pl	o-class masc nom sg	o-class masc nom sg	tVr-class masc nom sg	Vn-class masc gen pl	o-class masc nom sg

8	a	sākṣād	iva	Mánuh	svayám.	Táthāivā́sīd[236]	Vidarbhēṣu
	b	"	"	Mánus	"	Táthā ēva ásīt	"
	c	*clearly*	*as, like*	*Manu*	*himself*	*thus exactly be*	*people of Vidarbhan*
	d	adv	adv	u-class masc nom sg	indeclinable	adv, adv, 3sg imperf act class 3	Ø-class masc loc pl

9	a	Bhīmṓ,	bhīmáparākramah	śū́rah,	sarvaguṇāir	yuktáh,
	b	Bhīmás	bhīmáparākramas	śū́ras	sarvaguṇāis	yuktás
	c	*Bhīma*	*strong*	*bold*	*all virtues*	*yoke*
	d	o-class masc nom sg	o-class masc nom sg	o-class masc nom sg	compound, o-class masc instr pl	perf pass part o-class masc nom

10	**a**	prajā́kamah,	sa	cā́prajah.	Sa	prajārthē	páraṁ
	b	prajā́kamas	"	ca ā́prajas	"	"	páram
	c	*desirous of offspring*	*he*	*and childless*	*he*	*for offspring*	*extreme*
	d	o-class masc nom sg	pron nom sg	conj, o-class nom sg masc	pron nom sg	adv	o-class masc acc sg

11	**a**	yatnam	akarōt,	súsamāhitah.	Tam	abhyagacchad	brahmarṣir,
	b	"	"	súsamāhitas	"	abhi agacchat	brahmarṣis
	c	*effort*	*do*	*very intent*	*he*	*to go*	*priest-sage*
	d	o-class masc acc sg	3sg imperf class 2/5/8	o-class masc nom sg	pron acc sg	3sg imperf act class 1/2	compound, i-class masc nom sg

12	**a**	Damanō	nā́ma,	Bhā́rata.	Taṁ	sa	Bhīmáh,
	b	Damanas	"	"	Tam	"	Bhīmás
	c	*Damana*	*name*	*Bhārata*	*he*	*he*	*Bhīma*
	d	o-class masc nom sg	Vn-class neuter acc sg	o-class masc voc sg	pron acc sg masc	pron nom sg masc	o-class masc nom sg

13	**a**	prajā́kamas,	tōṣayā́m	āsa,	dhamarvít,	máhiṣyā	sahá
	b	"	"	"	dhamarvíts	"	"
	c	*desirous of offspring*	*receive*	*be*	*knowing the law*	*queen*	*with*
	d	o-class masc nom sg	periphrastic perf	3sg[237]	Ø-class masc nom sg	ī-class fem instr sg	prep

14	**a**	rājēndras,	satkārēṇa,	suvárcasam.	Tásmāi	prasannṓ	Damanah
	b	rāja indras	"	"	"	pra+sad+nás	Damanas
	c	*chief of kings*	*hospitality*	*glorious*	*he*	*be favorable to*	*Damana*
	d	o-class masc nom sg	o-class masc instr sg	Vs-class masc acc sg	pron dat sg masc	perf pass part o-class masc nom sg	o-class nom sg

15	a	sabhāryāya	váraṁ	dadāu,	kanyāratnaṁ	kumārā́ṁś	ca[238]
	b	"	váram	"	kanyāratnam	kumārā́n	"
	c	*having one's wife along*	*wish*	*give*	*girl-jewel*	*son*	*and*
	d	o-class masc nom sg	o-class masc dat sg	3sg perf act class 3	compound, o-class neuter acc sg	o-class masc acc pl	conj

16	a	trīn	udārān,	mahāyaśāh,	Damayantīṁ,	Damaṁ,	Dāntaṁ,
	b	"	"	mahāyaśās[239]	Damayantīm	Damam	Dāntam
	c	*three*	*excellent*	*famous*	*Damayantī*	*Dama*	*Dānta*
	d	masc acc pl	o-class masc acc pl	Vs-class masc acc pl	ī-class fem acc sg	o-class masc acc sg	Ø-class masc acc sg

17	a	Damanaṁ	ca	suvárcasam,	upapannān	guṇā́ih	sarvāir,
	b	Damanam	"	"	upa+pad+n+ān	guṇā́is	sarvāis
	c	*Damana*	*and*	*glorious*	*endow*	*quality*	*all*
	d	o-class masc acc sg	conj	Vs-class masc acc sg	perf pass part o-class masc acc pl	o-class masc instr pl	o-class masc instr pl

18	a	bhīmā́n,	bhīmáparākramān.
	b	"	"
	c	*awesome*	*strong*
	d	o-class masc acc pl	o-class masc acc pl

VII Key

(1) The Sanskrit forms are these: (a) aṁhú /aⁿhú-/, (b) bháran and bhárantas, (c) buddhá-, (d) dēváś śaknṓti, (e) dárśana- and kāraṇa-, (f) ábarad áśvān, (g) ájagrabham, (h) ḗti and áyati, (i) áśvō váhati, (j) árāikṣam, (k) gr̥hás, (l) gámbhan-, (m) gácchati, (n) gōbhiís and gavā́m, (o) yunákṣi and yuñjmás, (p) śrṓmatam, (q) cakrás, (r) cakr̥vā́n, (s) mánōbhyas, (t) nājati, (u) ájñāta-, (v) nīḍás, (w) ákṣṇas, (x) prāṇ, (y) rṓhita- and lṓhita-, (z) sḗnā, (aa) sácatē and ásakṣata, (bb) sahásram, (cc) śváśura-, (dd) taj jánam and tal lakṣám, (ee) upabdás, (ff) vŕ̥kāṁś ca, (gg) vāṇ mē.

(2) The Sanskrit forms and changes are these.

a. bhárēs. The derivation is 5a e(:)/o(:)-TO-a(:), 7a MON.
b. badhnā́mi. The derivation is 2b GRASSMANN, 2c SYL NAS.
c. dáśa. The derivation is 2a 1ST PAL, 2c SYL NAS, 5a e(:)/o(:)-TO-a(:).
d. dhr̥ṣṇṓti. The derivation is 4a RETRO 1 and 2, 5a e(:)/o(:)-TO-a(:), 7a MON.
e. duhitŕ̥-. The derivation is 2a 1ST PAL, 2b GRASSMANN, 8a ɟ^{h}-TO-h.
f. dadbhís. The derivation is lb OBSTR CL, 2c SYL NAS.
g. dvḗṣṭi. The derivation is 4a RETRO, 5a e(:)/o(:)-TO-a(:) 7a MON, 10 w-TO-v .
h. dviṣatḗ. The derivation is 2c SYL NAS, 4a RETRO, 7a MON, 10 w-TO-v .
i. áyāukṣma and áyāukta. The derivation is lb OBSTR CL, 4a RETRO, 5a e(:)/o(:)-TO-a(:).
j. áśvēṣu. The derivation is 2a 1ST PAL, 4a RETRO, 5a e(:)/o(:)-TO-a(:), 7a MON, 10 w-TO-v.
k. jṓṣati. The derivation is 2a 1ST PAL, 4a RETRO, 5a e(:)/o(:)-TO-a(:), 7a MON. ,
l. haṁsá-. The derivation is 2a 1ST PAL, 5a e(:)/o(:)-TO-a(:), 8a j^{h} -to-h, 9d NASAL DELE.
m. himás. The derivation is 2a 1ST PAL, 5a e(:)/o(:)-TO-a(:), 8a ɟ^{h}-TO-h.
n. juhṓmi. The derivation is 2a 1ST PAL, 2b GRASSMANN, 5a e(:)/o(:)-TO-a(:), 7a MON, 8a ɟ^{h}-TO-h.
o. jágat. The derivation is 2c SYL NAS, 3 DELAB , 4b 2ND PAL , 5a e(:)/o(:)-TO-a(:) .
p. yuñjati. The derivation is 2a 1ST PAL, 5a e(:)/o(:)-TO-a(:), 7b NASAL ASSIM.
q. śrutá-. The derivation is 2a 1ST PAL, 5a e(:)/o(:)-TO-a(:), 9b l/r ALT.
r. ca and kas. The derivation is 3 DELAB, 4b 2ND PAL , 5a e(:)/o(:)-TO-a(:).
s. cákṣus and cákṣuṣas. The derivation is 3 DELAB, 4a RETRO, 4b 2ND PAL, 5a e(:)/o(:)-TO-a(:).
t. cátuṣpat. The derivation is lb OBSTR CL, 3 DELAB, 4a RETRO, 4b 2ND PAL , 5a e(:)/o(:)-TO-a(:), 5c WF CL.
u. cōráyāmi. The derivation is 3 DELAB , 4b 2ND PAL , 5a e(:)/o(:)-TO-a(:), 7a MON.
v. máhattamas. The derivation is 2a 1ST PAL, 2c SYL NAS, 5a e(:)/o(:)-TO-a(:), 8a ɟ^{h}-TO-h.
w. āśú-. The derivation is 2a 1ST PAL, 5a e(:)/o(:)-TO-a(:).
x. ṓṣati. The derivation is 4a RETRO, 5a e(:)/o(:)-TO-a(:), 7a MON.
y. páñca. The derivation is 3 DELAB, 4b 2ND PAL , 5a e(:)/o(:)-TO-a(:), 7b NASAL ASSIM.
z. phēná-. The derivation is la LARYNGEALS, 5a e(:)/o(:)-TO-a(:), 7a MON.
aa. rā́jñas. The derivation is 2a 1ST PAL, 5a e(:)/o(:)-TO-a(:), 7b NASAL ASSIM.
bb. sáhatē. The derivation is 2a 1ST PAL, 5a e(:)/o(:)-TO-a(:). 7a MON, 8a ɟ^{h}-TO-h.
cc. viṁśatís. The derivation is 2a 1ST PAL, 2c SYL NAS, 9d NASAL DELE, 10 w-TO-v.

(3) The PIE forms are these.

a. *[V́, -high, -long] g$^{(w)}$ [V, -high, -long]ti, actually *ágeti.
b. *[V́, -high, -1ong]ug$^{(w)}$ [V, -high, -long]s-, actually *áugos-.
c. *k^{w}r̥n[V́, -high, -long]uti, actually *k^{w}r̥néuti.
d. *g$^{(h)w}$(á/ó)rb^{h}[V, -high, -long]-, actually *g^{w}ólbo-.
e. *g$^{(h)w}$ŕ̥d^{h}j[V,-high, -long]ti, actually *g^{hw}ŕ̥d^{h}jeti.
f. *g^{w} Ønā́- and *g^{w}éni- are the only possibilities.
g. *k^{w}etw[V́, -high, +long]r[V, -high, -long]-, actually *k^{w}etwṓro-.
h. *g^{hw}(a/o)rm[V́, -high, -long]-, actually *g^{hw}ormó-.
i. *g$^{(h)(w)}$[V́ -high, -long]mb^{h}[V, -high, -long]-, actually *gómb^{h}o-.
j. *n[V́, -high., +long]m([V, -high, -long] or n̥), actually *nṓmn̥.
k. *w[V́, -high, -long]rt[V, -high, -long]t[V, -high, -long]i, actually *wértetai.

(4) The early Germanic form must be *gr̥b-; and the PIE antecedent must be *gʰr̥bʰ-. The change 2b GRASSMANN applies in the derivation of the Sanskrit form.

(5) The two ablauting PIE forms are these: sg nom *diV́u+s (actually *diḗu+s); sg gen *diØu+és Their derivation is *diḗus and *diués (PIE 3.1.2c i-j/u-w ALT applying synchronically) → *djḗus and *diwés (5a e(:)/o(:)-TO-a(:), 10 w-TO-v) > Skt dyā́us and divás.

(6) The later forms stressed by 11.2 SKT STRESS are gúru-, garī́yaṁs-, gáriṣṭha- and jijī́viṣati.

(7) The PIE antecedents are these.

(a) The root is *bʰVndʰ-, where V = ablauting /e/ and Ø. The respective derivations are present *bʰØndʰ+nā́+ti (PIE 3.1.2g SYL SON applying synchronically) → *bn̥dhnā́ti (2b GRASSMANN, 2c SYL NAS, 5a e(:)/o(:)-TO-a(:)) > badhnā́ti; and future *bʰendʰ+s+jéti (1b OBSTR CL) > *bʰentsjéti (to which 2b GRASSMANN cannot apply, but by 5a e(:)/o(:)-TO-a(:)) > bhantsyáti.

(b) The root is *Vng⁽ʷ⁾- where V = ablauting /o/ or Ø. The respective derivations are the root *ongʷ- (3 DELAB, 4b 2ND PAL) > *onɟ- (5a e(:)/o(:)-TO-a(:), 7b NASAL ASSIM) > Skt añj-; and participle *Øngʷ+tó- (PIE 3.1.2g SYL SON applying synchronically) → *n̥gʷtó- (1b OBSTR CL) > *n̥kʷto- (2c SYL NAS) > *akʷtó- (3 DELAB) > *aktó- (5a e(:)/o(:)-TO-a(:)) > Skt aktá-.

(c) The antecedents are 1sg *gʰu+gʰéu+mi and 1pl *gʰu+gʰØu+més. The respective derivations are 1sg *gʰu+gʰéu+mi (2a 1ST PAL) > *ɟʰuɟʰéumi (2b GRASSMANN) > *ɟuɟʰéumi (5a e(:)/o(:)-TO-a(:), 7a MON) > *ɟuɟʰṓmi (8a ɟʰ-TO-h) > Skt juhṓmi; and 1pl *gʰu+gʰØu+més (2a 1ST PAL) > *ɟʰuɟʰumés (2b GRASSMANN) > *ɟuɟʰumés (5a e(:)/o(:)-TO-a(:)) > *ɟuɟʰumás > (8a ɟʰ-TO-h) > Skt juhumás.

(d) The respective antecedents are 3sg pres *gʰʷén+ti, 3pl pres *gʰʷØn+ónti and 3sg perf *gʰʷe+gʰʷṓn+e. The perfect root must be *gʰʷōn-: any other ablauting vowel besides /ō/ would result in a wrong Sanskrit form. Similarly, the present root must be *gʰʷen-: any other ablauting vowel besides /e/ would result in a wrong Sanskrit form. The respective derivations are these: 3sg pres *gʰʷén+ti (3 DELAB) > *gʰénti (4b 2ND PAL) > *ɟʰénti (5a e(:)/o(:)-TO-a(:)) > *ɟʰánti (8a ɟʰ-TO-h) > Skt hánti; 3pl pres *gʰʷØn+ónti (3 DELAB) > *gʰnónti (5a e(:)/o(:)-TO-a(:)) > Skt ghnánti; and 3sg perf *gʰʷe+gʰʷṓn+e (2b GRASSMANN) > *gʷegʰʷṓne (3 DELAB) > *gegʰṓne (4b 2ND PAL) > *ɟegʰṓne (5a e(:)/o(:)-TO-a(:)) > jaghā́na.

(8) The following is a translation of the text in section VI.

"Now the Nala episode.

"Br̥hadaśva spoke.

"'There was a king, Nala by name, the strong son of Vīrasēna, endowed with desirable qualities, handsome and skilled in horsemanship. Nala stood at the head of princes just like a lord of the gods and just as the sun-god is high above all others in splendor. He was pious, Veda-wise and bold. He was a king among the people of Niṣadha, lucky at gambling, truth-speaking and a great general. Nala was admired by both men and women, excellent, self-controlled and a protector. He was the best of bowmen, clearly like the god Manu himself.

"'Exactly like that was Bhīma among the Vidarbhan people. He was strong, bold and imbued with all virtues. He was desirous of offspring; yet he was childless. He made great efforts for offspring and was intent on this. A priest-sage, Damana by name, came to Bhīma. Listen now, Bhārata (to whom the narrator is speaking). So Bhīma, wanting offspring and knowing the law — Bhīma, the chief of kings — along with his wife, entertained Damana royally. Damana was favorable towards Bhīma and his wife; and he granted their wish — a jewel of a daughter and three excellent and famous sons. The daughter was Damayantī; the sons were Dama, Dānta and the glorious Damana. The sons were endowed with all virtues and were awesome and strong.'"

VIII Notes

[1] These are the customary romanizations of the Skt dēvanāgarī. The more usual symbols for these segments — and those we use to describe the pre-Sanskrit stages — are /č/ for <c>, /č^h/ for <ch>, /ɟ^h/ for <jh>, /ɟ/ for <j> and /š/ for <ś>, which is also found romanized as <ç>. The usual romanization of /ŋ/ is <ñ> or <ṅ>. Here we use <ŋ>. And Skt <y> is our pre-Skt /j/.

[2] We have assumed that the /h/ arising from 8a ɟ^h-TO-h and 9a b^h/d^h-TO-h is phonetically the same as the "visarga" /h/ arising from 8b s/r CHANGES. The former is usually romanized as <h>, the latter as <ḥ>.

[3] The nasalized allophone [l^n] of /l/ arises from 7b NASAL ASSIM.

[4] Whitney (1960: 10) considers the /a/ to have been phonetically the mid back [ə].

[5] Long /ē, ō/ arise by 7a MON from earlier /ai, au/. We mark their length in our Sanskrit transcriptions. In the usual romanization the macron is omitted.

[6] The +vocalic or +syllabic /r̥, l̥/ are inherited from PIE. The PIE syllabic nasals /m̥, n̥/ become Skt /a/ by 2c SYL NAS. The long syllabic /r̥̄/ occurs very rarely, almost exclusively in the tVr-class noun paradigm and is clearly a Sanskrit innovation. (See section 1.5.3 of the morphology.)

[7] The nasalized vowels arise from 9d NASAL DELE. The usual romanization is to write <ṁ> after the nasalized vowel. Hence /a^n/ is <aṁ>.

[8] After 7a MON the only remaining diphthongs are /āi/ and /āu/. We transcribe them with the macron; the usual romanization is <ai, au> without it.

[9] In most Sanskrit grammars the forms of this class are cited as having undergone 8b s/r CHANGES. Hence the nominative singular is given as <dēváḥ> with the visarga <ḥ> instead of our dēvas.

[10] As a result of 5a e(:)/o(:)-TO-a(:) it is not clear whether the PIE antecedent had /e(:)/ or /o(:)/. Hence these PIE endings may have been *ósjo and *-ói. Recall that /j/ in our PIE reconstructions equals Skt <y>.

[11] According to Burrow (1959: 255) the final -a in this word was an Indo-Aryan postposition. The derivation is then *deiwṓi (5a e(:)/o(:)-TO-a(:)) > *daiwā́i+a (PIE 3.1.2c i-j/u-w ALT, applying synchronically and persistently) → *daiwā́ja (7a MON) > *dēwā́ja (10 w-TO-v) > Skt dēvā́ya.

[12] According to Burrow (1959: 255), the instrumental singular is probably from the ending of the demonstrative pronoun tḗna 'this' < PIE *t+óino (see 5.3).

[13] The dual genitive and locative endings are according to Barrow (op. cit.) from the demonstrative pronoun táyōs 'these' < PIE *t+ójous.

[14] The derivation is *deiwṓns (5a e(:)/o(:)-TO-a(:)) > *daiwā́ns (5c WF CL) > *daiwā́n (7a MON, 10 w-TO-v) >Skt dēvā́n.

[15] According to Burrow (1959: 238-9), the Skt -ā́n- infix in the genitive plural is from the Vn-class (1.5.4).

[16] The derivation of these forms is *deiwóisu and *deiwṓis (4a RETRO applying only to the first form) > *deiwóiṣu and *deiwṓis (5a e(:)/o(:)-TO-a(:)) > *daiwáiṣu and *daiwā́is (7a MON, 10 w-TO-v) > Skt dēvḗṣu and dēvā́is.

[17] A later form is yugā́ni with the -ni from the Vn-class (1.5.4).

[18] The *-i in these forms may be a deictic particle. The origin of the short /a/ in the antecedent forms is not clear. The vocative singular may have been shortened already in PIE times: *séinā > *séina. Then the stem *séina- intruded into other cases as well. Another possibility is that the short /a/'s in the instrumental singular and dual forms were influenced by the short /o/ in the corresponding o-class forms. E.g., o-class gen dual *deiw+ój+ous 'god' vs. the corresponding ā-class form *séin+āj+ous (5a e(:)/o(:)-TO-a(:)) > *daiwájaus vs. *sáinājaus (7a MON) > *dēwájos vs. *sḗnājōs (analogizing of the ending *-ajōs) > *dēwájōs and *sḗnajōs (10 w-TO-v) > Skt dēváyōs and sḗnayōs.

[19] The origin of the -yā- in the Sanskrit endings is not clear. It may have come from the jā-class, on which see below.

[20] The antecedent of the -m in the Sanskrit ending is not clear. Burrow (1959: 254) notes that such an ending does not occur in Iranian. Hence its occurrence in Sanskrit is probably a post-PIE innovation.

[21] The Sanskrit accusative plural is from the PIE nom pl *séinās. Otherwise the derivation would be *séinān̄s (5a e(:)/o(:)-TO-a(:)) > *sáinān̄s (5c WF CL) > *sáinān (7a MON) > Skt **sḗnān instead of sḗnās.

[22] The -n- in this ending is from the Vn-class 1.5.4.

[23] These endings are formed on the analogy of those of the ā-class. The analogy is that /ī/ substitutes for /ā/. Hence the nom sg *séin+ā corresponds to *déiw+ī and the voc sg *séin+a corresponds to *déiw+i.

[24] In these forms the ā-class ending has been added to the stem *deiw+ī-. The genitive singular derivation is *deiwī+ā́s (the unusual sequence /īā́/ reformed to /jā́/, possibly under the influence of jā-class nouns like *konjā́ 'girl' cited above) >*deiwjā́s (5a e(:)/o(:)-TO-a(:), 7a MON, 10 w-TO-v) > Skt dēvyā́s. A contributory factor in the association of /ī/ with /j/ may have been the early application of PIE 3.1.2f SIEVERS, which was then later dropped from Sanskrit. Hence the derivation of a long-stem jā-class gen sg *deiw+j+ā́s (PIE 3.1.2f SIEVERS applying synchronically) → *deiwijā́s, which would also be the interpretation of original *deiwīā́s. (Mayerhofer 1965: 42 considers the PIE /ī/ in such forms to have been an ablaut grade of /j/.)

[25] These are root-class athematic endings.

[26] This ending is from the root class.

[27] These endings are from the ā-class.

[28] The derivation is *wedʰū+ā́s (the unusual sequence /ū ā́/ reformed to /wā́/) > *wedʰwā́s (5a e(:)/o(:)-TO-a(:)) > *wadʰwā́s (10 w-TO-v) > Skt vadhvā́s.

[29] These forms show ablaut: nom sg Ø-grade, voc sg e-grade and the final vowel in the instr sg a lengthened ē- or ō-grade. Recall that as far as Sanskrit is concerned, the ablauting vowel could be either /e(:)/ or /o(:)/ because of change 5a e(:)/o(:)-TO-a(:).

[30] This ending may have come from the u-class (1.4).

[31] The derivation is PIE *egnéi+ei (PIE 3.1.2c i-j/u-w ALT applying synchronically) → *egnéjei (2a 1ST PAL not applying perhaps because the form is an early borrowing from a dialect which did not undergo 2a, but 5a e(:)/o(:)-TO-a(:) applies) > *agnájai (7a MON) > Skt agnáyē.

[32] The long /ī/ in these forms is modeled on the long /ā/ in the corresponding endings of the o-class. It is probably a Sanskrit innovation.

[33] The /n/ in this ending is from the Vn-class. The long /ī/ was probably short in PIE. It was lengthened in Sanskrit on the model of the o-class gen pl dēvā́nām 'gods' and the ā-class gen pl sḗnānām 'armies'. Hence the genitive plural ending was probably thought of as being [any thematic V, +long]nām.

[34] The i-class endings like those of agnís also occur: gen gátēs, loc gátāu, dat gátayē, abl gátēs.

[35] The derivation is *gʷḿ̥ti+ās (PIE 3.1.2c i-j/u-w ALT applying as a persistent synchronic rule) → *gʷḿ̥tjās (2c SYL NAS) > *gʷátjās (3 DELAB) > Skt gátyās.

[36] For all cases except the nominative, vocative or accusative singular, the stem is vā́ri(:)n- plus the Vn-class neuter endings.

[37] The derivation is *wṓrines (4a RETRO) > *wṓriṇes (5a e(:)/o(:)-TO-a(:)) > *wā́riṇes (10 w-TO-v) > Skt vā́riṇas.

[38] The long /ī/ occurs only in the nominative/accusative plural. It was probably lengthened on the model of the long vowel in the corresponding forms of the Vn-class neuter noun nā́māni 'names' under 1.5.4 below.

[39] The derivation is *ókʷsnes (3 DELAB) > *óksnes (4a RETRO 1) > *ókṣnes (4a RETRO 2c) > *ókṣṇes (5a e(:)/o(:)-TO-a(:)) > Skt ákṣṇas.

[40] The changes from PIE to Sanskrit can produce different endings in the Sanskrit forms. E.g., i-class voc sg *égnei 'fire' vs. u-class voc sg *kótreu 'enemy' (2a 1ST PAL, 5a e(:)/o(:)-TO-a(:)) > *ágnai vs. *šátrau (7a MON) > Skt ágnē vs. śátrō.

[41] The derivation is *kótreu+ei (PIE 3.1.2c i-j/u-w ALT applying synchronically) → *kótrewei (2a 1ST PAL) > *šátrewei (5a e(:)/o(:)-TO-a(:)) > *šátrawai (7a MON, 10 w-TO-v) > Skt śátravē.

[42] The derivation is *dʰeinu+ā́s (IF 3.l.2c i-j/u-w ALT applying synchronically) → *dʰeinwā́s (5a e(:)/o(:)-TO-a(:) and 7a MON) > *dʰēnwā́s (10 w-TO-v) > Skt dhēnvā́s. The original u-class ending also occurs: PIE *dʰeinéus (ev) > Skt dhēnṓs.

[43] The u-class form also occurs: Skt dhēnā́u < PIE *dʰeinḗu.

[44] The derivation of the nominative singular is *pḗds (lb OBSTR CL 2) > *pḗts (5a e(:)/o(:)-TO-a(:)) > *pā́ts (5c WF CL) > Skt pā́t. The nominative singular can also occur as Skt pā́d by 7d STOP ASSIM part (a); and similarly the vocative singular may also occur as pā́t by the same rule. The underlying form is /pa(:)d/.

[45] The derivation is *pédm̥ (2c SYL NAS) > *péda (5a e(:)/o(:)-TO-a(:)) > *páda (addition of -m to this ending from the thematic paradigms where it regularly occurs) > Skt pádam.

[46] Note the ablaut /ē, e/ in the root as well as the endings in this paradigm. Recall that as a result of change 5a e(:)/o(:)-TO-a(:) it is not clear if the ablauting vowels were in fact /e(:)/ or /o(:)/.

[47] The stress in this paradigm is determined by 11.1 SKT STRESS I-V-C: namely that any monosyllabic-root noun of the Ø-class has root stress in the nominative/accusative/vocative and elsewhere ending stress. Hence one would expect here Skt **pádas or even **pā́das. The occurring form padás may have been influenced by the ablative singular.

[48] The derivation of these two forms is *wṓks vs. *wōkés (2a 1ST PAL) > *wṓks vs. *wōšés (5a e(:)/o(:)-TO-a(:)) > *wā́ks vs. *wāšás (5c WF CL) > *wā́k vs. *wāšás (10 w-TO-v) > Skt vā́k vs. **vāśás instead of the actually occurring vācás. Apparently the nominative singular in /k/ was associated by speakers with an alternation with /č/, which would have arisen by 4b 2ND PAL, instead of the historical 2a 1ST PAL.

[49] The stem shows Ø- vs. o-grade ablaut. The derivations are *gʷégʷn̥t vs. *gʷégʷontə (la LARYNGEALS) > *gʷégʷn̥t vs. *gʷégʷonti (2c SYL NAS) > *gʷégʷat vs. *gʷégʷonti (3 DELAB) > *gégat vs. *gégonti (4b 2ND PAL) > *ɟégat vs. *ɟégonti (5a e(:)/o(:)-TO-a(:)) > Skt jágat vs. jáganti. (Note that the only possible ablauting vowel here is /o/.)

[50] The occurrence of the Sanskrit ending -i vs. -a in the other IE languages constitutes a problem. Some posit as its antecedent a PIE -ə; some posit a laryngeal. (See change la LARYNGEALS.)

[51] The vocative singular is derived from the nominative.

[52] The respective derivations are *bʰū́+s and *bʰū+és (5a e(:)/o(:)-TO-a(:)) > *bʰū́s and *bʰūás (8c V-SON ALT b) > *bʰū́s and *bʰuwás (10 w-TO-v) > Skt bhū́s and bhuvás. Whenever the ending begins with a vowel, change 8c V-SON ALT (b) applies.

[53] The stress configuration here is determined by 11.1 SKT STRESS I-V-C, namely the same rule which determines the stress of the Ø-class pā́t 'foot' under 1.5.1 above. Further, the oblique feminine singular cases may take endings from the ā-class: e.g., the gen sg *bʰū+ā́s (ev) > Skt bhuvā́s.

[54] The derivation is *bʰū+sú (4a RETRO) > Skt bhūṣú.

[55] The derivation is *nāu+és (PIE 3.1.2c i-j/u-w ALT applying synchronically) → *nāwés (5a e(:)/o(:)-TO-a(:)) > *nāwás (10 w-TO-v) > Skt nāvás.

[56] The nominative singular has the /ē/-grade ablaut, the other eases the Ø-grade. The derivation is *diḗus (PIE 3.1.2c i-j/u-w ALT applying synchronically) → *djḗus (11.1 SKT STRESS, the PIE morph cond version) > *djḗus (5a e(:)/o(:)-TO-a(:)) > Skt dyā́us.

[57] The derivation is *diØu+és (PIE 3.1.2c i-j/u-w ALT applying synchronically) → *diwés (5a e(:)/o(:)-TO-a(:)) > *diwás (10 w-TO-v) > Skt divás.

[58] The derivation is *diØu+b^{h}jós (PIE 3.1.2c i-j/u-w ALT applying synchronically) → *djub^{h}jós (5a e(:)/o(:)-TO-a(:)) > *djub^{h}jás (a stress shift to the root, perhaps on the model of the nominative, vocative or accusative cases) > Skt dyúbhyas.

[59] The expected derivation would be *g^{w}ṓu+m̥ (PIE 3.1.2c i-j/u-w ALT) → *g^{w}ṓwm̥ (2c SYL NAS) > *g^{w}ṓwa (addition of -m from other declensions, 3 DELAB) > *gṓwam (5a e(:)/o(:)-TO-a(:), 10 w-TO-v) > Skt **gā́vam instead of gā́m.

[60] The derivation is *g^{w}ou+í (PIE 3.1.2c i-j/u-w ALT) → *g^{w}owí (3 DELAB) > *gowí (5a e(:)/o(:)-TO-a(:)) > *gawí (10 w-TO-v) > Skt gávi. The only problem here is the stress shift from the ending to the root.

[61] The /ī, ū/ are short before endings beginning with a vowel. The reason for this is not clear. The derivations may have been like this: gen sg *nedī́+es, *tenū́+es (5a e(:)/o(:)-TO-a(:)) > *nadī́as, *tanū́as (8c V-SON ALT (b)) > Skt nadíjas and tanúwas, possibly written as <nadías> and <tanúas>.

[62] The expected derivation would be *pətḗr+s (la LARYNGEALS) > *pitḗrs (5a e(:)/o(:)-TO-a(:)) > *pitā́rs (5c WF CL) > Skt **pitā́r instead of pitā́. The form pitā́ may have been constructed on the model of a Vn-class noun such as rā́jā 'king' under 1.5.4 below.

[63] The derivation here is not clear. If the ending were *-s, a possibility might be *pətŕ̥s (? substitution of /ur/ for /r̥/) > *pətúrs (la LARYNGEALS) > *pitúrs (5c WF CL) > Skt pitúr.

[64] The long /r̥̄/ in these forms is a Sanskrit innovation on the model of the long vowels in the corresponding o-class forms dēvā́n 'gods' and dēvā́nām, respectively.

[65] The derivation is *pətŕ̥su (la LARYNGEALS) > *pitŕ̥su (4a RETRO 1) > Skt pitŕ̥ṣu.

[66] If an ending begins with a vowel, an /n/ is inserted on the model of the Vn-class 1.5.4 below.

[67] The derivation is *dōtŕ̥nə (la LARYNGEALS) > *dōtŕ̥ni (4a RETRO) > *dōtŕ̥ṇi (5a e(:)/o(:)-TO-a(:)) > Skt dātŕ̥ṇi.

[68] The reason for the absence of /n/ from the Sanskrit form is not clear. The PIE antecedent may have been *rḗgōn. Then the /n/ may have been lost later on the model of the neuter noun nā́ma 'name', the derivation of which is described immediately below.

[69] The Skt -am is from the thematic declension.

[70] The derivation is *rḗgn+es (2a 1ST PAL) > *rḗɟnes (5a e(:)/o(:)-TO-a(:)) > *rā́ɟnas (7b NASAL ASSIM 2b) > Skt rā́jñas.

[71] The derivation of these forms is*rḗgn+n̥s and *rḗgn̥+b^{h}jos (2a 1ST PAL) > *rḗɟnn̥s and *rḗɟn̥b^{h}jos (2c SYL NAS) > *rḗɟnas and *rḗɟab^{h}jos (5a e(:)/o(:)-TO-a(:)) > *rā́ɟnas and *rā́ɟab^{h}jas (7b NASAL ASSIM) > Skt rā́jñas and rā́jabhyas.

[72] The derivation is *nṓm+n̥ (2c SYL NAS) > *nṓma (5a e(:)/o(:)-TO-a(:)) > Skt nā́ma.

[73] The suffix *-ēn may have been ablauting *-ōn.

[74] The original meaning of this word was 'hand'. The semantic development was 'hand' > 'elephant's trunk' > 'elephant'.

[75] The derivation of the vocative singular is *g^{h}éstj+n (PIE 3.1.2c i-j/u-w ALT applying synchronically) → *g^{h}éstin (2a 1ST PAL) > *ɟ^{h}éstin (5a e(:)/o(:)-TO-a(:)) > *ɟ^{h}ástin (8a ɟ^h-TO-h) > Skt hástin. The nom sg hastī́ with long /ī́/ was influenced by the long final /ā/ in the corresponding nom sg rā́jā 'king'.

[76] The expected derivation would be *g^{h}estj́+n+b^{h}jos (PIE 3.1.2c i-j/u-w ALT) → *g^{h}estínb^{h}jos (2a 1ST PAL, 5a e(:)/o(:)-TO-a(:)) > *ɟ^{h}astínb^{h}jas (7b NASAL ASSIM) > *ɟ^{h}astímb^{h}jas (8a ɟ^h-TO-h) > Skt **hastímbhyas instead of hastíbhyas. The occurrence of /i/ instead of /im/ is modeled on the corresponding form rā́jabhyas.

[77] The derivation is *b^{h}éronts (5a e(:)/o(:)-TO-a(:)) > *b^{h}árants (5c WF CL) > Skt bháran.

[78] The derivation is *b^{h}érn̥tes (2c SYL NAS) > *b^{h}érates (5a e(:)/o(:)-TO-a(:)) > Skt bháratas. The masculine nominative/vocative/accusative cases take the o-grade ablaut stem *-ont; the other masculine cases take the Ø-grade *-n̥t.

[79] The derivation is *b^{h}érn̥t (2c SYL NAS, 5a e(:)/o(:)-TO-a(:)) > Skt bhárat. The neuter forms devolve from *-n̥t in all forms except the nominative/vocative/accusative dual and plural, which come from *-ont. Hence nominative plural neuter *b^{h}érontə > Skt bháranti.

[80] Feminine nouns usually come from the *-ont ending. A few devolve from *-n̥t such as Skt tudatī́ 'pushing', which also occurs as tudántī.

[81] Only the nominative singular has the ō-grade of the –Vs suffix. The other forms devolve from short /e/ or /o/.

[82] The V in the –Vs suffix contained ablauting /e(:)/ or /o(:)/ as well as non-ablauting /i/ or /u/.

[83] The derivation is *g^{h}ewíses (2a 1ST PAL) > *ɟ^{h}ewíses (4a RETRO) > *ɟ^{h}ewíṣes (5a e(:)/o(:)-TO-a(:)) > *ɟ^{h}awíṣas (8a ɟ^h-TO-h) > *hawíṣas (10 w-TO-v) > Skt havíṣas.

[84] The long nasal vowel occurs only in the nominative/accusative/vocative plural neuter. The antecedent suffix *-Vns with /n/ may have been influenced by the Vn-class. The derivation of *mén+ōns+ə is (1a LARYNGEALS) > *ménōnsi (5a e(:)/o(:)-TO-a(:)) > *ménānsi (9d NASAL DELE) > Skt mánāṁsi /mánā^{n}si/.

[85] The long nasal vowels /ī^n, ū^n/ instead of the expected short nasal vowels are formed on the analogy of the long /ā^n/ in mánāṁsi.

[86] The derivation is *mén+os+b^{h}jos (5a e(:)/o(:)-TO-a(:)) > *mánas+b^{h}jas (8b s/r CHANGES (a)) > Skt mánōbhyas.

[87] The derivation is *g^{h}ewís+b^{h}jos (2a 1ST PAL, 4a RETRO, 5a e(:)/o(:)-TO-a(:)) > *ɟ^{h}awíṣb^{h}jas (8a ɟ^h-TO-h) > *hawíṣb^{h}jas (8b s/r CHANGES (d)) > *hawírb^{h}jas (10 w-TO-v) > Skt havírbhyas.

[88] The derivation is *ménos+su (5a e(:)/o(:)-TO-a(:)) > *mánassu (8b s/r CHANGES (e)) > Skt mánahsu.

[89] The derivation is *g^{h}ewíssu (2a 1ST PAL) > *ɟ^{h}ewíssu (4a RETRO 1) > *ɟ^{h}ewíṣṣu (5a e(:)/o(:)-TO-a(:)) > *ɟ^{h}awíṣṣu (8a ɟ^h-TO-h) > *hawíṣṣu (8b s/r CHANGES (e)) > *hawíhṣu (10 w-TO-v) > Skt havíhṣu.

[90] The derivation is *k^{w}étuspod+s (1b OBSTR CL) > *k^{w}étuspots (3 DELAB) > *kétuspots (4a RETRO) > *kétuṣpots (4b 2ND PAL) > *čétuṣpots (5a e(:)/o(:)-TO-a(:)) > *čátuṣpats (5c WF CL) > Skt cátuṣpat.

[91] The feminine nouns of this class take the ending in /ī/.

[92] The derivation is similar to that of cátuṣpat above, but without the changes 1b OBSTR CL and 5c WF CL.

[93] See on this derivation 1.5.3 above.

[94] The derivation is *d^{h}ō+tŕ (PIE rule 3.1.2g SYL SON) → *d^{h}ōtŕ̥ (5a e(:)/o(:)-TO-a(:)) > Skt dhātŕ̥.

[95] See the paradigm of hastī 'elephant' under 1.5.4 above.

[96] The ending is from the fem ā/ī-class.

[97] The derivation is *belj́ (PIE 3.1.2c i-j/u-w ALT) → *belí (5a e(:)/o(:)-TO-a(:)) > Skt balí.

[98] This as well as the comparative and superlative adjectives is o- and ā-class.

[99] Recall that by the early morph cond rule 11.1 SKT STRESS I-A-i, comparative and superlative forms are stressed on the first syllable.

[100] This is a Vnt-class adjective. The suffix *-Vnt has ō-Ø grade ablaut. The derivation is *meg^{h}ṓnts (2a 1ST PAL) > *meɟ^{h}ṓnts (5a e(:)/o(:)-TO-a(:)) > *maɟ^{h}ā́nts (5c WF CL) > *maɟ^{h}ā́n (8a ɟ^h-TO-h) > Skt mahā́n.

[101] The derivation is *még^{h}n̥tteros (2a 1ST PAL) > *méɟ^{h}n̥tteros (2c SYL NAS) > *méɟ^{h}atteros (5a e(:)/o(:)-TO-a(:)) > *máɟ^{h}attaras (8a ɟ^h-TO-h) > Skt máhattaras.

[102] This is a u-class adjective. Ø-grade ablaut occurs in the positive root. The derivation is *mldús (PIE 3.1.2g SYL SON applying synchronically) → *ml̥dús (9b l/r ALT) > Skt mr̥dús.

[103] e-grade ablaut appears in the comparative and superlative root. The antecedent of the comparative suffix is *-ījVns-, where the ablauting V is ō- or Ø-grade. The endings of the comparative are those of the Ø-class under 2.4 above. The derivation of the nominative is *mléd+ījōns+s (5a e(:)/o(:)-TO-a(:)) > *mládījānss (5c WF CL) > *mládījān (9b l/r ALT) > Skt mrádīyān.

[104] The derivation is *mléd+ījōns+m̥ (2c SYL NAS and addition of -m from other declensions) > *mlédījōnsam (5a e(:)/o(:)-TO-a(:)) > *mládījānsam (9b l/r ALT) > *mrádījānsam (9d NASAL DELE) > Skt mrádīyāṁsam.

[105] The derivation is *mléd+ījn̥s+es (2c SYL NAS) > *mlédījases (5a e(:)/o(:)-TO-a(:), 9b l/r ALT) > Skt mrádīyasas.

106 The /ṭh/ in the Sanskrit form may be the reflex of a PIE laryngeal. If so, the derivation is *mlédisthos (la LARYNGEALS) > *mlédist^{h}os (4a RETRO) > *mlédiṣṭ^{h}os (5a e(:)/o(:)-TO-a(:), 9b l/r ALT) > Skt mrádiṣṭhas.

107 This is the neuter of a (j)o- and ā-class adjective. The derivation is *sn̥tjóm (2c SYL NAS) > *satjóm (5a e(:)/o(:)-TO-a(:)) > Skt satyám.

108 This is from the interrogative pronoun in 5.6 below.

109 This is from an adjective meaning 'repeated'. The derivation is *kónek^{w}+ōis (2a 1ST PAL) > *šónek^{w}ōis (3 DELAB) > *šónekōis (5a e(:)/o(:)-TO-a(:)) > Skt śánakāis.

110 The endings are usually those of the i-class plural.

111 The feminine forms inflect like the plural of the tVr-class. The derivation is *tisr+és (4a RETRO not applying to produce /ṣ/ because of the following /r/, but 5a e(:)/o(:)-TO-a(:)) > Skt tisrás.

112 The masculine and neuter endings are those of the athematic Ø-class.

113 The antecedent stem has Ø-grade ablaut. The derivation is *k^{w}etwØr+n̥s (PIE 3.1.2c i-j/u-w ALT applying synchronically) → *k^{w}etúrn̥s (2c SYL NAS) > *kwetúras (3 DELAB) > *ketúras (4b 2ND PAL) > *četúras (5a e(:)/o(:)-TO-a(:)) > Skt catúras.

114 The feminine forms consist of the Sanskrit stem cátasr- plus the endings. The endings are of the fem tisrás '3' above.

115 The oblique-case endings for the numerals from '5' through '19' are those of the athematic Ø-class . The derivation is *penk^{w}é+b^{h}is (3 DELAB) > *penkéb^{h}is (4b 2ND PAL) > *penčéb^{h}is (7b NASAL ASSIM 1, inherited from PIE and applying as a persistent synchronic rule) → *peñčéb^{h}is (5a e(:)/o(:)-TO-a(:)) > Skt pañcábhis.

116 The somewhat problematical derivation is *seks (4a RETRO applying here even to word-final /s/ on the model of inflected forms like *seks+b^{h}ís below) > *sekṣ (5a e(:)/o(:)-TO-a(:)) > *sakṣ (5c WF CL , ? with /k/ changed to the corresponding retroflex /ṭ/) > *saṭ (7c s-ASSIM b) > Skt ṣaṭ. Uhlenbeck (1973: 323) posits an early Skt *kṣaṭ from a PIE *ksweks.

117 The derivation is early *ṣaṭ+b^{h}ís (lb OBSTR CL 2 applying as a persistent synchronic rule) → Skt ṣaḍbhís.

118 The derivation is *oktṓu alongside *ok+ī+t+ís '80' below (2a 1ST PAL) > *oktṓu and *ošītís (/oš-/ from '80' replacing /ok-/ in '8') > *ošṭṓu and *ošītís (4a RETRO 2a) > *oṣṭṓu and *ošītís (5a e(:)/o(:)-TO-a(:)) > Skt aṣṭā́u, and aśītís.

119 The masculine and feminine oblique-case endings are affixed to the stem aṣṭā-. The neuter stem is aṣṭa-.

120 The numerals from '11' through '19' consist of a form of the units-numeral plus *dekm̥.

121 The numerals '20' through '90' are i-class fem nouns, The derivation of '20' is *wi+n+km̥+t+ís = *wi- '2' plus *-n- perhaps from the Vn-class plus *-km̥- perhaps from *dkm̥- (an ablauting form of *dékm̥ '10') plus the noun suffix *-t- plus *-is, the i-class ending (2a 1ST PAL) > *winšm̥tís (2c SYL NAS) > *winšatís (9d NASAL DELE) > *wi^{n}šatís (10 w-TO-v) > Skt viṁśatís /vi^{n}šatís/.

122 The /ī/ in this numeral may have been a Ø-class neuter dual ending.

123 The numerals '100' and '1000' are o-class neuter nouns. Burrow (1959: 261) posits as the PIE antecedent *dkm̥tóm, "...a neuter collective noun meaning 'a decade (of tens)".

124 The PIE antecedents are *sm̥- '1' and *g^{h}éslom '1000'. The derivation is *sm̥g^{h}éslom (2a 1ST PAL) > *sm̥ɟ^{h}éslom (2c SYL NAS) > *saɟ^{h}éslom (5a e(:)/o(:)-TO-a(:)) > *saɟ^{h}áslam (8a ɟ^{h}-TO-h) > *sahāslam (9b l/r ALT) > Skt sahásram.

125 This suffix is that of the superlative.

126 There may have been an PIE laryngeal in this form.

127 The ordinals from '5th' through '10th' add -más to the bare cardinal numeral.

128 The ordinals from '11th' to '20th' add the adjective ending to the bare cardinal number.

129 This and the remaining ordinals either add the adjective ending directly to the cardinal or add the superlative suffix -tamás.

130 There may have been a PIE laryngeal in the antecedent form. Hence the derivation is *eghóm (la LARYNGEALS) > *eg^{h}óm (2a 1ST PAL) > *eɟ^{h}óm (5a e(:)/o(:)-TO-a(:)) > *aɟ^{h}ám (8a ɟ^{h}-TO-h) > Skt ahám. Otherwise without the /h/

in the antecedent, the derivation would be *egóm (2a 1ST PAL) > *eɟóm (5a e(:)/o(:)-TO-a(:)) > Skt **ajám instead of ahám.

[131] The other singular forms begin with m-.

[132] The precise antecedent here is not clear. The other dual forms begin with āv-.

[133] The derivation is *wei+óm (PIE 3.1.2c i-j/u-w ALT, applying synchronically) → *wejóm (5a e(:)/o(:)-TO-a(:)) > *wajám (10 w-TO-v) > Skt vayám.

[134] The other plural forms begin with asm-. The derivation is *n̥smṓns (2c SYL NAS) > *asmṓns (5a e(:)/o(:)-TO-a(:)) > *asmā́ns (5c WF CL) > Skt asmā́n.

[135] The other forms of the singular begin with t- or tv-.

[136] The other dual forms begin with yuv- or v-.

[137] The other plural forms begin with yuṣm-. The derivation is *jusmṓns (4a RETRO) > *juṣmṓns (5a e(:)/o(:)-TO-a(:)) > *juṣmāns (5c WF CL) > Skt yuṣmān.

[138] These endings are those of the masculine and neuter o-class nouns.

[139] These endings are pronominal.

[140] The derivation is *tṓns (5a e(:)/o(:)-TO-a(:), 5c WF CL) > Skt tān.

[141] The derivation is *tóisōm (4a RETRO) > *tóiṣōm (5a e(:)/o(:)-TO-a(:)) > *táiṣām (7a MON) > Skt tḗṣām.

[142] These endings are those of the fem ā-class nouns.

[143] Otherwise the feminine dual is like the masculine dual.

[144] The other neuter forms are like the masculine.

[145] These are from the same PIE root *i- with e- and Ø- ablaut.

[146] The derivations are *ei+óm and *ei+bʰís is (PIE 3.1.2c i-j/u-w ALT applying as a synchronic rule) → *ejóm and *eibʰís (5a e(:)/o(:)-TO-a(:)) > *ajám and *aibʰís (7a MON) > Skt ayám and ēbhís.

[147] This form consists of the acc sg *i+m plus the readded accusative singular masculine ending *-om.

[148] This form consists of the mere inflectional ending used pronominally.

[149] This form consists of *i- plus the neuter ending *-d plus the particle *-om.

[150] The *i- is an original deictic element. The derivation is *iós (PIE 3.1.2c i-j/u-w ALT) → *jós (5a e(:)/o(:)-TO-a(:)) > Skt yás.

[151] The expected derivation would be *kʷim (3 DELAB) > *kim (4b 2ND PAL) > Skt **cim instead of kim. The /k/ was reintroduced from other forms in the paradigm which did not undergo 4b 2ND PAL.

[152] The middle voice has the reflexive meaning 'to do for oneself or on one's own behalf'. There seems to be no verb occurring in the active which may not also occur in the middle. E.g., act yájati 'he offers a sacrifice (say, as a priest for someone else)' vs. mid yájatē 'he offers a sacrifice (for himself and on his own behalf)'.

[153] The subjunctive even at the time of the Vedic language was, according to Burrow (1939: 299), "the normal means of expressing the future". It remains in the classical language to function as a 1st singular imperative. The subjunctive is also used to express a wish or an obligation imposed by the speaker. E.g., śatam.. jīvāti śarádah 'he should or may he live 100 autumns'. The optative expresses a wish or a desire. E.g., yad bhūyāsur vibhūtayah 'there ought to be changes'. The optative is also found in conditional if-then sentences. Whitney (1960: 216) says of the subjunctive, imperative and optative (as far as the classical language is concerned) that "no sharp line of division exists between them; they are more or less exchangeable with one another, and combinable in co-ordinate clauses".

[154] The middle forms serve as passives in the perfect, pluperfect, aorist and future.

[155] The injunctive (inj) is a tenseless form, the use of which is described under 6.1.5 below.

[156] The conditional is derived morphologically from the future. Its use is described under 6.6.2 below.

[157] The imperfect, perfect and aorist are past tenses whose usages tend to merge. Whitney (1960: 328) says of the aorist of the classical language that "[t]he aorist of the later language is simply a preterite, equivalent to the imperfect and perfect". Burrow (1959: 295-300) notes of the aorist that it denotes a past event which has from the point of view of the speaker just been completed. Whitney (op. cit.) says that the aorist describes an event which has been personally experienced by the speaker. The perfect, on the other hand, may describe a past event not personally

witnessed by the speaker. It may also describe a present state which has arisen from an event in the past. E.g., perf bibhā́ya 'he got scared = is now frightened'.

158 The x's within the parentheses denote forms which are either extremely rare or occur only in the early language. We have not included them among the paradigms below.

159 These ten classes govern only the present and imperfect formations. Hence two verbs of the same class which form their present and imperfect paradigms similarly may form their aorist paradigms differently. E.g., 1st class 3sg pres pátati 'fly, fall' and bhájati 'divide' vs. 3sg reduplicated aorist ápaptat and sigmatic s-aorist ábhākṣīt.

160 The terms "thematic" and "athematic" refer to the presence vs. the absence of a vowel between a root and a verbal ending. E.g., the 3rd singular of the 1st class thematic verb bhárati 'carry' < PIE *bʰér+e+ti vs. the 2nd class athematic verb dvḗṣṭi 'hate' < PIE *dwéis+ti. The arrangement of the present and imperfect formations into ten classes is found in several sources including Whitney (1990). Almost all verbs can belong to more than one of these classes: e.g., thematic 1st class bhárati 'carry' < *bʰér+e+ti as well as the same verb in the athematic 3rd class bíbharti < *bʰ í+bʰer+ti.

161 The original PIE antecedent was the thematic form *bʰér+ō to which the athematic ending *-mi was added in pre-Sanskrit times.

162 The antecedent forms may have had a PIE laryngeal /h/. The derivation of the 2nd dual is *bʰér+e+thes (la LARYNGEALS 1 iii and la LARYNGEALS 2) > *bʰéretʰes (5a e(:)/o(:)-TO-a(:)) > Skt bhárathas.

163 The derivation is *dwéisti (4a RETRO) > *dwéiṣṭi (5a e(:)/o(:)-TO-a(:)) > *dwáiṣṭi (7a MON) > *dwḗṣṭi (10 w-TO-v) > Skt dvḗṣṭi.

164 The ending is from the thematic class. Otherwise the derivation would be *dwis+ńti (PIE 3.1.2g SYL SON applying synchronically) → *dwisń̥ti (2c SYL NAS) > *dwisáti (ev) > Skt **dviṣáti instead of dviṣánti.

165 The derivation is *gʰu+gʰéu+mi (2a 1ST PAL) > *ɟʰujʰéumi (2b GRASSMANN) > *ɟujʰéumi (5a e(:)/o(:)-TO-a(:)) > *ɟujʰáumi (7a MON) > *ɟujʰṓmi (8a ɟʰ-TO-h) > Skt juhṓmi.

166 The derivation is *nédʰ+j+ō+mi (5a e(:)/o(:)-TO-a(:)) > *nádʰjāmi (9a bʰ/dʰ-TO-h) > Skt náhyāmi.

167 The derivation is *junégmi (2a 1ST PAL) > *junéɟmi (5a e(:)/o(:)-TO-a(:)) > Skt yunájmi.

168 The derivation is *junégsi (lb OBSTR CL 2) > *junéksi (4a RETRO) > *junékṣi (5a e(:)/o(:)-TO-a(:)) > Skt yunákṣi.

169 The derivation is *jungwés (2a 1ST PAL) > *junɟwés (7b NASAL ASSIM 1, inherited from PIE and applying as a persistent synchronic rule) → *juñɟwés (5a e(:)/o(:)-TO-a(:)) > *juñɟwás (10 w-TO-v) > Skt yuñjvás.

170 The derivation is *tn̥néumi (2c SYL NAS) > *tanéumi (5a e(:)/o(:)-TO-a(:)) > *tanáumi (7a MON) > Skt tanṓmi.

171 The derivation is *tn̥nuwés (2c SYL NAS, 5a e(:)/o(:)-TO-a(:)) > *tanuwás (10 w-TO-v) > Skt tanuvás. The Ø-grade of the suffix *-nu- can occur without the /u/. Hence an alternate form is Skt tanvás.

172 The derivation is *bʰn̥dʰnā́mi (2b GRASSMANN) > *bn̥dʰnā́mi (2c SYL NAS) > Skt badhnā́mi.

173 Only -n- as opposed to –nī- occurs if the ending begins with a vowel. The antecedents of -nā́- and -nī- are not clear. Mayrhofer (1965: 82) posits antecedents with laryngeals.

174 The word may be a non-PIE borrowing. The derivation is *kʷeuréjōmi (3 DELAB) > *keuréjōmi (4b 2ND PAL) > *čeuréjōmi (5a e(:)/o(:)-TO-a(:), 7a MON) > Skt cōráyāmi.

175 The -i is from the indicative paradigm. It is optional in the 2nd and 3rd persons.

176 The derivation is *bʰérōnt (5a e(:)/o(:)-TO-a(:)) > *bʰárānt (5c WF CL) > Skt bhárān.

177 These are subjunctive forms.

178 This ending differs from that of the thematic classes. The derivation is not clear: one would expect *dwis+dʰí (1b OBSTR CL 2) > *dwizdʰí (4a RETRO 1 and 2a) > *dwiẓḍʰ í (5b VzC-TO-V̄C) > *dwīḍʰ í (10 w-TO-v) > **dvīḍhí instead of dviḍḍhí. The short /i/ might have been inserted here from the dual and plural forms where it occurs regularly.

179 The derivation of these forms in which the ending begins with a vowel are *bʰér+oi+om and *bʰér+oi+ur (PIE 3.1.2c i-j/u-w ALT applying synchronically) → *bʰérojom and *bʰérojur (5a e(:)/o(:)-TO-a(:)) > *bʰárajam and *bʰárajur (replacement of the /a/ preceding /j/ by /ē/, where it occurred regularly as in the 2sg bhárēs and elsewhere in the paradigm) > Skt bhárēyam and bhárēyur.

[180] The derivation is *b^{h}érois (5a e(:)/o(:)-TO-a(:)) > *b^{h}árais (7a MON) > Skt bhárēs.

[181] On the ending -ur see 6.3.1 below.

[182] Recall that the thematic marker was -oi-. Both thematic *-oi- and athematic *-jē- are probably ablauting versions of one and the same suffix *-(o)ī(ē)-, where /o/ and /ē/ could ablaut with the null-grade Ø. When *-oī- occurred, the PIE rule 3.1.2b DIPH applied producing the acceptable diphthong *-oi-. When *-īē- occurred, PIE 3.1.2c i-j/u-w ALT applied to produce *-jē-.

[183] The *-ai formative in all forms except the 1st singular is often posited as *-oi.

[184] The derivation is *b^{h}érōwod^{h}ai (5a e(:)/o(:)-TO-a(:)) > *b^{h}árāwad^{h}ai (7a MON) > *b^{h}árāwad^{h}ē (9a b^{h}/d^{h}-TO-h) > *b^{h}árāwahē (10 w-TO-v) > Skt bhárāvahē.

[185] The derivation is *dwissái (4a RETRO 1) > *dwiṣsái (4a RETRO 2b) > *dwikṣái (7a MON > *dwikṣḗ (10 w-TO-v) > Skt dvikṣḗ.

[186] The derivation is *dwistái (4a RETRO 1) > *dwiṣtái (4a RETRO 2a) > *dwiṣṭái (7a MON, 10 w-TO-v) > Skt dviṣṭḗ.

[187] The derivation is problematic. One would expect *dwisd^{h}wái (lb OBSTR CL 2) > *dwizd^{h}wái (4a RETRO) > *dwiẓḍ^{h}wái (7a MON) > *dwīḍwḗ (10 w-TO-v) > Skt **dvīḍhvḗ instead of the actually occurring dviḍḍhvḗ.

[188] The usual means of forming the subjunctive from the indicative by lengthening a short vowel in the ending was followed here in that the middle marker *-ai was lengthened to *-āi. This lengthening seems to have been optional in the 2nd and 3rd singular. The derivation of the two 2nd singular forms is *b^{h}érēsai and *b^{h}érēsāi (5a e(:)/o(:)-TO-a(:)) > *b^{h}árāsai and *b^{h}árāsāi (7a MON) > Skt bhárāsē and bhárāsāi.

[189] The derivations of these forms are analogous to those under 6.1.4 above.

[190] The derivation is *dwiṣīá (4a RETRO) > *dwiṣīá (8c V-SON ALT) > *dwiṣiyá (replacement of /i/ by /ī/ from the other endings where it occurred regularly) > *dwiṣīyá (10 w-TO-v) > Skt dviṣīyá.

[191] These forms have thematic endings. Otherwise they would occur as Skt **ádvēṣa and **ádviṣat, respectively. Their derivation is *é+dweis+om and *é+dwis+o+nt (4a RETRO) > *édweiṣom and *édwiṣont (5a e(:)/o(:)-TO-a(:)) > *ádwaiṣam and *ádwiṣant (5c WF CL) > *ádwaiṣam and *ádwiṣan (7a MON) > *ádwēṣam and *ádwiṣan (10 w-TO-v) > Skt ádvēṣam and ádviṣan.

[192] The derivation of these forms is *é+dweis+s and *é+dweis+t (4a RETRO 1) > *édweiṣs and *édweiṣṭ (4a RETRO 2b) > *édweiṭṣ and *édweiṣṭ (5a e(:)/o(:)-TO-a(:)) > *ádwaiṭṣ and *adwaiṣṭ (5c WF CL) > *ádwaiṭ and *ádwaiṣ (7a MON) > *ádwēṭ and *ádwēṣ (10 w-TO-v) > Skt ádvēṭ and ádvēṣ. At some point the 3rd singular **ádvēṣ was replaced by ádvēṭ, probably because the /ṭ/ looked more like a 3rd person ending.

[193] Like the present paradigm, the athematic imperfect has Ø-grade ablaut in the dual and plural.

[194] These are the only forms in this athematic paradigm with thematic vowels before the endings.

[195] Roots ending in a vowel (usually /a(:)/ add the particle -u to the ending: e.g., Skt 1sg dadhā́u 'set'. The probable derivation is PIE 1sg *d^{h}e+d^{h}ḗ+a (2b GRASSMAN) > *ded^{h}ḗa (5a e(:)/o(:)-TO-a(:)) > *dad^{h}ā́a (/ā́a/ restructured to /ā́/) > *dad^{h}ā́ (addition of -u) > Skt dadhā́u.

[196] In some verbs these endings occur without /i/. E.g., Skt 2sg cakártha 'you have done' from PIE *k^{w}e+k^{w}ór+tha.

[197] In some sources such as Whitney (1960: 288) these forms are listed with final /s/ as tutudáthus and tutudátus. The antecedent forms were as given with final /r/. The reason for this confusion would seem to be that after 8b s/r CHANGES, two underlying forms were possible, /tutudúr/ or /tutudús/, both of which would be realized as tutudúḥ. Hence it was unclear, probably even to native speakers, what the underlying form was.

[198] In some verbs the /i/ is lacking.

[199] The derivation is *é+g^{h}e+g^{h}rob^{h}+om (2a 1ST PAL not applying, possibly because the form is an early borrowing from a dialect not undergoing 1ST PAL, but 2b GRASSMANN does apply) > *égegrob^{h}om (4b 2ND PAL) > *éǰegrobhom (5a e(:)/o(:)-TO-a(:)) > Skt ájagrabham.

[200] Short /i/ occurs in certain forms. Mayrhofer (1965: 86) considers the antecedent of the /i(:)/ to have been a laryngeal.

[201] The derivation is *é+bheudh+īs+t (2b GRASSMANN) > *ébeudʰīst (4a RETRO) > *ébeudʰīṣṭ (5a e(:)/o(:)-TO-a(:)) > *ábaudʰīṣṭ (5c WF CL) > *ábaudʰīṣ (7a MON) > *ábōdʰīṣ (replacement of /ṣ/ by /t/ which is the usual 3rd singular ending) > Skt ábōdhīt.

[202] This aorist results from a conflation of the classes 6.5.1.4 and 6.5.1.5 above. The derivation is *é+jē+sis+t (4a RETRO) > *éjēsiṣṭ (5a e(:)/o(:)-TO-a(:)) > *ájāsiṣṭ (5c WF CL) > *ájāsiṣ (replacement of /s/ by /t/ which is the usual 3rd singular ending) > Skt áyāsit.

[203] The derivations are *bʰū+jḗ+s+s and *bʰū+jḗ+s+t (5a e(:)/o(:)-TO-a(:)) > *bʰūjā́ss and *bʰūjā́st (5c WF CL) > *bʰūjā́s and *bʰūjā́s for both forms (addition of the usual 3rd singular ending -t) > Skt bhūyā́s and bhūyā́t.

[204] This is a thematic ending.

[205] The derivation is *é+tēud+s+tom (lb OBSTR CL 2) > *étēutstom (lb OBSTR CL 3) > *étēuttom (5a e(:)/o(:)-TO-a(:)) > Skt átāuttam.

[206] The endings of this paradigm are generally those of the athematic imperfect active (6.2.1). However, the 3rd plural -ur is from the perfect active paradigm (6.3.1).

[207] The endings are those of the thematic imperfect middle indicative (6.2.2).

[208] The endings are those of the athematic imperfect middle indicative (6.2.2).

[209] The derivation is *é+teud+s+thās (la LARYNGEALS) > *éteudstʰās (lb OBSTR CL 2 and 3) > *éteuttʰās (5a e(:)/o(:)-TO-a(:), 7a MON) > Skt átōtthās.

[210] One would expect Skt **dātā́ssi from this antecedent.

[211] The 3rd person forms consist of only the noun.

[212] The meaning of the conditional is 'I was going to carry or give' or 'I would (under certain circumstances) carry or give'.

[213] The reduplicated syllable seems to have consisted of *de- plus the root vowel -ī- . The derivation is *déī+dīp+j+etai (PIE 3.1.2b DIPH, which changes /eī/ into a normal diphthong /ei/) > *déidīpjetai (5a e(:)/o(:)-TO-a(:)) > *dáidīpjatai (7a MON) > Skt dḗdīpyatē.

[214] The reduplicated syllable consists of the word-initial consonant plus the root vowel.

[215] The derivation is *gʷí+gʷīw+is+eti (3 DELAB) > *gígīwiseti (4a RETRO) > *gígīwiṣeti (4b 2ND PAL) > *ɟíɟīwiṣeti (5a e(:)/o(:)-TO-a(:)) > *ɟíɟīwiṣati (10 w-TO-v) > Skt jíjīviṣati.

[216] The vowel alternation of /a/ vs. /ū/ in Skt mar- vs. mūr- is not easy to explain. However, if one assumes a laryngeal in the PIE antecedent, one can posit a common kind of PIE ablaut. The derivation would then be unmarked *mérh+eti vs. desiderative *mú+mr̥h+s+eti (la LARYNGEALS 1-ii-a and 2) > *méreti and *múmūrseti (4a RETRO and 5a e(:)/o(:)-TO-a(:)) > Skt márati and múmūrṣati.

[217] These are u-class masculine nouns.

[218] This is a neuter Ø-class noun.

[219] This is an ablauting form of *bʰū-. Its derivation is *bʰéū+ont- (PIE 3.l.2b DIPH) → *bʰéu+ont- (PIE 3.l.2c i-j/u-w ALT) → *bʰéwont- (5a e(:)/o(:)-TO-a(:), 10 w-TO-v) > Skt bhávant-.

[220] This is a class 3 reduplicating verb (6.1.1.3 above). Its derivation is *gʰú+gʰu+n̥t- (PIE 3.l.2c i-j/u-w ALT) → *gʰúgʰwn̥t- (2a 1ST PAL) > *ɟʰúɟʰwn̥t- (2b GRASSMANN) > *ɟúɟʰwn̥t- (2c SYL NAS) > *ɟúɟʰwat- (8a ɟʰ-TO-h) > *ɟúhwat- (10 w-TO-v) > Skt júhvat-.

[221] The derivation is *bʰéromēno- (4a RETRO 2c) > *bʰéromēṇo- (5a e(:)/o(:)-TO-a(:)) > Skt bháramāṇa-.

[222] The derivation is *kʷekʷr̥+wṓns+s (3 DELAB) > *kekr̥wṓnss (4b 2ND PAL) > *čekr̥wṓnss (5a e(:)/o(:)-TO-a(:)) > *čakr̥wā́nss (5c WF CL) > *čakr̥wā́n (10 w-TO-v) > Skt cakr̥vā́n.

[223] The derivation is *kʷekʷr̥+wṓns+m̥ (2c SYL NAS, 3 DELAB , 4b 2ND PAL) > *čekr̥wṓnsa (addition of -m from the thematic declension) > *čekr̥wṓnsam (5a e(:)/o(:)-TO-a(:)) > *čakr̥wā́nsam (9d NASAL DELE, 10 w-TO-v) > Skt cakr̥vā́ṁsam.

[224] The derivation is *kʷekʷr̥+ws+es (PIE 3.1.2c i-j/u-w ALT applying synchronically) → *kʷekʷr̥úses (PIE 3.1.2g SYL SON now not applying, so [r] results instead of [r̥]) → *kʷekʷrúses (3 DELAB) > *kekrúses (4a RETRO) > *kekrúṣes (4b 2ND PAL) > *čekrúṣes (5a e(:)/o(:)-TO-a(:)) > Skt cakrúṣas.

225 The derivation is *kʷekʷr̥+wń̥t+bʰjos (lb OBSTR CL 2) > *kʷekʷr̥wń̥dbʰjos (2c SYL NAS) > *kʷekʷr̥wádbʰjos (3 DELAB, 4b 2ND PAL) > *čekr̥wádbʰjos (5a e(:)/o(:)-TO-a(:)) > *čakr̥wádbʰjas (10 w-TO-v) > Skt cakr̥vádbhyas.

226 The derivation is *kʷr̥+tó+wōnt+s (3 DELAB) > *kr̥tówōnts (5a e(:)/o(:)-TO-a(:)) > *kr̥táwānts (5c WF CL) > *kr̥táwān (10 w-TO-v) > Skt kr̥távān.

227 The derivation is *kʷīl+n+ó- (3 DELAB, 4b 2ND PAL for some reason not applying) > *kīlnó- (5a e(:)/o(:)-TO-a(:)) > *kīlná- (9b l/r ALT) > Skt kīrná-.

228 The derivation is *kʷor+enījó- (3 DELAB) > *korenījó- (4a RETRO 2c) > *koreṇījó- (5a e(:)/o(:)-TO-a(:)) > Skt karaṇīyá-.

229 The two meanings of this construction can be illustrated by these two sentences: "While *doing* this, they talk." and "After *having done* this, they talked."

230 The antecedent may have been an instrumental singular form.

231 The antecedent is an accusative singular o-class neuter ending.

232 Nala+upa+akhyānam (6 V##V-TO-V̄) → Nalaupākhyānam (7a MON) → Nalōpākhyānam.

233 upa+pad+n+nás (7d STOP ASSIM) → upapannás (8b s/r CHANGES) → upapannṓ.

234 upári upári (8c V-SON ALT) → upáry upári.

235 vēdavíts śū́ras (5c WF CL) → vēdavít śū́ras (7d STOP ASSIM) → vēdavíc śū́ras (a version of 4b 2ND PAL 2, applying as a persistent rule of sandhi) → vēdavic chū́ras (8b s/r CHANGES) → vēdavic chū́rō.

236 Táthā ēvá asīt (6 V##V-TO-V̄) → Táthāivā́sīt (7d STOP ASSIM) → Táthāivā́sīd.

237 This is a post-Vedic formation. It consists of the perfect of 'be' which is preceded by the accusative singular of a fem ā-class noun constructed from the perfect stem of the verb plus the suffix -ay-.

238 kurnārā́n ca (7c s-ASSIM) → kumārā́nś ca (9d NASAL DELE) → kumārā́ṁś ca.

239 The more frequently occurring form is mahāyaśasas.

Chapter 8

Hittite

I Introduction

Hittite is the most copiously attested of the Anatolian languages. (Other Anatolian languages are Hieroglyphic Hittite, Luwian, Palaic, Lydian and Lycian.) Hittite is preserved in cuneiform clay tablets written in a syllabary as described in section III Hittite Phonology below and dating from about 1650 to 1200 BC. After the discovery of the Hittite literary monuments in 1906 in Turkey, the language was able to be deciphered because some of the cuneiform Hittite texts were also written in Akkadian and Assyrian, two languages which were already known.

The position of Hittite within the PIE family has been a subject of some debate. According to the "Indo-Hittite hypothesis" proposed by Edgar Sturtevant, the PIE family tree was like this:

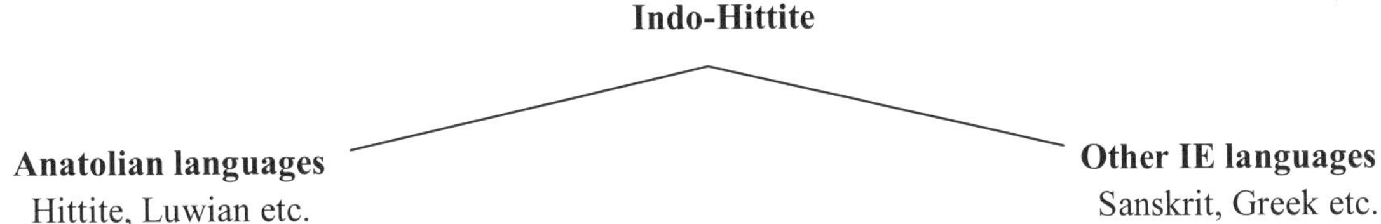

According to this theory Hittite reflects an earlier stage of PIE than do languages like Sanskrit, Greek and the others. We do not subscribe to this view here. Rather, we assume that our records of Hittite reflect an IE language which had undergone massive change from its PIE origins. Our reasons for this assumption are briefly these three.

First, it has been noted as an archaic feature of the language that Hittite has only a common (com) gender instead of masc and fem. In section IV, Historical Hittite Morphology, we argue that the development of the com gender was a Hittite innovation from an original masc vs. fem paradigm.

Second, the lack of oblique plural inflection in Hittite has been posited as an archaic PIE feature. In section IV we argue that traces of the earlier inflection can be found in Hittite, particularly of the genitive plural ending. The lack of oblique plural inflection in Hittite represents a Hittite innovation and not a retention from PIE.

Third, we assume that both the structure and the lexicon of Hittite were strongly influenced by the non-IE languages with which it came into contact. In this connection Kronasser (1956: 219) has noted that of some 1500 words of basic Hittite vocabulary, only about 20% are of IE origin. Indeed, even the name "Hatti" by which the Hittites called themselves was the name of a pre-IE population whom the Hittites displaced. Friedrich (1960: 15) suggests that the Hittites may have referred to their own language as "Nešili" /nésili/ after a placename in the area.

As described in section III Hittite phonology, we give the traditional Hittite orthography in brackets, e.g. <hu-u-ma-an-za> 'all'. Its phonemic transcription is /húmant^{h}s/, which forms we shall usually write without the slashes and without the indication of stress since — as we suggest in le HITTITE STRESS — Hittite stress fell invariably on the first syllable of a word.

II The Changes from PIE into Hittite

A. Overview of the Changes and their Chronology

The stages are ordered. The changes within each stage may have been in any order or roughly simultaneous. The beginning and terminal dates of the changes given below are from ca. 3000 BC to 1650 BC.

STAGE 1 (ca. 3000 BC or later)

STAGE 2

STAGE 3

STAGE 4

STAGE 5

STAGE 6

STAGE 7

B. The Changes

1a The Changes in Labiovelar Consonants (LABIOVEL)

These changes restructure the phonemic inventory of the language and are then dropped from the grammar. The changes are these:

(a) k^w, g^w, g^{hw} → k, g, g^h / ___[C, –sonorant]

(b) k^w, g^w → kw, gw / ___V

" " → ku, gu / ___[C, +sonorant]

(c) g^{hw} → w / ___ [V, +round]

" → g^hw / ___ [V, –round]

" → g^hu / ___ [C, +sonorant]

That is, (a) the PIE labiovelars lose the labial feature if followed by an obstruent consonant. (b) The unary segments /k^w/ and /g^w/ become bisegmental /kw/ and /gw/ before a vowel; and they become /ku/ and /gu/ before a sonorant consonant. (c) The unary segment /g^{hw}/ becomes /w/ before a round vowel, bisegmental /g^hw/ before a nonround vowel and /g^hu/ before a sonorant consonant.

E.g., (a) PIE 2sg perf *sok^w+ta 'you have seen' (LABIOVEL) > *sokta (2b OBSTR) > *so$k^h t^h$a (6 e/o-TO-a) > *so$k^h t^h$i (replacement of final -a by -i from the pres) > Hit sa$k^h t^h$i <sa-ak-ti> 'you know'. (b) PIE nom sg *$k^w$is 'who?' and *k^wod 'what?' (LABIOVEL) > *kwis and *kwod (2b OBSTR) > *k^hwis and *k^hwot (6 e/o-TO-a) > Hit k^hwis and k^hwat 'why'. And (c) PIE 3sg pass *g^{hw}or+oni 'is burnt' (LABIOVEL) > *woroni (6 e/o-TO-a) > Hit warani <wa-ra-a-ni>. (Given our formulation of LABIOVEL, LABIOVEL must precede 6 e/o-TO-a. LABIOVEL must also precede 2b OBSTR since the latter change conflates PIE /k^w/ and /g^{hw}/ to Hittite /k^{hw}/.) Also PIE 3sg pres *g^{hw}en+ti 'kill' vs. the Ø-grade ablauting 3pl *g^{hw}Øn+onti (LABIOVEL) > *g^hwenti and *g^hunonti (2b OBSTR) > *k^hwent^hi and *k^hunont^hi (3a t^h-TO-t^s) > *k^hent^si and *k^hunont^si (6 e/o-TO-a) > Hit k^hwent^si <ku-en-zi> and k^hunant^si <ku-na-an-zi>.

1b Some Possible Rules for Laryngeals (LARYNGEALS)

There are two views in the literature on the position of Hittite with regard to PIE laryngeals. Each view assumes a phonological rule in the development of Hittite from PIE. Whichever of these changes did in fact occur, either one of them would have restructured various lexical items as well as the phonemic inventory of the language and then would have dropped from the grammar.

According to the first view, one or more laryngeals existed in PIE. Certain of them were retained in Hittite and were reflected orthographically in words written with <ḫ>. (Here we shall write <h> without the subscript. We assume graphemic <h> can represent both /h/ as well as /x/ in some Hittite borrowings from non-IE languages. See on this note 2 in III Hittite Phonology below.)

Examples of Hittite words which under this view contain PIE laryngeals are haras 'eagle', hant^has 'front', the i-class adj harkis 'white' and the 1sg pres tehi 'I put, place' from PIE *horos, *hantos, *hargis (occurring also as an o-and ā-class Greek adj argós 'white') and *d^hēh+i, respectively. (We also designate the purported PIE laryngeals with "h".) However, given this view, there also occur Hittite words without /h/ whose PIE antecedents are reconstructed with laryngeals. E.g., Hittite 1sg pres etmi 'I eat', 1sg pres esmi 'I am', nom sg <e-es-har> eshar 'blood' vs. gen sg <e-es-na-as> esnas and ap^ha 'back, again' from PIE laryngeal forms *hedmi, *hesmi, *hesh+or vs. *hesh+nos and *hapo, respectively.

Hence under this view and given these Hittite forms and their PIE antecedents, one must posit a laryngeal-deletion rule which could apply to some of the PIE forms in their development into Hittite. The rule is something like this:

(i) h → Ø / in various environments

E.g., PIE 1sg pres *hedmi 'I eat' (LARYNGEALS i) > *edmi (2b OBSTR) > Hit etmi.

The second view constitutes a non-laryngealist account of the occurrence of /h/ in Hittite. Kronasser (1956: 75-97) is a proponent of this view and represents it as follows (op. cit.: 94): "The word-initial and word-internal intervocalic /h/ occurring in Hittite is ascribable to an avoidance of hiatus, i.e. to the tendency to pronounce contiguous vowels [in adjacent morphemes] with some sort of intermediary sound." (Translation my own: JV.)

This type of change has occurred in various languages. Kronasser cites several examples of it such as Vulgar Latin hinsidias 'ambushes' from Latin insidias, Umbrian pihaz 'venerated' and stahu 'I stand' from earlier *pi+āt+os and *stā+ō, and OHG bluohan 'to bloom' from Gmc. *blō+an. Additional examples of such glide-insertion rules occur in the present work: e.g., the Gothic change 9f j-INSERTION, Greek 8a h-ADD and OCS 4b PROTHESIS. Under this type of account, one must posit a laryngeal-insertion rule for pre-Hittite like the following — a rule which may in some instances have applied optionally:

(ii) Ø → h / (a) ## } ___ V or w
(b) V+
(c) C+

where ## is a word boundary and + a word-internal morpheme boundary.

That is, /h/ is inserted before a following vowel or if (a) word-initial, (b) if word-internal after a vowel and a morpheme boundary or (c) less frequently, if word-internal after a consonant and a morpheme boundary.

E.g., PIE *anti 'separately' (LARYNGEALS ii-a) > *hanti (2b OBSTR) > Hit <ha-an-ti> hant^{h}i; PIE acc sg *wr̥d^{h}ōim 'curse' (LARYNGEALS ii-a) > *hwr̥d^{h}ōim (1c SYL SON) > *hward^{h}ōim (2a m-TO-n) > *hward^{h}ōin (2b OBSTR) > *hwartōin (5 V-SHORT, 6 e/o-TO-a) > Hit <hu-ur-ta-in> hwartain. PIE nom sg *po+war 'fire' = root + suffix (LARYNGEALS ii-b) > *pohwar (2b OBSTR) > *p^{h}ohwar (6 e/o-TO-a) > Hit <pa-ah-hu-wa-ar> p^{h}ahwar. PIE nom sg *mē+ur 'measurement' = root + suffix (LARYNGEALS ii-b) > *mēhur (5 V-SHORT) > Hit mehur 'time'. PIE nom sg *es+os 'lord' = root + inflectional ending (LARYNGEALS ii-c) > *eshos (6 e/o-TO-a) > Hit eshas <is-ha-a-as>. Note here that LARYNGEALS does not apply in this form to the word-initial /e/. LARYNGEALS ii-a applies more frequently to words beginning with the +back vowels /a(:), o(:), u(:)/ or /w/ than to words beginning with the –back vowels /e(:), i(:)/. Finally, we note that in the following any PIE antecedent posited with a laryngeal /h/ may be posited without it if one assumes the application of LARYNGEALS ii.

1c Changes in Syllabic Sonorants (SYL SON)

This change restructures various lexical items and then is dropped from the grammar. Its precise formulation is not clear. An approximation is this:

m̥, n̥, l̥, r̥ → am or a, an, al, ar

That is, the PIE syllabic sonorants /m̥, n̥, l̥, r̥/ become Hit /am/ or sometimes /a/, and /an, al, ar/ respectively.

Sturtevant (1933: 104-7) assumes this change occurred only with the nasals /m̥, n̥/. Kronasser (1956: 52-3) assumes the change affected all the syllabic sonorant consonants.

E.g., PIE 3sg pres *sm̥+leg^h+ti 'lies with' (SYL SON) > *saleg^{h}ti (2b OBSTR) > *salekt^{h}i (3a t^h-TO-t^s) > Hit salekt^{s}i. PIE acc sg *humontm̥ 'all, whole' (SYL SON) > *humontam (2a m-TO-n) > *humontan (2b

OBSTR) > *humont^{h}an (6 e/o-TO-a) > Hit humant^{h}an. (Note in this derivation the necessary chronology SYL SON > 2a m-TO-n.) PIE *n̥+dō 'within' (SYL SON) > *andō (2b OBSTR) > *antō (5 V-SHORT) > *anto (6 e/o-TO-a) > Hit anta <an-da>. PIE nom sg *pl̥h+is 'broad' (SYL SON) > *palhis (2b OBSTR) > Hit p^{h}alhis. PIE nom sg *b^{h}r̥g^h+us 'high' (SYL SON) > *b^{h}arg^{h}us (2b OBSTR) > Hit parkuš.

1d The Change of /tt/ to /tst/ (tt-TO-tst)

This change consists of two parts, both of which remain in the grammar, the first as a phon cond rule and the second as a morph cond rule of Hittite. The first is early and is inherited from PIE:

$$(1)\quad \begin{bmatrix} \text{C, –sonorant} \\ \alpha\text{voiced} \end{bmatrix} \rightarrow [\beta\text{voiced}] \;/\; \_\_\_ \; [\text{C, –sonorant, } \beta\text{voiced}]$$

That is, an obstruent cluster must be voiced if its final segment is voiced and voiceless if its final segment is voiceless. To this rule was then added the following proviso:

$$(2)\quad \begin{array}{ccc} t & + & t \\ 1 & 2 & 3 \end{array} \rightarrow \begin{array}{ccccc} t & + & s & + & t \\ 1 & 2 & 4 & 2' & 3 \end{array}$$

where "+" is a word-internal morpheme boundary.

That is, the sequence /t+t/ becomes /t+s+t/.

E.g., PIE 3sg pres *ed+ti 'eats' (tt-TO-tst 1) > *et+ti (tt-TO-tst 2) > *etsti (3a t^h-TO-t^s applying here analogously from 3sg -t^{h}i to which it usually does apply) > Hit etst^{s}i <e-iz-za-az-zi>. We assume that tt-TO-tst 2 represents an early modification of the original PIE rule tt-TO-tst 1.

1e The Word-Stress Rule (HITTITE STRESS)

This change remained in the grammar as a phon cond rule:

$$V \rightarrow [\text{+stress}] \;/\; \#\#\, C_0 \,\_\_\_$$

That is, the first vowel in a word receives the stress.

E.g., PIE *apó 'back, behind' (HITTITE STRESS) > *ápo (2b OBSTR) > *áp^{h}o (6 e/o-TO-a) > Hit áp^{h}a <a-ap-pa>. (We will usually not mark the stress on Hittite words since it is invariably on the first syllable.)

In the Hittite writing system stress is not marked. We have assumed first-syllable stress for three reasons. First, a change like 2a m-TO-n below whereby word-final /m/ becomes /n/ is more likely to occur after an unstressed vowel. Hence a PIE ending like the gen pl *-ṓm, which was often stressed, might well have undergone a development like this: gen pl *at+ṓm 'fathers'' (HITTITE STRESS) > *átōm (2a m-TO-n) > *átōn (2b OBSTR) > *át^{h}ōn (5 V-SHORT) > *át^{h}on (6 e/o-TO-a) > Hit át^{h}an (see on this IV Historical Hittite Morphology, section 1.1). Recall in this connection that the Old Irish change 2c m-TO-n occurred after 1f IRISH STRESS had applied to move the stress away from the word-final syllable.

Second, although the stress was removed from word-final syllables, it still does not follow that it landed on the word's first syllable: it may have come to rest on the penultimate syllable. With this in mind, Kronasser (1956: 49) notes that the Hittite word for 'or' can appear either as nasuma <nas-su-ma> or as nasma <nas-ma>, the latter word with its penultimate syllable elided. Such an optional deletion is more likely to occur with an unstressed syllable than with a stressed one. Therefore we assume the word was stressed as násuma. In a similar vein, Friedrich (1960: 63) notes that the sequence of enclitics nu+mu+asta 'and me then' can also occur as nu+m+asta. This seems to indicate a stress pattern nú+mu+asta as opposed to nu+mú+asta.

Third, our final reason for assuming word-initial stress is touched upon by Pedersen (1938: 164): "Orthographic gemination of the vowel in a word-initial syllable of a polysyllabic word occurs frequently. This would seem to be a sign of vowel length in that syllable." (Translation my own: JV.) That is, a spelling like <a-ap-pa> 'back, behind' cited above occurs much more frequently than something like **<ap-pa-a>. The reason for this is that in languages where phonemic vowel length has been lost — as occurred in Hittite by 5 V-SHORT — stressed vowels are phonetically lengthened. And this is reflected in the Hittite orthography. Since in Hittite the vowels in first syllables evince by their orthographic doubling phonetic length, we assume that this indicates that this word-initial syllable was stressed.

2a The Change of Word-Final /m/ to /n/ (m-TO-n)

This change restructured certain lexical items and inflectional endings and was then dropped from the grammar.

m → n / —##

That is, word-final /m/ becomes /n/.

E.g., PIE nom sg *pedom 'place' (m-TO-n) > *pedon (2b OBSTR) > *p^heton (6 e/o-TO-a) > Hit p^hetan <pi-e-da-an>; PIE acc sg *māhlom 'apple tree' (m-TO-n) > *māhlon (5 V-SHORT) > *mahlon (6 e/o-TO-a) > Hit mahlan <ma-ah-la-an>; PIE acc sg *k^wi+m 'whom?' (la LABIOVEL) > *kwim (m-TO-n) > *kwin (2b OBSTR) > Hit k^hwin <ku-in>.

2b Changes in the Obstruent Stops (OBSTR)

These two rules were added to the grammar in the chronological order given below. Both changes restructure the phonemic inventory of the language and are then dropped as rules from the grammar. The two rules are these:

(1) (a) [C, –sonorant, αvoiced] → [–αaspirated]
(b) [C, –sonorant, -voiced] → [–aspirated] / s ___

(2) [C, –sonorant, +voiced] → [–voiced]

That is, (la) the PIE voiceless obstruents /p, t, k, k^w/ are aspirated to /p^h, t^h, k^h, k^{wh}/; and the voiced obstruents /b^h, b; d^h, d, etc./ are deaspirated to /b; d, etc./. And by (1b), the voiceless obstruent stops after /s/ remain un-aspirated: /sp^-, st^-, sk^-, sk^{w-}/. Hence at this stage after the application of OBSTR 1 the voiced obstruents /b, d, g, g^w / have two possible PIE sources, namely /b/ and /b^h/, /d/ and /d^h/, etc.

(2) The voiced stops /b, d, g, g^w/ become voiceless. They remain unaspirated. Hence /b, d, g, g^w/ > / p^-, t^-, k^-, k^{w-}/. These stops remain unaspirated because by this time OBSTR 1 has applied and then dropped from the grammar. So after OBSTR 2, the inventory of obstruent stops consists of only voiceless aspirated and voiceless unaspirated: /p^h/ vs. /p/, /t^h/ vs. /t/ etc.

E.g., (la) PIE *apo 'back, again' (OBSTR la) > *ap^ho (6 e/o-TO-a) > Hit ap^ha <a-ap-pa> or <a-ap-a>. PIE *kata 'with, down' (OBSTR la) > Hit k^hat^ha <kat-ta>. PIE 3sg pres *leuk+ti 'becomes light' (OBSTR la) > *$leuk^ht^hi$ (3a t^h-TO-t^s) > *$leuk^ht^si$ (4 MON) > *$l\bar{u}k^ht^si$ (5 V-SHORT) > Hit luk^ht^si <lu-uk-ki-iz-zi>. PIE 1 pl pres *ak^w+eni 'we drink' (la LABIOVEL) > *ak^weni (OBSTR la) > Hit ak^hweni <a-ku-e-ni>. (2) PIE 3pl pres *g^hrob^h+onti 'they devour' (OBSTR la) > *$grobont^hi$ (OBSTR 2) > *$kropont^hi$ (3a t^h-TO-t^s) > *$kropont^si$ (6 e/o-TO-a) > Hit $krapant^si$ <ka-ra-pa-an-zi>. PIE 1sg pres *$d^h\bar{e}$+h+i 'I put' (OBSTR la) > *dēhi (OBSTR 2) > *tēhi (5 V-SHORT) > Hit tehi <te-eh-hi>. PIE 1sg pres *ed+mi 'I eat' (OBSTR 2) > Hit etmi <e-it-mi>. And PIE nom sg *jugom 'yoke' and *genu 'knee' (2a m-TO-n) > *jugon and *genu (OBSTR 2) > *jukon and *kenu (6 e/o-TO-a) > Hit yukan <i-u-kan> and kenu <gi-e-nu>.

We have posited OBSTR 1 and 2 and the resulting Hittite obstruent stop inventory consisting of voiceless aspirated vs. unaspirated consonants for three reasons. First, Hittite has clearly lost the PIE distinction between voiced and voiceless stops. Both Sturtevant (1933: 67) and Kronasser (1956: 58) assume this on the basis of Hittite orthographic practice. As noted in III Hittite Phonology, the Hittite cuneiform syllabary was borrowed from Babylonian-Assyrian and Akkadian. Now both these linguistic communities did indeed distinguish between voiced and voiceless obstruent stops. But when their syllabaries were adapted for Hittite, this orthographic distinction was obliterated. That is why a form like the Hit nom pl at^has 'fathers' may be written as <ad-da-as> or <at-ta-as>. (See on this Sturtevant 1933: 178.)

Second, with the absence of a voiced-voiceless distinction in the Hittite obstruent series, we assume, as does Kronasser (1956), that all the obstruents were voiceless and that they differed in an aspirated vs. an unaspirated series, which Kronasser terms "fortis" and "lenis", respectively. According to Maddiesson (1987), most languages have at least two series of obstruent stops. Of such languages Maddieson (1987: 28) notes, "A language which contrasts only 2 series of stops typically has a plain voiceless/voiced contrast." Next in frequency are those languages like Hittite which "...have a contrast of plain voiceless and aspirated voiceless, or [unlike Hit] of plain voiced and aspirated voiceless." Hence our posited Hittite system is plausible.

Third and finally, the Hittite obstruent system posited here can be derived from that of PIE by changes which have been attested elsewhere and which are thus natural. These are OBSTR 1 by which voiceless stops are aspirated and voiced ones are unaspirated; and OBSTR 2 which devoices voiced obstruents.

In this connection Sturtevant has an interesting observation on one of the conventions of Hittite orthography (1933: 74): "In the case of the stops double writing has etymological value... The original [PIE] voiceless stops [p, t, k, k^w] tend to he written double, and frequently a non-phonetic vowel is introduced to make the double writing possible; whereas the original [PIE] voiced stops, including the voiced aspirates, [that is, b, b^h; d, d^h, etc.] are never written double except by analogy or on account of doubling in the course of word derivation or the construction of a phrase." (This observation is sometimes referred to as "Sturtevant' s Law".)

What Sturtevant's Law means is that the double spelling reflects the tense aspirated (and phonetically longer) consonants /p^h, t^h, k^h/ and that single spelling reflects the lax unaspirated (and phonetically shorter) unaspirated consonants /p, t, k/. Examples of Sturtevant's Law are these:

PIE *apo 'from, back' (OBSTR) > *ap^ho (6 e/o-TO-a) > Hit ap^ha, written <a-ap-pa> or <ap-pa> as opposed to PIE 3pl pres *g^hrob^honti 'they seize' (OBSTR 1) > *$grobont^hi$ (OBSTR 2) > *$kropont^hi$ (3a t^h-

TO-t^{s}) > *kropont^{s}i (6 e/o-TO-a) > Hit krapant^{s}i, written <ka-ra-pa-an-zi> and never as **<ka-ra-ap-pa-an-zi>. PIE *kata 'with, down' (OBSTR 1) > Hit k^{h}at^{h}a, written <kat-ta> vs. PIE 3pl pres *od+onti 'they eat' (OBSTR 1 and 2) > *otont^{h}i (3a t^{h}-TO-t^{s}) > *otant^{s}i (6 e/o-TO-a) > Hit atant^{s}i, written <a-da-an-zi> and never as **<a-ad-da-an-zi>. And PIE 3sg pres *pet+ti 'fly' (OBSTR) > *p^{h}et^{h}t^{h}i (3a t^{h}-TO-t^{s}) > Hit p^{h}et^{h}t^{s}i, written <pid-da-a-iz-zi> or <pi-it-ta-iz-zi>. Note that as described in III Hittite Phonology, given the structure of the Hittite syllabary, it is impossible to record aspiration by graphemic doubling word-initially, word-finally or word-internally after a consonant. In all such instances one must include a graphemic vowel of some sort. Hence a word-internal /p^{h}/ can be written as <ap-pa...>, while the possibility of a graphemic word-initial **<p-pa...> does not exist.

Finally, one of the few exceptions to Sturtevant's Law is the Hittite spelling of the adjective meaning 'great', namely <me-ig-ga-e-es>. This spelling would seem to indicate phonemic /mék^{h}is/. However, the generally assumed PIE antecedent is *megis; and one would expect the derivation *megis (OBSTR 2) > Hit **mekis, written **<me-ig-e-es> or the like.

3a The Change of /t^{h}/ to /t^{s}/ (t^{h}-TO-t^{s})

We posit here two changes which seem to represent one and the same process. Both changes restructure the phonemic inventory and certain lexical items of the language and are then dropped as rules from the grammar.

(a) t^{h} → t^{s} / ___ [+vocalic, –back] or j

(b) t → (? t^{s}i) → si / ## ___ j

That is, (a) /t^{h}/, which has been aspirated by 2b OBSTR, becomes the affricate /t^{s}/ when immediately followed by a front vowel /e(:), i(:)/ or by /j/. (We posit the output of this change as an affricate /t^{s}/. An alternative analysis would consider it a sequence /ts/.) (b) Unaspirated voiceless /t/ word-initially and followed by /j/ becomes /si/ (perhaps over an intermediate stage /t^{s}i/).

E.g., (a) PIE 3sg pres *b^{h}āi+ti 'goes' (2b OBSTR) > *pāit^{h}i (t^{h}-TO-t^{s}) > *pāit^{s}i (5 V-SHORT) > Hit pait^{s}i <pa-iz-zi>; PIE nom sg *te+g 'you' vs. acc sg *tu+g (2b OBSTR) > *t^{h}ek and *t^{h}uk (t^{h}-TO-t^{s}) > Hit t^{s}ek <zi-ik> and t^{h}uk <tu-uk>. The t^{h}-TO-t^{s} change seems not to apply to the /t/ in the cluster /st/, probably because by 2b OBSTR the /t/ here was unaspirated:

PIE nom sg *pl̥+ost+is 'breadth' (lb LARYNGEALS) > *pl̥h+ost+is (1c SYL SON) > *palhostis (2b OBSTR, 6 e/o-TO-a) > Hit p^{h}alhastis not **p^{h}alhast^{s}is. The t^{h}-TO-t^{s} change also does not apply to an unaspirated /t/ from PIE /d/ or /d^{h}/. E.g., PIE nom sg *kordis 'heart' (2b OBSTR) > *k^{h}ortis (ev) > Hit k^{h}artis, not **k^{h}art^{s}is. PIE 3sg pres *spond^{h}+i 'pours a libation' (ev) > Hit spanti <si-pa-an-ti>, not **spant^{s}i **<si-pa-an-zi>. Finally, PIE nom sg *d^{h}eb^{h}us 'small' (ev) > Hit tepus, not **t^{s}epus. In several paradigms the /t^{s}/ was analogized out by /t^{h}/. E.g., dat sg *humont+i 'all, whole' vs. gen sg *humont+os (ev) > Hit humant^{h}i and humant^{h}as, where one might expect dat sg **humant^{s}i.

Examples of (b) are PIE nom sg *dju+s 'god' (2b OBSTR) > *tjus (t^{h}-TO-t^{s}) > Hit siyus and PIE 3sg med *di+or+i 'show' (PIE 3.1.2c i-j/u-w ALT applying synchronically) → *djori (2b OBSTR) > *tjori (t^{h}-TO-t^{s}) > *sijori (6 e/o-TO-a) > Hit siyari <si-ya-a-ri>.

Note the two following chronologies. First, we have assumed that a more natural formulation of t^{h}-TO-t^{s} presumes that it applied to an aspirated /t^{h}/ and hence after 2b OBSTR. Second, consider the derivation of PIE 3sg mid *leuk+o+tai 'it dawns' (2b OBSTR) > *leuk^{h}ot^{h}ai (t^{h}-TO-t^{s} not applying, but 4

MON) > *lūk^{h}ot^{h}e (5 V-SHORT) > *luk^{h}ot^{h}e (6 e/o-TO-a) > Hit luk^{h}at^{h}e <lu-uk-kat-te>. If t^h-TO-t^s had applied after 4 MON, the Hittite form would be **luk^{h}at^{s}e.

3b Changes in Word-Final Consonant Clusters (WF CL)

We cite two of these rules below. Rule (a) restructures various inflectional endings and then is dropped as a rule from the grammar. Rule (b) remains as a phon cond rule of the language.

(a) ons → ūs / ___ ##

(b) t$^{(h)}$ → Ø / n ___ ##

That is, (a) word-final /ons/ becomes /ūs/ and (b) word-final /nt/ or /nt^h/ becomes /n/.

E.g., (a) acc pl *atons 'fathers' (2b OBSTR) > *at^{h}ons (3b WF CL) > *at^{h}ūs > (5 V-SHORT) > Hit at^{h}us. (We have assumed that a natural formulation of this rule presupposes a change of /ons/ to /ūs/. This assumes the chronologies WF CL > 5 V-SHORT and WF CL > 6 e/o-TO-a .) (b) PIE nom sg neuter *humont 'all' vs. gen sg *humontos (ev) > Hit human and humant^{h}as.

(4) Monophthongization (MON)

The rule for this change restructures the vocalic phonemic inventory of the language and then is dropped from the grammar. The rule is this:

$$\begin{bmatrix} +\text{vocalic} \\ -\text{high} \\ -\text{long} \end{bmatrix} \quad \begin{bmatrix} +\text{vocalic} \\ +\text{high} \\ \alpha\text{back} \\ -\text{long} \end{bmatrix} \quad \rightarrow \quad \begin{bmatrix} +\text{vocalic} \\ \alpha\text{high} \\ \alpha\text{back} \\ -\text{low} \\ +\text{long} \end{bmatrix}$$

That is, the PIE short diphthongs /ai, ei, oi/ → /ē/ and /au, eu, ou/ → /ū/.

E.g., PIE nom pl *k+oi 'these' (2b OBSTR) > *k^{h}oi (MON) > *k^{h}ē (5 V-SHORT) > Hit k^{h}e <ki-e>. PIE nom sg *g^{h}eimont+s 'winter' (2b OBSTR) > *keimont^{h}s (MON) > *kēmont^{h}s (5 V-SHORT) > *kemont^{h}s (6 e/o-TO-a) > Hit kemant^{h}s. Also PIE 1sg pres *au+h+i 'I see' (MON) > *ūhi (5 V-SHORT) > Hit uhi <u-uh-hi>; and PIE 3sg pres *eup+ti 'goes up' (2b OBSTR) > *eup^{h}t^{h}i (3a t^h-TO-t^s) > *eup^{h}t^{s}i (MON) > *ūp^{h}t^{s}i (5 V-SHORT) > Hit up^{h}t^{s}i. (We have assumed that the most natural version of a change like MON has long vowels as output. Thus the change must precede 5 V-SHORT.)

5 Shortening of Long Vowels (V-SHORT)

This change restructures the phonemic inventory of the language and then is dropped from the grammar:

[V, +long] → [–long]

That is, all long vowels — whether occurring singly or in the long diphthongs /āi, ēi, ōi; āu, ēu, ōu/ — are shortened.

E.g., PIE acc sg *hopādim 'vessel' (2a m-TO-n) > *hopādin (2b OBSTR) > *hop^{h}ātin (V-SHORT) > *hop^{h}atin (6 e/o-TO-a) > Hit hap^{h}atin <ha-pa-a-ti-in>. PIE 3sg pret *g^{h}rēb^h+s 'devour' (2a OBSTR) > *krēps (V-SHORT) > Hit kreps <ka-ri-pa-as>. PIE 3pl pres *dīj+onti 'come' (2b OBSTR) > *tījont^{h}i (3a t^h-TO-t^s) > *tījont^{s}i (V-SHORT) > *tijont^{s}i (6 e/o-TO-a) > Hit tiyant^{s}i <ti-ya-an-zi>. PIE nom sg *nōmn̥ 'name' (1c SYL SON) > *nōman (V-SHORT) > *noman (6 e/o-TO-a) > *naman (7a n-CHANGES) >

Hit laman <la-a-ma-an>. PIE nom sg *ūd^{h}noi 'country' (2b OBSTR) > *ūtnoi (4 MON) > *ūtnē (V-SHORT) > Hit utne <ud-ne-e>.

Examples of PIE long diphthongs are these: PIE 3sg pres *mol+ā+i 'breaks' (4 MON not applying, then V-SHORT) > *molai (6 e/o-TO-a) > Hit malai <ma-al-la-i>. (Note the necessary chronology 4 MON > V-SHORT.) PIE 3sg pres *d^{h}ē+i 'put, place' (2b OBSTR) > *tēi (V-SHORT) > *tei (6 e/o-TO-a) > Hit tai <da-a-i>. (Note the necessary chronology V-SHORT > 6 e/o-TO-a.) PIE dat sg *lutōi 'window' (2b OBSTR) > *lut^{h}ōi (V-SHORT) > *lut^{h}oi (6 e/o-TO-a) > Hit lut^{h}ai <lu-ut-ta-i>. Finally, PIE 3sg pres *āus+ti 'sees' (ev) > Hit aust^{s}i <a-us-zi>.

As described in section III Hittite Phonology below, the Hittite syllabary gives little indication of vowel length. In view of this, there seem to be three possibilities for interpreting the orthographic data: (1) There was in fact a consistently drawn phonemic distinction between long and short vowels, for which we have virtually no orthographic evidence. (2) There were only long vowels in Hittite. (3) There were only short vowels, which were very likely somewhat lengthened phonetically when stressed. (See on this the remarks under change 1e HITTITE STRESS.) Since there seems to be no graphemic evidence for proposition (1), we discount it. Since there seem to be no languages attested with only long vowels, we discount proposition (2). Therefore we have opted for (3).

6 The Change of /e/ and /o/ to /a/ (e/o-TO-a)

These changes restructure the phonemic inventory of the language and then drop from the grammar. There are two such changes, which seem to represent one and the same process in that both rules lower the –low vowels /e/ and /o/ to +low /a/. The rules are these:

(a) e → a / ___ { rC | i or u }

(b) o → a / everywhere

That is, (a) /e/ becomes /a/ if followed by /r/ plus a consonant or if in the diphthongs /ei/ or /eu/, which then become /ai/ and /au/. And (b) /o/ becomes /a/ in every occurrence.

E.g., (a) PIE 3sg pres *werb^h+ti 'wash' (2b OBSTR, 3a t^h-TO-t^s) > *werpt^{s}i (e/o-TO-a) > Hit warpt^{s}i <wa-ar-ap-zi>. (b) PIE nom sg *hostōi 'bone' (5 V-SHORT) > *hostoi (e/o-TO-a) > Hit hastai <ha-as-ta-i>. (Note that given our formulation of e/o-TO-a, it must follow 5 V-SHORT.) Also PIE nom sg *hornōus 'birthing chair' (ev) > Hit harnaus <har-na-a-us>. PIE *apo 'behind, back' (ev) > Hit ap^{h}a <a-ap-pa>. PIE *k^{w}od 'what?' (ev) > Hit k^{h}wat <ku-wa-at> 'to where? why?' PIE nom sg *nōmn̥ 'name' (1c SYL SON) > *nōman (5 V-SHORT) > *noman (e/o-TO-a) > *naman (7a n-CHANGES) > Hit laman <la-a-ma-an>.

7a Changes in /n/ (n-CHANGES).

These rules may have applied only optionally to some forms. The rules for these changes restructured certain lexical items and then dropped from the grammar. Two of the changes are these:

(a) n → Ø / ___m or m___

(b) n → l / ##___Vm

That is, (a) the sequences /mn/ and /nm/ lose the /n/. (b) Word-initial /n/ followed by a vowel and /m/ becomes /l/.

E.g., (a) PIE 1sg pres *memn+ō+i 'say' (5 V-SHORT) > *memnoi (6 e/o-TO-a) > *memnai (n-CHANGES)

> Hit memai <me-ma-a-i>; PIE 3sg pres *en+mejo+ti 'mixes' (2b OBSTR) > *enmejot^{h}i (3a t^h-TO-t^s) > *enmejot^{s}i (6 e/o-TO-a) > *enmejat^{s}i (n-CHANGES) > Hit emeyat^{s}i <im-mi-ya-az-zi>. (b) PIE nom sg *nōmn̥ 'name' (1c SYL SON) > *nōman (5 V-SHORT) > *noman (6 e/o-TO-a) > *naman (n-CHANGES) > Hit laman <la-a-ma-an>.

7b A Possible Change of /w/ to /m/ (w-TO-m)

This change, which may have been optional for some forms, remains in the grammar as a phon cond rule. Its basic form is this:

w → m / ## ... u + ___ V

> That is, word-internal /w/ preceded by /u/ plus a morpheme boundary and followed by a vowel becomes /m/.

Sturtevant (1933: 14-16) maintains that /w/ in several inflectional endings becomes /m/ if the root of the word ends in /u/. E.g., PIE 1pl pres *ernu+weni 'we bring' (6 e/o-TO-a) > *arnuweni (w-TO-m) > Hit arnumeni <ar-nu-um-me-ni> vs. 1pl pres *p^{h}ōi+weni 'we go' (2b OBSTR) > *p^{h}ōiweni (5 V-SHORT) > *p^{h}oiweni (6 e/o-TO-a, but w-TO-m not applying) > Hit p^{h}aiweni, not **p^{h}aimeni. We assume this change is late since it remained in Hittite as an optional phon cond rule: e.g., Hit nuwan 'never' alongside numan.

C. The Relative Chronology

The ">" means "must precede".

la LABIOVEL > 2b OBSTR (see la), > 6 e/o-TO-a (see la).

1b LARYNGEALS: probably early (see 1b).

lc SYL SON > 2a m-TO-n (see 1c).

1d tt-TO-tst: probably early (see 1d).

le HITTITE STRESS > 2a m-TO-n (see le).

2a m-TO-n > Ø.

2b OBSTR > 3a t^h-TO-t^s (see 3a).

3a t^h-TO-t^s > 4 MON (see 3a).

3b WF CL > 5 V-SHORT (see 3b), > 6 e/o-TO-a (see 3b).

4 MON > 5 V-SHORT (see 5).

5 V-SHORT > 6 e/o-TO-a (see 5 and 6).

6 e/o-TO-a > Ø.

7a n-CHANGES > Ø.

7b w-TO-m: probably late (see 7b).

III Hittite Phonology

The Hittite system of writing was a syllabary adapted from the syllabaries of Babylonian-Assyrian and of Akkadian, the latter a Semitic language. The system is called "cuneiform" because of the wedged-shaped marks which characterize it (Latin cuneus 'wedge'). The marks were made by pressing a stylus into wet clay; and our sources for Hittite are generally such clay tablets.

The Hittite writing system was a syllabary; and the signs, each of which consists of a configuration of wedges set at various angles, never stand for a single consonant. Rather, there are four different types of signs:

(a) CV

(b) VC

(c) CVC

(d) V

That is, sign (a) represents a consonant plus a vowel, (b) represents a vowel plus a consonant, (c) represents a consonant plus a vowel plus another consonant and (d) represents a single vowel. (The symbol C here includes the affricate /t^s/, which in the conventional transcription of the syllabary is written <z>, but always with adjacent vowels as in <ze>, <zi>, <uz>, etc.)

Under this system of writing, a word like the nom sg harnaus 'birthing chair' may be written as <har-na-u-us>, <har-na-a-us>, <ha-ar-na-us> or the like. Orthographic signs which do not represent one of the four types given above do not occur: hence the impossible spellings <ha-**rna-u-us> and <**h-ar-na-us>. Likewise, the representation of word-initial or word-final consonant clusters is orthographically impossible. Hence a word like the 3pl pres spiyant^{s}i 'they eat their fill' must be written as <is-pi-ya-an-zi> or <si-pi-ya-an-zi>; and the nom sg humants 'all' is written <hu-u-ma-an-za>, while <hu-u-ma-an-**z> would be impossible.

Another defect of this system is that cuneiform signs containing /e/ were rare. Held et al. (1988: 180-202) lists only ten signs such as <en> and <te> which contain /e/ while there are fifty-nine containing /a/ and forty-one with /i/. Thus a word like the nom sg utne 'land, country' is often written <ud-ni>; and the instrumental singular ending -et is frequently written <-it>. The presence of /e/ as opposed to /i/ can in some instances be inferred on the basis of etymological evidence. E.g., PIE *pedom as in Greek pédon 'ground, earth' (2a m-TO-n) > *pedon (2b OBSTR) > *p^{h}eton (6 e/o-TO-a) > Hit p^{h}etan 'place', written <pi-e-da-an>.

In our representation of Hittite orthography within <...> we have departed from three usually followed conventions. First, we represent /h/ with graphemic <h> instead of the usual <ḫ>. Second, we omit the accent marks and subscripts which are used to designate various signs for one and the same vowel. E.g., Hit nom sg harnaus 'birthing chair' is written <har-na-a-us> while the acc sg harnau is written <har-na-a-ú> in which the accent on <ú> indicates that a different orthographic sign is used for this /u/ than for the previous one. If in a text three different signs are used to represent /u/, the usual orthographic convention is to write them as <u, ú, ù>. If more than three different signs for /u/ occur, then they are designated orthographically by subscripts as <u_4, u_5> etc. The same convention is employed for the other vowels; we, however, do not follow this orthographic convention here and write all vowels uniformly as <u, e, a, i> without any other designations.

After the changes described in the previous section, the inventory of segments in the phonology of Hittite at about 1800 BC was as follows.

Obstruent Consonants

labial	dental	alveolar	velar	glottal
p^h	t^h		k^h	
p	t		k	
		s[1]	x[2]	h[2]
		t^s		

Sonorant Consonants

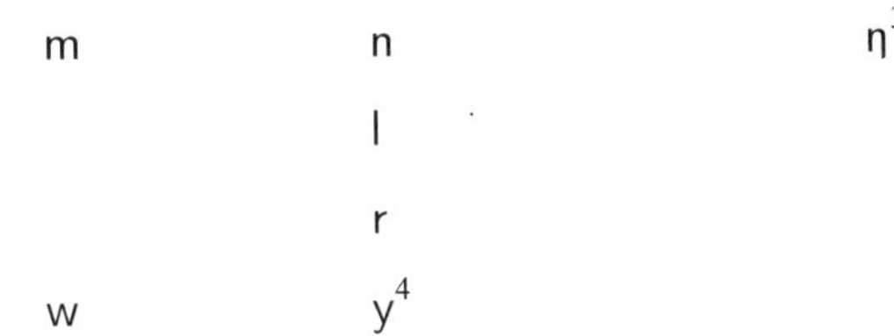

m	n	ŋ[3]
	l	
	r	
w	y[4]	

Vowels

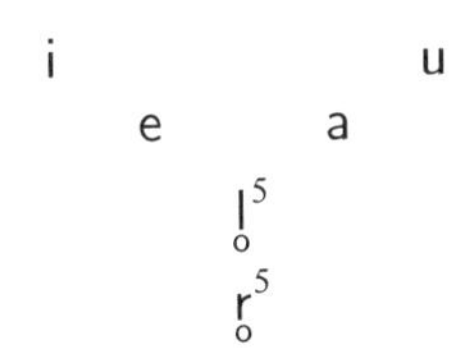

i u

e a

l̥[5]

r̥[5]

Diphthongs ai, au

Hittite Segments in Terms of Phonological Features

	p^h	t^h	k^h	p	t	k	s	x	h	t^s	m	n	ŋ	l	r	w	y	l̥	r̥	a	e	i	u
consonantal	+	+	+	+	+	+	+	+		+	+	+	+	+	+	−	−	−	−	−	−	−	−
sonorant	−	−	−	−	−	−	−	−		−	+	+	+	+	+	+	+	+	+	+	+	+	+
vocalic	−	−	−	−	−	−	−	−		−	−	−	−	−	−	−	−	+	+	+	+	+	+
high	−	−	+	−	−	+	−	+		−	−	−	+	−	−	+	+	−	−	−	−	+	+
back	−	−	+	−	−	+	−	+		−	−	−	+	−	−	+	−	−	−	+	−	−	+
low	−	−	−	−	−	−	−	−		−	−	−	−	−	−	−	−	−	−	+	−	−	−
anterior	+	+	−	+	+	−	+	−		+	+	+	−	+	+	−	−	+	+	−	−	−	−
coronal	−	+	−	−	+	−	+	−		+	−	+	−	+	+	−	−	+	+	−	−	−	−
voiced	−	−	−	−	−	−	−	−	−	−	+	+	+	+	+	+	+	+	+	+	+	+	+
continuant	−	−	−	−	−	−	+	+	+	−	−	−	−	+	+	+	+	+	+	+	+	+	+
nasal	−	−	−	−	−	−	−	−		−	+	+	+	−	−	−	−	−	−	−	−	−	−
strident	−	−	−	−	−	−	+	−		+	−	−	−	−	−	−	−	−	−	−	−	−	−
delayed release	−	−	−	−	−	−	−	−		+	−	−	−	−	−	−	−	−	−	−	−	−	−
round	−	−	−	−	−	−	−	−		−	−	−	−	−	−	+	−	−	−	−	−	−	+
lateral	−	−	−	−	−	−	−	−		−	−	−	−	+	−	−	−	+	−	−	−	−	−
palatal	−	−	−	−	−	−	−	−		−	−	−	−	−	−	−	+	−	−	−	−	+	−
aspirated	+	+	+	−	−	−	−	−	+	−	−	−	−	−	−	−	−	−	−	−	−	−	−
stressed	−	−	−	−	−	−	−	−		−	−	−	−	−	−	−	−	±	±	±	±	±	±
long	−	−	−	−	−	−	−	−		−	−	−	−	−	−	−	−	−	−	−	−	−	−

Certain of the changes have remained in the grammar of Hittite. Those below labeled “morph cond” are morphologically conditioned and apply either to lexically marked items or to morphosyntactically defined classes. Those marked “phon cond” are phonologically conditioned and apply more or less generally. The symbol “Ø” after a change means that it has restructured lexical items and/or changed the inventory of underlying segments and has then been dropped from the grammar. For those changes remaining as rules in the grammar we cite an illustrative derivation. Additional examples can be found in the discussions of the particular rules.

1a LABIOVEL: Ø

1b LARYNGEALS: Ø

1c SYL SON: Ø

1d tt-TO-tst (morph cond): 3sg pres /et+t^{s}i/ ‘eats’ → [etst^{s}i] <e-iz-za-az-zi>.

1e HITTITE STRESS (phon cond): nom sg /laman/ ‘name’ → [láman].

2a m-TO-n: Ø

2b OBSTR: Ø

3a t^{h}-TO-t^{s}: Ø

3b WF CL (phon cond): nom sg neuter /humant^{h}/ ‘all, every’ vs. gen sg /humant^{h}+as/ → [human] vs. [humant^{h}as].

4 MON: Ø

5 V-SHORT: Ø

6 e/o-TO-a: Ø

7a n-CHANGES: Ø

7b w-TO-m (phon cond): 1pl /arnu+weni/ ‘we bring’ → [arnumeni].

IV Historical Hittite Morphology

A. Overview

B. Hittite Morphology

In each paradigm below the Hittite forms of 1650 to 1200 BC are cited in the left-hand column and the PIE forms of about 3000 BC in the right-hand column. In the Hittite morphology we shall use a single word as representative of an entire paradigm, even when that particular word may not be attested in all its forms. We mark the unattested Hittite forms with an asterisk.

We cite our Hittite forms in phonemic transcription (minus the slashes). On occasion we supply the graphemic version of a form, which we enclose in brackets <...>. We do not mark Hittite stress: we assume it was word-initial by change le HITTITE STRESS.

1 Nouns

Hittite substantives (nouns, adjectives, pronouns) have only two genders, a neuter and a so-called "common" (com) gender. Sturtevant (1933: 162) assumes the Hittite com gender to have been a feature of PIE — or in his terms "Indo-Hittite" — which was retained in Hittite. Then in the other IE languages the original common gender split into the masculine and feminine.

We, on the other hand, assume that the original PIE distinction of masculine vs. feminine was lost in Hittite. The primary trigger for this merger was the occurrence of changes 5 V-SHORT and 6 e/o-TO-a. Because of these two changes virtually all of the endings of the masc o-class became identical with those of the fem ā-class. The development was like this: PIE masc o-class acc sg *newom 'new' vs. the fem ā-class acc sg *newām (2a m-TO-n) > *newon and *newān (5 V-SHORT) > *newon and *newan (6 e/o-TO-a) > Hit newan for both masculine and feminine accusative singular. And since in the other declensions such as the i-class and u-class the masculine and feminine endings were identical, with the merger of the masc o- with the fem ā-class in Hittite, the distinction between masculine and feminine declensions was completely lost.

Hittite nouns frequently fluctuate between common and neuter gender; the same noun can also occur in more than one declension. E.g., k^{h}art- 'heart' can occur in the genitive singular as an i-class k^{h}artiyas and in the ablative singular as an athematic Ø-class k^{h}artat^s. And the u-class 'birthing chair' is common gender in the nominative singular (harnaus) but is neuter in the accusative singular (harnau).

1.1 o- and jo-, ā- and jā-Class (Common, Neuter)

The antecedent PIE endings of the following noun were o-class masculine. The Hittite reflex is common gender.

		Hittite		PIE
sg	**nom**	at^{h}as	<at-ta-as> 'father'	*at+os[6]
	acc	at^{h}an		*at+om
	gen	at^{h}as		*at+os[7]
	dat	*at^{h}e		*at+oi[8]
	abl	*at^{h}at^s		*at+ōts[9]
	instr	*at^{h}et		*at+ed
pl	**nom**	at^{h}as		*at+ōs
		at^{h}es		*at+es[7]
	acc	at^{h}us		*at+ons[10]
	gen	at^{h}an		*at+ōm[11]
	obl	Same as the genitive singular.[12]		

Neuter nouns of the o- and jo-class have the same endings as those of the common gender except for these cases:

		Hittite		PIE
nom/acc	**sg**	yukan	'yoke'	*jug+om
	pl	*yuka		*jug+ā

There is one possible neuter dual form attested, namely the nom/acc sak^{h}wa 'two eyes', perhaps from PIE *sok^w+ō.

The jo- and jā-class nouns have the same endings as those of the o- and ā-classes. Most jV-class nouns are adjectives derived from nouns, verbs or other adjectives. E.g., the following nominative singular forms:

	Hittite		PIE
com	*anturiyas	'inner'	*n̥d^{h}ur+j+o/ā+s[13]
neuter	*anturiyan		*n̥d^{h}ur+j+om

1.2 i-Class (Common, Neuter)

The following is a common noun.

		Hittite		PIE
sg	**nom**	$t^{h}ut^{s}is$	<tu-uz-zi-is> 'army'	*touti+s[14]
	acc	$t^{h}ut^{s}in$		*touti+m
	gen	$t^{h}ut^{s}iyas$		*touti+os[15]
	dat	$t^{h}ut^{s}iya$		*touti+ō
	abl	$t^{h}ut^{s}iyat^{s}$		*touti+ōts
	instr	$t^{h}ut^{s}it$		*touti+d
pl	**nom**	$t^{h}ut^{s}iyes$		*touti+es
	acc	$t^{h}ut^{s}iyus$		*touti+ions[16]
	obl		Same as the genitive singular.	

The neuter i-class nouns have the same endings as those of the common gender except for the nominative/accusative cases, i.e.:

		Hittite		PIE
nom/acc	**sg**	talukasti	'length'	*dl̥ug+ost+i
	pl	*talukastiya		*dl̥ug+ost+i+ā[17]

Some i-class nouns and adjectives have endings with ō-grade ablaut. E.g., the following neuter noun:

		Hittite		PIE
sg	**nom/acc**	hastai	'bone'	*host+ō+i[18]
	gen	*hastayas		*host+ō+i+os[19]
	dat	*hastaya		*host+ō+i+ō
	abl	$*hastayat^{s}$		*host+ō+i+ōts
	instr	*hastait		*host+ō+i+d
pl	**nom/acc**	*hastaya		*host+ō+i+ā
	obl		Same as the genitive singular.	

Common gender i-class nouns with ō-grade ablaut have the same endings as the neuter except for the following forms:

		Hittite		PIE
sg	**nom**	*lenkais	'oath'	*leng+ō+i+s
	acc	lenkain		*leng+ō+i+m
pl	**nom**	*lenkayes		*leng+ō+i+es
	acc	*lenkayus		*leng+ō+i+ons

Kronasser (1966: 253) posits a Hit ē-class which is represented by the neuter noun utne <ud-ne-e> 'land'. We assume that this noun was originally i-class, but with the ablauting vowel /e/ instead of /ō/. Its paradigm is this:

		Hittite		PIE
sg	nom/acc	utne	'land'	*ūd^{h}n+e+i[20]
	gen	utneyas		*ūd^{h}n+e+i+os[21]
	dat	utni		*ūd^{h}n+i[22]
		utneya		*ūd^{h}n+e+i+ō
	abl	utneyat^s		*ūd^{h}n+e+i+ōts
	instr	*utnet		*ūd^{h}n+e+i+d
pl		Same as the genitive singular for the oblique cases.[23]		

1.3 u-Class (Common, Neuter)

The following is a noun of the common gender.

		Hittite		PIE
sg	nom	kenus	<gi-nu-us> 'knee'	*genu+s
	acc	*kenun		*genu+m
	gen	*kenuwas		*genu+os[24]
	dat	*kenuwa		*genu+ō[24]
	abl	*kenuwat^s		*genu+ōts[24]
	instr	*kenut		*genu+d
pl	nom	*kenuwes		*genu+es[24]
	acc	*kenus		*genu+ons[24,25]
	obl		Same as the genitive singular.	

Neuter nouns of this class have the same endings as the common declension except for the following. (We again cite Hit *kenu 'knee' as our example since it also occurs as a neuter noun.)

		Hittite		PIE
nom/acc	sg	*kenu		*genu
	pl	kenuwa	<gi-e-nu-wa>	*genu+ā

There are u-class nouns and adjectives whose endings have lengthened-grade ablaut. E.g., the common noun harnaus 'birthing chair'.

		Hittite		PIE
sg	nom	harnaus	<har-na-a-us>	*hornōu+s[26]
	acc	*harnaun		*hornōu+m
	gen	harnawas		*hornōu+os[27]
	dat	harnawi		*hornōu+i[28]
	abl	*harnawat^s		*hornōu+ōts
	instr	*harnaut		*hornōu+d
pl	nom	*harnawes		*hornōu+es
	acc	*harnaus		*hornōu+ons[29]
	obl		Same as the genitive singular.	

When Hit harnau 'birthing chair' occurs as a neuter noun, its endings are those of the com gender except for the following:

		Hittite	PIE
nom/acc	**sg**	harnau	*hornōu
	pl	*harnawa	*hornōu+ā

1.4 Athematic Classes

1.4.1 Ø-Class (Common, Neuter)

These nouns are referred to in the literature as "l-stems, r-stems, h-stems" and the like depending upon the final consonant of the stem. Most of these nouns are neuter. E.g., the following:

		Hittite		PIE
sg	**nom/acc**	kesar	<ki-es-sar> 'hand'	*g^hesor
	gen	*kesaras		*g^hesor+os
	dat	*kesari		*g^hesor+i
	abl	*kesarat^s		*g^hesor+ōts
	instr	*kesaret		*g^hesor+ed
pl	**nom/acc**	*kesar		*g^hesor[30]
	obl		Same as the genitive singular.	

The com Ø-class nouns have the same endings as the neuters except for the following:

		Hittite		PIE
sg	**nom**	*wet^hs	'year'	*wet+s
	acc	*wet^han		*wet+m̥[31]
pl	**nom**	*wet^hes		*wet+es
	acc	*wet^hus		*wet+ons[32]

1.4.2 r/n-Class (Neuter)

These nouns have stems ending in /r/ in the nominative and accusative and in/n/ in the oblique cases:

		Hittite		PIE
sg	**nom/acc**	watar	<wa-a-tar> 'water'	*wod+or[33]
	gen	wetenas	<u-ete-na-as>	*wed+en+os[34]
	dat	weteni		*wed+en+i
	abl	wetenat^s		*wed+en+ōts
	instr	wetenet		*wed+en+ed
pl	**nom/acc**	*watar		*wod+or[35]
	obl		Same as the genitive singular.	

There are four additional types of r/n-class nouns. These are as follows:

(i) Some nouns have no ablaut between the nominative/accusative and the oblique cases:

	Hittite		PIE
sg nom/acc	ut^{h}ar	<ut-tar> 'word'	*ut+or
gen	ut^{h}anas		*ut+on+os

(ii) Some nouns have Ø-grade ablaut in the derivative suffix in the oblique cases:

	Hittite		PIE
sg nom/acc	asawar	<a-sa-a-u-ar> 'sheepfold'	*osō+wor[36]
dat	asauni		*osō+wn+i[37]

(iii) Some nouns replace an entire derivative suffix containing /r/ with a single /n/ in the oblique cases:

	Hittite		PIE
sg nom/acc	ap^{h}at^{h}ar	<ap-pa-a-tar> 'act of taxing'	*apo+tor
gen	ap^{h}anas		*apo+n+os

(iv) Some nouns dispense with the /n/ suffix in the oblique cases:

	Hittite		PIE
sg nom/acc	tiyawar	<ti-ya-u-war> 'act of placing'	*d^{h}i+o+w+or
gen	tiyawas		*d^{h}i+o+w+os

1.4.3 Vn-Class (Common, Neuter)

Most nouns of this class are neuter. E.g., the following:

		Hittite		PIE
sg	**nom/acc**	laman	<la-a-ma-an> 'name'	*nōmn̥[38]
	gen	lamnas		*nōmn+os[39]
	dat	lamni		*nōmn+i
	abl	*lamnat^s		*nōmn+ōts
	instr	lamnet		*nōmn+ed
pl	**obl**		Same as the genitive singular.	

Some Vn-class neuter nouns have /o(:)/ in the -Vn- suffix throughout the paradigm:

		Hittite		PIE
nom/acc	**sg**	henkan	ß<hi-in-kan> 'fate'	*heng+o(:)n[40]
	pl	henkanas		*heng+o(:)n+os

The com Vn-class nouns take o- and ā-class endings in the nominative singular and possibly accusative singular. Otherwise the endings are those of the athematic class. The following is a jVn-class noun.

		Hittite		PIE
sg	**nom**	memiyas	'word'	*memj+os[41]
	acc	memiyan		*memj+m̥[42]
	gen	memiyanas		*memj+o(:)n+os
	dat	memiyani		*memj+o(:)n+i
	abl	memiyanat^{s}		*memj+o(:)n+ōts
	instr	memiyanet		*memj+o(:)n+ed
pl	**nom**	memiyanes		*memj+o(:)n+es
	acc	memiyanus		*memj+o(:)n+ons
	obl	Same as the genitive singular.		

1.4.4 Vnt-class (Common, Neuter)

As an example of this class we cite the Hittite adjective humant- 'all, whole' which occurs in common and neuter forms. (It is perhaps a non-IE borrowing; we posit a PIE antecedent for illustrative purposes.)

		Hittite		PIE
com sg	**nom**	humant^{h}s	<hu-u-ma-an-za>	*humont+s[43]
	acc	humant^{h}an		*humont+m̥
	gen	humant^{h}as		*humont+os
	dat	humant^{h}i		*humont+i[44]
	abl	humant^{h}at^{s}		*humont+ōts
	instr	*humant^{h}et		*humont+ed
pl	**nom**	humant^{h}es		*humont+es
	acc	humant^{h}us		*humont+ons
	obl	Same as the genitive singular.		
neuter sg	**nom/acc**	human		*humont[45]
pl		humant^{h}a		*humont+ā
		Otherwise the same as the common forms.		

1.4.5 Vs-Class (Neuter)

The endings are those of the neuter Ø-class in 1.4.1 above. E.g.,

	Hittite		PIE
sg nom/acc	nepes	<ne-pi-is> 'sky'	*neb^{h}+es
gen	nepesas		*neb^{h}+es+os

2 Adjectives

These paradigms are in virtually all forms identical to those of the corresponding noun classes.

2.1 Positive Forms

Since the paradigms are the same as those of the corresponding nouns, we cite only a few representative examples from each class.

2.1.1 o-, jo-, ā- and jā-Class

This adjective class corresponds to noun class 1.1. E.g.,

			Hittite		PIE
nom	**sg**	**com**	newas	'new'	*new+os
		neuter	*newan		*new+om

An example of the jo- and jā-class adjective is this:

			Hittite		PIE
nom	**sg**	**com**	*anturijas	'inner'	$^*\underset{\circ}{n}d^hur$+j+os

2.1.2 i-Class

This class corresponds to noun class 1.2. E.g.,

			Hittite		PIE
nom	**sg**	**com**	sup^his	'clean'	*sup+is
		neuter	sup^hi		*sup+i

Some adjectives of this class have ō-grade ablaut[46] in the endings. E.g.,

			Hittite		PIE
nom	**sg**	**com**	$^*mek^hais$	'great'	*meg+ōi+s[47]
		neuter	$^*mek^hai$		*meg+ōi

2.1.3 u-Class

This class corresponds to noun class 1.3. E.g.,

			Hittite		PIE
nom	**sg**	**com**	italus	'bad'	*idal+us
		neuter	*italu		*idal+u

The same adjective can also occur with ō-grade ablaut in the ending:

			Hittite		PIE
nom	**sg**	**com**	*italaus	'bad'	*idal+ōus
		neuter	*italau		*idal+ōu

2.1.4 Athematic Classes

These paradigms correspond to the noun classes under 1.4 above. Most adjectives of this type are of the Vnt-class under 1.4.4. A few of these adjectives are from other athematic declensions. The following are from the Ø- and r/n-classes, respectively:

			Hittite		PIE
sg	nom	com	*kururs	'unfriendly'	*gurur+s[48]
		neuter	*kurur		*gurur
		com	*kalars	'evil'	*galar+s
		neuter	*kalar		*galar
	gen	com	*kalanas		*galan+os

2.2 Comparison

The usual comparative and superlative consist of the positive form of the adjective plus a noun phrase in the dative (The following examples are constructed after Friedrich 1960: 127.)

comp *mek^{h}ais ane 'big (nom sg) + mother (dat sg)' = 'bigger than (another) mother'

sup *mek^{h}ais humant^{h}i ane 'big (nom sg) + every mother (dat sg)' = 'biggest of any mother'

Some comparative suffixes do occur in some adjectives E.g., the following forms. The first is an i-class adjective the second an adjective of the o/ā-class:

			Hittite		PIE
nom	sg	com	hant^{h}et^{s}is	'former, second'	*hant+et+is[49]
			k^{h}at^{h}eras	'lower'	*kat+er+os

3 Adverbs

These are generally formed from the neuter dative or accusative endings of the respective adjective. E.g.,

	Hittite		PIE
sg dat	hant^{h}et^{s}i	'firstly'	*hant+et+i
acc	mek^{h}i	'very'	*meg+i
pl acc	humant^{h}at^{s}iya	<hu-u-ma-an-ta-az-zi-ya> 'completely'	*humont+ot+j+ā[50]
	ap^{h}ant^{h}a	'backwards, later'	*ap+ont+ā[51]

Some advs. are formed with specific suffixes. E.g.,

	Hittite		PIE
(a)	k^{h}wapi	<ku-wa-pi> 'where, when?'	*k^{w}o+b^h+i[52]
(b)	xat^{h}ili	'in the Hittite language'	*xat+il+i[53]
(c)	X+ank^{h}i	'X times'	*numeral+n̥k+i[54]

4 Numerals

Hittite numerals can for the most part only be surmised since they are designated in texts by means of Akkadian logograms and hence are not spelled out with the syllabic graphemes. In the following we shall designate the Hittite numbers with Arabic numerals and give a phonemic transcription of the attested inflectional endings.

4.1 Cardinals

'1' The forms are singular.

		Hittite	**PIE**
com	**nom**	1+as	*1+os[55]
	acc	1+an	*1+om
	gen	1+el	*1+el[56]
	dat	1+etani	*1+ed+on+i
	abl	1+etat^s	*1+ed+ōts
neuter	**nom/acc**	1+an	*1+om

Otherwise like the common forms.

'2' The following numerical declensions are in the plural.

		Hittite	**PIE**
com	**nom**	2+us	*2+ons[57]
	acc	2+e	*2+oi
	obl	2+etas	*2+ed+os[58]
neuter	**nom/acc**	*2+a	*2+ā

'3' The following are plural forms.

		Hittite	**PIE**
com	**nom**	3+es	*3+es[59]
	acc	3+us	*3+ons
	obl	3+as	*3+os[60]
neuter	**nom/acc**	*3+a	*3+ā[61]

The other Hittite cardinals are not certain. A possible '4' is Hit *mewes, which would have a non-IE antecedent. A possible '7' is *sep^{h}t^{h}ames, which is attested as an i-class noun in the dat sg sep^{h}t^{h}amiya 'a drink with 7 ingredients'. (See on all these points Friedrich 1960: 71-3.)

4.2 Ordinals

The first two ordinals as listed below are attested graphemically in our Hittite texts. The succeeding ordinals are recorded with the usual Akkadian logograms, but with a suffix -anna, which was uninflected. I.e.,

	Hittite	**PIE**
'1st'	hant^{h}et^{h}is	*hant+et+is[62]
'2nd'	tan	*dō+n[63]
'3rd'	3+anna	*3+onnō[63,64]

5 Pronouns

5.1 First Person

		Hittite		PIE
sg	**nom**	uk, uka	‘I’	*eg(+ō)[65]
		amuk		*m̥+u+g[65,66]
	acc	amuk, amuka		*m̥+u+g(+ō)[65,67]
	gen	amel		*m̥+el[68]
	dat	amuk, amuka		*m̥+u+g(+ō)[69]
	abl	ametat^s		*m̥+ed+ōts
pl	**nom**	wes	‘we’	*weis
		ant^{s}as		*n̥s+ōs
	acc	ant^{s}as		*n̥s+ōs[70]
	gen	ant^{s}el		*n̥s+el
	dat	ant^{s}as		*n̥s+ōs
	abl	ant^{s}etat^s		*n̥s+ed+ōts

5.2 Second Person

		Hittite		PIE
sg	**nom**	t^{s}ek, t^{s}eka	‘you’	*te+g(+ō)[71,72]
	acc	t^{h}uk, t^{h}uka		*tu+g(+ō)[72]
	gen	t^{h}wel		*tu+el[73]
	dat	t^{h}uk, t^{h}uka		*tu+g(+ō)
	abl	t^{h}wetat^s		*tu+ed+ōts
pl	**nom**	sumes, sumas		*wsm+es[74]
	acc	" "		"
	gen	sumel		*wsm+el
	dat	sumes, sumas		*wsm+es[74]
	abl	sumetat^s		*wsm+ed+ōts

5.3 Third Person

		Hittite		PIE
com sg	**nom**	asi, sas	‘he, she’	*os+i, *s+os[75]
	acc	unin, san		*un+im, *s+om[76]
	gen	sel		*s+el
	dat	setani		*s+ed+on+i
	abl	set^s		*s+ets
pl	**nom**	uniyus, sus		*un+i+ons,[76] *s+ons[77]
	acc	" "		" "
	obl	Same as the genitive singular.		
neuter	**nom/acc sg**	eni, se	‘it’	*en+i, *so+i[78]
	pl	*ena, *sa		*en+ā, *s+ā

Otherwise the same as the common forms.

5.4 Demonstrative

There are three such pronouns: k^has ‘this, these’, apas ‘that, those’ and *etas ‘he, she, it, they’. Their declensions are as follows.

		Hittite		PIE
com sg	**nom**	k^has	‘this, these’	*k+os
	acc	k^han, k^hun		*k+om, *k+um[79]
	gen	k^hel		*k+el
	dat	k^hetani		*k+ed+on+i
		k^heti		*k+ed+i
	abl	k^het^s		*k+e+ts
	instr	k^het		*k+ed
		k^hetant^{h}a		*k+ed+ont+ō
pl	**nom**	k^he		*k+oi
	acc	k^hus		*k+ons
	gen	k^hent^{s}an		*k+ent+s+ōm
		k^hetas		*k+ed+os[80]
	obl	Same as the genitive singular.		
neuter	**nom/acc sg**	k^hi		*k+i
		k^he		*k+ai
		Otherwise the same as the common forms.		

The second demonstrative is this:

		Hittite		PIE
sg com	**nom**	apas	‘that, those’	*ob^h+os
sg neuter	**nom/acc**	apat		*ob^h+od

Otherwise the endings are those of Hit k^has above.

The third demonstrative meaning ‘he, she, it, they’ is defectively attested. I.e.,

		Hittite		PIE
com sg	**nom**	*etas	‘he’, etc.	*ed+os
	acc	*etan		*ed+om
	gen	etas		*ed+os
	dat	etani		*ed+on+i
	abl	etat^s		*ed+ōts
		etit^s		*ed+its
pl	**nom**	e		*oi
	acc	*us		*ons
	dat	etas		*ed+os[81]
neuter	**nom/acc sg**	*etat		*ed+od
	pl	*ete		*ed+ai

Otherwise the Hittite forms probably consist of et- plus the endings of k^has above.

5.5 Interrogative

The following is both a pronoun meaning ‘who, which, what?’ as well as an adjective meaning ‘what kind of?’.

		Hittite	PIE
com sg	**nom**	k^hwis	*k^w+is
	acc	k^hwin	*k^w+im
	gen	k^hwel	*k^w+el[82]
	dat	k^hwetani	*k^w+ed+on+i
	abl	k^hwet^s	*k^w+ets
com pl	**nom**	k^hwes	*k^w+es
		k^hwe	*k^w+oi[83]
	acc	k^hweus	*k^w+e+ons
	dat	k^hwetas	*k^w+ed+os
	obl	Same as the genitive singular.	
neuter	**nom/acc sg**	k^hwit	*k^w+id
	pl	k^hwe	*k^w+ai[83]

Otherwise the same as the common forms.

5.6 Relative and Indefinite

The relative pronouns are the same as the interrogatives immediately above. The indefinite pronouns are formed variously from the interrogative-relative pronoun. They mean ‘someone, whoever, whatever’. Examples of some indefinite formations are these nominative singular common forms:

Hittite	PIE
k^hwis k^hwis	*k^w+is *k^w+is[84]
k^hwisas k^hwis	*k^w+is+os *k^w+is[85]
k^hwis imma	*k^w+is *immō[86]
k^hwisk^{h}wi	*k^w+is *k^w+i[87]
k^hwis sa	*k^w+is *so[88]

5.7 Enclitic

These pronouns are suffixed to other parts of speech such as nouns and even to conjunctions like Hit nu ‘and’ and t^ha ‘idem’. As such, this represents a construction unlike that of any of the other early IE languages considered in the present work. It thus would seem to be a Semiticism adopted into Hittite.

In view of the preceding, an enclitic construction such as Hittite *nu+mu would mean ‘and to me’. Other examples of enclitics are to be found in the reading selection in section VI of this chapter; and in the following we cite additional examples of enclitic constructions.

These are enclitics in the dative and accusative, 1st, 2nd and 3rd persons:

		Hittite		PIE
sg	**1**	-mu	‘me’	*m+u
	2	-t^ha, -t^hu	‘you’	*t+ō, *tu
	3	-si	‘him, her, it’	*s+i
pl	**1**	-nas	‘us’	*n+ōs[89]
	2	-smas	‘you’	*ws+m+ōs[90]
	3	-smas	‘them’	*s+m+ōs[90]

The following 3rd person enclitics are attested mainly in the nominative and accusative. The PIE antecedents were the respective inflectional endings.

		Hittite		PIE
com sg	**nom**	-as	'he, she'	*-os[91]
	acc	-an	'him, her'	*-om
pl	**nom**	-e	'they'	*-oi
	acc	-us	'them'	*-ons
neuter	**nom/acc sg**	-at	'it'	*-od
	pl	-e	'they, them'	*-ai

The possessive enclitic pronouns are as follows. As our primary examples we cite the 1st person forms 'my, our':

			Hittite		PIE
1sg	**com sg**	**nom**	-mis	'my'	*-m+is[92,93]
		acc	-man		*-m+om[92,93]
			-mun		*-m+um[92]
		gen	-mas		*-m+os[93]
		dat	-ma		*-m+ō
			-mi		*-m+i
	pl	**nom**	-mes		*-m+es[93]
		acc	-mus		*-m+ons
		gen	-man		*-m+ōm
			Otherwise the same as the genitive singular.		
	neuter	**nom/acc sg**	-mit		*-m+id
		pl	-mit		*-m+id[94]
			Otherwise the same as the common forms.		
1pl	**com sg**	**nom**	-smis	'our'	*-s+m+is[93,95]
		acc	-sman, *-smin		*-s+m+om/im
		gen	-smas		*-s+m+os
		dat	-sma, *-smi		*-s+m+ō/i
	pl	**nom**	-smes		*-s+m+es[93]
		acc	-smus		*-s+m+ons
		gen	-sman		*-s+m+ōm
			Otherwise the same as the singular forms.		
	neuter	**nom/acc sg**	-smit		*-s+m+id
		pl	-smit		*-s+m+id[94]

The 2nd person possessive enclitics have the same endings as those of the 1st person. E.g.,

		Hittite		PIE
com sg	**nom 2sg**	-tis	'your'	*-t+is[96]
	2pl	*-smis	'your (pl)'	*-ws+m+is[96]

The 3rd person possessive enclitics also have the same endings as those of the 1st person. E.g.,

		Hittite		PIE
com sg/pl	**3sg nom**	-sis	'his, her, their'	*-s+is[97]
	acc	-san		*-s+om[97]
		-sin		*-s+im

6 Verbs

The features of the Hittite verb are given in the following two tables. Table i contains the variable features — namely those which can change contingent upon the context. Table ii shows the lexical or inherent features — namely those that are idiosyncratic. They indicate the particular form-class of the verb.

(i) Variable Features

The first section of this table lists the purely verbal features. The second gives the features of deverbative adjectives and nouns.

Verbal Inflection

(a) Person	(b) Number	(c) Voice	(d) Tense/Mood
1. 1st	1. singular	1. active	1. present
2. 2nd	2. plural	2. medial[98]	2. preterite
3. 3rd		3. passive[98]	3. imperative[99]

(e) Composite Tense/Mood

1. present or imperative perfective = participle + present or imperative form[100]
2. past perfective = participle + preterite form[100]

Adjectival and Nominal Inflection

(a) Person	(b) Number	(c) Voice	(d) Tense/Mood
Ø	1. singular	1. active	1. present
	2. plural	2. medial	2. preterite
		3. passive	

(e) Mood occurring in	Present	Preterite
1. infinitive[101]	active	
2. supine[102]	active	
3. verbal noun[101]	active	
4. participle[103]		active/passive

(ii) Inherent Features.

(a) Type	(b) Class
1. nondeponent	1. mi-conjugation[104]
2. deponent = medial/passive inflection	2. hi-conjugation[104]

In the above tables i and ii, the features in the columns are mutually exclusive. Not all the logical possibilities are realized: the notations in the (e) column of the table Adjectival and Nominal Inflection indicate which are.

6.1 The mi-Conjugation

				Hittite		PIE
act	**pres**	**sg**	**1**	*wesmi	'clothe'	*wes+mi
			2	*wessi, *west^hi		*wes+si, *wes+ta[105]
			3	*west^si		*wes+ti
		pl	**1**	*wesweni		*wes+we+n+i[106]
			2	*west^heni		*wes+te+n+i[106]
			3	*wesant^si		*wes+ont+i[107]
act	**pret**	**sg**	**1**	*wesun		*wes+u+m[108]
			2	*wess		*wes+s
				*west^h(a)		*wes+t(a)[109]
			3	*west^h(a)		*wes+t(a)[109]
		pl	**1**	*weswen		*wes+we+n
			2	*west^hen		*wes+te+n
			3	*weser		*wes+ēr
	imp	**sg**	**1**	*wesalu		*wes+Vl+u[110]
			2	*wes, *wesi,		*wes, *wes+i[111]
				*west^hu		*wes+t+u[111]
			3	*west^hu		*wes+t+u[111]
		pl	**1**	*wesweni		*wes+we+n+i[112]
			2	*west^hen		*wes+te+n[113]
			3	*wesant^hu		*wes+ont+u[114]
	inf			waswant^si	<wa-as-su-u-wa-an-zi>	*wos+won+ti[115]
				waswanna		*wos+onn+ō[115]
	supine			waswan		*wos+won[115]
	verbal noun			waswar	'clothes'	*wos+wor
pass	**pres**	**sg**	**1**	*wesha		*wes+ho[116,117]
				*weshahari		*wes+ho+ho+r+i
				*weshari		*wes+ho+r+i
			2	*west^ha		*west+to
				*west^hat^hi		*wes+to+ti[117]
			3	*west^ha		*wes+to
				*west^hari		*wes+to+ri

				Hittite		PIE
pass	**pres**	**pl**	**1**	*weswasta	'clothe'	*wes+wos+to
				*weswastat^{h}i		*wes+wos+to+t+i[117]
			2	*westuma		*wes+d^{h}um+o
				*westumari		*wes+d^{h}um+o+r+i
			3	*wesant^{h}a		*wes+ont+o
				*wesant^{h}ari		*wes+ont+o+r+i
	pret	**sg**	**1**	*weshat^h		*wes+ho+t
				*weshat^{h}i		*wes+ho+t+i[117]
				*weshahat^{h}i		*wes+ho+ho+t+i[117]
			2	*west^{h}a		*wes+to
				*west^{h}at^h		*wes+to+t
				*west^{h}at^{h}i		*wes+to+t+i[117]
			3		Same forms as the 2nd singular.	
		pl	**1**	*weswastat^h		*wes+wos+tot
			2	*westumat^h		*wes+d^{h}um+ot
			3	*wesant^{h}at^h		*wes+ont+ot
				*wesant^{h}at^{h}i		*wes+ont+ot+i[117]
	imp	**sg**	**1**	*wesharu		*wes+ho+r+u
				*weshaharu		*wes+ho+ho+r+u
			2	*weshut^h		*wes+hu+t
				*weshut^{h}i		*wes+hu+t+i[117]
			3	*west^{h}aru		*wes+to+r+u
		pl	**1**	*weswastat^{h}u		*wes+wos+to+t+u
			2	*westumat^h		*wes+d^{h}um+o+t
				*westumat^{h}i		*wes+d^{h}um+o+t+i[117]
			3	*wesant^{h}aru		*wes+ont+o+r+u
	part			*wasant^{h}s		*wes+ont+s

The following morphophonemic rules apply to mi-conjugation verbs:

a. 1d tt-TO-tst may apply to verbs whose stems end in /t/ or /t^h/. E.g., 3sg pres /et+t^{s}i/ 'eats' (ld tt-TO-tst) → [etst^{s}i].

b. 7a n-CHANGES may optionally apply to verb stems ending in a nasal consonant with endings beginning with /m/ or /s/. E.g., 1sg pres /kwen+mi/ 'I strike' vs. 3sg pres /kwen+t^{s}i/ 'he strikes' (7a n-CHANGES) → [kwemi] vs. [kwent^{s}i].

c. 7b w-TO-m may apply if the verb stem ends in /u/. E.g., 1pl pres /arnu+weni/ 'we bring' (7b w-TO-m) →> [arnumeni].

d. Some verbs whose stems end in /k/ delete it before endings beginning with a nonvocalic segment. E.g., 1sg pres /hark+mi/ 'have', 1pl pres /har+weni/, 3pl pres /hark+ant^{s}i/ → [harmi], [harweni], but [harkant^{s}i].

e. Some verbs show ablaut between the present singular vs. plural. E.g., PIE 3sg pres *g^{hw}en+ti 'strike' vs. 3pl pres *g^{hw}Øn+onti (PIE 3.1.2c i-j/u-w ALT applying synchronically) → *g^{hw}enti vs. *g^{h}unonti (1a LABIOVEL) > *g^{h}wenti vs. *g^{h}unonti (2b OBSTR) > *kwent^{h}i vs. *kunont^{h}i (3a t^{h}-TO-t^{s}) > *kwent^{s}i vs. *kunont^{s}i (6 e/o-TO-a) > Hit kwent^{s}i vs. kunant^{s}i.

Derivative suffixes forming mi-class verbs are the following. We give first the PIE antecedent, then the Hittite form.

a. *-āi- > -ai-. This suffix attaches to nouns, adjectives and other verbs. E.g., the deadjectival PIE 3sg pres *os+āi+ti 'is good' (2b OBSTR) > *osāit^{h}i (3a t^{h}-TO-t^{s}) > *osāit^{s}i (5 V-SHORT) > *osait^{s}i (6 e/o-TO-a) > Hit asait^{s}i.

b. *-es- > -es-. This suffix forms deadjectival verbs meaning 'become that adjective'. E.g., Hit 1sg pres *mak^{h}+es+mi 'I become great'.

c. *-jo- > -(i)ya-. This suffix forms verbs from adjectives, nouns and verbs. E.g., Hit 1sg pres *was+(i)ya+mi 'I put on clothes'.

d. *-nen- > -nen-, which is infixed within the verb root. This infix derives causative verbs from other verbs. E.g., Hit */nenk+mi/ 'I rise' plus infix /-nen-/ → Hit 1sg pres */ne+nen+nk+mi/ (ev) → *[nenenkmi] 'I raise'. Likewise, Hit */hwek^{h}+mi/ 'I bewitch' plus the infix /-nen-/ → *[hwenenk^{h}mi] 'I cause to bewitch'.

e. *-nu- > -nu-. This suffix derives causative verbs from other verbs. E.g., Hit 1sg pres es+mi 'I sit' vs. ablauting 1sg pres *as+nu+mi 'I cause to sit, set'.

f. *-s- > -s-. This suffix derives verbs from nouns, adjectives or other verbs. E.g., Hit 1sg pres *ke+mi 'I recline' as well as *ke+s+mi 'idem'.

g. *-sko- and *-ski- > -ska- and -ski-. This suffix forms iterative and durative verbs. E.g., hi-class 1sg pres ta+hi 'I take' vs. mi-class ta+ski+mi 'I take repeatedly'.

The Verb esmi 'be'

This verb follows the conjugation of the mi-class and occurs only in the active.

			Hittite	**PIE**
pres	**sg**	**1**	esmi	*es+mi
		2	essi	*es+si
		3	est^{s}i	*es+ti
	pl	**1**	*esweni	*es+weni
		2	*est^{h}eni	*es+teni
		3	asant^{s}i	*os+onti[118]
pret	**sg**	**1**	esun	*es+um
		2	est^{h}(a)	*es+t(a)
		3	est^{h}(a)	*es+t(a)

			Hittite	PIE
pret	**pl**	**1**	eswen	*es+wen
		2	est^{h}en	*es+ten
		3	eser	*es+ēr
imp	**sg**	**1**	asalu	*os+Vl+u[118]
		2	es	*es
		3	est^{h}u	*es+tu
	pl	**1**	*esweni	*es+weni
		2	*est^{h}en	*es+ten
		3	asantu	*os+ont+u[118]
inf			*eswant^{s}i	*es+wont+ti
			*eswanna	*es+wonn+ō
supine			*eswan	*es+won
verbal noun			*eswar	*es+wor
part			asant^{h}s	*os+ont+s[118]

6.2 The hi-Conjugation

This class is a Hittite development of an original PIE perfect system. As such it resembles the Germanic preterite-present verb class as described in Chapter 2 section 6.1.3 of Gothic morphology. In both these classes a past-tense form has taken on a present-tense meaning. (Example below; see also on this Sturtevant 1933: 239.) The endings are generally those of the mi-class.

				Hittite		PIE
act	**pres**	**sg**	**1**	sak^{h}ahi	<sa-ag-ga-ah-hi> 'know'	*sok^w+a+hi[119]
			2	sak^{h}t^{h}i		*sok^w+ta+i[120]
			3	sak^{h}i		*sok^w+e+i[120]
		pl	**1**	sek^{h}weni		*sēk^w+weni[121]
			2	sek^{h}teni		*sēk^w+teni
			3	sek^{h}ant^{s}i		*sēk^w+onti
act	**pret**	**sg**	**1**	sak^{h}hun		*sok^w+hum
			2	sak^{h}t^h(a)		*sok^w+t(a)[122]
			3	sak^{h}s		*sok^w+s[123]
				sek^{h}s		*sēk^w+s[123]
				*sak^{h}st^h(a)		*sok^w+s+t(a)[122]
				*sek^{h}st^h(a)		*sēk^w+s+t(a)[122]
		pl	**1**	*sek^{h}wen		*sēk^w+wen[121]
			2	*sek^{h}t^{h}en		*sēk^w+ten
			3	sek^{h}er		*sēk^w+ēr
	imp	**sg**	**1**	sek^{h}alu		*sēk^w+Vlu
			2	sak^h, sak^{h}i		*sok^w, *sok^w+i
			3	sak^{h}u		*sok^w+u
				sak^{h}t^{h}u		*sok^w+tu

				Hittite		PIE
	imp	**p**	**1**	*sek^{h}weni	'know'	*sēk^w+weni[121]
			2	sek^{h}t^{h}en		*sēk^w+ten
			3	sek^{h}antu		*sēk^w+ontu
	inf			*sek^{h}want^{s}i		*sēk^w+wonti
				*sek^{h}anna		*sēk^w+onnō
	supine			*sek^{h}wan		*sēk^w+won
	verbal noun			*sek^{h}war	'knowledge'	*sēk^w+wor
pass	**pres**	**sg**	**1**	*sak^{h}hahari		*sok^w+hohori
				*sak^{h}hari		*sok^w+hori
			2	*sak^{h}t^{h}a		*sok^w+to
				*sak^{h}t^{h}at^{h}i		*sok^w+toti
			3	*sak^{h}ari		*sok^w+ori
pass	**pres**	**pl**	**1**	*sek^{h}wasta		*sēk^w+wosto[121]
				*sek^{h}wastat^{h}i		*sēk^w+wostoti
			2	*sek^{h}wastuma		*sēk^w+wosd^{h}umo
				*sek^{h}wastumari		*sēk^w+wosd^{h}umori
			3	*sek^{h}ant^{h}a		*sēk^w+onto
				*sek^{h}ant^{h}ari		*sēk^w+ontori
	pret	**sg**	**1**	*sak^{h}hat^h		*sok^w+hot
				*sak^{h}hat^{h}i		*sok^w+hoti
				*sak^{h}hahat^{h}i		*sok^w+hohoti
			2	*sak^{h}t^{h}a		*sok^w+to
				*sak^{h}t^{h}at^h		*sok^w+tot
				*sak^{h}t^{h}at^{h}i		*sok^w+toti
			3	Same forms as the 2nd singular.		
		pl	**1**	*sek^{h}wastat^h		*sēk^w+wostot[121]
			2	*sek^{h}tumat^h		*sēk^w+d^{h}umot
			3	*sek^{h}ant^{h}at^h		*sēk^w+ontot
				*sek^{h}ant^{h}at^{h}i		*sēk^w+ontoti
	imp	**sg**	**1**	*sak^{h}haru		*sok^w+hor+u
				*sak^{h}haharu		*sok^w+hohor+u
			2	*sak^{h}hut^h		*sok^w+hut
				*sak^{h}hut^{h}i		*sok^w+huti
			3	*sak^{h}aru		*sok^w+oru
		pl	**1**	*sek^{h}wastat^{h}u		*sēk^w+wostotu[121]
			2	*sek^{h}tumat^h		*sēk^w+d^{h}umot
				*sek^{h}tumat^{h}i		*sēk^h+d^{h}umoti
			3	*sek^{h}ant^{h}aru		*sēk^w+ontoru
	part			sek^{h}ants	'known'	*sēk^w+ont+s

Derived hi-class verbs occur as follows:

a. *-nā- > -na-. This suffix forms intensive verbs. E.g., PIE *tr̥+nā+hi 'I put in' (lc SYL SON) > *tarnāhi (2b OBSTR) > *t^harnāhi (5 V-SHORT) > Hit *t^harnahi.

b. *-sō- > -sa-. This suffix forms intensive verbs. E.g., Hit mi-class *et+mi 'I eat' vs. hi-class *et+sa+hi 'I eat a lot'.

c. Some hi-class verbs are derived, but without a derivative suffix. E.g., Hit nom sg masc adj newa+s vs. the hi-class verb newa+hi 'I renew'.

Some hi-class verbs show ablaut between the 1st person present singular vs. the other forms of the paradigm. E.g.,

				Hittite		PIE
act	pres	sg	1	nehi	'lead'	*noi+hi[124]
				uhi	'see'	*ou+hi
			2	nait^{h}i		*nōi+ta+i[124]
				aut^{h}i		*ōu+ta+i

V Exercises

(1) Consider the following PIE forms and the changes which they underwent into Hittite. (We disregard here Hittite stress since it applies invariably word-initially.) What is the Hittite form? Give it in phonemic transcription (/.../) as well as in a possible graphemic transcription (<...>).

a. Nom sg *ak^w+tor+os 'a drinker' + la LABIOVEL, 2b OBSTR, 6 e/o-TO-a > Hittite?
b. Nom sg *antos 'front' + lb LARYNGEALS, 2b OBSTR, 6 e/o-TO-a > Hittite?
c. Acc pl *atons 'fathers' + 2b OBSTR, 3b WF CL, 5 V-SHORT > Hittite?
d. Nom sg u-class adj *b^{h}n̥g^{h}us 'all' + 1c SYL SON, 2b OBSTR > Hittite?
e. 1sg pres *d^{h}ē+i 'I put' + lb LARYNGEALS, 2b OBSTR, 5 V-SHORT > Hittite?
f. Nom sg *diu+s 'god' + PIE 3.l.2c i-j/u-w ALT applying synchronically, 2b OBSTR, 3a t^h-TO-t^s > Hittite?
g. Nom pl *dl̥+ug+ost+iā 'lengths' + PIE 3.l.2c i-j/u-w ALT applying synchronically, lc SYL SON, 2b OBSTR, 5 V-SHORT, 6 e/o-TO-a > Hittite?
h. 1sg pres *dō+i 'I give, (later) I take' + lb LARYNGEALS, 2b OBSTR, 5 V-SHORT, 6 e/o-TO-a > Hittite?
i. Nom sg *g^{h}esor 'hand' + 2b OBSTR, 6 e/o-TO-a > Hittite?
j. 1sg pres *g^{h}r̥b^h+mi 'I take' + lc SYL SON, 2b OBSTR > Hittite?
k. 3sg pres *g^{hw}enti 'kills' vs. ablauting 3pl pres *g^{hw}Ønonti + la LABIOVEL, 2b OBSTR, 3a t^h-TO-t^s > Hittite? and?
l. 3sg pass *g^{hw}or+on+i 'is burnt' + la LABIOVEL, 6 e/o-TO-a > Hittite?
m. 1sg pres *konk+a+hi 'I hang' + 2b OBSTR, 6 e/o-TO-a > Hittite?
n. Nom sg Vnt-class adj *makel+ont+s 'thin' + 2b OBSTR, 6 e/o-TO-a > Hittite?
o. Adv *n̥d^{h}o 'within, inside' + lc SYL SON, 2b OBSTR, 5 V-SHORT, 6 e/o-TO-a > Hittite?
p. 1sg pres *noi+i 'I lead' vs. ablauting 2sg pres *noi+t+i 'you lead' + lb LARYNGEALS, 2b OBSTR, 5 V-SHORT, 6 e/o-TO-a > Hittite? and?

q. Nom sg *nōmn̥ 'name' + 1c SYL SON, 5 V-SHORT, 6 e/o-TO-a, 7a n-CHANGES > Hittite?
r. Nom sg *opin+ont+s 'rich' + lb LARYNGEALS, 2b OBSTR, 6 e/o-TO-a > Hittite?
s. Nom sg *oros 'eagle' + lb LARYNGEALS, 6 e/o-TO-a > Hittite?
t. Nom sg neuter r/n-class *pet+or 'wing' + 2b OBSTR, 6 e/o-TO-a > Hittite?
u. 3sg pres *sm̥+legʰ+ti 'lies with' + lc SYL SON (producing /a/), 2b OBSTR, 3a tʰ-TO-tˢ > Hittite?
v. Nom sg *stom+or 'mouth' + 6 e/o-TO-a > Hittite?
w. 3sg pres *werbʰ+ti 'washes' + 2b OBSTR, 3a tʰ-TO-tˢ, 6 e/o-TO-a > Hittite?
x. Acc sg *wetm̥ 'year' + lc SYL SON, 2a m-TO-n, 2b OBSTR, 6 e/o-TO-a > Hittite?
y. Nom pl *wont+es 'winds' + lb LARYNGEALS, 2b OBSTR, 6 e/o-TO-a > Hittite?

(2) Given the following PIE forms, what will be the Hittite reflexes and what changes will they have undergone? Give the Hit forms in phonemic transcription (/.../) and in a possible graphemic transcription (<...>) — of which latter there are several.

a. Nom sg *albʰos 'white'.
b. Nom sg i-class *apo+i+t+is 'one who goes back, (later) last one'.
c. 3pl pres *ap+onti 'they seize'.
d. Nom sg masc *harg+is 'bright'.
e. Nom sg *bʰr̥gʰ+us 'high'.
f. 1sg pres *deik+us+ā+mi 'I show'.
g. Nom sg neuter u-class *doru 'wood'.
h. 3sg pres *eup+ti 'goes up'.
i. Nom sg *genu 'knee'.
j. Nom sg *gʰeim+ont+s 'winter'.
k. Nom sg *jugom 'yoke'.
l. 1sg pres *kors+mi 'I cut'.
m. Nom sg *kord+i 'heart'.
n. Acc sg *kʷim 'whom?'.
o. Nom/acc sg *kʷod 'what, why'.
p. 3sg pres mid *leuk+o+tai 'become light'.
q. Nom sg i-class adj *meg+is 'large, great'. (For some reason the Hittite reflex has /kʰ/.)
r. 3sg pres *ok+i 'kills'.
s. Nom sg i-class neuter *hostōi 'bone'.
t. Nom sg *porsnā+s 'thigh'.
u. 3pl pres *spondʰ+onti 'they sacrifice'.
v. Nom sg *te+g 'you' vs. acc sg *tu+g 'idem'.
w. Nom sg *trep+om 'plow'.
x. Nom sg *hwr̥d +ōi+m 'curse'

(3) Assume that the pre-Hittite PIE numerals were *som+os '1', *dw+oi '2', *tri+es '3', *kʷetwōr '4', *kʷinkʷe '5', *seks '6', *septm̥ '7', *oktōu '8', *nowm̥ '9', *dekm̥ '10'. What would be the Hittite reflexes and what changes would they have undergone?

(4) The following forms are given in the Hittite syllabic orthography. Give the Hittite form in phonemic transcription (/.../) and a possible PIE antecedent.

a. Adv <a-ap-pa> 'back, again'.
b. 1sg pres <e-it-mi> 'I eat', where <t> never occurs as <tt>.

c. Adv <kat-ta> 'down'.
d. 3sg pres <la-ga-a-ri> 'reclines', where <g> never occurs as <gg>.
e. 3sg pres <lu-uk-ki-iz-zi> 'becomes light'.
f. 3pl pres <ma-al-la-an-zi> 'they grind'.
g. Nom sg <ne-pi-is> 'sky', where <p> is never written as <pp>. Interpret the <i-i> as /e/.
h. Nom sg <ne-wa-as> 'new'.
i. Nom sg <ar-pa-as> 'loss, bad luck', where <p> never occurs as <pp>.
j. Nom sg <a-as-su-us> 'good'.
k. 3sg pres <a-us-zi> 'sees'.
l. Nom sg <pi-e-da-an> 'place', where <d> is never written as <dd> and <pi> is to be interpreted as /p^{h}e/.
m. Nom sg of i-class adj <pal-hi-is> 'broad'.
n. Acc sg <tu-uz-zi-in> 'army'.
o. Nom sg <ud-ne> 'city', where <d> never occurs as <dd>.
p. Nom sg <ut-tar> 'thing'.
q. 3sg pres <u-e-es-zi> 'lives'.

(5) Consider the glossed Hittite text in VI below. Give a smooth translation of this text.

VI A Hittite Text

Our text is taken from the Hittite legal code, which dates from about 1450-1200 BC. The text and the translation are based on the material in Held et al. (1988: 122–4 and 130).

In the text we give (a) the conventional transcription of the Hittite syllabary, (b) a phonemic transcription (where we do not mark word stress, which we assume was invariably word-initial), (c) a gloss and (d) a grammatical description of each form. The numbers in brackets on line (a) indicate the lines in the original cuneiform text. (We have also inserted here some of our own punctuation, namely periods, commas and semicolons.)

A word needs to be said about the conventions employed in line (a). As described in section III Hittite Phonology, the Hittite writing system was a syllabary. Most of any text is written in syllabic graphemes which are transcribed in lower-case letters, e.g. the first word in our text <tak-ku> 'if', phonemic /tak^{h}u/.

However, there also occur in Hittite texts logograms (also called ideograms) which may be borrowed from either the Sumerian or the Akkadian writing systems. These logograms are cuneiform symbols which stand for the Sumerian or the Akkadian word in its entirety. The usual transcriptional convention is to write Sumerian logograms in capitals and Akkadian ones in italicized capitals. (We assume that such logograms were pronounced as the corresponding Hittite words.)

For example:

(i) Sumerian LU 'man' = Hit /ant^{h}uhs-/.

(ii) Akkadian *EL* 'free' = Hit /araw-/.

Often the Hittite inflectional ending is added to these logograrns: e.g., nom <LU-as> 'man' = Hit /ant^{h}uhs+as/. Sometimes one and the same sign can function variously in a text as (i) a Sumerian logogram, (ii) an Akkadian logogram or (iii) a syllable designator.

For example:

(i) Sumerian <ŠU-as> = nom sg 'hand' = Hit /kesar+as/.

(ii) Akkadian <*ŠU*> = 'his' in word such as Hit <me-ne-*ŠU*> 'his face' = /menesit/.

(iii) Syllabic <šu> as in Hit 3sg pres <šu-u-ni-iz-zi> /sunit^{s}i/ 'sows'.

Up to now we have transcribed graphemic <š> as <s> since /s/ was clearly the phonetic value of the Hittite segment. In the following we shall use the more traditional grapheme <š>.

In the following text where these logograms occur we shall supply the Hittite equivalents. In those instances where no Hittite equivalent is attested — such as the numbers, for which Akkadian numerals are used — we reconstruct possible Hittite forms as they might have been derived from PIE. We prefix these Hittite forms with an asterisk, e.g. Hittite '1' *samas.

Many nouns in Hit texts may be preceded — and occasionally followed — by so-called "determinative" logograms. These mark the noun as belonging to a particular semantic or conceptual class. We assume that these determinatives were not pronounced. The usual transcriptional convention is to write deterrninatives before the word in superscript capitals. For example, in our text below, the sequence <^{GIŠ}APIN-an> 'plow' occurs. This is the accusative singular of the Hit /ap^{h}alas+an/. Here the superscripted <^{GIŠ} …> indicates an object made of wood.

Other determinatives are these:

<^{DINGIR} …> 'a god(dess)...'

<^{I} …> 'a masculine name...'

<^{KUR} …> 'a country...'

<^{LU} …> 'a masculine...'

<^{SAL} …> 'a feminine...'

<^{URU} …> 'a city or country...'

The text is as follows:

1	**a**	[1] tak-ku	NUMUN-ni	še-ir	NUMUN-an	ku-iš-ki	šu-u-ni-i-zi
	b	t^{h}ak^{h}u	warwala+ni	ser	warwal+an	k^{h}wiski	sunit^{s}i
	c	*if*	*seed*	*over*	*seed*	*anyone*	*sow*
	d	conj	dat sg neut	prep	acc sg neuter	nom sg	3sg pres
			Vn-class		Vn-class	com pron	act mi-class

2	**a**	[2] GU-*ŠU*	^{GIŠ}APIN-an	še-ir	ti-iz-zi	ta	*SI* [3]-*IM-TI*
	b	kut^{h}ar+sit	ap^{h}alas+an[125]	ser	tet^{s}i	t^{h}a	turan
	c	*neck his*	*plow*	*upon*	*put*	*then*	*team*
	d	acc sg neuter	acc sg neuter	prep	3sg pres	adv	acc sg neuter
		r/n-class	o/ā-class		act mi-class		o/ā-class

3	a	GUD-HI-A	tu-ri-ya-an-zi,	ki-e [4]-el	me-ne-iš-ši-it		du-wa-a-an
	b	*kuwawas[126]	turiyant^{s}i	k^{h}el	mene	+ sit	tuwan
	c	*ox*	*harness*	*this one*	*face*	*its*	*one way*
	d	gen pl com	3pl pres act	gen sg	acc sg,	acc sg neut	adv
		u-class	mi-class	pron	i-class neut	encl pron	

4	a	ki-e [5]-el-la		me-ne-iš-ši-it		du-wa-a-an	[6]ne-e-ya-an-zi.	LU-aš
	b	k^{h}el +	a	mene +	sit	tuwan	neyant^{s}i	ant^{h}uhsas
	c	*that one*	*and*	*face*	*its*	*another way*	*turn*	*man*
	d	gen sg	conj	acc sg	acc sg neut	adv	3pl pres act	nom sg com
		pron		i-class neut	encl pron		hi-class	o/ā-class

5	a	a-ki;	GUD-HI [7]-ya		ak-kan-zi	*U*	A-ŠA-*LAM*	ka[8]-ru-pit	
	b	ak^{h}i	kuwawes[126]	+ ya	ak^{h}ant^{s}i	t^{h}a	kweran	k^{h}aru	+ p^{h}it
	c	*die*	*ox*	*and*	*die*	*and*	*field*	*at first*	*then*
	d	3sg pres act	nom pl com	encl	3pl pres	conj	acc sg com	adv	enclit
		hi-class	u-class		act hi-class		o/ā-class		

6	a	ku-is	šu-u-ni-it	ta-az		[9]a-pa-a-aš	da-a-i.
	b	k^{h}wis	sunit^h	ta +	at^s	ap^{h}as	tai
	c	*whoever*	*sow*	*then*	*he*	*that one*	*take*
	d	nom sg	3sg pret	adv	abl sg	abl sg com	3sg pres
		com pron	act mi-class		encl pron	pron	act hi-class

7	a	ka-ru-u	ki-iš-ša[10]-an	e-eš-šir.	[11] ki-nu-na	1
	b	k^{h}aru	k^{h}isan	eser	k^{h}inuna	*samas[127]
	c	*formerly*	*thus*	*be*	*nowadays*	*one*
	d	adv	adv	3pl pret	adv	nom sg com
				act mi-class		

8	a	UDU	LU-na-aš	ka-aš-ša-aš-ša-aš		[12] hu-it-ti-an-ta,
	b	iyant^{h}s	ant^{h}usanas	k^{h}asas	+ sas	hwit^{h}ant^{h}a
	c	*sheep*	*man*	*instead of*	*he*	*bring*
	d	nom sg com	gen sg com	prep	gen sg com	3pl (!) pres
		Vnt-class	Vn-class		enclitic pron	pass mi-class

9	a	2	UDU-HI-A	GUD-HI-A	ka-aš-ša[13]-aš-ša-aš		hu-u-it-ti-an-ta.
	b	*twe	iyant^{h}es	kuwawas[126]	k^{h}asas	+ sas	hwit^{h}ant^{h}a
	c	*two*	*sheep*	*ox*	*instead of*	*they*	*bring*
	d	nom pl	nom pl com	gen pl com	prep	gen pl	3pl pres pass
		com	Vnt-class	u-class		encl pron	mi-class

10	a	30	NINDA-HI-A	3	DUG	KA[14]-KAK	pa-a-i;
	b	*t^{h}ri+tek^{h}anes	harsiyus	*t^{h}riyes	pullus	siyesanas[128]	pai
	c	*thirty*	*bread loaves*	*three*	*jug*	*beer*	*give*
	d	numeral, acc	acc pl	acc pl com	acc pl com	gen sg neuter	3sg pres
		pl com	com i-class	Ø-class	o/ā-class	r/n-class	act hi-class

11	a	ta	a-ap-pa	su-up-pi-ya-ah-hi	[15] *U*	A-ŠA-*LAM*
	b	t^{h}a	ap^{h}a	sup^{h}iyahi	t^{h}a	kweran
	c	*and*	*again*	*purify*	*and*	*field*
	d	conj	adv	3sg pres act	conj	acc sg com
				hi-class		o/ā-class

12	a	ka-ru-u-pit		ku-is	šu-u-ni [16]-e-it	ta-az	
	b	k^{h}aru	+ p^{h}it^h	k^{h}wis	sunit^h	t^{h}a	+ at^s
	c	*at first*	*then*	*whoever*	*sow*	*and*	*he*
	d	adv	enclitic	nom sg	3sg pres act	conj	abl sg
				com pron	mi-class		encl pron

13	a	a-pa-aš	wa-ar-aš-zi.	[17] tak-ku	A-ŠA-an	ZAG-an
	b	apas	warast^{s}i	t^{h}ak^{h}u	kweran	arhan
	c	*that one*	*harvest*	*if*	*field*	*boundary*
	d	nom sg	3sg pres	conj	acc sg com	acc sg
		com pron	act mi-class		o/ā-class	com o/ā-class

14	a	ku-is-ki	par-ši-ya		1	[18] ag-ga-la-an
	b	k^{h}wiski	p^{h}arsi	+ ya	*saman[127]	ak^{h}alan
	c	*anyone*	*break*	*and*	*one*	*furrow, plow*
	d	nom sg	3sg pres	conj	acc sg	acc sg com
		com pron	act hi-class		com	o/ā-class

15	a	pi-en-na-a-i,	EN	A-ŠA	[19] 1	gi-pi-eš-šar
	b	p^{h}enai	eshas	kweras	*saman[127]	kipesar
	c	*drive*	*owner*	*field*	*one*	*ell, unit of measure*
	d	3sg pres act	nom sg com	gen sg com	acc sg	acc sg neuter
		hi-class	o/ā-class	o/ā-class	neuter	r/n-class

16	a	kar-aš-zi	ta-az	[20] da-a-i.	ZAG-an	na
	b	k^{h}arst^{s}i	t^{h}a + at^{s}	tai	arhan	na
	c	*cut off*	*and* *he*	*take*	*boundary*	*and*
	d	3sg pres	conj abl sg	3sg pres	acc sg com	conj
		act mi-class	encl pron	act hi-class	o/ā-class	

17	a	ku-iš	par-ši-ya	1	[21] UDU	10
	b	k^{h}wis	p^{h}arsi + ya	*saman[127]	iyant^{h}an	*tek^{h}an
	c	*whoever*	*break* *and*	*one*	*sheep*	*ten*
	d	nom sg	3sg pres conj	acc sg	acc sg	numeral
		com pron	act hi-class	com	com Vnt-class	

18	a	NINDA-HI-A	1	DUG	KA-KAK
	b	harsiyus	*saman[127]	pullan	siyesanas [128]
	c	*loaf of bread*	*one*	*jug*	*beer*
	d	acc pl com	acc sg	acc sg com	gen sg neuter
		i-class	com	o/ā-class	r/n-class

19	a	pa-a-i.	ta	[22] A-ŠA-*LAM*	EGIR-pa	šu-up-pi-ya-ah-hi.
	b	pai	t^{h}a	kweran	ap^{h}a	sup^{h}iyahi
	c	*give*	*and*	*field*	*again*	*purify*
	d	3sg pres act	conj	acc sg com	adv	3sg pres act
		hi-class		o/ā-class		hi-class

20	a	[23] tak-ku	LU	*EL-LAM*	MUŠ-an	ku-en-zi
	b	t^{h}ak^{h}u	ant^{h}uhsas	arawas	illuyankan[129]	kwent^{s}i
	c	*if*	*man*	*free*	*snake*	*kill*
	d	conj	nom sg com	nom sg	acc sg com	3sg pres act
			Vn-class	com o/ā-class	o/ā-class	mi-class

21	**a**	da[24]-me-el-la		ŠUM-an	te-iz-zi,	1	MA-NA
	b	tamel	+ a	laman	tet^{s}i	*saman[127]	*manan
	c	*other*	*and*	*name*	*say*	*one*	*pound*
	d	gen sg	conj	acc sg neuter	3sg pres	acc sg	acc sg com
		pron		Vn-class	act hi-class	com	o/ā-class

22	**a**	KU-BABBAR	[25] pa-a-i.	tak-ku	IR-ša	a-pa-a-aš-pit		a-ki.
	b	hat^{h}as[130]	pai	t^{h}ak^{h}u	asiwant^{h}s[131]	apas +	p^{h}it^h	ak^{h}i
	c	*silver*	*give*	*if*	*slave*	*that*	*then*	*die*
	d	gen sg neuter	3sg pres act	conj	nom sg com	nom sg	encl	3sg pres
		o/ā-class	hi-class		Vnt-class	com pron		hi-class

VII Key

(1) The Hittite forms are these: (a) /ak^{h}ut^{h}aras/ <a-ku-ut-tar-as>, (b) /hantas/ <ha-an-da-as>, (c) /at^{h}us/ <at-tu-us>, (d) /pankus/ <pa-an-ku-us>, (e) /tehi/ <te-ih-hi>, (f) /siyus/ <si-u-us>, (g) /talukastiya/ <ta-lu-kas-ti-a>, (h) /tahi/ <da-ah-hi>, (i) /kesar/ <ki-es-sar>, (j) /karpmi/ <kar-ap-mi>, (k) /k^{h}went^{s}i/ and /k^{h}unant^{s}i/ <ku-en-zi> and <ku-na-an-zi>, (l) /warani/ <wa-a-ra-ni>, (m) /k^{h}ank^{h}ahi/ <kan-ga-ah-hi>, (n) /mak^{h}lant^{h}s/ <ma-ak-la-an-da-as>, (o) /anta/ <an-da-a>, (p) /nehi/ and /nait^{h}i/ <ne-hi> and <na-a-it-ti>, (q) /laman/ <la-a-ma-an>, (r) /hap^{h}inant^{s}s/ <ha-pi-na-an-tin-ta-za> (s) /haras/ <ha-a-ra-as>, (t) /p^{h}et^{h}ar/ <pit-tar>, (u) /salekt^{s}i/ <sa-lig-zi>, (v) /stamar/ <is-ta-ma-ar>, (w) /warpt^{s}i/ <wa-ar-ap-zi>, (x) /wet^{h}an/ <u-e-ta-an>, (y) /hwant^{h}es/ <hu-u-wa-an-te-es>.

(2) The Hittite forms and changes are these:

a. /alpas/ <al-pa-as>. The derivation is 2b OBSTR, 6 e/o-TO-a.
b. /ap^{h}et^{s}is/ <ap-pi-iz-zi-as>. The derivation is 2b OBSTR, 3a t^h-TO-t^s, 4 MON, 5 V-SHORT.
c. /ap^{h}ant^{s}i/ <ap-pa-an-zi>. The derivation is 2b OBSTR, 3a t^h-TO-t^s, 6 e/o-TO-a.
d. /harkis/ <har-ki-is>. The derivation is lb LARYNGEALS, 2b OBSTR.
e. /parkus/ <par-ku-us>. The derivation is lc SYL SON, 2b OBSTR.
f. /tek^{h}usami/ <te-ik-ku-us-sa-mi>, The derivation is 2b OBSTR, 4 MON, 5 V-SHORT.
g. /taru/ <ta-ru-u>. The derivation is 2b OBSTR, 6 e/o-TO-a .
h. /up^{h}t^{s}i/ <up-zi>. The derivation is 2b OBSTR, 3a t^h-TO-t^s, 4 MON, 5 V-SHORT.
i. /kenu/ <gi-e-nu>. The derivation is 2b OBSTR.
j. /kemant^{h}s/ <gi-im-ma-an-za>. The derivation is 2b OBSTR, 4 MON, 5 V-SHORT, 6 e/o-TO-a.
k. /yukan/ <i-u-kan>. The derivation is 2a m-TO-n, 2b OBSTR, 6 e/o-TO-a.
l. /k^{h}arsmi/ <kar-as-mi>. The derivation is 2b OBSTR, 6 e/o-TO-a .
m. /k^{h}arti/ <kar-di>. The derivation is 2b OBSTR, 6 e/o-TO-a .
n. /k^{h}win/ <ku-in>. The derivation is la LABIOVEL, 2a m-TO-n, 2b OBSTR.
o. /k^{h}wat/ <ku-wa-at>. The derivation is la LABIOVEL, 2b OBSTR, 6 e/o-TO-a.
p. /luk^{h}at^{h}e/ <lu-uk-kat-te>. The derivation is 2b OBSTR, 4 MON, 5 V-SHORT, 6 e/o-TO-a.
q. /mek^{h}is/ <mek-kis>. The derivation is only 2b OBSTR, which for some reason in this instance produces /k^h/ instead of the expected /k/.

r. /ak^{h}i/ <a-ki>. The derivation is 2b OBSTR, 6 e/o-TO-a.
s. /hastai/ <ha-as-ta-i>. The derivation is lb LARYNGEALS, 2b OBSTR (perhaps), 5 V-SHORT, 6 e/o-TO-a .
t. /p^{h}arsnas/ <pa-ar-si-na-as>. The derivation is 2b OBSTR, 5 V-SHORT, 6 e/o-TO-a.
u. /spantant^{s}i/ <is-pa-an-ta-an-zi>. The derivation is 2b OBSTR, 3a t^h-TO-t^s, 6 e/o-TO-a.
v. /t^{s}ek/<zi-ik> and /t^{h}uk/ <tu-uk>. The derivation is 2b OBSTR, 3a t^h-TO-t^s.
w. /t^{h}rep^{h}an/ <ta-ri-pa-an>. The derivation is 2a m-TO-n, 2b OBSTR, 6 e/o-TO-a.
x. /hwartain/ <hu-wa-ar-ta-in>. The derivation is lb LARYNGEALS, lc SYL SON, 2a m-TO-n, 2b OBSTR, 5 V-SHORT, 6 e/o-TO-a.

(3) The Hittite forms and their derivations are as follows:

'1' *samas. The derivation is 6 e/o-TO-a.
'2' *twe. The derivation is 2b OBSTR, 4 MON, 5 V-SHORT.
'3' *t^{h}riyes. The derivation is 2b OBSTR and possibly a glide-insertion rule whereby *t^{h}ries becomes *t^{h}riyes.
'4' *k^{h}wet^{h}war. The derivation is la LABIOVEL, 2b OBSTR, 5 V-SHORT, 6 e/o-TO-a .
'5' *k^{h}wink^{h}we, The derivation is la LABIOVEL, 2b OBSTR.
'6' *sek^{h}s. The derivation is 2b OBSTR.
'7' *sep^{h}t^{h}an. The derivation is lc SYL SON, 2a m-TO-n, 2b OBSTR.
'8' *ak^{h}t^{h}au. The derivation is 2b OBSTR, 5 V-SHORT, 6 e/o-TO-a.
'9' *nawan. The derivation is 1c SYL SON, 2a m-TO-n, 6 e/o-TO-a .
'10' *tek^{h}an. The derivation is lc SYL SON, 2a m-TO-n, 2b OBSTR.

(4) The Hittite form and. the possible PIE antecedents are as follows:

a. /ap^{h}a/ < *(a/o)p(a/o). The actual PIE form is *apo.
b. /etmi/ < *ed$^{(h)}$mi. The actual PIE form is *edmi.
c. /k^{h}at^{h}a/ < *k(a/o)t(a/o). The actual PIE form is *kata.
d. /lakari/ < *l(a/o)g$^{(h)}$(a/o)ri. The actual PIE form is *log^{h}ori.
e. /lukt^{s}i/ < *l(e/o/Ø)ukti, The actual PIE form is *leukti.
f. /malant^{s}i/ < *m(a/o)l(a/o)nti. The actual PIE form is *molonti.
g. /nepes/ < *neb$^{(h)}$es. The actual PIE form is *neb^{h}es.
h. /newas/ < *new(a/o)s, The actual PIE form is *newos.
i. /arpas/ < *(a/o)rb$^{(h)}$os. The actual PIE form is *orb^{h}os.
j. /asus/ < *(a/o)sus. The actual PIE form is *asus.
k. /aust^{s}i/ < *(ā/ō)us+ti, The actual PIE form is *ōus+ti.
l. /p^{h}etan/ < *ped$^{(h)}$(a/o)(m/n). The actual PIE form is *pedom.
m. /p^{h}alhis/ < *p(a/o/Ø)l(h)is. The actual PIE form is *pl̥(h)is.
n. /t^{h}ut^{s}in/ < PIE *t(a/o)uti(m/n). The actual PIE form is *t(o)utim.
o. /utne/ < *u(:)d$^{(h)}$ne(i). The actual PIE form is *ūd^{h}nei.
p. /ut^{h}ar/ < *u(:)t(a/o)r. The actual PIE form is *utor.
q. /west^{h}i/ < *west+ti, which is the PIE form.

(5) The following is a translation of the text in section VI.

"[1] If anyone sows seed over (previously planted) seed, one then puts that man's neck upon a plow. Then they harness a team of oxen; the face of one of them they turn one way and the face of the other of them the other way. [6] The man dies; and the oxen die. And then whoever at first sowed the field, he takes from him (the usurper) the field. Formerly they were thus. [11] Nowadays one sheep is brought instead of the man and two sheep are brought instead of the oxen. (And the usurper) gives up thirty loaves of bread (and) three jugs of beer; and (the usurper) purifies the field again. [15] And whoever at first had sowed the field harvests it. [17] If anyone breaks a field boundary and drives one furrow or plow (over the boundary), the owner of the field cuts off one ell and takes it from him (the usurper). And whoever breaks a boundary gives up one sheep, ten loaves of bread and one jug of beer. [22] And he purifies the field again. [23] (And) if a free man kills a snake and says the name of someone else (as a curse), he pays one pound of silver. If (the offender) is a slave, he dies."

VIII Notes

[1] We assume along with Friedrich (1960: 32) that the consonant represented orthographically as <š> was in fact phonemic /s/. On this Sturtevant (1933: 70) remarks, "There is then a probability that the Hittites learned cuneiform writing from speakers of Akkadian who pronounced <š> and <s> as [s]. The transliteration of Hittite names with Egyptian <s> instead of <š> ([Egyptian] <Mrsr> = [Hittite name] <Mur-ši-li-iš> ...) seems to settle the matter."

[2] The two phonemes /x/ and /h/ were both represented by graphemic <h>. The phoneme /h/ occurred in Hittite words of PIE provenience (and perhaps in some non-PIE words by change Ib LARYNGEALS); /x/ occurred exclusively in the many non-PIE borrowings into Hittite. Occurrences of /x/ as opposed to /h/ can be indicated graphemically. Examples of /x/ cited in Friedrich (1960: 32-3) are reflected in the graphemic alternations <tethessar> and <tetkissar>, which are two different spellings for the word /tetxesar/ 'story'. Similar alternations occur for the word /hamesxant^{h}s/ 'springtime', namely <hameshanza> and <hameskanza>. Another instance of /x/ probably occurs in the name of the Hittites, Hatti, itself a non-PIE Semitic borrowing and the name of the pre-Hittite population of the area. The Hittite pronunciation was probably /xat^{h}i/; the word occurs in Hebrew as /xati/. According to Friedrich (1960: 15) the Hittites themselves probably called their language "Nešili" /nesili/. Instances of /h/ are indicated by graphemic alternations such as these: /eshar/ 'blood' represented as <eshar> and <essar>; and /italawaht^{h}i/ 'you (sg) do evil' represented as <idalawahti> and <idalawatti>.

[3] The segment [ŋ] is an allophone of /n/ by the PIE rule 3.1.2d NASAL ASSIM, which remained in the grammar.

[4] We transcribe this segment as /j/ in the PIE forms and as /y/ in the Hittite forms since that is the usual transcription in the literature.

[5] Sturtevant (1933: 105-7) assumes that PIE syllabic [r̥] and [l̥] remained, in Hittite. If so, then they were allophonic variants of /r/ and /l/; and their distribution was determined by the PIE rule 3.1.2g SYL SON. (See also on this Ic SYL SON in this chapter.)

[6] The nominative singular is also used as a vocative. An original vocative cited in Kronasser (1956: 100) is the word esha 'lord' in the phrase esha+mi 'my lord'. The PIE antecedent ending may have been a PIE ā-class voc sg *esh+a. (If the antecedent had been the PIE o-class voc. *esh+e, one would expect Hit **eshe+mi.)

[7] These endings may come from the athematic class.

[8] The derivation is PIE *atoi (2b OBSTR) > *at^{h}oi (4 MON) > *at^{h}ē (5 V-SHORT) > Hit *at^{h}e. A Hittite dative singular in -ai is also attested: e.g., PIE *lut^{h}+ōi 'window' (2b OBSTR) > *lut^{h}ōi (5 V-SHORT) > *lut^{h}oi (6 e/o-TO-a) > Hit lut^{h}ai.

[9] The PIE ending *-ts may have been Ø-grade ablaut of an adverb suffix *-tos.

[10] The derivation is *atons (2b OBSTR) > *at^{h}ons (3b WF CL) > *at^{h}ūs (5 V-SHORT) > Hit at^{h}us.

[11] Usually the genitive plural is like the genitive singular. However, there is a Hittite remnant of the original PIE genitive plural cited in Friedrich (1952: 195) and in Kronasser (1966: 165). It occurs in the phrase siyunan ant^{h}usas 'a man of the gods, a seer'. The derivation of the genitive plural form is PIE *djun+ōm 'of the gods' (2a m-TO-n) > *djunōn (2b OBSTR) > *tjunōn (3a t^{h}-TO-t^{s}) > *sijunōn (5 V-SHORT, 6 e/o-TO-a) > Hit siyunan.

[12] By obl (oblique) cases we mean all the cases except nominative, vocative or accusative. The plural oblique case endings in Hittite have, except for rare exceptions like that described in the previous note, been replaced by the genitive singular.

[13] The derivation is PIE *n̥d^{h}urj(o/ā)s > (1c SYL SON) > *and^{h}urj(o/ā)s (2b OBSTR) > *anturj(o/ā)s (5 V-SHORT) > *anturj(o/a)s (6 e/o-TO-a) > Hit *anturyas (possibly *anturiyas).

[14] The PIE root must be either *tout- or ablauting *tut-. (If it were e-grade **teut-, the Hittite form would be **t^{s}ut^{s}- by change 3a t^{h}-TO-t^{s}.) The derivation from the first two possibilities is *toutis or *tutis (2b OBSTR) > *t^{h}out^{h}is or *t^{h}ut^{h}is (3a t^{h}-TO-t^{s}) > *t^{h}out^{s}is or *t^{h}ut^{s}is (4 MON) > *t^{h}ūt^{s}is or *t^{h}ut^{s}is (5 V-SHORT) > Hit t^{h}ut^{s}is in either event.

[15] The derivation is *touti+os (PIE 3.1.2c i-j/u-w ALT applying synchronically) > *toutjos (2b OBSTR, 3a t^{h}-TO-t^{s}, 4 MON, 5 V-SHORT) > *t^{h}ut^{s}jos (6 e/o-TO-a) > Hit t^{h}ut^{s}yas or possibly t^{h}ut^{s}iyas. If the latter form occurred, then Hittite had a glide-insertion rule like this:

Cy	→	Ciy
Cw		Cuw

In the following we shall record such Hittite forms with the intervening /i/ and /u/, although their occurrence may have been only orthographic.

[16] This ending is from the o-class.

[17] The derivation is *dl̥ug+ost+i+ā (PIE 3.1.2c i-j/u-w ALT applying synchronically) → *dl̥ugostjā (1c SYL SON) > *dalugostjā (2b OBSTR) > *talukostjā (5 V-SHORT) > *talukostja (6 e/o-TO-a) > Hit *talukastiya.

[18] The derivation is *hostōi (5 V-SHORT) > hostoi (6 e/o-TO-a) > Hit hastai. If one posits a laryngealless PIE ostōi, then lb LARYNGEALS must apply in the derivation.

[19] The derivation is *hostōjos (PIE 3.l.2c i-j/u-w ALT applying synchronically) → *hostōjos (5 V-SHORT, 6 e/o-TO-a) > Hit hastayas. If one posits a PIE ablauting /ē/ instead of /ō/ in the antecedent, then the derivation would be *hostējos (5 V-SHORT, 6 e/o-TO-a) > Hit **hasteyas.

[20] The derivation is *ūd^{h}nei (2b OBSTR) > *ūtnei (4 MON) > *ūtnē (5 V-SHORT) > Hit utne.

[21] The derivation is *ūd^{h}neios (PIE 3.l.2c i-j/u-w ALT applying synchronically) → *ūd^{h}nejos (2b OBSTR) > *ūtnejos (5 V-SHORT) > *utnejos (6 e/o-TO-a) > Hit utneyas.

[22] This ending is from the athematic class 1.4 below.

[23] All the oblique plural forms are apparently the same as those of the genitive singular. The PIE nominative/accusative plural was likely the derivation of which would be *ūd^{h}neiā (PIE 3.l.2c i-j/u-w ALT applying synchronically) → *ūd^{h}nejā (2b OBSTR, 5 V-SHORT) > Hit *utneya.

[24] These forms may have been Hittite *kenwas and the like without the intervening /u/. (See on this note 15 under 1.2 i-class t^{h}ut^{s}is 'army'.) The derivation of the genitive singular is PIE *genuos (PIE 3.1.2c i-j/u-w ALT applying synchronically) → *genwos (2b OBSTR) > *kenwos (6 e/o-TO-a) > Hit *kenwas or *kenuwas.

[25] This ending is from the o-class.

26 The word is probably non-PIE, but we consider it PIE for illustrative purposes. The derivation is *hornōus (5 V-SHORT, 6 e/o-TO-a) > Hit harnaus.

27 The derivation is *hornōuos (PIE 3.1.2c i-j/u-w ALT applying synchronically) → *hornōwos (5 V-SHORT) > *hornowos (6 e/o-TO-a) > Hit harnawas.

28 The ending here is from the athematic classes. There probably also existed a Hit dat sg *harnawa from PIE *hornōu+ō.

29 The ending is from the o-class.

30 Athematic nouns have no ending in the neuter nominative accusative plural. This is not the case with adjectives: e.g., nom/acc pl neuter hurnant^{h}a 'all, whole' as described under 1.4.4 below.

31 The derivation is *wetm̥ (1c SYL SON) > *wetam (2a m-TO-n) > *wetan (2b OBSTR) > Hit *wet^{h}an.

32 This ending is from the o-class.

33 Given the changes into Hittite, the PIE suffix could also have been ablauting *-ōr or *-r̥.

34 Note that this word has e-grade ablaut in the oblique cases in both the root and the derivational suffix.

35 The plural of this noun is not attested. We assume that it was like other athematic nouns in that it had identical singular and oblique plural forms.

36 The derivation is *osōwor (5 V-SHORT) > *osowor (6 e/o-TO-a) > Hit asawar.

37 The derivation is *osōwni (PIE 3.1.2c i-j/u-w ALT applying synchronically) → *osōuni (5 V-SHORT) > *osouni (6 e/o-TO-a) > Hit asauni.

38 The derivation is *nōmn (PIE 3.1.2g SYL SON applying synchronically) → *nōmn̥ (1c SYL SON) > *nōman (5 V-SHORT) > *noman (6 e/o-TO-a) > *naman (7a n-CHANGES) > Hit laman.

39 The derivation is like the preceding one except that the PIE synchronic rule 3.1.2g SYL SON cannot apply to the oblique case forms since the endings begin with vowels.

40 Hit henk- is a borrowing. We consider it PIE for illustrative purposes. The *-Vn- suffix may have contained either /o/ or /ō/. The derivation is *hengo(:)n (2b OBSTR) > *henko(:)n (5 V-SHORT) > *henkon (6 e/o-TO-a) > Hit henkan.

41 The Hittite form is written <me-mi-as> and <me-mi-ya-as>. This may represent memyas or memiyas.

42 The PIE antecedent ending could have been o-class *-om. In either event the derivation produces the same Hittite form: *memj+m̥/om (1c SYL SON) > *memjam and *memjom (2a m-TO-n) > *memjan and *memjon (6 e/o-TO-a) > Hit memiyan.

43 The bimorphemic sequence /t^{h}+s/ was probably the same phonetically as the affricate /t^{s}/.

44 The expected derivation would be *humonti (2b OBSTR) > *humont^{h}i (3a t^{h}-TO-t^{s}) > *humont^{s}i (6 e/o-TO-a) > Hit **humant^{s}i. The /t^{h}/ was restored here to Hit humant^{h}i from other forms in the paradigm which did not undergo 3a t^{h}-TO-t^{s}.

45 The derivation is *humont (3b WF CL) > humon (6 e/o-TO-a) > Hit human.

46 Some adjectives of this class occur with endings in either Ø- or ō-grade ablaut. E.g., the abl sg sup^{h}iyat^{s} 'clean' vs. sup^{h}ayat^{s} from PIE *supi+ōts vs. *supōi+ōts, respectively.

47 Given the PIE antecedent, one would expect the derivation *megōis (2b OBSTR) > *mekōis (5 V-SHORT, 6 e/o-TO-a) > Hit **mekais instead of *mek^{h}ais.

48 This adjective may be a non-PIE borrowing. It also occurs as a noun meaning 'enemy'.

49 The derivation is *hant+et+is (2b OBSTR) > *hant^{h}et^{h}is (3a t^{h}-TO-t^{s} applying only to the second /t^{h}/, perhaps because the first /t^{h}/ in /hant^{h}/ also occurred before back vowels) > Hit hant^{h}et^{s}is.

50 The antecedent form is a jo-class neuter plural.

51 The antecedent was probably a present active participle in the neuter plural.

52 The -i suffix may have been an original dative ending.

53 The noun *xat- 'Hatti' is a non-IE borrowing.

54 Most numerals are not recorded in Hittite (see on this the following section).

55 There are at least two possible PIE antecedents for Hit '1'. They are *oin- and *sem-. If the former, the Hit nom sg com is *enas; if the latter, the Hit nom sg com is *samas.
56 The antecedent of this genitive singular suffix is not clear. The same suffix is also found throughout the pronominal declension. Benveniste (1962: 67-8) suggests that the suffix -el may have originally been adverbial and possibly related to the suffix in Latin quālis 'what kind of' from PIE *k^{w}ā+l+is. Yet another possibility is that Hit -el may have been a borrowing from Semitic and as such perhaps related to the Hebrew preposition el 'to, toward'. (See also on this Kronasser 1956: 142.)
57 If the PIE antecedent is *dw-, then the Hittite forms are *twus, *twe, *twetas and *twa.
58 The *-os ending is an original genitive singular. It is used in Hittite as an oblique singular and plural ending.
59 If the PIE antecedent is *tri-, then the Hittite nominative plural is *t^{h}riyes.
60 This ending is again a genitive singular.
61 This ending is unattested.
62 This form is the nominative singular common of an i-class adjective.
63 These forms are uninflected.
64 The PIE antecedent of this suffix is not clear. The Hittite form may have been *t^{h}riyanna.
65 Sturtevant (1933: 192) assumes that the /u/ in these forms came from the 2nd person pronoun *tu 'you'.
66 This nominative form is from the accusative.
67 The derivation is *m̥ (oblique case form) + u (2sg 'you' vowel) + g(+ō) (1sg 'I' ending with optional /ō/) (1c SYL SON) > *amug(ō) (2b OBSTR) > *amuk(ō) (5 V-SHORT, 6 e/o-TO-a) > Hit amuk and amuka.
68 The antecedent of Hit -el is not clear. See on this note 56 above (under section 4.1).
69 This is an accusative form.
70 The expected derivation is *n̥sōs (1c SYL SON) > *ansōs (5 V-SHORT, 6 e/o-TO-a) > Hit *ansas. Why /t^{s}/ occurs here in the attested ant^{s}as is not clear.
71 The antecedent /g/ may be either from the 1sg 'I' or possibly from a PIE enclitic *-g(e).
72 The antecedent root *te- is an original accusative and *tu- a nominative. Respective derivations are nom *teg and acc *tug (2b OBSTR) > *t^{h}ek and *t^{h}uk (3a t^{h}-TO-t^{s}) > Hit t^{s}ek and t^{h}uk.
73 The derivation is *tu+el (PIE 3.1.2c i-j/u-w ALT applying synchronically) → *twel (2b OBSTR) > Hit t^{h}wel. On the provenience of -el, see note 56 above (under section 4.1).
74 The derivation is not clear: *ws+mes (PIE 3.1.2c i-j/u-w ALT applying synchronically) → *usmes (? metathesis) > Hit sumes.
75 The -i in this form is a deictic particle.
76 The endings are i-class and o-class, respectively.
77 The derivation is *s+ons (3b WF CL) > Hit sus.
78 The derivation is *so+i (4 MON) > *sē (5 V-SHORT) > Hit se. Yet another possibility is PIE *s+ai (ev) > Hit se.
79 The form *k+um has a u-class ending.
80 This was originally a genitive singular form.
81 This was originally a genitive singular form. It was presumably used for all plural oblique forms.
82 On the provenience of the suffix -el see note 56 above (under section 4.1).
83 The derivation of these forms is *k^{w}oi and *k^{w}ai (la LABIOVEL) > *kwoi and *kwai (2b OBSTR) > *k^{h}woi and *k^{h}wai (4 MON) > *k^{h}wē (5 V-SHORT) > Hit k^{h}we.
84 This formation consists of reduplication of the interrogative pronoun.
85 This formation consists of the interrogative pronoun plus nominative singular -os plus the interrogative pronoun again.
86 This formation consists of the interrogative pronoun plus an obscure formative.
87 This formation consists of the interrogative pronoun plus the enclitic *k^{w}- plus the deictic *-i.
88 This formation consists of the interrogative pronoun plus a 3sg pron *so.
89 A Hittite construction such as *nu+nas would mean 'and us' or 'and to us'.

90 A Hittite construction such as *nu+snas would mean 'and (to) you' or 'and (to) them'.

91 A Hittite construction such as *nu+as would mean 'and he or she'.

92 The structure of the antecedent consists of the 1sg pron *m- plus the respective inflectional ending. The nominative singular here is i-class and the accusative singular is o- or u-class .

93 The respective enclitics affixed to the noun at^{h}as 'father' are these: 'my father' in the nom sg *at^{h}asmis, acc sg *at^{h}anman, gen sg *at^{h}asmas, nom pl *at^{h}asmes 'my fathers'; nom sg *at^{h}assmis 'our father', nom pl *at^{h}assmes 'our fathers'.

94 This is an original singular form.

95 The PIE antecedent is not clear. It may have been *n̥s 'us' > *-s plus *m- 'me' plus the inflectional ending.

96 The respective enclitics affixed to the noun at^{h}as 'father' are these: 'your (sg) father' is *at^{h}astis; 'your (pl) father' is *at^{h}assmis.

97 The respective enclitics affixed to the noun at^{h}as 'father' are these: nom sg *at^{h}assis 'his, her, their father' and acc sg *at^{h}ansan 'idem'.

98 The medial (med) and passive (pass) endings are identical. Verbs in the medial (also called "middle" voice) mean 'to perform the action of the verb on one's own behalf'. E.g., Hit 3sg pres pass ney+ari 'he leads for himself'. This same construction can also have a passive meaning, namely 'he is led'. Finally in this connection, verbs which have the inherent feature deponent (dep) take the medial/passive endings, but have active meanings. E.g., Hit 3sg pres dep kis+ari '(s)he becomes'.

99 The so-called imperative (imp) occurs in all three persons in the singular and in the plural. As such it is not only an imperative, but also has an optative meaning 'may or should it happen that...' Hence we have labeled column (d) "Tense/Mood" since while present and preterite are clearly tenses, imperative is not.

100 The composite forms (which generally reflect perfective or stative tenses) are constructed from the participle plus the present, preterite or imperative of the verbs 'have' or 'be'. Examples of the present and imperative perfective are these (in the 1st singular unless otherwise noted). (a) Present perfective active with 'have': iyan harmi = accusative singular neuter of participle plus 1st singular present of 'have', 'I have made'. (b) Present perfective active with 'be': pant^{h}s esmi = nominative singular common of participle plus 1st singular present of 'be', 'I am gone, i.e. I have gone'. (c) Present perfective passive with 'be': *wasant^{h}s esmi = nominative singular common of participle plus 1st singular present of 'be', 'I am clothed'. (d) Imperative perfective passive 3rd plural with 'be': tant^{h}es asantu = nominative plural common of participle plus 3rd plural imperative of 'be', 'let them be taken, they should be taken'. Examples of the past perfective are these (all in the 1st singular). (a) Past perfective active with 'have': iyan hark^{h}un = accusative singular neuter of participle plus 1st singular preterite of 'have', 'I had made'. (b) Past perfective active with 'be': *pant^{h}s esun = nominative singular common of participle plus 1st singular preterite of 'be', 'I was gone'. (c) Past perfective passive with 'be': *wasant^{s} esun = nominative singular common of participle plus 1st singular preterite of 'be', 'I was clothed'.

101 The infinitive has a more direct and predictable semantic relationship to the verb than does the verbal noun. E.g., the infinitive is was+want^{s}i 'to clothe'; and the verbal noun is was+war 'clothes'.

102 The function of the supine is described by Sturtevant (1933: 268) as follows: "The supine in *-wan* is combined with forms of the verb *tai-* 'place' in a sense approximating 'begin and continue the action denoted by the verb'..." E.g., 3sg pres *waswan tai 'he is beginning to dress'.

103 The participle usually has an active meaning when the verb is intransitive and a passive meaning when the verb is transitive. E.g., the nom sg com *p+ant^{h}+s 'gone, having gone' vs. *was+ant^{h}+s 'clothed'.

104 There are two principal form classes of verbs, the mi-conjugation and the hi-conjugation. The designations are from the respective 1st singular present active endings. Many verbs can be conjugated in either paradigm. (In the following we shall as in the other paradigms use a single verb as illustrative of each form class.)

105 The PIE antecedent may have been the 2nd singular perfective ending *-ta. The /i/ on Hit *west^{h}i is from the other present forms.

106 The antecedents of these endings are not clear. The *-we- may be from the 1pl pron 'we'; the *-te- is from the 2nd plural ending *-te; the *-n- may be from the 3rd plural ending *-nti; and the *-i is from the other present endings.

107 The derivation is *wesonti (2b OBSTR) > *wesont^{h}i (3a t^h-TO-t^s) > *wesont^{s}i (6 e/o-TO-a) > Hit *wesant^{s}i.

108 The -u- in the Hittite form may have originally been an enclitic particle. The derivation is *wesum (2a m-TO-n) > Hit *wesun.

109 For these forms it is not clear if the word-final /a/ in the Hittite forms is really present or is merely a result of the Hittite syllabary which makes it impossible to record word-final consonant clusters.

110 The status of the antecedent *-Vl- is not clear. The *-u was probably a PIE enclitic.

111 Hit *wes is the original PIE form; *wesi has the *-i from other forms of the present indicative singular. The ending on Hit *west^{h}u may have been from the PIE 2sg pron *tu 'you'. The Hit 3sg imp *west^{h}u may have taken the /t^h/ from the 3rd singular present indicative and the /u/ from a PIE enclitic.

112 This is from the 1st plural present.

113 This is from the 2nd plural preterite.

114 The -u in the Hittite ending is from a PIE enclitic.

115 The infinitives may have original dative singular neuter endings. The *-i is an athematic class ending; the *-ō is from the o-class. The Hittite ending -anna is usually found with verbs that have ablaut within the paradigm. E.g., PIE *ed+mi 'I eat' vs. inf *od+onnō (ev) > Hit etmi vs. atanna. The infinitive ending *-won+ti may have been formed from the supine *-won plus the derivative suffix *-t.

116 The /h/ in the Hittite forms may either have been the reflex of a PIE laryngeal or inserted by change lb LARYNGEALS.

117 The final /-i/ in the Hittite forms comes from the present active paradigm. It must have been added to these forms after the time of change 3a t^h-TO-t^s. Otherwise one would expect, say, a 2sg pres pass **west^{h}at^{s}i instead of *west^{h}at^{h}i.

118 These forms have o-grade ablaut as opposed to the usual e-grade.

119 The meaning of the PIE *sok^{w}a was 'I have seen', which came to mean 'I do now know'. The derivation is *sok^{w}a to which the present-tense marker *-i was added: *sok^{w}a+i (la LABIOVEL applying to those forms in the paradigm where the ending begins with an obstruent consonant, then the change transferred throughout the paradigm) > *sokai (lb LARYNGEALS) > *sokahi (2b OBSTR) > *sok^{h}ahi (6 e/o-TO-a) > Hit sak^{h}ahi.

120 In these forms the original PIE word-final endings *-a and *-e were replaced by the present-tense marker *-i.

121 The plural forms have ē-grade ablaut as opposed to the other forms with o-grade.

122 The word-final /a/'s in the Hittite forms may be only apparent, resulting orthographically from the nature of the Hittite syllabary.

123 The -s in these forms may devolve from a PIE aorist.

124 The derivation of these forms is *noi+i and *nōi+t+i (lb LARYNGEALS) > *noihi and *nōiti (2b OBSTR) > *noihi and *nōit^{h}i (4 MON) > *nēhi and *nōit^{h}i (5 V-SHORT) > *nehi and *noit^{h}i (6 e/o-TO-a) > Hit nehi and nait^{h}i.

125 This is the form suggested in Tischler (1977: 43).

126 This form is a reconstruction suggested by Tischler (1983: 701). Its antecedent may have been PIE *g^{hw}ōu+os. The derivation would then have been *g^{hw}ōu+os (PIE 3.1.2c i-j/u-w ALT applying synchronically) → *g^{hw}ōwos (la LABIOVEL) > *g^{h}wōwos (2b OBSTR) > *kwōwos (5 V-SHORT) > *kwowos (6 e/o-TO-a) > Hit *kwawas instead of *kuwawas.

127 The form also may have been *asmas since the adv asma 'first, at first' is attested. If so, the PIE antecedent would have been an ablauting *osm+os.

128 This is the form given in Sturtevant (1936: 74).

129 This is the form suggested as a possibility in Tischler (1978: 355).

130 This is the form suggested as a possibility in Tischler (1978: 221).

131 This is the form suggested in Sturtevant (1936: 50).

References

Abbate, A. Scaffide. 1979. *Introduzione allo studio comparativo delle lingue germaniche antiche.* Bologna: Pàtron Editore.

Ambrosiani, Per. 1991. *On Church Slavonic accentuation.* Stockholm Slavic studies 21. Stockholm: Almqvist & Wiksell International.

Antilla, Raimo. 1989. *An introduction to historical and comparative linguistics.* New York: MacMillan.

Atkinson, B.F.C. 1952. *The Greek language.* (Second edition revised.) London: Faber & Faber Limited.

Auty, R. 1960. *Handbook of Old Church Slavonic. Part II. Texts and glossary.* London: University of London. Athlone Press.

Baldi, Philip. 1983. *An introduction to the Indo-European languages.* Carbondale, IL: Southern Illinois University Press.

———. 1999. *The foundations of Latin. Trends in linguistics.* Studies and monographs 117. Berlin: Mouton de Gruyter.

Bammesberger, Alfred. 1986. *Der Aufbau des germanischen Verbalsystems.* Heidelberg: Carl Winter Universitätsverlag.

Barrack, Charles M. 1975. *A diachronic phonology from Proto-Germanic to Old English stressing West-Saxon conditions.* The Hague: Mouton.

———. 1998. *Sievers' law in Germanic.* Berkeley insights in linguistics and semiotics, vol. 22. New York: Peter Lang.

———. 2000. "Gamkrelidze versus Grimm: Devoicing in Proto-Germanic." Paper delivered at the Berkeley Germanic Linguistics Round Table. Berkeley, CA.

———. 2001. "The glottalic controversy: Were there ejectives in the PIE obstruent system?" Paper delivered at the University of Washington Linguistics Society. Seattle.

———. 2002. "The Glottalic Theory revisited: A negative appraisal (part one)." *Indogermanische Forschungen* 107: 76–95.

———. 2003. "The Glottalic Theory revisited: A negative appraisal (part two)." *Indogermanische Forschungen* 108: 1–16.

Bazell, C.E. 1937. "IE final unaccented *ē* in Germanic." *Journal of English and Germanic philology* 36: 1–10.

Beade, Pedro. 1972. "Sievers' law in Gothic and other related matters." *Lingua* 30: 449–59.

Bech, Gunnar. 1963. *Die Entstehung des schwachen Präteritums.* Det Kongelige Danske Videnskabernes Selskab. Bind 40, nr. 4. Copenhagen: Munksgaard.

———. 1969. *Das germanische reduplizierte Präteritum.* Det Kongelige Danske Videnskabernes Selskab. Bind 44, nr. 1. Copenhagen: Munksgaard.

Beekes, R. 1969. *The development of the Proto-Indo-European laryngeals in Greek.* The Hague: Mouton.

———. 1995. *Comparative Indo-European linguistics.* Amsterdam: John Benjamins.

Benfey, Theodore. 1982. *Sanskrit-English dictionary.* New Delhi: Mohla, Milan Publication Services.

Benveniste, Émile. 1962. *Hittite et indo-européen.* Bibliothèque archéologique et historique de l'institut français d'archéologie d'Istanbul V. Paris: Librairie Adrien Maisonneuve.

Blust, Robert A. 1974. "A double counter universal in Kelabit." *Papers in linguistics* 7: 309–24.

Boisacq, Émile. 1923. *Dictionnaire étymologique de la langue grecque.* Heidelberg: Carl Winter Universitätsbuchhandlung, Paris: Librairie C. Klincksieck.

Bräuer, Herbert. 1961. *Slavische Sprachwissenschaft. Band I: Einleitung, Lautlehre. Band II: Akzent- und Intonationslehre, Wortbildungslehre.* Band III: *Formenlehre.* Berlin: Walter de Gruyter.

Brandenstein, Wilhelm. 1959. *Griechische Sprachwissenschaft. II Wortbildung und Formenlehre.* Sammlung Göschen Band 118/118a. Berlin: Walter de Gruyter.

Braune, Wilhelm. 1961. *Gotische Grammatik*. Tübingen: Max Niemeyer .

Brugmann, Karl and Berthold Delbrück. 1897–1918. *Grundriss der vergleichenden Grammatik der indogermanischen Sprachen.* 2 volumes. Strassburg: Karl J. Trübner.

Brugmann, Karl. 1930. *Kurze vergleichende Grammatik der indogermanischen Sprachen*. Berlin: Walter de Gruyter .

Buck, Carl Darling. 1949. *A dictionary of selected synonyms in the principal Indo-European languages*. Chicago: University of Chicago Press.

———. 1962. *Comparative grammar of Greek and Latin*. Chicago: University of Chicago Press.

Burrow, Thomas. 1959. *The Sanskrit language*. London: Faber and Faber.

Campbell, Lyle. 1999. *Historical linguistics: An introduction*. Cambridge, MA: MIT Press.

Carlton, Terence R. 1991. *Introduction to the phonological history of the Slavic languages*. Columbus, OH: Slavica Publishers.

Chadwick, John 1995. *The decipherment of linear B*. Cambridge: Cambridge University Press.

Chantraine, P. 1947. *Morphologie historique du grec*. (3rd edition.) Paris: Librairie C. Klincksieck.

———. 1961. *Morphologie historique du grec*. (2nd edition.) Paris: Librairie C. Klincksieck.

Collinge, N.E. 1985. *The laws of Indo-European*. Amsterdam: John Benjamins.

Costas, Procope S. 1936. *An outline of the history of the Greek language*. Chicago: Ares Publishers.

Cowgill, Warren and Manfred Mayrhofer. 1986. *Indogermanische Grammatik. Band I: 1. Einleitung. 2. Lautlehre*. Heidelberg: Carl Winter Universitätsverlag.

Debrunner, Albert and Anton Scherer. 1969. *Geschichte der griechischen Sprache*. II *Grundfragen und Grundzüge des nachklassischen Griechisch*. Sammlung Göschen Band 114/114a. Berlin: Walter de Gruyter.

Devine, A.M. and Laurence D. Stephens. 1994. *The prosody of Greek speech*. New York: Oxford University Press.

Diels, Paul. 1932 and 1934. *Altkirchenslavische Grammatik 1. Teil: Grammatik* [1932], *2. Teil: Ausgewählte Texte und Wörterbuch* [1934]. Heidelberg: Carl Winter Universitätsbuchhandlung.

Divry, G.C. and C.G. 1969. *English-Greek and Greek-English dictionary*. New York: D.C. Divry.

Edgerton, Franklin. 1934. "Sievers' law and IE weak-grade vocalism." *Language* 10: 235–66.

Ernout, A. 1945. *Morphologie historique du latin*. Paris: Librairie C. Klincksieck.

Ernout, A. and A. Meillet. 1951. *Dictionnaire étymologique de la langue latine*. (2 volumes.) Paris: Librairie C. Klincksieck.

Feist, Sigmund. 1939. *Vergleichendes Wörterbuch der gotischen Sprache*. (Dritte neubearbeitete und vermehrte Auflage.) Leiden: E.J. Brill.

Fox, Anthony. 1995. *Linguistic reconstruction: An introduction to theory and method*. New York: Oxford University Press.

Fortson, Benjamin W. 2004. *Indo-European language and culture*. Malden, MA: Blackwell Publishing.

Friedrich, Johannes. 1946. *Hethitisches Elementarbuch. 2. Teil, Lesestücke in Transkription*. Heidelberg: Carl Winter Universitätsverlag.

———. 1952. *Hethitisches Wörterbuch*. Heidelberg: Karl Winter Universitätsverlag.

———. 1960. *Hethitisches Elementarbuch*. 1. Teil, Kurzgefasste Grammatik. (Zweite, verbesserte und erweiterte Auflage.) Heidelberg: Carl Winter Universitätsverlag.

Gamkrelidze, Thomas and Vjacheslav Ivanov. 1973. "Sprachtypologie und die Rekonstruktion der gemeinindogermanischen Verschlüsse. Vorläufiger Bericht." *Phonetica* 27: 150–6.

———. 1984. *Indo-European and the Indo-Europeans. A reconstruction and historical typological analysis of a protolanguage and a protoculture*. Tbilisi: Publishing House of the Tbilisi State University.

Gamkrelidze, Thomas and Vjacheslav Ivanov. 1994 and 1995. *Indo-European and the Indo-Europeans. A reconstruction and historical analysis of a proto-language and proto-culture. Part I: The text. Part II: Bibliography and indexes.* (English-language edition.) New York: Mouton de Gruyter.

Garde, Paul. 1976. *Histoire de l'accentuation slave.* (2 volumes.) Paris: Institut d'Études Slaves.

Garry, Jane and Carl Rubino (eds.). 2001. *Facts about the world's languages.* New York: H.W. Wilson Company.

Gołąb, Zbigniew. 1972. "Kentum elements in Slavic." *Lingua Posnaniensis* 16: 53–82.

———. 1992. *The origins of the Slavs: A linguist's view.* Columbus, OH: Slavica.

Gonda, Jan. 1966. *A concise elementary grammar of the Sanskrit language.* (Trans. Gordon B. Ford, Jr.) Birmingham: University of Alabama Press.

Goodwin, William Watson and Gulick, Charles Burton. 1930. *Greek grammar.* Boston: Ginn and Company.

Green, Antony. 1995. *Old Irish verbs and vocabulary.* Somerville, ME: Cascadilla Press.

Greenberg, Joseph (ed.). 1963. *Universals of language.* Cambridge, MA: M.I.T. Press.

Greenough, J.B. et al. (eds.). 1931. *Allen and Greenough's new Latin grammar.* New York: Ginn.

Guchmann, M. M. et al. (eds.). 1962–6. *Sravitelnaya grammatika germanskich yazikov.* 4 volumes. Moscow: Izdatel'stvo Akademii nauk SSSR.

Halle, Morris. 1971. "Remarks on Slavic accentology." *Linguistic inquiry* 2: 1–21.

———. 1973. "The accentuation of Russian words." *Language* 49: 312–49.

———. 1995. "Feature geometry and feature spreading." *Linguistic inquiry* 26: 1–47.

———. 1997. "On stress and accent in Indo-European." *Language* 73: 275–314.

Held, Warren H. Jr., William R. Schmalstieg, and Jane E. Gertz. 1988. *Beginning Hittite.* Columbus, OH: Slavica Publishers.

Hirt, Hermann. 1912. *Handbuch der griechischen Laut- und Formenlehre.* Heidelberg: Carl Winter Universitätsbuchhandlung.

———. 1931, 1932, 1934. *Handbuch des Urgermanischen.* (3 parts.) Heidelberg: Carl Winter Universitätsbuchhandlung.

———. 1927–37. *Indogermanische Grammatik.* 7 volumes. Heidelberg: Carl Winter Universitätsbuchhandl ung.

———. 1939. *Die Hauptprobleme der indogermanischen Sprachwissenschaft.* Halle/Saale: Max Niemeyer .

Hogg, Richard and C. B. McCully. 1987. *Metrical phonology: A coursebook.* Cambridge: Cambridge University Press.

Hooker, J.T. 1980. Linear B. *An introduction.* Bristol: Bristol Classical Press.

Hopper, Paul J. 1973. "Glottalized and murmured occlusives in Indo-European." *Glossa* 7: 141–67.

———. 1977. "Indo-European consonantism and the new look." *Orbis* 26: 57–72.

Horrocks, Geoffrey. 1997. *Greek: A history of the language and its speakers.* London: Longman.

Hymen, Larry H. 1975. *Phonology: Theory and analysis.* New York: Holt, Rinehart and Winston.

Jakobson, Roman. 1963. *Slavic languages: A condensed survey.* New York: King's Crown Press.

Jasanoff, Jay H. 1973. "The Germanic third weak class." *Language* 49: 850–71.

Jellinek, Max Hermann. 1926. *Geschichte der gotischen Sprache.* Berlin: Walter de Gruyter .

Jones, Asburg Wesley. 1979. "Gothic final syllables: A new look at the phonological and morphological developments from Germanic." Ph.D. dissertation, University of North Carolina at Chapel Hill.

Kenstowicz, Michael and Charles Kisseberth. 1979. *Generative phonology. Description and theory.* New York: Academic Press.

Kent, Roland G. 1940. *The sounds of Latin.* (2nd edition.) Baltimore: Linguistic Society of America.

———. 1946. *The forms of Latin.* Baltimore: Linguistic Society of America.

Kieckers, Ernst. 1928. *Handbuch der vergleichenden gotischen Grammatik.* Munich: Max Hueber .

———. 1960. *Historische lateinische Grammatik. Erster Teil: Lautlehre. Zweiter Teil: Formenlehre.* Munich: Max Hueber .

Kiliaan, H.N. 1911. *Nadoereesche Spraakkunst. Erst stuk: Inleiding en klankleer.* Amsterdam: H. A. Benjamins.

Kimball, Sara E. 1999. *Hittite historical phonology.* Innsbruck: Innsbrucker Beiträge zur Sprachwissenschaft.

Kiparsky, Paul. 1968. "Tense and. mood in Indo-European syntax." *Foundations of language* 4: 30–58.

———. 1982. "Lexical morphology and phonology." *Linguistics in the Morning Calm*, pp. 3–91. Seoul: Hanshin Publishing.

Kiparsky, Valentin. 1962. *Der Wortakzent der russischen Schriftsprache.* Heidelberg: Carl Winter Universitätsverlag.

Kortlandt, Frederick. 1994. "From Proto-Indo-European to Slavic." *Journal of Indo-European studies* 22: 91–113.

Krahe, Hans. 1958, 1959. *Indogermanische Sprachwissenschaft. I. Einleitung und Lautlehre. II. Formenlehre.* Walter de Gruyter . Berlin: Sammlung Göschen.

Krause, Wolfgang. 1953. *Handbuch des Gotischen.* Munich: C.H. Beck'sche Verlagsbuchhandlung.

Kretschmer, Paul. 1970. *Einleitung in die Geschichte der griechischen Sprache.* Göttingen: Vandenhoeck & Ruprecht.

Kronasser, Heinz. 1956. *Vergleichende Laut- und Formenlehre des Hethitischen.* Heidelberg: Carl Winter Universitätsverlag.

———. 1966. *Etymologie der hethitischen Sprache.* Wiesbaden: Otto Harrassowitz.

Kuryłowicz, Jerzy. 1956. *L'Apophonie en indo-européen.* Zakład Narodowy Imienia Ossolińskich.
Wrocław: Wydawnictwo Polskiej Akademii Nauk.

———. 1958. *L'Accentuation des langues indo-européennes.* Zakład Narodowy Imienia Ossolińskich. Wrocław: Wydawnictwo Polskiej Akademii Nauk.

———. 1964. *The inflectional categories of Indo-European.* Heidelberg: Carl Winter Universitätsverlag.

———. 1968. *Indogermanische Grammatik. Band II: Akzent. Ablaut.* Heidelberg: Carl Winter Universitätsverlag.

Labov, William 1994. *Principles of linguistic change. Volume 1: Internal factors.* Oxford: Blackwell.

Ladefoged, Peter and Ian Maddieson. 1996. *The sounds of the world's languages.* Cambridge, MA: Blackwell Publishers Inc.

Lanman, Charles Rockwell. 1959. *A Sanskrit reader.* Cambridge: Harvard University Press.

Lehmann, Winfred P. 1955. *Proto-Indo-European phonology.* Austin: University of Texas Press.

———. 1974. *Proto-Indo-European syntax.* Austin: University of Texas Press.

———. 1993. *Theoretical bases of Indo-European linguistics.* London: Routledge.

———. 1999. "Review of *Encyclopedia of Indo-European culture.*" Ed. by James P. Mallory and Douglas Q. Adams. 1997. *Language* 75: 154–58.

Lehmann, W.P. and R.P.M Lehmann. 1975. *An introduction to Old Irish.* New York: Modern Language Association of America.

Leskien, A. 1922. *Handbuch der altbulgarischen (altkirchenslavischen) Sprache.* Heidelberg: Carl Winter Universitätsbuchhandlung.

Leumann, Manu. 1977. *Lateinische Laut- und Formenlehre.* Munich: C.H. Beck'sche Verlagsbuchhandlung.

Lewis, Henry and Holger Pedersen. 1937. *A concise comparative Celtic grammar.* Göttingen: Vandenhoeck & Ruprecht.

Liddell, H.G. 1959. *An intermediate Greek-English lexicon.* (Founded upon the 7th edition of Liddell and Scott's Greek-English lexicon.) Oxford: Clarendon Press.

Lindeman, Fredrik Otto. 1987. *Introduction to the "laryngeal theory".* Oslo: Norwegian University Press.

Lindsay, W.M. 1894. *The Latin language.* Oxford: Clarendon Press.

———. 1915. *A short historical Latin grammar.* Oxford: Clarendon Press.

Lunt, Horace G. 2001. *Old Church Slavonic grammar.* Berlin: Mouton de Gruyter.

Luraghi, Silvia. 1990. *Old Hittite sentence structure.* London: Routledge.

MacAulay, Donald. 1992. *The Celtic languages.* Cambridge: Cambridge University Press.

Macdonell, Arthur Anthony. 1969. *A practical Sanskrit dictionary.* Oxford: Oxford University Press.

Maddieson, Ian. 1987. *Patterns of sounds.* Cambridge: Cambridge University Press.

Mallory, J. P. 1991. *In search of the Indo-Europeans.* New York: Thanes and Hudson.

Marchant, E. C. (trans.). 1953. *Xenophon: Memorabilia and oeconomicus.* Loeb Classical Library. Cambridge, MA: Harvard University Press.

Mayrhofer, Manfred. 1965. *Sanskrit-Grammatik mit sprachvergleichenden Erläuterungen.* (2. Auflage.) Berlin: Walter de Gruyter.

McCone, Kim. 1987. *The early Irish verb.* Kildare: An Sagart Maynooth.

———. 1996. *Towards a relative chronology of ancient and medieval Celtic sound change.* Maynooth Studies in Celtic Linguistics I. Maynooth: Cardinal Press.

Meid, Wolfgang. 1963. *Die indogermanischen Grundlagen der altirischen absoluten und konjunkten Verbalflexion.* Wiesbaden: Otto Harrassowitz.

Meier-Brügger, Michael. 2000. *Indogermanische Sprachwissenschaft.* Berlin: Walter de Gruyter.

Meillet, Antoine. 1902. *Études sur l'étymologie et le vocabulaire du vieux slave 1.* Paris: Bibliothèque de l'école des hautes études.

———. 1905. *Études sur l'étymologie et le vocabulaire du vieux slave 2.* Paris: Bibliothèque de l'école des hautes études.

———. 1934. *Le Slave commun.* Paris: Librairie Ancienne Honoré Champion.

———. 1948. *Esquisse d'une histoire de la langue latine.* Paris: Librairie Hachette.

———. 1964. *Introduction a l'étude comparative des langues indo-européennes.* Birmingham: University of Alabama Press.

———. 1965. *Aperçu d'une histoire de la langue grecque.* (7e édition.) Paris: Librairie C. Klincksieck.

Meillet, A. and J. Vendryes. 1948. *Traits de grammaire comparée des langues classiques.* (2nd edition.) Paris: Librairie Ancienne Honoré Champion.

Melchert, H. Craig. 1984. *Studies in Hittite historical phonology.* Göttingen: Vandenhoeck & Ruprecht.

Monier-Williams, Monier. 1970. *A Sanskrit-English dictionary.* (First Indian edition.) Delhi: Motilal Banarsidass.

Moulton, William G. 1948. "The phonemes of Gothic." *Language* 24: 76–87.

Mylius, Klaus. 1987. *Wörterbuch Sanskrit-Deutsch.* (3. Auflage.) Leipzig: VEB Verlag Enzyklopädie.

Nahtigal, Rajko. 1961. *Die slavischen Sprachen.* Wiesbaden: Otto Harrassowitz.

Nandriș, Grigore. 1959. *Handbook of Old Church Slavonic, Part I. Old Church Slavonic grammar.* London: Athlone Press.

Ó Dochartaigh, Cathair. 1992. "The Irish language." MacAulay, Donald (ed.), *The Celtic languages*, pp. 11–100. Cambridge: Cambridge University Press.

O'Reilly, Edward. 1910. *An Irish-English dictionary.* Dublin: James Duffy and Co.

Ó Siadhail, Mícheál. 1988. *Learning Irish: An introductory self-tutor.* New Haven: Yale University Press.

Oettinger, Norbert. 1979. *Die Stammbildung des hethitischen Verbums.* Nuremberg: Verlag Hans Carl.

Orr, Robert. 2000a. *Common Slavic nominal morphology: A new synthesis.* Indiana: Slavica.

Orr, Robert. 2000b. "Filling in the gaps — the reflexes of IE *ag- in Slavic." Ilona Janyšková & Helena Karlikova, eds. *Studia Etymologica Brunensia* 1: 311–316.

———. 2002. "Demythologising Celtic — Celtic as non-exotic compared with other linguistic systems." *Journal of Celtic Language Learning* 7: 5–44.

Oswald, James L. 1984. *Wiros and deiwos: He who would be god. The story of the Indo-Europeans. (A historical novel.)* Seattle: Waldos Press.

Palmer, L.R. 1954. *The Latin language*. London: Faber and Faber Limited.

Pedersen, Holger. 1909 and 1913. *Vergleichende Grammatik der keltischen Sprachen. (1) Erster Band: Einleitung und Lautlehre. (2) Zweiter Band: Bedeutungslehre (Wortlehre)*. Göttingen: Vandenhoeck und Ruprecht.

———. 1938. *Hittitisch und die anderen indoeuropäischen Sprachen*. Det Kgl. Danske Videnskabernes Selskab. Historiskfilologiske Meddelelser. XXV, 2. Copenhagen: Levin & Munksgaard.

———. 1962. *The discovery of language. Linguistic science in the nineteenth century*. (Trans., John Webster Spargo.) Bloomington, IN: Indiana University Press.

Perry, Edward Delavan. 1959. *A Sanskrit primer*. (4th edition.) New York: Columbia University Press.

Peters, Martin. 1980. *Untersuchungen zur Vertretung der indogermanischen Laryngale im Griechischen*. Vienna: Verlag der Österreichischen Akademie der Wissenschaften.

Pieraccioni, Dino. 1966. *Morfologia storica della lingua greca*. Florence: Vallecchi.

Pisani, Vittore. 1962. *Storia della lingua latina. Parte prima. Le origini, et la lingua letterana fino a Virgilio e Orazio*. Turin: Rosenberg & Sellier.

———. 1973. *Manuale storico della lingua greca*. (Seconda edizione.) Brescia: Paideia.

Pokorny, Julius. 1914. *A concise Old Irish grammar and reader*. Halle/Saale: Max Niemeyer.

———. 1959 and 1969. *Indogermanisches etymologisches Wörterbuch*. 2 volumes. Berne: Francke .

———. 1969. *Altirische Grammatik*. (2. Auflage.) Sammlung Göschen Band 896. Berlin: Walter de Gruyter .

Porzig, Walter. 1954. *Die gliederung des indogermanischen Sprachgebiets*. Heidelberg: Carl Winter Universitätsverlag.

Prokosch, Eduard. 1939. *A comparative Germanic grammar*. Philadelphia: Linguistic Society of America.

Puhvel, Jaan 1984, 1991, 1997. *Hittite etymological dictionary*. Vol. 1, vol. 2 (1984), vol. 3 (1991), vol. 4 (1997). Berlin: Mouton Publishers.

Rackham, H. (trans.). 1979. *Cicero: De natura deorum, Academica*. (Loeb Classical Library 19.) Cambridge: Harvard University Press.

Ramat, Anna Giacalone and Paolo Ramat (eds.). 1993. *Le lingue indoeuropee*. Bologna: Società editrice il Mulino.

Renou, Louis. 1956. *Histoire de la langue sanskrite*. Lyon: Éditions IAC.

Robinson, Orrin W. 1992. *Old English and its closest relatives: A survey of the earliest Germanic languages*. Stanford: Stanford University Press.

Rockel, Martin. 1989. *Grundzüge einer Geschichte der irischen Sprache*. Vienna: Verlag der österreichischen Akademie der Wissenschaften.

Russell, Paul. 1995. *An introduction to the Celtic languages*. London: Longman.

Sadnik, L. and R. Aitzetmüller. 1955. *Handwörterbuch zu den altkirchenslavischen Texten*. Heidelberg: Carl Winter Universitätsverlag.

Safarewicz, Jan. 1969. *Historische lateinische Grammatik*. Halle/Saale: VEB Max Niemeyer .

Scharfe, H. 1985. "The Vedic word for 'king'." *Journal of the American Oriental Society*. 105: 543–48.

Schmalstieg, William R. 1980. *Indo-European linguistics: A new synthesis*. University Park, PA: Pennsylvania State University Press.

Schmalstieg, William R. 1983. *An introduction to Old Church Slavic*. (Second edition revised and expanded.) Columbus, OH: Slavica Publishers.

Seebold, Elmar. 1967. "Die Vertretung idg. g^{hw} im Germanischen." *Zeitschrift für vergleichende Sprachforschung* 81: 104–33.

Sen, Subhadva Kumar (ed.). 1994. "Proto-Indo-European: A multiangular view." *Journal of Indo-European Studies* 22: 67–91.

Sen, Sukumar. 1958. *History and pre-history of Sanskrit*. Mysore: Government Branch Press.

Shevelov, George Y. 1965. *A prehistory of Slavic*. New York: Columbia University Press.

Sievers, Eduard. 1878. "Zur Akzent- und Lautlehre der germanischen Sprachen." *Zeitschrift für vergleichende Sprachforschung* 5: 63–164.

Sihler, Andrew L. 1995. *New comparative grammar of Greek and Latin*. New York: Oxford University Press.

Smyth, Herbert Weir. 1959. *Greek grammar*. (2nd printing of edition of 1920.) Cambridge, MA: Harvard University Press.

Sommer, Ferdinand. 1948. *Handbuch der lateinischen Laut- und Formenlehre*. Heidelberg: Carl Winter Universitätsverlag.

———. 1977. *Handbuch der lateinischen Laut- und Formenlehre*. (4th edition, Raimund Pfister, ed.) Heidelberg: Carl Winter Universitätsverlag.

Sommerstein, Alan H. 1973. *The sound pattern of Ancient Greek*. Oxford: Basil Blackwell.

Stang, Christian S. 1942. *Das slavische und baltische Verbum*. Skrifter utgitt av Det Norske Videnskaps-Akademi i Oslo. Oslo: Jacob Dybwad.

———. 1957. *Slavonic accentuation*. Skrifter utgitt av Det Norske Videnskaps-Akademi i Oslo. Oslo: W. Nygaard.

Stevens, Alan M. 1968. *Madurese phonology and morphology*. New Haven: American Oriental Society.

Strachan, John. 1905. *Old-Irish paradigms*. Dublin: Hodges, Figgis & Co.

Streitberg, William. 1920. *Gotisches Elementarbuch*. Heidelberg: Carl Winter Universitätsbuchhandlung.

———. 1943. *Urgermanische Grammatik*. Heidelberg: Carl Winter Universitätsbuchhandlung.

Strunk, Klaus. 1994. "Relative chronology and the Indo-European verb-system: The case of present and aorist stems." *Journal of Indo-European studies* 22: 417–35.

Sturtevant, Edgar H. 1933. *A comparative grammar of the Hittite language*. Philadelphia: Linguistic Society of America.

———. 1936. *A Hittite glossary*. Philadelphia: Linguistic Society of America.

———. 1939. *Supplement to a Hittite glossary*. Philadelphia: Linguistic Society of America.

———. 1940. *The pronunciation of Greek and Latin*. (Second edition.) Philadelphia: Linguistic Society of America.

———. 1942. *The Indo-Hittite laryngeals*. Linguistic Society of America. Baltimore: Waverly Press.

Sturtevant, Edgar H. and George Bechtel. 1935. *A Hittite chrestomathy*. Philadelphia: Linguistic Society of America.

Szemerényi, Oswald. 1967. "The new look of Indo-European." *Phonetica* 17: 65–99.

———. 1970. *Einführung in die vergleichende Sprachwissenschaft*. Darmstadt: Wissenschaftliche Buchgesellschaft.

———. 1990. *Introduction to Indo-European linguistics*. (4th edition.) Oxford: Oxford University Press.

Thurneysen, Rudolf. 1898. "Spirantenwechsel im Gotischen." *Indogermanische Forschungen* 8: 208–14.

———. 1909. *Handbuch des Alt-Irischen. I. Teil: Grammatik. II. Teil: Texte mit Wörterbuch*. Heidelberg: Carl Winter Universitätsbuchhandlung.

Tischler, Johann. 1977, 1978, 1980, 1983. *Hethitisches etymologisches Glossar*. Innsbruck: Innsbrucker Beiträge zur Sprachwissenschaft. Band 20.

Toporov, V. N. 1963. "K ètimologija slav. *myslь*." *Ètimologija*. 1963: 5–13.

Tops, Guy A. 1974. *The origin of the Germanic dental preterite. A critical research history since 1912*. Leiden: E.J. Brill.

Tornow, Siegfried. 1984. *Die häufigsten Akzenttypen in der russischen Flexion*. Wiesbaden: Otto Harrassowitz.

Townsend, Charles E. and Laura A. Janda. 1996. *Common and comparative Slavic: Phonology and inflection*. Columbus, OH: Slavica Publishers.

Trubačev, O. N. ed. 1974. *Ètimologičeskij slovarь slavjanskix jazykov*. Moscow: Nauka.

Uhlenbeck, C.C. 1973. *Kurzgefasstes etymologisches Wörterbuch der altindischen Sprache*. (Neudruck der Ausgabe von 1898–1899.) Osnabrück: Otto Zeller .

Vaillant, André. 1950–1977. *Grammaire comparée des langues slaves. Tome 1. Phonétique* (1950), *Tome 2. Morphologie*, Éditions IAC, Lyon. *Tome 3. Le verbe* (1966), *Tome 4. La formation des noms* (1974), *Tome 5. La syntaxe* (1977). Paris: Éditions Klincksieck.

van Coetsem, Frans. 1956. *Das System der starken Verba und die Periodisierung im älteren Germanischen*. Amsterdam: Mededelingen der Koninklijke Nederlandse Akademie van Wetenschappen, Afdeling Letterkunde.

van Coetsem, Frans and Herbert Kufner (eds.). 1972. *Toward a grammar of Proto-Germanic*. Tübingen: Max Niemeyer .

van Wijk, Nicolaas. 1931. *Geschichte der altkirchenslavischen Sprache. Erster Band: Laut- und Formenlehre*. Berlin: Walter de Gruyter.

Vendryes, Joseph. 1908. *Grammaire du vieil-irlandais*. Paris: Librairie Orientale & Américaine.

Ventris, Michael and John Chadwick. 1953. "Evidence for Greek dialect in the Mycenaean archives." *The Journal of Hellenic studies* 73: 84–103.

Voyles, Joseph. 1974. "Ancient Greek accentuation." *Glotta* 52: 65–92.

———. 1980. "Reduplicating verbs in North-West Germanic." *Lingua* 52: 89–123.

———. 1989. "Bifurcational Germanic and glottonic Indo-European: A critique." *Zeitschrift für vergleichende Sprachforschung* 111: 16–35.

———. 1992. *Early Germanic grammar: Pre-, Proto- and Post-Germanic languages*. San Diego: Academic Press.

———. 2002. "The status of linear B in the history of Ancient Greek." *Studia Anglica Resovensia 1. Seria Filologiczna* Nr. 6: 99–110. Rzeszów, Poland: Wydawníctwo Universytetu Rzeszówskiego.

Watkins, Calvert. 1962. *Indo-European origins of the Celtic verb. The sigmatic aorist*. Dublin: Dublin Institute for Advanced Studies.

———. 1969. *Indogermanische Grammatik. Band III: Formenlehre. Erster Teil: Geschichte der indogermanischen Verbalflexion*. Heidelberg: Carl Winter Universitätsverlag.

———. (ed.). 2000. *The American heritage dictionary of Indo-European roots*. Boston: Houghton Mifflin.

Whitney, William Dwight. 1960. *Sanskrit grammar*. Cambridge: Harvard University Press.

———. 1990. *The root verb-forms and primary derivatives of the Sanskrit language*. Delhi: Bodhi Leaves Corporation.

Wright, Joseph. 1954. *Grammar of the Gothic language*. Oxford: Clarendon Press.

Ziegler, Sabine. 1994. *Die Sprache der altirischen Ogam-Inschriften*. Göttingen: Vandenhoeck & Ruprecht.

Word Indices

The index of words from our eight principal languages (including PIE) is selective in that, first, we usually do not cite intermediate stages in derivations; second, we do not usually cite pronouns, numerals or other words which are easily locatable in the paradigms or in the exercises (unless they occur in significant derivations); and third, we do not cite those words occurring solely in the reading text of our eight languages.

We do cite "key" or crucial words, namely those which occur in significant and enlightening derivations. (In such instances we occasionally cite more than one form of a single lexical item.) Further, we may on occasion cite two or more PIE forms for a single lexical item. This occurs for three main reasons. First, there are laryngeal vs. nonlaryngeal etymologies: e.g., 'mill' can be *moleh$_1$ or *molā. Second, the development of PIE into the daughter languages was gradual and in some instances evinced different roots. Hence a pre-Latin PIE word can differ from, say, a pre-Greek PIE word. E.g., pre-Latin PIE *reg- 'king' vs. pre-Greek PIE *g^{w}m̥til- 'king'. (This is particularly evident in the later PIE numerals such as pre-Gmc PIE *sepń̥t '7', pre-Latin PIE *septm̥ 'idem' and pre-OIr PIE *septōm 'idem'.) Third, later forms can enter into different inflectional classes. E.g., pre-Latin PIE *just+os 'just' (o-class) vs. pre-Old Irish PIE *just+jos 'idem' (jo-class).

All references below are to pages (and notes where indicated). The abbreviation *f* signifies that both the indicated page and the following page should be examined. The abbreviation *n* refers to the numbered note on the given page.

Proto-Indo-European

*adtendō 'attend' 127
*ageti 'drives' 479, 484
*agnis 'act of giving' 331, 368
*agrā 'massacre' 331
*agros 'field' 137, 160, 193
*ag^{w}nos, 'lamb'124, 192, 231, 316
*aiskṓm 'I seek' 410
*ákmōn, *akmū 'stone' 402, 417, 430
*ákros 'sharp' 403, 452
*ak^{w}eni 'we drink' 569
*ak^{w}toros 'one who drinks' 597
*ala##aljos 'other' 315, 327
*alb^{h}os 'white' 598
*ald^{h}jā́ 'boat' 427, 462n32
*alg^{hw}eti 'is worth' 483
*alg^{hw}+ó- 'price' 483
*aljā 'other' 327
*aljos 'another' 226
*amb^{h}í, *m̥b^{h}í 'around' 10
*ang^{h}- 'narrow' 10, 33, 35
*áng^{h}os- 'narrowness' 479
*ang^{h}ú- 'narrow' 495, 543
*ángulos 'angle' 396, 452
*ánso- 'shoulder' 495
*anti 'separately 566
*antos 'front' 597
*apo 'back, again' 569, 572
*apodeukō 'remove' 127, 195
*apoitis 'one who goes back' 598
*aponti 'they seize' 598
*apotor 'act of taxing' 582
*apterṓd 'from behind' 56f, 106
*ardōs 'ardor' 128, 136
*ardsai 'burned' 130, 132
*āridos 'arid' 128
*asus 'good' 599
*atnos 'year' 129, 143
*atṓm 'fathers' 567
*atons 'fathers' 571, 597
*atos 'father' 578
*auhi 'I see' 571
*āusti 'sees' 572
*áutrom 'morning' 407
*b^{h}ab^{h}ā 'bean' 124
*b^{h}āgā 'beech, (later) book' 52
*b^{h}ā́g^{h}us 'elbow' 10, 33, 35

*phoinó- 'foam' 545, 476
*ph$_2$tēr 'father' 217
*phtŕ̥- 'father' 475
*pikā́tei 'write' 404, 414, 450
*pilis 'much, many' 314
*pjuō 'spit' 226
*plā́kātei 'weep' 414
*pl̥(h)is 'broad' 567
*pl̥hnó- 'full' 476
*pl̥nos 'full' 51
*plōis 'more' 50
*pl̥ostis 'breadth' 570
*plóutei 'swim' 412
*plusmos 'bare' 326, 371, 376
*pod-, *pódm̥, *pōds 'foot' 15, 248
*pōiweni 'we go' 573
*póljom 'field' 411, 426
*poljos 'every' 346, 371
*pōmn̥tís 'memory' 396, 453
*porgāti 'slays' 364, 369
*porgonā 'slaughter' 364
*póronom 'travel' 52
*porsnās 'thigh' 598
*pórsos 'dust' 404, 454
*pṓun 'fire' 50, 60, 75, 107
*powar 'fire' 566
*prijós 'dear' 517
*prismos 'first' 131
*prōnk^{w}s 'forward-looking, eastern' 544
*prṓwos 'right' 398
*ptērsnā 'heel' 218
*radtrom 'rake' 132
*rḗgō(n), *rēgs 'king' 13, 21, 127, 162, 194, 327, 342f, 485, 514
*reg^{w}os 'darkness' 229
*rēim 'thing' 125
*répepulai 'I repelled' 136
*r(e)ud^{h}os 'red' 124
*róth$_2$e-, *roteh$_2$ 'wagon' 477
*róud^{h}ito-, *rud^{h}iró- 'red' 493f, 544
*roud^{h}os 'red' 329
*róuseitei 'destroy' 410
*rud^{h}ros 'red' 229
*sáusjā 'dryness' 414
*sausós 'dry' 416, 454
*sā́welios 'sun' 286
*sēdjṓm 'sit' 444
*sedno- 'having sat' 491
*sedō 'sit' 44, 97
*sedtos 'set' 11
*ség^{h}etai 'prevail' 545
*seg^{h}ō 'get, have' 229
*sḗiātei 'to sow' 395
*séilā 'strength' 397
*séinā 'army' 477, 508f
*séineh$_2$ 'army' 477, 544
*sḗitom 'sieve' 395
*seks '6' 318, 350, 369
*sekskn̥toi '600' 131, 169
*sek^{w}emā 'a following' 364
*sék^{w}etai 'follow' 482f, 544
*sek^{w}ītorai 'follows' 364
*sék^{w}ō 'see' 52, 107
*sek^{w}omai 'follow' 231, 287
*sek^{w}ōr 'follow' 369
*selb^{h} 'self' 52
*selpís- 'butter' 494
*sēment 'seed' 397, 431, 454
*seng^{hw}ō 'sing' 106
*séng^{hw}onom 'sing' 50
*senism̥- 'oldest' 348
*senjōs 'older' 320, 323, 348, 369
*senotūts 'old age' 322
*sentikī 'wife' 341
*sentus 'way' 324, 329, 371
*sepń̥t '7' 15
*septḿ̥ '7' 15
*septōm '7' 314, 350
*sirpā 'sickle' 327
*sisteh$_2$mi 'stand' 217
*sistēmi 'stand' 237
*skándeti 'jump' 483
*skepjomai 'look at' 226
*skindéti 'cut off' 483
*skoubṓm 'I rip' 395
*sk^{w}etlom 'story' 331, 338
*sleimos 'slime' 130
*slṓbos 'weak' 464n60
*smerus 'marrow' 371
*sm̥g^{h}éslom '1000' 519, 544
*sm̥leg^{h}ti 'lies with' 567, 598
*sm̥ōs 'somehow' 219

*sm̥paks 'once' 219, 258, 262
*snáisos 'laughter' 404
*sneig^{hw}eti 'it snows' 229, 231
*sn̥htó- 'won' 476
*snig^{hw}eti 'it snows' 316, 371
*snig^{hw}- 'snow' 125, 130, 193
*snoig^{hw}-, *snóig^{hw}- 'snow' 44, 50, 72, 106, 394, 403, 454
*sn̥tjóm 'truly' 518
*sodjagīōr 'I set' 357
*sodjagītjos 'placed, set' 365
*sodjom 'seat' 317, 322
*sok^{w}ahi 'I know' 595
*sok^{w}jos 'friend' 160
*sok^{w}ta 'you have seen' 565
*som##g^{w}m̥skonti 'they come together' 495
*som##jougo- 'union' 495
*song^{hw}ā, *song^{hw}ā́ 'song, oracle' 231, 294, 287
*sopnos 'sleep' 314
*spenjā 'breast' 314
*spespondai 'promised' 133
*sph$_2$erja 'ball' 217
*sphr̥héti 'throbs' 476
*spond^{h}i 'pours a libation' 570
*spond^{h}onti 'they sacrifice' 598
*srewō 'flow' 229
*sréwono- 'flowing' 482
*srīgos 'cold' 130
*sroumos 'stream' 51
*srutus 'stream' 322, 329, 371
*stad^{h}lom 'stable' 123, 128
*stad^{h}los 'stall' 51
*-stāō 'stand' 329
*stā́rējis 'older' 398, 434
*steh$_2$- 'stand' 14
*steig^{h}- 'climb, go' 15, 218, 326, 329
*steljō 'put' 227
*sterkā- 'love' 363, 371
*steros 'star' 326
*sth$_2$- 'stand' 477
*sth̥$_2$tis 'act of standing' 217
*stolós 'chair' 397
*stomor 'mouth' 598
*stratos 'valley' 326, 369
*suhs 'pig' 14
*suménos 'well-disposed' 515
*sunéumi 'press' 13
*súnous, *sū́nus 'son' 53, 73, 428f
*supis 'clean' 584
*súpnos 'sleep' 406
*supsā́tei 'to suck' 406
*swādús 'sweet' 254, 257, 287
*swékuro- 'father-in-law' 490
*swepnos 'sleep' 129, 140, 145, 193
*swesōr 'sister' 344, 372
*taidros 'foul' 130
*tarstom 'thirst' 315, 326
*teg 'you (sg)' 609n72
*tegesos, *tegos 'house' 317, 346, 371
*tek^{w}eti 'flees' 361
*temnō, *témnō 'cut' 26, 266, 305n161
*tenús 'thin' 513
*tenū́s 'body' 347,372
*tepents 'hot' 347, 372
*terrāis 'lands' 125
*tetéuda 'pushed' 29
*tetudwṓts 'having pushed' 10,30
*teutāb^{h}is 'people' 317
*teutās 'nations' 317f
*tl̥onom 'tolerate' 53
*tn̥gjonom 'seem' 53
*tod 'this' 328, 370
*tolnō 'bear up' 128
*tongj-'think' 43, 97, 112f
*tonkatom 'happiness' 324
*torsējō 'burn' 130, 194
*toutis 'army' 607n14
*trag^{h}ets 'foot' 343
*trepom 'plow' 598
*tris '3 times' 137, 171
*trisú '3' 481
*trónktos 'guard' 405
*tr̥stos 'thirst' 315, 371
*tu 'you (sg)' 230
*tØulā- 'scales' 488
*ū́d^{h}ment 'udder' 406, 453
*ūd^{h}nei, *ūd^{h}noi 'country' 572
*udōr 'water' 238
*ulktos 'avenged' 132
*upeitéi 'cry out' 407
*upopdós 'act of trampling' 478

Gothic

Latin

Greek

t^{h}etós 'placed' 217
t^{h}ríks 'hair' 234, 237, 288
t^{h}ȳmós 'smoke' 218
tīmɔ̄̂men 'we honor' 232
tīmɔ̄̂ 'honor' 222
tīmɔ̄̂ntes 'honoring' 218
tís 'who?' 288
tít^{h}ɛ̄mi 'put' 217f, 222
tó 'that' 220
treîs '3' 236, 259
trī́bɔ̄ 'rub' 234, 242
týp^{h}ɔ̄ 'smoke' 327
zéɔ̄ 'seethe' 227
Zeús (name) 226, 235, 249, 288
zygón, zygós 'yoke' 223, 227, 236, 246

Old Irish

a(i)gid 'drives' 364
aile 'other' 327
áin 'act of going' 331
ainm(m)^n 'name' 345
aithir, ath(a)ir 'father' 313f, 317, 320, 343
aláile 'other' 315
amm 'I am' 317, 330
apstol 'apostle' 314, 331
ár 'massacre' 331
asbeir 'says' 322f, 330
asbiur 'I say' 322f
baile 'place' 330
bece 'small' 348
ben, mná 'woman' 316
benaid 'strikes' 355
-ber, berid, biur 'carry' 312, 319, 324, 355, 364, 375, 387
bláth 'flower' 321, 375
bó 'cow' 316, 381n59
bongid 'breaks' 355
breth 'act of bearing' 314
brith 'act of carrying' 365
brithem 'judge' 344
cacht 'slave, servant' 314
caera 'sheep' 314
caich 'blind' 329, 376
fid 'wood' 322
-car- 327, 360, 363 'love'
car(a)e 'friend' 330, 336, 345
carsu 'I loved' 360
cechan 'I sang' 361, 367
ceimm 'a walk' 364
césad 'suffering' 331
cét '100' 315, 350
céte 'sung' 365
ceth(a)ir '4' 324f, 330, 350
charat 'friend' 318
cia 'who?' 353
cingid 'walks' 364, 391n220
cleth- 'which should be hidden' 324f, 365
clithe 'hidden' 365, 376
cóic '5' 317, 325, 350, 376
coll 'hazel tree' 327, 376
commaith 'well' 348, 383n100
cona 'dogs' 324, 328, 344, 382n68
cor 'throw' 363
crú 'blood' 330, 375
cú 'dog' 320, 344
cumachte 'might, power' 331
da 'two' 325, 378n15, 383n100
dán 'gift' 321
dech 'best' 348
deich '10' 317, 320, 350, 375
déinithir 'just as fast as' 347
dét 'tooth' 317, 346, 375
dia 'god' 329, 335f
dobeir 'carry' 315
doformagar 'is increased' 315
doirsea, ndoirsea 'doors' 320, 331
do-lleicet 'they leave' 318
domoinether 'thinks' 364
dorus 'door' 312, 316, 320, 342, 375
dub 'black' 347, 383n87
epir 'say' 315
-epir 'bring forth' 327
fáith 'prophet' 323, 341, 375
fedb 'widow' 325, 377
fén 'wagon' 377
fer^n 'man' 319, 338
ferr 'better' 348, 383n95
fiche '20' 350
fiched 'fights' 361
find 'white' 322

fír 'true' 313, 325
firu 'men' 320, 327f, 338
fiur 'man' 319, 321, 338, 377
fiur, siur 'sister' 377, 378n6, 382n64
fius 'knowledge' 313, 364, 376
flaith 'rulership' 314, 341, 377
géis 'swan' 324
giun 'mouth' 341f
gort 'garden' 312, 375
guidid 'asks' 316, 361
guin 'act of killing' 312, 316
hil 'much, many' 314
hillab 'syllable' 318
huisse 'just' 327, 329, 375
imb 'butter' 316, 375
ingen 'daughter' 317, 375
ingnáth 'unknown' 315
insce^{l} 'speech' 340
ís 'under' 327
karait 'friends' 324
kride^{n} 'heart' 339
lécid 'leaves' 355
lomm 'bare' 326, 376
lugam 'smallest' 348
lugu 'smaller' 348
maccu 'sons' 318
maith 'good' 347f
messa 'worse' 348
messam 'worst' 348
mí 'month' 370, 376
midithir 'judges (3 sg pres)' 355
mligid 'milk' 375
móraid 'magnifies' 355, 387n157
muce^{l} 'pig' 340
muir^{n} 'sea' 341, 375
naithir 'fathers' 319f, 377
nau 'ship' 321
net 'nest' 33, 327
ocht, ocht^{n} '8' 317, 320, 350
oin '1' 329, 349
oirdnide, oirdnithe 'gives orders' 317
olc 'bad' 348
org(a)id 'slays' 364
orgon 'slaughter' 364
peccad, peccath 'sin' 317
phreceptóri 'preacher(s)' 318
rí 'king' 327, 335, 343, 345
ruad 'red' 329
scél, scél^{n} 'story' 331, 338, 379n20
sé '6' 318, 350, 321, 369
sechem 'a following' 364, 391n223
sechither 'follows' 364
secht, secht^{n} '7' 314, 319f, 377
sechur 'follow' 324, 330, 375
seirc 'love' 323
sen 'old' 318
sentu 'old age' 322
ser 'star' 326
serc 'love' 363, 377
serr 'sickle' 327
sét 'way' 324, 329, 376
sétig^{l} 'wife' 341, 379
sethar, siur 'sister' 344, 352, 372, 377
sine 'breast' 314
sinem 'oldest' 348, 383
siniu 'older' 320, 323, 348, 375
smiur 'marrow' 376
snigit 'it snows' 316, 371
srath 'valley' 322, 329
srotho 'stream' 322, 329
sruth 'stream' 322, 376
suan 'sleep' 314
suide 'seat' 317, 322, 363
suidigthe 'placed, set' 357
suidigur 'I set' 357f
tart 'thirst' 377, 315
-tā̃u, -tó 'stand' 329
té 'hot' 347
techid 'flees' 361
teg^{n} 'house' 346
thuatha, tuatha 'nations' 317f, 335
tiagu 'go' 326, 329
tige 'house' 317, 383n83
tige 'houses' 320
tó 'this' 328f, 375
tó 'thus, yes' 330
tocad 'happiness' 324
toimtiu 'opinion' 315, 345, 364
traig 'foot' 343
tuathaib 'people' 317
uan 'lamb' 316
uile 'every' 346, 376

Old Church Slavic

ágnę 'lamb' 431
bě́gati 'flee' 403
berǫ́ 'I carry' 394, 443f
berǫ́štɪ 'carrying' 422
berý 'carrying' 402, 422
bǫdǫ́ 'I will be' 448
bógʊ 'god' 410, 423
božɪstvó 'divinity' 397
brátrʊ 'brother' 397, 430, 458
bytí 'be' 417, 419, 447f
čásʊ 'period of time' 410
cěná 'price' 416
cěsarɪ 'emperor' 416
cę́ta 'coin' 413
čisló 'number' 405
črědá 'herd' 409
críky, crʊ́ky 'church' 417, 429
črɪnʊ́ 'black' 398
čúdo 'wonder' 412, 415
dámɪ 'I give' 444
datí 'give' 408
dělátelji 'worker' 429
désętɪ 'ten' 396, 437
désnʊ 'right-handed' 404
dě́ti 'put' 408
dómʊ 'house' 408
drágyi 'dear' 398
dręzgá 'forest' 416
dʊšá 'soul' 411f, 427, 432
dʊ́ždɪ 'rain' 411, 452
dvígnǫ 'I move' 399, 444
dvizáti 'move often' 418, 423
dzě́lo, zě́lo 'very' 416
gǫ́sɪ 'goose' 396, 452
gospoždá 'mistress' 397
góstɪ 'guest' 413, 428, 454
grádi 'cities' 412
grádiskʊ 'of a city, urban' 398
graždanínʊ 'citizen' 431
grebǫ́ 'dig' 406, 423, 455
grómʊ 'thunder' 94
ígo 'yoke' 411, 459
imǫ́ 'I take' 407, 413
iskǫ́ 'I seek' 410
jásti 'eat' 410
jésmɪ 'I am' 444, 447
jętí 'take' 407, 413, 423
jútro 'morning' 407
kámy 'stone' 417, 402, 430
klonítì 'lean' 396
koló 'wheel' 403, 454
koráblɪ 'ship' 397
kričáti 'scream' 409
kʊ́nęzɪ 'king' 418
kúpiti 'buy' 412
kúsiti 'test' 404
ladɪjí 'boat' 427, 437
lákʊtʊ 'elbows' 429, 458
lě́vʊ 'left' 412, 454
ležáti 'recline' 409
listí 'leaves' 419
lɪ́sti 'deceptions' 419
ljubíti 'love' 415
ljubʊ́ 'dear' 412, 458
ljúdɪskʊ 'of people' 416
luná 'moon' 405
lʊ́ža 'a lie' 414
lʊ́žɪ 'lying, medacious' 432, 434
máti 'mother' 430, 463n48
mečɪ́ 'sword' 397
médʊ 'honey' 394
mestí 'throw' 403, 406, 422
mě́sto 'place' 397, 425, 432
meždá 'middle' 415, 453
mɪně́ti 'think' 396, 423
mɪzdá 'reward' 403
mlětí 'grind' 416f, 423
mogǫ́ 'be able' 399, 445
molíti 'pray, request' 406, 450
móljęšta 'asking' 411, 451
mórje 'sea' 397, 415, 458
mózgʊ 'brain' 410
mǫ́žɪ 'man' 425f, 432
mýsliti 'think' 403, 415
mýšɪ 'mouse' 404
mýtarji 'toll-taker' 429
nagʊ́ 'naked' 459
nasʊ́ 'of us' 419
nesʊ́ 'having carried' 419
nóštɪ 'night' 395, 398, 413, 415

Sanskrit

múrmūrṣati 'want to die' 539
mūṣ- 'mouse' 481
muṣṇāti 'steal' 482
nadī́s 'stream, river' 497, 513
náhyati 'ties' 524
nákti- 'night' 479
nā́ma 'name' 515, 544
nāsti 'is not' 486
matá- 'considered' 480
nā́us 'ship' 492, 513
nāyati 'leads' 488
nīḍá-, nīḍás 'nest' 11, 481, 485
nr̥pas 'king' 492
ṓjas 'power' 545
páñca '5' 504, 518
pāpás 'evil' 516
pā́patati 'fall a lot' 539
paptima 'we fly, fall' 488
pāt 'foot' 486
pátati 'fall' 9, 539f
pātáyati 'cause to fall' 9, 488
patsú 'feet' 478, 512
pávati 'cleanses' 488
phēná- 'foam' 476
pitā́-, pitŕ̥- 'father' 475, 497, 514
pitár 'father' 35
prāṇ 'forward-looking, eastern' 488, 549
priyás 'dear' 517
pūrná- 'full' 476
rā́jā 'king' 485, 514
rátha- 'wagon' 477
riṇákti 'leaves' 494
rṓhita-, rudhirá- 'red' 493f
sácatē 'follow' 503, 549, 582f
sáhatē 'prevail' 550
saṁgacchanti 'they come together' 495
saṁyōga- 'union' 495
śánakāis 'slowly' 518
sanna- 'having sat' 491
sarpíṣ- 'butter' 494
ṣaṭ '6' 490, 518
sātá- 'won' 476
śatám '100' 12, 478, 484, 519
śátrus 'enemy' 511
sattás 'set' 11
satyám 'truly' 518, 557n107
sḗnā 'army' 477, 508f
śíras-, śīr̥ṣán- 'head' 476
skándati 'jump' 483
sphuráti 'throbs' 476
sphū́rjati 'gasp' 476
śrṓmatam 'blessing' 485
srávaṇa- 'flowing' 482
śrutá- 'heard' 479, 491, 544
sthā- 'stand' 477
sthagati 'covers' 484
stighnōti 'mount' 484
śúcis 'pure' 516
sumánās 'well-disposed' 516f
sunṓmi 'press' 13, 499, 526
sunṓti 'presses out' 524, 526f
svādús 'sweet' 34
śván- 'dog' 478f
śváśura- 'father-in-law' 490
tanṓti 'stretches' 524, 527
tanús 'thin' 516
tanū́s 'body' 513
triṣú '3' 481
tudáti 'pushes' 526, 534
tulā- 'scales' 488
upabdá-, upabdás 'act of trampling' 11, 478, 544
uvaca 'spoke' 492
vadhū́s 'woman' 509
vāgbhís 'words' 478
vāk 'word' 485, 504
vā́ri 'water' 497, 510f
várṣman- 'summit' 481
vártatē 'turns' 545
vḗda 'I know' 485, 534
vḗttha 'you know' 476
vḗvētti 'know well' 539
viṁśatís '20' 519, 557n121
viṭ 'house' 482
vr̥ṣṭí- 'rain' 481
yaktá- 'joined' 478f
yugám 'yoke' 507
yujatē 'join' 473
yuktá- 'yoked, joined' 11, 479
yunákti 'joined' 524, 526

Hittite